W9-BHW-837

SAS/ETS® User's Guide

Version 6
Second Edition

SAS Institute Inc.
SAS Campus Drive
Cary, NC 27513

The correct bibliographic citation for this manual is as follows: SAS Institute Inc., *SAS/ETS® User's Guide, Version 6, Second Edition*, Cary, NC: SAS Institute Inc., 1993. 1,022 pp.

SAS/ETS® User's Guide, Version 6, Second Edition

Copyright © 1993 by SAS Institute Inc., Cary, NC, USA.

ISBN 1-55544-554-3

All rights reserved. Printed in the United States of America. No part of this publication may be reproduced, stored in a retrieval system, or transmitted, in any form or by any means, electronic, mechanical, photocopying, or otherwise, without the prior written permission of the publisher, SAS Institute Inc.

1st printing, September 1993

The SAS® System is an integrated system of software providing complete control over data access, management, analysis, and presentation. Base SAS software is the foundation of the SAS System. Products within the SAS System include SAS/ACCESS® SAS/AF® SAS/ASSIST® SAS/CALC® SAS/CONNECT® SAS/CPE® SAS/DMI® SAS/EIS® SAS/ENGLISH® SAS/ETS® SAS/FSP® SAS/GRAPH® SAS/IML® SAS/IMS-DL/I® SAS/INSIGHT® SAS/LAB® SAS/OR® SAS/PH-Clinical® SAS/QC® SAS/REPLAY-CICS® SAS/SHARE® SAS/STAT® SAS/TOOLKIT® SAS/TUTOR® SAS/DB2™ SAS/LOOKUP™ SAS/NVISION™ and SAS/SQL-DS™ software. Other SAS Institute products are SYSTEM 2000® Data Management Software, with basic SYSTEM 2000, CREATE™ Multi-User™ QueX™ Screen Writer™ and CICS interface software; NeoVisuals® software; JMP® JMP IN® JMP Serve® and JMP *Design®* software; SAS/RTERM® software; and the SAS/C® Compiler and the SAS/CX® Compiler. MultiVendor Architecture™ and MVA™ are trademarks of SAS Institute Inc. SAS Video Productions™ and the SVP logo are service marks of SAS Institute Inc. SAS Institute also offers SAS Consulting® Ambassador Select™ and On-Site Ambassador™ services. *Authorline® Observations® SAS Communications® SAS Training® SAS Views®* and the SASware Ballot® are published by SAS Institute Inc. All trademarks above are registered trademarks or trademarks of SAS Institute Inc. in the USA and other countries. ® indicates USA registration.

The Institute is a private company devoted to the support and further development of its software and related services.

Other brand and product names are registered trademarks or trademarks of their respective companies.

Table of Contents

Credits

Documentation

Writing	Gul Ege, Donald J. Erdman, R. Bart Killam, Minbo Kim, Charles C. Lin, Mark R. Little, Meltem A. Narter, H. Jin Park
Editing	Juile A. LaBarr, Mark R. Little, Donna M. Sawyer, Maura E. Stokes, Robert Tschudi
Review	Jackie F. Allen, Brent Cohen, Mark Craver, Gul Ege, Anwar El-Jawhari, Donald J. Erdman, R. Bart Killam, Minbo Kim, Tae Yoon Lee, Meltem A. Narter, David M. Price, Jim Seabolt, Donna E. Woodward
Copyediting	Patsy Blessis, Susan McCoy, Curtis Yeo
Cover Design and Production Support	Design, Production, and Printing Services

Software Development

The procedures in SAS/ETS software were implemented by the Econometrics and Time Series Research and Development department.

Substantial contributions and support were given to the project by the other members of the Application Division.

In the following list, the SAS Institute staff member currently having primary responsibility for the procedure is indicated with an asterisk; others have contributed previously.

ARIMA	H. Jin Park*
AUTOREG	Minbo Kim*, John P. Sall
CITIBASE	Richard D. Langston, Mark R. Little, Meltem A. Narter*
COMPUTAB	Alan R. Eaton*, David F. Ross
DATASOURCE	Kelly F. Frost*, Meltem A. Narter
EXPAND	Mark R. Little*
FORECAST	Menqiong G. Liou*, Mark R. Little, John P. Sall
LOAN	Gul Ege*
MODEL	Donald J. Erdman*, Mark R. Little, John P. Sall

MORTGAGE	Gul Ege*, R. Bart Killam, Richard D. Langston
PDLREG	Leigh A. Ihnen, Minbo Kim*
SIMLIN	Mark R. Little*, John P. Sall
SPECTRA	Donald J. Erdman*, H. Jin Park, John P. Sall
STATESPACE	H. Jin Park*
SYSLIN	Leigh A. Ihnen, Charles C. Lin*, John P. Sall
TSCSREG	Minbo Kim*, Meltem A. Narter
X11	Leigh A. Ihnen, R. Bart Killam*, Richard D. Langston
Forecasting Menu System	Gul Ege, Menqiong G. Liou*
Help menus	Gul Ege*, Sandy B. Emerson, Kathy J. Roggenkamp, Melissa Stevenson, Maura E. Stokes
Testing	Ming-Chun Chang, David M. Price, Kim Sherrill

Support Groups

Quality Assurance	Mark Craver, Anwar El-Jawhari, Tae Yoon Lee, Kathy DeRusso
Technical Support	Thomas J. Hahl, Tina Keene, Cathy Maahs-Fladung, Donna E. Woodward

Acknowledgments

Hundreds of people have helped the SAS System in many ways since its inception. The individuals listed below have been especially helpful in the development of the procedures in SAS/ETS software. Acknowledgments for the SAS System generally are in base SAS documentation and SAS/STAT documentation.

David Amick	Idaho Office of Highway Safety
David M. DeLong	Duke University
David Dickey	North Carolina State University
Douglas J. Drummond	Center for Survey Statistics
William Fortney	Boeing Computer Services
Wayne Fuller	Iowa State University
A. Ronald Gallant	North Carolina State University
Phil Hanser	Sacramento Municipal Utilities District
Marvin Jochimsen	Mississippi R&O Center
George McCollister	San Diego Gas & Electric
Brian Monsell	U.S. Census Bureau
Robert Parks	Washington University
Gregory Sali	Idaho Office of Highway Safety
Terry J. Woodfield	Risk Data Corporation
Mary Young	Salt River Project

The final responsibility for the SAS System lies with SAS Institute alone. We hope you will always let us know your opinions about the SAS System and its documentation. It is through your participation that the progress of SAS software has been accomplished.

Chapter 1
Introduction

Chapter Table of Contents

Chapter 1
Introduction

Overview of SAS/ETS Software

SAS/ETS software, a component of the SAS System, provides SAS procedures for

- econometric analysis
- time series analysis
- forecasting time series
- systems modeling and simulation
- seasonal adjustment
- financial analysis and reporting
- access to economic and financial databases
- time series data management

Uses of SAS/ETS Software

SAS/ETS software provides tools for a wide variety of applications in business, government, and academia. Major uses of SAS/ETS procedures are economic analysis, forecasting, economic and financial modeling, time series analysis, financial reporting, and manipulation of time series data.

The common theme relating the many applications of the software is time series data: SAS/ETS software is useful whenever it is necessary to analyze or predict processes that take place over time or to analyze processes that involve simultaneous relationships.

Although SAS/ETS software is most closely associated with business and economics, time series data also arise in many other fields. SAS/ETS software is useful whenever time dependencies, simultaneous relationships, or dynamic processes complicate data analysis. For example, an environmental quality study might use SAS/ETS software's time series analysis tools to analyze pollution emissions data. A pharmacokinetic study might use SAS/ETS software's features for nonlinear systems to model the dynamics of drug metabolism in different tissues.

The diversity of problems for which econometrics and time series analysis tools are needed is reflected in the applications reported by SAS users. The following are some applications of SAS/ETS software presented by SAS users at past annual conferences of the SAS Users Group International (SUGI):

- forecasting oil prices (Dennis, Fraiman, and Mohl 1982)
- analyzing the effect of drunk driving laws on highway accident rates (Starks, Elizandro, and Classen 1983)
- predicting prison population (Davis 1984)
- forecasting aggregate industrial production (Bailey 1984)
- forecasting monthly total electricity demand (Jacob 1984)
- forecasting daily peak load electricity demand (Jacob 1985)
- forecasting the demand for natural gas (Brand and Funk 1985)
- forecasting health insurance claims (Hanumara and Salzillo 1986)
- inventory planning (Cardamone and Brauer 1987)
- monitoring the environmental impact of nuclear power plant thermal emissions on fish populations (Bireley 1987)
- analyzing the usefulness of the composite index of leading economic indicators for forecasting the economy (Lin and Myers 1988)
- analyzing Dow Jones stock index trends (Early, Sweeney, and Zekavat 1989)
- learning curve analysis for predicting manufacturing costs of aircraft (Le Bouton 1989)
- predicting the gloss of coated aluminum products subject to weathering (Khan 1990)
- forecasting dairy milk yields and composition (Benseman 1990)
- evaluating the theory of input separability in the production function of U.S. manufacturing (Hisnanick 1991)
- estimating tree biomass for measurement of forestry yields (Parresol and Thomas 1991)

Contents of SAS/ETS Software

SAS/ETS software includes the following SAS procedures:

ARIMA	ARIMA (Box-Jenkins) and ARIMAX (Box-Tiao) modeling and forecasting
AUTOREG	regression analysis with autocorrelated errors and ARCH and GARCH modeling
CITIBASE	access to CITIBASE database files
COMPUTAB	spreadsheet calculations and financial report generation
DATASOURCE	access to financial and economic databases
EXPAND	time series interpolation and frequency conversion, and transformation of time series
FORECAST	automatic forecasting
LOAN	loan analysis and comparison

MODEL   nonlinear simultaneous equations regression and nonlinear systems modeling and simulation

MORTGAGE   mortgage amortization tables

PDLREG   polynomial distributed lag regression (Almon lags)

SIMLIN   linear systems simulation

SPECTRA   spectral analysis and cross spectral analysis

STATESPACE   state space modeling and automated forecasting of multivariate time series

SYSLIN   linear simultaneous equations models

TSCSREG   time series cross-sectional regression analysis

X11   seasonal adjustment (Census X-11 and X-11-ARIMA)

SAS/ETS software also includes the following SAS macros:

%AR   generates statements to define autoregressive error models for the MODEL procedure

%BOXCOXAR   investigates Box-Cox transformations useful for modeling and forecasting a time series

%DFPVALUE   computes probabilities for Dickey-Fuller test statistics

%DFTEST   performs Dickey-Fuller tests for unit roots in a time series process

%LOGTEST   tests to see if a log transformation is appropriate for modeling and forecasting a time series

%MA   generates statements to define moving average error models for the MODEL procedure

%PDL   generates statements to define polynomial distributed lag models for the MODEL procedure

These macros are part of the SAS AUTOCALL facility and are automatically available for use in your SAS program. (Refer to *SAS Guide to Macro Processing, Version 6, Second Edition* for information about the SAS macro facility.)

Some of the features of SAS/ETS software are also available through menu driven interfaces provided by SAS/ASSIST software. (Both SAS/ASSIST software and SAS/ETS software must be licensed for you to use these features.)

The following components of SAS/ASSIST software enable you to use SAS/ETS procedures through a menu interface:

- loan analysis (uses PROC LOAN)
- regression with correction for autocorrelation (uses PROC AUTOREG)
- seasonal adjustment (uses PROC X11)
- convert frequency of time series data (uses PROC EXPAND)

About This Book

This book is a user's guide to Release 6.08 SAS/ETS software. If you have a later release of the SAS System, your system may have additional features not documented in this book. You can find out about any new features added since the publication of this book by using the online help facility.

From the SAS Display Manager command line, enter the command `help etsnews`. Alternatively, if you are using the SAS display manager with pull-down menus instead of a command line, you can pull down the `Help` menu, and make the following selections:

`SAS System` ▸ `INDEX` ▸ `SAS/ETS` ▸ `ETSNEWS`

Since SAS/ETS software is a part of the SAS System, this book assumes that you are familiar with base SAS software and have the books *SAS Language: Reference, Version 6, First Edition* and the *SAS Procedures Guide, Version 6, Third Edition* available for reference. It also assumes that you are familiar with the SAS data set, the SAS DATA step, and with basic SAS procedures such as PROC PRINT and PROC SORT. Chapter 2, "Working with Time Series Data," in this book summarizes the aspects of base SAS software most relevant to the use of SAS/ETS software.

Chapter Organization

This book is organized as follows.

Chapter 1 provides an overview of SAS/ETS software and summarizes related SAS Institute publications, products, and services.

Chapter 2, "Working with Time Series Data," discusses the use of SAS data management and programming features for time series data.

Subsequent chapters explain the SAS procedures that make up SAS/ETS software. These chapters appear in alphabetic order by procedure name.

The chapters documenting the SAS/ETS procedures are organized as follows:

1. Each chapter begins with an *Overview* section that gives a brief description of the procedure.

2. The *Getting Started* section provides a tutorial introduction on how to use the procedure.

3. The *Syntax* section is a reference to the SAS statements and options that control the procedure.

4. The *Details* section discusses various technical details.

5. The *Examples* section contains examples of the use of the procedure.

6. The *References* section contains technical references on methodology.

Following the chapters on the SAS/ETS procedures, Chapter 20, "SAS Macros," documents SAS macros provided with SAS/ETS software. These macros use

SAS/ETS procedures to perform Dickey-Fuller tests, test for the need for log transformations, or select optimal Box-Cox transformations.

Chapter 21, "Date Intervals, Formats, and Functions," provides a quick reference to some base SAS features useful to users of SAS/ETS software. This chapter consolidates material found in various sections of *SAS Language: Reference.*

Chapter 22, "Changes and Enhancements," summarizes the new features added to SAS/ETS software since the publication of *SAS/ETS User's Guide, Version 6, First Edition.* If you have used SAS/ETS software in the past, you may want to skim Chapter 22 to see what's new.

Typographical Conventions

This book uses several type styles for presenting information. The following list explains the meaning the typographical conventions used in this book:

roman	is the standard type style used for most text.
UPPERCASE ROMAN	is used for SAS statements, options, variable names, and other SAS language elements when they appear in the text. However, you can enter these elements in your own SAS programs in lowercase, uppercase, or a mixture of the two.
UPPERCASE BOLD	is used in the "Syntax" sections for SAS keywords such as the names of statements and options.
oblique	is used for user-supplied values for options (for example, **INTERVAL=***interval*).
bold	is used to refer to matrices and vectors
italic	is used for terms that are defined in the text, for emphasis, and for references to publications.
`monospace`	is used to show examples of SAS statements. In most cases, this book uses lowercase type for SAS statements. You can enter your own SAS statements in lowercase, uppercase, or a mixture of the two. The SAS System always changes your variable names to uppercase, but character variable values remain in lowercase if you have entered them that way. Enter any titles and footnotes exactly as you want them to appear on your output.

Output of Examples

For each example, the procedure output is numbered consecutively starting with 1, and each output is given a title. Each page of output produced by a procedure is enclosed in a box. Most of the output shown in this book was produced using the SAS System options LINESIZE=80, PAGESIZE=40, NOPAGE, and NODATE. In some cases, if you run the examples, you will get slightly different output. This is a function of the SAS system options you use and of the precision used for floating-point calculations by your computer, rather than a problem with the software. In all situations, any differences should be very small.

Where to Turn for More Information

This section describes other sources of information about SAS/ETS software.

Online Help System

You can access online help information about SAS/ETS software in two ways, depending on whether you are using the SAS Display Manager System in the command line mode or the pull down menu mode.

If you are using a command line, you can access the SAS/ETS help menus by typing **help ets** on the display manager command line. If you are using the display manager with pull-down menus instead of a command line, you can pull down the | Help | menu and make the following selections:

| SAS System | ▶ | SAS SYSTEM HELP: Main Menu | ▶ | INDEX | ▶ | SAS/ETS |

The | SAS SYSTEM HELP: SAS/ETS | menu contains three parts: procedure help, SAS/ETS news, and a general review of the software.

Procedure Help

The SAS/ETS Help menu contains an entry for each SAS/ETS procedure. To access the help information for a procedure, select the entry with the procedure name. For example, to get help on the ARIMA procedure, select | ARIMA |. The help material given for each procedure is abstracted from this book.

The help menu for each procedure contains three items: | Introduction |, | Syntax |, and | Additional Topics |. The | Introduction | contains a few paragraphs describing the procedure. The | Syntax | item provides a quick reminder of the syntax of the statements and options that control the procedure. The | Additional Topics | item contains additional information and tips on using the procedure.

ETSNEWS: New Features in SAS/ETS Software

Select the | ETSNEWS | item for information on features that have been added to SAS/ETS software in recent releases of the product. (The | ETSNEWS | help can also be accessed directly from the display manager command line by typing the command **help etsnews**.)

New versions of SAS/ETS software may be released more frequently than new editions of this user's guide are published. Therefore, your version of SAS/ETS software may contain additional features not documented in this book. The | ETSNEWS | help menus update you on any features added since this book was published. You should also check the | ETSNEWS | help menus whenever you begin using a new release of the SAS System.

About SAS/ETS

The `About SAS/ETS` entry provides a general overview of SAS/ETS software. It contains information abstracted from this chapter.

Other Related SAS Institute Publications

In addition to this user's guide, SAS Institute publishes other books on using SAS/ETS software. The following books are companions to this user's guide:

- *SAS/ETS Software: Applications Guide 1, Version 6, First Edition*
- *SAS/ETS Software: Applications Guide 2, Version 6, First Edition*

The first volume, *SAS/ETS Software: Applications Guide 1*, discusses features of SAS/ETS software for time series modeling and forecasting, financial reporting, and loan analysis. The second volume, *SAS/ETS Software: Applications Guide 2*, discusses features of SAS/ETS software for econometric modeling and simulation.

SAS System for Forecasting Time Series, 1986 Edition, discusses forecasting using SAS/ETS software.

SAS Institute Short Courses

SAS Institute offers the following short courses on using SAS/ETS software:

Forecasting Techniques Using SAS/ETS Software focuses on the practical application of forecasting techniques in SAS/ETS software. The course covers

- exponential smoothing
- seasonal adjustment
- seasonal exponential smoothing
- regression models with autoregressive errors
- graphical presentation of forecasts
- forecast confidence limits
- testing for nonstationarity
- Box-Jenkins ARIMA modeling
- transfer function and intervention models
- multivariate time series analysis
- spectral analysis

Econometric Modeling Using SAS/ETS Software explains the use of the SYSLIN, SIMLIN, and MODEL procedures for analyzing systems of simultaneous equations. The course covers

- statistical problems caused by dependent regressors and simultaneous relationships
- methods of estimating simultaneous equations
- simulation and forecasting of simultaneous systems
- fitting nonlinear autoregressive models with PROC MODEL
- fitting distributed lag models with PROC MODEL
- tests on parameter estimates in simultaneous systems

- Monte Carlo simulation of equation systems

SAS Institute Technical Support Services

As with all SAS Institute products, the SAS Institute Technical Support staff is available to respond to problems and answer technical questions regarding the use of SAS/ETS software.

Major Features of SAS/ETS Software

The following sections briefly summarize major features of SAS/ETS software. See the chapters on individual procedures for more detailed information.

Regression with Autocorrelated and Heteroscedastic Errors

The AUTOREG procedure provides regression analysis and forecasting of linear models with autocorrelated or conditional heteroscedastic errors. The AUTOREG procedure includes the following features:

- estimation and prediction of linear regression models with autoregressive errors
- any order autoregressive or subset autoregressive process
- optional stepwise selection of autoregressive parameters
- choice of the following estimation methods:
  - exact maximum likelihood
  - exact nonlinear least squares
  - Yule-Walker
  - iterated Yule-Walker
- forecasts with confidence limits
- estimation and forecasting of ARCH (autoregressive conditional heteroscedasticity), GARCH (generalized autoregressive conditional heteroscedasticity), I-GARCH (integrated GARCH), E-GARCH (exponential GARCH), and GARCH-M (GARCH in mean) models
- ARCH and GARCH models can be combined with autoregressive models, with or without regressors
- variety of model diagnostic information including
  - autocorrelation plots
  - partial autocorrelation plots
  - Durbin-Watson test statistic and generalized Durbin-Watson tests to any order
  - Durbin h and Durbin t statistics
  - Akaike information criterion
  - Schwarz information criterion
  - tests for ARCH errors
- exact significance levels (p-values) for the Durbin-Watson, Durbin t, and Durbin h statistics
- embedded missing values

Simultaneous Systems Linear Regression

The SYSLIN procedure provides regression analysis of a simultaneous system of linear equations. The SYSLIN procedure includes the following features:

- estimation of parameters in simultaneous systems of linear equations
- full range of estimation methods including
  - ordinary least squares (OLS)
  - two-stage least squares (2SLS)
  - three-stage least squares (3SLS)
  - iterated 3SLS
  - seemingly unrelated regression (SUR)
  - iterated SUR
  - limited-information maximum-likelihood (LIML)
  - full-information maximum-likelihood (FIML)
  - minimum-expected-loss (MELO)
  - general K-class estimators
- weighted regression
- restrictions for any linear combination of coefficients, within a single model or across equations; any number of restrictions easily specified
- tests for any linear hypothesis, for the parameters of a single model or across equations
- wide range of model diagnostics and statistics including
  - usual ANOVA tables and R^2 statistics
  - Durbin-Watson statistics
  - standardized coefficients
  - test for over-identifying restrictions
  - residual plots
  - standard errors and T tests
  - covariance and correlation matrices of parameter estimates and equation errors
- predicted values, residuals, parameter estimates, and variance-covariance matrices saved in output SAS data sets

Linear Systems Simulation

The SIMLIN procedure performs simulation and multiplier analysis for simultaneous systems of linear regression models. The SIMLIN procedure includes the following features:

- reduced form coefficients
- interim multipliers
- total multipliers
- dynamic forecasts and simulations
- goodness-of-fit statistics
- processes equation system coefficients estimated by the SYSLIN procedure

Polynomial Distributed Lag Regression

The PDLREG procedure provides regression analysis for linear models with polynomial distributed (Almon) lags. The PDLREG procedure includes the following features:

- any number of regressors may enter as a polynomial lag distribution, and any number of covariates may be used
- any order lag length and degree polynomial for lag distribution may be used
- optional upper and lower endpoint restrictions
- any number of linear restrictions may be placed on covariates
- option to repeat analysis over a range of degrees for the lag distribution polynomials
- support for autoregressive errors to any lag
- forecasts with confidence limits

Nonlinear Systems Regression and Simulation

The MODEL procedure provides parameter estimation, simulation, and forecasting of dynamic nonlinear simultaneous equation models. The MODEL procedure includes the following features:

- nonlinear regression analysis for systems of simultaneous equations, including weighted nonlinear regression
- full range of parameter estimation methods including
  - nonlinear ordinary least squares (OLS)
  - nonlinear seemingly unrelated regression (SUR)
  - nonlinear two-stage least squares (2SLS)
  - nonlinear three-stage least squares (3SLS)
  - iterated SUR
  - iterated 3SLS
  - generalized method of moments (GMM)
  - nonlinear full information maximum likelihood (FIML)
- supports dynamic multi-equation nonlinear models of any size or complexity
- uses the full power of the SAS programming language for model definition
- vector autoregressive error processes and polynomial lag distributions easily specified for the nonlinear equations
- computes goal-seeking solutions of nonlinear systems to find input values needed to produce target outputs
- dynamic, static, or n-period-ahead-forecast simulation modes
- simultaneous solution or single equation solution modes
- Monte Carlo simulation using parameter estimate covariance and across-equation residuals covariance matrices or user specified random functions
- a variety of diagnostic statistics including
  - model R^2 statistics
  - Durbin-Watson statistics
  - asymptotic standard errors and T tests

  - first stage R^2 statistics
  - covariance estimates
  - collinearity diagnostics
  - simulation goodness-of-fit statistics
  - Theil inequality coefficient decompositions
  - Theil relative change forecast error measures
- block structure and dependency structure analysis for the nonlinear system
- listing and cross reference of fitted model
- automatic calculation of needed derivatives using exact analytic formula
- efficient sparse matrix methods used for model solution; choice of other solution methods
- model definition, parameter estimation, simulation, and forecasting may be performed interactively in a single SAS session or models can also be stored in files and reused and combined in later runs

ARIMA (Box-Jenkins) and ARIMAX (Box-Tiao) Modeling and Forecasting

The ARIMA procedure provides the identification, parameter estimation, and forecasting of autoregressive integrated moving average (Box-Jenkins) models, seasonal ARIMA models, transfer function models, and intervention models. The ARIMA procedure includes the following features:

- complete ARIMA (Box-Jenkins) modeling with no limits on the order of autoregressive or moving average processes
- model identification diagnostics, including plots of the following functions:
  - autocorrelation
  - partial autocorrelation
  - inverse autocorrelation
  - cross-correlation
- intervention analysis
- regression with ARMA errors
- transfer function modeling with fully general rational transfer functions
- seasonal ARIMA models
- ARIMA model-based interpolation of missing values
- several parameter estimation methods including
  - exact maximum likelihood
  - conditional least squares
  - exact nonlinear unconditional least squares
- forecasts and confidence limits for all models
- forecasting tied to parameter estimation methods: finite memory forecasts for models estimated by maximum likelihood or exact nonlinear least squares methods and infinite memory forecasts for models estimated by conditional least squares
- a variety of model diagnostic statistics including
  - Akaike's information criterion (AIC)
  - Schwarz's Bayesian criterion (SBC or BIC)

- Box-Ljung chi-square test statistics for white noise residuals
- autocorrelation function of residuals
- partial autocorrelation function of residuals
- inverse autocorrelation function of residuals

The %DFTEST macro performs Dickey-Fuller tests for simple unit roots or seasonal unit roots in a time series. The %DFTEST macro is useful to test for stationarity and determine the order of differencing needed for the ARIMA modeling of a time series.

State Space Modeling and Forecasting

The STATESPACE procedure provides automatic model selection, parameter estimation, and forecasting of state space models. (*State space models* encompass an alternative general formulation of multivariate ARIMA models.) The STATESPACE procedure includes the following features:

- multivariate ARIMA modeling using the general state space representation of the stochastic process
- automatic model selection using Akaike's information criterion (AIC)
- user-specified state space models including restrictions
- transfer function models with random inputs
- any combination of simple and seasonal differencing; input series can be differenced to any order for any lag lengths
- forecasts with confidence limits
- can save selected and fitted model in a data set and reuse for forecasting
- wide range of output options; print any statistics concerning the data and their co-variance structure, the model selection process, and the final model fit

Spectral Analysis

The SPECTRA procedure provides spectral analysis and cross-spectral analysis of time series. The SPECTRA procedure includes the following features:

- efficient calculation of periodogram and smoothed periodogram using fast finite Fourier transform and Chirp algorithms
- multiple spectral analysis, including raw and smoothed spectral and cross-spectral function estimates, with user-specified window weights
- outputs the following spectral estimates to a SAS data set:
  - Fourier sine and cosine coefficients
  - periodogram
  - smoothed periodogram
  - cospectrum
  - quadrature spectrum
  - amplitude
  - phase spectrum
  - squared coherency
- Fisher's Kappa and Bartlett's Kolmogorov-Smirnov test statistic for testing a null hypothesis of white noise

Seasonal Adjustment Using X-11 and X-11 ARIMA Methods

The X11 procedure provides seasonal adjustment of time series using the Census X-11 or X-11 ARIMA method. The X11 procedure is based on the U.S. Bureau of the Census X-11 seasonal adjustment program and also supports the X-11 ARIMA method developed by Statistics Canada. The X11 procedure includes the following features:

- decomposition of monthly or quarterly series into seasonal, trend, trading day, and irregular components
- both multiplicative and additive form of the decomposition
- includes all the features of the Census Bureau program
- supports the X-11 ARIMA method
- processes any number of variables at once with no maximum length for a series
- can optionally print or store in SAS data sets the individual X11 tables showing the various components at different stages of the computation. Full control over what is printed or output
- can project seasonal component one year ahead enabling reintroduction of seasonal factors for an extrapolated series

Time Series Cross-Sectional Regression Analysis

The TSCSREG procedure provides combined time series cross-sectional regression analysis. The TSCSREG procedure includes the following features:

- estimation of the regression parameters under three common error structures:
    - Fuller and Battese method (variance component model)
    - Parks method (autoregressive model)
    - Da Silva method (mixed variance component moving-average model)
- any number of model specifications
- variety of estimates and statistics including
    - underlying error components estimates
    - regression parameter estimates
    - standard errors of estimates
    - *t*-tests
    - degrees of freedom
    - correlation matrix of estimates
    - covariances matrix of estimates
    - autoregressive parameter estimate
    - cross-sectional components estimates
    - autocovariance estimates

This procedure is a translation of the procedure written by D. Drummond and A. R. Gallant and available in the SUGI Supplemental Library for Version 5 and earlier releases of the SAS system.

Automatic Time Series Forecasting

The FORECAST procedure provides forecasting of univariate time series using automatic trend extrapolation. PROC FORECAST is an easy-to-use procedure for automatic forecasting that uses simple popular methods that do not require statistical modeling of the time series, such as exponential smoothing, time trend with autoregressive errors, and the Holt-Winters method.

The FORECAST procedure supplements the powerful forecasting capabilities of the econometric and time series analysis procedures described above. You can use PROC FORECAST when you have many series to forecast and want to extrapolate trends without going to the trouble of developing a model for each series.

The FORECAST procedure includes the following features:

- choice of the following four forecasting methods:
  - exponential smoothing: single, double, triple, or Holt two-parameter smoothing
  - stepwise autoregressive models with constant, linear, or quadratic trend and autoregressive errors to any order
  - Holt-Winters forecasting method with constant, linear, or quadratic trend
  - additive variant of the Holt-Winters method
- support for up to three levels of seasonality for Holt-Winters method: time-of-year, day-of-week, or time-of-day
- ability to forecast any number of variables at once
- forecast confidence limits for all methods

Time Series Interpolation and Frequency Conversion

The EXPAND procedure provides time interval conversion and missing value interpolation for time series. The EXPAND procedure includes the following features:

- conversion of time series frequency; for example, constructing quarterly estimates from annual series or aggregating quarterly values to annual values
- conversion of irregular observations to periodic estimates
- interpolation of missing values in time series
- conversion of observation types; for example, estimate stocks from flows and vice versa. All possible conversions supported between
  - beginning of period
  - end of period
  - period midpoint
  - period total
  - period average
- conversion of time series phase shift; for example, conversion between fiscal years and calendar years
- choice of four interpolation methods:
  - cubic splines
  - linear splines
  - step functions
  - simple aggregation

- ability to transform series before and after interpolation (or without interpolation) using any combination of the following:
  - shift by constant
  - scale by constant
  - change sign
  - absolute value
  - reciprocate
  - logarithm
  - exponential
  - square root
  - square
  - logistic
  - inverse logistic
  - upper bounds
  - lower bounds
  - lags
  - leads
  - differences
  - cumulative sum
  - moving sum
  - moving average
  - reverse series

- support for a wide range of time series frequencies:
  - YEAR
  - SEMIYEAR
  - QUARTER
  - MONTH
  - SEMIMONTH
  - TENDAY
  - WEEK
  - WEEKDAY
  - DAY
  - HOUR
  - MINUTE
  - SECOND

- The basic interval types can be repeated or shifted to define a great variety of different frequencies, such as fiscal years, biennial periods, work shifts, and so forth.

Access to Financial and Economic Databases

The DATASOURCE procedure provides a convenient way to read time series data from data files supplied by a variety of different commercial and governmental data vendors. The DATASOURCE procedure includes the following features:

- support for data files distributed by the following data vendors:
  - Citicorp Database Services (CITIBASE)
  - Haver Analytics
  - Standard & Poors Compustat Service
  - Center for Research in Security Prices (CRSP)
  - International Monetary Fund
  - U.S. Bureau of Labor Statistics
  - U.S. Bureau of Economic Analysis
  - Organization for Economic Cooperation and Development (OECD)
- ability to select the series, time range, and cross sections of data extracted
- can create an output data set containing descriptive information on the series available in the data file
- can read EBCDIC tapes on ASCII systems and vice versa

The CITIBASE procedure provides a convenient way to read time series from CITIBASE data files and Haver Analytics data files. The CITIBASE procedure has been superseded by the DATASOURCE procedure but is supported for compatibility with previous releases of SAS/ETS software. The CITIBASE procedure includes the following features:

- reads CITIBASE or Haver Analytics database files and creates SAS data sets containing annual, quarterly, monthly, or weekly data series
- reads both tape and diskette format CITIBASE files
- reads EBCDIC tapes on ASCII systems and vice versa
- ability to select the series and the time range read
- optionally creates an output data set containing descriptive information

Spreadsheet Calculations and Financial Report Generation

The COMPUTAB procedure generates tabular reports using a programmable data table.

The COMPUTAB procedure is especially useful when you need both the power of a programmable spreadsheet and a report generation system, and you want to set up a program to run in batch mode and generate routine reports. The COMPUTAB procedure includes the following features:

- report generation facility for creating tabular reports such as income statements, balance sheets, and other row and column reports for analyzing business or time series data
- can tailor report format to almost any desired specification
- uses the SAS programming language to provide complete control of the calculation and format of each item of the report
- reports definition in terms of a data table on which programming statements operate
- a single reference to a row or column brings the entire row or column into a calculation
- can create new rows and columns (such as totals, subtotals, and ratios) with a single programming statement
- access to individual table values is available when needed
- built-in features to provide consolidation reports over summarization variables

Loan Analysis, Comparison, and Amortization

The LOAN procedure provides analysis and comparison of mortgages and other installment loans. The LOAN procedure includes the following features:

- contract terms for any number of different loans may be input and various financing alternatives analyzed and compared
- analysis of four different types of loan contracts including
  - fixed rate
  - buydown rate
  - adjustable rate
  - balloon payment
- full control over adjustment terms for adjustable rate loans: life caps, adjustment frequency, and maximum and minimum rates
- support for a wide variety of payment and compounding intervals
- loan calculations can incorporate initialization costs, discount points, down payments, and prepayments (uniform or lump-sum)
- analysis of different rate adjustment scenarios for variable rate loans including
  - worst case
  - fixed rate case
  - best case
  - estimated case
- can make loan comparisons at different points in time
- can make loan comparisons at each analysis date on the basis of five different economic criteria
  - present worth of cost (net present value of all payments to date)
  - true interest rate (internal rate of return to date)

- current periodic payment
- total interest paid to date
- outstanding balance
- can base loan comparisons on either after-tax or before-tax analysis
- reports best alternative when loans of equal amount are compared
- amortization schedules for each loan contract
- when starting date is specified, output shows payment dates rather than just payment sequence numbers
- can optionally print or output to SAS data sets the amortization schedules, loan summaries, and loan comparison information
- can specify rounding of payments to any number of decimal places

The MORTGAGE procedure provides amortization schedules for fixed rate mortgages. The MORTGAGE procedure has been superseded by the LOAN procedure but is supported for compatibility with previous releases of SAS/ETS software. The MORTGAGE procedure includes the following features:

- fixed rate mortgage calculations and amortization schedules
- loan amount, payment, interest rate, or length of loan computed given the other three items
- supports a wide variety of payment and compounding intervals
- payment schedule with principal and interest division and ending balance printed or output to a data set

Related SAS Software

Many features not found in SAS/ETS software are available in other parts of the SAS System. If you don't find something you need in SAS/ETS software, try looking for the feature in the following SAS software products.

Base SAS Software

The features provided by SAS/ETS software are in addition to the features provided by base SAS software. Many data management and reporting capabilities you will need are part of base SAS software. Refer to *SAS Language: Reference* and the *SAS Procedures Guide* for documentation of base SAS software.

The following sections summarize base SAS software features of interest to users of SAS/ETS software. See Chapter 2 for further discussion of some of these topics as they relate to time series data and SAS/ETS software.

SAS DATA Step

The DATA step is your primary tool for reading and processing data in the SAS System. The DATA step provides a powerful general purpose programming language that enables you to perform all kinds of data processing tasks. The DATA step is documented in *SAS Language: Reference*.

Base SAS Procedures

Base SAS software includes many useful SAS procedures. Base SAS procedures are documented in the *SAS Procedures Guide*. The following is a list of base SAS procedures you may find useful:

CATALOG	for managing SAS catalogs
CHART	for printing charts and histograms
COMPARE	for comparing SAS data sets
CONTENTS	for displaying the contents of SAS data sets
COPY	for copying SAS data sets
CORR	for computing correlations
CPORT	for moving SAS data libraries between computer systems
DATASETS	for deleting or renaming SAS data sets
FREQ	for computing frequency crosstabulations
PLOT	for printing scatter plots
PRINT	for printing SAS data sets
RANK	for computing rankings or order statistics
SORT	for sorting SAS data sets
SQL	for processing SAS data sets with Structured Query Language
STANDARD	for standardizing variables to a fixed mean and variance
MEANS	for computing descriptive statistics and summarizing or collapsing data over cross sections
TABULATE	for printing descriptive statistics in tabular format
TIMEPLOT	for plotting variables over time
TRANSPOSE	for transposing SAS data sets
UNIVARIATE	for computing descriptive statistics

Global Statements

Global statements can be specified anywhere in your SAS program, and they remain in effect until changed. Global statements are documented in *SAS Language: Reference*. You may find the following SAS global statements useful:

FILENAME	for accessing data files
FOOTNOTE	for printing footnote lines at the bottom of each page
%INCLUDE	for including files of SAS statements
LIBNAME	for accessing SAS data libraries
OPTIONS	for setting various SAS system options
RUN	for executing the preceding SAS statements

TITLE   for printing title lines at the top of each page

X   for issuing host operating system commands from within your SAS session

Some base SAS statements can be used with any SAS procedure, including SAS/ETS procedures. These statements are not global, and they only affect the SAS procedure they are used with. These statements are documented in *SAS Language: Reference*.

The following base SAS statements are useful with SAS/ETS procedures:

BY   for computing separate analyses for groups of observations

FORMAT   for assigning formats to variables

LABEL   for assigning descriptive labels to variables

WHERE   for subsetting data to restrict the range of data processed or to select or exclude observations from the analysis

SAS Functions

SAS functions can be used in DATA step programs and in the COMPUTAB and MODEL procedures. The following kinds of functions are available:

- character functions for manipulating character strings
- date and time functions, for performing date and calendar calculations
- financial functions, for performing financial calculations such as depreciation, net present value, periodic savings, and internal rate of return
- lagging and differencing functions, for computing lags and differences
- mathematical functions, for computing data transformations and other mathematical calculations
- probability functions, for computing quantiles of statistical distributions and the significance of test statistics
- random number functions, for simulation experiments
- sample statistics functions, for computing means, standard deviations, kurtosis, and so forth

SAS functions are documented in *SAS Language: Reference*. Chapter 2 discusses the use of date and time and lagging and differencing functions. Chapter 21, "Date Intervals, Formats, and Functions," contains a reference list of date and time functions.

Formats, Informats, and Time Intervals

Base SAS software provides formats to control the printing of data values, informats to read data values, and time intervals to define the frequency of time series. See Chapter 21 for more information.

SAS/GRAPH Software

SAS/GRAPH software includes procedures that create two- and three-dimensional high resolution color graphics plots and charts. You can generate output that graphs the relationship of data values to one another, enhance existing graphs, or simply create graphics output that is not tied to data. SAS/GRAPH software can produce

- charts
- plots
- maps
- text
- three-dimensional graphs

With SAS/GRAPH software you can produce high-resolution color graphics plots of time series data.

SAS/STAT Software

SAS/STAT software includes procedures for a wide range of statistical methodologies including

- logistic regression
- censored regression
- principal component analysis
- structural equation models using covariance structure analysis
- factor analysis
- survival analysis
- discriminant analysis
- cluster analysis
- categorical data analysis; log-linear and conditional logistic models
- general linear models
- mixed linear models
- generalized linear models
- response surface analysis

SAS/STAT software is of interest to users of SAS/ETS software because many econometric and other statistical methods not included in SAS/ETS software are provided in SAS/STAT software. The section "Econometric Methods in Other SAS Software" later in this chapter discusses these method in greater detail.

SAS/IML Software

SAS/IML software gives you access to a powerful and flexible programming language (Interactive Matrix Language) in a dynamic, interactive environment. The fundamental object of the language is a data matrix. You can use SAS/IML software interactively (at the statement level) to see results immediately, or you can store statements in a module and execute them later. The programming is dynamic because necessary activities such as memory allocation and dimensioning of matrices are done automatically.

You can access built-in operators and call routines to perform complex tasks such as matrix inversion or eigenvector generation. You can define your own functions and subroutines using SAS/IML modules. You can perform operations on an entire data matrix. For example, the statement

```
x=x+1;
```

can be used to add 1 to a single value X, or to add 1 to all elements of a matrix X.

You have access to a wide choice of data management commands. You can read, create, and update SAS data sets from inside SAS/IML software without ever using the DATA step.

SAS/IML software is of interest to users of SAS/ETS software because it enables you to program your own econometric and time series methods in the SAS System. It contains subroutines for time series operators and for general function optimization. If you need to perform a statistical calculation not provided as an automated feature by SAS/ETS or other SAS software, you can use SAS/IML software to program the matrix equations for the calculation.

SAS/INSIGHT Software

SAS/INSIGHT software is a highly interactive tool for data analysis. You can explore data through a variety of interactive graphs including bar charts, scatter plots, box plots, and three-dimensional rotating plots. You can examine distributions and perform parametric and nonparametric regression, analyze general linear models and generalized linear models, examine correlation matrixes, and perform principal component analyses. Any changes you make to your data show immediately in all graphs and analyses. You can also configure SAS/INSIGHT software to produce graphs and analyses tailored to the way you work.

SAS/INSIGHT software is an integral part of the SAS System. You can use it to examine output from a SAS procedure, and you can use any SAS procedure to analyze results from SAS/INSIGHT software.

SAS/INSIGHT software includes features for both displaying and analyzing data interactively. A data window displays a SAS data set as a table with columns of the table displaying variables and rows displaying observations. Data windows provide data management features for editing, transforming, subsetting, and sorting data. A graph window displays different types of graphs: bar charts, scatter plots, box plots, and rotating plots. Graph windows provide interactive exploratory techniques such as data brushing and highlighting. Analysis windows display statistical analyses in the form of graphs and tables. Analysis window features include

- univariate statistics
- robust estimates
- density estimates
- cumulative distribution functions

- theoretical quantile-quantile plots
- multiple regression analysis with numerous diagnostic capabilities
- general linear models
- generalized linear models
- smoothing spline estimates
- kernel density estimates
- correlations
- principal components

SAS/INSIGHT software may be of interest to users of SAS/ETS software for interactive graphical viewing of data, editing data, exploratory data analysis, and checking distributional assumptions.

SAS/CALC Software

SAS/CALC software provides all-purpose spreadsheet capabilities for information management. In addition to standard spreadsheet features, SAS/CALC software has an important advantage: its direct link to the SAS System. To define relationships among the rows and columns of the spreadsheet, you can use cell formulas or SAS/CALC software's own programming language (similar to the DATA step language). SAS/CALC software can transform SAS data sets into spreadsheets and create SAS data sets from spreadsheets for further processing by other SAS procedures or a DATA step.

You can build two- and three-dimensional spreadsheet applications using features such as formulas, linked spreadsheets, what-if and goal-seeking analysis, and the powerful programming language. You can also review your links with the drilldown function. Function keys, the point and click and pull-down windowing enviroment, interface to SAS/AF software, and help windows make SAS/CALC software easy to use and easy to provide users with turnkey applications.

SAS/OR Software

SAS/OR software provides SAS procedures for operations research and project planning and includes a menu driven system for project management. SAS/OR software has features for

- solving transportation problems
- linear, integer, and mixed-integer programming
- nonlinear programming
- scheduling projects
- plotting Gantt charts
- drawing network diagrams
- solving optimal assignment problems
- network flow programming

SAS/OR software may be of interest to users of SAS/ETS software for its mathematical programming features. In particular, the NLP procedure in SAS/OR software solves nonlinear programming problems and can be used for constrained and unconstrained maximization of user-defined likelihood functions.

SAS/QC Software

SAS/QC software provides a variety of procedures for statistical quality control and quality improvement. SAS/QC software includes procedures for

- Shewhart control charts
- cumulative sum control charts
- moving average control charts
- process capability analysis
- Ishikawa diagrams
- Pareto charts
- experimental design

SAS/QC software also includes the SQC menu system for interactive application of statistical quality control methods and the ADX menu system for experimental design.

Econometric Methods in Other SAS Software

Many econometric methods overlap statistical methodology used in other fields. In the SAS System, these methods are included in SAS/STAT software. General function optimization tools are included in SAS/OR software and in SAS/IML software.

The following features of SAS/STAT software complement SAS/ETS software for econometric analysis.

Qualitative Dependent Variables and Logistic Regression

The LOGISTIC procedure in SAS/STAT software fits linear logistic regression models for binary or ordinal response data by the method of maximum likelihood. Subsets of explanatory variables can be chosen by various model-selection methods. Regression diagnostics can be displayed for the binary response model. The logit link function in the logistic regression models can be replaced by the normit (probit) function or the complementary log-log function.

Limited Dependent Variables and Censored Regression

The LIFEREG procedure in SAS/STAT software fits parametric models to failure time or other kinds of duration data that may be right-, left-, or interval-censored. The models for the response variable consist of a linear effect composed of the exogenous covariables together with a random disturbance term. The distribution of the random disturbance can be taken from a class of distributions that includes the extreme value, normal and logistic distributions and (by using a log transformation) exponential, Weibull, lognormal, loglogistic, and gamma distributions.

While PROC LIFEREG is tailored for survival analysis, the same kinds of censoring arises in econometric data. PROC LIFEREG is a powerful tool for censored regression, including Tobit analysis.

Cox Proportional Hazards Model

The PHREG procedure in SAS/STAT software performs regression analysis of survival or duration data based on the Cox proportional hazards model. Cox's semiparametric model is widely used in the analysis of survival time, failure time, or other duration data to explain the effect of exogenous explanatory variables.

The population under study may consist of a number of subpopulations, each of which has its own baseline hazard function. PROC PHREG performs a stratified analysis to adjust for such subpopulation differences. The Cox model also allows time-dependent explanatory variables. A time-dependent variable is one whose value for any given individual can change over time. Time-dependent variables have many useful applications in survival analysis.

PROC PHREG includes the following features:

- tests of linear hypotheses about the regression parameters
- conditional logistic regression analysis for matched case-control studies
- creates an output SAS data set containing survivor function estimates and residuals
- creates a SAS data set containing estimates of the survivor function at all event times for a given realization of the explanatory variables
- four model selection methods: forward selection, backward selection, stepwise selection, and best subset selection
- several methods for handling ties

PROC PHREG is also useful for the econometric analysis of discrete choice models.

Random Effects Models and the Analysis of Panel Data

SAS/STAT software contains two procedures for fitting general linear models to panel data. The GLM procedure fits general linear models involving fixed effects. The more general MIXED procedure fits mixed linear models containing both fixed and random effects.

The MIXED procedure provides easy accessibility to a variety of mixed models useful in many common statistical analyses, including split-plot designs, repeated measures, random coefficients, best linear unbiased predictions, shrinkage estimators, and heterogeneous variances. In the style of the GLM procedure, PROC MIXED fits the specified mixed linear model and produces appropriate statistics.

Some features of PROC MIXED are

- covariance structures, including simple random effects, compound symmetry, unstructured, AR(1), Toeplitz, and spatial
- syntax similar to that of PROC GLM, using the MODEL, RANDOM, and REPEATED statements for model specification, and the CONTRAST, ESTIMATE, and LSMEANS statements for inferences

- appropriate standard errors for all specified estimable linear combinations of fixed and random effects, and corresponding *t*- and *F*-tests
- subject and group effects that enable blocking and heterogeneity
- REML and ML estimation methods
- capacity to handle unbalanced data
- ability to create a SAS data set corresponding to any printed table

Covariance Structure Analysis of Linear Structural Models

The CALIS procedure (Covariance Analysis and Linear Structural Equations) in SAS/STAT software estimates parameters and tests the appropriateness of linear structural equation models using covariance structure analysis.

The CALIS procedure can be used to estimate parameters and test hypotheses for constrained and unconstrained problems such as

- multiple and multivariate linear regression
- path analysis and causal modeling
- simultaneous equations models with reciprocal causation
- exploratory and confirmatory factor analysis of any order
- three-mode factor analysis
- canonical correlation
- a wide variety of other linear and nonlinear latent variables models

Principal Components

The PRINCOMP procedure in SAS/STAT software performs principal components analysis. Output data sets containing eigenvalues, eigenvectors, and standardized or unstandardized principal components scores can be created.

MLE for User-Defined Likelihood Functions

There are three SAS procedures that enable you to do maximum likelihood estimation of parameters in an arbitrary model with a likelihood function that you define: PROC MODEL, PROC NLP, and PROC IML.

Maximum likelihood can often be cast as an equivalent least squares problem through the use of appropriate transformations. The MODEL procedure in SAS/ETS software enables you to minimize a sum of squares function. If you can write a sum of squares function that is minimized when the likelihood function is maximized, then you can use the MODEL procedure in SAS/ETS software.

The NLP procedure in SAS/OR software is a general nonlinear programming procedure that can maximize a general function subject to linear equality or inequality constraints. You can use PROC NLP to maximize a user-defined likelihood function.

You can use the IML procedure in SAS/IML software for maximum likelihood problems. The optimization routines used by PROC NLP are available through IML subroutines. You can write the likelihood function in the SAS/IML matrix language and call the nonlinear programming subroutines to maximize the likelihood function with respect to the parameter vector.

Other Statistical Tools

Many other statistical tools are available in base SAS, SAS/STAT, SAS/OR, SAS/QC, SAS/INSIGHT, and SAS/IML software. If you don't find something you need in SAS/ETS software, try looking in SAS/STAT software and in base SAS software. If you still don't find it, look in other SAS software products or contact the SAS Institute Technical Support staff.

References

Bailey, C.T. (1984), "Forecasting Industrial Production—1981–1984," *Proceedings of the Ninth Annual SAS Users Group International Conference*, 50–57. Cary, NC: SAS Institute Inc.

Benseman, B. (1990), "Better Forecasting with SAS/ETS Software," *Proceedings of the Fifteenth Annual SAS Users Group International Conference*, 494–497. Cary, NC: SAS Institute Inc.

Bireley, L.E. (1987), "Application of Intervention Analysis to Power Plant Monitoring Data," *Proceedings of the Twelfth Annual SAS Users Group International Conference*, 340–348. Cary, NC: SAS Institute Inc.

Brand, J. and Funk, J. (1985), "Forecasting Residential, Commercial, and Industrial Gas Demand," *Proceedings of the Tenth Annual SAS Users Group International Conference*, 92–97. Cary, NC: SAS Institute Inc.

Cardamone, P. and Brauer, D. (1987), "A SAS/ETS Software Forecasting and Inventory Planning System," *Proceedings of the Twelfth Annual SAS Users Group International Conference*, 313–318. Cary, NC: SAS Institute Inc.

Davis, S. (1984), "Predicting Prison Population with the SAS/ETS Product," *Proceedings of the Ninth Annual SAS Users Group International Conference*, 64–69. Cary, NC: SAS Institute Inc.

Dennis, R., Fraiman, N.M., and Mohl M. (1982), "Strategic Analysis for Commodity Hedging," *Proceedings of the Seventh Annual SAS Users Group International Conference*, 134–141. Cary, NC: SAS Institute Inc.

Early, J., Sweeney, J., and Zekavat, S.M. (1989), "PROC ARIMA and the Dow Jones Stock Index," *Proceedings of the Fourteenth Annual SAS Users Group International Conference*, 371–375. Cary, NC: SAS Institute Inc.

Hanumara, R.C. and Salzillo, M. (1986), "Use of SAS Software to Forecast Claims," *Proceedings of the Eleventh Annual SAS Users Group International Conference*, 82–87. Cary, NC: SAS Institute Inc.

Hisnanick, J.J. (1991), "Evaluating Input Separability in a Model of of the U.S. Manufacturing Sector," *Proceedings of the Sixteenth Annual SAS Users Group International Conference*, 688–693. Cary, NC: SAS Institute Inc.

Jacob, M.F. (1984), "Residential Energy Forecasting: A Pragmatic Application of Box-Jenkins," *Proceedings of the Ninth Annual SAS Users Group International Conference*, 44–49. Cary, NC: SAS Institute Inc.

Jacob, M.F. (1985), "A Time Series Approach to Modeling Daily Peak Electricity Demands," *Proceedings of the Tenth Annual SAS Users Group International Conference*, 44–49. Cary, NC: SAS Institute Inc.

Khan, M.H. (1990), "Transfer Function Model for Gloss Prediction of Coated Aluminum Using the ARIMA Procedure," *Proceedings of the Fifteenth Annual SAS Users Group International Conference*, 517–522. Cary, NC: SAS Institute Inc.

Le Bouton, K.J. (1989), "Performance Function for Aircraft Production Using PROC SYSLIN and L^2 Norm Estimation," *Proceedings of the Fourteenth Annual SAS Users Group International Conference*, 424–426. Cary, NC: SAS Institute Inc.

Lin, L. and Myers, S.C. (1988), "Forecasting the Economy using the Composite Leading Index, Its Components, and a Rational Expectations Alternative," *Proceedings of the Thirteenth Annual SAS Users Group International Conference*, 181–186. Cary, NC: SAS Institute Inc.

Parresol, B.R. and Thomas, C.E. (1991), "Econometric Modeling of Sweetgum Stem Biomass Using the IML and SYSLIN Procedures," *Proceedings of the Sixteenth Annual SAS Users Group International Conference*, 694–699. Cary, NC: SAS Institute Inc.

Starks, S.O., Elizandro, D.W., and Classen R.J. (1983), "Time Series Analysis of Highway Accident Data," *Proceedings of the Eighth Annual SAS Users Group International Conference*, 92–94. Cary, NC: SAS Institute Inc.

Chapter 2
Working with Time Series Data

Chapter Table of Contents

Chapter 2
Working with Time Series Data

This chapter discusses working with time series data in the SAS System. The following topics are included:

- dating time series and working with SAS date and datetime values
- subsetting data and selecting observations
- storing time series data in SAS data sets
- specifying time series periodicity and time intervals
- plotting time series
- using calendar and time interval functions
- computing lags and other functions across time
- transforming time series
- transposing time series data sets
- interpolating time series
- reading time series data recorded in different ways

In general, this chapter focuses on using features of the SAS programming language and not on features of SAS/ETS software. However, since SAS/ETS procedures are used to analyze time series, understanding how to use the SAS programming language to work with time series data is important for the effective use of SAS/ETS software.

You do not need to read this chapter to use SAS/ETS procedures. If you are already familiar with SAS programming you may want to skip this chapter, or you may refer to sections of this chapter for help on specific time series data processing questions.

Time Series and SAS Data Sets

Introduction

For you to analyze data with the SAS System, data values must be stored in a SAS data set. A SAS data set is a matrix of data values organized into variables and observations.

The *variables* in a SAS data set label the columns of the data matrix and the observations in a SAS data set are the rows of the data matrix. You can also think of a SAS data set as a kind of file, with the observations representing records in the file and the variables representing fields in the records. (Refer to *SAS Language: Reference, Version 6, First Edition* for more information about SAS data sets.)

Usually, each observation represents the measurement of one or more variables for the individual subject or item observed. Often, the values of some of the variables in the data set are used to identify the individual subjects or items that the observations measure. These identifying variables are referred to as *ID variables*.

For many kinds of statistical analysis, only relationships among the variables are of interest, and the identity of the observations does not matter. ID variables may not be relevant in such a case.

However, for time series data the identity and order of the observations are crucial. A time series is a set of observations made at a succession of equally spaced points in time.

For example, if the data are monthly sales of a company's product, the variable measured is sales of the product and the thing observed is the operation of the company during each month. These observations can be identified by year and month. If the data are quarterly gross national product, the variable measured is total production and the thing observed is the economy during each quarter. These observations can be identified by year and quarter.

For time series data, the observations are identified and related to each other by their position in time. Since the SAS system does not assume any particular structure to the observations in a SAS data set, there are some special considerations needed when storing time series in a SAS data set.

The main considerations are how to associate dates with the observations and how to structure the data set so that SAS/ETS procedures and other SAS procedures will recognize the observations of the data set as constituting time series. These issues are discussed in following sections.

Reading a Simple Time Series

Time series data can be recorded in many different ways. The section "Reading Time Series Data" later in this chapter discusses some of the possibilities. The following example shows a simple case.

The following SAS statements read monthly values of the U.S. Consumer Price Index for June 1990 through July 1991. The data set USCPI is shown in Figure 2.1.

```
data uscpi;
   input year month cpi;
cards;
90  6 129.9
90  7 130.4
90  8 131.6
90  9 132.7
90 10 133.5
90 11 133.8
90 12 133.8
91  1 134.6
91  2 134.8
91  3 135.0
91  4 135.2
91  5 135.6
91  6 136.0
91  7 136.2
;

proc print data=uscpi;
```

```
run;
```

```
        OBS    YEAR    MONTH    CPI
         1      90       6      129.9
         2      90       7      130.4
         3      90       8      131.6
         4      90       9      132.7
         5      90      10      133.5
         6      90      11      133.8
         7      90      12      133.8
         8      91       1      134.6
         9      91       2      134.8
        10      91       3      135.0
        11      91       4      135.2
        12      91       5      135.6
        13      91       6      136.0
        14      91       7      136.2
```

Figure 2.1. Time Series Data

When a time series is stored in observations of a variable in a SAS data set in the manner shown by this example, the terms *series* and *variable* can be used interchangeably.

Dating Observations

The SAS System supports special date, datetime, and time values, which make it easy to represent dates, perform calendar calculations, and identify the time period of observations in a data set.

The preceding example used the ID variables YEAR and MONTH to identify the time periods of the observations. For a quarterly data set, you might use YEAR and QTR as ID variables. A daily data set might have the ID variables YEAR, MONTH, and DAY. Clearly, it would be more convenient to have a single ID variable that could be used to identify the time period of observations, regardless of their frequency.

The following section, "SAS Date, Datetime, and Time Values," discusses how the SAS System represents dates and times internally and how to specify date, datetime, and time values in a SAS program. The section "Reading Date and Datetime Values with Informats" discusses how to control the display of date and datetime values in SAS output and how to read in date and time values from data records. Later sections discuss other issues concerning date and datetime values, specifying time intervals, data periodicity, and calendar calculations.

SAS date and datetime values and the other features discussed in the following sections are also described in *SAS Language: Reference*. Reference documentation on these features is also provided in Chapter 21, "Date Intervals, Formats, and Functions."

SAS Date, Datetime, and Time Values

SAS Date Values

The SAS System represents dates as a number of days since a reference date. The reference date, or date zero, used for SAS date values is 1 January 1960. Thus, for example, 3 February 1960 is represented by the SAS System as 33. The SAS date for 17 October 1991 is 11612.

Dates represented in this way are called SAS *date values*. Any numeric variable in a SAS data set whose values represent dates in this way is called a SAS *date variable*.

Representing dates as the number of days from a reference date makes it easy for the computer to store them and perform calendar calculations, but these numbers are not meaningful to users. However, you never have to use SAS date values directly, since SAS automatically converts between this internal representation and ordinary ways of expressing dates, provided that you indicate the format with which you want the date values to be displayed. (Formatting of date values is explained in a following section.)

SAS Date Constants

SAS date values are written in a SAS program by placing the dates in single quotes followed by a D. The date is represented by the day of the month, the three letter abbreviation of the month name, and the year.

For example, SAS reads the value '17OCT91'D the same as 11612, the SAS date value for 17 October 1991. Thus, the following SAS statements print DATE=11612.

```
data _null_;
  date = '17oct91'd;
  put date=;
run;
```

The year value can be given with two or four digits, so '17OCT91'D is the same as '17OCT1991'D. (The century assumed for a two-digit year value can be controlled with the YEARCUTOFF= option in the OPTIONS statement. Refer to the *SAS Language: Reference* for information on YEARCUTOFF=.)

SAS Datetime Values and Datetime Constants

To represent both the time of day and the date, the SAS System uses *datetime values*. SAS datetime values represent the date and time as the number of seconds the time is from a reference time. The reference time, or time zero, used for SAS datetime values is midnight, 1 January 1960. Thus, for example, the SAS datetime value for 17 October 1991 at 2:45 in the afternoon is 1003329900.

To specify datetime constants in a SAS program, write the date and time in single quotes followed by DT. To write the date and time in a SAS datetime constant, write the date part using the same syntax as for date constants, and follow the date part with the hours, the minutes, and the seconds, separating the parts with colons. The seconds are optional.

For example, in a SAS program you would write 17 October 1991 at 2:45 in the afternoon as '17OCT91:14:45'DT. SAS reads this as 1003329900. Table 2.1 shows some other examples of datetime constants.

Table 2.1. Examples of Datetime Constants

Datetime Constant	Time
'17OCT91:14:45:32'DT	32 seconds past 2:45 p.m., 17 October 1991
'17OCT91:12:5'DT	12:05 p.m., 17 October 1991
'17OCT91:2:0'DT	2 AM, 17 October 1991
'17OCT91:0:0'DT	midnight, 17 October 1991

SAS Time Values

The SAS System also supports *time values*. SAS time values are just like datetime values, except that the date part is not given. To write a time value in a SAS program, write the time the same as for a datetime constant but use T instead of DT. For example, 2:45:32 p.m. is written '14:45:32'T. Time values are represented by a number of seconds since midnight, so SAS reads '14:45:32'T as 53132.

SAS time values are not very useful for identifying time series, since usually both the date and the time of day are needed. Time values are not discussed further in this book.

Reading Date and Datetime Values with Informats

The SAS System provides a selection of *informats* for reading SAS date and datetime values from date and time values recorded in ordinary notations.

A SAS informat is a program that converts the values from a character string representation into the internal numerical value of a SAS variable. Date informats convert dates from ordinary notations used to enter them to SAS date values; datetime informats convert date and time from ordinary notation to SAS datetime values.

For example, the following SAS statements read monthly values of the U.S. Consumer Price Index. Since the data are monthly, you could identify the date with the variables YEAR and MONTH, as in the previous example. Instead, in this example the time periods are coded as a three-letter month abbreviation followed by the year. The informat MONYY is used to read month-year dates coded this way and to express them as SAS date values for the first day of the month, as shown in the following instream data:

```
data uscpi;
   input date monyy. cpi;
cards;
jun90 129.9
jul90 130.4
aug90 131.6
sep90 132.7
oct90 133.5
nov90 133.8
dec90 133.8
jan91 134.6
```

```
feb91 134.8
mar91 135.0
apr91 135.2
may91 135.6
jun91 136.0
jul91 136.2
;
```

The SAS System provides informats for most common notations for dates and times. See Chapter 21 for more information on the date and datetime informats available.

Formatting Date and Datetime Values

The SAS System provides *formats* to convert the internal representation of date and datetime values used by SAS to ordinary notations for dates and times. Several different formats are available for displaying dates and datetime values in most of the commonly used notations.

A SAS format is a program that converts the internal numerical value of a SAS variable to a character string that can be printed or displayed. Date formats convert SAS date values to a readable form; datetime formats convert SAS datetime values to a readable form.

In the preceding example, the variable DATE was set to the SAS date value for the first day of the month for each observation. If the data set USCPI were printed or otherwise displayed, the values shown for DATE would be the number of days since 1 January 1960. (See the DATE0 column in Figure 2.2.) To display date values appropriately, use the FORMAT statement.

The following example processes the data set USCPI to make several copies of the variable DATE and uses a FORMAT statement to give different formats to these copies. The format cases shown are the MONYY format (for the DATE variable), the DATE format (for the DATE1 variable), and no format (for the DATE0 variable). The PROC PRINT output in Figure 2.2 shows the effect of the different formats on how the date values are printed.

```
data fmttest;
   set uscpi;
   date0 = date;
   date1 = date;
   label date  = "DATE with MONYY. format"
         date1 = "DATE with DATE. format"
         date0 = "DATE with no format";
   format date monyy. date1 date.;
run;

proc print data=fmttest label;
run;
```

```
                   DATE with                            DATE with
                     MONYY.              DATE with         DATE.
         OBS         format       CPI    no format       format
          1          JUN90       129.9     11109         01JUN90
          2          JUL90       130.4     11139         01JUL90
          3          AUG90       131.6     11170         01AUG90
          4          SEP90       132.7     11201         01SEP90
          5          OCT90       133.5     11231         01OCT90
          6          NOV90       133.8     11262         01NOV90
          7          DEC90       133.8     11292         01DEC90
          8          JAN91       134.6     11323         01JAN91
          9          FEB91       134.8     11354         01FEB91
         10          MAR91       135.0     11382         01MAR91
```

Figure 2.2. SAS Date Values Printed with Different Formats

The appropriate format to use for SAS date or datetime valued ID variables depends on the sampling frequency or periodicity of the time series. Table 2.2 shows recommended formats for common data sampling frequencies and shows how the date '17OCT91'D or the datetime value '17OCT91:14:45:32'DT is displayed by these formats.

Table 2.2. Formats for Different Sampling Frequencies

ID values	Periodicity	FORMAT	Example
SAS Date	Annual	YEAR4.	1991
	Quarterly	YYQC6.	1991:4
	Monthly	MONYY7.	OCT1991
	Weekly	WEEKDATX23. DATE9.	Thursday, 17 Oct 1991 17OCT1991
	Daily	DATE9.	17OCT1991
SAS Datetime	Hourly	DATETIME10.	17OCT91:14
	Minutes	DATETIME13.	17OCT91:14:45
	Seconds	DATETIME16.	17OCT91:14:45:32

See Chapter 21 for more information on the date and datetime formats available.

The Variables DATE and DATETIME

SAS/ETS procedures enable you to identify time series observations any way you like. As discussed in preceding sections, you can use a combination of several ID variables, such as YEAR and MONTH for monthly data.

However, using a single SAS date or datetime ID variable is more convenient and enables you to take advantage of some features SAS/ETS procedures provide for processing dating variables. One such feature is automatic extrapolation of the ID variable to identify forecast observations. These features are discussed in following sections.

Thus, it is a good practice to include a SAS date or datetime ID variable in all the time series SAS data sets you create. It is also a good practice to always give the date or datetime ID variable a format appropriate for the data periodicity.

You can name a SAS date or datetime valued ID variable anything you like. However, you may find working with time series data in SAS easier and less confusing if you adopt the practice of always using the same name for the SAS date or datetime ID variable.

This book always names the dating ID variable "DATE" if it contains SAS date values or "DATETIME" if it contains SAS datetime values. This makes it easy to recognize the ID variable and also makes it easy to recognize whether this ID variable uses SAS date or datetime values.

Sorting by Time

Many SAS/ETS procedures assume the data are in chronological order. If the data are not in time order, you can use the SORT procedure to sort the data set. For example

```
proc sort data=a;
   by date;
run;
```

There are many ways of coding the time ID variable or variables, and some ways do not sort correctly. If you use SAS date or datetime ID values as suggested in the preceding section, you do not need to be concerned with this issue. But if you encode date values in nonstandard ways, you need to consider whether your ID variables will sort.

SAS date and datetime values always sort correctly, as do combinations of numeric variables like YEAR, MONTH, and DAY used together. Julian dates also sort correctly. (Julian dates are numbers of the form *yyddd*, where *yy* is the year and *ddd* is the day of the year. For example 17 October 1991 has the Julian date value 91290.)

Calendar dates such as numeric values coded as *mmddyy* or *ddmmyy* do not sort correctly. Character variables containing display values of dates, such as dates in the notation produced by SAS date formats, generally do not sort correctly.

Subsetting Data and Selecting Observations

It is often necessary to subset data for analysis. You may need to subset data to

- restrict the time range. For example, you want to perform a time series analysis using only recent data and ignoring observations from the distant past.

- select cross sections of the data. (See the section "Cross-sectional Dimensions and BY Groups" later in this chapter.) For example, you have a data set with observations over time for each of several states, and you want to analyze the data for a single state.

- select particular kinds of time series from an interleaved form data set. (See the section "Interleaved Time Series and the _TYPE_ Variable" later in this chapter.) For example, you have an output data set produced by the FORECAST procedure that contains both forecast and confidence limits observations, and you want to extract only the forecast observations.

- exclude particular observations. For example, you have an outlier in your time series, and you want to exclude this observation from the analysis.

You can subset data either by using the DATA step to create a subset data set or by using a WHERE statement with the SAS procedure that analyzes the data. Refer to *SAS Language: Reference* for information on the WHERE statement.

Subsetting SAS Data Sets

To create a subset data set, specify the name of the subset data set on the DATA statement, bring in the full data set with a SET statement, and specify the subsetting criteria with either subsetting IF statements or WHERE statements.

For example, suppose you have a data set containing time series observations for each of several states. The following DATA step uses a WHERE statement to exclude observations with dates before 1970 and uses a subsetting IF statement to select observations for the state NC:

```
data subset;
   set full;
   where date >= '1jan1970'd;
   if state = 'NC';
run;
```

In this case, it makes no difference whether the WHERE statement or the IF statement is used, and you can combine several conditions on one subsetting statement. The following statements produce the same results as the previous example:

```
data subset;
   set full;
   if date >= '1jan1970'd & state = 'NC';
run;
```

The WHERE statement acts on the input data sets specified in the SET statement before observations are processed by the DATA step program, whereas the IF statement is executed as part of the DATA step program. If the input data set is indexed, using the WHERE statement can be more efficient than using the IF statement. However, the WHERE statement can only refer to variables in the input data set, not to variables computed by the DATA step program.

To subset the variables of a data set, use KEEP or DROP statements or use KEEP= or DROP= data set options. Refer to *SAS Language: Reference* for information on KEEP and DROP statements and SAS data set options.

For example, suppose you want to subset the data set as in the preceding example, but you want to include in the subset data set only the variables DATE, X, and Y. You could use the following statements:

```
data subset;
   set full;
   if date >= '1jan1970'd & state = 'NC';
   keep date x y;
run;
```

Using the WHERE Statement with SAS Procedures

Use the WHERE statement with SAS procedures to process only a subset of the input data set. For example, suppose you have a data set containing monthly observations for each of several states, and you want to use the AUTOREG procedure to analyze data since 1970 for the state NC. You could use the following:

```
proc autoreg data=full;
   where date >= '1jan1970'd & state = 'NC';
   ... additional statements ...
run;
```

You can specify any number of conditions on the WHERE statement. For example, suppose that a strike created an outlier in May 1975, and you want to exclude that observation. You could use the following:

```
proc autoreg data=full;
   where date >= '1jan1970'd & state = 'NC'
       & date ^= '1may1975'd;
   ... additional statements ...
run;
```

Using SAS Data Set Options

You can use the OBS= and FIRSTOBS= data set options to subset the input data set. (These options cannot be used in conjunction with the WHERE statement.) For example, the following statements print observations 20 through 25 of the data set FULL.

```
proc print data=full(firstobs=20 obs=25);
run;
```

You can use KEEP= and DROP= data set options to exclude variables from the input data set. Refer to *SAS Language: Reference* for information on SAS data set options.

Storing Time Series in a SAS Data Set

This section discusses aspects of storing time series in SAS data sets. The topics discussed are the standard form of a time series data set, storing several series with different time ranges in the same data set, omitted observations, cross-sectional dimensions and BY groups, and interleaved time series.

Any number of time series can be stored in a SAS data set. Normally, each time series is stored in a separate variable. For example, the following statements augment the USCPI data set read in the previous example with values for the producer price index.

```
data usprice;
   input date monyy. cpi ppi;
   format date monyy.;
   label cpi = "Consumer Price Index"
         ppi = "Producer Price Index";
cards;
jun90 129.9 114.3
jul90 130.4 114.5
aug90 131.6 116.5
sep90 132.7 118.4
oct90 133.5 120.8
nov90 133.8 120.1
dec90 133.8 118.7
jan91 134.6 119.0
feb91 134.8 117.2
mar91 135.0 116.2
apr91 135.2 116.0
may91 135.6 116.5
jun91 136.0 116.3
jul91 136.2 116.0
;

proc print data=usprice;
run;
```

OBS	DATE	CPI	PPI
1	JUN90	129.9	114.3
2	JUL90	130.4	114.5
3	AUG90	131.6	116.5
4	SEP90	132.7	118.4
5	OCT90	133.5	120.8
6	NOV90	133.8	120.1
7	DEC90	133.8	118.7
8	JAN91	134.6	119.0
9	FEB91	134.8	117.2
10	MAR91	135.0	116.2
11	APR91	135.2	116.0
12	MAY91	135.6	116.5
13	JUN91	136.0	116.3
14	JUL91	136.2	116.0

Figure 2.3.   Time Series Data Set Containing Two Series

Standard Form of a Time Series Data Set

The simple way the CPI and PPI time series are stored in the USPRICE data set in the preceding example is termed the *standard form* of a time series data set. A time series data set in standard form has the following characteristics:

- The data set contains one variable for each time series.

- The data set contains one observation for each time period and contains only these observations.

- The data set contains an ID variable or variables that identify the time period of each observation.

- The data set is sorted by the dating ID variables, so the observations are in time sequence.

- The data are equally spaced in time. That is, successive observations are a fixed time interval apart, so the data set can be described by a single sampling interval such as hourly, daily, monthly, quarterly, yearly, and so forth. This means that time series with different sampling frequencies are not mixed in the same SAS data set.

Most SAS/ETS procedures that process time series expect the input data set to contain time series in this standard form, and this is the simplest way to store time series in SAS data sets. There are more complex ways to represent time series in SAS data sets.

You can incorporate cross-sectional dimensions with BY groups, so that each BY group is like a standard form time series data set. This method is discussed in the section "Cross-sectional Dimensions and BY Groups."

You can interleave time series, with several observations for each time period identified by another ID variable. Interleaved time series data sets are used to store several series in the same SAS variable. Interleaved time series data sets are often used to store series of actual values, predicted values, and residuals, or series of forecast values and confidence limits for the forecasts. This is discussed in the section "Interleaved Time Series and the _TYPE_ Variable" later in this chapter.

Several Series with Different Ranges

Different time series can have values recorded over different time ranges. Since a SAS data set must have the same observations for all variables, when time series with different ranges are stored in the same data set, missing values must be used for the periods in which a series is not available.

Suppose that in the previous example you did not record values for CPI before August 1990 and did not record values for PPI after June 1991. The USPRICE data set could be read with the following statements:

```
data usprice;
   input date monyy. cpi ppi;
   format date monyy.;
cards;
jun90      . 114.3
jul90      . 114.5
aug90 131.6 116.5
sep90 132.7 118.4
oct90 133.5 120.8
nov90 133.8 120.1
dec90 133.8 118.7
jan91 134.6 119.0
feb91 134.8 117.2
mar91 135.0 116.2
apr91 135.2 116.0
may91 135.6 116.5
jun91 136.0 116.3
jul91 136.2      .
;
```

The decimal points with no digits in the data records represent missing data and are read by the SAS System as missing value codes.

In this example, the time range of the USPRICE data set is June 1990 through July 1991, but the time range of the CPI variable is August 1990 through July 1991, and the time range of the PPI variable is June 1990 through June 1991.

SAS/ETS procedures ignore missing values at the beginning or end of a series. That is, the series is considered to begin with the first nonmissing value and end with the last nonmissing value.

Missing Values and Omitted Observations

Missing data can also occur within a series. Missing values that appear after the beginning of a time series and before the end of the time series are called *embedded missing values.*

Suppose that in the preceding example you did not record values for CPI for November 1990 and did not record values for PPI for both November 1990 and March 1991. The USPRICE data set could be read with the following statements:

```
data usprice;
   input date monyy. cpi ppi;
   format date monyy.;
cards;
jun90      . 114.3
jul90      . 114.5
aug90 131.6 116.5
sep90 132.7 118.4
oct90 133.5 120.8
nov90      .     .
dec90 133.8 118.7
jan91 134.6 119.0
feb91 134.8 117.2
mar91 135.0      .
apr91 135.2 116.0
may91 135.6 116.5
jun91 136.0 116.3
```

```
jul91 136.2     .
;
```

In this example, the series CPI has one embedded missing value, and the series PPI has two embedded missing values. The ranges of the two series are the same as before.

Note that the observation for November 1990 has missing values for both CPI and PPI; there is no data for this period. This is an example of a *missing observation.*

You might ask why the data record for this period is included in the example at all, since the data record contains no data. However, if the data record for November 1990 were deleted from the example, this would cause an *omitted observation* in the USPRICE data set. SAS/ETS procedures expect input data sets to contain observations for a contiguous time sequence. If you omit observations from a time series data set and then try to analyze the data set with SAS/ETS procedures, the omitted observations will cause errors. When all data are missing for a period, a missing observation should be included in the data set to preserve the time sequence of the series.

Cross-sectional Dimensions and BY Groups

Often, a collection of time series are related by a cross-sectional dimension. For example, the national average U.S. consumer price index data shown in the previous example can be disaggregated to show price indexes for major cities. In this case there are several related time series: CPI for New York, CPI for Chicago, CPI for Los Angeles, and so forth. When these time series are considered one data set, the city whose price level is measured is a cross-sectional dimension of the data.

There are two basic ways to store such related time series in a SAS data set. The first way is to use a standard form time series data set with a different variable for each series.

For example, the following statements read CPI series for three major U.S. cities:

```
data citycpi;
    input date monyy7. cpiny cpichi cpila;
    format date monyy7.;
cards;
nov1989   133.200   126.700   130.000
dec1989   133.300   126.500   130.600
jan1990   135.100   128.100   132.100
feb1990   135.300   129.200   133.600
mar1990   136.600   129.500   134.500
apr1990   137.300   130.400   134.200
may1990   137.200   130.400   134.600
jun1990   137.100   131.700   135.000
jul1990   138.400   132.000   135.600
;
```

The second way is to store the data in a time series cross-sectional form. In this form, the series for all cross sections are stored in one variable and a cross-section ID variable is used to identify observations for the different series. The observations are sorted by the cross-section ID variable and by time within each cross section.

The following statements indicate how to read the CPI series for U.S. cities in time series cross-sectional form:

```
data cpicity;
   input city $11. date monyy7. cpi;
   format date monyy7.;
cards;
Chicago       nov1989  126.700
Chicago       dec1989  126.500
Chicago       jan1990  128.100
Chicago       feb1990  129.200
Chicago       mar1990  129.500
Chicago       apr1990  130.400
Chicago       may1990  130.400
Chicago       jun1990  131.700
Chicago       jul1990  132.000
Los Angeles   nov1989  130.000
Los Angeles   dec1989  130.600
Los Angeles   jan1990  132.100
   ... etc. ...
New York      may1990  137.200
New York      jun1990  137.100
New York      jul1990  138.400
;

proc sort data=cpicity;
   by city date;
run;
```

When processing a time series cross-section-form data set with most SAS/ETS procedures, use the cross-section ID variable in a BY statement to process the time series separately. The data set must be sorted by the cross-section ID variable and sorted by date within each cross section. The PROC SORT step in the preceding example ensures that the CPICITY data set is correctly sorted.

When the cross-section ID variable is used in a BY statement, each BY group in the data set is like a standard form time series data set. Thus, SAS/ETS procedures that expect a standard form time series data set can process time series cross-sectional data sets when a BY statement is used, producing an independent analysis for each cross section.

It is also possible to analyze time series cross-sectional data jointly. The TSCSREG procedure expects the input data to be in the time series cross-sectional form described here. See Chapter 18, "The TSCSREG Procedure," for more information.

Interleaved Time Series and the _TYPE_ Variable

Normally, a time series data set has only one observation for each time period, or one observation for each time period within a cross section for a time series cross-sectional form data set. However, it is sometimes useful to store several related time series in the same variable when the different series do not correspond to levels of a cross-sectional dimension of the data.

In this case, the different time series can be interleaved. An interleaved time series data set is similar to a time series cross-sectional data set, except that the observations are sorted differently, and the ID variable that distinguishes the different time series does not represent a cross-sectional dimension.

Some SAS/ETS procedures produce interleaved output data sets. The interleaved time series form is a convenient way to store procedure output when the results consist of several different kinds of series for each of several input series. (Interleaved time series are also easy to process with plotting procedures. See the section "Plotting Time Series" later in this chapter.)

For example, the FORECAST procedure fits a model to each input time series and computes predicted values and residuals from the model. The FORECAST procedure then uses the model to compute forecast values beyond the range of the input data and also to compute upper and lower confidence limits for the forecast values.

Thus, the output from PROC FORECAST consists of five related time series for each variable forecast. The five resulting time series for each input series are stored in a single output variable with the same name as the input series being forecast. The observations for the five resulting series are identified by values of the ID variable _TYPE_. These observations are interleaved in the output data set with observations for the same date grouped together.

The following statements show the use of PROC FORECAST to forecast the variable CPI in the USCPI data set. Figure 2.4 shows part of the output data set produced by PROC FORECAST and illustrates the interleaved structure of this data set.

```
proc forecast data=uscpi interval=month lead=12
              out=foreout outfull outresid;
   var cpi;
   id date;
run;

proc print data=foreout;
run;
```

OBS	DATE	_TYPE_	_LEAD_	CPI
37	JUN91	ACTUAL	0	136.000
38	JUN91	FORECAST	0	136.146
39	JUN91	RESIDUAL	0	-0.146
40	JUL91	ACTUAL	0	136.200
41	JUL91	FORECAST	0	136.566
42	JUL91	RESIDUAL	0	-0.366
43	AUG91	FORECAST	1	136.856
44	AUG91	L95	1	135.723
45	AUG91	U95	1	137.990
46	SEP91	FORECAST	2	137.443
47	SEP91	L95	2	136.126
48	SEP91	U95	2	138.761

Figure 2.4. Output Data Set Produced by PROC FORECAST

Observations with _TYPE_=ACTUAL contain the values of CPI read from the input data set. Observations with _TYPE_=FORECAST contain one-step-ahead predicted values for observations with dates in the range of the input series, and contain forecast values for observations for dates beyond the range of the input series. Observations with _TYPE_=RESIDUAL contain the difference between the actual and one-step-ahead predicted values. Observations with _TYPE_=U95 and _TYPE_=L95 contain the upper and lower bounds of the 95% confidence interval for the forecasts.

Using Interleaved Data Sets as Input to SAS/ETS Procedures

Interleaved time series data sets are not directly accepted as input by SAS/ETS procedures. However, it is easy to use a WHERE statement with any procedure to subset the input data and select one of the interleaved time series as the input.

For example, to analyze the residual series contained in the PROC FORECAST output data set with another SAS/ETS procedure, include a WHERE_TYPE_='RESIDUAL'; statement. The following statements perform a spectral analysis of the residuals produced by PROC FORECAST in the preceding example:

```
proc spectra data=foreout out=spectout;
   var cpi;
   where _type_='RESIDUAL';
run;
```

Combined Cross Sections and Interleaved Time Series Data Sets

Interleaved time series output data sets produced from BY-group processing of time series cross-sectional input data sets have a complex structure combining a cross-sectional dimension, a time dimension, and the values of the _TYPE_ variable. For example, consider the PROC FORECAST output data set produced by the following statements:

```
data cpicity;
   input city $11. date monyy7. cpi;
   format date monyy7.;
cards;
Chicago      nov1989  126.700
Chicago      dec1989  126.500
Chicago      jan1990  128.100
   ... etc. ...
New York     may1990  137.200
New York     jun1990  137.100
New York     jul1990  138.400
;

proc sort data=cpicity;
   by city date;
run;

proc forecast data=cpicity interval=month lead=2
              out=foreout outfull outresid;
   var cpi;
   id date;
   by city;
run;
```

The output data set FOREOUT contains many different time series in the single variable CPI. BY groups identified by the variable CITY contain the result series for the different cities. Within each value of CITY, the actual, forecast, residual, and confidence limits series are stored in interleaved form, with the observations for the different series identified by the values of _TYPE_.

Output Data Sets of SAS/ETS Procedures

Some SAS/ETS procedures produce interleaved output data sets (like PROC FORE-CAST), while other SAS/ETS procedures produce standard form time series data sets. The form a procedure uses depends on whether the procedure is normally used to produce multiple result series for each of many input series in one step (as PROC FORECAST does).

For example, the ARIMA procedure can output actual series, forecast series, residual series, and confidence limit series just as the FORECAST procedure does. The PROC ARIMA output data set uses the standard form because PROC ARIMA is designed for the detailed analysis of one series at a time and so only forecasts one series at a time.

The following statements show the use of the ARIMA procedure to forecast the USCPI data set. Figure 2.5 shows part of the output data set produced by the ARIMA procedure's FORECAST statement. (The printed output from PROC ARIMA is not shown.) Compare the PROC ARIMA output data set shown in Figure 2.5 with the PROC FORECAST output data set shown in Figure 2.4.

```
proc arima data=uscpi;
    identify var=cpi(1);
    estimate q=1;
    forecast id=date interval=month lead=12 out=arimaout;
run;

proc print data=arimaout;
run;
```

OBS	DATE	CPI	FORECAST	STD	L95	U95	RESIDUAL
13	JUN91	136.0	136.078	0.36160	135.369	136.787	-0.07816
14	JUL91	136.2	136.437	0.36160	135.729	137.146	-0.23725
15	AUG91	.	136.574	0.36160	135.865	137.283	.
16	SEP91	.	137.042	0.62138	135.824	138.260	.

Figure 2.5. Output Data Set Produced by PROC ARIMA

The output data set produced by the ARIMA procedure's FORECAST statement stores the actual values in a variable with the same name as the input series, stores the forecast series in a variable named FORECAST, stores the residuals in a variable named RESIDUAL, stores the confidence limits in variables named L95 and U95, and stores the standard error of the forecast in the variable STD.

This method of storing several different result series as a standard form time series data set is simple and convenient. However, it only works well for a single input series. The forecast of a single series can be stored in the variable FORECAST, but if two series are forecast, two different FORECAST variables are needed.

The STATESPACE procedure handles this problem by generating forecast variable names FOR1, FOR2, and so forth. The SPECTRA procedure uses a similar method. Names like FOR1, FOR2, RES1, RES2, and so forth are awkward and require you to remember the order in which the input series are listed. This is why PROC FORE-

CAST, which is designed to forecast a whole list of input series at once, stores its results in interleaved form.

Other SAS/ETS procedures are often used for a single input series but can also be used to process several series in a single step. Thus, they are not clearly like PROC FORECAST nor clearly like PROC ARIMA in the number of input series they are designed to work with. These procedures use a third method for storing multiple result series in an output data set. These procedures store output time series in standard form (like PROC ARIMA does) but require an OUTPUT statement to give names to the result series.

The way different SAS/ETS procedures store result series in output data sets is summarized in Figure 2.6.

Procedures producing standard form output data sets with fixed names for result series:
- ARIMA
- SPECTRA
- STATESPACE

Procedures producing standard form output data sets with result series named by an OUTPUT statement:

- AUTOREG
- PDLREG
- SIMLIN
- SYSLIN
- X11

Procedures producing interleaved form output data sets:

- FORECAST
- MODEL

Figure 2.6.   Form of Output Data Set for SAS/ETS Procedures

See the chapters for these procedures for details on the output data sets they create.

Time Series Periodicity and Time Intervals

A fundamental characteristic of time series data is how frequently the observations are spaced in time. How often the observations of a time series occur is called the *sampling frequency* or the *periodicity* of the series. For example, a time series with one observation each month has a monthly sampling frequency or monthly periodicity and so is called a monthly time series.

In the SAS System, data periodicity is described by specifying periodic *time intervals* into which the dates of the observations fall. For example, the SAS time interval MONTH divides time into calendar months.

Several SAS/ETS procedures enable you to specify the periodicity of the input data set with the INTERVAL= option. For example, specifying INTERVAL=MONTH indicates that the procedure should expect the ID variable to contain SAS date values, and that the date value for each observation should fall in a separate calendar month. The EXPAND procedure uses interval name values with the FROM= and TO= options to control the interpolation of time series from one periodicity to another.

The SAS System also uses time intervals in several other ways. In addition to indicating the periodicity of time series data sets, time intervals are used with the interval functions INTNX and INTCK, and for controlling the plot axis and reference lines for plots of data over time.

Specifying Time Intervals

Time intervals are specified in SAS Software using *interval names* like YEAR, QTR, MONTH, DAY, and so forth. Table 2.3 summarizes the basic types of intervals.

Table 2.3. Basic Interval Types

Interval Name	Periodicity
YEAR	Yearly
SEMIYEAR	Semiannual
QTR	Quarterly
MONTH	Monthly
SEMIMONTH	1st and 16th of each month
TENDAY	1st, 11th, and 21st of each month
WEEK	Weekly
WEEKDAY	Daily ignoring weekend days
DAY	Daily
HOUR	Hourly
MINUTE	Every Minute
SECOND	Every Second

Interval names can be abbreviated in various ways. For example, you could specify monthly intervals as MONTH, MONTHS, MONTHLY, or just MON. The SAS System accepts all these forms as equivalent.

Interval names can also be qualified with a multiplier to indicate multiperiod intervals. For example, biennial intervals are specified as YEAR2.

Interval names can also be qualified with a shift index to indicate intervals with different starting points. For example, fiscal years starting in July are specified as YEAR.7.

Time intervals are classified as either date intervals or datetime intervals. Date intervals are used with SAS date values, while datetime intervals are used with SAS datetime values. The interval types YEAR, SEMIYEAR, QTR, MONTH, SEMIMONTH, TENDAY, WEEK, WEEKDAY, and DAY are date intervals. HOUR, MINUTE, and SECOND are datetime intervals. Date intervals can be turned into datetime intervals for use with datetime values by prefixing the interval name with 'DT'. Thus DTMONTH intervals are like MONTH intervals but are used with datetime ID values instead of date ID values.

See Chapter 21 for more information about specifying time intervals and for a detailed reference to the different kinds of intervals available.

Using Time Intervals with SAS/ETS Procedures

The ARIMA, FORECAST, and STATESPACE procedures use time intervals with the INTERVAL= option to specify the periodicity of the input data set. The EXPAND procedure uses time intervals with the FROM= and TO= options to specify the periodicity of the input and the output data sets. The DATASOURCE and CITIBASE procedures use the INTERVAL= option to control the periodicity of time series extracted from time series databases.

The INTERVAL= option (FROM= option for PROC EXPAND) is used with the ID statement to fully describe the observations that make up the time series. SAS/ETS procedures use the time interval specified by the INTERVAL= option and the ID variable in the following ways:

- to validate the data periodicity. The ID variable is used to check the data and verify that successive observations have valid ID values corresponding to successive time intervals.

- to check for gaps in the input observations. For example, if INTERVAL=MONTH and an input observation for January 1990 is followed by an observation for April 1990, there is a gap in the input data with two omitted observations.

- to label forecast observations in the output data set. The values of the ID variable for the forecast observations after the end of the input data set are extrapolated according to the frequency specifications of the INTERVAL= option.

Plotting Time Series

This section discusses SAS procedures available for plotting time series data. This section assumes you are generally familiar with SAS plotting procedures and only discusses certain aspects of the use of these procedures with time series data.

The GPLOT procedure produces high resolution color graphics plots. Refer to *SAS/GRAPH Software: Reference, Version 6, First Edition, Volume 1 and Volume 2* for information about the GPLOT procedure, SYMBOL statements, and other SAS/GRAPH features.

The PLOT procedure and the TIMEPLOT procedure produce low resolution line printer type plots. Refer to the *SAS Procedures Guide, Version 6, Third Edition* for information about these procedures.

Using PROC GPLOT

The following statements use the GPLOT procedure to plot CPI in the USCPI data set against DATE. (The USCPI data set was shown in a previous example; the data set plotted in the following example contains more observations than shown previously.) The SYMBOL statement is used to draw a smooth line between the plotted points and to specify the plotting character.

```
proc gplot data=uscpi;
    symbol i=spline v=star h=2;
    plot cpi * date;
run;
```

The plot is shown in Figure 2.7.

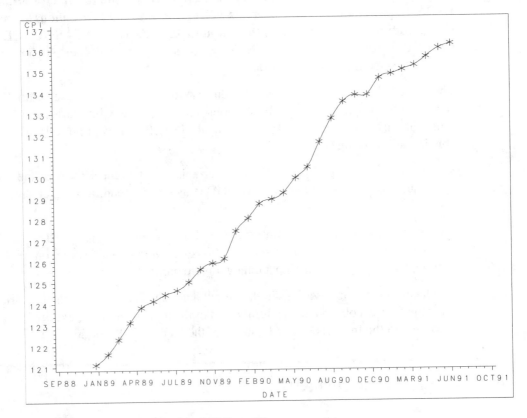

Figure 2.7. Plot of Monthly CPI Over Time

Controlling the Time Axis: Tick Marks and Reference Lines

In the preceding example, the spacing of values on the time axis looks a bit odd. Since DATE is a SAS date variable, the GPLOT procedure needs additional instruction on how to place the time axis tick marks.

The following statements use the HAXIS= option to tell PROC GPLOT to mark the axis at the start of each quarter. (The GPLOT procedure prints a warning message indicating that the intervals on the axis are not evenly spaced. This message simply reflects the fact that there is a different number of days in each quarter. This warning message can be ignored.)

```
proc gplot data=uscpi;
   symbol i=spline v=star h=2;
   plot cpi * date /
        haxis= '1jan89'd to '1jul91'd by qtr;
run;
```

The plot is shown in Figure 2.8.

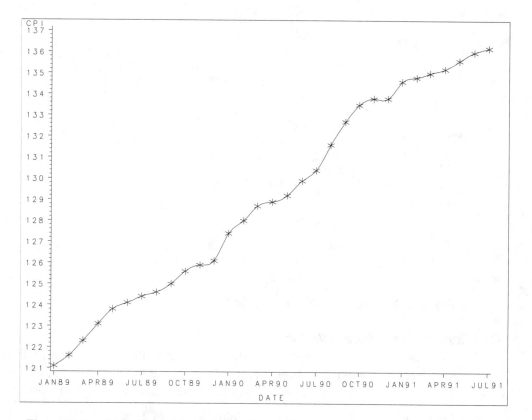

Figure 2.8. Plot of Monthly CPI Over Time

The following example changes the plot by using year and quarter value to label the tick marks. The FORMAT statement causes PROC GPLOT to use the YYQC format to print the date values. This example also shows how to place reference lines on the plot with the HREF= option. Reference lines are drawn to mark the boundary between years.

```
proc gplot data=uscpi;
   symbol i=spline v=star h=2;
   plot cpi * date /
        haxis= '1jan89'd to '1jul91'd by qtr
        href= '1jan90'd to '1jan91'd by year;
   format date yyqc4.;
run;
```

The plot is shown in Figure 2.9.

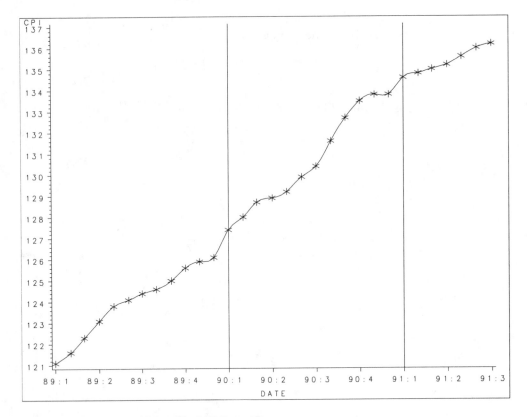

Figure 2.9. Plot of Monthly CPI Over Time

Overlay Plots of Different Variables

You can plot two or more series on the same graph. Plot series stored in different variables by specifying multiple plot requests on one PLOT statement, and use the OVERLAY option. Specify a different SYMBOL statement for each plot.

For example, the following statements plot the CPI, FORECAST, L95, and U95 variables produced by PROC ARIMA in a previous example. The SYMBOL1 statement is used for the actual series. Values of the actual series are labeled with a star, and the points are not connected. The SYMBOL2 statement is used for the forecast series. Values of the forecast series are labeled with an open circle, and the points are connected with a smooth curve. The SYMBOL3 statement is used for the upper and lower confidence limits series. Values of the upper and lower confidence limits points are not plotted, but a broken line is drawn between the points. A reference line is drawn to mark the start of the forecast period. Quarterly tick marks with MONYY format date values are used.

```
proc arima data=uscpi;
   identify var=cpi(1);
   estimate q=1;
   forecast id=date interval=month lead=12 out=arimaout;
run;

proc gplot data=arimaout;
   symbol1 i=none    v=star h=2;
   symbol2 i=spline v=circle h=2;
   symbol3 i=spline l=5;
   plot cpi * date = 1 forecast * date = 2 ( l95 u95 ) * date = 3 /
         overlay
         haxis= '1jan89'd to '1jul92'd by qtr
         href= '15jul91'd ;
run;
```

The plot is shown in Figure 2.10.

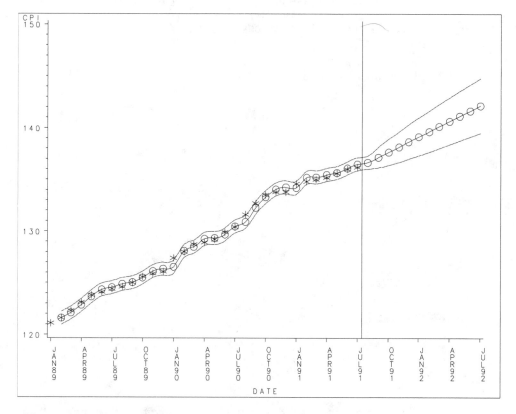

Figure 2.10.   Plot of ARIMA Forecast

Overlay Plots of Interleaved Series

You can also plot several series on the same graph when the different series are stored in the same variable in interleaved form. Plot interleaved time series by using the values of the ID variable to distinguish the different series and by selecting different SYMBOL statements for each plot.

The following example plots the output data set produced by PROC FORECAST in a previous example. Since the residual series has a different scale than the other series, it is excluded from the plot with a WHERE statement.

The _TYPE_ variable is used on the PLOT statement to identify the different series and to select the SYMBOL statements to use for each plot. The first SYMBOL statement is used for the first sorted value of _TYPE_, which is _TYPE_=ACTUAL. The second SYMBOL statement is used for the second sorted value of the _TYPE_ variable (_TYPE_=FORECAST), and so forth.

```
proc forecast data=uscpi interval=month lead=12
              out=foreout outfull outresid;
   var cpi;
   id date;
run;

proc gplot data=foreout;
   symbol1 i=none   v=star h=2;
   symbol2 i=spline v=circle h=2;
   symbol3 i=spline l=20;
   symbol4 i=spline l=20;
   plot cpi * date = _type_ /
       haxis= '1jan89'd to '1jul92'd by qtr
       href= '15jul91'd ;
   where _type_ ^= 'RESIDUAL';
run;
```

The plot is shown in Figure 2.11.

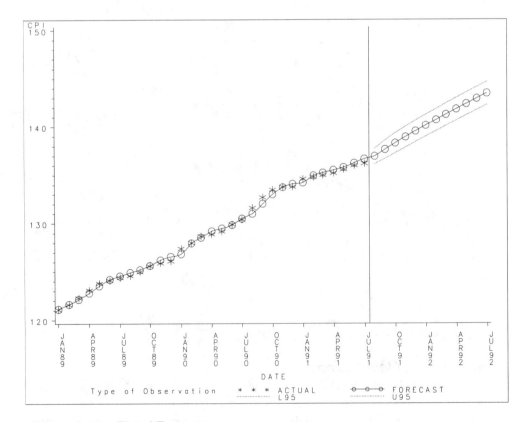

Figure 2.11.   Plot of Forecast

Residuals Plots

The following example plots the residuals series that was excluded from the plot in the previous example. The SYMBOL statement specifies a needle plot, so that each residual point is plotted as a vertical line showing deviation from zero.

```
proc gplot data=foreout;
   symbol1 i=needle width=6;
   plot cpi * date /
        haxis= '1jan89'd to '1jul91'd by qtr ;
   where _type_ = 'RESIDUAL';
run;
```

The plot is shown in Figure 2.12.

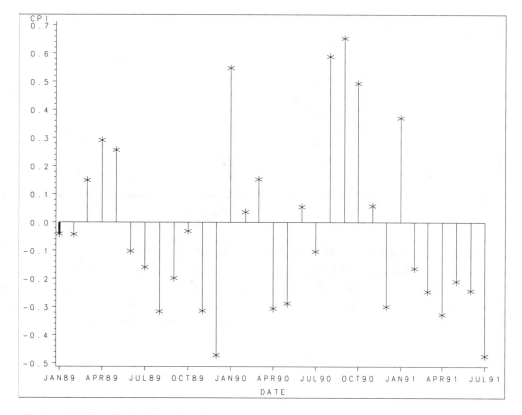

Figure 2.12. Plot of Residuals

Using PROC PLOT

The following statements use the PLOT procedure to plot CPI in the USCPI data set against DATE. (The data set plotted contains more observations than shown in the previous examples.) The plotting character used is a plus sign (+).

```
proc plot data=uscpi;
   plot cpi * date = '+';
run;
```

The plot is shown in Figure 2.13.

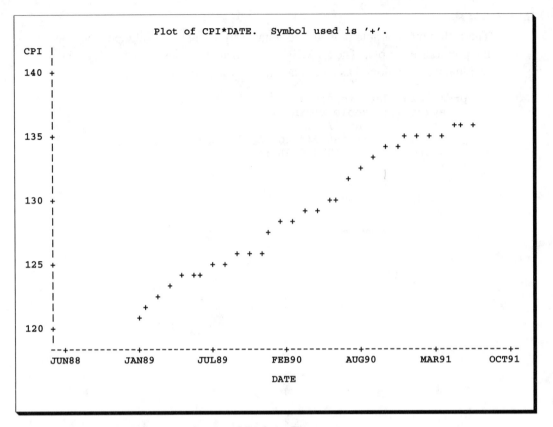

Figure 2.13. Plot of Monthly CPI Over Time

Controlling the Time Axis: Tick Marks and Reference Lines

In the preceding example, the spacing of values on the time axis looks a bit odd. Since DATE is a SAS date variable, the PLOT procedure needs additional instruction on how to place the time axis tick marks. The following statements use the HAXIS= option to tell PROC PLOT to mark the axis at the start of each quarter.

```
proc plot data=uscpi;
   plot cpi * date = '+' /
         haxis= '1jan89'd to '1jul91'd by qtr;
run;
```

The plot is shown in Figure 2.14.

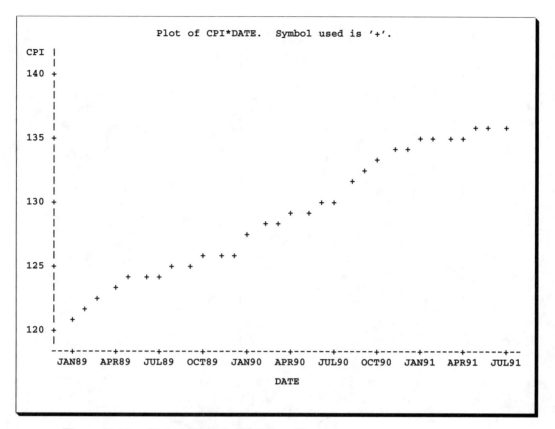

Figure 2.14. Plot of Monthly CPI Over Time

The following example improves the plot by placing tick marks every year and adds quarterly reference lines to the plot using the HREF= option. The FORMAT statement tells PROC PLOT to print just the year part of the date values on the axis. The plot is shown in Figure 2.15.

```
proc plot data=uscpi;
   plot cpi * date = '+' /
        haxis= '1jan89'd to '1jan92'd by year
        href=  '1apr89'd to '1apr91'd by qtr ;
   format date year4.;
run;
```

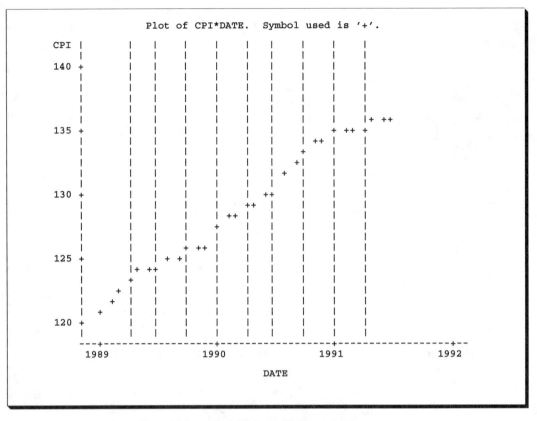

Figure 2.15. Plot of Monthly CPI Over Time

Marking the Subperiod of Points

In the preceding example, it is a little hard to tell which month each point is, although the quarterly reference lines help some. The following example shows how to set the plotting symbol to the first letter of the month name. A DATA step first makes a copy of DATE and gives this variable PCHAR a MONNAME1. format. The variable PCHAR is used in the PLOT statement to supply the plotting character.

This example also changes the plot by using quarterly tick marks and by using the YYQC format to print the date values. This example also changes the HREF= option to use annual reference lines. The plot is shown in Figure 2.16.

```
data temp;
   set uscpi;
   pchar = date;
   format pchar monname1.;
run;

proc plot data=temp;
   plot cpi * date = pchar /
        haxis= '1jan89'd to '1jul91'd by qtr
        href= '1jan90'd to '1jan91'd by year;
   format date yyqc4.;
run;
```

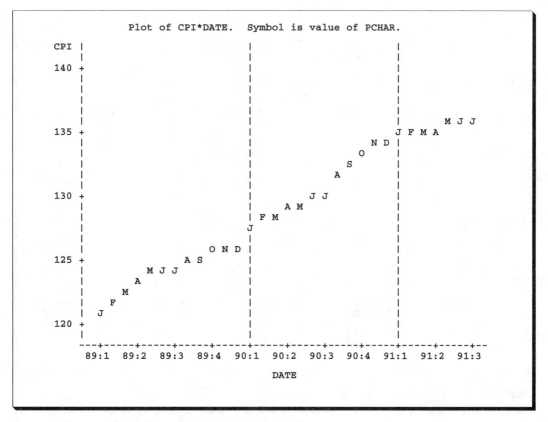

Figure 2.16. Plot of Monthly CPI Over Time

Overlay Plots of Different Variables

Plot different series in different variables by specifying the different plot requests, each with its own plotting character, on the same PLOT statement, and use the OVERLAY option.

For example, the following statements plot the CPI, FORECAST, L95, and U95 variables produced by PROC ARIMA in a previous example. The actual series CPI is labeled with the plot character plus (+). The forecast series is labeled with the plot character F. The upper and lower confidence limits are labeled with the plot character period (.). The plot is shown in Figure 2.17.

```
proc arima data=uscpi;
    identify var=cpi(1);
    estimate q=1;
    forecast id=date interval=month lead=12 out=arimaout;
run;

proc plot data=arimaout;
    plot cpi * date = '+' forecast * date = 'F'
        ( l95 u95 ) * date = '.' /
        overlay
        haxis= '1jan89'd to '1jul92'd by qtr
        href= '1jan90'd to '1jan92'd by year ;
run;
```

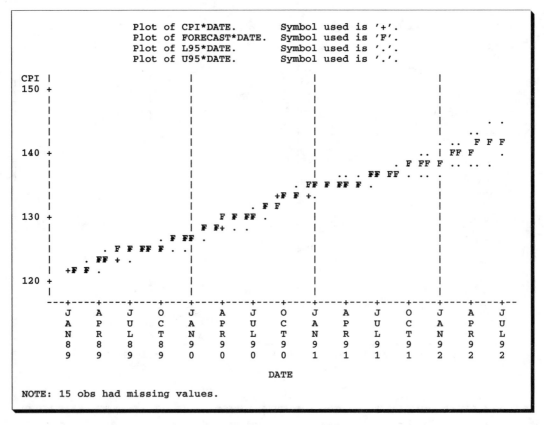

Figure 2.17. Plot of ARIMA Forecast

Overlay Plots of Interleaved Series

Plot interleaved time series by using the first character of the ID variable to distinguish the different series as the plot character.

The following example plots the output data set produced by PROC FORECAST in a previous example. The _TYPE_ variable is used on the PLOT statement to supply plotting characters to label the different series.

The actual series is plotted with A, the forecast series is plotted with F, the lower confidence limit is plotted with L, and the upper confidence limit is plotted with U. Since the residual series has a different scale than the other series, it is excluded from the plot with a WHERE statement. The plot is shown in Figure 2.18.

```
proc forecast data=uscpi interval=month lead=12
              out=foreout outfull outresid;
   var cpi;
   id date;
run;

proc plot data=foreout;
   plot cpi * date = _type_ /
        haxis= '1jan89'd to '1jul92'd by qtr
        href= '1jan90'd to '1jan92'd by year ;
   where _type_ ^= 'RESIDUAL';
run;
```

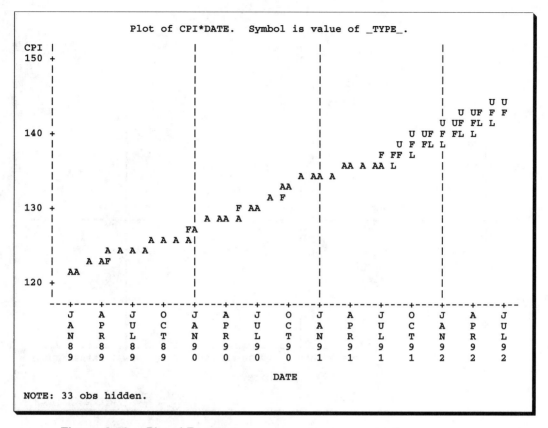

Figure 2.18. Plot of Forecast

Residuals Plots

The following example plots the residual series that was excluded from the plot in the previous example. The VREF=0 option is used to draw a reference line at 0 on the vertical axis. The plot is shown in Figure 2.19.

```
proc plot data=foreout;
   plot cpi * date = '*' /
        vref=0
        haxis= '1jan89'd to '1jul91'd by qtr
        href= '1jan90'd to '1jan91'd by year ;
   where _type_ = 'RESIDUAL';
run;
```

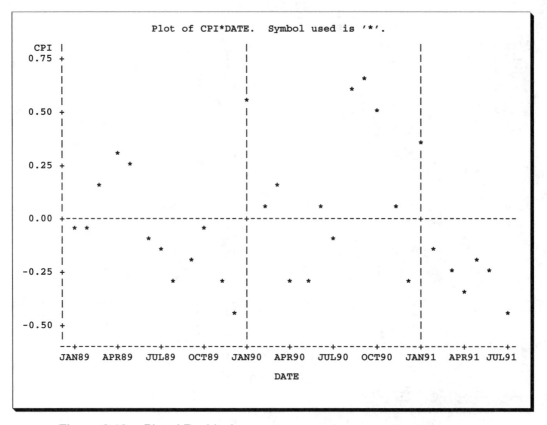

Figure 2.19. Plot of Residuals

Using PROC TIMEPLOT

The TIMEPLOT procedure plots time series data vertically on the page instead of horizontally across the page as the PLOT procedure does. PROC TIMEPLOT can also print the data values as well as plot them.

The following statements use the TIMEPLOT procedure to plot CPI in the USCPI data set. Only the last 14 observations are included in this example. The plot is shown in Figure 2.20.

```
proc timeplot data=uscpi;
   plot cpi;
   id date;
   where date >= '1jun90'd;
run;
```

```
 DATE         CPI      min                                                  max
                       129.9                                              136.2
                      *----------------------------------------------------*
 JUN90      129.90    |C                                                   |
 JUL90      130.40    |     C                                              |
 AUG90      131.60    |              C                                     |
 SEP90      132.70    |                       C                            |
 OCT90      133.50    |                            C                       |
 NOV90      133.80    |                              C                     |
 DEC90      133.80    |                              C                     |
 JAN91      134.60    |                                   C                |
 FEB91      134.80    |                                    C               |
 MAR91      135.00    |                                     C              |
 APR91      135.20    |                                      C             |
 MAY91      135.60    |                                        C           |
 JUN91      136.00    |                                          C  |
 JUL91      136.20    |                                             C|
                      *----------------------------------------------------*
```

Figure 2.20.   Output Produced by PROC TIMEPLOT

The TIMEPLOT procedure has several interesting features not discussed here. Refer to "The TIMEPLOT Procedure" in the *SAS Procedures Guide* for more information.

Calendar and Time Functions

Calendar and time functions convert calendar and time variables like YEAR, MONTH, DAY, and HOUR, MINUTE, SECOND into SAS date or datetime values, and vice versa.

The SAS calendar and time functions are DATEJUL, DATEPART, DAY, DHMS, HMS, HOUR, JULDATE, MDY, MINUTE, MONTH, QTR, SECOND, TIMEPART, WEEKDAY, YEAR, and YYQ. Refer to *SAS Language Reference* for more details about these functions.

Computing Dates from Calendar Variables

The MDY function converts MONTH, DAY, and YEAR values to a SAS date value. For example, MDY(10,17,91) returns the SAS date value '17OCT91'D.

The YYQ function computes the SAS date for the first day of a quarter. For example, YYQ(91,4) returns the SAS date value '1OCT91'D.

The DATEJUL function computes the SAS date for a Julian date. For example, DATEJUL(91290) returns the SAS date '17OCT91'D.

The YYQ and MDY functions are useful for creating SAS date variables when the ID values recorded in the data are year and quarter; year and month; or year, month, and day, instead of dates that can be read with a date informat.

For example, the following statements read quarterly estimates of the gross national product of the U.S. from 1990:I to 1991:II from data records on which dates are coded as separate year and quarter values. The YYQ function is used to compute the variable DATE.

```
data usecon;
   input year qtr gnp;
   date = yyq( year, qtr );
   format date yyqc.;
cards;
1990 1 5375.4
1990 2 5443.3
1990 3 5514.6
1990 4 5527.3
1991 1 5557.7
1991 2 5615.8
;
```

The monthly USCPI data shown in a previous example contained time ID values represented in the MONYY format. If the data records instead contain separate year and month values, the data can be read in and the DATE variable computed with the following statements:

```
data uscpi;
   input month year cpi;
   date = mdy( month, 1, year );
   format date monyy.;
cards;
6 90 129.9
7 90 130.4
8 90 131.6
 ... etc. ...
;
```

Computing Calendar Variables from Dates

The functions YEAR, MONTH, DAY, WEEKDAY, and JULDATE compute calendar variables from SAS date values.

Returning to the example of reading the USCPI data from records containing date values represented in the MONYY format, you can find the month and year of each observation from the SAS dates of the observations using the following statements.

```
data uscpi;
   input date monyy. cpi;
   format date monyy.;
   year  = year( date );
   month = month( date );
cards;
jun90 129.9
jul90 130.4
aug90 131.6
sep90 132.7
 ... etc. ...
;
```

Converting between Date, Datetime, and Time Values

The DATEPART function computes the SAS date value for the date part of a SAS datetime value. The TIMEPART function computes the SAS time value for the time part of a SAS datetime value.

The HMS function computes SAS time values from HOUR, MINUTE, and SECOND time variables. The DHMS function computes a SAS datetime value from a SAS date value and HOUR, MINUTE, and SECOND time variables.

Computing Datetime Values from Calendar and Time Variables

To compute datetime ID values from calendar and time variables, first compute the date and then compute the datetime with DHMS.

For example, suppose you read trihourly temperature data with time recorded as YEAR, MONTH, DAY, and HOUR. The following statements show how to compute the ID variable DATETIME:

```
data weather;
   input year month day hour temp;
   datetime = dhms( mdy( month, day, year ), hour, 0, 0 );
   format datetime datetime10.;
cards;
91 10 16 21  61
91 10 17  0  56
91 10 17  3  53
91 10 17  6  54
91 10 17  9  65
91 10 17 12  72
 ... etc. ...
;
```

Computing Calendar and Time Variables from Datetime Values

The functions HOUR, MINUTE, and SECOND compute time variables from SAS datetime values. The DATEPART function and the date-to-calendar variables functions can be combined to compute calendar variables from datetime values.

For example, suppose the date and time of the trihourly temperature data in the preceding example were recorded as datetime values in the datetime format. The following statements show how to compute the YEAR, MONTH, DAY, and HOUR of each observation and include these variables in the SAS data set:

```
data weather;
   input datetime datetime10. temp;
   format datetime datetime10.;
   hour = hour( datetime );
   date = datepart( datetime );
   year = year( date );
   month = month( date );
   day = day( date );
cards;
16oct91:21  61
17oct91:00  56
17oct91:03  53
17oct91:06  54
17oct91:09  65
17oct91:12  72
 ... etc. ...
;
```

Interval Functions INTNX and INTCK

The SAS interval functions INTNX and INTCK perform calculations with date and datetime values and time intervals. They can be used for calendar calculations with SAS date values, to count time intervals between dates, and to increment dates or datetime values by intervals.

The INTNX function increments dates by intervals. INTNX computes the date or datetime of the start of the interval a specified number of intervals from the interval containing a given date or datetime value.

The form of the INTNX function is

INTNX(*interval, from, n*)

where:

interval   is a character constant or variable containing an interval name

from   is a SAS date value (for date intervals) or datetime value (for datetime intervals)

n   is the number of intervals to increment from the interval containing the *from* value.

The number of intervals to increment, *n*, can be positive, negative, or zero.

For example, the statement NEXTMON = INTNX('MONTH',DATE,1); assigns to the variable NEXTMON the date of the first day of the month following the month containing the value of DATE.

The INTCK function counts the number of interval boundaries between two dates or between two datetime values.

The form of the INTCK function is

INTCK(*interval, from, to*)

where:

interval   is a character constant or variable containing an interval name

from   is the starting date (for date intervals) or datetime value (for datetime intervals)

to   is the ending date (for date intervals) or datetime value (for datetime intervals).

For example, the statement NEWYEARS = INTCK('YEAR',DATE1,DATE2); assigns to the variable NEWYEARS the number of New Year's Days between the two dates.

Incrementing Dates by Intervals

Use the INTNX function to increment dates by intervals. For example, suppose you want to know the date of the start of the week that is six weeks from the week of 17 October 1991. The function INTNX('WEEK','17OCT91'D,6) returns the SAS date value '24NOV1991'D.

One practical use of the INTNX function is to generate periodic date values. For example, suppose the monthly U.S. Consumer Price Index data in a previous example were recorded without any time identifier on the data records. Given that you know the first observation is for June 1990, the following statements use the INTNX function to compute the ID variable DATE for each observation:

```
data uscpi;
   input cpi;
   date = intnx( 'month', '1jun90'd, _n_-1 );
   format date monyy.;
cards;
129.9
130.4
131.6
132.7
 ... etc. ...
;
```

The automatic variable _N_ counts the number of times the DATA step program has executed, and in this case _N_ contains the observation number. Thus _N_-1 is the increment needed from the first observation date. Alternatively, we could increment from the month before the first observation, in which case the INTNX function in this example would be written INTNX('MONTH','1MAY90'D,_N_).

Normalizing Dates to the Start of a Time Interval

Any date within the time interval corresponding to an observation of a periodic time series can serve as an ID value for the observation. For example, the USCPI data in a previous example might have been recorded with dates at the 15th of each month. The person recording the data might reason that since the CPI values are monthly averages, midpoints of the months might be the appropriate ID values.

However, as far as SAS/ETS procedures are concerned, what is important about monthly data is the month of each observation, not the exact date of the ID value. If you indicate that the data are monthly (with an INTERVAL=MONTH) option, SAS/ETS procedures ignore the day of the month in processing the ID variable. The MONYY format also ignores the day of the month.

Thus, you could read in the monthly USCPI data with midmonth DATE values using the following statements:

```
data uscpi;
   input date date. cpi;
   format date monyy.;
cards;
15jun90 129.9
15jul90 130.4
15aug90 131.6
15sep90 132.7
 ... etc. ...
;
```

The results of using this version of the USCPI data set for analysis with SAS/ETS procedures would be the same as with first-of-month values for DATE. Although you can use any date within the interval as an ID value for the interval, you may find working with time series in SAS less confusing if you always use date ID values normalized to the start of the interval.

SAS/ETS procedures that extrapolate date values to identify forecast observations always produce normalized dates. The EXPAND procedure always uses normalized dates to identify interpolated observations.

To normalize date values to the start of intervals, use the INTNX function with a 0 increment. The INTNX function with an increment of 0 computes the date of the first day of the interval (or the first second of the interval for datetime values).

For example, INTNX('MONTH','17OCT91'D,0) returns the date '1OCT91'D .

The following statements show how the preceding example can be changed to normalize the mid-month DATE values to first-of-month values:

```
data uscpi;
   input date date. cpi;
   format date monyy.;
   date = intnx( 'month', date, 0 );
cards;
15jun90 129.9
15jul90 130.4
15aug90 131.6
15sep90 132.7
 ... etc. ...
 ;
```

Computing the Width of a Time Interval

To compute the width of a time interval, subtract the ID value of the start of the next interval from the ID value of the start of the current interval. If the ID values are SAS dates, the width will be in days. If the ID values are SAS datetime values, the width will be in seconds.

For example, the following statements show how to add a variable WIDTH to the USCPI data set that contains the number of days in the month for each observation:

```
data uscpi;
   input date date. cpi;
   format date monyy.;
   width = intnx( 'month', date, 1 ) - intnx( 'month', date, 0 );
cards;
15jun90 129.9
15jul90 130.4
15aug90 131.6
15sep90 132.7
 ... etc. ...
 ;
```

Computing the Ending Date or Midpoint of a Time Interval

To compute the ending date of an interval, compute the beginning date of the next interval and subtract 1. Since SAS dates are recorded as a number of days, subtracting 1 from a date value shifts the date back one day. For datetime values, subtracting 1 from the datetime of the start of the next interval gives the datetime of the last second in the interval.

For example, the following statements add the variable MONTHEND to the monthly USCPI data set:

```
data uscpi;
   set uscpi;
   monthend = intnx( 'month', date, 1 ) - 1;
   format monthend date.;
run;
```

To compute the midpoint date of an interval, you can average the date for the first day of the interval and the first day of the next interval. This may produce fractional date values.

For example, the following statements add the variable MIDMONTH to the monthly USCPI data set. The variable MIDMONTH gives the time point, with time measured in days since 1 January 1960, exactly in the middle of the month.

```
data uscpi;
   set uscpi;
   midmonth = ( intnx('month',date,1) + intnx('month',date,0) ) / 2;
run;
```

Since MIDMONTH is a point in time and not an exact date value, no format is given in this example. Date formats can be used for fractional date values; however, the formats ignore fractional parts of date values.

If you want to compute the date of a particular day within an interval, you can use calendar functions, or you can increment the starting date of the interval by a number of days. To compute the 15th day of the month, you can also use the INTNX function with the SEMIMONTH interval type. The following example shows four ways to compute the 15th day of the month:

```
data test;
   set uscpi;
   mon15_1 = mdy( month(date), 15, year(date) );
   date = intnx( 'month', date, 0 ); /* ensure date is normalized */
   mon15_2 = date + 14;
   mon15_3 = intnx( 'day', date, 14 );
   mon15_4 = intnx( 'semimonth', date, 1 ) - 1;
run;
```

Computing the Ceiling of an Interval

To shift a date to the start of the next interval if not already at the start of an interval, subtract 1 from the date and use INTNX to increment the date by 1 interval.

For example, the following statements add the variable NEWYEAR to the monthly USCPI data set. The variable NEWYEAR contains the date of the next New Year's Day. NEWYEAR contains the same value as DATE when the DATE value is the start of year and otherwise contains the date of the start of the next year.

```
data test;
   set uscpi;
   newyear = intnx( 'year', date - 1, 1 );
   format newyear date.;
run;
```

Counting Time Intervals

Use the INTCK function to count the number of interval boundaries between two dates.

Note that the INTCK function counts the number of times the beginning of an interval is reached in moving from the first date to the second. It does not count the number of complete intervals between two dates.

For example, the function INTCK('MONTH','1JAN91'D,'31JAN91'D) returns 0, since the two dates are within the same month.

The function INTCK('MONTH','31JAN91'D,'1FEB91'D) returns 1, since the two dates lie in different months that are one month apart.

When the first date is later than the second date, INTCK returns a negative count. For example, the function INTCK('MONTH','1FEB91'D,'31JAN91'D) returns -1.

The following example shows how to use the INTCK function to count the number of Sundays, Mondays, Tuesdays, and so forth, in each month. The variables NSUNDAY, NMONDAY, NTUESDAY, and so forth, are added to the USCPI data set.

```
data uscpi;
   set uscpi;
   d0 = intnx( 'month', date, 0 ) - 1;
   d1 = intnx( 'month', date, 1 ) - 1;
   nsunday  = intck( 'week.1', d0, d1 );
   nmonday  = intck( 'week.2', d0, d1 );
   ntuesday = intck( 'week.3', d0, d1 );
   nwedday  = intck( 'week.4', d0, d1 );
   nthurday = intck( 'week.5', d0, d1 );
   nfriday  = intck( 'week.6', d0, d1 );
   nsatday  = intck( 'week.7', d0, d1 );
   drop d0 d1;
run;
```

Since the INTCK function counts the number of interval beginning dates between two dates, the number of Sundays is computed by counting the number of week boundaries between the last day of the previous month and the last day of the current month. To count Mondays, Tuesdays, and so forth, shifted week intervals are used. The interval type WEEK.2 specifies weekly intervals starting on Mondays, WEEK.3 specifies weeks starting on Tuesdays, and so forth.

Checking Data Periodicity

Suppose you have a time series data set, and you want to verify that the data periodicity is correct, the observations are dated correctly, and the data set is sorted by date. You can use the INTCK function to compare the date of the current observation with the date of the previous observation and verify that the dates fall into consecutive time intervals.

For example, the following statements verify that the data set USCPI is a correctly dated monthly data set. The RETAIN statement is used to hold the date of the previous observation, and the automatic variable _N_ is used to start the verification process with the second observation.

```
data _null_;
   set uscpi;
   retain prevdate;
   if _n_ > 1 then
      if intck( 'month', prevdate, date ) ^= 1 then
         put "Bad date sequence at observation number " _n_;
   prevdate = date;
run;
```

Filling in Omitted Observations in a Time Series Data Set

Recall that most SAS/ETS procedures expect input data to be in the standard form, with no omitted observations in the sequence of time periods. When data are missing for a time period, the data set should contain a missing observation, in which all variables except the ID variables have missing values.

You can replace omitted observations in a time series data set with missing observations by merging the data set with a data set containing a complete sequence of dates.

The following statements create a monthly data set, OMITTED, from data lines containing records for an intermittent sample of months. (Data values are not shown.) This data set is converted to a standard form time series data set in four steps.

First, the OMITTED data set is sorted to make sure it is in time order. Second, the first and last date in the data set are determined and stored in the data set RANGE. Third, the data set DATES is created containing only the variable DATE and containing monthly observations for the needed time span. Finally, the data sets OMITTED and DATES are merged to produce a standard form time series data set with missing observations inserted for the omitted records.

```
data omitted;
   input date monyy7. x y z;
   format date monyy7.;
cards;
jan1991 ...
mar1991 ...
apr1991 ...
jun1991 ...
;

proc sort data=omitted;
   by date;
run;

data range;
   retain from to;
   set omitted end=lastobs;
   if _n_ = 1 then from = date;
   if lastobs then do;
      to = date;
      output;
      end;
run;

data dates;
   set range;
   date = from;
   do while( date <= to );
```

```
        output;
        date = intnx( 'month', date, 1 );
        end;
    keep date;
run;

data standard;
    merge omitted dates;
    by date;
run;
```

Using Interval Functions for Calendar Calculations

With a little thought, you can come up with a formula involving INTNX and INTCK functions and different interval types to perform almost any calendar calculation.

For example, suppose you want to know the date of the third Wednesday in the month of October 1991. The answer can be computed as

```
intnx( 'week.4', '1oct91'd - 1, 3 )
```

which returns the SAS date value '16OCT91'D.

Consider this more complex example: how many weekdays are there between 17 October 1991 and the second Friday in November 1991, inclusive? The following formula computes the number of weekdays between the date value contained in the variable DATE and the second Friday of the following month (including the ending dates of this period):

```
n = intck( 'weekday', date - 1,
            intnx( 'week.6', intnx( 'month', date, 1 ) - 1, 2 ) + 1 );
```

Setting DATE to '17OCT91'D and applying this formula produces the answer, N=17.

Lags, Leads, Differences, and Summations

When working with time series data, you sometimes need to refer to the values of a series in previous or future periods. For example, the usual interest in the consumer price index series shown in previous examples is how fast the index is changing, rather than the actual level of the index. To compute a percent change, you need both the current and the previous values of the series. When modeling a time series, you may want to use the previous values of other series as explanatory variables.

This section discusses how to use the DATA step to perform operations over time: lags, differences, leads, summations over time, and percent changes.

The EXPAND procedure can also be used to perform many of these operations; see Chapter 8, "The EXPAND Procedure," for more information. See also the section "Transforming Time Series" later in this chapter.

The LAG and DIF Functions

The DATA step provides two functions, LAG and DIF, for accessing previous values of a variable or expression. These functions are useful for computing lags and differences of series.

For example, the following statements add the variables CPILAG and CPIDIF to the USCPI data set. The variable CPILAG contains lagged values of the CPI series. The variable CPIDIF contains the changes of the CPI series from the previous period; that is, CPIDIF is CPI minus CPILAG. The new data set is shown in part in Figure 2.21.

```
data uscpi;
   set uscpi;
   cpilag = lag( cpi );
   cpidif = dif( cpi );
run;

proc print data=uscpi;
run;
```

OBS	DATE	CPI	CPILAG	CPIDIF
1	JUN90	129.9	.	.
2	JUL90	130.4	129.9	0.5
3	AUG90	131.6	130.4	1.2
4	SEP90	132.7	131.6	1.1
5	OCT90	133.5	132.7	0.8
6	NOV90	133.8	133.5	0.3
7	DEC90	133.8	133.8	0.0
8	JAN91	134.6	133.8	0.8

Figure 2.21. USCPI Data Set with Lagged and Differenced Series

Understanding the DATA Step LAG and DIF Functions

When used in this simple way, LAG and DIF act as lag and difference functions. However, it is important to keep in mind that, despite their names, the LAG and DIF functions available in the DATA step are not true lag and difference functions.

Rather, LAG and DIF are queuing functions that remember and return argument values from previous calls. The LAG function remembers the value you pass to it and returns as its result the value you passed to it on the previous call. The DIF function works the same way but returns the difference between the current argument and the remembered value. (LAG and DIF return a missing value the first time the function is called.)

A true lag function does not return the value of the argument for the "previous call," as do the DATA step LAG and DIF functions. Instead, a true lag function returns the value of its argument for the "previous observation," regardless of the sequence of previous calls to the function. Thus, for a true lag function to be possible, it must be clear what the "previous observation" is.

The DATA step is a powerful tool that can read any number of observations from any number of input files or data sets, can create any number of output data sets, and can write any number of output observations to any of the output data sets, all in the same program. Thus, in general, it is not clear what "previous observation" means in a DATA step program. In a DATA step program, the "previous observation" exists only if you write the program in a simple way that makes this concept meaningful.

Since, in general, the previous observation is not clearly defined, it is not possible to make true lag or difference functions for the DATA step. Instead, the DATA step provides queuing functions that make it easy to compute lags and differences.

Pitfalls of DATA Step LAG and DIF Functions

The LAG and DIF functions compute lags and differences provided that the sequence of calls to the function corresponds to the sequence of observations in the output data set. However, any complexity in the DATA step that breaks this correspondence causes the LAG and DIF functions to produce unexpected results.

For example, suppose you want to add the variable CPILAG to the USCPI data set, as in the previous example, and you also want to subset the series to 1991 and later years. You might use the following statements:

```
data subset;
   set uscpi;
   if date >= '1jan91'd;
   cpilag = lag( cpi );   /* WRONG PLACEMENT! */
run;
```

If the subsetting IF statement comes before the LAG function call, the value of CPI-LAG will be missing for January 1991, even though a value for December 1990 is available in the USCPI data set. To avoid losing this value, you must rearrange the statements to ensure that the LAG function is actually executed for the December 1990 observation.

```
data subset;
   set uscpi;
   cpilag = lag( cpi );
   if date >= '1jan91'd;
run;
```

In other cases, the subsetting statement should come before the LAG and DIF functions. For example, the following statements subset the FOREOUT data set shown in a previous example to select only _TYPE_=RESIDUAL observations and also to compute the variable LAGRESID.

```
data residual;
   set foreout;
   if _type_ = "RESIDUAL";
   lagresid = lag( cpi );
run;
```

Another pitfall of LAG and DIF functions arises when they are used to process time series cross-sectional data sets. For example, suppose you want to add the variable CPILAG to the CPICITY data set shown in a previous example. You might use the following statements:

```
data cpicity;
   set cpicity;
   cpilag = lag( cpi );
run;
```

However, these statements do not yield the desired result. In the data set produced by these statements, the value of CPILAG for the first observation for the first city is missing (as it should be), but in the first observation for all later cities, CPILAG contains the last value for the previous city. To correct this, set the lagged variable to missing at the start of each cross section, as follows:

```
data cpicity;
   set cpicity;
   by city date;
   cpilag = lag( cpi );
   if first.city then cpilag = .;
run;
```

LAG and DIF Functions in PROC MODEL

The preceding discussion of LAG and DIF functions applies to LAG and DIF functions used in the DATA step. However, LAG and DIF functions are also used in the MODEL procedure.

The MODEL procedure LAG and DIF functions do not work like the DATA step LAG and DIF functions. The LAG and DIF functions supported by PROC MODEL are true lag and difference functions, not queuing functions.

Unlike the DATA step, the MODEL procedure processes observations from a single input data set, so the "previous observation" is always clearly defined in a PROC MODEL program. Therefore, PROC MODEL is able to define LAG and DIF as true lagging functions that operate on values from the previous observation. See Chapter 11, "The MODEL Procedure," for more information on LAG and DIF functions in the MODEL procedure.

Alternatives to LAG and DIF Functions

You can also calculate lags and differences in the DATA step without using LAG and DIF functions. For example, the following statements add the variables CPILAG and CPIDIF to the USCPI data set:

```
data uscpi;
   set uscpi;
   retain cpilag;
   cpidif = cpi - cpilag;
   output;
   cpilag = cpi;
run;
```

The RETAIN statement prevents the DATA step from reinitializing CPILAG to a missing value at the start of each iteration and thus allows CPILAG to retain the value of CPI assigned to it in the last statement. The OUTPUT statement causes the output observation to contain values of the variables before CPILAG is reassigned the current value of CPI in the last statement.

You can also use the EXPAND procedure to compute lags and differences. For example, the following statements compute lag and difference variables for CPI:

```
proc expand data=uscpi out=uscpi method=none;
   id date;
   convert cpi=cpilag / transform=( lag 1 );
   convert cpi=cpidif / transform=( dif 1 );
run;
```

Multiperiod Lags and Higher-Order Differencing

To compute lags at a lagging period greater than 1, add the lag length to the end of the LAG keyword to specify the lagging function needed. For example, the LAG2 function returns the value of its argument two calls ago, the LAG3 function returns the value of its argument three calls ago, and so forth.

To compute differences at a lagging period greater than 1, add the lag length to the end of the DIF keyword. For example, the DIF2 function computes the differences between the value of its argument and the value of its argument two calls ago.

The following statements add the variables CPILAG12 and CPIDIF12 to the USCPI data set. CPILAG12 contains the value of CPI from the same month one year ago. CPIDIF12 contains the change in CPI from the same month one year ago. (In this case, the first 12 values of CPILAG12 and CPIDIF12 will be missing.)

```
data uscpi;
   set uscpi;
   cpilag12 = lag12( cpi );
   cpidif12 = dif12( cpi );
run;
```

To compute second differences, take the difference of the difference. To compute higher-order differences, nest DIF functions to the order needed. For example, the following statements compute the second difference of CPI:

```
data uscpi;
   set uscpi;
   cpi2dif = dif( dif( cpi ) );
run;
```

Multiperiod lags and higher-order differencing can be combined. For example, the following statements compute monthly changes in the inflation rate, with inflation rate computed as percent change in CPI from the same month one year ago:

```
data uscpi;
   set uscpi;
   infchng = dif( 100 * dif12( cpi ) / lag12( cpi ) );
run;
```

Percent Change Calculations

There are several common ways to compute the percent change in a time series. This section illustrates the use of LAG and DIF functions by showing SAS statements for various kinds of percent change calculations.

Computing Period-to-Period Change

To compute percent change from the previous period, divide the difference of the series by the lagged value of the series and multiply by 100.

```
data uscpi;
   set uscpi;
   pctchng = dif( cpi ) / lag( cpi ) * 100;
   label pctchng = "Monthly Percent Change, At Monthly Rates";
run;
```

Often, changes from the previous period are expressed at annual rates. This is done by exponentiation of the current-to-previous period ratio to the number of periods in a year and expressing the result as a percent change. For example, the following statements compute the month-over-month change in CPI as a percent change at annual rates:

```
data uscpi;
   set uscpi;
   pctchng = ( ( cpi / lag( cpi ) ) ** 12 - 1 ) * 100;
   label pctchng = "Monthly Percent Change, At Annual Rates";
run;
```

Computing Year-over-Year Change

To compute percent change from the same period in the previous year, use LAG and DIF functions with a lagging period equal to the number of periods in a year. (For quarterly data, use LAG4 and DIF4. For monthly data, use LAG12 and DIF12.)

For example, the following statements compute monthly percent change in CPI from the same month one year ago:

```
data uscpi;
   set uscpi;
   pctchng = dif12( cpi ) / lag12( cpi ) * 100;
   label pctchng = "Percent Change from One Year Ago";
run;
```

To compute year-over-year percent change measured at a given period within the year, subset the series of percent changes from the same period in the previous year to form a yearly data set. Use an IF or WHERE statement to select observations for the period within each year on which the year-over-year changes are based.

For example, the following statements compute year-over-year percent change in CPI from December of the previous year to December of the current year:

```
data annual;
   set uscpi;
   pctchng = dif12( cpi ) / lag12( cpi ) * 100;
   label pctchng = "Percent Change: December to December";
   if month( date ) = 12;
   format date year4.;
run;
```

Computing Percent Change in Yearly Averages

To compute changes in yearly averages, first aggregate the series to an annual series using the EXPAND procedure, and then compute the percent change of the annual series. (See Chapter 8, "The EXPAND Procedure," for more information on PROC EXPAND.)

For example, the following statements compute percent changes in the annual averages of CPI:

```
proc expand data=uscpi out=annual from=month to=year;
   convert cpi / observed=average method=aggregate;
run;

data annual;
   set annual;
   pctchng = dif( cpi ) / lag( cpi ) * 100;
   label pctchng = "Percent Change in Yearly Averages";
run;
```

It is also possible to compute percent change in the average over the most recent yearly span. For example, the following statements compute monthly percent change in the average of CPI over the most recent 12 months from the average over the previous 12 months:

```
data uscpi;
   retain sum12 0;
   drop sum12 ave12 cpilag12;
   set uscpi;
   sum12 = sum12 + cpi;
   cpilag12 = lag12( cpi );
   if cpilag12 ^= . then sum12 = sum12 - cpilag12;
   if lag11( cpi ) ^= . then ave12 = sum12 / 12;
   pctchng = dif12( ave12 ) / lag12( ave12 ) * 100;
   label pctchng = "Percent Change in 12 Month Moving Ave.";
run;
```

This example is a complex use of LAG and DIF functions that requires care in handling the initialization of the moving-window averaging process. The LAG12 of CPI is checked for missing values to determine when more than 12 values have been accumulated, and older values must be removed from the moving sum. The LAG11 of CPI is checked for missing values to determine when at least 12 values have been accumulated; AVE12 will be missing when LAG11 of CPI is missing. The DROP statement prevents temporary variables from being added to the data set.

Note that the DIF and LAG functions must execute for every observation or the queues of remembered values will not operate correctly. The CPILAG12 calculation must be separate from the IF statement. The PCTCHNG calculation must not be conditional on the IF statement.

The EXPAND procedure provides an alternative way to compute moving averages.

Leading Series

The SAS System does not provide a function to look ahead at the "next" value of a series. However, it is simple to compute lead series in SAS software by lagging the time ID variable, renaming the series, and merging the result data set back with the original data set.

For example, the following statements add the variable CPILEAD to the USCPI data set. The variable CPILEAD contains the value of CPI in the following month. (The value of CPILEAD will be missing for the last observation, of course.)

```
data temp;
   set uscpi;
   keep date cpi;
   rename cpi = cpilead;
   date = lag( date );
   if date ^= .;
run;

data uscpi;
   merge uscpi temp;
   by date;
run;
```

To compute leads at different lead lengths, you must create one temporary data set for each lead length. For example, the following statements compute CPILEAD1 and CPILEAD2, which contain leads of CPI for 1 and 2 periods, respectively:

```
data temp1(rename=(cpi=cpilead1)) temp2(rename=(cpi=cpilead2));
   set uscpi;
   keep date cpi;
   date = lag( date );
   if date ^= . then output temp1;
   date = lag( date );
   if date ^= . then output temp2;
run;

data uscpi;
   merge uscpi temp1 temp2;
   by date;
run;
```

An easier way to compute leads is to use the EXPAND procedure. For example

```
proc expand data=uscpi out=uscpi method=none;
   id date;
   convert cpi=cpilead1 / transform=( lead 1 );
   convert cpi=cpilead2 / transform=( lead 2 );
run;
```

Summing Series

Time series summation is the inverse of differencing. Simple cumulative sums are easy to compute using SAS sum statements. The following statements show how to compute the running sum of variable X in data set A, adding XSUM to the data set.

```
data a;
   set a;
   xsum + x;
run;
```

The SAS sum statement automatically retains the variable XSUM and initializes it to 0, and the sum statement treats missing values as 0. The sum statement is equivalent to using a RETAIN statement and the SUM function. The previous example could also be written as follows:

```
data a;
   set a;
   retain xsum;
   xsum = sum( xsum, x );
run;
```

You can also use the EXPAND procedure to compute summations. For example

```
proc expand data=a out=a method=none;
   convert x=xsum / transform=( sum );
run;
```

Like differencing, summation can be done at different lags and can be repeated to produce higher-order sums. To compute sums over observations separated by lags greater than 1, use the LAG and SUM functions together, and use a RETAIN statement that initializes the summation variable to zero.

For example, the following statements add the variable XSUM2 to data set A. XSUM2 contains the sum of every other observation, with even-numbered observations containing a cumulative sum of values of X from even observations, and odd-numbered observations containing a cumulative sum of values of X from odd observations.

```
data a;
   set a;
   retain xsum2 0;
   xsum2 = sum( lag( xsum2 ), x );
run;
```

Assuming that A is a quarterly data set, the following statements compute running sums of X for each quarter. XSUM4 contains the cumulative sum of X for all observations for the same quarter as the current quarter. Thus, for a first-quarter observation, XSUM4 contains a cumulative sum of current and past first-quarter values.

```
data a;
   set a;
   retain xsum4 0;
   xsum4 = sum( lag3( xsum4 ), x );
run;
```

To compute higher-order sums, repeat the preceding process and sum the summation variable. For example, the following statements compute the first and second summations of X:

```
data a;
   set a;
   xsum + x;
   x2sum + xsum;
run;
```

The following statements compute the second order four-period sum of X:

```
data a;
   set a;
   retain xsum4 x2sum4 0;
   xsum4 = sum( lag3( xsum4 ), x );
   x2sum4 = sum( lag3( x2sum4 ), xsum4 );
run;
```

Transforming Time Series

It is often useful to transform time series for analysis or forecasting. Many time series analysis and forecasting methods are most appropriate for time series with an unrestricted range, linear trend, and constant variance. Series that do not conform to these assumptions can often be transformed to series for which the methods are appropriate.

Transformations can be useful for the following:

- range restrictions. Many time series cannot have negative values or may be limited by a maximum possible value. You can often create a transformed series with an unbounded range.

- nonlinear trends. Many economic time series grow exponentially. Exponential growth corresponds to linear growth in the logarithms of the series.

- series variability that changes over time. Various transformations can be used to stabilize the variance.

Log Transformation

The logarithmic transformation is often useful for series that must be greater than zero and that grow exponentially. For example, Figure 2.22 shows a plot of an airline passenger miles series. Notice that the series has exponential growth and the variability of the series increases over time.

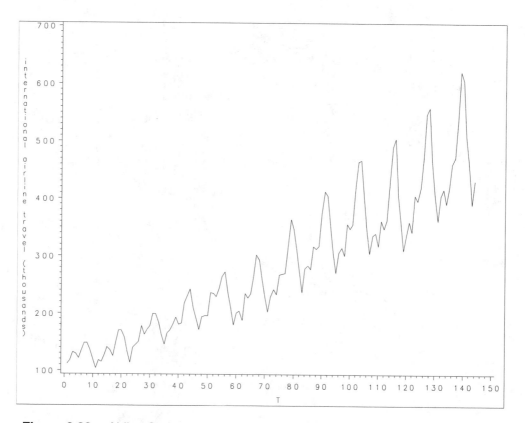

Figure 2.22. Airline Series

The following statements compute the logarithms of the airline series:

```
data a;
   set a;
   logair = log( air );
run;
```

Figure 2.23 shows a plot of the log transformed airline series. Notice that the log series has a linear trend and constant variance.

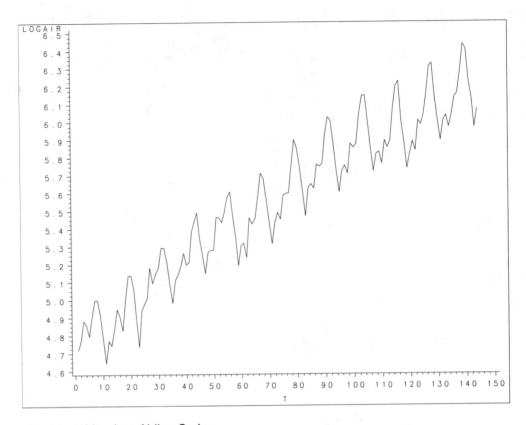

Figure 2.23.   Log Airline Series

The %LOGTEST macro can help you decide if a log transformation is appropriate for a series. See Chapter 20, "SAS Macros," for more information on the %LOGTEST macro.

Other Transformations

The Box-Cox transformation is a general class of transformations that includes the logarithm as a special case. The %BOXCOXAR macro can be used to find an optimal Box-Cox transformation for a time series. See Chapter 20 for more information on the %BOXCOXAR macro.

The logistic transformation is useful for variables with both an upper and a lower bound, such as market shares. The logistic transformation is useful for proportions, percent values, relative frequencies, or probabilities. The logistic function transforms values between 0 and 1 to values that can range from $-\infty$ to $+\infty$.

For example, the following statements transform the variable SHARE from percent values to an unbounded range:

```
data a;
   set a;
   lshare = log( share / ( 100 - share ) );
run;
```

Many other data transformation can be used. You can create virtually any desired data transformation using DATA step statements.

The EXPAND Procedure and Data Transformations

The EXPAND procedure provides a convenient way to transform series. For example, the following statements add variables for the logarithm of AIR and the logistic of SHARE to data set A:

```
proc expand data=a out=a method=none;
   convert air=logair  / transform=( log );
   convert share=lshare / transform=( / 100 logit );
run;
```

See Table 8.1 in Chapter 8 for a complete list of transformations supported by PROC EXPAND.

Manipulating Time Series Data Sets

This section discusses merging, splitting, and transposing time series data sets and interpolating time series data to a higher or lower sampling frequency.

Merging and Splitting Variables

In some cases, you may want to separate several time series contained in one data set into different data sets. In other cases, you may want to combine time series from different data sets into one data set.

To split a time series data set into two or more data sets containing subsets of the series, use a DATA step to create the new data sets and use the KEEP= data set option to control which series are included in each new data set. The following statements split the USPRICE data set shown in a previous example into two data sets, USCPI and USPPI:

```
data uscpi(keep=date cpi)
     usppi(keep=date ppi);
   set usprice;
run;
```

If the series have different time ranges, you can subset the time ranges of the output data sets accordingly. For example, if you know that CPI in USPRICE has the range August 1990 through the end of the data set, while PPI has the range from the beginning of the data set through June 1991, you could write the previous example as follows:

```
data uscpi(keep=date cpi)
    usppi(keep=date ppi);
  set usprice;
  if date >= '1aug90'd then output uscpi;
  if date <= '1jun91'd then output usppi;
run;
```

To combine time series from different data sets into one data set, list the data sets to be combined in a MERGE statement and specify the dating variable in a BY statement. The following statements show how to combine the USCPI and USPPI data sets to produce the USPRICE data set. It is important to use the BY DATE; statement so observations are matched by time before merging.

```
data usprice;
  merge uscpi usppi;
  by date;
run;
```

Transposing Data

The TRANSPOSE procedure is used to transpose data sets from one form to another. The TRANSPOSE procedure can transpose variables and observations, or transpose variables and observations within BY groups. This section discusses some applications of the TRANSPOSE procedure relevant to time series data sets. Refer to the *SAS Procedures Guide* for more information on PROC TRANSPOSE.

Transposing from Interleaved to Standard Time Series Form

The following statements transpose part of the interleaved form output data set FOREOUT, produced by PROC FORECAST in a previous example, to a standard form time series data set. To reduce the volume of output produced by the example, a WHERE statement is used to subset the input data set.

Observations with _TYPE_=ACTUAL are stored in the new variable ACTUAL; observations with _TYPE_=FORECAST are stored in the new variable FORECAST; and so forth. Note that the method used in this example only works for a single variable.

```
title "Original Data Set";
proc print data=foreout;
  where date > '1may91'd & date < '1oct91'd;
run;

proc transpose data=foreout out=trans(drop=_name_ _label_);
  var cpi;
  id _type_;
  by date;
  where date > '1may91'd & date < '1oct91'd;
run;

title "Transposed Data Set";
proc print data=trans;
run;
```

The TRANSPOSE procedure adds the variables _NAME_ and _LABEL_ to the output data set. These variables contain the names and labels of the variables that were transposed. In this example, there is only one transposed variable, so _NAME_ has the value CPI for all observations. Thus, _NAME_ and _LABEL_ are of no interest and are dropped from the output data set using the DROP= data set option. (If none of the variables transposed have a label, PROC TRANSPOSE does not output the _LABEL_ variable and the DROP=_LABEL_ option produces a warning message. You can ignore this message, or you can prevent the message by omitting _LABEL_ from the DROP= list.)

The original and transposed data sets are shown in Figure 2.24. (The observation numbers for the original data set reflect the operation of the WHERE statement.)

```
                           Original Data Set

           OBS      DATE     _TYPE_      _LEAD_         CPI

            37     JUN91     ACTUAL         0        136.000
            38     JUN91     FORECAST       0        136.146
            39     JUN91     RESIDUAL       0         -0.146
            40     JUL91     ACTUAL         0        136.200
            41     JUL91     FORECAST       0        136.566
            42     JUL91     RESIDUAL       0         -0.366
            43     AUG91     FORECAST       1        136.856
            44     AUG91     L95            1        135.723
            45     AUG91     U95            1        137.990
            46     SEP91     FORECAST       2        137.443
            47     SEP91     L95            2        136.126
            48     SEP91     U95            2        138.761
```

```
                          Transposed Data Set

     OBS     DATE     ACTUAL    FORECAST    RESIDUAL      L95        U95

      1     JUN91     136.0     136.146    -0.14616        .          .
      2     JUL91     136.2     136.566    -0.36635        .          .
      3     AUG91       .       136.856        .        135.723    137.990
      4     SEP91       .       137.443        .        136.126    138.761
```

Figure 2.24.   Original and Transposed Data Sets

Transposing Cross-sectional Dimensions

The following statements transpose the variable CPI in the CPICITY data set shown in a previous example from time series cross-sectional form to a standard form time series data set. (Only a subset of the data shown in the previous example is used here.) Note that the method shown in this example only works for a single variable.

```
title "Original Data Set";
proc print data=cpicity;
run;

proc sort data=cpicity out=temp;
   by date city;
run;

proc transpose data=temp out=citycpi(drop=_name_ _label_);
   var cpi;
   id city;
   by date;
run;

title "Transposed Data Set";
proc print data=citycpi;
run;
```

The names of the variables in the transposed data sets are taken from the first eight characters of the city names in the ID variable CITY. The original and the transposed data sets are shown in Figure 2.25.

```
                          Original Data Set

             OBS     CITY            DATE        CPI

              1      Chicago         JAN90       128.1
              2      Chicago         FEB90       129.2
              3      Chicago         MAR90       129.5
              4      Chicago         APR90       130.4
              5      Chicago         MAY90       130.4
              6      Chicago         JUN90       131.7
              7      Chicago         JUL90       132.0
              8      Los Angeles     JAN90       132.1
              9      Los Angeles     FEB90       133.6
             10      Los Angeles     MAR90       134.5
             11      Los Angeles     APR90       134.2
             12      Los Angeles     MAY90       134.6
             13      Los Angeles     JUN90       135.0
             14      Los Angeles     JUL90       135.6
             15      New York        JAN90       135.1
             16      New York        FEB90       135.3
             17      New York        MAR90       136.6
             18      New York        APR90       137.3
             19      New York        MAY90       137.2
             20      New York        JUN90       137.1
             21      New York        JUL90       138.4
```

```
                        Transposed Data Set

        OBS     DATE      CHICAGO    LOS_ANGE    NEW_YORK

         1      JAN90      128.1      132.1       135.1
         2      FEB90      129.2      133.6       135.3
         3      MAR90      129.5      134.5       136.6
         4      APR90      130.4      134.2       137.3
         5      MAY90      130.4      134.6       137.2
         6      JUN90      131.7      135.0       137.1
         7      JUL90      132.0      135.6       138.4
```

Figure 2.25. Original and Transposed Data Sets

The following statements transpose the CITYCPI data set back to the original form of the CPICITY data set. The variable _NAME_ is added to the data set to tell PROC TRANSPOSE the name of the variable in which to store the observations in the transposed data set. (If the (DROP=_NAME_ _LABEL_) option were omitted from the first PROC TRANSPOSE step, this would not be necessary. PROC TRANSPOSE assumes ID _NAME_ by default.)

The NAME=CITY option in the PROC TRANSPOSE statement causes PROC TRANSPOSE to store the names of the transposed variables in the variable CITY. Because PROC TRANSPOSE recodes the values of the CITY variable to create valid SAS variable names in the transposed data set, the values of the variable CITY in the retransposed data set are not the same as the original. The retransposed data set is shown in Figure 2.26.

```
data temp;
   set citycpi;
   _name_ = 'CPI';
run;

proc transpose data=temp out=retrans name=city;
   by date;
run;

proc sort data=retrans;
   by city date;
run;

title "Retransposed Data Set";
proc print data=retrans;
run;
```

```
                    Retransposed Data Set

         OBS     DATE      CITY        CPI

           1     JAN90     CHICAGO     128.1
           2     FEB90     CHICAGO     129.2
           3     MAR90     CHICAGO     129.5
           4     APR90     CHICAGO     130.4
           5     MAY90     CHICAGO     130.4
           6     JUN90     CHICAGO     131.7
           7     JUL90     CHICAGO     132.0
           8     JAN90     LOS_ANGE    132.1
           9     FEB90     LOS_ANGE    133.6
          10     MAR90     LOS_ANGE    134.5
          11     APR90     LOS_ANGE    134.2
          12     MAY90     LOS_ANGE    134.6
          13     JUN90     LOS_ANGE    135.0
          14     JUL90     LOS_ANGE    135.6
          15     JAN90     NEW_YORK    135.1
          16     FEB90     NEW_YORK    135.3
          17     MAR90     NEW_YORK    136.6
          18     APR90     NEW_YORK    137.3
          19     MAY90     NEW_YORK    137.2
          20     JUN90     NEW_YORK    137.1
          21     JUL90     NEW_YORK    138.4
```

Figure 2.26.   Data Set Transposed Back to Original Form

Time Series Interpolation

The EXPAND procedure interpolates time series. This section provides a brief summary of the use of PROC EXPAND for different kinds of time series interpolation problems. Most of the issues discussed in this section are explained in greater detail in Chapter 8.

By default, the EXPAND procedure performs interpolation by first fitting cubic spline curves to the available data and then computing needed interpolating values from the fitted spline curves. Other interpolation methods can be requested.

Note that interpolating values of a time series does not add any real information to the data. While time series interpolation can sometimes be useful, care is needed in analyzing time series containing interpolated values.

Interpolating Missing Values

To use the EXPAND procedure to interpolate missing values in a time series, specify the input and output data sets on the PROC EXPAND statement, and specify the time ID variable in an ID statement. For example, the following statements cause PROC EXPAND to interpolate values for missing values of all numeric variables in the data set USPRICE:

```
proc expand data=usprice out=interpl;
   id date;
run;
```

Interpolated values are computed only for embedded missing values in the input time series. Missing values before or after the range of a series are ignored by the EX-PAND procedure.

In the preceding example, PROC EXPAND assumes that all series are measured at points in time given by the value of the ID variable. In fact, the series in the USPRICE data set are monthly averages. PROC EXPAND may produce a better interpolation if this is taken into account. The following example uses the FROM=MONTH option to tell PROC EXPAND that the series is monthly and uses the CONVERT statement with the OBSERVED=AVERAGE to specify that the series values are averages over each month:

```
proc expand data=usprice out=interpl from=month;
   id date;
   convert cpi ppi / observed=average;
run;
```

Interpolating to a Higher or Lower Frequency

You can use PROC EXPAND to interpolate values of time series at a higher or lower sampling frequency than the input time series. To change the periodicity of time series, specify the time interval of the input data set with the FROM= option, and specify the time interval for the desired output frequency with the TO= option. For example, the following statements compute interpolated weekly values of the monthly CPI and PPI series:

```
proc expand data=usprice out=interpl from=month to=week;
   id date;
   convert cpi ppi / observed=average;
run;
```

Interpolating between Stocks and Flows, Levels and Rates

A distinction is made between variables that are measured at points in time and variables that represent totals or averages over an interval. Point-in-time values are often called *stocks* or *levels*. Variables that represent totals or averages over an interval are often called *flows* or *rates*.

For example, the annual series Gross National Product represents the total value of production over the year and also the yearly average rate of production. However, the monthly variable Inventory represents the cost of a stock of goods at the end of the month.

The EXPAND procedure can convert between point-in-time values and period average or total values. To convert observation characteristics, specify the input and output characteristics with the OBSERVED= option in the CONVERT statement. For example, the following statements use the monthly average price index values in US-PRICE to compute interpolated estimates of the price index levels at the midpoint of each month.

```
proc expand data=usprice out=midpoint from=month;
   id date;
   convert cpi ppi / observed=(average,middle);
run;
```

Reading Time Series Data

Time series data can be coded in many different ways. The SAS System can read time series data recorded in almost any form. Earlier sections of this chapter show how to read time series data coded in several commonly used ways. This section shows how to read time series data from data records coded in two other commonly used ways not previously introduced.

Several time series databases distributed by major data vendors can be read into SAS data sets by the DATASOURCE procedure. See Chapter 7, "The DATASOURCE Procedure," for more information.

Reading a Simple List of Values

Time series data can be coded as a simple list of values without dating information and with an arbitrary number of observations on each data record. In this case, the INPUT statement must use the trailing "@@" option to retain the current data record after reading the values for each observation, and the time ID variable must be generated with programming statements.

For example, the following statements read the USPRICE data set from data records containing pairs of values for CPI and PPI. This example assumes you know that the first pair of values is for June 1990.

```
data usprice;
   input cpi ppi @@;
   date = intnx( 'month', '1jun90'd, _n_-1 );
   format date monyy.;
cards;
129.9 114.3   130.4 114.5   131.6 116.5
132.7 118.4   133.5 120.8   133.8 120.1 133.8 118.7
134.6 119.0   134.8 117.2   135.0 116.2 135.2 116.0
135.6 116.5   136.0 116.3   136.2 116.0
;
```

Reading Fully Described Time Series in Transposed Form

Data for several time series can be coded with separate groups of records for each time series. Data files coded this way are transposed from the form required by SAS procedures. Time series data can also be coded with descriptive information about the series included with the data records.

The following example reads time series data for the USPRICE data set coded with separate groups of records for each series. The data records for each series consist of a series description record and one or more value records. The series description record gives the series name, starting month and year of the series, number of values in the series, and a series label. The value records contain the observations of the time series.

The data are first read into a temporary data set that contains one observation for each value of each series. This data set is sorted by date and series name, and the TRANSPOSE procedure is used to transpose the data into a standard form time series data set.

```
data temp;
   length _name_ $8 _label_ $40;
   keep _name_ _label_ date value;
   format date monyy.;
   input _name_ month year nval _label_ &;
   date = mdy( month, 1, year );
   do i = 1 to nval;
      input value @;
      output;
      date = intnx( 'month', date, 1 );
   end;
cards;
cpi       8 90  12  Consumer Price Index
131.6 132.7 133.5 133.8 133.8 134.6 134.8 135.0
135.2 135.6 136.0 136.2
ppi       6 90  13  Producer Price Index
114.3 114.5 116.5 118.4 120.8 120.1 118.7 119.0
117.2 116.2 116.0 116.5 116.3
;

proc sort data=temp;
   by date _name_;
run;

proc transpose data=temp out=usprice(drop=_name_ _label_);
   by date;
   var value;
run;

proc contents data=usprice;
run;

proc print data=usprice;
run;
```

The final data set is shown in Figure 2.27.

```
                         CONTENTS PROCEDURE
        Data Set Name: WORK.USPRICE          Observations:           14
        Member Type:   DATA                  Variables:              3
        Engine:        SASEB                 Indexes:                0
        Created:       DDMMMYY:00:00:00      Observation Length:     24
        Last Modified: DDMMMYY:00:00:00      Deleted Observations:   0
        Protection:                          Compressed:             NO
        Data Set Type:                       Sorted:                 NO
        Label:

             -----Alphabetic List of Variables and Attributes-----

        #     Variable   Type    Len    Pos    Format    Label
        -------------------------------------------------------------------
        3     CPI        Num     8      16               Consumer Price Index
        1     DATE       Num     8      0      MONYY.
        2     PPI        Num     8      8               Producer Price Index
```

```
              OBS      DATE      PPI      CPI
               1       JUN90    114.3       .
               2       JUL90    114.5       .
               3       AUG90    116.5     131.6
               4       SEP90    118.4     132.7
               5       OCT90    120.8     133.5
               6       NOV90    120.1     133.8
               7       DEC90    118.7     133.8
               8       JAN91    119.0     134.6
               9       FEB91    117.2     134.8
              10       MAR91    116.2     135.0
              11       APR91    116.0     135.2
              12       MAY91    116.5     135.6
              13       JUN91    116.3     136.0
              14       JUL91        .     136.2
```

Figure 2.27. USPRICE Data Set

Chapter 3
The ARIMA Procedure

Chapter Table of Contents

Chapter 3
The ARIMA Procedure

Overview

The ARIMA procedure analyzes and forecasts equally spaced univariate time series data, transfer function data, and intervention data using the **AutoR**egressive **I**ntegrated **M**oving-**A**verage (ARIMA) or autoregressive moving-average (ARMA) model. An ARIMA model predicts a value in a response time series as a linear combination of its own past values, past errors (also called shocks or innovations), and current and past values of other time series.

The ARIMA approach was first popularized by Box and Jenkins, and ARIMA models are often referred to as Box-Jenkins models. The general transfer function model employed by the ARIMA procedure was discussed by Box and Tiao (1975). When an ARIMA model includes other time series as input variables, the model is sometimes referred to as an ARIMAX model. Pankratz (1991) refers to the ARIMAX model as *dynamic regression.*

The ARIMA procedure provides a comprehensive set of tools for univariate time series model identification, parameter estimation, and forecasting, and it offers great flexibility in the kinds of ARIMA or ARIMAX models that can be analyzed. The ARIMA procedure supports seasonal, subset, and factored ARIMA models; intervention or interrupted time series models; multiple regression analysis with ARMA errors; and rational transfer function models of any complexity.

The design of PROC ARIMA closely follows the Box-Jenkins strategy for time series modeling with features for the identification, estimation and diagnostic checking, and forecasting steps of the Box-Jenkins method.

Before using PROC ARIMA, you should be familiar with Box-Jenkins methods, and you should exercise care and judgment when using the ARIMA procedure. The ARIMA class of time series models is complex and powerful, and some degree of expertise is needed to use them correctly.

If you are unfamiliar with the principles of ARIMA modeling, refer to textbooks on time series analysis. Also refer to *SAS/ETS Software: Applications Guide 1, Version 6, First Edition.* You might consider attending the SAS Training Courses "Forecasting Techniques Using SAS/ETS Software" and "Advanced Forecasting Techniques Using SAS/ETS Software." These courses provide in-depth training on ARIMA modeling using PROC ARIMA, as well as training on the use of other forecasting tools available in SAS/ETS software.

Getting Started

This section outlines the use of the ARIMA procedure and gives a cursory description of the ARIMA modeling process for readers less familiar with these methods.

The Three Stages of ARIMA Modeling

The analysis performed by PROC ARIMA is divided into three stages, corresponding to the stages described by Box and Jenkins (1976). The IDENTIFY, ESTIMATE, and FORECAST statements perform these three stages, which are summarized below.

1. In the *identification* stage, you use the IDENTIFY statement to specify the response series and identify candidate ARIMA models for it. The IDENTIFY statement reads time series that are to be used in later statements, possibly differencing them, and computes autocorrelations, inverse autocorrelations, partial autocorrelations, and cross correlations. The analysis of this output usually suggests one or more ARIMA models that could be fit.

2. In the *estimation and diagnostic checking* stage, you use the ESTIMATE statement to specify the ARIMA model to fit to the variable specified in the previous IDENTIFY statement, and to estimate the parameters of that model. The ESTIMATE statement also produces diagnostic statistics to help you judge the adequacy of the model.

   Significance tests for parameter estimates indicate whether some terms in the model may be unnecessary. Goodness-of-fit statistics aid in comparing this model to others. Tests for white noise residuals indicate whether the residual series contains additional information that might be utilized by a more complex model. If the diagnostic tests indicate problems with the model, you try another model, then repeat the estimation and diagnostic checking stage.

3. In the *forecasting* stage you use the FORECAST statement to forecast future values of the time series and to generate confidence intervals for these forecasts from the ARIMA model produced by the preceding ESTIMATE statement.

These three steps are explained further and illustrated through an extended example in the following sections.

Identification Stage

Suppose you have a variable called SALES that you want to forecast. The following example illustrates ARIMA modeling and forecasting using a simulated data set TEST containing a time series SALES generated by an ARIMA(1,1,1) model. The output produced by this example is explained in the following sections. The simulated SALES series is shown in Figure 3.1.

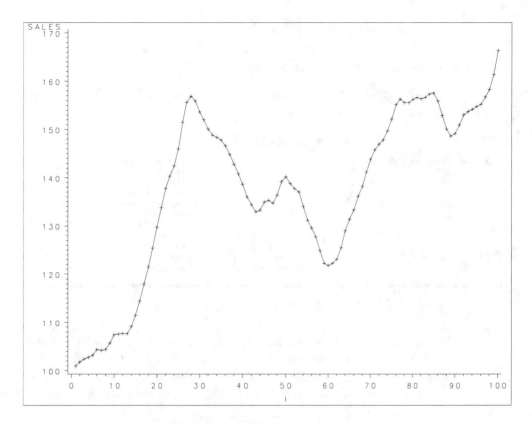

Figure 3.1. Simulated ARIMA(1,1,1) Series SALES

Using the IDENTIFY Statement

You first specify the input data set in the PROC ARIMA statement. Then, you use an IDENTIFY statement to read in the SALES series and plot its autocorrelation function. You do this using the following statements:

```
proc arima data=test;
   identify var=sales nlag=8;
   run;
```

Descriptive Statistics

The IDENTIFY statement first prints descriptive statistics for the SALES series. This part of the IDENTIFY statement output is shown in Figure 3.2.

```
                    ARIMA Procedure

     Name of variable = SALES.

     Mean of working series = 137.3662
     Standard deviation     = 17.36385
     Number of observations =      100
```

Figure 3.2. IDENTIFY Statement Descriptive Statistics Output

Autocorrelation Function Plots

The IDENTIFY statement next prints three plots of the correlations of the series with its past values at different lags. These are the

- sample autocorrelation function plot
- partial autocorrelation function plot
- inverse autocorrelation function plot

The sample autocorrelation function plot output of the IDENTIFY statement is shown in Figure 3.3.

```
                            Autocorrelations

Lag Covariance Correlation -1 9 8 7 6 5 4 3 2 1 0 1 2 3 4 5 6 7 8 9 1
  0   301.503    1.00000   |                    |********************|
  1   288.454    0.95672   |                  . |******************* |
  2   273.437    0.90691   |                 .  |******************  |
  3   256.787    0.85169   |                .   |*****************   |
  4   238.518    0.79110   |              .     |****************    |
  5   219.033    0.72647   |             .      |**************      |
  6   198.617    0.65876   |            .       |*************       |
  7   177.150    0.58755   |           .        |************        |
  8   154.914    0.51381   |          .         |**********  .       |
                      "." marks two standard errors
```

Figure 3.3.   IDENTIFY Statement Autocorrelations Plot

The autocorrelation plot shows how values of the series are correlated with past values of the series. For example, the value 0.95672 in the "Correlation" column for the Lag 1 row of the plot means that the correlation between SALES and the SALES value for the previous period is .95672. The rows of asterisks show the correlation values graphically.

These plots are called autocorrelation functions because they show the degree of correlation with past values of the series as a function of the number of periods in the past (that is, the lag) at which the correlation is computed.

The NLAG= option controls the number of lags for which autocorrelations are shown. By default, the autocorrelation functions are plotted to lag 24; in this example the NLAG=8 option is used, so only the first 8 lags are shown.

Most books on time series analysis explain how to interpret autocorrelation plots and partial autocorrelation plots. See the section "The Inverse Autocorrelation Function" later in this chapter for a discussion of inverse autocorrelation plots.

By examining these plots, you can judge whether the series is *stationary* or *nonstationary*. (See the section "Stationarity" later in this chapter.) In this case, the autocorrelation function plot indicates that the SALES series is nonstationary.

The inverse and partial autocorrelation plots are printed after the autocorrelation plot. These plots have the same form as the autocorrelation plots, but display inverse and partial autocorrelation values instead of autocorrelations and autocovariances. Since the autocorrelations clearly show that the SALES series is nonstationary, the partial and inverse autocorrelation plots are not shown.

White Noise Test

The last part of the IDENTIFY statement output is the check for white noise. This is an approximate statistical test of the hypothesis that none of the autocorrelations of the series up to a given lag are significantly different from 0. If this is true for all lags, then there is no information in the series to model, and no ARIMA model is needed for the series.

The autocorrelations are checked in groups of 6, and the number of lags checked depends on the NLAG= option. The check for white noise output is shown in Figure 3.4.

```
                Autocorrelation Check for White Noise

   To   Chi                        Autocorrelations
  Lag  Square DF    Prob
    6  426.44  6   0.000   0.957   0.907   0.852   0.791   0.726   0.659
```

Figure 3.4. IDENTIFY Statement Check for White Noise

In this case, the white noise hypothesis is rejected very strongly, which is expected since the series is nonstationary. The p value for the test of the first six autocorrelations is printed as 0.000, which means the p value is less than .0005.

Identification of the Differenced Series

Since the series is nonstationary, the next step is to transform it to a stationary series by differencing. That is, instead of modeling the SALES series itself, you model the change in SALES from one period to the next. To difference the SALES series, use another IDENTIFY statement and specify that the first difference of SALES be analyzed, as shown in the following statements:

```
identify var=sales(1) nlag=8;
run;
```

The second IDENTIFY statement produces the same information as the first but for the change in SALES from one period to the next rather than for the total sales in each period. The summary statistics output from this IDENTIFY statement is shown in Figure 3.5. Note that the period of differencing is given as 1, and one observation was lost through the differencing operation.

```
                        ARIMA Procedure

             Name of variable = SALES.

             Period(s) of Differencing = 1.
             Mean of working series = 0.660589
             Standard deviation     = 2.011543
             Number of observations =       99
             NOTE: The first observation was eliminated by
                   differencing.
```

Figure 3.5. IDENTIFY Statement Output for Differenced Series

The autocorrelation plot for the differenced series is shown in Figure 3.6.

```
                              Autocorrelations

Lag Covariance Correlation -1 9 8 7 6 5 4 3 2 1 0 1 2 3 4 5 6 7 8 9 1
  0  4.046306    1.00000   |                     |********************|
  1  3.351258    0.82823   |                .    |****************    |
  2  2.390895    0.59088   |                .    |************        |
  3  1.838925    0.45447   |                .    |*********          |
  4  1.494253    0.36929   |                .    |*******.           |
  5  1.135753    0.28069   |                .    |******ͮ.            |
  6  0.801319    0.19804   |                .    |****  .            |
  7  0.610543    0.15089   |                .    |***   .            |
  8  0.326495    0.08069   |                .    |**    .            |
                           "." marks two standard errors
```

Figure 3.6. Autocorrelations Plot for Change in SALES

The autocorrelation plot indicates that the change in SALES is stationary. The next step is to examine the patterns in the autocorrelation plot to choose an ARMA model to fit to the data.

The partial and inverse autocorrelation function plots are also useful aids in identifying appropriate ARMA models for the series. The partial and inverse autocorrelation function plots are shown in Figure 3.7 and Figure 3.8.

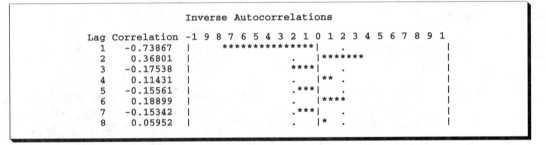

```
                        Inverse Autocorrelations

Lag Correlation -1 9 8 7 6 5 4 3 2 1 0 1 2 3 4 5 6 7 8 9 1
  1   -0.73867  |     ***************|   .                  |
  2    0.36801  |                 .  |*******               |
  3   -0.17538  |                ****|  .                   |
  4    0.11431  |                 .  |** .                  |
  5   -0.15561  |                .***|  .                   |
  6    0.18899  |                 .  |****                  |
  7   -0.15342  |                .***|  .                   |
  8    0.05952  |                 .  |*  .                  |
```

Figure 3.7. Inverse Autocorrelation Function Plot for Change in SALES

```
                        Partial Autocorrelations

Lag Correlation -1 9 8 7 6 5 4 3 2 1 0 1 2 3 4 5 6 7 8 9 1
  1    0.82823  |                 .  |*****************     |
  2   -0.30275  |           ******|  .                     |
  3    0.23722  |                 .  |*****                 |
  4   -0.07450  |                 . *|  .                   |
  5   -0.02654  |                 . *|  .                   |
  6   -0.01012  |                 .  |  .                   |
  7    0.04189  |                 .  |* .                   |
  8   -0.17668  |               ****|  .                    |
```

Figure 3.8. Partial Autocorrelation Plot for Change in SALES

In the usual Box and Jenkins approach to ARIMA modeling, the sample autocorrelation function, inverse autocorrelation function, and partial autocorrelation function are compared with the theoretical correlation functions expected from different kinds of ARMA models. This matching of theoretical autocorrelation functions of different ARMA models to the sample autocorrelation functions computed from the response series is the heart of the identification stage of Box-Jenkins modeling. Most textbooks on time series analysis discuss the theoretical autocorrelation functions for different kinds of ARMA models.

Since the input data is only a limited sample of the series, the sample autocorrelation functions computed from the input series will only approximate the true autocorrelation functions of the process generating the series. This means that the sample autocorrelation functions will not exactly match the theoretical autocorrelation functions for any ARMA model and may have a pattern similar to that of several different ARMA models.

The check for white noise residuals, shown in Figure 3.9, indicates that the change in sales is highly autocorrelated.

```
                 Autocorrelation Check for White Noise

     To    Chi                      Autocorrelations
    Lag  Square DF  Prob
     6   154.44  6  0.000  0.828  0.591  0.454  0.369  0.281  0.198
```

Figure 3.9. IDENTIFY Statement Check for White Noise

Estimation and Diagnostic Checking Stage

Having identified some possible ARIMA models to try, you move on to the estimation and diagnostic checking stage. In this case, the autocorrelation plots suggest a mixed ARMA model for the change in SALES. You can also try fitting simpler models, such as an AR(1) or MA(1) model, and check the diagnostic statistics to see if the simple model is adequate. In this example, the AR(1) model is tried first.

Estimating an AR(1) Model

The following statements fit an AR(1) model (an autoregressive model of order 1), which predicts the change in sales as an average change, plus some fraction of the previous change, plus a random error. To estimate an AR model, you specify the order of the autoregressive model with the P= option on an ESTIMATE statement, as shown in the following statements:

```
estimate p=1;
run;
```

The ESTIMATE statement fits the model to the data and prints parameter estimates and various diagnostic statistics that indicate how well the model fits the data. The first part of the ESTIMATE statement output, the table of parameter estimates, is shown in Figure 3.10.

```
              Conditional Least Squares Estimation

                                  Approx.
          Parameter    Estimate   Std Error   T Ratio  Lag
          MU           0.90280     0.65984      1.37    0
          AR1,1        0.86847     0.05485     15.83    1

          Constant Estimate  = 0.11874944
```

Figure 3.10. Parameter Estimates for AR(1) Model

The table of parameter estimates is headed with "Conditional Least Squares Estimation." The title indicates the estimation method used. You can request different estimation methods with the METHOD= option.

The table of parameter estimates lists the parameters in the model; for each parameter, the table shows the estimated value and the standard error and *t* ratio for the estimate. The table also indicates the lag at which the parameter appears in the model.

In this case, there are two parameters in the model. The mean term is labeled MU; its estimated value is .90280. The autoregressive parameter is labeled AR1,1; this is the coefficient of the lagged value of the change in SALES, and its estimate is .86847.

The *t* ratios provide significance tests for the parameter estimates and indicate whether some terms in the model may be unnecessary. In this case, the *t* ratio for the autoregressive parameter is 15.83, so this term is highly significant. The *t* ratio for MU indicates that the mean term adds little to the model.

The standard error estimates are based on large sample theory. Thus, the standard errors are labeled as approximate, and the standard errors and *t* ratios may not be reliable in small samples.

The constant term of the model can be expressed as a function of the mean term MU and the autoregressive parameters. This form of the model constant term is printed as "Constant Estimate." See the section "General Notation for ARIMA Models" later in this chapter for an explanation of the constant estimate.

The next part of the ESTIMATE statement output is a table of goodness-of-fit statistics, which aid in comparing this model to others. This output is shown in Figure 3.11.

```
Variance   Estimate = 1.15793962
Std Error Estimate = 1.07607603
AIC                = 297.446933*
SBC                = 302.637173*
Number of Residuals=        99
* Does not include log determinant.
```

Figure 3.11.   Goodness-of-Fit Statistics for AR(1) Model

The "Variance Estimate" is the variance of the residual series, which estimates the innovation variance. The item labeled "Std Error Estimate" is the square root of the variance estimate. The section "Estimation Details" later in this chapter explains the AIC and SBC statistics.

The ESTIMATE statement next prints a table of correlations of the parameter estimates, as shown in Figure 3.12. This table can help judge the extent to which collinearity may have influenced the results. If two parameter estimates are very highly correlated, you might consider dropping one of them from the model.

```
                Correlations of the Estimates

        Parameter           MU          AR1,1

        MU               1.000          0.114
        AR1,1            0.114          1.000
```

Figure 3.12. Correlations of the Estimates for AR(1) Model

The next part of the ESTIMATE statement output is a check of the autocorrelations of the residuals. This output has the same form as the autocorrelation check for white noise that the IDENTIFY statement prints for the response series. The autocorrelation check of residuals is shown in Figure 3.13.

```
                Autocorrelation Check of Residuals

     To    Chi                    Autocorrelations
     Lag  Square DF   Prob
      6   19.09   5  0.002   0.327 -0.220 -0.128  0.068 -0.002 -0.096
     12   22.90  11  0.018   0.072  0.116 -0.042 -0.066  0.031 -0.091
     18   31.63  17  0.017  -0.233 -0.129 -0.024  0.056 -0.014 -0.008
     24   32.83  23  0.084   0.009 -0.057 -0.057 -0.001  0.049 -0.015
```

Figure 3.13. Check for White Noise Residuals for AR(1) Model

The χ^2 test statistics for the residuals series indicate whether the residuals are uncorrelated (white noise) or contain additional information that might be utilized by a more complex model. In this case, the test statistics reject the no-autocorrelation hypothesis at a high level of significance. ($p = 0.002$ for the first six lags.) This means that the residuals are not white noise, and so the AR(1) model is not a fully adequate model for this series.

The final part of the ESTIMATE statement output is a listing of the estimated model using the back shift notation. This output is shown in Figure 3.14.

```
            Model for variable SALES

            Estimated Mean = 0.90279892
            Period(s) of Differencing = 1.

            Autoregressive Factors
            Factor 1: 1 - 0.86847 B**(1)
```

Figure 3.14. Estimated ARIMA(1,1,0) Model for SALES

This listing combines the differencing specification given in the IDENTIFY statement with the parameter estimates of the model for the change in sales. Since the AR(1) model is for the change in sales, the final model for sales is an ARIMA(1,1,0) model. The mathematical form of the estimated model shown in this output is as follows:

$$(1 - B)sales_t = 0.90279892 + \frac{1}{(1 - 0.86847\,B)}\,a_t$$

See the section "General Notation for ARIMA Model" later in this chapter for further explanation of this notation.

Estimating an ARMA(1,1) Model

The IDENTIFY statement plots suggest a mixed autoregressive and moving average model, and the previous ESTIMATE statement check of residuals indicates that an AR(1) model is not sufficient. You now try estimating an ARMA(1,1) model for the change in SALES.

An ARMA(1,1) model predicts the change in SALES as an average change, plus some fraction of the previous change, plus a random error, plus some fraction of the random error in the preceding period. An ARMA(1,1) model for the change in sales is the same as an ARIMA(1,1,1) model for the level of sales.

To estimate a mixed autoregressive moving average model, you specify the order of the moving average part of the model with the Q= option on an ESTIMATE statement in addition to specifying the order of the autoregressive part with the P= option. The following statements fit an ARMA(1,1) model to the differenced SALES series:

```
estimate p=1 q=1;
run;
```

The parameter-estimates table and goodness-of-fit statistics for this model are shown in Figure 3.15.

```
              Conditional Least Squares Estimation

                              Approx.
    Parameter    Estimate    Std Error    T Ratio   Lag
    MU            0.89288      0.49391       1.81     0
    MA1,1        -0.58935      0.08988      -6.56     1
    AR1,1         0.74755      0.07785       9.60     1

    Constant Estimate  = 0.22540938

    Variance  Estimate = 0.90403418
    Std Error Estimate = 0.95080712
    AIC                = 273.915513*
    SBC                = 281.700872*
    Number of Residuals=        99
    * Does not include log determinant.
```

Figure 3.15. Estimated ARMA(1,1) Model for Change in SALES

The moving average parameter estimate, labeled "MA1,1", is -0.58935. Both the moving average and the autoregressive parameters have significant t ratios. Note that the variance estimate, AIC, and SBC are all smaller than they were for the AR(1) model, indicating that the ARMA(1,1) model fits the data better.

The check for white noise residuals is shown in Figure 3.16. The χ^2 tests show that we cannot reject the hypothesis that the residuals are uncorrelated. Thus, you conclude that the ARMA(1,1) model is adequate for the change in sales series, and there is no point in trying more complex models.

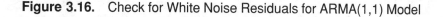

```
                 Autocorrelation Check of Residuals
  To    Chi                    Autocorrelations
  Lag  Square DF   Prob
   6    3.95   4   0.413   0.016 -0.044 -0.068  0.145  0.024 -0.094
  12    7.03  10   0.723   0.088  0.087 -0.037 -0.075  0.051 -0.053
  18   15.41  16   0.495  -0.221 -0.033 -0.092  0.086 -0.074 -0.005
  24   16.96  22   0.766   0.011 -0.066 -0.022 -0.032  0.062 -0.047
```

Figure 3.16.   Check for White Noise Residuals for ARMA(1,1) Model

The output showing the form of the estimated ARIMA(1,1,1) model for SALES is shown in Figure 3.17.

```
              Model for variable SALES

              Estimated Mean = 0.89287527
              Period(s) of Differencing = 1.

              Autoregressive Factors
              Factor 1: 1 - 0.74755 B**(1)


              Moving Average Factors
              Factor 1: 1 + 0.58935 B**(1)
```

Figure 3.17.   Estimated ARIMA(1,1,1) Model for SALES

The estimated model shown in this output is

$$(1 - B)sales_t = 0.89287527 + \frac{(1 + 0.58935\,B)}{(1 - 0.74755\,B)}\,a_t$$

Since the model diagnostic tests show that all the parameter estimates are significant and the residual series is white noise, the estimation and diagnostic checking stage is complete. You can now proceed to forecasting the SALES series with this ARIMA(1,1,1) model.

Forecasting Stage

To produce the forecast, use a FORECAST statement after the ESTIMATE statement for the model you decide is best. If the last model fit were not the best, then repeat the ESTIMATE statement for the best model before using the FORECAST statement.

Suppose that the SALES series is monthly, that you wish to forecast one year ahead from the most recently available sales figure, and that the dates for the observations are given by a variable DATE in the input data set TEST. You use the following FORECAST statement:

```
forecast lead=12 interval=month id=date out=results;
run;
```

The LEAD= option specifies how many periods ahead to forecast (12 months, in this case). The ID= option specifies the ID variable used to date the observations of the SALES time series. The INTERVAL= option indicates that data are monthly and enables PROC ARIMA to extrapolate DATE values for forecast periods. The OUT=

option writes the forecasts to an output data set RESULTS. See the section "OUT= Data Set" later in this chapter for information on the contents of the output data set.

By default, the FORECAST statement also prints the forecast values, as shown in Figure 3.18. This output shows for each forecast period the observation number, forecast value, standard error estimate for the forecast value, and lower and upper limits for a 95% confidence interval for the forecast.

```
Forecasts for variable SALES

Obs    Forecast Std Error    Lower 95%    Upper 95%
101    171.0320    0.9508    169.1684     172.8955
102    174.7534    2.4168    170.0165     179.4903
103    177.7608    3.9879    169.9445     185.5770
104    180.2343    5.5658    169.3256     191.1430
105    182.3088    7.1033    168.3866     196.2310
106    184.0850    8.5789    167.2707     200.8993
107    185.6382    9.9841    166.0698     205.2066
108    187.0247   11.3173    164.8433     209.2061
109    188.2866   12.5807    163.6289     212.9443
110    189.4553   13.7784    162.4501     216.4605
111    190.5544   14.9153    161.3209     219.7879
112    191.6014   15.9964    160.2491     222.9538
```

Figure 3.18. Estimated ARIMA(1,1,1) Model for SALES

Normally, you want the forecast values stored in an output data set, and you are not interested in seeing this printed list of the forecast. You can use the NOPRINT option on the FORECAST statement to suppress this output.

Using ARIMA Procedure Statements

The IDENTIFY, ESTIMATE, and FORECAST statements are related in a hierarchy. An IDENTIFY statement brings in a time series to be modeled; several ESTIMATE statements can follow to estimate different ARIMA models for the series; for each model estimated, several FORECAST statements can be used. Thus, a FORECAST statement must be preceded at some point by an ESTIMATE statement, and an ESTIMATE statement must be preceded at some point by an IDENTIFY statement. Additional IDENTIFY statements can be used to switch to modeling a different response series or to change the degree of differencing used.

The ARIMA procedure can be used interactively in the sense that all ARIMA procedure statements can be executed any number of times without reinvoking PROC ARIMA. You can execute ARIMA procedure statements singly or in groups by following the single statement or group of statements with a RUN statement. The output for each statement or group of statements is produced when the RUN statement is entered.

A RUN statement does not terminate the PROC ARIMA step but tells the procedure to execute the statements given so far. You can end PROC ARIMA by submitting a DATA step, another PROC step, an ENDSAS statement, or a QUIT statement.

The example in the preceding section illustrates the interactive use of ARIMA procedure statements. The complete PROC ARIMA program for that example is as follows:

```
proc arima data=test;
   identify var=sales nlag=8;
   run;
   identify var=sales(1) nlag=8;
   run;
   estimate p=1;
   run;
   estimate p=1 q=1;
   run;
   forecast lead=12 interval=month id=date out=results;
   run;
quit;
```

General Notation for ARIMA Models

ARIMA is an acronym for autoregressive integrated moving-average. The order of an ARIMA model is usually denoted by the notation ARIMA(p,d,q), where

p is the order of the autoregressive part

d is the order of the differencing

q is the order of the moving-average process

If no differencing is done $(d = 0)$, the models are usually referred to as ARMA(p,q) models. The final model in the preceding example is an ARIMA(1,1,1) model since the IDENTIFY statement specified $d = 1$, and the final ESTIMATE statement specified $p = 1$ and $q = 1$.

Notation for Pure ARIMA Models

Mathematically the pure ARIMA model is written as

$$\mathbf{W}_t = \mu + \frac{\theta(\mathrm{B})}{\phi(\mathrm{B})} a_t$$

where

t indexes time

$\mathbf{W}_t$ is the response series $\mathbf{Y}_t$ or a difference of the response series

μ is the mean term

B   is the backshift operator; that is, $\mathrm{B}\mathbf{X}_t = \mathbf{X}_{t-1}$

$\phi(\mathrm{B})$ is the autoregressive operator, represented as a polynomial in the back shift operator: $\phi(\mathrm{B}) = 1 - \phi_1 \mathrm{B} - \ldots - \phi_p \mathrm{B}^p$

$\theta(\mathrm{B})$ is the moving-average operator, represented as a polynomial in the back shift operator: $\theta(\mathrm{B}) = 1 - \theta_1 \mathrm{B} - \ldots - \theta_q \mathrm{B}^q$

a_t is the independent disturbance, also called the random error

The series $\mathbf{W}_t$ is computed by the IDENTIFY statement and is the series processed by the ESTIMATE statement. Thus, $\mathbf{W}_t$ is either the response series $\mathbf{Y}_t$ or a difference of $\mathbf{Y}_t$ specified by the differencing operators in the IDENTIFY statement.

For simple (nonseasonal) differencing, $\mathbf{W}_t = (1 - \mathrm{B})^d \mathbf{Y}_t$. For seasonal differencing $\mathbf{W}_t = (1 - B)^d (1 - B^s)^D \mathbf{Y}_t$, where d is the degree of nonseasonal differencing, D is the degree of seasonal differencing, and s is the length of the seasonal cycle.

For example, the mathematical form of the ARIMA(1,1,1) model estimated in the preceding example is

$$(1 - B)\mathbf{Y}_t = \mu + \frac{(1 - \theta_1 B)}{(1 - \phi_1 B)} a_t$$

Model Constant Term

The ARIMA model can also be written as

$$\phi(B)(\mathbf{W}_t - \mu) = \theta(B)a_t$$

or

$$\phi(B)\mathbf{W}_t = const + \theta(B)a_t$$

where

$$const = \phi(B)\mu = \mu - \phi_1\mu - \phi_2\mu - \ \ldots \ - \phi_p\mu$$

Thus, when an autoregressive operator and a mean term are both included in the model, the constant term for the model can be represented as $\phi(B)\mu$. This value is printed with the label "Constant Estimate" in the ESTIMATE statement output.

Notation for Transfer Function Models

The general ARIMA model with input series, also called the ARIMAX model, is written as

$$\mathbf{W}_t = \mu + \sum_i \frac{\omega_i(B)}{\delta_i(B)} B^{k_i} \mathbf{X}_{i,t} + \frac{\theta(B)}{\phi(B)} a_t$$

where

$\mathbf{X}_{i,t}$ is the ith input time series or a difference of the ith input series at time t

k_i is the pure time delay for the effect of the ith input series

$\omega_i(B)$ is the numerator polynomial of the transfer function for the ith input series

$\delta_i(B)$ is the denominator polynomial of the transfer function for the ith input series

The model can also be written more compactly as

$$\mathbf{W}_t = \mu + \sum_i \Psi_i(B)\mathbf{X}_{i,t} + n_t$$

where

$\Psi_i(B)$ is the transfer function weights for the ith input series modeled as a ratio of the ω and δ polynomials: $\Psi_i(B) = (\omega_i(B)/\delta_i(B))B^{k_i}$

n_t is the noise series: $n_t = (\theta(\mathrm{B})/\phi(\mathrm{B}))a_t$

This model expresses the response series as a combination of past values of the random shocks and past values of other series (called input series). The response series is also called the *dependent series* or *output series*. An input time series is also referred to as an *independent series* or a *predictor series*. Response variable, dependent variable, independent variable, or predictor variable are other terms often used.

Notation for Factored Models

ARIMA models are sometimes expressed in a factored form. This means that the ϕ, θ, ω, or δ polynomials are expressed as products of simpler polynomials. For example, we could express the pure ARIMA model as

$$\mathbf{W}_t = \mu + \frac{\theta_1(\mathrm{B})\theta_2(\mathrm{B})}{\phi_1(\mathrm{B})\phi_2(\mathrm{B})}a_t$$

where $\phi_1(\mathrm{B})\phi_2(\mathrm{B}) = \phi(\mathrm{B})$ and $\theta_1(\mathrm{B})\theta_2(\mathrm{B}) = \theta(\mathrm{B})$.

When an ARIMA model is expressed in factored form, the order of the model is usually expressed using a factored notation also. The order of an ARIMA model expressed as the product of two factors is denoted as ARIMA(p,d,q) × (P,D,Q).

Notation for Seasonal Models

ARIMA models for time series with regular seasonal fluctuations often use differencing operators and autoregressive and moving average parameters at lags that are multiples of the length of the seasonal cycle. When all the terms in an ARIMA model factor refer to lags that are a multiple of a constant s, the constant is factored out and suffixed to the ARIMA(p,d,q) notation.

Thus, the general notation for the order of a seasonal ARIMA model with both seasonal and nonseasonal factors is ARIMA(p,d,q) × (P,D,Q)$_s$. The term (p,d,q) gives the order of the nonseasonal part of the ARIMA model; the term (P,D,Q)$_s$ gives the order of the seasonal part. The value of s is the number of observations in a seasonal cycle: 12 for monthly series, 4 for quarterly series, 7 for daily series with day-of-week effects, and so forth.

For example, the notation ARIMA($0,1,2$) × ($0,1,1$)$_{12}$ describes a seasonal ARIMA model for monthly data with the following mathematical form:

$$(1 - \mathrm{B})\left(1 - \mathrm{B}^{12}\right)\mathbf{Y}_t = \mu + \left(1 - \theta_{1,1}\mathrm{B} - \theta_{1,2}\mathrm{B}^2\right)\left(1 - \theta_{2,1}\mathrm{B}^{12}\right)a_t$$

Stationarity

The noise series for an ARMA model must be *stationary*, which means that both the expected values of the series and its autocovariance function are independent of time.

The standard way to check for nonstationarity is to plot the series and its autocorrelation function. You can visually examine a graph of the series over time to see if it has a visible trend or if its variability changes noticeably over time. If the series is nonstationary, its autocorrelation function will usually decay slowly.

Most time series are nonstationary and must be transformed to a stationary series before the ARIMA modeling process can proceed. If the series has a nonstationary variance, taking the log of the series may help. You can compute the log values in a DATA step and then analyze the log values with PROC ARIMA.

If the series has a trend over time, seasonality, or some other nonstationary pattern, the usual solution is to take the difference of the series from one period to the next and then analyze this differenced series. Sometimes a series may need to be differenced more than once or differenced at lags greater than one period. (If the trend or seasonal effects are very regular, the introduction of explanatory variables may be an appropriate alternative to differencing.)

Differencing

Differencing of the response series is specified with the VAR= option of the IDENTIFY statement by placing a list of differencing periods in parentheses after the variable name. For example, to take a simple first difference of the series SALES, use the statement

```
identify var=sales(1);
```

In this example, the change in SALES from one period to the next will be analyzed.

A deterministic seasonal pattern will also cause the series to be nonstationary, since the expected value of the series will not be the same for all time periods but will be higher or lower depending on the season. When the series has a seasonal pattern, you may want to difference the series at a lag corresponding to the length of the cycle of seasons. For example, if SALES is a monthly series, the statement

```
identify var=sales(12);
```

takes a seasonal difference of SALES, so that the series analyzed is the change in SALES from its value in the same month one year ago.

To take a second difference, add another differencing period to the list. For example, the following statement takes the second difference of SALES:

```
identify var=sales(1,1);
```

That is, SALES is differenced once at lag 1 and then differenced again, also at lag 1. The statement

```
identify var=sales(1,12);
```

takes a second-order difference of SALES, so that the series analyzed is the difference between the current period-to-period change in SALES and the change 12 periods ago. You might want to do this if the series had both a trend over time and a seasonal pattern.

There is no limit to what you can specify for the order of differencing and the degree of lagging for each difference.

Differencing not only affects the series used for the IDENTIFY statement output but also applies to any following ESTIMATE and FORECAST statements. ESTIMATE statements fit ARMA models to the differenced series. FORECAST statements forecast the differences and automatically sum these differences back to undo the differencing operation specified by the IDENTIFY statement, thus producing the final forecast result.

Differencing of input series is specified by the CROSSCORR= option and works just like differencing of the response series. For example, the statement

```
identify var=y(1) crosscorr=(x1(1) x2(1));
```

takes the first difference of Y, the first difference of X1, and the first difference of X2. Whenever X1 and X2 are used in INPUT= options in following ESTIMATE statements, these names refer to the differenced series.

Subset, Seasonal, and Factored ARMA Models

The simplest way to specify an ARMA model is to give the order of the AR and MA parts with the P= and Q= options. When you do this, the model has parameters for the AR and MA parts for all lags through the order specified. However, you can control the form of the ARIMA model exactly as shown in the following section.

Subset Models

You can control which lags have parameters by specifying the P= or Q= option as a list of lags in parentheses. A model like this that includes parameters for only some lags is sometimes called a *subset model*. For example, consider the following two ESTIMATE statements:

```
identify var=sales;
estimate p=4;
estimate p=(1 4);
```

Both specify AR(4) models, but the first has parameters for lags 1, 2, 3, and 4, while the second has parameters for lags 1 and 4, with the coefficients for lags 2 and 3 constrained to 0. The mathematical form of the autoregressive models produced by these two specifications is shown in Table 3.1.

Table 3.1.   Saturated versus Subset Models

P= Option	Autoregressive Operator
P=4	$\left(1 - \phi_1 B - \phi_2 B^2 - \phi_3 B^3 - \phi_4 B^4\right)$
P=(1 4)	$\left(1 - \phi_1 B - \phi_4 B^4\right)$

Seasonal Models

One particularly useful kind of subset model is a *seasonal model*. When the response series has a seasonal pattern, the values of the series at the same time of year in previous years may be important for modeling the series. For example, if the series SALES is observed monthly, the statements

```
identify var=sales;
estimate p=(12);
```

model SALES as an average value plus some fraction of its deviation from this average value a year ago, plus a random error. Although this is an AR(12) model, it has only one autoregressive parameter.

Factored Models

A factored model represents the ARIMA model as a product of simpler ARIMA models. For example, you might model SALES as a combination of an AR(1) process reflecting short term dependencies and an AR(12) model reflecting the seasonal pattern.

It might seem that the way to do this is with the option P=(1 12), but the AR(1) process also operates in past years; you really need autoregressive parameters at lags 1, 12, and 13. You can specify a subset model with separate parameters at these lags, or you can specify a factored model that represents the model as the product of an AR(1) model and an AR(12) model. Consider the following two ESTIMATE statements:

```
identify var=sales;
estimate p=(1 12 13);
estimate p=(1)(12);
```

The mathematical form of the autoregressive models produced by these two specifications are shown in Table 3.2.

Table 3.2.   Subset versus Factored Models

P= Option	Autoregressive Operator
P=(1 12 13)	$\left(1 - \phi_1 B - \phi_{12} B^{12} - \phi_{13} B^{13}\right)$
P=(1)(12)	$\left(1 - \phi_1 B\right)\left(1 - \phi_{12} B^{12}\right)$

Both models fit by these two ESTIMATE statements predict SALES from its values 1, 12, and 13 periods ago, but they use different parameterizations. The first model has three parameters, whose meanings may be hard to interpret.

The factored specification P=(1)(12) represents the model as the product of two different AR models. It has only two parameters: one that corresponds to recent effects and one that represents seasonal effects. Thus the factored model is more parsimonious, and its parameter estimates are more clearly interpretable.

Input Variables and Regression with ARMA Errors

In addition to past values of the response series and past errors, you can also model the response series using the current and past values of other series, called *input series*.

Several different names are used to describe ARIMA models with input series. *Transfer function model*, *intervention model*, *interrupted time series model*, *regression model with ARMA errors*, *Box-Tiao model*, and *ARIMAX model* are all different names for ARIMA models with input series. Pankratz (1991) refers to these models as *dynamic regression*.

Using Input Series

To use input series, list the input series in a CROSSCORR= option on the IDENTIFY statement and specify how they enter the model with an INPUT= option on the ESTIMATE statement. For example, you might use a series called PRICE to help model SALES, as shown in the following statements:

```
proc arima data=a;
    identify var=sales crosscorr=price;
    estimate input=price;
    run;
```

This example performs a simple linear regression of SALES on PRICE, producing the same results as PROC REG or another SAS regression procedure. The mathematical form of the model estimated by these statements is

$$\mathbf{Y}_t = \mu + \omega_0 \mathbf{X}_t + a_t$$

The parameter estimates table for this example (using simulated data) is shown in Figure 3.19. The intercept parameter is labeled MU. The regression coefficient for PRICE is labeled NUM1. (See the section "Naming of Model Parameters" later in this chapter for information on how parameters for input series are named.)

```
                  Conditional Least Squares Estimation

                              Approx.
     Parameter    Estimate   Std Error   T Ratio   Lag   Variable   Shift
     MU           199.84459    0.48757    409.88     0    SALES        0
     NUM1          -9.99151    0.03276   -304.98     0    PRICE        0
```

Figure 3.19. Parameter Estimates Table for Regression Model

Any number of input variables can be used in a model. For example, the following statements fit a multiple regression of SALES on PRICE and INCOME:

```
proc arima data=a;
    identify var=sales crosscorr=(price income);
    estimate input=(price income);
    run;
```

The mathematical form of the regression model estimated by these statements is

$$\mathbf{Y}_t = \mu + \omega_{1,0}\mathbf{X}_{1,t} + \omega_{2,0}\mathbf{X}_{2,t} + a_t$$

Lagging and Differencing Input Series

You can also difference and lag the input series. For example, the following statements regress the change in SALES on the change in PRICE lagged by one period.

```
proc arima data=a;
    identify var=sales(1) crosscorr=price(1);
    estimate input=( 1 $ price );
    run;
```

These statements estimate the model

$$(1 - \mathrm{B})\mathbf{Y}_t = \mu + \omega_0(1 - \mathrm{B})\mathbf{X}_{t-1} + a_t$$

Regression with ARMA Errors

You can combine input series with ARMA models for the errors. For example, the following statements regress SALES on INCOME and PRICE but with the error term of the regression model (called the *noise series* in ARIMA modeling terminology) assumed to be an ARMA(1,1) process.

```
proc arima data=a;
    identify var=sales crosscorr=(price income);
    estimate p=1 q=1 input=(price income);
    run;
```

These statements estimate the model

$$\mathbf{Y}_t = \mu + \omega_{1,0}\mathbf{X}_{1,t} + \omega_{2,0}\mathbf{X}_{2,t} + \frac{(1 - \theta_1\mathrm{B})}{(1 - \phi_1\mathrm{B})}a_t$$

Stationarity and Input Series

Note that the requirement of stationarity applies to the noise series. If there are no input variables, the response series (after differencing and minus the mean term) and the noise series are the same. However, if there are inputs, the noise series is the residual after the effect of the inputs is removed.

There is no requirement that the input series be stationary. If the inputs are nonstationary, the response series will be nonstationary, even though the noise process may be stationary.

When nonstationary input series are used, you can fit the input variables first with no ARMA model for the errors and then consider the stationarity of the residuals before identifying an ARMA model for the noise part.

Identifying Regression Models with ARMA Errors

Previous sections described the ARIMA modeling identification process using the autocorrelation function plots produced by the IDENTIFY statement. This identification process does not apply when the response series depends on input variables. This is because it is the noise process for which we need to identify an ARIMA model, and when input series are involved the response series adjusted for the mean is no longer an estimate of the noise series.

However, if the input series are independent of the noise series, you can use the residuals from the regression model as an estimate of the noise series, then apply the ARIMA modeling identification process to this residual series. This assumes that the noise process is stationary.

The PLOT option on the ESTIMATE statement produces for the model residuals the same plots as the IDENTIFY statement produces for the response series. The PLOT option prints an autocorrelation function plot, an inverse autocorrelation function plot, and a partial autocorrelation function plot for the residual series.

The following statements show how the PLOT option is used to identify the ARMA(1,1) model for the noise process used in the preceding example of regression with ARMA errors:

```
proc arima data=a;
    identify var=sales crosscorr=(price income) noprint;
    estimate input=(price income) plot;
    run;
    estimate p=1 q=1 input=(price income) plot;
    run;
```

In this example, the IDENTIFY statement includes the NOPRINT option since the autocorrelation plots for the response series are not useful when you know that the response series depends on input series.

The first ESTIMATE statement fits the regression model with no model for the noise process and includes the PLOT option to produce autocorrelation, inverse autocorrelation, and partial autocorrelation function plots for the residual series of the regression on PRICE and INCOME.

By examining the PLOT option output for the residual series, you verify that the residual series is stationary and identify an ARMA(1,1) model for the noise process. The second ESTIMATE statement fits the final model.

Although this discussion addresses regression models, the same remarks apply to identifying an ARIMA model for the noise process in models that include input series with complex transfer functions.

Intervention Models and Interrupted Time Series

One special kind of ARIMA model with input series is called an *intervention model* or *interrupted time series* model. In an intervention model, the input series is an indicator variable containing discrete values that flag the occurrence of an event affecting the response series. This event is an intervention in or an interruption of the normal evolution of the response time series, which, in the absence of the intervention, is usually assumed to be a pure ARIMA process.

Intervention models can be used both to model and forecast the response series and to analyze the impact of the intervention. When the focus is on estimating the effect of the intervention, the process is often called *intervention analysis* or *interrupted time series analysis*.

Impulse Interventions

The intervention can be a one-time event. For example, you might want to study the effect of a short-term advertising campaign on the sales of a product. In this case, the input variable has the value of 1 for the period during which the advertising campaign took place and the value 0 for all other periods. Intervention variables of this kind are sometimes called *impulse functions* or *pulse functions.*

Suppose that SALES is a monthly series, and a special advertising effort was made during the month of March 1992. The following statements estimate the effect of this intervention assuming an ARMA(1,1) model for SALES. The model is specified just like the regression model, but the intervention variable AD is constructed in the DATA step as a zero-one indicator for the month of the advertising effort.

```
data a;
   set a;
   ad = date = '1mar1992'd;
run;

proc arima data=a;
   identify var=sales crosscorr=ad;
   estimate p=1 q=1 input=ad;
run;
```

Continuing Interventions

Other interventions can be continuing, in which case the input variable flags periods before and after the intervention. For example, you might want to study the effect of a change in tax rates on some economic measure. Another example is a study of the effect of a change in speed limits on the rate of traffic fatalities. In this case, the input variable has the value 1 after the new speed limit went into effect and the value 0 before. Intervention variables of this kind are called *step functions.*

Another example is the effect of news on product demand. Suppose it was reported in March 1992 that consumption of the product prevents heart disease (or causes cancer), and SALES is consistently higher (or lower) thereafter. The following statements model the effect of this news intervention:

```
data a;
   set a;
   news = date >= '1mar1992'd;
run;

proc arima data=a;
   identify var=sales crosscorr=news;
   estimate p=1 q=1 input=news;
run;
```

Interaction Effects

You can include any number of intervention variables in the model. Intervention variables can have any pattern—impulse and continuing interventions are just two possible cases. You can mix discrete valued intervention variables and continuous regressor variables in the same model.

You can also form interaction effects by multiplying input variables and including the product variable as another input. Indeed, as long as the dependent measure forms a regular time series, you can use PROC ARIMA to fit any general linear model in conjunction with an ARMA model for the error process by using input variables that correspond to the columns of the design matrix of the linear model.

Rational Transfer Functions and Distributed Lag Models

How an input series enters the model is called its *transfer function*. Thus, ARIMA models with input series are sometimes referred to as transfer function models.

In the preceding regression and intervention model examples, the transfer function is a single scale parameter. However, you can also specify complex transfer functions composed of numerator and denominator polynomials in the backshift operator. These transfer functions operate on the input series in the same way that the ARMA specification operates on the error term.

Numerator Factors

For example, suppose you want to model the effect of PRICE on SALES as taking place gradually with the impact distributed over several past lags of PRICE. This is illustrated by the following statements:

```
proc arima data=a;
   identify var=sales crosscorr=price;
   estimate input=( (1 2 3) price );
   run;
```

These statements estimate the model

$$\mathbf{Y}_t = \mu + \left(\omega_0 - \omega_1 B - \omega_2 B^2 - \omega_3 B^3\right)\mathbf{X}_t + a_t$$

This example models the effect of PRICE on SALES as a linear function of the current and three most recent values of PRICE. It is equivalent to a multiple linear regression of SALES on PRICE, LAG(PRICE), LAG2(PRICE), and LAG3(PRICE).

This is an example of a transfer function with one *numerator factor*. The numerator factors for a transfer function for an input series are like the MA part of the ARMA model for the noise series.

Denominator Factors

You can also use transfer functions with *denominator factors*. The denominator factors for a transfer function for an input series are like the AR part of the ARMA model for the noise series. Denominator factors introduce exponentially weighted, infinite distributed lags into the transfer function.

To specify transfer functions with denominator factors, place the denominator factors after a slash (/) in the INPUT= option. For example, the following statements estimate the PRICE effect as an infinite distributed lag model with exponentially declining weights:

```
proc arima data=a;
   identify var=sales crosscorr=price;
   estimate input=( / (1) price );
   run;
```

The transfer function specified by these statements is as follows:

$$\frac{\omega_0}{(1 - \delta_1 B)} X_t$$

This transfer function also can be written in the following equivalent form:

$$\omega_0 \left(1 + \sum_{i=1}^{\infty} \delta_1^i B^i \right) X_t$$

This transfer function can be used with intervention inputs. When it is used with a pulse function input, the result is an intervention effect that dies out gradually over time. When it is used with a step function input, the result is an intervention effect that increases gradually to a limiting value.

Rational Transfer Functions

By combining various numerator and denominator factors in the INPUT= option, you can specify *rational transfer functions* of any complexity. To specify an input with a general rational transfer function of the form

$$\frac{\omega(B)}{\delta(B)} B^k X_t$$

use an INPUT= option in the ESTIMATE statement of the form

```
input=( k $ ( ω-lags ) / ( δ-lags ) x )
```

See the section "Specifying Inputs and Transfer Functions" later in this chapter for more information.

Identifying Transfer Function Models

The CROSSCORR= option of the IDENTIFY statement prints sample cross-correlation functions showing the correlations between the response series and the input series at different lags. The sample cross-correlation function can be used to help identify the form of the transfer function appropriate for an input series. See textbooks on time series analysis for information on using cross-correlation functions to identify transfer function models.

For the cross-correlation function to be meaningful, the input and response series must be filtered with a prewhitening model for the input series. See the section "Prewhitening" later in this chapter for more information on this issue.

Forecasting with Input Variables

To forecast a response series using an ARIMA model with inputs, you need values of the input series for the forecast periods. You can supply values for the input variables for the forecast periods in the DATA= data set, or you can have PROC ARIMA forecast the input variables.

If you do not have future values of the input variables in the input data set used by the FORECAST statement, the input series must be forecast before the ARIMA procedure can forecast the response series. If you fit an ARIMA model to each of the input series you need forecasts for before fitting the model for the response series, the FORECAST statement automatically uses the ARIMA models for the input series to generate the needed forecasts of the inputs.

For example, suppose you want to forecast SALES for the next 12 months. In this example, we predict the change in SALES as a function of the lagged change in PRICE, plus an ARMA(1,1) noise process. To forecast SALES using PRICE as an input, you also need to fit an ARIMA model for PRICE.

The following statements fit an AR(2) model to the change in PRICE before fitting and forecasting the model for SALES. The FORECAST statement automatically forecasts PRICE using this AR(2) model to get the future inputs needed to produce the forecast of SALES.

```
proc arima data=a;
   identify var=price(1);
   estimate p=2;
   identify var=sales(1) crosscorr=price(1);
   estimate p=1 q=1 input=price;
   forecast lead=12 interval=month id=date out=results;
run;
```

Fitting a model to the input series is also important for identifying transfer functions. (See the section "Prewhitening" later in this chapter for more information.)

Input values from the DATA= data set and input values forecast by PROC ARIMA can be combined. For example, a model for SALES might have three input series: PRICE, INCOME, and TAXRATE. For the forecast, you assume that the tax rate will be unchanged. You have a forecast for INCOME from another source but only for the first few periods of the SALES forecast you want to make. You have no future values for PRICE, which needs to be forecast as in the preceding example.

In this situation, you include observations in the input data set for all forecast periods, with SALES and PRICE set to a missing value, with TAXRATE set to its last actual value, and with INCOME set to forecast values for the periods you have forecasts for and set to missing values for later periods. In the PROC ARIMA step, you estimate ARIMA models for PRICE and INCOME before estimating the model for SALES, as shown in the following statements:

```
proc arima data=a;
   identify var=price(1);
   estimate p=2;
   identify var=income(1);
   estimate p=2;
   identify var=sales(1) crosscorr=( price(1) income(1) taxrate );
   estimate p=1 q=1 input=( price income taxrate );
   forecast lead=12 interval=month id=date out=results;
   run;
```

In forecasting SALES, the ARIMA procedure uses as inputs the value of PRICE forecast by its ARIMA model, the value of TAXRATE found in the DATA= data set, and the value of INCOME found in the DATA= data set, or, when the INCOME variable is missing, the value of INCOME forecast by its ARIMA model. (Because SALES is missing for future time periods, the estimation of model parameters is not affected by the forecast values for PRICE, INCOME, or TAXRATE.)

Data Requirements

PROC ARIMA can handle time series of moderate size; there should be at least 30 observations. With 30 or fewer observations, the parameter estimates may be poor. With thousands of observations, the method requires considerable computer time and memory.

Syntax

The ARIMA procedure uses the following statements:

PROC ARIMA *options*;
    BY *variables*;
        IDENTIFY VAR= *variable options*;
        ESTIMATE *options*;
        FORECAST *options*;

Functional Summary

The statements and options controlling the ARIMA procedure are summarized in the following table.

Description	Statement	Option
Data Set Options		
specify the input data set	PROC ARIMA	DATA=
	IDENTIFY	DATA=
specify the output data set	PROC ARIMA	OUT=
	FORECAST	OUT=
include only forecasts in the output data set	FORECAST	NOOUTALL
write autocovariances to output data set	IDENTIFY	OUTCOV=
write parameter estimates to an output data set	ESTIMATE	OUTEST=
write correlation of parameter estimates	ESTIMATE	OUTCORR
write covariance of parameter estimates	ESTIMATE	OUTCOV
write estimated model to an output data set	ESTIMATE	OUTMODEL=
Options for Identifying the Series		
difference time series and plot autocorrelations	IDENTIFY	
specify response series and differencing	IDENTIFY	VAR=

Description	Statement	Option
specify and cross correlate input series	IDENTIFY	CROSSCORR=
center data by subtracting the mean	IDENTIFY	CENTER
exclude missing values	IDENTIFY	NOMISS
delete previous models and start fresh	IDENTIFY	CLEAR

Options for Defining and Estimating the Model

Description	Statement	Option
specify and estimate ARIMA models	ESTIMATE	
specify autoregressive part of model	ESTIMATE	P=
specify moving average part of model	ESTIMATE	Q=
specify input variables and transfer functions	ESTIMATE	INPUT=
drop mean term from the model	ESTIMATE	NOINT
specify the estimation method	ESTIMATE	METHOD=
use alternative form for transfer functions	ESTIMATE	ALTPARM
suppress degrees-of-freedom correction in variance estimates	ESTIMATE	NODF

Printing Control Options

Description	Statement	Option
limit number of lags shown in correlation plots	IDENTIFY	NLAG=
plot autocorrelation functions of the residuals	ESTIMATE	PLOT
print log likelihood around the estimates	ESTIMATE	GRID
control spacing for GRID option	ESTIMATE	GRIDVAL=
print details of the iterative estimation process	ESTIMATE	PRINTALL
suppress printed output for estimation	ESTIMATE	NOPRINT
suppress printing of the forecast values	FORECAST	NOPRINT
print the one-step forecasts and residuals	FORECAST	PRINTALL

Options to Specify Parameter Values

Description	Statement	Option
specify autoregressive starting values	ESTIMATE	AR=
specify moving average starting values	ESTIMATE	MA=
specify a starting value for the mean parameter	ESTIMATE	MU=
specify starting values for transfer functions	ESTIMATE	INITVAL=

Options to Control the Iterative Estimation Process

Description	Statement	Option
specify convergence criterion	ESTIMATE	CONVERGE=
specify the maximum number of iterations	ESTIMATE	MAXITER=
specify criterion for checking for singularity	ESTIMATE	SINGULAR=
suppress the iterative estimation process	ESTIMATE	NOEST
omit initial observations from objective	ESTIMATE	BACKLIM=
specify perturbation for numerical derivatives	ESTIMATE	DELTA=
omit stationarity and invertibility checks	ESTIMATE	NOSTABLE

Description	Statement	Option
Options for Forecasting		
forecast the response series	FORECAST	
specify how many periods to forecast	FORECAST	LEAD=
specify the ID variable	FORECAST	ID=
specify the periodicity of the series	FORECAST	INTERVAL=
specify size of forecast confidence limits	FORECAST	ALPHA=
start forecasting before end of the input data	FORECAST	BACK=
BY Groups		
specify BY group processing	BY	

PROC ARIMA Statement

PROC ARIMA *options*;

The following options can be used in the PROC ARIMA statement:

DATA= *SAS-data-set*

specifies the name of the SAS data set containing the time series. If different DATA= specifications appear in the PROC ARIMA and IDENTIFY statements, the one in the IDENTIFY statement is used. If the DATA= option is not specified in either the PROC ARIMA or IDENTIFY statement, the most recently created SAS data set is used.

OUT= *SAS-data-set*

specifies a SAS data set to which the forecasts are output. If different OUT= specifications appear in the PROC ARIMA and FORECAST statement, the one in the FORECAST statement is used.

BY Statement

BY *variables*;

A BY statement can be used in the ARIMA procedure to process a data set in groups of observations defined by the BY variables. Note that all IDENTIFY, ESTIMATE, and FORECAST statements specified are applied to all BY groups.

Because of the need to make data-based model selections, BY-group processing is not usually done with PROC ARIMA. You usually want different models for the different series contained in different BY-groups, and the PROC ARIMA BY statement does not let you do this.

Using a BY statement imposes certain restrictions. The BY statement must appear before the first RUN statement. If a BY statement is used, the input data must come from the data set specified in the PROC statement; that is, no input data sets can be specified in IDENTIFY statements.

When a BY statement is used with PROC ARIMA, interactive processing only applies to the first BY group. Once the end of the PROC ARIMA step is reached, all ARIMA statements specified are executed again for each of the remaining BY groups in the input data set.

IDENTIFY Statement

IDENTIFY VAR= *variable options*;

The IDENTIFY statement specifies the time series to be modeled, differences the series if desired, and computes statistics to help identify models to fit. Use an IDENTIFY statement for each time series that you want to model.

If other time series are to be used as inputs in a subsequent ESTIMATE statement, they must be listed in a CROSSCORR= list in the IDENTIFY statement.

The following options are used in the IDENTIFY statement. The VAR= option is required.

CENTER
> centers each time series by subtracting its sample mean. The analysis is done on the centered data. Later, when forecasts are generated, the mean is added back. Note that centering is done after differencing. The CENTER option is normally used in conjunction with the NOCONSTANT option of the ESTIMATE statement.

CLEAR
> deletes all old models. This option is useful when you want to delete old models so that the input variables are not prewhitened. (See the section "Prewhitening" later in this chapter for more information.)

CROSSCORR= *variable* (*d11, d12, ..., d1k*)
CROSSCORR= (*variable* (*d11, d12, ..., d1k*) ... *variable* (*d21, d22, ..., d2k*))
> names the variables cross correlated with the response variable given by the VAR= specification.

> Each variable name can be followed by a list of differencing lags in parentheses, the same as for the VAR= specification. If differencing is specified for a variable in the CROSSCORR= list, the differenced series is cross correlated with the VAR= option series, and the differenced series is used when the ESTIMATE statement INPUT= option refers to the variable.

DATA= *SAS-data-set*
> specifies the input SAS data set containing the time series. If the DATA= option is omitted, the DATA= data set specified in the PROC ARIMA statement is used; if the DATA= option is omitted from the PROC ARIMA statement as well, the most recently created data set is used.

NLAG= *number*

indicates the number of lags to consider in computing the autocorrelations and cross correlations. To obtain preliminary estimates of an ARIMA(p,d,q) model, the NLAG= value must be at least $p + q + d$. The number of observations must be greater than or equal to the NLAG= value. The default value for NLAG= is 24 or one-fourth the number of observations, whichever is less. Even though the NLAG= value is specified, the NLAG= value can be changed according to the data set.

NOMISS

uses only the first continuous sequence of data with no missing values. By default, all observations are used.

NOPRINT

suppresses the normal printout (including the correlation plots) generated by the IDENTIFY statement.

OUTCOV= *SAS-data-set*

writes the autocovariances, autocorrelations, inverse autocorrelations, partial autocorrelations, and cross covariances to an output SAS data set. If the OUTCOV= option is not specified, no covariance output data set is created. See the section "OUTCOV= Data Set" later in this chapter for more information.

VAR= *variable*
VAR= *variable* (*d1, d2, ..., dk*)

names the variable containing the time series to analyze. The VAR= option is required.

A list of differencing lags can be placed in parentheses after the variable name to request that the series be differenced at these lags. For example, VAR=X(1) takes the first differences of X. VAR=X(1,1) requests that X be differenced twice, both times with lag 1, producing a second difference series, which is $\left(\mathbf{X}_t - \mathbf{X}_{t-1} \right) - \left(\mathbf{X}_{t-1} - \mathbf{X}_{t-2} \right) = \mathbf{X}_t - 2\mathbf{X}_{t-1} - \mathbf{X}_{t-2}$. VAR=X(2) differences X once at lag two $\left(\mathbf{X}_t - \mathbf{X}_{t-2} \right)$.

If differencing is specified, it is the differenced series that is processed by any subsequent ESTIMATE statement.

ESTIMATE Statement

ESTIMATE *options*;

The ESTIMATE statement specifies an ARMA model or transfer function model for the response variable specified in the previous IDENTIFY statement, and produces estimates of its parameters. The ESTIMATE statement also prints diagnostic information by which to check the model. Include an ESTIMATE statement for each model that you want to estimate.

Options used in the ESTIMATE statement are described in the following sections.

Options for Defining the Model and Controlling Diagnostic Statistics

The following options are used to define the model to be estimated and to control the output that is printed.

ALTPARM

specifies the alternative parameterization of the overall scale of transfer functions in the model. See the section "Alternative Model Parameterization" later in this chapter for details.

INPUT= *variable*
INPUT= (*transfer-function variable* ...)

specifies input variables and their transfer functions.

The variables used on the INPUT= option must be included in the CROSS-CORR= list in the previous IDENTIFY statement. If any differencing is specified in the CROSSCORR= list, then the differenced series is used as the input to the transfer function.

The transfer function specification for an input variable is optional. If no transfer function is specified, the input variable enters the model as a simple regressor. If specified, the transfer function specification has the following syntax:

$$\mathbf{S} \, \$ \, \left(\mathbf{L}_{1,1}, \mathbf{L}_{1,2}, ... \right) \left(\mathbf{L}_{2,1}, ... \right) ... / \left(\mathbf{L}_{j,1}, ... \right) ...$$

Here, S is a shift or lag of the input variable, the terms before the slash (/) are numerator factors, and the terms after the slash (/) are denominator factors of the transfer function. All three parts are optional. See the section "Specifying Inputs and Transfer Functions" later in this chapter for details.

METHOD= ML
METHOD= ULS
METHOD= CLS

specifies the estimation method to use. METHOD=ML specifies the maximum likelihood method. METHOD=ULS specifies the unconditional least-squares method. METHOD=CLS specifies the conditional least-squares method. METHOD=CLS is the default. See the section "Estimation Details" later in this chapter for more information.

NOCONSTANT
NOINT

suppresses the fitting of a constant (or intercept) parameter in the model. (That is, the parameter μ is omitted.)

NODF

estimates the variance by dividing the error sum of squares (SSE) by the number of residuals. The default is to divide the SSE by the number of residuals minus the number of free parameters in the model.

NOPRINT

suppresses the normal printout generated by the ESTIMATE statement.

P= *order*
P= (*lag, ..., lag*) ... (*lag, ..., lag*)

specifies the autoregressive part of the model. By default, no autoregressive parameters are fit.

P=($l_1, l_2, ..., l_k$) defines a model with autoregressive parameters at the specified lags. P=*order* is equivalent to P=(1, 2, ..., *order*).

A concatenation of parenthesized lists specifies a factored model. For example, P=(1,2,5)(6,12) specifies the autoregressive model

$$\left(1 - \phi_{1,1}B - \phi_{1,2}B^2 - \phi_{1,3}B^5\right)\left(1 - \phi_{2,1}B^6 - \phi_{2,2}B^{12}\right)$$

PLOT

plots the residual autocorrelation functions. The sample autocorrelation, the sample inverse autocorrelation, and the sample partial autocorrelation functions of the model residuals are plotted.

Q= *order*
Q= (*lag, ..., lag*) ... (*lag, ..., lag*)

specifies the moving-average part of the model. By default, no moving-average part is included in the model.

Q=($l_1, l_2, ..., l_k$) defines a model with moving-average parameters at the specified lags. Q=*order* is equivalent to Q=(1, 2, ..., *order*). A concatenation of parenthesized lists specifies a factored model. The interpretation of factors and lags is the same as for the P= option.

Options for Output Data Sets

The following options are used to store results in SAS data sets:

OUTEST= *SAS-data-set*

writes the parameter estimates to an output data set. If the OUTCORR or OUTCOV option is used, the correlations or covariances of the estimates are also written to the OUTEST= data set. See the section "OUTEST= Data Set" later in this chapter for a description of the OUTEST= output data set.

OUTCORR

writes the correlations of the parameter estimates to the OUTEST= data set.

OUTCOV

writes the covariances of the parameter estimates to the OUTEST= data set.

OUTMODEL= *SAS-data-set*

writes the model and parameter estimates to an output data set. If OUTMODEL= is not specified, no model output data set is created. See the section "OUTMODEL= Data Set" for a description of the OUTMODEL= output data set.

OUTSTAT= *SAS-data-set*

writes the model diagnostic statistics to an output data set. If OUTSTAT= is not specified, no statistics output data set is created. See the section "OUTSTAT= Data Set" later in this chapter for a description of the OUTSTAT= output data set.

Options to Specify Parameter Values

The following options enable you to specify values for the model parameters. These options can provide starting values for the estimation process, or you can specify fixed parameters for use in the FORECAST stage and suppress the estimation process with the NOEST option. By default, the ARIMA procedure finds initial parameter estimates and uses these estimates as starting values in the iterative estimation process.

If values for any parameters are specified, values for all parameters should be given. The number of values given must agree with the model specifications.

AR= *value* ...

lists starting values for the autoregressive parameters. See "Initial Values" later in this chapter for more information.

INITVAL= (*initializer-spec variable* ...)

specifies starting values for the parameters in the transfer function parts of the model. See "Initial Values" later in this chapter for more information.

MA= *value* ...

lists starting values for the moving-average parameters. See "Initial Values" later in this chapter for more information.

MU= *value*

specifies the MU parameter.

NOEST

uses the values specified with the AR=, MA=, INITVAL=, and MU= options as final parameter values. The estimation process is suppressed except for estimation of the residual variance. The specified parameter values are used directly by the next FORECAST statement. When NOEST is specified, standard errors, *t* ratios, and the correlations between estimates are displayed as 0 or missing. (The NOEST option is useful, for example, when you wish to generate forecasts corresponding to a published model.)

Options to Control the Iterative Estimation Process

The following options can be used to control the iterative process of minimizing the error sum of squares or maximizing the log likelihood function. These tuning options are not usually needed but may be useful if convergence problems arise.

BACKLIM= *-n*

omits the specified number of initial residuals from the sum of squares or likelihood function. Omitting values can be useful for suppressing transients in transfer function models that are sensitive to start-up values.

CONVERGE= *value*

specifies the convergence criterion. Convergence is assumed when the largest change in the estimate for any parameter is less that the CONVERGE= option value. If the absolute value of the parameter estimate is greater than 0.01, the relative change is used; otherwise, the absolute change in the estimate is used. The default is CONVERGE=.001.

DELTA= *value*

specifies the perturbation value for computing numerical derivatives. The default is DELTA=.001.

GRID

prints the error sum of squares (SSE) or concentrated log likelihood surface in a small grid of the parameter space around the final estimates. For each pair of parameters, the SSE is printed for the nine parameter-value combinations formed by the grid, with a center at the final estimates and with spacing given by the GRIDVAL= specification. The GRID option may help you judge whether the estimates are truly at the optimum, since the estimation process does not always converge. For models with a large number of parameters, the GRID option produces voluminous output.

GRIDVAL= *number*

controls the spacing in the grid printed by the GRID option. The default is GRIDVAL=0.005.

MAXITER= *n*
MAXIT= *n*

specifies the maximum number of iterations allowed. The default is MAXITER=50. (The default was 15 in previous releases of SAS/ETS software.)

NOLS

begins the maximum likelihood or unconditional least-squares iterations from the preliminary estimates rather than from the conditional least-squares estimates that are produced after four iterations. See the section "Estimation Details" later in this chapter for details.

NOSTABLE

specifies that the autoregressive and moving-average parameter estimates for the noise part of the model not be restricted to the stationary and invertible regions, respectively. See the section "Stationarity and Invertibility" later in this chapter for more information.

PRINTALL

prints preliminary estimation results and the iterations in the final estimation process.

SINGULAR= *value*

specifies the criterion for checking singularity. If a pivot of a sweep operation is less than the SINGULAR= value, the matrix is deemed singular. Sweep operations are performed on the Jacobian matrix during final estimation and on the covariance matrix when preliminary estimates are obtained. The default is SINGULAR=1E-7.

FORECAST Statement

FORECAST *options*;

The FORECAST statement generates forecast values for a time series using the parameter estimates produced by the previous ESTIMATE statement. See the section "Forecasting Details" later in this chapter for more information on calculating forecasts.

The following options can be used in the FORECAST statement:

ALPHA= *value*

sets the size of the forecast confidence limits. The ALPHA= value must be between 0 and 1. When you specify ALPHA=α, the upper and lower confidence limits will have a $1 - \alpha$ confidence level. The default is ALPHA=.05, which produces 95% confidence intervals.

BACK= *n*

specifies the number of observations before the end of the data that the multistep forecasts are to begin. The BACK= option value must be less than or equal to the number of observations minus the number of parameters.

The default is BACK=0, which means that the forecast starts at the end of the available data. The end of the data is the last observation for which a noise value can be calculated. If there are no input series, the end of the data is the last nonmissing value of the response time series. If there are input series, this observation can precede the last nonmissing value of the response variable, since there may be missing values for some of the input series.

ID= *variable*

names a variable in the input data set that identifies the time periods associated with the observations. The ID= variable is used in conjunction with the INTERVAL= option to extrapolate ID values from the end of the input data to identify forecast periods in the OUT= data set.

If the INTERVAL= option specifies an interval type, the ID variable must be a SAS date or datetime variable with the spacing between observations indicated by the INTERVAL= value. If the INTERVAL= option is not used, the last input value of the ID= variable is incremented by one for each forecast period to extrapolate the ID values for forecast observations.

INTERVAL= *interval*
INTERVAL= *n*

specifies the time interval between observations. See Chapter 21, "Date Intervals, Formats, and Functions," for information on valid INTERVAL= values.

The value of the INTERVAL= option is used by PROC ARIMA to extrapolate the ID values for forecast observations and to check that the input data are in order with no missing periods. See the section "Specifying Series Periodicity" later in this chapter for more details.

LEAD= *n*

specifies the number of multistep forecast values to compute. For example, if LEAD=10, PROC ARIMA forecasts for ten periods beginning with the end of the input series (or earlier if BACK= is specified). (It is possible to obtain fewer than the requested number of forecasts if a transfer function model is specified and insufficient data are available to compute the forecast.) The default is LEAD=24.

NOOUTALL

includes only the final forecast observations in the output data set, not the one-step forecasts for the data before the forecast period.

NOPRINT

suppresses the normal printout of the forecast and associated values.

OUT= *SAS-data-set*

writes the forecast (and other values) to an output data set. If OUT= is not specified, the OUT= data set specified in the PROC ARIMA statement is used. If OUT= is also not specified in the PROC ARIMA statement, no output data set is created. See the section "OUT= Data Set" later in this chapter for more information.

PRINTALL

prints the FORECAST computation throughout the whole data set. The forecast values for the data before the forecast period (specified by the BACK= option) are one-step forecasts.

Details

The Inverse Autocorrelation Function

The sample inverse autocorrelation function (SIACF) plays much the same role in ARIMA modeling as the sample partial autocorrelation function (SPACF) but generally indicates subset and seasonal autoregressive models better than the SPACF.

Additionally, the SIACF may be useful for detecting over-differencing. If the data come from a nonstationary or nearly nonstationary model, the SIACF has the characteristics of a noninvertible moving average. Likewise, if the data come from a model with a noninvertible moving average, then the SIACF has nonstationary characteristics. In particular, if the data have been over-differenced, the SIACF looks like a SACF from a nonstationary process.

The inverse autocorrelation function is not often discussed in textbooks, so a brief description is given here. More complete discussions can be found in Cleveland (1972), Chatfield (1980), and Priestly (1981).

Let $\mathbf{W}_t$ be generated by the ARMA(p,q) process

$$\phi(\mathrm{B})\mathbf{W}_t = \theta(\mathrm{B})a_t$$

where a_t is a white noise sequence. If $\theta(\mathrm{B})$ is invertible (that is, if θ considered as a polynomial in B has no roots less than or equal to 1 in magnitude), then the model

$$\theta(\mathrm{B})\mathbf{Z}_t = \phi(\mathrm{B})a_t$$

is also a valid ARMA(q,p) model. This model is sometimes referred to as the dual model. The autocorrelation function (ACF) of this dual model is called the inverse autocorrelation function (IACF) of the original model.

Notice that if the original model is a pure autoregressive model, then the IACF is an ACF corresponding to a pure moving-average model. Thus, it cuts off sharply when the lag is greater than p; this behavior is similar to the behavior of the partial autocorrelation function (PACF).

The sample inverse autocorrelation function (SIACF) is estimated in the ARIMA procedure by the following steps. A high-order autoregressive model is fit to the data by means of the Yule-Walker equations. The order of the autoregressive model used to calculate the SIACF is the minimum of the NLAG= value and one-half the number of observations after differencing. The SIACF is then calculated as the autocorrelation function that corresponds to this autoregressive operator when treated as a moving-average operator. That is, the autoregressive coefficients are convolved with themselves and treated as autocovariances.

Under certain conditions, the sampling distribution of the SIACF can be approximated by the sampling distribution of the SACF of the dual model (Bhansali 1980). In the plots generated by ARIMA, the confidence limit marks (.) are located at $\pm 2/\sqrt{n}$. These limits bound an approximate 95% confidence interval for the hypothesis that the data are from a white noise process.

The Partial Autocorrelation Function

The approximation for a standard error for the estimated partial autocorrelation function at lag k is based on a null hypothesis that a pure autoregressive Gaussian process of order $k-1$ generated the time series. This standard error is $1/\sqrt{n}$ and is used to produce the approximate 95% confidence intervals depicted by the dots in the plot.

The Cross-Correlation Function

The autocorrelation and partial and inverse autocorrelation functions described in the preceding sections help when you want to model a series as a function of its past values and past random errors. When you want to include the effects of past and current values of other series in the model, the correlations of the response series and the other series must be considered.

The CROSSCORR= option on the IDENTIFY statement computes cross correlations of the VAR= series with other series and makes these series available for use as inputs in models specified by later ESTIMATE statements.

When the CROSSCORR= option is used, PROC ARIMA prints a plot of the cross-correlation function for each variable in the CROSSCORR= list. This plot is similar in format to the other correlation plots, but shows the correlation between the two series at both lags and leads. For example

```
identify var=y crosscorr=x ...;
```

plots the cross-correlation function of Y and X, $\text{Cor}(y_t, x_{t-s})$, for $s = -L$ to L, where L is the value of the NLAG= option.

Study of the cross-correlation functions can indicate the transfer functions through which the input series should enter the model for the response series.

The cross-correlation function is computed after any specified differencing has been done. If differencing is specified for the VAR= variable or for a variable in the CROSSCORR= list, it is the differenced series that is cross correlated (and the differenced series is processed by any following ESTIMATE statement).

For example,

```
identify var=y(1) crosscorr=x(1);
```

computes the cross correlations of the changes in Y with the changes in X. Any following ESTIMATE statement models changes in the variables rather than the variables themselves.

Prewhitening

If, as is usually the case, an input series is autocorrelated, the direct cross-correlation function between the input and response series gives a misleading indication of the relation between the input and response series.

One solution to this problem is called *prewhitening*. You first fit an ARIMA model for the input series sufficient to reduce the residuals to white noise; then, filter the input series with this model to get the white noise residual series. You then filter the response series with the same model and cross correlate the filtered response with the filtered input series.

The ARIMA procedure performs this prewhitening process automatically when you precede the IDENTIFY statement for the response series with IDENTIFY and ESTIMATE statements to fit a model for the input series. If a model with no inputs was previously fit to a variable specified by the CROSSCORR= option, then that model is used to prewhiten both the input series and the response series before the cross correlations are computed for the input series.

For example,

```
proc arima data=in;
   identify var=x;
   estimate p=1 q=1;
   identify var=y crosscorr=x;
```

Both X and Y are filtered by the ARMA(1,1) model fit to X before the cross correlations are computed.

Note that prewhitening is done to estimate the cross-correlation function; the unfiltered series are used in any subsequent ESTIMATE or FORECAST statements, and the correlation functions of Y with its own lags are computed from the unfiltered Y series. But initial values in ESTIMATE statement are obtained with prewhitened data; therefore, the result with prewhitening can be different from the result without prewhitening.

To suppress prewhitening for all input variables, use the CLEAR option on the IDENTIFY statement to make PROC ARIMA forget all previous models.

Prewhitening and Differencing

If the VAR= and CROSSCORR= options specify differencing, the series are differenced before the prewhitening filter is applied. When the differencing lists specified on the VAR= option for an input and on the CROSSCORR= option for that input are not the same, PROC ARIMA combines the two lists so that the differencing operators used for prewhitening include all differences in either list (in the least common multiple sense).

Identifying Transfer Function Models

With more than one input series, unless the input series are uncorrelated with each other, the cross-correlation functions may be misleading as an indication of the appropriate transfer functions. Any dependencies among two or more input series will confound their cross correlations with the response series.

The prewhitening technique assumes that the input variables do not depend on past values of the response variable. If there is feedback from the response variable to an input variable, both the input and the response variables need to be prewhitened before meaningful cross correlations can be computed.

PROC ARIMA cannot handle feedback models. You can use several PROC ARIMA steps passing residual series through output data sets to implement the double prewhitening technique described in some textbooks. However, once you identify the transfer functions, you still cannot estimate a feedback model with PROC ARIMA. The STATESPACE procedure is more appropriate for models with feedback.

Missing Values and Autocorrelations

To compute the sample autocorrelation function when missing values are present, PROC ARIMA uses only cross products that do not involve missing values and employs divisors that reflect the number of cross products used rather than the total length of the series. Sample partial autocorrelations and inverse autocorrelations are then computed using the sample autocorrelation function. If necessary, a taper is employed to transform the sample autocorrelations into a positive definite sequence before calculating the partial autocorrelation and inverse correlation functions. The confidence intervals produced for these functions may not be valid when there are missing values. The distributional properties for sample correlation functions are not clear for finite samples. See Dunsmuir (1984) for some asymptotic properties of the sample correlation functions.

Estimation Details

The ARIMA procedure uses, for the most part, the computational methods outlined by Box and Jenkins. Marquardt's method is used for the nonlinear least-squares iterations. Numerical approximations of the derivatives of the sum-of-squares function are taken using a fixed delta (controlled by the DELTA= option).

The methods do not always converge successfully for a given set of data, particularly if the starting values for the parameters are not close to the least-squares estimates.

Back-forecasting

The unconditional sum of squares is computed exactly; thus, back-forecasting is not performed. Early versions of SAS/ETS software used the back-forecasting approximation and allowed a positive value of the BACKLIM= option to control the extent of the back-forecasting. In the current version, requesting a positive number of back-forecasting steps with the BACKLIM= option has no effect.

Preliminary Estimation

If an autoregressive or moving-average operator is specified with no missing lags, preliminary estimates of the parameters are computed using the autocorrelations computed in the IDENTIFY stage. Otherwise, the preliminary estimates are arbitrarily set to values that produce stable polynomials.

When preliminary estimation is not performed by PROC ARIMA, then initial values of the coefficients for any given autoregressive or moving average factor are set to 0.1 if the degree of the polynomial associated with the factor is 9 or less. Otherwise, the coefficients are determined by expanding the polynomial $(1 - 0.1B)$ to an appropriate power using a recursive algorithm.

These preliminary estimates are the starting values in an iterative algorithm to compute estimates of the parameters.

Estimation Methods

The likelihood function for METHOD=ML is calculated using a Kalman filter algorithm suggested by Morf, Sidhu, and Kailath (1974) (see also Pearlman 1980).

The likelihood function is maximized via nonlinear least squares using Marquardt's method.

The maximum likelihood estimates are more expensive to compute than the conditional least-squares estimates. In some cases, however, they may be preferable (Ansley and Newbold 1980; Davidson 1981).

The maximum likelihood estimates are computed as follows. Let the univariate ARMA model be

$$\phi(\mathrm{B})(\mathbf{W}_t - \mu_t) = \theta(\mathrm{B})a_t$$

where a_t is an independent sequence of normally distributed innovations with mean 0 and variance σ^2. Here μ_t is the mean parameter μ plus the transfer function inputs.

The log likelihood function can be written as follows:

$$-\frac{1}{2\sigma^2}\mathbf{x}'\Omega^{-1}\mathbf{x} - \frac{1}{2}\ln(|\Omega|) - \frac{n}{2}\ln(\sigma^2)$$

In this equation, n is the number of observations, $\sigma^2\Omega$ is the variance of $\mathbf{x}$ as a function of the ϕ and θ parameters, and $|\,\bullet\,|$ denotes the determinant. The vector $\mathbf{x}$ is the time series $\mathbf{W}_t$ minus the structural part of the model μ_t, written as a column vector, as follows:

$$\mathbf{x} = \begin{bmatrix} \mathbf{W}_1 \\ \mathbf{W}_2 \\ \vdots \\ \mathbf{W}_n \end{bmatrix} - \begin{bmatrix} \mu_1 \\ \mu_2 \\ \vdots \\ \mu_n \end{bmatrix}$$

The maximum likelihood estimate (MLE) of σ^2 is

$$s^2 = \frac{1}{n}\mathbf{x}'\Omega^{-1}\mathbf{x}$$

Note that the default estimator of the variance divides by $n - r$ (where r is the number of parameters in the model) instead of by n. Specifying the NODF option causes a divisor of n to be used.

The log likelihood concentrated with respect to σ^2 can be taken up to additive constants as

$$-\frac{n}{2}\ln(\mathbf{x}'\Omega^{-1}\mathbf{x}) - \frac{1}{2}\ln(|\Omega|)$$

Let $\mathbf{H}$ be the lower triangular matrix with positive elements on the diagonal such that $\mathbf{HH}' = \Omega$. Let $\mathbf{e}$ be the vector $\mathbf{H}^{-1}\mathbf{x}$. The concentrated log likelihood is

$$-\frac{n}{2}\ln(\mathbf{e}'\mathbf{e}) - \ln(|\mathbf{H}|)$$

or

$$-\frac{n}{2}\ln(|\mathbf{H}|^{1/n}\mathbf{e}'\mathbf{e}|\mathbf{H}|^{1/n})$$

The MLE is produced by using a Marquardt algorithm to minimize the following sum of squares:

$$|\mathbf{H}|^{1/n}\mathbf{e}'\mathbf{e}|\mathbf{H}|^{1/n}$$

The subsequent analysis of the residuals is done using $\mathbf{e}$ as the vector of residuals.

The METHOD=ULS option produces unconditional least-squares estimates. The ULS method is also referred to as the *exact least-squares* (ELS) method. For METHOD=ULS, the estimates minimize

$$\sum_{t=1}^{n} \tilde{a}_t^2 = \sum_{t=1}^{n} \left(x_t - \mathbf{C}_t \mathbf{V}_t^{-1} \left(x_1, \cdots , x_{t-1} \right)' \right)^2$$

where $\mathbf{C}_t$ is the covariance matrix of x_t and $(x_1, \cdots , x_{t-1})$, and $\mathbf{V}_t$ is the variance matrix of $(x_1, \cdots , x_{t-1})$. In fact, $\sum_{t=1}^{n} \tilde{a}_t^2$ is the same as $\mathbf{x}' \Omega^{-1} \mathbf{x}$ and, hence, $\mathbf{e}' \mathbf{e}$. Therefore, the unconditional least-squares estimates are obtained by minimizing the sum of squared residuals rather than using the log likelihood as the criterion function.

The METHOD=CLS option produces conditional least-squares estimates. The CLS estimates are conditional on the assumption that the past unobserved errors are equal to 0. The series x_t can be represented in terms of the previous observations, as follows:

$$x_t = a_t + \sum_{i=1}^{\infty} \pi_i x_{t-i}$$

The π weights are computed from the ratio of the ϕ and θ polynomials, as follows:

$$\frac{\phi(\mathrm{B})}{\theta(\mathrm{B})} = 1 - \sum_{i=1}^{\infty} \pi_i \mathrm{B}^i.$$

The CLS method produces estimates minimizing

$$\sum_{t=1}^{n} \hat{a}_t^2 = \sum_{t=1}^{n} \left(x_t - \sum_{i=1}^{\infty} \hat{\pi}_i x_{t-i} \right)^2$$

where the unobserved past values of x_t are set to 0 and $\hat{\pi}_i$ are computed from the estimates of ϕ and θ at each iteration.

For METHOD=ULS and METHOD=ML, initial estimates are computed using the METHOD=CLS algorithm.

Start-up for Transfer Functions

When computing the noise series for transfer function and intervention models, the start-up for the transferred variable is done assuming that past values of the input series are equal to the first value of the series. The estimates are then obtained by applying least squares or maximum likelihood to the noise series. Thus, for transfer function models, the ML option does not generate the full (multivariate ARMA) maximum likelihood estimates, but it uses only the univariate likelihood function applied to the noise series.

Because PROC ARIMA uses all of the available data for the input series to generate the noise series, other start-up options for the transferred series can be implemented by prefixing an observation to the beginning of the real data. For example, if you fit a transfer function model to the variable Y with the single input X, then you can employ a start-up using 0 for the past values by prefixing to the actual data an observation with a missing value for Y and a value of 0 for X.

Information Criteria

PROC ARIMA computes and prints two information criteria, Akaike's information criterion (AIC) (Akaike 1974; Harvey 1981) and Schwarz's Bayesian criterion (SBC) (Schwarz 1978). The AIC is computed as

$$-2 \ln(L) + 2k$$

where L is the likelihood function and k is the number of free parameters. The SBC is computed as

$$-2 \ln(L) + \ln(n) k$$

where n is the number of residuals that can be computed for the time series. Sometimes Schwarz's Bayesian criterion is called BIC.

If METHOD=CLS is used to do the estimation, an approximation value of L is used, where L is based on the conditional sum of squares instead of the exact sum of squares, and a Jacobian factor is left out.

Tests of Residuals

A table of test statistics for the hypothesis that the model residuals are white noise is printed as part of the ESTIMATE statement output. The chi-square statistics used in the test for lack of fit are computed using the Ljung-Box formula

$$\chi^2_m = n\,(n+2) \sum_{k=1}^{m} \frac{r_k^2}{(n-k)}$$

where

$$r_k = \frac{\sum_{t=1}^{n-k} a_t\, a_{t+k}}{\sum_{t=1}^{n} a_t^2}$$

and a_t is the residual series.

This formula has been suggested by Ljung and Box (1978) as yielding a better fit to the asymptotic chi-square distribution than the Box-Pierce Q statistic. Some simulation studies of the finite sample properties of this statistic are given by Davies, Triggs, and Newbold (1977) and by Ljung and Box (1978).

Each chi-square statistic is computed for all lags up to the indicated lag value and is not independent of the preceding chi-square values.

t statistics

The t statistics reported in the table of parameter estimates are approximations whose accuracy depends on the validity of the model, the nature of the model, and the length of the observed series. When the length of the observed series is short and the number of estimated parameters is large with respect to the series length, the t approximation is usually poor. Consequently, probability values corresponding to a t distribution are not displayed because they may be misleading.

Cautions

The ARIMA procedure uses a general nonlinear least-squares estimation method that can yield problematic results if your data do not fit the model. Output should be examined carefully. The GRID option can be used to ensure the validity and quality of the results. Problems you may encounter include the following:

- Preliminary moving-average estimates may not converge. Should this occur, preliminary estimates are derived as described previously in "Preliminary Estimation." You can supply your own preliminary estimates with the ESTIMATE statement options.

- The estimates can lead to an unstable time series process, which can cause extreme forecast values or overflows in the forecast.

- The Jacobian matrix of partial derivatives may be singular; usually, this happens because not all the parameters are identifiable. Removing some of the parameters or using a longer time series may help.

- The iterative process may not converge. PROC ARIMA's estimation method stops after n iterations, where n is the value of the MAXITER= option. If an iteration does not improve the SSE, the Marquardt parameter is increased by a factor of ten until parameters that have a smaller SSE are obtained or until the limit value of the Marquardt parameter is exceeded.

- For METHOD=CLS, the estimates may converge but not to least-squares estimates. The estimates may converge to a local minimum, the numerical calculations may be distorted by data whose sum-of-squares surface is not smooth, or the minimum may lie outside the region of invertibility or stationarity.

- If the data are differenced and a moving-average model fit, the parameter estimates may try to converge exactly on the invertibility boundary. In this case, the standard error estimates that are based on derivatives may be inaccurate.

Specifying Inputs and Transfer Functions

Input variables and transfer functions for them may be specified using the INPUT= option on the ESTIMATE statement. The variables used on the INPUT= option must be included in the CROSSCORR= list in the previous IDENTIFY statement. If any differencing is specified in the CROSSCORR= list, then the differenced variable is used as the input to the transfer function.

General Syntax of the INPUT= Option

The general syntax of the INPUT= option is

ESTIMATE ... INPUT= (*transfer-function variable ...* **)**

The transfer function for an input variable is optional. The name of a variable by itself can be used to specify a pure regression term for the variable.

If specified, the syntax of the transfer function is

$$S \$ \left(L_{1,1}, L_{1,2}, \ldots \right)\left(L_{2,1}, \ldots \right) \ldots / \left(L_{i,1}, L_{i,2}, \ldots \right)\left(L_{i+1,1}, \ldots \right) \ldots$$

S is the number of periods of time delay (lag) for this input series. Each term in parentheses specifies a polynomial factor with parameters at the lags specified by the $L_{i,j}$ values. The terms before the slash (/) are numerator factors. The terms after the slash (/) are denominator factors. All three parts are optional.

Commas can optionally be used between input specifications to make the INPUT= option more readable. The $ sign after the shift is also optional.

Except for the first numerator factor, each of the terms $L_{i,1}, L_{i,2}, \ldots, L_{i,k}$ indicates a factor of the form

$$\left(1 - \omega_{i,1} B^{L_{i,1}} - \omega_{i,2} B^{L_{i,2}} - \ldots - \omega_{i,k} B^{L_{i,k}}\right)$$

The form of the first numerator factor depends on the ALTPARM option. By default, in the first numerator factor the constant 1 is replaced with a free parameter ω_0.

Alternative Model Parameterization

When the ALTPARM option is specified, the ω_0 parameter is factored out so it multiplies the entire transfer function, and the first numerator factor has the same form as the other factors.

The ALTPARM option does not materially affect the results; it just presents the results differently. Some people prefer to see the model written one way, while others prefer the alternative representation. Table 3.3 illustrates the effect of the ALTPARM option.

Table 3.3. The ALTPARM Option

INPUT= Option	ALTPARM	Model
INPUT=((1 2)(12)/(1)X);	No	$\left(\omega_0 - \omega_1 B - \omega_2 B^2\right)\left(1 - \omega_3 B^{12}\right)/\left(1 - \delta_1 B\right)X_t$
	Yes	$\omega_0\left(1 - \omega_1 B - \omega_2 B^2\right)\left(1 - \omega_3 B^{12}\right)/\left(1 - \delta_1 B\right)X_t$

Differencing and Input Variables

If you difference the response series and use input variables, take care that the differencing operations do not change the meaning of the model. For example, if you want to fit the model

$$Y_t = \frac{\omega_0}{\left(1 - \delta_1 B\right)} X_t + \frac{\left(1 - \theta_1 B\right)}{\left(1 - B\right)\left(1 - B^{12}\right)} a_t$$

then the IDENTIFY statement must read

```
identify var=y(1,12) crosscorr=x(1,12);
estimate q=1 input=(/(1)x) noconstant;
```

If instead you specify the differencing as

```
identify var=y(1,12) crosscorr=x;
estimate q=1 input=(/(1)x) noconstant;
```

then the model being requested is

$$Y_t = \frac{\omega_0}{\left(1 - \delta_1 B\right)\left(1 - B\right)\left(1 - B^{12}\right)} X_t + \frac{\left(1 - \theta_1 B\right)}{\left(1 - B\right)\left(1 - B^{12}\right)} a_t$$

which is a very different model.

The point to remember is that a differencing operation requested for the response variable specified by the VAR= option is applied only to that variable and not to the noise term of the model.

Initial Values

The syntax for giving initial values to transfer function parameters in the the INITVAL= option parallels the syntax of the INPUT= option. For each transfer function in the INPUT= option, the INITVAL= option should give an initialization specification followed by the input series name. The initialization specification for each transfer function has the form

$$C \, \$ \, \left(V_{1,1}, V_{1,2}, \ \dots \ \right)\left(V_{2,1}, \ \dots \ \right) \ \dots \ / \ \left(V_{i,1}, \ \dots \ \right) \ \dots$$

where C is the lag 0 term in the first numerator factor of the transfer function (or the overall scale factor if the ALTPARM option is specified), and $V_{i,j}$ is the coefficient of the $L_{i,j}$ element in the transfer function.

To illustrate, suppose you want to fit the model

$$Y_t = \mu + \frac{\left(\omega_0 - \omega_1 B - \omega_2 B^2\right)}{\left(1 - \delta_1 B - \delta_2 B^2 - \delta_3 B^3\right)} X_{t-3} + \frac{1}{\left(1 - \phi_1 B - \phi_2 B^3\right)} a_t$$

and start the estimation process with the initial values $\mu = 10, \omega_0 = 1, \omega_1 = .5,$ $\omega_2 = .03, \delta_1 = .8, \delta_2 = -.1, \delta_3 = .002, \phi_1 = .1, \phi_2 = .01.$ (These are arbitrary values for illustration only.) You would use the following statements:

```
identify var=y crosscorr=x;
estimate p=(1,3) input=(3$(1,2)/(1,2,3)x)
         mu=10 ar=.1 .01 initval=(1$(.5,.03)/(.8,-.1,.002)x);
```

Note that the lags specified for a particular factor will be sorted, so initial values should be given in sorted order. For example, if the P= option had been entered as P=(3,1) instead of P=(1,3), the model would be the same and so would the AR= option. Sorting is done within all factors, including transfer function factors, so initial values should always be given in order of increasing lags.

Here is another illustration, showing initialization for a factored model with multiple inputs. The model is

$$Y_t = \mu + \frac{\omega_{1,0}}{\left(1 - \delta_{1,1} B\right)} W_t + \left(\omega_{2,0} - \omega_{2,1} B\right) X_{t-3}$$

$$+ \frac{1}{\left(1 - \phi_1 B\right)\left(1 - \phi_2 B^6 - \phi_3 B^{12}\right)} a_t$$

and the initial values are $\mu = 10$, $\omega_{1,0} = 5$, $\delta_{1,1} = .8$, $\omega_{2,0} = 1$, $\omega_{1,1} = .5$, $\phi_1 = .1$, $\phi_2 = .05$, and $\phi_3 = .01$. You would use the following statements:

```
identify var=y crosscorr=(w x);
estimate p=(1)(6,12) input=(/(1)w, 3$(1)x)
         mu=10 ar=.1 .05 .01 initval=(5$/(.8)w 1$(.5)x);
```

Stationarity and Invertibility

By default PROC ARIMA requires that the parameter estimates for the AR and MA parts of the model always remain in the stationary and invertible regions, respectively. The NOSTABLE option removes this restriction and for high-order models may save some computer time. Note that using the NOSTABLE option does not necessarily result in an unstable model being fit, since the estimates may leave the stable region for some iterations, but still ultimately converge to stable values.

Naming of Model Parameters

In the table of parameter estimates produced by the ESTIMATE statement, model parameters are referred to using the naming convention described in this section.

The parameters in the noise part of the model are named as AR$i,j$ or MA$i,j$, where AR refers to autoregressive parameters and MA to moving-average parameters. The subscript i refers to the particular polynomial factor, and the subscript j refers to the jth term within the ith factor. These terms are sorted in order of increasing lag within factors, so the subscript j refers to the jth term after sorting.

When inputs are used in the model, the parameters of each transfer function are named NUMi,j and DENi,j. The jth term in the ith factor of a numerator polynomial is named NUMi,j. The jth term in the ith factor of a denominator polynomial is named DENi,j.

This naming process is repeated for each input variable, so if there are multiple inputs, parameters in transfer functions for different input series have the same name. The table of parameter estimates shows in the "Variable" column the input with which each parameter is associated. The parameter name shown in the "Parameter" column and the input variable name shown in the "Variable" column must be combined to fully identify transfer function parameters.

The lag 0 parameter in the first numerator factor for the first input variable is named NUM1. For subsequent input variables, the lag 0 parameter in the first numerator factor is named NUMk, where k is the position of the input variable in the INPUT= option list. If the ALTPARM option is specified, the NUMk parameter is replaced by an overall scale parameter named SCALEk.

For the mean and noise process parameters, the response series name is shown in the "Variable" column. The "Lag" and "Shift" for each parameter are also shown in the table of parameter estimates when inputs are used.

Missing Values and Estimation and Forecasting

Estimation and forecasting are carried out in the presence of missing values by forecasting the missing values with the current set of parameter estimates. The maximum likelihood algorithm employed was suggested by Jones (1980) and is used for both unconditional least-squares (ULS) and conditional least-squares (CLS) estimation.

The CLS algorithm simply fills in missing values with infinite memory forecast values, computed by forecasting ahead from the nonmissing past values as far as required by the structure of the missing values. These artificial values are then employed in the nonmissing value CLS algorithm. Artificial values are updated at each iteration along with parameter estimates.

For models with input variables, embedded missing values (that is, missing values other than at the beginning or end of the series) are not generally supported. Embedded missing values in input variables are supported for the special case of a multiple regression model having ARIMA errors. A multiple regression model is specified by an INPUT= option that simply lists the input variables (possibly with lag shifts) without any numerator or denominator transfer function factors. One-step-ahead forecasts are not available for the response variable when one or more of the input variables have missing values.

When embedded missing values are present for a model with complex transfer functions, PROC ARIMA uses the first continuous nonmissing piece of each series to do the analysis. That is, PROC ARIMA skips observations at the beginning of each series until it encounters a nonmissing value and then uses the data from there until it encounters another missing value or until the end of the data is reached. This makes the current version of PROC ARIMA compatible with earlier releases that did not allow embedded missing values.

Forecasting Details

If the model has input variables, a forecast beyond the end of the data for the input variables is possible only if univariate ARIMA models have previously been fit to the input variables.

If input variables are used, the forecast standard errors and confidence limits of the response depend on the estimated forecast error variance of the predicted inputs. If several input series are used, the forecast errors for the inputs should be independent; otherwise, the standard errors and confidence limits for the response series will not be accurate.

The forecasts are generated using forecasting equations consistent with the method used to estimate the model parameters. Thus, the estimation method specified on the ESTIMATE statement also controls the way forecasts are produced by the FORECAST statement.

If METHOD=CLS is used, the forecasts are *infinite memory forecasts*, also called *conditional forecasts*. The term *conditional* is used because the forecasts are computed by assuming that the unknown values of the response series before the start of the data are equal to the mean of the series. Thus, the forecasts are conditional on this assumption.

The series x_t can be represented as

$$x_t = a_t + \sum_{i=1}^{\infty} \pi_i x_{t-i}$$

where $\phi(B)/\theta(B) = 1 - \sum_{i=1}^{\infty} \pi_i B^i$.

The k-step forecast of x_{t+k} is computed as

$$\hat{x}_{t+k} = \sum_{i=1}^{k-1} \hat{\pi}_i \hat{x}_{t+k-i} + \sum_{i=k}^{\infty} \hat{\pi}_i x_{t+k-i}$$

where unobserved past values of x_t are set to zero, and $\hat{\pi}_i$ is obtained from the estimated parameters $\hat{\phi}$ and $\hat{\theta}$.

For METHOD=ULS or METHOD=ML, the forecasts are *finite memory forecasts*, also called *unconditional forecasts*. For finite memory forecasts, the covariance function of the ARMA model is used to derive the best linear prediction equation. That is, the k-step forecast of x_{t+k}, given $(x_1, \cdots, x_{t-1})$, is

$$\tilde{x}_{t+k} = \mathbf{C}_{k,t} \mathbf{V}_t^{-1} (x_1, \cdots, x_{t-1})'$$

where $\mathbf{C}_{k,t}$ is the covariance of x_{t+k} and $(x_1, \cdots, x_{t-1})$, and $\mathbf{V}_t$ is the covariance matrix of the vector $(x_1, \cdots, x_{t-1})$. $\mathbf{C}_{k,t}$ and $\mathbf{V}_t$ are derived from the estimated parameters.

Finite memory forecasts minimize the mean-squared error of prediction if the parameters of the ARMA model are known exactly. (In most cases, the parameters of the ARMA model are estimated, so the predictors are not true best linear forecasts.)

If the response series is differenced, the final forecast is produced by summing the forecast of the differenced series. This summation, and thus the forecast, is conditional on the initial values of the series. Thus, when the response series is differenced, the final forecasts are not true finite memory forecasts because they are derived assuming that the differenced series begins in a steady-state condition. Thus, they fall somewhere between finite memory and infinite memory forecasts. In practice, there is seldom any practical difference between these forecasts and true finite memory forecasts.

Forecasting Log Transformed Data

The log transformation is often used to convert time series that are nonstationary with respect to the innovation variance into stationary time series. The usual approach is to take the log of the series in a DATA step and then apply PROC ARIMA to the transformed data. A DATA step is then used to transform the forecasts of the logs back to the original units of measurement. The confidence limits are also transformed using the exponential function.

As one alternative, you can simply exponentiate the forecast series. This procedure gives a forecast for the median of the series, but the antilog of the forecast log series underpredicts the mean of the original series. If you want to predict the expected value of the series, you need to take into account the standard error of the forecast, as shown in the following example, which uses an AR(2) model to forecast the log of a series Y:

```
data in;
    set in;
    ylog = log( y );
run;

proc arima data=in;
    identify var=ylog;
    estimate p=2;
    forecast lead=10 out=out;
run;

data out;
    set out;
    y    = exp( ylog );
    l95 = exp( l95 );
    u95 = exp( u95 );
    forecast = exp( forecast + std*std/2 );
run;
```

Specifying Series Periodicity

The INTERVAL= option is used together with the ID= variable to describe the observations that make up the time series. For example, INTERVAL=MONTH specifies a monthly time series in which each observation represents one month. See Chapter 21 for details on the interval values supported.

The variable specified by the ID= option in the PROC ARIMA statement identifies the time periods associated with the observations. Usually, SAS date or datetime values are used for this variable. PROC ARIMA uses the ID= variable in the following ways:

- to validate the data periodicity. When the INTERVAL= option is specified, PROC ARIMA uses the ID variable to check the data and verify that successive observations have valid ID values corresponding to successive time intervals. When the INTERVAL= option is not used, PROC ARIMA verifies that the ID values are nonmissing and in ascending order.

- to check for gaps in the input observations. For example, if INTERVAL=MONTH and an input observation for April 1970 follows an observation for January 1970, there is a gap in the input data with two omitted observations (namely February and March 1970). A warning message is printed when a gap in the input data is found.

- to label the forecast observations in the output data set. PROC ARIMA extrapolates the values of the ID variable for the forecast observations from the ID value at the end of the input data according to the frequency specifications of the INTERVAL= option. If the INTERVAL= option is not specified, PROC ARIMA extrapolates the ID variable by incrementing the ID variable value for the last observation in the input data by 1 for each forecast period. Values of the ID variable over the range of the input data are copied to the output data set.

OUT= Data Set

The output data set produced by the OUT= option of the PROC ARIMA or FORE-CAST statements contains the following variables:

- the BY variables

- the ID variable

- the variable specified by the VAR= option in the IDENTIFY statement, which contains the actual values of the response series

- FORECAST, a numeric variable containing the forecast values

- STD, a numeric variable containing the standard errors of the forecasts

- a numeric variable containing the lower confidence limits of the forecast. This variable is named L95 by default but has a different name if the ALPHA= option specifies a different size for the confidence limits.

- RESIDUAL, a numeric variable containing the differences between actual and forecast values

- a numeric variable containing the upper confidence limits of the forecast. This variable is named U95 by default but has a different name if the ALPHA= option specifies a different size for the confidence limits.

The ID variable, the BY variables, and the time series variable are the only ones copied from the input to the output data set.

Unless the NOOUTALL option is specified, the data set contains the whole time series. The FORECAST variable has the one-step forecasts (predicted values) for the input periods, followed by *n* forecast values, where *n* is the LEAD= value. The actual and RESIDUAL values are missing beyond the end of the series.

If you specify the same OUT= data set on different FORECAST statements, the latter FORECAST statements overwrite the output from the previous FORECAST statements. If you want to combine the forecasts from different FORECAST statements in the same output data set, specify the OUT= option once on the PROC ARIMA statement and omit the OUT= option on the FORECAST statements.

When a global output data set is created by the OUT= option in the PROC ARIMA statement, the variables in the OUT= data set are defined by the first FORECAST statement that is executed. Thus, if no ID variable is specified in the first FORECAST statement that is executed, no ID variable appears in the output data set, even if one is specified in a later FORECAST statement. If an ID variable is specified in the first FORECAST statement that is executed but not in a later FORECAST statement, the value of the ID variable is the same as the last value processed for the ID variable for all observations created by the later FORECAST statement. Furthermore, even if the response variable changes in subsequent FORECAST statements, the response variable name in the output data set will be that of the first response variable analyzed.

OUTCOV= Data Set

The output data set produced by the OUTCOV= option of the IDENTIFY statement contains the following variables:

- LAG, a numeric variable containing the lags corresponding to the values of the covariance variables. The values of LAG range from 0 to N for covariance functions and from $-N$ to N for cross-covariance functions, where N is the value of the NLAG= option.

- VAR, a character variable containing the name of the variable specified by the VAR= option

- CROSSVAR, a numeric variable containing the name of the variable specified in the CROSSCORR= option, which labels the different cross-covariance functions. The CROSSVAR variable is blank for the autocovariance observations. When there is no CROSSCORR= option, this variable is not created.

- N, a numeric variable containing the number of observations used to calculate the current value of the covariance or cross-covariance function

- COV, a numeric variable containing the autocovariance or cross-covariance function values. COV contains the autocovariances of the VAR= variable when the value of the CROSSVAR variable is blank. Otherwise COV contains the cross covariances between the VAR= variable and the variable named by the CROSSVAR variable.

- CORR, a numeric variable containing the autocorrelation or cross-correlation function values. CORR contains the autocorrelations of the VAR= variable when the value of the CROSSVAR variable is blank. Otherwise CORR contains the cross correlations between the VAR= variable and the variable named by the CROSSVAR variable.

- STDERR, a numeric variable containing the standard errors of the autocorrelations. The standard error estimate is based on the hypothesis that the process generating the time series is a pure moving-average process of order LAG-1. For the cross correlations, STDERR contains the value $1/\sqrt{n}$, which approximates the standard error under the hypothesis that the two series are uncorrelated.

- INVCORR, a numeric variable containing the inverse autocorrelation function values of the VAR= variable. For cross-correlation observations, (that is, when the value of the CROSSVAR variable is not blank), INVCORR contains missing values.

- PARTCORR, a numeric variable containing the partial autocorrelation function values of the VAR= variable. For cross-correlation observations (that is, when the value of the CROSSVAR variable is not blank), PARTCORR contains missing values.

OUTEST= Data Set

PROC ARIMA writes the parameter estimates for a model to an output data set when the OUTEST= option is specified in the ESTIMATE statement. The OUTEST= data set contains the following variables:

- the BY variables

- _NAME_, a character variable containing the name of the parameter for the covariance or correlation observations, or blank for the observations containing the parameter estimates. (This variable is not created if neither OUTCOV nor OUTCORR is specified.)

- _TYPE_, a character variable that identifies the type of observation

- variables for model parameters

The variables for the model parameters are named as follows:

ERRORVAR   This variable contains the variance estimate. The _TYPE_=EST observation for this variable contains the estimated error variance, and the remaining observations are missing.

MU   This variable contains values for the mean parameter for the model. (This variable is not created if NOCONSTANT is specified.)

MAj_k These variables contain values for the moving average parameters. The variables for moving average parameters are named MAj_k, where j is the factor number, and k is the index of the parameter within a factor.

ARj_k These variables contain values for the autoregressive parameters. The variables for autoregressive parameters are named ARj_k, where j is the factor number, and k is the index of the parameter within a factor.

Ij_k These variables contain values for the transfer function parameters. Variables for transfer function parameters are named Ij_k, where j is the number of the INPUT variable associated with the transfer function component, and k is the number of the parameter for the particular INPUT variable. INPUT variables are numbered according to the order in which they appear in the INPUT= list.

The value of the _TYPE_ variable for each observation indicates the kind of value contained in the variables for model parameters for the observation. The OUTEST= data set contains observations with the following _TYPE_ values:

EST   the observation contains parameter estimates

STD   the observation contains approximate standard errors of the estimates

CORR   the observation contains correlations of the estimates. OUTCORR must be specified to get these observations.

COV   the observation contains covariances of the estimates. OUTCOV must be specified to get these observations.

FACTOR   the observation contains values that identify for each parameter the factor that contains it

LAG   the observation contains values that identify the lag associated with each parameter

SHIFT   the observation contains values that identify the shift associated with the input series for the parameter

The values given for _TYPE_=FACTOR, _TYPE_=LAG, or _TYPE_=SHIFT observations enable you to reconstruct the model employed when provided with only the OUTEST= data set.

OUTEST= Examples

This section clarifies how model parameters are stored in the OUTEST= data set with two examples.

Consider the following example:

```
proc arima data=input;
    identify var=y cross=(x1 x2);
    estimate p=(1)(6) q=(1,3)(12) input=(x1 x2) outest=est;
quit;
proc print data=est;
run;
```

The model specified by these statements is

$$Y_t = \mu + \omega_{1,0} X_{1,t} + \omega_{2,0} X_{2,t} + \frac{\left(1 - \theta_{11} B - \theta_{12} B^3\right)\left(1 - \theta_{21} B^{12}\right)}{\left(1 - \phi_{11} B\right)\left(1 - \phi_{21} B^6\right)} a_t$$

The OUTEST= data set contains the values shown in Table 3.4.

Table 3.4. OUTEST= Data Set for First Example

Obs	_TYPE_	ERRORVAR	MU	MA1_1	MA1_2	MA2_1	AR1_1	AR2_1	I1_1	I2_1
1	EST	σ^2	μ	θ_{11}	θ_{12}	θ_{21}	ϕ_{11}	ϕ_{21}	$\omega_{1,0}$	$\omega_{2,0}$
2	STD	.	se μ	se θ_{11}	se θ_{12}	se θ_{21}	se ϕ_{11}	se ϕ_{21}	se $\omega_{1,0}$	se $\omega_{2,0}$
3	FACTOR	.	0	1	1	2	1	2	1	1
4	LAG	.	0	1	3	12	1	6	0	0
5	SHIFT	.	0	0	0	0	0	0	0	0

Next, consider the following example:

```
proc arima data=input;
    identify var=y cross=(x1(2) x2(1));
    estimate p=1 q=1 input=(2 $ (1)/(1,2)x1 1 $ /(1)x2) outest=est;
quit;
proc print data=est;
run;
```

The model specified by these statements is

$$Y_t = \mu + \frac{\omega_{10} - \omega_{11}B}{1 - \delta_{11}B - \delta_{12}B^2}X_{1,t-2} + \frac{\omega_{20}}{1 - \delta_{21}B}X_{2,t-1} + \frac{(1 - \theta_1 B)}{(1 - \phi_1 B)}a_t$$

The OUTEST= data set contains the values shown in Table 3.5.

Table 3.5. OUTEST= Data Set for Second Example

Obs	_TYPE_	ERRORVAR	MU	MA1_1	AR1_1	I1_1	I1_2	I1_3	I1_4	I2_1	I2_2
1	EST	σ^2	μ	θ_1	ϕ_1	ω_{10}	ω_{11}	δ_{11}	δ_{12}	ω_{20}	δ_{21}
2	STD	.	se μ	se θ_1	se ϕ_1	se ω_{10}	se ω_{11}	se δ_{11}	se δ_{12}	se ω_{20}	se δ_{21}
3	FACTOR	.	0	1	1	1	1	-1	-1	1	-1
4	LAG	.	0	1	1	0	1	1	2	0	1
5	SHIFT	.	0	0	0	2	2	2	2	1	1

OUTMODEL= Data Set

The OUTMODEL= option in the ESTIMATE statement writes an output data set that enables you to reconstruct the model. The OUTMODEL= data set contains much the same information as the OUTEST= data set but in a transposed form that may be more useful for some purposes. In addition, the OUTMODEL= data set includes the differencing operators.

The OUTMODEL data set contains the following variables:

- the BY variables

- _NAME_, a character variable containing the name of the response or input variable for the observation

- _TYPE_, a character variable that contains the estimation method that was employed. The value of _TYPE_ can be CLS, ULS, or ML.

- _PARM_, a character variable containing the name of the parameter given by the observation. _PARM_ takes on the values ERRORVAR, MU, AR, MA, NUM, DEN, and DIF.

- _VALUE_, a numeric variable containing the value of the estimate defined by the _PARM_ variable

- _STD_, a numeric variable containing the standard error of the estimate

- _FACTOR_, a numeric variable indicating the number of the factor to which the parameter belongs

- _LAG_, a numeric variable containing the number of the term within the factor containing the parameter

- _SHIFT_, a numeric variable containing the shift value for the input variable associated with the current parameter

The values of _FACTOR_ and _LAG_ identify which particular MA, AR, NUM, or

DEN parameter estimate is given by the _VALUE_ variable. The _NAME_ variable contains the response variable name for the MU, AR, or MA parameters. Otherwise, _NAME_ contains the input variable name associated with NUM or DEN parameter estimates. The _NAME_ variable contains the appropriate variable name associated with the current DIF observation as well. The _VALUE_ variable is 1 for all DIF observations, and the _LAG_ variable indicates the degree of differencing employed.

The observations contained in the OUTMODEL= data set are identified by the _PARM_ variable. A description of the values of the _PARM_ variable follows:

NUMRESID   _VALUE_ contains the number of residuals

NPARMS   _VALUE_ contains the number of parameters in the model

NDIFS   _VALUE_ contains the sum of the differencing lags employed for the response variable

ERRORVAR   _VALUE_ contains the estimate of the innovation variance

MU   _VALUE_ contains the estimate of the mean term

AR   _VALUE_ contains the estimate of the autoregressive parameter indexed by the _FACTOR_ and _LAG_ variable values

MA   _VALUE_ contains the estimate of a moving average parameter indexed by the _FACTOR_ and _LAG_ variable values

NUM   _VALUE_ contains the estimate of the parameter in the numerator factor of the transfer function of the input variable indexed by the _FACTOR_, _LAG_, and _SHIFT_ variable values

DEN   _VALUE_ contains the estimate of the parameter in the denominator factor of the transfer function of the input variable indexed by the _FACTOR_, _LAG_, and _SHIFT_ variable values

DIF   _VALUE_ contains the difference operator defined by the difference lag given by the value in the _LAG_ variable

OUTSTAT= Data Set

PROC ARIMA writes the diagnostic statistics for a model to an output data set when the OUTSTAT= option is specified in the ESTIMATE statement. The OUTSTAT data set contains the following variables:

- the BY variables

- _TYPE_, a character variable that contains the estimation method used. _TYPE_ can have the value CLS, ULS, or ML.

- _STAT_, a character variable containing the name of the statistic given by the _VALUE_ variable in this observation. _STAT_ takes on the values AIC, SBC, LOGLIK, SSE, NUMRESID, NPARMS, and NDIFS.

- _VALUE_, a numeric variable containing the value of the statistic named by the _STAT_ variable

The observations contained in the OUTSTAT= data set are identified by the _STAT_ variable. A description of the values of the _STAT_ variable follows:

AIC   Akaike's information criterion

SBC   Schwarz's Bayesian criterion

LOGLIK   the log likelihood, if METHOD=ML or METHOD=ULS is specified

SSE   the sum of the squared residuals

NUMRESID   the number of residuals

NPARMS   the number of parameters in the model

NDIFS   the sum of the differencing lags employed for the response variable

ERRORVAR   the estimate of the innovation variance

MU   the estimate of the mean term

Printed Output

The ARIMA procedure produces printed output for each of the IDENTIFY, ESTIMATE, and FORECAST statements. The output produced by each ARIMA statement is described in the following sections.

IDENTIFY Statement Printed Output

The printed output of the IDENTIFY statement consists of the following:

1. a table of summary statistics, including the name of the response variable, any specified periods of differencing, the mean and standard deviation of the response series after differencing, and the number of observations after differencing

2. a plot of the sample autocorrelation function for lags up to and including the NLAG= option value. Standard errors of the autocorrelations also appear to the right of the autocorrelation plot if the value of LINESIZE= option is sufficiently large. The standard errors are derived using Bartlett's approximation (Box and Jenkins 1976, p. 177). The approximation for a standard error for the estimated autocorrelation function at lag k is based on a null hypothesis that a pure moving-average Gaussian process of order k-1 generated the time series. The relative position of an approximate 95% confidence interval under this null hypothesis is indicated by the dots in the plot, while the asterisks represent the relative magnitude of the autocorrelation value.

3. a plot of the sample inverse autocorrelation function. See the section "The Inverse Autocorrelation Function" for more information on the inverse autocorrelation function.

4. a plot of the sample partial autocorrelation function

5. a table of test statistics for the hypothesis that the series is white noise. These test statistics are the same as the tests for white noise residuals produced by the ESTIMATE statement and are described in the section "Estimation Details" later in this chapter.

6. if the CROSSCORR= option is used, a plot of the sample cross-correlation function for each series specified in the CROSSCORR= option. If a model was previously estimated for a variable in the CROSSCORR= list, the cross correlations for that series are computed for the prewhitened input and response series. For each input variable with a prewhitening filter, the cross-correlation report for the input series includes

   a. a table of test statistics for the hypothesis of no cross correlation between the input and response series

   b. the prewhitening filter used for the prewhitening transformation of the predictor and response variables

ESTIMATE Statement Printed Output

The printed output of the ESTIMATE statement consists of the following:

1. when the PRINTALL option is specified, the preliminary parameter estimates and an iteration history showing the sequence of parameter estimates tried during the fitting process

2. a table of parameter estimates showing the following for each parameter: the parameter name, the parameter estimate, the approximate standard error (Approx. Std Error), *t* ratio (T Ratio), the lag for the parameter, the input variable name for the parameter, and the lag or "Shift" for the input variable

3. the estimates of the constant term, the innovation variance (Variance Estimate), the innovation standard deviation (Std Error Estimate), Akaike's information criterion (AIC), Schwarz's Bayesian criterion (SBC), and the number of residuals

4. the correlation matrix of the parameter estimates

5. a table of test statistics for hypothesis that the residuals of the model are white noise titled "Autocorrelation Check of Residuals"

6. if the PLOT option is specified, autocorrelation, inverse autocorrelation, and partial autocorrelation function plots of the residuals

7. if an INPUT variable has been modeled in such a way that prewhitening is performed in the IDENTIFY step, a table of test statistics titled "Crosscorrelation Check of Residuals." The test statistic is based on the chi-square approximation suggested by Box and Jenkins (1976, pp. 395–396). The cross-correlation function is computed using the residuals from the model as one series and the prewhitened input variable as the other series.

8. if the GRID option is specified, the sum-of-squares or likelihood surface over a grid of parameter values near the final estimates

9. a summary of the estimated model showing the autoregressive factors, moving average factors, and transfer function factors in back shift notation with the estimated parameter values.

FORECAST Statement Printed Output

The printed output of the FORECAST statement consists of the following:

1. a summary of the estimated model

2. a table of forecasts, with columns for the observation numbers (Obs), the forecast values (Forecast), the forecast standard errors (Std Error), lower limits of the approximate 95% confidence interval (Lower 95%), and upper limits of the approximate 95% confidence interval (Upper 95%). If the PRINTALL option is specified, the forecast table also includes columns for the actual values of the response series (Actual) and the residual values (Residual), and the table includes the input observations used to estimate the model.

Examples

Example 3.1. Simulated IMA Model

This example illustrates the ARIMA procedure results for a case where the true model is known. An integrated moving average model is used for this illustration.

The following DATA step generates a pseudo-random sample of 100 periods from the ARIMA(0,1,1) process $u_t = u_{t-1} + a_t - .8a_{t-1}$, $a_t \sim$ iid $N(0,1)$.

```
title1 'Simulated IMA(1,1) Series';
data a;
   u1 = 0.9; a1 = 0;
   do i = -50 to 100;
      a = rannor( 32565 );
      u = u1 + a - .8 * a1;
      if i > 0 then output;
      a1 = a;
      u1 = u;
      end;
run;
```

The following ARIMA procedure statements identify and estimate the model.

```
proc arima data=a;
   identify var=u nlag=15;
   run;
   identify var=u(1) nlag=15;
   run;
   estimate q=1 ;
   run;
quit;
```

The results of the first IDENTIFY statement are shown in Output 3.1.1. The output shows the behavior of the sample autocorrelation function when the process is nonstationary. Note that in this case the estimated autocorrelations are not very high, even at small lags. Nonstationarity is reflected in a pattern of significant autocorrelations that do not decline quickly with increasing lag, not in the size of the autocorrelations.

Output 3.1.1. Output from the First IDENTIFY Statement

```
                        Simulated IMA(1,1) Series

                           ARIMA Procedure


                   Name of variable = U.

                   Mean of working series = 0.099637
                   Standard deviation      = 1.115604
                   Number of observations =      100

                         Autocorrelations

Lag Covariance Correlation -1 9 8 7 6 5 4 3 2 1 0 1 2 3 4 5 6 7 8 9 1
  0  1.244572    1.00000  |                    |********************|
  1  0.547457    0.43988  |                    .|********            |
  2  0.534787    0.42970  |                    .|********            |
  3  0.569849    0.45787  |                   .|*********            |
  4  0.384428    0.30888  |                    .|******              |
  5  0.405137    0.32552  |                    .|*******             |
  6  0.253617    0.20378  |                    .|****  .             |
  7  0.321830    0.25859  |                   .|*****  .             |
  8  0.363871    0.29237  |                   .|******.             |
  9  0.271180    0.21789  |                   .|****  .             |
 10  0.419208    0.33683  |                   .|*******             |
 11  0.298127    0.23954  |                   .|*****  .             |
 12  0.186460    0.14982  |                   .|***   .             |
 13  0.313270    0.25171  |                   .|*****  .             |
 14  0.314594    0.25277  |                  .|*****  .             |
 15  0.156329    0.12561  |                   .|***   .             |
                    "." marks two standard errors
```

```
                        Simulated IMA(1,1) Series

                           ARIMA Procedure


                       Inverse Autocorrelations

Lag Correlation -1 9 8 7 6 5 4 3 2 1 0 1 2 3 4 5 6 7 8 9 1
  1  -0.12382  |                    . **|  .                 |
  2  -0.17396  |                    .***|  .                 |
  3  -0.19966  |                   ****|  .                 |
  4  -0.01476  |                    .  |  .                 |
  5  -0.02895  |                    . *|  .                 |
  6   0.20612  |                    . |****                 |
  7   0.01258  |                    . |  .                 |
  8  -0.09616  |                    . **|  .                 |
  9   0.00025  |                    . |  .                 |
 10  -0.16879  |                   .***|  .                 |
 11   0.05680  |                    . |*  .                 |
 12   0.14306  |                    . |***.                 |
 13  -0.02466  |                    . |  .                 |
 14  -0.15549  |                   .***|  .                 |
 15   0.08247  |                    . |** .                 |


                       Partial Autocorrelations

Lag Correlation -1 9 8 7 6 5 4 3 2 1 0 1 2 3 4 5 6 7 8 9 1
  1   0.43988  |                    . |*********            |
  2   0.29287  |                    . |******              |
  3   0.26499  |                    . |*****               |
  4  -0.00728  |                    . |  .                 |
  5   0.06473  |                    . |*  .                 |
```

Example 3.1. Simulated IMA Model □ □ □ 161

Output 3.1.1. (Continued)

```
         6    -0.09926  |              .  **|    .        |
         7     0.10048  |              .    |**  .        |
         8     0.12872  |              .    |***.        |
         9     0.03286  |              .    |*   .        |
        10     0.16034  |              .    |***.        |
        11    -0.03794  |              .   *|    .        |
        12    -0.14469  |              .***|    .        |
        13     0.06415  |              .    |*   .        |
        14     0.15482  |              .    |***.        |
        15    -0.10989  |              .  **|    .        |
```

```
                    Simulated IMA(1,1) Series

                         ARIMA Procedure


              Autocorrelation Check for White Noise

        To   Chi                    Autocorrelations
       Lag  Square  DF   Prob
         6   87.22   6  0.000  0.440  0.430  0.458  0.309  0.326  0.204
        12  131.39  12  0.000  0.259  0.292  0.218  0.337  0.240  0.150
```

The second IDENTIFY statement differences the series. The results of the second IDENTIFY statement are shown in Output 3.1.2. This output shows autocorrelation, inverse autocorrelation, and partial autocorrelation functions typical of MA(1) processes.

Output 3.1.2. Output from the Second IDENTIFY Statement

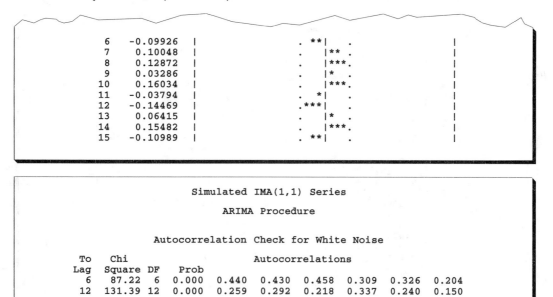

```
                        Simulated IMA(1,1) Series

                            ARIMA Procedure


                  Name of variable = U.

                  Period(s) of Differencing = 1.
                  Mean of working series = 0.019752
                  Standard deviation      = 1.160921
                  Number of observations =        99
                  NOTE: The first observation was eliminated by
                        differencing.

                         Autocorrelations

Lag Covariance Correlation -1 9 8 7 6 5 4 3 2 1 0 1 2 3 4 5 6 7 8 9 1
  0   1.347737    1.00000  |                   |********************|
  1  -0.699404   -0.51895  |         **********|    .               |
  2  -0.036142   -0.02682  |              .   *|    .               |
  3   0.245093    0.18186  |              .    |****.               |
  4  -0.234167   -0.17375  |              . ***|    .               |
  5   0.181778    0.13488  |              .    |***  .              |
  6  -0.184601   -0.13697  |              . ***|    .               |
  7   0.0088659   0.00658  |              .    |    .               |
  8   0.146372    0.10861  |              .    |**  .               |
  9  -0.241579   -0.17925  |              .****|    .               |
 10   0.240512    0.17846  |              .    |****.               |
 11   0.031005    0.02301  |              .    |    .               |
 12  -0.250954   -0.18620  |              . ****|    .              |
 13   0.095295    0.07071  |              .    |*   .               |
 14   0.194110    0.14403  |              .    |***  .              |
 15  -0.219688   -0.16300  |              . ***|    .               |
                  "." marks two standard errors
```

Output 3.1.2. (Continued)

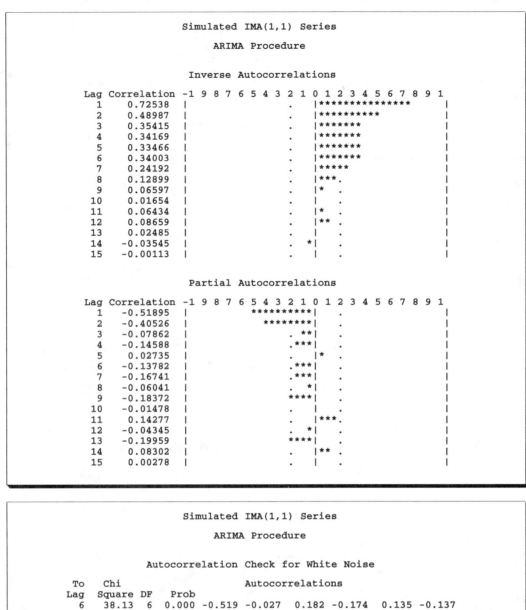

```
                           Simulated IMA(1,1) Series

                               ARIMA Procedure

                          Inverse Autocorrelations

       Lag Correlation -1 9 8 7 6 5 4 3 2 1 0 1 2 3 4 5 6 7 8 9 1
        1    0.72538   |                        .  |***************  |
        2    0.48987   |                        .  |*********        |
        3    0.35415   |                        .  |*******          |
        4    0.34169   |                        .  |*******          |
        5    0.33466   |                        .  |*******          |
        6    0.34003   |                        .  |*******          |
        7    0.24192   |                        .  |*****            |
        8    0.12899   |                        .  |***.             |
        9    0.06597   |                        .  |*  .             |
       10    0.01654   |                        .  |   .             |
       11    0.06434   |                        .  |*  .             |
       12    0.08659   |                        .  |** .             |
       13    0.02485   |                        .  |   .             |
       14   -0.03545   |                        . *|   .             |
       15   -0.00113   |                        .  |   .             |

                          Partial Autocorrelations

       Lag Correlation -1 9 8 7 6 5 4 3 2 1 0 1 2 3 4 5 6 7 8 9 1
        1   -0.51895   |         *********|   .                      |
        2   -0.40526   |          ********|   .                      |
        3   -0.07862   |              . **|   .                      |
        4   -0.14588   |              .***|   .                      |
        5    0.02735   |              .   |*  .                      |
        6   -0.13782   |              .***|   .                      |
        7   -0.16741   |              .***|   .                      |
        8   -0.06041   |              . *|   .                       |
        9   -0.18372   |             ****|   .                       |
       10   -0.01478   |              .   |   .                      |
       11    0.14277   |              .   |***.                      |
       12   -0.04345   |              . *|   .                       |
       13   -0.19959   |             ****|   .                       |
       14    0.08302   |              .   |** .                      |
       15    0.00278   |              .   |   .                      |
```

```
                           Simulated IMA(1,1) Series

                               ARIMA Procedure

                   Autocorrelation Check for White Noise

       To   Chi                        Autocorrelations
      Lag  Square DF   Prob
       6    38.13  6  0.000  -0.519  -0.027   0.182  -0.174   0.135  -0.137
      12    50.62 12  0.000   0.007   0.109  -0.179   0.178   0.023  -0.186
```

The ESTIMATE statement fits an ARIMA(0,1,1) model to the simulated data. Note that in this case the parameter estimates are reasonably close to the values used to generate the simulated data. ($\mu = 0$, $\hat{\mu} = .02$. $\theta_1 = .8$, $\hat{\theta}_1 = .79$. $\sigma^2 = 1$, $\hat{\sigma}^2 = .82$.) The ESTIMATE statement results are shown in Output 3.1.3.

Example 3.1. Simulated IMA Model □ □ □ 163

Output 3.1.3. Output from Fitting ARIMA(0,1,1) Model

```
                    Simulated IMA(1,1) Series

                        ARIMA Procedure


               Conditional Least Squares Estimation

                               Approx.
          Parameter    Estimate    Std Error    T Ratio   Lag
          MU            0.02056      0.01972       1.04    0
          MA1,1         0.79142      0.06474      12.22    1

          Constant Estimate   =    0.020558

          Variance  Estimate  = 0.81980707
          Std Error Estimate  = 0.90543198
          AIC                 = 263.259412*
          SBC                 = 268.449652*
          Number of Residuals=        99
          * Does not include log determinant.

                 Correlations of the Estimates


             Parameter             MU         MA1,1

             MU                  1.000        -0.124
             MA1,1             -0.124         1.000


              Autocorrelation Check of Residuals

     To    Chi                    Autocorrelations
    Lag  Square DF   Prob
      6    6.48   5  0.262 -0.033  0.030  0.153 -0.096  0.013 -0.163
     12   13.11  11  0.286 -0.048  0.046 -0.086  0.159  0.027 -0.145
     18   20.12  17  0.268  0.069  0.130 -0.099  0.006  0.164 -0.013
     24   24.73  23  0.364  0.064  0.032  0.076 -0.077 -0.075  0.114



             Model for variable U

             Estimated Mean =    0.020558
             Period(s) of Differencing = 1.

             Moving Average Factors
             Factor 1: 1 - 0.79142 B**(1)
```

Example 3.2. Seasonal Model for the Airline Series

The airline passenger data, given as Series G in Box and Jenkins (1976), has been used in time series analysis literature as an example of a nonstationary seasonal time series. This example uses PROC ARIMA to fit the "airline model," ARIMA$(0,1,1) \times (0,1,1)_{12}$, to Box and Jenkins' Series G.

The following statements read the data and log transform the series. The PROC
GPLOT step plots the series, as shown in Output 3.2.1.

```
title1 'International Airline Passengers';
title2 '(Box and Jenkins Series-G)';
data seriesg;
   input x @@;
   xlog = log( x );
   date = intnx( 'month', '31dec1948'd, _n_ );
   format date monyy.;
   cards;
112 118 132 129 121 135 148 148 136 119 104 118
115 126 141 135 125 149 170 170 158 133 114 140
145 150 178 163 172 178 199 199 184 162 146 166
171 180 193 181 183 218 230 242 209 191 172 194
196 196 236 235 229 243 264 272 237 211 180 201
204 188 235 227 234 264 302 293 259 229 203 229
242 233 267 269 270 315 364 347 312 274 237 278
284 277 317 313 318 374 413 405 355 306 271 306
315 301 356 348 355 422 465 467 404 347 305 336
340 318 362 348 363 435 491 505 404 359 310 337
360 342 406 396 420 472 548 559 463 407 362 405
417 391 419 461 472 535 622 606 508 461 390 432
;

symbol1 i=join  v=star;
proc gplot data=seriesg;
   plot x * date = 1 / haxis= '1jan49'd to '1jan61'd by year;
run;
```

Output 3.2.1. Plot of Data

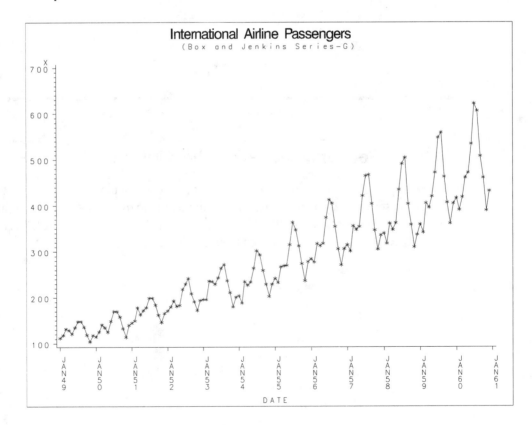

Example 3.2. Seasonal Model for the Airline Series ▫ ▫ ▫ 165

The following PROC ARIMA step fits an ARIMA$(0,1,1) \times (0,1,1)_{12}$ model without a mean term to the logarithms of the airline passengers series. The model is forecast, and the results stored in the data set B.

```
proc arima data=seriesg;
   identify var=xlog(1,12) nlag=15;
   run;
   estimate q=(1)(12) noconstant method=uls;
   run;
   forecast out=b lead=24 id=date interval=month noprint;
quit;
```

The printed output from the IDENTIFY statement is shown in Output 3.2.2. The autocorrelation plots shown are for the twice differenced series $(1-B)(1-B^{12})X$. Note that the autocorrelation functions have the pattern characteristic of a first-order moving average process combined with a seasonal moving average process with lag 12.

Output 3.2.2. IDENTIFY Statement Output

```
              International Airline Passengers
                 (Box and Jenkins Series-G)

                      ARIMA Procedure


          Name of variable = XLOG.

          Period(s) of Differencing = 1,12.
          Mean of working series = 0.000291
          Standard deviation      = 0.045673
          Number of observations =      131
          NOTE: The first 13 observations were eliminated by
                differencing.

                      Autocorrelations

Lag Covariance Correlation -1 9 8 7 6 5 4 3 2 1 0 1 2 3 4 5 6 7 8 9 1
 0   0.0020860    1.00000   |                    |********************|
 1  -0.0007116   -0.34112   |             *******|  .                 |
 2   0.00021913   0.10505   |                 .  |**  .               |
 3  -0.0004217   -0.20214   |              ****|  .                    |
 4   0.00004456   0.02136   |                 .  |  .                  |
 5   0.0001161    0.05565   |                 .  |*  .                 |
 6   0.00006426   0.03080   |                 .  |*  .                 |
 7  -0.0001159   -0.05558   |                 .  *|  .                 |
 8  -1.5867E-6   -0.00076   |                 .  |  .                  |
 9   0.00036791   0.17637   |                 .  |****                 |
10  -0.0001593   -0.07636   |                 . **|  .                 |
11   0.00013431   0.06438   |                 .  |*  .                 |
12  -0.0008065   -0.38661   |            *******|  .                   |
13   0.00031624   0.15160   |                 .  |***  .               |
14  -0.0001202   -0.05761   |                 .  *|  .                 |
15   0.000312     0.14957   |                 .  |***  .               |
              "." marks two standard errors
```

Output 3.2.2. (Continued)

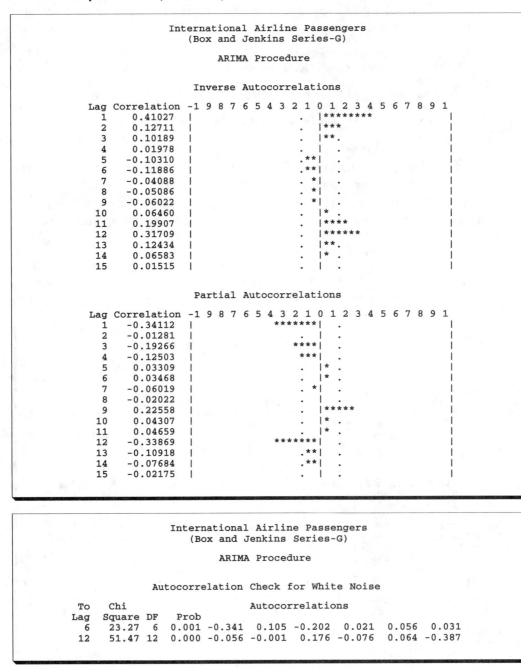

```
                International Airline Passengers
                   (Box and Jenkins Series-G)

                        ARIMA Procedure


                    Inverse Autocorrelations

Lag Correlation  -1 9 8 7 6 5 4 3 2 1 0 1 2 3 4 5 6 7 8 9 1
  1    0.41027   |                    .  |********          |
  2    0.12711   |                    .  |***               |
  3    0.10189   |                    .  |**.               |
  4    0.01978   |                    .  |  .               |
  5   -0.10310   |                  .**|  .                 |
  6   -0.11886   |                  .**|  .                 |
  7   -0.04088   |                  . *|  .                 |
  8   -0.05086   |                  . *|  .                 |
  9   -0.06022   |                  . *|  .                 |
 10    0.06460   |                  .  |* .                 |
 11    0.19907   |                    .  |****              |
 12    0.31709   |                    .  |******            |
 13    0.12434   |                    .  |**.               |
 14    0.06583   |                    .  |* .               |
 15    0.01515   |                    .  |  .               |


                    Partial Autocorrelations

Lag Correlation  -1 9 8 7 6 5 4 3 2 1 0 1 2 3 4 5 6 7 8 9 1
  1   -0.34112   |              *******|  .                 |
  2   -0.01281   |                    .  |  .               |
  3   -0.19266   |                ****|  .                 |
  4   -0.12503   |                 ***|  .                 |
  5    0.03309   |                    .  |* .               |
  6    0.03468   |                    .  |* .               |
  7   -0.06019   |                  . *|  .                 |
  8   -0.02022   |                    .  |  .               |
  9    0.22558   |                    .  |*****             |
 10    0.04307   |                    .  |* .               |
 11    0.04659   |                    .  |* .               |
 12   -0.33869   |              *******|  .                 |
 13   -0.10918   |                  .**|  .                 |
 14   -0.07684   |                  .**|  .                 |
 15   -0.02175   |                    .  |  .               |
```

```
                International Airline Passengers
                   (Box and Jenkins Series-G)

                        ARIMA Procedure


              Autocorrelation Check for White Noise

  To   Chi                     Autocorrelations
 Lag  Square DF  Prob
   6  23.27   6  0.001 -0.341  0.105 -0.202  0.021  0.056  0.031
  12  51.47  12  0.000 -0.056 -0.001  0.176 -0.076  0.064 -0.387
```

Example 3.2.   Seasonal Model for the Airline Series   □ □ □   167

The results of the ESTIMATE statement are shown in Output 3.2.3.

Output 3.2.3.   ESTIMATE Statement Output

```
                International Airline Passengers
                    (Box and Jenkins Series-G)

                        ARIMA Procedure


             Unconditional Least Squares Estimation

                               Approx.
        Parameter    Estimate    Std Error    T Ratio   Lag
        MA1,1         0.39594      0.08149       4.86     1
        MA2,1         0.61331      0.07961       7.70    12


        Variance  Estimate = 0.00136313
        Std Error Estimate = 0.03692065
        AIC                = -484.75494
        SBC                = -479.00455
        Number of Residuals=          131

                 Correlations of the Estimates


             Parameter        MA1,1         MA2,1

             MA1,1            1.000        -0.055
             MA2,1           -0.055         1.000


             Autocorrelation Check of Residuals

        To    Chi                 Autocorrelations
        Lag  Square DF   Prob
         6    5.56   4  0.235   0.022   0.024  -0.125  -0.129   0.057   0.065
        12    8.49  10  0.582  -0.065  -0.042   0.102  -0.060   0.023   0.007
        18   13.23  16  0.656   0.022   0.039   0.045  -0.162   0.035   0.001
        24   24.99  22  0.298  -0.106  -0.104  -0.037  -0.027   0.219   0.040



        Model for variable XLOG

        No mean term in this model.
        Period(s) of Differencing = 1,12.

        Moving Average Factors
        Factor 1: 1 - 0.39594 B**(1)
        Factor 2: 1 - 0.61331 B**(12)
```

The following statements retransform the forecast values to get forecasts in the original scales. See the section "Forecasting Log Transformed Data" earlier in this chapter for more information.

```
data c;
   set b;
   x        = exp( xlog );
   forecast = exp( forecast + std*std/2 );
   l95      = exp( l95 );
   u95      = exp( u95 );
run;
```

The forecasts and their confidence limits are plotted using the following PROC GPLOT step. The plot is shown in Output 3.2.4.

```
symbol1 i=none  v=star;
symbol2 i=join  v=plus;
symbol3 i=join  v=none l=3;
proc gplot data=c;
   where date >= '1jan58'd;
   plot x * date = 1 forecast * date = 2
        195 * date = 3 u95 * date = 3 /
        overlay haxis= '1jan58'd to '1jan62'd by year;
run;
```

Output 3.2.4. Plot of the Forecast for the Original Series

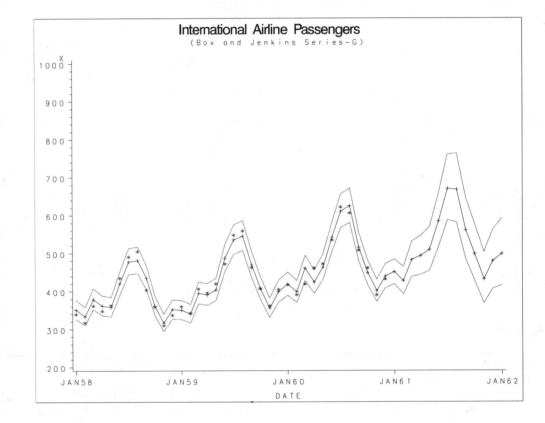

Example 3.3.   Model for Series J Data from Box and Jenkins

This example uses the Series J data from Box and Jenkins (1976). First the input series, X, is modeled with a univariate ARMA model. Next, the dependent series, Y, is cross correlated with the input series. Since a model has been fit to X, both Y and X are prewhitened by this model before the sample cross correlations are computed. Next, a transfer function model is fit with no structure on the noise term. The residuals from this model are identified by means of the PLOT option; then, the full model, transfer function and noise is fit to the data.

Example 3.3. Model for Series J Data from Box and Jenkins □□□ 169

The following statements read data input gas rate and output CO_2 from a gas furnace. (Data values are not shown. See "Series J" in Box and Jenkins (1976) for the values.)

```
title1 'Gas Furnace Data';
title2 '(Box and Jenkins, Series J)';
data seriesj;
   input x y @@;
   label x = 'Input Gas Rate'
         y = 'Output CO2';
cards;
;
```

The following statements produce Output 3.3.1 through Output 3.3.5.

```
proc arima data=seriesj;

   /*--- Look at the input process ------------------*/
   identify var=x nlags=10;
   run;

   /*--- Fit a model for the input ------------------*/
   estimate p=3;
   run;

   /*--- Crosscorrelation of prewhitened series ------*/
   identify var=y crosscorr=(x) nlags=10;
   run;

   /*--- Fit transfer function - look at residuals ---*/
   estimate input=( 3$ (1,2)/(1,2) x ) plot;
   run;

   /*--- Estimate full model ------------------------*/
   estimate p=2 input=( 3$ (1,2)/(1) x );
   run;

quit;
```

The results of the first IDENTIFY statement for the input series X are shown in Output 3.3.1.

Output 3.3.1. IDENTIFY Statement Results for X

```
                         Gas Furnace Data
                     (Box and Jenkins, Series J)

                         ARIMA Procedure


                 Name of variable = X.

                 Mean of working series = -0.05683
                 Standard deviation     = 1.070952
                 Number of observations =      296

                         Autocorrelations

Lag Covariance Correlation -1 9 8 7 6 5 4 3 2 1 0 1 2 3 4 5 6 7 8 9 1
  0   1.146938    1.00000   |                    |*******************|
  1   1.092430    0.95247   |                 .  |*******************  |
  2   0.956652    0.83409   |              .     |****************     |
  3   0.782051    0.68186   |            .       |**************       |
  4   0.609291    0.53123   |          .         |**********          |
  5   0.467380    0.40750   |          .         |********            |
  6   0.364957    0.31820   |          .         |******              |
  7   0.298427    0.26019   |          .         |*****.              |
  8   0.260943    0.22751   |          .         |*****.              |
  9   0.244378    0.21307   |          .         |****  .             |
```

Output 3.3.1. (Continued)

```
10   0.238942    0.20833  |              .             |**** .              |
                              "." marks two standard errors


                            Inverse Autocorrelations

         Lag Correlation -1 9 8 7 6 5 4 3 2 1 0 1 2 3 4 5 6 7 8 9 1
          1   -0.71090  |      **************|  .                      |
          2    0.26217  |                    .  |*****                 |
          3   -0.13005  |                 ***|  .                      |
          4    0.14777  |                    .  |***                   |
          5   -0.06803  |                    .*|  .                    |
          6   -0.01147  |                    .  |  .                   |
          7   -0.01649  |                    .  |  .                   |
          8    0.06108  |                    .  |*.                    |
          9   -0.04490  |                    .*|  .                    |
         10    0.01100  |                    .  |  .                   |
```

```
                            Gas Furnace Data
                      (Box and Jenkins, Series J)

                            ARIMA Procedure


                         Partial Autocorrelations

         Lag Correlation -1 9 8 7 6 5 4 3 2 1 0 1 2 3 4 5 6 7 8 9 1
          1    0.95247  |                    .  |******************* |
          2   -0.78796  |      ***************|  .                   |
          3    0.33897  |                    .  |*******             |
          4    0.12121  |                    .  |**                  |
          5    0.05896  |                    .  |*.                  |
          6   -0.11147  |                  **|  .                    |
          7    0.04862  |                    .  |*.                  |
          8    0.09945  |                    .  |**                  |
          9    0.01587  |                    .  |  .                 |
         10   -0.06973  |                    .*|  .                  |


                   Autocorrelation Check for White Noise

      To   Chi                    Autocorrelations
      Lag  Square DF  Prob
       6   786.35  6  0.000  0.952  0.834  0.682  0.531  0.408  0.318
```

The ESTIMATE statement results for the AR(3) model for the input series X are shown in Output 3.3.2.

Output 3.3.2. Estimates of the AR(3) Model for X

```
                            Gas Furnace Data
                      (Box and Jenkins, Series J)

                            ARIMA Procedure


                  Conditional Least Squares Estimation

                                    Approx.
            Parameter   Estimate   Std Error   T Ratio   Lag
            MU          -0.12280    0.10902     -1.13     0
            AR1,1        1.97607    0.05499     35.94     1
            AR1,2       -1.37499    0.09967    -13.80     2
            AR1,3        0.34336    0.05502      6.24     3

            Constant Estimate  = -0.0068229

            Variance  Estimate = 0.03579652
```

Example 3.3.   Model for Series J Data from Box and Jenkins □ □ □   171

Output 3.3.2.   (Continued)

```
              Std Error Estimate = 0.18919968
              AIC               = -141.66743*
              SBC               =  -126.906*
              Number of Residuals=      296
              * Does not include log determinant.

                     Correlations of the Estimates

         Parameter        MU      AR1,1      AR1,2      AR1,3

         MU            1.000    -0.017      0.014     -0.016
         AR1,1        -0.017     1.000     -0.941      0.790
         AR1,2         0.014    -0.941      1.000     -0.941
         AR1,3        -0.016     0.790     -0.941      1.000

                  Autocorrelation Check of Residuals

    To   Chi                    Autocorrelations
    Lag  Square DF   Prob
     6   10.30   3  0.016 -0.042  0.068  0.056 -0.145 -0.009  0.059
    12   19.89   9  0.019  0.014  0.002 -0.055  0.035  0.143 -0.079
    18   27.92  15  0.022  0.099  0.043 -0.082  0.017  0.066 -0.052
    24   31.05  21  0.073 -0.078  0.024  0.015  0.030  0.045  0.004
    30   34.58  27  0.150 -0.007 -0.004  0.073 -0.038 -0.062  0.003
    36   38.84  33  0.223  0.010  0.002  0.082  0.045  0.056 -0.023
    42   41.18  39  0.375  0.002  0.033 -0.061 -0.003 -0.006 -0.043
```

```
                      Gas Furnace Data
                 (Box and Jenkins, Series J)

                      ARIMA Procedure


   Model for variable X

   Estimated Mean = -0.1228034

   Autoregressive Factors
   Factor 1: 1 - 1.9761 B**(1) + 1.375 B**(2) - 0.34336 B**(3)
```

The IDENTIFY statement results for the dependent series Y cross correlated with the input series X is shown in Output 3.3.3. Since a model has been fit to X, both Y and X are prewhitened by this model before the sample cross correlations are computed.

Output 3.3.3. IDENTIFY Statement for Y Cross Correlated with X

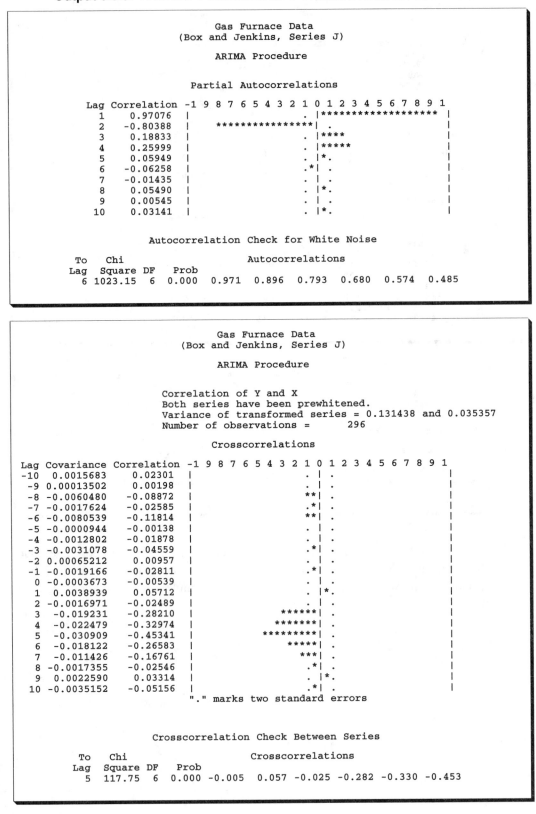

```
                          Gas Furnace Data
                    (Box and Jenkins, Series J)

                          ARIMA Procedure


                     Partial Autocorrelations

        Lag Correlation  -1 9 8 7 6 5 4 3 2 1 0 1 2 3 4 5 6 7 8 9 1
         1    0.97076    |                    . |******************** |
         2   -0.80388    |      ****************| .                   |
         3    0.18833    |                    . |****                 |
         4    0.25999    |                    . |*****                |
         5    0.05949    |                    . |*.                   |
         6   -0.06258    |                    .*| .                   |
         7   -0.01435    |                    . | .                   |
         8    0.05490    |                    . |*.                   |
         9    0.00545    |                    . | .                   |
        10    0.03141    |                    . |*.                   |


                Autocorrelation Check for White Noise

      To    Chi                    Autocorrelations
      Lag  Square DF   Prob
       6  1023.15   6  0.000    0.971   0.896   0.793   0.680   0.574   0.485
```

```
                          Gas Furnace Data
                    (Box and Jenkins, Series J)

                          ARIMA Procedure


              Correlation of Y and X
              Both series have been prewhitened.
              Variance of transformed series = 0.131438 and 0.035357
              Number of observations =       296

                          Crosscorrelations

  Lag Covariance Correlation  -1 9 8 7 6 5 4 3 2 1 0 1 2 3 4 5 6 7 8 9 1
  -10  0.0015683    0.02301   |                    . | .                   |
   -9  0.00013502   0.00198   |                    . | .                   |
   -8 -0.0060480   -0.08872   |                    **| .                   |
   -7 -0.0017624   -0.02585   |                    .*| .                   |
   -6 -0.0080539   -0.11814   |                    **| .                   |
   -5 -0.0000944   -0.00138   |                    . | .                   |
   -4 -0.0012802   -0.01878   |                    . | .                   |
   -3 -0.0031078   -0.04559   |                    .*| .                   |
   -2  0.00065212   0.00957   |                    . | .                   |
   -1 -0.0019166   -0.02811   |                    .*| .                   |
    0 -0.0003673   -0.00539   |                    . | .                   |
    1  0.0038939    0.05712   |                    . |*.                   |
    2 -0.0016971   -0.02489   |                    . | .                   |
    3 -0.019231    -0.28210   |              ******| .                   |
    4 -0.022479    -0.32974   |             *******| .                   |
    5 -0.030909    -0.45341   |            ********| .                   |
    6 -0.018122    -0.26583   |              *****| .                   |
    7 -0.011426    -0.16761   |                ***| .                   |
    8 -0.0017355   -0.02546   |                .*| .                   |
    9  0.0022590    0.03314   |                    . |*.                   |
   10 -0.0035152   -0.05156   |                    .*| .                   |
                     "." marks two standard errors


                Crosscorrelation Check Between Series

      To    Chi                    Crosscorrelations
      Lag  Square DF   Prob
       5   117.75   6  0.000   -0.005   0.057  -0.025  -0.282  -0.330  -0.453
```

Example 3.3. Model for Series J Data from Box and Jenkins ▢ ▢ ▢ 173

Output 3.3.3. (Continued)

```
                        Gas Furnace Data
                  (Box and Jenkins, Series J)

                        ARIMA Procedure


    Both variables have been prewhitened by the following filter:

    Prewhitening Filter


    Autoregressive Factors
    Factor 1:  1 - 1.9761 B**(1) + 1.375 B**(2) - 0.34336 B**(3)
```

The ESTIMATE statement results for the transfer function model with no structure on the noise term is shown in Output 3.3.4. The PLOT option prints the residual autocorrelation functions from this model.

Output 3.3.4. Estimates of the Transfer Function Model

```
                        Gas Furnace Data
                  (Box and Jenkins, Series J)

                        ARIMA Procedure


              Conditional Least Squares Estimation

                                  Approx.
        Parameter    Estimate    Std Error    T Ratio   Lag   Variable   Shift
        MU           53.32237     0.04932     1081.24    0    Y           0
        NUM1         -0.62868     0.25385       -2.48    0    X           3
        NUM1,1        0.47258     0.62253        0.76    1    X           3
        NUM1,2        0.73660     0.81006        0.91    2    X           3
        DEN1,1        0.15411     0.90483        0.17    1    X           3
        DEN1,2        0.27774     0.57345        0.48    2    X           3

        Constant Estimate   = 53.3223702

        Variance  Estimate  = 0.70424109
        Std Error Estimate  = 0.83919073
        AIC                 =    729.72486*
        SBC                 =  751.764799*
        Number of Residuals=        291
        * Does not include log determinant.

                    Correlations of the Estimates
```

Variable	Parameter	Y MU	X NUM1	X NUM1,1	X NUM1,2	X DEN1,1	X DEN1,2
Y	MU	1.000	0.013	0.002	-0.002	0.004	-0.006
X	NUM1	0.013	1.000	0.755	-0.447	0.089	-0.065
X	NUM1,1	0.002	0.755	1.000	0.121	-0.538	0.565
X	NUM1,2	-0.002	-0.447	0.121	1.000	-0.892	0.870
X	DEN1,1	0.004	0.089	-0.538	-0.892	1.000	-0.998
X	DEN1,2	-0.006	-0.065	0.565	0.870	-0.998	1.000

Output 3.3.4. (Continued)

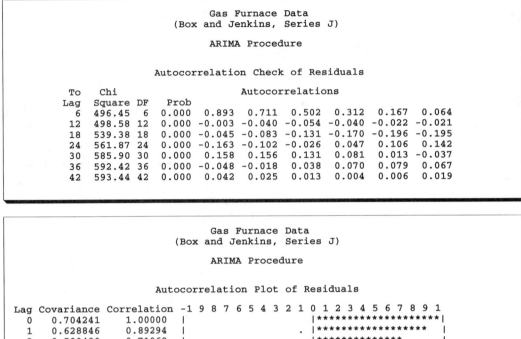

```
                         Gas Furnace Data
                    (Box and Jenkins, Series J)

                         ARIMA Procedure


                 Autocorrelation Check of Residuals

    To   Chi                    Autocorrelations
    Lag  Square DF   Prob
     6   496.45  6   0.000   0.893  0.711  0.502  0.312  0.167  0.064
    12   498.58 12   0.000  -0.003 -0.040 -0.054 -0.040 -0.022 -0.021
    18   539.38 18   0.000  -0.045 -0.083 -0.131 -0.170 -0.196 -0.195
    24   561.87 24   0.000  -0.163 -0.102 -0.026  0.047  0.106  0.142
    30   585.90 30   0.000   0.158  0.156  0.131  0.081  0.013 -0.037
    36   592.42 36   0.000  -0.048 -0.018  0.038  0.070  0.079  0.067
    42   593.44 42   0.000   0.042  0.025  0.013  0.004  0.006  0.019
```

```
                         Gas Furnace Data
                    (Box and Jenkins, Series J)

                         ARIMA Procedure


                 Autocorrelation Plot of Residuals

Lag Covariance Correlation -1 9 8 7 6 5 4 3 2 1 0 1 2 3 4 5 6 7 8 9 1
  0  0.704241   1.00000   |                    |*******************|
  1  0.628846   0.89294   |                   .|*****************  |
  2  0.500490   0.71068   |                 .  |*************      |
  3  0.353404   0.50182   |                 .  |**********         |
  4  0.219895   0.31224   |                 .  |******             |
  5  0.117330   0.16660   |                 .  |***  .             |
  6  0.044967   0.06385   |                 .  |*    .             |
  7 -0.0023551 -0.00334   |                 .  |     .             |
  8 -0.028030  -0.03980   |                 .  *|    .             |
  9 -0.037891  -0.05380   |                 .  *|    .             |
 10 -0.028378  -0.04030   |                 .  *|    .             |
                   "." marks two standard errors


                    Inverse Autocorrelations

 Lag Correlation -1 9 8 7 6 5 4 3 2 1 0 1 2 3 4 5 6 7 8 9 1
   1   -0.57346   |        ***********|  .                        |
   2    0.02264   |                  .|  .                        |
   3    0.03631   |                  .| *.                        |
   4    0.03941   |                  .| *.                        |
   5   -0.01256   |                  .|  .                        |
   6   -0.01618   |                  .|  .                        |
   7    0.02680   |                  .| *.                        |
   8   -0.05895   |                 .*|  .                        |
   9    0.07043   |                  .| *.                        |
  10   -0.02987   |                 .*|  .                        |
```

```
                         Gas Furnace Data
                    (Box and Jenkins, Series J)

                         ARIMA Procedure


                    Partial Autocorrelations

 Lag Correlation -1 9 8 7 6 5 4 3 2 1 0 1 2 3 4 5 6 7 8 9 1
   1    0.89294   |                  .|*****************         |
   2   -0.42765   |           ********|  .                       |
   3   -0.13463   |               ***|  .                        |
   4    0.02199   |                  .| .                        |
   5    0.03891   |                  .|*.                        |
   6   -0.02219   |                  .| .                        |
   7   -0.02249   |                  .| .                        |
   8    0.01538   |                  .| .                        |
   9    0.00634   |                  .| .                        |
```

Example 3.3. Model for Series J Data from Box and Jenkins □ □ □ 175

Output 3.3.4. (Continued)

```
       10    0.07737  |                        .  |**                    |


             Crosscorrelation Check of Residuals with Input X
      To    Chi                      Crosscorrelations
     Lag  Square DF   Prob
       5    0.48   2  0.785 -0.009 -0.005  0.026  0.013 -0.017 -0.022
      11    0.93   8  0.999 -0.006  0.008  0.022  0.023 -0.017 -0.013
      17    2.63  14  1.000  0.012  0.035  0.037  0.039 -0.005 -0.040
      23   19.19  20  0.509 -0.076 -0.108 -0.122 -0.122 -0.094 -0.041
      29   20.12  26  0.786 -0.039 -0.013  0.010 -0.020 -0.031 -0.005
      35   24.22  32  0.836 -0.022 -0.031 -0.074 -0.036  0.014  0.076
      41   30.66  38  0.795  0.108  0.091  0.046  0.018  0.003  0.009



     Model for variable Y

     Estimated Intercept = 53.3223702

     Input Number 1 is X with a shift of 3.

     The Numerator Factors are
     Factor 1: -0.6287 - 0.47258 B**(1) - 0.7366 B**(2)


     The Denominator Factors are
     Factor 1: 1 - 0.15411 B**(1) - 0.27774 B**(2)
```

The ESTIMATE statement results for the final transfer function model with AR(2) noise are shown in Output 3.3.5.

Output 3.3.5. Estimates of the Final Model

```
                            Gas Furnace Data
                        (Box and Jenkins, Series J)

                            ARIMA Procedure


                  Conditional Least Squares Estimation

                             Approx.
        Parameter   Estimate  Std Error   T Ratio  Lag  Variable Shift
        MU          53.26307    0.11926    446.63   0    Y          0
        AR1,1        1.53292    0.04754     32.25   1    Y          0
        AR1,2       -0.63297    0.05006    -12.64   2    Y          0
        NUM1        -0.53522    0.07482     -7.15   0    X          3
        NUM1,1       0.37602    0.10287      3.66   1    X          3
        NUM1,2       0.51894    0.10783      4.81   2    X          3
        DEN1,1       0.54842    0.03822     14.35   1    X          3

     Constant Estimate  = 5.32937102

     Variance  Estimate = 0.05882782
     Std Error Estimate = 0.24254447
     AIC                = 8.29281119*
     SBC                = 34.0060741*
     Number of Residuals=      291
     * Does not include log determinant.

                    Correlations of the Estimates


                           Y        Y        Y        X        X        X
     Variable  Parameter   MU     AR1,1    AR1,2    NUM1    NUM1,1   NUM1,2

     Y          MU        1.000   -0.063    0.047   -0.008   -0.016    0.017
     Y          AR1,1    -0.063    1.000   -0.927   -0.003    0.007   -0.002
     Y          AR1,2     0.047   -0.927    1.000    0.023   -0.005    0.005
```

Output 3.3.5. (Continued)

X	NUM1	-0.008	-0.003	0.023	1.000	0.713	-0.178
X	NUM1,1	-0.016	0.007	-0.005	0.713	1.000	-0.467
X	NUM1,2	0.017	-0.002	0.005	-0.178	-0.467	1.000
X	DEN1,1	-0.049	0.015	-0.022	-0.013	-0.039	-0.720

```
                         Gas Furnace Data
                     (Box and Jenkins, Series J)

                         ARIMA Procedure


                                          X
              Variable   Parameter     DEN1,1

                 Y        MU           -0.049
                 Y        AR1,1         0.015
                 Y        AR1,2        -0.022
                 X        NUM1         -0.013
                 X        NUM1,1       -0.039
                 X        NUM1,2       -0.720
                 X        DEN1,1        1.000
```

Autocorrelation Check of Residuals

To Lag	Chi Square	DF	Prob	Autocorrelations					
6	8.61	4	0.072	0.024	0.055	-0.073	-0.054	-0.054	0.119
12	15.43	10	0.117	0.032	0.028	-0.081	0.047	0.022	0.107
18	21.13	16	0.173	-0.038	0.052	-0.093	-0.013	-0.073	-0.005
24	27.52	22	0.192	-0.118	-0.002	-0.007	0.076	0.024	-0.004
30	36.94	28	0.120	0.034	-0.021	0.020	0.094	-0.118	0.065
36	44.26	34	0.112	-0.025	-0.057	0.113	0.022	0.030	0.065
42	45.62	40	0.250	-0.017	-0.036	-0.029	-0.013	-0.033	0.017

Crosscorrelation Check of Residuals with Input X

To Lag	Chi Square	DF	Prob	Crosscorrelations					
5	0.93	3	0.819	0.008	0.004	0.010	0.008	-0.045	0.030
11	6.60	9	0.678	0.075	-0.024	-0.019	-0.026	-0.111	0.013
17	13.86	15	0.537	0.050	0.043	0.014	0.014	-0.141	-0.028
23	18.55	21	0.614	-0.074	-0.078	0.023	-0.016	0.021	0.060
29	27.99	27	0.411	-0.071	-0.001	0.038	-0.156	0.031	0.035
35	35.18	33	0.365	-0.014	0.015	-0.039	0.028	0.046	0.142
41	37.15	39	0.554	0.031	-0.029	-0.070	-0.006	0.012	-0.004

```
                         Gas Furnace Data
                     (Box and Jenkins, Series J)

                         ARIMA Procedure


         Model for variable Y

         Estimated Intercept = 53.2630713

         Autoregressive Factors
         Factor 1: 1 - 1.5329 B**(1) + 0.63297 B**(2)


         Input Number 1 is X with a shift of 3.

         The Numerator Factors are
         Factor 1: -0.5352 - 0.37602 B**(1) - 0.51894 B**(2)


         The Denominator Factors are
         Factor 1: 1 - 0.54842 B**(1)
```

Example 3.4. An Intervention Model for Ozone Data □□□ 177

Example 3.4. An Intervention Model for Ozone Data

This example fits an intervention model to ozone data as suggested by Box and Tiao (1975). Notice that since the response variable, OZONE, is differenced, the innovation, X1, must also be differenced to generate a step function change in the response. If X1 had not been differenced, the change in the response caused by X1 would be a (seasonal) ramp and not a step function. Notice that the final model for the differenced data is a multiple regression model with a moving-average structure assumed for the residuals.

The model is fit by maximum likelihood. The seasonal moving-average parameter and its standard error are fairly sensitive to which method is chosen to fit the model, in agreement with the observations of Davidson (1981) and Ansley and Newbold (1980); thus, fitting the model by the unconditional or conditional least squares methods produce somewhat different estimates for these parameters.

Some missing values are appended to the end of the input data to generate additional values for the independent variables. Since the independent variables are not modeled, values for them must be available for any times at which predicted values are desired. In this case, predicted values are requested for 12 periods beyond the end of the data. Thus, values for X1, WINTER, and SUMMER must be given for 12 periods ahead.

The following statements read in the data and compute dummy variables for use as intervention inputs:

```
title1 'Intervention Data for Ozone Concentration';
title2 '(Box and Tiao, JASA 1975 P.70)';

data air;
   input ozone @@;
   label ozone  = 'Ozone Concentration'
         x1      = 'Intervention for post 1960 period'
         summer = 'Summer Months Intervention'
         winter = 'Winter Months Intervention';
   date = intnx( 'month', '31dec54'd, _n_ );
   format date monyy.;
   month = month( date );
   year = year( date );
   x1 = year >= 1960;
   summer = ( 5 < month < 11 ) * ( year > 1965 );
   winter = ( year > 1965 ) - summer;
cards;
2.7  2.0  3.6  5.0  6.5  6.1  5.9  5.0  6.4  7.4  8.2  3.9
4.1  4.5  5.5  3.8  4.8  5.6  6.3  5.9  8.7  5.3  5.7  5.7
3.0  3.4  4.9  4.5  4.0  5.7  6.3  7.1  8.0  5.2  5.0  4.7
3.7  3.1  2.5  4.0  4.1  4.6  4.4  4.2  5.1  4.6  4.4  4.0
2.9  2.4  4.7  5.1  4.0  7.5  7.7  6.3  5.3  5.7  4.8  2.7
1.7  2.0  3.4  4.0  4.3  5.0  5.5  5.0  5.4  3.8  2.4  2.0
2.2  2.5  2.6  3.3  2.9  4.3  4.2  4.2  3.9  3.9  2.5  2.2
2.4  1.9  2.1  4.5  3.3  3.4  4.1  5.7  4.8  5.0  2.8  2.9
1.7  3.2  2.7  3.0  3.4  3.8  5.0  4.8  4.9  3.5  2.5  2.4
1.6  2.3  2.5  3.1  3.5  4.5  5.7  5.0  4.6  4.8  2.1  1.4
2.1  2.9  2.7  4.2  3.9  4.1  4.6  5.8  4.4  6.1  3.5  1.9
1.8  1.9  3.7  4.4  3.8  5.6  5.7  5.1  5.6  4.8  2.5  1.5
1.8  2.5  2.6  1.8  3.7  3.7  4.9  5.1  3.7  5.4  3.0  1.8
2.1  2.6  2.8  3.2  3.5  3.5  4.9  4.2  4.7  3.7  3.2  1.8
2.0  1.7  2.8  3.2  4.4  3.4  3.9  5.5  3.8  3.2  2.3  2.2
```

```
1.3  2.3  2.7  3.3  3.7  3.0  3.8  4.7  4.6  2.9  1.7  1.3
1.8  2.0  2.2  3.0  2.4  3.5  3.5  3.3  2.7  2.5  1.6  1.2
1.5  2.0  3.1  3.0  3.5  3.4  4.0  3.8  3.1  2.1  1.6  1.3
 .    .    .    .    .    .    .    .    .    .    .    .
;
```

The following statements produce Output 3.4.1 and Output 3.4.2:

```
proc arima data=air;

   /*--- Identify and seasonally difference ozone series ---*/
   identify var=ozone(12) crosscorr=( x1(12) summer winter ) noprint;

   /*--- Fit a multiple regression with a seasonal MA model ---*/
   /*---     by the maximum likelihood method ---*/
   estimate q=(1)(12) input=( x1 summer winter )
            noconstant method=ml itprint;

   /*--- Forecast ---*/
   forecast  lead=12 id=date interval=month;

run;
```

The ESTIMATE statement results are shown in Output 3.4.1.

Output 3.4.1. Parameter Estimates

```
                 Intervention Data for Ozone Concentration
                     (Box and Tiao, JASA 1975 P.70)

                            ARIMA Procedure

                         Preliminary Estimation

                       Initial Moving Average Estimates
                        1        -0.29241

                       Initial Moving Average Estimates
                       12         0.40740

               White Noise Variance Est = 0.944969
```

```
                 Intervention Data for Ozone Concentration
                     (Box and Tiao, JASA 1975 P.70)

                            ARIMA Procedure


                  Conditional Least Squares Estimation

Iteration   SSE       MA1,1     MA2,1      NUM1      NUM2      NUM3    Lambda
   0    154.53372   -0.2924    0.4074   -1.1349   -0.1173   0.05581  0.00001
   1    146.19630   -0.2926    0.5984   -1.2029   -0.2978   -0.1157  1E-6
   2    145.87909   -0.3007    0.5924   -1.2617   -0.2625  -0.08247  1E-7
   3    145.87883   -0.2998    0.5924   -1.2625   -0.2615  -0.08197  1E-8
   4    145.87883   -0.2998    0.5923   -1.2624   -0.2615  -0.08196  1E-9


                  Maximum Likelihood Estimation

Iter    Loglike     MA1,1     MA2,1      NUM1      NUM2      NUM3    Lambda
   0  -249.07778   -0.2998    0.5923   -1.2624   -0.2615  -0.08196  0.00001
   1  -245.89135   -0.2683    0.7663   -1.3449   -0.2398  -0.07578  1E-6
   2  -245.88484   -0.2665    0.7662   -1.3305   -0.2394  -0.08025  1E-7
   3  -245.88482   -0.2669    0.7666   -1.3307   -0.2394  -0.08020  1E-8
   4  -245.88481   -0.2668    0.7666   -1.3306   -0.2394  -0.08021  1E-9
```

Example 3.4. An Intervention Model for Ozone Data ▢ ▢ ▢ 179

Output 3.4.1. (Continued)

```
                    ARIMA Estimation Optimization Summary

Estimation Method:                          Maximum Likelihood
Parameters Estimated:                                       5
Termination Criteria:       Maximum Relative Change in Estimates
Iteration Stopping Value:                               0.001
Criteria Value:                                    0.00019544
Alternate Criteria:         Relative Change in Objective Function
Alternate Criteria Value:                          1.24707E-8
Maximum Absolute Value of Gradient:               0.00712034
R-Square (Relative Change in Regression SSE) from Last Iteration
    Step:                                          5.36232E-9
Objective Function:             Log Gaussian Likelihood
Objective Function Value:                         -245.88481
Marquardt's Lambda Coefficient:                         1E-9
Numerical Derivative Perturbation Delta:               0.001
Iterations:                                                4
```

```
                Intervention Data for Ozone Concentration
                    (Box and Tiao, JASA 1975 P.70)

                          ARIMA Procedure


                    Maximum Likelihood Estimation

                         Approx.
Parameter    Estimate    Std Error    T Ratio   Lag   Variable   Shift
MA1,1        -0.26684     0.06710      -3.98     1    OZONE        0
MA2,1         0.76665     0.05973      12.83    12    OZONE        0
NUM1         -1.33062     0.19236      -6.92     0    X1           0
NUM2         -0.23936     0.05952      -4.02     0    SUMMER       0
NUM3         -0.08021     0.04978      -1.61     0    WINTER       0

Variance  Estimate = 0.63450562
Std Error Estimate = 0.79655861
AIC              = 501.769629
SBC              = 518.360229
Number of Residuals=      204
```

```
                    Correlations of the Estimates

                        OZONE     OZONE       X1    SUMMER    WINTER
Variable   Parameter    MA1,1     MA2,1     NUM1      NUM2      NUM3

OZONE      MA1,1        1.000     0.090    -0.039    0.062    -0.034
OZONE      MA2,1        0.090     1.000    -0.169    0.211     0.022
X1         NUM1        -0.039    -0.169     1.000   -0.124    -0.107
SUMMER     NUM2         0.062     0.211    -0.124    1.000     0.097
WINTER     NUM3        -0.034     0.022    -0.107    0.097     1.000
```

```
                 Autocorrelation Check of Residuals

  To   Chi                    Autocorrelations
 Lag  Square DF   Prob
   6   7.47   4  0.113   0.017  0.054  0.043  0.101 -0.022  0.140
  12  10.21  10  0.422  -0.024 -0.059 -0.047  0.014  0.032  0.072
  18  14.53  16  0.559   0.054  0.006 -0.110  0.028 -0.042  0.043
  24  19.99  22  0.583   0.003 -0.074 -0.074  0.098 -0.038  0.043
  30  27.00  28  0.518  -0.072 -0.035  0.023 -0.028 -0.107  0.100
  36  32.65  34  0.534   0.022 -0.099 -0.006  0.087 -0.046  0.053
```

Output 3.4.1. (Continued)

```
              Intervention Data for Ozone Concentration
                    (Box and Tiao, JASA 1975 P.70)

                          ARIMA Procedure


         Model for variable OZONE

         No mean term in this model.
         Period(s) of Differencing = 12.

         Moving Average Factors
         Factor 1: 1 + 0.26684 B**(1)
         Factor 2: 1 - 0.76665 B**(12)


         Input Number 1 is X1.
         Period(s) of Differencing = 12.
         Overall Regression Factor  = -1.33062

         Input Number 2 is SUMMER.
         Overall Regression Factor  = -0.23936

         Input Number 3 is WINTER.
         Overall Regression Factor  = -0.08021
```

The FORECAST statement results are shown in Output 3.4.2.

Output 3.4.2. Forecasts

```
              Intervention Data for Ozone Concentration
                    (Box and Tiao, JASA 1975 P.70)

                          ARIMA Procedure


    Forecasts for variable OZONE

      Obs    Forecast Std Error    Lower 95%    Upper 95%
      217      1.4205    0.7966      -0.1407       2.9817
      218      1.8446    0.8244       0.2287       3.4604
      219      2.4567    0.8244       0.8408       4.0725
      220      2.8590    0.8244       1.2431       4.4748
      221      3.1501    0.8244       1.5342       4.7659
      222      2.7211    0.8244       1.1053       4.3370
      223      3.3147    0.8244       1.6989       4.9306
      224      3.4787    0.8244       1.8629       5.0946
      225      2.9405    0.8244       1.3247       4.5564
      226      2.3587    0.8244       0.7429       3.9746
      227      1.8588    0.8244       0.2429       3.4746
      228      1.2898    0.8244      -0.3260       2.9057
```

References

Akaike, H. (1974), "A New Look at the Statistical Model Identification," *IEEE Transaction on Automatic Control*, AC-19, 716–723.

Anderson, T.W. (1971), *The Statistical Analysis of Time Series*, New York: John Wiley & Sons, Inc.

Andrews and Herzberg (1985), *A collection of problems from many fields for the student and research worker*, New York: Springer Verlag.

Ansley, C. (1979), "An Algorithm for the Exact Likelihood of a Mixed Autoregressive-Moving Average Process," *Biometrika*, 66, 59.

Ansley, C. and Newbold, P. (1980), "Finite Sample Properties of Estimators for Autoregressive Moving Average Models," *Journal of Econometrics*, 13, 159.

Bhansali, R.J. (1980), "Autoregressive and Window Estimates of the Inverse Correlation Function," *Biometrika*, 67, 551–566.

Box, G.E.P. and Jenkins, G.M. (1976), *Time Series Analysis: Forecasting and Control*, San Francisco: Holden-Day.

Box, G.E.P. and Tiao, G.C. (1975), "Intervention Analysis with Applications to Economic and Environmental Problems," *JASA*, 70, 70–79.

Brocklebank, J.C. and Dickey, D.A. (1986), *SAS System for Forecasting Time Series, 1986 Edition*, Cary, North Carolina: SAS Institute Inc.

Chatfield, C. (1980), "Inverse Autocorrelations," *Journal of the Royal Statistical Society*, A142, 363–377.

Cleveland, W.S. (1972), "The Inverse Autocorrelations of a Time Series and Their Applications," *Technometrics*, 14, 277.

Davidson, J. (1981), "Problems with the Estimation of Moving Average Models," *Journal of Econometrics*, 16, 295.

Davies, N., Triggs, C.M., and Newbold, P. (1977), "Significance Levels of the Box-Pierce Portmanteau Statistic in Finite Samples," *Biometrika*, 64, 517–522.

Dunsmuir, William (1984), "Large sample properties of estimation in time series observed at unequally spaced times," in *Time Series Analysis of Irregularly Observed Data*, Emanuel Parzen, ed., New York: Springer-Verlag.

Fuller, W.A. (1976), *Introduction to Statistical Time Series*, New York: John Wiley & Sons, Inc.

Harvey, A.C. (1981), *Time Series Models*, New York: John Wiley & Sons, Inc.

Jones, Richard H. (1980), "Maximum Likelihood Fitting of ARMA Models to Time Series with Missing Observations," *Technometrics*, 22, 389–396.

Ljung, G.M. and Box, G.E.P. (1978), "On a Measure of Lack of Fit in Time Series Models," *Biometrika*, 65, 297–303.

Montgomery, D.C. and Johnson, L.A. (1976), *Forecasting and Time Series Analysis*, New York: McGraw-Hill Book Co.

Morf, M., Sidhu, G.S., and Kailath, T. (1974), "Some New Algorithms for Recursive Estimation on Constant Linear Discrete Time Systems," *I.E.E.E. Transactions on Automatic Control*, AC-19, 315–323.

Nelson, C.R. (1973), *Applied Time Series for Managerial Forecasting*, San Francisco: Holden-Day.

Newbold, P. (1981), "Some Recent Developments in Time Series Analysis," *International Statistical Review*, 49, 53–66.

Newton, H. Joseph and Pagano, Marcello (1983), "The Finite Memory Prediction of Covariance Stationary Time Series," *SIAM Journal of Scientific and Statistical Computing*, 4, 330–339.

Pankratz, Alan (1983), *Forecasting with Univariate Box-Jenkins Models: Concepts and Cases*, New York: John Wiley & Sons, Inc.

Pankratz, Alan (1991), *Forecasting with Dynamic Regression Models*, New York: John Wiley & Sons, Inc.

Pearlman, J.G. (1980), "An Algorithm for the Exact Likelihood of a High-order Autoregressive-Moving Average Process," *Biometrika*, 67, 232–233.

Priestly, M.B. (1981), *Spectra Analysis and Time Series, Volume 1: Univariate Series*, New York: Academic Press, Inc.

Schwarz, G. (1978), "Estimating the Dimension of a Model," *Annals of Statistics*, 6, 461–464.

Woodfield, T.J. (1987), "Time Series Intervention Analysis Using SAS Software," *Proceedings of the Twelfth Annual SAS Users Group International Conference*, 331–339. Cary, NC: SAS Institute Inc.

Chapter 4
The AUTOREG Procedure

Chapter Table of Contents

Chapter 4
The AUTOREG Procedure

Overview

The AUTOREG procedure estimates and forecasts linear regression models for time series data when the errors are autocorrelated or heteroscedastic. The autoregressive error model is used to correct for autocorrelation, and the generalized autoregressive conditional heteroscedasticity (GARCH) model and its variants are used to model and correct for heteroscedasticity.

When time series data are used in regression analysis, often the error term is not independent through time. Instead, the errors are *serially correlated* or *autocorrelated*. If the error term is autocorrelated, the efficiency of ordinary least-squares (OLS) parameter estimates is adversely affected and standard error estimates are biased.

The autoregressive error model corrects for serial correlation. The AUTOREG procedure can fit autoregressive error models of any order and can fit subset autoregressive models. You can also specify stepwise autoregression to select the autoregressive error model automatically.

To diagnose autocorrelation, the AUTOREG procedure produces generalized Durbin-Watson (DW) statistics and their marginal probabilities. Exact *p*-values are reported for generalized DW tests to any specified order. For models with lagged dependent regressors, PROC AUTOREG performs the Durbin *t*-test and the Durbin *h*-test for first-order autocorrelation and reports their marginal significance levels.

Ordinary regression analysis assumes that the error variance is the same for all observations. When the error variance is not constant, the data are said to be *heteroscedastic*, and ordinary least-squares estimates are inefficient. Heteroscedasticity also affects the accuracy of forecast confidence limits. More efficient use of the data and more accurate prediction error estimates can be made by models that take the heteroscedasticity into account.

To test for heteroscedasticity, the AUTOREG procedure uses the portmanteau test statistics and the Engle Lagrange multiplier tests. Test statistics and significance *p*-values are reported for conditional heteroscedasticity at lags 1 through 12. The Bera-Jarque normality test statistic and its significance level are also reported to test for conditional nonnormality of residuals.

The family of GARCH models provides a means of estimating and correcting for the changing variability of the data. The GARCH process assumes that the errors, although uncorrelated, are not independent and models the conditional error variance as a function of the past realizations of the series.

The AUTOREG procedure supports the following variations of the GARCH models:

- generalized ARCH (GARCH)

- integrated GARCH (IGARCH)

- exponential GARCH (EGARCH)

- GARCH-in-mean (GARCH-M)

For GARCH-type models, the AUTOREG procedure produces the conditional prediction error variances as well as parameter and covariance estimates.

The AUTOREG procedure can also analyze models that combine autoregressive errors and GARCH-type heteroscedasticity. PROC AUTOREG can output predictions of the conditional mean and variance for models with autocorrelated disturbances and changing conditional error variances over time.

Four estimation methods are supported for the autoregressive error model:

- Yule-Walker

- iterated Yule-Walker

- unconditional least squares

- exact maximum likelihood

The maximum likelihood method is used for GARCH models and for mixed AR-GARCH models.

The AUTOREG procedure produces forecasts and forecast confidence limits when future values of the independent variables are included in the input data set. PROC AUTOREG is a useful tool for forecasting because it uses the time series part of the model as well as the systematic part in generating predicted values. The autoregressive error model takes into account recent departures from the trend in producing forecasts.

The AUTOREG procedure permits embedded missing values for the independent or dependent variables. The procedure should be used only for ordered and equally spaced time series data.

Getting Started

Regression with Autocorrelated Errors

Ordinary regression analysis is based on several statistical assumptions. One key assumption is that the errors are independent of each other. However, with time series data, the ordinary regression residuals usually are correlated over time. It is not desirable to use ordinary regression analysis for time series data since the assumptions on which the classical linear regression model is based will usually be violated.

Violation of the independent errors assumption has three important consequences for ordinary regression. First, statistical tests of the significance of the parameters and the confidence limits for the predicted values are not correct. Second, the estimates of the regression coefficients are not as efficient as they would be if the autocorrelation were taken into account. Third, since the ordinary regression residuals are not independent, they contain information that can be used to improve the prediction of future values.

The AUTOREG procedure solves this problem by augmenting the regression model with an autoregressive model for the random error, thereby accounting for the autocorrelation of the errors. Instead of the usual regression model, the following autoregressive error model is used:

$$y_t = \mathbf{x}_t' \beta + v_t$$
$$v_t = -\varphi_1 v_{t-1} - \varphi_2 v_{t-2} - \ldots - \varphi_m v_{t-m} + \epsilon_t$$
$$\epsilon_t \sim \text{IN}\left(0, \sigma^2\right)$$

The notation $\epsilon_t \sim \text{IN}\left(0, \sigma^2\right)$ indicates that each ϵ_t is normally and independently distributed with mean 0 and variance σ^2.

By simultaneously estimating the regression coefficients β and the autoregressive error model parameters φ_i, the AUTOREG procedure corrects the regression estimates for autocorrelation. Thus, this kind of regression analysis is often called *autoregressive error correction* or *serial correlation correction*.

Example of Autocorrelated Data

A simulated time series is used to introduce the AUTOREG procedure. The following statements generate a simulated time series Y with second-order autocorrelation:

```
data a;
   ul = 0; ull = 0;
   do time = -10 to 36;
      u = + 1.3 * ul - .5 * ull + 2*rannor(12346);
      y = 10 + .5 * time + u;
      if time > 0 then output;
      ull = ul; ul = u;
      end;
run;
```

The series Y is a time trend plus a second-order autoregressive error. The model simulated is

$$y_t = 10 + .5\,t + v_t$$
$$v_t = 1.3\,v_{t-1} - .5\,v_{t-2} + \epsilon_t$$
$$\epsilon_t \sim \text{IN}(0,4)$$

The following statements plot the simulated time series Y. A linear regression trend line is shown for reference. (The regression line is produced by plotting the series a second time using the regression interpolation feature of the SYMBOL statement. Refer to *SAS/GRAPH Software: Reference, Version 6, First Edition, Volume 1* for further explanation.)

```
title "Autocorrelated Time Series";
proc gplot data=a;
   symbol1 v=star i=join;
   symbol2 v=none i=r;
   plot y * time = 1 y * time = 2 / overlay;
run;
```

The plot of series Y and the regression line are shown in Figure 4.1.

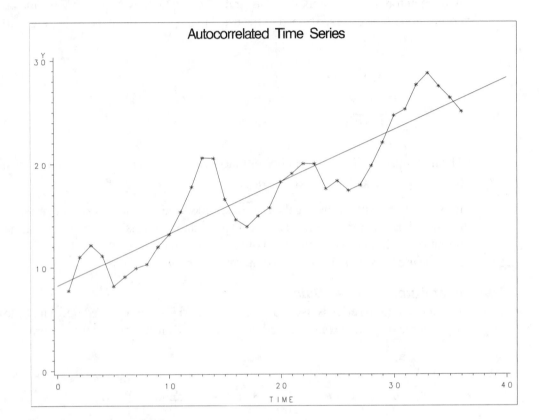

Figure 4.1.   Autocorrelated Time Series

Note that when the series is above (or below) the OLS regression trend line, it tends to remain above (below) the trend for several periods.   This pattern is an example of *positive autocorrelation.*

Time series regression usually involves independent variables other than a time-trend.   However, the simple time-trend model is convenient for illustrating regression with autocorrelated errors, and the series Y shown in Figure 4.1 is used in the following introductory examples.

Ordinary Least-Squares Regression

To use the AUTOREG procedure, specify the input data set in the PROC AUTOREG statement and specify the regression model in a MODEL statement.   Specify the model by first naming the dependent variable and then listing the regressors after an equal sign, as is done in other SAS regression procedures.   The following statements regress Y on TIME using ordinary least squares:

```
proc autoreg data=a;
   model y = time;
run;
```

The AUTOREG procedure output is shown in Figure 4.2.

```
                        Autocorrelated Time Series
                           Autoreg Procedure

Dependent Variable = Y

                     Ordinary Least Squares Estimates
              SSE           214.9534    DFE                34
              MSE            6.32216    Root MSE     2.514391
              SBC           173.6591    AIC          170.4921
              Reg Rsq         0.8200    Total Rsq      0.8200
              Durbin-Watson   0.4752


        Variable      DF      B Value    Std Error    t Ratio Approx Prob

        Intercept      1    8.23075782     0.85590      9.616     0.0001
        TIME           1    0.50210974     0.04034     12.447     0.0001
```

Figure 4.2. AUTOREG Results for OLS estimation

The output first shows statistics for the model residuals. The model root mean square error (Root MSE) is 2.51, and the model R^2 is .82. Notice that two R^2 statistics are shown, one for the regression model (Reg Rsq) and one for the full model (Total Rsq) that includes the autoregressive error process, if any. In this case, an autoregressive error model is not used, so the two R^2 statistics are the same.

Other statistics shown are the sum of square errors (SSE), mean square error (MSE), error degrees of freedom (DFE, the number of observations minus the number of parameters), the information criteria SBC and AIC, and the Durbin-Watson statistic. (Durbin-Watson statistics and SBC and AIC are discussed in the "Details" section later in this chapter.)

The output then shows a table of regression coefficients, with standard errors and t-tests. The estimated model is

$$y_t = 8.23 + .502\,t + \epsilon_t$$
$$\text{Est. Var}(\epsilon_t) = 6.32$$

The OLS parameter estimates are reasonably close to the true values, but the estimated error variance, 6.32, is much larger than the true value, 4.

Autoregressive Error Model

The following statements regress Y on TIME with the errors assumed to follow a second-order autoregressive process. The order of the autoregressive model is specified by the NLAG=2 option. The Yule-Walker estimation method is used by default. The example uses the METHOD=ML option to specify the exact maximum likelihood method instead.

```
proc autoreg data=a;
   model y = time / nlag=2 method=ml;
run;
```

The first part of the results are shown in Figure 4.3. The initial OLS results are produced first, followed by estimates of the autocorrelations computed from the OLS residuals. The autocorrelations are also displayed graphically.

```
                         Autocorrelated Time Series

                            Autoreg Procedure

Dependent Variable = Y


                       Ordinary Least Squares Estimates

                  SSE           214.9534    DFE                  34
                  MSE            6.32216     Root MSE       2.514391
                  SBC           173.6591     AIC            170.4921
                  Reg Rsq         0.8200     Total Rsq        0.8200
                  Durbin-Watson   0.4752


          Variable      DF      B Value    Std Error    t Ratio  Approx Prob

          Intercept     1     8.23075782     0.85590      9.616     0.0001
          TIME          1     0.50210974     0.04034     12.447     0.0001


                       Estimates of Autocorrelations

   Lag   Covariance   Correlation  -1 9 8 7 6 5 4 3 2 1 0 1 2 3 4 5 6 7 8 9 1

    0     5.970929     1.000000   |                      |********************|
    1     4.516919     0.756485   |                      |***************     |
    2     2.024114     0.338995   |                      |*******             |


                          Preliminary MSE = 1.794304
```

Figure 4.3.   Preliminary Estimate for AR(2) Error Model

The maximum likelihood estimates are shown in Figure 4.4. Figure 4.4 also shows the preliminary Yule-Walker estimates used as starting values for the iterative computation of the maximum likelihood estimates.

```
                        Autocorrelated Time Series

                            Autoreg Procedure

                 Estimates of the Autoregressive Parameters

            Lag    Coefficient        Std Error          t Ratio
             1     -1.16905667        0.14817234        -7.889844
             2      0.54537934        0.14817234         3.680709


                      Maximum Likelihood Estimates

            SSE             54.7493    DFE                    32
            MSE            1.710916    Root MSE          1.30802
            SBC           133.4765    AIC              127.1424
            Reg Rsq         0.7280    Total Rsq          0.9542
            Durbin-Watson   2.2761


   Variable       DF        B Value    Std Error    t Ratio Approx Prob

   Intercept       1     7.88333847       1.1693      6.742      0.0001
   TIME            1     0.50955285       0.0551      9.254      0.0001
   A(1)            1    -1.24642817       0.1385     -9.001      0.0001
   A(2)            1     0.62828534       0.1366      4.600      0.0001


        Autoregressive parameters assumed given.


   Variable       DF        B Value    Std Error    t Ratio Approx Prob

   Intercept       1     7.88333847       1.1678      6.750      0.0001
   TIME            1     0.50955285       0.0551      9.255      0.0001
```

Figure 4.4. Maximum Likelihood Estimates of AR(2) Error Model

The tables of diagnostic statistics and parameter estimates in Figure 4.4 have the same form as in the OLS output, but the values shown are for the autoregressive error model. The MSE for the autoregressive model is 1.71, which is much smaller than the true value of 4. In small samples, the autoregressive error model tends to underestimate σ^2, while the OLS MSE overestimates σ^2.

Notice that the total R^2 statistic computed from the autoregressive model residuals is .954, reflecting the improved fit from the use of past residuals to help predict the next Y value. The Reg Rsq value .728 is the R^2 statistic for a regression of transformed variables adjusted for the estimated autocorrelation. (This is not the R^2 for the estimated trend line. For details, see "R2 Statistics and Other Measures of Fit" later in this chapter.)

The parameter estimates table shows the ML estimates of the regression coefficients and includes two additional rows for the estimates of the autoregressive parameters, labeled A(1) and A(2). The estimated model is

$$y_t = 7.88 + .5096\,t + v_t$$
$$v_t = 1.25\,v_{t-1} - .628\,v_{t-2} + \epsilon_t$$
$$\text{Est. Var}(\epsilon_t) = 1.71$$

Note that the signs of the autoregressive parameters shown in this equation for v_t are the reverse of the estimates shown in the AUTOREG procedure output. Figure 4.4 also shows the estimates of the regression coefficients with the standard errors recomputed on the assumption that the autoregressive parameter estimates equal the true values.

Predicted Values and Residuals

The AUTOREG procedure can produce two kinds of predicted values and corresponding residuals and confidence limits. The first kind of predicted value is obtained from only the structural part of the model, $x_t'\,b$. This is an estimate of the unconditional mean of the response variable at time t. For the time trend model, these predicted values trace the estimated trend. The second kind of predicted values include both the structural part of the model and the predicted values of the autoregressive error process. The full model (conditional) predictions are used to forecast future values.

Use the OUTPUT statement to store predicted values and residuals in a SAS data set and to output other values such as confidence limits and variance estimates. The P= option specifies an output variable to contain the full model predicted values. The PM= option names an output variable for the predicted mean. The R= and RM= options specify output variables for the corresponding residuals, computed as the actual value minus the predicted value.

The following statements store both kinds of predicted values in the output data set. (The printed output is the same as previously shown in Figure 4.3 and Figure 4.4.)

```
proc autoreg data=a;
   model y = time / nlag=2 method=ml;
   output out=p p=yhat pm=trendhat;
run;
```

The following statements plot the predicted values from the regression trend line and from the full model together with the actual values.

```
title "Predictions for Autocorrelation Model";
proc gplot data=p;
   symbol1 v=star i=none;
   symbol2 v=plus i=join;
   symbol3 v=none i=join;
   plot y * time = 1 yhat * time = 2
        trendhat * time = 3 / overlay ;
run;
```

The plot of predicted values is shown in Figure 4.5.

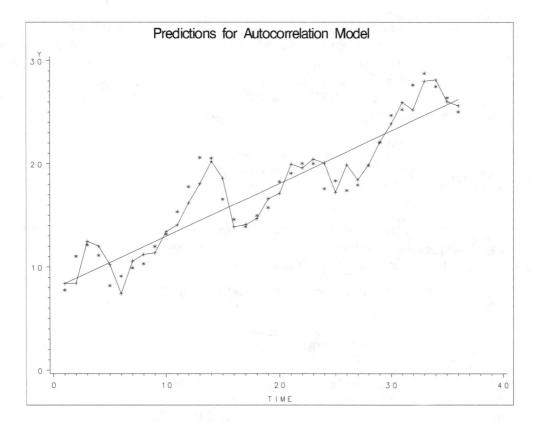

Figure 4.5. PROC AUTOREG Predictions

In Figure 4.5 the straight line is the autocorrelation corrected regression line, traced out by the structural predicted values TRENDHAT. The jagged line traces the full model prediction values. The actual values are marked by asterisks. This plot graphically illustrates the improvement in fit provided by the autoregressive error process for highly autocorrelated data.

Forecasting Autoregressive Error Models

To produce forecasts for future periods, include observations for the forecast periods in the input data set. The forecast observations must provide values for the independent variables and have missing values for the response variable.

For the time trend model, the only regressor is time. The following statements add observations for time periods 37 through 46 to the data set A to produce an augmented data set B:

```
data b;
   y = .;
   do time = 37 to 46; output; end;
run;

data b; merge a b; by time; run;
```

To produce the forecast, use the augmented data set as input to PROC AUTOREG, and specify the appropriate options in the OUTPUT statement. The following statements produce forecasts for the time trend with autoregressive error model. The output data set includes all the variables in the input data set, the forecast values (YHAT), the predicted trend (YTREND), and the upper (UCL) and lower (LCL) 95% confidence limits.

```
proc autoreg data=b;
   model y = time / nlag=2 method=ml;
   output out=p p=yhat pm=ytrend
                lcl=lcl ucl=ucl;
run;
```

The following statements plot the predicted values and confidence limits, and they also plot the trend line for reference. The actual observations are shown for periods 16 through 36, and a reference line is drawn at the start of the out-of-sample forecasts.

```
title "Forecasting Autocorrelated Time Series";
proc gplot data=p;
   plot y*time=1 yhat*time=2 ytrend*time=3
        lcl*time=3 ucl*time=3 /
        overlay href=36.5;
   where time >= 16;
   symbol1 v=star i=none;
   symbol2 v=plus i=join;
   symbol3 v=none i=join;
run;
```

The plot is shown in Figure 4.6. Notice that the forecasts take into account the recent departures from the trend but converge back to the trend line for longer forecast horizons.

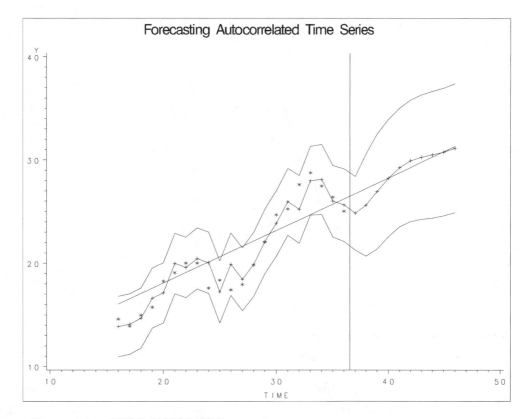

Figure 4.6. PROC AUTOREG Forecasts

Testing for Autocorrelation

In the preceding section, it is assumed that the order of the autoregressive process is known. In practice, you need to test for the presence of autocorrelation.

The Durbin-Watson test is a widely used method of testing for autocorrelation. The first-order Durbin-Watson statistic is printed by default. This statistic can be used to test for first-order autocorrelation. Use the DWPROB option to print the significance level (*p*-values) for the Durbin-Watson tests. (Since the Durbin-Watson *p*-values are computationally expensive, they are not reported by default.)

You can use the DW= option to request higher-order Durbin-Watson statistics. Since the ordinary Durbin-Watson statistic only tests for first-order autocorrelation, the Durbin-Watson statistics for higher-order autocorrelation are called *generalized Durbin-Watson statistics.*

The following statements perform the Durbin-Watson test for autocorrelation in the OLS residuals for orders 1 through 4. The DWPROB option prints the marginal significance levels (*p*-values) for the Durbin-Watson statistics.

```
proc autoreg data=a;
   model y = time / dw=4 dwprob;
run;
```

The AUTOREG procedure output is shown in Figure 4.7. In this case, the first-order Durbin-Watson test is highly significant, with p < .0001 for the hypothesis of no first-order autocorrelation. Thus, autocorrelation correction is needed.

```
                         Autoreg Procedure
Dependent Variable = Y

                  Ordinary Least Squares Estimates
             SSE          214.9534    DFE              34
             MSE           6.32216    Root MSE   2.514391
             SBC         173.6591     AIC        170.4921
             Reg Rsq        0.8200    Total Rsq    0.8200

                     Durbin-Watson Statistics
                    Order     DW      PROB<DW
                     1      0.4752     0.0001
                     2      1.2935     0.0137
                     3      2.0694     0.6545
                     4      2.5544     0.9818

     Variable     DF      B Value    Std Error    t Ratio Approx Prob

     Intercept     1    8.23075782    0.85590       9.616     0.0001
     TIME          1    0.50210974    0.04034      12.447     0.0001
```

Figure 4.7.   Durbin-Watson Test Results for OLS Residuals

Using the Durbin-Watson test, you can decide if autocorrelation correction is needed. However, generalized Durbin-Watson tests should not be used to decide on the autoregressive order. The higher-order tests assume the absence of lower-order autocorrelation. If the ordinary Durbin-Watson test indicates no first-order autocorrelation, you can use the second-order test to check for second-order autocorrelation. Once autocorrelation is detected, further tests at higher orders are not appropriate. In Figure 4.7, since the first-order Durbin-Watson test is significant, the order 2, 3, and 4 tests can be ignored.

When using Durbin-Watson tests to check for autocorrelation, you should specify an order at least as large as the order of any potential seasonality, since seasonality produces autocorrelation at the seasonal lag. For example, for quarterly data use DW=4, and for monthly data use DW=12.

Lagged Dependent Variables

The Durbin-Watson tests are not valid when the lagged dependent variable is used in the regression model. In this case, the Durbin *h*-test or Durbin *t*-test can be used to test for first-order autocorrelation.

For the Durbin *h*-test, specify the name of the lagged dependent variable in the LAGDEP= option. For the Durbin *t*-test, specify the LAGDEP option without giving the name of the lagged dependent variable.

For example, the following statements add the variable YLAG to the data set A and regress Y on YLAG instead of TIME.

```
data b;
   set a;
   ylag = lag1( y );
run;

proc autoreg data=b;
   model y = ylag / lagdep=ylag;
run;
```

The results are shown in Figure 4.8. The Durbin *h* statistic 2.78 is significant with a *p*-value of .0027, indicating autocorrelation.

```
                       Autoreg Procedure

Dependent Variable = Y


                   Ordinary Least Squares Estimates

            SSE            97.71123   DFE                33
            MSE            2.960946   Root MSE      1.72074
            SBC            142.3698   AIC           139.2591
            Reg Rsq          0.9109   Total Rsq      0.9109
            Durbin h       2.781442   PROB>h         0.0027


    Variable      DF      B Value    Std Error   t Ratio Approx Prob

    Intercept      1   1.57422227      0.93004     1.693      0.0999
    YLAG           1   0.93755916      0.05105    18.366      0.0001
```

Figure 4.8.   Durbin *h*-Test With a Lagged Dependent Variable

Stepwise Autoregression

Once you determine that autocorrelation correction is needed, you must select the order of the autoregressive error model to use. One way to select the order of the autoregressive error model is *stepwise autoregression*. The stepwise autoregression method initially fits a high-order model with many autoregressive lags and then sequentially removes autoregressive parameters until all remaining autoregressive parameters have significant *t*-tests.

To use stepwise autoregression, specify the BACKSTEP option, and specify a large order with the NLAG= option. The following statements show the stepwise feature, using an initial order of 5:

```
proc autoreg data=a;
   model y = time / method=ml nlag=5 backstep;
run;
```

The results are shown in Figure 4.9.

```
                          Autoreg Procedure

Dependent Variable = Y


                    Ordinary Least Squares Estimates

              SSE          214.9534    DFE                34
              MSE           6.32216    Root MSE     2.514391
              SBC          173.6591    AIC          170.4921
              Reg Rsq        0.8200    Total Rsq      0.8200
              Durbin-Watson  0.4752


        Variable     DF      B Value   Std Error    t Ratio Approx Prob

        Intercept     1   8.23075782     0.85590      9.616     0.0001
        TIME          1   0.50210974     0.04034     12.447     0.0001


                    Estimates of Autocorrelations

   Lag   Covariance   Correlation  -1 9 8 7 6 5 4 3 2 1 0 1 2 3 4 5 6 7 8 9 1

    0     5.970929     1.000000  |                   |********************|
    1     4.516919     0.756485  |                   |***************     |
    2     2.024114     0.338995  |                   |*******             |
    3    -0.44021     -0.073725  |                 *|                     |
    4    -2.11748     -0.354632  |            *******|                     |
    5    -2.85343     -0.477887  |          *********|                     |


              Backward Elimination of Autoregressive Terms

              Lag    Estimate    t-Ratio     Prob
               4    -0.052908    -0.1983    0.8442
               3     0.115986     0.5746    0.5698
               5     0.131734     1.2139    0.2340
```

Figure 4.9. Stepwise Autoregression

The estimates of the autocorrelations are shown for 5 lags. The backward elimination of autoregressive terms report shows that the autoregressive parameters at lags 3, 4, and 5 were insignificant and eliminated, resulting in the second-order model shown previously in Figure 4.4. By default, retained autoregressive parameters must be significant at the .05 level, but you can control this with the SLSTAY= option. The remainder of the output from this example is the same as that in Figure 4.3 and Figure 4.4, and it is not repeated here.

The stepwise autoregressive process is performed using the Yule-Walker method. The maximum likelihood estimates are produced after the order of the model is determined from the significance tests of the preliminary Yule-Walker estimates.

When using stepwise autoregression, it is a good idea to specify an NLAG= option value larger than the order of any potential seasonality, since seasonality produces autocorrelation at the seasonal lag. For example, for monthly data use NLAG=13, and for quarterly data use NLAG=5.

Subset and Factored Models

In the previous example, the BACKSTEP option dropped lags 3, 4, and 5, leaving an order 2 model. However, in other cases a parameter at a longer lag may be kept while some smaller lags are dropped. For example, the stepwise autoregression method might drop lags 2, 3, and 5 but keep lags 1 and 4. This is called a *subset model*, since the number of estimated autoregressive parameters is smaller than the order of the model.

Subset models are common for seasonal data and often correspond to *factored* autoregressive models. A factored model is the product of simpler autoregressive models. For example, the best model for seasonal monthly data may be the combination of a first-order model for recent effects with a twelfth-order subset model for the seasonality, with a single parameter at lag 12. This results in an order 13 subset model with nonzero parameters at lags 1, 12, and 13. See Chapter 3, "The ARIMA Procedure," for further discussion of subset and factored autoregressive models.

You can specify subset models with the NLAG= option. List the lags to include in the autoregressive model within parentheses. The following statements show an example of specifying the subset model resulting from the combination of a first-order process for recent effects with a fourth-order seasonal process:

```
proc autoreg data=a;
   model y = time / nlag=(1 4 5);
run;
```

The MODEL statement specifies the following fifth-order autoregressive error model:

$$y_t = a + b t + v_t$$
$$v_t = -\varphi_1 v_{t-1} - \varphi_4 v_{t-4} - \varphi_5 v_{t-5} + \epsilon_t$$

Testing for Heteroscedasticity

One of the key assumptions of the ordinary regression model is that the errors have the same variance throughout the sample. This is also called the *homoscedasticity* model. If the error variance is not constant, the data are said to be *heteroscedastic*.

Since ordinary least-squares regression assumes constant error variance, heteroscedasticity causes the OLS estimates to be inefficient. Models that take into account the changing variance can make more efficient use of the data. Also, heteroscedasticity can make the OLS forecast error variance inaccurate since the predicted forecast variance is based on the average variance instead of the variability at the end of the series.

To illustrate heteroscedastic time series, the following statements re-create the simulated series Y. The variable Y has an error variance that changes from 1 to 4 in the middle part of the series. The length of the series is also extended 120 observations.

```
data a;
   ul = 0; ull = 0;
   do time = -10 to 120;
      s = 1 + (time >= 60 & time < 90);
      u = + 1.3 * ul - .5 * ull + s*rannor(12346);
      y = 10 + .5 * time + u;
      if time > 0 then output;
      ull = ul; ul = u;
      end;
run;

title "Heteroscedastic Autocorrelated Time Series";
```

```
proc gplot data=a;
   symbol1 v=star i=join;
   symbol2 v=none i=r;
   plot y * time = 1 y * time = 2 / overlay;
run;
```

The simulated series is plotted in Figure 4.10.

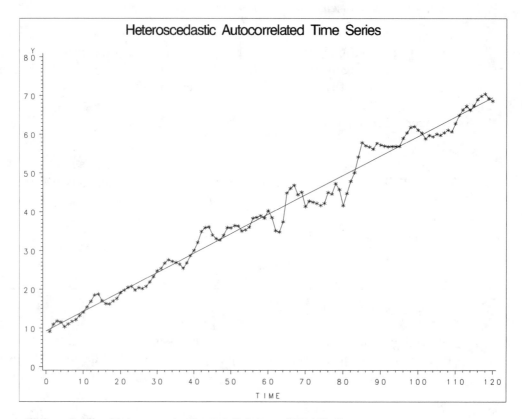

Figure 4.10.   Heteroscedastic and Autocorrelated Series

To test for heteroscedasticity with PROC AUTOREG, specify the ARCHTEST option. The following statements regress Y on TIME and use the ARCHTEST option to test for heteroscedastic OLS residuals. The DWPROB option is also used to test for autocorrelation.

```
proc autoreg data=a;
   model y = time / nlag=2 archtest dwprob;
   output out=r r=yresid;
run;
```

The PROC AUTOREG output is shown in Figure 4.11. The Q statistics test for changes in variance across time using lag windows ranging from 1 through 12. (See "Heteroscedasticity and Normality Tests" for details.) The p-values for the test statistics are given in parentheses. These tests strongly indicate heteroscedasticity, with p<.0001 for all lag windows.

The Lagrange multiplier (LM) tests also indicate heteroscedasticity. These tests can also help determine the order of the ARCH model appropriate for modeling the heteroscedasticity, assuming that the changing variance follows an autoregressive conditional heteroscedasticity model.

```
                         Autoreg Procedure

Dependent Variable = Y


                 Ordinary Least Squares Estimates

         SSE              690.266    DFE                  118
         MSE             5.849712    Root MSE        2.418618
         SBC             560.0705    AIC             554.4955
         Reg Rsq           0.9814    Total Rsq         0.9814
         Durbin-Watson     0.4060    PROB<DW           0.0001

           Q and LM Tests for ARCH Disturbances

         Order        Q       Prob>Q           LM      Prob>LM

            1    37.5445      0.0001       37.0072      0.0001
            2    40.4245      0.0001       40.9189      0.0001
            3    41.0753      0.0001       42.5032      0.0001
            4    43.6893      0.0001       43.3822      0.0001
            5    55.3846      0.0001       48.2511      0.0001
            6    60.6617      0.0001       49.7799      0.0001
            7    62.9655      0.0001       52.0126      0.0001
            8    63.7202      0.0001       52.7083      0.0001
            9    64.2329      0.0001       53.2393      0.0001
           10    66.2778      0.0001       53.2407      0.0001
           11    68.1923      0.0001       53.5924      0.0001
           12    69.3725      0.0001       53.7559      0.0001


     Variable    DF     B Value   Std Error   t Ratio Approx Prob

     Intercept    1  9.22171095     0.44435    20.753      0.0001
     TIME         1  0.50242021     0.00637    78.825      0.0001
```

Figure 4.11.   Heteroscedasticity Tests

Heteroscedasticity and GARCH Models

There are several approaches to dealing with heteroscedasticity. If the error variance at different times is known, weighted regression is a good method. If, as is usually the case, the error variance is unknown and must be estimated from the data, you can model the changing error variance.

The *generalized autoregressive conditional heteroscedasticity* (GARCH) model is one approach to modeling time series with heteroscedastic errors. The GARCH regression model with autoregressive errors is

$$y_t = \mathbf{x}_t' \beta + v_t$$
$$v_t = \epsilon_t - \varphi_1 v_{t-1} - \dots - \varphi_m v_{t-m}$$
$$\epsilon_t = \sqrt{h_t}\, e_t$$
$$h_t = \omega + \sum_{i=1}^{q} \alpha_i \epsilon_{t-i}^2 + \sum_{j=1}^{p} \gamma_j h_{t-j}$$
$$e_t \sim \text{IN}(0,1)$$

This model combines the mth-order autoregressive error model with the GARCH(p,q) variance model. It is denoted as the AR(m)-GARCH(p,q) regression model.

The Lagrange multiplier (LM) tests shown in Figure 4.11 can help determine the order of the ARCH model appropriate for the data. The tests are significant ($p < .0001$) through order 12, which indicates that a very high-order ARCH model is needed to model the heteroscedasticity.

The basic ARCH(q) model ($p = 0$) is a *short memory* process in that only the most recent q squared residuals are used to estimate the changing variance. The GARCH model ($p > 0$) allows *long memory* processes, which use all the past squared residuals to estimate the current variance. The LM tests in Figure 4.11 suggest the use of the GARCH model ($p > 0$) instead of the ARCH model.

The GARCH(p,q) model is specified with the GARCH=(P=p,Q=q) option in the MODEL statement. The basic ARCH(q) model is the same as the GARCH($0,q$) model and is specified with the GARCH=(Q=q) option.

The following statements fit an AR(2)-GARCH(1,1) model for the Y series regressed on TIME. The GARCH=(P=1,Q=1) option specifies the GARCH(1,1) conditional variance model. The NLAG=2 option specifies the AR(2) error process. Only the maximum likelihood method is supported for GARCH models; therefore, the METHOD= option is not needed. The CEV= option in the OUTPUT statement stores the estimated conditional error variance at each time period in the variable VHAT in an output data set named OUT.

```
proc autoreg data=a;
   model y = time / nlag=2 garch=(q=1,p=1) maxit=50;
   output out=out cev=vhat;
run;
```

The results for the GARCH model are shown in Figure 4.12. (The preliminary estimates are not shown.)

```
                      Autoreg Procedure

                      GARCH Estimates

            SSE          218.8459    OBS               120
            MSE          1.823716    UVAR          1.82567
            Log L         -187.452   Total Rsq      0.9941
            SBC          408.4156    AIC           388.9032
            Normality Test   0.0878  Prob>Chi-Sq    0.9570


    Variable      DF      B Value   Std Error   t Ratio Approx Prob

    Intercept      1    8.92855101   0.51862    17.216    0.0001
    TIME           1    0.50747825   0.00869    58.391    0.0001
    A(1)           1   -1.22986252   0.08732   -14.084    0.0001
    A(2)           1    0.50204655   0.08959     5.604    0.0001
    ARCH0          1    0.08337304   0.06696     1.245    0.2131
    ARCH1          1    0.21711705   0.07699     2.820    0.0048
    GARCH1         1    0.73721587   0.08772     8.405    0.0001
```

Figure 4.12.   AR(2)-GARCH(1,1) Model

The normality test is not significant ($p = .957$), which is consistent with the hypothesis that the residuals from the GARCH model, $\epsilon_t / \sqrt{h_t}$, are normally distributed. The parameter estimates table includes rows for the GARCH parameters. ARCH0 represents the estimate for the parameter ω, ARCH1 represents α_1, and GARCH1 represents γ_1.

The following statements transform the estimated conditional error variance series VHAT to the estimated standard deviation series SHAT. Then, they plot SHAT together with the true standard deviation S used to generate the simulated data.

```
data out;
   set out;
   shat = sqrt( vhat );
run;

title "Predicted and Actual Standard Deviations";
proc gplot data=out;
   plot s*time=1 shat*time=2 / overlay;
   symbol1 v=star i=none;
   symbol2 v=none i = join;
run;
```

The plot is shown in Figure 4.13.

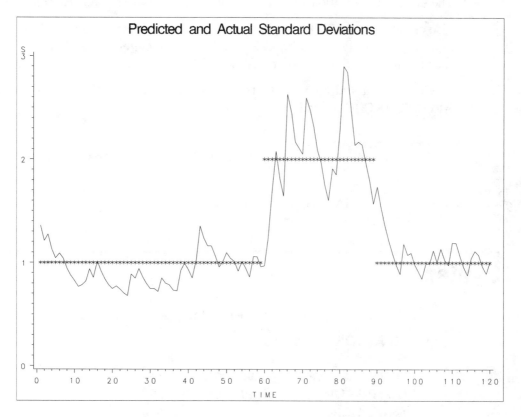

Figure 4.13.   Estimated and Actual Error Standard Deviation Series

Note that in this example the form of heteroscedasticity used in generating the simulated series Y does not fit the GARCH model. The GARCH model assumes *conditional* heteroscedasticity, with homoscedastic unconditional error variance. That is, the GARCH model assumes that the changes in variance are a function of the realizations of preceding errors and that these changes represent temporary and random departures from a constant unconditional variance. The data generating process used to simulate series Y, contrary to the GARCH model, has exogenous unconditional heteroscedasticity that is independent of past errors.

Nonetheless, as shown in Figure 4.13, the GARCH model does a reasonably good job of approximating the error variance in this example, and some improvement in the efficiency of the estimator of the regression parameters can be expected.

The GARCH model may perform better in cases where theory suggests that the data generating process produces true autoregressive conditional heteroscedasticity. This is the case in some economic theories of asset returns, and GARCH-type models are often used for analysis of financial markets data.

EGARCH, IGARCH, GARCH-M Models

The AUTOREG procedure supports several variations of the generalized conditional heteroscedasticity model.

Using the TYPE= suboption of the GARCH= option, you can control the constraints placed on the estimated GARCH parameters. You can specify unconstrained, non-negativity constrained (default), stationarity constrained, or integration constrained. The integration constraint produces the integrated GARCH or IGARCH model.

You can also use the TYPE= option to specify the exponential form of the GARCH model, called the EGARCH model. The MEAN suboption of the GARCH= option specifies the GARCH-in-mean or GARCH-M model.

The following statements illustrate the use of the TYPE= option to fit an AR(2)-EGARCH(1,1) model to the series Y. (Output is not shown.)

```
proc autoreg data=a;
   model y = time / nlag=2 garch=(p=1,q=1,type=exp);
run;
```

See the section "GARCH, IGARCH, EGARCH, and GARCH-M Models" later in this chapter for details.

Syntax

The AUTOREG procedure is controlled by the following statements:

> **PROC AUTOREG** *options* ;
>   **BY** *variables* ;
>   **MODEL** *dependent* = *regressors / options* ;
>   **OUTPUT OUT** = *SAS data set options* ;

At least one MODEL statement must be specified. One OUTPUT statement can follow each MODEL statement.

Functional Summary

The statements and options used with the AUTOREG procedure are summarized in the following table:

Description	Statement	Option
Data Set Options		
specify the input data set	AUTOREG	DATA=
write parameter estimates to an output data set	AUTOREG	OUTEST=
include covariances in the OUTEST= data set	AUTOREG	COVOUT
write predictions, residuals, and confidence limits to an output data set	OUTPUT	OUT=
Declaring the Role of Variables		
specify BY-group processing	BY	
Printing Control Options		
request all printing options	MODEL	ALL
print transformed coefficients	MODEL	COEF
print correlation matrix of the estimates	MODEL	CORRB
print covariance matrix of the estimates	MODEL	COVB
print DW statistics up to order j	MODEL	DW=j
print marginal probability of DW statistics	MODEL	DWPROB
print inverse of Toeplitz matrix	MODEL	GINV
print details at each iteration step	MODEL	ITPRINT
print the Durbin t statistic	MODEL	LAGDEP
print the Durbin h statistic	MODEL	LAGDEP=
print tests for ARCH process	MODEL	ARCHTEST
suppress printed output	MODEL	NOPRINT
print partial autocorrelations	MODEL	PARTIAL
Model Estimation Options		
specify the order of autoregressive process	MODEL	NLAG=
center the dependent variable	MODEL	CENTER
suppress the intercept parameter	MODEL	NOINT
remove nonsignificant AR parameters	MODEL	BACKSTEP
specify significance level for BACKSTEP	MODEL	SLSTAY=
specify the convergence criterion	MODEL	CONVERGE=
specify iterative Yule-Walker method	MODEL	ITER
specify maximum number of iterations	MODEL	MAXITER=
specify the estimation method	MODEL	METHOD=

Description	Statement	Option
use only first sequence of nonmissing data	MODEL	NOMISS

GARCH Related Options

Description	Statement	Option
specify order of GARCH process	MODEL	GARCH=(Q=,P=)
specify type of GARCH model	MODEL	GARCH=(... ,TYPE=)
specify GARCH-M model	MODEL	GARCH=(... ,MEAN)
suppress GARCH intercept parameter	MODEL	GARCH=(... ,NOINT)
specify the trust region method	MODEL	GARCH=(... ,TR)
output conditional error variance	OUTPUT	CEV=
output conditional prediction error variance	OUTPUT	CPEV=

Output Control Options

Description	Statement	Option
specify confidence limit size	OUTPUT	ALPHACLI=
specify confidence limit size for structural predicted values	OUTPUT	ALPHACLM=
output transformed intercept variable	OUTPUT	CONSTANT=
output lower confidence limit	OUTPUT	LCL=
output lower confidence limit for structural predicted values	OUTPUT	LCLM=
output predicted values	OUTPUT	P=
output predicted values of structural part	OUTPUT	PM=
output residuals	OUTPUT	R=
output residuals from structural predictions	OUTPUT	RM=
output transformed variables	OUTPUT	TRANSFORM=
output upper confidence limit	OUTPUT	UCL=
output upper confidence limit for structural predicted values	OUTPUT	UCLM=

PROC AUTOREG Statement

> **PROC AUTOREG** *options* **;**

The following options can be used in the PROC AUTOREG statement:

DATA= *SAS-data-set*
> specifies the input SAS data set. If the DATA= option is not specified, PROC AUTOREG uses the most recently created SAS data set.

OUTEST= *SAS-data-set*

writes the parameter estimates to an output data set. See "OUTEST= Data Set" later in this chapter for information on the contents of this data set.

COVOUT

writes the covariance matrix for the parameter estimates to the OUTEST= data set. This option is valid only if the OUTEST= option is specified.

In addition, any of the following MODEL statement options can be specified in the PROC AUTOREG statement, which is equivalent to specifying the option for every MODEL statement: ALL, ARCHTEST, BACKSTEP, CENTER, COEF, CONVERGE=, CORRB, COVB, DW=, DWPROB, GINV, ITER, ITPRINT, MAXITER=, METHOD=, NOINT, NOMISS, NOPRINT, and PARTIAL.

BY Statement

> **BY** *variables*;

A BY statement can be used with PROC AUTOREG to obtain separate analyses on observations in groups defined by the BY variables.

MODEL Statement

> **MODEL** *dependent* = *regressors* / *options* ;

The MODEL statement specifies the dependent variable and independent regressor variables for the regression model. If no independent variables are specified in the MODEL statement, only the mean is fitted. (This is a way to obtain autocorrelations of a series.)

Models can be given labels of up to eight characters. Model labels are used in the printed output to identify the results for different models. The model label is specified as follows:

> *label* **: MODEL ... ;**

The following options can be used in the MODEL statement after a slash (/).

CENTER

centers the dependent variable by subtracting its mean and suppresses the intercept parameter from the model. This option is only valid when the model does not have regressors (explanatory variables).

NOINT

suppresses the intercept parameter.

Autoregressive Error Options

NLAG= *number*
NLAG= (*number-list*)

specifies the order of the autoregressive error process or the subset of autoregressive error lags to be fitted. Note that NLAG=3 is the same as NLAG=(1 2 3). If the NLAG= option is not specified, PROC AUTOREG does not fit an autoregressive model.

GARCH Estimation Options

GARCH= (*option-list*)

Specifies a GARCH-type conditional heteroscedasticity model. The GARCH= option in the MODEL statement specifies the family of ARCH models to be estimated. The GARCH(1,1) regression model is specified in the following statement:

```
model y = x1 x2 / garch=(q=1,p=1);
```

When you want to estimate the subset of ARCH terms, for example, ARCH(1 3), you can write the SAS statement as follows:

```
model y = x1 x2 / garch=(q=(1 3));
```

With the TYPE= option, you can specify various GARCH models. The IGARCH(2,1) model without trend in variance is estimated as follows:

```
model y = / garch=(q=2,p=1,type=integ,noint);
```

The following options can be used in the GARCH=( ) option. The options are listed within parentheses and separated by commas.

Q= *number*
Q= (*number-list*)

specifies the order of the process or the subset of ARCH terms to be fitted.

P= *number*
P= (*number-list*)

specifies the order of the process or the subset of GARCH terms to be fitted. If only the P= option is specified, Q=1 is assumed.

TYPE= *value*

specifies the type of GARCH models. The following option values are allowed:

NOINEQ	specifies the unconstrained GARCH model
NONNEGATIVE NONNEG	specifies the GARCH model with nonnegativity constraints
STATIONARY STN	constrains the sum of GARCH coefficients to be less than 1
INTEGRATED INTEG	specifies the integrated GARCH or IGARCH model
EXP	specifies the exponential GARCH or EGARCH model

The default is TYPE=NONNEG.

MEAN

specifies the GARCH-M model. For example, the following statement specifies the GARCH(1,1)-M model:

```
model y = x1 x2 / garch=(q=1,p=1,mean);
```

NOINT

suppresses the intercept parameter in the conditional variance model. This option is valid only with the TYPE=INTEG option.

TR

uses the trust region method for GARCH estimation. This algorithm is numerically stable, though computation is expensive. The dual quasi-Newton method is the default.

Printing Options

ALL

requests all printing options.

ARCHTEST

requests the Q and LM statistics testing for the absence of ARCH effects.

COEF

prints the transformation coefficients for the first p observations. These coefficients are formed from a scalar multiplied by the inverse of the Cholesky root of the Toeplitz matrix of autocovariances.

CORRB

prints the estimated correlations of the parameter estimates.

COVB

prints the estimated covariances of the parameter estimates.

DW= n

prints Durbin-Watson statistics up to the order n. The default is DW=1. When the LAGDEP option is specified, the Durbin-Watson statistic is not printed unless the DW= option is explicitly specified.

DWPROB

prints the p-value of the Durbin-Watson statistic. The DWPROB option is ignored when the degrees of freedom for error is greater than 300. See "Generalized Durbin-Watson Tests" later in this chapter for details.

GINV

prints the inverse of the Toeplitz matrix of autocovariances for the Yule-Walker solution. See "Computational Methods" later in this chapter for details.

ITPRINT

prints the objective function and parameter estimates at each iteration. The objective function is the log likelihood function for the maximum likelihood method, while the error sum of squares is produced as the objective function of unconditional least squares. For the ML method, the ITPRINT option prints the value of the full log likelihood function, not the concentrated likelihood.

LAGDEP
LAGDV

prints the Durbin *t* statistic, which is used to detect residual autocorrelation in the presence of lagged dependent variables. See "Generalized Durbin-Watson Tests" later in this chapter for details.

LAGDEP= *name*
LAGDV= *name*

prints the Durbin *h* statistic for testing the presence of first-order autocorrelation when regressors contain the lagged dependent variable whose name is specified as LAGDEP=*name*. If the Durbin *h* statistic cannot be computed, the asymptotically equivalent *t* statistic is printed instead. See "Generalized Durbin-Watson Tests" for details.

When the regression model contains several lags of the dependent variable, specify the lagged dependent variable for the smallest lag in the LAGDEP= option, for example,

```
model y = x1 x2 ylag2 ylag3 / lagdep=ylag2;
```

NOPRINT

suppresses all printed output.

PARTIAL

prints partial autocorrelations.

Stepwise Selection Options

BACKSTEP

removes insignificant autoregressive parameters. The parameters are removed in order of least significance. This backward elimination is done only once on the Yule-Walker estimates computed after the initial ordinary least-squares estimation. The BACKSTEP option can be used with all estimation methods since the initial parameter values for other estimation methods are estimated using the Yule-Walker method.

SLSTAY= *value*

specifies the significance level criterion to be used by the BACKSTEP option. The default is SLSTAY=.05.

Estimation Control Options

CONVERGE= *value*

specifies the convergence criterion. If the maximum absolute value of the change in the autoregressive parameter estimates between iterations is less than this amount, then convergence is assumed. The default is CONVERGE=.001.

MAXITER= *number*

sets the maximum number of iterations allowed. The default is MAXITER=50.

METHOD= *value*

requests the type of estimates to be computed. The values of the METHOD= option are

METHOD=ML   specifies maximum likelihood estimates

METHOD=ULS   specifies unconditional least-squares estimates

METHOD=YW   specifies Yule-Walker estimates

METHOD=ITYW specifies iterative Yule-Walker estimates

If the GARCH= or LAGDEP option is specified, the default is METHOD=ML. Otherwise, the default is METHOD=YW.

NOMISS

requests the estimation to the first contiguous sequence of data with no missing values. Otherwise, all complete observations are used.

OUTPUT Statement

> **OUTPUT OUT**= *SAS-data-set keyword* = *options* ... ;

The OUTPUT statement creates an output SAS data set as specified by the following options:

OUT= *SAS-data-set*

names the output SAS data set containing the predicted and transformed values. If the OUT= option is not specified, the new data set is named according to the DATA*n* convention.

ALPHACLI= *number*

sets the confidence limit size for the estimates of future values of the response time series. The ALPHACLI= value must be between 0 and 1. The resulting confidence interval has 1-*number* confidence. The default is ALPHACLI=.05, corresponding to a 95% confidence interval.

ALPHACLM= *number*

sets the confidence limit size for the estimates of the structural or regression part of the model. The ALPHACLM= value must be between 0 and 1. The resulting confidence interval has 1-*number* confidence. The default is ALPHACLM=.05, corresponding to a 95% confidence interval.

The following options are of the form *KEYWORD=name*, where *KEYWORD* specifies the statistic to include in the output data set and *name* gives the name of the variable in the OUT= data set containing the statistic.

CEV= *variable*

writes the conditional error variance to the output data set. The CEV= option is only relevant when a GARCH model is estimated. See "Predicted Values" later in this chapter for details.

CPEV= *variable*

writes the conditional prediction error variance to the output data set. The value of conditional prediction error variance is equal to that of the conditional error variance when there are no autoregressive parameters. For the exponential GARCH model, conditional prediction error variance cannot be calculated. See "Predicted Values" later in this chapter for details.

CONSTANT= *variable*

writes the transformed intercept to the output data set. The details of the transformation are described in "Computational Methods" later in this chapter.

LCL= *name*

writes the lower confidence limit for the predicted value (specified in the PREDICTED= option) to the output data set. The size of the confidence interval is set by the ALPHACLI= option. When a GARCH model is estimated, the lower confidence limit is calculated assuming that the disturbances have homoscedastic conditional variance. See "Predicted Values" later in this chapter for details.

LCLM= *name*

writes the lower confidence limit for the structural predicted value (specified in the PREDICTEDM= option) to the output data set under the name given. The size of the confidence interval is set by the ALPHACLM= option.

PREDICTED= *name*
P= *name*

writes the predicted values to the output data set. These values are formed from both the structural and autoregressive parts of the model. See "Predicted Values" later in this chapter for details.

PREDICTEDM= *name*
PM= *name*

writes the structural predicted values to the output data set. These values are formed from only the structural part of the model. See "Predicted Values" later in this chapter for details.

RESIDUAL= *name*
R= *name*

writes the residuals from the predicted values based on both the structural and time series parts of the model to the output data set.

RESIDUALM= *name*
RM= *name*

writes the residuals from the structural prediction to the output data set.

TRANSFORM= *variables*

transforms the specified variables from the input data set by the autoregressive model and writes the transformed variables to the output data set. The details of the transformation are described in "Computational Methods" later in this chapter. If you need to reproduce the data suitable for reestimation, you must also transform an intercept variable. To do this, use the CONSTANT= option.

UCL= *name*

writes the upper confidence limit for the predicted value (specified in the PREDICTED= option) to the output data set. The size of the confidence interval is set by the ALPHACLI= option. When the GARCH model is estimated, the upper confidence limit is calculated assuming that the disturbances have homoscedastic conditional variance. See "Predicted Values" later in this chapter for details.

UCLM= *name*

writes the upper confidence limit for the structural predicted value (specified in the PREDICTEDM= option) to the output data set. The size of the confidence interval is set by the ALPHACLM= option.

Details

Missing Values

PROC AUTOREG skips any missing values at the beginning of the data set. If the NOMISS option is specified, the first contiguous set of data with no missing values is used; otherwise, all data with nonmissing values for the independent and dependent variables are used. Note, however, that the observations containing missing values are still needed to maintain the correct spacing in the time series. PROC AUTOREG can generate predicted values when the dependent variable is missing.

Autoregressive Error Model

The regression model with autocorrelated disturbances is as follows:

$$y_t = \mathbf{x}_t' \beta + \nu_t$$
$$\nu_t = \epsilon_t - \varphi_1 \nu_{t-1} - \ldots - \varphi_m \nu_{t-m}$$
$$\epsilon_t \sim N(0, \sigma^2)$$

In these equations, y_t are the dependent values, $\mathbf{x}_t$ is a column vector of regressor variables, β is a column vector of structural parameters, and ϵ_t is normally and independently distributed with a mean of 0 and a variance of σ^2. Note that in this parameterization, the signs of the autoregressive parameters are reversed from the parameterization documented in most of the literature.

PROC AUTOREG offers four estimation methods for the autoregressive error model. The default method, Yule-Walker (YW) estimation, is the fastest computationally. The Yule-Walker method used by PROC AUTOREG is described in Gallant and Goebel (1976). Harvey (1981) calls this method the *two-step full transform method*. The other methods are iterated YW, unconditional least squares (ULS), and maximum likelihood (ML). The ULS method is also referred to as nonlinear least squares (NLS) or exact least squares (ELS).

You can use all of the methods with data containing missing values, but you should use ML estimation if the missing values are plentiful. See the section "Alternative Autocorrelation Correction Methods" later in this chapter for further discussion of the advantages of different methods.

The Yule-Walker Method

Let φ represent the vector of autoregressive parameters

$$\varphi = (\varphi_1, \varphi_2, \ldots, \varphi_m)'$$

and let the variance matrix of the error vector $v = (v_1, \ldots, v_N)'$ be Σ

$$E(vv') = \Sigma = \sigma^2 V$$

If the vector of autoregressive parameters φ is known, the matrix V can be computed from the autoregressive parameters. Given V, efficient estimates of the regression parameters β can be computed using generalized least squares (GLS). These GLS estimates then yield unbiased estimate of the variance σ^2.

The Yule-Walker method alternates estimation of β using generalized least squares with estimation of φ using the Yule-Walker equations applied to the sample autocorrelation function. The YW method starts by forming the OLS estimate of β. Next, φ is estimated from the sample autocorrelation function of the OLS residuals using the Yule-Walker equations. Then V is estimated from the estimate of φ, and Σ is estimated from V and the GLS estimate of σ^2. The autocorrelation corrected estimates of the regression parameters β are computed by GLS using the estimated V matrix. These are the Yule-Walker estimates.

If the METHOD=ITYW option is specified, the Yule-Walker residuals are used to form a new sample autocorrelation function, the new autocorrelation function is used to form a new estimate of φ and V, and the GLS estimates are recomputed using the new variance matrix. This alternation of estimates continues until either the maximum change in the $\widehat{\varphi}$ estimate between iterations is less than the value specified by the CONVERGE= option or the maximum number of allowed iterations is reached. This produces the Iterated Yule-Walker estimates. Iteration of the estimates may not yield much improvement.

The Yule-Walker equations, solved to obtain $\widehat{\varphi}$ and a preliminary estimate of σ^2, are

$$R\widehat{\varphi} = -r$$

Here $r = (r_1, \ldots, r_m)'$, where r_i is the lag i sample autocorrelation. The matrix R is the Toeplitz matrix whose (i,j)th element is $r_{|i-j|}$. If you specify a subset model, then only the rows and columns of R and r corresponding to the subset of lags specified are used.

If the BACKSTEP option is specified, for purposes of significance testing, the matrix $[R \ r]$ is treated as a sum-of-squares-and-crossproducts matrix arising from a simple regression with $N - k$ observations, where k is the number of estimated parameters.

The Unconditional Least Squares and Maximum Likelihood Methods

Define the transformed error, e, as

$$e = L^{-1}n$$
$$n = y - X\beta$$

The unconditional sum of squares for the model, $\mathbf{S}$, is

$$\mathbf{S} = \mathbf{n}' \mathbf{V}^{-1} \mathbf{n} = \mathbf{e}' \mathbf{e}$$

The ULS estimates are computed by minimizing $\mathbf{S}$ with respect to the parameters β and φ_i.

The full log likelihood function for the autoregressive error model is

$$l = -\frac{N}{2}\ln(2\pi) - \frac{N}{2}\ln(\sigma^2) - \frac{1}{2}\ln(|\mathbf{V}|) - \frac{\mathbf{S}}{2\sigma^2}$$

where $|\mathbf{V}|$ denotes determinant of $\mathbf{V}$. For the ML method, the likelihood function is maximized by minimizing an equivalent sum-of-squares function.

Maximizing l with respect to σ^2 (and concentrating σ^2 out of the likelihood) and dropping the constant term $-\frac{N}{2}[\ln(2\pi) + 1 - \ln(N)]$ produces the concentrated log likelihood function

$$l_c = -\frac{N}{2}\ln(\mathbf{S}|\mathbf{V}|^{1/N})$$

Rewriting the terms within the logarithm gives

$$\mathbf{S}_{ml} = |\mathbf{L}|^{1/N} \mathbf{e}' \mathbf{e} |\mathbf{L}|^{1/N}$$

PROC AUTOREG computes the ML estimates by minimizing the objective function $\mathbf{S}_{ml} = |\mathbf{L}|^{1/N} \mathbf{e}' \mathbf{e} |\mathbf{L}|^{1/N}$.

The maximum likelihood estimates may not exist for some data sets (Anderson and Mentz 1980). This is the case for very regular data sets, such as an exact linear trend.

Computational Methods

Sample Autocorrelation Function

The sample autocorrelation function is computed from the structural residuals or noise $n_t = y_t - \mathbf{x}_t' \mathbf{b}$, where $\mathbf{b}$ is the current estimate of β. The sample autocorrelation function is the sum of all available lagged products of n_t of order j divided by $\ell + j$, where ℓ is the number of such products.

If there are no missing values, then $\ell + j = N$, the number of observations. In this case, the Toeplitz matrix of autocorrelations, $\mathbf{R}$, is at least positive semidefinite. If there are missing values, these autocorrelation estimates, r_i, can yield an $\mathbf{R}$ matrix that is not positive semidefinite. If such estimates occur, a warning message is printed, and the estimates are tapered by exponentially declining weights until $\mathbf{R}$ is positive definite.

Data Transformation and the Kalman Filter

The calculation of $\mathbf{V}$ from φ for the general AR(m) model is complicated, and the size of $\mathbf{V}$ depends on the number of observations. Instead of actually calculating $\mathbf{V}$ and performing GLS in the usual way, in practice a Kalman filter algorithm is used to transform the data and compute the GLS results through a recursive process.

In all of the estimation methods, the original data are transformed by the inverse of the Cholesky root of $\mathbf{V}$. Let $\mathbf{L}$ denote the Cholesky root of $\mathbf{V}$, that is $\mathbf{V} = \mathbf{LL}'$ with $\mathbf{L}$ lower triangular. For an AR(m) model, $\mathbf{L}^{-1}$ is a band diagonal matrix with m anomalous rows at the beginning and the autoregressive parameters along the remaining rows. Thus, if there are no missing values, after the first m observations the data are transformed as

$$z_t = x_t + \widehat{\varphi}_1 x_{t-1} + \ \dots \ + \widehat{\varphi}_m x_{t-m}$$

The transformation is carried out using a Kalman filter, and the lower triangular matrix $\mathbf{L}$ is never directly computed. The Kalman filter algorithm, as it applies here, is described in Harvey and Phillips (1979) and Jones (1980). Although $\mathbf{L}$ is not computed explicitly, for ease of presentation the remaining discussion is in terms of $\mathbf{L}$. If there are missing values, then the submatrix of $\mathbf{L}$ consisting of the rows and columns with nonmissing values is used to generate the transformations.

Gauss-Marquardt Algorithms

The ULS and ML estimates employ a Gauss-Marquardt algorithm to minimize the sum of squares and maximize the log likelihood, respectively. The relevant optimization is performed simultaneously for both the regression and AR parameters. The OLS estimates of β and the Yule-Walker estimates of φ are used as starting values for these methods.

The Gauss-Marquardt algorithm requires the derivatives of $\mathbf{e}$ or $|\mathbf{L}|^{1/N}\mathbf{e}$ with respect to the parameters. The derivatives with respect to the parameter vector β are

$$\frac{\partial \mathbf{e}}{\partial \beta'} = -\mathbf{L}^{-1}\mathbf{X}$$

$$\frac{\partial |\mathbf{L}|^{1/N}\mathbf{e}}{\partial \beta'} = -|\mathbf{L}|^{1/N}\mathbf{L}^{-1}\mathbf{X}$$

These derivatives are computed by the transformation described previously. The derivatives with respect to φ are computed by differentiating the Kalman filter recurrences and the equations for the initial conditions.

Variance Estimates and Standard Errors

For the Yule-Walker method, the estimate of the error variance, s^2, is the error sum of squares from the last application of GLS, divided by the error degrees of freedom (number of observations N minus the number of free parameters).

The variance-covariance matrix for the components of $\mathbf{b}$ is taken as $s^2(\mathbf{X}'\mathbf{V}^{-1}\mathbf{X})^{-1}$ for the Yule-Walker method. For the ULS and ML methods, the variance-covariance matrix of the parameter estimates is computed as $s^2(\mathbf{J}'\mathbf{J})^{-1}$. For the ULS method, $\mathbf{J}$ is the matrix of derivatives of $\mathbf{e}$ with respect to the parameters. For the ML method, $\mathbf{J}$ is the matrix of derivatives of $|\mathbf{L}|^{1/N}\mathbf{e}$ divided by $|\mathbf{L}|^{1/N}$. The estimate of the variance-covariance matrix of $\mathbf{b}$ assuming that φ is known is $s^2(\mathbf{X}'\mathbf{V}^{-1}\mathbf{X})^{-1}$.

Park and Mitchell (1980) investigated the small sample performance of the standard error estimates obtained from some of these methods. In particular, simulating an AR(1) model for the noise term, they found that the standard errors calculated using

GLS with an estimated autoregressive parameter underestimated the true standard errors. These estimates of standard errors are the ones calculated by PROC AUTOREG with the Yule-Walker method.

The estimates of the standard errors calculated with the ULS or ML methods take into account the joint estimation of the AR and the regression parameters and may give more accurate standard-error values than the YW method. At the same values of the autoregressive parameters, the ULS and ML standard errors will always be larger than those computed from Yule-Walker. However, simulations of the models used by Park and Mitchell suggest that the ULS and ML standard error estimates can also be underestimates. Caution is advised, especially when the estimated autocorrelation is high and the sample size is small.

High autocorrelation in the residuals is a symptom of lack of fit. An autoregressive error model should not be used as a nostrum for models that simply do not fit. It is often the case that time series variables tend to move as a random walk. This means that an AR(1) process with a parameter near one absorbs a great deal of the variation. See Example 4.3 later in this chapter, which fits a linear trend to a sine wave.

For ULS or ML estimation, the joint variance-covariance matrix of all the regression and autoregression parameters is computed. For the Yule-Walker method, the variance-covariance matrix is computed only for the regression parameters.

Lagged Dependent Variables

The Yule-Walker estimation method is not directly appropriate for estimating models that include lagged dependent variables among the regressors. Therefore, the maximum likelihood method is the default when the LAGDEP or LAGDEP= option is specified in the MODEL statement. However, when lagged dependent variables are used, the maximum likelihood estimator is not exact maximum likelihood but is conditional on the first few values of the dependent variable.

Alternative Autocorrelation Correction Methods

Autocorrelation correction in regression analysis has a long history, and various approaches have been suggested. Moreover, the same method may be referred to by different names.

Pioneering work in the field was done by Cochrane and Orcutt (1949). The *Cochrane-Orcutt method* refers to a more primitive version of the Yule-Walker method that drops the first observation. The Cochrane-Orcutt method is like the Yule-Walker method for first-order autoregression, except that the Yule-Walker method retains information from the first observation. The iterative Cochrane-Orcutt method is also in use.

The Yule-Walker method used by PROC AUTOREG is also known by other names. Harvey (1981) refers to the Yule-Walker method as the *two-step full transform method*. The Yule-Walker method can be considered as generalized least squares using the OLS residuals to estimate the covariances across observations, and Judge et al. (1985) use the term *estimated generalized least squares* (EGLS) for this method. For a first-order AR process, the Yule-Walker estimates are often termed *Prais-Winsten estimates* (Prais and Winsten 1954). There are variations to these methods that use different estimators of the autocorrelations or the autoregressive parameters.

The unconditional least squares (ULS) method, which minimizes the error sum of squares for all observations, is referred to as the nonlinear least squares (NLS) method by Spitzer (1979).

The *Hildreth-Lu* method (Hildreth and Lu 1960) uses nonlinear least squares to jointly estimate the parameters with an AR(1) model, but it omits the first transformed residual from the sum of squares. Thus, the Hildreth-Lu method is a more primitive version of the ULS method supported by PROC AUTOREG in the same way Cochrane-Orcutt is a more primitive version of Yule-Walker.

The maximum likelihood method is also widely cited in the literature. Although the maximum likelihood method is well defined, some early literature refers to estimators that are called maximum likelihood but are not full unconditional maximum likelihood estimates. The AUTOREG procedure produces full unconditional maximum likelihood estimates.

Harvey (1981) and Judge et al. (1985) summarize the literature on various estimators for the autoregressive error model. Although asymptotically efficient, the various methods have different small sample properties. Several Monte Carlo experiments have been conducted, although usually for the AR(1) model.

Harvey and McAvinchey (1978) found that for a one-variable model, when the independent variable is trending, methods similar to Cochrane-Orcutt are inefficient in estimating the structural parameter. This is not surprising since a pure trend model is well modeled by an autoregressive process with a parameter close to 1.

Harvey and McAvinchey (1978) also made the following conclusions:

- The Yule-Walker method appears to be about as efficient as the maximum likelihood method. Although Spitzer (1979) recommended ML and NLS, the Yule-Walker method (labeled Prais-Winsten) did as well or better in estimating the structural parameter in Spitzer's Monte Carlo study (table A2 in their article) when the autoregressive parameter was not too large. Maximum likelihood tends to do better when the autoregressive parameter is large.

- For small samples, it is important to use a full transformation (Yule-Walker) rather than the Cochrane-Orcutt method, which loses the first observation. This was also demonstrated by Maeshiro (1976), Chipman (1979), and Park and Mitchell (1980).

- For large samples (Harvey used 100), losing the first few observations does not make much difference.

GARCH, IGARCH, EGARCH, and GARCH-M Models

Consider the series y_t, which follows the GARCH process. The conditional distribution of the series Y for time t is written

$$y_t \mid \Psi_{t-1} \sim N(0, h_t)$$

where Ψ_{t-1} denotes all available information at time $t-1$.

The conditional variance h_t is

$$h_t = \omega + \sum_{i=1}^{q} \alpha_i \, y_{t-i}^2 + \sum_{j=1}^{p} \gamma_j \, h_{t-j}$$

where

$$p \geq 0, q > 0$$
$$\omega > 0, \alpha_i \geq 0, \gamma_j \geq 0$$

The GARCH(p,q) model reduces to the ARCH(q) process when $p = 0$. At least one of the ARCH parameters must be nonzero ($q > 0$). The GARCH regression model can be written

$$y_t = \mathbf{x}_t' \beta + \epsilon_t$$
$$\epsilon_t = \sqrt{h_t} e_t$$

$$h_t = \omega + \sum_{i=1}^{q} \alpha_i \, \epsilon_{t-i}^2 + \sum_{j=1}^{p} \gamma_j h_{t-j}$$

where $e_t \sim \text{IN}(0, 1)$.

In addition, you can consider the model with disturbances following an autoregressive process and with the GARCH errors. The AR(m)-GARCH(p,q) regression model is denoted

$$y_t = \mathbf{x}_t' \beta + \nu_t$$
$$\nu_t = \epsilon_t - \varphi_1 \nu_{t-1} - \cdots - \varphi_m \nu_{t-m}$$
$$\epsilon_t = \sqrt{h_t} e_t$$

$$h_t = \omega + \sum_{i=1}^{q} \alpha_i \, \epsilon_{t-i}^2 + \sum_{j=1}^{p} \gamma_j h_{t-j}$$

IGARCH and Stationary GARCH Model

The condition $\sum_{i=1}^{q} \alpha_i + \sum_{j=1}^{p} \gamma_j < 1$ implies that the GARCH process is weakly stationary since the mean, variance, and autocovariance are finite and constant over time. However, this condition is not sufficient for weak stationarity in the presence of autocorrelation. For example, the stationarity condition for an AR(1)-GARCH(p, q) process is

$$\frac{1}{1 - \varphi_1^2} \sum_{i=1}^{q} \alpha_i + \sum_{j=1}^{p} \gamma_j < 1$$

When the GARCH process is stationary, the unconditional variance of ϵ_t is

$$\mathbf{V}(\epsilon_t) = \frac{\omega}{1 - \sum_{i=1}^{q} \alpha_i - \sum_{j=1}^{p} \gamma_j}$$

where $\epsilon_t = \sqrt{h_t}\, e_t$ and h_t is the GARCH(p,q) conditional variance.

Sometimes, the multistep forecasts of the variance do not approach the unconditional variance when the model is integrated in variance; that is, $\sum_{i=1}^{q} \alpha_i + \sum_{j=1}^{p} \gamma_j = 1$. The unconditional variance for the IGARCH model does not exist. However, it is interesting that the IGARCH model can be strongly stationary even though it is not weakly stationary. Refer to Nelson (1990) for details.

EGARCH Model

The EGARCH model was proposed by Nelson (1991). Nelson and Cao (1992) argue that the nonnegativity constraints in the linear GARCH model are too restrictive. The GARCH model imposes the nonnegative constraints on the parameters, α_i and γ_j, while there are no restrictions on these parameters in the EGARCH model. In the EGARCH model, the conditional variance, h_t, is an asymmetric function of lagged disturbances ϵ_{t-i}:

$$\ln(h_t) = \omega + \sum_{i=1}^{q} \alpha_i g(z_{t-i}) + \sum_{j=1}^{p} \gamma_j \ln(h_{t-j})$$

where

$$g(z_t) = \theta z_t + \gamma [\,|z_t| - \mathrm{E}|z_t|\,]$$
$$z_t = \epsilon_t / \sqrt{h_t}$$

The coefficient of the second term in $g(z_t)$ is set to be 1 ($\gamma = 1$) in our formulation. Note that $\mathrm{E}|z_t| = (2/\pi)^{1/2}$ if $z_t \sim \mathrm{N}(0,1)$. The properties of the EGARCH model are summarized as follows:

- The function $g(z_t)$ is linear in z_t with slope coefficient $\theta + 1$ if z_t is positive while $g(z_t)$ is linear in z_t with slope coefficient $\theta - 1$ if z_t is negative

- Suppose that $\theta = 0$. Large innovations increase the innovation in the variance $g(z_t)$ if $[\,|z_t| - \mathrm{E}|z_t|\,] > 0$ and decrease the innovation in the variance if $[\,|z_t| - \mathrm{E}|z_t|\,] < 0$.

- Suppose that $\theta < 1$. The innovation in variance, $g(z_t)$, is positive if the innovations z_t are less than $(2/\pi)^{1/2}/(\theta - 1)$. Therefore, the negative innovations in returns, ϵ_t, cause the innovation to the conditional variance to be positive if θ is much less than 1.

GARCH-in-Mean

The GARCH-M model has the added regressor that is the conditional standard deviation:

$$y_t = \mathbf{x}_t' \beta + \delta \sqrt{h_t} + \epsilon_t$$
$$\epsilon_t = \sqrt{h_t} e_t$$

where h_t follows the ARCH or GARCH process.

Maximum Likelihood Estimation

The family of GARCH models are estimated using the maximum likelihood method. The log-likelihood function is computed from the product of all conditional densities of the prediction errors.

$$l = \sum_{t=1}^{N} \frac{1}{2} \left[-\ln(2\pi) - \ln(h_t) - \frac{\epsilon_t^2}{h_t} \right]$$

where $\epsilon_t = y_t - x_t' \beta$ and h_t is the conditional variance. When the GARCH(p, q)-M model is estimated, $\epsilon_t = y_t - x_t' \beta - \delta\sqrt{h_t}$. When there are no regressors, the residuals ϵ_t are denoted as y_t or $y_t - \delta\sqrt{h_t}$.

The likelihood function is maximized via either the dual quasi-Newton or trust region algorithm. The default is the dual quasi-Newton algorithm. The starting values for the regression parameters β are obtained from the OLS estimates. When there are autoregressive parameters in the model, the initial values are obtained from the Yule-Walker estimates. The starting value 1E-6 is used for the GARCH process parameters.

The variance-covariance matrix is computed using the Hessian matrix. The dual quasi-Newton method approximates the Hessian matrix while the quasi-Newton method gets an approximation of the inverse of Hessian. The trust region method uses the Hessian matrix obtained using numerical differentiation. When there are active constraints, that is, $q(\theta) = 0$, the variance-covariance matrix is given by

$$V(\hat{\theta}) = H^{-1} \left[I - Q' \left(Q H^{-1} Q' \right)^{-1} Q H^{-1} \right]$$

where $H = -\partial^2 l / \partial\theta\partial\theta'$ and $Q = \partial q(\theta) / \partial\theta'$. Therefore, the variance-covariance matrix without active constraints reduces to $V(\hat{\theta}) = H^{-1}$.

R² Statistics and Other Measures of Fit

This section discusses various goodness-of-fit statistics produced by the AUTOREG procedure.

Total R²

The total R^2 statistic (Total Rsq) is computed as

$$R_{\text{tot}}^2 = 1 - \frac{SSE}{SST}$$

where *SST* is the sum of squares for the original response variable corrected for the mean and *SSE* is the final error sum of squares. The Total Rsq is a measure of how well the next value can be predicted using the structural part of the model and the past values of the residuals. If the NOINT option is specified, *SST* is the uncorrected sum of squares.

Regression R²

The regression R^2 (Reg RSQ) is computed as

$$R^2_{\text{reg}} = 1 - \frac{TSSE}{TSST}$$

where $TSST$ is the total sum of squares of the transformed response variable corrected for the transformed intercept, and $TSSE$ is the error sum of squares for this transformed regression problem. If the NOINT option is requested, no correction for the transformed intercept is made. The Reg RSQ is a measure of the fit of the structural part of the model after transforming for the autocorrelation and is the R^2 for the transformed regression.

The regression R^2 and the total R^2 should be the same when there is no autocorrelation correction (OLS regression).

Information Criteria AIC and SBC

The Akaike's information criterion (AIC) and the Schwarz's Bayesian information criterion (SBC) are computed as follows:

$$AIC = -2\ln(L) + 2k$$
$$SBC = -2\ln(L) + \ln(N)k$$

In these formulas, L is the value of the likelihood function evaluated at the parameter estimates, N is the number of observations, and k is the number of estimated parameters. Refer to Judge et al. (1985) and Schwarz (1978) for additional details.

Generalized Durbin-Watson Tests

Consider the following linear regression model:

$$\mathbf{Y} = \mathbf{X}\beta + \nu$$

where $\mathbf{X}$ is an $N \times k$ data matrix, β is a $k \times 1$ coefficient vector, and ν is a $N \times 1$ disturbance vector. The error term ν is assumed to be generated by the jth order autoregressive process $\nu_t = \epsilon_t - \varphi_j \nu_{t-j}$ where $\left| \varphi_j \right| < 1$, ϵ_t is a sequence of independent normal error terms with mean 0 and variance σ^2. Usually, the Durbin-Watson statistic is used to test the null hypothesis H_0: $\varphi_1 = 0$ against H_1: $-\varphi_1 > 0$. Vinod (1973) generalized the Durbin-Watson statistic:

$$d_j = \frac{\sum_{t=j+1}^{N} \left(\hat{\nu}_t - \hat{\nu}_{t-j} \right)^2}{\sum_{t=1}^{N} \hat{\nu}_t^2}$$

where $\hat{\nu}$ are OLS residuals. Using matrix notation,

$$d_j = \frac{\nu' \mathbf{M} \mathbf{A}_j' \, \mathbf{A}_j \mathbf{M} \nu}{\nu' \mathbf{M} \nu}$$

where $\mathbf{M} = \mathbf{I}_N - \mathbf{X}(\mathbf{X}'\mathbf{X})^{-1}\mathbf{X}'$ and $\mathbf{A}_j$ is a $(N-j) \times N$ matrix:

$$\mathbf{A}_j = \begin{bmatrix} -1 & 0 & \cdots & 0 & 1 & 0 & \cdots & 0 \\ 0 & -1 & 0 & \cdots & 0 & 1 & 0 & \cdots \\ \vdots & \vdots & \vdots & \vdots & \vdots & \vdots & \vdots & \vdots \\ 0 & \cdots & 0 & -1 & 0 & \cdots & 0 & 1 \end{bmatrix}$$

and there are $j-1$ zeros between -1 and 1 in each row of matrix $\mathbf{A}_j$.

The QR factorization of the design matrix $\mathbf{X}$ yields a $N \times N$ orthogonal matrix $\mathbf{Q}$

$$\mathbf{X} = \mathbf{QR}$$

where $\mathbf{R}$ is a $N \times k$ upper triangular matrix. There exists a $N \times (N-k)$ submatrix of $\mathbf{Q}$ such that $\mathbf{Q}_1\mathbf{Q}_1' = \mathbf{M}$ and $\mathbf{Q}_1'\mathbf{Q}_1 = \mathbf{I}_{N-k}$. Consequently, the generalized Durbin-Watson statistic is stated as a ratio of two quadratic forms:

$$d_j = \frac{\sum_{l=1}^{n} \lambda_{jl}\xi_l^2}{\sum_{l=1}^{n} \xi_l^2}$$

where $\lambda_{j1} \dots \lambda_{jn}$ are upper n eigenvalues of $\mathbf{MA}_j'\mathbf{A}_j\mathbf{M}$ and ξ_l is a standard normal variate, and $n = \min(N-k, N-j)$. These eigenvalues are obtained by a singular value decomposition of $\mathbf{Q}_1'\mathbf{A}_j'$ (Golub and Loan 1989; Savin and White 1978).

The marginal probability (or p-value) for d_j given c_0 is

$$\text{Prob}\left(\frac{\sum_{l=1}^{n} \lambda_{jl}\xi_l^2}{\sum_{l=1}^{n} \xi_l^2} < c_0 \right) = \text{Prob}(q_j < 0)$$

where

$$q_j = \sum_{l=1}^{n} \left(\lambda_{jl} - c_0 \right)\xi_l^2$$

When the null hypothesis H_0: $\varphi_j = 0$ holds, the quadratic form q_j has the characteristic function

$$\phi_j(t) = \prod_{l=1}^{n} \left(1 - 2\left(\lambda_{jl} - c_0\right) it \right)^{-1/2}$$

The distribution function is uniquely determined by this characteristic function:

$$\text{F}(x) = \frac{1}{2} + \frac{1}{2\pi}\int_0^{\infty} \frac{1}{it} \left(e^{itx}\phi_j(-t) - e^{-itx}\phi_j(t) \right) dt$$

For example, to test H_0: $\varphi_4 = 0$ given $\varphi_1 = \varphi_2 = \varphi_3 = 0$ against H_1: $-\varphi_4 > 0$, the marginal probability (p-value) can be used:

$$\text{F}(0) = \frac{1}{2} + \frac{1}{2\pi}\int_0^{\infty} \frac{1}{it}(\phi_4(-t) - \phi_4(t))\, dt$$

where

$$\phi_4(t) = \prod_{l=1}^{n} \left(1 - 2\left(\lambda_{4l} - \hat{d}_4\right)it\right)^{-1/2}$$

and $\hat{d}_4$ is the calculated value of the fourth-order Durbin-Watson statistic.

In the Durbin-Watson test, the marginal probability indicates positive autocorrelation $(-\varphi_j > 0)$ if it is less than the level of significance (α), while you can conclude that a negative autocorrelation $(-\varphi_j < 0)$ exists if the marginal probability based on the computed Durbin-Watson statistic is greater than $1 - \alpha$. Wallis (1972) presented tables for bounds tests of fourth-order autocorrelation and Vinod (1973) has given tables for a five percent significance level for orders two to four. Using the AUTOREG procedure, you can calculate the exact p-values for the general order of Durbin-Watson test statistics. Tests for the absence of autocorrelation of order p can be performed sequentially; at the jth step, test H_0: $\varphi_j = 0$ given $\varphi_1 = \ldots = \varphi_{j-1} = 0$ against $\varphi_j \neq 0$. However, the size of the sequential test is not known.

The Durbin-Watson statistic is computed from the OLS residuals, while that of the autoregressive error model uses residuals that are the difference between the predicted values and the actual values. When you use the Durbin-Watson test from the residuals of the autoregressive error model, you must be aware that this test is only an approximation. See "Regression with Autoregressive Errors" earlier in this chapter. If there are missing values, the Durbin-Watson statistic is computed using all the nonmissing values and ignoring the gaps caused by missing residuals. This does not affect the significance level of the resulting test, although the power of the test against certain alternatives may be adversely affected. Savin and White (1978) have examined the use of the Durbin-Watson statistic with missing values.

Tests for Serial Correlation with Lagged Dependent Variables

When regressors contain lagged dependent variables, the Durbin-Watson statistic (d_1) for the first-order autocorrelation is biased toward 2 and has reduced power. Wallis (1972) shows that the bias in the Durbin-Watson statistic (d_4) for the fourth-order autocorrelation is smaller than the bias in d_1 in the presence of a first-order lagged dependent variable. Durbin (1970) proposed two alternative statistics (Durbin h and t) that are asymptotically equivalent. The h statistic is written as

$$h = \hat{\rho}\left(\frac{N}{1 - N\hat{V}}\right)^{1/2}$$

where $\hat{\rho} = \sum_{t=2}^{N} \hat{v}_t \hat{v}_{t-1} / \sum_{t=1}^{N} \hat{v}_t^2$ and $\hat{V}$ is the least-squares variance estimate for the coefficient of the lagged dependent variable. Durbin's t-test consists of regressing the OLS residuals $\hat{v}_t$ on explanatory variables and $\hat{v}_{t-1}$ and testing the significance of the estimate for coefficient of $\hat{v}_{t-1}$.

Inder (1984) shows that the Durbin-Watson test for the absence of first-order autocorrelation is generally more powerful than the h-test in finite samples. Refer to Inder (1986) and King and Wu (1991) for the Durbin-Watson test in the presence of lagged dependent variables.

Heteroscedasticity and Normality Tests

Portmanteau Q-Test

For nonlinear time series models, the portmanteau test statistic based on squared residuals is used to test for independence of the series (McLeod and Li 1983):

$$Q(q) = N(N + 2) \sum_{i=1}^{q} \frac{r\left(i ; \hat{v}_t^2\right)}{(N - i)}$$

where

$$r\left(i ; \hat{v}_t^2\right) = \frac{\sum_{t=i+1}^{N} \left(\hat{v}_t^2 - \hat{\sigma}^2\right) \left(\hat{v}_{t-i}^2 - \hat{\sigma}^2\right)}{\sum_{t=1}^{N} \left(\hat{v}_t^2 - \hat{\sigma}^2\right)^2}$$

$$\hat{\sigma}^2 = \frac{1}{N} \sum_{t=1}^{N} \hat{v}_t^2$$

This Q statistic is used to test the nonlinear effects (for example, GARCH effects) present in the residuals. The GARCH(p, q) process can be considered as an ARMA($\max(p, q), p$) process. See the section "Predicting the Conditional Variance" later in this chapter. Therefore, the Q statistic calculated from the squared residuals can be used to identify the order of the GARCH process.

Lagrange Multiplier Test for ARCH Disturbances

Engle (1982) proposed a Lagrange multiplier test for ARCH disturbances. The test statistic is asymptotically equivalent to the test used by Breusch and Pagan (1979). Engle's Lagrange multiplier test for the qth order ARCH process is written

$$LM(q) = \frac{N \mathbf{W}' \mathbf{Z} (\mathbf{Z}' \mathbf{Z})^{-1} \mathbf{Z}' \mathbf{W}}{\mathbf{W}' \mathbf{W}}$$

where

$$\mathbf{W} = \left(\frac{\hat{v}_1^2}{\hat{\sigma}^2}, \ \ldots, \ \frac{\hat{v}_N^2}{\hat{\sigma}^2} \right)'$$

and

$$\mathbf{Z} = \begin{bmatrix} 1 & \hat{v}_0^2 & \cdots & \hat{v}_{-q+1}^2 \\ \vdots & \vdots & \vdots & \vdots \\ \vdots & \vdots & \vdots & \vdots \\ 1 & \hat{v}_{N-1}^2 & \cdots & \hat{v}_{N-q}^2 \end{bmatrix}$$

The presample values $(v_0^2, \ldots, v_{-q+1}^2)$ have been set to 0. Note that the $LM(q)$ tests may have different finite sample properties depending on the presample values, though they are asymptotically equivalent regardless of the presample values. The

LM and *Q* statistics are computed from the OLS residuals assuming that disturbances are white noise. The *Q* and *LM* statistics have an approximate $\chi^2_{(q)}$ distribution under the white-noise null hypothesis.

Normality Test

Based on skewness and kurtosis, Bera and Jarque (1982) calculated the test statistic

$$T_N = \left[\frac{N}{6} b_1^2 + \frac{N}{24} (b_2 - 3)^2 \right]$$

where

$$b_1 = \frac{\sqrt{N} \sum_{t=1}^{N} \hat{u}_t^3}{\left(\sum_{t=1}^{N} \hat{u}_t^2 \right)^{\frac{3}{2}}}$$

$$b_2 = \frac{N \sum_{t=1}^{N} \hat{u}_t^4}{\left(\sum_{t=1}^{N} \hat{u}_t^2 \right)^2}$$

The $\chi^2(2)$-distribution gives an approximation to the normality test T_N.

When the GARCH model is estimated, the normality test is obtained using the standardized residuals $\hat{u}_t = \hat{\epsilon}_t / \sqrt{h_t}$. The normality test can be used to detect misspecification of the family of ARCH models.

Predicted Values

The AUTOREG procedure can produce two kinds of predicted values for the response series and corresponding residuals and confidence limits. The residuals in both cases are computed as the actual value minus the predicted value. In addition, when GARCH models are estimated, the AUTOREG procedure can output predictions of the conditional error variance.

Predicting the Unconditional Mean

The first type of predicted value is obtained from only the structural part of the model, $\mathbf{x}_t' \mathbf{b}$. These are useful in predicting values of new response time series, which are assumed to be described by the same model as the current response time series. The predicted values, residuals, and upper and lower confidence limits for the structural predictions are requested by specifying the PREDICTEDM=, RESIDUALM=, UCLM=, or LCLM= options in the OUTPUT statement. The ALPHACLM= option controls the confidence level for UCLM= and LCLM=. These confidence limits are for estimation of the mean of the dependent variable, $\mathbf{x}_t' \mathbf{b}$, where $\mathbf{x}_t$ is the column vector of independent variables at observation t.

The predicted values are computed as

$$\hat{y}_t = \mathbf{x}_t' \mathbf{b}$$

and the upper and lower confidence limits as

$$\hat{u}_t = \hat{y}_t + t_{\alpha/2}\, v$$

$$\hat{l}_t = \hat{y}_t - t_{\alpha/2}\, v$$

where v^2 is an estimate of the variance of $\hat{y}_t$ and $t_{\alpha/2}$ is the upper $\alpha/2$ percentage point of the t distribution.

$$\text{Prob}\left(T > t_{\alpha/2}\right) = \frac{\alpha}{2}$$

where T is an observation from a t distribution with q degrees of freedom. The value of α can be set with the ALPHACLM= option. The degrees of freedom parameter, q, is taken to be the number of observations minus the number of free parameters in the regression and autoregression parts of the model. For the YW estimation method, the value of v is calculated as

$$v = \sqrt{s^2 \mathbf{x}_t' \left(\mathbf{X}'\mathbf{V}^{-1}\mathbf{X}\right)^{-1} \mathbf{x}_t}$$

where s^2 is the error sum of squares divided by q. For the ULS and ML methods, it is calculated as

$$v = \sqrt{s^2 \mathbf{x}_t' \, \mathbf{W}\mathbf{x}_t}$$

where $\mathbf{W}$ is the $k \times k$ submatrix of $\left(\mathbf{J}'\mathbf{J}\right)^{-1}$ that corresponds to the regression parameters. For details, see "Computational Methods" earlier in this chapter.

Predicting Future Series Realizations

The other predicted values use both the structural part of the model and the predicted values of the error process. These conditional mean values are useful in predicting future values of the current response time series. The predicted values, residuals, and upper and lower confidence limits for future observations conditional on past values are requested by the PREDICTED=, RESIDUAL=, UCL=, or LCL= options in the OUTPUT statement. The ALPHACLI= option controls the confidence level for UCL= and LCL=. These confidence limits are for the predicted value,

$$\tilde{y}_t = \mathbf{x}_t' \mathbf{b} + \nu_{t|t-1}$$

where $\mathbf{x}_t$ is the vector of independent variables and $\nu_{t|t-1}$ is the minimum variance linear predictor of the error term given the available past values of $\nu_{t-j}, j = 1,2, \ldots,$ $t - 1$, and the autoregressive model for ν_t. If the m previous values of the structural residuals are available, then

$$\nu_{t|t-1} = -\hat{\varphi}_1 \nu_{t-1} - \cdots - \hat{\varphi}_m \nu_{t-m}$$

where $\hat{\varphi}_1, \ldots, \hat{\varphi}_m$ are the estimated AR parameters. The upper and lower confidence limits are computed as

$$\tilde{u}_t = \tilde{y}_t + t_{\alpha/2}\, v$$

$$\tilde{l}_t = \tilde{y}_t - t_{\alpha/2}\, v$$

where v, in this case, is computed as

$$v = \sqrt{s^2 \left(\mathbf{x}_t' \left(\mathbf{X}' \mathbf{V}^{-1} \mathbf{X} \right)^{-1} \mathbf{x}_t + r \right)}$$

where the value rs^2 is the estimate of the variance of $v_{t|t-1}$. At the start of the series, and after missing values, r is generally greater than 1. See "Predicting the Conditional Variance" for computational details of r. The plot of residuals and confidence limits in Example 4.4 later in this chapter illustrates this behavior.

Except to adjust the degrees of freedom for the error sum of squares, the preceding formulas do not account for the fact that the autoregressive parameters are estimated. In particular, the confidence limits are likely to be somewhat too narrow. In large samples, this is probably not an important effect, but it may be appreciable in small samples. Refer to Harvey (1981) for some discussion of this problem for AR(1) models.

Note that at the beginning of the series (the first m observations, where m is the value of the NLAG= option) and after missing values, these residuals do not match the residuals obtained by using OLS on the transformed variables. This is because, in these cases, the predicted noise values must be based on less than a complete set of past noise values and, thus, have larger variance. The GLS transformation for these observations includes a scale factor as well as a linear combination of past values. Put another way, the $\mathbf{L}^{-1}$ matrix defined in the section "Computational Methods" has the value 1 along the diagonal, except for the first m observations and after missing values.

Predicting the Conditional Variance

The GARCH process can be written

$$\epsilon_t^2 = \omega + \sum_{i=1}^{n} (\alpha_i + \gamma_i) \epsilon_{t-i}^2 - \sum_{j=1}^{p} \gamma_j \eta_{t-j} + \eta_t$$

where $\eta_t = \epsilon_t^2 - h_t$ and $n = \max(p, q)$. This representation shows that the squared residual ϵ_t^2 follows an ARMA(n, p) process.

Then for any $d > 0$, the conditional expectations are as follows:

$$\mathrm{E}\left(\epsilon_{t+d}^2 \mid \Psi_t \right) = \omega + \sum_{i=1}^{n} (\alpha_i + \gamma_i) \, \mathrm{E}\left(\epsilon_{t+d-i}^2 \mid \Psi_t \right) \\ - \sum_{j=1}^{p} \gamma_j \mathrm{E}\left(\eta_{t+d-j} \mid \Psi_t \right)$$

The d-step-ahead prediction error, $\xi_{t+d} = y_{t+d} - y_{t+d|t}$, has the conditional variance

$$\mathrm{Var}\left(\xi_{t+d} \mid \Psi_t \right) = \sum_{j=0}^{d-1} g_j^2 \sigma_{t+d-j|t}^2$$

where

$$\sigma^2_{t+d-j|t} = E\left(\epsilon^2_{t+d-j} \mid \Psi_t\right)$$

Coefficients in the conditional d-step prediction error variance are calculated recursively using the following formula:

$$g_j = -\varphi_1 g_{j-1} - \cdots - \varphi_m g_{j-m}$$

where $g_0 = 1$ and $g_j = 0$ if $j < 0$; $\varphi_1, \ldots, \varphi_m$ are autoregressive parameters. Since the parameters are not known, the conditional variance is computed using the estimated autoregressive parameters. The d-step-ahead prediction error variance is simplified when there are no autoregressive terms:

$$\text{Var}(\xi_{t+d} \mid \Psi_t) = \sigma^2_{t+d|t}$$

Therefore, the one-step-ahead prediction error variance is equivalent to the conditional error variance defined in the GARCH process:

$$h_t = E\left(\epsilon^2_t \mid \Psi_{t-1}\right) = \sigma^2_{t|t-1}$$

Note that the conditional prediction error variance of the EGARCH and GARCH-M models cannot be calculated using the preceding formula. Therefore, the confidence intervals for the predicted values are computed assuming the homoscedastic conditional error variance. That is, the conditional prediction error variance is identical to the unconditional prediction error variance:

$$\text{Var}(\xi_{t+d} \mid \Psi_t) = \text{Var}(\xi_{t+d}) = \sigma^2 \sum_{j=0}^{d-1} g_j^2$$

since $\sigma^2_{t+d-j|t} = \sigma^2$. You can compute $s^2 r$, which is the second term of the variance for the predicted value $\tilde{y}_t$ explained previously in "Predicting Future Series Realizations," using the formula $\sigma^2 \sum_{j=0}^{d-1} g_j^2$; r is estimated from $\sum_{j=0}^{d-1} g_j^2$ using the estimated autoregressive parameters.

Consider the following conditional prediction error variance:

$$\text{Var}(\xi_{t+d} \mid \Psi_t) = \sigma^2 \sum_{j=0}^{d-1} g_j^2 + \sum_{j=0}^{d-1} g_j^2 (\sigma^2_{t+d-j|t} - \sigma^2)$$

The second term in the preceding equation can be interpreted as the noise from using the homoscedastic conditional variance when the errors follow the GARCH process. However, it is expected that if the GARCH process is covariance stationary, the difference between the conditional prediction error variance and the unconditional prediction error variance disappears as the forecast horizon d increases.

OUT= Data Set

The output SAS data set produced by the OUTPUT statement contains all the variables in the input data set and the new variables specified by the OUTPUT statement options. See the section "OUTPUT Statement" earlier in this chapter for information on the output variables that can be created. The output data set contains one observation for each observation in the input data set.

OUTEST= Data Set

The OUTEST= data set contains all the variables used in any MODEL statement. Each regressor variable contains the estimate for the corresponding regression parameter in the corresponding model. In addition, the OUTEST= data set contains the following variables:

_A_i	the ith order autoregressive parameter estimate. There are m such variables _A_1 through _A_m, where m is the value of the NLAG= option.
_AH_i	the ith order ARCH parameter estimate, if the GARCH= option is specified. There are q such variables _AH_1 through _AH_q, where q is the value of the Q= option. The variable _AH_0 contains the estimate of ω.
DELTA	the estimated mean parameter for the GARCH-M model, if a GARCH-in-mean model is specified
DEPVAR	the name of the dependent variable
_GH_i	the ith order GARCH parameter estimate, if the GARCH= option is specified. There are p such variables _GH_1 through _GH_p, where p is the value of the P= option.
INTERCEP	the intercept estimate. INTERCEP contains a missing value for models for which the NOINT option is specified.
METHOD	the estimation method that is specified in the METHOD= option
MODEL	the label of the MODEL statement if one is given, or blank otherwise
MSE	the value of the mean square error for the model
NAME	the name of the row of covariance matrix for the parameter estimate, if the COVOUT option is specified
LIKL	the log likelihood value of the GARCH model
SSE	the value of the error sum of squares
STDERR	standard error of the parameter estimate, if the COVOUT option is specified
THETA	the estimate of the θ parameter in the EGARCH model, if an EGARCH model is specified

TYPE   OLS for observations containing parameter estimates, or COV for observations containing covariance matrix elements.

The OUTEST= data set contains one observation for each MODEL statement giving the parameter estimates for that model. If the COVOUT option is specified, the OUTEST= data set includes additional observations for each MODEL statement giving the rows of the covariance of parameter estimates matrix. For covariance observations, the value of the _TYPE_ variable is COV, and the _NAME_ variable identifies the parameter associated with that row of the covariance matrix.

Printed Output

The AUTOREG procedure prints the following items:

1. the name of the dependent variable

2. the ordinary least-squares estimates

3. estimates of autocorrelations, which include the estimates of the autocovariances, the autocorrelations, and (if there is sufficient space) a graph of the autocorrelation at each LAG

4. if the PARTIAL option is specified, the partial autocorrelations

5. the preliminary MSE, which results from solving the Yule-Walker equations. This is an estimate of the final MSE.

6. the estimates of the autoregressive parameters (Coefficient), their standard errors (Std Error), and the ratio of estimate to standard error (*t* Ratio)

7. the statistics of fit are printed for the final model. These include the error sum of squares (SSE), the degrees of freedom for error (DFE), the mean square error (MSE), the root mean square error (Root MSE), the Schwarz information criterion (SBC), the Akaike information criterion (AIC), the regression R^2 (Reg Rsq), and the total R^2 (Total Rsq). For GARCH models, the following additional items are printed:

   - the value of the log likelihood function

   - the number of observations that are used in estimation (OBS)

   - the unconditional variance (UVAR)

   - the normality test statistic and its *p*-value

8. the parameter estimates for the structural model (B Value), a standard error estimate (Std Error), the ratio of estimate to standard error (*t* Ratio), and an approximation to the significance probability for the parameter being 0 (Approx Prob)

9. the regression parameter estimates, printed again assuming that the autoregressive parameter estimates are known to be correct. The Std Error and related statistics for the regression estimates will, in general, be different when the autoregressive parameters are assumed to be given.

Examples

Example 4.1.   Analysis of Real Output Series

In this example, the annual real output series is analyzed over the period 1901 to 1983 (Gordon 1986, pp 781-783). With the DATA step, the original data is transformed using the natural logarithm, and the differenced series DY is created for further analysis. The log of real output is plotted in Output 4.1.1.

```
title 'Analysis of Real GNP';
data gnp;
   date = intnx( 'year', '01jan01'd, _n_-1 );
   format date year4.;
   input x @@;
   y  = log(x);
   dy = dif(y);
   t  = _n_;
   label y  = 'Real GNP'
         dy = 'First Difference of Y'
         t  = 'Time Trend';
cards;
 ... data lines omitted ...
;

proc gplot data=gnp;
   plot y * date /
       haxis='01jan01'd '01jan11'd '01jan21'd '01jan31'd
             '01jan41'd '01jan51'd '01jan61'd '01jan71'd
             '01jan81'd '01jan91'd;
   symbol i=join;
run;
```

Example 4.1. Analysis of Real Output Series ☐ ☐ ☐ 233

Output 4.1.1. Real Output Series: 1901 - 1983

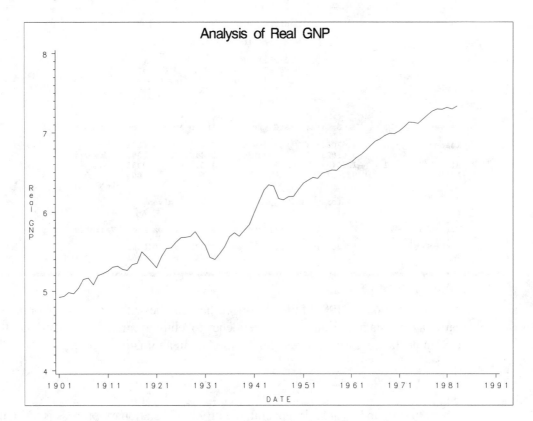

The (linear) trend-stationary process is estimated using the following form:

$$y_t = \beta_0 + \beta_1 t + \nu_t$$

where

$$\nu_t = \epsilon_t - \varphi_1 \nu_{t-1} - \varphi_2 \nu_{t-2}$$
$$\epsilon_t \sim \text{IN}(0, \sigma_\epsilon)$$

The preceding trend-stationary model assumes that uncertainty over future horizons is bounded since the error term, ν_t, has a finite variance. The maximum likelihood AR estimates are shown in Output 4.1.2.

```
proc autoreg data=gnp;
   model y = t / nlag=2 method=ml;
run;
```

Output 4.1.2. Estimating the Linear Trend Model

```
                        Autoreg Procedure

                   Maximum Likelihood Estimates

             SSE            0.239543   DFE              79
             MSE            0.003032   Root MSE   0.055065
             SBC           -230.394    AIC        -240.069
             Reg Rsq         0.8645    Total Rsq    0.9947
             Durbin-Watson   1.9935


Variable    DF      B Value   Std Error   t Ratio Approx Prob  Variable Label

Intercept    1   4.82064463    0.06615     72.878     0.0001
T            1   0.03022224    0.00135     22.448     0.0001   Time Trend
A(1)         1  -1.20409107    0.10398    -11.580     0.0001
A(2)         1   0.37479682    0.10392      3.607     0.0005


             Autoregressive parameters assumed given.


Variable    DF      B Value   Std Error   t Ratio Approx Prob  Variable Label

Intercept    1   4.82064463    0.06615     72.878     0.0001
T            1   0.03022224    0.00135     22.448     0.0001   Time Trend
```

Nelson and Plosser (1982) failed to reject the hypothesis that macroeconomic time series are nonstationary and have no tendency to return to a trend line. In this context, the simple random walk process can be used as an alternative process:

$$y_t = \beta_0 + y_{t-1} + \nu_t$$

where $\nu_t = \epsilon_t$ and $y_0 = 0$. In general, the difference-stationary process is written as

$$\phi(B)(1 - B)y_t = \beta_0 \phi(1) + \theta(B) \epsilon_t$$

where B is the back shift (lag) operator. You can observe that the class of a difference-stationary process should have at least one unit root in the AR polynomial $\phi(B)(1 - B)$.

The Dickey-Fuller procedure is used to test the null hypothesis that the series has a unit root in the AR polynomial. Consider the following equation for the augmented Dickey-Fuller test:

$$\Delta y_t = \beta_0 + \delta t + \beta_1 y_{t-1} + \sum_{i=1}^{m} \gamma_i \Delta y_{t-i} + \epsilon_t$$

where $\Delta = 1 - B$. The test statistic τ_τ is the usual t ratio for the parameter estimate $\hat{\beta}_1$, but the τ_τ does not follow a t distribution.

The %DFTEST macro computes the test statistic τ_τ and its p-value to perform the Dickey-Fuller test. The default value of m is 3, but you can specify m with the AR= option. The option TREND=2 implies that the Dickey-Fuller test equation contains linear time trend. See Chapter 20, "SAS Macros," for details.

Example 4.1. Analysis of Real Output Series □ □ □ 235

```
%dftest(gnp,y,trend=2,outstat=stat1)

proc print data=stat1;
run;
```

The augmented Dickey-Fuller test indicates that the output series may have a difference-stationary process. The statistic _TAU_ has a value of -2.61903 and its *p*-value is 0.29104. See Output 4.1.3.

Output 4.1.3. Augmented Dickey-Fuller Test Results

OBS	_TYPE_	_DEPVAR_	_NAME_	_MSE_	INTERCEP	AR_V	TIME	DLAG_V	AR_V1
1	OLS	AR_V		.0031985	0.76919	-1	0.0048162	-0.15629	0.37194
2	COV	AR_V	INTERCEP	.0031985	0.08085	.	0.0005133	-0.01695	0.00549
3	COV	AR_V	TIME	.0031985	0.00051	.	0.0000034	-0.00011	0.00004
4	COV	AR_V	DLAG_V	.0031985	-0.01695	.	-.0001085	0.00356	-0.00120
5	COV	AR_V	AR_V1	.0031985	0.00549	.	0.0000360	-0.00120	0.01242
6	COV	AR_V	AR_V2	.0031985	0.00842	.	0.0000542	-0.00180	-0.00346
7	COV	AR_V	AR_V3	.0031985	0.01056	.	0.0000677	-0.00226	0.00209

OBS	AR_V2	AR_V3	_NOBS_	_TAU_	_TREND_	_DLAG_	_PVALUE_
1	0.025483	-0.082422	79	-2.61903	2	1	0.29104
2	0.008422	0.010556	79	-2.61903	2	1	0.29104
3	0.000054	0.000068	79	-2.61903	2	1	0.29104
4	-0.001798	-0.002265	79	-2.61903	2	1	0.29104
5	-0.003455	0.002095	79	-2.61903	2	1	0.29104
6	0.014238	-0.002910	79	-2.61903	2	1	0.29104
7	-0.002910	0.013538	79	-2.61903	2	1	0.29104

The AR(1) model for the differenced series DY is estimated using the maximum likelihood method for the period 1902 to 1983. The difference-stationary process is written

$$\Delta y_t = \beta_0 + v_t$$
$$v_t = \epsilon_t - \varphi_1 v_{t-1}$$

The estimated value of φ_1 is -0.297 and that of β_0 is 0.0293. All estimated values are statistically significant.

```
proc autoreg data=gnp;
   model dy = / nlag=1 method=ml;
run;
```

Output 4.1.4. Estimating the Differenced Series with AR(1) Error

```
                     Autoreg Procedure

                 Maximum Likelihood Estimates

        SSE            0.271077    DFE                80
        MSE            0.003388    Root MSE      0.05821
        SBC            -226.778    AIC          -231.592
        Reg Rsq          0.0000    Total Rsq      0.0900
        Durbin-Watson    1.9268


Variable     DF      B Value    Std Error    t Ratio Approx Prob

Intercept     1   0.029319273     0.00909       3.224      0.0018
A(1)          1  -0.296650656     0.10666      -2.781      0.0067


           Autoregressive parameters assumed given.


Variable     DF      B Value    Std Error    t Ratio Approx Prob

Intercept     1   0.029319273     0.00909       3.224      0.0018
```

Example 4.2. Comparing Estimates and Models

In this example, the Grunfeld series are estimated using different estimation methods. Refer to Maddala (1977) for details of the Grunfeld investment data set. For comparison, the Yule-Walker method, the ULS method, and maximum likelihood method estimates are shown. With the DWPROB option, the *p*-value of the Durbin-Watson statistic is printed. The Durbin-Watson test indicates the positive autocorrelation of the regression residuals.

```
title 'Grunfeld''s Investment Models Fit with Autoregressive Errors';
data grunfeld;
   input year gei gef gec;
   label gei = 'Gross investment GE'
         gec = 'Lagged Capital Stock GE'
         gef = 'Lagged Value of GE shares';
cards;
 ... data lines omitted ...
;

proc autoreg data=grunfeld;
   model gei = gef gec / nlag=1 dwprob;
   model gei = gef gec / nlag=1 method=uls;
   model gei = gef gec / nlag=1 method=ml;
run;
```

The printed output produced by each of the MODEL statements is shown in Output 4.2.1 through Output 4.2.4.

Example 4.2. Comparing Estimates and Models ☐ ☐ ☐   237

Output 4.2.1. OLS Analysis of Residuals

```
            Grunfeld's Investment Models Fit with Autoregressive Errors
                             Autoreg Procedure

Dependent Variable = GEI        Gross investment GE


                        Ordinary Least Squares Estimates

                    SSE            13216.59    DFE                 17
                    MSE            777.4463    Root MSE      27.88272
                    SBC            195.6147    AIC           192.6275
                    Reg Rsq          0.7053    Total Rsq       0.7053
                    Durbin-Watson    1.0721    PROB<DW         0.0038


    Variable      DF     B Value    Std Error    t Ratio  Approx Prob  Variable Label

    Intercept      1  -9.95630645      31.374     -0.317       0.7548
    GEF            1   0.02655119       0.016      1.706       0.1063  Lagged Value of GE shares
    GEC            1   0.15169387       0.026      5.902       0.0001  Lagged Capital Stock GE


                          Estimates of Autocorrelations

      Lag  Covariance  Correlation  -1 9 8 7 6 5 4 3 2 1 0 1 2 3 4 5 6 7 8 9 1

       0    660.8294    1.000000  |                    |********************|
       1    304.5546    0.460867  |                    |*********           |


                          Preliminary MSE = 520.4701
```

Output 4.2.2. Regression Results Using Default Yule-Walker Method

```
            Grunfeld's Investment Models Fit with Autoregressive Errors
                             Autoreg Procedure

                   Estimates of the Autoregressive Parameters

            Lag     Coefficient       Std Error        t Ratio
             1      -0.46086726      0.22186727      -2.077221


                           Yule-Walker Estimates

                    SSE             10238.3    DFE                 16
                    MSE            639.8934    Root MSE      25.29612
                    SBC            193.7424    AIC           189.7595
                    Reg Rsq          0.5717    Total Rsq       0.7717
                    Durbin-Watson    1.3321    PROB<DW         0.0232


    Variable      DF     B Value    Std Error    t Ratio  Approx Prob  Variable Label

    Intercept      1  -18.2317775      33.251     -0.548       0.5911
    GEF            1    0.0331996       0.016      2.096       0.0523  Lagged Value of GE shares
    GEC            1    0.1391942       0.038      3.632       0.0022  Lagged Capital Stock GE
```

Output 4.2.3. Regression Results Using Unconditional Least Squares Method

```
            Grunfeld's Investment Models Fit with Autoregressive Errors

                               Autoreg Procedure

                    Estimates of the Autoregressive Parameters

              Lag    Coefficient      Std Error       t Ratio
               1     -0.46086726     0.22186727     -2.077221


                      Unconditional Least Squares Estimates

              SSE           10220.85     DFE                16
              MSE           638.8028     Root MSE     25.27455
              SBC           193.7567     AIC          189.7738
              Reg Rsq         0.5511     Total Rsq      0.7721
              Durbin-Watson   1.3523


   Variable     DF      B Value    Std Error   t Ratio Approx Prob  Variable Label

   Intercept     1  -18.6581577       34.810    -0.536      0.5993
   GEF           1    0.0338724        0.018     1.891      0.0769   Lagged Value of GE shares
   GEC           1    0.1368992        0.045     3.052      0.0076   Lagged Capital Stock GE
   A(1)          1   -0.4996199        0.259    -1.928      0.0718


                    Autoregressive parameters assumed given.


   Variable     DF      B Value    Std Error   t Ratio Approx Prob  Variable Label

   Intercept     1  -18.6581577       33.757    -0.553      0.5881
   GEF           1    0.0338724        0.016     2.135      0.0486   Lagged Value of GE shares
   GEC           1    0.1368992        0.040     3.389      0.0037   Lagged Capital Stock GE
```

Output 4.2.4. Regression Results Using Maximum Likelihood Method

```
            Grunfeld's Investment Models Fit with Autoregressive Errors

                               Autoreg Procedure

                    Estimates of the Autoregressive Parameters

              Lag    Coefficient      Std Error       t Ratio
               1     -0.46086726     0.22186727     -2.077221


                        Maximum Likelihood Estimates

              SSE           10229.23     DFE                16
              MSE           639.3269     Root MSE     25.28491
              SBC           193.7389     AIC          189.7559
              Reg Rsq         0.5656     Total Rsq      0.7719
              Durbin-Watson   1.3385


   Variable     DF      B Value    Std Error   t Ratio Approx Prob  Variable Label

   Intercept     1  -18.3750736       34.594    -0.531      0.6026
   GEF           1    0.0334051        0.018     1.870      0.0799   Lagged Value of GE shares
   GEC           1    0.1385257        0.043     3.233      0.0052   Lagged Capital Stock GE
   A(1)          1   -0.4727583        0.258    -1.831      0.0858


                    Autoregressive parameters assumed given.


   Variable     DF      B Value    Std Error   t Ratio Approx Prob  Variable Label

   Intercept     1  -18.3750736       33.393    -0.550      0.5897
   GEF           1    0.0334051        0.016     2.108      0.0512   Lagged Value of GE shares
   GEC           1    0.1385257        0.039     3.559      0.0026   Lagged Capital Stock GE
```

Example 4.3. Lack of Fit Study □ □ □ 239

Example 4.3. Lack of Fit Study

Many time series exhibit high positive autocorrelation, having the smooth appearance of a random walk. This behavior can be explained by the partial adjustment and adaptive expectation hypotheses.

Short-term forecasting applications often use autoregressive models because these models absorb the behavior of this kind of data. In the case of a first-order AR process where the autoregressive parameter is exactly 1 (a *random walk*), the best prediction of the future is the immediate past.

PROC AUTOREG can often greatly improve the fit of models, not only by adding additional parameters but also by capturing the random walk tendencies. Thus, PROC AUTOREG can be expected to provide good short-term forecast predictions.

However, good forecasts do not necessarily mean that your structural model contributes anything worthwhile to the fit. In the following example, random noise is fit to part of a sine wave. Notice that the structural model does not fit at all, but the autoregressive process does quite well and is very nearly a first difference (A(1) = -.976).

```
title1 'Lack of Fit Study';
title2 'Fitting White Noise Plus Autoregressive Errors to a Sine Wave';

data a;
   pi=3.14159;
   do time = 1 to 75;
      if time > 75 then y = .;
      else y = sin( pi * ( time / 50 ) );
      x = ranuni( 1234567 );
      output;
      end;
run;

proc autoreg data=a;
   model y = x / nlag=1;
   output out=b p=pred pm=xbeta;
run;

proc gplot data=b;
   plot y*time=1 pred*time=2 xbeta*time=3 / overlay;
   symbol1  v='none' i=spline;
   symbol2  v='X';
   symbol3  v=plus;
run;
```

The printed output produced by PROC AUTOREG is shown in Output 4.3.1 and Output 4.3.2. Plots of observed and predicted values are shown in Output 4.3.3.

Output 4.3.1. Results of OLS Analysis: No Autoregressive Model Fit

```
                          Lack of Fit Study
            Fitting White Noise Plus Autoregressive Errors to a Sine Wave

                            Autoreg Procedure

Dependent Variable = Y


                     Ordinary Least Squares Estimates

                SSE             34.8061    DFE              73
                MSE            0.476796    Root MSE    0.690504
                SBC           163.8986    AIC         159.2636
                Reg Rsq         0.0008    Total Rsq     0.0008
                Durbin-Watson   0.0057


        Variable      DF      B Value     Std Error    t Ratio Approx Prob

        Intercept      1    0.238326817     0.15837      1.505     0.1367
        X              1   -0.066526216     0.27706     -0.240     0.8109


                     Estimates of Autocorrelations

   Lag  Covariance  Correlation  -1 9 8 7 6 5 4 3 2 1 0 1 2 3 4 5 6 7 8 9 1

    0    0.464081    1.000000  |                    |********************|
    1    0.453122    0.976386  |                    |*******************|


                     Preliminary MSE = 0.021659
```

Output 4.3.2. Regression Results with AR(1) Error Correction

```
                          Lack of Fit Study
            Fitting White Noise Plus Autoregressive Errors to a Sine Wave

                            Autoreg Procedure

                  Estimates of the Autoregressive Parameters

            Lag    Coefficient      Std Error        t Ratio
             1    -0.97638591      0.02545981     -38.350083


                         Yule-Walker Estimates

                SSE            0.183043    DFE              72
                MSE           0.002542    Root MSE    0.050421
                SBC          -222.306     AIC        -229.259
                Reg Rsq         0.0001    Total Rsq     0.9947
                Durbin-Watson   0.0942


        Variable      DF      B Value     Std Error    t Ratio Approx Prob

        Intercept      1   -0.147298080     0.17023     -0.865     0.3898
        X              1   -0.001219092     0.01414     -0.086     0.9315
```

Example 4.3. Lack of Fit Study □ □ □ 241

Output 4.3.3. Plot of Autoregressive Prediction

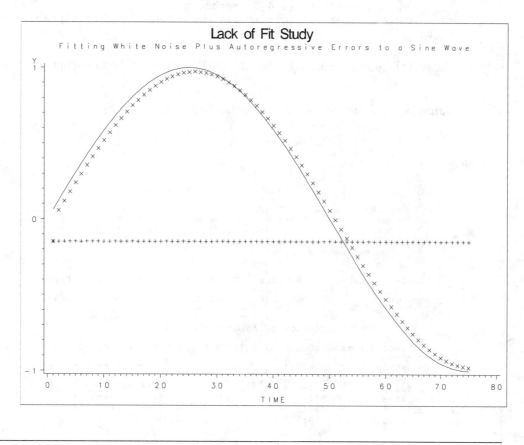

Example 4.4. Missing Values

In this example, a pure autoregressive error model with no regressors is used to generate 50 values of a time series. Approximately fifteen percent of the values are randomly chosen and set to missing. The following statements generate the data.

```
title  'Simulated Time Series with Roots:';
title2 ' (X-1.25)(X**4-1.25)';
title3 'With 15% Missing Values';
data ar;
   do i=1 to 550;
      e = rannor(12345);
      n = sum( e, .8*n1, .8*n4, -.64*n5 ); /* ar process  */
      y = n;
      if ranuni(7890) > .85 then y = .;    /* 15% missing */
      n5=n4; n4=n3; n3=n2; n2=n1; n1=n;    /* set lags    */
      if i>500 then output;
      end;
run;
```

The model is estimated using maximum likelihood, and the residuals are plotted with 99% confidence limits. The PARTIAL option prints the partial autocorrelations. The following statements fit the model:

```
proc autoreg data=ar partial;
    model y = / nlag=(1 4 5) method=ml;
    output out=a predicted=p residual=r ucl=u lcl=l alphacli=.01;
run;
```

The printed output produced by the AUTOREG procedure is shown in Output 4.4.1.

Output 4.4.1.   Autocorrelation-Corrected Regression Results

```
                         Autoreg Procedure

Dependent Variable = Y


                   Ordinary Least Squares Estimates

              SSE           218.9039    DFE                42
              MSE           5.211997    Root MSE      2.28298
              SBC           195.7695    AIC           194.0083
              Reg Rsq         0.0000    Total Rsq      0.0000
              Durbin-Watson   0.4141


       Variable     DF      B Value    Std Error    t Ratio Approx Prob

       Intercept     1    1.06387366     0.34815      3.056      0.0039


                   Estimates of Autocorrelations

    Lag   Covariance   Correlation  -1 9 8 7 6 5 4 3 2 1 0 1 2 3 4 5 6 7 8 9 1

      0    5.090788     1.000000  |                     |********************|
      1    4.193243     0.823692  |                     |****************    |
      2    3.601517     0.707458  |                     |**************      |
      3    3.21282      0.631105  |                     |************        |
      4    3.306776     0.649561  |                     |*************       |
      5    2.166853     0.425642  |                     |*********           |


                     Partial Autocorrelations
                        1   0.823692
                        4   0.215594
                        5  -0.676511
```

```
                         Autoreg Procedure

                  Preliminary MSE = 0.810499

            Estimates of the Autoregressive Parameters

        Lag    Coefficient      Std Error        t Ratio
         1     -0.83348161     0.08620247       -9.668883
         4     -0.68078321     0.11558431       -5.889928
         5      0.67651074     0.11792362        5.736855


                  Expected Autocorrelations

                     Lag Autocorr
                      0   1.0000
                      1   0.8349
                      2   0.7319
                      3   0.6833
                      4   0.6855
                      5   0.4632


                  Maximum Likelihood Estimates

              SSE           33.95524    DFE                39
              MSE           0.870647    Root MSE      0.933085
              SBC           137.3552    AIC           130.3104
              Reg Rsq         0.0000    Total Rsq      0.8449
              Durbin-Watson   2.8264
```

Example 4.4. Missing Values □ □ □ 243

Output 4.4.1. (Continued)

Variable	DF	B Value	Std Error	t Ratio	Approx Prob
Intercept	1	0.327989298	1.2201	0.269	0.7895
A(1)	1	-0.777510232	0.0987	-7.879	0.0001
A(4)	1	-0.765128825	0.1016	-7.529	0.0001
A(5)	1	0.645737600	0.1223	5.282	0.0001

```
                    Autoreg Procedure

                Expected Autocorrelations

                    Lag  Autocorr
                     0   1.0000
                     1   0.8074
                     2   0.7153
                     3   0.7120
                     4   0.7974
                     5   0.5920


           Autoregressive parameters assumed given.
```

Variable	DF	B Value	Std Error	t Ratio	Approx Prob
Intercept	1	0.327989298	1.1524	0.285	0.7774

The following statements plot the residuals and confidence limits:

```
data reshape1;
   set a;
   miss = .;
   if r=. then do;
      miss = p;
      p = .;
      end;
run;

title 'Predicted Values and Confidence Limits';
proc gplot data=reshape1;
   plot l*i=1 miss*i=2 p*i=3 u*i=4 / overlay;
   symbol1  i=join v=none l=2;
   symbol2  i=needle v='X';
   symbol3  i=needle v=circle;
   symbol4  i=join v=none l=2;
run;
```

The plot of the predicted values and the upper and lower confidence limits is shown in Output 4.4.2. Note that the confidence interval is wider at the beginning of the series (when there are no past noise values to use in the forecast equation) and after missing values where, again, there is an incomplete set of past residuals.

Output 4.4.2. Plot of Residuals and Confidence Interval

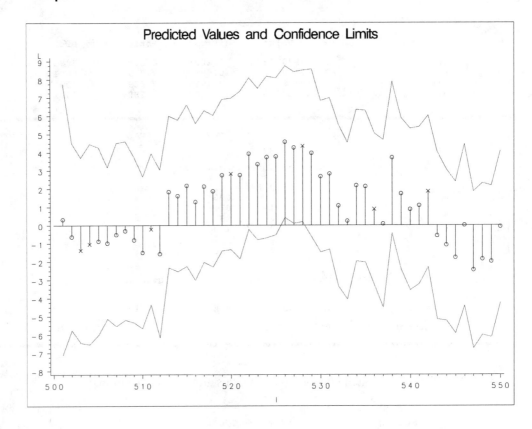

Example 4.5.   Money Demand Model

The following example estimates the log-log money demand equation using the maximum likelihood method. The money demand model contains four explanatory variables. The lagged nominal money stock M1 is divided by the current price level GDF to calculate a new variable M1CP since the money stock is assumed to follow the partial adjustment process. The variable M1CP is then used to estimate the coefficient of adjustment. All variables are transformed using the natural logarithm with a DATA step. Refer to Balke and Gordon (1986) for data description.

The first eight observations are printed using the PRINT procedure and are shown in Output 4.5.1. Note that the first observation of the variables M1CP and INFR are missing. Therefore, the money demand equation is estimated for the period 1968:2 to 1983:4 since PROC AUTOREG ignores the first missing observation.

```
data money;
   date = intnx( 'qtr', '01jan1968'd, _n_-1 );
   format date yyqc6.;
   input m1 gnp gdf ycb @@;
   m = log( 100 * m1 / gdf );
   m1cp = log( 100 * lag(m1) / gdf );
   y = log( gnp );
   intr = log( ycb );
   infr = 100 * log( gdf / lag(gdf) );
   label m    = 'Real Money Stock (M1)'
         m1cp = 'Lagged M1/Current GDF'
```

Example 4.5. Money Demand Model □ □ □ 245

```
            y    = 'Real GNP'
            intr = 'Yield on Corporate Bonds'
            infr = 'Rate of Prices Changes';
cards;
  ... data lines omitted ...
;
```

Output 4.5.1. Money Demand Data Series — First 8 Observations

```
OBS  DATE   M1      GNP     GDF   YCB   M        M1CP     Y        INTR     INFR
  1 1968:1 187.15 1036.22 81.18 6.84 5.44041  .        6.94333 1.92279  .
  2 1968:2 190.63 1056.02 82.12 6.97 5.44732 5.42890 6.96226 1.94162 1.15127
  3 1968:3 194.30 1068.72 82.80 6.98 5.45815 5.43908 6.97422 1.94305 0.82465
  4 1968:4 198.55 1071.28 84.04 6.84 5.46492 5.44328 6.97661 1.92279 1.48648
  5 1969:1 201.73 1084.15 84.97 7.32 5.46980 5.45391 6.98855 1.99061 1.10054
  6 1969:2 203.18 1088.73 86.10 7.54 5.46375 5.45659 6.99277 2.02022 1.32112
  7 1969:3 204.18 1091.90 87.49 7.70 5.45265 5.44774 6.99567 2.04122 1.60151
  8 1969:4 206.10 1085.53 88.62 8.22 5.44917 5.43981 6.98982 2.10657 1.28331
```

The money demand equation is first estimated using OLS. The DW=4 option produces generalized Durbin-Watson statistics up to the fourth order. Their exact marginal probabilities (*p*-values) are also calculated with the DWPROB option. The Durbin-Watson test indicates positive first-order autocorrelation at, say, the 10% confidence level. You can use the Durbin-Watson table, which is available only for 1% and 5% significance points. The relevant upper (d_U) and lower (d_L) bounds are $d_U = 1.731$ and $d_L = 1.471$, respectively, at 5% significance level. However, the bounds test is inconvenient since sometimes you may get the statistic in the inconclusive region.

```
title 'Partial Adjustment Money Demand Equation';
title2 'Quarterly Data - 1968:2 to 1983:4';

proc autoreg data=money outest=est covout;
   model m = m1cp y intr infr / dw=4 dwprob;
run;
```

Output 4.5.2. OLS Estimation of the Partial Adjustment Money Demand Equation

```
              Partial Adjustment Money Demand Equation
                    Quarterly Data - 1968:2 to 1983:4

                          Autoreg Procedure

Dependent Variable = M        Real Money Stock (M1)


                      Ordinary Least Squares Estimates

              SSE         0.002719   DFE            58
              MSE         0.000047   Root MSE  0.006847
              SBC         -433.687   AIC       -444.403
              Reg Rsq       0.9546   Total Rsq   0.9546

                      Durbin-Watson Statistics

                    Order    DW      PROB<DW
                      1     1.7355    0.0607
                      2     2.1058    0.5519
                      3     2.0286    0.5002
                      4     2.2835    0.8880


   Variable    DF   B Value    Std Error  t Ratio Approx Prob Variable Label

   Intercept   1  0.308350999   0.23586    1.307     0.1963
```

Output 4.5.2. (Continued)

M1CP	1	0.895221876	0.04393	20.378	0.0001	Lagged M1/Current GDF
Y	1	0.047571130	0.01223	3.891	0.0003	Real GNP
INTR	1	-0.023813622	0.00793	-3.002	0.0040	Yield on Corporate Bonds
INFR	1	-0.005645942	0.00158	-3.564	0.0007	Rate of Prices Changes

The autoregressive model is estimated using the maximum likelihood method. Though the Durbin-Watson test statistic is calculated after correcting the autocorrelation, it should be used with care since the test based on this statistic is not justified theoretically.

```
proc autoreg data=money;
    model m = m1cp y intr infr / nlag=1 method=ml maxit=50;
    output out=a p=p pm=pm r=r rm=rm ucl=ucl lcl=lcl
                uclm=uclm lclm=lclm;
run;

proc print data=a(obs=8);
    var p pm r rm ucl lcl uclm lclm;
run;
```

A difference is shown between the OLS estimates in Output 4.5.2 and the AR(1)-ML estimates in Output 4.5.3. The estimated autocorrelation coefficient is significantly negative (-0.88345). Note that the negative coefficient of A(1) should be interpreted as a positive autocorrelation.

Two predicted values are produced — predicted values computed for the structural model and predicted values computed for the full model. The full model includes both the structural and error-process parts. The predicted values and residuals are stored in the output data set A, as are the upper and lower 95% confidence limits for the predicted values. Part of the data set A is shown in Output 4.5.4. The first observation is missing since the explanatory variables, M1CP and INFR, are missing for the corresponding observation.

Output 4.5.3. Estimated Partial Adjustment Money Demand Equation

```
            Partial Adjustment Money Demand Equation
                Quarterly Data - 1968:2 to 1983:4

                     Autoreg Procedure

         Estimates of the Autoregressive Parameters

         Lag    Coefficient      Std Error       t Ratio
          1     -0.12627330     0.13139301     -0.961035


                 Maximum Likelihood Estimates

         SSE           0.002267    DFE              57
         MSE           0.00004     Root MSE    0.006307
         SBC           -439.477    AIC         -452.335
         Reg Rsq       0.6954      Total Rsq     0.9621
         Durbin-Watson 2.1778
```

Variable	DF	B Value	Std Error	t Ratio	Approx Prob	Variable Label
Intercept	1	2.41206983	0.48796	4.943	0.0001	
M1CP	1	0.40858733	0.09084	4.498	0.0001	Lagged M1/Current GDF
Y	1	0.15088108	0.04111	3.670	0.0005	Real GNP

Example 4.5. Money Demand Model □ □ □ 247

Output 4.5.3. (Continued)

```
   INTR        1    -0.11010986    0.01590    -6.925    0.0001  Yield on Corporate Bonds
   INFR        1    -0.00634812    0.00183    -3.462    0.0010  Rate of Prices Changes
   A(1)        1    -0.88345377    0.06856   -12.886    0.0001


                   Autoregressive parameters assumed given.


   Variable    DF      B Value   Std Error  t Ratio Approx Prob  Variable Label

   Intercept   1     2.41206983    0.46846     5.149    0.0001
   M1CP        1     0.40858733    0.08398     4.865    0.0001  Lagged M1/Current GDF
   Y           1     0.15088108    0.04024     3.750    0.0004  Real GNP
   INTR        1    -0.11010986    0.01555    -7.081    0.0001  Yield on Corporate Bonds
   INFR        1    -0.00634812    0.00183    -3.473    0.0010  Rate of Prices Changes
```

Output 4.5.4. Partial List of the Predicted Values

```
                  Partial Adjustment Money Demand Equation
                     Quarterly Data - 1968:2 to 1983:4

 OBS      P         PM          R         RM        UCL       LCL       UCLM      LCLM

  1       .         .          .          .          .         .         .         .
  2    5.45962   5.45962   -0.012301  -0.012301   5.49319   5.42606   5.47962   5.43962
  3    5.45663   5.46750    0.001511  -0.009356   5.47987   5.43340   5.48700   5.44800
  4    5.45934   5.46761    0.005574  -0.002691   5.48267   5.43601   5.48723   5.44799
  5    5.46636   5.46874    0.003442   0.001064   5.48903   5.44369   5.48757   5.44991
  6    5.46675   5.46581   -0.002994  -0.002054   5.48925   5.44424   5.48444   5.44718
  7    5.45672   5.45854   -0.004074  -0.005889   5.47882   5.43462   5.47667   5.44040
  8    5.44404   5.44924    0.005136  -0.000066   5.46604   5.42203   5.46726   5.43122
```

Example 4.6.   Estimation of ARCH(2) Process

Stock returns show a tendency for small changes to be followed by small changes while large changes are followed by large changes. The plot of daily price changes of the IBM common stock (Box and Jenkins 1976, p 527) are shown in Output 4.6.1. The time series look serially uncorrelated, but the plot makes us skeptical of their independence.

With a DATA step, the stock (capital) returns are computed from the closing prices. To forecast the conditional variance, an additional 46 observations with missing values are generated.

```
title 'IBM Stock Returns (daily)';
title2 '29jun1959 - 30jun1960';

data ibm;
   infile cards eof=last;
   input x @@;
   r = dif( log( x ) );
   time = _n_-1;
   output;
   return;
last:
   do i = 1 to 46;
      r = .;
      time + 1;
      output;
   end;
```

```
      return;
cards;
   ... data lines omitted ...
;

proc gplot data=ibm;
   plot r*time / vref=0;
   symbol1 i=join v=none;
run;
```

Output 4.6.1. IBM Stock Returns: Daily

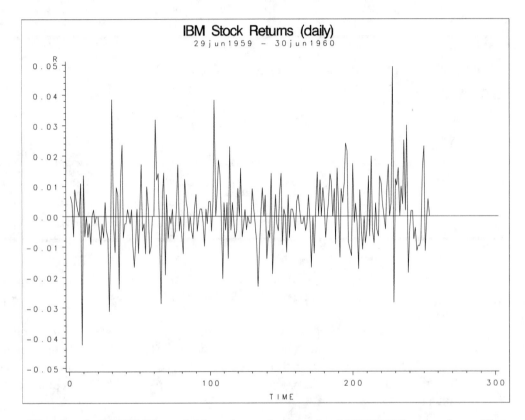

The simple ARCH(2) model is estimated using the AUTOREG procedure. The MODEL statement option GARCH=(Q=2) specifies the ARCH(2) model. The OUTPUT statement with the CEV= option produces the conditional variances V. The conditional variance and its forecast is calculated using parameter estimates:

$$h_t = \widehat{\omega} + \widehat{\alpha}_1\, \epsilon^2_{t-1} + \widehat{\alpha}_2\, \epsilon^2_{t-2}$$

$$\mathrm{E}\!\left(\epsilon^2_{t+d} \mid \Psi_t\right) = \widehat{\omega} + \sum_{i=1}^{2} \widehat{\alpha}_i\, \mathrm{E}\!\left(\epsilon^2_{t+d-i} \mid \Psi_t\right)$$

where $d > 1$.

Example 4.6.   Estimation of ARCH(2) Process   □ □ □   249

```
proc autoreg data=ibm maxit=50;
   model r = / noint garch=(q=2);
   output out=a cev=v;
run;
```

The parameter estimates for ω, α_1, and α_2 are 0.00011, 0.04136, and 0.06976, respectively. The normality test indicates that the conditional normal distribution may not fully explain the leptokurtosis in the stock returns (Bollerslev 1987).

The ARCH model estimates are shown in Output 4.6.2, and conditional variances are also shown in Output 4.6.3.

Output 4.6.2.   ARCH(2) Estimation Results

```
                        Autoreg Procedure

Dependent Variable = R


                 Ordinary Least Squares Estimates

           SSE            0.032143    DFE               254
           MSE            0.000127    Root MSE     0.011249
           SBC             -1558.8    AIC            -1558.8
           Reg Rsq         0.0000     Total Rsq       0.0000
           Durbin-Watson        .

NOTE: No intercept term is used. R-squares are redefined.




                        GARCH Estimates

           SSE            0.032143    OBS               254
           MSE            0.000127    UVAR         0.000126
           Log L         781.0174     Total Rsq       0.0000
           SBC           -1545.42     AIC            -1556.03
           Normality Test 105.8616    Prob>Chi-Sq     0.0001


     Variable    DF      B Value    Std Error   t Ratio Approx Prob

     ARCH0        1   0.000112282   0.000012      9.018     0.0001
     ARCH1        1   0.041357618   0.03899       1.061     0.2889
     ARCH2        1   0.069759883   0.05489       1.271     0.2038
```

Output 4.6.3.　Conditional Variance for IBM Stock Prices

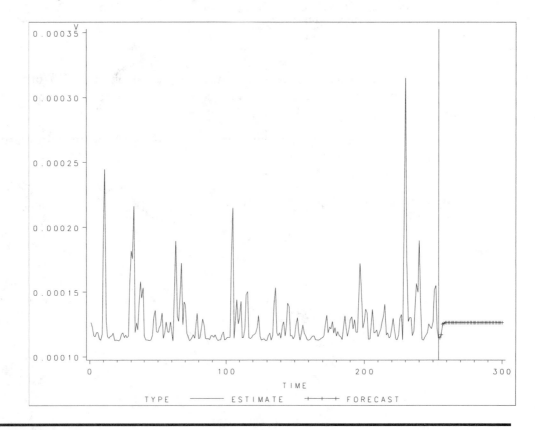

References

Anderson, T.W. and Mentz, R.P. (1980), "On the Structure of the Likelihood Function of Autoregressive and Moving Average Models," *Journal of Time Series*, 1, 83–94.

Baillie, R.T. and Bollerslev, T. (1992), "Prediction in Dynamic Models with Time-Dependent Conditional Variances," *Journal of Econometrics*, 52, 91–113.

Balke, N.S. and Gordon, R.J. (1986) "Historical Data," in *The American Business Cycle*, ed. R.J. Gordon, Chicago: The University of Chicago Press, 781–850.

Beach, C.M. and MacKinnon, J.G. (1978), "A Maximum Likelihood Procedure for Regression with Autocorrelated Errors," *Econometrica*, 46, 51–58.

Bollerslev, T. (1986), "Generalized Autoregressive Conditional Heteroskedasticity," *Journal of Econometrics*, 31, 307–327.

Bollerslev, T. (1987), "A Conditionally Heteroskedastic Time Series Model for Speculative Prices and Rates of Return," *The Review of Economics and Statistics*, 69, 542–547.

Box, G.E.P. and Jenkins, G.M. (1976), *Time Series Analysis: Forecasting and Control*, Revised Edition, San Francisco: Holden-Day.

Breusch, T.S. and Pagan, A.R. (1979), "A Simple Test for Heteroscedasticity and Random Coefficient Variation," *Econometrica*, 47, 1287–1294.

Chipman, J.S. (1979), "Efficiency of Least Squares Estimation of Linear Trend When Residuals Are Autocorrelated," *Econometrica*, 47, 115–128.

Cochrane, D. and Orcutt, G.H. (1949), "Application of Least Squares Regression to Relationships Containing Autocorrelated Error Terms," *Journal of the American Statistical Association*, 44, 32–61.

Durbin, J. (1970), "Testing for Serial Correlation in Least-Squares Regression When Some of the Regressors Are Lagged Dependent Variables," *Econometrica*, 38, 410–421.

Engle, R.F. (1982), "Autoregressive Conditional Heteroscedasticity with Estimates of the Variance of United Kingdom Inflation," *Econometrica*, 50, 987–1007.

Engle, R.F. and Bollerslev, T. (1986), "Modelling the Persistence of Conditional Variances," *Econometric Review*, 5, 1–50.

Engle, R.F.; Lilien, D.M.; and Robins, R.P. (1987), "Estimating Time Varying Risk in the Term Structure: The ARCH-M Model," *Econometrica*, 55, 391–407.

Fuller, W. (1978), *Introduction to Time Series*, New York: John Wiley & Sons, Inc.

Gallant, A.R. and Goebel, J.J. (1976), "Nonlinear Regression with Autoregressive Errors," *Journal of the American Statistical Association*, 71, 961–967.

Golub, G.H. and Loan, C.F. (1989), *Matrix Computations*, Baltimore: The Johns Hopkins University Press.

Harvey, A.C. (1981), *The Econometric Analysis of Time Series*, New York: John Wiley & Sons, Inc., Chapter 6.

Harvey, A.C. and McAvinchey, I.D. (1978), "The Small Sample Efficiency of Two-Step Estimators in Regression Models with Autoregressive Disturbances," Discussion Paper No. 78–10, University of British Columbia, April, 1978.

Harvey, A.C. and Phillips, G.D.A. (1979), "Maximum Likelihood Estimation of Regression Models with Autoregressive-Moving Average Disturbances," *Biometrika*, 66, 49–58.

Hildreth, C. and Lu, J.Y. (1960), "Demand Relations with Autocorrelated Disturbances," Michigan State University Agricultural Experiment Station Technical Bulletin 276, East Lansing, MI.

Inder, B.A. (1984), "Finite-Sample Power of Tests for Autocorrelation in Models Containing Lagged Dependent Variables," *Economics Letters*, 14, 179–185.

Inder, B.A. (1986), "An Approximation to the Null Distribution of the Durbin-Watson Statistic in Models Containing Lagged Dependent Variables," *Econometric Theory*, 2, 413–428.

Johnston, J. (1972), *Econometric Methods*, Second Edition, New York: McGraw-Hill, Inc.

Jones, R.H. (1980), "Maximum Likelihood Fitting of ARMA Models to Time Series with Missing Observations," *Technometrics*, 22, 389–395.

Judge, G.G.; Griffiths, W.E.; Hill, R.C.; Lütkepohl, H.; and Lee, T.C. (1985), *The Theory and Practice of Econometrics*, Second Edition, New York: John Wiley & Sons, Inc.

King, M.L. and Wu, P.X. (1991), "Small-Disturbance Asymptotics and the Durbin-Watson and Related Tests in the Dynamic Regression Model," *Journal of Econometrics*, 47, 145–152.

L'Esperance, W.L.; Chall, D.; and Taylor, D. (1976), "An Algorithm for Determining the Distribution Function of the Durbin-Watson Test Statistic," *Econometrica*, 44, 1325–1326.

Maddala, G.S. (1977), *Econometrics*, New York: McGraw-Hill, 280–281.

Maeshiro, A. (1976), "Autoregressive Transformation, Trended Independent Variables and Autocorrelated Disturbance Terms," *Review of Economics and Statistics*, 58, 497–500.

McLeod, A.I. and Li, W.K. (1983), "Diagnostic Checking ARMA Time Series Models Using Squared-Residual Autocorrelations," *Journal of Time Series Analysis*, 4, 269–273.

Nelson, C.R. and Plosser, C.I. (1982), "Trends and Random Walks in Macroeconomic Time Series: Some Evidence and Implications." *Journal of Monetary Economics*, 10, 139–162.

Nelson, D.B. (1990), "Stationarity and Persistence in the GARCH(1,1) Model," *Econometric Theory*, 6, 318–334.

Nelson, D.B. (1991), "Conditional Heteroskedasticity in Asset Returns: A New Approach," *Econometrica*, 59, 347–370.

Nelson, D.B. and Cao, C.Q. (1992), "Inequality Constraints in the Univariate GARCH Model," *Journal of Business & Economic Statistics*, 10, 229–235.

Park, R.E. and Mitchell, B.M. (1980), "Estimating the Autocorrelated Error Model with Trended Data," *Journal of Econometrics*, 13, 185–201.

Prais, S.J. and Winsten, C.B. (1954), "Trend Estimators and Serial Correlation," Cowles Commission Discussion Paper No. 383.

Savin, N.E. and White, K.J. (1978), "Testing for Autocorrelation with Missing Observations," *Econometrica*, 46, 59–66.

Schwarz, G. (1978), "Estimating the Dimension of a Model," *Annals of Statistics*, 6, 461–464.

Spitzer, John J. (1979), "Small-Sample Properties of Nonlinear Least Squares and Maximum Likelihood Estimators in the Context of Autocorrelated Errors," *Journal of the American Statistical Association*, 74, 41–47.

Vinod, H.D. (1973), "Generalization of the Durbin-Watson Statistic for Higher Order Autoregressive Process," *Communications in Statistics*, 2, 115–144.

Wallis, K.F. (1972), "Testing for Fourth Order Autocorrelation in Quarterly Regression Equations," *Econometrica*, 40, 617–636.

Chapter 5
The CITIBASE Procedure

Chapter Table of Contents

Chapter 5
The CITIBASE Procedure

Overview

The CITIBASE procedure reads time series from a CITIBASE file and stores them in a SAS data set. CITIBASE is the economic database distributed on magnetic tape or on diskettes by the Citicorp Database Services.

The CITIBASE database contains economic and financial indicators of the U.S. and international economies gathered from various government and private sources by the Citicorp Database Services. There are over 8,000 yearly, quarterly, monthly, weekly, and daily time series. The CITIBASE Directory, the document accompanying the data files, has complete descriptions of the series supplied in the data files.

The CITIBASE procedure reads the CITIBASE files and converts the data into a SAS data set containing a numeric variable for each series requested. PROC CITIBASE can also create an output data set containing information on the contents of the CITIBASE database.

PROC CITIBASE can read

- tape-format CITIBASE data files

- diskette format CITIBASE database

- Haver Analytics data files

The CITIBASE procedure can handle only one of the following data types at a time: yearly, quarterly, monthly, or weekly. The daily CITIBASE files cannot be processed with this release of the CITIBASE procedure. If you want to read daily CITIBASE files, use the DATASOURCE procedure instead. (See Chapter 7, "The DATA-SOURCE Procedure," for more information.) In addition to the CITIBASE files containing data of any frequency, the DATASOURCE procedure can also read many other kinds of data files and provides many additional features.

Getting Started

Reading Tape Format Data Files

If you want to extract all the monthly series contained in a tape format CITIBASE data file, use the following statements:

```
proc citibase infile=citifile type=month out=dataset;
run;
```

The INFILE= option names the fileref assigned to the CITIBASE tape format data
file. Since CITIFILE is the default fileref, you could have omitted this option from
the PROC CITIBASE statement. The OUT= option names the SAS data set to contain all the series of the frequency TYPE=MONTH. Note that the OUT= data set
can contain data only of the same frequency.

Subsetting Input Data Files

When only a subset of a data file is needed, extracting all the data and then subsetting
it in a subsequent DATA step would be very inefficient. Instead, you can use the
CITIBASE procedure options and statements to extract only needed information
from the data file.

The CITIBASE procedure offers the following subsetting capabilities:

- SELECT statement to extract a subset of time series variables

- BEGINYR= and ENDYR= options to restrict the time range of data

If you are interested only in some specific series, list their names in a SELECT statement. For example, the following statements extract monthly exchange rates for Germany (EXRGER), Japan (EXRJAN), and the United Kingdom (EXRUK) from CITI-
FILE:

```
proc citibase infile=citifile type=month out=exchange;
   select exrger exrjan exruk;
run;
```

If you are not interested in all the historical data contained in CITIFILE for the series
EXRGER, EXRJAN, and EXRUK, specify the range to be output to the OUT= data
set using the BEGINYR= and ENDYR= options. The following statements extract
only the data corresponding to 1986:

```
proc citibase out=exchange beginyr=1986 endyr=1986 noprint;
   select exrger exrjan exruk;
run;

title1 'Printout of the OUT= Data Set';
proc print data=exchange noobs;
run;
```

```
                    Printout of the OUT= Data Set

        YEAR     MONTH       DATE      EXRGER      EXRJAN      EXRUK

        1986       1       JAN1986     2.43840     199.890     142.440
        1986       2       FEB1986     2.33170     184.850     142.970
        1986       3       MAR1986     2.27520     178.690     146.740
        1986       4       APR1986     2.27320     175.090     149.850
        1986       5       MAY1986     2.22770     167.030     152.110
        1986       6       JUN1986     2.23370     167.540     150.850
        1986       7       JUL1986     2.15170     158.610     150.710
        1986       8       AUG1986     2.06210     154.180     148.610
        1986       9       SEP1986     2.04150     154.730     146.980
        1986      10       OCT1986     2.00540     156.470     142.640
        1986      11       NOV1986     2.02430     162.850     142.380
        1986      12       DEC1986     1.98800     162.050     143.930
```

Figure 5.1.   Subsetting CITIBASE Data Files

Notice that the last example omits the INFILE= and the TYPE= options. This is legit-
imate because the INFILE= option defaults to CITIFILE, and the TYPE= option defaults to the frequency of the first selected series, and the variable EXRGER is monthly.

Obtaining Descriptive Information

In order to list variables in a SELECT statement, you need to know the names of the
series available in your CITIBASE file. The OUTCONT= option lists out all the series and gives descriptive information about each, including the frequency, label, and
the dates of the first and last observations. For example, Figure 5.2 lists some of
the monthly series available in CITIFILE, extracted by the following statements:

```
proc citibase type=month outcont=moninfo outselect noprint;
run;

title1 'Some Monthly Series Available in CITIFILE';
proc print data=moninfo( where=(index(label,'EXCHANGE')) );
run;
```

Here, the OUTSELECT option limits the observations in the OUTCONT= data set
to only the selected series. In this case, only monthly series observations are extracted. If you omit this option, you get information on all the series contained in
CITIFILE.

Figure 5.2 shows the output produced by PROC PRINT.

```
                 Some Monthly Series Available in CITIFILE

                             S
                             E
                             L       V
                             E       A                          L
             N       F       C       R                          A
    O        A       R       T       N                          B
    B        M       E       E       U                          E
    S        E       Q       D       M                          L

    6     EXRGER     2       1       9     FOREIGN EXCHANGE RATE: GERMANY (DEUTSCHE
    7     EXRJAN     2       1      10     FOREIGN EXCHANGE RATE: JAPAN (YEN PER U.
    8     EXRUK      2       1      11     FOREIGN EXCHANGE RATE: UNITED KINGDOM (C
    9     EXVUS      2       1      12     WEIGHTED-AVERAGE EXCHANGE VALUE OF U.S.D
```

```
      C
      I       C                           C
      T       I                           I
      I       T                           T
      C       I                           I
  O   O       N                           D
  B   D       U                           E
  S   E       M                           S
                                          C

  6 EXRGER 33 FOREIGN EXCHANGE RATE: GERMANY (DEUTSCHE MARK PER U.S.$)
  7 EXRJAN 34 FOREIGN EXCHANGE RATE: JAPAN (YEN PER U.S.$)
  8 EXRUK  35 FOREIGN EXCHANGE RATE: UNITED KINGDOM (CENTS PER POUND)
  9 EXVUS  36 WEIGHTED-AVERAGE EXCHANGE VALUE OF U.S.DOLLAR(MAR.1973=100)

            S           O                   F
      S     T           B                   I        L
      T     A           S                   R        A
      A     R           E                   S        S
      R     T     N     R     N             T        T
  O   T     P     O     V     D             O        O
  B   Y     E     B     E     E             B        B
  S   R     R     S     D     C             S        S

  6 1951    1     435   1     3     01JAN1951    01MAR1987
  7 1957    1     363   1     3     01JAN1957    01MAR1987
  8 1947    1     483   1     3     01JAN1947    01MAR1987
  9 1967    1     243   1     3     01JAN1967    01MAR1987
```

Figure 5.2. Partial Listing of the OUTCONT= Data Set

Reading a Diskette Format Database

A CITIBASE diskette format database consists of three files that have the same file name but different extensions: .KEY, .IND, and .DB. The .KEY file contains the list of series contained in the database; the .IND file contains series descriptive information and indices to the .DB file; and the .DB file contains the actual data. The diskette format database is distributed on floppy disks.

To read a diskette format database, specify the fully qualified name of the database (the *dbname*) using the DBNAME= option. For example, if on a PC system the files ABC.KEY, ABC.IND, and ABC.DB of a CITIBASE diskette format database "ABC" are contained in the directory \CITIBASE of a disk in drive A, you could use the following statements:

```
proc citibase  dbname="a:\citibase\abc";
run;
```

Note that the DBNAME= and INFILE= options are mutually exclusive. Depending on which format data files you have, you need to specify one or the other. When neither is specified, PROC CITIBASE attempts to read a tape format data file, whose fileref is CITIFILE.

Syntax

The CITIBASE procedure uses two statements:

PROC CITIBASE *options*;
    SELECT *specifications*;

Functional Summary

The statements and options used by the CITIBASE procedure are summarized in the following table.

Description	Statement	Option
Input Data File Options		
specify the fileref of the input data file	PROC CITIBASE	INFILE=
specify the pathname of the database	PROC CITIBASE	DBNAME=
specify the format of the data file	PROC CITIBASE	FORMAT=
Output Data Set Options		
specify the output data set	PROC CITIBASE	OUT=
output descriptive information	PROC CITIBASE	OUTCONT=
restrict descriptive information to selected series	PROC CITIBASE	OUTSELECT
Subsetting		
specify the periodicity of series extracted	PROC CITIBASE	TYPE=
specify the time series variables extracted	SELECT	
specify time range of observations extracted	PROC CITIBASE	BEGINYR=
	PROC CITIBASE	ENDYR=
Assigning Attributes		
control the lengths of the series variables	PROC CITIBASE	LENGTH=

PROC CITIBASE Statement

PROC CITIBASE *options*;

The following options can be used in the PROC CITIBASE statement:

BEGINYR= *n*

specifies the starting year for the observations in the OUT= data set. Use the BEGINYR= option if you want to restrict the range of the time series output to start no earlier than the first period of the specified year. The beginning year can be given as either a two- or four-digit value. For example, BEGINYR=47 and BEGINYR=1947 are equivalent. If you do not use the BEGINYR= option, the observations in the OUT= data set begin with the first period of the earliest year for which data are available for any of the series selected.

DBNAME= *"pathname"*

specifies the qualified name of the diskette format database to read the input series from. The INFILE= option cannot be used if the DBNAME= option is used.

ENDYR= *n*

specifies the ending year for the observations in the OUT= data set. Use the ENDYR= option if you want to restrict the range of the time series output to end no later than the last period of the specified year. The ending year can be given as either a two- or four-digit value. For example, ENDYR=82 and ENDYR=1982 are equivalent. If you do not use the ENDYR= option, the observations in the OUT= data set end with the last period of the latest year for which data are available for any of the series selected.

FORMAT= HAVER

specifies that the input file given in the INFILE= option is a Haver Analytics data file, rather than a CITIBASE tape format data file. This option will be ignored if used together with the DBNAME= option.

FORMAT= OLD

specifies that the input file (given in the INFILE= option) or the database (given in the DBNAME= option) is in the old format. Use this option to read CITIBASE data tapes distributed before May 1987, or to read CITIBASE diskettes distributed before May 1991.

INFILE= *fileref*

specifies the fileref assigned to the CITIBASE tape format data file. This file is usually either the actual nonlabeled tape distributed by Citicorp Database Services or a copy thereof, either on disk or tape. See "Control Language for Input Data Files" later in this chapter for more information. The default is INFILE=CITIFILE. The DBNAME= option cannot be used if the INFILE= option is used.

LENGTH= *n*

specifies the number of bytes of storage used for each data value in the OUT= data set. This option is equivalent to using a LENGTH statement for the output variables in a DATA step. The default is LENGTH=5.

NOPRINT

suppresses the printed output.

OUT= *SAS-data-set*

names the output data set to contain the selected time series. If you omit the OUT= option, PROC CITIBASE names the output data set according to the DATA*n* convention, unless the OUTCONT= option is used, in which case no OUT= data set is created unless OUT= is specified.

OUTCONT= *SAS-data-set*

names the output data set that contains contents information on all of the series contained in the data file. If you omit the OUTCONT= option, no contents data set is created.

OUTSELECT

writes file contents information to the OUTCONT= data set only for those series selected for output to the OUT= data set. The OUTSELECT option is only relevant when OUTCONT= is specified.

TYPE= *frequency*

specifies the frequency of series selected for output to the OUT= data set. The value of *frequency* can be YEAR, QTR, MONTH, or WEEK. (These values can be abbreviated as Y, Q, M, or W, respectively.) If TYPE= is not specified, the type is determined by the frequency of the first selected series. Only one type of series can be output by each invocation of PROC CITIBASE.

SELECT Statement

SELECT *specifications*;

The SELECT statement specifies the time series to be extracted from the CITIBASE file. The SELECT keyword is followed by a series of name, range, or prefix specifications. If omitted, all series of the specified frequency are selected.

There are four forms of SELECT statement specifications:

- a name (for example, PZU)

- an alphabetic range (for example, PW111-PW117)

- an order range (for example, GLR72–GLRD72)

- a prefix specification (for example, IP:)

Name Specification

To select a single CITIBASE series, specify it by its code. For example, to select the series PZU (consumer price index), use the following statement:

```
select pzu;
```

Alphabetic Range

To select all names within a given alphabetic range, specify the beginning and ending names of the range, separated by a hyphen. For example, the following statement selects all series in the alphabetic range PW–PZ.

```
select pw-pz;
```

Note that nothing beyond PZ (for example, PZU) is selected.

Order Range

To select all series of a given type between two series in the database, specify the beginning and ending series, separated by two hyphens. For example, to select all of the series in the data file found between GLR72 and GLRD72 (inventories), use the statement:

```
select glr72--glrd72;
```

To determine the order of series in a CITIBASE data file, run PROC CITIBASE with the OUTCONT= option and print the output data set. (In the tape format database files, the order of series may vary from one release of the CITIBASE database to the next.)

Prefix Specification

To select all names that start with a certain combination of letters, specify the prefix, followed by a colon. For example, all series starting with the prefix IP (industrial production) can be selected by the following statement:

```
select ip: ;
```

Note: Different specifications can be combined in the same SELECT statement. For example:

```
select pzu ip: pw112-pw117;
```

Details

Missing Values

PROC CITIBASE generates missing values when data are not present for a period because the series was not recorded for that period, or when missing values occur within a series.

Control Language for Input Data Files

The CITIBASE database is currently distributed on a nonlabeled tape and on diskettes. If your copy is on a nonlabeled tape rather than on a labeled tape or a disk, you must include a statement in the control language appropriate for your operating system to access the data.

1. **CMS:** You need DCB information for a Fixed Blocked (FB) file on disk if the filemode number is 4. Otherwise, the procedure reads only the first record in each block.

   ```
   FILEDEF fileref TAP1 (RECFM FB LRECL 80 BLKSIZE 8640)
   ```

   In addition, if you are using the SAS System under CMS and the data are stored in an FB file on disk with a filemode number of 4, you must supply DCB information; otherwise, PROC CITIBASE reads only the first record in each block.

2. **OS:** If you are reading an FB file residing on a tape with *xxxxxx* volume number, give the following DD JCL card:

   ```
   //fileref DD UNIT=TAPE,VOL=SER=xxxxxx,LABEL=(1,NL),
   //      DCB=(RECFM=FB,LRECL=80,BLKSIZE=8640)
   ```

3. **VMS:** If you are reading an FB file residing on a tape created under OS, give the following operating system commands followed by a SAS FILENAME statement:

   ```
   qtape/wait/char=6250
   qtape/alloc
   mount/foreign tape: volser/blocksize=8640/recordsize=80/comment="..."
   set magtape/rewind tape:

   filename tape 'tape:' recfm=f lrecl=80 blksize=8640;
   ```

   If the FB CITIBASE file is stored on a disk, you can directly give a FILENAME statement.

4. **VSE:** If you are using the SAS System under VSE, refer to *SAS Companion for the VSE Environment, Version 6, First Edition* before using this procedure.

   The following VSE command can be used to assign a tape drive *xxx* to a CITIBASE tape to be read:

   ```
   //  ASSGN SYS021,xxx;
   ```

For all the other operating sytems not listed previously, such as UNIX based O/S, DOS, and OS/2, no operating system commands are required. However, you should give a FILENAME statement to assign a fileref to the tape format disk file you want to read.

OUT= Data Set

The OUT= data set contains a numeric variable for each of the series selected in a SELECT statement and variables to identify the time periods of the observations. The identifying variables are DATE, YEAR, and (unless TYPE=YEAR) a variable indicating the period within the year. The period variable is named QTR, MONTH, and WEEK depending on the TYPE= option specification.

The variable DATE contains the SAS date value for the first day of the period of the observation. Note that for TYPE=WEEK data, the DATE values are the dates of Sundays, with the periods counted from the week of January 1 of the earliest year of the data set. For example, for TYPE=WEEK and BEGINYR=1969, the DATE of the first observation in the OUT= data set is 29DEC1968, the date of the Sunday of the week of 1JAN1969.

The format of DATE depends on the type of the series selected: YYMMDD2. for yearly, YYQ6. for quarterly, MONYY5. for monthly, and DATE9. for weekly.

The variable names of the series in the OUT= data set are the same as the CITIBASE series codes. The variable labels consist of the first 40 characters of the 72-character CITIBASE series description.

OUTCONT= Data Set

The OUTCONT= data set contains the information read from the series definition records in the input data file (or from the .KEY and .IND files for diskette format databases). This data set contains one observation for each series contained in the database, unless the OUTSELECT option is used, in which case the OUTCONT= data set contains one observation for each selected series.

The OUTCONT= data set contains the following variables:

CITICODE   a character variable containing the CITIBASE series code of the series (same as NAME)

CITIDESC   a character variable containing the 72-character CITIBASE series description

CITINUM   a numeric variable containing the sequence number of the series in the input data file. (CITINUM is 1 for the first series in the file, 2 for the second, and so on.)

DOW   a numeric variable indicating the "ending day of week." This variable is added only if TYPE=WEEK. A value of 1 is used for Mondays (when FREQ=41), 2 for Tuesdays (when FREQ=42), and so on. The DATE variable in the OUT= data set reports the dates of Sundays marking the beginning of the weeks that contain the observation.

FIRSTOBS

a numeric variable containing the SAS date value of the first period for which data are available for the series. FIRSTOBS is computed as

$$\text{INTNX}(\textit{interval}, \text{MDY}(1,1,\text{STARTYR}), \text{STARTPER-1})$$

where *interval* depends on the frequency specified in the TYPE= option. INTNX is a SAS function that returns the date STARTPER-1 intervals later than the date MDY(1,1,STARTYR). (Refer to *SAS Language: Reference, Version 6, First Edition* for more information.)

FREQ

a numeric variable containing the frequency code for the series (series type). For tape format input files, the FREQ codes are 1=quarterly, 2=monthly, 3=yearly, and 4,41–46=weekly. For diskette format databases, FREQ codes are 3=monthly, 4=quarterly, and 5=yearly.

LABEL

a character variable containing the SAS variable label for the series. This is the first 40 characters of the CITIBASE series description (CITIDESC).

LASTOBS

a numeric variable containing the SAS date of the last period for which data are available for the series. LASTOBS is computed as

$$\text{INTNX}(\textit{interval}, \text{FIRSTOBS}, \text{NOBS-1})$$

where *interval* is the value of the TYPE= option.

NAME

a character variable containing the eight-character SAS variable name for the series (same as the first eight characters of the CITICODE)

NDEC

a numeric variable that for tape format files contains the "number of decimal places" of the series, as defined by the Citicorp Database Services. For diskette format files, the value labeled "precision value" in the .IND file documentation is stored in the NDEC variable.

NOBS

a numeric variable containing the number of data values available for the series

OBSERVED

a numeric variable containing the "observed" attribute code for the series. For tape format input files, the codes are 1=averaged, 2=summed, 3=end, 4=averaged, and 5=midperiod. For diskette format files, the value labeled "aggregation value" in the .IND file documentation is stored in the OBSERVED variable.

SELECTED

a numeric variable indicating whether the series was selected for output to the OUT= data set: 0=no, 1=yes. When OUTSELECT is specified, only observations with SELECTED=1 are output.

STARTPER

a numeric variable containing the first period within the STARTYR year for which data are available for the series

STARTYR   a numeric variable containing the first year for which data are available for the series

VARNUM   a numeric variable containing the variable number of the variable in the OUT= data set if the series is selected or a missing value if the series is not selected

Printed Output

The printed output includes summary information about the number of series and records read, number of variables and observations output, and the time range (beginning and ending years) of the observations output. You can suppress the printed output by using the NOPRINT option.

Examples

Example 5.1.   CITIBASE Tape Format Data File

This example demonstrates how to extract Standard & Poor's weekly bond yields (WSP:) and petroleum, refined oil prices (FCPOIL) for the year 1990 from a CITIBASE tape format file CITIDEMO.

```
proc citibase infile=citidemo out=spbonds outcont=desc outselect
          type=week beginyr=90 endyr=1990 noprint;
   select wsp: fcpoil;
run;

title1 'Listing of Series Description Data Set';
proc print data=desc( drop=label );
run;

title1 'Contents of Output Data Set';
proc contents data=spbonds;
run;

title1 'Listing of Output Data Set';
proc print data=spbonds;
run;
```

The OUTCONT= data set is shown in Output 5.1.1. Output 5.1.2 shows printed output produced by PROC CONTENTS for the OUT= data set. A listing of the OUT= data set is shown in Output 5.1.3.

Example 5.1. CITIBASE Tape Format Data File ▫ ▫ ▫ 269

Output 5.1.1. PROC PRINT Listing of the OUTCONT= Data Set

```
                Listing of Series Description Data Set

   OBS    NAME    FREQ   DOW   SELECTED   VARNUM   CITICODE   CITINUM

    1    WSPCA      4     3       1          4      WSPCA        37
    2    WSPUA      4     3       1          5      WSPUA        38
    3    WSPIA      4     3       1          6      WSPIA        39
    4    WSPGLT     4     3       1          7      WSPGLT       40
    5    FCPOIL     4     5       1          8      FCPOIL       41

   OBS                         CITIDESC

    1    STANDARD & POOR'S WEEKLY BOND YIELD: COMPOSITE, A
    2    STANDARD & POOR'S WEEKLY BOND YIELD: UTILITIES, A
    3    STANDARD & POOR'S WEEKLY BOND YIELD:INDUSTRIALS, A
    4    STANDARD & POOR;S WEEKLY BOND YIELD: GOV'T LONG TERM
    5    PETROLEUM, REFINED OIL PRICES: FUEL OIL, NO. 2 NY GAL.

   OBS   STARTYR   STARTPER   NOBS   OBSERVED   NDEC   FIRSTOBS    LASTOBS

    1     1986        1        271       1        2    29DEC1985  03MAR1991
    2     1986        1        271       1        2    29DEC1985  03MAR1991
    3     1986        1        271       1        2    29DEC1985  03MAR1991
    4     1986        1        271       1        2    29DEC1985  03MAR1991
    5     1986        1        271       1        4    29DEC1985  03MAR1991
```

Output 5.1.2. PROC CONTENTS Output for the OUT= Data Set

```
                  Contents of Output Data Set
                     CONTENTS PROCEDURE

Data Set Name: WORK.SPBONDS            Observations:        52
Member Type:   DATA                    Variables:           8
Engine:        V608                    Indexes:             0
Created:       17:35 Thursday, Oct 22, 1992   Observation Length:  36
Last Modified: 17:35 Thursday, Oct 22, 1992   Deleted Observations: 0
Protection:                            Compressed:          NO
Data Set Type:                         Sorted:              NO
Label:         CITIBASE Weekly Series.

           -----Engine/Host Dependent Information-----

            Data Set Page Size:         4096
            Number of Data Set Pages:   1
            File Format:                607
            First Data Page:            1
            Max Obs per Page:           112
            Obs in First Data Page:     52
            FILETYPE:                   REGULAR

        -----Alphabetic List of Variables and Attributes-----

# Variable Type Len Pos Format Label
-------------------------------------------------------------------------
3 DATE     Num   4   7 DATE9. Date of Observation
8 FCPOIL   Num   5  31        PETROLEUM, REFINED OIL PRICES: FUEL OIL,
2 WEEK     Num   3   4        Period of Observation within Year
4 WSPCA    Num   5  11        STANDARD & POOR'S WEEKLY BOND YIELD: COM
7 WSPGLT   Num   5  26        STANDARD & POOR;S WEEKLY BOND YIELD: GOV
6 WSPIA    Num   5  21        STANDARD & POOR'S WEEKLY BOND YIELD:INDU
5 WSPUA    Num   5  16        STANDARD & POOR'S WEEKLY BOND YIELD: UTI
1 YEAR     Num   4   0        Year of Observation
```

Output 5.1.3.   PROC PRINT Listing of the OUT= Data Set

```
                        Listing of Output Data Set

OBS   YEAR   WEEK      DATE    WSPCA    WSPUA    WSPIA    WSPGLT    FCPOIL

  1   1990     1   31DEC1989   9.4700   9.3900   9.5500   8.22000   0.91850
  2   1990     2   07JAN1990   9.5300   9.4400   9.6100   8.27000   0.79750
  3   1990     3   14JAN1990   9.6500   9.5600   9.7400   8.42000   0.64700
  4   1990     4   21JAN1990   9.7800   9.6900   9.8700   8.60000   0.60000
  5   1990     5   28JAN1990   9.9100   9.8200  10.0100   8.66000   0.59500
  6   1990     6   04FEB1990   9.9700   9.8700  10.0600   8.77000   0.54900
  7   1990     7   11FEB1990   9.7900   9.7000   9.8900   8.65000   0.57600
  8   1990     8   18FEB1990  10.0100   9.9200  10.1000   8.92000   0.58350
  9   1990     9   25FEB1990   9.9000   9.7800  10.0300   8.77000   0.57000
 10   1990    10   04MAR1990  10.0400   9.9100  10.1700   8.84000   0.56000
 11   1990    11   11MAR1990  10.0800   9.9600  10.2100   8.88000   0.58350
 12   1990    12   18MAR1990   9.9500   9.8400  10.0700   8.74000   0.58100
 13   1990    13   25MAR1990   9.8600   9.7400   9.9900   8.71000   0.59000
 14   1990    14   01APR1990   9.9900   9.8500  10.1200   8.78000   0.59100
 15   1990    15   08APR1990   9.9400   9.8200  10.0700   8.83000   0.62500
 16   1990    16   15APR1990  10.1600  10.0300  10.2800   9.11000   0.57750
 17   1990    17   22APR1990  10.3100  10.1900  10.4000   9.23000   0.56650
 18   1990    18   29APR1990  10.3600  10.2100  10.5000   9.26000   0.55500
 19   1990    19   06MAY1990  10.1900  10.0600  10.3200   9.09000   0.55100
 20   1990    20   13MAY1990   9.9800   9.8600  10.0900   8.89000   0.53400
 21   1990    21   20MAY1990   9.9300   9.8100  10.0400   8.82000   0.50000
 22   1990    22   27MAY1990   9.9400   9.8100  10.0600   8.84000   0.49000
 23   1990    23   03JUN1990   9.7800   9.6600   9.9100   8.67000   0.48000
 24   1990    24   10JUN1990   9.7700   9.6600   9.8700   8.63000   0.48520
 25   1990    25   17JUN1990   9.8500   9.7500   9.9400   8.77000   0.48750
 26   1990    26   24JUN1990   9.8400   9.7700   9.9200   8.73000   0.48500
 27   1990    27   01JUL1990   9.8000   9.7400   9.8600   8.63000   0.48100
 28   1990    28   08JUL1990   9.9100   9.8500   9.9600   8.80000   0.53000
 29   1990    29   15JUL1990   9.9100   9.8500   9.9600   8.77000   0.55000
 30   1990    30   22JUL1990   9.9300   9.8800   9.9800   8.96700   0.65000
 31   1990    31   29JUL1990   9.7700   9.7100   9.8200   8.53000   0.65350
 32   1990    32   05AUG1990  10.2200  10.1700  10.2700   9.07000   0.71500
 33   1990    33   12AUG1990  10.1500  10.1000  10.2100   8.98000   0.79350
 34   1990    34   19AUG1990  10.3600  10.3000  10.4100   9.24000   0.89750
 35   1990    35   26AUG1990  10.3700  10.3000  10.4300   9.16000   0.74350
 36   1990    36   02SEP1990  10.3300  10.2300  10.4200   9.18000   0.82500
 37   1990    37   09SEP1990  10.2700  10.1900  10.3400   9.15000   0.81000
 38   1990    38   16SEP1990  10.3700  10.3000  10.4400   9.20000   0.96000
 39   1990    39   23SEP1990  10.4300  10.3600  10.5000   9.32000   1.04000
 40   1990    40   30SEP1990  10.1700  10.1000  10.2400   9.02000   1.01000
 41   1990    41   07OCT1990  10.3100  10.2400  10.3800   9.20000   1.04000
 42   1990    42   14OCT1990  10.2100  10.1400  10.2800   9.07000   0.87000
 43   1990    43   21OCT1990  10.0900  10.0200  10.1600   8.97000   0.86750
 44   1990    44   28OCT1990  10.1200  10.0400  10.1900   9.01000   0.85650
 45   1990    45   04NOV1990  10.0000   9.8800  10.1100   8.88000   0.89000
 46   1990    46   11NOV1990   9.9100   9.8100  10.0100   8.67000   0.83800
 47   1990    47   18NOV1990   9.7900   9.6900   9.8900   8.63000   0.83800
 48   1990    48   25NOV1990   9.7700   9.6600   9.8700   8.62000   0.85350
 49   1990    49   02DEC1990   9.7500   9.6400   9.8500   8.47000   0.81100
 50   1990    50   09DEC1990   9.5900   9.4800   9.6900   8.22000   0.75100
 51   1990    51   16DEC1990   9.6200   9.5100   9.7200   8.35000   0.78750
 52   1990    52   23DEC1990   9.7000   9.6000   9.8000   8.48000   0.79450
```

Example 5.2.   CITIBASE Diskette Format Database

This example demonstrates how to extract Personal Consumption Expenditures series from a diskette format database BASE.

The following initial run of PROC CITIBASE produces a listing of quarterly series contained in the BASE database:

Example 5.2.   CITIBASE Diskette Format Database   □ □ □   271

```
proc citibase dbname="base" type=qtr
             outcont=qtrvars outselect noprint;
run;

title1 'Quarterly Series Contained in the BASE Database';
proc print data=qtrvars( drop=label );
run;
```

Output 5.2.1.   PROC PRINT Listing of the OUTCONT= Data Set

```
                Quarterly Series Contained in the BASE Database

  OBS  NAME     FREQ     SELECTED     VARNUM     CITICODE     CITINUM

    1  BPB        4          1           4          BPB          6
    2  BPCR       4          1           5          BPCR         7
    3  GC         4          1           6          GC           8
    4  GCQ        4          1           7          GCQ          9
    5  GCD        4          1           8          GCD         10
    6  GCDQ       4          1           9          GCDQ        11
    7  GD         4          1          10          GD          12
    8  GDP        4          1          11          GDP         13
    9  GDPQ       4          1          12          GDPQ        14
   10  GNP        4          1          13          GNP         15
   11  GNPQ       4          1          14          GNPQ        16
   12  GY         4          1          15          GY          17
   13  GYD        4          1          16          GYD         18
   14  GYDQ       4          1          17          GYDQ        19

  OBS  CITIDESC

    1  BAL OF P'MENT:BALANCE ON MERCHANDISE TRADE,MIL.$ SA
    2  BAL OF P'MENT:BAL ON CURRENT A/C(INC REINV EARN INC AFFIL)MIL$SA
    3  PERSONAL CONSUMPTION EXPENDITURES
    4  PERSONAL CONSUMPTION EXPENDITURES (BIL. 1987$)(T.1.2)
    5  PERSONAL CONS. EXPENDITURES, DURABLE GOODS
    6  PERSONAL CONSUMPTION EXPENDITURES:DUR GOODS(BIL. 1987$)(T.1.2)
    7  IMPLICIT PR DEFLATOR: GROSS NATIONAL PRODUCT
    8  GROSS DOMESTIC PRODUCT (BIL.$,SAAR)(T.1.1)
    9  GROSS DOMESTIC PRODUCT (BIL. 1987$)(T.1.2)
   10  GROSS NATIONAL PRODUCT, TOTAL
   11  GROSS NATIONAL PRODUCT (BILL.1987$)(T1.10)
   12  NATIONAL INCOME, TOTAL
   13  PERSN'L INCOME: DISPOSABLE PERSONAL INCOME
   14  DISPOSABLE PERSONAL INCOME: TOTAL (BIL.87$)(T.2.1)

  OBS  STARTYR   STARTPER   NOBS   OBSERVED   NDEC   FIRSTOBS    LASTOBS

    1   1980         1       47        2        0   01JAN1980   01JUL1991
    2   1980         1       47        2        0   01JAN1980   01JUL1991
    3   1980         1       48        1        1   01JAN1980   01OCT1991
    4   1980         1       48        1        0   01JAN1980   01OCT1991
    5   1980         1       48        1        1   01JAN1980   01OCT1991
    6   1980         1       48        1        0   01JAN1980   01OCT1991
    7   1980         1       47        1        1   01JAN1980   01JUL1991
    8   1980         1       48        1        0   01JAN1980   01OCT1991
    9   1980         1       48        1        0   01JAN1980   01OCT1991
   10   1980         1       47        1        1   01JAN1980   01JUL1991
   11   1980         1       47        1        0   01JAN1980   01JUL1991
   12   1980         1       47        1        1   01JAN1980   01JUL1991
   13   1980         1       48        3        1   01JAN1980   01OCT1991
   14   1980         1       48        1        0   01JAN1980   01OCT1991
```

In Output 5.2.1, you can see that all the Personal Consumption Expenditures series begin with GC. Therefore, these series starting from year 1987 can be extracted by the following statements:

```
proc citibase dbname="base" out=pce type=qtr beginyr=87;
   select gc:;
run;

title1 'Personal Consumption Expenditures';
proc print data=pce noobs;
run;
```

The same series could also have been selected by the following order range specification:

```
select gc--gcdq;
```

or by the following alphabetic range specification:

```
select gc-gcdq;
```

Output 5.2.2. Printed Output Produced by PROC CITIBASE

```
                    CITIBASE Procedure

                     Input Summary

        Input Database: base.
        First Year Read: 1980.
        Last Year Read:   1991.
        Total Number of Series Read: 37.
        Total Input Records Read: 266.

        Beginning Year Output: 1987.
        Ending Year Output:    1991.
        Periods Per Year: 4.
        Number of Selected Variables:    4.
        Number of Observations Output:   20.
```

Output 5.2.3. PROC PRINT Listing of the OUT= Data Set

```
            Personal Consumption Expenditures
YEAR   QTR    DATE      GC       GCQ       GCD       GCDQ

1987    1    1987Q1   2962.80   3011.50   384.900   389.400
1987    2    1987Q2   3030.10   3046.80   401.400   403.100
1987    3    1987Q3   3091.40   3075.80   419.700   417.700
1987    4    1987Q4   3124.60   3074.70   408.800   404.700
1988    1    1988Q1   3199.10   3128.20   428.800   425.100
1988    2    1988Q2   3260.50   3147.80   433.100   426.900
1988    3    1988Q3   3326.60   3170.60   433.500   423.800
1988    4    1988Q4   3398.20   3202.90   452.900   439.200
1989    1    1989Q1   3436.50   3200.90   449.400   433.600
1989    2    1989Q2   3490.60   3208.60   457.200   439.900
1989    3    1989Q3   3551.70   3241.10   474.500   454.300
1989    4    1989Q4   3592.80   3241.60   458.000   435.600
1990    1    1990Q1   3667.30   3258.80   479.900   452.700
1990    2    1990Q2   3706.00   3258.60   464.600   438.700
1990    3    1990Q3   3785.20   3281.20   467.100   440.300
1990    4    1990Q4   3812.00   3251.80   451.900   424.000
1991    1    1991Q1   3827.70   3241.10   440.700   410.800
1991    2    1991Q2   3868.50   3252.40   440.000   408.900
1991    3    1991Q3   3916.40   3271.20   452.900   418.300
1991    4    1991Q4   3934.40   3262.20   447.200   412.100
```

References

Citibank(1978), *CITIBASE: Citibank Economic Database (Machine-Readable Magnetic Data File), 1946–Present*, New York, NY.

Citibank (1990), *CITIBASE Directory*, New York, NY.

Citibank(1978), *CITIBASE-WEEKLY: Citibank Economic Database (Machine-Readable Magnetic Data File), 1975–Present*, New York, NY.

Chapter 6
The COMPUTAB Procedure

Chapter Table of Contents

Chapter 6
The COMPUTAB Procedure

Overview

The COMPUTAB procedure (**COMPU**ting and **TAB**ular reporting) produces tabular reports generated using a programmable data table.

The COMPUTAB procedure is especially useful when you need both the power of a programmable spreadsheet and a report generation system, but you want to set up a program to run in a batch mode and generate routine reports.

With PROC COMPUTAB, you can select a subset of observations from the input data set, define the format of a table, operate on its row and column values, and create new columns and rows. Access to individual table values is available when needed.

The COMPUTAB procedure can tailor reports to almost any desired specification and provide consolidation reports over summarization variables. The generated report values can be stored in an output data set. It is especially useful in creating tabular reports such as income statements, balance sheets, and other row and column reports.

Getting Started

The following example shows the different types of reports that can be generated by PROC COMPUTAB.

Suppose a company has monthly expense data on three of its divisions and wants to produce the year-to-date expense report shown in Figure 6.1. This section starts out with the default report produced by the COMPUTAB procedure and modifies it until the desired report is achieved.

```
                   Year to Date Expenses

                       Division  Division  Division        All
                              A         B         C  Divisions
Travel Expenses within U.S.    18700    211000     12800   $242,500
Advertising                    18500    176000     34500   $229,000
Permanent Staff Salaries      186000   1270000    201000 $1,657,000
Benefits Including Insurance    3900     11100     17500    $32,500
                            ========  ========  ======== ==========
Total                         227100   1668100    265800 $2,161,000
```

Figure 6.1. Year to Date Expense Report

Producing a Simple Report

Without any specifications, the COMPUTAB procedure transposes and prints the input data set. The variables in the input data set become rows in the report, and the observations in the input data set become columns. The variable names are used as the row titles. The column headings default to COL1 through COLn. For example, the following input data set contains the monthly expenses reported by different divisions of the company:

```
data report;
    input compdiv $ date:date7. salary travel insure advrtise;
    format date date7.;
    label travel   = 'Travel Expenses within U.S.'
          advrtise = 'Advertising'
          salary   = 'Permanent Staff Salaries'
          insure   = 'Benefits Including Insurance';
    cards;
A 31JAN89 95000 10500  2000 6500
B 31JAN89 668000 112000 5600 90000
C 31JAN89 105000 6800 9000 18500
A 28FEB89 91000 8200 1900 12000
B 28FEB89 602000 99000 5500 86000
C 28FEB89 96000 6000 8500 16000
;
```

You can get a listing of the data set by using the PRINT procedure, as follows:

```
title 'Listing of Monthly Divisional Expense Data';
proc print data=report;
run;
```

```
              Listing of Monthly Divisional Expense Data

    OBS     COMPDIV      DATE      SALARY     TRAVEL     INSURE     ADVRTISE

     1         A       31JAN89     95000      10500      2000        6500
     2         B       31JAN89    668000     112000      5600       90000
     3         C       31JAN89    105000       6800      9000       18500
     4         A       28FEB89     91000       8200      1900       12000
     5         B       28FEB89    602000      99000      5500       86000
     6         C       28FEB89     96000       6000      8500       16000
```

Figure 6.2. Listing of Data Set by PROC PRINT

To get a simple, transposed report of the same data set, use the following PROC COMPUTAB statement:

```
title 'Monthly Divisional Expense Report';
proc computab data=report;
run;
```

```
                   Monthly Divisional Expense Report
             COL1       COL2       COL3       COL4       COL5       COL6

 COMPDIV        A          B          C          A          B          C
 DATE       31JAN89    31JAN89    31JAN89    28FEB89    28FEB89    28FEB89
 SALARY    95000.00  668000.00  105000.00   91000.00  602000.00   96000.00
 TRAVEL    10500.00  112000.00    6800.00    8200.00   99000.00    6000.00
 INSURE     2000.00    5600.00    9000.00    1900.00    5500.00    8500.00
 ADVRTISE   6500.00   90000.00   18500.00   12000.00   86000.00   16000.00
```

Figure 6.3. Listing of Data Set by PROC COMPUTAB

Using PROC COMPUTAB

The COMPUTAB procedure is best understood by examining the following features:

- definition of the report layout with ROWS and COLUMNS statements
- input block
- row blocks
- column blocks

PROC COMPUTAB builds a table according to the specifications in the ROWS and COLUMNS statements. Row names and column names define the rows and columns of the table. Options in the ROWS and COLUMNS statements control titles, spacing, and formatting.

The input block places input observations into the appropriate columns of the report. It consists of programming statements used to select observations to be included in the report, to determine the column into which the observation should be placed, and to calculate row and column values that are not in the input data set.

Row blocks and column blocks perform operations on the values of rows and columns of the report after the input block has executed. Row blocks are a block of programming statements labeled ROW*xxxxx*: that create or modify row values; column blocks are a block of programming statements labeled COL*xxxxx*: that create or modify column values. Row and column blocks can make multiple passes through the report for final calculations.

For most reports, these features are sufficient. More complicated applications may require knowledge of the program data vector and the COMPUTAB data table. These topics are discussed in the section "Details" later in this chapter.

Defining Report Layout

ROWS and COLUMNS statements define the rows and columns of the report. The order of row and column names on these statements determines the order of rows and columns in the report. Additional ROWS and COLUMNS statements can be used to specify row and column formatting options.

The following statements select and order the variables from the input data set and produce the report in Figure 6.4:

```
proc computab data=report;
   rows travel advrtise salary insure;
run;
```

	COL1	COL2	COL3	COL4	COL5	COL6
TRAVEL	10500.00	112000.00	6800.00	8200.00	99000.00	6000.00
ADVRTISE	6500.00	90000.00	18500.00	12000.00	86000.00	16000.00
SALARY	95000.00	668000.00	105000.00	91000.00	602000.00	96000.00
INSURE	2000.00	5600.00	9000.00	1900.00	5500.00	8500.00

Figure 6.4. Report Produced Using a ROWS Statement

When a COLUMNS statement is not specified, each observation becomes a new column. If you use a COLUMNS statement, you must specify to which column each observation belongs by using program statements for column selection. When more than one observation is selected for the same column, values are summed.

The following statements produce Figure 6.5:

```
proc computab data= report;
   rows travel advrtise salary insure;
   columns a b c;
   *----select column for company division,
        based on value of compdiv----*;
   a = compdiv = 'A';
   b = compdiv = 'B';
   c = compdiv = 'C';
run;
```

The statement A=COMPDIV='A'; illustrates the use of logical operators as a selection technique. If COMPDIV='A', then the current observation is added to the A column. Refer to *SAS Language: Reference, Version 6, First Edition* for more information on logical operators.

	A	B	C
TRAVEL	18700.00	211000.00	12800.00
ADVRTISE	18500.00	176000.00	34500.00
SALARY	186000.00	1270000.0	201000.00
INSURE	3900.00	11100.00	17500.00

Figure 6.5. Report Produced Using ROWS and COLUMNS Statements

Adding Computed Rows and Columns

In addition to the variables and observations in the input data set, you can create additional rows or columns by using SAS programming statements in PROC COMPUTAB. You can

- modify input data and select columns in the input block
- create or modify columns in column blocks
- create or modify rows in row blocks

The following statements add one computed row (SUM) and one computed column (TOTAL) to the report in Figure 6.5. In the input block the logical operators indicate the observations corresponding to each column of the report. After the input block reads in the values from the input data set, the column block creates the column variable TOTAL by summing the columns A, B, and C. The additional row variable, SUM, is calculated as the sum of the other rows. The result is shown in Figure 6.6.

```
proc computab data= report;
   rows travel advrtise salary insure sum;
   columns a b c total;
   a = compdiv = 'A';
   b = compdiv = 'B';
   c = compdiv = 'C';
   colblk: total = a + b + c;
   rowblk: sum   = travel + advrtise + salary + insure;
run;
```

	A	B	C	TOTAL
TRAVEL	18700.00	211000.00	12800.00	242500.00
ADVRTISE	18500.00	176000.00	34500.00	229000.00
SALARY	186000.00	1270000.0	201000.00	1657000.0
INSURE	3900.00	11100.00	17500.00	32500.00
SUM	227100.00	1668100.0	265800.00	2161000.0

Figure 6.6.   Report Produced Using Row and Column Blocks

Enhancing the Report

To enhance the appearance of the final report, you can use

• TITLE and LABEL statements
• column headings
• row titles
• row and column spacing control
• overlining and underlining
• formats

The following example enhances the report in the previous example. The enhanced report is shown in Figure 6.7.

The TITLE statement assigns the report title. The column headings in Figure 6.7 (Division A, Division B, and Division C) are assigned in the first COLUMNS statement by 'Division' _name_ specification. The second COLUMNS statement assigns the column heading ('All' 'Divisions'), sets the spacing (+4), and formats the values in the TOTAL column.

Similarly, the first ROWS statement uses previously assigned variable labels for row labels by specifying the _LABEL_ option. The DUL option in the second ROWS statement double underlines the INSURE row. The third ROWS statement assigns the row label TOTAL to the SUM row.

```
      title 'Year to Date Expenses';

  proc computab cwidth=8 cdec=0;

      columns a  b  c / 'Division' _name_;
      columns total / 'All' 'Divisions' +4 f=dollar10.0;

      rows travel advrtise salary insure / _label_;
      rows insure / dul;
      rows sum / 'Total';

      a = compdiv = 'A';
      b = compdiv = 'B';
      c = compdiv = 'C';

      colblk: total = a + b + c;
      rowblk: sum   = travel + advrtise + salary + insure;
  run;
```

```
                    Year to Date Expenses

                         Division  Division  Division        All
                            A         B         C       Divisions
Travel Expenses within U.S.   18700    211000     12800    $242,500
Advertising                   18500    176000     34500    $229,000
Permanent Staff Salaries     186000   1270000    201000  $1,657,000
Benefits Including Insurance   3900     11100     17500     $32,500
                           ========  ========  ========  ==========
Total                        227100   1668100    265800  $2,161,000
```

Figure 6.7. Report Produced by PROC COMPUTAB Using Enhancements

Syntax

The following statements are used with the COMPUTAB procedure:

> **PROC COMPUTAB** *options*;
>   **BY** *variables*;
>   **COLUMNS** *names* / *options*;
>   **ROWS** *names* / *options*;
>   **CELL** *names* / **FORMAT**= *format*;
>   **INIT** *anchor-name* [*locator-name*] *values* [*locator-name values*];
>   *programming statements*;
>   **SUMBY** *variables*;

The PROC COMPUTAB statement is the only required statement. The COLUMNS, ROWS, and CELL statements define the COMPUTAB table. The INIT statement initializes the COMPUTAB table values. Programming statements process COMPUTAB table values. The BY and SUMBY statements provide BY-group processing and consolidation (roll up) tables.

Functional Summary

COMPUTAB procedure statements and options are summarized in the following table:

Description	Statement	Option
Statements		
specify BY-group processing	BY	
specify the format for printing a particular cell	CELL	
define columns of the report	COLUMNS	
initialize values in the COMPUTAB data table	INIT	
define rows of the report	ROWS	
produce consolidation tables	SUMBY	
Data Set Options		
specify the input data set	COMPUTAB	DATA=
specify an output data set	COMPUTAB	OUT=
Input Options		
specify a value to use when testing for 0	COMPUTAB	FUZZ=
initialize the data table to missing	COMPUTAB	INITMISS
prevent the transposition of the input data set	COMPUTAB	NOTRANS
Printing Control Options		
suppress printing of the listed columns	COLUMNS	NOPRINT
suppress all printed output	COMPUTAB	NOPRINT
suppress printing of the listed rows	ROWS	NOPRINT
suppress columns with all 0 or missing values	COLUMNS	NOZERO
suppress rows with all 0 or missing values	ROWS	NOZERO
list option values	COMPUTAB	OPTIONS
overprint titles, values, overlining, and under- lining associated with listed rows	ROWS	OVERPRINT
print only consolidation tables	COMPUTAB	SUMONLY
Report Formatting Options		
specify number of decimal places to print	COMPUTAB	CDEC=
specify number of spaces between columns	COMPUTAB	CSPACE=
specify column width for the report	COMPUTAB	CWIDTH=
overlines the listed rows with double lines	ROWS	DOL
underline the listed rows with double lines	ROWS	DUL
specify a format for printing the cell values	CELL	FORMAT=

Description	Statement	Option
specify a format for printing column values	COLUMNS	FORMAT=
specify a format for printing the row values	ROWS	FORMAT=
left align the column headings	COLUMNS	LJC
left-justify character rows in each column	ROWS	LJC
specify indentation from the margin	ROWS	+n
suppress printing of row titles on later pages	COMPUTAB	NORTR
overlines the listed rows with a single line	ROWS	OL
starts a new page before printing the listed rows	ROWS	_PAGE_
specify number of spaces before row titles	COMPUTAB	RTS=
print a blank row	ROWS	SKIP
underline the listed rows with a single line	ROWS	UL
specify text to print if column is 0 or missing	COLUMNS	ZERO=
specify text to print if row is 0 or missing	ROWS	ZERO=

Row and Column Type Options

Description	Statement	Option
specify that columns contain character data	COLUMNS	CHAR
specify that rows contain character data	ROWS	CHAR

Options for Column Headings

Description	Statement	Option
specify literal column headings	COLUMNS	'column heading'
use variable labels in column headings	COLUMNS	_LABEL_
specify a master title centered over columns	COLUMNS	MTITLE=
use column names in column headings	COLUMNS	_NAME_

Options for Row Titling

Description	Statement	Option
use labels in row titles	ROWS	_LABEL_
use row names in row titles	ROWS	_NAME_
specify literal row titles	ROWS	'row title'

PROC COMPUTAB Statement

PROC COMPUTAB *options*;

The following options can be used in the PROC COMPUTAB statement:

Input Options

DATA= *SAS-data-set*

names the SAS data set containing the input data. If this option is not specified, the last created data set is used. If you are not reading a data set, use DATA=_NULL_.

FUZZ= *value*

specifies the criterion to use when testing for 0. If a number is within the FUZZ= value of 0, the number is set to 0.

INITMISS

initializes the COMPUTAB data table to missing rather than to 0. The COMPUTAB data table is discussed further in the section "Details" later in this chapter.

NOTRANSPOSE
NOTRANS

prevents the transposition of the input data set in building the COMPUTAB report tables. The NOTRANS option causes input data set variables to appear among the columns of the report rather than among the rows.

Report Formatting Options

The formatting options specify default values. Many of the formatting options can be modified for specific columns in COLUMNS statements and for rows in ROWS statements.

CDEC= *d*

specifies the default number of decimal places for printing. The default is CDEC=2. See the FORMAT= option in the sections on COLUMN, ROWS, and CELL statements later in this chapter.

CSPACE= *n*

specifies the default number of spaces to insert between columns. The value of the CSPACE= option is used as the default value for the +n option in the COLUMNS statement. The default is CSPACE=2.

CWIDTH= *w*

specifies a default column width for the report. The default is CWIDTH=9. The width must be in the range of 1-32.

NORTR

suppresses the printing of row titles on each page. The NORTR (no row-title repeat) option is useful to suppress row titles when report pages are to be joined together in a larger report.

RTS= *n*

specifies the default number of spaces to be inserted before row titles when row titles appear after the first printed column. The default row-title spacing is RTS=2.

Output Options

NOPRINT

suppresses all printed output. Use the NOPRINT option with the OUT= option to produce an output data set but no printed reports.

OPTIONS

lists PROC COMPUTAB option values. The option values appear on a separate page preceding the procedure's normal output.

OUT= *SAS-data-set*

names the SAS data set to contain the output data. See the section "Details" for a description of the structure of the output data set.

SUMONLY

suppresses printing of detailed reports. When the SUMONLY option is used, PROC COMPUTAB generates and prints only consolidation tables as specified in the SUMBY statement.

COLUMNS Statement

COLUMNS *column-list / options*;

COLUMNS statements define the columns of the report. The COLUMNS statement can be abbreviated COLUMN, COLS, or COL.

The specified column names must be valid SAS names. Abbreviated lists, as described in *SAS Language: Reference*, can also be used.

You can use as many COLUMNS statements as you need. A COLUMNS statement can describe more than one column, and one column of the report can be described with several different COLUMNS statements. The order of the columns on the report is determined by the order of appearance of column names in COLUMNS statements. The first occurrence of the name determines where in the sequence of columns a particular column is located.

The following options can be used in the COLUMNS statement:

Option for Column Type

CHAR

indicates that the columns contain character data.

Options for Column Headings

You can specify as many lines of column headings as needed. If no options are specified, the column names from the COLUMNS statement are used as column headings. Any or all of the following options can be used in a column heading:

'*column heading*'

specifies that the characters enclosed in quotes is to be used in the column heading for the variable or variables listed in the COLUMNS statement. Each quoted string appears on a separate line of the heading.

LABEL

uses labels, if provided, in the heading for the column or columns listed in the COLUMNS statement. If a label has not been provided, the name of the column is used. Refer to *SAS Language: Reference* for information on the LABEL statement.

MTITLE= '*text*'

specifies that the string of characters enclosed in quotes is a master title to be centered over all the columns listed in the COLUMNS statement. The list of columns must be consecutive. Special characters ('+', '*', '=', and so forth) placed on either side of the text expand to fill the space. The MTITLE= option can be abbreviated M=.

NAME

uses column names in column headings for the columns listed in the COLUMNS statement. This option allows headings ('*text*') and names to be combined in a heading.

Options for Column Print Control

+*n*

inserts *n* spaces before each column listed in the COLUMNS statement. The default spacing is given by the CSPACE= option in the PROC COMPUTAB statement.

NOPRINT

suppresses printing of columns listed in the COLUMNS statement. This option enables you to create columns to be used for intermediate calculations without having those columns printed.

NOZERO

suppresses printing of columns when all the values in a column are 0 or missing. Numbers within the FUZZ= value of 0 are treated as 0.

PAGE

starts a new page of the report before printing each of the columns in the list that follows.

TITLES

prints row titles before each column in the list. The _TITLES_ option can be abbreviated as _TITLE_.

Options for Column Formatting

Column formats override row formats for particular table cells only when the input data set is not transposed (when the NOTRANS option is specified).

FORMAT= *format*

specifies a format for printing the values of the columns listed in the COLUMNS statement. The FORMAT= option can be abbreviated F=.

LJC

left-justifies the column headings for the columns listed. By default, columns are right-justified. When the LJC (left-justify character) option is used, any character row values in the column are also left-justified rather than right-justified.

ZERO= '*text*'

substitutes *text* when the value in the column is 0 or missing.

ROWS Statement

ROWS *row-list | options*;

ROWS statements define the rows of the report. The ROWS statement can be abbreviated ROW.

The specified row names must be valid SAS names. Abbreviated lists, as described in *SAS Language: Reference*, can also be used.

You can use as many ROWS statements as you need. A ROWS statement can describe more than one row, and one row of the report can be described with several different ROWS statements. The order of the rows in the report is determined by the order of appearance of row names in ROWS statements. The first occurrence of the name determines where the row is located.

The following options can be used in the ROWS statement:

Option for Row Type
CHAR

indicates that the rows contain character data.

Options for Row Titling

You can specify as many lines of row titles as needed. If no options are specified, the names from the ROWS statement are used as row titles. Any or all of the following options can be used in a row title:

LABEL

uses labels as row titles for the row or rows listed in the ROWS statement. If a label is not provided, the name of the row is substituted. Refer to *SAS Language: Reference* for more information on the LABEL statement.

NAME

uses row names in row titles for the row or rows listed in the ROWS statement.

'*row title*'

specifies that the string of characters enclosed in quotes is to be used in the row title for the row or rows listed in the ROWS statement. Each quoted string appears on a separate line of the heading.

Options for Row Print Control

+*n*

indents *n* spaces from the margin for the rows in the ROWS statement.

DOL

overlines the rows listed in the ROWS statement with double lines. Overlines are printed on the line before any row titles or data for the row.

DUL

underlines the rows listed in the ROWS statement with double lines. Underlines are printed on the line after the data for the row. A row can have both an underline and an overline option.

NOPRINT

suppresses printing of the rows listed in the ROWS statement. This option enables you to create rows to be used for intermediate calculations without having those rows printed.

NOZERO

suppresses the printing of a row when all the values are 0 or missing.

OL

overlines the rows listed in the ROWS statement with a single line. Overlines are printed on the line before any row titles or data for the row.

OVERPRINT

overprints titles, values, overlining, and underlining associated with rows listed in the ROWS statement. The OVERPRINT option can be abbreviated OVP. This option is valid only when the system option OVP is in effect. Refer to *SAS Language: Reference* for more information about the OVP option.

PAGE

starts a new page of the report before printing these rows.

SKIP

prints a blank line after the data lines for these rows.

UL

underlines the rows listed in the ROWS statement with a single line. Underlines are printed on the line after the data for the row. A row can have both an underline and an overline option.

Options for Row Formatting

Row formatting options take precedence over column-formatting options when the input data set is transposed. Row print width can never be wider than column width. Character values are truncated on the right.

FORMAT= *format*

specifies a format for printing the values of the rows listed in the ROWS statement. The FORMAT= option can be abbreviated as F=.

LJC

left-justifies character rows in each column.

ZERO= *'text'*

substitutes *text* when the value in the row is 0 or missing.

CELL Statement

CELL *cell_names* / **FORMAT**= *format*;

The CELL statement specifies the format for printing a particular cell in the COMPUTAB data table. Cell variable names are compound SAS names of the form *name1.name2*, where *name1* is the name of a row variable and *name2* is the name of a column variable. Formats specified with the FORMAT= option in CELL statements override formats specified in ROWS and COLUMNS statements.

INIT Statement

INIT *anchor-name* [*locator-name*] *values* [*locator-name values*];

The INIT statement initializes values in the COMPUTAB data table at the beginning of each execution of the procedure and at the beginning of each BY group if a BY statement is present.

The INIT statement in the COMPUTAB procedure is similar in function to the RETAIN statement in the DATA step, which initializes values in the program data vector. The INIT statement can be used at any point after the variable to which it refers has been defined in COLUMNS or ROWS statements. Each INIT statement initializes one row or column. Any number of INIT statements can be used.

The first term after the keyword INIT, *anchor-name*, anchors initialization to a row or column. If *anchor-name* is a row name, then all *locator-name* values in the statement are columns of that row. If *anchor-name* is a column name, then all *locator-name* values in the statement are rows of that column.

The following terms appear in the INIT statement:

anchor-name   names the row or column in which values are to be initialized. This term is required.

locator-name   identifies the starting column in the row (or starting row in the column) into which values are to be placed. For example, in a table with a row SALES and a column for each month of the year, the following statement initializes values for columns JAN, FEB, and JUN:

```
init sales jan 500 feb 600 jun 800;
```

If you do not specify *locator-name* values, the first value is placed into the first row or column, the second value into the second row or column, and so on. For example,

```
init sales 500 600 450;
```

assigns 500 to column JAN, 600 to FEB, and 450 to MAR.

+n   specifies the number of columns in a row (or rows in a column) that
            are to be skipped when initializing values. For example, the state-
            ment

```
init sales jan 500 +5 900;
```

assigns 500 to JAN and 900 to JUL.

n*value   assigns *value* to n columns in the row (or rows in the column). For
            example, the statement

```
init sales jan 6*500 jul 6*1000;
```

and the statement

```
init sales 6*500 6*1000;
```

both assign 500 to columns JAN through JUN and 1000 to JUL
through DEC.

Programming Statements

You can use most SAS programming statements the same way you use them in the
DATA step. Also, all DATA step functions can be used in the COMPUTAB procedure.

Lines written by the PUT statement are not integrated with the COMPUTAB report.
PUT statement output is written to the SAS log.

The automatic variable _N_ can be used; its value is the number of observations read
or the number read in the current BY group, if a BY statement is used. FIRST.*variable* and LAST.*variable* references cannot be used.

The following statements are also available in PROC COMPUTAB:

ABORT	FORMAT
ARRAY	GOTO
ATTRIB	IF-THEN/ELSE
assignment statement	LABEL
CALL	LINK
DELETE	PUT
DO	RETAIN
iterative DO	SELECT
DO UNTIL	STOP
DO WHILE ·	sum statement
END	TITLE
FOOTNOTE	

The programming statements can be assigned labels ROW*xxxxx*: or COL*xxxxx*: to
indicate the start of a row and column block, respectively. Statements in a row block

create or change values in all the columns in the specified rows. Similarly, statements in a column block create or change values in all the rows in the specified columns.

There is an implied RETURN statement before each new row or column block. Thus, the flow of execution does not leave the current row (column) block before the block repeats for all columns (rows.) Row and column variables and nonretained variables are initialized prior to each execution of the block.

The next COL*xxxxx*: label, ROW*xxxxx*: label, or the end of the PROC COMPUTAB step signals the end of a row (column) block. Column blocks and row blocks can be mixed in any order. In some cases, performing calculations in different orders can lead to different results.

See "Program Flow Example," "Order of Calculations," and "Controlling Execution within Row and Column Blocks" in the section "Details" for more information.

BY Statement

BY *variables*;

A BY statement can be used with PROC COMPUTAB to obtain separate reports for observations in groups defined by the BY variables. At the beginning of each BY group, before PROC COMPUTAB reads any observations, all table values are set to 0 unless the INITMISS option or an INIT statement is specified.

SUMBY Statement

SUMBY *variables*;

The SUMBY statement produces consolidation tables for variables whose names are in the SUMBY list. Only one SUMBY statement can be used.

To use a SUMBY statement, you must use a BY statement. The SUMBY and BY variables must be in the same relative order in both statements, for example:

```
by a b c;
sumby a b;
```

This SUMBY statement produces tables that consolidate over values of C within levels of B and over values of B within levels of A. Suppose A has values 1,2; B has values 1,2; and C has values 1,2,3. Table 6.1 indicates the consolidation tables produced by the SUMBY statement.

Table 6.1. Consolidation Tables Produced by the SUMBY Statement

SUMBY Consolidations	Consolidated BY Groups		
A=1,B=1	C=1	C=2	C=3
A=1,B=2	C=1	C=2	C=3
A=1	B=1,C=1 B=2,C=1	B=1,C=2 B=2,C=2	B=1,C=3 B=2,C=3
A=2,B=1	C=1	C=2	C=3
A=2,B=2	C=1	C=2	C=3
A=2	B=1,C=1 B=2,C=1	B=1,C=2 B=2,C=2	B=1,C=3 B=2,C=3

Two consolidation tables for B are produced for each value of A. The first table consolidates the three tables produced for the values of C while B is 1; the second table consolidates the three tables produced for C while B is 2.

Tables are similarly produced for values of A. Nested consolidation tables are produced for B (as described previously) for each value of A. Thus, this SUMBY statement produces a total of six consolidation tables in addition to the tables produced for each BY group.

To produce a table that consolidates the entire data set (the equivalent of using PROC COMPUTAB with neither BY nor SUMBY statements), use the special name _TOTAL_ as the first entry in the SUMBY variable list, for example,

```
sumby _total_ a b;
```

PROC COMPUTAB then produces consolidation tables for SUMBY variables as well as a consolidation table for all observations.

To produce only consolidation tables, use the SUMONLY option in the PROC COMPUTAB statement.

Details

NOTRANS Option

The NOTRANS option in the PROC COMPUTAB statement prevents the transposition of the input data set. NOTRANS affects the input block, the precedence of row and column options, and the structure of the output data set if the OUT= option is specified.

When the input data set is transposed, input variables are among the rows of the COMPUTAB report, and observations compose columns. The reverse is true if the data set is not transposed; therefore, the input block must select rows to receive data values, and input variables are among the columns.

Variables from the input data set dominate the format specification and data type. When the input data set is transposed, input variables are among the rows of the report, and row options take precedence over column options. When the input data set is not transposed, input variables are among the columns, and column options take precedence over row options.

Variables for the output data set are taken from the dimension (row or column) that contains variables from the input data set. When the input data set is transposed, this dimension is the row dimension; otherwise, the output variables come from the column dimension.

Program Flow Example

This example shows how the COMPUTAB procedure processes observations in the program working storage and the COMPUTAB data table (CDT).

Assume you have three years of sales and cost of goods sold (CGS) figures, and you want to determine total sales and cost of goods sold and calculate gross profit and the profit margin.

```
data example;
   input year sales cgs;
   cards;
1988    83      52
1989    106     85
1990    120     114
;

proc computab data=example;

   columns c88 c89 c90 total;
   rows sales cgs gprofit pctmarg;

   /* calculate gross profit */
   gprofit = sales - cgs;

   /* select a column */
   c88 = year = 1988;
   c89 = year = 1989;
```

```
c90 = year = 1990;

/* calculate row totals for sales */
/* and cost of goods sold */
col: total = c88 + c89 + c90;

/* calculate profit margin */
row: pctmarg = gprofit / cgs * 100;
run;
```

Table 6.2 shows the CDT before any observation is read in. All the columns and rows are defined with the values initialized to 0.

Table 6.2. CDT Before any Input

	C88	C89	C90	TOTAL
SALES	0	0	0	0
CGS	0	0	0	0
GPROFIT	0	0	0	0
PCTMARG	0	0	0	0

When the first input is read in (year=1988, sales=83, and cgs=52), the input block puts the values for SALES and CGS in the C88 column since year=1988. Also the value for the gross profit for that year (GPROFIT) is calculated as indicated in the following:

```
gprofit = sales-cgs;
c88 = year = 1988;
c89 = year = 1989;
c90 = year = 1990;
```

Table 6.3 shows the CDT after the first observation is input.

Table 6.3. CDT After First Observation Input (C88=1)

	C88	C89	C90	TOTAL
SALES	83	0	0	0
CGS	52	0	0	0
GPROFIT	31	0	0	0
PCTMARG	0	0	0	0

Similarly, the second observation (year=1989, sales=106, cgs=85) is put in the second column and the GPROFIT is calculated to be 21. The third observation (year=1990, sales=120, cgs=114) is put in the third column and the GPROFIT is calculated to be 6. Table 6.4 shows the CDT after all observations are input.

Table 6.4. CDT After All Observations Input

	C88	C89	C90	TOTAL
SALES	83	106	120	0
CGS	52	85	114	0
GPROFIT	31	21	6	0
PCTMARG	0	0	0	0

After the input block is executed for each observation in the input data set, the first row or column block is processed. In this case, the column block is

```
col: total = c88 + c89 + c90;
```

The column block executes for each row, calculating the TOTAL column for each row. Table 6.5 shows the CDT after the column block has executed for the first row (total=83 + 106 + 120). The total sales for the three years is 309.

Table 6.5. CDT After Column Block Executed for First Row

	C88	C89	C90	TOTAL
SALES	83	106	120	309
CGS	52	85	114	0
GPROFIT	31	21	6	0
PCTMARG	0	0	0	0

Table 6.6 shows the CDT after the column block has executed for all rows and the values for total cost of goods sold and total gross profit have been calculated.

Table 6.6. CDT After Column Block Executed for All Rows

	C88	C89	C90	TOTAL
SALES	83	106	120	309
CGS	52	85	114	251
GPROFIT	31	21	6	58
PCTMARG	0	0	0	0

Once the column block has been executed for all rows, the next block is processed. The row block is

```
row: pctmarg = gprofit / cgs * 100;
```

The row block executes for each column, calculating the PCTMARG for each year and the total (TOTAL column) for three years. Table 6.7 shows the CDT after the row block has executed for all columns.

Table 6.7. CDT After Row Block Executed for All Columns

	C88	C89	C90	TOTAL
SALES	83	106	120	309
CGS	52	85	114	251
GPROFIT	31	21	6	58
PCTMARG	59.62	24.71	5.26	23.11

Order of Calculations

The COMPUTAB procedure provides alternative programming methods for performing most calculations. New column and row values are formed by adding values from the input data set, directly or with modification, into existing columns or rows. New columns can be formed in the input block or in column blocks. New rows can be formed in the input block or in row blocks.

This example illustrates the different ways to collect totals. Table 6.8 is the total sales report for two products, SALES1 and SALES2, during the years 1988-1990. The values for SALES1 and SALES2 in columns C88, C89, and C90 come from the input data set.

Table 6.8. Total Sales Report

	C88	C89	C90	SALESTOT
SALES1	15	45	80	140
SALES2	30	40	50	120
YRTOT	45	85	130	260

The new column SALESTOT, which is the total sales for each product over three years, can be computed in several different ways:

- in the input block by selecting SALESTOT for each observation

```
salestot = 1;
```

- in a column block

```
coltot: salestot = c88 + c89 + c90;
```

In a similar fashion, the new row YRTOT, which is the total sales for each year, can be formed as follows:

- in the input block

```
yrtot = sales1 + sales2;
```

- in a row block

```
rowtot: yrtot = sales1 + sales2;
```

Performing some calculations in PROC COMPUTAB in different orders can yield different results, since many operations are not commutative. Be sure to perform calculations in the proper sequence. It may take several column and row blocks to produce the desired report values.

Notice that in the previous example, the grand total for all rows and columns is 260 and is the same whether it is calculated from row subtotals or column subtotals. It makes no difference in this case whether you compute the row block or the column block first.

However, consider the following example where a new column and a new row are formed:

Table 6.9.   Report Sensitive to Order of Calculations

	STORE1	STORE2	STORE3	MAX
PRODUCT1	12	13	27	27
PRODUCT2	11	15	14	15
TOTAL	23	28	41	?

The new column MAX contains the maximum value in each row, and the new row TOTAL contains the column totals. MAX is calculated in a column block:

```
col: max = max(store1,store2,store3);
```

TOTAL is calculated in a row block:

```
row: total = product1 + product2;
```

Notice that either of two values, 41 or 42, is possible for the element in column MAX and row TOTAL. If the row block is first, the value is the maximum of the column totals (41). If the column block is first, the value is the sum of the MAX values (42). Whether to compute a column block before a row block can be a critical decision.

Column Selection

The following discussion assumes that the NOTRANS option has not been specified. When NOTRANS is specified, this section applies to rows rather than columns.

If a COLUMNS statement appears in PROC COMPUTAB, a target column must be selected for the incoming observation. If there is no COLUMNS statement, a new column is added for each observation. When a COLUMNS statement is present and the selection criteria fail to designate a column, the current observation is ignored. Faulty column selection can result in columns or entire tables of 0s (or missing values if the INITMISS option is specified).

During execution of the input block, when an observation is read, its values are copied into row variables in the Program Data Vector (PDV).

To select columns, use either the column variable names themselves or the special variable _COL_. Use the column names by setting a column variable equal to some nonzero value. The example in the section "Getting Started" earlier in this chapter uses the logical expression COMPDIV=*value* which is evaluated to produce 0 or 1, and the result is assigned to the corresponding column variable.

```
a = compdiv = 'A';
b = compdiv = 'B';
c = compdiv = 'C';
```

IF statements can also be used to select columns. The following statements are equivalent to the preceding example:

```
if      compdiv = 'A' then a = 1;
else if compdiv = 'B' then b = 1;
else if compdiv = 'C' then c = 1;
```

At the end of the input block for each observation, PROC COMPUTAB multiplies numeric input values by any nonzero selector values and adds the result to selected columns. Character values simply overwrite the contents already in the table. If more than one column is selected, the values are added to each of the selected columns.

Use the _COL_ variable to select a column by assigning the column number to it. The COMPUTAB procedure automatically initializes column variables and sets the _COL_ variable to 0 at the start of each execution of the input block. At the end of the input block for each observation, PROC COMPUTAB examines the value of

COL. If the value is nonzero and within range, the row variable values are added to the CDT cells of the _COL_th column, for example,

```
data rept;
   input div sales cgs;
   cards;
2   106     85
3   120    114
1    83     52
;

proc computab data=rept;
   row div sales cgs;
   columns div1 div2 div3;
   _col_ = div;
run;
```

The code in this example places the first observation (DIV=2) in column 2 (DIV2), the second observation (DIV=3) in column 3 (DIV3), and the third observation (DIV=1) in column 1 (DIV1).

Controlling Execution within Row and Column Blocks

Row names, column names, and the special variables _ROW_ and _COL_ can be used to limit the execution of programming statements to selected rows or columns. A row block operates on all columns of the table for a specified row unless restricted in some way. Likewise, a column block operates on all rows for a specified column. Use column names or _COL_ in a row block to execute programming statements conditionally; use row names or _ROW_ in a column block.

For example, consider a simple column block consisting of only one statement:

```
col: total = qtr1 + qtr2 + qtr3 + qtr4;
```

This column block assigns a value to each row in the TOTAL column. As each row participates in the execution of a column block,

- its row variable in the program data vector is set to 1

- the value of _ROW_ is the number of the participating row

- the value from each column of the row is copied from the COMPUTAB data table to the program data vector

To avoid calculating TOTAL on particular rows, use row names or _ROW_, for example,

```
col: if sales|cost then total = qtr1 + qtr2 + qtr3 + qtr4;
```

or

```
col: if _row_ < 3  then total = qtr1 + qtr2 + qtr3 + qtr4;
```

Row and column blocks can appear in any order, and rows and columns can be selected in each block.

Program Flow

This section describes in detail the different steps in PROC COMPUTAB execution.

Step 1: Define Report Organization and Set Up the COMPUTAB Data Table

Before the COMPUTAB procedure reads in data or executes programming statements, the columns list from the COLUMNS statements and the rows list from the ROWS statements are used to set up a matrix of all columns and rows in the report. This matrix is called the COMPUTAB data table (CDT). When you define columns and rows of the CDT, the COMPUTAB procedure also sets up corresponding variables in working storage called the program data vector (PDV) for programming statements. Data values reside in the CDT but are copied into the program data vector as they are needed for calculations.

Step 2: Select Input Data with Input Block Programming Statements

The input block copies input observations into rows or columns of the CDT. By default, observations go to columns; if the data set is not transposed (NOTRANS option), observations go to rows of the report table. The input block consists of all executable statements before any ROW*xxxxx*: or COL*xxxxx*: statement label. Use programming statements to perform calculations and select a given observation to be added into the report.

Input Block

The input block is executed once for each observation in the input data set. If there is no input data set, the input block is not executed. The program logic of the input block is as follows:

1. Determine which variables, row or column, are selector variables and which are data variables. Selector variables determine which rows or columns receive values at the end of the block. Data variables contain the values that the selected rows or columns receive. By default, column variables are selector variables and row variables are data variables. If the input data set is not transposed (NOTRANS option), the roles are reversed.

2. Initialize nonretained program variables (including selector variables) to 0 (or missing if the INITMISS option is specified). Selector variables are temporarily associated with a numeric data item supplied by the procedure. Using these variables to control row and column selection does not affect any other data values.

3. Transfer data from an observation in the data set to data variables in the PDV.

4. Execute the programming statements in the input block using values from the PDV and storing results in the PDV.

5. Transfer data values from the PDV into the appropriate columns of the CDT. If a selector variable for a row or column has a nonmissing, nonzero value, multiply each PDV value for variables used in the report by the selector variable and add

the results to the selected row or column of the CDT.

Step 3: Calculate Final Values Using Column Blocks and Row Blocks

Column Blocks

A column block is executed once for each row of the CDT. The program logic of a column block is as follows:

1. Indicate the current row by setting the corresponding row variable in the PDV to 1 and the other row variables to missing. Assign the current row number to the special variable _ROW_.

2. Move values from the current row of the CDT to the respective column variables in the PDV.

3. Execute programming statements in the column block using the column values in the PDV. Here, new columns can be calculated and old ones adjusted.

4. Move the values back from the PDV to the current row of the CDT.

Row Blocks

A row block is executed once for each column of the CDT. The program logic of a row block is as follows:

1. Indicate the current column by setting the corresponding column variable in the PDV to 1 and the other column variables to missing. Assign the current column number to the special variable _COL_.

2. Move values from the current column of the CDT to the respective row variables in the PDV.

3. Execute programming statements in the row block using the row values in the PDV. Here new rows can be calculated and old ones adjusted.

4. Move the values back from the PDV to the current column of the CDT.

See "Controlling Execution within Row and Column Blocks" later in this chapter for details.

Any number of column blocks and row blocks can be used. Each may include any number of programming statements.

The values of row variables and column variables are determined by the order in which different row-block and column-block programming statements are processed. These values can be modified throughout the COMPUTAB procedure, and final values are printed in the report.

Direct Access to Table Cells

You can insert or retrieve numeric values from specific table cells using the special reserved name TABLE with row and column subscripts. References to the TABLE have the form

```
TABLE[ row-index, column-index ]
```

where *row-index* and *column-index* can be numbers, character literals, numeric variables, character variables, or expressions that produce a number or a name. If an index is numeric, it must be within range; if it is character, it must name a row or column.

References to TABLE elements can appear on either side of an equal sign in an assignment statement and can be used in a SAS expression.

Reserved Words

Certain words are reserved for special use by the COMPUTAB procedure, and using these words as variable names can lead to syntax errors or warnings. They are:

- COLUMN
- COLUMNS
- COL
- COLS
- _COL_
- ROW
- ROWS
- _ROW_
- INIT
- _N_
- TABLE

Missing Values

Missing values for variables in programming statements are treated in the same way that missing values are treated in the DATA step; that is, missing values used in expressions propagate missing values to the result. Refer to *SAS Language: Reference* for more information about missing values.

Missing values in the input data are treated as follows in the COMPUTAB report table. At the end of the input block, either one or more rows or one or more columns may have been selected to receive values from the program data vector (PDV). Numeric data values from variables in the PDV are added into selected report table rows or columns. If a PDV value is missing, the values already in the selected rows or columns for that variable are unchanged by the current observation. Other values from the current observation are added to table values as usual.

OUT= Data Set

The output data set contains the following variables:

- BY variables
- a numeric variable _TYPE_
- a character variable _NAME_
- the column variables from the COMPUTAB data table

The BY variables contain values for the current BY group. For observations in the output data set from consolidation tables, the consolidated BY variables have missing values.

The special variable _TYPE_ is a numeric variable that can have one of three values: 1, 2, or 3. _TYPE_= 1 indicates observations from the normal report table produced for each BY group; _TYPE_= 2 indicates observations from the _TOTAL_ consolidation table; _TYPE_= 3 indicates observations from other consolidation tables. _TYPE_= 2 and 3 observations have one or more BY variables with missing values.

The special variable _NAME_ is a character variable of length 8 that contains the row or column name associated with the observation from the report table. If the input data set is transposed, _NAME_ contains column names; otherwise, _NAME_ contains row names.

If the input data set is transposed, the remaining variables in the output data set are row variables from the report table. They are column variables if the input data set is not transposed.

Examples

Example 6.1.   Using Programming Statements

This example illustrates two ways of operating on the same input variables and producing the same tabular report. To simplify the example, no report enhancements are shown.

The manager of a hotel chain wants a report that shows the number of bookings at its hotels in each of four cities, the total number of bookings in the current quarter, and the percentage of the total coming from each location for each quarter of the year. Input observations contain the following variables: REPTDATE (report date), LA (number of bookings in Los Angeles), ATL (number of bookings in Atlanta), CH (number of bookings in Chicago), and NY (number of bookings in New York).

The following DATA step creates the SAS data set BOOKINGS:

```
data bookings;
   input reptdate date7. la atl ch ny;
   cards;
01JAN89 100 110 120 130
01FEB89 140 150 160 170
01MAR89 180 190 200 210
01APR89 220 230 240 250
01MAY89 260 270 280 290
01JUN89 300 310 320 330
01JUL89 340 350 360 370
01AUG89 380 390 400 410
01SEP89 420 430 440 450
01OCT89 460 470 480 490
01NOV89 500 510 520 530
01DEC89 540 550 560 570
;
```

Example 6.1. Using Programming Statements □ □ □ 305

The following PROC COMPUTAB statements select columns by setting _COL_ to an appropriate value. The PCT1, PCT2, PCT3, and PCT4 columns represent the percentage contributed by each city to the total for the quarter. These statements produce Output 6.1.1.

```
proc computab data=bookings cspace=1 cwidth=6;

    columns qtr1 pct1 qtr2 pct2 qtr3 pct3 qtr4 pct4;
    columns qtr1-qtr4 / format=6.;
    columns pct1-pct4 / format=6.2;
    rows la atl ch ny total;

    /* column selection */
    _col_ = qtr( reptdate ) * 2 - 1;

    /* copy qtr column values temporarily into pct columns */
    colcopy:
        pct1 = qtr1;
        pct2 = qtr2;
        pct3 = qtr3;
        pct4 = qtr4;

    /* calculate total row for all columns */
    /* calculate percentages for all rows in pct columns only  */
    rowcalc:
        total = la + atl + ch + ny;
        if mod( _col_, 2 ) = 0 then do;
            la  = la  / total * 100;
            atl = atl / total * 100;
            ch  = ch  / total * 100;
            ny  = ny  / total * 100;
            total = 100;
            end;
run;
```

Output 6.1.1. Quarterly Report of Hotel Bookings

	QTR1	PCT1	QTR2	PCT2	QTR3	PCT3	QTR4	PCT4
LA	420	22.58	780	23.64	1140	24.05	1500	24.27
ATL	450	24.19	810	24.55	1170	24.68	1530	24.76
CH	480	25.81	840	25.45	1200	25.32	1560	25.24
NY	510	27.42	870	26.36	1230	25.95	1590	25.73
TOTAL	1860	100.00	3300	100.00	4740	100.00	6180	100.00

Using the same input data, the next set of statements shows the usefulness of arrays in allowing PROC COMPUTAB to work in two directions at once. Arrays in larger programs can both reduce the amount of program source code and simplify otherwise complex methods of referring to rows and columns. The same report as in Output 6.1.1 is produced.

```
proc computab data=bookings cspace=1 cwidth=6;

    columns qtr1 pct1 qtr2 pct2 qtr3 pct3 qtr4 pct4;
    columns qtr1-qtr4 / format=6.;
    columns pct1-pct4 / format=6.2;
    rows la atl ch ny total;

    array pct[4] pct1-pct4;
    array qt[4] qtr1-qtr4;
    array rowlist[5] la atl ch ny total;
```

```
/* column selection */
_col_ = qtr(reptdate) * 2 - 1;

/* copy qtr column values temporarily into pct columns */
colcopy:
   do i = 1 to 4;
      pct[i] = qt[i];
      end;

/* calculate total row for all columns */
/* calculate percentages for all rows in pct columns only */

rowcalc:
   total = la + atl + ch + ny;
   if mod(_col_,2) = 0 then
      do i = 1 to 5;
         rowlist[i] = rowlist[i] / total * 100;
      end;
run;
```

Example 6.2.   Enhancing a Report

The following example shows how a report can be enhanced from a simple listing to a complex report. The simplest COMPUTAB report is a transposed listing of the data in the SAS data set INCOMREP shown in Output 6.2.1. To produce this output, nothing is specified except the PROC COMPUTAB statement and a TITLE statement.

```
data incomrep;
   input type :$6. date :monyy5.
         sales retdis tcos selling randd
         general admin deprec other taxes;
   format date monyy5.;
cards;
BUDGET JAN89 4600 300 2200 480 110 500 210 14 -8 510
BUDGET FEB89 4700 330 2300 500 110 500 200 14  0 480
BUDGET MAR89 4800 360 2600 500 120 600 250 15  2 520
ACTUAL JAN89 4900 505 2100 430 130 410 200 14 -8 500
ACTUAL FEB89 5100 480 2400 510 110 390 230 15  2 490
;
title 'Computab Report without Any Specifications';
proc computab data=incomrep;
run;
```

Example 6.2. Enhancing a Report □ □ □ 307

Output 6.2.1. Simple Report

```
              Computab Report without Any Specifications

                    COL1       COL2       COL3       COL4       COL5

         TYPE      BUDGET     BUDGET     BUDGET     ACTUAL     ACTUAL
         DATE       JAN89      FEB89      MAR89      JAN89      FEB89
         SALES    4600.00    4700.00    4800.00    4900.00    5100.00
         RETDIS    300.00     330.00     360.00     505.00     480.00
         TCOS     2200.00    2300.00    2600.00    2100.00    2400.00
         SELLING   480.00     500.00     500.00     430.00     510.00
         RANDD     110.00     110.00     120.00     130.00     110.00
         GENERAL   500.00     500.00     600.00     410.00     390.00
         ADMIN     210.00     200.00     250.00     200.00     230.00
         DEPREC     14.00      14.00      15.00      14.00      15.00
         OTHER      -8.00       0.00       2.00      -8.00       2.00
         TAXES     510.00     480.00     520.00     500.00     490.00
```

To exclude the budgeted values from your report, select columns for ACTUAL observations only. To remove unwanted variables, specify the variables you want in a ROWS statement.

```
title 'Column Selection by Month';

proc computab data=incomrep;
    rows sales--other;
    columns jana feba mara;
    mnth = month(date);
    if type = 'ACTUAL';
        jana = mnth = 1;
        feba = mnth = 2;
        mara = mnth = 3;
run;
```

The report is shown in Output 6.2.2.

Output 6.2.2. Report Using Column Selection Techniques

```
              Column Selection by Month

                     JANA       FEBA       MARA

         SALES     4900.00    5100.00       0.00
         RETDIS     505.00     480.00       0.00
         TCOS      2100.00    2400.00       0.00
         SELLING    430.00     510.00       0.00
         RANDD      130.00     110.00       0.00
         GENERAL    410.00     390.00       0.00
         ADMIN      200.00     230.00       0.00
         DEPREC      14.00      15.00       0.00
         OTHER       -8.00       2.00       0.00
```

To complete the report, compute new rows from existing rows. This is done in a row block (although it can also be done in the input block). Add a new column (QTR1) that accumulates all the actual data. The NOZERO option suppresses the zero column for March. The output produced by these statements is shown in Output 6.2.3.

```
proc computab data=incomrep;

    /* add a new column to be selected */
    /* qtr1 column will be selected several times */
    columns actual1-actual3 qtr1 / nozero;
    array collist[3] actual1-actual3;
    rows sales retdis netsales tcos grosspft selling randd general
        admin deprec operexp operinc other taxblinc taxes netincom;

    if type='ACTUAL';
    i = month(date);
    if i <= 3 then qtr1 = 1;
    collist[i]=1;

    rowcalc:
        if sales = . then return;
        netsales = sales - retdis;
        grosspft = netsales - tcos;
        operexp  = selling + randd + general + admin + deprec;
        operinc  = grosspft - operexp;
        taxblinc = operinc + other;
        netincom = taxblinc - taxes;
run;
```

Output 6.2.3. Report Using Techniques to Compute New Rows

```
                    Column Selection by Month

                    ACTUAL1      ACTUAL2        QTR1

        SALES       4900.00      5100.00     10000.00
        RETDIS       505.00       480.00       985.00
        NETSALES    4395.00      4620.00      9015.00
        TCOS        2100.00      2400.00      4500.00
        GROSSPFT    2295.00      2220.00      4515.00
        SELLING      430.00       510.00       940.00
        RANDD        130.00       110.00       240.00
        GENERAL      410.00       390.00       800.00
        ADMIN        200.00       230.00       430.00
        DEPREC        14.00        15.00        29.00
        OPEREXP     1184.00      1255.00      2439.00
        OPERINC     1111.00       965.00      2076.00
        OTHER         -8.00         2.00        -6.00
        TAXBLINC    1103.00       967.00      2070.00
        TAXES        500.00       490.00       990.00
        NETINCOM     603.00       477.00      1080.00
```

Now that you have all the numbers calculated, add specifications to improve the report's appearance. Specify titles, row and column labels, and formats. The report produced by these statements is shown in Output 6.2.4.

```
/* now get the report to look the way we want it */
title  'Pro Forma Income Statement';
title2 'XYZ Computer Services, Inc.';
title3 'Period to Date Actual';
title4 'Amounts in Thousands';

proc computab data=incomrep;

    columns actual1-actual3 qtr1 / nozero f=comma7. +3 ' ';
    array collist[3] actual1-actual3;
    columns actual1 / 'Jan';
    columns actual2 / 'Feb';
    columns actual3 / 'Mar';
    columns qtr1 / 'Total' 'Qtr 1';
```

Example 6.2. Enhancing a Report □ □ □ 309

```
        rows sales    / ' '
                        'Gross Sales ';
        rows retdis   / 'Less Returns & Discounts';
        rows netsales / 'Net Sales'                    +3 ol;
        rows tcos     / ' '
                        'Total Cost of Sales';
        rows grosspft / ' '
                        'Gross Profit';
        rows selling  / ' '
                        'Operating Expenses:'
                        '    Selling';
        rows randd    / '    R & D';
        rows general  / +3;
        rows admin    / '    Administrative';
        rows deprec   / '    Depreciation'            ul;
        rows operexp  / ' '                           skip;
        rows operinc  / 'Operating Income';
        rows other    / 'Other Income/-Expense'       ul;
        rows taxblinc / 'Taxable Income';
        rows taxes    / 'Income Taxes'                ul;
        rows netincom / '    Net Income'              dul;

        if type = 'ACTUAL';
        i = month( date );
        collist[i] = 1;

        colcalc:
           qtr1 = actual1 + actual2 + actual3;

        rowcalc:
           if sales = . then return;
           netsales = sales - retdis;
           grosspft = netsales - tcos;
           operexp = selling + randd + general + admin + deprec;
           operinc = grosspft - operexp;
           taxblinc = operinc + other;
           netincom = taxblinc - taxes;
     run;
```

Output 6.2.4. Specifying Titles, Row and Column Labels, and Formats

```
                      Pro Forma Income Statement
                      XYZ Computer Services, Inc.
                          Period to Date Actual
                          Amounts in Thousands


                                                      Total
                                  Jan        Feb      Qtr 1

     Gross Sales                 4,900      5,100     10,000
     Less Returns & Discounts      505        480        985
                                ---------  ---------  ---------
        Net Sales               4,395      4,620      9,015

     Total Cost of Sales        2,100      2,400      4,500

     Gross Profit               2,295      2,220      4,515

     Operating Expenses:
        Selling                   430        510        940
        R & D                     130        110        240
        GENERAL                   410        390        800
        Administrative            200        230        430
        Depreciation               14         15         29
                                ---------  ---------  ---------
                                1,184      1,255      2,439
```

Output 6.2.4. (Continued)

```
                    Pro Forma Income Statement
                    XYZ Computer Services, Inc.
                       Period to Date Actual
                       Amounts in Thousands

        Operating Income            1,111         965       2,076
        Other Income/-Expense          -8           2          -6
                                 ---------   ---------   ---------
        Taxable Income              1,103         967       2,070
        Income Taxes                  500         490         990
                                 ---------   ---------   ---------
           Net Income                603         477       1,080
                                 =========   =========   =========
```

Example 6.3.   Comparison of Actual and Budget

This example shows a more complex report that compares the actual data with the budgeted values. The same input data as in the previous example is used.

The report produced by these statements is shown in Output 6.3.1. The report shows the values for the current month and the year-to-date totals for budgeted amounts, actual amounts, and the actuals as a percentage of the budgeted amounts. The data have the values for January and February. Therefore, the CURMO variable (current month) in the RETAIN statement is set to 2. The values for the observations where the month of the year is 2 (February) are accumulated for the Current Month values. The year-to-date values are accumulated from those observations where the month of the year is less than or equal to 2 (January and February).

```
/* do a more complex report */
title  'Pro Forma Income Statement';
title2 'XYZ Computer Services, Inc.';
title3 'Budget Analysis';
title4 'Amounts in Thousands';

proc computab data=incomrep;

   columns cmbud cmact cmpct ytdbud ytdact ytdpct /
           zero=' ';
   columns cmbud--cmpct / mtitle='- Current Month: February -';
   columns ytdbud--ytdpct / mtitle='- Year To Date -';
   columns cmbud ytdbud / 'Budget' f=comma6.;
   columns cmact ytdact / 'Actual' f=comma6.;
   columns cmpct ytdpct / '%  ' f=7.2;
   columns cmbud--ytdpct / '-';
   columns ytdbud / _titles_;
   retain curmo 2; /* current month: February */
   rows sales     / ' '
                    'Gross Sales';
   rows retdis    / 'Less Returns & Discounts';
   rows netsales / 'Net Sales'                  +3 ol;
   rows tcos      / ' '
                    'Total Cost of Sales';
   rows grosspft / ' '
                    'Gross Profit'              +3;
   rows selling  / ' '
                    'Operating Expenses:'
                    '   Selling';
   rows randd     / '   R & D';
```

Example 6.3.   Comparison of Actual and Budget   □□□   311

```
rows general  / +3;
rows admin    / '    Administrative';
rows deprec   / '    Depreciation'              ul;
rows operexp  / ' ';
rows operinc  / 'Operating Income'             ol;
rows other    / 'Other Income/-Expense'         ul;
rows taxblinc / 'Taxable Income';
rows taxes    / 'Income Taxes'                   ul;
rows netincom / '   Net Income'                dul;

cmbud = type = 'BUDGET' & month(date) = curmo;
cmact = type = 'ACTUAL' & month(date) = curmo;
ytdbud = type = 'BUDGET' & month(date) <= curmo;
ytdact = type = 'ACTUAL' & month(date) <= curmo;

rowcalc:
   if cmpct | ytdpct then return;
   netsales = sales - retdis;
   grosspft = netsales - tcos;
   operexp  = selling + randd + general + admin + deprec;
   operinc  = grosspft - operexp;
   taxblinc = operinc + other;
   netincom = taxblinc - taxes;

colpct:
   if cmbud  & cmact  then cmpct  = 100 * cmact  / cmbud;
   if ytdbud & ytdact then ytdpct = 100 * ytdact / ytdbud;
run;
```

Output 6.3.1.   Report Using Specifications to Tailor Output

```
                            Pro Forma Income Statement
                            XYZ Computer Services, Inc.
                                 Budget Analysis
                               Amounts in Thousands

--- Current Month: February ---                    -------- Year To Date ---------
  Budget    Actual      %                            Budget    Actual       %
 --------- --------- ---------                       --------- --------- ---------

    4,700     5,100    108.51  Gross Sales             9,300    10,000    107.53
      330       480    145.45  Less Returns & Discounts  630       985    156.35
 --------- --------- ---------                       --------- --------- ---------
    4,370     4,620    105.72    Net Sales             8,670     9,015    103.98

    2,300     2,400    104.35  Total Cost of Sales     4,500     4,500    100.00

    2,070     2,220    107.25    Gross Profit          4,170     4,515    108.27

                               Operating Expenses:
      500       510    102.00    Selling                 980       940     95.92
      110       110    100.00    R & D                   220       240    109.09
      500       390     78.00    GENERAL               1,000       800     80.00
      200       230    115.00    Administrative          410       430    104.88
       14        15    107.14    Depreciation             28        29    103.57
 --------- --------- ---------                       --------- --------- ---------
    1,324     1,255     94.79                          2,638     2,439     92.46
 --------- --------- ---------                       --------- --------- ---------
      746       965    129.36  Operating Income        1,532     2,076    135.51
                  2            Other Income/-Expense      -8        -6     75.00
 --------- --------- ---------                       --------- --------- ---------
      746       967    129.62  Taxable Income          1,524     2,070    135.83
      480       490    102.08  Income Taxes              990       990    100.00
 --------- --------- ---------                       --------- --------- ---------
      266       477    179.32    Net Income              534     1,080    202.25
 ========= ========= =========                       ========= ========= =========
```

Example 6.4.   Consolidations

This example consolidates product tables by region and region tables by corporate division. Output 6.4.1 shows the North Central and Northeast regional summaries for the Equipment division for the first quarter. Output 6.4.2 shows the profit summary for the Equipment division. Similar tables for the Publishing division are produced but not shown here.

```
data product;
    input pcode div region month sold revenue recd cost;
cards;
1 1 1 1 56 5600 29 2465
1 1 1 2 13 1300 30 2550
1 1 1 3 17 1700 65 5525
2 1 1 1  2  240 50 4900
2 1 1 2 82 9840 17 1666
more data lines
;

proc format;
    value divfmt 1='Equipment'
                 2='Publishing';
    value regfmt 1='North Central'
                 2='Northeast'
                 3='South'
                 4='West';
run;

proc sort data=product;
    by div region pcode;
run;

title1 '      XYZ Development Corporation        ';
title2 ' Corporate Headquarters: New York, NY ';
title3 '             Profit Summary             ';
title4 '                                        ';

proc computab data=product sumonly;
    by div region pcode;
    sumby _total_ div region;

    format div    divfmt.;
    format region regfmt.;
    label  div = 'DIVISION';

    /* specify order of columns and column titles */
    columns jan feb mar qtr1 / mtitle='- first quarter -' ' '  nozero;
    columns apr may jun qtr2 / mtitle='- second quarter -' ' '  nozero;
    columns jul aug sep qtr3 / mtitle='- third quarter -' ' '  nozero;
    columns oct nov dec qtr4 / mtitle='- fourth quarter -' ' '  nozero;
    column  jan  / ' ' 'January' '=';
    column  feb  / ' ' 'February' '=';
    column  mar  / ' ' 'March' '=';
    column  qtr1 / 'Quarter' 'Summary' '=';

    column  apr  / ' ' 'April' '=' _page_;
    column  may  / ' ' 'May' '=';
    column  jun  / ' ' 'June' '=';
    column  qtr2 / 'Quarter' 'Summary' '=';

    column  jul  / ' ' 'July' '=' _page_;
    column  aug  / ' ' 'August' '=';
    column  sep  / ' ' 'September' '=';
```

Example 6.4. Consolidations □ □ □ 313

```
column   qtr3 / 'Quarter' 'Summary' '=';

column   oct  / ' ' 'October' '=' _page_;
column   nov  / ' ' 'November' '=';
column   dec  / ' ' 'December' '=';
column   qtr4 / 'Quarter' 'Summary' '=';

/* specify order of rows and row titles */
row      sold    / ' ' 'Number Sold' f=8.;
row      revenue / ' ' 'Sales Revenue';
row      recd    / ' ' 'Number Received' f=8.;
row      cost    / ' ' 'Cost of' 'Items Received';
row      profit  / ' ' 'Profit' 'Within Period' ol;
row      pctmarg / ' ' 'Profit Margin' dul;

/* select column for appropriate month */
_col_ = month + ceil( month / 3 ) - 1;

/* calculate quarterly summary columns */
colcalc:
   qtr1 = jan + feb + mar;
   qtr2 = apr + may + jun;
   qtr3 = jul + aug + sep;
   qtr4 = oct + nov + dec;

/* calculate profit rows */
 rowcalc:
   profit = revenue - cost;
   if cost > 0 then pctmarg = profit / cost * 100;
run;
```

Output 6.4.1. Summary by Regions for the Equipment Division

```
                  XYZ Development Corporation
              Corporate Headquarters: New York, NY
                         Profit Summary

-----------SUMMARY TABLE:  DIVISION=Equipment REGION=North Central------------

                    ------------- first quarter ---------------

                                                        Quarter
                     January    February      March     Summary
                    =========   =========   =========  =========

   Number Sold          140         128         102         370

   Sales Revenue    16250.00    15690.00    12320.00    44260.00

   Number Received      176         170         145         491

   Cost of
   Items Received   17003.00    15888.00    13880.00    46771.00
                    ---------   ---------   ---------  ---------

   Profit
   Within Period     -753.00     -198.00    -1560.00    -2511.00

   Profit Margin       -4.43       -1.25      -11.24       -5.37
                    =========   =========   =========  =========
```

Output 6.4.1. (Continued)

```
                    XYZ Development Corporation
                  Corporate Headquarters: New York, NY
                            Profit Summary

--------------SUMMARY TABLE:  DIVISION=Equipment REGION=Northeast--------------

                        ------------- first quarter --------------

                                                            Quarter
                          January   February     March      Summary
                         =========  =========  =========  =========

        Number Sold             82        180        183        445

        Sales Revenue     9860.00   21330.00   21060.00   52250.00

        Number Received        162         67        124        353

        Cost of
        Items Received   16374.00    6325.00   12333.00   35032.00
                         ---------  ---------  ---------  ---------

        Profit
        Within Period    -6514.00   15005.00    8727.00   17218.00

        Profit Margin      -39.78     237.23      70.76      49.15
                         =========  =========  =========  =========
```

Output 6.4.2. Profit Summary for the Equipment Division

```
                    XYZ Development Corporation
                  Corporate Headquarters: New York, NY
                            Profit Summary

-----------------------SUMMARY TABLE:  DIVISION=Equipment----------------------

                        ------------- first quarter --------------

                                                            Quarter
                          January   February     March      Summary
                         =========  =========  =========  =========

        Number Sold            222        308        285        815

        Sales Revenue    26110.00   37020.00   33380.00   96510.00

        Number Received        338        237        269        844

        Cost of
        Items Received   33377.00   22213.00   26213.00   81803.00
                         ---------  ---------  ---------  ---------

        Profit
        Within Period    -7267.00   14807.00    7167.00   14707.00

        Profit Margin      -21.77      66.66      27.34      17.98
                         =========  =========  =========  =========
```

Output 6.4.3 shows the consolidation report of profit summary over both divisions and regions.

Example 6.4. Consolidations □ □ □ 315

Output 6.4.3. Profit Summary

```
                        XYZ Development Corporation
                   Corporate Headquarters: New York, NY
                              Profit Summary

-----------------------------SUMMARY TABLE:   TOTALS----------------------------

                       ------------- first quarter --------------

                                                              Quarter
                        January     February      March       Summary
                       =========    =========    =========   =========

     Number Sold            532          588          610        1730

     Sales Revenue     35950.00     44770.00     43100.00   123820.00

     Number Received       577          626          669        1872

     Cost of
     Items Received    38995.00     31143.00     34599.00   104737.00
                       ---------    ---------    ---------   ---------

     Profit
     Within Period     -3045.00     13627.00      8501.00    19083.00

     Profit Margin        -7.81        43.76        24.57       18.22
                       =========    =========    =========   =========
```

Example 6.5.   Creating an Output Data Set

This example uses data and reports similar to those in Example 6.3 to illustrate the creation of an output data set.

```
data product;
    input pcode div region month sold revenue recd cost;
    cards;
1 1 1 1 56 5600 29 2465
1 1 1 2 13 1300 30 2550
1 1 1 3 17 1700 65 5525
2 1 1 1  2  240 50 4900
2 1 1 2 82 9840 17 1666
more data lines
;

proc sort data=product out=sorted;
   by div region;
run;

/* create data set, profit */
proc computab data=sorted notrans out=profit noprint;
   by div region;
   sumby div;

   /* specify order of rows and row titles */
   row     jan feb mar qtr1;
   row     apr may jun qtr2;
   row     jul aug sep qtr3;
   row     oct nov dec qtr4;

   /* specify order of columns and column titles */
   columns sold revenue recd cost profit pctmarg;

   /* select row for appropriate month */
   _row_ = month + ceil( month / 3 ) - 1;
```

```
/* calculate quarterly summary rows */
rowcalc:
   qtr1 = jan + feb + mar;
   qtr2 = apr + may + jun;
   qtr3 = jul + aug + sep;
   qtr4 = oct + nov + dec;

/* calculate profit columns */
colcalc:
   profit = revenue - cost;
   if cost > 0 then pctmarg = profit / cost * 100;
run;

/* make a partial listing of the output data set */
proc print data=profit (obs=10) noobs;
run;
```

Since the NOTRANS option is specified, column names become variables in the data set. REGION has missing values in the output data set for observations associated with consolidation tables. The output data set PROFIT, in conjunction with the option NOPRINT, illustrates how you can use the computational features of PROC COMPUTAB for creating additional rows and columns as in a spread sheet without producing a report. Output 6.5.1 shows a partial listing of the output data set PROFIT.

Output 6.5.1. Partial Listing of the PROFIT Data Set

DIV	REGION	_TYPE_	_NAME_	SOLD	REVENUE	RECD	COST	PROFIT	PCTMARG
1	1	1	JAN	140	16250	176	17003	-753	-4.429
1	1	1	FEB	128	15690	170	15888	-198	-1.246
1	1	1	MAR	102	12320	145	13880	-1560	-11.239
1	1	1	QTR1	370	44260	491	46771	-2511	-5.369
1	1	1	APR	82	9860	162	16374	-6514	-39.783
1	1	1	MAY	180	21330	67	6325	15005	237.233
1	1	1	JUN	183	21060	124	12333	8727	70.761
1	1	1	QTR2	445	52250	353	35032	17218	49.149
1	1	1	JUL	194	23210	99	10310	12900	125.121
1	1	1	AUG	153	17890	164	16704	1186	7.100

Example 6.6.   A What-If Market Analysis

PROC COMPUTAB can be used with other SAS/ETS procedures and with macros to implement commonly needed decision support tools for financial and marketing analysis.

The following input data set reads quarterly sales figures:

```
data market;
   input date :yyq4. units @@;
   cards;
80Q1   3608.9   80Q2   5638.4   80Q3   6017.9   80Q4   4929.6   81Q1   4962.0
81Q2   5804.6   81Q3   5498.6   81Q4   7687.1   82Q1   6864.1   82Q2   7625.8
82Q3   7919.7   82Q4   8294.7   83Q1   8151.6   83Q2  10992.7   83Q3  10671.4
83Q4  10643.2   84Q1  10215.1   84Q2  10795.5   84Q3  14144.4   84Q4  11623.1
85Q1  14445.3   85Q2  13925.2   85Q3  16729.3   85Q4  16125.3   86Q1  15232.6
86Q2  16272.2   86Q3  16816.7   86Q4  17040.0   87Q1  17967.8   87Q2  14727.2
87Q3  18797.3   87Q4  18258.0   88Q1  20041.5   88Q2  20181.0   88Q3  20061.7
```

Example 6.6.   A What-If Market Analysis   □□□   317

```
88Q4 21670.1  89Q1 21844.3  89Q2 23524.1  89Q3 22000.6  89Q4 24166.7
;
```

PROC FORECAST makes a total market forecast for the next four quarters.

```
/* forecast the total number of units to be */
/* sold in the next four quarters */
proc forecast out=outcome trend=2 interval=qtr lead=4;
   id date;
   var units;
   run;
```

The macros WHATIF and SHOW build a report table and provide the flexibility of examining alternate what-if situations. The row and column calculations of PROC COMPUTAB compute the income statement. With macros stored in a macro library, the only statements required with PROC COMPUTAB are macro invocations and TITLE statements.

```
/* set up rows and columns of report and initialize */
/* market share and program constants */
%macro whatif(mktshr=,price=,ucost=,taxrate=,numshar=,overhead=);

   columns mar / ' ' 'March';
   columns jun / ' ' 'June';
   columns sep / ' ' 'September';
   columns dec / ' ' 'December';
   columns total / 'Calculated' 'Total';
   rows mktshr / 'Market Share'           f=5.2;
   rows tunits / 'Market Forecast';
   rows units  / 'Items Sold';
   rows sales  / 'Sales';
   rows cost   / 'Cost of Goods';
   rows ovhd   / 'Overhead';
   rows gprof  / 'Gross Profit';
   rows tax    / 'Tax';
   rows pat    / 'Profit After Tax';
   rows earn   / 'Earnings per Share';

   rows mktshr--earn / skip;
   rows sales--earn  / f=dollar12.2;
   rows tunits units / f=comma12.2;

   /* initialize market share values */
   init mktshr &mktshr;

   /* define constants */
   retain price &price ucost &ucost taxrate &taxrate numshar &numshar;

   /* retain overhead and sales from previous quarter */
   retain prevovhd &overhead prevsale;
%mend whatif;

/* perform calculations and print the specified rows */
%macro show(rows);

   /* initialize list of row names */
   %let row1 = mktshr;
   %let row2 = tunits;
   %let row3 = units;
   %let row4 = sales;
   %let row5 = cost;
   %let row6 = ovhd;
   %let row7 = gprof;
```

```
%let row8  = tax;
%let row9  = pat;
%let row10 = earn;

/* find parameter row names in list and eliminate */
/* them from the list of noprint rows */
%let n = 1;
%let word = %scan(&rows,&n);
%do %while(&word NE );
   %let i = 1;
   %let row11 = &word;
   %do %while(&&row&i NE &word);
      %let i = %eval(&i+1);
      %end;
   %if &i<11 %then %let row&i = ;
   %let n = %eval(&n+1);
   %let word = %scan(&rows,&n);
%end;

rows &row1 &row2 &row3 &row4 &row5 &row6 &row7 &row8 &row9 &row10
    dummy / noprint;

/* select column using lead values from proc forecast */
mar = _lead_ = 1;
jun = _lead_ = 2;
sep = _lead_ = 3;
dec = _lead_ = 4;

rowreln:;
   /* inter-relationships */
   share  = round( mktshr, 0.01 );
   tunits = units;
   units  = share * tunits;
   sales  = units * price;
   cost   = units * ucost;

   /* calculate overhead */
   if mar then prevsale = sales;
   if sales > prevsale
      then ovhd = prevovhd + .05 * ( sales - prevsale );
      else ovhd = prevovhd;
   prevovhd = ovhd;
   prevsale = sales;
   gprof = sales - cost - ovhd;
   tax   = gprof * taxrate;
   pat   = gprof - tax;
   earn  = pat / numshar;

coltot:;
   if mktshr
      then total = ( mar + jun + sep + dec ) / 4;
      else total = mar + jun + sep + dec;
%mend show;
run;
```

The following PROC COMPUTAB statements use the PROC FORECAST output data set with invocations of the macros defined previously to perform a what-if analysis of the predicted income statement. The report is shown in Output 6.6.1.

Example 6.6. A What-If Market Analysis □ □ □ 319

```
title1 'Fleet Footwear, Inc.';
title2 'Marketing Analysis Income Statement';
title3 'Based on Forecasted Unit Sales';
title4 'All Values Shown';

proc computab data=outcome cwidth=12;

    %whatif(mktshr=.02 .07 .15 .25,price=38.00,
            ucost=20.00,taxrate=.48,numshar=15000,overhead=5000);

    %show(mktshr tunits units sales cost ovhd gprof tax pat earn);
run;
```

Output 6.6.1. PROC COMPUTAB Report Using Macro Invocations

```
                          Fleet Footwear, Inc.
                    Marketing Analysis Income Statement
                      Based on Forecasted Unit Sales
                            All Values Shown

                                                              Calculated
                       March        June    September    December     Total
Market Share            0.02        0.07        0.15        0.25      0.12

Market Forecast     23,663.94   24,169.61   24,675.27   25,180.93  97,689.75

Items Sold             473.28    1,691.87    3,701.29    6,295.23  12,161.67

Sales              $17,984.60  $64,291.15 $140,649.03 $239,218.83 $462,143.61

Cost of Goods       $9,465.58  $33,837.45  $74,025.80 $125,904.65 $243,233.48

Overhead            $5,000.00   $7,315.33  $11,133.22  $16,061.71  $39,510.26

Gross Profit        $3,519.02  $23,138.38  $55,490.00  $97,252.47 $179,399.87

Tax                 $1,689.13  $11,106.42  $26,635.20  $46,681.19  $86,111.94

Profit After Tax    $1,829.89  $12,031.96  $28,854.80  $50,571.28  $93,287.93

Earnings per Share      $0.12       $0.80       $1.92       $3.37       $6.22
```

The following statements produce a similar report for different values of market share and unit costs. The report in Output 6.6.2 displays the values for the market share, market forecast, sales, after tax profit, and earnings per share.

```
title3 'Revised';
title4 'Selected Values Shown';

proc computab data=outcome cwidth=12;
    %whatif(mktshr=.01 .06 .12 .20,price=38.00,
            ucost=23.00,taxrate=.48,numshar=15000,overhead=5000);
    %show(mktshr tunits sales pat earn);
run;
```

Output 6.6.2.   Report Using Macro Invocations for Selected Values

```
                          Fleet Footwear, Inc.
                    Marketing Analysis Income Statement
                                Revised
                          Selected Values Shown

                                                               Calculated
                  March        June     September    December      Total
Market Share       0.01        0.06        0.12        0.20         0.10

Market Forecast  23,663.94   24,169.61   24,675.27   25,180.93   97,689.75

Sales            $8,992.30  $55,106.70  $112,519.22 $191,375.06 $367,993.28

Profit After Tax  $-754.21   $7,512.40   $17,804.35  $31,940.30  $56,502.84

Earnings per Share  $-0.05      $0.50       $1.19       $2.13       $3.77
```

Example 6.7.   Cash Flows

The COMPUTAB procedure can be used to model cash flows from one time period
to the next. The RETAIN statement is useful for enabling a row or column to contribute one of its values to its successor. Financial functions such as IRR (internal
rate of return) and NPV (net present value) can be used on PROC COMPUTAB table
values to provide a more comprehensive report. The following statements produce
Output 6.7.1:

```
data cashflow;
    input date date7. netinc depr borrow invest tax div adv ;
    cards;
30MAR82 65 42 32 126 43 51 41
30JUN82 68 47 32 144 45 54 46
30SEP82 70 49 30 148 46 55 47
30DEC82 73 49 30 148 48 55 47
;

title1 'Blue Sky Endeavors';
title2 'Financial Summary';
title4 '(Dollar Figures in Thousands)';

proc computab data=cashflow;

    cols qtr1 qtr2 qtr3 qtr4 / 'Quarter' f=7.1;
    col  qtr1 / 'One';
    col  qtr2 / 'Two';
    col  qtr3 / 'Three';
    col  qtr4 / 'Four';
    row  begcash / 'Beginning Cash';
    row  netinc  / 'Income' '   Net income';
    row  depr    / 'Depreciation';
    row  borrow;
    row  subtot1 / 'Subtotal';
    row  invest  / 'Expenditures' '   Investment';
    row  tax     / 'Taxes';
    row  div     / 'Dividend';
    row  adv     / 'Advertising';
    row  subtot2 / 'Subtotal';
    row  cashflow/  skip;
    row  irret   / 'Internal Rate' 'of Return' zero=' ';
    rows depr borrow subtot1 tax div adv subtot2 / +3;

    retain cashin -5;
```

Example 6.7. Cash Flows □ □ □ 321

```
        _col_ = qtr( date );

    rowblock:
        subtot1 = netinc + depr + borrow;
        subtot2 = tax + div + adv;
        begcash = cashin;
        cashflow = begcash + subtot1 - subtot2;
        irret = cashflow;
        cashin = cashflow;

    colblock:
        if begcash then cashin = qtr1;
        if irret then do;
            temp = irr( 4, cashin, qtr1, qtr2, qtr3, qtr4 );
            qtr1 = temp;
            qtr2 = 0; qtr3 = 0; qtr4 = 0;
            end;
run;
```

Output 6.7.1. Report Using a RETAIN Statement and the IRR Financial Function

```
                        Blue Sky Endeavors
                        Financial Summary

                  (Dollar Figures in Thousands)

                     Quarter    Quarter    Quarter    Quarter
                       One        Two       Three       Four
   Beginning Cash      -5.0       -1.0       1.0        2.0
   Income
       Net income      65.0       68.0      70.0       73.0
       Depreciation    42.0       47.0      49.0       49.0
       BORROW          32.0       32.0      30.0       30.0
       Subtotal       139.0      147.0     149.0      152.0
   Expenditures
       Investment     126.0      144.0     148.0      148.0
       Taxes           43.0       45.0      46.0       48.0
       Dividend        51.0       54.0      55.0       55.0
       Advertising     41.0       46.0      47.0       47.0
       Subtotal       135.0      145.0     148.0      150.0
   CASHFLOW            -1.0        1.0       2.0        4.0

   Internal Rate
   of Return           20.9
```

Chapter 7
The DATASOURCE Procedure

Chapter Table of Contents

Chapter 7
The DATASOURCE Procedure

Overview

The DATASOURCE procedure extracts time series data from many different kinds of data files distributed by various data vendors and stores them in a SAS data set. Once stored in a SAS data set, the time series variables can be processed by other SAS procedures.

The DATASOURCE procedure has statements and options to extract only a subset of time series data from an input data file. It gives you control over the frequency of data to be extracted, time series variables to be selected, cross sections to be included, and the time range of data to be output.

The DATASOURCE procedure can create auxiliary data sets containing descriptive information on the time series variables and cross sections. More specifically, the OUTCONT= data set contains information on time series variables, the OUTBY= data set reports information on the cross-sectional variables, and the OUTALL= data set combines both time series variables and cross-sectional information.

The output variables in the output and auxiliary data sets can be assigned various attributes by the DATASOURCE procedure. These attributes are labels, formats, new names, and lengths. While the first three attributes in this list are used to enhance the output, the length attribute is used to control the memory and disk-space usage of the DATASOURCE procedure.

Data files currently supported by the DATASOURCE procedure include

- U.S. Bureau of Economic Analysis data files:

  - National Income and Product Accounts tapes
  - National Income and Product Accounts diskettes
  - S-page diskettes

- U.S. Bureau of Labor Statistics data files:

  - Consumer Price Index Surveys
  - Producer Price Index Survey
  - National Employment, Hours, and Earnings Survey
  - State and Area Employment, Hours, and Earnings Survey

- Standard & Poor's Compustat Services Financial Database Files:

  - COMPUSTAT Annual
  - COMPUSTAT 48 Quarter

- FAME Software Corporation's CITIBASE data files

- Center for Research in Security Prices (CRSP) data files:

  - Daily Binary Format Files
  - Monthly Binary Format Files
  - Daily Character Format Files
  - Monthly Character Format Files
  - Daily IBM Binary Format Files
  - Monthly IBM Binary Format Files

- Haver Analytics data files

- International Monetary Fund data files:

  - International Financial Statistics
  - Direction of Trade Statistics
  - Balance of Payment Statistics
  - Government Finance Statistics

- Organization for Economic Cooperation and Development:

  - Annual National Accounts
  - Quarterly National Accounts
  - Main Economic Indicators

Getting Started

Structure of a SAS Data Set Containing Time Series Data

SAS procedures require time series data to be in a specific form recognizable by the SAS System. This form is a two-dimensional array, called a SAS data set, whose columns correspond to series variables and whose rows correspond to measurements of these variables at certain time periods.

The time periods at which observations are recorded can be included in the data set as a time ID variable. The DATASOURCE procedure does include a time ID variable by the name of DATE.

For example, the following data set, extracted from a CITIBASE data file, gives the foreign exchange rates for Japan, Switzerland, and the United Kingdom, respectively.

Time ID variable	Time Series Variables		
DATE	EXRJAN	EXRSW	EXRUK
SEP1987	143.290	1.50290	164.460
OCT1987	143.320	1.49400	166.200
NOV1987	135.400	1.38250	177.540
DEC1987	128.240	1.33040	182.880
JAN1988	127.690	1.34660	180.090
FEB1988	129.170	1.39160	175.820

Figure 7.1.   The Form of SAS Data Sets Required by Most SAS/ETS Procedures

Reading Data Files

The DATASOURCE procedure is designed to read data from many different files and to place them in a SAS data set. For example, if you have a tape format CITIBASE data file you want to read, use the following statements:

```
proc datasource filetype=citibase infile=citifile out=dataset;
run;
```

Here, the FILETYPE= option indicates that you want to read a tape format CITIBASE file, the INFILE= option specifies the fileref CITIFILE of the external file you want to read, and the OUT= option names the SAS data set to contain the time series data.

Subsetting Input Data Files

When only a subset of a data file is needed, it is inefficient to extract all the data and then subset it in a subsequent DATA step. Instead, you can use the DATASOURCE procedure options and statements to extract only needed information from the data file.

The DATASOURCE procedure offers the following subsetting capabilities:

- the INTERVAL= option controls the frequency of data output
- the KEEP or DROP statements selects a subset of time series variables
- the RANGE statement restricts the time range of data
- the WHERE statement selects a subset of cross sections

Controlling the Frequency of Data — The INTERVAL= Option

The OUT= data set can only contain data with the same frequency. If the data file you want to read contains time series data with several frequencies, you can indicate the frequency of data you want to extract with the INTERVAL= option. For example, the following statements extract all monthly time series from the CITIBASE file CITIFILE:

```
proc datasource filetype=citibase infile=citifile
                interval=month  out=dataset;
run;
```

When the INTERVAL= option is not given, the default frequency defined for the FILETYPE= type file is used. For example, the statements in the previous section extract yearly series since INTERVAL=YEAR is the default frequency for CITIBASE files.

To extract data for several frequencies, you need to execute the DATASOURCE procedure once for each frequency.

Selecting Time Series Variables — The KEEP and DROP Statements

If you want to include specific series in the OUT= data set, list them in a KEEP statement. If, on the other hand, you want to exclude some variables from the OUT= data set, list them in a DROP statement. For example, the following statements extract monthly foreign exchange rates for Japan (EXRJAN), Switzerland (EXRSW), and the United Kingdom (EXRUK) from a CITIBASE file CITIFILE:

```
proc datasource filetype=citibase infile=citifile
                interval=month  out=dataset;
   keep  exrjan exrsw exruk;
run;
```

Obviously, to be able to use KEEP and DROP statements, you need to know the name of time series variables available in the data file. The OUTCONT= option gives you this information. More specifically, the OUTCONT= option creates a data set containing descriptive information on the same frequency time series. This descriptive information includes series names, a flag indicating if the series is selected for output, series variable types, lengths, position of series in the OUT= data set, labels, format names, format lengths, format decimals, and a set of FILETYPE= specific descriptor variables. For example, the following statements list some of the monthly series available in the CITIFILE:

```
filename citifile 'host-specific-file-name' <host-options>;
proc datasource filetype=citibase infile=citifile
                interval=month  outcont=vars;
run;

title1 'Some Time Series Variables Available in CITIFILE';
proc print data=vars noobs;
run;
```

```
        Some Time Series Variables Available in CITIFILE

NAME    SELECTED   TYPE   LENGTH   VARNUM              LABEL

EXRJAN     1         1      5        .     FOREIGN EXCHANGE RATE: JAPAN (YEN PER U.
EXRSW      1         1      5        .     FOREIGN EXCHANGE RATE: SWITZERLAND (SWIS
EXRUK      1         1      5        .     FOREIGN EXCHANGE RATE: UNITED KINGDOM (C

                     DESCRIPT

FOREIGN EXCHANGE RATE: JAPAN (YEN PER U.S.$)
FOREIGN EXCHANGE RATE: SWITZERLAND (SWISS FRANC PER U.S.$)
FOREIGN EXCHANGE RATE: UNITED KINGDOM (CENTS PER POUND)

FORMAT    FORMATL    FORMATD     CODE

            0          0        EXRJAN
            0          0        EXRSW
            0          0        EXRUK
```

Figure 7.2. Partial Listing of the OUTCONT= Data Set

Controlling the Time Range of Data — The RANGE Statement

The RANGE statement is used to control the time range of observations included in the output data set. For example, if you want to extract the foreign exchange rates from September, 1987 to February, 1988, you can use the following statements:

```
filename citifile 'host-specific-file-name' <host-options>;
proc datasource filetype=citibase infile=citifile
                interval=month  out=dataset;
   keep  exrjan exrsw exruk;
   range from 1987:9 to 1988:2;
run;

title1 'Printout of the OUT= Data Set';
proc print data=dataset noobs;
run;
```

```
                  Printout of the OUT= Data Set

             DATE      EXRJAN       EXRSW        EXRUK

            SEP1987    143.290     1.50290      164.460
            OCT1987    143.320     1.49400      166.200
            NOV1987    135.400     1.38250      177.540
            DEC1987    128.240     1.33040      182.880
            JAN1988    127.690     1.34660      180.090
            FEB1988    129.170     1.39160      175.820
```

Figure 7.3. Subset Obtained by KEEP and RANGE Statements

Reading in Data Files Containing Cross Sections

Some data files group time series data with respect to cross-section identifiers; for example, International Financial Statistics files, distributed by IMF, group data with respect to countries (COUNTRY). Within each country, data are further grouped by Control Source Code (CSC), Partner Country Code (PARTNER), and Version Code (VERSION).

If a data file contains cross-section identifiers, the DATASOURCE procedure adds them to the output data set as BY variables. For example, the data set in Figure 7.4 contains three cross sections:

- the first one is identified by (COUNTRY='112' CSC='F' PARTNER=' ' VERSION='Z')

- the second one is identified by (COUNTRY='146' CSC='F' PARTNER=' ' VERSION='Z')

- the third one is identified by (COUNTRY='158' CSC='F' PARTNER=' ' VERSION='Z').

BY Variables				Time ID Variable	Time Series Variables	
COUNTRY	CSC	PARTNER	VERSION	DATE	EFFEXR	EXRINDEX
112	F		Z	SEP1987	9326	12685
112	F		Z	OCT1987	9393	12813
112	F		Z	NOV1987	9626	13694
112	F		Z	DEC1987	9675	14099
112	F		Z	JAN1988	9581	13910
112	F		Z	FEB1988	9493	13549
146	F		Z	SEP1987	12046	16192
146	F		Z	OCT1987	12067	16266
146	F		Z	NOV1987	12558	17596
146	F		Z	DEC1987	12759	18301
146	F		Z	JAN1988	12642	18082
146	F		Z	FEB1988	12409	17470
158	F		Z	SEP1987	13841	16558
158	F		Z	OCT1987	13754	16499
158	F		Z	NOV1987	14222	17505
158	F		Z	DEC1987	14768	18423
158	F		Z	JAN1988	14933	18565
158	F		Z	FEB1988	14915	18331

Figure 7.4. The Form of a SAS Data Set Containing BY Variables

Note that the data sets in Figure 7.1 and Figure 7.4 are two different ways of representing the same data, namely foreign exchange rates for three different countries: the United Kingdom (COUNTRY='112'), Switzerland (COUNTRY='146') and Japan (COUNTRY='158'). The first representation (Figure 7.1) incorporates country names into the series names, while the second representation (Figure 7.4) represents countries as different cross sections. See "Time Series and SAS Data Sets" in Chapter 2, "Working with Time Series Data."

Obtaining Descriptive Information on Cross Sections

If you want to know the unique set of values BY variables assume for each cross section in the data file, use the OUTBY= option. For example, the following statements list some of the cross sections available for an IFS file.

```
filename ifsfile 'host-specific-file-name' <host-options>;
proc datasource filetype=imfifsp infile=ifsfile
              interval=month outby=xsection;
run;

title1 'Some Cross Sections Available in IFSFILE';
proc print data=xsection noobs;
run;
```

```
              Some Cross Sections Available in IFSFILE

                                  E
   C        P   V        S        N              N    N
   O        A   E        T        D              S    S    C
   U        R   R        _        _     N        E    E    _
   N        T   S        D        D     T    N   R    L    N
   T    C   N   I        A        A     I    O   I    E    A
   R    S   E   O        T        T     M    B   E    C    M
   Y    C   R   N        E        E     E    S   S    S    T    E

   1    F  900  Z        .        .     .    0   0    0    WORLD
   1    F       Z   JAN1957   DEC1989  396  396  46   23   WORLD
   1    T       Z   JAN1957   DEC1989  396  396  16    8   WORLD
  10    F       Z   JAN1957   DEC1989  396  396  32   16   ALL COUNTRIES
  10    F  900  Z        .        .     .    0   0    0    ALL COUNTRIES
  10    M       Z   JAN1957   NOV1989  395  395   2    1   ALL COUNTRIES
  10    T       Z   JAN1957   DEC1989  396  396  18    9   ALL COUNTRIES
  16    F       Z   JAN1970   SEP1989  237  237  12    6   OFFSHORE BNKING CTRS
  16    F  900  Z        .        .     .    0   0    0    OFFSHORE BNKING CTRS
  24    F       Z   JAN1962   JUL1989  331  331   2    1   ACP COUNTRIES
```

Figure 7.5.   Partial Listing of the OUTBY= Data Set

The OUTBY= data set reports the total number of series, NSERIES, defined in each cross section, NSELECT of which represent the selected variables. If you want to see the descriptive information on each of these NSELECT variables for each cross section, specify the OUTALL= option. For example, the following statements print descriptive information on the eight series defined for cross section (COUNTRY='1' CSC='T' PARTNER=' ' and VERSION='Z'):

```
filename ifsfile 'host-specific-file-name' <host-options>;
proc datasource filetype=imfifsp infile=ifsfile interval=month
                outall=ifsall;
run;

title1 'Time Series Defined in Cross Section';
title2 "COUNTRY='1'  CSC='T'  PARTNER=' '  VERSION='Z'";
proc print data=ifsall noobs;
   where country='1' and csc='T' and  partner=' ' and version='Z';
run;
```

Figure 7.6 shows a partial listing of the OUTALL= data set. Note that only those time series defined in the cross section are represented.

```
              Time Series Defined in Cross Section
              COUNTRY='1'  CSC='T'  PARTNER=' '  VERSION='Z'

                              S
   C        P   V            E                                           F
   O        A   E            L        L   V   B                      F   O
   U        R   R            E        E   A   L    L                 O   R
   N        T   S        N   K    C   T   N   R    A                 R   M
   T    C   N   I        A   E    C   T   Y   G    N    B            M   A
   R    S   E   O        M   P    E   P   T   U    U    B            A   T
   Y    C   R   N        E   T    D   E   H   M    M    L            T   L

   1    T       Z   F__2KS   1    1   1   5   .    26   TOTAL PURCHASES     0
   1    T       Z   F__2LA   1    1   1   5   .    27   REPMTS.BY REPUR.IN PERIOD  0
   1    T       Z   F__2MS   1    1   1   5   .    28   TOTAL PURCHASES BY OTHERS  0
   1    T       Z   F__2NS   1    1   1   5   .    29   TOTAL REPURCHASES BY OTHERS 0
   1    T       Z   F_C2KS   1    1   1   5   .    30   TOTAL PURCHASES,CUM.       0
   1    T       Z   F_C2LA   1    1   1   5   .    31   REPAYMENTS BY REPURCHASE,CUM. 0
   1    T       Z   F_C2MS   1    1   1   5   .    32   TOTAL PURCHASES BY OTHERS,CUM 0
   1    T       Z   F_C2NS   1    1   1   5   .    33   TOTAL REP.BY OTHERS,CUM.   0

             E                        D                        B
```

F O R M A T D	S T _ D A T E	N D _ D A T E	N D T I M E	N O B S	C _ N A M E	S U B J E C T	A S C A Y P A	D T U _ C O D E	D U _ N A M E	A S E N D E C	S O U R C E
0	JAN1957	DEC1989	396	396	WORLD		F	S	MILLIONS OF SDRS	1	T
0	JAN1957	DEC1989	396	396	WORLD		F	S	MILLIONS OF SDRS	2	T
0	JAN1957	DEC1989	396	396	WORLD		F	S	MILLIONS OF SDRS	1	T
0	JAN1957	DEC1989	396	396	WORLD		F	S	MILLIONS OF SDRS	2	T
0	JAN1957	NOV1986	359	359	WORLD	C	S	S	MILLIONS OF SDRS	1	
0	JAN1957	DEC1989	396	396	WORLD	C	S	S	MILLIONS OF SDRS	1	
0	JAN1957	NOV1986	359	359	WORLD	C	S	S	MILLIONS OF SDRS	1	
0	JAN1957	DEC1989	396	396	WORLD	C	S	S	MILLIONS OF SDRS	1	

Figure 7.6.   Partial Listing of the OUTALL= Data Set

The OUTCONT= data set contains one observation for each time series variable with the descriptive information summarized over BY groups. When the data file contains no cross sections, the OUTCONT= and OUTALL= data sets are equivalent, except that the OUTALL= data set also reports time ranges for which data are available. The OUTBY= data set in this case contains a single observation reporting the number of series and time ranges for the whole data file.

Subsetting a Data File Containing Cross Sections

Data files containing cross sections can be subsetted by controlling which cross sections to include in the output data set. Selecting a subset of cross sections is accomplished using the WHERE statement. The WHERE statement gives a condition the BY variables must satisfy for a cross section to be selected. For example, the following statements extract the monthly effective exchange rate (F_X_AM) and exchange rate index (F_X_AF) for the United Kingdom (COUNTRY='112'), Switzerland (COUNTRY='146'), and Japan (COUNTRY='158') for the period from September, 1987 to February, 1988.

```
filename ifsfile 'host-specific-file-name' <host-options>;
proc datasource filetype=imfifsp infile=ifsfile interval=month
                out=exchange;
    where country in ('112','146','158') and partner=' ';
    keep  f_x_ah f_x_am;
    range from '01sep87'd to '01feb88'd;
run;

title1 'Printout of the OUT= Data Set';
proc print data=exchange noobs;
run;
```

```
              Printout of the OUT= Data Set

 COUNTRY    CSC    PARTNER    VERSION      DATE    F_X_AH    F_X_AM

    112      F                   Z      SEP1987    12685      9326
    112      F                   Z      OCT1987    12813      9393
    112      F                   Z      NOV1987    13694      9626
    112      F                   Z      DEC1987    14099      9675
    112      F                   Z      JAN1988    13910      9581
    112      F                   Z      FEB1988    13549      9493
    146      F                   Z      SEP1987    16192     12046
    146      F                   Z      OCT1987    16266     12067
    146      F                   Z      NOV1987    17596     12558
    146      F                   Z      DEC1987    18301     12759
    146      F                   Z      JAN1988    18082     12642
    146      F                   Z      FEB1988    17470     12409
    158      F                   Z      SEP1987    16558     13841
    158      F                   Z      OCT1987    16499     13754
    158      F                   Z      NOV1987    17505     14222
    158      F                   Z      DEC1987    18423     14768
    158      F                   Z      JAN1988    18565     14933
    158      F                   Z      FEB1988    18331     14915
```

Figure 7.7.   Subset Obtained by WHERE, KEEP, and RANGE Statements

Renaming Time Series Variables

Sometimes the time series variable names as given by data vendors are not descriptive enough, or you may prefer a different naming convention. In such cases, you can use the RENAME statement to assign more meaningful names to time series variables. You can also use LABEL statements to associate descriptive labels with your series variables.

For example, the series names for effective exchange rate (F_X_AM) and exchange rate index (F_X_AH) used by IMF can be given more descriptive names and labels by the following statements:

```
filename ifsfile 'host-specific-file-name' <host-options>;
proc datasource filetype=imfifsp infile=ifsfile interval=month
            out=exchange outcont=exchvars;
   where country in ('112','146','158') and partner=' ';
   keep  f_x_ah f_x_am;
   range from '01jun87'd to '01feb88'd;
   rename  f_x_ah=exrindex f_x_am=effexr;
   label   f_x_ah='F_X_AH: Exchange Rate Index 1985=100'
           f_x_am='F_X_AM: Effective Exchange Rate(MERM)';
run;

title1 'Printout of OUTCONT= Showing New NAMEs and LABELs';
proc print data=exchvars noobs;
   var  name label length;
run;

title1 'Contents of OUT= Showing New NAMEs and LABELs';
proc contents data=exchange;
run;
```

```
                    Printout of OUTCONT= Showing New NAMEs and LABELs

           NAME                         LABEL                        LENGTH

        EFFEXR         F_X_AM: Effective Exchange Rate(MERM)          5
        EXRINDEX       F_X_AH: Exchange Rate Index 1985=100          5
```

```
                    Contents of OUT= Showing New NAMEs and LABELs

                              CONTENTS PROCEDURE

Data Set Name: WORK.EXCHANGE                     Observations:          18
Member Type:   DATA                              Variables:             7
Engine:        V608                              Indexes:               0
Created:       12:37 Wednesday, August 12, 1992  Observation Length:    22
Last Modified: 12:37 Wednesday, August 12, 1992  Deleted Observations:  0
Protection:                                      Compressed:            NO
Data Set Type:                                   Sorted:                NO
Label:

                    -----Engine/Host Dependent Information-----

                    Data Set Page Size:          4096
                    Number of Data Set Pages: 1
                    File Format:                 607
                    First Data Page:             1
                    Max Obs per Page:            184
                    Obs in First Data Page:      18
                    FILETYPE:                    REGULAR

             -----Alphabetic List of Variables and Attributes-----

   #  Variable  Type  Len  Pos  Format   Label
   ------------------------------------------------------------------------
   3  COUNTRY   Char   3    10           COUNTRY CODE
   4  CSC       Char   1    13           CONTROL SOURCE CODE
   7  DATE      Num    4    18   MONYY7. Date of Observation
   2  EFFEXR    Num    5     5           F_X_AM: Effective Exchange Rate(MERM)
   1  EXRINDEX  Num    5     0           F_X_AH: Exchange Rate Index 1985=100
   5  PARTNER   Char   3    14           PARTNER COUNTRY CODE
   6  VERSION   Char   1    17           VERSION CODE
```

Figure 7.8.   Renaming and Labeling Variables

Notice that even though you changed the names of F_X_AH and F_X_AM to
EXRINDEX and EFFEXR, respectively, you still used their old names in the KEEP
and LABEL statements because renaming takes place at the output stage.

Changing the Lengths of Numeric Variables

The length attribute indicates the number of bytes the SAS System uses for storing
the values of variables in output data sets. Therefore, the shorter the variable lengths,
the more efficient the disk-space usage. However, there is a trade-off. The lengths
of numeric variables are closely tied to their precision, and reducing their lengths arbitrarily can cause precision loss.

The DATASOURCE procedure uses default lengths for series variables appropriate
to each file type. For example, the default lengths for numeric variables are 5 for
IMFIFSP type files (see the LENGTH variable in Figure 7.7). In some cases, however, you may want to assign different lengths. Assigning lengths less than the defaults
reduces memory and disk-space usage at the expense of reduced precision. Specifying lengths longer than the defaults increases the precision but causes the DATA-
SOURCE procedure to use more memory and disk space. The following statements

define a default length of 4 for all numeric variables in the IFSFILE and then assign a length of 6 to the exchange rate index:

```
filename ifsfile 'host-specific-file-name' <host-options>;
proc datasource filetype=imfifsp infile=ifsfile interval=month
              out=exchange outcont=exchvars;
    where country in ('112','146','158') and partner='   ';
    keep  f_x_am f_x_ah;
    range from '01jun87'd to '01feb88'd;
    rename  f_x_ah=exrindex  f_x_am=effexr;
    label   f_x_ah='F_X_AH: Exchange Rate Index 1985=100'
            f_x_am='F_X_AM: Effective Exchange Rate(MERM)';
    length _numeric_ 4; length f_x_ah 6;
run;

title1 'Printout of OUTCONT= Showing LENGTH Variable';
proc print data=exchvars noobs;
    var  name label length;
run;

title1 'Contents of the OUT= Data Set Showing LENGTHs';
proc contents data=exchange;
run;
```

```
                 Printout of OUTCONT= Showing LENGTH Variable

         NAME                      LABEL                          LENGTH

         EFFEXR      F_X_AM: Effective Exchange Rate(MERM)          4
         EXRINDEX    F_X_AH: Exchange Rate Index 1985=100           6
```

```
                 Contents of the OUT= Data Set Showing LENGTHs

                             CONTENTS PROCEDURE

Data Set Name: WORK.EXCHANGE                    Observations:          18
Member Type:   DATA                             Variables:             7
Engine:        V608                             Indexes:               0
Created:       12:46 Wednesday, August 12, 1992 Observation Length:    22
Last Modified: 12:46 Wednesday, August 12, 1992 Deleted Observations:  0
Protection:                                     Compressed:            NO
Data Set Type:                                  Sorted:                NO
Label:

                -----Engine/Host Dependent Information-----

                Data Set Page Size:        4096
                Number of Data Set Pages:  1
                File Format:               607
                First Data Page:           1
                Max Obs per Page:          184
                Obs in First Data Page:    18
                FILETYPE:                  REGULAR

        -----Alphabetic List of Variables and Attributes-----

# Variable  Type  Len  Pos  Format  Label
---------------------------------------------------------------------------
3  COUNTRY  Char   3   10           COUNTRY CODE
4  CSC      Char   1   13           CONTROL SOURCE CODE
7  DATE     Num    4   18  MONYY7.  Date of Observation
2  EFFEXR   Num    4    6           F_X_AM: Effective Exchange Rate(MERM)
1  EXRINDEX Num    6    0           F_X_AH: Exchange Rate Index 1985=100
5  PARTNER  Char   3   14           PARTNER COUNTRY CODE
6  VERSION  Char   1   17           VERSION CODE
```

Figure 7.9. Changing the Lengths of Numeric Variables

The default lengths of the character variables are set to the minimum number of characters that can hold the longest possible value.

Syntax

The DATASOURCE procedure uses the following statements:

PROC DATASOURCE *options*;
    KEEP *variable-list*;
    DROP *variable-list*;
    KEEPEVENT *event-list*;
    DROPEVENT *event-list*;
    WHERE *where-expression*;
    RANGE FROM *from* **TO** *to*;
    ATTRIBUTE *variable-list attribute-list* ... ;
    FORMAT *variable-list format* ... ;
    LABEL *variable=* "*label*" ... ;
    LENGTH *variable-list length* ... ;
    RENAME *old-name= new-name* ... ;

The PROC DATASOURCE statement is required. All the rest of the statements are optional.

The DATASOURCE procedure uses two kinds of statements:

1. subsetting statements, which control what time series, time periods, and cross sections are extracted from the input data file

2. attribute statements, which control the attributes of the variables in the output SAS data set

The subsetting statements are the KEEP, DROP, KEEPEVENT, and DROPEVENT statements (which select output variables); the RANGE statement (which selects time ranges); and the WHERE statement (which selects cross sections). The attribute statements are the ATTRIBUTE, FORMAT, LABEL, LENGTH, and RENAME statements.

The statements and options used by PROC DATASOURCE are summarized in Table 7.1.

Table 7.1. Summary of Syntax

Description	Statement	Option
Input Data File Options		
specify the type of input data file to read	PROC DATASOURCE	FILETYPE=
specify the fileref(s) of the input data file(s)	PROC DATASOURCE	INFILE=
Output Data Set Options		
write the extracted time series data	PROC DATASOURCE	OUT=
output the descriptive information on the time series variables and cross sections	PROC DATASOURCE	OUTALL=
output the descriptive information on the cross sections	PROC DATASOURCE	OUTBY=
output the descriptive information on the time series variables	PROC DATASOURCE	OUTCONT=
write event-oriented data	PROC DATASOURCE	OUTEVENT=
control whether all or only selected series and cross sections be reported	PROC DATASOURCE	OUTSELECT=
create single indexes from BY variables for the OUT= data set	PROC DATASOURCE	INDEX
Subsetting		
specify the periodicity of series to be extracted	PROC DATASOURCE	INTERVAL=
specify the time series variables to be included in the OUT= data set	KEEP	
specify the time series variables to be excluded from the OUT= data set	DROP	
specify the events to be included in the OUTEVENT= data set	KEEPEVENT	
specify the events to be excluded from the OUTEVENT= data set	DROPEVENT	
select cross sections for output	WHERE	
specify the time range of observations to be output	RANGE	
Assigning Attributes		
assign formats to the output variables	FORMAT	
	ATTRIBUTE	FORMAT=
assign labels to variables in the output data sets	LABEL	
	ATTRIBUTE	LABEL=
control the lengths of the output variables	LENGTH	
	ATTRIBUTE	LENGTH=

Description	Statement	Option
assign new names to the output variables	RENAME	

PROC DATASOURCE Statement

PROC DATASOURCE *options*;

The following options can be used in the PROC DATASOURCE statement:

FILETYPE= *entry*
DBTYPE= *dbtype*

specifies the kind of input data file to process. See "Supported File Types" later in this chapter for a list of supported file types. The FILETYPE= option is required.

INDEX

creates a set of single indexes from BY variables for the OUT= data set. Under some circumstances, creating indexes for a SAS data set may increase the efficiency in locating observations when BY or WHERE statements are used in subsequent steps. Refer to *SAS Language: Reference, Version 6, First Edition* for more information on SAS indexes. The INDEX option is ignored when no OUT= data set is created or when the data file does not contain any BY variables. The INDEX= data set option can be used to override the index variable definitions.

INFILE= *fileref*
INFILE= (*fileref1 fileref2 ... filerefn*)

specifies the *fileref* assigned to the input data file. The default value is DATAFILE. The fileref used in INFILE= option (or if no INFILE= option is specified, the fileref DATAFILE) must be associated with the physical data file in a FILENAME statement. (On some operating systems, the fileref assignment can be made with the system's control language, and a FILENAME statement may not be needed. Refer to *SAS Language: Reference, Version 6, First Edition* for more details on the FILENAME statement). Physical data files can reside on tapes, disks, diskettes, CD-ROM, or other media.

For some file types, the data are distributed over several files. In this case, the INFILE= option is required, and it lists in parentheses the filerefs for each of the files making up the database. The order in which these filerefs are listed is important and must conform to the specifics of each file type as explained in "Supported File Types" later in this chapter.

INTERVAL= *interval*
FREQUENCY= *interval*
TYPE= *interval*

specifies the periodicity of series selected for output to the OUT= data set. The OUT= data set created by PROC DATASOURCE can contain only time series with the same periodicity. Some data files contain time series with different periodicities; for example, a file may contain both monthly series and quarterly series. Use the INTERVAL= option to indicate which periodicity you want. If you want to extract series with different periodicities, use different PROC DATASOURCE invocations with the desired INTERVAL= options.

Common values for INTERVAL= are YEAR, QUARTER, MONTH, WEEK, and DAY. The values allowed, as well as the default value of the INTERVAL= option, depend on the file type. See "Supported File Types" later in this chapter for the INTERVAL= values appropriate to the data file type you are reading.

OUT= *SAS-data-set*

names the output data set for the time series extracted from the data file. If none of the output data set options are specified, including the OUT= data set itself, an OUT= data set is created and named according to the DATA*n* convention. However, when you create any of the other output data sets, such as OUT-CONT=, OUTBY=, OUTALL=, or OUTEVENT=, you must explicitly specify the OUT= data set; otherwise, it will not be created. See "OUT= Data Set" later in this chapter for further details.

OUTALL= *SAS-data-set*

writes information on the contents of the input data file to an output data set. The OUTALL= data set includes descriptive information, time ranges, and observation counts for all the time series within each BY group. By default, no OUT-ALL= data set is created.

The OUTALL= data set contains the Cartesian product of the information output by the OUTCONT= and OUTBY= options. In data files for which there are no cross sections, the OUTALL= and OUTCONT= data sets are almost equivalent, except that OUTALL= data set also reports time ranges and observation counts of series. See "OUTALL= Data Set" later in this chapter for further details.

OUTBY= *SAS-data-set*

writes information on the BY variables to an output data set. The OUTBY= data set contains the list of cross sections in the database delimited by the unique set of values that the BY variables assume. Unless the OUTSELECT=OFF option is present, only the selected BY groups get written to the OUTBY= data set. If you omit the OUTBY= option, no OUTBY= data set is created. See "OUTBY= Data Set" later in this chapter for further details.

OUTCONT= *SAS-data-set*

writes information on the contents of the input data file to an output data set. By default, the OUTCONT= data set includes descriptive information on all of the unique series of the selected periodicity in the data file. When the OUTSE-LECT=OFF option is omitted, the OUTCONT= data set includes observations only for the series selected for output to the OUT= data set. By default, no OUT-CONT= data set is created. See "OUTCONT= Data Set" later in this chapter for further details.

OUTEVENT= *SAS-data-set*

names the output data set to output event-oriented time series data. This option can only be used when CRSP stock files are being processed. For all other file types, it will be ignored. See "OUTEVENT= Data Set" later in this chapter for further details.

OUTSELECT= OFF
OUTSELECT= ON

determines whether to output all observations (OUTSELECT=OFF) or only those corresponding to the selected time series and selected BY groups (OUTSE-LECT=ON) to OUTCONT=, OUTBY=, and OUTALL= data sets. The default is OUTSELECT=ON. The OUTSELECT= option is only relevant when any one of the auxiliary data sets is specified.

KEEP Statement

KEEP *variable-list*;

The KEEP statement specifies which variables in the data file are to be included in the OUT= data set. Only the time series and event variables can be specified in a KEEP statement. All the BY variables and the time ID variable DATE are always included in the OUT= data set; they cannot be referenced in a KEEP statement. If they are referenced, a warning message is given and the reference is ignored.

The variable list can contain variable names or name range specifications. See "Variable Lists" later in this chapter for details.

There is a default KEEP list for each file type. Usually, descriptor type variables, like footnotes, are not included in the default KEEP list. If you give a KEEP statement, the default list becomes undefined.

Only one KEEP or one DROP statement can be used. KEEP and DROP are mutually exclusive.

You can also use the KEEP= data set option to control which variables to include in the OUT= data set. However, the KEEP statement differs from the KEEP= data set option in several aspects:

• The KEEP statement selection is applied before variables are read from the data file, while the KEEP= data set option selection is applied after variables are read and as they are written to the OUT= data set. Therefore, using the KEEP statement instead of the KEEP= data set option is much more efficient.

• If the KEEP statement causes no series variables to be selected, then no observations are output to the OUT= data set.

• The KEEP statement variable specifications are applied to each cross section independently. This behavior may produce different variables than those produced by the KEEP= data set option when order-range variable list specifications are used.

DROP Statement

DROP *variable-list*;

The DROP statement specifies that some variables be excluded from the OUT= data set. Only the time series and event variables can be specified in a DROP statement. None of the BY variables or the time ID variable DATE can be excluded from the OUT= data set. If they are referenced in a DROP statement, a warning message is given and the reference is ignored. Use the WHERE statement for selection based on BY variables, and use the RANGE statement for date selections.

The variable list can contain variable names or name range specifications. See "Variable Lists" later in this chapter for details.

Only one DROP or one KEEP statements can be used. KEEP and DROP are mutually exclusive.

There is a default KEEP list for each file type. Usually, descriptor type variables, like footnotes, are not included in the default KEEP list. If you specify a DROP statement, the default list becomes undefined.

You can also use the DROP= data set option to control which variables to exclude from the OUT= data set. However, the DROP statement differs from the DROP= data set option in several aspects:

- The DROP statement selection is applied before variables are read from the data file, while the DROP= data set option selection is applied after variables are read and as they are written to the OUT= data set. Therefore, using the DROP statement instead of the DROP= data set option is much more efficient.

- If the DROP statement causes all series variables to be excluded, then no observations are output to the OUT= data set.

- The DROP statement variable specifications are applied to each cross section independently. This behavior may produce different variables than those produced by the DROP= data set option when order-range variable list specifications are used.

KEEPEVENT Statement

KEEPEVENT *variable-list*;

The KEEPEVENT statement specifies which event variables in the data file are to be included in the OUTEVENT= data set. As a result, the KEEPEVENT statement is valid only for data files containing event-oriented time series data, that is, only for CRSP files. All the BY variables, the time ID variable DATE and the event-grouping variable EVENT are always included in the OUTEVENT= data set. These variables can not be referenced in the KEEPEVENT statement. If any of these variables are referenced, a warning message is given and the reference is ignored.

The variable list can contain variable names or name range specifications. See "Variable Lists" later in this chapter for details.

Only one KEEPEVENT or one DROPEVENT statement can be used. KEEPEVENT and DROPEVENT are mutually exclusive.

You can also use the KEEP= data set option to control which event variables to include in the OUTEVENT= data set. However, the KEEPEVENT statement differs from the KEEP= data set option in several aspects:

- The KEEPEVENT statement selection is applied before variables are read from the data file, while the KEEP= data set option selection is applied after variables are read and as they are written to the OUTEVENT= data set. Therefore, using the KEEPEVENT statement instead of the KEEP= data set option is much more efficient.

- If the KEEPEVENT statement causes no event variables to be selected, then no observations are output to the OUTEVENT= data set.

DROPEVENT Statement

DROPEVENT *variable-list*;

The DROPEVENT statement specifies that some event variables be excluded from the OUTEVENT= data set. As a result, the DROPEVENT statement is valid only for data files containing event-oriented time series data, that is, only for CRSP files. All the BY variables, the time ID variable DATE, and the event-grouping variable EVENT are always included in the OUTEVENT= data set. These variables cannot be referenced in the DROPEVENT statement. If any of these variables are referenced, a warning message is given and the reference is ignored.

The variable list can contain variable names or name range specifications. See "Variable Lists" later in this chapter for details.

Only one DROPEVENT or one KEEPEVENT statement can be used. DROPEVENT and KEEPEVENT are mutually exclusive.

You can also use the DROP= data set option to control which event variables to exclude from the OUTEVENT= data set. However, the DROPEVENT statement differs from the DROP= data set option in several aspects:

- The DROPEVENT statement selection is applied before variables are read from the data file, while the DROP= data set option selection is applied after variables are read and as they are written to the OUTEVENT= data set. Therefore, using the DROPEVENT statement instead of the DROP= data set option is much more efficient.

- If the DROPEVENT statement causes all series variables to be excluded, then no observations are output to the OUTEVENT= data set.

WHERE Statement

WHERE *where-expression*;

The WHERE statement specifies conditions that BY variables must satisfy in order for a cross section to be included in the OUT= and OUTEVENT= data sets. By default, all BY groups are selected.

The *where-expression* must refer only to BY variables defined for the file type you are reading. The section "Supported File Types" later in this chapter lists the names of the BY variables for each file type.

For example, DOTS (Direction of Trade Statistics) files, distributed by International Monetary Fund, have four BY variables: COUNTRY, CSC, PARTNER, and VERSION. Both COUNTRY and PARTNER are three-digit country codes. To select the direction of trade statistics of the United States (COUNTRY='111') with Turkey (COUNTRY='186'), Japan (COUNTRY='158'), and the oil exporting countries group (COUNTRY='985'), you should specify

```
where country='111' and partner in ('186','158','985');
```

You can use any SAS language operators and special WHERE expression operators in the WHERE statement condition. Refer to *SAS Language: Reference, Version 6, First Edition* for a more detailed discussion of WHERE expressions.

If you want to see the names of the BY variables and the values they assume for each cross section, you can first run PROC DATASOURCE with only the OUTBY= option. The information contained in the OUTBY= data set will aid you in selecting the appropriate BY groups for subsequent PROC DATASOURCE steps.

RANGE Statement

RANGE FROM *from* TO *to*;

The RANGE statement selects the time range of observations written to the OUT= and OUTEVENT= data sets. The *from* and *to* values can be SAS date, time, or date-time constants, or they can be specified as *year* or *year* : *period*, where *year* is a two-digit or four-digit year, and *period* (when specified) is a period within the year corresponding to the INTERVAL= option. (For example, if INTERVAL=QTR, then *period* refers to quarters.) When *period* is omitted, the beginning of the year is assumed for the *from* value, and the end of the year is assumed for the *to* value.

The RANGE option restricts the time range output but does not cause the full range specified to be output when the data availability for all the selected series is shorter.

Both the FROM and TO specifications are optional, and both the FROM and TO keywords are optional. If the FROM limit is omitted, the output observations start with the minimum date for which data is available for any selected series. Similarly, if the TO limit is omitted, the output observations end with the maximum date for which data are available.

The following are some examples of RANGE statements:

```
range from 1980 to 1990;
range 1980 - 1990;
range from 1980;
range 1980;
range to 1990;
range to 1990:2;
range from '31aug89'd to '28feb1990'd;
```

The RANGE statement applies to each BY group independently. If all the selected series contain no data in the specified range for a given BY group, then there will be no observations for that BY group in the OUT= and OUTEVENT= data sets.

If you want to know the time ranges for which periodic time series data is available, you can first run PROC DATASOURCE with the OUTBY= or OUTALL= options. OUTBY= data set reports the union of the time ranges over all the series within each BY group, while the OUTALL= data set gives time ranges for each series separately in each BY group.

ATTRIBUTE Statement

> **ATTRIBUTE** *variable-list attribute-list* ... ;

The ATTRIBUTE statement assigns formats, labels, and lengths to variables in the output data sets.

The *variable-list* can contain variable names and variable name range specifications. See "Variable Lists" later in this chapter for details. The attributes specified in the following attribute list apply to all variables in the variable list:

An *attribute-list* consists of one or more of the following options:

FORMAT= *format*

associates a format with variables in *variable-list*. The *format* can be either a standard SAS format or a format defined with the FORMAT procedure. The default formats for variables depend on the file type.

LABEL= *"label"*

assigns a label to the variables in the variable list. The default labels for variables depend on the file type.

LENGTH= *length*

specifies the number of bytes used to store the values of variables in the variable list. The default lengths for numeric variables depend on the file type. Usually default lengths are set to 5 bytes. (For CRSP files, the default lengths are 6 bytes).

The length specification also controls the amount of memory that PROC DATA-SOURCE uses to hold variable values while processing the input data file. Thus, specifying a LENGTH= value smaller than the default will reduce both the disk space taken up by the output data sets and the amount of memory used by the PROC DATASOURCE step, at the cost of reduced precision of output data values.

FORMAT Statement

> **FORMAT** *variable-list format* ... ;

The FORMAT statement assigns formats to variables in output data sets. The *variable-list* can contain variable names and variable name range specifications. See "Variable Lists" later in this chapter for details. The format specified applies to all variables in the variable list.

A single FORMAT statement can assign the same format to several variables or different formats to different variables. The FORMAT statement can use standard SAS formats or formats defined using the FORMAT procedure.

Any later format specification for a variable, using either the FORMAT statement or the FORMAT= option in the ATTRIBUTE statement, always overrides the previous one.

LABEL Statement

LABEL *variable* = "*label*" ... ;

The LABEL statement assigns SAS variable labels to variables in the output data sets. You can give labels for any number of variables in a single LABEL statement. The default labels for variables depend on the file type.

Any later label specification for a variable, using either the LABEL statement or the LABEL= option in the ATTRIBUTE statement, always overrides the previous one.

LENGTH Statement

LENGTH *variable-list length* ... ;

The LENGTH statement, like the LENGTH= option in the ATTRIBUTE statement, specifies the number of bytes used to store values of variables in output data sets. The default lengths for numeric variables depend on the file type. Usually default lengths are set to 5 bytes. (For CRSP files, the default lengths are 6 bytes).

The default lengths of character variables are defined as the minimum number of characters that can hold the longest possible value.

For some file types, the LENGTH statement also controls the amount of memory used to store values of numeric variables while processing the input data file. Thus, specifying LENGTH values smaller than the default will reduce both the disk space taken up by the output data sets and the amount of memory used by the PROC DATA-SOURCE step, at the cost of reduced precision of output data values.

Any later length specification for a variable, using either the LENGTH statement or the LENGTH= option in the ATTRIBUTE statement, always overrides the previous one.

RENAME Statement

RENAME *old-name* = *new-name* ... ;

The RENAME statement is used to change the names of variables in the output data sets. Any number of variables can be renamed in a single RENAME statement. The most recent RENAME specification overrides any previous ones for a given variable.

For some data files, variables have long names. Due to the eight-character name restriction in SAS software, PROC DATASOURCE truncates those long names in an attempt to generate unique names within each BY group. Sometimes the truncation does not generate unique names. In such cases, you will get a list of warnings in the log indicating the duplicate names. You can resolve this problem by changing the conflicting old names to valid SAS names. For example, in OECD Annual National Accounts files, both the names P0DISCGDPE and P5DISCGDPE become SCGDPE by truncating the first 4 bytes. In this case, the following RENAME statement will assign the valid SAS name P0DIGDPE to P0DISCGDPE:

```
rename p0discgdpe=p0digdpe;
```

Note that P5DISCGDPE keeps the name SCGDPE unless you choose to rename it also.

Renaming of variables is done at the output stage. Therefore, you need to use the old variable names in all other PROC DATASOURCE statements. For example, the series variable names DATA1-DATA350 used with annual COMPUSTAT files are not very descriptive, so you may choose to rename them to reflect the financial aspect they represent. You may rename "DATA51" to "INVESTTAX" with the RENAME statement

```
rename data51=investtax;
```

since it contains investment tax credit data. However, in all other DATASOURCE statements, you must use the old name, DATA51.

Details

Variable Lists

Variable lists used in PROC DATASOURCE statements can consist of any combination of variable names and name range specifications. Items in variable lists can have the following forms:

- a name, for example, PZU

- an alphabetic range *name1-name2*. For example, A-DZZZZZZZ specifies all variables with names starting with A, B, C, or D.

- a prefix range *prefix:*. For example, IP: selects all variables with names starting with the letters IP.

- an order range *name1--name2*. For example, GLR72--GLRD72 specifies all variables in the input data file between GLR72 and GRLD72 inclusive.

- a numeric order range *name1*-NUMERIC-*name2*. For example, GLR72-NUMERIC-GLRD72 specifies all numeric variables between GLR72 and GRLD72 inclusive.

- a character order range *name1*-CHARACTER-*name2*. For example, GLR72-CHARACTER-GLRD72 specifies all character variables between GLR72 and GRLD72 inclusive.

- one of the keywords _NUMERIC_, _CHARACTER_, or _ALL_. _NUMERIC_ specifies all numeric variables. _CHARACTER_ specifies all character variables. _ALL_ specifies all variables.

To determine the order of series in a data file, run PROC DATASOURCE with the OUTCONT= option, and print the output data set. Note that order and alphabetic range specifications are inclusive, meaning that the beginning and ending names of the range are also included in the variable list.

For order ranges, the names used to define the range must actually name variables in the input data file. For alphabetic ranges, however, the names used to define the range need not be present in the data file.

Note that variable specifications are applied to each cross section independently. This may cause the order-range variable list specification to behave differently than its DATA step and data set option counterparts. This is because PROC DATASOURCE knows which variables are defined for which cross sections, while the DATA step applies order range specification to the whole collection of time series variables.

If the ending variable name in an order range specification is not in the current cross section, all variables starting from the beginning variable to the last variable defined in that cross section get selected. If the first variable is not in the current cross section, then order range specification has no effect for that cross section.

The variable names used in variable list specifications can refer to either series names appearing in the input data file or to the SAS names assigned to series data fields internally if the series names are not recorded to the INFILE= file. When the latter is the case, internally defined variable names are listed in the section "Data Files" later in this chapter.

The following are examples of the use of variable lists:

```
keep  ip: pw112-pw117 pzu;
drop  data1-data99  data151-data350;
length data1-numeric-aftnt350  ucode 4;
```

The first statement keeps all the variables starting with IP:, all the variables between PW112 and PW117 including the PW112 and PW117 themselves, and a single variable PZU. The second statement drops all the variables that fall alphabetically between DATA1 and DATA99, and DATA151 and DATA350. Finally, the third statement assigns a length of 4 bytes to all the numeric variables defined between DATA1 and AFTNT350, and UCODE.

OUT= Data Set

The OUT= data set can contain the following variables:

- the BY variables, which identify cross-sectional dimensions when the input data file contains time series replicated for different values of the BY variables. Use the BY variables in a WHERE statement to process the OUT= data set by cross sections. The order in which BY variables are defined in the OUT= data set corresponds to the order in which the data file is sorted.

- DATE, a SAS date-, time-, or datetime- valued variable that reports the time period of each observation. The values of the DATE variable may span different time ranges for different BY groups. The format of the DATE variable depends on the INTERVAL= option.

- the periodic time series variables, which are included in the OUT= data set only if they have data in at least one selected BY group and they are not discarded by a KEEP or DROP statement

- the event variables, which are included in the OUT= data set if they are not discarded by a KEEP or DROP statement. By default, these variables are not output to OUT= data set.

The values of BY variables remain constant in each cross section. Observations within each BY group correspond to the sampling of the series variables at the time periods indicated by the DATE variable.

You can create a set of single indexes for the OUT= data set by using the INDEX option, provided there are BY variables. Under some circumstances, this may increase the efficiency of subsequent PROC and DATA steps that use BY and WHERE statements. However, there is a cost associated with creation and maintenance of indexes. The *SAS Language: Reference, Version 6, First Edition* lists the conditions under which the benefits of indexes outweigh the cost.

With data files containing cross sections, there can be various degrees of overlap among the series variables. One extreme is when all the series variables contain data for all the cross sections. In this case, the output data set is very compact. In the other extreme case, however, the set of time series variables are unique for each cross section, making the output data set very sparse, as depicted in Figure 7.10.

BY Variables BY1 ... BYP	Series in first BY group F1 F2 F3 ... FN	Series in second BY group S1 S2 S3 ... SM	... ...	Series in last BY group T1 T2 T3 ... TK
BY group 1				
BY group 2				data is missing everywhere except in these boxes
⋮			⋮	
BY group N				

Figure 7.10. The OUT= Data Set containing unique Series for each BY Group

The data in Figure 7.10 can be represented more compactly if cross-sectional information is incorporated into series variable names.

OUTCONT= Data Set

The OUTCONT= data set contains descriptive information for the time series variables. This descriptive information includes various attributes of the time series variables. The OUTCONT= data set contains the following variables:

- NAME, a character variable that contains the series name

- KEPT, a numeric variable that indicates whether the series was selected for output by the DROP or KEEP statements, if any. KEPT will usually be the same as SELECTED, but may differ if a WHERE statement is used.

- SELECTED, a numeric variable that indicates whether the series is selected for output to the OUT= data set. The series is included in the OUT= data set (SELECT-

ED=1) if it is kept (KEPT=1) and it has data for at least one selected BY group.

- TYPE, a numeric variable that indicates the type of the time series variable. TYPE=1 for numeric series; TYPE=2 for character series.

- LENGTH, a numeric variable that gives the number of bytes allocated for the series variable in the OUT= data set

- VARNUM, a numeric variable that gives the variable number of the series in the OUT= data set. If the series variable is not selected for output (SELECTED=0), then VARNUM has a missing value. Likewise, if no OUT= option is given, VAR-NUM has all missing values.

- LABEL, a character variable that contains the label of the series variable. LABEL contains only the first 40 characters of the labels. If they are longer than 40 charac-ters, then an additional variable, DESCRIPT, is defined to hold the whole length of series labels. Note that if a data file assigns different labels to the same series variable within different cross sections, only the first occurrence of labels will be transferred to the LABEL column.

- the variables FORMAT, FORMATL, and FORMATD, which give the format name, length, and number of format decimals, respectively

- the GENERIC variables, whose values may vary from one series to another, but whose values remain constant across BY groups for the same series

By default, the OUTCONT= data set contains observations for only the selected se-ries, that is, for series where SELECTED=1. If the OUTSELECT=OFF option is specified, the OUTCONT= data set contains one observation for each unique series of the specified periodicity contained in the input data file.

If you do not know what series are in the data file, you can run PROC DATA-SOURCE with the OUTCONT= option and OUTSELECT=OFF. The information contained in the OUTCONT= data set can then help you to determine which time series data you want to extract.

OUTBY= Data Set

The OUTBY= data set contains information on the cross sections contained in the input data file. These cross sections are represented as BY groups in the OUT= data set. The OUTBY= data set contains the following variables:

- the BY variables, whose values identify the different cross sections in the data file. The BY variables depend on the file type.

- BYSELECT, a numeric variable that reports the outcome of the WHERE statement condition for the BY variable values for this observation. The value of BYSE-LECT is 1 for BY groups selected by the WHERE statement for output to the OUT= data set and is 0 for BY groups that are excluded by the WHERE statement. BYSELECT is added to the data set only if a WHERE statement is given. When there is no WHERE statement, then all the BY groups are selected.

- ST_DATE, a numeric variable that gives the starting date for the BY group. The starting date is the earliest of the starting dates of all the series that have data for the current BY group.

- END_DATE, a numeric variable that gives the ending date for the BY group. The ending date is the latest of the ending dates of all the series that have data for the BY group.

- NTIME, a numeric variable that gives the number of time periods between ST_DATE and END_DATE, inclusive. Usually, this is the same as NOBS, but they may differ when time periods are not equally spaced and when the OUT= data set is not specified. NTIME is a maximum limit on NOBS.

- NOBS, a numeric variable that gives the number of time series observations in OUT= data set between ST_DATE and END_DATE, inclusive. When a given BY group is discarded by a WHERE statement, the NOBS variable corresponding to this BY group becomes 0, since the OUT= data set does not contain any observations for this BY group. Note that BYSELECT=0 for every discarded BY group.

- NINRANGE, a numeric variable that gives the number of observations in the range (*from,to*) defined by the RANGE statement. This variable is only added to the OUTBY= data set when the RANGE statement is specified.

- NSERIES, a numeric variable that gives the total number of unique time series variables having data for the BY group

- NSELECT, a numeric variable that gives the total number of selected time series variables having data for the BY group

- the generic variables, whose values remain constant for all the series in the current BY group

In this list, you can only control the attributes of the BY and GENERIC variables.

The variables NOBS, NTIME, and NINRANGE give observation counts, while the variables NSERIES and NSELECT give series counts.

By default, observations for only the selected BY groups (where BYSELECT=1) are output to the OUTBY= data set, and the date and time range variables are computed over only the selected time series variables. If the OUTSELECT=OFF option is specified, the OUTBY= data set contains an observation for each BY group, and the date and time range variables are computed over all the time series variables.

For file types that have no BY variables, the OUTBY= data set contains one observation giving ST_DATE, END_DATE, NTIME, NOBS, NINRANGE, NSERIES, and NSELECT for all the series in the file.

If you do not know the BY variable names or their possible values, you can do an initial run of PROC DATASOURCE with the OUTBY= option. The information contained in the OUTBY= data set can help you design your WHERE expression and RANGE statement for the subsequent executions of PROC DATASOURCE to obtain different subsets of the same data file.

OUTALL= Data Set

The OUTALL= data set combines and expands the information provided by the OUTCONT= and OUTBY= data sets. That is, the OUTALL= data set contains the OUTCONT= information separately for each BY group and contains the OUTBY= information separately for each series. Each observation in the OUTBY= data set gets expanded to NSERIES or NSELECT observations in the OUTALL= data set, depending on whether the OUTSELECT=OFF option is specified.

By default, only the selected BY groups and series are included in the OUTALL= data set. If the OUTSELECT=OFF option is specified, then all the series within all the BY groups are reported.

The OUTALL= data set contains all the variables defined in the OUTBY= and OUT-CONT= data sets and also contains the GENERIC variables (whose values may vary from one series to another and also from one BY group to another). Another additional variable is BLKNUM, which gives the data block number in the data file containing the series variable.

The OUTALL= data set is useful when BY groups do not contain the same time series variables or when the time ranges for series change across BY groups.

You should be careful in using the OUTALL= option, since the OUTALL= data set can get very large for many file types. Some file types have the same series and time ranges for each BY group; the OUTALL= option should not be used with these file types. For example, you should not specify the OUTALL= option with COMPUS-TAT files, since all the BY groups contain the same series variables.

The OUTALL= and OUTCONT= data sets are equivalent when there are no BY variables, except that the OUTALL= data set contains extra information about the time ranges and observation counts of the series variables.

OUTEVENT= Data Set

The OUTEVENT= data set is used to output event-oriented time series data. Events occurring at discrete points in time are recorded along with the date they occurred. Only CRSP stock files contain event-oriented time series data. For all other types of files, the OUTEVENT= option is ignored.

The OUTEVENT= data set contains the following variables:

- the BY variables, which identify cross-sectional dimensions when the input data file contains time series replicated for different values of the BY variables. Use the BY variables in a WHERE statement to process the OUTEVENT= data set by cross sections. The order in which BY variables are defined in the OUTEVENT= data set corresponds to the order in which the data file is sorted.

- DATE, a SAS date-, time- or datetime- valued variable that reports the discrete time periods at which events occurred. The format of the DATE variable depends on the INTERVAL= option.

- EVENT, a character variable that contains the event group name. The EVENT variable acts like yet another cross-sectional variable.

- the event variables, which are included in the OUTEVENT= data set only if they have data in at least one selected BY group and they are not discarded by a KEEP-EVENT or DROPEVENT statement.

Note that each event group contains a nonoverlapping set of event variables; therefore, the OUTEVENT= data set is very sparse. You should exercise care when selecting event variables to be included in the OUTEVENT= data set.

Also note that even though the OUTEVENT= data set can not contain any periodic time series variables, the OUT= data set can contain event variables if they are explicitly specified in a KEEP statement. In other words, you can specify event variables in a KEEP statement, but you cannot specify periodic time series variables in a KEEP-EVENT statement.

While variable selection for OUT= and OUTEVENT= data sets are controlled by a different set of statements (KEEP versus KEEPEVENT or DROP versus DROPEVENT), cross-section and range selections are controlled by the same statements. In other words, the WHERE and the RANGE statements are effective for both output data sets.

Supported File Types

PROC DATASOURCE can process only certain kinds of data files. For certain time series databases, the DATASOURCE procedure has built-in information on the layout of files comprising the database. PROC DATASOURCE knows how to read only these kinds of data files. To access these databases, you must indicate the data file type in the FILETYPE= option. For more detailed information, see the corresponding document for each filetype. See the section "References" later in this chapter.

The currently supported file types are summarized in Table 7.2.

Table 7.2. Supported File Types

Supplier	FILETYPE=	Description
BEA	BEANIPA	National Income and Product Accounts Tape Format
	BEANIPAD	National Income and Product Accounts Diskette Format
BLS	BLSCPI	Consumer Price Index Surveys
	BLSWPI	Producer Price Index Survey
	BLSEENA	National Employment, Hours, and Earnings Survey
	BLSEESA	State and Area Employment Hours and Earnings Survey
FAME	CITIBASE	Tape Format CITIBASE Data Files
	CITIOLD	Old format CITIBASE Data Files
	CITIDISK	PC Diskette format CITIBASE Databases
CRSP	CRSPDBS	CRSP Daily Binary Security File Format
	CRSPDBI	CRSP Daily Binary Calendar/Indices File Format
	CRSPDBA	CRSP Daily Binary File Annual Data Format
	CRSPMBS	CRSP Monthly Binary Security File Format

Supplier	FILETYPE=	Description
	CRSPMBI	CRSP Monthly Binary Calendar/Indices File Format
	CRSPMBA	CRSP Monthly Binary File Annual Data Format
	CRSPDCS	CRSP Daily Character Security File Format
	CRSPDCI	CRSP Daily Character Calendar/Indices File Format
	CRSPDCA	CRSP Daily Character File Annual Data Format
	CRSPMCS	CRSP Monthly Character Security File Format
	CRSPMCI	CRSP Monthly Character Calendar/Indices File Format
	CRSPMCA	CRSP Monthly Character File Annual Data Format
	CRSPDIS	CRSP Daily IBM Binary Security File Format
	CRSPDII	CRSP Daily IBM Binary Calendar/Indices File Format
	CRSPDIA	CRSP Daily IBM Binary File Annual Data Format
	CRSPMIS	CRSP Monthly IBM Binary Security File Format
	CRSPMII	CRSP Monthly IBM Binary Calendar/Indices File Format
	CRSPMIA	CRSP Monthly IBM Binary File Annual Data Format
Haver	HAVER	Haver Analytics Data Files
IMF	IMFIFSP	International Financial Statistics, Packed Format
	IMFDOTSP	Direction of Trade Statistics, Packed Format
	IMFBOPSP	Balance of Payment Statistics, Packed Format
	IMFGFSP	Government Finance Statistics, Packed Format
OECD	OECDANA	OECD Annual National Accounts Tape Format
	OECDQNA	OECD Quarterly National Accounts Tape Format
	OECDMEI	OECD Main Economic Indicators Tape Format
S&P	CSAIBM	COMPUSTAT Annual, IBM 360/370 Format
	CS48QIBM	COMPUSTAT 48 Quarter, IBM 360/370 Format
	CSAUC	COMPUSTAT Annual, Universal Character Format
	CS48QUC	COMPUSTAT 48 Quarter, Universal Character Format

Data supplier abbreviations used in Table 7.2 are

Abbreviation	Supplier
BEA	Bureau of Economic Analysis, U.S. Department of Commerce
BLS	Bureau of Labor Statistics, U.S. Department of Labor
FAME	FAME Software Corporation
CRSP	Center for Research in Security Prices
Haver	Haver Analytics Inc.
IMF	International Monetary Fund
OECD	Organization for Economic Cooperation and Development
S&P	Standard & Poor's Compustat Services Inc.

BEA Data Files

The Bureau of Economic Analysis, U.S. Department of Commerce, supplies national income, product accounting, and various other macro economic data at the regional, national, and international levels in the form of data files with various formats and on various media.

The following BEA data file types are supported:

FILETYPE= BEANIPA—National Income and Product Accounts Tape Format

Data Files	Database is stored in a single tape file.	
INTERVAL=	YEAR (default), QUARTER, MONTH	
BY variables	PARTNO	Part Number of Publication, Integer Portion of the Table Number, 1-9 (character)
	TABNUM	Table Number Within Part, Decimal Portion of the Table Number, 1-24 (character)
Series Variables	Series variable names are constructed by concatenating table number suffix, line and column numbers within each table. An underscore (_) prefix is also added to make series names valid SAS names.	

FILETYPE= BEANIPAD—National Income and Product Accounts Diskette Format

The diskette format National Income and Product Accounts files contain the same information as the tape format files described previously.

Data Files	Database is stored in a single diskette file.	
INTERVAL=	YEAR (default), QUARTER, MONTH	
BY variables	PARTNO	Part Number of Publication, Integer Portion of the Table Number, 1-9 (character)
	TABNUM	Table Number Within Part, Decimal Portion of the Table Number, 1-24 (character)
Series Variables	Series variable names are constructed by concatenating table number suffix, line and column numbers within each table. An underscore (_) prefix is also added to make series names valid SAS names.	

BLS Data Files

The Bureau of Labor Statistics, U.S. Department of Labor, compiles and distributes data on employment, expenditures, prices, productivity, injuries and illnesses, and wages. These data are available either on tapes or on diskettes.

The following BLS file types are supported:

FILETYPE= BLSCPI—Consumer Price Index Surveys (= CU,CW)

Data Files	Database is stored in a single tape file.	
INTERVAL=	YEAR, SEMIYEAR1.6, MONTH (default)	
BY variables	SURVEY	Survey type: CU=All Urban Consumers, CW=Urban Wage Earners and Clerical Workers (character)

	SEASON	Seasonality: S=Seasonally adjusted, U=Unadjusted (character)
	AREA	Geographic Area (character)
	BASPTYPE	Index Base Period Type, S=Standard, A=Alternate Reference (character)
	BASEPER	Index Base Period (character)
Series Variables	Series variable names are the same as consumer item codes listed in the Series Directory shipped with the data tapes.	
Missing Codes	A data value of 0 is interpreted as MISSING.	

FILETYPE= BLSWPI—*Producer Price Index Survey (WP)*

Data Files	Database is stored in a single tape file.	
INTERVAL=	YEAR, MONTH (default)	
BY variables	SEASON	Seasonality: S=Seasonally adjusted, U=Unadjusted (character)
	MAJORCOM	Major Commodity Group (character)
Sorting Order	BY SEASON MAJORCOM	
Series Variables	Series variable names are the same as commodity codes but prefixed by an underscore (_).	
Missing Codes	A data value of 0 is interpreted as MISSING.	

FILETYPE= BLSEENA—*National Employment, Hours, and Earnings Survey*

Data Files	Database is stored in a single tape file.	
INTERVAL=	YEAR, QUARTER, MONTH (default)	
BY variables	SEASON	Seasonality: S=Seasonally adjusted, U=Unadjusted (character)
	DIVISION	Major Industrial Division (character)
	INDUSTRY	Industry Code (character)
Sorting Order	BY SEASON DIVISION INDUSTRY	
Series Variables	Series variable names are the same as data type codes prefixed by EE.	
	EE01	Total Employment
	EE02	Employment of Women
	EE03	Employment of Production or Nonsupervisory Workers
	EE04	Average Weekly Earnings of Production Workers
	EE05	Average Weekly Hours of Production Workers
	EE06	Average Hourly Earnings of Production Workers
	EE07	Average Weekly Overtime Hours of Production Workers
	EE40	Index of Aggregate Weekly Hours
	EE41	Index of Aggregate Weekly Payrolls
	EE47	Hourly Earnings Index; 1977 Weights; Current Dollars
	EE48	Hourly Earnings Index; 1977 Weights; Base 1977 Dollars
	EE49	Average Hourly Earnings; Base 1977 Dollars
	EE50	Gross Average Weekly Earnings; Current Dollars
	EE51	Gross Average Weekly Earnings; Base 1977 Dollars
	EE52	Spendable Average Weekly Earnings; No Dependents; Current Dollars
	EE53	Spendable Average Weekly Earnings; No Dependents; Base 1977 Dollars
	EE54	Spendable Average Weekly Earnings; 3 Dependents; Cur-

		rent Dollars
	EE55	Spendable Average Weekly Earnings; 3 Dependents; Base 1977 Dollars
	EE60	Average Hourly Earnings Excluding Overtime
	EE61	Index of Diffusion; 1-month Span; Base 1977
	EE62	Index of Diffusion; 3-month Span; Base 1977
	EE63	Index of Diffusion; 6-month Span; Base 1977
	EE64	Index of Diffusion; 12-month Span; Base 1977
Missing Codes	Series data values are set to MISSING when their status codes are 1.	

FILETYPE= BLSEESA—State and Area Employment, Hours, and Earnings Survey

Data Files	Database is stored in a single tape file.	
INTERVAL=	YEAR, MONTH (default)	
BY variables	STATE	State FIPS codes (numeric)
	AREA	Area Codes (character)
	DIVISION	Major Industrial Division (character)
	INDUSTRY	Industry Code (character)
	DETAIL	Private/Government Detail
Sorting Order	BY STATE AREA DIVISION INDUSTRY DETAIL	
Series Variables	Series variable names are the same as data type codes prefixed by SA.	
	SA1	All employees
	SA2	Women workers
	SA3	Production Workers
	SA4	Average weekly earnings
	SA5	Average weekly hours
Missing Codes	Series data values are set to MISSING when their status codes are 1.	

CITIBASE Data Files

The CITIBASE database contains economic and financial indicators of the U.S. and international economies gathered from various government and private sources by FAME Software Corporation. There are over 8000 yearly, quarterly, monthly, weekly, and daily time series. The CITIBASE Directory, the document accompanying the data files, has complete descriptions of the series supplied in the data files.

FAME distributes data files in either tape format or diskette format. There are no key fields by which data is organized. Series names are constructed from series codes reported in the CITIBASE directory. Note that if there is a series code starting with a digit, it must be preceded by an underscore (_) to convert it to a valid SAS variable name.

The following CITIBASE file types are supported:

FILETYPE= CITIBASE—Tape Format CITIBASE Data Files

Data Files	Database is stored in a single file.
INTERVAL=	YEAR (default), QUARTER, MONTH, WEEK, WEEK1.1, WEEK1.3, WEEK1.4, WEEK1.5, WEEK1.6, WEEK1.7, WEEKDAY
BY variables	None
Series Variables	Variable names are taken from the series descriptor records in the data file and are the same as the series codes reported in the *CITIBASE Directory*. Note that for daily series, series codes could be longer than 8 bytes. In these cases the first four characters of the series codes are truncated.
Missing Codes	MISSING=('1.000000E9'=. 'NA'-'ND'=.)

Note that when you specify the INTERVAL=WEEK option, all the weekly series will be aggregated, and the DATE variable in the OUT= data set will be set to the date of Sundays. The date of first observation for each series is the Sunday marking the beginning of the week that contains the starting date of that variable.

FILETYPE= CITIOLD—Old format CITIBASE data files

This file type is used for CITIBASE data tapes distributed prior to May, 1987. The contents of the data file are similar to those of FILETYPE=CITIBASE described previously.

Data Files	Database is stored in a single file.
INTERVAL=	YEAR (default), QUARTER, MONTH
BY variables	None
Series Variables	Variable names are taken from the series descriptor records in the data file and are the same as the series codes reported in the *CITIBASE Directory*.
Missing Codes	1.0E9=.

FILETYPE= CITIDISK—PC Diskette Format CITIBASE Databases

Data Files	Database is stored in groups of three associated files having the same file name but different extensions: KEY, IND, or DB. The INFILE= option should contain three filerefs in the following order: INFILE=(*keyfile indfile dbfile*)
INTERVAL=	YEAR (default), QUARTER, MONTH
BY variables	None
Series Variables	Series variable names are the same as series codes reported in the *CITIBASE Directory*.
Missing Codes	1.0E9=.

COMPUSTAT Data Files

COMPUSTAT data files, distributed by Standard and Poor's Compustat Services, Inc., consist of a collection of financial, statistical, and market information covering several thousand industrial and nonindustrial companies. Data are available in both an IBM 360/370 format and a "Universal Character" format, both of which further subdivide into annual and quarterly formats.

The BY variables are used to select individual companies or a group of companies. Individual companies can be selected by their unique six-digit CUSIP issuer code (CNUM). A number of specific groups of companies can be extracted from the tape by the following key fields:

FILE   specifies the file identification code used to group companies by files

ZLIST   specifies the exchange listing code that can be used to group companies by exchange

DNUM   is used to extract companies in a specific SIC industry group

Series names are internally constructed from the data array names documented in the COMPUSTAT manual. Each column of data array is treated as a SAS variable. The names of these variables are generated by concatenating the corresponding column numbers to the array name.

FILETYPE= CSAIBM—COMPUSTAT Annual, IBM 360/370 Format

Data Files	Database is stored in a single file.	
INTERVAL=	YEAR (default)	
BY Variables	DNUM	Industry Classification Code (numeric)
	CNUM	CUSIP Issuer Code (character)
	CIC	CUSIP Issue Number and Check Digit (numeric)
	FILE	File Identification Code (numeric)
	ZLIST	Exchange Listing and S&P Index Code (numeric)
	SMBL	Stock Ticker Symbol (character)
	XREL	S&P Industry Index Relative Code (numeric)
	STK	Stock Ownership Code (numeric)
	STATE	Company Location Identification Code - State (numeric)
	COUNTY	Company Location Identification Code - County (numeric)
	FINC	Incorporation Code - Foreign (numeric)
	EIN	Employer Identification Number (character)
Sorting order	BY DNUM CNUM CIC	
Series Variables	DATA1-DATA350 UCODE SOURCE AFTNT1-AFTNT70	
Default KEEP List	KEEP DATA1-DATA318 UCODE SOURCE AFTNT1-AFTNT45;	
Missing Codes	0.0001=. 0.0004=.C 0.0008=.I 0.0002=.S 0.0003=.A	

FILETYPE= CS48QIBM—COMPUSTAT 48-Quarter, IBM 360/370 Format

Data Files	Database is stored in a single file.	
INTERVAL=	QUARTER (default)	
BY Variables	DNUM	Industry Classification Code (numeric)
	CNUM	CUSIP Issuer Code (character)
	CIC	CUSIP Issue Number and Check Digit (numeric)
	FILE	File Identification Code (numeric)
	EIN	Employer Identification Number (character)
	STK	Stock Ownership Code (numeric)
	SMBL	Stock Ticker Symbol (character)
	ZLIST	Exchange Listing and S&P Index Code (numeric)
	XREL	S&P Industry Index Relative Code (numeric)
	FINC	Incorporation Code - Foreign (numeric)
	SINC	Incorporation Code - State (numeric)

	STATE	Company Location Identification Code - State (numeric)
	COUNTY	Company Location Identification Code - County (numeric)
Sorting order	BY DNUM CNUM CIC;	
Series Variables	DATA1 - DATA232	Data Array
	QFTNT1 - QFTNT60	Data Footnotes
	FSCYR	Fiscal Year-end Month of Data
	SPCSCYR	SPCS Calendar Year
	SPCSCQTR	SPCS Calendar Quarter
	UCODE	Update Code
	SOURCE	Source Document Code
	BONDRATE	S&P Bond Rating
	DEBTCL	S&P Class of Debt
	CPRATE	S&P Commercial Paper Rating
	STOCK	S&P Common Stock Ranking
	MIC	S&P Major Index Code
	REPORTDT	Report Date of Quarterly Earnings
	FORMAT	Flow of Funds Statement Format Code
	CS	Comparability Status
	CSA	Company Status Alert
Default KEEP List	DROP DATA118-DATA232 QFTNT22-QFTNT60;	
Missing Codes	0.0001=. 0.0004=.C 0.0008=.I 0.0002=.S 0.0003=.A	

FILETYPE= CSAUC—COMPUSTAT Annual, Universal Character Format

Data Files	Database is stored in a single file.	
INTERVAL=	YEAR (default)	
BY variables	DNUM	Industry Classification Code (numeric)
	CNUM	CUSIP Issuer Code (character)
	CIC	CUSIP Issue Number and Check Digit (character)
	FILE	File Identification Code (numeric)
	ZLIST	Exchange Listing and S&P Index Code (numeric)
	SMBL	Stock Ticker Symbol (character)
	XREL	S&P Industry Index Relative Code (numeric)
	STK	Stock Ownership Code (numeric)
	STATE	Company Location Identification Code - State (numeric)
	COUNTY	Company Location Identification Code - County (numeric)
	FINC	Incorporation Code - Foreign (numeric)
	EIN	Employer Identification Number (character)
Sorting order	BY DNUM CNUM CIC	
Series Variables	DATA1-DATA350 UCODE SOURCE AFTNT1-AFTNT70	
Default KEEP List	KEEP DATA1-DATA318 UCODE SOURCE AFTNT1-AFTNT45;	
Missing Codes	-0.001=. -0.004=.C -0.008=.I -0.002=.S -0.003=.A	

FILETYPE= CS48QUC—COMPUSTAT 48 Quarter, Universal Character Format

Data Files	Database is stored in a single file.	
INTERVAL=	QUARTER (default)	
BY Variables	DNUM	Industry Classification Code (numeric)
	CNUM	CUSIP Issuer Code (character)
	CIC	CUSIP Issue Number and Check Digit (character)
	FILE	File Identification Code (numeric)
	EIN	Employer Identification Number (character)
	STK	Stock Ownership Code (numeric)
	SMBL	Stock Ticker Symbol (character)
	ZLIST	Exchange Listing and S&P Index Code (numeric)
	XREL	S&P Industry Index Relative Code (numeric)
	FINC	Incorporation Code - Foreign (numeric)
	SINC	Incorporation Code - State (numeric)
	STATE	Company Location Identification Code - State (numeric)
	COUNTY	Company Location Identification Code - County (numeric)
Sorting order	BY DNUM CNUM CIC	
Series Variables	DATA1 - DATA232	Data Array
	QFTNT1 - QFTNT60	Data Footnotes
	FSCYR	Fiscal Year-end Month of Data
	SPCSCYR	SPCS Calendar Year
	SPCSCQTR	SPCS Calendar Month
	UCODE	Update Code
	SOURCE	Source Document Code
	BONDRATE	S&P Bond Rating
	DEBTCL	S&P Class of Debt
	CPRATE	S&P Commercial Paper Rating
	STOCK	S&P Common Stock Ranking
	MIC	S&P Major Index Code
	IIC	S&P Industry Index Code
	REPORTDT	Report Date of Quarterly Earnings
	FORMAT	Flow of Funds Statement Format Code
Default KEEP List	DROP DATA118-DATA232 QFTNT22-QFTNT60;	
Missing Codes	-0.001=. -0.004=.C -0.008=.I -0.002=.S -0.003=.A	

CRSP Stock Files

The Center for Research in Security Prices provides comprehensive security price data via two primary stock files, the NYSE/AMEX file and the NASDAQ file. These files are composed of master and return components, available separately or combined. CRSP stock files are further differentiated by the frequency at which prices and returns are reported, daily or monthly. Both daily and monthly files contain annual data fields.

CRSP data files come either in binary or character tape format.

CRSP stock data are provided in two tape files, a main data file containing security information and a calendar/indices file containing a list of trading dates and market information associated with those trading dates. If security data do not fit on one tape, they are split into two or more files, each one of which resides on a different self-contained tape. The calendar/indices file is on the first tape only.

The file types for CRSP stock files are constructed by concatenating CRSP with a D or M to indicate the frequency of data, followed by B,C, or I to indicate file formats. B is for host binary, C is for character, and I is for IBM binary formats. The last character in the file type indicates if you are reading the Calendar/Indices file (I), or if you are extracting the security (S) or annual data (A). For example, the file type for the daily NYSE/AMEX combined tape in IBM binary format is CRSPDIS. Its calendar/indices file can be read by CRSPDII, and its annual data can be extracted by CRSPDIA.

If you use utility routines supplied by CRSP to convert a character format file to a binary format file on a given host, then you need to use host binary file types to read those files in. Note that you can not do the conversion on one host and transfer and read the file on another host.

For CRSP file types, the INFILE= option must be of the form

```
INFILE=( calfile securty1 < securty2 ... > )
```

where *calfile* is the fileref assigned to the calendar/indices file, and *securty1 < securty2 ... >* are the filerefs given to the security files, in the order in which they should be read.

CRSP Calendar/Indices Files

Data Files	Database is stored in a single file.	
INTERVAL=	DAY	for products DR, DM, DX, EX, EZ, NR, NM, and NX
	MONTH	for products MR, MM, MX, MT, MO, MZ, QR, QM, and QX
BY variables	None	
Series Variables	VWRETD	Value-Weighted Return (including all distributions)
	VWRETX	Value-Weighted Return (excluding dividends)
	EWRETD	Equal-Weighted Return (including all distributions)
	EWRETX	Equal-Weighted Return (excluding dividends)
	TOTVAL	Total Market Value
	TOTCNT	Total Market Count
	USDVAL	Market Value of Securities Used
	USDCNT	Count of Securities Used
	SPINDX	Level of the Standard & Poor's Composite Index
	SPRTRN	Return on the Standard & Poor's Composite Index
	NCINDX	NASDAQ Composite Index
	NCRTRN	NASDAQ Composite Return
Default KEEP List	All variables will be kept.	

CRSP Daily Security Files

Data Files	INFILE=(calfile securty1 < securty2 … >)		
INTERVAL=	DAY		
BY variables	CUSIP	CUSIP Identifier (character)	
	PERMNO	CRSP Permanent Number (numeric)	
	COMPNO	NASDAQ Company Number (numeric)	
	ISSUNO	NASDAQ Issue Number (numeric)	
	HEXCD	Header Exchange Code (numeric)	
	HSICCD	Header SIC Code (numeric)	
Sorting Order	BY CUSIP		
Series Variables	BIDLO	Bid or Low	
	ASKHI	Ask or High	
	PRC	Closing Price of Bid/Ask Average	
	VOL	Share Volume	
	RET	Holding Period Return	
	BXRET	Beta Excess Return	
	SXRET	Standard Deviation Excess Return	
Events	NAMES	NCUSIP	Name CUSIP
		TICKER	Exchange Ticker Symbol
		COMNAM	Company Name
		SHRCLS	Share Class
		SHRCD	Share Code
		EXCHCD	Exchange Code
		SICCD	Standard Industrial Classification Code
	DIST	DISTCD	Distribution Code
		DIVAMT	Dividend Cash Amount
		FACPR	Factor to Adjust Price
		FACSHR	Factor to Adjust Shares Outstanding
		EXDT	Ex-distribution Date
		RCRDDT	Record Date
		PAYDT	Payment Date
	SHARES	SHROUT	Number of Shares Outstanding
		SHRFLG	Share Flag
	DELIST	DLSTCD	Delisting Code
		NWPERM	New CRSP Permanent Number
		NEXTDT	Date of Next Available Information
		DLBID	Delisting Bid
		DLASK	Delisting Ssk
		DLPRC	Delisting Price
		DLVOL	Delisting Volume
		DLRET	Delisting Return
	NASDIN	TRTSCD	Traits Code
		NMSIND	National Market System Indicator
		MMCNT	Market Maker Count
		NSDINX	NASD Index
	Default KEEP Lists	All periodic series variables will be output to the OUT= data set and all event variables will be output to the OUTEVENT= data set.	

CRSP Monthly Security Files

Data Files	INFILE=(calfile securty1 < securty2 … >)		
INTERVAL=	MONTH		
BY variables	CUSIP	CUSIP Identifier (character)	
	PERMNO	CRSP Permanent Number (numeric)	
	COMPNO	NASDAQ Company Number (numeric)	
	ISSUNO	NASDAQ Issue Number (numeric)	
	HEXCD	Header Exchange Code (numeric)	
	HSICCD	Header SIC Code (numeric)	
Sorting Order	BY CUSIP		
Series Variables	BIDLO	Bid or Low	
	ASKHI	Ask or High	
	PRC	Closing Price of Bid/Ask average	
	VOL	Share Volume	
	RET	Holding Period Return	
	RETX	Return Without Dividends	
	PRC2	Secondary Price	
Events	NAMES	NCUSIP	Name CUSIP
		TICKER	Exchange Ticker Symbol
		COMNAM	Company Name
		SHRCLS	Share Class
		SHRCD	Share Code
		EXCHCD	Exchange Code
		SICCD	Standard Industrial Classification Code
	DIST	DISTCD	Distribution Code
		DIVAMT	Dividend Cash Amount
		FACPR	Factor to Adjust Price
		FACSHR	Factor to Adjust Shares Outstanding
		EXDT	Ex-distribution Date
		RCRDDT	Record Date
		PAYDT	Payment Date
	SHARES	SHROUT	Number of Shares Outstanding
		SHRFLG	Share Flag
	DELIST	DLSTCD	Delisting Code
		NWPERM	New CRSP Permanent Number
		NEXTDT	Date of Next Available Information
		DLBID	Delisting Bid
		DLASK	Delisting Ssk
		DLPRC	Delisting Price
		DLVOL	Delisting Volume
		DLRET	Delisting Return
	NASDIN	TRTSCD	Traits Code
		NMSIND	National Market System Indicator
		MMCNT	Market Maker Count
		NSDINX	NASD Index
	Default KEEP Lists	All periodic series variables will be output to the OUT= data set and all event variables will be output to the OUT-EVENT= data set.	

CRSP Annual Data

Data Files	INFILE=(securty1 < securty2 ... >)	
INTERVAL=	YEAR	
BY variables	CUSIP	CUSIP Identifier (character)
	PERMNO	CRSP Permanent Number (numeric)
	COMPNO	NASDAQ Company Number (numeric)
	ISSUNO	NASDAQ Issue Number (numeric)
	HEXCD	Header Exchange Code (numeric)
	HSICCD	Header SIC Code (numeric)
Sorting Order	BY CUSIP	
Series Variables	CAPV	Year End Capitalization
	SDEVV	Annual Standard Deviation
	BETAV	Annual Beta
	CAPN	Year End Capitalization Portfolio Assignment
	SDEVN	Standard Deviation Portfolio Assignment
	BETAN	Beta Portfolio Assignment
Default KEEP Lists	All variables will be kept.	

Haver Analytics Data Files

Haver Analytics offers a broad range of economic, financial, and industrial data for the U.S. and other countries. The format of Haver Analytics data files is similar to the CITIBASE format.

FILETYPE= HAVER—Haver Analytics Data Files

Data Files	Database is stored in a single file.
INTERVAL=	YEAR (default), QUARTER, MONTH
BY variables	None
Series Variables	Variable names are taken from the series descriptor records in the data file.
Missing Codes	1.0E9=.

IMF Data Files

The International Monetary Fund offers tape subscriptions for their International Financial Statistics (IFS), Direction of Trade Statistics (DOTS), Balance of Payment Statistics (BOPS), and the Government Finance Statistics (GFS) databases. The first three contain annual, quarterly, and monthly data, while the GFS file has only annual data.

IMF data tapes are available for IBM mainframe systems (EBCDIC character coding) in both a "packed" and an "unpacked" format. PROC DATASOURCE supports only the "packed" format at this time.

FILETYPE= IMFIFSP—*International Financial Statistics, Packed format*

The IFS data files contain over 23,000 time series including interest and exchange rates, national income and product accounts, price and production indexes, money and banking, export commodity prices, and balance of payments for nearly 200 countries and regional aggregates.

Data Files	Database is stored in a single file.	
INTERVAL=	YEAR (default), QUARTER, MONTH	
BY variables	COUNTRY	Country Code (character, three-digits)
	CSC	Control Source Code (character)
	PARTNER	Partner Country Code (character, three-digits)
	VERSION	Version Code (character)
Sorting Order	BY COUNTRY CSC PARTNER VERSION	
Series Variables	Series variable names are the same as series codes reported in *IMF Documentation* prefixed by F for data and F_F for footnote indicators.	
Default KEEP List	By default all the footnote indicators will be dropped.	

FILETYPE= IMFDOTSP—*Direction of Trade Statistics, Packed Format*

The DOTS files contain time series on the distribution of exports and imports for about 160 countries and country groups by partner country and areas.

Data Files	Database is stored in a single file.	
INTERVAL=	YEAR (default), QUARTER, MONTH	
BY variables	COUNTRY	Country Code (character, three-digits)
	CSC	Control Source Code (character)
	PARTNER	Partner Country Code (character, three-digits)
	VERSION	Version Code (character)
Sorting Order	BY COUNTRY CSC PARTNER VERSION	
Series Variables	Series variable names are the same as series codes reported in *IMF Documentation* prefixed by D for data and F_D for footnote indicators.	
Default KEEP List	By default all the footnote indicators will be dropped.	

FILETYPE= IMFBOPSP—*Balance of Payment Statistics, Packed Format*

The BOPS data files contain approximately 43,000 time series on balance of payments for about 120 countries.

Data Files	Database is stored in a single file.	
INTERVAL=	YEAR (default), QUARTER, MONTH	
BY variables	COUNTRY	Country Code (character, three-digits)
	CSC	Control Source Code (character)
	PARTNER	Partner Country Code (character, three-digits)
	VERSION	Version Code (character)
Sorting Order	BY COUNTRY CSC PARTNER VERSION	
Series Variables	Series variable names are the same as series codes reported in *IMF Documentation* prefixed by B for data F_B for footnote indicators.	

Default KEEP List	By default all the footnote indicators will be dropped.

FILETYPE= IMFGFSP—Government Finance Statistics, Packed Format

The GFS data files encompass approximately 28,000 time series that give a detailed picture of federal government revenue, grants, expenditures, lending minus repayment financing and debt, and summary data of state and local governments, covering 128 countries.

Data Files	Database is stored in a single file.	
INTERVAL=	YEAR (default)	
BY variables	COUNTRY	Three-digit country code (character)
	CSC	Control Source Code (character)
	PARTNER	Three-digit partner country code (character)
	VERSION	Version Code (character)
Sorting Order	BY COUNTRY CSC PARTNER VERSION	
Series Variables	Series variable names are the same as series codes reported in *IMF Documentation* prefixed by G for data and F_G for footnote indicators.	
Default KEEP List	By default all the footnote indicators will be dropped.	

OECD Data Files

The Organization for Economic Cooperation and Development compiles and distributes statistical data, including National Accounts and Main Economic Indicators.

FILETYPE= OECDANA—Annual National Accounts

The ANA data files contain both main national aggregates accounts (Volume I) and detailed tables for each OECD Member country (Volume II).

Data Files	Database is stored on a single tape file.	
INTERVAL=	YEAR (default),SEMIYR1.6,QUARTER,MONTH,WEEK,WEEKDAY	
BY variables	PREFIX	Table number prefix (character)
	CNTRYZ	Country Code (character)
Series Variables	Series variable names are the same as the mnemonic name of the element given on the element 'E' record. They are taken from the value 'V' record time series identifier. In cases where this identifier is longer than 8 bytes, the first 4 bytes will be truncated. However, this requires that the following variables be renamed to generate unique variable names within BY groups:	

```
.fontsize 9pt
rename p0discgdpe=p0digdpe;
rename doll2gdpe=dol2gdpe;
rename doll3gdpe=dol3gdpe;
rename doll1gdpe=dol1gdpe;
rename ppp1gdpd=pp1gdpd;
rename ppp1gdpd1=pp1gdpd1;
```

Missing Codes	A data value of * is interpreted as MISSING.

FILETYPE= OECDQNA—*Quarterly National Accounts*

The QNA tape contains the main aggregates of quarterly national accounts for 16 OECD Member Countries and on a selected number of aggregates for 4 groups of member countries: OECD-Total, OECD-Europe, EEC, and the 7 major countries.

Data Files	Database is stored on a single tape file.	
INTERVAL=	QUARTER(default),YEAR	
BY variables	COUNTRY	Country Code (character)
	SEASON	Seasonality
		S=Seasonally adjusted
		0=raw data, not seasonally adjusted
	PRICETAG	Prices C=data at current prices
		R,L,M=data at constant prices
		P,K,J,V=implicit price index or volume index
Series Variables	Subject code used to distinguish series within countries.	
Missing Codes	A data value of + or - is interpreted as MISSING.	

FILETYPE= OECDMEI—*Main Economic Indicators*

The MEI tape contains all series found in Parts 1 and 2 of the publication *Main Economic Indicators*.

Data Files	Database is stored on a single tape file.	
INTERVAL=	YEAR(default),QUARTER,MONTH	
BY variables	COUNTRY	Country Code (character)
	CURRENCY	Unit of expression of the series.
	ADJUST	Adjustment 0,H,S,A,L=no adjustment
		1,I=calendar or working day adjusted
		2,B,J,M=seasonally adjusted by National Authorities
		3,K,D=seasonally adjusted by OECD
Series Variables	Series variables are prefixed by _ for data, C for control codes, and D for relative date in weeks since last updated.	
Missing Codes	A data value of + or - is interpreted as MISSING.	

Examples

Example 7.1.   BEA National Income and Product Accounts

In this example, exports and imports of goods and services are extracted to demonstrate how to work with a National Income and Product Accounts Tape file.

From the "Statistical Tables" published by the United States Department of Commerce, Bureau of Economic Analysis, exports and imports of goods and services are given in the second table (TABNUM='02') of the "Foreign Transactions" section (PARTNO='4'). This table does not have any table suffix A or B. Moreover, the first line in the table gives exports, while the eighth gives imports. Therefore, the series names for exports and imports are __00100 and __00800, where the first underscore is inserted by the procedure, the second underscore is the place holder for the table suffix, the following three digits are the line numbers, and the last two digits are the column numbers.

The following statements put this information together to extract quarterly exports and imports from a BEANIPA type file:

```
filename  datafile 'host-specific-path-name' host-options;
proc datasource filetype=beanipa infile=datafile
                interval=qtr out=foreign;
   keep __00100 __00800;
   where partno='4' and tabnum='02';
   label __00100='Exports of Goods and Services';
   label __00800='Imports of Goods and Services';
   rename __00100=exports __00800=imports;
run;
```

The plot of EXPORTS and IMPORTS against DATE is shown in Output 7.1.1.

Output 7.1.1. Plot of Time Series in the OUT= Data Set for FILETYPE=BEANIPA

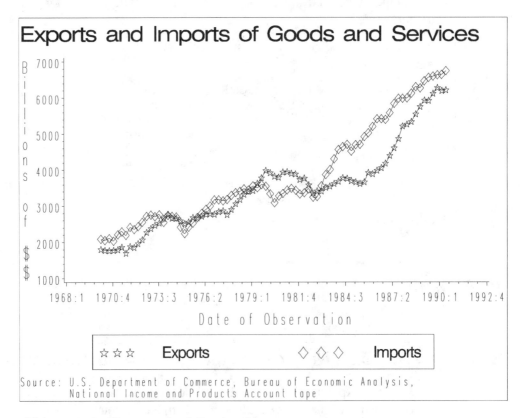

This example illustrates the following features:

• You need to know the series variables names used by a particular vendor in order to construct the KEEP statement.

• You need to know the BY variable names and their values for the required cross sections.

Example 7.1. BEA National Income and Product Accounts □ □ □ 369

- You can use RENAME and LABEL statements to associate more meaningful names and labels with your selected series variables.

Example 7.2. BLS Consumer Price Index Surveys

This example compares changes of the prices in medical care services with respect to different regions for all urban consumers (SURVEY='CU') since May, 1975. The source of data is the Consumer Price Index Surveys distributed by the U.S. Department of Labor, Bureau of Labor Statistics.

An initial run of PROC DATASOURCE gives the descriptive information on different regions available (the OUTBY= data set), as well as the series variable name corresponding to medical care services (the OUTCONT= data set).

```
filename datafile 'host-specific-file-name' <host-options>;
proc datasource filetype=blscpi interval=month
                outby=cpikey outcont=cpicont;
   where survey='CU';
run;

title1 'Partial Listing of the OUTBY= Data Set';
proc print data=cpikey noobs;
   where upcase(areaname) in ('NORTHEAST','NORTH CENTRAL','SOUTH','WEST');
run;

title1 'Partial Listing of the OUTCONT= Data Set';
proc print data=cpicont noobs;
   where index( upcase(label), 'MEDICAL CARE' );
run;
```

The OUTBY= data set in Output 7.2.1 lists all cross sections available for the four geographical regions: Northeast (AREA='0100'), North Central (AREA='0200'), Southern (AREA='0300'), and Western (AREA='0400'). The OUTCONT= data set gives the variable names for medical care related series.

Output 7.2.1. Partial Listings of the OUTBY= and OUTCONT= Data Sets

```
                  Partial Listing of the OUTBY= Data Set

  SURVEY    SEASON    AREA    BASPTYPE    BASEPER              ST_DATE    END_DATE

    CU        U       0100       A        DECEMBER 1977=100    DEC1966    JUL1990
    CU        U       0100       S        1982-84=100          DEC1966    JUL1990
    CU        U       0100       S        DECEMBER 1982=100    DEC1982    JUL1990
    CU        U       0100       S        DECEMBER 1986=100    DEC1986    JUL1990
    CU        U       0200       A        DECEMBER 1977=100    DEC1966    JUL1990
    CU        U       0200       S        1982-84=100          DEC1966    JUL1990
    CU        U       0200       S        DECEMBER 1982=100    DEC1982    JUL1990
    CU        U       0200       S        DECEMBER 1986=100    DEC1986    JUL1990
    CU        U       0300       A        DECEMBER 1977=100    DEC1966    JUL1990
    CU        U       0300       S        1982-84=100          DEC1966    JUL1990
    CU        U       0300       S        DECEMBER 1982=100    DEC1982    JUL1990
    CU        U       0300       S        DECEMBER 1986=100    DEC1986    JUL1990
    CU        U       0400       A        DECEMBER 1977=100    DEC1966    JUL1990
    CU        U       0400       S        1982-84=100          DEC1966    JUL1990
    CU        U       0400       S        DECEMBER 1982=100    DEC1982    JUL1990
    CU        U       0400       S        DECEMBER 1986=100    DEC1986    JUL1990

  NTIME     NOBS     NSERIES    NSELECT      SURTITLE          AREANAME

    284      284        1          1       ALL URBAN CONSUM    NORTHEAST
    284      284        90         90      ALL URBAN CONSUM    NORTHEAST
```

Output 7.2.1.   (Continued)

```
   92        92        7         7       ALL URBAN CONSUM    NORTHEAST
   44        44        1         1       ALL URBAN CONSUM    NORTHEAST
  284       284        1         1       ALL URBAN CONSUM    NORTH CENTRAL
  284       284       90        90       ALL URBAN CONSUM    NORTH CENTRAL
   92        92        7         7       ALL URBAN CONSUM    NORTH CENTRAL
   44        44        1         1       ALL URBAN CONSUM    NORTH CENTRAL
  284       284        1         1       ALL URBAN CONSUM    SOUTH
  284       284       90        90       ALL URBAN CONSUM    SOUTH
   92        92        7         7       ALL URBAN CONSUM    SOUTH
   44        44        1         1       ALL URBAN CONSUM    SOUTH
  284       284        1         1       ALL URBAN CONSUM    WEST
  284       284       90        90       ALL URBAN CONSUM    WEST
   92        92        7         7       ALL URBAN CONSUM    WEST
   44        44        1         1       ALL URBAN CONSUM    WEST
```

```
                  Partial Listing of the OUTCONT= Data Set
                 S
                 E
                 L        L   V                              F    F
                 E        E   A   L                          O    O
         N       C    T   N   R   A                          R    R
         A       T    Y   G   N   B                          M    M
         M       E    P   T   U   E                          A    A
         E       D    E   H   M   L                          T    T
                                                             L    D

       ASL5      1    1   5   .   SERVICES LESS MEDICAL CARE      0    0
       A0L5      1    1   5   .   ALL ITEMS LESS MEDICAL CARE     0    0
       A5        1    1   5   .   MEDICAL CARE                    0    0
       A51       1    1   5   .   MEDICAL CARE COMMODITIES        0    0
       A512      1    1   5   .   MEDICAL CARE SERVICES           0    0
```

The following statements make use of this information to extract the data for A512 and descriptive information on cross sections containing A512:

```
proc format;
   value $areafmt '0100' = 'Northeast Region'
                  '0200' = 'North Central Region'
                  '0300' = 'Southern Region'
                  '0400' = 'Western Region';
run;

filename datafile 'host-specific-file-name' <host-options>;
proc datasource filetype=blscpi interval=month
                out=medical outall=medinfo;
   where survey='CU' and area in ( '0100','0200','0300','0400' );
   keep a512;
   range  from 1980:5;
   format area $areafmt.;
   rename a512=medcare;
run;

title1 'Information on Medical Care Service';
proc print data=medinfo;
run;
```

Example 7.2. BLS Consumer Price Index Surveys □ □ □ 371

Output 7.2.2. Printout of the OUTALL= Data Set

```
                   Information on Medical Care Service

OBS SURVEY    SEASON   AREA                    BASPTYPE     BASEPER      LENGTH

 1   CU         U      Northeast Region           S        1982-84=100     5
 2   CU         U      North Central Region       S        1982-84=100     5
 3   CU         U      Southern Region            S        1982-84=100     5
 4   CU         U      Western Region             S        1982-84=100     5

OBS BYSELECT   NAME   KEPT  SELECTED  TYPE  VARNUM  BLKNUM        LABEL

 1     1      MEDCAR    1       1       1      7     3479   MEDICAL CARE SERVICES
 2     1      MEDCAR    1       1       1      7     3578   MEDICAL CARE SERVICES
 3     1      MEDCAR    1       1       1      7     3677   MEDICAL CARE SERVICES
 4     1      MEDCAR    1       1       1      7     3776   MEDICAL CARE SERVICES

OBS FORMAT FORMATL FORMATD ST_DATE END_DATE NTIME NOBS NINRANGE    SURTITLE

 1             0       0    DEC1977  JUL1990  152   152    123   ALL URBAN CONSUM
 2             0       0    DEC1977  JUL1990  152   152    123   ALL URBAN CONSUM
 3             0       0    DEC1977  JUL1990  152   152    123   ALL URBAN CONSUM
 4             0       0    DEC1977  JUL1990  152   152    123   ALL URBAN CONSUM

OBS AREANAME           S_CODE        UNITS    NDEC

 1  NORTHEAST       CUUR0100SA512               1
 2  NORTH CENTRAL   CUUR0200SA512               1
 3  SOUTH           CUUR0300SA512               1
 4  WEST            CUUR0400SA512               1
```

Note that only the cross sections with BASEPER='1982-84=100' are listed in the OUTALL= data set (see Output 7.2.2). This is because only those cross sections contain data for MEDCARE.

The OUTALL= data set indicates that data values are stored with one decimal place (see the NDEC variable). Therefore, they need to be rescaled, as follows:

```
data medical;
   set medical;
   medcare = medcare * 0.1;
run;
```

The variation of MEDCARE against DATE with respect to different geographic regions can be demonstrated graphically, as follows:

Output 7.2.3. Plot of Time Series in the OUT= Data Set for FILETYPE=BLSCPI

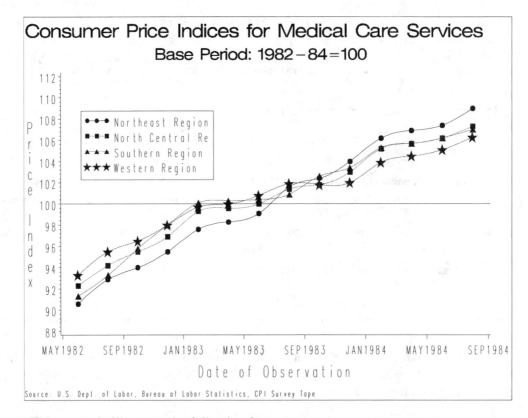

This example illustrates the following features:

- Descriptive information needed to write KEEP and WHERE statements can be obtained with an initial run of the DATASOURCE procedure.

- The OUTCONT= and OUTALL= data sets may contain information on how data values are stored, such as the precision, the units, and so on.

- The OUTCONT= and OUTALL= data sets report the new series names assigned by the RENAME statement, not the old names (see the NAME variable in Output 7.2.2).

- You can use PROC FORMAT to define formats for series or BY variables to enhance your output. Note that PROC DATASOURCE associated a permanent format, $AREAFMT., with the BY variable AREA. As a result, the formatted values are displayed in the printout of the OUTALL=MEDINFO data set (see Output 7.2.2) and in the legend created by PROC GPLOT.

- The base period for all the geographical areas is the same (BASEPER='1982-84=100') as indicated by the intersections of plots with the horizontal reference line drawn at 100. This makes comparisons meaningful.

Example 7.3.   BLS State and Area, Employment, Hours and Earnings Surveys

This example illustrates how to extract specific series from a State and Area, Employment, Hours and Earnings Survey. The series to be extracted is total employment in manufacturing industries with respect to states as of March, 1990.

The State and Area, Employment, Hours and Earnings survey designates the totals for manufacturing industries by DIVISION='3', INDUSTRY='0000', and DETAIL='1'. Also, statewide figures are denoted by AREA='0000'.

The data type code for total employment is reported to be 1. Therefore, the series name for this variable is SA1, since series names are constructed by adding an SA prefix to the data type codes given by BLS.

The following statements extract statewide figures for total employment (SA1) in manufacturing industries for March, 1990:

```
filename datafile 'host-specific-file-name' <host-options>;
proc datasource filetype=blseesa out=totemp;
   where division='3' and industry='0000' and detail='1' and
         area='0000';
   keep sa1;
   range from 1990:3 to 1990:3;
   rename sa1=totemp;
run;
```

Variations of women workers in manufacturing industries with respect to states can best be demonstrated on a map of the United States, as shown in Output 7.3.1.

Output 7.3.1.   Map of the Series in the OUT= Data Set for FILETYPE=BLSEESA

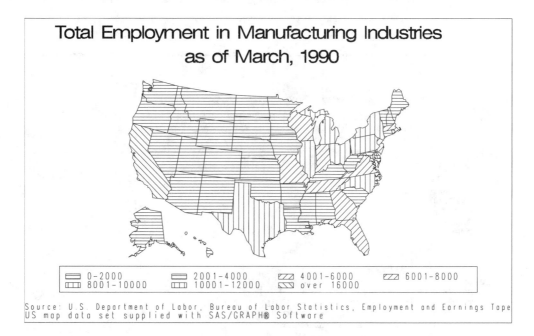

Note the following for the preceding example:

- The INFILE= option is omitted, since the fileref assigned to the BLSEESA file is the default value DATAFILE.

- When the FROM and TO values in the RANGE statement are the same, only one observation for each cross section is extracted. This observation corresponds to a monthly data point since the INTERVAL= option defaults to MONTH.

Example 7.4. Tape Format CITIBASE Files

This example illustrates how to extract daily series from a sample CITIBASE file. Also, it shows how the OUTSELECT= option affects the contents of the auxiliary data sets.

The daily series contained in the sample data file CITIDEMO are listed by the following statements:

```
proc datasource filetype=citibase infile=citidemo interval=weekday
                outall=citiall outby=citikey;
run;

title1 'Summary Information on Daily Data for CITIDEMO File';
proc print data=citikey noobs;
run;

title1 'Daily Series Available in CITIDEMO File';
proc print data=citiall( drop=label );
run;
```

Output 7.4.1. Printout of the OUTBY= and OUTALL= Data Sets

```
          Summary Information on Daily Data for CITIDEMO File

   OBS     ST_DATE     END_DATE     NTIME     NOBS     NSERIES     NSELECT

    1     01JAN1988   14MAR1991      835       835        10          10
```

```
              Daily Series Available in CITIDEMO File

OBS NAME       SELECTED    TYPE    LENGTH    VARNUM    BLKNUM

  1 SNYDJCM       1         1         5         .        42
  2 SNYSECM       1         1         5         .        43
  3 DSIUSWIL      1         1         5         .        44
  4 DFXWCAN       1         1         5         .        45
  5 DFXWUK90      1         1         5         .        46
  6 DSIUKAS       1         1         5         .        47
  7 DSIJPND       1         1         5         .        48
  8 DCP05         1         1         5         .        49
  9 DCD1M         1         1         5         .        50
 10 DTBD3M        1         1         5         .        51

OBS DESCRIPT                                                       FORMAT

  1 STOCK MKT INDEX:NY DOW JONES COMPOSITE, (WSJ)
  2 STOCK MKT INDEX:NYSE COMPOSITE, (WSJ)
  3 STOCK MKT INDEX:WILSHIRE 500, (WSJ)
  4 FOREIGN EXCH RATE WSJ:CANADA,CANADIAN $/U.S. $,NSA
  5 FOREIGN EXCH RATE WSJ:U.K.,CENTS/POUND(90 DAY FORWARD),NSA
  6 STOCK MKT INDEX:U.K. - ALL SHARES
  7 STOCK MKT INDEX:JAPAN - NIKKEI-DOW
  8 INT.RATE:5-DAY COMM.PAPER, SHORT TERM YIELD
```

Example 7.4. Tape Format CITIBASE Files ▢ ▢ ▢   375

Output 7.4.1. (Continued)

```
    9 INT.RATE:1MO CERTIFICATES OF DEPOSIT, SHORT TERM YIELD (FBR H.15)
   10 INT.RATE:3MO T-BILL, DISCOUNT YIELD (FRB H.15)

  OBS FORMATL FORMATD    ST_DATE   END_DATE NTIME NOBS CODE        ATTRIBUT NDEC

    1     0       0     04JAN1988 14MAR1991  834   834 DSIUSNYDJCM      1    2
    2     0       0     04JAN1988 14MAR1991  834   834 DSIUSNYSECM      1    2
    3     0       0     04JAN1988 14MAR1991  834   834 DSIUSWIL         1    2
    4     0       0     01JAN1988 14MAR1991  835   835 DFXWCAN          1    4
    5     0       0     01JAN1988 14MAR1991  835   835 DFXWUK90         1    2
    6     0       0     01JAN1988 14MAR1991  835   835 DSIUKAS          1    2
    7     0       0     01JAN1988 14MAR1991  835   835 DSIJPND          1    2
    8     0       0     04JAN1988 24FEB1989  300   300 DCP05            2    2
    9     0       0     04JAN1988 08MAR1991  830   830 DCD1M            1    2
   10     0       0     04JAN1988 08MAR1991  830   830 DTBD3M           1    2
```

Note the following from Output 7.4.1:

- The OUTALL= data set reports the time ranges of variables.

- Generally, series names (NAME) are the same as the series codes (CODE) reported in the OUTALL= data set. However, for series codes longer than 8 characters, series names are extracted by truncating the first 4 characters. For example, series names become SNYDJCM for DSIUSNYDJCM and SNYSECM for DSIUSNY-SECM.

- There are ten observations in the OUTALL= data set, the same number as reported by NSERIES and NSELECT variables in the OUTBY= data set.

- The VARNUM variable contains all MISSING values, since no OUT= data set is created.

The next step is to demonstrate how the OUTSELECT= option affects the contents of the OUTBY= and OUTALL= data sets when a KEEP statement is present. First, set the OUTSELECT= option to OFF.

```
    proc datasource filetype=citibase infile=citidemo interval=weekday
                 outall=alloff outby=keyoff outselect=off;
       keep dsiusnysecm dc:;
    run;

    title1 'Summary Information on Daily Data for CITIDEMO File';
    proc print data=keyoff;
    run;

    title1 'Daily Series Available in CITIDEMO File';
    proc print data=alloff( keep=name kept selected st_date
                                 end_date ntime nobs code );
    run;
```

Output 7.4.2. Printout of the OUTBY= and OUTALL= Data Sets with OUTSELECT=OFF

```
            Summary Information on Daily Data for CITIDEMO File

   OBS      ST_DATE      END_DATE     NTIME      NOBS     NSERIES     NSELECT

    1      01JAN1988    14MAR1991      835       834        10          3
```

```
              Daily Series Available in CITIDEMO File

 OBS  NAME       KEPT   SELECTED    ST_DATE    END_DATE    NTIME   NOBS   CODE

  1   SNYDJCM     0        0       04JAN1988   14MAR1991    834    834    DSIUSNYDJCM
  2   SNYSECM     1        1       04JAN1988   14MAR1991    834    834    DSIUSNYSECM
  3   DSIUSWIL    0        0       04JAN1988   14MAR1991    834    834    DSIUSWIL
  4   DFXWCAN     0        0       01JAN1988   14MAR1991    835    835    DFXWCAN
  5   DFXWUK90    0        0       01JAN1988   14MAR1991    835    835    DFXWUK90
  6   DSIUKAS     0        0       01JAN1988   14MAR1991    835    835    DSIUKAS
  7   DSIJPND     0        0       01JAN1988   14MAR1991    835    835    DSIJPND
  8   DCP05       1        1       04JAN1988   24FEB1989    300    300    DCP05
  9   DCD1M       1        1       04JAN1988   08MAR1991    830    830    DCD1M
 10   DTBD3M      0        0       04JAN1988   08MAR1991    830    830    DTBD3M
```

Then, set the OUTSELECT= option ON.

```
proc datasource filetype=citibase infile=citidemo interval=weekday
                outall=allon outby=keyon outselect=on;
   keep dsiusnysecm dc:;
run;

title1 'Summary Information on Daily Data for CITIDEMO File';
proc print data=keyon;
run;

title1 'Daily Series Available in CITIDEMO File';
proc print data=allon( keep=name kept selected st_date
                            end_date ntime nobs code );

run;
```

Output 7.4.3. Printout of the OUTBY= and OUTALL= Data Sets with OUTSELECT=ON

```
            Summary Information on Daily Data for CITIDEMO File

   OBS      ST_DATE      END_DATE     NTIME      NOBS     NSERIES     NSELECT

    1      04JAN1988    14MAR1991      834       834        10          3
```

```
              Daily Series Available in CITIDEMO File

 OBS   NAME      KEPT   SELECTED    ST_DATE    END_DATE    NTIME   NOBS   CODE

  1   SNYSECM     1        1       04JAN1988   14MAR1991    834    834    DSIUSNYSECM
  2   DCP05       1        1       04JAN1988   24FEB1989    300    300    DCP05
  3   DCD1M       1        1       04JAN1988   08MAR1991    830    830    DCD1M
```

Comparison of Output 7.4.2 and Output 7.4.3 reveals the following:

- The OUTALL= data set contains ten (NSERIES) observations when OUTSE-LECT=OFF, and three (NSELECT) observations when OUTSELECT=ON.

Example 7.4. Tape Format CITIBASE Files □□□ 377

- The observations in OUTALL=ALLON are those for which SELECTED=1 in OUTALL=ALLOFF.

- The time ranges in the OUTBY= data set are computed over all the variables (selected or not) for OUTSELECT=OFF, resulting in ST_DATE='01JAN88'd and END_DATE='14MAR91'd; and over only the selected variables for OUTSELECT=ON, resulting in ST_DATE='04JAN88'd and END_DATE='14MAR91'd. This corresponds to computing time ranges over all the series reported in the OUTALL= data set.

- The variable NTIME is the number of time periods between ST_DATE and END_DATE, while NOBS is the number of observations the OUT= data set is to contain. Thus, NTIME is different depending on whether the OUTSELECT= option is set to ON or OFF, while NOBS stays the same.

Also the use of the KEEP statement in the last two examples illustrates the following points:

- The variable names used in the KEEP statement are the series codes (CODE), not series variable names (NAME). Therefore, they are not limited to 8 characters.

- The OUTALL= data sets in Output 7.4.2 and Output 7.4.3 contain an additional variable, KEPT, which reports the outcome of the KEEP statement. This variable is not added to the OUTALL= data set when there is not a KEEP statement, as shown in Output 7.4.1.

Adding the RANGE statement to the last example generates the data sets in Output 7.4.4:

```
proc datasource filetype=citibase infile=citidemo interval=weekday
                outby=keyrange out=citiday outselect=on;
   keep dsiusnysecm dc:;
   range to '12jan88'd;
run;

title1 'Summary Information on Daily Data for CITIDEMO File';
proc print data=keyrange;
run;

title1 'Daily Data in CITIDEMO File';
proc print data=citiday;
run;
```

Output 7.4.4. Printout of the OUT=CITIDAY Data Set for FILETYPE=CITIBASE

			Daily Series Available in CITIDEMO File				
OBS	ST_DATE	END_DATE	NTIME	NOBS	NINRANGE	NSERIES	NSELECT
1	04JAN1988	14MAR1991	834	834	7	10	3

		Daily Data in CITIDEMO File		
OBS	DATE	SNYSECM	DCP05	DCD1M
1	04JAN1988	142.900	6.81000	6.89000
2	05JAN1988	144.540	6.84000	6.85000
3	06JAN1988	144.820	6.79000	6.87000
4	07JAN1988	145.890	6.77000	6.88000
5	08JAN1988	137.030	6.73000	6.88000
6	11JAN1988	138.810	6.81000	6.89000
7	12JAN1988	137.740	6.73000	6.83000

The OUTBY= data set in this last example contains an additional variable NIN-RANGE. This variable is added since there is a RANGE statement. Its value, 7, is the number of observations in the OUT= data set. In this case, NOBS gives the number of observations the OUT= data set would contain if there were not a RANGE statement.

Note that the OUT= data set does not contain data for 09JAN1988 and 10JAN1988. This is because the WEEKDAY interval skips over weekends.

Example 7.5. PC Diskette Format CITIBASE Database

This example uses a diskette format CITIBASE database (FILETYPE=CITIDISK) to extract annual population estimates for females and males with respect to various age groups since 1980.

Population estimate series for females with five-year age intervals are given by PANF1 through PANF16, where PANF1 is for females under 5 years of age, PANF2 is for females between 5 and 9 years of age, and so on. Similarly, PANM1 through PANM16 gives population estimates for males with five-year age intervals.

The following statements extract the required population estimates series:

```
filename keyfile 'host-specific-key-file-name' <host-options>;
filename indfile 'host-specific-ind-file-name' <host-options>;
filename dbfile  'host-specific-db-file-name'  <host-options>;
proc datasource filetype=citidisk  infile=( keyfile indfile dbfile )
                out=popest outall=popinfo;
   keep panf1-panf16 panm1-panm16;
   range from 1980;
run;
```

This example demonstrates the following:

- The INFILE= options lists the filerefs of the key, index, and database files, in that order.

Example 7.5. PC Diskette Format CITIBASE Database □ □ □ **379**

- The INTERVAL= option is omitted since the default interval for CITIDISK type files is YEAR.

Example 7.6. Quarterly COMPUSTAT Data Files

This example shows how to extract data from a 48-quarter Compustat Database File. For COMPUSTAT data files, the series variable names are constructed by concatenating the name of the data array DATA and the column number containing the required information. For example, for quarterly files the common stock data is in column 56. Therefore, the variable name for this series is DATA56. Similarly, the series variable names for quarterly footnotes are constructed by adding the column number to the array name, QFTNT. For example, the variable name for common stock footnotes is QFTNT14 since the 14th column of the QFTNT array contains this information.

The following example extracts common stock series (DATA56) and its footnote (QFTNT14) for Computer Programming Service Companies (DNUM=7371) and Prepackaged Software Companies (DNUM=7370) whose stocks are traded over-the-counter and not in the S&P 500 Index (ZLIST=06) and whose data reside in the over-the-counter file (FILE=06).

```
filename compstat 'host-specific-Compustat-file-name' <host-options>;
proc datasource filetype=cs48qibm infile=compstat
                out=stocks outby=company;
   keep data56 qftnt14;
   rename data56=comstock  qftnt14=ftcomstk;
   label  data56='Common Stock'
          qftnt14='Footnote for Common Stock';
   where dnum in (7370,7371) and zlist=06 and file=06;
run;

/*- add company name to the out= data set     */
data stocks;
   merge stocks company( keep=dnum cnum cic coname );
   by dnum cnum cic;
run;

title1 'Common Stocks for Software Companies for 1990';
proc print data=stocks noobs;
   where date between '01jan90'd and '31dec90'd;
run;
```

The Output 7.6.1 contains a partial listing of the STOCKS data set.

Output 7.6.1. Partial Listing of the OUT=STOCKS Data Set

```
                Common Stocks for Software Companies for 1990

DNUM    CNUM    CIC    FILE    EIN        STK    SMBL    ZLIST    XREL    FINC    SINC    STATE

7370    027352   103    6     54-0856778   0     AMSY     6        0       0      10      51
7370    027352   103    6     54-0856778   0     AMSY     6        0       0      10      51
7370    027352   103    6     54-0856778   0     AMSY     6        0       0      10      51
7370    027352   103    6     54-0856778   0     AMSY     6        0       0      10      51
7370    553412   107    6     73-1064024   0     MPSG     6        0       0      10      40
7370    553412   107    6     73-1064024   0     MPSG     6        0       0      10      40
7370    553412   107    6     73-1064024   0     MPSG     6        0       0      10      40
7370    553412   107    6     73-1064024   0     MPSG     6        0       0      10      40
7371    032681   108    6     41-0905408   0     ANLY     6        0       0      27      27
7371    032681   108    6     41-0905408   0     ANLY     6        0       0      27      27
7371    032681   108    6     41-0905408   0     ANLY     6        0       0      27      27
7371    032681   108    6     41-0905408   0     ANLY     6        0       0      27      27
7371    458816   105    6     04-2448936   0     IMET     6        0       0      25      25
7371    458816   105    6     04-2448936   0     IMET     6        0       0      25      25
7371    458816   105    6     04-2448936   0     IMET     6        0       0      25      25
7371    458816   105    6     04-2448936   0     IMET     6        0       0      25      25

COUNTY      DATE     COMSTOCK    FTCOMSTK     CONAME

   13      1990:1    0.11500                 AMERICAN MANAGEMENT SYSTEMS
   13      1990:2    0.11600                 AMERICAN MANAGEMENT SYSTEMS
   13      1990:3    0.12200                 AMERICAN MANAGEMENT SYSTEMS
   13      1990:4    0.11700                 AMERICAN MANAGEMENT SYSTEMS
  143      1990:1    0.42400                 MPSI SYSTEMS INC
  143      1990:2    0.42400                 MPSI SYSTEMS INC
  143      1990:3    0.42400                 MPSI SYSTEMS INC
  143      1990:4    0.42300                 MPSI SYSTEMS INC
   53      1990:1      .                     ANALYSTS INTERNATIONAL CORP
   53      1990:2      .                     ANALYSTS INTERNATIONAL CORP
   53      1990:3      .                     ANALYSTS INTERNATIONAL CORP
   53      1990:4    0.46000                 ANALYSTS INTERNATIONAL CORP
   17      1990:1    0.03600                 INTERMETRICS INC
   17      1990:2    0.03600                 INTERMETRICS INC
   17      1990:3    0.03600                 INTERMETRICS INC
   17      1990:4      .                     INTERMETRICS INC
```

```
                Common Stocks for Software Companies for 1990

DNUM    CNUM    CIC    FILE    EIN        STK    SMBL    ZLIST    XREL    FINC    SINC    STATE

7371    834021   107    6     04-2453033   0     SOFT     6        0       0      25      25
7371    834021   107    6     04-2453033   0     SOFT     6        0       0      25      25
7371    834021   107    6     04-2453033   0     SOFT     6        0       0      25      25
7371    834021   107    6     04-2453033   0     SOFT     6        0       0      25      25
7371    872885   108    6     13-2635899   0     TSRI     6        0       0      10      36
7371    872885   108    6     13-2635899   0     TSRI     6        0       0      10      36
7371    872885   108    6     13-2635899   0     TSRI     6        0       0      10      36
7371    872885   108    6     13-2635899   0     TSRI     6        0       0      10      36
7371    878351   105    6     41-0918564   0     TECN     6        0       0      27      27
7371    878351   105    6     41-0918564   0     TECN     6        0       0      27      27
7371    878351   105    6     41-0918564   0     TECN     6        0       0      27      27
7371    878351   105    6     41-0918564   0     TECN     6        0       0      27      27

COUNTY      DATE     COMSTOCK    FTCOMSTK     CONAME

   17      1990:1    0.38700                 SOFTECH INC
   17      1990:2    0.38700                 SOFTECH INC
   17      1990:3      .                     SOFTECH INC
   17      1990:4      .                     SOFTECH INC
  103      1990:1    0.02500                 TSR INC
  103      1990:2    0.02500                 TSR INC
  103      1990:3      .                     TSR INC
  103      1990:4      .                     TSR INC
   53      1990:1    0.21500                 TECHNALYSIS CORP
   53      1990:2    0.21600                 TECHNALYSIS CORP
   53      1990:3    0.21600                 TECHNALYSIS CORP
   53      1990:4    0.21600                 TECHNALYSIS CORP
```

Note that quarterly Compustat data are also available in Universal Character format.

Example 7.6. Quarterly COMPUSTAT Data Files □ □ □ 381

If you have this type of file instead of IBM 360/370 General format, use the FILE-TYPE=CS48QUC option instead.

Example 7.7. Annual COMPUSTAT Data Files

This example shows how to extract a subset of cross sections when the required cross sections are listed in an external file. In the case of a COMPUSTAT file, the required cross sections are a list of companies. For example, you may want to extract annual data for a list of companies whose industry classification codes (DNUM), CUSIP issuer codes (CNUM), and CUSIP issue number and check digits (CIC) are given in an external file, COMPLIST, as follows:

```
2640    346377    104
3714    017634    106
5812    171583    107
6025    446150    104
8051    087851    101
```

When the required companies are listed in an external file, you can either use the SAS macro processor to construct your WHERE statement expression or restructure your data file and include it after the WHERE key word.

The following steps use the first approach to construct the WHERE statement expression in the macro variable WHEXPR:

```
filename compfile 'host-specific-file-name' <host-options>;
%macro whstmt( fileref );
   %global whexpr;
   data _null_;
      infile &fileref end=last;
      length cnum $ 6;
      input  dnum cnum cic;
      call symput( 'dnum'||left(_n_), left(dnum) );
      call symput( 'cnum'||left(_n_), cnum );
      call symput( 'cic' ||left(_n_), left(cic) );
      if last then call symput( 'n', left(_n_) );
   run;
   %do i = 1 %to &n;
      %let whexpr = &whexpr (DNUM=&&dnum&i and CNUM="&&cnum&i" and CIC=&&cic&i);
      %if &i ^= &n %then %let whexpr = &whexpr or;
      %end;
   %mend whstmt;
%whstmt( compfile );
filename compustat 'host-specific-Compustat-file-name' <host-options>;
proc datasource filetype=csaibm infile=compstat
                outby=company  out=dataset;
   where &whexpr;
run;
```

The same result can also be obtained by creating an external file, WHEXPR, from the COMPFILE and including it after the WHERE key word, as shown in the following statements:

```
filename whexpr 'host-specific-WHEXPR-file-name' <host-options>;
data _null_;
   infile compfile end=last; file   whexpr;
   length cnum $ 6;
   input   dnum cnum cic;
   put "( " dnum= "and CNUM='" cnum $6. "' and " cic= ")" @;
   if not last then put ' or'; else put ';' ;
run;

filename compstat 'host-specific-Compustat-file-name' <host-options>;
proc datasource filetype=csaibm infile=compustat
             outby=company  out=dataset;
   where %inc 'host-specific-WHEXPR-file-name';
run;

title1 'Information on Selected Companies';
proc print data=company;
run;
```

The Output 7.7.1 shows the OUTBY= data set created by the preceding statements. As you can see, the companies listed in the COMPLIST file are reported in this data set.

Output 7.7.1. Printout of the OUTBY= Data Set Listing Selected Companies

```
                    Information on Selected Companies
 OBS  DNUM    CNUM    CIC    FILE    ZLIST    SMBL    XREL    STK    STATE    COUNTY

  1   2640   346377   104     3       4       FOR      0      0      34       31
  2   3714   017634   106     1       4       ALN      0      0      36       103
  3   5812   171583   107    11       1       CHU    5812     0      48       29
  4   6025   446150   104     3       6       HBAN     0      0      39       49
  5   8051   087851   101    11       1       BEV    8050     0       6       37

 OBS  FINC       EIN       BYSELECT    ST_DATE    END_DATE    NTIME    NOBS    NSERIES

  1    0     34-1046753       1         1968        1987       20      20       423
  2    0     38-0290950       1         1968        1987       20      20       423
  3    0     74-1507270       1         1968        1987       20      20       423
  4    0     31-0724920       1         1968        1987       20      20       423
  5    0     95-4100309       1         1968        1987       20      20       423

 OBS  NSELECT    REC    INAME                                 CONAME

  1    366        1     CONVRT,PAPRBRD PD,EX CONTAIN          FORMICA CORP
  2    366        1     MOTOR VEHICLE PART,ACCESSORY          ALLEN GROUP
  3    366        1     EATING PLACES                         CHURCH'S FRIED CHICKEN INC
  4    366        1     NATL BANKS-FED RESERVE SYS            HUNTINGTON BANCSHARES
  5    366        1     SKILLED NURSING CARE FAC              BEVERLY ENTERPRISES

 OBS  DUP    DNUM2    CNUM2    CIC2    REC2    FILE2

  1    0     2640    346377    104      2       3
  2    0     3714    017634    106      2       1
  3    0     5812    171583    107      2       11
  4    0     6025    446150    104      2       3
  5    0     8051    087851    101      2       11
```

Note that annual COMPUSTAT data are available in either IBM 360/370 General format or the Universal Character format. The first example expects an IBM 360/370 General format file since the FILETYPE= is set to CSAIBM, while the second example uses a Universal Character format file (FILETYPE=CSAUC).

Example 7.8. CRSP Daily NYSE/AMEX Combined Stocks □ □ □ 383

Example 7.8.   CRSP Daily NYSE/AMEX Combined Stocks

This example reads all the data on a three-volume daily NYSE/AMEX combined character data set. Assume that the following filerefs are assigned to the calendar/indices file and security files comprising this database:

Fileref	VOLSER	File Type
calfile	UDXAA1	calendar
secfile1	UDXAA1	security file on volume 1
secfile2	UDXAA2	security file on volume 2
secfile3	UDXAA3	security file on volume 3

The data set CALDATA is created by the following statements to contain the calendar/indices file:

```
proc datasource filetype=crspdci infile=calfile out=caldata;
run;
```

Here the FILETYPE=CRSPDCI indicates that you are reading a character format (indicated by a C in the 6th position) daily (indicated by a D in the 5th position) calendar/indices file (indicated by an I in the 7th position).

The annual data in security files can be obtained by the following statements:

```
proc datasource filetype=crspdca
                infile=( secfile1 secfile2 secfile3 )
                out=annual;
run;
```

Similarly, the data sets to contain the daily security data (the OUT= data set) and the event data (the OUTEVENT= data set) are obtained by the following statements:

```
proc datasource filetype=crspdcs
                infile=( calfile secfile1 secfile2 secfile3 )
                out=periodic index outevent=events;
run;
```

Note that the FILETYPE= has an S at the 7th position, since you are reading the security files. Also, the INFILE= option first expects the fileref of the calendar/indices file since the dating variable (CALDT) is contained in that file. Following the fileref of calendar/indices file, you give the list of security files in the order you want to read them.

The Output 7.8.1 is generated by the following statements:

```
title1 'First 5 Observations in the Calendar/Indices File';
proc print data=caldata( obs=5 );
run;

title1 'Last 5 Observations in the Calendar/Indices File';
proc print data=caldata( firstobs=6659 ) noobs;
run;

title1 "Periodic Series for CUSIP='09523220'";
title2 "DATE >= '22dec88'd";
proc print data=periodic;
```

```
          where cusip='09523220' and date >= '22dec88'd;
       run;

       title1 "Events for CUSIP='09523220'";
       proc print data=events;
          where cusip='09523220';
       run;
```

Output 7.8.1. Partial Listing of the Output Data Sets

```
              First 5 Observations in the Calendar/Indices File

   OBS      DATE       VWRETD       VWRETX       EWRETD       EWRETX       TOTVAL

    1    02JUL1962    -99.0000     -99.0000     -99.0000     -99.0000    319043897
    2    03JUL1962      0.0113       0.0112       0.0131       0.0130    322929231
    3    05JUL1962      0.0060       0.0059       0.0069       0.0068    324750979
    4    06JUL1962     -0.0107      -0.0107      -0.0064      -0.0064    321302641
    5    09JUL1962      0.0067       0.0067       0.0018       0.0018    323221296

   OBS      TOTCNT       USDVAL       USDCNT       SPINDX       SPRTRN

    1        2036             0            0        55.86     -99.0000
    2        2040     319043897         2036        56.49       0.0113
    3        2031     322838977         2031        56.81       0.0057
    4        2031     324699079         2022        56.17      -0.0113
    5        2029     320935790         2019        56.55       0.0068
```

```
              Last 5 Observations in the Calendar/Indices File

      DATE        VWRETD       VWRETX       EWRETD       EWRETX       TOTVAL

   23DEC1988    0.0042154    0.0028936     0.005104     0.003588   2367541510
   27DEC1988   -.0029128    -.0029624    -0.001453    -0.001585   2360680550
   28DEC1988    0.0015624    0.0015249     0.001575     0.001484   2364369540
   29DEC1988    0.0067816    0.0066433     0.005578     0.005469   2379932980
   30DEC1988   -.0027338    -.0029144     0.010736     0.010572   2362374030

   TOTCNT       USDVAL       USDCNT       SPINDX        SPRTRN

    2563     2360655540      2561        277.87       0.0036118
    2565     2367496320      2562        276.83      -.0037429
    2568     2360668370      2564        277.08       0.0009031
    2565     2364169480      2563        279.40       0.0083724
    2567     2379932980      2565        277.72      -.0060126
```

```
                   Periodic Series for CUSIP='09523220'
                         DATE >= '22dec88'd

                  P   C I     H
          C       E   O S H   S                 B       A                       S B
          U       R   M S E   I         D       I       S                       X X
   O      S       M   P U X   C         A       D       K       P       V   R   R R
   B      I       N   N N C   C         T       L       H       R       O   E   E E
   S      P       O   O O D   D         E       O       I       C       L   T   T T

   3 09523220 75285 0 0 1 7361 22DEC1988 15.00 15.375 15.375 54300  0.016529 . .
   4 09523220 75285 0 0 1 7361 23DEC1988 15.50 15.750 15.625 17700  0.016260 . .
   5 09523220 75285 0 0 1 7361 27DEC1988 15.50 15.750 15.625 10600  0.000000 . .
   6 09523220 75285 0 0 1 7361 28DEC1988 15.50 15.500 15.500 10600 -0.008000 . .
   7 09523220 75285 0 0 1 7361 29DEC1988 15.25 15.500 15.375  7000 -0.008065 . .
   8 09523220 75285 0 0 1 7361 30DEC1988 15.00 15.250 15.000 13700 -0.024390 . .
```

Example 7.8.   CRSP Daily NYSE/AMEX Combined Stocks   □ □ □   385

Output 7.8.1. (Continued)

```
                       Events for CUSIP='09523220'
OBS   CUSIP    PERMNO COMPNO ISSUNO HEXCD HSICCD EVENT       DATE    NCUSIP

 1  09523220   75285    0      0      1    7361   NAMES   03MAY1988 09523220
 2  09523220   75285    0      0      1    7361   DIST    18JUL1988
 3  09523220   75285    0      0      1    7361   SHARES  03MAY1988
 4  09523220   75285    0      0      1    7361   SHARES  30SEP1988
 5  09523220   75285    0      0      1    7361   SHARES  30DEC1988
 6  09523220   75285    0      0      1    7361   DELIST  30DEC1988

OBS TICKER      COMNAM     SHRCLS SHRCD EXCHCD SICCD DISTCD  DIVAMT FACPR

 1   BAW    BLUE ARROW PLC           3     1    7361    .      .       .
 2                                   .     .     .    1212  0.13376   0
 3                                   .     .     .      .      .       .
 4                                   .     .     .      .      .       .
 5                                   .     .     .      .      .       .
 6                                   .     .     .      .      .       .

OBS FACSHR   DCLRDT   RCRDDT    PAYDT    SHROUT   SHRFLG  DLSTCD  NWPERM   NEXTDT

 1    .        .        .         .        .        .       .       .        .
 2    0     13JUL88   22JUL88  26AUG88     .        .       .       .        .
 3    .        .        .         .      72757      0       .       .        .
 4    .        .        .         .     706842      0       .       .        .
 5    .        .        .         .     706842      0       .       .        .
 6    .        .        .         .        .        .     100       0        .

OBS DLBID   DLASK   DLPRC   DLVOL   DLRET   TRTSCD  NMSIND  MMCNT  NSDINX

 1    .       .       .       .       .       .       .       .       .
 2    .       .       .       .       .       .       .       .       .
 3    .       .       .       .       .       .       .       .       .
 4    .       .       .       .       .       .       .       .       .
 5    .       .       .       .       .       .       .       .       .
 6    .       .       0       .       A       .       .       .       .
```

This example illustrates the following points:

- When data span more than one physical volume, the filerefs of the security files residing on each volume must be given following the fileref of the calendar/indices file. The DATASOURCE procedure reads each of these files in the order they are specified. Therefore, you can request that all three volumes be mounted to the same tape drive, if you choose to do so.

- The INDEX option in the second PROC DATASOURCE run creates an index file for the OUT=PERIODIC data set. This index file provides random access to the OUT= data set and may increase the efficiency of the subsequent PROC and DATA steps that use BY and WHERE statements. The index variables are CUSIP, CRSP permanent number (PERMNO), NASDAQ company number (COMPNO), NASDAQ issue number (ISSUNO), header exchange code (HEXCD) and header SIC code (HSICCD). Each one of these variables forms a different key, that is, a single index. If you want to form keys from a combination of variables (composite indexes) or use some other variables as indexes, you should use the INDEX= data set option for the OUT= data set.

- The OUTEVENT=EVENTS data set is sparse. In fact, for each EVENT type, a unique set of event variables are defined. For example, for EVENT='SHARES', only the variables SHROUT and SHRFLG are defined, and they have missing values for all other EVENT types. Pictorially, this structure is similar to the data set shown in Figure 7.10. Because of this sparse representation, you should create the

OUTEVENT= data set only when you need a subset of securities and events.

By default, the OUT= data set contains only the periodic data. However, you may also want to include the event-oriented data in the OUT= data set. This is accomplished by listing the event variables together with periodic variables in a KEEP statement. For example, if you want to extract the historical CUSIP (NCUSIP), number of shares outstanding (SHROUT), and dividend cash amount (DIVAMT) together with all the periodic series, use the following statements:

```
proc datasource filetype=crspdcs
                infile=( calfile secfile1 secfile2 secfile3 )
                out=both outevent=events;
   where cusip='09523220';
   keep  bidlo askhi prc vol ret sxret bxret ncusip shrout divamt;
run;

title1 "Printout of the First 4 Observations";
title2 "CUSIP = '09523220'";
proc print data=both noobs;
   var  cusip date vol ncusip divamt shrout;
   where cusip='09523220' and date <= '08may88'd;
run;

title1 "Printout of the Observations centered Around 18jul88";
title2 "CUSIP = '09523220'";
proc print data=both noobs;
   var  cusip date vol ncusip divamt shrout;
   where cusip='09523220' and
         date between '14jul88'd and '20jul88'd;
run;

title1 "Printout of the Observations centered Around 30sep88";
title2 "CUSIP = '09523220'";
proc print data=both noobs;
   var  cusip date vol ncusip divamt shrout;
   where cusip='09523220' and
         date between '28sep88'd and '04oct88'd;
run;
```

Output 7.8.2.   Including Event Variables in the OUT= Data Set

```
              Printout of the First 4 Observations
                     CUSIP = '09523220'

   CUSIP        DATE       VOL     NCUSIP    DIVAMT    SHROUT

   09523220   03MAY1988   296100   09523220     .      72757
   09523220   04MAY1988   139200   09523220     .      72757
   09523220   05MAY1988     9000   09523220     .      72757
   09523220   06MAY1988     7900   09523220     .      72757
```

Example 7.8. CRSP Daily NYSE/AMEX Combined Stocks ☐ ☐ ☐ 387

Output 7.8.2. (Continued)

```
        Printout of the Observations centered Around 18jul88
                        CUSIP = '09523220'

    CUSIP         DATE        VOL       NCUSIP      DIVAMT      SHROUT

   09523220    14JUL1988    62000     09523220        .          72757
   09523220    15JUL1988   106800     09523220        .          72757
   09523220    18JUL1988    32100     09523220     0.13376       72757
   09523220    19JUL1988     8600     09523220        .          72757
   09523220    20JUL1988    10700     09523220        .          72757
```

```
        Printout of the Observations centered Around 30sep88
                        CUSIP = '09523220'

    CUSIP         DATE        VOL       NCUSIP      DIVAMT      SHROUT

   09523220    28SEP1988    33000     09523220        .          72757
   09523220    29SEP1988    55200     09523220        .          72757
   09523220    30SEP1988    40700     09523220        .         706842
   09523220    03OCT1988    13400     09523220        .         706842
   09523220    04OCT1988   110600     09523220        .         706842
```

Events referring to distributions and delistings have entries only in observations whose dates match the event dates. For example, DIVAMT has a value for only 18JUL88, as shown in the second printout in Output 7.8.2. The NAME and SHARES events refer to a date of change, therefore their values are expanded such that there is a value for each observation. For example, the date of NAMES record is 03MAY88, therefore NCUSIP has the same value from that date on. The SHROUT on the other hand changes its value three times once on 03MAY88, the other time on 30SEP88, and the last one on 30DEC88. The third listing shows how the value of SHROUT remains constant at 72757 from 03MAY88 to 30SEP88, at which date it changes to 706842.

The events occurring on days other than the trading dates are not output to the OUT= data set.

The KEEP statement in the preceding example has no effect on the event variables output to the OUTEVENT= data set. If you want to extract only a subset of event variables, you need to use the KEEPEVENT statement. For example, the following code outputs only NCUSIP and SHROUT to the OUTEVENT= data set for CUSIP='09523220':

```
proc datasource filetype=crspdxc
                infile=( calfile secfile1 secfile2 secfile3 )
                outevent=subevts;
   where cusip='09523220';
   keepevent  ncusip shrout;
run;

title1 "NCUSIP and SHROUT for CUSIP='09523220'";
proc print data=subevts noobs;
run;
```

Output 7.8.3. Listing of the OUTEVENT= Data Set with a KEEPEVENT Statement

```
                    NCUSIP and SHROUT for CUSIP='09523220'

 CUSIP     PERMNO COMPNO ISSUNO HEXCD HSICCD EVENT      DATE   NCUSIP    SHROUT

09523220   75285    0      0      1    7361  NAMES   03MAY1988 09523220     .
09523220   75285    0      0      1    7361  SHARES  03MAY1988            72757
09523220   75285    0      0      1    7361  SHARES  30SEP1988           706842
09523220   75285    0      0      1    7361  SHARES  30DEC1988           706842
```

The OUTEVENT= data set in Output 7.8.3 is missing observations for which the EVENT variable is DIST or DELIST, since these event groups do not contain any selected events.

Example 7.9. IMF Direction of Trade Statistics

This example illustrates how to extract data from a Direction of Trade Statistics (DOTS) data file. The DOTS data files contain only two series, EXPORTS and IMPORTS, for various sets of countries. The foreign trade figures between any two countries can be extracted by specifying their three-digit codes for COUNTRY and PARTNER BY variables. The following statements can then be used to extract quarterly EXPORTS and IMPORTS between the United States of America (COUNTRY='111') and Japan (PARTNER='158').

```
filename dotsfile 'host-specific-gfs-file-name' <host-options>;
proc datasource filetype=imfdotsp infile=dotsfile interval=qtr
               out=foreign outall=forngvar;
   where country='111' and partner='158';
run;
```

Example 7.10. IMF Government Finance Statistics

This example demonstrates how to work with a Government Finance Statistics (GFS) data file. The expenditures of the U.S. Central Government are extracted and grouped with respect to political parties.

The series names used with GFS-type files are the subject codes assigned by IMF prefixed by a G. According to IMF documentation, the expenditures recorded for the federal government consolidated account have subject codes starting with 8H2. Output 7.10.1, obtained by the following statements, list these series.

```
filename gfsfile 'host-specific-gfs-file-name' <host-options>;
proc datasource filetype=imfgfsp infile=gfsfile outall=expvars;
   where country='111';
   keep g8h2:;
run;

proc print data=expvars( where=(length(name)<=5) );
   var name label st_date end_date du_name ndec;
run;
```

Example 7.10. IMF Government Finance Statistics □ □ □ 389

Output 7.10.1. Listing of Expenditure Series for the Federal Government
Consolidated Account

```
OBS NAME   LABEL                        ST_DATE END_DATE    DU_NAME     NDEC

  1 G8H2   TOTAL EXPENDITURE (C.II)       4383    10593  BILLIONS OF US$   2
  3 G8H2A  GENERAL PUBLIC SERVICES        4383    10227  BILLIONS OF US$   2
  5 G8H2B  DEFENSE                        4383    10227  BILLIONS OF US$   2
  6 G8H2C  EDUCATION                      4383    10227  BILLIONS OF US$   2
 10 G8H2D  HEALTH                         4383    10227  BILLIONS OF US$   2
 13 G8H2E  SOCIAL SECURITY & WELFARE      4383    10227  BILLIONS OF US$   2
 16 G8H2F  HOUSING & COMMUN. AMENITIES    4383    10227  BILLIONS OF US$   2
 20 G8H2G  RECR.,CULTR.,RELIG.AFFRS.      4383    10227  BILLIONS OF US$   2
 21 G8H2H  ECON. AFFAIRS & SERVICES       4383    10227  BILLIONS OF US$   2
 31 G8H2K  OTHER EXPENDITURES             4383    10227  BILLIONS OF US$   2
 32 G8H2N  EXPENDITURE ON GOODS & SERV.   4383    10227  BILLIONS OF US$   2
 46 G8H2R  CURRENT EXPENDITURE (C.III)    4383    10227  BILLIONS OF US$   2
 49 G8H2T  OF WHICH: FROM CENTRAL GOVT.   4383    10227  BILLIONS OF US$   2
 50 G8H2U  CAPITAL TRANSFERS              4383    10227  BILLIONS OF US$   2
 56 G8H2V  CAPITAL EXPENDITURE (C.IV)     4383    10227  BILLIONS OF US$   2
 60 G8H2W  ADJ. TO TOTAL EXPENDITURE      4383    10227  BILLIONS OF US$   2
 61 G8H2Z  TOTAL EXP.& LEND-REPAY(C.I)    4383    10593  BILLIONS OF US$   2
```

From Output 7.10.1, you can obtain series variable names for defense, education,
health, social security and welfare, housing and community amenities, recreational,
cultural and religious affairs, economic affairs and services, and expenditures on
goods and services. Once these names are known, their data can be extracted by the
following statements:

```
proc datasource filetype=imfgfsp infile=gfsfile
               out=expend;
   where country='111';
   keep g8h2 g8h2b g8h2c g8h2d g8h2e g8h2f g8h2g g8h2h g8h2n;
   rename g8h2=total    g8h2b=defense g8h2c=educat
          g8h2d=health g8h2e=socsec  g8h2f=housing
          g8h2g=recraff g8h2h=econaff g8h2n=goods;
run;
```

Note that in PROC DATASOURCE statements, the INTERVAL= option is omitted,
since the default interval for IMFGFSP type files is YEAR.

References

Bureau of Economic Analysis (1986), *The National Income and Product Accounts of the United States, 1929–82*, U.S. Dept of Commerce, Washington D.C.

Bureau of Economic Analysis (1987), *Index of Items Appearing in the National Income and Product Accounts Tables*, U.S. Dept of Commerce, Washington D.C.

Bureau of Economic Analysis (1991), *Survey of Current Business*, U.S. Dept of Commerce, Washington D.C.

Center for Research in Security Prices (1992), *CRSP Stock File Guide*, Chicago, IL.

Citibank (1990), *CITIBASE Directory*, New York, NY.

Citibank (1991), *CITIBASE-Weekly*, New York, NY.

Citibank (1991), *CITIBASE-Daily*, New York, NY.

International Monetary Fund (1984), *IMF Documentation on Computer Tape Subscription*, Washington, D.C.

Organization For Economic Cooperation and Development (1992) *Annual National Accounts: Volume I. Main Aggregates Content Documentation for Magnetic Tape Subscription*, Paris, France.

Organization For Economic Cooperation and Development (1992) *Annual National Accounts: Volume II. Detailed Tables Technical Documentation for Magnetic Tape Subscription*, Paris, France.

Organization For Economic Cooperation and Development (1992) *Main Economic Indicators Database Note*, Paris, France.

Organization For Economic Cooperation and Development (1992) *Main Economic Indicators Inventory*, Paris, France.

Organization For Economic Cooperation and Development (1992) *Main Economic Indicators OECD Statistics on Magnetic Tape Document*, Paris, France.

Organization For Economic Cooperation and Development (1992) *OECD Statistical Information Research and Inquiry System Magnetic Tape Format Documentation*, Paris, France.

Organization For Economic Cooperation and Development (1992) *Quarterly National Accounts Inventory of Series Codes*, Paris, France.

Organization For Economic Cooperation and Development (1992) *Quarterly National Accounts Technical Documentation*, Paris, France.

Standard & Poor's Compustat Services Inc. (1991), *COMPUSTAT II Documentation*, Englewood, CO.

Chapter 8
The EXPAND Procedure

Chapter Table of Contents

Chapter 8
The EXPAND Procedure

Overview

The EXPAND procedure converts time series from one sampling interval or frequency to another and interpolates missing values in time series. Using PROC EXPAND, you can collapse time series data from higher frequency intervals to lower frequency intervals, or expand data from lower frequency intervals to higher frequency intervals. For example, quarterly estimates can be interpolated from an annual series, or quarterly values can be aggregated to produce an annual series.

Time series frequency conversion is useful when you need to combine series with different sampling intervals into a single data set. For example, if you need as input to a monthly model a series that is only available quarterly, you might use PROC EXPAND to interpolate the needed monthly values.

You can also interpolate missing values in time series, either without changing series frequency or in conjunction with expanding or collapsing series.

You can convert between any combination of input and output frequencies that can be specified by SAS time interval names. (See Chapter 21, "Date Intervals, Formats, and Functions," for a complete description of SAS interval names.) When the "from" and "to" intervals are specified, PROC EXPAND automatically accounts for calendar effects such as the differing number of days in each month and leap years.

The EXPAND procedure also handles conversions of frequencies that cannot be defined by standard interval names. Using the FACTOR= option, you can interpolate any number of output observations for each group of a specified number of input observations. For example, if you specify the option FACTOR=(13:2), 13 equally spaced output observations are interpolated for each pair of input observations.

You can also convert aperiodic series, observed at arbitrary points in time, into periodic estimates. For example, a series of randomly timed quality control spot-check results might be interpolated to form estimates of monthly average defect rates.

The EXPAND procedure can also change the observation characteristics of time series. Time series observations can measure beginning-of-period values, end-of-period values, midpoint values, or period averages or totals. PROC EXPAND can convert between these cases. You can construct estimates of interval averages from end-of-period values of a variable, estimate beginning-of-period or midpoint values from interval averages, or compute averages from interval totals, and so forth.

By default, the EXPAND procedure fits cubic spline curves to the nonmissing values of variables to form continuous-time approximations of the input series. Output series are then generated from the spline approximations. Several alternate conversion methods are described in the section "Conversion Methods" later in this chapter.

You can also interpolate estimates of the rate of change of time series by differentiating the interpolating spline curve.

Various transformation can be applied to the input series prior to interpolation and to the interpolated output series. For example, the interpolation process can be modified by transforming the input series, interpolating the transformed series, and applying the inverse of the input transformation to the output series. PROC EXPAND can also be used to apply transformations to time series without interpolation or frequency conversion.

The results of the EXPAND procedure are stored in a SAS data set. No printed output is produced.

Getting Started

Converting to Higher Frequency Series

To create higher frequency estimates, specify the input and output intervals with the FROM= and TO= options, and list the variables to be converted in a CONVERT statement. For example, suppose variables X, Y, and Z in the data set ANNUAL are annual time series, and you want monthly estimates. You can interpolate monthly estimates by using the following statements:

```
proc expand data=annual out=monthly from=year to=month;
   convert x y z;
run;
```

Using the ID Statement

An ID statement is normally used with PROC EXPAND to specify a SAS date or datetime variable to identify the time of each input observation. An ID variable allows PROC EXPAND to do the following:

- identify the observations in the output data set

- determine the time span between observations and detect gaps in the input series caused by omitted observations

- account for calendar effects such as the number of days in each month and leap years

Assuming that the data set ANNUAL contains a SAS date variable called DATE that identifies the year for each observation, the preceding example should be modified to include an ID statement as follows:

```
proc expand data=annual out=monthly from=year to=month;
   id date;
   convert x y z;
run;
```

If you do not specify an ID variable with SAS date or datetime values, PROC

EXPAND makes default assumptions (see the section "ID Statement" later in this chapter for details) that are probably not what you want.

Specifying Observation Characteristics

It is important to distinguish between variables that are measured at points in time and variables that represent totals or averages over an interval. Point-in-time values are often called *stocks* or *levels*. Variables that represent totals or averages over an interval are often called *flows* or *rates*.

For example, the annual series "U.S. Gross Domestic Product" represents the total value of production over the year and also the yearly average rate of production in dollars per year. However, a monthly variable *inventory* may represent the cost of a stock of goods as of the end of the month.

When the data represent periodic totals or averages, the process of interpolation to a higher frequency is sometimes called *distribution*, and the total values of the larger intervals are said to be *distributed* to the smaller intervals. The process of interpolating periodic total or average values to lower frequency estimates is sometimes called *aggregation*.

By default, PROC EXPAND assumes that all time series represent beginning-of-period point-in-time values. If a series does not measure beginning-of-period point-in-time values, interpolation of the data values using this assumption is not appropriate, and you should specify the correct observation characteristics of the series. The observation characteristics of series are specified with the OBSERVED= option on the CONVERT statement.

For example, suppose that the data set ANNUAL contains variables A, B, and C that measure yearly totals, while the variables X, Y, and Z measure first-of-year values. The following statements estimate the contribution of each month to the annual totals in A, B, and C and interpolate first-of-month estimates of X, Y, and Z.

```
proc expand data=annual out=monthly from=year to=month;
   id date;
   convert x y z;
   convert a b c / observed=total;
run;
```

The EXPAND procedure supports five different observation characteristics. The OBSERVED= option values for these five observation characteristics are

BEGINNING	beginning-of-period values
MIDDLE	period midpoint values
END	end-of-period values
TOTAL	period totals
AVERAGE	period averages

The interpolation of each series is adjusted appropriately for its observation characteristics. When OBSERVED=TOTAL or AVERAGE is specified, the interpolating curve is fit to the data values so that the area under the curve within each input interval equals the value of the series. For OBSERVED=MIDDLE or END, the curve is fit through the data points, with the time position of each data value placed at the specified offset from the start of the interval.

See the section "The OBSERVED= Option" later in this chapter for details.

Combining Time Series with Different Frequencies

One important use of PROC EXPAND is to combine time series measured at different sampling frequencies. For example, suppose you have data on monthly money stocks (M1), quarterly gross domestic product (GDP), and weekly interest rates (INTEREST), and you want to perform an analysis of a model that uses all these variables. To perform the analysis, you first need to convert the series to a common frequency and combine the variables into one data set.

The following statements illustrate this process for the three data sets QUARTER, MONTHLY, and WEEKLY. The data sets QUARTER and WEEKLY are converted to monthly frequency using two PROC EXPAND steps, and the three data sets are then merged using a DATA step MERGE statement to produce the data set COMBINED.

```
proc expand data=quarter out=temp1 from=qtr to=month;
   id date;
   convert gdp / observed=total;
run;

proc expand data=weekly out=temp2 from=week to=month;
   id date;
   convert interest / observed=average;
run;

data combined;
   merge monthly temp1 temp2;
   by date;
run;
```

See Chapter 2, "Working with Time Series Data," for further discussion of time series periodicity, time series dating, and time series interpolation.

Interpolating Missing Values

To interpolate missing values in time series without converting the observation frequency, leave off the TO= option. For example, the following statements interpolate any missing values in the time series in the data set ANNUAL:

```
proc expand data=annual out=new from=year;
   id date;
   convert x y z;
   convert a b c / observed=total;
run;
```

To interpolate missing values in variables observed at specific points in time, omit both the FROM= and TO= options and use the ID statement to supply time values for the observations. The observations do not need to be periodic or form regular time series, but the data set must be sorted by the ID variable. For example, the following statements interpolate any missing values in the numeric variables in data set A:

```
proc expand data=a out=b;
    id date;
run;
```

If the observations are equally spaced in time, and all the series are observed as beginning-of-period values, you need to specify only the input and output data sets. For example, the following statements interpolate any missing values in the numeric variables in data set A, assuming that the observations are at equally spaced points in time:

```
proc expand data=a out=b;
run;
```

Converting Observation Characteristics

The EXPAND procedure can be used to interpolate values for output series with observation characteristics different from the input series. To change observation characteristics, specify two values in the OBSERVED= option. The first value specifies the observation characteristics of the input series; the second value specifies the observation characteristics of the output series.

For example, the following statements convert the period total variable A in the data set ANNUAL to yearly midpoint estimates. This example does not change the series frequency, and the other variables in the data set are copied to the output data set unchanged.

```
proc expand data=annual out=new from=year;
    id date;
    convert a / observed=(total,middle);
run;
```

Creating New Variables

You can use the CONVERT statement to name a new variable to contain the results of the conversion. Using this feature, you can create several different versions of a series in a single PROC EXPAND step. Specify the new name after the input variable name and an equal sign:

```
convert variable=newname ... ;
```

For example, suppose you are converting quarterly data to monthly and you want both first-of-month and midmonth estimates for a beginning-of-period variable X. The following statements perform this task:

```
proc expand data=a out=b from=qtr to=month;
   id date;
   convert x=x_begin   / observed=beginning;
   convert x=x_mid     / observed=(beginning,middle);
run;
```

Requesting Different Interpolation Methods

By default, a cubic spline curve is fit to the input series, and the output is computed from this interpolating curve. Other interpolation methods can be specified with the METHOD= option on the CONVERT statement. The section "Conversion Methods" later in this chapter explains the available methods.

For example, the following statements convert annual series to monthly series using linear interpolation instead of cubic spline interpolation:

```
proc expand data=annual out=monthly from=year to=month;
   id date;
   convert x y z / method=join;
run;
```

Transforming Series

The interpolation methods used by PROC EXPAND assume that there are no restrictions on the range of values that series can have. This assumption can sometimes cause problems if the series must be within a certain range.

For example, suppose you are converting monthly sales figures to weekly estimates. Sales estimates should never be less than zero, but since the spline curve ignores this restriction some interpolated values may be negative. One way to deal with this problem is to transform the input series before fitting the interpolating spline and then reverse transform the output series.

You can apply various transformations to the input series using the TRANS-FORMIN= option on the CONVERT statement. (The TRANSFORMIN= option can be abbreviated as TRANSFORM= or TIN=.) You can apply transformations to the output series using the TRANSFORMOUT= option. (The TRANSFORMOUT= option can be abbreviated as TOUT=.)

For example, you might use a logarithmic transformation of the input sales series and exponentiate the interpolated output series. The following statements fit a spline curve to the log of SALES and then exponentiate the output series:

```
proc expand data=a out=b from=month to=week;
   id date;
   convert sales / observed=total
                   transformin=(log) transformout=(exp);
run;
```

As another example, suppose you are interpolating missing values in a series of market share estimates. Market shares must be between 0% and 100%, but applying a spline interpolation to the raw series can produce estimates outside of this range.

The following statements use the logistic transformation to transform proportions in the range 0 to 1 to values in the range $-\infty$ to $+\infty$. The TIN= option first divides the market shares by 100 to rescale percent values to proportions and then applies the LOGIT function. The TOUT= option applies the inverse logistic function ILOGIT to the interpolated values to convert back to proportions and then multiplies by 100 to rescale back to percentages.

```
proc expand data=a out=b;
   id date;
   convert mshare / tin=( / 100 logit ) tout=( ilogit * 100 );
run;
```

You can also use the TRANSFORM= (or TRANSFORMOUT=) option as a convenient way to do calculations normally performed with the DATA step. For example, the following statements add the lead of X to data set A. The METHOD=NONE option is used to suppress interpolation.

```
proc expand data=a method=none;
   id date;
   convert x=xlead / transform=(lead);
run;
```

Any number of operations can be listed in the TRANSFORMIN= and TRANSFORMOUT= options. See Table 8.1 for a list of the transformation operations supported.

Aggregating to Lower Frequency Series

PROC EXPAND provides two ways to convert from a higher frequency to a lower frequency. When a curve fitting method is used, converting to a lower frequency is no different than converting to a higher frequency—you just specify the desired output frequency with the TO= option. This provides for interpolation of missing values and allows conversion from non-nested intervals, such as converting from weekly to monthly values.

Alternatively, you can specify simple aggregation or selection without interpolation of missing values. This might be useful, for example, if you wanted to add up monthly values to produce annual totals but wanted the annual output data set to contain values only for complete years.

To perform simple aggregation, use the METHOD=AGGREGATE option in the CONVERT statement. For example, the following statements aggregate monthly values to yearly values:

```
proc expand data=monthly out=annual from=month to=year;
   convert x y z / method=aggregate;
   convert a b c / observed=total method=aggregate;
   id date;
run;
```

Note that the AGGREGATE method can be used only if the input intervals are nested within the output intervals, as when converting from daily to monthly or from monthly to yearly frequency.

Syntax

The EXPAND procedure uses the following statements:

PROC EXPAND *options* ;
    BY *variables* ;
    CONVERT *variables* / *options* ;
    ID *variable* ;

Functional Summary

The statements and options controlling the EXPAND procedure are summarized in the following table:

Description	Statement	Option
Statements		
specify BY-group processing	BY	
specify conversion options	CONVERT	
specify the ID variable	ID	
Data Set Options		
specify the input data set	PROC EXPAND	DATA=
specify the output data set	PROC EXPAND	OUT=
write interpolating functions to a data set	PROC EXPAND	OUTEST=
extrapolate values before or after input series	PROC EXPAND	EXTRAPOLATE
Input and Output Frequencies		
specify input frequency	PROC EXPAND	FROM=
specify output frequency	PROC EXPAND	TO=
specify frequency conversion factor	PROC EXPAND	FACTOR=
Interpolation Control Options		
specify interpolation method	CONVERT	METHOD=
specify observation characteristics	CONVERT	OBSERVED=
specify transformations of the input series	CONVERT	TRANSIN=
specify transformations of the output series	CONVERT	TRANSOUT=

PROC EXPAND Statement

PROC EXPAND *options*;

The following options can be used with the PROC EXPAND statement:

Data Set Options

DATA= *SAS-data-set*

names the input data set. If the DATA= option is omitted, the most recently created SAS data set is used.

OUT= *SAS-data-set*

names the output data set containing the result time series. If OUT= is not specified, the data set is named using the DATA*n* convention. See the section "OUT= Data Set" later in this chapter for details.

OUTEST= *SAS-data-set*

names an output data set containing the coefficients of the spline curves fit to the input series. If the OUTEST= option is not specified, the spline coefficients are not output. See the section "OUTEST= Data Set" later in this chapter for details.

Options That Define Input and Output Frequencies

FACTOR= *n*
FACTOR= (*n:m*)
FACTOR= (*n,m*)

specifies the number of output observations to be created from the input observations. FACTOR=(*n:m*) specifies that *n* output observations are to be produced for each group of *m* input observations. FACTOR=*n* is the same as FACTOR=(*n*:1).

The FACTOR= option cannot be used if the TO= option is used. The default value is FACTOR=(1:1). For more information, see the section "Frequency Conversion" later in this chapter.

FROM= *interval*

specifies the time interval between observations in the input data set. Examples of FROM= values are YEAR, QTR, MONTH, DAY, and HOUR. See Chapter 21, "Date Intervals, Formats, and Functions," for a complete description and examples of interval specification.

TO= *interval*

specifies the time interval between observations in the output data set. By default, the TO= interval is generated from the combination of the FROM= and the FACTOR= values or is set to be the same as the FROM= value if FACTOR= is not specified. See Chapter 21 for a description of interval specifications.

Options to Control the Interpolation

METHOD= *option*

> specifies the method used to convert the data series. The methods supported are SPLINE, JOIN, STEP, AGGREGATE, and NONE. The METHOD= option specified on the PROC EXPAND statement can be overridden for particular series by the METHOD= option on the CONVERT statement. The default is METHOD=SPLINE.

OBSERVED= *value*

OBSERVED= (*from-value*, *to-value*)

> indicates the observation characteristics of the input time series and of the output series. Specifying the OBSERVED= option on the PROC EXPAND statement sets the default OBSERVED= value for subsequent CONVERT statements. See the sections "CONVERT Statement" and "The OBSERVED= Option" later in this chapter for details. The default is OBSERVED=BEGINNING.

EXTRAPOLATE

> specifies that missing values at the beginning or end of input series be replaced with values produced by a linear extrapolation of the interpolating curve fit to the input series. See the section "Extrapolation" later in this chapter for details.

> By default, PROC EXPAND avoids extrapolating values beyond the first or last input value for a series and only interpolates values within the range of the non-missing input values. Note that the extrapolated values are often not accurate, and for the SPLINE method the EXTRAPOLATE option results are often unreasonable. The EXTRAPOLATE option is not normally used.

BY Statement

> **BY** *variables*;

A BY statement can be used with PROC EXPAND to obtain separate analyses on observations in groups defined by the BY variables. The input data set must be sorted by the BY variables and be sorted by the ID variable within each BY group.

Use a BY statement when you want to interpolate or convert time series within levels of a cross-sectional variable. For example, suppose you have a data set STATE containing annual estimates of average disposable personal income per capita (DPI) by state and you want quarterly estimates by state. These statements convert the DPI series within each state:

```
proc sort data=state;
   by state date;
run;

proc expand data=state out=stateqtr from=year to=qtr;
   convert dpi;
   by state;
   id date;
run;
```

CONVERT Statement

CONVERT *variable= newname ... / options*;

The CONVERT statement lists the variables to be processed. Only numeric variables can be processed.

For each of the variables listed, a new variable name can be specified after an equal sign to name the variable in the output data set that contains the converted values. If a name for the output series is not given, the variable in the output data set has the same name as the input variable.

Any number of CONVERT statements can be used. If no CONVERT statement is used, all the numeric variables in the input data set except those appearing in the BY and ID statements are processed.

The following options can be used with the CONVERT statement:

METHOD= *option*

> specifies the method used to convert the data series.
>
> The methods supported are SPLINE, JOIN, STEP, AGGREGATE, and NONE.
>
> The default is the value specified for the METHOD= option on the PROC EXPAND statement, if any, or else the default is METHOD=SPLINE. See the section "Conversion Methods" later in this chapter for more information about these methods.

OBSERVED= *value*
OBSERVED= (*from-value, to-value*)

> indicates the observation characteristics of the input time series and of the output series. The values supported are TOTAL, AVERAGE, BEGINNING, MIDDLE, and END. In addition, DERIVATIVE can be specified as the *to-value* when the SPLINE method is used. See the section "The OBSERVED= Option" later in this chapter for details.
>
> The default is the value specified for the OBSERVED= option on the PROC EXPAND statement, if any, or else the default value is OBSERVED=BEGINNING.

TRANSFORMIN= (*operation ...*)

> specifies a list of transformations to be applied to the input series before the interpolating function is fit. The operations are applied in the order listed. See the section "Transformation Operations" later in this chapter for the operations that can be specified. The TRANSFORMIN= option can be abbreviated as TRANSIN=, TIN=, or TRANSFORM=.

TRANSFORMOUT= (*operation ...*)

> specifies a list of transformations to be applied to the output series. The operations are applied in the order listed. See the section "Transformation Operations" later in this chapter for the operations that can be specified. The TRANSFORMOUT= option can be abbreviated as TRANSOUT=, or TOUT=.

ID Statement

ID *variable*;

The ID statement names a numeric variable that identifies observations in the input and output data sets. The ID variable's values are assumed to be SAS date or datetime values.

The input data must form time series. This means that the observations in the input data set must be sorted by the ID variable (within the BY variables, if any). Moreover, there should be no duplicate observations, and no two observations should have ID values within the same time interval as defined by the FROM= option.

If the ID statement is omitted, SAS date or datetime values are generated to label the input observations. These ID values are generated by assuming that the input data set starts at a SAS date value of 0, that is, 1 January 1960. This default starting date is then incremented for each observation by the FROM= interval (using the INTNX function). If the FROM= option is not specified, the ID values are generated as the observation count minus 1. When the ID statement is not used, an ID variable is added to the output data set named either DATE or DATETIME, depending on the value specified in the TO= option. If neither the TO= option nor the FROM= option is given, the ID variable in the output data set is named TIME.

Details

Frequency Conversion

Frequency conversion is controlled by the FROM=, TO=, and FACTOR= options. The possible combinations of these options are explained in this section.

None Used
If FROM=, TO=, and FACTOR= are not specified, no frequency conversion is done. The data are processed to interpolate any missing values and perform any specified transformations. Each input observation produces one output observation.

FACTOR=(n:m)
FACTOR=(*n:m*) specifies that *n* output observations are produced for each group of *m* input observations. The fraction *m/n* is reduced first: thus FACTOR=(10:6) is equivalent to FACTOR=(5:3). Note that if *m/n*=1, the result is the same as the case given previously under "None Used."

FROM=interval
The FROM= option used alone establishes the frequency and interval widths of the input observations. Missing values are interpolated, and any specified transformations are performed, but no frequency conversion is done.

TO=interval
When the TO= option is used without the FROM= option, output observations with

the TO= frequency are generated over the range of input ID values. The first output observation is for the TO= interval containing the ID value of the first input observation; the last output observation is for the TO= interval containing the ID value of the last input observation. The input observations are not assumed to form regular time series and may represent aperiodic points in time. An ID variable is required to give the date or datetime of the input observations.

FROM=interval TO=interval
When both the FROM= and TO= options are used, the input observations have the frequency given by the FROM= interval, and the output observations have the frequency given by the TO= interval.

FROM=interval FACTOR=(n:m)
When both the FROM= and FACTOR= options are used, a TO= interval is inferred from the combination of the FROM=*interval* and the FACTOR=(*n:m*) values specified. For example, FROM=YEAR FACTOR=4 is the same as FROM=YEAR TO=QTR. Also, FROM=YEAR FACTOR=(3:2) is the same as FROM=YEAR used with TO=MONTH8. Once the implied TO= interval is determined, this combination operates the same as if FROM= and TO= had been specified. If no valid TO= interval can be constructed from the combination of the FROM= and FACTOR= options, an error is produced.

TO=interval FACTOR=(n:m)
The combination of the TO= option and the FACTOR= option is not allowed and produces an error.

Converting to a Lower Frequency
When converting to a lower frequency, the results are either exact or approximate, depending on whether the input intervals nest within the output intervals and depending on the need to interpolate missing values within the series. If the TO= interval is nested within the FROM= interval (as when converting monthly to yearly), and if there are no missing input values or partial periods, the results are exact.

When values are missing or the FROM= intervals are not nested within the TO= intervals (as when aggregating weekly to monthly), the results depend on an interpolation. The METHOD=AGGREGATE option always produces exact results, never an interpolation. However, this method cannot be used unless the FROM= interval is nested within the TO= interval.

Identifying Observations

The variable specified in the ID statement is used to identify the observations. Usually, SAS date or datetime values are used for this variable. PROC EXPAND uses the ID variable to do the following:

- identify the time interval of the input values
- validate the input data set observations
- compute the ID values for the observations in the output data set

Identifying the Input Time Intervals

When the FROM= option is specified, observations are understood to refer to the whole time interval and not to a single time point. The ID values are interpreted as identifying the FROM= time interval containing the value. In addition, the widths of these input intervals are used by the OBSERVED= cases TOTAL, AVERAGE, MIDDLE, and END.

For example, if FROM=MONTH is specified, then each observation is for the whole calendar month containing the ID value for the observation, and the width of the time interval covered by the observation is the number of days in that month. Therefore, if FROM=MONTH, the ID value '31MAR92'D is equivalent to the ID value '1MAR92'D—both of these ID values identify the same interval, March, 1992.

Widths of Input Time Intervals

When the FROM= option is not specified, the ID variable values are usually interpreted as referring to points in time. However, if an OBSERVED= option is specified that assumes the observations refer to whole intervals and also requires interval widths, then, in the absence of the FROM= specification, interval widths are assumed to be the time span between ID values. For the last observation, the interval width is assumed to be the same as for the next to last observation. (If neither the FROM= option nor the ID statement are specified, interval widths are assumed to be 1.0.) A note is printed in the SAS log warning that this assumption is made.

Validating the Input Data Set Observations

The ID variable is used to verify that successive observations read from the input data set correspond to sequential FROM= intervals. When the FROM= option is not used, PROC EXPAND verifies that the ID values are nonmissing and in ascending order. An error message is produced and the observation is ignored when an invalid ID value is found in the input data set.

ID Values for Observations in the Output Data Set

The time unit used for the ID variable in the output data set is controlled by the interval value specified by the TO= option. If you specify a date interval for the TO= value, the ID variable values in the output data set are SAS date values. If you specify a datetime interval for the TO= value, the ID variable values in the output data set are SAS datetime values.

Range of Output Observations

If no frequency conversion is done, the range of output observations is the same as in the input data set.

When frequency conversion is done, the observations in the output data set range from the earliest start of any result series to the latest end of any result series. Observations at the beginning or end of the input range for which all result values are missing are not written to the OUT= data set.

When the EXTRAPOLATE option is not used, the range of the nonmissing output results for each series is as follows. The first result value is for the TO= interval that contains the ID value of the start of the FROM= interval containing the ID value of the first nonmissing input observation for the series. The last result value is for the TO= interval that contains the end of the FROM= interval containing the ID value of the last nonmissing input observation for the series.

When the EXTRAPOLATE option is used, result values for all series are computed for the full time range covered by the input data set.

Extrapolation

The spline functions fit by the EXPAND procedure are very good at approximating continuous curves within the time range of the input data but poor at extrapolating beyond the range of the data. The accuracy of the results produced by PROC EXPAND may be somewhat less at the ends of the output series than at time periods for which there are several input values at both earlier and later times. The curves fit by PROC EXPAND should not be used for forecasting.

PROC EXPAND normally avoids extrapolation of values beyond the time range of the nonmissing input data for a series, unless the EXTRAPOLATE option is used. However, if the start or end of the input series does not correspond to the start or end of an output interval, some output values may depend in part on an extrapolation.

For example, if FROM=YEAR, TO=WEEK, and OBSERVED=BEGINNING, the first observation output for a series is for the week of 1 January of the first nonmissing input year. If 1 January of that year is not a Sunday, the beginning of this week falls before the date of the first input value; therefore, a beginning-of-period output value for this week is extrapolated.

This extrapolation is made only to the extent needed to complete the terminal output intervals that overlap the endpoints of the input series and is limited to no more than the width of one FROM= interval or one TO= interval, whichever is less. This restriction of the extrapolation to complete terminal output intervals is applied to each series separately, and it takes into account the OBSERVED= option for the input and output series.

When you use the EXTRAPOLATE option, the normal restriction on extrapolation is overridden. Output values are computed for the full time range covered by the input data set.

For the SPLINE method, extrapolation is performed by a linear projection of the trend of the cubic spline curve fit to the input data, not by extrapolation of the first and last cubic segments.

The OBSERVED= Option

The values of the CONVERT statement OBSERVED= option are as follows:

BEGINNING   indicates that the data are beginning-of-period values. OBSERVED=BEGINNING is the default.

MIDDLE   indicates that the data are period midpoint values.

ENDING   indicates that the data represent end-of-period values.

TOTAL indicates that the data values represent period totals for the time interval corresponding to the observation.

AVERAGE indicates that the data values represent period averages.

DERIVATIVE specifies that the output series be the derivatives of the cubic spline curve fit to the input data by the SPLINE method.

If only one value is specified in the OBSERVED= option, that value applies to both the input and the output series. For example, OBSERVED=TOTAL is the same as OBSERVED=(TOTAL,TOTAL), which indicates both that the input values represent totals over the time intervals corresponding to the input observations and that the converted output values also represent period totals. The value DERIVATIVE can be used only as the second OBSERVED= option value, and it can be used only when METHOD=SPLINE is specified or is the default method.

Since the TOTAL, AVERAGE, MIDDLE, and END cases require that the width of each input interval be known, both the FROM= option and an ID statement are normally required if one of these observation characteristics is specified for any series. However, if the FROM= option is not specified, each input interval is assumed to extend from the ID value for the observation to the ID value of the next observation, and the width of the interval for the last observation is assumed to be the same as the width for the next to last observation.

Scale of OBSERVED= AVERAGE Values

The average values are assumed to be expressed in the time units defined by the FROM= or TO= option. That is, the product of the average value for an interval and the width of the interval is assumed to equal the total value for the interval. For purposes of interpolation, OBSERVED=AVERAGE values are first converted to OBSERVED=TOTAL values using this assumption; then, the interpolated totals are converted back to averages by dividing by the widths of the output intervals. For example, suppose the options FROM=MONTH, TO=HOUR, and OBSERVED=AVERAGE are specified.

Since FROM=MONTH in this example, each input value is assumed to represent an average rate per day such that the product of the value and the number of days in the month is equal to the total for the month. The input values are assumed to represent a per-day rate because FROM=MONTH implies SAS date ID values that measure time in days; therefore, the widths of MONTH intervals are measured in days. If FROM=DTMONTH is used instead, the values are assumed to represent a per-second rate, because the widths of DTMONTH intervals are measured in seconds.

Since TO=HOUR in this example, the output values are scaled as an average rate per second such that the product of each output value and the number of seconds in an hour (3600) is equal to the interpolated hourly total. A per-second rate is used because TO=HOUR implies SAS datetime ID values that measure time in seconds; therefore, the widths of HOUR intervals are measured in seconds.

Note that the scale assumed for OBSERVED=AVERAGE data is important only when converting between AVERAGE and another OBSERVED= option, or when converting between SAS date and SAS datetime ID values. When both the input and the output series are AVERAGE values, and the units for the ID values are not changed, the scale assumed does not matter.

For example, suppose you are converting a series gross domestic product (GDP) from quarterly to monthly. The GDP values are quarterly averages measured at annual rates. If you want the interpolated monthly values also to be measured at annual rates, then the option OBSERVED=AVERAGE works fine. Since there is no change of scale involved in this problem, it makes no difference that PROC EXPAND assumes daily rates instead of annual rates.

However, suppose you want to convert GDP from quarterly to monthly and also convert from annual rates to monthly rates, so that the result is total gross domestic product for the month. Using the option OBSERVED=(AVERAGE,TOTAL) would fail because PROC EXPAND assumes the average is scaled to daily, not annual, rates.

One solution is to rescale to quarterly totals and treat the data as totals. You could use the options TRANSFORMIN=(/ 4) OBSERVED=TOTAL. Alternatively, you could treat the data as averages but first convert to daily rates. In this case, you would use the options TRANSFORMIN=(/ 365.25) OBSERVED=AVERAGE.

Results of the OBSERVED= DERIVATIVE Option

If the first value of the OBSERVED= option is BEGINNING, TOTAL, or AVERAGE, the result is the derivative of the spline curve evaluated at first-of-period ID values for the output observation. For OBSERVED=(MIDDLE,DERIVATIVE), the derivative of the function is evaluated at output interval midpoints. For OBSERVED=(END,DERIVATIVE), the derivative is evaluated at end-of-period ID values.

Conversion Methods

The SPLINE Method

The SPLINE method fits a cubic spline curve to the input values. A cubic spline is a segmented function consisting of third-degree (cubic) polynomial functions joined together so that the whole curve and its first and second derivatives are continuous.

For point-in-time input data, the spline curve is constrained to pass through the given data points. For interval total or average data, the definite integrals of the spline over the input intervals are constrained to equal the given interval totals.

For boundary constraints, the *not-a-knot* condition is used (de Boor 1981). This means that the first two spline pieces are constrained to be part of the same cubic curve, as are the last two pieces. Thus, the spline used by PROC EXPAND is not the same as the commonly used natural spline, which uses zero second-derivative endpoint constraints.

For OBSERVED=BEGINNING, MIDDLE, and END series, the spline knots are placed at the beginning, middle, and end of each input interval, respectively. For total or averaged series, the spline knots are set at the start of the first interval, at the end of the last interval, and at the interval midpoints, except that there are no knots for the first two and last two midpoints.

Once the cubic spline curve is fit to the data, the spline is extended by adding linear segments at the beginning and end. These linear segments are used for extrapolating values beyond the range of the input data.

For point-in-time output series, the spline function is evaluated at the appropriate points. For interval total or average output series, the spline function is integrated over the output intervals.

The JOIN Method

The JOIN method fits a continuous curve to the data by connecting successive straight line segments. (This produces a linear spline.) For point-in-time data, the JOIN method connects successive nonmissing input values with straight lines. For interval total or average data, interval midpoints are used as the break points, and ordinates are chosen so that the integrals of the piecewise linear curve agree with the input totals.

For point-in-time output series, the JOIN function is evaluated at the appropriate points. For interval total or average output series, the JOIN function is integrated over the output intervals.

The STEP Method

The STEP method fits a discontinuous piecewise constant curve. For point-in-time input data, the resulting step function is equal to the most recent input value. For interval total or average data, the step function is equal to the average value for the interval.

For point-in-time output series, the step function is evaluated at the appropriate points. For interval total or average output series, the step function is integrated over the output intervals.

The AGGREGATE Method

The AGGREGATE method performs simple aggregation of time series without interpolation of missing values.

If the input data are totals or averages, the results are the sums or averages, respectively, of the input values for observations corresponding to the output observations. That is, if either TOTAL or AVERAGE is specified for the OBSERVED= option, the METHOD=AGGREGATE result is the sum or mean of the input values corresponding to the output observation. For example, suppose METHOD=AGGREGATE, FROM=MONTH, and TO=YEAR. For OBSERVED=TOTAL series, the result for each output year is the sum of the input values over the months of that year. If any input value is missing, the corresponding sum or mean is also a missing value.

If the input data are point-in-time values, the result value of each output observation equals the input value for a selected input observation determined by the OB-SERVED= attribute. For example, suppose METHOD=AGGREGATE, FROM=MONTH, and TO=YEAR. For OBSERVED=BEGINNING series, January observations are selected as the annual values. For OBSERVED=MIDDLE series, July observations are selected as the annual values. For OBSERVED=END series, December observations are selected as the annual values. If the selected value is missing, the output annual value is missing.

The AGGREGATE method can be used only when the FROM= intervals are nested within the TO= intervals. For example, you can use METHOD=AGGREGATE when FROM=MONTH and TO=QTR because months are nested within quarters. You cannot use METHOD=AGGREGATE when FROM=WEEK and TO=QTR because weeks are not nested within quarters.

In addition, the AGGREGATE method cannot convert between point-in-time data and interval total or average data. Conversions between TOTAL and AVERAGE data are allowed, but conversions between BEGINNING, MIDDLE, and END are not.

Missing input values produce missing result values for METHOD=AGGREGATE. However, gaps in the sequence of input observations are not allowed. For example, if FROM=MONTH, you may have a missing value for a variable in an observation for a given February. But if an observation for January is followed by an observation for March, there is a gap in the data, and METHOD=AGGREGATE cannot be used.

When the AGGREGATE method is used, there is no interpolating curve; therefore, the EXTRAPOLATE option is not allowed.

METHOD= NONE

The option METHOD=NONE specifies that no interpolation be performed. This option is normally used in conjunction with the TRANSFORMIN= or TRANSFORMOUT= option.

When METHOD=NONE is specified, there is no difference between the TRANSFORMIN= and TRANSFORMOUT= options; if both are specified, the TRANSFORMIN= operations are performed first, followed by the TRANSFORMOUT= operations. TRANSFORM= can be used as an abbreviation for TRANSFORMIN=.

METHOD=NONE cannot be used when frequency conversion is specified.

Transformation Operations

The operations that can be used in the TRANSFORMIN= and TRANSFORMOUT= options are shown in Table 8.1. Operations are applied to each value of the series. Each value of the series is replaced by the result of the operation.

In Table 8.1, x_t or x represents the value of the series at a particular time period t before the transformation is applied. The notation [n] indicates that the argument n is optional and has a default of 1.

Table 8.1. Transformation Operations

Syntax	Result
+ *number*	adds the specified *number*: $x + number$
− *number*	subtracts the specified *number*: $x - number$
* *number*	multiplies by the specified *number*: $x \times number$
/ *number*	divides by the specified *number*: $x / number$
NEG	changes the sign: $-x$
RECIPROCAL	reciprocal: $1/x$
LOG	natural logarithm: $\log(x)$
EXP	exponential function: $\exp(x)$
SQRT	square root: $\sqrt{x}$
SQUARE	square: x^2

Syntax	Result
LOGIT	logistic function: $\log\left(\frac{x}{1-x}\right)$
ILOGIT	inverse logistic function: $\frac{\exp(x)}{1+\exp(x)}$
MIN *number*	minimum of x and *number*: $\min(x, number)$
MAX *number*	maximum of x and *number*: $\max(x, number)$
> *number*	missing value if $x \leq number$, else x
>= *number*	missing value if $x < number$, else x
= *number*	missing value if $x \neq number$, else x
^= *number*	missing value if $x = number$, else x
< *number*	missing value if $x \geq number$, else x
<= *number*	missing value if $x > number$, else x
ABS	absolute value: $\lvert x \rvert$
SIGN	$-1, 0$, or 1 as x is $< 0, = 0$, or > 0, respectively
FLOOR	largest integer less than or equal to x: $\mathrm{floor}(x)$
CEIL	smallest integer greater than or equal to x: $\mathrm{ceil}(x)$
LAG [*n*]	value of the series n periods earlier: x_{t-n}
LEAD [*n*]	value of the series n periods later: x_{t+n}
DIF [*n*]	lag n difference: $x_t - x_{t-n}$
SUM	cumulative sum: $\sum_{j=1}^{t} x_j$
SUM *n*	cumulative sum of n-period lags: $x_t + x_{t-n} + x_{t-2n} + \dots$
MOVSUM *n*	moving sum: $\sum_{j=t-n+1}^{t} x_j$
MOVAVE *n*	moving average of n neighboring values: $\frac{1}{n}\sum_{j=0}^{n-1} x_{t-j}$
MOVAVE($w_1 \dots$)	weighted moving average of neighboring values: $\left(\sum_{j=1}^{n} w_j x_{t-j+1}\right) / \left(\sum_{j=1}^{n} w_j\right)$
REVERSE	reverse the series: x_{N-t}

OUT= Data Set

The OUT= output data set contains the following variables:

- the BY variables, if any

- an ID variable that identifies the time period for each output observation

- the result variables

- if no frequency conversion is performed (so that there is one output observation corresponding to each input observation), all the other variables in the input data set are copied to the output data set

The ID variable in the output data set is named as follows:

- If an ID statement is used, the new ID variable has the same name as the variable used in the ID statement.

- If no ID statement is used, but the FROM= option is used, then the name of the ID variable is either DATE or DATETIME, depending on whether the TO= option indicates SAS date or SAS datetime values.

- If neither an ID statement nor the TO= option is used, the ID variable is named TIME.

OUTEST= Data Set

The OUTEST= data set contains the coefficients of the spline curves fit to the input series. The OUTEST= data set is of interest only if you want to verify the interpolating curve PROC EXPAND uses, or if you want to use this function in another context, (for example, in a SAS/IML program).

The OUTEST= data set contains the following variables:

- the BY variables, if any

- VARNAME, a character variable containing the name of the input variable to which the coefficients apply

- METHOD, a character variable containing the value of the METHOD= option used to fit the series

- OBSERVED, a character variable containing the first letter of the OBSERVED= option name for the input series

- the ID variable that contains the lower breakpoint (or *knot*) of the spline segment to which the coefficients apply. The ID variable has the same name as the variable used in the ID statement. If an ID statement is not used, but the FROM= option is used, then the name of the ID variable is DATE or DATETIME, depending on whether the FROM= option indicates SAS date or SAS datetime values. If neither an ID statement nor the FROM= option is used, the ID variable is named TIME.

- CONSTANT, the constant coefficient for the spline segment

- LINEAR, the linear coefficient for the spline segment

- QUAD, the quadratic coefficient for the spline segment

- CUBIC, the cubic coefficient for the spline segment

For each BY group, the OUTEST= data set contains observations for each polynomial segment of the spline curve fit to each input series. To obtain the observations defining the spline curve used for a series, select the observations where the value of VARNAME equals the name of the series.

The observations for a series in the OUTEST= data set encode the spline function fit to the series as follows. Let $a_i, b_i, c_i,$ and d_i be the values of the variables CUBIC, QUAD, LINEAR, and CONSTANT, respectively, for the ith observation for the series. Let x_i be the value of the ID variable for the ith observation for the series. Let n be the number of observations in the OUTEST= data set for the series. The value of the spline function evaluated at a point x is

$$\mathrm{f}(x) = a_i(x - x_i)^3 + b_i(x - x_i)^2 + c_i(x - x_i) + d_i$$

where the segment number i is selected as follows:

$$
i = \begin{cases}
i & \text{such that } x_i \leq x < x_{i+1}, \, 1 \leq i < n \\
1 & \text{if } x < x_1 \\
n & \text{if } x \geq x_n
\end{cases}
$$

In other words, if x is between the first and last ID values ($x_1 \leq x < x_n$), use the observation from the OUTEST= data set with the largest ID value less than or equal to x. If x is less than the first ID value x_1, then $i = 1$. If x is greater than or equal to the last ID value ($x \geq x_n$), then $i = n$.

For METHOD=JOIN, the curve is a linear spline, and the values of CUBIC and QUAD are 0. For METHOD=STEP, the curve is a constant spline, and the values of CUBIC, QUAD, and LINEAR are 0. For METHOD=AGGREGATE, no coefficients are output.

Note that for METHOD=SPLINE, the first and last observations for a curve are linear segments appended to the curve for use in extrapolating beyond the range the input data. The cubic spline fit to the input data is represented by the remaining observations.

Examples

Example 8.1.   Combining Monthly and Quarterly Data

This example combines monthly and quarterly data sets by interpolating monthly values for the quarterly series. The series are extracted from two small sample data sets stored in the SASHELP library. These data sets were contributed by Citicorp Data Base Services and contain selected U.S. macroeconomic series.

The quarterly series gross domestic product (GDP) and implicit price deflator (GD) are extracted from SASHELP.CITIQTR. The monthly series industrial production index (IP) and unemployment rate (LHUR) are extracted from SASHELP.CITIMON. Only observations for the years 1990 and 1991 are selected. PROC EXPAND is then used to interpolate monthly estimates for the quarterly series, and the interpolated series are merged with the monthly data.

The following statements extract and print the quarterly data, shown in Output 8.1.1:

```
data qtrly;
   set sashelp.citiqtr;
   where date >= '1jan1990'd &
         date <  '1jan1992'd ;
   keep date gdp gd;
run;

title "Quarterly Data";
proc print data=qtrly;
run;
```

Example 8.1. Combining Monthly and Quarterly Data ▫ ▫ ▫   415

Output 8.1.1.   Quarterly Data Set

```
                     Quarterly Data

        OBS     DATE       GD        GDP

         1     1990:1    111.100    5422.40
         2     1990:2    112.300    5504.70
         3     1990:3    113.600    5570.50
         4     1990:4    114.500    5557.50
         5     1991:1    115.900    5589.00
         6     1991:2    116.800    5652.60
         7     1991:3    117.400    5709.20
         8     1991:4      .        5736.60
```

The following statements extract and print the monthly data, shown in Output 8.1.2:

```
data monthly;
   set sashelp.citimon;
   where date >= '1jan1990'd &
         date <  '1jan1992'd ;
   keep date ip lhur;
run;

title "Monthly Data";
proc print data=monthly;
run;
```

Output 8.1.2.   Monthly Data Set

```
                      Monthly Data

        OBS     DATE        IP         LHUR

         1     JAN1990    107.500     5.30000
         2     FEB1990    108.500     5.30000
         3     MAR1990    108.900     5.20000
         4     APR1990    108.800     5.40000
         5     MAY1990    109.400     5.30000
         6     JUN1990    110.100     5.20000
         7     JUL1990    110.400     5.40000
         8     AUG1990    110.500     5.60000
         9     SEP1990    110.600     5.70000
        10     OCT1990    109.900     5.80000
        11     NOV1990    108.300     6.00000
        12     DEC1990    107.200     6.10000
        13     JAN1991    106.600     6.20000
        14     FEB1991    105.700     6.50000
        15     MAR1991    105.000     6.70000
        16     APR1991    105.500     6.60000
        17     MAY1991    106.400     6.80000
        18     JUN1991    107.300     6.90000
        19     JUL1991    108.100     6.80000
        20     AUG1991    108.000     6.80000
        21     SEP1991    108.400     6.80000
        22     OCT1991    108.200     6.90000
        23     NOV1991    108.000     6.90000
        24     DEC1991    107.800     7.10000
```

The following statements interpolate monthly estimates for the quarterly series and merge the interpolated series with the monthly data. The resulting combined data set is then printed, as shown in Output 8.1.3.

```
proc expand data=qtrly out=temp from=qtr to=month;
   convert gdp gd / observed=average;
   id date;
run;

data combined;
   merge monthly temp;
   by date;
run;

title "Combined Data Set";
proc print data=combined;
run;
```

Output 8.1.3.   Combined Data Set

```
                            Combined Data Set

         OBS      DATE       IP       LHUR       GDP        GD

           1     JAN1990   107.500    5.30000   5409.69   110.879
           2     FEB1990   108.500    5.30000   5417.67   111.048
           3     MAR1990   108.900    5.20000   5439.39   111.367
           4     APR1990   108.800    5.40000   5470.58   111.802
           5     MAY1990   109.400    5.30000   5505.35   112.297
           6     JUN1990   110.100    5.20000   5538.14   112.801
           7     JUL1990   110.400    5.40000   5563.38   113.264
           8     AUG1990   110.500    5.60000   5575.69   113.641
           9     SEP1990   110.600    5.70000   5572.49   113.905
          10     OCT1990   109.900    5.80000   5561.64   114.139
          11     NOV1990   108.300    6.00000   5553.83   114.451
          12     DEC1990   107.200    6.10000   5556.92   114.909
          13     JAN1991   106.600    6.20000   5570.06   115.452
          14     FEB1991   105.700    6.50000   5588.18   115.937
          15     MAR1991   105.000    6.70000   5608.68   116.314
          16     APR1991   105.500    6.60000   5630.81   116.600
          17     MAY1991   106.400    6.80000   5652.92   116.812
          18     JUN1991   107.300    6.90000   5674.06   116.988
          19     JUL1991   108.100    6.80000   5693.43   117.164
          20     AUG1991   108.000    6.80000   5710.54   117.380
          21     SEP1991   108.400    6.80000   5724.11   117.665
          22     OCT1991   108.200    6.90000   5733.65      .
          23     NOV1991   108.000    6.90000   5738.46      .
          24     DEC1991   107.800    7.10000   5737.75      .
```

Example 8.2.   Interpolating Irregular Observations

This example shows the interpolation of a series of values measured at irregular points in time.   The data are hypothetical.   Assume that a series of randomly timed quality control inspections are made and defect rates for a process are measured.   The problem is to produce two reports: estimates of monthly average defect rates for the months within the period covered by the samples and a plot of the interpolated defect rate curve over time.

Example 8.2. Interpolating Irregular Observations □ □ □ 417

The following statements read and print the input data, as shown in Output 8.2.1:

```
data samples;
   input date : date. defects @@;
   label defects = "Defects per 1000 units";
   format date date.;
cards;
13jan92    55     27jan92    73     19feb92    84      8mar92    69
27mar92    66      5apr92    77     29apr92    63     11may92    81
25may92    89      7jun92    94     23jun92   105     11jul92    97
15aug92   112     29aug92    89     10sep92    77     27sep92    82
;

title "Sampled Defect Rates";
proc print data=samples;
run;
```

Output 8.2.1. Measured Defect Rates

```
                        Sampled Defect Rates

                OBS      DATE      DEFECTS

                 1      13JAN92       55
                 2      27JAN92       73
                 3      19FEB92       84
                 4      08MAR92       69
                 5      27MAR92       66
                 6      05APR92       77
                 7      29APR92       63
                 8      11MAY92       81
                 9      25MAY92       89
                10      07JUN92       94
                11      23JUN92      105
                12      11JUL92       97
                13      15AUG92      112
                14      29AUG92       89
                15      10SEP92       77
                16      27SEP92       82
```

To compute the monthly estimates, use PROC EXPAND with the TO=MONTH option and specify OBSERVED=(BEGINNING,AVERAGE). The following statements interpolate the monthly estimates:

```
proc expand data=samples out=monthly to=month;
   id date;
   convert defects / observed=(beginning,average);
run;

title "Estimated Monthly Average Defect Rates";
proc print data=monthly;
run;
```

The results are printed in Output 8.2.2.

Output 8.2.2. Monthly Average Estimates

```
       Estimated Monthly Average Defect Rates

          OBS       DATE     DEFECTS

           1      JAN1992     59.323
           2      FEB1992     82.000
           3      MAR1992     66.909
           4      APR1992     70.205
           5      MAY1992     82.762
           6      JUN1992     99.701
           7      JUL1992    101.564
           8      AUG1992    105.491
           9      SEP1992     79.206
```

To produce the plot, first use PROC EXPAND with TO=DAY to interpolate a full
set of daily values, naming the interpolated series INTERPOL. Then merge this data
set with the samples so you can plot both the measured and the interpolated values
on the same graph. PROC GPLOT is used to plot the curve. The actual sample points
are plotted with asterisks. The following statements interpolate and plot the defects
rate curve:

```
proc expand data=samples out=daily to=day;
  id date;
  convert defects = interpol;
run;

data daily;
  merge daily samples;
  by date;
run;

title "Plot of Interpolated Defect Rate Curve";
proc gplot data=daily;
   symbol1 i=none v=star h=2;
   symbol2 i=join v=none;
   plot defects * date = 1 interpol * date = 2 / overlay;
run;
```

Example 8.2. Interpolating Irregular Observations □ □ □ **419**

The plot is shown in Output 8.2.3.

Output 8.2.3. Interpolated Defects Rate Curve

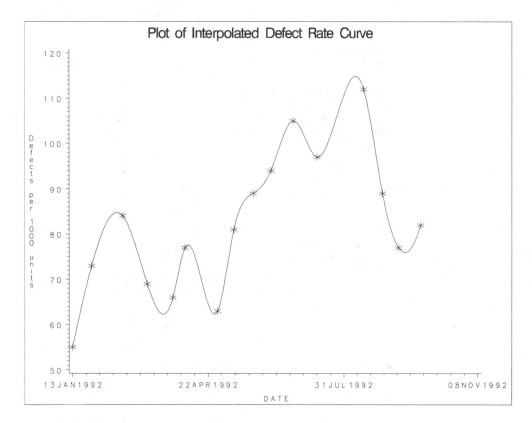

Example 8.3.   Using Transformations

This example shows the use of PROC EXPAND to perform various transformations of time series. The following statements read in monthly values for a variable X:

```
data test;
    input year qtr x;
    date = yyq( year, qtr );
    format date yyqc.;
cards;
1989 3 5238
1989 4 5289
1990 1 5375
1990 2 5443
1990 3 5514
1990 4 5527
1991 1 5557
1991 2 5615
;
```

The following statements use PROC EXPAND to compute lags and leads and a 3-period moving average of the X series:

```
proc expand data=test out=out method=none;
   id date;
   convert x = x_lag2   / transform=(lag 2);
   convert x = x_lag1   / transform=(lag 1);
   convert x;
   convert x = x_lead1  / transform=(lead 1);
   convert x = x_lead2  / transform=(lead 2);
   convert x = x_movave / transform=(movave 3);
run;

title "Transformed Series";
proc print data=out;
run;
```

Since there are no missing values to interpolate and no frequency conversion, the METHOD=NONE option is used to prevent PROC EXPAND from performing unnecessary computations. Since no frequency conversion is done, all variables in the input data set are copied to the output data set. The CONVERT X; statement is included to control the position of X in the output data set. This statement can be omitted, in which case X is copied to the output data set following the new variables computed by PROC EXPAND.

The results are shown in Output 8.3.1.

Output 8.3.1. Output Data Set with Transformed Variables

```
                            Transformed Series

   OBS    DATE    X_LAG2   X_LAG1    X    X_LEAD1  X_LEAD2  X_MOVAVE   YEAR   QTR

    1    1989:3      .        .     5238    5289    5375        .      1989    3
    2    1989:4      .      5238    5289    5375    5443     5300.67   1989    4
    3    1990:1    5238     5289    5375    5443    5514     5369.00   1990    1
    4    1990:2    5289     5375    5443    5514    5527     5444.00   1990    2
    5    1990:3    5375     5443    5514    5527    5557     5494.67   1990    3
    6    1990:4    5443     5514    5527    5557    5615     5532.67   1990    4
    7    1991:1    5514     5527    5557    5615       .     5566.33   1991    1
    8    1991:2    5527     5557    5615       .       .        .      1991    2
```

References

de Boor, Carl (1981), *A Practical Guide to Splines*, New York: Springer-Verlag.

Chapter 9
The FORECAST Procedure

Chapter Table of Contents

Chapter 9
The FORECAST Procedure

Overview

The FORECAST procedure provides a quick and automatic way to generate forecasts for many time series in one step. The procedure can forecast hundreds of series at a time, with the series organized into separate variables or across BY groups. PROC FORECAST uses extrapolative forecasting methods where the forecasts for a series are functions only of time and past values of the series, not of other variables.

You can use the following forecasting methods. For each of these methods, you can specify linear, quadratic, or no trend.

- The stepwise autoregressive method is used by default. This method combines time trend regression with an autoregressive model and uses a stepwise method to select the lags to use for the autoregressive process.

- The exponential smoothing method produces a time trend forecast, but in fitting the trend, the parameters are allowed to change gradually over time, and earlier observations are given exponentially declining weights. Single, double, and triple exponential smoothing are supported, depending on whether no trend, linear trend, or quadratic trend is specified. Holt two-parameter linear exponential smoothing is supported as a special case of the Holt-Winters method without seasons.

- The Winters method (also called Holt-Winters) combines a time trend with multiplicative seasonal factors to account for regular seasonal fluctuations in a series. Like the exponential smoothing method, the Winters method allows the parameters to change gradually over time, with earlier observations given exponentially declining weights. You can also specify the additive version of the Winters method, which uses additive instead of multiplicative seasonal factors. When seasonal factors are omitted, the Winters method reduces to the Holt two-parameter version of double exponential smoothing.

The FORECAST procedure writes the forecasts and confidence limits to an output data set, and can write parameter estimates and fit statistics to an output data set. The FORECAST procedure does not produce printed output.

PROC FORECAST is an extrapolation procedure useful for producing practical results efficiently. However, in the interest of speed, PROC FORECAST uses some shortcuts that cause some statistical results (such as confidence limits) to be only approximate. For many time series, the FORECAST procedure, with appropriately chosen methods and weights, can yield satisfactory results. Other SAS/ETS procedures can produce better forecasts but at greater computational expense.

You can perform the stepwise autoregressive forecasting method with the AUTOREG procedure. You can perform exponential smoothing with statistically optimal weights as an ARIMA model using the ARIMA procedure. Seasonal ARIMA models can be used for forecasting seasonal series for which the Winters and additive Winters methods might be used.

Getting Started

To use PROC FORECAST, specify the input and output data sets and the number of periods to forecast in the PROC FORECAST statement, then list the variables to forecast in a VAR statement.

For example, suppose you have monthly data on the sales of some product, as shown in Figure 9.1, and you want to forecast sales for the next 10 months.

OBS	DATE	SALES
1	JUL89	9.5161
2	AUG89	9.6994
3	SEP89	9.2644
4	OCT89	9.6837
5	NOV89	10.0784
6	DEC89	9.9005
7	JAN90	10.2375
8	FEB90	10.6940
9	MAR90	10.6290
10	APR90	11.0332
11	MAY90	11.0270
12	JUN90	11.4165
13	JUL90	11.2918
14	AUG90	11.3475
15	SEP90	11.2913
16	OCT90	11.3771
17	NOV90	11.5457
18	DEC90	11.6433
19	JAN91	11.9293
20	FEB91	11.9752
21	MAR91	11.9283
22	APR91	11.8985
23	MAY91	12.0419
24	JUN91	12.3537
25	JUL91	12.4546

Figure 9.1. Example Data Set PAST

The following statements forecast 10 observations for the variable SALES using the default STEPAR method and write the results to the output data set PRED:

```
proc forecast data=past lead=10 out=pred;
   var sales;
run;
```

The following statements use the PRINT procedure to print the data set PRED:

```
proc print data=pred;
run;
```

The PROC PRINT listing of the forecast data set PRED is shown in Figure 9.2.

```
        OBS      _TYPE_     _LEAD_      SALES

          1    FORECAST        1      12.6205
          2    FORECAST        2      12.7665
          3    FORECAST        3      12.9020
          4    FORECAST        4      13.0322
          5    FORECAST        5      13.1595
          6    FORECAST        6      13.2854
          7    FORECAST        7      13.4105
          8    FORECAST        8      13.5351
          9    FORECAST        9      13.6596
         10    FORECAST       10      13.7840
```

Figure 9.2. Forecast Data Set PRED

Giving Dates to Forecast Values

Normally, your input data set has an ID variable that gives dates to the observations, and you want the forecast observations to have dates also. Usually, the ID variable has SAS date values. (See Chapter 2, "Working with Time Series Data," for information on using SAS date values.) The ID statement specifies the identifying variable.

If the ID variable contains SAS date values, the INTERVAL= option should be used on the PROC FORECAST statement to specify the time interval between observations. (See Chapter 21, "Date Intervals, Formats, and Functions," for more information on time intervals.) The FORECAST procedure uses the INTERVAL= option to generate correct dates for forecast observations.

The data set PAST, shown in Figure 9.1, has monthly observations and contains an ID variable DATE with SAS date values identifying each observation. The following statements produce the same forecast as the preceding example and also include the ID variable DATE in the output data set. Monthly SAS date values are extrapolated for the forecast observations.

```
proc forecast data=past interval=month lead=10 out=pred;
   var sales;
   id date;
run;
```

Computing Confidence Limits

Depending on the output options specified, multiple observations are written to the OUT= data set for each time period. The different parts of the results are contained in the VAR statement variables in observations identified by the character variable _TYPE_ and by the ID variable.

For example, the following statements use the OUTLIMIT option to write forecasts and 95% confidence limits for the variable SALES to the output data set PRED. This data set is printed with the PRINT procedure.

```
proc forecast data=past interval=month lead=10
              out=pred outlimit;
   var sales;
   id date;
run;

proc print data=pred;
run;
```

The output data set PRED is shown in Figure 9.3.

OBS	DATE	_TYPE_	_LEAD_	SALES
1	AUG91	FORECAST	1	12.6205
2	AUG91	L95	1	12.1848
3	AUG91	U95	1	13.0562
4	SEP91	FORECAST	2	12.7665
5	SEP91	L95	2	12.2808
6	SEP91	U95	2	13.2522
7	OCT91	FORECAST	3	12.9020
8	OCT91	L95	3	12.4001
9	OCT91	U95	3	13.4039
10	NOV91	FORECAST	4	13.0322
11	NOV91	L95	4	12.5223
12	NOV91	U95	4	13.5421
13	DEC91	FORECAST	5	13.1595
14	DEC91	L95	5	12.6435
15	DEC91	U95	5	13.6755
16	JAN92	FORECAST	6	13.2854
17	JAN92	L95	6	12.7637
18	JAN92	U95	6	13.8070
19	FEB92	FORECAST	7	13.4105
20	FEB92	L95	7	12.8830
21	FEB92	U95	7	13.9379
22	MAR92	FORECAST	8	13.5351
23	MAR92	L95	8	13.0017
24	MAR92	U95	8	14.0686
25	APR92	FORECAST	9	13.6596
26	APR92	L95	9	13.1200
27	APR92	U95	9	14.1993
28	MAY92	FORECAST	10	13.7840
29	MAY92	L95	10	13.2380
30	MAY92	U95	10	14.3301

Figure 9.3. Output Data Set

Form of the OUT= Data Set

The OUT= data set PRED, shown in Figure 9.3, contains three observations for each of the 10 forecast periods. Each of these three observations has the same value of the ID variable DATE, the SAS date value for the month and year of the forecast.

The three observations for each forecast period have different values of the variable _TYPE_. For the _TYPE_=FORECAST observation, the value of the variable SALES is the forecast value for the period indicated by the DATE value. For the _TYPE_=L95 observation, the value of the variable SALES is the lower limit of the 95% confidence interval for the forecast. For the _TYPE_=U95 observation, the value of the variable SALES is the upper limit of the 95% confidence interval.

You can control the types of observations written to the OUT= data set with the PROC FORECAST statement options OUTLIMIT, OUTRESID, OUTACTUAL, OUT1STEP, OUTSTD, OUTFULL, and OUTALL. For example, the OUTFULL option outputs the confidence limit values, the one-step-ahead predictions, and the actual data, in addition to the forecast values. See the sections "Syntax" and "OUT= Data Set" later in this chapter for more information.

Plotting Forecasts

The forecasts, confidence limits, and actual values can be plotted on the same graph with the GPLOT procedure. Use the appropriate output control options on the PROC FORECAST statement to include in the OUT= data set the series you want to plot. Use the _TYPE_ variable in the GPLOT procedure PLOT statement to separate the observations for the different plots.

For example, the following statements plot the forecast with confidence limits in context with the historical data:

```
proc forecast data=past interval=month lead=10
              out=pred outfull;
    id date;
    var sales;
run;

proc gplot data=pred;
    plot sales * date = _type_ /
        haxis= '1jan90'd to '1jan93'd by qtr
        href='15jul91'd;
    symbol1 i=none    v=star h=2; /* for _type_=ACTUAL */
    symbol2 i=spline v=circle;   /* for _type_=FORECAST */
    symbol3 i=spline l=3;        /* for _type_=L95 */
    symbol4 i=spline l=3;        /* for _type_=U95 */
    where date >= '1jan90'd;
run;
```

The _TYPE_ variable is used in the GPLOT procedure's PLOT statement to make separate plots over time for each type of value. A reference line marks the start of the forecast period. (Refer to *SAS/GRAPH Software: Reference, Volume 2, Version 6, First Edition* for more information on using PROC GPLOT.) The WHERE statement restricts the range of the actual data shown in the plot. In this example, the variable SALES has monthly data from July 1989 through July 1991, but only the data for 1990 and 1991 are shown in the plot. The plot is shown in Figure 9.4.

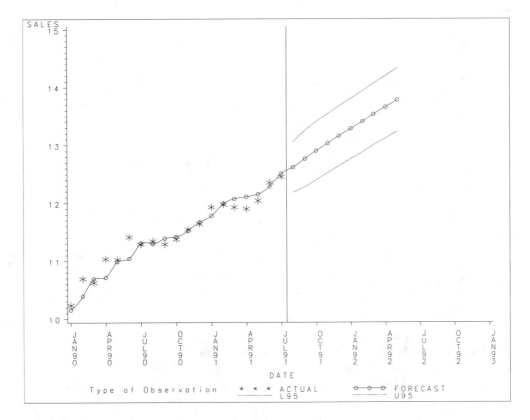

Figure 9.4. Plot of Forecast with Confidence Limits

Plotting Residuals

You can plot the residuals from the forecasting model used by specifying the OUTRESID or OUTALL option and using a WHERE statement to select only residual type observations in the PROC GPLOT step. The following example adds the OUTRESID option to the preceding example and plots the residuals:

```
proc forecast data=past interval=month lead=10
              out=pred outfull outresid;
   id date;
   var sales;
run;

proc gplot data=pred;
   where _type_='RESIDUAL';
   plot sales * date /
        haxis= '1jan89'd to '1oct91'd by qtr;
   symbol1 i=needle;
run;
```

The plot of residuals is shown in Figure 9.5.

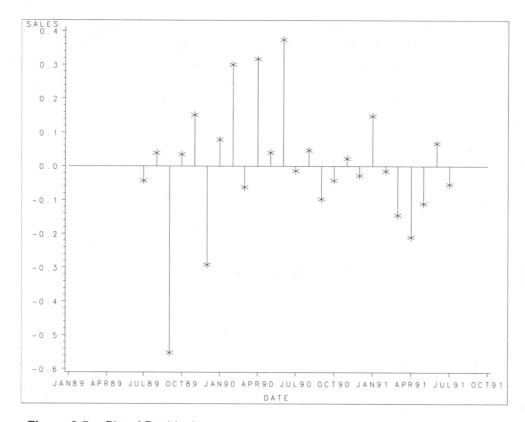

Figure 9.5. Plot of Residuals

Model Parameters and Goodness-of-Fit Statistics

You can write the parameters of the forecasting models used, as well as statistics measuring how well the forecasting models fit the data, to an output SAS data set using the OUTEST= option. The options OUTFITSTATS, OUTESTTHEIL, and OUTESTALL control what goodness-of-fit statistics are added to the OUTEST= data set.

For example, the following statements add the OUTEST= and OUTFITSTATS options to the previous example to create the output statistics data set EST for the results of the default stepwise autoregressive forecasting method:

```
proc forecast data=past interval=month lead=10
              out=pred outfull outresid
              outest=est outfitstats;
   id date;
   var sales;
run;

proc print data=est;
run;
```

The PRINT procedure prints the OUTEST= data set, as shown in Figure 9.6.

OBS	_TYPE_	DATE	SALES
1	N	JUL91	25
2	NRESID	JUL91	25
3	DF	JUL91	22
4	SIGMA	JUL91	0.2001613
5	CONSTANT	JUL91	9.4348822
6	LINEAR	JUL91	0.1242648
7	AR1	JUL91	0.5206294
8	AR2	JUL91	.
9	AR3	JUL91	.
10	AR4	JUL91	.
11	AR5	JUL91	.
12	AR6	JUL91	.
13	AR7	JUL91	.
14	AR8	JUL91	.
15	SST	JUL91	21.28342
16	SSE	JUL91	0.8793714
17	MSE	JUL91	0.0399714
18	RMSE	JUL91	0.1999286
19	MAPE	JUL91	1.2280089
20	MPE	JUL91	-0.050139
21	MAE	JUL91	0.1312115
22	ME	JUL91	-0.001811
23	MAXE	JUL91	0.3732328
24	MINE	JUL91	-0.551605
25	MAXPE	JUL91	3.2692294
26	MINPE	JUL91	-5.954022
27	RSQUARE	JUL91	0.9586828
28	ADJRSQ	JUL91	0.9549267
29	RW_RSQ	JUL91	0.2657801
30	ARSQ	JUL91	0.9474145
31	APC	JUL91	0.044768
32	AIC	JUL91	-77.68559
33	SBC	JUL91	-74.02897
34	CORR	JUL91	0.9791313

Figure 9.6.   The OUTEST= Data Set for STEPAR Method

In the OUTEST= data set, the DATE variable contains the ID value of the last observation in the data set used to fit the forecasting model. The variable SALES contains the statistic indicated by the value of the _TYPE_ variable. The _TYPE_=N, NRESID, and DF observations contain, respectively, the number of observations read from the data set, the number of nonmissing residuals used to compute the goodness-of-fit statistics, and the number of nonmissing observations minus the number of parameters used in the forecasting model.

The _TYPE_=SIGMA observation gives the estimate of the standard deviation of the one-step prediction error computed from the residuals. The _TYPE_=CONSTANT and _TYPE_=LINEAR give the coefficients of the time trend regression. The

TYPE=AR1, AR2, ..., AR7 observations give the estimated autoregressive parameters. A missing autoregressive parameter indicates that the autoregressive term at that lag was not included in the model by the stepwise model selection method. (See the section "STEPAR Method" later in this chapter for more information.)

The other observations in the OUTEST= data set contain various goodness-of-fit statistics that measure how well the forecasting model used fits the given data. See "OUTEST= Data Set" later in this chapter for details.

Controlling the Forecasting Method

The METHOD= option controls which forecasting method is used. The TREND= option controls the degree of the time trend model used. For example, the following statements produce forecasts of SALES as in the preceding example but use the double exponential smoothing method instead of the default STEPAR method:

```
proc forecast data=past interval=month lead=10
              method=expo trend=2
              out=pred outfull outresid
              outest=est outfitstats;
   var sales;
   id date;
run;

proc print data=est;
run;
```

The PRINT procedure prints the OUTEST= data set for the EXPO method, as shown in Figure 9.7.

OBS	_TYPE_	DATE	SALES
1	N	JUL91	25
2	NRESID	JUL91	25
3	DF	JUL91	23
4	WEIGHT	JUL91	0.1055728
5	S1	JUL91	11.427657
6	S2	JUL91	10.316473
7	SIGMA	JUL91	0.2545069
8	CONSTANT	JUL91	12.538841
9	LINEAR	JUL91	0.1311574
10	SST	JUL91	21.28342
11	SSE	JUL91	1.4897965
12	MSE	JUL91	0.0647738
13	RMSE	JUL91	0.2545069
14	MAPE	JUL91	1.9121204
15	MPE	JUL91	-0.816886
16	MAE	JUL91	0.2101358
17	ME	JUL91	-0.094941
18	MAXE	JUL91	0.3127332
19	MINE	JUL91	-0.460207
20	MAXPE	JUL91	2.9243781
21	MINPE	JUL91	-4.967478
22	RSQUARE	JUL91	0.930002
23	ADJRSQ	JUL91	0.9269586
24	RW_RSQ	JUL91	-0.243886
25	ARSQ	JUL91	0.9178285
26	APC	JUL91	0.0699557
27	AIC	JUL91	-66.50591
28	SBC	JUL91	-64.06816
29	CORR	JUL91	0.9772418

Figure 9.7. The OUTEST= Data Set for METHOD=EXPO

See the "Syntax" section later in this chapter for other options that control the forecasting method. See "Introduction to Forecasting Methods" and "Forecasting Methods" later in this chapter for an explanation of the different forecasting methods.

Introduction to Forecasting Methods

This section briefly introduces the forecasting methods used by the FORECAST procedure. Refer to textbooks on forecasting and see "Forecasting Methods" later in this chapter for more detailed discussions of forecasting methods.

The FORECAST procedure combines three basic models to fit time series:

- time trend models for long-term, deterministic change
- autoregressive models for short-term fluctuations
- seasonal models for regular seasonal fluctuations

Two approaches to time series modeling and forecasting are *time trend models* and *time series methods*.

Time Trend Models

Time trend models assume that there is some permanent deterministic pattern across time. These models are best suited to data that are not dominated by random fluctuations.

Examining a graphical plot of the time series you want to forecast is often very useful in choosing an appropriate model. The simplest case of a time trend model is one in which you assume the series is a constant plus purely random fluctuations that are independent from one time period to the next. Figure 9.8 shows how such a time series might look.

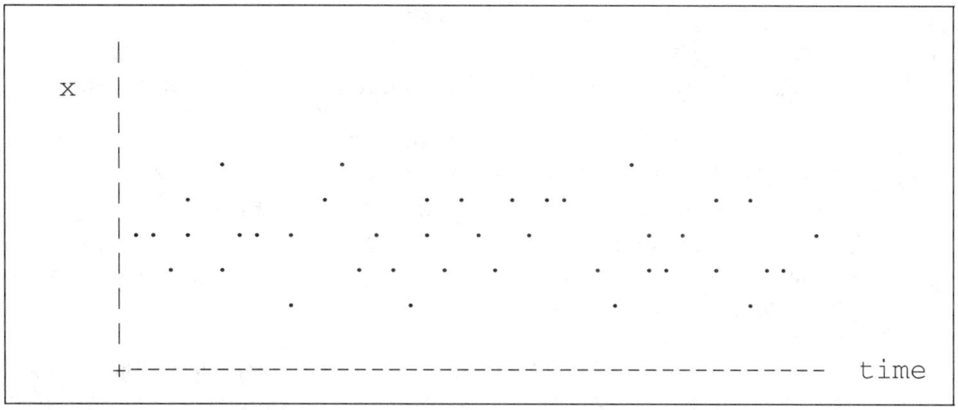

Figure 9.8. Time Series without Trend

The x_t values are generated according to the equation

$$x_t = b_0 + \epsilon_t$$

where ϵ_t is an independent, zero-mean, random error, and b_0 is the true series mean.

Suppose that the series exhibits growth over time, as shown in Figure 9.9.

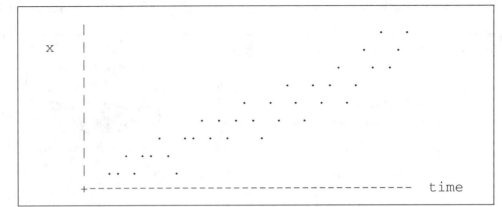

Figure 9.9. Time Series with Linear Trend

A linear model is appropriate for this data. For the linear model, assume the x_t values are generated according to the equation

$$x_t = b_0 + b_1 t + \epsilon_t$$

The linear model has two parameters. The predicted values for the future are the points on the estimated line. The extension of the polynomial model to three parameters is the quadratic (which forms a parabola). This allows for a constantly changing slope, where the x_t values are generated according to the equation

$$x_t = b_0 + b_1 t + b_2 t^2 + \epsilon_t$$

PROC FORECAST can fit three types of time trend models: constant, linear, and quadratic. For other kinds of trend models, other SAS procedures can be used.

Exponential smoothing fits a time trend model using a smoothing scheme in which the weights decline geometrically as you go backward in time. The forecasts from exponential smoothing are a time trend, but the trend is based mostly on the recent observations instead of on all the observations equally. How well exponential smoothing works as a forecasting method depends on choosing a good smoothing weight for the series.

Use the METHOD=EXPO option to specify the exponential smoothing method. Single exponential smoothing produces forecasts with a constant trend (that is, no trend). Double exponential smoothing produces forecasts with a linear trend, and triple exponential smoothing produces a quadratic trend. Use the TREND= option with the METHOD=EXPO option to select single, double, or triple exponential smoothing.

The time trend model can be modified to account for regular seasonal fluctuations of the series about the trend. To capture seasonality, the trend model includes a seasonal parameter for each season. Seasonal models can be additive or multiplicative.

$$x_t = b_0 + b_1 t + s(t) + \epsilon_t \quad \text{(Additive)}$$
$$x_t = (b_0 + b_1 t)\, s(t) + \epsilon_t \quad \text{(Multiplicative)}$$

where $s(t)$ is the seasonal parameter for the season corresponding to time t.

The Winters method is similar to exponential smoothing, but includes seasonal factors. The Winters method can use either additive or multiplicative seasonal factors. Like exponential smoothing, good results with the Winters method depend on choosing good smoothing weights for the series to be forecast.

Use the METHOD=WINTERS or METHOD=ADDWINTERS option to specify the multiplicative or additive version of the Winters method, and use the SEASONS= option to specify the seasonal factors to include in the model.

Many observed time series do not behave like constant, linear, or quadratic time trends. However, you can partially compensate for the inadequacies of the trend models by fitting time series models to the departures from the time trend, as described in the following sections.

Time Series Methods

Time series models assume the future value of a variable to be a linear function of past values. If the model is a function of past values for a finite number of periods, it is an *autoregressive model* and is written as follows:

$$x_t = a_0 + a_1 x_{t-1} + a_2 x_{t-2} + \dots + a_p x_{t-p} + \epsilon_t$$

The coefficients a_i are *autoregressive parameters*. One of the simplest cases of this model is the random walk, where the series dances around in purely random jumps. This is illustrated in Figure 9.10.

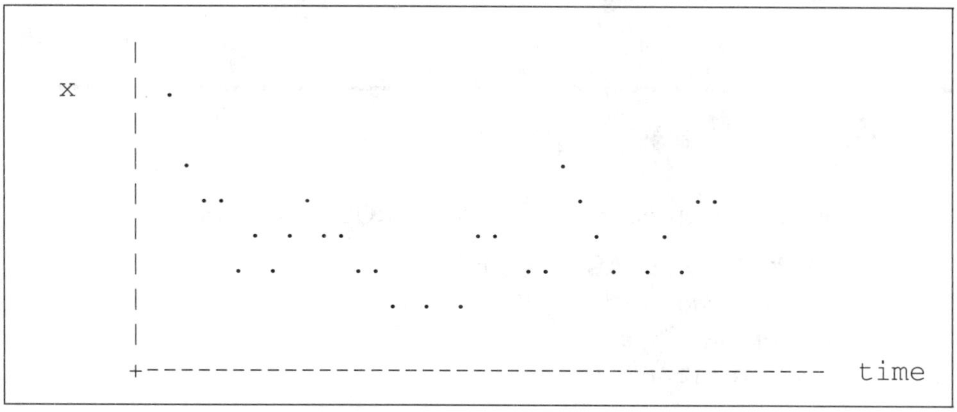

Figure 9.10. Random Walk Series

The x_t values are generated by the equation

$$x_t = x_{t-1} + \epsilon_t$$

In this type of model, the best forecast of a future value is the present value. However, with other autoregressive models, the best forecast is a weighted sum of recent values. Pure autoregressive forecasts always damp down to a constant (assuming the process is stationary).

Autoregressive time series models can also be used to predict seasonal fluctuations.

Combining Time Trend with Autoregressive Models

Trend models are suitable for capturing long-term behavior, whereas autoregressive models are more appropriate for capturing short-term fluctuations. One approach to forecasting is to combine a deterministic time trend model with an autoregressive model.

The *stepwise autoregressive method* (STEPAR method) combines a time-trend regression with an autoregressive model for departures from trend. The combined time-trend and autoregressive model is written as follows:

$$x_t = b_0 + b_1 t + b_2 t^2 + u_t$$
$$u_t = a_1 u_{t-1} + a_2 u_{t-2} + ... + a_p u_{t-p} + \epsilon_t$$

The autoregressive parameters included in the model for each series are selected by a stepwise regression procedure, so that autoregressive parameters are only included at those lags at which they are statistically significant.

The stepwise autoregressive method is fully automatic and, unlike the exponential smoothing and Winters methods, does not depend on choosing smoothing weights. However, the STEPAR method assumes that the long-term trend is stable; that is, the time trend regression is fit to the whole series with equal weights for the observations.

The stepwise autoregressive model is used when you specify the METHOD=STEPAR option or do not specify any METHOD= option. Use the TREND= option to select a constant, linear, or quadratic trend for the time-trend part of the model.

Syntax

The following statements are used with PROC FORECAST:

PROC FORECAST *options*;
    BY *variables*;
    ID *variables*;
    VAR *variables*;

Functional Summary

The statements and options controlling the FORECAST procedure are summarized in the following table:

Description	Statement	Option
Statements		
specify BY-group processing	BY	
identify observations	ID	
specify the variables to forecast	VAR	
Input Data Set Options		
specify the input SAS data set	PROC FORECAST	DATA=
specify frequency of the input time series	PROC FORECAST	INTERVAL=
	PROC FORECAST	INTPER=
specify seasonality	PROC FORECAST	SEASONS=
specify number of periods in a season	PROC FORECAST	SINTPER=
treat zeros at beginning of series as missing	PROC FORECAST	ZEROMISS
Output Data Set Options		
specify the number of periods ahead to forecast	PROC FORECAST	LEAD=
name output data set containing the forecasts	PROC FORECAST	OUT=
write actual values to the OUT= data set	PROC FORECAST	OUTACTUAL
write confidence limits to the OUT= data set	PROC FORECAST	OUTLIMIT
write residuals to the OUT= data set	PROC FORECAST	OUTRESID
write standard errors of the forecasts to the OUT= data set	PROC FORECAST	OUTSTD
write one-step-ahead predicted values to the OUT= data set	PROC FORECAST	OUT1STEP
write predicted, actual, and confidence limit values to the OUT= data set	PROC FORECAST	OUTFULL
write all available results to the OUT= data set	PROC FORECAST	OUTALL
specify significance level for confidence limits	PROC FORECAST	ALPHA=
Parameters and Statistics Output Data Set Options		
write parameter estimates and goodness-of-fit statistics to an output data set	PROC FORECAST	OUTEST=
write additional statistics to OUTEST= data set	PROC FORECAST	OUTESTALL
write Theil statistics to OUTEST= data set	PROC FORECAST	OUTESTTHEIL
write forecast accuracy statistics to OUTEST= data set	PROC FORECAST	OUTFITSTATS
Forecasting Method Options		
specify the forecasting method	PROC FORECAST	METHOD=
specify degree of the time trend model	PROC FORECAST	TREND=
specify smoothing weights	PROC FORECAST	WEIGHT=

Description	Statement	Option
specify order of the autoregressive model	PROC FORECAST	AR=
specify significance level for adding AR lags	PROC FORECAST	SLENTRY=
specify significance level for keeping AR lags	PROC FORECAST	SLSTAY=
start forecasting before the end of data	PROC FORECAST	START=
specify criterion for judging singularity	PROC FORECAST	SINGULAR=
Initializing Smoothed Values		
specify number of beginning values to use in calculating starting values	PROC FORECAST	NSTART=
specify number of beginning values to use in calculating initial seasonal parameters	PROC FORECAST	NSSTART=
specify starting values for constant term	PROC FORECAST	ASTART=
specify starting values for linear trend	PROC FORECAST	BSTART=
specify starting values for the quadratic trend	PROC FORECAST	CSTART=

PROC FORECAST Statement

> **PROC FORECAST** *options*;

The following options can be specified in the PROC FORECAST statement:

ALPHA= *value*

> specifies the significance level to use in computing the confidence limits of the forecast. The value of the ALPHA= option must be between .01 and .99. You should use only two digits for the ALPHA= option because PROC FORECAST rounds the value to the nearest percent (ALPHA=.101 is the same as ALPHA=.10). The default is ALPHA=.05, which produces 95% confidence limits.

AR= *n*
NLAGS= *n*

> specifies the maximum order of the autoregressive model. The AR= option is only valid for METHOD=STEPAR. The default value of *n* depends on the INTERVAL= option and on the number of observations in the DATA= data set. See "STEPAR Method" later in this chapter for details.

ASTART= *value*
ASTART= (*value ...*)

> specifies starting values for the constant term for the exponential smoothing, Winters, and additive Winters methods. This option is ignored if METHOD=STEPAR. See "Starting Values for EXPO, WINTERS, and ADDWINTERS Methods" later in this chapter for details.

BSTART= *value*
BSTART= (*value ...*)

specifies starting values for the linear trend for the exponential smoothing, Winters, and additive Winters methods. This option is ignored if METHOD=STEPAR or TREND=1. See "Starting Values for EXPO, WINTERS, and ADDWINTERS Methods" later in this chapter for details.

CSTART= *value*
CSTART= (*value ...*)

specifies starting values for the quadratic trend for the exponential smoothing, Winters, and additive Winters methods. This option is ignored if METHOD=STEPAR or TREND=1 or 2. See "Starting Values for EXPO, WINTERS, and ADDWINTERS Methods" later in this chapter for details.

DATA= *SAS-data-set*

names the SAS data set containing the input time series for the procedure to forecast. If the DATA= option is not specified, the most recently created SAS data set is used.

INTERVAL= *interval*

specifies the frequency of the input time series. For example, if the input data set consists of quarterly observations, then INTERVAL=QTR should be used. See Chapter 21, "Date Intervals, Formats, and Functions," for more details on the intervals available.

INTPER= *n*

when the INTERVAL= option is not used, INTPER= specifies an increment (other than 1) to use in generating the values of the ID variable for the forecast observations in the output data set.

LEAD= *n*

specifies the number of periods ahead to forecast. The default is LEAD=12.

The LEAD= value is relative to the last observation in the input data set and not to the end of a particular series. Thus, if a series has missing values at the end, the actual number of forecasts computed for that series will be greater than the LEAD= value.

METHOD= *method-name*

specifies the method to use to model the series and generate the forecasts.

METHOD=STEPAR	specifies the stepwise autoregressive method.
METHOD=EXPO	specifies the exponential smoothing method.
METHOD=WINTERS	specifies the Holt-Winters exponentially smoothed trend-seasonal method.
METHOD=ADDWINTERS	specifies the additive seasonal factors variant of the Winters method.

For more information, see the section "Forecasting Methods" later in this chapter. The default is METHOD=STEPAR.

NSTART= *n*
NSTART= MAX

specifies the number of beginning values of the series to use in calculating starting values for the trend parameters in the exponential smoothing, Winters, and additive Winters methods. This option is ignored if METHOD=STEPAR.

For METHOD=EXPO, *n* beginning values of the series are used in forming the exponentially smoothed values S1, S2, and S3, where *n* is the value of the NSTART= option. The parameters are initialized by fitting a time trend regression to the first *n* nonmissing values of the series.

For METHOD=WINTERS or METHOD=ADDWINTERS, *n* beginning complete seasonal cycles are used to compute starting values for the trend parameters. For example, for monthly data the seasonal cycle is one year, and NSTART=2 specifies that the first 24 observations at the beginning of each series are used for the time trend regression used to calculate starting values.

When NSTART=MAX is specified, all the observations are used. The default for METHOD=EXPO is NSTART=8; the default for METHOD=WINTERS or METHOD=ADDWINTERS is NSTART=2. See "Starting Values for EXPO, WINTERS, and ADDWINTERS Methods" later in this chapter for details.

NSSTART= *n*
NSSTART= MAX

specifies the number of beginning values of the series to use in calculating starting values for seasonal parameters for METHOD=WINTERS or METHOD=ADDWINTERS. The seasonal parameters are initialized by averaging over the first *n* values of the series for each season, where *n* is the value of the NSSTART= option. When NSSTART=MAX is specified, all the observations are used.

If NSTART= is specified, but NSSTART= is not, NSSTART= defaults to the value specified for NSTART=. If neither NSTART= nor NSSTART= is specified, then the default is NSSTART=2. This option is ignored if METHOD=STEPAR or METHOD=EXPO. See "Starting Values for EXPO, WINTERS, and ADDWINTERS Methods" later in this chapter for details.

OUT= *SAS-data-set*

names the output data set to contain the forecasts. If the OUT= option is not specified, the data set is named using the DATA*n* convention. See "OUT= Data Set" later in this chapter for details.

OUTACTUAL

writes the actual values to the OUT= data set.

OUTALL

provides all the output control options (OUTLIMIT, OUT1STEP, OUTACTUAL, OUTRESID, and OUTSTD).

OUTEST= *SAS-data-set*

names an output data set to contain the parameter estimates and goodness-of-fit statistics. When the OUTEST= option is not specified, the parameters and goodness-of-fit statistics are not stored. See "OUTEST= Data Set" later in this chapter for details.

OUTESTALL

writes additional statistics to the OUTEST= data set. This option is the same as specifying both OUTESTTHEIL and OUTFITSTATS.

OUTESTTHEIL

writes Theil forecast accuracy statistics to the OUTEST= data set.

OUTFITSTATS

writes various R^2-type forecast accuracy statistics to the OUTEST= data set.

OUTFULL

provides OUTACTUAL, OUT1STEP, and OUTLIMIT output control options in addition to the forecast values.

OUTLIMIT

writes the forecast confidence limits to the OUT= data set.

OUTRESID

writes the residuals (when available) to the OUT= data set.

OUTSTD

writes the standard errors of the forecasts to the OUT= data set.

OUT1STEP

writes the one-step-ahead predicted values to the OUT= data set.

SEASONS= *interval*
SEASONS= (*interval1* [*interval2* [*interval3*]])
SEASONS= *n*
SEASONS= (*n1* [*n2* [*n3*]])

specifies the seasonality for seasonal models. The *interval* can be QTR, MONTH, DAY, or HOUR, or multiples of these (QTR2, MONTH2, MONTH3, MONTH4, MONTH6, HOUR2, HOUR3, HOUR4, HOUR6, HOUR8, HOUR12).

Alternatively, seasonality can be specified by giving the length of the seasonal cycles. For example, SEASONS=3 means that every group of three observations forms a seasonal cycle. The SEASONS= option is valid only for METHOD=WINTERS or METHOD=ADDWINTERS. See "Specifying Seasonality" later in this chapter for details.

SINGULAR= *value*

gives the criterion for judging singularity. The default depends on the precision of the computer that you run SAS programs on.

SINTPER= *m*
SINTPER= (*m1* [*m2* [*m3*]])

specifies the number of periods to combine in forming a season. For example, SEASONS=3 SINTPER=2 specifies that each group of two observations forms a season and that the seasonal cycle repeats every six observations. The SINTPER= option is valid only when the SEASONS= option is used. See "Specifying Seasonality" later in this chapter for details.

SLENTRY= *value*

controls the significance levels for entry of autoregressive parameters in the STEPAR method. The value of the STEPAR= option must be between 0 and 1. The default is SLENTRY=0.2. See "STEPAR Method" later in this chapter for details.

SLSTAY= *value*

controls the significance levels for removal of autoregressive parameters in the STEPAR method. The value of the SLSTAY= option must be between 0 and 1. The default is SLSTAY=0.05. See "STEPAR Method" later in this chapter for details.

START= *n*

uses the first *n* observations to fit the model and begins forecasting with the $n + 1$ observation.

TREND= *n*

specifies the degree of the time trend model. The value of the TREND= option must be 1, 2, or 3. TREND=1 selects the constant trend model; TREND=2 selects the linear trend model; and TREND=3 selects the quadratic trend model. The default is TREND=2, except for METHOD=EXPO, for which the default is TREND=3.

WEIGHT= *w*
WEIGHT= (*w1* [*w2* [*w3*]])

specifies the smoothing weights for the EXPO, WINTERS, and ADDWINTERS methods. For the EXPO method, only one weight can be specified. For the WINTERS or ADDWINTERS method, *w1* gives the weight for updating the constant component, *w2* gives the weight for updating the linear and quadratic trend components, and *w3* gives the weight for updating the seasonal component. The *w2* and *w3* values are optional. Each value in the WEIGHT= option must be between 0 and 1. For default values, see "EXPO Method" and "WINTERS Method" later in this chapter.

ZEROMISS

treats zeros at the beginning of a series as missing values. For example, a product may be introduced at a date after the date of the first observation in the data set, and the sales variable for the product may be recorded as zero for the observations prior to the introduction date. The ZEROMISS option says to treat these initial zeros as missing values.

BY Statement

BY *variables*;

A BY statement can be used with PROC FORECAST to obtain separate analyses on observations in groups defined by the BY variables.

ID Statement

> **ID** *variables*;

The first variable listed in the ID statement identifies observations in the input and output data sets. Usually, the first ID variable is a SAS date or datetime variable. Its values are interpreted and extrapolated according to the values of the INTER-VAL= option. See "Data Periodicity and Time Intervals" later in this chapter for details.

If more than one ID variable is specified in the ID statement, only the first is used to identify the observations; the rest are just copied to the OUT= data set and will have missing values for forecast observations.

VAR Statement

> **VAR** *variables*;

The VAR statement specifies the variables in the input data set that you want to forecast. If no VAR statement is specified, the procedure forecasts all numeric variables except the ID and BY variables.

Details

Missing Values

The treatment of missing values varies by method. For METHOD=STEPAR, missing values are tolerated in the series; the autocorrelations are estimated from the available data and tapered, if necessary. For the EXPO, WINTERS, and ADDWINTERS methods, missing values after the start of the series are replaced with one-step-ahead predicted values, and the predicted values are applied to the smoothing equations. For the WINTERS method, negative or zero values are treated as missing.

Data Periodicity and Time Intervals

The INTERVAL= option is used to establish the frequency of the time series. For example, INTERVAL=MONTH specifies that each observation in the input data set represents one month. If INTERVAL=MONTH2, each observation represents two months. Thus, there is a two-month time interval between each pair of successive observations, and the data frequency is bimonthly.

See Chapter 21, "Date Intervals, Formats, and Functions," for details on the interval values supported.

The INTERVAL= option is used together with the ID statement to fully describe the observations that make up the time series. The first variable specified in the ID statement is used to identify the observations. Usually, SAS date or datetime values are used for this variable. PROC FORECAST uses the ID variable in the following ways:

- to validate the data periodicity. When the INTERVAL= option is specified, the ID variable is used to check the data and verify that successive observations have valid ID values corresponding to successive time intervals. When the INTERVAL= option is not used, PROC FORECAST verifies that the ID values are non-missing and in ascending order. A warning message is printed when an invalid ID value is found in the input data set.

- to check for gaps in the input observations. For example, if INTERVAL=MONTH and an input observation for January 1970 is followed by an observation for April 1970, there is a gap in the input data, with two observations omitted. When a gap in the input data is found, a warning message is printed, and PROC FORECAST processes missing values for each omitted input observation.

- to label the forecast observations in the output data set. The values of the ID variable for the forecast observations after the end of the input data set are extrapolated according to the frequency specifications of the INTERVAL= option. If the INTERVAL= option is not specified, the ID variable is extrapolated by incrementing the ID variable value for the last observation in the input data set by the INTPER= value, if specified, or by one.

Forecasting Methods

This section explains the forecasting methods used by PROC FORECAST.

STEPAR Method

In the STEPAR method, PROC FORECAST first fits a time trend model to the series and takes the difference between each value and the estimated trend. (This process is called *detrending*.) Then, the remaining variation is fit using an autoregressive model.

The STEPAR method fits the autoregressive process to the residuals of the trend model using a backwards-stepping method to select parameters. Since the trend and autoregressive parameters are fit in sequence rather than simultaneously, the parameter estimates are not optimal in a statistical sense; however, the estimates are usually close to optimal, and the method is computationally inexpensive.

The STEPAR Algorithm

The STEPAR method consists of the following computational steps:

1. Fit the trend model as specified by the TREND= option using ordinary least-squares regression. This step detrends the data. The default trend model for the STEPAR method is TREND=2, a linear trend model.

2. Take the residuals from step 1 and compute the autocovariances to the number of lags specified by the NLAGS= option.

3. Regress the current values against the lags, using the autocovariances from step 2 in a Yule-Walker framework. Do not bring in any autoregressive parameter that is not significant at the level specified by the SLENTRY= option. (The default is SLENTRY=0.20.)

4. Find the autoregressive parameter that is least significant. If the significance level

is greater than the SLSTAY= value, remove the parameter from the model. (The default is SLSTAY=0.05.) Continue this process until only significant autoregressive parameters remain. If the OUTEST= option is specified, write the estimates to the OUTEST= data set.

5. Generate the forecasts using the estimated model and output to the OUT= data set. Form the confidence limits by combining the trend variances with the autoregressive variances.

Missing values are tolerated in the series; the autocorrelations are estimated from the available data and tapered if necessary.

This method requires at least three passes through the data: two passes to fit the model and a third pass to initialize the autoregressive process and write to the output data set.

Default Value of the NLAGS= Option

If the NLAGS= option is not specified, the default value of the NLAGS= option is chosen based on the data frequency specified by the INTERVAL= option and on the number of observations in the input data set, if this can be determined in advance. (PROC FORECAST cannot determine the number of input observations before reading the data when a BY statement or a WHERE statement is used or if the data are from a tape format SAS data set or external database. The NLAGS= value must be fixed before the data are processed.)

If the INTERVAL= option is specified, the default NLAGS= value includes lags for up to three years plus one, subject to the maximum of 13 lags or one third of the number of observations in your data set, whichever is less. If the number of observations in the input data set cannot be determined, the maximum NLAGS= default value is 13. If the INTERVAL= option is not specified, the default is NLAGS=13 or one-third the number of input observations, whichever is less.

For example, for INTERVAL=QTR, the default is NLAGS=13 (that is, $4 \times 3 + 1$) provided that there are at least 39 observations. The NLAGS= option default is always at least 3.

EXPO Method

Exponential smoothing is used when the METHOD=EXPO option is specified. The term *exponential smoothing* is derived from the computational scheme developed by Brown and others (Brown and Meyers 1961; Brown 1962). Estimates are computed with updating formulas that are developed across time series in a manner similar to smoothing.

The EXPO method fits a trend model such that the most recent data are weighted more heavily than data in the early part of the series. The weight of an observation is a geometric (exponential) function of the number of periods that the observation extends into the past relative to the current period. The weight function is

$$w_\tau = \omega(1 - \omega)^{t-\tau}$$

where τ is the observation number of the past observation, t is the current observation number, and ω is the weighting constant specified with the WEIGHT= option.

You specify the model with the TREND= option as follows:

- TREND=1 specifies single exponential smoothing (a constant model)

- TREND=2 specifies double exponential smoothing (a linear trend model)

- TREND=3 specifies triple exponential smoothing (a quadratic trend model)

Updating Equations

The single exponential smoothing operation is expressed by the formula

$$S_t = \omega x_t + (1 - \omega)S_{t-1}$$

where S_t is the smoothed value at the current period, t is the time index of the current period, and x_t is the current actual value of the series. The smoothed value S_t is the forecast of x_{t+1} and is calculated as the smoothing constant ω times the value of the series, x_t, in the current period plus $(1 - \omega)$ times the previous smoothed value S_{t-1}, which is the forecast of x_t computed at time $t - 1$.

Double and triple exponential smoothing are derived by applying exponential smoothing to the smoothed series, obtaining smoothed values as follows:

$$S_t^{[2]} = \omega S_t + (1 - \omega)S_{t-1}^{[2]}$$
$$S_t^{[3]} = \omega S_t^{[2]} + (1 - \omega)S_{t-1}^{[3]}$$

Missing values after the start of the series are replaced with one-step-ahead predicted values, and the predicted value is then applied to the smoothing equations.

The polynomial time trend parameters CONSTANT, LINEAR, and QUAD in the OUTEST= data set are computed from S_T, $S_T^{[2]}$, and $S_T^{[3]}$, the final smoothed values at observation T, the last observation used to fit the model. In the OUTEST= data set, the values of S_T, $S_T^{[2]}$, and $S_T^{[3]}$ are identified by _TYPE_=S1, _TYPE_=S2, and _TYPE_=S3, respectively.

Smoothing Weights

Exponential smoothing forecasts are forecasts for an integrated moving-average process; however, the weighting parameter is specified by the user rather than estimated from the data. Experience has shown that good values for the WEIGHT= option are between .05 and .3. As a general rule, smaller smoothing weights are appropriate for series with a slowly changing trend, while larger weights are appropriate for volatile series with a rapidly changing trend. If unspecified, the weight defaults to $\left(1 - .8^{1/trend}\right)$, where *trend* is the value of the TREND= option. This produces defaults of WEIGHT=.2 for TREND=1, WEIGHT=.10557 for TREND=2, and WEIGHT=.07168 for TREND=3.

Confidence Limits

The confidence limits for exponential smoothing forecasts are calculated as they would be for an exponentially weighted time-trend regression, using the simplifying assumption of an infinite number of observations. The variance estimate is computed using the mean square of the unweighted one-step-ahead forecast residuals.

More detailed descriptions of the forecast computations can be found in Montgomery and Johnson (1976) and Brown (1962).

Exponential Smoothing as an ARIMA Model

The traditional description of exponential smoothing given in the preceding section is standard in most books on forecasting, and so this traditional version is employed by PROC FORECAST.

However, the standard exponential smoothing model is, in fact, a special case of an ARIMA model (McKenzie 1984). Single exponential smoothing corresponds to an ARIMA(0,1,1) model; double exponential smoothing corresponds to an ARIMA(0,2,2) model; and triple exponential smoothing corresponds to an ARIMA(0,3,3) model.

The traditional exponential smoothing calculations can be viewed as a simple and computationally inexpensive method of forecasting the equivalent ARIMA model. The exponential smoothing technique was developed in the 1960s before computers were widely available and before ARIMA modeling methods were developed.

If you use exponential smoothing as a forecasting method, you might consider using the ARIMA procedure to forecast the equivalent ARIMA model as an alternative to the traditional version of exponential smoothing used by PROC FORECAST. The advantages of the ARIMA form are:

- The optimal smoothing weight is automatically computed as the estimate of the moving average parameter of the ARIMA model.

- For double exponential smoothing, the optimal pair of two smoothing weights are computed. For triple exponential smoothing, the optimal three smoothing weights are computed by the ARIMA method. Most implementations of the traditional exponential smoothing method (including PROC FORECAST) use the same smoothing weight for each stage of smoothing.

- The problem of setting the starting smoothed value is automatically handled by the ARIMA method. This is done in a statistically optimal way when the maximum likelihood method is used.

- The statistical estimates of the forecast confidence limits have a sounder theoretical basis.

See Chapter 3, "The ARIMA Procedure," for information on forecasting with ARIMA models.

WINTERS Method

The WINTERS method uses updating equations similar to exponential smoothing to fit parameters for the model

$$x_t = (a + bt) s(t) + \epsilon_t$$

where a and b are the trend parameters, and the function $s(t)$ selects the seasonal parameter for the season corresponding to time t.

The WINTERS method assumes that the series values are positive. If negative or zero values are found in the series, a warning is printed and the values are treated as missing.

The preceding standard WINTERS model uses a linear trend. However, PROC FORECAST can also fit a version of the WINTERS method that uses a quadratic trend. When TREND=3 is specified for METHOD=WINTERS, PROC FORECAST fits the following model:

$$x_t = \left(a + bt + ct^2\right) s(t) + \epsilon_t$$

The quadratic trend version of the Winters method is often unstable, and its use is not recommended.

When TREND=1 is specified, the following constant trend version is fit:

$$x_t = a\,s(t) + \epsilon_t$$

The default for the WINTERS method is TREND=2, which produces the standard linear trend model.

Seasonal Factors

The notation $s(t)$ represents the selection of the seasonal factor used for different time periods. For example, if INTERVAL=DAY and SEASONS=MONTH, there are 12 seasonal factors, one for each month in the year, and the time index t is measured in days. For any observation, t is determined by the ID variable and $s(t)$ selects the seasonal factor for the month that t falls in. For example, if t is 9 February 1993 then $s(t)$ is the seasonal parameter for February.

When there are multiple seasons specified, $s(t)$ is the product of the parameters for the seasons. For example, if SEASONS=(MONTH DAY), then $s(t)$ is the product of the seasonal parameter for the month corresponding to the period t, and the seasonal parameter for the day of the week corresponding to period t. When the SEASONS= option is not specified, the seasonal factors $s(t)$ are not included in the model. See the section "Specifying Seasonality" later in this chapter for more information on specifying multiple seasonal factors.

Updating Equations

This section shows the updating equations for the Winters method. In the following formula, x_t is the actual value of the series at time t; a_t is the smoothed value of the series at time t; b_t is the smoothed trend at time t; c_t is the smoothed quadratic trend at time t; $s_{t-1}(t)$ selects the old value of the seasonal factor corresponding to time t before the seasonal factors are updated.

The estimates of the constant, linear, and quadratic trend parameters are updated using the following equations:

For TREND=3,

$$a_t = \omega_1 \frac{x_t}{s_{t-1}(t)} + \left(1 - \omega_1\right) \left(a_{t-1} + b_{t-1} + c_{t-1}\right)$$

$$b_t = \omega_2 \left(a_t - a_{t-1} + c_{t-1}\right) + \left(1 - \omega_2\right) \left(b_{t-1} + 2c_{t-1}\right)$$

$$c_t = \omega_2 \tfrac{1}{2}\left(b_t - b_{t-1}\right) + \left(1 - \omega_2\right) c_{t-1}$$

For TREND=2,

$$a_t = \omega_1 \frac{x_t}{s_{t-1}(t)} + (1 - \omega_1)(a_{t-1} + b_{t-1})$$

$$b_t = \omega_2 (a_t - a_{t-1}) + (1 - \omega_2) b_{t-1}$$

For TREND=1,

$$a_t = \omega_1 \frac{x_t}{s_{t-1}(t)} + (1 - \omega_1) a_{t-1}$$

In this updating system, the trend polynomial is always centered at the current period so that the intercept parameter of the trend polynomial for predicted values at times after t is always the updated intercept parameter a_t. The predicted value for τ periods ahead is

$$x_{t+\tau} = (a_t + b_t \tau) s_t(t + \tau)$$

The seasonal parameters are updated when the season changes in the data, using the mean of the ratios of the actual to the predicted values for the season. For example, if SEASONS=MONTH and INTERVAL=DAY, then, when the observation for the first of February is encountered, the seasonal parameter for January is updated using the formula

$$s_t(t - 1) = \omega_3 \frac{1}{31} \sum_{i=t-31}^{t-1} \frac{x_i}{a_i} + (1 - \omega_3) s_{t-1}(t - 1)$$

where t is February 1 of the current year and $s_t(t - 1)$ is the seasonal parameter for January updated with the data available at time t.

When multiple seasons are used, $s_t(t)$ is a product of seasonal factors. For example, if SEASONS=(MONTH DAY) then $s_t(t)$ is the product of the seasonal factors for the month and for the day of the week: $s_t(t) = s_t^m(t) s_t^d(t)$. The factor $s_t^m(t)$ is updated at the start of each month using the preceding formula, and the factor $s_t^d(t)$ is updated at the start of each week using the following formula:

$$s_t^d(t - 1) = \omega_3 \frac{1}{7} \sum_{i=t-7}^{t-1} \frac{x_i}{a_i} + (1 - \omega_3) s_{t-1}^d(t - 1)$$

Missing values after the start of the series are replaced with one-step-ahead predicted values, and the predicted value is substituted for x_i and applied to the updating equations.

Normalization

The parameters are normalized so that the seasonal factors for each cycle have a mean of 1.0. This normalization is performed after each complete cycle and at the end of the data. Thus, if INTERVAL=MONTH and SEASONS=MONTH are specified, and a series begins with a July value, then the seasonal factors for the series are normalized at each observation for July and at the last observation in the data set. The normalization is performed by dividing each of the seasonal parameters, and multiplying each of the trend parameters, by the mean of the unnormalized seasonal parameters.

Smoothing Weights

The weight for updating the seasonal factors, ω_3, is given by the third value specified in the WEIGHT= option. If the WEIGHT= option is not used, then ω_3 defaults to 0.25; if the WEIGHT= option is used but does not specify a third value, then ω_3 defaults to ω_2. The weight for updating the linear and quadratic trend parameters, ω_2, is given by the second value specified in the WEIGHT= option; if the WEIGHT= option does not specify a second value, then ω_2 defaults to ω_1. The updating weight for the constant parameter, ω_1, is given by the first value specified in the WEIGHT= option. As a general rule, smaller smoothing weights are appropriate for series with a slowly changing trend, while larger weights are appropriate for volatile series with a rapidly changing trend.

If the WEIGHT= option is not used, then ω_1 defaults to $(1 - .8^{1/trend})$, where *trend* is the value of the TREND= option. This produces defaults of WEIGHT=.2 for TREND=1, WEIGHT=.10557 for TREND=2, and WEIGHT=.07168 for TREND=3.

Confidence Limits

A method for calculating exact forecast confidence limits for the WINTERS method is not available. Therefore, the approach taken in PROC FORECAST is to assume that the true seasonal factors have small variability about a set of fixed seasonal factors and that the remaining variation of the series is small relative to the mean level of the series. The equations are written

$$s_t(t) = I(t)(1 + \delta_t)$$
$$x_t = \mu I(t)(1 + \gamma_t)$$
$$a_t = \xi(1 + \alpha_t)$$

where μ is the mean level and $I(t)$ are the fixed seasonal factors. Assuming that α_t and δ_t are small, the forecast equations can be linearized and only first-order terms in δ_t and α_t kept. In terms of forecasts for γ_t, this linearized system is equivalent to a seasonal ARIMA model. Confidence limits for γ_t are based on this ARIMA model and converted into confidence limits for x_t using $s_t(t)$ as estimates of $I(t)$.

The exponential smoothing confidence limits are based on an approximation to a weighted regression model, whereas the preceding Winters confidence limits are based on an approximation to an ARIMA model. You can use METHOD=WINTERS without the SEASONS= option to do exponential smoothing and get confidence limits for the EXPO forecasts based on the ARIMA model approximation. These are generally more pessimistic than the weighted regression confidence limits produced by METHOD=EXPO.

ADDWINTERS Method

The ADDWINTERS method is like the WINTERS method except that the seasonal parameters are added to the trend instead of multiplied with the trend. The default TREND=2 model is as follows:

$$x_t = a + bt + s(t) + \epsilon_t$$

The WINTERS method for updating equation and confidence limits calculations described in the preceding section are modified accordingly for the additive version.

Holt Two-Parameter Exponential Smoothing

If the seasonal factors are omitted (that is, if the SEASONS= option is not specified), the WINTERS (and ADDWINTERS) method reduces to the Holt two-parameter version of exponential smoothing. Thus, the WINTERS method is often referred to as the Holt-Winters method.

Double exponential smoothing is a special case of the Holt two-parameter smoother. The double exponential smoothing results can be duplicated with METHOD=WINTERS by omitting the SEASONS= option and appropriately setting the WEIGHT= option. Letting $\alpha = \omega(2 - \omega)$ and $\beta = \omega / (2 - \omega)$, the following statements produce the same forecasts:

```
proc forecast method=expo    trend=2 weight=ω ... ;

proc forecast method=winters trend=2 weight=(α,β) ... ;
```

Although the forecasts are the same, the confidence limits are computed differently.

Choice of Weights for EXPO, WINTERS, and ADDWINTERS Methods

For the EXPO, WINTERS, and ADDWINTERS methods, properly chosen smoothing weights are of critical importance in generating reasonable results. There are several factors to consider in choosing the weights.

The noisier the data, the lower should be the weight given to the most recent observation. Another factor to consider is how quickly the mean of the time series is changing. If the mean of the series is changing rapidly, relatively more weight should be given to the most recent observation. The more stable the series over time, the lower should be the weight given to the most recent observation.

Note that the smoothing weights should be set separately for each series; weights that produce good results for one series may be poor for another series. Since PROC FORECAST does not have a feature to use different weights for different series, when forecasting multiple series with the EXPO, WINTERS, or ADDWINTERS method it may be desirable to use different PROC FORECAST steps with different WEIGHT= options.

For the Winters method, many combinations of weight values may produce unstable *noninvertible* models, even though all three weights are between 0 and 1. When the model is noninvertible, the forecasts depend strongly on values in the distant past, and predictions are determined largely by the starting values. Unstable models usually produce poor forecasts. The Winters model may be unstable even if the weights are optimally chosen to minimize the in-sample MSE. Refer to Archibald (1990) for a detailed discussion of the unstable region of the parameter space of the Winters model.

Optimal weights and forecasts for exponential smoothing models can be computed using the ARIMA procedure. For more information, see "Exponential Smoothing as an ARIMA Model" earlier in this chapter.

The ARIMA procedure can also be used to compute optimal weights and forecasts for seasonal ARIMA models similar to the Winters type methods. In particular, an ARIMA(0,1,1) × (0,1,1)S model may be a good alternative to the additive version of the Winters method. The ARIMA(0,1,1) × (0,1,1)S model fit to the logarithms of the series may be a good alternative to the multiplicative Winters method. See Chapter 3, "The ARIMA Procedure," for information on forecasting with ARIMA models.

Starting Values for EXPO, WINTERS, and ADDWINTERS Methods

The exponential smoothing method requires starting values for the smoothed values S_0, $S_0^{[2]}$, and $S_0^{[3]}$. The Winters and additive Winters methods require starting values for the trend coefficients and seasonal factors.

By default, starting values for the trend parameters are computed by a time-trend regression over the first few observations for the series. Alternatively, you can specify the starting value for the trend parameters with the ASTART=, BSTART=, and CSTART= options.

The number of observations used in the time-trend regression for starting values depends on the NSTART= option. For METHOD=EXPO, NSTART= beginning values of the series are used, and the coefficients of the time-trend regression are then used to form the initial smoothed values S_0, $S_0^{[2]}$, and $S_0^{[3]}$.

For METHOD=WINTERS or METHOD=ADDWINTERS, n complete seasonal cycles are used to compute starting values for the trend parameter, where n is the value of the NSTART= option. For example, for monthly data the seasonal cycle is one year, so NSTART=2 specifies that the first 24 observations at the beginning of each series are used for the time trend regression used to calculate starting values.

The starting values for the seasonal factors for the WINTERS and ADDWINTERS methods are computed from seasonal averages over the first few complete seasonal cycles at the beginning of the series. The number of seasonal cycles averaged to compute starting seasonal factors is controlled by the NSSTART= option. For example, for monthly data with SEASONS=12 or SEASONS=MONTH, the first n January values are averaged to get the starting value for the January seasonal parameter, where n is the value of the NSSTART= option.

The $s_0(i)$ seasonal parameters are set to the ratio (for WINTERS) or difference (for ADDWINTERS) of the mean for the season to the overall mean for the observations used to compute seasonal starting values.

For example, if METHOD=WINTERS, INTERVAL=DAY, SEASON=(MONTH DAY), and NSTART=2 (the default), the initial seasonal parameter for January is the ratio of the mean value over days in the first two Januarys after the start of the series (that is, after the first nonmissing value), to the mean value for all days read for initialization of the seasonal factors. Likewise, the initial factor for Sundays is the ratio of the mean value for Sundays to the mean of all days read.

For the ASTART=, BSTART=, and CSTART= options, the values specified are associated with the variables in the VAR statement in the order in which the variables are listed (the first value with the first variable, the second value with the second variable, and so on). If there are fewer values than variables, default starting values are used for the later variables. If there are more values than variables, the extra values are ignored.

Specifying Seasonality

Seasonality of a time series is a regular fluctuation about a trend. This is called seasonality because the time of year is the most common source of periodic variation. For example, sales of home heating oil are regularly greater in winter than during other times of the year.

Seasonality can be caused by many things other than weather. In the United States, sales of nondurable goods are greater in December than in other months because of the Christmas shopping season. The term seasonality is also used for cyclical fluctuation at periods other than a year. Often, certain days of the week cause regular fluctuation in daily time series, such as increased spending on leisure activities during weekends.

Three kinds of seasonality are supported in PROC FORECAST: time-of-year, day-of-week, and time-of-day. The seasonal part of the model is specified using the SEASONS= option. The values for the SEASONS= option are listed in Table 9.1.

Table 9.1. The SEASONS= Option

SEASONS= Value	Cycle Length	Type of Seasonality
QTR	yearly	time of year
MONTH	yearly	time of year
DAY	weekly	day of week
HOUR	daily	time of day

The three kinds of seasonality can be combined. For example, SEASONS=(MONTH DAY HOUR) specifies that 24 hour-of-day seasons are nested within 7 day-of-week seasons, which in turn are nested within 12 month-of-year seasons. The different kinds of intervals can be listed in the SEASONS= option in any order. Thus, SEASONS=(HOUR DAY MONTH) is the same as SEASONS=(MONTH DAY HOUR). Note that the Winters method smoothing equations may be less stable when multiple seasonal factors are used.

Multiple period seasons can also be used. For example, SEASONS=QTR2 specifies two semiannual time-of-year seasons. The grouping of observations into multiple period seasons starts with the first interval in the seasonal cycle. Thus, MONTH2 seasons are January-February, March-April, and so on. (There is no provision for shifting seasonal intervals; thus, there is no way to specify December-January, February-March, April-May, and so on seasons.)

For multiple period seasons, the number of intervals combined to form the seasons must evenly divide and be less than the basic cycle length. For example, with SEASONS=MONTH*n*, the basic cycle length is 12, so MONTH2, MONTH3, MONTH4, and MONTH6 are valid SEASONS= values (since 2, 3, 4, and 6 evenly divide 12 and are less than 12), but MONTH5 and MONTH12 are not valid SEASONS= values.

The frequency of the seasons must not be greater than the frequency of the input data. For example, you cannot specify SEASONS=MONTH if INTERVAL=QTR or SEA-

SONS=MONTH if INTERVAL=MONTH2. You also cannot specify two seasons of the same basic cycle. For example, SEASONS=(MONTH QTR) or SEASONS=(MONTH2 MONTH4) is not allowed.

Alternatively, the seasonality can be specified by giving the number of seasons in the SEASONS= option. SEASONS=n specifies that there are n seasons, with observations 1, $n + 1$, $2n + 1$, and so on in the first season, observations 2, $n + 2$, $2n + 2$, and so on in the second season, and so forth.

The options SEASONS=n and SINTPER=m cause PROC FORECAST to group the input observations into n seasons, with m observations to a season, which repeat every nm observations. The options SEASONS=$(n_1 \ n_2)$ and SINTPER=$(m_1 \ m_2)$ produce n_1 seasons with m_1 observations to a season nested within n_2 seasons with $n_1 m_1 m_2$ observations to a season.

If the SINTPER=m option is used with the SEASONS= option, the SEASONS= interval is multiplied by the SINTPER= value. For example, specifying both SEASONS=(QTR HOUR) and SINTPER=(2 3) is the same as specifying SEASONS=(QTR2 HOUR3) and also the same as specifying SEASONS=(HOUR3 QTR2).

Data Requirements

You should have ample data for the series that you forecast using PROC FORECAST. However, the results may be poor unless you have a good deal more than the minimum amount of data the procedure allows. The minimum number of observations required for the different methods is as follows:

- If METHOD=STEPAR is used, the minimum number of nonmissing observations required for each series forecast is the TREND= option value plus the value of the NLAGS= option. For example, using NLAGS=13 and TREND=2, at least 15 nonmissing observations are needed.

- If METHOD=EXPO is used, the minimum is the TREND= option value.

- If METHOD=WINTERS or ADDWINTERS is used, the minimum number of observations is either the number of observations in a complete seasonal cycle or the TREND= option value, whichever is greater. (However, there should be data for several complete seasonal cycles, or the seasonal factor estimates may be poor.) For example, for the seasonal specifications SEASONS=MONTH, SEASONS=(QTR DAY), or SEASONS=(MONTH DAY HOUR), the longest cycle length is one year, so at least one year of data is required.

OUT= Data Set

The FORECAST procedure writes the forecast to the output data set named by the OUT= option. The OUT= data set contains the following variables:

- the BY variables

- _TYPE_, a character variable that identifies the type of observation

- _LEAD_, a numeric variable that indicates the number of steps ahead in the forecast. The value of _LEAD_ is 0 for the one-step-ahead forecasts before the start of the forecast period.

- the ID statement variables

- the VAR statement variables, which contain the result values as indicated by the _TYPE_ variable value for the observation

The FORECAST procedure processes each of the input variables listed in the VAR statement and writes several observations for each forecast period to the OUT= data set. The observations are identified by the value of the _TYPE_ variable. The options OUTACTUAL, OUTALL, OUTLIMIT, OUTRESID, OUT1STEP, OUTFULL, and OUTSTD control which types of observations are included in the OUT= data set.

The values of the variable _TYPE_ are as follows:

ACTUAL   The VAR statement variables contain actual values from the input data set. The OUTACTUAL option writes the actual values. By default, only the observations for the forecast period are output.

FORECAST   The VAR statement variables contain forecast values. The OUT1STEP option writes the one-step-ahead predicted values for the observations used to fit the model.

RESIDUAL   The VAR statement variables contain residuals. The residuals are computed by subtracting the forecast value from the actual value (*residual = actual − forecast*). The OUTRESID option writes observations for the residuals.

L*nn*   The VAR statement variables contain lower *nn%* confidence limits for the forecast values. The value of *nn* depends on the ALPHA= option; with the default ALPHA=0.05, the _TYPE_ value is L95 for the lower confidence limit observations. The OUTLIMIT option writes observations for the upper and lower confidence limits.

U*nn*   The VAR statement variables contain upper *nn%* confidence limits for the forecast values. The value of *nn* depends on the ALPHA= option; with the default ALPHA=0.05, the _TYPE_ value is U95 for the upper confidence limit observations. The OUTLIMIT option writes observations for the upper and lower confidence limits.

STD   The VAR statement variables contain standard errors of the forecast values. The OUTSTD option writes observations for the standard errors of the forecast.

If no output control options are specified, PROC FORECAST outputs only the forecast values for the forecast periods.

The _TYPE_ variable can be used to subset the OUT= data set. For example, the following data step splits the OUT= data set into two data sets, one containing the forecast series and the other containing the residual series. For example

```
proc forecast out=out outresid ...;
    ...
run;

data fore resid;
    set out;
    if _TYPE_='FORECAST' then output fore;
    if _TYPE_='RESIDUAL' then output resid;
run;
```

See Chapter 2, "Working with Time Series Data," for more information on processing time series data sets in this format.

OUTEST= Data Set

The FORECAST procedure writes the parameter estimates and goodness-of-fit statistics to an output data set when the OUTEST= option is specified. The OUTEST=
data set contains the following variables:

- the BY variables

- the first ID variable, which contains the value of the ID variable for the last observation in the input data set used to fit the model

- _TYPE_, a character variable that identifies the type of each observation

- the VAR statement variables, which contain statistics and parameter estimates for
  the input series. The values contained in the VAR statement variables depend on
  the _TYPE_ variable value for the observation.

The observations contained in the OUTEST= data set are identified by the _TYPE_
variable. The OUTEST= data set may contain observations with the following
TYPE values:

AR1–AR*n*   The observation contains estimates of the autoregressive parameters
            for the series. Two-digit lag numbers are used if the value of the
            NLAGS= option is 10 or more; in that case these _TYPE_ values
            are AR01–AR*n*. These observations are output for the STEPAR
            method only.

CONSTANT   The observation contains the estimate of the constant or intercept pa-
            rameter for the time-trend model for the series. The trend model is
            centered (that is, $t = 0$) at the last observation used for the fit, so the
            value for the _TYPE_=CONSTANT observation is the predicted
            value for the series at the observation with the ID variable value giv-
            en.

LINEAR   The observation contains the estimate of the linear or slope parame-
            ter for the time-trend model for the series. This observation is output
            only if you specify TREND=2 or TREND=3.

N   The observation contains the number of nonmissing observations
            used to fit the model for the series.

QUAD   The observation contains the estimate of the quadratic parameter for
```
```

the time-trend model for the series. This observation is output only if you specify TREND=3.

SIGMA
: The observation contains the estimate of the standard deviation of the error term for the series.

S1–S3
: The observation contains exponentially smoothed values at the last observation. _TYPE_=S1 is the final smoothed value of the single exponential smooth. _TYPE_=S2 is the final smoothed value of the double exponential smooth. _TYPE_=S3 is the final smoothed value of the triple exponential smooth. These observations are output for METHOD=EXPO only.

S_name
: The observation contains estimates of the seasonal parameters. For example, if SEASONS=MONTH, the OUTEST= data set will contain observations with _TYPE_=S_JAN, _TYPE_=S_FEB, _TYPE_=S_MAR, and so forth.

: For multiple-period seasons, the names of the first and last interval of the season are concatenated to form the season name. Thus, for SEASONS=MONTH4, the OUTEST= data set will contain observations with _TYPE_=S_JANAPR, _TYPE_=S_MAYAUG, and _TYPE_=S_SEPDEC.

: When the SEASONS= option specifies numbers, the seasonal factors are labeled _TYPE_=S_i_j. For example, SEASONS=(2 3) produces observations with _TYPE_ values of S_1_1, S_1_2, S_2_1, S_2_2, and S_2_3. The observation with _TYPE_=S_i_j contains the seasonal parameters for the *j*th season of the *i*th seasonal cycle.

: These observations are output only for METHOD=WINTERS or METHOD=ADDWINTERS.

WEIGHT
: The observation contains the smoothing weight used for exponential smoothing. This is the value of the WEIGHT= option. This observation is output for METHOD=EXPO only.

WEIGHT1
WEIGHT2
WEIGHT3
: The observation contains the weights used for smoothing the WINTERS or ADDWINTERS method parameters (specified by the WEIGHT= option). _TYPE_=WEIGHT1 is the weight used to smooth the CONSTANT parameter. _TYPE_=WEIGHT2 is the weight used to smooth the LINEAR and QUAD parameters. _TYPE_=WEIGHT3 is the weight used to smooth the seasonal parameters. These observations are output only for the WINTERS and ADDWINTERS methods.

NRESID
: The observation contains the number of nonmissing residuals, *n*, used to compute the goodness-of-fit statistics. The residuals are obtained by subtracting the one-step-ahead predicted values from the observed values.

SST
: The observation contains the total sum of squares for the series, corrected for the mean. $SST = \sum_{t=0}^{n} (y_t - \bar{y})^2$, where $\bar{y}$ is the series mean.

SSE   The observation contains the sum of the squared residuals, uncorrected for the mean. $SSE = \sum_{t=0}^{n} (y_t - \hat{y}_t)^2$, where $\hat{y}$ is the one-step predicted value for the series.

MSE   The observation contains the mean squared error, calculated from one-step-ahead forecasts. $MSE = \frac{1}{n-k} SSE$, where k is the number of parameters in the model.

RMSE   The observation contains the root mean square error. $RMSE = \sqrt{MSE}$.

MAPE   The observation contains the mean absolute percent error. $MAPE = \frac{100}{n} \sum_{t=0}^{n} \left| (y_t - \hat{y}_t) / y_t \right|$.

MPE   The observation contains the mean percent error. $MPE = \frac{100}{n} \sum_{t=0}^{n} (y_t - \hat{y}_t) / y_t$.

MAE   The observation contains the mean absolute error. $MAE = \frac{1}{n} \sum_{t=0}^{n} \left| y_t - \hat{y}_t \right|$.

ME   The observation contains the mean error. $ME = \frac{1}{n} \sum_{t=0}^{n} (y_t - \hat{y}_t)$.

MAXE   The observation contains the maximum error (the largest residual).

MINE   The observation contains the minimum error (the smallest residual).

MAXPE   The observation contains the maximum percent error.

MINPE   The observation contains the minimum percent error.

RSQUARE   The observation contains the R^2 statistic, $R^2 = 1 - SSE/SST$. If the model fits the series badly, the model error sum of squares SSE may be larger than SST and the R^2 statistic will be negative.

ADJRSQ   The observation contains the adjusted R^2 statistic. $ADJRSQ = 1 - \left[\left(\frac{n-1}{n-k} \right) \left(1 - R^2 \right) \right]$.

ARSQ   The observation contains Amemiya's adjusted R^2 statistic. $ARSQ = 1 - \left[\left(\frac{n+k}{n-k} \right) \left(1 - R^2 \right) \right]$.

RW_RSQ   The observation contains the random walk R^2 statistic (Harvey's R_D^2 statistic using the random walk model for comparison). $RW\_RSQ = 1 - \left(\frac{n-1}{n} \right) SSE / RWSSE$, where $RWSSE = \sum_{t=2}^{n} (y_t - y_{t-1} - \mu)^2$, and $\mu = \frac{1}{n-1} \sum_{t=2}^{n} (y_t - y_{t-1})$.

AIC   The observation contains Akaike's information criterion. $AIC = n \ln(MSE) + 2k$.

SBC   The observation contains Schwarz's Bayesian criterion. $SBC = n \ln(MSE) + k \ln(n)$.

APC   The observation contains Amemiya's prediction criterion. $APC = \frac{1}{n} SST \left(\frac{n+k}{n-k} \right) \left(1 - R^2 \right) = \left(\frac{n+k}{n-k} \right) \frac{1}{n} SSE$.

CORR   The observation contains the correlation coefficient between the actual values and the one-step-ahead predicted values.

THEILU	The observation contains Theil's U statistic using original units. Refer to Maddala (1977, pp. 344–345), and Pindyck and Rubinfeld (1981, pp. 364–365) for more information on Theil statistics.
RTHEILU	The observation contains Theil's U statistic calculated using relative changes.
THEILUM	The observation contains the bias proportion of Theil's U statistic.
THEILUS	The observation contains the variance proportion of Theil's U statistic.
THEILUC	The observation contains the covariance proportion of Theil's U statistic.
THEILUR	The observation contains the regression proportion of Theil's U statistic.
THEILUD	The observation contains the disturbance proportion of Theil's U statistic.
RTHEILUM	The observation contains the bias proportion of Theil's U statistic, calculated using relative changes.
RTHEILUS	The observation contains the variance proportion of Theil's U statistic, calculated using relative changes.
RTHEILUC	The observation contains the covariance proportion of Theil's U statistic, calculated using relative changes.
RTHEILUR	The observation contains the regression proportion of Theil's U statistic, calculated using relative changes.
RTHEILUD	The observation contains the disturbance proportion of Theil's U statistic, calculated using relative changes.

Examples

Example 9.1. Forecasting Auto Sales

This example uses the Winters method to forecast the monthly U.S. sales of passenger cars series (VEHICLES) from the data set SASHELP.USECON. These data are taken from *Business Statistics*, published by the U.S. Bureau of Economic Analysis.

The following statements plot the series; the plot is shown in Output 9.1.1:

```
title1 "Sales of Passenger Cars";

symbol1 i=spline v=plus;
proc gplot data=sashelp.usecon;
   plot vehicles * date = 1 /
        haxis= '1jan80'd to '1jan92'd by year;
   where date >= '1jan80'd;
   format date year4.;
run;
```

Output 9.1.1. Monthly Passenger Car Sales

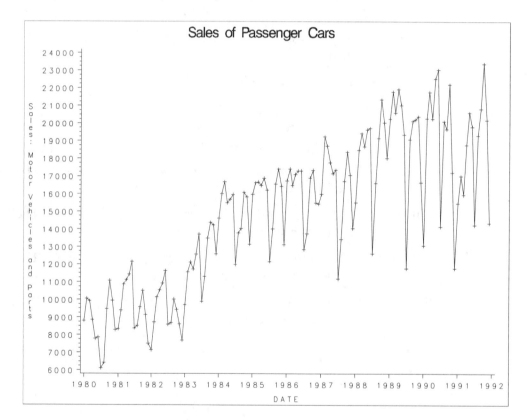

The following statements produce the forecast:

```
proc forecast data=sashelp.usecon interval=month
              method=winters seasons=month lead=12
              out=out outfull outresid outest=est;
   id date;
   var vehicles;
   where date >= '1jan80'd;
run;
```

The INTERVAL=MONTH option indicates that the data are monthly, and the ID DATE statement gives the dating variable. The METHOD=WINTERS specifies the Winters smoothing method. The LEAD=12 option forecasts 12 months ahead. The OUT=OUT option specifies the output data set, while the OUTFULL and OUT-RESID options include in the OUT= data set the predicted and residual values for the historical period and the confidence limits for the forecast period. The OUTEST=

Example 9.1. Forecasting Auto Sales □ □ □   459

option stores various statistics in an output data set. The WHERE statement is used to include only data from 1980 on.

The following statements print the OUT= data set:

```
title2 'The OUT= Data Set';
proc print data=out;
run;
```

The listing of the output data set produced by PROC PRINT is shown in part in Output 9.1.2.

Output 9.1.2. The OUT= Data Set Produced by PROC FORECAST

```
                      Sales of Passenger Cars
                         The OUT= Data Set

         OBS    DATE    _TYPE_     _LEAD_      VEHICLES

         421    SEP91   ACTUAL       0         20827.00
         422    SEP91   FORECAST     0         18266.20
         423    SEP91   RESIDUAL     0          2560.79
         424    OCT91   ACTUAL       0         23388.00
         425    OCT91   FORECAST     0         19913.88
         426    OCT91   RESIDUAL     0          3474.11
         427    NOV91   ACTUAL       0         20181.00
         428    NOV91   FORECAST     0         18294.58
         429    NOV91   RESIDUAL     0          1886.41
         430    DEC91   ACTUAL       0         14344.00
         431    DEC91   FORECAST     0         15172.36
         432    DEC91   RESIDUAL     0          -828.36
         433    JAN92   FORECAST     1         16555.17
         434    JAN92   L95          1         13514.26
         435    JAN92   U95          1         19596.08
         436    FEB92   FORECAST     2         19516.83
         437    FEB92   L95          2         15908.52
         438    FEB92   U95          2         23125.16
         439    MAR92   FORECAST     3         19607.89
         440    MAR92   L95          3         15954.55
         441    MAR92   U95          3         23261.22
```

The following statements print the OUTEST= data set:

```
title2 'The OUTEST= Data Set: WINTERS Method';
proc print data=est;
run;
```

The PROC PRINT listing of the OUTEST= data set is shown in Output 9.1.3.

Output 9.1.3. The OUTEST= Data Set Produced by PROC FORECAST

```
                    Sales of Passenger Cars
              The OUTEST= Data Set: WINTERS Method

          OBS     _TYPE_       DATE      VEHICLES

           1     N            DEC91           144
           2     NRESID       DEC91           144
           3     DF           DEC91           130
           4     WEIGHT1      DEC91     0.1055728
           5     WEIGHT2      DEC91     0.1055728
           6     WEIGHT3      DEC91          0.25
           7     SIGMA        DEC91      1741.481
           8     CONSTANT     DEC91     18577.368
           9     LINEAR       DEC91      4.804732
          10     S_JAN        DEC91     0.8909173
          11     S_FEB        DEC91     1.0500278
          12     S_MAR        DEC91     1.0546539
          13     S_APR        DEC91      1.074955
          14     S_MAY        DEC91     1.1166121
          15     S_JUN        DEC91     1.1012972
          16     S_JUL        DEC91     0.7418297
          17     S_AUG        DEC91     0.9633888
          18     S_SEP        DEC91      1.051159
          19     S_OCT        DEC91     1.1399126
          20     S_NOV        DEC91     1.0132126
          21     S_DEC        DEC91      0.802034
          22     SST          DEC91     2.63312E9
          23     SSE          DEC91     394258270
          24     MSE          DEC91     3032755.9
          25     RMSE         DEC91      1741.481
          26     MAPE         DEC91     9.4800217
          27     MPE          DEC91     -1.049956
          28     MAE          DEC91     1306.8534
          29     ME           DEC91     -42.95376
          30     RSQUARE      DEC91     0.8502696
```

The following statements plot the residuals. The plot is shown in Output 9.1.4.

```
title2 'Plot of Residuals';
symbol1 i=needle;
proc gplot data=out;
   plot vehicles * date = 1 / vref=0
        haxis= '1jan80'd to '1jan92'd by year;
   where _type_ = 'RESIDUAL';
   format date year4.;
run;
```

Example 9.1. Forecasting Auto Sales □ □ □ 461

Output 9.1.4. Residuals from Winters Method

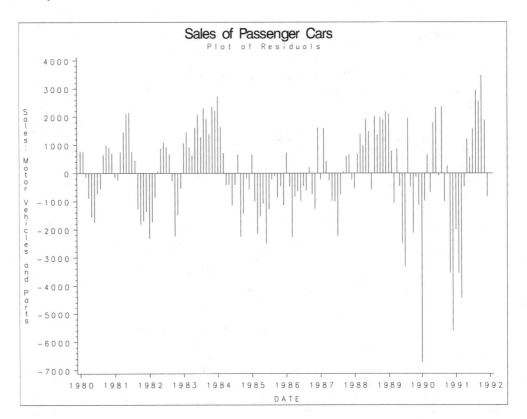

The following statements plot the forecast and confidence limits. The last two years of historical data are included in the plot to provide context for the forecast plot. A reference line is drawn at the start of the forecast period.

```
title2 'Plot of Forecast from WINTERS Method';
symbol1 i=none   v=star h=2; /* for _type_=ACTUAL */
symbol2 i=spline v=plus h=2; /* for _type_=FORECAST */
symbol3 i=spline l=3;        /* for _type_=L95 */
symbol4 i=spline l=3;        /* for _type_=U95 */

proc gplot data=out;
   plot vehicles * date = _type_ /
        href= '15dec91'd
        haxis= '1jan90'd to '1jan93'd by qtr;
   where _type_ ^= 'RESIDUAL' & date >= '1jan90'd;
run;
```

The plot is shown in Output 9.1.5.

Output 9.1.5.　Forecast of Passenger Car Sales

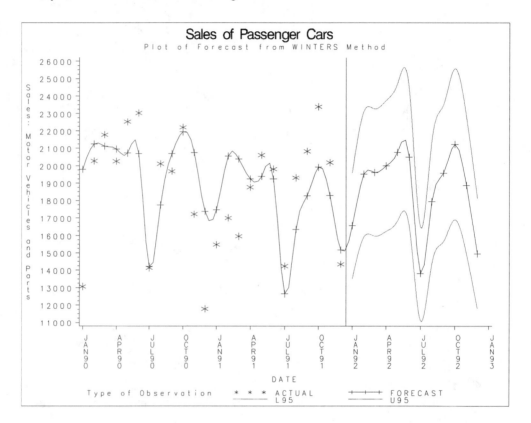

Example 9.2.　Forecasting Retail Sales

This example uses the stepwise autoregressive method to forecast the monthly U.S. sales of durable goods (DURABLES) and nondurable goods (NONDUR) from the SASHELP.USECON data set. The data are from *Business Statistics* published by the U.S. Bureau of Economic Analysis. The following statements plot the series:

```
symbol1 i=spline v=plus;
proc gplot data=sashelp.usecon;
   plot ( durables nondur ) * date = 1 /
        haxis= '1jan80'd to '1jan92'd by year;
   where date >= '1jan80'd;
   format date year4.;
run;
```

The plots are shown in Output 9.2.1 and Output 9.2.2.

Example 9.2.   Forecasting Retail Sales   □ □ □   463

Output 9.2.1.   Durable Goods Sales

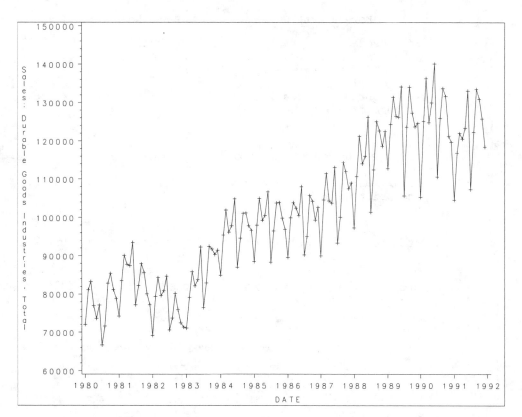

Output 9.2.2.   Nondurable Goods Sales

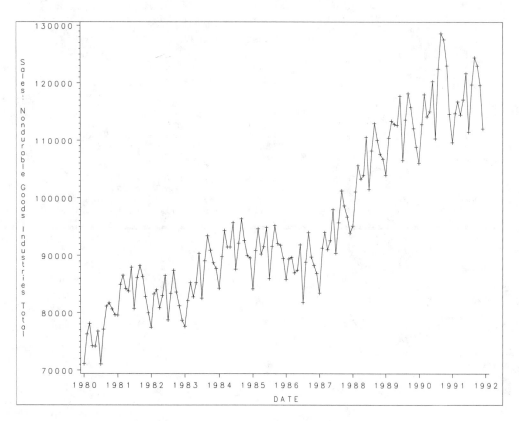

The following statements produce the forecast:

```
title1 "Forecasting Sales of Durable and Nondurable Goods";

proc forecast data=sashelp.usecon interval=month
              method=stepar trend=2 lead=12
              out=out outfull outest=est;
   id date;
   var durables nondur;
   where date >= '1jan80'd;
run;
```

The following statements print the OUTEST= data set.

```
title2 'OUTEST= Data Set: STEPAR Method';
proc print data=est;
run;
```

The PROC PRINT listing of the OUTEST= data set is shown in Output 9.2.3.

Output 9.2.3. The OUTEST= Data Set Produced by PROC FORECAST

```
        Forecasting Sales of Durable and Nondurable Goods
               OUTEST= Data Set: STEPAR Method

     OBS     _TYPE_       DATE      DURABLES        NONDUR

      1      N            DEC91          144           144
      2      NRESID       DEC91          144           144
      3      DF           DEC91          137           139
      4      SIGMA        DEC91     4519.451     2452.2642
      5      CONSTANT     DEC91    71884.597    73190.812
      6      LINEAR       DEC91    400.90106     308.5115
      7      AR01         DEC91    0.5844515    0.8243265
      8      AR02         DEC91            .             .
      9      AR03         DEC91            .             .
     10      AR04         DEC91            .             .
     11      AR05         DEC91            .             .
     12      AR06         DEC91    0.2097977             .
     13      AR07         DEC91            .             .
     14      AR08         DEC91            .             .
     15      AR09         DEC91            .             .
     16      AR10         DEC91    -0.119425             .
     17      AR11         DEC91            .             .
     18      AR12         DEC91    0.6138699    0.8050854
     19      AR13         DEC91    -0.556707    -0.741854
     20      SST          DEC91     4.923E10    2.8331E10
     21      SSE          DEC91    1.88157E9    544657337
     22      MSE          DEC91     13734093    3918398.1
     23      RMSE         DEC91    3705.9538    1979.4944
     24      MAPE         DEC91    2.9252601    1.6555935
     25      MPE          DEC91    -0.253607    -0.085357
     26      MAE          DEC91     2866.675    1532.8453
     27      ME           DEC91    -67.87407    -29.63026
     28      RSQUARE      DEC91    0.9617803    0.9807752
```

Example 9.2. Forecasting Retail Sales ☐ ☐ ☐ 465

The following statements plot the forecasts and confidence limits. The last two years of historical data are included in the plots to provide context for the forecast. A reference line is drawn at the start of the forecast period.

```
title1 'Plot of Forecasts from STEPAR Method';

symbol1 i=none   v=star h=2; /* for _type_=ACTUAL */
symbol2 i=spline v=plus h=2; /* for _type_=FORECAST */
symbol3 i=spline l=3;        /* for _type_=L95 */
symbol4 i=spline l=3;        /* for _type_=U95 */

proc gplot data=out;
   plot ( durables nondur ) * date = _type_ /
        href= '15dec91'd
        haxis= '1jan90'd to '1jan93'd by qtr;
   where date >= '1jan90'd;
run;
```

The plots are shown in Output 9.2.4 and Output 9.2.5.

Output 9.2.4. Forecast of Durable Goods Sales

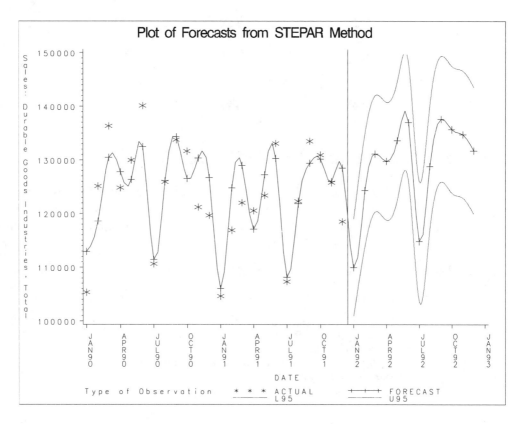

Output 9.2.5.   Forecast of Nondurable Goods Sales

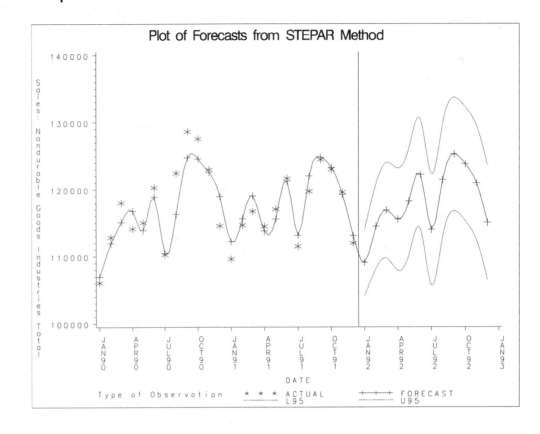

Example 9.3.   Forecasting Petroleum Sales

This example uses the double exponential smoothing method to forecast the monthly U.S. sales of petroleum and related products series (PETROL) from the data set SASHELP.USECON. These data are taken from *Business Statistics*, published by the U.S. Bureau of Economic Analysis.

The following statements plot the PETROL series:

```
title1 "Sales of Petroleum and Related Products";

symbol1 i=spline v=plus;
proc gplot data=sashelp.usecon;
   plot petrol * date = 1 /
        haxis= '1jan80'd to '1jan92'd by year;
   where date >= '1jan80'd;
   format date year4.;
run;
```

Example 9.3.   Forecasting Petroleum Sales   □ □ □   467

The plot is shown in Output 9.3.1.

Output 9.3.1.   Sales of Petroleum and Related Products

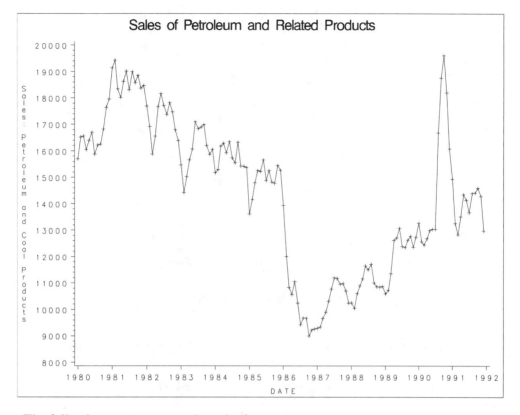

The following statements produce the forecast:

```
proc forecast data=sashelp.usecon interval=month
              method=expo trend=2 lead=12
              out=out outfull outest=est;
   id date;
   var petrol;
   where date >= '1jan80'd;
run;
```

The following statements print the OUTEST= data set:

```
title2 'OUTEST= Data Set: EXPO Method';
proc print data=est;
run;
```

The PROC PRINT listing of the output data set is shown in Output 9.3.2.

Output 9.3.2. The OUTEST= Data Set Produced by PROC FORECAST

```
                 Sales of Petroleum and Related Products
                     OUTEST= Data Set: EXPO Method

            OBS     _TYPE_       DATE         PETROL

             1      N           DEC91              144
             2      NRESID      DEC91              144
             3      DF          DEC91              142
             4      WEIGHT      DEC91        0.1055728
             5      S1          DEC91        14165.259
             6      S2          DEC91        13933.435
             7      SIGMA       DEC91        1281.0945
             8      CONSTANT    DEC91        14397.084
             9      LINEAR      DEC91        27.363164
            10      SST         DEC91        1.17001E9
            11      SSE         DEC91        233050838
            12      MSE         DEC91        1641203.1
            13      RMSE        DEC91        1281.0945
            14      MAPE        DEC91        6.5514467
            15      MPE         DEC91        -0.147168
            16      MAE         DEC91        891.04243
            17      ME          DEC91        8.2148584
            18      RSQUARE     DEC91        0.8008122
```

The plot of the forecast is shown in Output 9.3.3.

Output 9.3.3. Forecast of Petroleum and Related Products

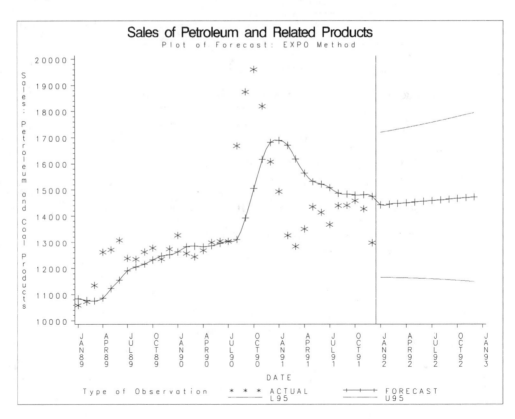

References

Ahlburg, D. A. (1984). "Forecast evaluation and improvement using Theil's decomposition." *Journal of Forecasting*, 3, 345–351.

Aldrin, M. and Damsleth, E. (1989). "Forecasting non-seasonal time series with missing observations." *Journal of Forecasting*, 8, 97–116.

Archibald, B.C. (1990), "Parameter space of the Holt-Winters' model." *International Journal of Forecasting*, 6, 199–209.

Bails, D.G. and Peppers, L.C. (1982), *Business Fluctuations: Forecasting Techniques and Applications,* New Jersey: Prentice-Hall.

Bartolomei, S.M. and Sweet, A.L. (1989). "A note on the comparison of exponential smoothing methods for forecasting seasonal series." *International Journal of Forecasting*, 5, 111–116.

Bureau of Economic Analysis, U.S. Department of Commerce (1992 and earlier editions), *Business Statistics*, 27th and earlier editions, Washington: U.S. Government Printing Office.

Bliemel, F. (1973). "Theil's forecast accuracy coefficient: a clarification." *Journal of Marketing Research*, 10, 444–446.

Bowerman, B.L. and O'Connell, R.T. (1979), *Time Series and Forecasting: An Applied Approach,* North Scituate, Massachusetts: Duxbury Press.

Box, G.E.P. and Jenkins, G.M. (1976), *Time Series Analysis: Forecasting and Control,* Revised Edition, San Francisco: Holden-Day.

Bretschneider, S.I., Carbone, R., and Longini, R.L. (1979). "An adaptive approach to time series forecasting." *Decision Sciences*, 10, 232–244.

Brown, R.G. (1962), *Smoothing, Forecasting and Prediction of Discrete Time Series*, New York: Prentice-Hall.

Brown, R.G. and Meyer, R.F. (1961). "The fundamental theorem of exponential smoothing." *Operations Research*, 9, 673–685.

Chatfield, C. (1978). "The Holt-Winters forecasting procedure." *Applied Statistics*, **27**, 264–279.

Chatfield, C., and Prothero, D.L. (1973). "Box-Jenkins seasonal forecasting: problems in a case study." *Journal of the Royal Statistical Society, Series A*, 136, 295–315.

Chow, W.M. (1965). "Adaptive control of the exponential smoothing constant." *Journal of Industrial Engineering*, September–October 1965.

Cogger, K.O. (1974). "The optimality of general-order exponential smoothing." *Operations Research*, 22, 858-.

Cox, D. R. (1961). "Prediction by exponentially weighted moving averages and related methods." *Journal of the Royal Statistical Society, Series B*, 23, 414–422.

Fair, R.C. (1986). "Evaluating the predictive accuracy of models." In *Handbook of Econometrics*, Vol. 3., Griliches, Z. and Intriligator, M.D., eds. New York: North Holland.

Fildes, R. (1979). "Quantitative forecasting —- the state of the art: extrapolative models." *Journal of Operational Research Society*, 30, 691–710.

Gardner, E.S. (1984). "The strange case of the lagging forecasts." *Interfaces*, 14, 47–50.

Gardner, E.S., Jr. (1985). "Exponential smoothing: the state of the art." *Journal of Forecasting*, 4, 1–38.

Granger, C.W.J. and Newbold, P. (1977), *Forecasting Economic Time Series*, New York: Academic Press, Inc.

Harvey, A.C. (1984). "A unified view of statistical forecasting procedures." *Journal of Forecasting*, 3, 245–275.

Ledolter, J. and Abraham, B. (1984). "Some comments on the initialization of exponential smoothing." *Journal of Forecasting*, 3, 79–84.

Maddala, G.S. (1977), *Econometrics*, New York: McGraw-Hill Book Co.

Makridakis, S., Wheelwright, S.C., and McGee, V.E. (1983). *Forecasting: Methods and Applications, 2nd Ed.* New York: John Wiley and Sons.

McKenzie, Ed (1984). "General exponential smoothing and the equivalent ARMA process." *Journal of Forecasting*, 3, 333–344.

Montgomery, D.C. and Johnson, L.A. (1976), *Forecasting and Time Series Analysis*, New York: McGraw-Hill Book Co.

Muth, J.F. (1960). "Optimal properties of exponentially weighted forecasts." *Journal of the American Statistical Association*, 55, 299–306.

Pierce, D.A. (1979). "R^2 Measures for Time Series." *Journal of the American Statistical Association*, 74, 901–910.

Pindyck, R.S. and Rubinfeld, D.L. (1981), *Econometric Models and Economic Forecasts*, Second Edition, New York: McGraw-Hill Book Co.

Raine, J.E. (1971). "Self-adaptive forecasting reconsidered." *Decision Sciences*, 2, 181–191.

Roberts, S.A. (1982). "A general class of Holt-Winters type forecasting models." *Management Science*, 28, 808–820.

Theil, H. (1966). *Applied Economic Forecasting*. Amsterdam: North Holland.

Trigg, D.W., and Leach, A.G. (1967). "Exponential smoothing with an adaptive response rate." *Operational Research Quarterly*, 18, 53–59.

Winters, P.R. (1960). "Forecasting sales by exponentially weighted moving averages." *Management Science*, 6, 324–342.

Chapter 10
The LOAN Procedure

Chapter Table of Contents

Chapter 10
The LOAN Procedure

Overview

The LOAN procedure analyzes and compares fixed rate, adjustable rate, buydown, and balloon payment loans. The LOAN procedure computes the loan parameters and outputs the loan summary information for each loan.

Multiple loans can be processed and compared in terms of economic criteria such as after-tax or before-tax present worth of cost and true interest rate, breakeven of periodic payment and of interest paid, and outstanding balance at different periods in time. PROC LOAN selects the best alternative in terms of the specified economic criterion for each loan comparison period.

The LOAN procedure allows various payment and compounding intervals (including continuous compounding) and uniform or lump sum prepayments for each loan. Down payments, discount points, and other initialization costs can be included in the loan analysis and comparison.

Getting Started

PROC LOAN supports four types of loans. You specify each type of loan using the corresponding statement: FIXED, BALLOON, ARM, and BUYDOWN.

- FIXED - Fixed rate loans have a constant interest rate and periodic payment throughout the life of the loan.

- BALLOON - Balloon payment loans are fixed rate loans with lump sum payments in certain payment periods in addition to the constant periodic payment.

- ARM - Adjustable rate loans are those in which the interest rate and periodic payment vary over the life of the loan. The future interest rates of an adjustable rate loan are not known with certainty, but they will vary within specified limits according to terms stated in the loan agreement. In practice, the rate adjustment terms vary. PROC LOAN offers a flexible set of options to capture a wide variety of rate adjustment terms.

- BUYDOWN - Buydown rate loans are similar to adjustable rate loans, but the interest rate adjustments are predetermined at the initialization of the loan, usually by paying interest points at the time of loan initialization.

Analyzing Fixed Rate Loans

The most common loan analysis is the calculation of the periodic payment when the loan amount, life, and interest rate are known. The following PROC LOAN statements analyze a 15-year (180 monthly payments) fixed rate loan for $100,000 with an annual nominal interest rate of 13%:

```
proc loan;
   fixed amount=100000 rate=13 life=180;
run;
```

Another parameter PROC LOAN can compute is the maximum amount you can borrow given the periodic payment you can afford and the rates available in the market. The following SAS statements analyze a loan for 180 monthly payments of $1250, with a nominal annual rate of 13%:

```
proc loan;
   fixed payment=1250 rate=13 life=180;
run;
```

Assume that you want to borrow $100,000 and can pay $1250 a month. You know that the lender charges a 13% nominal interest rate compounded monthly. To determine how long it will take you to pay off your debt, use the following statements:

```
proc loan;
   fixed amount=100000 payment=1250 rate=13;
run;
```

Sometimes, a loan is expressed in terms of the amount borrowed and the amount and number of periodic payments. In this case, you want to calculate the annual nominal rate charged on the loan to compare it to other alternatives. The following statements analyze a loan of $100,000 paid in 180 monthly payments of $1250:

```
proc loan;
   fixed amount=100000 payment=1250 life=180;
run;
```

There are four basic parameters that define a loan: life (number of periodic payments), principal amount, interest rate, and the periodic payment amount. PROC LOAN calculates the missing parameter among these four. Loan analysis output includes a loan summary table and an amortization schedule.

You can use the START= and LABEL= options to enhance your output. The START= option specifies the date of loan initialization and dates all the output accordingly. The LABEL= specification is used to label all output corresponding to a particular loan and is especially useful when multiple loans are analyzed. For example, the preceding statements for the first fixed rate loan are revised to include the START= and LABEL= options as follows:

```
proc loan start=1992:12;
   fixed amount=100000 rate=13 life=180
         label='BANK1, Fixed Rate';
run;
```

Loan Summary Table

The loan summary table is produced by default and contains loan analysis information. It shows the principal amount, the costs at the time of loan initialization (downpayment, discount points, and other loan initialization costs), the total payment and interest, the initial nominal and effective interest rates, payment and compounding intervals, the length of the loan in the time units specified, the start and end dates (if specified), a list of nominal and effective interest rates, and periodic payments throughout the life of the loan.

Figure 10.1 shows the loan summary table for the fixed rate loan labeled "BANK1, Fixed Rate."

```
                    Fixed Rate Loan Summary

                      BANK1, Fixed Rate


   Downpayment:               0.00   Principal Amount:     100000.00
   Initialization:            0.00   Points:                    0.00

   Total Interest:       127744.33   Nominal Rate:            13.00%
   Total Payment:        227744.33   Effective Rate:          13.80%

   Pay Interval:           MONTHLY   Compounding:            MONTHLY
   No. of payments:            180   No. of compoundings:        180

   Start date:             DEC1992   End date:               DEC2007


        List of Rates and Payments for BANK1, Fixed Rate

      Date      Nominal Rate  Effective Rate     Payment

      DEC1992      13.00%         13.80%         1265.24
```

Figure 10.1. Fixed Rate Loan Summary

The loan is initialized in December, 1992 and paid off in December, 2007. The monthly payment is calculated to be $1265.24, and the effective interest rate is 13.8%. Over the 15 years, $127,744.33 is paid for interest charges on the loan.

Analyzing Balloon Payment Loans

You specify balloon payment loans like fixed rate loans, with the additional specification of the balloon payments. Assume you have an alternative to finance the $100,000 investment with a 15-year balloon payment loan. The annual nominal rate is 13%, as in the fixed rate loan. The terms of the loan require two balloon payments of $2000 and $1000 at the 15th and 48th payment periods, respectively. These balloon payments keep the periodic payment lower than that of the fixed rate loan. The balloon payment loan is defined by the following BALLOON statement:

```
proc loan start=1992:12;
   balloon amount=100000 rate=13 life=180
           balloonpayment=(15=2000 48=1000)
           label='BANK2, with Balloon Payment';
run;
```

List of Balloon Payments

In addition to the information for the fixed rate loan, the "Loan Summary Table" for the balloon payment loan includes a list of balloon payments in the "List of Rates and Payments." For example, the balloon payment loan described previously includes two balloon payments, as shown in Figure 10.2.

```
        List of Rates and Payments for BANK2, with Balloon Payment

      Date       Nominal Rate  Effective Rate      Payment

      DEC1992       13.00%         13.80%          1236.17

                  Balloon Period      Payment

                    MAR1994          2000.00
                    DEC1996          1000.00
```

Figure 10.2.   List of Rates and Payments for a Balloon Payment Loan

The periodic payment for the balloon payment loan is $29.07 less than that of the fixed rate loan.

Analyzing Adjustable Rate Loans

In addition to specifying the basic loan parameters, you need to specify the terms of the rate adjustments for an adjustable rate loan. There are many ways of stating the rate adjustment terms, and PROC LOAN facilitates all of them. For details, see the "Rate Adjustment Terms Options" in the "ARM Statement" section later in this chapter.

Assume that you have an alternative to finance the $100,000 investment with a 15-year adjustable rate loan with an initial annual nominal interest rate of 11%. The rate adjustment terms specify a 0.5% annual cap, a 2.5% life cap, and a rate adjustment every 12 months. *Annual cap* refers to the maximum increase in interest rate per adjustment period, and *life cap* refers to the maximum increase over the life of the loan. The following ARM statement specifies this adjustable rate loan assuming the interest rate adjustments will always increase by the maximum allowed by the terms of the loan. These assumptions are specified by the WORSTCASE and CAPS= options, as shown in the following statements:

```
proc loan start=1992:12;
   arm amount=100000 rate=11 life=180 worstcase
       caps=(0.5, 2.5)
       label='BANK3, Adjustable Rate';
run;
```

List of Rates and Payments for Adjustable Rate Loans

The "List of Rates and Payments" in the loan summary table for the adjustable rate loans reflects the changes in the interest rates and payments, as well as the dates these changes become effective. For the adjustable rate loan described previously, Figure 10.3 shows the "List of Rates and Payments" indicating five annual rate adjustments in addition to the initial rate and payment.

```
       List of Rates and Payments for BANK3, Adjustable Rate

       Date      Nominal Rate  Effective Rate      Payment

       DEC1992      11.00%         11.57%          1136.60
       JAN1994      11.50%         12.13%          1166.74
       JAN1995      12.00%         12.68%          1195.72
       JAN1996      12.50%         13.24%          1223.43
       JAN1997      13.00%         13.80%          1249.75
       JAN1998      13.50%         14.37%          1274.55
```

Figure 10.3. List of Rates and Payments for an Adjustable Rate Loan

Notice that the periodic payment of the adjustable rate loan as of January 1998 ($1274.55) exceeds that of the fixed rate loan ($1265.24).

Analyzing Buydown Rate Loans

A 15-year buydown rate loan is another alternative to finance the $100,000 investment. The nominal annual interest rate is 12% initially and will increase to 14% and 16% as of the 24th and 48th payment periods, respectively. The nominal annual interest rate is lower than that of the fixed rate alternative, at the cost of a 1% discount point ($1000) paid at the initialization of the loan. The following BUYDOWN statement represents this loan alternative:

```
proc loan start=1992:12;
   buydown amount=100000 rate=12 life=180
           buydownrates=(24=14 48=16) pointpct=1
           label='BANK4, Buydown';
run;
```

List of Rates and Payments for Buydown Rate Loans

Figure 10.4 shows the "List of Rates and Payments" in the loan summary table. It reflects the two rate adjustments and the corresponding monthly payments as well as the initial values for these parameters. As of December 1994, the periodic payment of the buydown loan exceeds the periodic payment for any of the other alternatives.

```
          List of Rates and Payments for BANK4, Buydown

     Date     Nominal Rate  Effective Rate      Payment

     DEC1992      12.00%         12.68%          1200.17
     DEC1994      14.00%         14.93%          1320.31
     DEC1996      16.00%         17.23%          1432.33
```

Figure 10.4.   List of Rates and Payments for a Buydown Rate Loan

Loan Repayment Schedule

In addition to the loan summary, you can print a loan repayment (amortization) schedule for each loan. For each payment period, this schedule contains the year and period within the year (or date, if the START= option is specified), the principal balance at the beginning of the period, the total payment, interest payment, principal repayment for the period, and the principal balance at the end of the period.

To print the first year of the amortization schedule for the fixed rate loan shown in Figure 10.5, use the following statements:

```
proc loan start=1992:12;
   fixed amount=100000 rate=13 life=180
         label='BANK1, Fixed Rate'
         schedule=1;
run;
```

```
                       Loan Repayment Schedule

                         BANK1, Fixed Rate

             Beginning                Interest   Principal      Ending
   Date     Outstanding    Payment     Payment   Repayment   Outstanding

   DEC1992   100000.00        0.00        0.00        0.00    100000.00

   DEC1992   100000.00        0.00        0.00        0.00    100000.00

   JAN1993   100000.00     1265.24     1083.33      181.91     99818.09
   FEB1993    99818.09     1265.24     1081.36      183.88     99634.21
   MAR1993    99634.21     1265.24     1079.37      185.87     99448.34
   APR1993    99448.34     1265.24     1077.36      187.88     99260.46
   MAY1993    99260.46     1265.24     1075.32      189.92     99070.54
   JUN1993    99070.54     1265.24     1073.26      191.98     98878.56
   JUL1993    98878.56     1265.24     1071.18      194.06     98684.50
   AUG1993    98684.50     1265.24     1069.08      196.16     98488.34
   SEP1993    98488.34     1265.24     1066.96      198.28     98290.06
   OCT1993    98290.06     1265.24     1064.81      200.43     98089.63
   NOV1993    98089.63     1265.24     1062.64      202.60     97887.03
   DEC1993    97887.03     1265.24     1060.44      204.80     97682.23

   DEC1993   100000.00    15182.88    12865.11     2317.77     97682.23
```

Figure 10.5.   Loan Repayment Schedule for the First Two Years

The principal balance at the end of two years is $95,044.54. The total payment for both years is the same, but the principal repayment increases from $2317.77 the first year to $2637.69 the second year.

You can also print the amortization schedule with annual summary information or for a specified number of years. The SCHEDULE=YEARLY option produces an annual summary loan amortization schedule, which is useful for loans with long life.

For example, to print the annual summary loan repayment schedule for the buydown loan shown in Figure 10.6, use the following statements:

```
proc loan start=1992:12;
    buydown amount=100000 rate=12 life=180
            buydownrates=(24=14 48=16) pointpct=1
            schedule=yearly
            label='BANK4, Buydown';
run;
```

```
                            Loan Repayment Schedule

                               BANK4,  Buydown

             Beginning                  Interest   Principal       Ending
    Year   Outstanding    Payment        Payment   Repayment   Outstanding

    1992   100000.00      1000.00           0.00        0.00    100000.00
    1993   100000.00     14402.04       11863.39     2538.65     97461.35
    1994    97461.35     14522.18       11699.51     2822.67     94638.68
    1995    94638.68     15843.72       13076.31     2767.41     91871.27
    1996    91871.27     15955.74       12811.27     3144.47     88726.80
    1997    88726.80     17187.96       13966.84     3221.12     85505.68
    1998    85505.68     17187.96       13411.96     3776.00     81729.68
    1999    81729.68     17187.96       12761.44     4426.52     77303.16
    2000    77303.16     17187.96       11998.90     5189.06     72114.10
    2001    72114.10     17187.96       11104.96     6083.00     66031.10
    2002    66031.10     17187.96       10057.05     7130.91     58900.19
    2003    58900.19     17187.96        8828.61     8359.35     50540.84
    2004    50540.84     17187.96        7388.53     9799.43     40741.41
    2005    40741.41     17187.96        5700.35    11487.61     29253.80
    2006    29253.80     17187.96        3721.38    13466.58     15787.22
    2007    15787.22     17188.72        1401.50    15787.22         0.00
```

Figure 10.6.   Annual Summary Loan Repayment Schedule

Loan Comparison

The LOAN procedure can compare alternative loans on the basis of different economic criteria and help select the most desirable loan. You can compare alternative loans through different points in time. The economic criteria offered by PROC LOAN are

- outstanding principal balance, that is, the unpaid balance of the loan

- present worth of cost, that is, before-tax or after-tax net value of the loan cash flow through the comparison period. The cash flow includes all payments, discount points, initialization costs, down payment, and the outstanding principal balance at the comparison period.

- true interest rate, that is, before-tax or after-tax effective annual interest rate charged on the loan. The cash flow includes all payments, discount points, initialization costs, and the outstanding principal balance at the specified comparison period.

- periodic payment

- the total interest paid on the loan

The figures for present worth of cost, true interest rate, and interest paid are reported on the cash flow through the comparison period. The reported outstanding principal balance and the periodic payment are the values as of the comparison period.

The COMPARE statement specifies the type of comparison and the periods of comparison. For each period specified in the compare statement, a loan comparison report is printed that also indicates the best alternative. Different criteria may lead to selection of different alternatives. Also, the period of comparison may change the desirable alternative. See the section "Loan Comparison Details" later in this chapter for further information.

Comparison of 15-Year versus 30-Year Loan Alternatives

An issue that arises in the purchase of a house is the length of the loan life. In the U.S., residential home loans are usually for 15 or 30 years. Ordinarily, 15-year loans have a lower interest rate but higher periodic payments than 30-year loans. A comparison of both loans might point out which one better suits your needs and means. The following SAS statements compare two such loans:

```
proc loan start=1992:12 amount=100000;
    fixed rate=13 life=360 label='30 year loan';
    fixed rate=12.5 life=180 label='15 year loan';
    compare;
run;
```

Default Loan Comparison Report

The default loan comparison report in Figure 10.7 shows the ending outstanding balance, periodic payment, interest paid, and before-tax true rate at the end of 30 years. In the case of the default loan comparison, the selection of the best alternative is based on minimization of the true rate.

```
                  Loan Comparison Report

                 Analysis through DEC2022

                      Ending              Interest    True
        Loan Label  Outstanding  Payment     Paid     Rate

        30 year loan       0.00  1105.57  298231.37  13.80
        15 year loan       0.00  1233.78  121854.86  13.24

Note: "15 year loan" is the best alternative based on true rate analysis
      through DEC2022.
```

Figure 10.7. Default Loan Comparison Report

The best alternative based on true rate is reported as the 15-year loan. However, if the objective were to minimize the periodic payment, the 30-year loan would be the more desirable.

Comparison of Fixed Rate and Adjustable Rate Loans

Suppose you want to compare a fixed rate loan to an adjustable rate alternative. The nominal interest rate on the adjustable rate loan is initially 1.5% lower than the fixed rate loan. The future rates of the adjustable rate loan are calculated using the worst case scenario.

According to current U.S. tax laws, the loan for a family home qualifies the interest paid on the loan as a tax deduction. The TAXRATE=33 (income tax rate) option on the compare statement bases the calculations of true interest rate on the after-tax cash flow. Assume, also, that you are uncertain as to how long you will keep this property. The AT=(60 120) option, as shown in the following example, produces two loan comparison reports through the end of the 5th and the 10th years:

```
proc loan start=1992:12 amount=100000 life=360;
   fixed rate=13 label='BANK1, Fixed Rate' ;
   arm  rate=11.5 worstcase caps=(0.5, 2.5)
        label='BANK3, Adjustable Rate';
   compare taxrate=33 at=(60 120);

run;
```

After-Tax Loan Comparison Reports

The two loan comparison reports in Figure 10.8 and Figure 10.9 show the ending outstanding balance, periodic payment, interest paid, and after-tax true rate at the end of five years and ten years, respectively.

```
                        Loan Comparison Report

                    Analysis through DEC1997

                            Ending                Interest    True
   Loan Label           Outstanding    Payment        Paid    Rate

   BANK1, Fixed Rate       98081.66    1106.20    64453.66    9.07
   BANK3, Adjustable Rate  97897.43    1141.14    61848.19    8.64

Note: "BANK3, Adjustable Rate" is the best alternative based on true rate
      analysis through DEC1997.
```

Figure 10.8.   Loan Comparison Report as of December 1997

```
                        Loan Comparison Report

                    Analysis through DEC2002

                            Ending                Interest    True
   Loan Label           Outstanding    Payment        Paid    Rate

   BANK1, Fixed Rate       94419.82    1106.20   127163.82    9.07
   BANK3, Adjustable Rate  94767.36    1178.45   129425.12    9.08

Note: "BANK1, Fixed Rate" is the best alternative based on true rate
      analysis through DEC2002.
```

Figure 10.9.   Loan Comparison Report as of December 2002

The loan comparison report through December 1997 picks the adjustable rate loan as the best alternative, whereas the report through December 2002 shows the fixed rate loan as the better alternative. This implies that if you intend to keep the loan for 10 years or longer, you should probably opt for the fixed rate alternative. Otherwise, the adjustable rate loan is the better alternative in spite of the worst-case scenario. Further analysis shows that the actual breakeven of true interest rate occurs at August 2002. That is, the desirable alternative switches from the adjustable rate loan to the fixed rate loan in August 2002.

Note that, under the assumption of worst-case scenario for the rate adjustments, the periodic payment for the adjustable rate loan already exceeds that of the fixed rate loan on December 1997 (as of the rate adjustment on January 1997 to be exact). If the objective were to minimize the periodic payment, the fixed rate loan would have been more desirable as of December 1997. However, all of the other criteria at that point still favor the adjustable rate loan.

Syntax

The following statements are used with PROC LOAN:

PROC LOAN *options* ;
    FIXED *options* ;
    BALLOON *options* ;
    ARM *options* ;
    BUYDOWN *options* ;
    COMPARE *options* ;

Functional Summary

The statements and options controlling the LOAN procedure are summarized in the following table:

Description	Statement	Option
Statements		
specify an adjustable rate loan	ARM	
specify a balloon payment loan	BALLOON	
specify a buydown rate loan	BUYDOWN	
specify loan comparisons	COMPARE	
specify a fixed rate loan	FIXED	
Data Set Options		
specify output data set for loan summary	PROC LOAN	OUTSUM=
specify output data set for repayment schedule	FIXED	OUT=
specify output data set for loan comparison	COMPARE	OUTCOMP=
Printing Control Options		
suppress printing of loan summary report	FIXED	NOSUMMARYPRINT
suppress all printed output	FIXED	NOPRINT
print amortization schedule	FIXED	SCHEDULE=
suppress printing of loan comparison report	COMPARE	NOCOMPRINT
Required Specifications		
specify the loan amount	FIXED	AMOUNT=
specify life of loan as number of payments	FIXED	LIFE=
specify the periodic payment	FIXED	PAYMENT=
specify the initial annual nominal interest rate	FIXED	RATE=

Description	Statement	Option
Loan Specifications Options		
specify loan amount as percentage of price	FIXED	AMOUNTPCT=
specify time interval between compoundings	FIXED	COMPOUND=
specify down payment at loan initialization	FIXED	DOWNPAYMENT=
specify down payment as percentage of price	FIXED	DOWNPAYPCT=
specify amount paid for loan initialization	FIXED	INITIAL=
specify initialization costs as a percent	FIXED	INITIALPCT=
specify time interval between payments	FIXED	INTERVAL=
specify label for the loan	FIXED	LABEL=
specify amount paid for discount points	FIXED	POINTS=
specify discount points as a percent	FIXED	POINTPCT=
specify uniform or lump sum prepayments	FIXED	PREPAYMENTS=
specify the purchase price	FIXED	PRICE=
specify number of decimal places for rounding	FIXED	ROUND=
specify the date of loan initialization	FIXED	START=
Balloon Payment Loan Specification Option		
specify the list of balloon payments	BALLOON	BALLOONPAYMENT=
Rate Adjustment Terms Options		
specify frequency of rate adjustments	ARM	ADJUSTFREQ=
specify periodic and life cap on rate adjustment	ARM	CAPS=
specify maximum rate adjustment	ARM	MAXADJUST=
specify maximum annual nominal interest rate	ARM	MAXRATE=
specify minimum annual nominal interest rate	ARM	MINRATE=
Rate Adjustment Case Options		
specify best-case (optimistic) scenario	ARM	BESTCASE
specify predicted interest rates	ARM	ESTIMATEDCASE=
specify constant rate	ARM	FIXEDCASE
specify worst case (pessimistic) scenario	ARM	WORSTCASE
Buydown Rate Loan Specification Option		
specify list of nominal interest rates	BUYDOWN	BUYDOWNRATES=
Loan Comparison Options		
specify all comparison criteria	COMPARE	ALL
specify the loan comparison periods	COMPARE	AT=
specify breakeven analysis of the interest paid	COMPARE	BREAKINTEREST
specify breakeven analysis of periodic payment	COMPARE	BREAKPAYMENT

Description	Statement	Option
specify minimum attractive rate of return	COMPARE	MARR=
specify present worth of cost analysis	COMPARE	PWOFCOST
specify the income tax rate	COMPARE	TAXRATE=
specify true interest rate analysis	COMPARE	TRUEINTEREST

PROC LOAN Statement

PROC LOAN *options* ;

The following output option can be used in the PROC LOAN statement. In addition, the following FIXED statement options can be specified in the PROC LOAN statement to be used as defaults for all loans unless otherwise specified for a given loan: AMOUNT=, LIFE=, PAYMENT=, RATE=, AMOUNTPCT, COMPOUND=, DOWNPAYMENT=, DOWNPAYPCT=, INITIAL=, INITIALPCT=, INTERVAL=, LABEL=, POINTS=, POINTPCT=, PREPAYMENTS=, PRICE=, ROUND=, START=, NOSUMMARYPRINT, NOPRINT, and SCHEDULE options (all FIXED statement options other than the OUT= and LABEL= options, which are specific to individual loans).

Output Option

OUTSUM= *SAS-data-set*

creates an output data set containing loan summary information for all loans other than those for which a different OUTSUM= output data set is specified.

FIXED Statement

FIXED *options* ;

The FIXED statement specifies a fixed rate and periodic payment loan. It can be specified using the options that are common to all loan statements. The FIXED statement options are listed in this section.

You must specify three of the following options in each loan statement: AMOUNT=, LIFE=, RATE=, and PAYMENT=. The LOAN procedure calculates the fourth parameter based on the values you give the other three. If you specify all four of the options, the PAYMENT= specification is ignored, and the periodic payment is recalculated for consistency.

As an alternative to specifying the AMOUNT= option, you can specify the PRICE= option along with one of the following options to facilitate the calculation of the loan amount: AMOUNTPCT=, DOWNPAYMENT=, or DOWNPAYPCT=.

Required Specifications

AMOUNT= *amount*

specifies the loan amount (the outstanding principal balance at the initialization of the loan).

The AMOUNT= option can be abbreviated A=.

LIFE= *n*

gives the life of the loan in number of payments. (The payment frequency is specified by the INTERVAL= option.) For example, if the life of the loan is 10 years with monthly payments, use LIFE=120 and INTERVAL=MONTH (default) to indicate a 10-year loan in which 120 monthly payments are made.

The LIFE= option can be abbreviated L=.

PAYMENT= *amount*

specifies the periodic payment. For ARM and BUYDOWN loans where the periodic payment might change, the PAYMENT= option specifies the initial amount of the periodic payment.

The PAYMENT= option can be abbreviated P=.

RATE= *rate*

specifies the initial annual (nominal) interest rate in percent notation. The rate specified must be in the range 0% to 120%. For example, use RATE=12.75 for a 12.75% loan. For ARM and BUYDOWN loans, where the rate might change over the life of the loan, the RATE= option specifies the initial annual interest rate.

The RATE= option can be abbreviated R=.

Specification Options

AMOUNTPCT= *value*

specifies the loan amount as a percentage of the purchase price (PRICE= option). The AMOUNTPCT= specification is used to calculate the loan amount if the AMOUNT= option is not specified. The value specified must be in the range 1% to 100%.

If both the AMOUNTPCT= and DOWNPAYPCT= options are specified and the sum of their values is not equal to 100, the value of the downpayment percentage is set equal to 100 minus the value of the amount percentage.

The AMOUNTPCT= option can be abbreviated APCT=.

COMPOUND= *time-unit*

specifies the time interval between compoundings. The default is the time unit given by the INTERVAL= option. If the INTERVAL= option is not used, then the default is COMPOUND=MONTH. The following time units are valid COMPOUND= values: CONTINUOUS, DAY, SEMIMONTH, MONTH, QUARTER, SEMIYEAR, and YEAR. The compounding interval is used to calculate the simple interest rate per payment period from the nominal annual interest rate or vice versa.

DOWNPAYMENT= *amount*

specifies the down payment at the initialization of the loan. The down payment is included in the calculation of the present worth of cost but not in the calculation of the true interest rate. The after-tax analysis assumes that the down payment is not tax-deductible. (Specify after-tax analysis with the TAXRATE= option in the COMPARE statement.)

The DOWNPAYMENT= option can be abbreviated DP=.

DOWNPAYPCT= *value*

specifies the down payment as a percentage of the purchase price (PRICE= option). The DOWNPAYPCT= specification is used to calculate the down payment amount if you do not specify the DOWNPAYMENT= option. The value you specify must be in the range 0% to 99%.

If you specified both the AMOUNTPCT= and DOWNPAYPCT= options, and the sum of their values is not equal to 100, the value of the downpayment percentage is set equal to 100 minus the value of the amount percentage.

The DOWNPAYPCT= option can be abbreviated DPCT=.

INITIAL= *amount*

specifies the amount paid for loan initialization other than the discount points and down payment. This amount is included in the calculation of the present worth of cost and the true interest rate. The after-tax analysis assumes that the initial amount is not tax-deductible. (After-tax analysis is specified by the TAXRATE= option in the COMPARE statement.)

The INITIAL= option can be abbreviated INIT=.

INITIALPCT= *value*

specifies the initialization costs as a percentage of the loan amount (AMOUNT= option). The INITIALPCT= specification is used to calculate the amount paid for loan initialization if you do not specify the INITIAL= option. The value you specify must be in the range of 0% to 100%.

The INITIALPCT= option can be abbreviated INITPCT=.

INTERVAL= *time-unit*

gives the time interval between periodic payments. The default is INTERVAL=MONTH. The following time units are valid INTERVAL values: SEMIMONTH, MONTH, QUARTER, SEMIYEAR, and YEAR.

LABEL= *'loan-label'*

specifies a label for the loan. If you specify the LABEL= option, all output related to the loan is labeled accordingly. If you do not specify the LABEL= option, the loan is labeled by sequence number.

POINTS= *amount*

specifies the amount paid for discount points at the initialization of the loan. This amount is included in the calculation of the present worth of cost and true interest rate. The amount paid for discount points is assumed to be tax-deductible in after-tax analysis (that is, if the TAXRATE= option is specified in the COMPARE statement).

The POINTS= option can be abbreviated PNT=.

POINTPCT= *value*

specifies the discount points as a percentage of the loan amount (AMOUNT= option). The POINTPCT= specification is used to calculate the amount paid for discount points if you do not specify the POINTS= option. The value you specify must be in the range of 0% to 100%.

The POINTPCT= option can be abbreviated PNTPCT=.

PREPAYMENTS= *amount*
PREPAYMENTS= (*date1= prepayment1 date2= prepayment2 ...*)
PREPAYMENTS= (*period1= prepayment1 period2= prepayment2 ...*)

specifies either a uniform prepayment p throughout the life of the loan or lump sum prepayments. A uniform prepayment, p, is assumed to be paid with each periodic payment. Specify lump sum prepayments by pairs of periods (or dates) and respective prepayment amounts.

You can specify the prepayment periods as dates if you specify the START= option. Prepayment periods or dates and the respective prepayment amounts must be in time sequence. The prepayments are treated as principal payments, and the outstanding principal balance is adjusted accordingly. In the adjustable rate and buydown rate loans, if there is a rate adjustment after prepayments, the adjusted periodic payment is calculated based on the outstanding principal balance. The prepayments do not result in periodic payment amount adjustments in fixed rate and balloon payment loans.

The PREPAYMENTS= option can be abbreviated PREP=.

PRICE= *amount*

specifies the purchase price, which is the loan amount plus the down payment. If you specify the PRICE= option along with the loan amount (AMOUNT= option) or the down payment (DOWNPAYMENT= option), the value of the other one is calculated.

If you specify the PRICE= option with the AMOUNTPCT= or DOWN-PAYPCT= options, the loan amount and the downpayment are calculated.

The PRICE= option can be abbreviated PRC=.

ROUND= *n*
ROUND= **NONE**

specifies the number of decimal places to which the monetary amounts are rounded for the loan. Valid values for *n* are integers from 0 to 6. If you specify ROUND=NONE, the values are not rounded off internally, but the printed output is rounded off to two decimal places. The default is ROUND=2.

START= *SAS-date*
START= *yyyy:per*

gives the date of loan initialization. The first payment is assumed to be one payment interval after the start date. For example, you can specify the START= option as '1APR1990'd or as 1990:3 where 3 is the third payment interval. If IN-TERVAL=QUARTER, 3 refers to the third quarter. If you specify the START= option, all output involving the particular loan is dated accordingly.

The START= option can be abbreviated S=.

Output Options

NOSUMMARYPRINT

suppresses the printing of the loan summary report. The NOSUMMARYPRINT option is usually used when an OUTSUM= data set is created to store loan summary information.

The NOSUMMARYPRINT option can be abbreviated NOSUMPR.

NOPRINT

suppresses all printed output for the loan.

The NOPRINT option can be abbreviated NOP.

OUT= *SAS-data-set*

writes the loan amortization schedule to an output data set.

OUTSUM= *SAS-data-set*

writes the loan summary for the individual loan to an output data set.

SCHEDULE
SCHEDULE= *nyears*
SCHEDULE= YEARLY

prints the amortization schedule for the loan. SCHEDULE=*nyears* specifies the number of years the printed amortization table covers. If you omit the number of years or specify a period longer than the loan life, the schedule is printed for the full term of the loan. SCHEDULE=YEARLY prints yearly summary information in the amortization schedule rather than the full amortization schedule. SCHEDULE=YEARLY is useful for long-term loans.

The SCHEDULE option can be abbreviated SCHED.

BALLOON Statement

> **BALLOON** *options*;

The BALLOON statement specifies a fixed rate loan with scheduled balloon payments in addition to the periodic payment. In addition to the required specifications and options listed under the FIXED statement, the following option is used in the BALLOON statement:

BALLOONPAYMENT= (*date1*= *payment1 date2*= *payment2 ...*)
BALLOONPAYMENT= (*period1*= *payment1 period2*= *payment2 ...*)

specifies pairs of periods and amounts of balloon (lump sum) payments in excess of the periodic payment during the life of the loan. You can also specify the balloon periods as dates if you specify the START= option.

If you do not specify this option, the calculations are identical to a loan specified in a FIXED statement. Balloon periods (or dates) and the respective balloon payments must be in time sequence.

The BALLOONPAYMENT= option can be abbreviated BPAY=.

ARM Statement

> **ARM** *options*;

The ARM statement specifies an adjustable rate loan where the future interest rates are not known with certainty but will vary within specified limits according to the terms stated in the loan agreement. In practice, the adjustment terms vary. Adjustments in the interest rate can be captured using the ARM statement options.

In addition to the required specifications and options listed under the FIXED statement, you can use the following options with the ARM statement:

Rate Adjustment Terms Options

ADJUSTFREQ= *n*

specifies the number of periods (in terms of the INTERVAL= specification) between rate adjustments. INTERVAL=MONTH ADJUSTFREQ=6 indicates that the nominal interest rate can be adjusted every six months until the life cap or maximum rate (whichever is specified) is reached. The default is ADJUSTFREQ=12. The periodic payment is adjusted every adjustment period even if there is no rate change; therefore, if prepayments are made (as specified with the PREPAYMENTS= option), the periodic payment might change even if the nominal rate does not.

The ADJUSTFREQ= option can be abbreviated ADF=.

CAPS= (*periodic-cap*, *life-cap*)

specifies the maximum interest rate adjustment (in percent notation) allowed by the loan agreement. The *periodic cap* specifies the maximum adjustment allowed at each adjustment period. The *life cap* specifies the maximum total adjustment over the life of the loan. For example, a loan specified with CAPS=(0.5, 2) indicates that the nominal interest rate can change by 0.5% each adjustment period, and the annual nominal interest rate throughout the life of the loan will be within a 2% range of the initial annual nominal rate.

MAXADJUST= *rate*

specifies the maximum rate adjustment (in percent notation) allowed at each adjustment period. Use the MAXADJUST= option with the MAXRATE= and MINRATE= options. The initial nominal rate plus the maximum adjustment should not exceed the specified MAXRATE= value. The initial nominal rate minus the maximum adjustment should not be less than the specified MINRATE= value.

The MAXADJUST= option can be abbreviated MAXAD=.

MAXRATE= *rate*

specifies the maximum annual nominal rate (in percent notation) that might be charged on the loan. The maximum annual nominal rate should be greater than or equal to the initial annual nominal rate (the RATE= option value, if specified).

The MAXRATE= option can be abbreviated MAXR=.

MINRATE= *rate*

specifies the minimum annual nominal rate (in percent notation) that might be charged on the loan. The minimum annual nominal rate should be less than or equal to the initial annual nominal rate (the RATE= option value, if specified).

The MINRATE= option can be abbreviated MINR=.

Rate Adjustment Case Options

PROC LOAN supports four rate adjustment scenarios for analysis of adjustable rate loans: pessimistic (WORSTCASE), optimistic (BESTCASE), no-change (FIXED-CASE), and estimated (ESTIMATEDCASE). The estimated case enables you to analyze the adjustable rate loan using your predictions of future interest rates. The default is worst-case analysis. If more than one case is specified, worst-case analysis is performed. You can specify options for adjustable rate loans as follows:

BESTCASE

specifies a best-case analysis. The best-case analysis assumes the interest rate charged on the loan will reach its minimum allowed limits at each adjustment period and over the life of the loan. If you use the BESTCASE option, you must specify either the CAPS= option or the MINRATE= and MAXADJUST= options.

The BESTCASE option can be abbreviated B.

ESTIMATEDCASE= (*date1= rate1 date2= rate2 ...*)
ESTIMATEDCASE= (*period1= rate1 period2= rate2 ...*)

specifies an estimated case analysis that indicates the rate adjustments will follow the rates you predict. This option specifies pairs of periods and estimated nominal interest rates.

The ESTIMATEDCASE= option can be abbreviated ESTC=.

The ESTIMATEDCASE= option can specify adjustments that cannot fit into the BESTCASE, WORSTCASE, or FIXEDCASE specifications, or "what-if" type analysis. If you specify the START= option, you can also specify the estimation periods as dates. Estimated rates and the respective periods must be in time sequence.

If the estimated period falls between two adjustment periods (determined by AD-JUSTFREQ= option), the rate is adjusted in the next adjustment period. The nominal interest rate charged on the loan is constant between two adjustment periods.

If any of the MAXRATE=, MINRATE=, CAPS=, and MAXADJUST= options are specified to indicate the rate adjustment terms of the loan agreement, these specifications are used to bound the rate adjustments. By using the ESTIMAT-EDCASE= option, you are predicting what the annual nominal rates in the market will be at different points in time, not necessarily the interest rate on your particular loan. For example, if the initial nominal rate (RATE= option) is 10, ADJUST-FREQ=6, MAXADJUST=0.5, and the ESTIMATEDCASE=(6=10.5, 12=10.8), the actual nominal rates charged on the loan would be 10.0% initially, 10.5% for the sixth through the eleventh periods, and 10.8% for the twelfth period on.

FIXEDCASE

specifies a fixed case analysis that assumes the rate will stay constant. The FIXEDCASE option calculates the ARM loan values similar to a fixed rate loan, but the payments are updated every adjustment period even if the rate does not change, leading to minor differences between the two methods. One such difference is in the way prepayments are handled. In a fixed rate loan, the rate and the payments are never adjusted; therefore, the payment stays the same over the life of the loan even when prepayments are made (instead, the life of the loan is shortened). In an ARM loan with the FIXEDCASE option, on the other hand, if prepayments are made, the payment is adjusted in the following adjustment period (leaving the life of the loan constant).

The FIXEDCASE option can be abbreviated FIXCASE.

WORSTCASE

specifies a worst-case analysis. The worst-case analysis assumes the interest rate charged on the loan will reach its maximum allowed limits at each rate adjustment period and over the life of the loan. If the WORSTCASE option is used, either the CAPS= option or the MAXRATE= and MAXADJUST= options must be specified. The WORSTCASE option can be abbreviated W.

BUYDOWN Statement

> **BUYDOWN** *options*;

The BUYDOWN statement specifies a buydown rate loan. The buydown rate loans are similar to ARM loans, but the interest rate adjustments are predetermined at the initialization of the loan (usually by paying interest points at the time of loan initialization).

You can use all the required specifications and options listed under the FIXED statement with the BUYDOWN statement. The following option is specific to the BUYDOWN statement and is required:

BUYDOWNRATES= (*date1*= *rate1 date2*= *rate2* ...)
BUYDOWNRATES= (*period1*= *rate1 period2*= *rate2* ...)

specifies pairs of periods and the predetermined nominal interest rates that will be charged on the loan starting at the corresponding time periods.

You can also specify the buydown periods as dates if you specify the START=option. Buydown periods (or dates) and the respective buydown rates must be in time sequence.

The BUYDOWNRATES= option can be abbreviated BDR=.

COMPARE Statement

> **COMPARE** *options* ;

The COMPARE statement compares multiple loans and it can be used with a single loan. You can use only one COMPARE statement. COMPARE statement options specify the periods and desired types of analysis for loan comparison. The default analysis reports the outstanding principal balance, breakeven of payment, breakeven of interest paid, and before-tax true interest rate. The default comparison period corresponds to the first LIFE= option specification. If the LIFE= option is not specified for any loan, the loan comparison period defaults to the first calculated life.

You can use the following options with the COMPARE statement. For more detailed information on loan comparison, see the section "Loan Comparison Details" later in this chapter.

Analysis Options

ALL

is equivalent to specifying the BREAKINTEREST, BREAKPAYMENT, PWOFCOST, and TRUEINTEREST options. The loan comparison report includes all the criteria. You need to specify the MARR= option for present worth of cost calculation.

AT= (*date1 date2 ...*)
AT= (*period1 period2 ...*)

specifies the periods for loan comparison reports. If you specify the START= option in the PROC LOAN statement, you can specify the AT= option as a list of dates instead of periods. The comparison periods do not need to be in time sequence. If you do not specify the AT= option, the comparison period defaults to the first LIFE= option specification. If you do not specify the LIFE= option for any of the loans, the loan comparison period defaults to the first calculated life.

BREAKINTEREST

specifies breakeven analysis of the interest paid. The loan comparison report includes the interest paid for each loan through the specified comparison period (AT= option).

The BREAKINTEREST option can be abbreviated BI.

BREAKPAYMENT

specifies breakeven analysis of payment. The periodic payment for each loan is reported for every comparison period specified in the AT=option.

The BREAKPAYMENT option can be abbreviated BP.

MARR= *rate*

specifies the MARR (**M**inimum **A**ttractive **R**ate of **R**eturn) in percent notation. MARR reflects the cost of capital or the opportunity cost of money. The MARR= option is used in calculating the present worth of cost.

PWOFCOST

calculates the present worth of cost (net present value of costs) for each loan based on the cash flow through the specified comparison periods. The calculations account for down payment, initialization costs and discount points, as well as the payments and outstanding principal balance at the comparison period. If you specify the TAXRATE= option, the present worth of cost is based on after-tax cash flow. Otherwise, before-tax present worth of cost is calculated. You need to specify the MARR= option for present worth of cost calculations.

The PWOFCOST option can be abbreviated PWC.

TAXRATE= *rate*

specifies income tax rate in percent notation for the after-tax calculations of the true interest rate and present worth of cost for those assets that qualify for tax deduction. If you specify this option, the amount specified in the POINTS= option and the interest paid on the loan are assumed to be tax-deductible. Otherwise, it is assumed that the asset does not qualify for tax deductions, and the cash flow is not adjusted for tax savings.

The TAXRATE= option can be abbreviated TAX=.

TRUEINTEREST

calculates the true interest rate (effective interest rate based on the cash flow of all payments, initialization costs, discount points, and the outstanding principal balance at the comparison period) for all the specified loans through each comparison period. If you specify the TAXRATE= option, the true interest rate is based on after-tax cash flow. Otherwise, the before-tax true interest rate is calculated.

The TRUEINTEREST option can be abbreviated TI.

Output Options
NOCOMPRINT

suppresses the printing of the loan comparison report. The NOCOMPRINT option is usually used when an OUTCOMP= data set is created to store loan comparison information.

The NOCOMPRINT option can be abbreviated NOCP.

OUTCOMP= *SAS-data-set*

writes the loan comparison report to an output data set.

Details

Computational Details

These terms are used in the formulas that follow:

p periodic payment

a principal amount

r_a nominal annual rate

f compounding frequency (per year)

f' payment frequency (per year)

r periodic rate

r_e effective interest rate

n total number of payments

The periodic rate, or the simple interest applied during a payment period, is given by

$$r = \left(1 + \frac{r_a}{f}\right)^{f/f'} - 1$$

Note that the interest calculation is performed at each payment period rather than at the compound period. This is done by adjusting the nominal rate. Refer to Muksian (1984) for details.

Note that when $f = f'$, that is, when the payment and compounding frequency coincide, the preceding expression reduces to the familiar form:

$$r = \frac{r_a}{f}$$

The periodic rate for continuous compounding can be obtained from this general expression by taking the limit as the compounding frequency f goes to infinity. The resulting expression is

$$r = \exp\left(\frac{r_a}{f'}\right) - 1$$

The effective interest rate, or annualized percentage rate (APR), is that rate which, if compounded once per year, is equivalent to the nominal annual rate compounded f times per year. Thus,

$$(1 + r_e) = (1 + r)^f = \left(1 + \frac{r_a}{f}\right)^f$$

or

$$r_e = \left(1 + \frac{r_a}{f}\right)^f - 1$$

For continuous compounding, the effective interest rate is given by

$$r_e = \exp(r_a) - 1$$

Refer to Muksian (1984) for details.

The payment is calculated as

$$p = \frac{a\,r}{1 - \frac{1}{(1+r)^n}}$$

The amount is calculated as

$$a = \frac{p}{r}\left(1 - \frac{1}{(1+r)^n}\right)$$

Both the payment and amount are rounded to the nearest hundredth (cent) unless the ROUND= specification is different than the default, 2.

The total number of payments n is calculated as

$$n = \frac{-\ln\left(1 - \frac{ar}{p}\right)}{\ln(1 + r)}$$

The total number of payments is rounded up to the nearest integer.

The nominal annual rate is calculated using the bisection method, with a as the objective and r starting in the interval between 8×10^{-6} and .1 with an initial midpoint .01 and successive midpoints bisecting.

Loan Comparison Details

In order to compare the costs of different alternatives, the input cash flow for the alternatives must be represented in equivalent values. The equivalent value of a cash flow accounts for the time-value of money. That is, it is preferable to pay the same amount of money later than to pay it now, since the money can earn interest while you keep it. The MARR (**M**inimum **A**ttractive **R**ate of **R**eturn) reflects the cost of capital or the opportunity cost of money, that is, the interest that would have been earned on the savings that is foregone by making the investment. The MARR is used to discount the cash flow of alternatives into equivalent values at a fixed point in time. The MARR can vary for each investor and for each investment. Therefore, the MARR= option must be specified in the COMPARE statement if present worth of cost (PWOFCOST option) comparison is specified.

Present worth of cost reflects the equivalent amount at loan initialization of the loan cash flow discounted at MARR, not accounting for inflation. Present worth of cost accounts for the down payment, initialization costs, discount points, periodic payments, and the principal balance at the end of the report period. Therefore, it reflects the present worth of cost of the asset, not the loan. It is only meaningful to use minimization of present worth of cost as a selection criterion if the assets (down payment plus loan amount) are of the same value.

Another economic selection criterion is the rate of return (internal rate of return) of the alternatives. If interest is being earned by an alternative, the objective would be to maximize the rate of return. If interest is being paid, as in loan alternatives, the best alternative is the one that minimizes the rate of return. The true interest rate reflects the effective annual rate charged on the loan based on the cash flow, including the initialization cost and the discount points.

The effects of taxes on different alternatives must be accounted for when these vary among different alternatives. Since interest costs on certain loans are tax-deductible, the comparisons for those loans are made based on the after-tax cash flows. The cost of the loan is reduced by the tax benefits it offers through the loan life if the TAXRATE= option is specified. The present worth of cost and true interest rate are calculated based on the after-tax cash flow of the loan. The down payment on the loan and initialization costs are assumed to be not tax-deductible in after-tax analysis. Discount points and the interest paid in each periodic payment are assumed to be tax-deductible if the TAXRATE= option is specified. If the TAXRATE= option is not specified, the present worth of cost and the true interest rate are based on before-tax cash flow, assuming that the interest paid on the specified loan does not qualify for tax benefits.

The other two selection criteria are breakeven analysis of periodic payment and interest paid. If the objective is to minimize the periodic payment, the best alternative would be the one with the minimum periodic payment. If the objective is to minimize the interest paid on the principal, then the best alternative is the one with the least interest paid.

Another criterion might be the minimization of the outstanding balance of the loan at a particular point in time. For example, if you plan to sell a house before the end of the loan life (which is often the case), you might want to select the loan with the minimum principal balance at the time of the sale, since this balance must be paid at that time. The outstanding balance of the alternative loans is calculated for each loan comparison period by default.

If you specified the START= option in the PROC LOAN statement, the present worth of cost reflects the equivalent amount for each loan at that point in time. Any loan that has a START= specification different from the one in the PROC LOAN statement is not processed in the loan comparison.

The loan comparison report for each comparison period contains for each loan the loan label, outstanding balance, and any of the following measures if requested in the COMPARE statement: periodic payment (BREAKPAY option), total interest paid to date (BREAKINTEREST option), present worth of cost (PWOFCOST option), and true interest rate (TRUEINTEREST option). The best loan is selected on the basis of present worth of cost or true interest rate. If both PWOFCOST and TRUEINTEREST options are specified, present worth of cost is the basis for the selection of the best loan.

You can use the OUTCOMP= option in the COMPARE statement to write the loan comparison report to a data set. The NOCOMPRINT option suppresses the printing of a loan comparison report.

OUT= Data Set

The OUT= option writes the loan amortization schedule to an output data set. The OUT= data set contains one observation for each payment period (or one observation for each year if you specified the SCHEDULE=YEARLY option). If you specified the START= option, the DATE variable denotes the date of the payment. Otherwise, YEAR and period variable (SEMIMONTH, MONTH, QUARTER, or SEMIYEAR) denote the payment year and period within the year.

The OUT= data set contains the following variables:

- DATE, date of the payment. DATE is included in the OUT= data set only when you specify the START= option.

- YEAR, year of the payment period. YEAR is included in the OUT= data set only when you do not specify the START= option.

- PERIOD, period within the year of the payment period. The name of the period variable matches the INTERVAL= specification (SEMIMONTH, MONTH, QUARTER, or SEMIYEAR.) The PERIOD variable is included in the OUT= data set only when you do not specify the START= option.

- BEGPRIN, beginning principal balance

- PAYMENT, payment

- INTEREST, interest payment

- PRIN, principal repayment

- ENDPRIN, ending principal balance

OUTCOMP= Data Set

The OUTCOMP= option in the COMPARE statement writes the loan comparison analysis results to an output data set. If you specified the START= option, the DATE variable identifies the date of the loan comparison. Otherwise, the PERIOD variable identifies the comparison period.

The OUTCOMP= data set contains one observation for each loan for each loan comparison period. The OUTCOMP= data set contains the following variables:

- DATE, date of loan comparison report. The DATE variable is included in the OUTCOMP= data set only when you specify the START= option.

- PERIOD, period of the loan comparison for the observation. The PERIOD variable is included in the OUTCOMP= data set only when you do not specify the START= option.

- LABEL, label string for the loan

- TYPE, type of the loan

- PAYMENT, periodic payment at the time of report. The PAYMENT is included in the OUTCOMP= data set if you specified the BREAKPAYMENT or ALL option or if you used default criteria.

- INTPAY, interest paid through the time of report. The INTPAY variable is included in the OUTCOMP= data set if you specified the BREAKINTEREST or ALL option or if you used default criteria.

- TRUERATE, true interest rate charged on the loan. The TRUERATE variable is included in the OUTCOMP= data set if you specified the TRUERATE or ALL option or if you used default criteria.

- PWOFCOST, present worth of cost. The PWOFCOST variable is included in the OUTCOMP= data set only if you specified the PWOFCOST or ALL option.

- BALANCE, outstanding principal balance at the time of report

OUTSUM= Data Set

The OUTSUM= option writes the loan summary to an output data set. If you specified this option in the PROC LOAN statement, the loan summary information for all loans will be written to the specified data set, except for those loans for which you specified a different OUTSUM= data set on the ARM, BALLOON, BUYDOWN, or FIXED statement.

You can also specify the OUTSUM=option in individual loan statements, in which case the loan summary information of the individual loan is written to the specified data set. The OUTSUM= data set contains one observation for each loan and contains the following variables:

- TYPE, type of loan

- LABEL, loan label

- PAYMENT, periodic payment

- AMOUNT, loan principal

- DOWNPAY, down payment. DOWNPAY is included in the OUTSUM= data set only when you specify a down payment.

- INITIAL, loan initialization costs. INITIAL is included in the OUTSUM= data set only when you specify initialization costs.

- POINTS, discount points. POINTS is included in the OUTSUM= data set only when you specify discount points.

- TOTAL, total payment

- INTEREST,total interest paid

- RATE, nominal annual interest rate

- EFFRATE, effective interest rate

- INTERVAL, payment interval

- COMPOUND, compounding interval

- LIFE, loan life (that is, the number of payment intervals)

- NCOMPND, number of compounding intervals

- COMPUTE, computed loan parameter: life, amount, payment, or rate

If you specified the START= option either in the PROC LOAN statement or for the individual loan, the OUTSUM= data set also contains the following variables:

- BEGIN, start date

- END, loan termination date

Printed Output

The output from PROC LOAN consists of the loan summary table, loan amortization schedule, and loan comparison report.

Loan Summary Table

The loan summary table shows the total payment and interest, the initial nominal annual and effective interest rates, payment and compounding intervals, the length of the loan in the time units specified, the start and end dates (if specified), a list of nominal and effective interest rates, and periodic payments throughout the life of the loan.

A list of balloon payments for balloon payment loans and a list of prepayments (if specified) are printed with their respective periods (or dates).

The loan summary table is printed for each loan by default. The NOSUMMARYPRINT option specified in the PROC LOAN statement will suppress the printing of the loan summary table for all loans. The NOSUMMARYPRINT option can be specified in individual loan statements to selectively suppress the printing of the loan summary table.

Loan Repayment Schedule

The amortization schedule contains for each payment period the year and period within the year (or date, if you specified the START= option), principal balance at the beginning of the period, total payment, interest payment and principal payment for the period, and the principal balance at the end of the period. If you specified the SCHEDULE=YEARLY option, the amortization will contain a summary for each year instead of for each payment period.

The amortization schedule is not printed by default. The SCHEDULE option in the PROC LOAN statement requests the printing of amortization tables for all loans. You can specify the SCHEDULE option in individual loan statements to selectively request the printing of the amortization schedule.

Loan Comparison Report

The loan comparison report is processed for each report period and contains the results of economic analysis of the loans. The quantities reported can include the outstanding principal balance, after-tax or before-tax present worth of cost and true interest rate, periodic payment, and the interest paid through the report period for each loan. The best alternative is selected if the asset value (down payment plus loan amount) is the same for each alternative.

The loan comparison report is printed by default. The NOCOMPRINT option specified in the COMPARE statement suppresses the printing of the loan comparison report.

Examples

Example 10.1. Discount Points for Lower Interest Rates

This example illustrates the comparison of two $100,000 loans. The major difference between the two loans is that the nominal interest rate in the second one is lower than the first with the added expense of paying discount points at the time of initialization.

Both alternatives are 30-year loans. The first loan is labeled "8.25% - no discount points" and the second one is labeled "8% - 1 discount point."

Assume that the interest paid qualifies for a tax deduction, and you are in the 33% tax bracket. Also, your Minimum Attractive Rate of Return (MARR) for an alternative investment is 4% (adjusted for tax rate.)

You use the following statements to find the breakeven point in the life of the loan for your preference between the loans:

```
proc loan start=1992:1 nosummaryprint amount=100000 life=360;
    fixed rate=8.25 label='8.25% - no discount points';
    fixed rate=8 points=1000 label='8% - 1 discount point';
    compare at=(48 54 60) all taxrate=33 marr=4;
run;
```

Output 10.1.1 shows the loan comparison reports as of January 1996 (48th period), July 1996 (54th period), and January 1997(60th period.)

Output 10.1.1. Loan Comparison Reports for Discount Point Breakeven

```
                         LOAN Procedure

                      Loan Comparison Report

                    Analysis through JAN1996

                          Ending   P.W. of            Interest   True
Loan Label                Outstanding  Cost   Payment    Paid     Rate

8.25% - no discount points  96388.09 105546.17  751.27  32449.05  5.67
8% - 1 discount point        96219.32 105604.05  733.76  31439.80  5.69

  Note: "8.25% - no discount points" is the best alternative based on present
        worth of cost analysis through JAN1996.

                      Loan Comparison Report

                    Analysis through JUL1996

                          Ending   P.W. of            Interest   True
Loan Label                Outstanding  Cost   Payment    Paid     Rate

8.25% - no discount points  95847.27 106164.97  751.27  36415.85  5.67
8% - 1 discount point        95656.22 106153.97  733.76  35279.26  5.67

  Note: "8% - 1 discount point" is the best alternative based on present
        worth of cost analysis through JUL1996.
```

Example 10.1. Discount Points for Lower Interest Rates □ □ □ 501

Output 10.1.1. (Continued)

```
                        LOAN Procedure

                    Loan Comparison Report

                  Analysis through JAN1997

                        Ending   P.W. of             Interest   True
Loan Label              Outstanding  Cost   Payment     Paid    Rate

8.25% - no discount points  95283.74 106768.07   751.27  40359.94   5.67
8% - 1 discount point       95070.21 106689.80   733.76  39095.81   5.66

    Note: "8% - 1 discount point" is the best alternative based on present
          worth of cost analysis through JAN1997.
```

Notice that the breakeven point for present worth of cost and true rate both happen on July 1996. This indicates that if you intend to keep the loan for 4.5 years or more, it is better to pay the discount points for the lower rate. If your objective is to minimize the interest paid or the periodic payment, the "8% - 1 discount point" loan is the preferred choice.

Example 10.2. Refinancing a Loan

Assume that you obtained a fixed rate 15-year loan in June 1990 for $78,500 with a nominal annual rate of 10%. By early 1992, the market offers a 7.5% interest rate, and you are considering whether to refinance your loan.

Use the following statements to find out the status of the loan on February 1992. Output 10.2.1 shows the results:

```
proc loan start=1990:6;
   fixed life=180 rate=10 amount=78500 noprint
        label='Original loan';
   compare at=('10FEB92'd) ;
run;
```

Output 10.2.1. Loan Comparison Report for Original Loan

```
                        LOAN Procedure

                    Loan Comparison Report

                  Analysis through FEB1992

                        Ending            Interest   True
        Loan Label      Outstanding  Payment    Paid    Rate

        Original loan    74396.51    843.57  12767.91   10.47
```

The monthly payment on the original loan is $843.57. The ending outstanding principal balance as of February is $74,396.51. At this point, you might want to refinance your loan with another 15-year loan. The alternate loan has a 7.5% nominal annual rate. The initialization costs are $1,419.00. Use the following statements to compare your alternatives:

```
proc loan start=1992:2 amount=74396.51;
    fixed rate=10 payment=843.57
          label='Keep the original loan' noprint;
    fixed life=180  rate=7.5 init=1419
          label='Refinance at 7.5%' noprint;
    compare at=(14 15) taxrate=33 marr=4 all;
run;
```

Output 10.2.2.   Loan Comparison Report for Refinancing Decision

```
                      LOAN Procedure

                  Loan Comparison Report

                 Analysis through APR1993

                        Ending   P.W. of              Interest   True
Loan Label              Outstanding  Cost   Payment      Paid    Rate

Keep the original loan  71090.78  76636.65   843.57   8504.25    6.91
Refinance at 7.5%       71119.93  76666.00   689.66   6378.66    6.98

  Note: "Keep the original loan" is the best alternative based on present
        worth of cost analysis through APR1993.

                  Loan Comparison Report

                 Analysis through MAY1993

                        Ending   P.W. of              Interest   True
Loan Label              Outstanding  Cost   Payment      Paid    Rate

Keep the original loan  70839.63  76788.82   843.57   9096.67    6.91
Refinance at 7.5%       70874.77  76723.79   689.66   6823.16    6.86

  Note: "Refinance at 7.5%" is the best alternative based on present worth of
        cost analysis through MAY1993.
```

The comparison reports of April 1993 and May 1993 in Output 10.2.2 illustrate the breakeven between the two alternatives. If you intend to keep the loan through May 1993 or longer, your initialization costs for the refinancing are justified. The periodic payment of the refinanced loan is $689.66.

Example 10.3.   Prepayments on a Loan

This example compares a 30-year loan with and without prepayments. Assume the 30-year loan has an 8.25% nominal annual rate. Use the following statements to see the effect of making uniform prepayments of $500 with periodic payment:

```
proc loan start=1992:12 rate=8.25 amount=240000 life=360;
    fixed label='No prepayments';
    fixed label='With Prepayments' prepay=500 ;
    compare at=(120) taxrate=33 marr=4 all;
run;
```

Example 10.3. Prepayments on a Loan ▫ ▫ ▫ 503

Output 10.3.1. Loan Summary Reports and Loan Comparison Report

```
                           LOAN Procedure

                      Fixed Rate Loan Summary

                         No prepayments


  Downpayment:              0.00   Principal Amount:     240000.00
  Initialization:           0.00   Points:                    0.00

  Total Interest:      409094.17   Nominal Rate:              8.25%
  Total Payment:       649094.17   Effective Rate:            8.57%

  Pay Interval:         MONTHLY     Compounding:            MONTHLY
  No. of payments:          360     No. of compoundings:        360

  Start date:          DEC1992      End date:              DEC2022


          List of Rates and Payments for No prepayments

       Date     Nominal Rate  Effective Rate     Payment

       DEC1992       8.25%         8.57%          1803.04
```

```
                           LOAN Procedure

                      Fixed Rate Loan Summary

                        With Prepayments


  Downpayment:              0.00   Principal Amount:     240000.00
  Initialization:           0.00   Points:                    0.00

  Total Interest:      183650.70   Nominal Rate:              8.25%
  Total Payment:       423650.70   Effective Rate:            8.57%

  Pay Interval:         MONTHLY     Compounding:            MONTHLY
  No. of payments:          184     No. of compoundings:        184

  Start date:          DEC1992      End date:              APR2008


         List of Rates and Payments for With Prepayments

       Date     Nominal Rate  Effective Rate     Payment

       DEC1992       8.25%         8.57%          2303.04
```

```
                           LOAN Procedure

                      Loan Comparison Report

                     Analysis through DEC2002

                         Ending    P.W. of              Interest    True
  Loan Label         Outstanding      Cost   Payment        Paid    Rate

  No prepayments      211608.05  268762.31   1803.04   187972.85    5.67
  With Prepayments    118848.23  264149.25   2303.04   155213.03    5.67

  Note: "With Prepayments" is the best alternative based on present worth of
        cost analysis through DEC2002.
```

Notice that with prepayments you pay off the loan in slightly more than 15 years.
Also, the total payments and total interest are considerably lower with the prepay-

ments. If you can afford the prepayments of $500 each month, another alternative you should consider is using a 15-year loan, which is generally offered at a lower nominal interest rate.

Example 10.4.   Output Data Sets

This example shows the analysis and comparison of five alternative loans. Initialization cost, discount points, and both lump sum and periodic payments are included in the specification of these loans. No printed output is produced. The OUTSUM= and OUTCOMP= data sets store the loan summary and loan comparison information, respectively. Output 10.4.1 illustrates the contents of the output data sets.

```
proc loan start=1992:12 noprint outsum=loans
        amount=100000 life=360;

   fixed rate=13 life=180  prepayment=200
        label='BANK1, Fixed Rate';

   arm rate=10.5 estimatedcase=(12=11.5 18=12)
       label='BANK1, Adjustable Rate';

   buydown rate=12 interval=semimonth  init=15000
          bdrates=(3=14 10=16)  label='BANK2, Buydown';

   arm rate=10.8 worstcase caps=(0.5, 2.5)
       adjustfreq=6 label='BANK3, Adjustable Rate'
       prepayments=(12=2000 36=5000);

   balloon rate=13 life=480
           points=1100 balloonpayment=(15=2000 48=1000)
           label='BANK4, with Balloon Payment';

   compare at=(120 360) all marr=12 tax=33 outcomp=comp;
run;

proc print data=loans;
run;

proc print data=comp;
run;
```

Output 10.4.1. OUTSUM= and OUTCOMP= Data Sets

OBS	TYPE	LABEL	PAYMENT	AMOUNT	INITIAL
1	FIXED	BANK1, Fixed Rate	1465.24	100000	0
2	ARM	BANK1, Adjustable Rate	914.74	100000	0
3	BUYDOWN	BANK2, Buydown	599.55	100000	15000
4	ARM	BANK3, Adjustable Rate	937.24	100000	0
5	BALLOON	BANK4, with Balloon Payment	1064.48	100000	0

OBS	POINTS	TOTAL	INTEREST	RATE	EFFRATE	INTERVAL
1	0	182845.49	82845.49	0.130	0.13803	MONTHLY
2	0	367829.20	267829.20	0.105	0.11020	MONTHLY
3	0	262965.77	162965.77	0.120	0.12716	SEMIMONTHLY
4	0	382789.77	282789.77	0.108	0.11351	MONTHLY
5	1100	513955.78	413955.78	0.130	0.13803	MONTHLY

Example 10.4. Output Data Sets □ □ □ 505

Output 10.4.1. (Continued)

OBS	COMPOUND	LIFE	NCOMPND	COMPUTE	START	END
1	MONTHLY	125	125	PAYMENT	DEC1992	MAY2003
2	MONTHLY	360	360	PAYMENT	DEC1992	DEC2022
3	SEMIMONTHLY	360	360	PAYMENT	DEC1992	DEC2007
4	MONTHLY	360	360	PAYMENT	DEC1992	DEC2022
5	MONTHLY	480	480	PAYMENT	DEC1992	DEC2032

OBS	DATE	TYPE	LABEL	PAYMENT
1	DEC2002	FIXED	BANK1, Fixed Rate	1465.24
2	DEC2002	ARM	BANK1, Adjustable Rate	1026.73
3	DEC2002	BUYDOWN	BANK2, Buydown	732.51
4	DEC2002	ARM	BANK3, Adjustable Rate	1046.81
5	DEC2002	BALLOON	BANK4, with Balloon Payment	1064.48
6	DEC2022	FIXED	BANK1, Fixed Rate	1155.73

OBS	INTEREST	TRUERATE	PWOFCOST	BALANCE
1	82629.51	0.09066	86219.64	6800.71
2	114661.68	0.08143	76281.06	93246.64
3	135439.05	0.14623	107791.10	60374.65
4	119300.98	0.08888	80958.61	87745.00
5	126966.27	0.09189	82001.89	96228.67
6	82845.49	0.09066	86203.45	0.00

OBS	DATE	TYPE	LABEL	PAYMENT
7	DEC2022	ARM	BANK1, Adjustable Rate	1026.76
8	DEC2022	BUYDOWN	BANK2, Buydown	732.68
9	DEC2022	ARM	BANK3, Adjustable Rate	1046.79
10	DEC2022	BALLOON	BANK4, with Balloon Payment	1064.48

OBS	INTEREST	TRUERATE	PWOFCOST	BALANCE
7	267829.20	0.08209	69197.06	0.00
8	162965.77	0.14368	107249.24	0.00
9	282789.77	0.09011	75684.48	0.00
10	357507.19	0.09145	75031.89	71294.39

References

DeGarmo, E.P., Sullivan, W.G., and Canada, J.R. (1984), *Engineering Economy*, Seventh Edition, New York: Macmillan Publishing Company.

Muksian, R. (1984), *Financial Mathematics Handbook*, Englewood Cliffs: Prentice-Hall.

Newnan, D.G. (1988), *Engineering Economic Analysis*, Third Edition, San Jose, California: Engineering Press.

Riggs, J.L. and West, T.M. (1986), *Essentials of Engineering Economics*, Second Edition, New York: McGraw Hill, Inc.

Chapter 11
The MODEL Procedure

Chapter Table of Contents

Chapter 11
The MODEL Procedure

Overview

The MODEL procedure analyzes models in which the relationships among the variables comprise a system of one or more nonlinear equations. Primary uses of the MODEL procedure are estimation, simulation, and forecasting of nonlinear simultaneous equation models.

PROC MODEL features include

- SAS programming statements to define simultaneous systems of nonlinear equations

- tools to analyze the structure of the simultaneous equation system

- ARIMA, PDL, and other dynamic modeling capabilities

- the following methods for parameter estimation for nonlinear systems of equations:

  - Ordinary Least Squares (OLS)
  - Two-Stage Least Squares (2SLS)
  - Seemingly Unrelated Regression (SUR) and iterative SUR (ITSUR)
  - Three-Stage Least Squares (3SLS) and iterative 3SLS (IT3SLS)
  - Generalized Method of Moments (GMM)
  - Full Information Maximum Likelihood (FIML)

- simulation and forecasting capabilities

- Monte Carlo simulation of the model

- goal seeking solutions

A system of equations can be nonlinear in the parameters, nonlinear in the observed variables, or nonlinear in both the parameters and the variables. *Nonlinear* in the parameters means that the mathematical relationship between the variables and parameters is not required to have a linear form. (A linear model is a special case of a nonlinear model.) A general nonlinear system of equations can be written as

$$q_1\left(y_{1,t}, y_{2,t}, \ \cdots \ , y_{g,t}, x_{1,t}, x_{2,t}, \ \cdots \ , x_{m,t}, \theta_1, \theta_2, \ \cdots \ , \theta_p\right) = \epsilon_{1,t}$$

$$q_2\left(y_{1,t}, y_{2,t}, \ \cdots \ , y_{g,t}, x_{1,t}, x_{2,t}, \ \cdots \ , x_{m,t}, \theta_1, \theta_2, \ \cdots \ , \theta_p\right) = \epsilon_{2,t}$$

$$\vdots$$

$$q_g\left(y_{1,t}, y_{2,t}, \ \cdots \ , y_{g,t}, x_{1,t}, x_{2,t}, \ \cdots \ , x_{m,t}, \theta_1, \theta_2, \ \cdots \ , \theta_p\right) = \epsilon_{g,t}$$

where $y_{i,t}$ is an endogenous variable, $x_{i,t}$ is an exogenous variable, θ_i is a parameter, and ϵ_i is the unknown error. The subscript t represents time or some index to the data. In econometrics literature, the observed variables are either *endogenous* (dependent) variables or *exogenous* (independent) variables. This system can be written more succinctly in vector form as

$$\mathbf{q}(\mathbf{y}_t, \mathbf{x}_t, \theta) = \epsilon_t$$

This system of equations is in *general form* because the error term is by itself on one side of the equality. Systems can also be written in *normalized form* by placing the endogenous variable on one side of the equality, with each equation defining a predicted value for a unique endogenous variable. A normalized form equation system can be written in vector notation as

$$\mathbf{y}_t = \mathbf{f}(\mathbf{y}_t, \mathbf{x}_t, \theta) + \epsilon_t$$

PROC MODEL handles equations written in both forms.

Econometric models often explain the current values of the endogenous variables as functions of past values of exogenous and endogenous variables. These past values are referred to as *lagged* values, and the variable x_{t-i} is called lag i of the variable x_t. Using lagged variables, you can create a *dynamic*, or time-dependent, model. In the preceding model systems, the lagged exogenous and endogenous variables are included as part of the exogenous variables.

If the data are time series, so that t indexes time (see Chapter 2, "Working with Time Series Data," for more information on time series), it is possible that ϵ_t depends on ϵ_{t-i} or, more generally, the ϵ_t's are not identically and independently distributed. If the errors of a model system are autocorrelated, the standard error of the estimates of the parameters of the system will be inflated.

Sometimes the ϵ_i's are not identically distributed because the variance of ϵ is not constant. This is known as *heteroscedasticity*. Heteroscedasticity in an estimated model can also inflate the standard error of the estimates of the parameters. Using a weighted estimation can sometimes eliminate this problem. If the proper weighting scheme is difficult to determine, generalized methods of moments (GMM) estimation can be used to determine parameter estimates that are asymptotically more efficient than the OLS parameter estimates.

Other problems may also arise when estimating systems of equations. Consider the system of equations:

$$y_{1,t} = \theta_1 + \left(\theta_2 + \theta_3 \, \theta_4^t\right)^{-1} + \theta_5 y_{2,t} + \epsilon_{1,t}$$
$$y_{2,t} = \theta_6 + \left(\theta_7 + \theta_8 \, \theta_9^t\right)^{-1} + \theta_{10} y_{1,t} + \epsilon_{2,t}$$

which is nonlinear in its parameters and cannot be estimated with linear regression. This system of equations represents a rudimentary predator-prey process with y_1 as the prey and y_2 as the predator (the second term in both equations is a logistics curve). The two equations must be estimated simultaneously because of the cross dependency of y's. Nonlinear ordinary least-squares estimation of these equations will produce biased and inconsistent parameter estimates. This is called *simultaneous equation bias.*

One method to remove simultaneous equation bias, in the linear case, is to replace the endogenous variables on the right-hand side of the equations with predicted values that are uncorrelated with the error terms. These predicted values can be obtained through a preliminary, or first stage, *instrumental variable regression. Instrumental variables*, which are uncorrelated with the error term, are used as regressors to model the predicted values. The parameter estimates are obtained by a second regression using the predicted values of the regressors. This process is called *two-stage least squares.*

In the nonlinear case, nonlinear ordinary least-squares estimation is performed iteratively using a linearization of the model with respect to the parameters. The instrumental solution to simultaneous equation bias in the nonlinear case is the same as the linear case except the linearization of the model with respect to the parameters is predicted by the instrumental regression. Nonlinear two-stage least squares is one of several instrumental variables methods available in the MODEL procedure to handle simultaneous equation bias.

When you have a system of several regression equations, the random errors of the equations can be correlated. In this case, the large-sample efficiency of the estimation can be improved by using a joint generalized least-squares method that takes the cross-equation correlations into account. If the equations are not simultaneous (no dependent regressors), then *seemingly unrelated regression* (SUR) can be used. The SUR method requires an estimate of the cross-equation error covariance matrix, Σ. The usual approach is to first fit the equations using OLS, compute an estimate $\hat{\Sigma}$ from the OLS residuals, and then perform the SUR estimation based on $\hat{\Sigma}$. The MODEL procedure estimates Σ by default, or you can supply your own estimate of Σ.

If the equation system is simultaneous, you can combine the 2SLS and SUR methods to take into account both simultaneous equation bias and cross-equation correlation of the errors. This is called *three-stage least squares* or 3SLS.

A different approach to the simultaneous equation bias problem is the full information maximum likelihood, or FIML, estimation method. FIML does not require instrumental variables, but it assumes that the equation errors have a multivariate normal distribution. 2SLS and 3SLS estimation do not assume a particular distribution for the errors.

Once a nonlinear model has been estimated, it can be used to obtain forecasts. If the model is linear in the variables you want to forecast, a simple linear solve can generate the forecasts. If the system is nonlinear, an iterative procedure must be used. The preceding example system is linear in its endogenous variables. The MODEL procedure's SOLVE statement is used to forecast nonlinear models.

One of the main purposes of creating models is to obtain an understanding of the relationship among the variables. There are usually only a few variables in a model you can control (for example, the amount of money spent on advertising). Often you want to determine how to change the variables under your control to obtain some target goal. This process is called *goal seeking.* PROC MODEL enables you to solve for any subset of the variables in a system of equations given values for the remaining variables.

The nonlinearity of a model creates two problems with the forecasts: the forecast errors are not normally distributed with zero mean, and no formula exits to calculate the forecast confidence intervals. PROC MODEL provides Monte Carlo techniques, which, when used with the covariance of the parameters and error covariance matrix, can produce approximate error bounds on the forecasts.

Getting Started

This section introduces the MODEL procedure and shows how to use PROC MODEL for several kinds of nonlinear regression analysis and nonlinear systems simulation problems.

Nonlinear Regression Analysis

One of the most important uses of PROC MODEL is to estimate unknown parameters in a nonlinear model. A simple nonlinear model has the form

$$y = f(\mathbf{x}, \theta) + \epsilon$$

where $\mathbf{x}$ is a vector of exogenous variables. To estimate unknown parameters using PROC MODEL, do the following:

1. Specify the input SAS data set containing y and $\mathbf{x}$, the observed values of the variables with a DATA= option in a PROC MODEL statement.

2. Write the equation for the model using SAS programming statements, leaving off the unobserved error component, ϵ.

3. Use a FIT statement to fit the model equation to the input data to determine the unknown parameters, θ.

An Example

The SASHELP library contains the data set CITIMON, which contains the variable LHUR, the monthly unemployment figures, and the variable IP, the monthly industrial production index. You suspect that the unemployment rates are inversely proportional to the industrial production index. Assume that these variables are related by the following nonlinear equation:

$$lhur = \frac{1}{a\,ip + b} + c + \epsilon$$

In this equation a, b, and c are unknown coefficients and ϵ is an unobserved random error.

The following statements illustrate how to use PROC MODEL to estimate values for *a*, *b*, and *c* from the data in SASHELP.CITIMON.

```
proc model data=sashelp.citimon;
   lhur = 1/(a * ip + b) + c;
   fit lhur;
run;
```

Notice that the model equation is written as a SAS assignment statement. The variable LHUR is assumed to be the dependent variable because it is named in the FIT statement and is on the left-hand side of the assignment.

PROC MODEL determines that LHUR and IP are observed variables because they are in the input data set. A, B, and C are treated as unknown parameters to be estimated from the data because they are not in the input data set. If the data set contained a variable named A, B, or C, you would need to explicitly declare the parameters with a PARMS statement.

In response to the FIT statement, PROC MODEL estimates values for A, B, and C using nonlinear least squares and prints the results. The first part of the output is a "Model Summary" table, shown in Figure 11.1.

```
                        Model Summary

              Model Variables          1
              Parameters               3
              Equations                1

              Number of Statements     1

                Model Variables: LHUR

                Parameters: A B C

                Equations: LHUR
```

Figure 11.1.   Model Summary Report

This table details the size of the model, including the number of programming statements defining the model, and lists the dependent variables (LHUR in this case), the unknown parameters (A, B, and C), and the model equations. In this case, the equation is named for the dependent variable, LHUR.

PROC MODEL then prints a summary of the estimation problem, as shown in Figure 11.2.

```
              The Equation to Estimate is:

                 LHUR = F( A, B, C(1) )
```

Figure 11.2.   Estimation Problem Report

The notation used in the summary of the estimation problem indicates that LHUR is a function of A, B, and C, which are to be estimated by fitting the function to the data. If the partial derivative of the equation with respect to a parameter is a simple variable or constant, the derivative is shown in parentheses after the parameter name. In this case, the derivative with respect to the intercept C is 1. The derivatives with respect to A and B are complex expressions and so are not shown.

Next, PROC MODEL prints an estimation summary as shown in Figure 11.3.

```
                    MODEL Procedure
                    OLS Estimation

                 OLS Estimation Summary

         Data set Option        Data set
         DATA=             SASHELP.CITIMON

         Parameters Estimated         3

                Minimization Summary
         Method                    GAUSS
         Iterations                   10

         Final  Convergence  Criteria
         R                    0.00073651
         PPC(B)                0.003943
         RPC(B)                0.00968
         Object              4.78441E-6
         Trace(S)             0.53332525
         Objective Value      0.52221431

             Observations Processed
         Read                       145
         Solved                     145
         Used                       144
         Missing                      1
```

Figure 11.3.   Estimation Summary Report

The estimation summary provides information on the iterative process used to compute the estimates. The heading "OLS Estimation Summary" indicates that the nonlinear ordinary least-squares (OLS) estimation method is used. This table indicates that all 3 parameters were estimated successfully using 144 nonmissing observations from the data set SASHELP.CITIMON. Calculating the estimates required 10 iterations of the GAUSS method. Various measures of how well the iterative process converged are also shown. For example, the "RPC(B)" value 0.00968 means that on the final iteration the largest relative change in any estimate was for parameter B, which changed by .968 percent. See the section "Convergence Criteria" later in this chapter for details.

PROC MODEL then prints the estimation results. The first part of this table is the summary of residual errors, shown in Figure 11.4.

```
           Nonlinear OLS Summary of Residual Errors

              DF   DF
Equation   Model Error      SSE        MSE     Root MSE  R-Square  Adj R-Sq

LHUR          3   141    75.19886   0.53333   0.73029    0.7472    0.7436
```

Figure 11.4.   Summary of Residual Errors Report

This table lists the sum of squared errors (SSE), the mean square error (MSE), the root mean square error (Root MSE), and the R^2 and adjusted R^2 statistics. The R^2 value of .7472 means that the estimated model explains approximately 75 percent more of the variability in LHUR than a mean model explains.

Following the summary of residual errors is the parameter estimates table, shown in Figure 11.5.

```
            Nonlinear OLS Parameter Estimates

                                Approx.      'T'     Approx.
    Parameter     Estimate      Std Err     Ratio   Prob>|T|

        A         0.00904632   0.0034343     2.63    0.0094
        B        -0.570595     0.26167      -2.18    0.0309
        C         3.337151     0.72966       4.57    0.0001
```

Figure 11.5. Parameter Estimates

Because the model is nonlinear, the standard error of the estimate, the T ratio, and its significance level are only approximate. These values are computed using asymptotic formulas that are correct for large sample sizes but only approximately correct for smaller samples. Thus, you should use caution in interpreting these statistics for nonlinear models, especially for small sample sizes. For linear models, these results are exact and are the same as standard linear regression.

The last part of the output produced by the FIT statement is shown in Figure 11.6.

```
        Number of Observations      Statistics for System
        Used               144      Objective        0.5222
        Missing              1      Objective*N     75.1989
```

Figure 11.6. System Summary Statistics

This table lists the objective value for the estimation of the nonlinear system, which is a weighted system mean square error. This statistic can be used for testing cross-equation restrictions in multiple-equation regression problems. See the section "Restrictions and Bounds on Parameters" later in this chapter for details. Since there is only a single equation in this case, the objective value is the same as the residual MSE for LHUR except that the objective value does not include a degrees of freedom correction. This can be seen in the fact that "Objective*N" equals the residual SSE, 75.1989. N is 144, the number of observations used.

Convergence and Starting Values

Computing parameter estimates for nonlinear equations requires an iterative process. Starting with an initial guess for the parameter values, PROC MODEL tries different parameter values until the objective function of the estimation method is minimized. (The objective function of the estimation method is sometimes called the *fitting function*.) This process does not always succeed, and whether it does succeed depends greatly on the starting values used. By default, PROC MODEL uses the starting value .0001 for all parameters.

Consequently, to use PROC MODEL for nonlinear regression analysis, you need to know two things: how to recognize convergence failure and interpret diagnostic output, and how to specify reasonable starting values. The MODEL procedure includes alternate iterative techniques and grid search capabilities to aid in finding estimates. See the section "Troubleshooting Convergence Problems" later in this chapter for more details.

Nonlinear Systems Regression

If a model has more than one endogenous variable, several facts need to be considered in the choice of an estimation method. If the model has endogenous regressors, then an instrumental variables method such as 2SLS or 3SLS can be used to avoid simultaneous equation bias. Instrumental variables must be provided to use these methods. A discussion of possible choices for instrumental variables is provided in "Choice of Instruments" later in this chapter.

The following is an example of the use of 2SLS and the INSTRUMENTS statement:

```
proc model data=test2 ;
   exogenous x1 x2;
   parms a1 a2 b2 2.5 c2 55 d1;

   y1 = a1 * y2 + b2 * x1 * x1 + d1;
   y2 = a2 * y1 + b2 * x2 * x2 + c2 / x2 + d1;

   fit y1 y2 / 2sls;
   instruments b2 c2 _exog_;
run;
```

The estimation method selected is added after the slash (/) in the FIT statement. The INSTRUMENTS statement follows the FIT statement and, in this case, selects all the exogenous variables as instruments with the _EXOG_ keyword. The parameters B2 and C2 in the instruments list request that the derivatives with respect to B2 and C2 be additional instruments.

Full information maximum likelihood (FIML) can also be used to avoid simultaneous equation bias. FIML is computationally more expensive than an instrumental variables method and assumes that the errors are normally distributed. On the other hand, FIML does not require the specification of instruments. FIML is selected with the FIML option in the FIT statement.

The preceding example is estimated with FIML using the following statements:

```
proc model data=test2 ;
   exogenous x1 x2;
   parms a1 a2 b2 2.5 c2 55 d1;

   y1 = a1 * y2 + b2 * x1 * x1 + d1;
   y2 = a2 * y1 + b2 * x2 * x2 + c2 / x2 + d1;

   fit y1 y2 / fiml;
run;
```

General Form Models

The single equation example shown in the preceding section was written in normalized form and specified as an assignment of the regression function to the dependent variable LHUR. However, sometimes it is impossible or inconvenient to write a nonlinear model in normalized form.

To write a general form equation, give the equation a name with the prefix "EQ." .

This EQ.-prefixed variable represents the equation error. Write the equation as an assignment to this variable.

For example, suppose you have the following nonlinear model relating the variables x and y:

$$\epsilon = a + b \ln(c\, y + d\, x)$$

Naming this equation ONE, you can fit this model with the following statements:

```
proc model data=xydata;
   eq.one = a + b * log( c * y + d * x );
   fit one;
run;
```

The use of the EQ. prefix tells PROC MODEL that the variable is an error term and that it should not expect actual values for the variable ONE in the input data set.

Demand and Supply Models

General form specifications are often useful when you have several equations for the same dependent variable. This is common in demand and supply models, where both the demand equation and the supply equation are written as predictions for quantity as functions of price.

For example, consider the following demand-and-supply system:

$$\text{(demand)} \quad quantity = \alpha_1 + \alpha_2\, price + \alpha_3\, income + \epsilon_1$$

$$\text{(supply)} \quad quantity = \beta_1 + \beta_2\, price + \epsilon_2$$

Assume the *quantity* of interest is the amount of energy consumed in the U.S.; the *price* is the price of gasoline, and the *income* variable is the consumer debt. When the market is at equilibrium, these equations determine the market price and the equilibrium quantity. These equations are written in general form as

$$\epsilon_1 = quantity - (\alpha_1 + \alpha_2\, price + \alpha_3\, income)$$

$$\epsilon_2 = quantity - (\beta_1 + \beta_2\, price)$$

Note that the endogenous variables *quantity* and *price* depend on two error terms so that OLS should not be used. The following example uses three-stage least-squares estimation:

Data for this model is obtained from the SASHELP.CITIMON data set.

```
title1 'Supply-Demand Model using General-form Equations';
proc model data=sashelp.citimon;
   endogenous eegp eec;
   exogenous exvus cciutc;
   parameters a1 a2 a3 b1 b2 ;
   label eegp   = 'Gasoline Retail Price'
         eec    = 'Energy Consumption'
         cciutc = 'Consumer Debt';

   /* -------- Supply equation ------------- */
   eq.supply = eec - (a1 + a2 * eegp + a3 * cciutc);

   /* -------- Demand equation ------------- */
   eq.demand = eec - (b1 + b2 * eegp );

   /* -------- Instrumental variables -------*/
   lageegp = lag(eegp); lag2eegp=lag2(eegp);

         /* -------- Estimate parameters --------- */
   fit supply demand / n3sls fsrsq;
   instruments _EXOG_ lageegp lag2eegp;
run;
```

The FIT statement specifies the two equations to estimate and the method of estimation, N3SLS. Note that 3SLS is an alias for N3SLS. The option FSRSQ is selected to get a report of the first stage R^2 to determine the viability of the selected instruments.

Since three-stage least squares is an instrumental variables method, instruments are specified with the INSTRUMENTS statement. The instruments selected are all the exogenous variables, selected with the _EXOG_ option, and two lags of the variable EEGP, L and L2.

The data set CITIMON has four observations that generate missing values because values for either EEGP, EEC, or CCIUTC are missing. This is revealed in Figure 11.7, which shows output for the supply-demand observations processed. Missing values are also generated when the equations cannot be computed for a given observation. Missing observations are not used in the estimation.

```
           Observations Processed
           Read                145
           Solved              143
           First                 3
           Last                145
           Used                139
           Missing               4
           Lagged                2
```

Figure 11.7. Supply-Demand Observations Processed

The lags used to create the instruments also reduce the number of observations used. In this case, the first 2 observations were used to fill the lags of EEGP.

The data set has a total of 145 observations, of which four generated missing values and two were used to fill lags, which left 139 observations for the estimation. In the estimation summary, in Figure 11.8, the total degrees of freedom for the model and error is 139.

```
                Supply-Demand Model using General-form Equations

                              MODEL Procedure
                              3SLS Estimation

                  Nonlinear 3SLS Summary of Residual Errors

                  DF      DF
     Equation  Model    Error        SSE         MSE      Root MSE  R-Square  Adj R-Sq

     SUPPLY       3      136     39.57914     0.29102      0.53947
     DEMAND       2      137     43.26774     0.31582      0.56198



                    Nonlinear 3SLS Parameter Estimates

                                    Approx.     'T'    Approx.   1st Stage
         Parameter     Estimate     Std Err    Ratio   Prob>|T|  R-Square


         A1           6.821960     0.37881     18.01    0.0001    1.0000
         A2          -0.00614093   0.0030344   -2.02    0.0450    0.9617
         A3           9.000004E-7  3.16477E-7   2.84    0.0051    1.0000
         B1           7.309520     0.37990     19.24    0.0001    1.0000
         B2          -0.00852965   0.0032793   -2.60    0.0103    0.9617
```

Figure 11.8. Supply-Demand Parameter Estimates

One disadvantage of specifying equations in general form is that there are no actual values associated with the equation, and so the R^2 statistic cannot be computed.

Solving Simultaneous Nonlinear Equation Systems

You can use a SOLVE statement to solve the nonlinear equation system for some variables when the values of other variables are given.

Consider the demand-and-supply model shown in the preceding example. The following statement computes equilibrium price (EEGP) and quantity (EEC) values for given observed cost (CCIUTC) values and stores them in the output data set EQUI-LIB.

```
title1 'Supply-Demand Model using General-form Equations';
proc model data=sashelp.citimon;
   endogenous eegp eec;
   exogenous exvus cciutc;
   parameters a1 a2 a3 b1 b2 ;
   label eegp   = 'Gasoline Retail Price'
         eec    = 'Energy Consumption'
         cciutc = 'Consumer Debt';

   /* -------- Supply equation ------------- */
   eq.supply = eec - (a1 + a2 * eegp + a3 * cciutc);

   /* -------- Demand equation ------------- */
   eq.demand = eec - (b1 + b2 * eegp );

   /* -------- Instrumental variables -------*/
   lageegp = lag(eegp); lag2eegp=lag2(eegp);

        /* -------- Estimate parameters --------- */
   instruments _EXOG_ lageegp lag2eegp;
   fit supply demand / n3sls ;
   solve eegp eec / out=equilib;
run;
```

As a second example, suppose you want to compute points of intersection between the square root function and hyperbolas of the form $a + b/x$; that is, you want to solve the system

(square root) $y = \sqrt{x}$

(hyperbola) $y = a + \dfrac{b}{x}$

The following statements read parameters for several hyperbolas in the input data set TEST and solve the nonlinear equations. The SOLVEPRINT option in the SOLVE statement prints the solution values. The ID statement is used to include the values of A and B in the output of the SOLVEPRINT option.

```
data test;
  input a b @@;
  cards;
  0 1   1 1   1 2
;

proc model data=test;
  eq.sqrt       = sqrt(x) - y;
  eq.hyperbola = a + b / x - y;
  solve x y / solveprint;
  id a b;
run;
```

The printed output produced by this example consists of a model summary report, a listing of the solution values for each observation, and a solution summary report. The model summary for this example is shown in Figure 11.9.

```
                           Model Summary

                    Model Variables         2
                    ID Variables            2
                    Equations               2

                    Number of Statements    2

                    Model Variables: X Y

                    Equations: SQRT HYPERBOLA
```

Figure 11.9. Model Summary Report

The output produced by the SOLVEPRINT option is shown in Figure 11.10.

```
Observation 1. A=0 B=1.000000 NEWTON Iterations=17 CC=9.176E-9(EQ.HYPERBOLA=9.18E-9)

Solution Values:
X:    1.0000 Y:    1.0000

Observation 2. A=1.000000 B=1.000000 NEWTON Iterations=5 CC=1.243E-14(EQ.HYPERBOLA=1.24E-14)

Solution Values:
X:    2.1479 Y:    1.4656

Observation 3. A=1.000000 B=2.000000 NEWTON Iterations=4 CC=4.416E-13(EQ.HYPERBOLA=4.42E-13)

Solution Values:
X:    2.8751 Y:    1.6956
```

Figure 11.10.   Solution Values for Each Observation

For each observation, a heading line is printed that lists the values of the ID variables for the observation and information on the iterative process used to compute the solution. Following the heading line for the observation, the solution values are printed.

The heading line shows the solution method used (Newton's method by default), the number of iterations required, and the convergence measure, labeled CC=. This convergence measure indicates the maximum error by which solution values fail to satisfy the equations. When this error is small enough (as determined by the CONVERGE= option), the iterations terminate. The equation with the largest error is indicated in parentheses. For example, for observation 3 the HYPERBOLA equation has an error of 4.42×10^{-13}, while the error of the SQRT equation is even smaller.

The last part of the SOLVE statement output is the solution summary report shown in Figure 11.11. This report summarizes the iteration history and the model solved.

```
                         Solution Summary

                 Data set Option        Data set
                 DATA=                   TEST

                 Variables Solved          2
                    Implicit Equations     2

                 Solution Method         NEWTON
                 CONVERGE=               1E-8
                 Maximum CC                0
                 Maximum Iterations       17
                 Total Iterations         26
                 Average Iterations     8.67

                    Observations Processed
                 Read                      3
                 Solved                    3

            Variables Solved For: X Y

            Equations Solved: SQRT HYPERBOLA
```

Figure 11.11. Solution Summary Report

Monte Carlo Simulation

The RANDOM= option is used to request Monte Carlo (or stochastic) simulation to generate confidence intervals for a forecast. The confidence intervals are implied by the model's relationship to the implicit random error term ϵ and the parameters.

The Monte Carlo simulation generates a random set of additive error values, one for each observation and each equation, and computes one set of perturbations of the parameters. These new parameters, along with the additive error terms, are then used to compute a new forecast that satisfies this new simultaneous system. Then a new set of additive error values and parameter perturbations is computed, and the process is repeated the requested number of times.

Consider the following exchange rate model for the U.S. dollar with the German mark and the Japanese yen:

$$rate\_jp = a_1 + b_1 im\_jp + c_1 di\_jp;$$

$$rate\_wg = a_2 + b_2 im\_wg + c_1 di\_wg;$$

where *rate_jp* and *rate_wg* are the exchange rate of the Japanese yen and the German mark versus the U.S. dollar respectively; *im_jp* and *im_wg* are the imports from Japan and Germany in 1984 dollars respectively; and *di_jp* and *di_wg* are the differences in the inflation rate of Japan and the U.S., and Germany and the U.S., respectively. The Monte Carlo capabilities of the MODEL procedure are used to generate error bounds on a forecast using this model.

```
proc model data=exchange;
   endo im_jp im_wg;
   exo di_jp di_wg;
   parms a1 a2 b1 b2 c1 c2;
   label rate_jp = 'Exchange Rate of Yen/$'
         rate_wg = 'Exchange Rate of Gm/$'
         im_jp = 'Imports to US from Japan in 1984 $'
         im_wg = 'Imports to US from WG in 1984 $'
         di_jp = 'Difference in Inflation Rates US-JP'
         di_wg = 'Difference in Inflation Rates US-WG';

   rate_jp = a1 + b1*im_jp + c1*di_jp;
   rate_wg = a2 + b2*im_wg + c2*di_wg;

            /* Fit the EXCHANGE data */
   fit rate_jp rate_wg / sur outest=xch_est outcov outs=s;

            /* Solve using the WHATIF data set */
   solve rate_jp rate_wg / data=whatif estdata=xch_est sdata=s
         random=100 seed=123 out=monte forecast;
   id yr;
   range yr=1986;
run;
```

Data for the EXCHANGE data set was obtained from the Department of Commerce and the yearly "Economic Report of the President."

First, the parameters are estimated using SUR selected by the SUR option in the FIT statement. The OUTEST= option is used to create the XCH_EST data set that contains the estimates of the parameters. The OUTCOV option adds the covariance matrix of the parameters to the XCH_EST data set. The OUTS= option is used to save the covariance of the equation error in the data set S.

Next, Monte Carlo simulation is requested using the RANDOM= option in the SOLVE statement. The data set WHATIF, shown in Figure 11.12, is used to drive the forecasts. The ESTDATA= option reads in the XCH_EST data set that contains the parameter estimates and covariance matrix. Because the parameter covariance matrix is included, perturbations of the parameters are performed. The SDATA= option causes the Monte Carlo simulation to use the equation error covariance in the S data set to perturb the equation errors. The SEED= option selects the number 123 as seed value for the random number generator. The output of the Monte Carlo simulation is written to the data set MONTE selected by the OUT= option.

```
                     /* data for simulation */
          data whatif;
             input yr rate_jp rate_wg imn_jp imn_wg emp_us emp_jp emp_wg
                prod_us / prod_jp prod_wg cpi_us cpi_jp cpi_wg;
             label cpi_us = 'US CPI 1982-1984 = 100'
                   cpi_jp = 'JP CPI 1982-1984 = 100'
                   cpi_wg = 'WG CPI 1982-1984 = 100';
             im_jp = imn_jp/cpi_us;
             im_wg = imn_wg/cpi_us;
             ius = 100*(cpi_us-(lag(cpi_us)))/(lag(cpi_us));
             ijp = 100*(cpi_jp-(lag(cpi_jp)))/(lag(cpi_jp));
             iwg = 100*(cpi_wg-(lag(cpi_wg)))/(lag(cpi_wg));
             di_jp = ius - ijp;
             di_wg = ius - iwg;
          cards;
          1980 226.63 1.8175 30714 11693 103.3 101.3 100.4 101.7
                125.4 109.8  .824  .909  .868
          1981 220.63 2.2631 35000 11000 102.8 102.2  97.9 104.6
                126.3 112.8  .909  .954  .922
          1982 249.06 2.4280 40000 12000  95.8 101.4  95.0 107.1
                146.8 113.3  .965  .980  .970
          1983 237.55 2.5539 45000 13100  94.4 103.4  91.1 111.6
                152.8 116.8  .996  .999 1.003
          1984 237.45 2.8454 50000 14300  99.0 105.8  90.4 118.5
                152.2 124.7 1.039 1.021 1.027
          1985 238.47 2.9419 55000 15600  98.1 107.6  91.3 124.2
                161.1 128.5 1.076 1.042 1.048
          1986   .      .    60000 17000  96.8 107.3  92.7 128.8
                163.8 130.7 1.096 1.049 1.047
          1987   .      .    65000 18500  97.1 106.1  92.8 132.0
                176.5 129.9 1.136 1.050 1.049
          1988   .      .    70000 20000  99.6 108.8  92.7 136.2
                190.0 135.9 1.183 1.057 1.063
          ;
```

Figure 11.12. The WHATIF Data Set

To generate a confidence interval plot for the forecast, use PROC UNIVARIATE to generate percentile bounds and PROC GPLOT to plot the graph. The following SAS statements produce the graph in Figure 11.13.

```
proc sort data=monte;
   by yr;
run;

proc univariate data=monte noprint;
   by yr;
   var rate_jp rate_wg;
   output out=bounds mean=mean p5=p5 p95=p95;
run;

title "Monte Carlo Generated Confidence Intervals on a Forecast";
proc gplot data=bounds;
   plot mean*yr p5*yr p95*yr /overlay;
   symbol1 i=join value=triangle;
   symbol2 i=join value=square l=4;
   symbol3 i=join value=square l=4;
run;
```

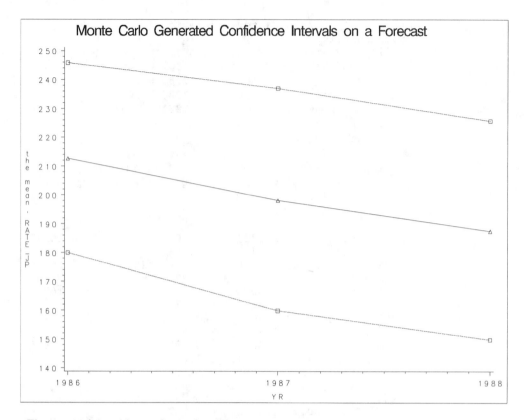

Figure 11.13.   Monte Carlo Confidence Interval Plot

Syntax

The following statements can be used with the MODEL procedure:

> **PROC MODEL** *options*;
>   **ABORT** ;
>   **ARRAY** *arrayname variables* **...** ;
>   **ATTRIB** *variable-list attribute-list* [*variable-list attribute-list*];
>   **BY** *variables*;
>   **CALL** *name* [**(** *expression* [**,** *expression* **...**] **)**] ;
>   **CONTROL** *variable* [*value*] **...** ;
>   **DELETE** ;
>   **DO** [*variable* **=** *expression* [**TO** *expression*] [**BY** *expression*]
>   [**,** *expression* [**TO** *expression*] [**BY** *expression*] **...**]]
>   [**WHILE** *expression*] [**UNTIL** *expression*] ;
>   **END** ;
>   **DROP** *variable* **...** ;
>   **ENDOGENOUS** *variable* [*initial values*] **...** ;
>   **EXOGENOUS** *variable* [*initial values*] **...** ;
>   **FIT** *equations* [**PARMS=** (*parameter values* **...**)]
>   [**START=** (*parameter values* **...**)]
>   [**DROP=** (*parameters*)] [**/** *options*];
>   **FORMAT** *variables* [*format*] [**DEFAULT =** *default-format*];

GOTO *statement_label* ;
ID *variables*;
IF *expression* ;
IF *expression* **THEN** *programming_statement* ;
  ELSE *programming_statement* ;
variable = *expression* ;
variable + *expression* ;
INCLUDE *model files* ... ;
INSTRUMENTS [*instruments*] [**_EXOG_**]
    [**EXCLUDE**= (*parameters*)] [/ *options*] ;
KEEP *variable* ... ;
LABEL *variable* = '*label*' ... ;
LENGTH *variables* [**$**] *length* ... [**DEFAULT**= *length*];
LINK *statement_label* ;
OUTVARS *variable* ... ;
PARAMETERS *variable* [*value*] *variable* [*value*] ... ;
PUT *print_item* ... [**@**] [**@@**] ;
RANGE *variable* [= *first*] [**TO** *last*];
RENAME *old-name* = *new-name* ... [*old-name*= *new-name*];
RESET *options*;
RETAIN *variables values* [*variables values*...] ;
RETURN ;
SOLVE *variables* [**SATISFY**= (*equations*)] [/ *options*] ;
SUBSTR(*variable, index, length*) = *expression* ;
SELECT [(*expression*)] ;
  OTHERWISE *programming_statement* ;
STOP ;
VAR *variable* [*initial values*] ... ;
WEIGHT *variable*;
WHEN (*expression*) *programming_statement* ;

Functional Summary

The statements and options in the MODEL procedure are summarized in the following table.

Description	Statement	Option
Data Set Options		
specify the input data set for the variables	FIT, SOLVE	DATA=
specify the input data set for parameters	FIT, SOLVE	ESTDATA=
specify the input data set for parameters	MODEL	PARMSDATA=
specify the output data set for residual, predicted, or actual values	FIT	OUT=

Description	Statement	Option
specify the output data set for solution mode results	SOLVE	OUT=
write the actual values to OUT= data set	FIT	OUTACTUAL
select all output options	FIT	OUTALL
write the covariance matrix of the estimates	FIT	OUTCOV
write the parameter estimates to a data set	FIT	OUTEST=
write the parameter estimates to a data set	MODEL	OUTPARMS=
write the observations used to start the lags	SOLVE	OUTLAGS
write the predicted values to the OUT= data set	FIT	OUTPREDICT
write the residual values to the OUT= data set	FIT	OUTRESID
write the covariance matrix of the equation errors to a data set	FIT	OUTS=
write the **S** matrix used in the objective function definition to a data set	FIT	OUTSUSED=
write the estimate of the variance matrix of the moment generating function	FIT	OUTV=
read the covariance matrix of the equation errors	FIT, SOLVE	SDATA=
read the covariance matrix for GMM and ITG-MM	FIT	VDATA=
select the estimation type to read	FIT, SOLVE	TYPE=

Printing Options for FIT Tasks

print collinearity diagnostics	FIT	COLLIN
print the correlation matrices	FIT	CORR
print the correlation matrix of the parameters	FIT	CORRB
print the correlation matrix of the residuals	FIT	CORRS
print the covariance matrices	FIT	COV
print the covariance matrix of the parameters	FIT	COVB
print the covariance matrix of the residuals	FIT	COVS
print Durbin-Watson d statistics	FIT	DW
print first-stage R^2 statistics	FIT	FSRSQ
specify all the printing options	FIT	PRINTALL

Options to Control FIT Iteration Output

print the inverse of the crossproducts Jacobian matrix	FIT	I
print a summary iteration listing	FIT	ITPRINT
print a detailed iteration listing	FIT	ITDETAILS
print the crossproduct Jacobian matrix	FIT	XPX

Description	Statement	Option
specify all the iteration printing-control options	FIT	ITALL

Options to Control the Minimization Process

Description	Statement	Option
specify the convergence criteria	FIT	CONVERGE=
specify the number of minimization iterations to perform at each grid point	FIT	STARTITER=
select the Hessian approximation used for FIML	FIT	HESSIAN=
specify the maximum number of iterations allowed	FIT	MAXITER=
specify the maximum number of subiterations allowed	FIT	MAX-SUBITER=
select the iterative minimization method to use	FIT	METHOD=
modify the iterations for estimation methods that iterate the **S** matrix or the **V** matrix	FIT	NESTIT
specify a weight variable	WEIGHT	

Options to Read and Write Model Files

Description	Statement	Option
read a model from one or more input model files	INCLUDE	MODEL=
suppress the default output of the model file	MODEL, RESET	NOSTORE
specify the name of an output model file	MODEL, RESET	OUTMODEL=
delete the current model	RESET	PURGE

Options to List or Analyze the Structure of the Model

Description	Statement	Option
print a dependency structure of a model	MODEL	BLOCK
print a graph of the dependency structure of a model	MODEL	GRAPH
print the model program and variable lists	MODEL	LIST
print the derivative tables and compiled model program code	MODEL	LISTCODE
print a dependency list	MODEL	LISTDEP
print a table of derivatives	MODEL	LISTDER
print a cross-reference of the variables	MODEL	XREF

General Printing Control Options

Description	Statement	Option
expand parts of the printed output	FIT, SOLVE	DETAILS
print a message for each statement as it is executed	FIT, SOLVE	FLOW
select the maximum number of execution errors that can be printed	FIT, SOLVE	MAXER-RORS=

Description	Statement	Option
select the number of decimal places shown in the printed output	FIT, SOLVE	NDEC=
suppress the normal printed output	FIT, SOLVE	NOPRINT
specify all the noniteration printing options	FIT, SOLVE	PRINTALL
print the result of each operation as it is executed	FIT, SOLVE	TRACE

Statements that Declare Variables

Description	Statement	Option
associate a name with a list of variables and constants	ARRAY	
declare a variable to have a fixed value	CONTROL	
declare a variable to be a dependent or endogenous variable	ENDOGENOUS	
declare a variable to be an independent or exogenous variable	EXOGENOUS	
specify identifying variables	ID	
assign a label to a variable	LABEL	
select additional variables to be output	OUTVARS	
declare a variable to be a parameter	PARAMETERS	
force a variable to hold its value from a previous observation	RETAIN	
declare a model variable	VAR	
declare an instrumental variable	INSTRUMENTS	
omit the default intercept term in the instruments list	INSTRUMENTS	NOINT

General FIT Statement Options

Description	Statement	Option
omit parameters from the estimation	FIT	DROP=
specify the parameters to estimate	FIT	PARMS=
select a grid search	FIT	START=

Options to Control the Estimation Method Used

Description	Statement	Option
specify nonlinear ordinary least squares	FIT	OLS
specify iterated nonlinear ordinary least squares	FIT	ITOLS
specify seemingly unrelated regression	FIT	SUR
specify iterated seemingly unrelated regression	FIT	ITSUR
specify two-stage least squares	FIT	2SLS
specify iterated two-stage least squares	FIT	IT2SLS
specify three-stage least squares	FIT	3SLS
specify iterated three-stage least squares	FIT	IT3SLS
specify full information maximum likelihood	FIT	FIML

Description	Statement	Option
select the variance-covariance estimator used for FIML	FIT	COVBEST=
specify generalized method of moments	FIT	GMM
specify the kernel for GMM and ITGMM	FIT	KERNEL=
specify iterated generalized method of moments	FIT	ITGMM
specify the denominator for computing variances and covariances	FIT	VARDEF=

Solution Mode Options

Description	Statement	Option
select a subset of the model equations	SOLVE	SATISFY=
solve only for missing variables	SOLVE	FORECAST
solve for all solution variables	SOLVE	SIMULATE

Solution Mode Options: Lag Processing

Description	Statement	Option
use solved values in the lag functions	SOLVE	DYNAMIC
use actual values in the lag functions	SOLVE	STATIC
produce successive forecasts to a fixed forecast horizon	SOLVE	NAHEAD=
select the observation to start dynamic solutions	SOLVE	START=

Solution Mode Options: Numerical Methods

Description	Statement	Option
specify the maximum number of iterations allowed	SOLVE	MAXITER=
specify the maximum number of subiterations allowed	SOLVE	MAXSUBITER=
specify the convergence criteria	SOLVE	CONVERGE=
compute a simultaneous solution using a Jacobi-like iteration	SOLVE	JACOBI
compute a simultaneous solution using a Gauss-Seidel-like iteration	SOLVE	SEIDEL
compute a simultaneous solution using Newton's method	SOLVE	NEWTON
compute a nonsimultaneous solution	SOLVE	SINGLE

Monte Carlo Simulation Options

Description	Statement	Option
repeat the solution multiple times	SOLVE	RANDOM=
initialize the pseudo-random number generator	SOLVE	SEED=

Description	Statement	Option
Solution Mode Printing Options		
print the solution approximation and equation errors	SOLVE	ITPRINT
print the solution values and residuals at each observation	SOLVE	SOLVEPRINT
print various summary statistics	SOLVE	STATS
print tables of Theil inequality coefficients	SOLVE	THEIL
specify all printing control options	SOLVE	PRINTALL
Miscellaneous Statements		
specify the range of observations to be used	RANGE	
specify BY-group processing	BY	

PROC MODEL Statement

> **PROC MODEL** *options*;

The following options can be specified in the PROC MODEL statement. All of the nonassignment options (the options that do not accept a value after an equal sign) can have NO prefixed to the option name in the RESET statement to turn the option off. The default case is not explicitly indicated in the discussion that follows. Thus, for example, the option DETAILS is documented in the following, but NODETAILS is not documented since it is the default. Also, the NOSTORE option is documented because STORE is the default.

Data Set Options

DATA= *SAS-data-set*
> names the input data set. Variables in the model program are looked up in the DATA= data set and, if found, their attributes (type, length, label, format) are set to be the same as those in the input data set (if not previously defined otherwise). The values for the variables in the program are read from the input data set when the model is estimated or simulated by FIT and SOLVE statements.

OUTPARMS= *SAS-data-set*
> writes the parameter estimates to a SAS data set. See "Output Data Sets" later in this chapter for details.

PARMSDATA= *SAS-data-set*
> names the SAS data set that contains the parameter estimates. See "Input Data Sets" later in this chapter for details.

Options to Read and Write Model Files

MODEL= *model-name*
MODEL= (*model-list*)

> reads the model from one or more input model files created by previous PROC MODEL executions. Model files are written by the OUTMODEL= option.

NOSTORE

> suppresses the default output of the model file. This option is only applicable when FIT or SOLVE statements are not used, when the MODEL= option is not used, and when a model is specified.

OUTMODEL= *model-name*

> specifies the name of an output model file to which the model is to be written. Model files are stored as members of a SAS catalog, with the type MODEL.

V5MODEL= *model-name*

> reads model files written by Version 5 of SAS/ETS software

Options to List or Analyze the Structure of the Model

These options produce reports on the structure of the model or list the programming statements defining the models. These options are automatically reset (turned off) after the reports are printed. To turn these options back on after a RUN statement has been entered, use the RESET statement or specify the options in a FIT or SOLVE statement.

BLOCK

> prints an analysis of the structure of the model given by the assignments to model variables appearing in the model program. This analysis includes a classification of model variables into endogenous (dependent) and exogenous (independent) groups based on the presence of the variable on the left-hand side of an assignment statement. The endogenous variables are grouped into simultaneously determined blocks. The dependency structure of the simultaneous blocks and exogenous variables is also printed. The BLOCK option cannot analyze dependencies implied by general form equations.

GRAPH

> prints the graph of the dependency structure of the model. The GRAPH option also invokes the BLOCK option and produces a graphical display of the information listed by the BLOCK option.

LIST

> prints the model program and variable lists, including the statements added by PROC MODEL and macros

LISTALL

> selects the LIST, LISTDEP, LISTDER, and LISTCODE options

LISTCODE

> prints the derivative tables and compiled model program code. LISTCODE is a debugging feature and is not normally needed.

LISTDEP

prints a report that lists for each variable in the model program the variables that depend on it and that it depends on. These lists are given separately for current-period values and for lagged values of the variables.

The information displayed is the same as that used to construct the BLOCK report but differs in that the information is listed for all variables (including parameters, control variables, and program variables), not just the model variables. Classification into endogenous and exogenous groups and analysis of simultaneous structure is not done by the LISTDEP report.

LISTDER

prints a table of derivatives for FIT and SOLVE tasks. (The LISTDER option is only applicable for the default NEWTON method for SOLVE tasks.) The derivatives table shows each nonzero derivative computed for the problem. The derivative listed can be a constant, a variable in the model program, or a special derivative variable created to hold the result of the derivative expression. This option is turned on by the LISTCODE and PRINTALL options.

XREF

prints a cross-reference of the variables in the model program showing where each variable was referenced or given a value. The XREF option is normally used in conjunction with the LIST option. A more detailed description is given in "Diagnostics and Debugging" later in this chapter.

General Printing Control Options

DETAILS

specifies the detailed printout. Parts of the printed output are expanded when the DETAILS option is specified.

FLOW

prints a message for each statement in the model program as it is executed. This debugging option is needed very rarely and produces voluminous output.

MAXERRORS= *n*

specifies the maximum number of execution errors that can be printed. The default is MAXERRORS=50.

NDEC= *n*

specifies the precision of the format that PROC MODEL uses when printing various numbers. The default is NDEC=3, which means that PROC MODEL attempts to print values using the D format but ensures that at least three significant digits are shown. If the NDEC= value is greater than nine, the BEST. format is used. The smallest value allowed is NDEC=2.

The NDEC= option affects the format of most, but not all, of the floating point numbers that PROC MODEL can print. For some values (such as parameter estimates), a precision limit one or two digits greater than the NDEC= value is used. This option does not apply to the precision of the variables in the output data set.

NOPRINT

suppresses the normal printed output but does not suppress error listings. Using any other print option turns the NOPRINT option off. The PRINT option can be used with the RESET statement to turn off NOPRINT.

PRINTALL

turns on all the printing control options. The options set by PRINTALL are DETAILS; the model information options LIST, LISTDEP, LISTDER, XREF, BLOCK, and GRAPH; the FIT task printing options FSRSQ, COVB, CORRB, COVS, CORRS, DW, and COLLIN; and the SOLVE task printing options STATS, THEIL, SOLVEPRINT, and ITPRINT.

TRACE

prints the result of each operation in each statement in the model program as it is executed, in addition to the information printed by the FLOW option. This debugging option is needed very rarely and produces voluminous output.

FIT Task Options

The following options are used in the FIT statement (parameter estimation) and can also be used in the PROC MODEL statement: COLLIN, CONVERGE=, CORR, CORRB, CORRS, COVB, COVBEST=, COVS, DW, FIML, FSRSQ, GMM, HESSIAN=, I, ITALL, ITDETAILS, ITGMM, ITPRINT, ITOLS, ITSUR, IT2SLS, IT3SLS, KERNEL=, MAXITER=, MAXSUBITER=, METHOD=, NESTIT, N2SLS, N3SLS, OLS, OUTPREDICT, OUTRESID, OUTACTUAL, OUTLAGS, OUTERRORS, OUTALL, OUTCOV, SINGULAR=, STARTITER=, SUR, VARDEF, and XPX. See the syntax section in "FIT Statement" later in this chapter for a description of these options.

When used in the PROC MODEL or RESET statement, these are default options for subsequent FIT statements. For example, the statement

```
proc model n2sls ... ;
```

makes two-stage least squares the default parameter estimation method for FIT statements that do not specify an estimation method.

SOLVE Task Options

The following options used in the SOLVE statement can also be used in the PROC MODEL statement: CONVERGE=, DYNAMIC, FORECAST, ITPRINT, JACOBI, MAXITER=, MAXSUBITER=, NAHEAD=, NEWTON, OUTPREDICT, OUTRESID, OUTACTUAL, OUTLAGS, OUTERRORS, OUTALL, SEED=, SEIDEL, SIMULATE, SINGLE, SINGULAR=, SOLVEPRINT, START=, STATIC, STATS, THEIL, and TYPE=. See the syntax section in "SOLVE Statement" later in this chapter for a description of these options.

When used in the PROC MODEL or RESET statement, these options provide default values for subsequent SOLVE statements.

BY Statement

> **BY** *variables*;

A BY statement is used with the FIT statement to obtain separate estimates for observations in groups defined by the BY variables. Note that if an output model file is written using the OUTMODEL= option, the parameter values stored are those from the last BY group processed. To save parameter estimates for each BY group, use the OUTEST= option in the FIT statement.

A BY statement is used with the SOLVE statement to obtain solutions for observations in groups defined by the BY variables. The BY statement only applies to the DATA= data set.

BY-group processing is done separately for the FIT and the SOLVE tasks. It is not possible to use the BY statement to estimate and solve a model for each instance of a BY variable. If BY-group processing is done for the FIT and the SOLVE tasks, the parameters obtained from the last BY group processed by the FIT statement are used by the SOLVE statement for all of the BY groups.

CONTROL Statement

> **CONTROL** *variable* [*value*] ... ;

The CONTROL statement declares control variables and specifies their values. A control variable is like a parameter except that it has a fixed value and is not estimated from the data. You can use control variables for constants in model equations that you may want to change in different solution cases. You can use control variables to vary the program logic.

ENDOGENOUS Statement

> **ENDOGENOUS** *variable* [*initial-values*] ... ;

The ENDOGENOUS statement declares model variables and identifies them as endogenous. You can declare model variables with an ENDOGENOUS statement instead of with a VAR statement to help document the model or to indicate the default solution variables. The variables declared endogenous are solved when a SOLVE statement does not indicate which variables to solve. Valid abbreviations for the ENDOGENOUS statement are ENDOG and ENDO.

The ENDOGENOUS statement optionally provides initial values for lagged dependent variables. See "Lag Logic" in the section "Functions Across Time" for more information.

EXOGENOUS Statement

EXOGENOUS *variable* [*initial-values*] ... ;

The EXOGENOUS statement declares model variables and identifies them as exogenous. You can declare model variables with an EXOGENOUS statement instead of with a VAR statement to help document the model or to indicate the default instrumental variables. The variables declared exogenous are used as instruments when an instrumental variables estimation method is requested (such as N2SLS or N3SLS) and an INSTRUMENTS statement is not used. Valid abbreviations for the EXOGENOUS statement are EXOG and EXO.

The EXOGENOUS statement optionally provides initial values for lagged exogenous variables. See "Lag Logic" in the section "Functions Across Time" for more information.

FIT Statement

FIT [*equations*] [**PARMS**= (*parameter* [*values*] ...)]
   [**START**= (*parameter values* ...)]
   [**DROP**= (*parameter* ...)]
   [/ *options*] ;

The FIT statement estimates model parameters by fitting the model equations to input data and optionally selects the equations to be fit. If the list of equations is omitted, all model equations containing parameters are fit.

The following options can be used in the FIT statement:

DROP= (*parameters* ...)
   specifies that the named parameters not be estimated. All the parameters in the equations fit are estimated except those listed in the DROP= option. The dropped parameters retain their previous values and are not changed by the estimation.

PARMS= (*parameters* [*values*] ...)
   selects a subset of the parameters for estimation. When the PARMS= option is used, only the named parameters are estimated. Any parameters not specified in the PARMS= list retain their previous values and are not changed by the estimation.

START= (*parameter values* ...)
   supplies starting values for the parameter estimates. If the START= option specifies more than one starting value for one or more parameters, a grid search is performed over all combinations of the values, and the best combination is used to start the iterations. For more information, see the STARTITER= option.

Options to Control the Estimation Method Used

COVBEST= GLS | CROSS | FDA

specifies the variance-covariance estimator used for FIML. COVBEST=GLS selects the generalized least-squares estimator. COVBEST=CROSS selects the crossproducts estimator. COVBEST=FDA selects the inverse of the finite difference approximation to the Hessian. The default is COVBEST=CROSS.

FIML

specifies full information maximum likelihood estimation

GMM

specifies generalized method of moments estimation

ITGMM

specifies iterated generalized method of moments estimation

ITOLS

specifies iterated ordinary least-squares estimation. This is the same as OLS unless there are cross-equation parameter restrictions.

ITSUR

specifies iterated seemingly unrelated regression estimation

IT2SLS

specifies iterated two-stage least-squares estimation. This is the same as 2SLS unless there are cross-equation parameter restrictions.

IT3SLS

specifies iterated three-stage least-squares estimation

KERNEL= (PARZEN | BART | QS, [*c*], [*e*])
KERNEL= PARZEN | BART | QS

specifies the kernel to be used for GMM and ITGMM. PARZEN selects the Parzen kernel, BART selects the Bartlett kernel, and QS selects the Quadratic Spectral kernel. $e \geq 0$ and $c \geq 0$ are used to compute the bandwidth parameter. The default is KERNEL=(PARZEN, 1, 0.2). See "Estimation Methods" later in this chapter for more details.

N2SLS | 2SLS

specifies nonlinear two-stage least-squares estimation. This is the default when an INSTRUMENTS statement is used.

N3SLS | 3SLS

specifies nonlinear three-stage least-squares estimation

OLS

specifies ordinary least-squares estimation. This is the default when no INSTRUMENTS statement is used.

SUR

specifies seemingly unrelated regression estimation

VARDEF= N | WGT | DF | WDF

specifies the denominator to be used in computing variances and covariances. VARDEF=N specifies that the number of nonmissing observations be used. VARDEF=WGT specifies that the sum of the weights be used. VARDEF=DF specifies that the number of nonmissing observations minus the model degrees of freedom (number of parameters) be used. VARDEF=WDF specifies that the sum of the weights minus the model degrees of freedom be used. The default is VARDEF=DF. VARDEF=N is used for FIML estimation.

Data Set Options

DATA= *SAS-data-set*

specifies the input data set. Values for the variables in the program are read from this data set. If the DATA= option is not specified in the FIT statement, the data set specified by the DATA= option in the PROC MODEL statement is used.

ESTDATA= *SAS-data-set*

specifies a data set whose first observation provides initial values for some or all of the parameters

OUT= *SAS-data-set*

names the SAS data set to contain the residuals, predicted values, or actual values from each estimation. Only the residuals are output by default.

OUTACTUAL

writes the actual values of the endogenous variables of the estimation to the OUT= data set. This option is applicable only if the OUT= option is specified.

OUTALL

selects the OUTACTUAL, OUTERRORS, OUTLAGS, OUTPREDICT, and OUTRESID options

OUTCOV
COVOUT

writes the covariance matrix of the estimates to the OUTEST= data set in addition to the parameter estimates. The OUTCOV option is applicable only if the OUT-EST= option is also specified.

OUTEST= *SAS-data-set*

names the SAS data set to contain the parameter estimates and, optionally, the covariance of the estimates

OUTLAGS

writes the observations used to start the lags to the OUT= data set. This option is applicable only if the OUT= option is specified.

OUTPREDICT

writes the predicted values to the OUT= data set. This option is applicable only if OUT= is specified.

OUTRESID

writes the residual values computed from the parameter estimates to the OUT= data set. The OUTRESID option is the default if neither OUTPREDICT nor OUTACTUAL is specified. This option is applicable only if the OUT= option is specified.

OUTS= *SAS-data-set*

names the SAS data set to contain the estimated covariance matrix of the equation errors. This is the covariance of the residuals computed from the parameter estimates.

OUTSUSED= *SAS-data-set*

names the SAS data set to contain the S matrix used in the objective function definition. The OUTSUSED= data set is the same as the OUTS= data set for the methods that iterate the S matrix.

OUTV= *SAS-data-set*

names the SAS data set to contain the estimate of the variance matrix for GMM and ITGMM

SDATA= *SAS-data-set*

specifies a data set that provides the covariance matrix of the equation errors. The matrix read from the SDATA= data set is used for the equation covariance matrix (S matrix) in the estimation. (The SDATA= S matrix is used to provide only the initial estimate of S for the methods that iterate the S matrix.)

TYPE= *name*

specifies the estimation type to read from the SDATA= and ESTDATA= data sets. The name specified in the TYPE= option is compared to the _TYPE_ variable in the ESTDATA= and SDATA= data sets to select observations to use in constructing the covariance matrices. When the TYPE= option is omitted, the last estimation type in the data set is used. Valid values are the estimation methods used in PROC MODEL.

VDATA= *SAS-data-set*

specifies a data set containing a variance matrix for GMM and ITGMM estimation

Printing Options for FIT Tasks

COLLIN

prints collinearity diagnostics for the Jacobian crossproducts matrix (XPX) after the parameters have converged. Collinearity diagnostics are also automatically printed if the estimation fails to converge.

CORR

prints the correlation matrices of the residuals and parameters. Using CORR is the same as using both CORRB and CORRS.

CORRB

prints the correlation matrix of the parameter estimates

CORRS

prints the correlation matrix of the residuals

COV

prints the covariance matrices of the residuals and parameters. Specifying COV is the same as specifying both COVB and COVS.

COVB

prints the covariance matrix of the parameter estimates

COVS

prints the covariance matrix of the residuals

DW

prints Durbin-Watson d statistics, which measure autocorrelation of the residuals. When the residual series is interrupted by missing observations, the Durbin-Watson statistic calculated is d' as suggested by Savin and White (1978). This is the usual Durbin-Watson computed by ignoring the gaps. Savin and White show that it has the same null distribution as the DW with no gaps in the series and can be used to test for autocorrelation using the standard tables. The Durbin-Watson statistic is not valid for models containing lagged endogenous variables.

FSRSQ

prints the first-stage R^2 statistics for instrumental estimation methods. These R^2s measure the proportion of the variance retained when the Jacobian columns associated with the parameters are projected through the instruments space.

PRINTALL

specifies the printing options COLLIN, CORRB, CORRS, COVB, COVS, DETAILS, DW, and FSRSQ

Options to control iteration output

Details of the output produced are discussed in the section "Iteration History" later in this chapter.

I

prints the inverse of the crossproducts Jacobian matrix at each iteration

ITALL

specifies all iteration printing control options (I, ITDETAILS, ITPRINT, and XPX). ITALL also prints the crossproducts matrix (labeled CROSS), the parameter change vector, and the estimate of the cross-equation covariance of residuals matrix at each iteration.

ITDETAILS

prints a detailed iteration listing. This includes the ITPRINT information and additional statistics.

ITPRINT

prints the parameter estimates, objective function value, and convergence criteria at each iteration. The parameter estimates, objective function value, and convergence criteria are printed in a column format if the line size (controlled by option LINESIZE=) is wide enough.

XPX

prints the crossproducts Jacobian matrix at each iteration

Options to Control the Minimization Process

The following options may be helpful when you experience a convergence problem:

CONVERGE= *value1*
CONVERGE= (*value1, value2*)

specifies the convergence criteria. The convergence measure must be less than *value1* before convergence is assumed. *value2* is the convergence criterion for the **S** and **V** matrices for **S** and **V** iterated methods. *value2* defaults to *value1*. See "The Convergence Criteria" later in this chapter for details. The default value is CONVERGE=.001.

HESSIAN= CROSS | GLS | FDA

specifies the Hessian approximation used for FIML. HESSIAN=CROSS selects the crossproducts approximation to the Hessian, HESSIAN=GLS selects the generalized least-squares approximation to the Hessian, and HESSIAN=FDA selects the finite difference approximation to the Hessian. HESSIAN=GLS is the default.

MAXITER= *n*

specifies the maximum number of iterations allowed. The default is MAXITER=40.

MAXSUBITER= *n*

specifies the maximum number of subiterations allowed for an iteration. For the GAUSS method, the MAXSUBITER= option limits the number of step halvings. For the MARQUARDT method, the MAXSUBITER= option limits the number of times λ can be increased. The default is MAXSUBITER=20. See "Minimization Methods" later in this chapter for details.

METHOD= GAUSS | MARQUARDT

specifies the iterative minimization method to use. METHOD=GAUSS specifies the Gauss-Newton method, and METHOD=MARQUARDT specifies the Marquardt-Levenberg method. The default is METHOD=GAUSS. See "Minimization Methods" for details.

NESTIT

changes the way the iterations are performed for estimation methods that iterate the estimate of the equation covariance (**S** matrix). The NESTIT option is relevant only for the methods that iterate the estimate of the covariance matrix (ITG-MM, ITOLS, ITSUR, IT2SLS, IT3SLS). See "Details on the Covariance of Equation Errors" later in this chapter for an explanation of NESTIT.

SINGULAR= *value*

specifies the smallest pivot value allowed. The default is the machine epsilon.

STARTITER= *n*

specifies the number of minimization iterations to perform at each grid point. The default is STARTITER=0, which implies that no minimization is performed at the grid points. See "Using the STARTITER option" for more details.

Other Options

Other options that can be used in the FIT statement to list and analyze the model include the following:

- BLOCK
- GRAPH
- LIST
- LISTCODE
- LISTDEP
- LISTDER
- XREF

The following printing control options are also available:

- DETAILS
- FLOW
- MAXERRORS=
- NOPRINT
- PRINTALL
- TRACE

For complete descriptions of these options, see the section "PROC MODEL Statement" earlier in this chapter.

ID Statement

ID *variables* **;**

The ID statement specifies variables to identify observations in error messages or other listings and in the OUT= data set. The ID variables are normally SAS date or date-time variables. If more than one ID variable is used, the first variable is used to identify the observations; the remaining variables are added to the OUT= data set.

INCLUDE Statement

INCLUDE *model-names* **... ;**

The INCLUDE statement reads model files and inserts their contents into the current model. However, instead of replacing the current model as the RESET MODEL= option does, the contents of included model files are inserted into the model program at the position that the INCLUDE statement appears.

INSTRUMENTS Statement

The INSTRUMENTS statement specifies the instrumental variables to be used in the N2SLS, N3SLS, IT2SLS, IT3SLS, GMM, and ITGMM estimation methods. There are two forms of the INSTRUMENTS statement:

INSTRUMENTS *variables* [**_EXOG_**] ;

INSTRUMENTS [*instruments*] [**_EXOG_**]
[**EXCLUDE**= (*parameters*)] [/ *options*] ;

The first form of the INSTRUMENTS statement is used only before a FIT statement and defines the default instruments list. The items specified as instruments can be variables or the special keyword _EXOG_. _EXOG_ indicates that all the model variables declared EXOGENOUS are to be added to the instruments list.

The second form of the INSTRUMENTS statement is used only after the FIT statement and before the next RUN statement. The items specified as instruments for the second form can be variables, names of parameters to be estimated, or the special keyword _EXOG_. If you specify the name of a parameter in the instruments list, the partial derivatives of the equations with respect to the parameter (that is, the columns of the Jacobian matrix associated with the parameter) are used as instruments. The parameter itself is not used as an instrument. These partial derivatives should not depend on any of the parameters to be estimated. Only the names of parameters to be estimated can be specified.

EXCLUDE= (*parameters*)

specifies that the derivatives of the equations with respect to all of the parameters to be estimated, except the parameters listed in the EXCLUDE list, be used as instruments, in addition to the other instruments specified. If you use the EXCLUDE= option, you should be sure that the derivatives with respect to the non-excluded parameters in the estimation are independent of the endogenous variables and not functions of the parameters estimated.

The following option is specified in the INSTRUMENTS statement following a slash (/):

NOINTERCEPT
NOINT

excludes the constant of 1.0 (intercept) from the instruments list. An intercept is always included as an instrument unless NOINTERCEPT is specified.

When a FIT statement specifies an instrumental variables estimation method and no INSTRUMENTS statement accompanies the FIT statement, the default instruments are used. If no default instruments list has been specified, all the model variables declared EXOGENOUS are used as instruments.

See "Choice of Instruments" later in this chapter for more details.

LABEL Statement

LABEL *variable*= '*label*' ... ;

The LABEL statement specifies a label of up to 255 characters for parameters and other variables used in the model program. Labels are used to identify parts of the printout of FIT and SOLVE tasks. The labels will be displayed in the output if the LINESIZE= option is large enough. Labels for variables written to output data sets are truncated to 40 characters and are included in the output data set. Note that PROC MODEL allows a longer label in its label statement than the DATA step does.

OUTVARS Statement

OUTVARS *variables*;

The OUTVARS statement specifies additional variables defined in the model program to be output to the OUT= data sets. The OUTVARS statement is not needed unless the variables to be added to the output data set are not referred to by the model, or unless you want to include parameters or other special variables in the OUT= data set. The OUTVARS statement includes additional variables, whereas the KEEP statement excludes variables.

PARAMETERS Statement

PARAMETERS *variable* [*value*] [*variable* [*value*]] ... ;

The PARAMETERS statement declares the parameters of a model and optionally sets their values. Valid abbreviations are PARMS and PARM.

Each parameter has a single value associated with it, which is the same for all observations. Lagging is not relevant for parameters. If a value is not specified in the PARMS statement (or by the PARMS= option of a FIT statement), the value defaults to 0.0001 for FIT tasks and to a missing value for SOLVE tasks.

RANGE Statement

RANGE *variable* [= *first*] [**TO** *last*];

The RANGE statement specifies the range of observations to be read from the DATA= data set. For FIT tasks, the RANGE statement controls the period of fit for the estimation. For SOLVE tasks, the RANGE statement controls the simulation period or forecast horizon.

The RANGE variable must be a numeric variable in the DATA= data set that identifies the observations, and the data set must be sorted by the RANGE variable. The first observation in the range is identified by *first*, and the last observation is identified by *last*.

PROC MODEL uses the first l observations prior to *first* to initialize the lags, where l is the maximum number of lags needed to evaluate any of the equations to be fit or solved, or the maximum number of lags needed to compute any of the instruments when an instrumental variables estimation method is used. There should be at least l observations in the data set before *first*. If *last* is not specified, all the nonmissing observations starting with *first* are used.

If *first* is omitted, the first l observations are used to initialize the lags, and the rest of the data, until *last*, is used. If a RANGE statement is used but both *first* and *last* are omitted, the RANGE statement variable is used to report the range of observations processed.

The RANGE variable should be nonmissing for all observations. Observations containing missing RANGE values are deleted.

The following are examples of RANGE statements:

```
range year = 1971 to 1988;                      /* yearly  data  */
range date = '1feb73'd to '1nov82'd;            /* monthly data  */
range time = 60.5;                              /* time in years */
range year to 1977;                    /* use all years through 1977 */
range date;        /* use values of date to report period-of-fit */
```

RESET Statement

> **RESET** *options*;

All of the options of the PROC MODEL statement can be reset by the RESET statement. In addition, the RESET statement supports one additional option:

PURGE

deletes the current model so a new model can be defined.

When the MODEL= option is used in the RESET statement, the current model is deleted before the new model is read.

SOLVE Statement

> **SOLVE** [*variables*] [**SATISFY** = *equations*] [/ *options*];

The SOLVE statement specifies that the model be simulated or forecast for input data values and optionally selects the variables to be solved. If the list of variables is omitted, all of the model variables declared ENDOGENOUS are solved. If no model variables are declared ENDOGENOUS, then all model variables are solved.

The following specification can be used in the SOLVE statement:

SATISFY= *equation*
SATISFY= (*equations*)

specifies a subset of the model equations that the solution values are to satisfy. If the SATISFY= option is not used, the solution is computed to satisfy all the model equations. Note that the number of equations must equal the number of variables solved.

Data Set Options

DATA= *SAS-data-set*

names the input data set. The model is solved for each observation read from the DATA= data set. If the DATA= option is not specified in the SOLVE statement, the data set specified by the DATA= option in the PROC MODEL statement is used.

ESTDATA= *SAS-data-set*

names a data set whose first observation provides values for some or all of the parameters and whose additional observations (if any) give the covariance matrix of the parameter estimates. The covariance matrix read from the ESTDATA= data set is used to generate multivariate normal pseudo-random shocks to the model parameters when the RANDOM= option requests Monte Carlo simulation.

OUT= *SAS-data-set*

outputs the predicted (solution) values, residual values, actual values, or equation errors from the solution to a data set. Only the solution values are output by default.

OUTACTUAL

outputs the actual values of the solved variables read from the input data set to the OUT= data set. This option is applicable only if the OUT= option is specified.

OUTALL

specifies the OUTACTUAL, OUTERRORS, OUTLAGS, OUTPREDICT, and OUTRESID options

OUTERRORS

writes the equation errors to the OUT= data set. These values are normally very close to zero when a simultaneous solution is computed; they can be used to double-check the accuracy of the solution process. It is applicable only if the OUT= option is specified.

OUTLAGS

writes the observations used to start the lags to the OUT= data set. This option is applicable only if the OUT= option is specified.

OUTPREDICT

writes the solution values to the OUT= data set. This option is relevant only if the OUT= option is specified. The OUTPREDICT option is the default unless one of the other output options is used.

OUTRESID

writes the residual values computed as the difference of the solution values and the values for the solution variables read from the input data set to the OUT= data set. This option is applicable only if the OUT= option is specified.

PARMSDATA= *SAS-data-set*

specifies a data set that contains the parameter estimates. See "Input Data Sets" later in this chapter for more details.

SDATA= *SAS-data-set*

specifies a data set that provides the covariance matrix of the equation errors. The covariance matrix read from the SDATA= data set is used to generate multivariate normal pseudo-random shocks to the equations when the RANDOM= option requests Monte Carlo simulation.

TYPE= *name*

specifies the estimation type. The name specified in the TYPE= option is compared to the _TYPE_ variable in the ESTDATA= and SDATA= data sets to select observations to use in constructing the covariance matrices. When the TYPE= option is omitted, the last estimation type in the data set is used.

Solution Mode Options: Lag Processing

DYNAMIC

specifies a dynamic solution. In the dynamic solution mode, solved values are used by the lagging functions. DYNAMIC is the default.

NAHEAD= *n*

specifies a simulation of *n*-period-ahead dynamic forecasting. The NAHEAD= option is used to simulate the process of using the model to produce successive forecasts to a fixed forecast horizon, with each forecast using the historical data available at the time the forecast is made.

Note that NAHEAD=1 produces a static (one-step-ahead) solution. NAHEAD=2 produces a solution using one-step-ahead solutions for the first lag (LAG1 functions return static predicted values) and actual values for longer lags. NA-HEAD=3 produces a solution using NAHEAD=2 solutions for the first lags, NA-HEAD=1 solutions for the second lags, and actual values for longer lags. In general, NAHEAD=*n* solutions use NAHEAD=*n*-1 solutions for LAG1, NA-HEAD=*n*-2 solutions for LAG2, and so forth.

START= *s*

specifies static solutions until the *s*th observation and then changes to dynamic solutions. If the START=*s* option is specified, the first observation in the range in which LAG*n* delivers solved predicted values is *s* + *n*, while LAG*n* returns actual values for earlier observations.

STATIC

specifies a static solution. In static solution mode, actual values of the solved variables from the input data set are used by the lagging functions.

Solution Mode Options: Use of Available Data

FORECAST

specifies that the actual value of a solved variable is used as the solution value (instead of the predicted value from the model equations) whenever nonmissing data are available in the input data set. That is, in FORECAST mode, PROC MODEL solves only for those variables that are missing in the input data set.

SIMULATE

specifies that PROC MODEL always solves for all solution variables as a function of the input values of the other variables, even when actual data for some of the solution variables are available in the input data set. SIMULATE is the default.

Solution Mode Options: Numerical Solution Method

JACOBI

computes a simultaneous solution using a Jacobi-like iteration. The JACOBI option can only be used to solve normalized-form equation systems and cannot be used for goal-seeking solutions.

NEWTON

computes a simultaneous solution using Newton's method. When the NEWTON option is selected, the analytic derivatives of the equation errors with respect to the solution variables are computed and memory-efficient sparse matrix techniques are used for factoring the Jacobian matrix.

The NEWTON option can be used to solve both normalized-form and general-form equations and can compute goal-seeking solutions. NEWTON is the default.

SEIDEL

computes a simultaneous solution using a Gauss-Seidel-like method. The SEIDEL option cannot be used with the FORECAST or SDATA= options. The SEIDEL option can only be used to solve normalized-form equation systems and cannot be used for goal-seeking solutions.

SINGLE
ONEPASS

specifies a single-equation (nonsimultaneous) solution. The model is executed once to compute predicted values for the variables from the actual values of the other endogenous variables. The SINGLE option can only be used for normalized-form equations and cannot be used for goal-seeking solutions.

For more information on these options, see "Solution Modes" later in this chapter.

Monte Carlo Simulation Options

RANDOM= *n*

repeats the solution *n* times for each BY group, with different random perturbations of the equation errors if the SDATA= option is used; with different random perturbations of the parameters if the ESTDATA= option is used and the ESTDATA= data set contains a parameter covariance matrix; and with different values returned from the random-number generator functions, if any are used in the model program. If RANDOM=0, the random-number generator functions always return zero. See "Monte Carlo Simulation" earlier in this chapter for details. The default is RANDOM=0.

SEED= *n*

specifies an integer to use as the seed in generating pseudo-random numbers to shock the parameters and equations when the ESTDATA= or the SDATA= options are specified. If *n* is negative or 0, the time of day from the computer's clock is used as the seed. The SEED= option is only relevant if the RANDOM= option is used. The default is SEED=0.

Options for Controlling the Numerical Solution Process

The following options are useful when you have difficulty converging to the simultaneous solution.

CONVERGE= *value*

specifies the convergence criterion for the simultaneous solution. Convergence of the solution is judged by comparing the CONVERGE= value to the maximum over the equations of

$$\frac{|\epsilon_i|}{|y_i| + 1\text{E}-6}$$

if it is computable, otherwise

$$|\epsilon_i|$$

where ϵ_i represents the equation error and y_i represents the solution variable corresponding to the ith equation for normalized-form equations. The default is CONVERGE=1E-8.

MAXITER= *n*

specifies the maximum number of iterations allowed for computing the simultaneous solution for any observation. The default is MAXITER=50.

MAXSUBITER= *n*

specifies the maximum number of damping subiterations that are performed in solving a nonlinear system when using the NEWTON solution method. Damping is disabled by setting MAXSUBITER=0. The default is MAXSUBITER=10.

Printing Options

ITPRINT

prints the solution approximation and equation errors at each iteration for each observation. This option can produce voluminous output.

PRINTALL

specifies the printing control options DETAILS, ITPRINT, SOLVEPRINT, STATS, and THEIL

SOLVEPRINT

prints the solution values and residuals at each observation

STATS

prints various summary statistics for the solution values

THEIL

prints tables of Theil inequality coefficients and Theil relative change forecast error measures for the solution values. See "Summary Statistics" in the "Simulation Details" section later in this chapter for more information.

Other Options

Other options that can be used on the SOLVE statement include the following that list and analyze the model:

- BLOCK
- GRAPH
- LIST
- LISTCODE

- LISTDEP
- LISTDER
- XREF

The following printing control options are also available:

- DETAILS
- FLOW
- MAXERRORS=
- NOPRINT
- TRACE

For complete descriptions of these options, see the PROC MODEL statement options described earlier in this chapter.

VAR Statement

VAR *variables* [*initial_values*] ... ;

The VAR statement declares model variables and optionally provides initial values for the variables' lags. See "Lag Logic" in the section "Functions Across Time" later in this chapter for more information.

WEIGHT Statement

WEIGHT *variable*;

The WEIGHT statement specifies a variable to supply weighting values to use for each observation in estimating parameters. The WEIGHT statement must follow a FIT statement.

If the weight of an observation is nonpositive, that observation is not used for the estimation. *variable* must be a numeric variable in the input data set.

An alternate weighting method is to use an assignment statement to give values to the special variable _WEIGHT_. The _WEIGHT_ variable must not depend on the parameters being estimated. If both weighting specifications are given, the weights are multiplied together.

Compatibility with Version 5

The following information is provided for compatibility with Release 5.18 and earlier versions of SAS/ETS software.

The PROC SYSNLIN and PROC SIMNLIN statements are another way to invoke the MODEL procedure. They have the general form

PROC SYSNLIN *options*;

PROC SIMNLIN *options*;

These statements are supported to provide compatibility with earlier versions of SAS/ETS software in which the parameter estimation features of the FIT statement were contained in a separate procedure, PROC SYSNLIN, and the simulation and forecasting features of the SOLVE statement were contained in a separate procedure, PROC SIMNLIN. The features of the old SYSNLIN and SIMNLIN procedures are now incorporated in the MODEL procedure. The PROC SYSNLIN statement invokes PROC MODEL with a default FIT statement. The PROC SIMNLIN statement invokes PROC MODEL with a default SOLVE statement.

The PROC SYSNLIN statement accepts the same options as are used after the slash (/) in the FIT statement. In addition, the MODEL= and OUTMODEL= options can be used in the PROC SYSNLIN statement.

The PROC SIMNLIN statement accepts the same options as are used after a slash (/) in the SOLVE statement. In addition, the MODEL= and OUTMODEL= options can be used in the PROC SIMNLIN statement.

Estimation Details

Estimation Methods

Consider the general nonlinear model:

$$\epsilon_t = \mathbf{q}(\mathbf{y}_t, \mathbf{x}_t, \theta)$$
$$\mathbf{z}_t = \mathbf{Z}(\mathbf{x}_t)$$

where $\mathbf{q} \in \Re^g$ is a real vector valued function, $\mathbf{y}_t \in \Re^g$, $\mathbf{x}_t \in \Re^l$, $\theta \in \Re^p$, g is the number of equations, l is the number of exogenous variables (lagged endogenous variables are considered exogenous here), p is the number of parameters and t ranges from 1 to n. $\mathbf{z}_t \in \Re^k$ is a vector of instruments. ϵ_t is an unobservable disturbance vector with the following properties:

$$E(\epsilon_t) = 0$$
$$E(\epsilon_t \epsilon_t') = \Sigma$$

All of the methods implemented in PROC MODEL aim to minimize an *objective function*. The following table summarizes the objective functions defining the estimators and the corresponding estimator of the covariance of the parameter estimates for each method.

Table 11.1. Summary of PROC MODEL Estimation Methods

Method	Instruments	Objective Function	Covariance of θ
OLS	no	$\mathbf{r}'\mathbf{r}/n$	$\left(\mathbf{X}'\left(\text{diag}(\mathbf{S})^{-1}\otimes\mathbf{I}\right)\mathbf{X}\right)^{-1}$
ITOLS	no	$\mathbf{r}'\left(\text{diag}(\mathbf{S})^{-1}\otimes\mathbf{I}\right)\mathbf{r}/n$	$\left(\mathbf{X}'\left(\text{diag}(\mathbf{S})^{-1}\otimes\mathbf{I}\right)\mathbf{X}\right)^{-1}$
SUR	no	$\mathbf{r}'\left(\mathbf{S}_{\text{OLS}}^{-1}\otimes\mathbf{I}\right)\mathbf{r}/n$	$\left(\mathbf{X}'\left(\mathbf{S}^{-1}\otimes\mathbf{I}\right)\mathbf{X}\right)^{-1}$
ITSUR	no	$\mathbf{r}'\left(\mathbf{S}^{-1}\otimes\mathbf{I}\right)\mathbf{r}/n$	$\left(\mathbf{X}'\left(\mathbf{S}^{-1}\otimes\mathbf{I}\right)\mathbf{X}\right)^{-1}$
N2SLS	yes	$\mathbf{r}'\left(\mathbf{I}\otimes\mathbf{W}\right)\mathbf{r}/n$	$\left(\mathbf{X}'\left(\text{diag}(\mathbf{S})^{-1}\otimes\mathbf{W}\right)\mathbf{X}\right)^{-1}$
IT2SLS	yes	$\mathbf{r}'\left(\text{diag}(\mathbf{S})^{-1}\otimes\mathbf{W}\right)\mathbf{r}/n$	$\left(\mathbf{X}'\left(\text{diag}(\mathbf{S})^{-1}\otimes\mathbf{W}\right)\mathbf{X}\right)^{-1}$
N3SLS	yes	$\mathbf{r}'\left(\mathbf{S}_{\text{N2SLS}}^{-1}\otimes\mathbf{W}\right)\mathbf{r}/n$	$\left(\mathbf{X}'\left(\mathbf{S}^{-1}\otimes\mathbf{W}\right)\mathbf{X}\right)^{-1}$
IT3SLS	yes	$\mathbf{r}'\left(\mathbf{S}^{-1}\otimes\mathbf{W}\right)\mathbf{r}/n$	$\left(\mathbf{X}'\left(\mathbf{S}^{-1}\otimes\mathbf{W}\right)\mathbf{X}\right)^{-1}$
GMM	yes	$\left[n\mathbf{m}_n(\theta)\right]'\widehat{\mathbf{V}}_{\text{N2SLS}}^{-1}\left[n\mathbf{m}_n(\theta)\right]$	$\left[(\mathbf{YX})'\widehat{\mathbf{V}}^{-1}(\mathbf{YX})\right]^{-1}$
ITGMM	yes	$\left[n\mathbf{m}_n(\theta)\right]'\widehat{\mathbf{V}}^{-1}\left[n\mathbf{m}_n(\theta)\right]$	$\left[(\mathbf{YX})'\widehat{\mathbf{V}}^{-1}(\mathbf{YX})\right]^{-1}$
FIML	no	$constant + \frac{n}{2}\ln(\det(\mathbf{S}))$ $-\sum_1^n\ln\lvert\det(\mathbf{J}_t)\rvert$	$\left[\widehat{\mathbf{Z}}'\left(\mathbf{S}^{-1}\otimes\mathbf{I}\right)\widehat{\mathbf{Z}}\right]^{-1}$

The "Instruments" column identifies the estimation methods that require instruments. The variables used in this table and the remainder of this chapter are defined as follows:

$$\mathbf{r} = \begin{bmatrix} r_1 \\ r_2 \\ \vdots \\ r_g \end{bmatrix} \text{ is the } ng \times 1 \text{ vector of residuals for the } g \text{ equations stacked together.}$$

$$\mathbf{r}_i = \begin{bmatrix} \mathbf{q}_i(\mathbf{y}_1,\ \mathbf{x}_1,\ \theta) \\ \mathbf{q}_i(\mathbf{y}_2,\ \mathbf{x}_2,\ \theta) \\ \vdots \\ \mathbf{q}_i(\mathbf{y}_n,\ \mathbf{x}_n,\ \theta) \end{bmatrix} \text{ is the } n \times 1 \text{ column vector of residuals for the } i\text{th equation.}$$

$\mathbf{S}$ is a $g \times g$ matrix that estimates Σ, the covariances of the errors across equations (referred to as the $\mathbf{S}$ matrix).

$\mathbf{X}$ is an $ng \times p$ matrix of partial derivatives of the residual with respect to the parameters.

$\mathbf{W}$ is an $n \times n$ matrix, $\mathbf{Z}(\mathbf{Z}'\mathbf{Z})^{-1}\mathbf{Z}'$.

$\mathbf{Z}$ is an $n \times k$ matrix of instruments.

$\mathbf{Y}$ is a $gk \times ng$ matrix of instruments. $\mathbf{Y} = \mathbf{I}_g \otimes \mathbf{Z}'$.

$\widehat{\mathbf{Z}}$ $\widehat{\mathbf{Z}} = \left(\widehat{\mathbf{Z}}_1, \widehat{\mathbf{Z}}_2, \dots, \widehat{\mathbf{Z}}_p \right)$ is an $ng \times p$ matrix. $\widehat{\mathbf{Z}}_i$ is a $ng \times 1$ column vector obtained from stacking the columns of

$$\mathbf{U} \frac{1}{n} \sum_{t=1}^{n} \left(\frac{\partial\, \mathbf{q}(\mathbf{y}_t, \mathbf{x}_t, \theta)\,'}{\partial\, \mathbf{y}_t} \right)^{-1} \frac{\partial^2\, \mathbf{q}(\mathbf{y}_t, \mathbf{x}_t, \theta)\,'}{\partial\, \mathbf{y}_t\, \partial\, \theta_i} - \mathbf{Q}_i$$

$\mathbf{U}$ is an $n \times g$ matrix of residual errors. $\mathbf{U} = \left[\epsilon_1, \epsilon_2, \dots, \epsilon_n \right]'$

$\mathbf{Q}$ is the $n \times g$ matrix $\left[\mathbf{q}(\mathbf{y}_1, \mathbf{x}_1, \theta), \mathbf{q}(\mathbf{y}_2, \mathbf{x}_2, \theta), \dots, \mathbf{q}(\mathbf{y}_n, \mathbf{x}_n, \theta) \right]'$.

$\mathbf{Q}_i$ is an $n \times g$ matrix $\partial\, \mathbf{Q} / \partial\, \theta_i$.

$\mathbf{I}$ is an $n \times n$ identity matrix.

$\mathbf{J}_t$ is $\partial\, \mathbf{q}(\mathbf{y}_t, \mathbf{x}_t, \theta) / \partial\, \mathbf{y}_t'$ which is a $g \times g$ Jacobian matrix.

$\mathbf{m}_n$ is first moment of the crossproduct $\mathbf{q}(\mathbf{y}_t, \mathbf{x}_t, \theta) \otimes \mathbf{z}_t$.
         $\mathbf{m}_n = \frac{1}{n} \sum_{t=1}^{n} \mathbf{q}(\mathbf{y}_t, \mathbf{x}_t, \theta) \otimes \mathbf{z}_t$

$\mathbf{z}_t$ is a k column vector of instruments for observation t. $\mathbf{z}_t'$ is also the tth row of $\mathbf{Z}$.

$\widehat{\mathbf{V}}$ is the $gk \times gk$ matrix representing the variance of the moment functions.

k is the number of instrumental variables used.

constant is the constant $\frac{ng}{2} \left(1 + \ln(2\pi) \right)$.

$\otimes$ is the notation for Kronecker product.

All vectors are column vectors unless otherwise noted. Other estimates of the covariance matrix for FIML are also available.

Dependent Regressors and Two-Stage Least Squares

Ordinary regression analysis is based on several assumptions. A key assumption is that the independent variables are in fact statistically independent of the unobserved error component of the model. If this assumption is not true—if the regressor varies systematically with the error—then ordinary regression produces inconsistent results. The parameter estimates are *biased*.

Regressors may fail to be independent variables because they are dependent variables in a larger simultaneous system. For this reason, the problem of dependent regressors is often called *simultaneous equation bias*. For example, consider the following two-equation system.

$$y_1 = a_1 + b_1\, y_2 + c_1\, x_1 + \epsilon_1$$
$$y_2 = a_2 + b_2\, y_1 + c_2\, x_2 + \epsilon_2$$

In the first equation, y_2 is a dependent, or *endogenous*, variable. As shown by the second equation, y_2 is a function of y_1, which by the first equation is a function of ϵ_1, and therefore y_2 depends on ϵ_1. Likewise, y_1 depends on ϵ_2 and is a dependent regressor in the second equation. This is an example of a *simultaneous equation* system; y_1 and y_2 are a function of all the variables in the system.

Using the ordinary least squares (OLS) estimation method to estimate these equations produces biased estimates. One solution to this problem is to replace y_1 and y_2 on the right-hand side of the equations with predicted values, thus changing the regression problem to the following:

$$y_1 = a_1 + b_1 \hat{y}_2 + c_1 x_1 + \epsilon_1$$
$$y_2 = a_2 + b_2 \hat{y}_1 + c_2 x_2 + \epsilon_2$$

This method requires estimating the predicted values $\hat{y}_1$ and $\hat{y}_2$ through a preliminary, or first-stage, *instrumental regression*. An instrumental regression is a regression of the dependent regressors on a set of *instrumental variables*, which can be any independent variables useful for predicting the dependent regressors. In this example, the equations are linear and the exogenous variables for the whole system are known. Thus, the best choice for instruments are the variables x_1 and x_2.

This method is known as *two-stage least squares* or 2SLS, or more generally as the *instrumental variables method*. The 2SLS method for linear models is discussed in Pindyck (1981, p. 191-192). For nonlinear models this situation is more complex, but the idea is the same. In nonlinear 2SLS, the derivatives of the model with respect to the parameters are replaced with predicted values. See "Choice of Instruments" later in this chapter for further discussion of the use of instrumental variables in nonlinear regression.

To perform nonlinear 2SLS estimation with PROC MODEL, specify the instrumental variables with an INSTRUMENTS statement and specify the 2SLS or N2SLS option in the FIT statement. The following statements show how to estimate the first equation in the preceding example with PROC MODEL.

```
proc model data=in;
   y1 = a1 + b1 * y2 + c1 * x1;
   fit y1 / 2sls;
   instruments x1 x2;
run;
```

The 2SLS or instrumental variables estimator can be computed using a first-stage regression on the instrumental variables as described previously. However, PROC MODEL actually uses the equivalent, but computationally more appropriate, technique of projecting the regression problem into the linear space defined by the instruments. Thus PROC MODEL does not produce any first-stage results when you use 2SLS. If you specify the FSRSQ option in the FIT statement, PROC MODEL prints "first-stage R^2" statistic for each parameter estimate.

Formally, the $\hat{\theta}$ that minimizes

$$\hat{\mathbf{S}}_n = \frac{1}{n} \left(\sum_{t=1}^{n} \mathbf{q}(\mathbf{y}_t, \mathbf{x}_t, \theta) \otimes \mathbf{z}_t \right)' \left(\sum_{t=1}^{n} \mathbf{I} \otimes \mathbf{z}_t \mathbf{z}_t' \right)^{-1} \left(\sum_{t=1}^{n} \mathbf{q}(\mathbf{y}_t, \mathbf{x}_t, \theta) \otimes \mathbf{z}_t \right)$$

is the N2SLS estimator of the parameters. The estimate of Σ at the final iteration is used in the covariance of the parameters given in Table 11.1. Refer to Amemiya (1985, p. 250) for details on the properties of nonlinear two-stage least squares.

Seemingly Unrelated Regression

If the regression equations are not simultaneous, so there are no dependent regressors, *seemingly unrelated regression* (SUR) can be used to estimate systems of equations with correlated random errors. The large-sample efficiency of an estimation can be improved if these cross-equation correlations are taken into account. SUR is also known as *joint generalized least squares* or *Zellner regression*. Formally, the $\hat{\theta}$ that minimizes

$$\hat{S}_n = \frac{1}{n} \sum_{t=1}^{n} q(y_t, x_t, \theta)' \, \hat{\Sigma}^{-1} \, q(y_t, x_t, \theta)$$

is the SUR estimator of the parameters.

The SUR method requires an estimate of the cross-equation covariance matrix, Σ. PROC MODEL first performs an OLS estimation, computes an estimate $\hat{\Sigma}$ from the OLS residuals, and then performs the SUR estimation based on $\hat{\Sigma}$. The OLS results are not printed unless you specify the OLS option in addition to the SUR option.

You can specify the $\hat{\Sigma}$ to use for SUR by storing the matrix in a SAS data set and naming that data set in the SDATA= option. You can also feed the $\hat{\Sigma}$ computed from the SUR residuals back into the SUR estimation process by specifying the ITSUR option. You can print the estimated covariance matrix $\hat{\Sigma}$ using the COVS option on the FIT statement.

The SUR method requires estimation of the Σ matrix, and this increases the sampling variability of the estimator for small sample sizes. The efficiency gain SUR has over OLS is a large sample property, and you must have a reasonable amount of data to realize this gain. For a more detailed discussion of SUR, refer to Pindyck (1981, p. 331-333).

Three-Stage Least-Squares Estimation

If the equation system is simultaneous, you can combine the 2SLS and SUR methods to take into account both dependent regressors and cross-equation correlation of the errors. This is called *three-stage least squares* (3SLS).

Formally, the $\hat{\theta}$ that minimizes

$$\hat{S}_n = \frac{1}{n} \left(\sum_{t=1}^{n} q(y_t, x_t, \theta) \otimes z_t \right)' \left(\sum_{t=1}^{n} \hat{\Sigma} \otimes z_t z_t' \right)^{-1} \left(\sum_{t=1}^{n} q(y_t, x_t, \theta) \otimes z_t \right)$$

is the 3SLS estimator of the parameters. For more details on 3SLS, refer to Gallant (1987, p. 435).

Residuals from the 2SLS method are used to estimate the Σ matrix required for 3SLS. The results of the preliminary 2SLS step are not printed unless the 2SLS option is also specified.

To use the three-stage least-squares method, specify an INSTRUMENTS statement and use the 3SLS or N3SLS option in either the PROC MODEL statement or the FIT statement.

Generalized Method of Moments - GMM

For systems of equations with heteroscedastic errors, generalized method of moments (GMM) can be used to obtain efficient estimates of the parameters. See "Heteroscedasticity" later in this chapter for alternatives to GMM.

Consider the nonlinear model

$$\epsilon_t = \mathbf{q}(\mathbf{y}_t, \mathbf{x}_t, \theta)$$
$$\mathbf{z}_t = \mathbf{Z}(\mathbf{x}_t)$$

where $\mathbf{z}_t$ is a vector of instruments and ϵ_t as an unobservable disturbance vector that can be serially correlated and nonstationary.

In general, the following orthogonality condition is desired:

$$\mathrm{E}(\epsilon_t \otimes \mathbf{z}_t) = 0$$

which states that the expected crossproducts of the unobservable disturbances, ϵ_t, and functions of the observable variables are set to 0. The first moment of the crossproducts is

$$\mathbf{m}_n = \frac{1}{n} \sum_{t=1}^{n} \mathbf{m}(\mathbf{y}_t, \mathbf{x}_t, \theta)$$
$$\mathbf{m}(\mathbf{y}_t, \mathbf{x}_t, \theta) = \mathbf{q}(\mathbf{y}_t, \mathbf{x}_t, \theta) \otimes \mathbf{z}_t$$

where $\mathbf{m}(\mathbf{y}_t, \mathbf{x}_t, \theta) \in \Re^{gk}$. The case where $gk > p$ is considered here, where p is the number of parameters.

Estimate the true parameter vector θ^0 by the value of $\hat{\theta}$ that minimizes

$$\mathbf{S}(\theta, \mathbf{V}) = [n\mathbf{m}_n(\theta)]' \, \mathbf{V}^{-1} \, [n\mathbf{m}_n(\theta)]$$

where

$$\mathbf{V} = \mathrm{Cov}\left([n\mathbf{m}_n(\theta^0)], [n\mathbf{m}_n(\theta^0)]' \right)$$

The parameter vector that minimizes this objective function is the GMM estimator. GMM estimation is requested in the FIT statement with the GMM option.

The variance of the moment functions, $\mathbf{V}$, can be expressed as

$$\mathbf{V} = \mathrm{E}\left(\sum_{t=1}^{n} \epsilon_t \otimes \mathbf{z}_t \right) \left(\sum_{s=1}^{n} \epsilon_s \otimes \mathbf{z}_s \right)'$$
$$= \sum_{t=1}^{n} \sum_{s=1}^{n} \mathrm{E}\left[(\epsilon_t \otimes \mathbf{z}_t)(\epsilon_s \otimes \mathbf{z}_s)' \right]$$
$$= n\mathbf{S}_n^0$$

where $\mathbf{S}_n^0$ is estimated as

$$\hat{\mathbf{S}}_n = \frac{1}{n} \sum_{t=1}^{n} \sum_{s=1}^{n} \left(\mathbf{q}(\mathbf{y}_t, \mathbf{x}_t, \theta) \otimes \mathbf{z}_t\right) \left(\mathbf{q}(\mathbf{y}_s, \mathbf{x}_s, \theta) \otimes \mathbf{z}_s\right)'$$

Note that $\hat{\mathbf{S}}_n$ is a $gk \times gk$ matrix. Because $\text{Var}\left(\hat{\mathbf{S}}_n\right)$ will not decrease with increasing n, estimators of $\mathbf{S}_n^0$ are considered of the form:

$$\hat{\mathbf{S}}_n(1(n)) = \sum_{\tau=-n+1}^{n-1} w\left(\frac{\tau}{1(n)}\right) \mathbf{D}\, \hat{\mathbf{S}}_{n,\tau}\, \mathbf{D}$$

$$\hat{\mathbf{S}}_{n,\tau} = \begin{cases} \sum_{t=1+\tau}^{n} \left[\mathbf{q}\left(\mathbf{y}_t, \mathbf{x}_t, \theta^{\#}\right) \otimes \mathbf{z}_t\right]\left[\mathbf{q}\left(\mathbf{y}_{t-\tau}, \mathbf{x}_{t-\tau}, \theta^{\#}\right) \otimes \mathbf{z}_{t-\tau}\right]' & \tau \geq 0 \\[2mm] \left(\hat{\mathbf{S}}_{n,-\tau}\right)' & \tau < 0 \end{cases}$$

where $1(n)$ is a scalar function that computes the bandwidth parameter, $w(\cdot)$ is a scalar valued kernel, and the diagonal matrix $\mathbf{D}$ is used for a small sample degrees of freedom correction (Gallant 1987). The initial $\theta^{\#}$ used for the estimation of $\hat{\mathbf{S}}_n$ is obtained from a 2SLS estimation of the system. The degrees of freedom correction is handled by the VARDEF= option as for the $\mathbf{S}$ matrix estimation.

The following kernels are supported by PROC MODEL. They are listed with their default bandwidth functions:

Bartlett: KERNEL=BART

$$w(x) = \begin{cases} 1 - |x| & |x| \leq 1 \\ 0 & \text{otherwise} \end{cases}$$

$$1(n) = \frac{1}{2}\, n^{1/3}$$

Parzen: KERNEL=PARZEN

$$w(x) = \begin{cases} 1 - 6|x|^2 + 6|x|^3 & 0 \leq |x| \leq \frac{1}{2} \\ 2(1 - |x|)^3 & \frac{1}{2} \leq |x| \leq 1 \\ 0 & \text{otherwise} \end{cases}$$

$$1(n) = n^{1/5}$$

Quadratic Spectral: KERNEL=QS

$$w(x) = \frac{25}{12\pi^2\, x^2} \left(\frac{\sin(6\pi x/5)}{6\pi x/5} - \cos(6\pi x/5)\right)$$

$$1(n) = \frac{1}{2}\, n^{1/5}$$

Details of the properties of these and other kernels are given in Andrews (1991). Kernels are selected with the KERNEL= option; KERNEL=PARZEN is the default. The general form of the KERNEL= option is

```
KERNEL=( PARZEN | QS | BART, c, e )
```

where the $e \geq 0$ and $c \geq 0$ are used to compute the bandwidth parameter as

$$l(n) = c\, n^e$$

The bias of the standard error estimates increases for large bandwidth parameters. A warning message is produced for bandwidth parameters greater than $n^{1/3}$. For a discussion of the computation of the optimal $l(n)$, refer to Andrews (1991).

Andrews (1992) has shown that using prewhitening in combination with GMM can improve confidence interval coverage and reduce over-rejection of t-statistics at the cost of inflating the variance and MSE of the estimator. Prewhitening can be performed using the %AR macros.

For the special case that the errors are not serially correlated, that is

$$\mathrm{E}\big[(e_t \otimes \mathbf{z}_t)(e_s \otimes \mathbf{z}_s)\big] = 0 \qquad t \neq s$$

the estimate for $\mathbf{S}_n^0$ reduces to

$$\hat{\mathbf{S}}_n = \tfrac{1}{n} \sum_{t=1}^{n} \big[\mathbf{q}(\mathbf{y}_t, \mathbf{x}_t, \theta) \otimes \mathbf{z}_t\big] \big[\mathbf{q}(\mathbf{y}_t, \mathbf{x}_t, \theta) \otimes \mathbf{z}_t\big]'$$

The option KERNEL=(*kernel*,0) is used to select this type of estimation when using GMM.

Testing Over-Identifying Restrictions

Let r be the number of unique instruments times the number of equations. The value r represents the number of orthogonality conditions imposed by the GMM method. Under the assumptions of the GMM method, $r - p$ linearly independent combinations of the orthogonality should be close to 0. The GMM estimates are computed by setting these combinations to 0. When r exceeds the number of parameters to be estimated, the OBJECTIVE*N, reported at the end of the estimation, is an asymptoticly valid statistic to test the null hypothesis that the over-identifying restrictions of the model are valid. The OBJECTIVE*N is distributed as a chi-square with $r - p$ degrees of freedom (Hansen 1982, p. 1049).

Iterated Generalized Method of Moments - ITGMM

Iterated generalized method of moments is similar to the iterated versions of 2SLS, SUR, and 3SLS. The variance matrix for GMM estimation is reestimated at each iteration with the parameters determined by the GMM estimation. The iteration terminates when the variance matrix for the equation errors change less than the CONVERGE= value. Iterated generalized method of moments is selected by the ITGMM option in the FIT statement. For some indication of the small sample properties of ITGMM, refer to Ferson (1993).

Full Information Maximum Likelihood Estimation - FIML

A different approach to the simultaneous equation bias problem is the full information maximum likelihood (FIML) estimation method (Amemiya 1977).

Compared to the instrumental variables methods (2SLS and 3SLS), the FIML method has these advantages and disadvantages:

- FIML does not require instrumental variables.

- FIML requires that the model include the full equation system, with as many equations as there are endogenous variables. With 2SLS or 3SLS, you can estimate some of the equations without specifying the complete system.

- FIML assumes that the equations errors have a multivariate normal distribution.If the errors are not normally distributed, the FIML method may produce poor results. 2SLS and 3SLS do not assume a specific distribution for the errors.

- The FIML method is computationally expensive.

The full information maximum likelihood estimators of θ and σ are the $\hat{\theta}$ and $\hat{\sigma}$ that minimize the negative log likelihood function:

$$1_n(\theta, \sigma) = \frac{ng}{2} \ln(2\pi) - \sum_{t=1}^{n} \ln\left(\left|\frac{\partial \mathbf{q}(\mathbf{y}_t, \mathbf{x}_t, \theta)}{\partial \mathbf{y}_t'}\right|\right) + \frac{n}{2} \ln(|\Sigma(\sigma)|)$$
$$+ \frac{1}{2} \text{trace}\left(\Sigma(\sigma)^{-1} \sum_{t=1}^{n} \mathbf{q}(\mathbf{y}_t, \mathbf{x}_t, \theta) \mathbf{q}(\mathbf{y}_t, \mathbf{x}_t, \theta)'\right)$$

The option FIML requests full information maximum likelihood estimation. If the errors are distributed normally, FIML produces efficient estimators of the parameters. If instrumental variables are not provided, the starting values for the estimation are obtained from a SUR estimation. If instrumental variables are provided, then the starting values are obtained from a 3SLS estimation. The negative log likelihood value and the l_2 norm of the gradient of the negative log likelihood function are shown in the estimation summary.

FIML Details

To compute the minimum of $l_n(\theta, \sigma)$, this function is *concentrated* using the relation

$$\Sigma(\theta) = \frac{1}{n} \sum_{t=1}^{n} \mathbf{q}(\mathbf{y}_t, \mathbf{x}_t, \theta) \mathbf{q}(\mathbf{y}_t, \mathbf{x}_t, \theta)'$$

This results in the concentrated negative log likelihood function

$$1_n(\theta) = \frac{ng}{2}(1 + \ln(2\pi)) - \sum_{t=1}^{n} \ln\left(\left|\frac{\partial \mathbf{q}(\mathbf{y}_t, \mathbf{x}_t, \theta)}{\partial \mathbf{y}_t'}\right|\right)$$
$$+ \frac{n}{2} \ln(|\Sigma(\theta)|)$$

The gradient of the negative log likelihood function is

$$\frac{\partial \, \mathbf{l}_n(\theta)}{\partial \, \theta_i} = \sum_{t=1}^{n} \nabla_i(t)$$

$$\nabla_i(t) = -\text{trace}\left(\left(\frac{\partial \, \mathbf{q}(\mathbf{y}_t, \mathbf{x}_t, \theta)}{\partial \, y'} \right)^{-1} \frac{\partial^2 \, \mathbf{q}(\mathbf{y}_t, \mathbf{x}_t, \theta)}{\partial \mathbf{y}_t' \, \partial \, \theta_i} \right)$$

$$+ \frac{1}{2} \text{trace}\left(\Sigma(\theta)^{-1} \frac{\partial}{\partial \, \theta_i} \Sigma(\theta) \right.$$

$$\left. \left[\mathbf{I} - \Sigma(\theta)^{-1} \, \mathbf{q}(\mathbf{y}_t, \mathbf{x}_t, \theta) \, \mathbf{q}(\mathbf{y}_t, \mathbf{x}_t, \theta)' \right] \right)$$

$$+ \, \mathbf{q}(\mathbf{y}_t, \mathbf{x}_t, \theta)' \, \Sigma(\theta)^{-1} \frac{\partial \, \mathbf{q}(\mathbf{y}_t, \mathbf{x}_t, \theta)}{\partial \, \theta_i}$$

where

$$\frac{\partial \, \Sigma(\theta)}{\partial \, \theta_i} = \frac{2}{n} \sum_{t=1}^{n} \mathbf{q}(\mathbf{y}_t, \mathbf{x}_t, \theta) \frac{\partial \, \mathbf{q}(\mathbf{y}_t, \mathbf{x}_t, \theta)'}{\partial \, \theta_i}$$

The estimator of the variance-covariance of $\hat{\theta}$ (COVB) for FIML can be selected with the COVBEST= option with the following arguments:

CROSS   selects the crossproducts estimator of the covariance matrix (default) (Gallant 1987, p. 473):

$$\mathbf{C} = \left(\frac{1}{n} \sum_{t=1}^{n} \nabla(t) \, \nabla(t)' \right)^{-1}$$

where $\nabla(t) = \left[\nabla_1(t), \nabla_2(t), \dots, \nabla_p(t) \right]'$

GLS   selects the generalized least-squares estimator of the covariance matrix. This is computed as (Dagenais 1978)

$$\mathbf{C} = \left[\hat{\mathbf{Z}}' \left(\Sigma(\theta)^{-1} \otimes \mathbf{I} \right) \hat{\mathbf{Z}} \right]^{-1}$$

where $\hat{\mathbf{Z}} = \left(\hat{\mathbf{Z}}_1, \hat{\mathbf{Z}}_2, \dots, \hat{\mathbf{Z}}_p \right)$ is $ng \times p$ and each $\hat{\mathbf{Z}}_i$ column vector is obtained from stacking the columns of

$$\mathbf{U} \frac{1}{n} \sum_{t=1}^{n} \left(\frac{\partial \, \mathbf{q}(\mathbf{y}_t, \mathbf{x}_t, \theta)'}{\partial \, y} \right)^{-1} \frac{\partial^2 \, \mathbf{q}(\mathbf{y}_t, \mathbf{x}_t, \theta)'}{\partial \, \mathbf{y}_n' \partial \, \theta_i} - \mathbf{Q}_i$$

$\mathbf{U}$ is an $n \times g$ matrix of residual errors and $\mathbf{Q}_i$ is an $n \times g$ matrix $\frac{\partial \, \mathbf{Q}}{\partial \, \theta_i}$.

FDA   selects the inverse of concentrated likelihood Hessian as an estimator of the covariance matrix. The Hessian is computed numerically, so for a large problem, this is computationally expensive.

The HESSIAN= option controls which approximation to the Hessian is used in the minimization procedure. Alternate approximations are used to improve convergence and execution time. The choices are

CROSS   The crossproducts approximation is used.

GLS   The generalized least-squares approximation is used (default).

FDA   The Hessian is computed numerically by finite differences.

HESSIAN=GLS has better convergence properties in general, but COVBEST=CROSS produces the most pessimistic standard error bounds. When the HESSIAN= option is used, the default estimator of the variance-covariance of $\hat{\theta}$ is the inverse of the Hessian selected.

Properties of the Estimates

All of the methods are consistent. Small sample properties may not be good for non-linear models. The tests and standard errors reported are based on the convergence of the distribution of the estimates to a normal distribution in large samples.

These nonlinear estimation methods reduce to the corresponding linear systems regression methods if the model is linear. If this is the case, PROC MODEL produces the same estimates as PROC SYSLIN.

Except for GMM, the estimation methods assume that the equation errors for each observation are identically and independently distributed with a 0 mean vector and positive definite covariance matrix Σ consistently estimated by S. For FIML, the errors need to be normally distributed. There are no other assumptions concerning the distribution of the errors for the other estimation methods.

The consistency of the parameter estimates relies on the assumption that the S matrix is a consistent estimate of Σ. These standard error estimates are asymptotically valid, but for nonlinear models they may not be reliable for small samples.

The S matrix used for the calculation of the covariance of the parameter estimates is the best estimate available for the estimation method selected. For S-iterated methods, this is the most recent estimation of Σ. For OLS and 2SLS, an estimate of the S matrix is computed from OLS or 2SLS residuals and used for the calculation of the covariance matrix. For a complete list of the S matrix used for the calculation of the covariance of the parameter estimates, see Table 11.1.

Missing Values

An observation is excluded from the estimation if any variable used for FIT tasks is missing, if the weight for the observation is not greater than 0 when weights are used, or if a DELETE statement is executed by the model program. Variables used for FIT tasks include the equation errors for each equation; the instruments, if any; and the derivatives of the equation errors with respect to the parameters estimated. Note that variables can become missing as a result of computational errors or calculations with missing values.

The number of usable observations can change when different parameter values are used; some parameter values can be invalid and cause execution errors for some observations. PROC MODEL keeps track of the number of usable and missing observations at each pass through the data; and if the number of missing observations counted during a pass exceeds the number that was obtained using the previous parameter vector, the pass is terminated and the new parameter vector is considered infeasible. PROC MODEL never takes a step that produces more missing observations than the current estimate does.

The values used to compute the Durbin-Watson, R^2, and other statistics of fit are from the observations used in calculating the objective function and do not include any observation for which any needed variable was missing (residuals, derivatives, and instruments).

Details on the Covariance of Equation Errors

There are several **S** matrices that can be involved in the various estimation methods and in forming the estimate of the covariance of parameter estimates. These **S** matrices are estimates of Σ, the true covariance of the equation errors. Apart from the choice of instrumental or noninstrumental methods, many of the methods provided by PROC MODEL differ in the way the various **S** matrices are formed and used.

All of the estimation methods result in a final estimate of Σ, which is included in the output if the COVS option is specified. The final **S** matrix of each method provides the initial **S** matrix for any subsequent estimation.

This estimate of the covariance of equation errors is defined as

$$\mathbf{S} = \mathbf{D}(\mathbf{R}'\mathbf{R})\mathbf{D}$$

where $\mathbf{R} = (\mathbf{r}_1, \ldots, \mathbf{r}_g)$ is composed of the equation residuals computed from the current parameter estimates in an $n \times g$ matrix and **D** is a diagonal matrix that depends on the VARDEF= option.

For VARDEF=N, the diagonal elements of **D** are $n^{-1/2}$ where n is the number of non-missing observations. For VARDEF=WGT, n is replaced with the sum of the weights. For VARDEF=WDF, n is replaced with the sum of the weights minus the model degrees of freedom. For the default VARDEF=DF, the ith diagonal element of **D** is $(n - df_i)^{-1/2}$, where df_i is the degrees of freedom (number of parameters) for the ith equation. Binkley and Nelson (1984) show the importance of using a degrees-of-freedom correction in estimating Σ. Their results indicate that the DF method produces more accurate confidence intervals for N3SLS parameter estimates in the linear case than the alternative approach they tested. VARDEF=N is always used for the computation of the FIML estimates.

For the fixed **S** methods, the OUTSUSED= option writes the **S** matrix used in the estimation to a data set. This **S** matrix is either the estimate of the covariance of equation errors matrix from the preceding estimation, or a prior Σ estimate read in from a data set when the SDATA= option is specified. For the diagonal **S** methods, all of the off-diagonal elements of the **S** matrix are set to 0 for the estimation of the parameters and for the OUTSUSED= data set, but the output data set produced by the OUTS= option will contain the off-diagonal elements. For the OLS and N2SLS methods, there is no previous estimate of the covariance of equation errors matrix, and the option OUTSUSED= will save an identity matrix unless a prior Σ estimate is supplied by the SDATA= option. For FIML the OUTSUSED= data set contains the **S** matrix computed with VARDEF=N. The OUTS= data set contains the **S** matrix computed with the selected VARDEF= option. If the COVS option is used, the method is not S-iterated, and **S** is not an identity, the OUTSUSED= matrix is included in the printed output.

For the methods that iterate the covariance of equation errors matrix, the **S** matrix is iteratively reestimated from the residuals produced by the current parameter estimates. This **S** matrix estimate iteratively replaces the previous estimate until both the parameter estimates and the estimate of the covariance of equation errors matrix converge. The final OUTS= matrix and OUTSUSED= matrix are thus identical for the S-iterated methods.

Nested Iterations

By default, for S-iterated methods, the **S** matrix is held constant until the parameters converge once. Then the **S** matrix is reestimated. One iteration of the parameter estimation algorithm is performed, and the **S** matrix is again reestimated. This latter process is repeated until convergence of both the parameters and the **S** matrix. Since the objective of the minimization depends on the **S** matrix, this has the effect of chasing a moving target.

When the NESTIT option is specified, iterations are performed to convergence for the structural parameters with a fixed **S** matrix. The **S** matrix is then reestimated, the parameter iterations are repeated to convergence, and so on until both the parameters and the **S** matrix converge. This has the effect of fixing the objective function for the inner parameter iterations. It is more reliable, but usually more expensive, to nest the iterations.

R^2

For unrestricted linear models with an intercept successfully estimated by OLS, R^2 is always between 0 and 1. However, nonlinear models do not necessarily encompass the dependent mean as a special case and can produce negative R^2 statistics. Negative R^2 values can also be produced even for linear models when an estimation method other than OLS is used and no intercept term is in the model.

R^2 is defined for normalized equations as

$$R^2 = 1 - \frac{SSE}{SSA - \overline{y}^2}$$

where SSA is the sum of the squares of the actual y's and $\overline{y}$ are the actual means. R^2 cannot be computed for models in general form because of the need for an actual Y.

Minimization Methods

PROC MODEL currently supports two methods for minimizing the objective function. These methods are described in the following sections.

GAUSS

The Gauss-Newton parameter-change vector for a system with g equations, n non-missing observations, and p unknown parameters is

$$\Delta = (\mathbf{X}'\mathbf{X})^{-1}\mathbf{X}'\mathbf{r}$$

where Δ is the change vector, $\mathbf{X}$ is the stacked $ng \times p$ Jacobian matrix of partial derivatives of the equation errors with respect to the parameters, and $\mathbf{r}$ is an $ng \times 1$ vector of the stacked residuals. The components of $\mathbf{X}$ and $\mathbf{r}$ are weighted by the $\mathbf{S}^{-1}$ matrix. When instrumental methods are used, $\mathbf{X}$ and $\mathbf{r}$ are the projections of the Jacobian matrix and residuals vector in the instruments space and not the Jacobian and residuals themselves. In the preceding formula, $\mathbf{S}$ and $\mathbf{W}$ are suppressed.

If instrumental variables are used, then the change vector becomes:

$$\Delta = \left(\mathbf{X}'\left(\mathbf{S}^{-1} \otimes \mathbf{W}\right)\mathbf{X}\right)^{-1}\mathbf{X}'\left(\mathbf{S}^{-1} \otimes \mathbf{W}\right)\mathbf{r}$$

This vector is computed at the end of each iteration. The objective function is then computed at the changed parameter values at the start of the next iteration. If the objective function is not improved by the change, the Δ vector is reduced by one-half and the objective function is reevaluated. The change vector will be halved up to MAXSUBITER= times until the objective function is improved.

For FIML the $\mathbf{X}'\mathbf{X}$ matrix is substituted with one of three choices for approximations to the Hessian. See "Full Information Maximun Likelihood Estimation-FIML" earlier in this chapter.

MARQUARDT

The Marquardt-Levenberg parameter change vector is

$$\Delta = \left(\mathbf{X}'\mathbf{X} + \lambda\mathrm{diag}(\mathbf{X}'\mathbf{X})\right)^{-1}\mathbf{X}'\mathbf{r}$$

where Δ is the change vector, and $\mathbf{X}$ and $\mathbf{r}$ are the same as for the Gauss-Newton method, described in the preceding section. Before the iterations start, λ is set to a small value (1E-6). At each iteration, the objective function is evaluated at the parameters changed by Δ. If the objective function is not improved, λ is increased to 10λ and the step is tried again. λ can be increased up to MAXSUBITER= times to a maximum of 1E15 (whichever comes first) until the objective function is improved. For the start of the next iteration, λ is reduced to $\max\left(\lambda/10, 10^{-10}\right)$.

Convergence Criteria

There are a number of measures that could be used as convergence or stopping criteria. PROC MODEL computes five convergence measures labeled R, S, PPC, RPC, and OBJECT.

When an estimation technique that iterates estimates of Σ is used (that is, IT3SLS), two convergence criteria are used. The termination values can be specified with the CONVERGE=(p,s) option in the FIT statement. If the second value, s, is not specified, it defaults to p. The criterion labeled S (given in the following) controls the convergence of the **S** matrix. When S is less than *s*, the **S** matrix has converged. The criterion labeled R is compared to the *p*-value to test convergence of the parameters.

The R convergence measure cannot be computed accurately in the special case of singular residuals (when all the residuals are close to 0) or in the case of a 0 objective value. When either the trace of the **S** matrix computed from the current residuals (Trace(**S**)) or the objective value is less than the value of the SINGULAR= option, convergence is assumed.

The various convergence measures are explained in the following:

R   is the primary convergence measure for the parameters. It measures the degree to which the residuals are orthogonal to the Jacobian columns, and it approaches 0 as the gradient of the objective function becomes small. R is defined as the square root of

$$\frac{\mathbf{r}'\left(\mathbf{S}^{-1}\otimes\mathbf{W}\right)\mathbf{X}\left(\mathbf{X}'\left(\mathbf{S}^{-1}\otimes\mathbf{W}\right)\mathbf{X}\right)^{-1}\mathbf{X}'\left(\mathbf{S}^{-1}\otimes\mathbf{W}\right)\mathbf{r}}{\mathbf{r}'\left(\mathbf{S}^{-1}\otimes\mathbf{W}\right)\mathbf{r}}$$

where **X** is the Jacobian matrix and **r** is the residuals vector. R is similar to the relative offset orthogonality convergence criterion proposed by Bates and Watts (1981).

In the univariate case, the R measure has several equivalent interpretations:

- the cosine of the angle between the residuals vector and the column space of the Jacobian matrix. When this cosine is 0, the residuals are orthogonal to the partial derivatives of the predicted values with respect to the parameters, and the gradient of the objective function is 0.

- the square root of the R^2 for the current linear pseudo-model in the residuals

- a norm of the gradient of the objective function, where the norming matrix is proportional to the current estimate of the covariance of the parameter estimates. Thus, using R, convergence is judged when the gradient becomes small in this norm.

- the prospective relative change in the objective function value expected from the next GAUSS step, assuming that the current linearization of the model is a good local approximation.

In the multivariate case, R is somewhat more complicated, but it is designed to go to 0 as the gradient of the objective becomes small and can still be given the previous interpretations for the aggregation of the equations weighted by $\mathbf{S}^{-1}$.

PPC   is the prospective parameter change measure. PPC measures the maximum relative change in the parameters implied by the parameter-change vector computed for the next iteration. At the kth iteration, PPC is the maximum over the parameters

$$\frac{\left| \theta_i^{k+1} - \theta_i^k \right|}{\left| \theta_i^k \right| + 10^{-6}}$$

where θ_i^k is the current value of the ith parameter and θ_i^{k+1} is the prospective value of this parameter after adding the change vector computed for the next iteration. The parameter with the maximum prospective relative change is printed with the value of PPC, unless the PPC is nearly 0.

RPC   is the retrospective parameter change measure. RPC measures the maximum relative change in the parameters from the previous iteration. At the kth iteration, RPC is the maximum over i of

$$\frac{\left| \theta_i^k - \theta_i^{k-1} \right|}{\left| \theta_i^{k-1} \right| + 10^{-6}}$$

where θ_i^k is the current value of the ith parameter and θ_i^{k-1} is the previous value of this parameter. The name of the parameter with the maximum retrospective relative change is printed with the value of RPC, unless the RPC is nearly 0.

OBJECT measures the relative change in the objective function value between iterations:

$$\frac{\left| O^k - O^{k-1} \right|}{O^{k-1} + 10^{-6}}$$

where O^{k-1} is the value of the objective function (O^k) from the previous iteration.

S   measures the relative change in the $\mathbf{S}$ matrix. S is computed as the maximum over i, j of

$$\frac{\left| \mathbf{S}_{ij}^k - \mathbf{S}_{ij}^{k-1} \right|}{\left| \mathbf{S}_{ij}^{k-1} \right| + 10^{-6}}$$

where $\mathbf{S}^{k-1}$ is the previous $\mathbf{S}$ matrix. The S measure is relevant only for estimation methods that iterate the $\mathbf{S}$ matrix.

An example of the convergence criteria output is as follows:

```
                Minimization Summary
            Method               GAUSS
            Iterations               5

            Final  Convergence  Criteria
            R                 0.00023969
            PPC(C2)             0.000046
            RPC(C2)             0.000398
            Object            0.00004896
            Trace(S)          4920.12012
            Objective Value   0.04686739
            S                 0.00041448
```

Figure 11.14. Convergence Criteria Output

This output indicates the total number of iterations required by the Gauss minimization for all the **S** matrices was 5. The "Trace(S)" is the trace (the sum of the diagonal elements) of the **S** matrix computed from the current residuals. This row is labeled MSE if there is only one equation.

Troubleshooting Convergence Problems

As with any nonlinear estimation routine, there is no guarantee that the estimation will be successful for a given model and data. If the equations are linear with respect to the parameters, the parameter estimates always converge in one iteration. The methods that iterate the **S** matrix must iterate further for the **S** matrix to converge. Nonlinear models may not necessarily converge.

Convergence can be expected only with fully identified parameters, adequate data, and starting values sufficiently close to solution estimates.

Convergence and the rate of convergence may depend primarily on the choice of starting values for the estimates. This does not mean that a great deal of effort should be invested in choosing starting values. First, try the default values. If the estimation fails with these starting values, examine the model and data and rerun the estimation using reasonable starting values. It is usually not necessary that the starting values be good, just that they not be bad; choose values that seem plausible for the model and data.

An Example of Requiring Starting Values

Suppose you want to regress a variable Y on a variable X, assuming that the variables are related by the following nonlinear equation:

$$y = a + b\,x^c + \epsilon$$

In this equation, Y is linearly related to a power transformation of X. The unknown parameters are a, b, and c. ϵ is an unobserved random error. Some simulated data were generated using the following SAS statements. In this simulation, $a = 10$, $b = 2$, and the use of the SQRT function corresponds to $c = .5$.

```
data test;
  do i = 1 to 20;
     x = 5 * ranuni(1234);
     y = 10 + 2 * sqrt(x) + .1 * rannor(2345);
     output;
     end;
run;
```

The following statements specify the model and give descriptive labels to the model parameters. Then the FIT statement attempts to estimate A, B, and C using the default starting value .0001.

```
proc model data=test;
   y = a + b * x ** c;
   label a = "Intercept"
         b = "Coefficient of Transformed X"
         c = "Power Transformation Parameter";
   fit y;
run;
```

PROC MODEL prints model summary and estimation problem summary reports and then prints the output shown in Figure 11.15.

```
                           OLS Estimation
ERROR: After 20 halvings of the GAUSS method parameter change vector the objective
       function was not improved.
       With the change vector below reduced by the factor 9.5367432E-7, the OBJECTIVE=
       4586843415.1, which is not less than the previous OBJECTIVE=155.23721009.

Failed GAUSS Method Change Vector At OLS Iteration 1
A:  -6999834 B:   6999822 C:  -7011011


ERROR: The parameter estimates failed to converge for OLS after 1 iterations using
       CONVERGE=0.001 as the convergence criteria.

OLS Iteration 1: N=20 Objective=155.23721009 MSE=182.63201187 Nsubit=20 R=0.9998251532
                 PPC=69415946768(C)
                 A: 0.0001 B: 0.0001 C: 0.0001

   GAUSS Method Parameter Change Vector At OLS Iteration 1
   A:  -6999834 B:   6999822 C:  -7011011
```

Figure 11.15. Diagnostics for Convergence Failure

By using the default starting values, PROC MODEL was unable to take even the first step in iterating to the solution. The change in the parameters that the Gauss-Newton method computes is extreme and makes the objective values worse instead of better. Even when this step is shortened by a factor of a million, the objective function is still worse, and PROC MODEL fails.

The problem is caused by the starting value of C. Using the default starting value C=.0001, the first iteration attempts to compute better values of A and B by what is, in effect, a linear regression of Y on the 10,000th root of X, which is almost the same as the constant 1. Thus the matrix that is inverted to compute the changes is nearly singular and affects the accuracy of the computed parameter changes.

This is also illustrated by the next part of the output, which displays collinearity diagnostics for the crossproducts matrix of the partial derivatives with respect to the parameters, shown in Figure 11.16.

```
WARNING: Singularities or near singularities have caused grossly large variance
         calculations. To provide diagnostics, the eigenvalues are inflated to a minimum
         of 1e-12.


                              Collinearity Diagnostics

                             Condition  Var Prop  Var Prop  Var Prop
            Number  Eigenvalue   Number     A         B         C
                 1   2.03043    1.0000    0.0000    0.0000    0.0000
                 2   0.96957    1.4471    0.0000    0.0000    0.0002
                 3     1E-12   1424932    1.0000    1.0000    0.9998
```

Figure 11.16. Collinearity Diagnostics

This output shows that the matrix is singular and that the partials of A, B, and C with respect to the residual are collinear at the point $(0.0001, 0.0001, 0.0001)$ in the parameter space. See "Linear Dependencies" later in this chapter for a full explanation of the collinearity diagnostics.

The MODEL procedure next prints the note shown in Figure 11.17, which suggests that you try different starting values.

```
NOTE: The parameter estimation is abandoned. Check your model and data. If the model is
      correct and the input data are appropriate, try rerunning the parameter estimation
      using different starting values for the parameter estimates.
      PROC MODEL continues as if the parameter estimates had converged.
```

Figure 11.17. Estimation Failure Note

PROC MODEL then produces the usual printout of results for the nonconverged parameter values. The estimation summary is shown in Figure 11.18. The heading includes the reminder (Not Converged).

```
                        OLS Estimation

             OLS Estimation Summary (Not Converged)

                Data set Option        Data set
                DATA=                     TEST

                Parameters Estimated (    3)

                       Minimization Summary
                Method                   GAUSS
                Iterations                   1
                Subiterations               20

                Final  Convergence  Criteria
                R               0.99982515
                PPC(C)             6.942E10
                RPC                        .
                Object                     .
                Trace(S)          182.632012
                Objective Value   155.23721

                     Observations Processed
                Read                      20
                Solved                    20
```

Figure 11.18. Nonconverged Estimation Summary

The nonconverged estimation results are shown in Figure 11.19.

```
                              OLS Estimation

        Nonlinear OLS Summary of Residual Errors (Estimates Not Converged)

                   DF    DF
        Equation Model Error        SSE        MSE    Root MSE  R-Square  Adj R-Sq

        Y            1    19       3105   163.40759   12.78310  -126.322  -126.322


               Nonlinear OLS Parameter Estimates (Not Converged)

                             Approx.    'T'   Approx.
        Parameter  Estimate  Std Err   Ratio  Prob>|T|  Label

        A          0.00010000  4.77797   0.00   1.0000  Intercept
        B          0.00010000       0  <-------- Biased  Coefficient of transformed X
        C          0.00010000       0  <-------- Biased  Power transformation parameter

        NOTE: The model was singular. Some estimates are marked 'Biased'.
```

Figure 11.19. Nonconverged Results

Note that the R^2 statistic is negative. An $R^2 < 0$ results when the residual mean square error for the model is larger than the variance of the dependent variable. Negative R^2 statistics can be produced when either the parameter estimates fail to converge correctly, as in this case, or when the correctly estimated model fits the data poorly.

Note that some of the parameter estimates are marked 'biased.' This means that the parameter is not uniquely estimable.

Controlling Starting Values

To fit the preceding model you must specify a better starting value for C. In this example, a starting value of 1 for C will make the model linear in X, so 1 is a good choice. Alternatively, you can plot the data to get an idea of the appropriate transformation needed for X and make a guess at a good C value. In any case, avoid starting values of C that are either very large or close to 0. For starting values of A and B, you can either specify values, use the default, or have PROC MODEL fit starting values for them conditional on the starting value for C.

Starting values are specified with the START= option of the FIT statement or in a PARMS statement. For example, the following statements estimate the model parameters using the starting values A=.0001, B=.0001, and C=1.

```
proc model data=test;
   y = a + b * x ** c;
   label a = "Intercept"
         b = "Coefficient of Transformed X"
         c = "Power Transformation Parameter";
   fit y start=(c=1);
run;
```

Using these starting values, the estimates converge in 12 iterations. The results are shown in Figure 11.20. Note that since the START= option explicitly declares parameters, the parameter C is placed first in the table.

```
                              OLS Estimation

                   Nonlinear OLS Summary of Residual Errors

                 DF   DF
      Equation  Model Error      SSE        MSE     Root MSE  R-Square  Adj R-Sq

         Y        3    17      0.18089    0.01064    0.10315   0.9926    0.9917



                     Nonlinear OLS Parameter Estimates

                            Approx.    'T'    Approx.
      Parameter   Estimate  Std Err   Ratio  Prob>|T|  Label

      C           0.465513  0.04771    9.76   0.0001   Power Transformation Parameter
      A           9.750613  0.25656   38.00   0.0001   Intercept
      B           2.287272  0.27445    8.33   0.0001   Coefficient of Transformed X
```

Figure 11.20.   Converged Results

Using the STARTITER Option

PROC MODEL can compute starting values for some parameters conditional on starting values you specify for the other parameters. You supply starting values for some parameters and specify the STARTITER option in the FIT statement.

For example, the following statements set C to 1 and compute starting values for A and B by estimating these parameters conditional on the fixed value of C. With C=1 this is equivalent to computing A and B by linear regression on X. A PARMS statement is used to declare the parameters in alphabetical order. The ITPRINT option is used to print the parameter values at each iteration.

```
proc model data=test;
   parms a b c;
   y = a + b * x ** c;
   label a = "Intercept"
         b = "Coefficient of Transformed X"
         c = "Power Transformation Parameter";
   fit y start=(c=1) / startiter itprint;
run;
```

With better starting values, the estimates converge in only 5 iterations. Counting the 2 iterations required to compute the starting values for A and B, this is 5 fewer than the 12 iterations required without the STARTITER option. The iteration history listing is shown in Figure 11.21.

```
                              OLS Estimation

Estimates at Each START= Iteration

Iter    N Criterion Objective Subit          A         B          C
   0   20    0.9998  155.2352     0     0.0001    0.0001   1.000000
   1   20         0 0.0656414     0  11.083736  0.791944   1.000000


OLS Estimates at Each GAUSS Iteration

Iter    N Criterion Objective Subit          A         B          C
   0   20    0.9167 0.0656414     0  11.083736  0.791944   1.000000
   1   20    0.8947 0.0461593     1  10.759953  1.176620   0.709682
   2   20    0.8580 0.0343697     1  10.399248  1.583781   0.566538
   3   20    0.6638 0.0161703     0   9.829853  2.206472   0.450860
   4   20    0.0216 0.0090487     0   9.752423  2.285496   0.466454
   5   20 0.0000508 0.0090445     0   9.750700  2.287177   0.465525
NOTE: At OLS Iteration 5 CONVERGE=0.001 Criteria Met.
```

Figure 11.21. ITPRINT Listing

The results produced in this case are almost the same as the results shown in Figure 11.20, except that the PARMS statement causes the Parameter Estimates table to be ordered A, B, C instead of C, A, B. They are not exactly the same because the different starting values caused the iterations to converge at a slightly different place. This effect is controlled by changing the convergence criterion with the CONVERGE= option.

By default, the STARTITER option only performs one iteration to find starting values for the parameters not given values. In this case, the model is linear in A and B, so only one iteration is needed. If A or B were nonlinear, you could specify more than one starting-values iteration by specifying a number for the STARTITER= option.

Finding Starting Values by Grid Search

PROC MODEL can try various combinations of parameter values and use the combination producing the smallest objective function value as starting values. (For OLS the objective function is the residual mean square.) This is known as a preliminary *grid search*. You can combine the STARTITER option with a grid search.

For example, the following statements try 5 different starting values for C: 2, 1, .5, -.5, -1. For each value of C, values for A and B are estimated. The combination of A, B, and C values producing the smallest residual mean square is then used to start the iterative process.

```
proc model data=test;
   parms a b c;
   y = a + b * x ** c;
   label a = "Intercept"
         b = "Coefficient of Transformed X"
         c = "Power Transformation Parameter";
   fit y start=(c=2 1 .5 -.5 -1) / startiter itprint;
run;
```

The iteration history listing is shown in Figure 11.22. Using the best starting values found by the grid search, the OLS estimation only requires 2 iterations. However, since the grid search required 10 iterations, the total iterations in this case is 12.

```
                            OLS Estimation

Estimates at Each START= Iteration

Iter    N Criterion Objective Subit          A          B          C
   0   20    0.9990  155.2269     0      0.0001     0.0001   2.000000
   1   20         0  0.296706     0   11.733944   0.145627   2.000000
   0   20    0.9673  1.021194     0   11.733944   0.145627   1.000000
   1   20         0 0.0656414     0   11.083736   0.791944   1.000000
   0   20    0.9926  0.631313     0   11.083736   0.791944   0.500000
   1   20         0 0.0093181     0    9.918700   2.104367   0.500000
   0   20    0.9772  4.882620     0    9.918700   2.104367  -0.500000
   1   20         0  0.220510     0   14.360454  -1.838053  -0.500000
   0   20    0.9487  4.235745     0   14.360454  -1.838053  -1.000000
   1   20         0  0.423242     0   13.264446  -0.600889  -1.000000


OLS Estimates at Each GAUSS Iteration

Iter    N  Criterion Objective Subit          A          B          C
   0   20     0.1706 0.0093181     0    9.918700   2.104367   0.500000
   1   20     0.0644 0.0090821     0    9.763422   2.274195   0.465707
   2   20  0.0000345 0.0090445     0    9.750655   2.287225   0.465516
NOTE: At OLS Iteration 2 CONVERGE=0.001 Criteria Met.
```

Figure 11.22. ITPRINT Listing

Since no initial values for A or B were provided in the PARAMETERS statement or were read in with a PARMSDATA= or ESTDATA= option, A and B were given the default value of 0.0001 for the first iteration. At the second grid point, C=1, the values of A and B obtained from the previous iterations are used for the initial iteration. If initial values are provided for parameters, the parameters start at those initial values at each grid point.

Guessing Starting Values from the Logic of the Model

Example 11.1 of the logistic growth curve model of the U.S. population illustrates the need for reasonable starting values. This model can be written

$$pop = \frac{a}{1 + \exp(b - c(t - 1790))}$$

where t is time in years. The model is estimated using decennial census data of the U.S. population in millions. If this simple but highly nonlinear model is estimated using the default starting values, the estimation fails to converge.

To find reasonable starting values, first consider the meaning of a and c. Taking the limit as time increases, a is the limiting or maximum possible population. So, as a starting value for a, several times the most recent population known can be used, for example, one billion (1000 million).

Dividing the time derivative by the function to find the growth rate and taking the limit as t moves into the past, you can determine that c is the initial growth rate. You can examine the data and compute an estimate of the growth rate for the first few decades, or you can pick a number that sounds like a plausible population growth rate figure, such as 2%.

To find a starting value for b, let t equal the base year used, 1790, which causes c to drop out of the formula for that year, and then solve for the value of b that is consistent with the known population in 1790 and with the starting value of a. This yields $b = \ln(a/3.9 - 1)$ or about 5.5, where a is 1000 and 3.9 is roughly the population for 1790 given in the data. The estimates converge using these starting values.

Convergence Problems

When estimating nonlinear models, you may encounter some of the following convergence problems.

Unable to Improve

The optimization algorithm may be unable to find a step that improves the objective function. If this happens in the Gauss-Newton method, the step size is halved to find a change vector for which the objective improves. In the Marquardt method, λ will be increased to find a change vector for which the objective improves. If, after MAX-SUBITER= step-size halvings or increases in λ, the change vector still does not produce a better objective value, the iterations are stopped and an error message is printed. An example error message for the Gauss-Newton method is shown in Figure 11.23.

```
ERROR: After 20 halvings of the GAUSS method parameter change vector the
       objective function was not improved.
       With the change vector below reduced by the factor 9.5367432E-7, the
       OBJECTIVE=23.004554885, which is not less than the previous OBJECTIVE=
       23.004554885.
```

Figure 11.23. Convergence Error Message

Failure of the algorithm to improve the objective value can be caused by a CON-VERGE= value that is too small. Look at the convergence measures reported at the point of failure. If the estimates appear to be approximately converged, you can accept the NOT CONVERGED results reported, or you can try rerunning the FIT task with a larger CONVERGE= value.

If the procedure fails to converge because it is unable to find a change vector that improves the objective value, check your model and data to ensure that all parameters are identified and data values are reasonably scaled. Then, rerun the model with different starting values. Also, consider using the Marquardt method if Gauss-Newton fails; the Gauss-Newton method can get into trouble if the Jacobian matrix is nearly singular or ill-conditioned. Keep in mind that a nonlinear model can be well-identified and well-conditioned for parameter values close to the solution values but unidentified or numerically ill-conditioned for other parameter values. The choice of starting values can make a big difference.

Nonconvergence

The estimates can diverge into areas where the program overflows or they can go into areas where function values are illegal or too badly scaled for accurate calculation. The estimation can also take steps that are too small or that make only marginal improvement in the objective function and, thus, fail to converge within the iteration limit.

When the estimates fail to converge, collinearity diagnostics for the Jacobian crossproducts matrix are printed if there are 20 or fewer parameters estimated. See "Linear Dependencies" later in this section for an explanation of these diagnostics.

Inadequate Convergence Criterion

If convergence is obtained, the resulting estimates will only approximate a minimum point of the objective function. The statistical validity of the results is based on the exact minimization of the objective function, and for nonlinear models the quality of the results depends on the accuracy of the approximation of the minimum. This is controlled by the convergence criterion used.

There are many nonlinear functions for which the objective function is quite flat in a large region around the minimum point so many different parameter vectors may satisfy a weak convergence criterion. By using different starting values, different convergence criteria, or different minimization methods, you can produce very different estimates for such models.

You can guard against this by running the estimation with different starting values and different convergence criteria and checking that the estimates produced are essentially the same. If they are not, use a smaller CONVERGE= value.

Local Minimum

You may have converged to a local minimum rather than a global one. This problem is difficult to detect because the procedure will appear to have succeeded. You can guard against this by running the estimation with different starting values or with a different minimization technique. The START= option can be used to automatically perform a grid search to aid in the search for a global minimum.

Discontinuities

The computational methods assume that the model is a continuous and smooth function of the parameters. If this is not the case, the methods may not work.

If the model equations or their derivatives contain discontinuities, the estimation will usually succeed, provided that the final parameter estimates lie in a continuous interval and that the iterations do not produce parameter values at points of discontinuity or parameter values that try to cross asymptotes.

One common case of discontinuities causing estimation failure is that of an asymptotic discontinuity between the final estimates and the initial values. For example, consider the following model, which is basically linear but is written with one parameter in reciprocal form:

```
y = a + b * x1 + x2 / c;
```

By placing the parameter C in the denominator, a singularity is introduced into the parameter space at C=0. This is not necessarily a problem, but if the correct estimate of C is negative while the starting value is positive (or vice versa), the asymptotic discontinuity at 0 will lie between the estimate and the starting value. This means that the iterations have to pass through the singularity to get to the correct estimates. The situation is shown in Figure 11.24.

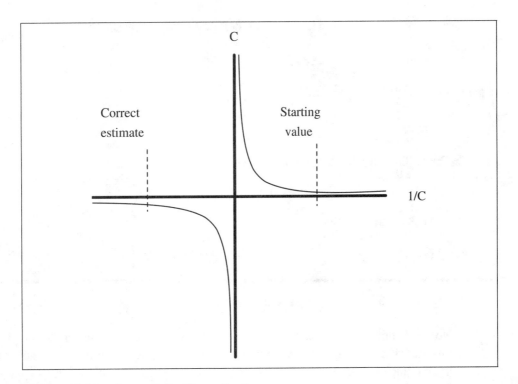

Figure 11.24. Asymptotic Discontinuity

Because of the incorrect sign of the starting value, the C estimate goes off towards positive infinity in a vain effort to get past the asymptote and onto the correct arm of the hyperbola. As the computer is required to work with ever closer approximations to infinity, the numerical calculations break down and an "objective function was not improved" convergence failure message is printed. At this point, the iterations terminate with an extremely large positive value for C. When the sign of the starting value for C is changed, the estimates converge quickly to the correct values.

Linear Dependencies

In some cases, the Jacobian matrix may not be of full rank; parameters may not be fully identified for the current parameter values with the current data. When linear dependencies occur among the derivatives of the model, some parameters appear with a standard error of 0 and with the word BIASED printed in place of the *t* statistic. When this happens, collinearity diagnostics for the Jacobian crossproducts matrix are printed if the DETAILS option is specified and there are twenty or fewer parameters estimated. Collinearity diagnostics are also printed out automatically when a minimization method fails, or when the COLLIN option is specified.

For each parameter, the proportion of the variance of the estimate accounted for by each *principal component* is printed. The principal components are constructed from the eigenvalues and eigenvectors of the correlation matrix (scaled covariance matrix). When collinearity exists, a principal component is associated with proportion of the variance of more than one parameter. The numbers reported are proportions, so they will remain between 0 and 1. If two or more parameters have large proportion values associated with the same principle component, then two problems can occur: the computation of the parameter estimates are slow or nonconvergent; and the parameter estimates have inflated variances (Belsley 1980, p. 105-117).

For example, the following cubic model is fit to a quadratic data set:

```
proc model data=test3;
   exogenous x1 ;
   parms b1 a1 c1 ;
   y1 = a1 * x1 + b1 * x1 * x1  + c1 * x1 * x1 *x1;
   fit y1/ collin ;
run;
```

The collinearity diagnostics are shown in Figure 11.25.

```
                 Collinearity Diagnostics

                        Condition  Var Prop  Var Prop  Var Prop
       Number  Eigenvalue  Number        B1        A1        C1

            1     2.91421   1.0000    0.0002    0.0011    0.0005
            2     0.08467   5.8668    0.0002    0.0671    0.0221
            3     0.00112  50.9370    0.9996    0.9318    0.9774
```

Figure 11.25.   Collinearity Diagnostics

Notice that the proportions associated with the smallest eigenvalue are almost 1. For this model, removing any of the parameters will decrease the variances of the remaining parameters.

In many models, the collinearity may not be clear cut. Collinearity is not necessarily something you remove. A model may need to be reformulated to remove the redundant parameterization or the limitations on the estimatability of the model can be accepted.

Collinearity diagnostics are also useful when an estimation does not converge. The diagnostics provide insight into the numerical problems and can suggest which parameters need better starting values. These diagnostics are based on the approach of Belsley, Kuh, and Welsch (1980).

Iteration History

The options ITPRINT, ITDETAILS, XPX, I, and ITALL specify a detailed listing of each iteration of the minimization process.

ITPRINT Option

The ITPRINT information is selected whenever any iteration information is requested. An example of the ITPRINT output for the MODEL program:

```
proc model data=test2 ;
   y1 = a1 * x2 * x2 - exp( d1*x1);
   y2 = a2 * x1 * x1 + b2 * exp( d2*x2);
   fit y1 y2 / itprint ;
run;
```

is shown in Figure 11.26.

```
OLS Iteration 0: N=50 Objective=151361.08307 Trace(S)=157745.12349 Nsubit=0 R=
                 0.9979800182
                 A1: 0.0001 D1: 0.0001 A2: 0.0001 B2: 0.0001 D2: 0.0001

OLS Iteration 1: N=50 Objective=151282.57326 Trace(S)=157663.19695 Nsubit=12 R=
                 0.9979651255
                 A1: -0.000386686 D1: 0.0002050242 A2: -0.000362408
                 B2: -0.000686288 D2: 0.3033921694
```

Figure 11.26. A Portion of the ITPRINT Output

If ITPRINT is selected by itself and the page is wide enough to print the parameters in columns (the LINESIZE= option in the OPTIONS statement), the output will be a tabular output, as shown in Figure 11.27.

```
Iter   N Criterion Objective Subit       A1         D1         A2         B2        D2
  0   50  0.9980   151361.1    0       0.0001     0.0001     0.0001     0.0001    0.0001
  1   50  0.9980   151282.6   12    -0.0003867  0.00020502 -0.0003624 -0.0006863  0.303392
  2   50  0.9977   133249.9    4    -0.124948   0.0270765  -0.124725   0.00138091 0.436958
  3   50  0.2136   643.2317    0    -1.992828   0.397328   -1.982484   0.0001768  0.428796
```

Figure 11.27. A Portion of the ITPRINT Output in Tabular Form

The following information is displayed for each iteration:

N   the number of usable observations

Objective   the corrected objective function value

Trace(S)   the trace of the **S** matrix

subit   the number of subiterations required to find a λ or a damping factor that reduces the objective function

R   the R convergence measure

The estimates for the parameters at each iteration are also printed.

ITDETAILS Option

If the same estimation is run with the ITDETAILS option, the output shown in Figure 11.28 is produced.

```
OLS Iteration 0: N=50 Objective=151361.08307 Trace(S)=157745.12349 Nsubit=0
                 Theta=89.905612158 R=0.9979800182 PPC=12299848.769(D2)
                 A1: 0.0001 D1: 0.0001 A2: 0.0001 B2: 0.0001 D2: 0.0001

At   Iteration 0.Observation 6.
     ERROR: 1 execution errors for this observation: 2(17:32):#temp4=EXP(
     18048.367983)

At   Iteration 0.Observation 10.
     ERROR: 1 execution errors for this observation: 2(17:32):#temp4=EXP(
     13891.866445)

WARNING:  At OLS Iteration 1 a total of 2 execution errors occurred for 23
          observations.

OLS Iteration 1, Subiteration 0: N=27 Nmiss=2 Objective=151361.08307
                                 Trace(S)=157745.12349 Theta=89.905612158
                                 Stepsize=1 PPC=12299848.769(D2)
                   A1: -1.993365346 D1: 0.4302789353 A2: -1.893924247 B2:
                   -3.220534649 D2: 1242.2848257

OLS Iteration 1, Subiteration 1: N=5 Nmiss=1 Objective=151361.08307 Trace(S)=
                                 157745.12349 Theta=89.905612158 Stepsize=0.5
                                 PPC=6149924.3845(D2)
```

```
        A1: -0.996632673 D1: 0.2151894677 A2: -0.946912124 B2:
        -1.610217325 D2: 621.14246283

OLS Iteration 1, Subiteration 2: N=5 Nmiss=1 Objective=151361.08307 Trace(S)=
                    157745.12349 Theta=89.905612158
                    Stepsize=0.25 PPC=3074962.1922(D2)
        A1: -0.498266337 D1: 0.1076447338 A2: -0.473406062 B2:
        -0.805058662 D2: 310.57128142
```

Figure 11.28. A Portion of the ITDETAILS Option Output

The additional values printed for the ITDETAILS option are

Theta   is the angle in degrees between Δ, the parameter change vector, and the negative gradient of the objective function.

Phi   is the directional derivative of the objective function in the Δ direction scaled by the objective function

Stepsize   is the value of the damping factor used to reduce Δ if the Gauss-Newton method is used.

Lambda   is the value of λ if the Marquardt method is used

Rank(XPX)   If the projected Jacobian crossproducts matrix is singular, the rank of the $\mathbf{X}'\mathbf{X}$ matrix is output.

The definitions of PPC and R are explained in "Convergence Criteria" earlier in this chapter. When the values of PPC are large, the parameter associated with the criteria is displayed in parentheses after the value.

XPX and I Options

The XPX and the I options select the printing of the augmented $\mathbf{X}'\mathbf{X}$ matrix and the augmented $\mathbf{X}'\mathbf{X}$ matrix after a *sweep* operation (Goodnight 1979) has been performed on it. An example of the output from:

```
proc model data=test2 ;
   y1 = a1 * x2 * x2 - exp( d1*x1);
   y2 = a2 * x1 * x1 + b2 * exp( d2*x2);
   fit y1 y2 / XPX I ;
run;
```

is shown in Figure 11.29.

```
              Cross Products for System At OLS Iteration 0
    XPX           A1         D1         A2         B2          D2     Residual

    A1        1839468     -33818          0          0           0      3681465
    D1         -33818       1276          0          0           0       -67965
    A2              0          0      42925       1275      0.1547        85216
    B2              0          0       1275    50.0076    0.003867         2571
    D2              0          0     0.1547   0.003867   0.0000641       0.2259
    Residual  3681465     -67965      85216       2571      0.2259      7568054

              XPX Inverse for System At OLS Iteration 0

    I             A1         D1         A2         B2          D2     Residual

    A1      1.0599E-6  0.0000281          0          0           0       1.9935
    D1      0.0000281   0.001527          0          0           0      -0.4302
    A2              0          0  0.0000965  -0.002455     -0.0849       1.8940
```

B2	0	0	-0.002455	0.0825	0.9476	3.2206
D2	0	0	-0.0849	0.9476	15747	-1242
Residual	1.9935	-0.4302	1.8940	3.2206	-1242	30544

Figure 11.29. XPX and I Options Output

The first matrix, labeled "Cross Products," for OLS estimation is

$$\begin{bmatrix} \mathbf{X'X} & \mathbf{X'r} \\ \mathbf{r'X} & \mathbf{r'r} \end{bmatrix}$$

The column labeled "Residual" in the output is the vector $\mathbf{X'r}$, which is the gradient of the objective function. The diagonal scalar value $\mathbf{r'r}$ is the objective function uncorrected for degrees of freedom. The second matrix, labeled "XPX Inverse," is created through a sweep operation on the augmented $\mathbf{X'X}$ matrix to get

$$\begin{bmatrix} (\mathbf{X'X})^{-1} & (\mathbf{X'X})^{-1}\mathbf{X'r} \\ (\mathbf{X'r})'(\mathbf{X'X})^{-1} & \mathbf{r'r} - (\mathbf{X'r})'(\mathbf{X'X})^{-1}\mathbf{X'r} \end{bmatrix}$$

Note that the residual column is the change vector used to update the parameter estimates at each iteration. The corner scalar element is used to compute the R convergence criteria.

ITALL Option

The ITALL option, in addition to causing the output of all of the preceding options, outputs the S matrix, the inverse of the S matrix, the CROSS matrix, and the swept CROSS matrix. An example of a portion of the CROSS matrix for the preceding example is shown in Figure 11.30.

```
                 Crossproducts Matrix At OLS Iteration 0

Cross                       1    @PRED.Y1/@A1   @PRED.Y1/@D1   @PRED.Y2/@A2

1                  50.000000     6409.079154    -239.163337    1275.000000
@PRED.Y1/@A1     6409.079154        1839468         -33818         187766
@PRED.Y1/@D1     -239.163337         -33818    1276.450599   -7252.996714
@PRED.Y2/@A2     1275.000000         187766   -7252.996714          42925
@PRED.Y2/@B2       50.003771    6409.883889    -239.189345    1275.153800
@PRED.Y2/@D2        0.003803       0.813934      -0.026177       0.154739
RESID.Y1              12836        3681465         -67965         378250
RESID.Y2         2571.200557         382603         -14492          85216

                 Crossproducts Matrix At OLS Iteration 0

Cross          @PRED.Y2/@B2   @PRED.Y2/@D2        RESID.Y1       RESID.Y2

1                 50.003771       0.003803           12836    2571.200557
@PRED.Y1/@A1    6409.883889       0.813934         3681465         382603
@PRED.Y1/@D1    -239.189345      -0.026177          -67965         -14492
@PRED.Y2/@A2    1275.153800       0.154739          378250          85216
@PRED.Y2/@B2      50.007606       0.003867           12838    2571.424539
@PRED.Y2/@D2       0.003867    0.000064107        1.766211       0.225895
RESID.Y1              12838       1.766211         7393601         772309
RESID.Y2        2571.424539       0.225895          772309         174453
```

Figure 11.30. ITALL Option Cross-Products Matrix Output

Computer Resource Requirements

If you are estimating large systems, you need to be aware of how PROC MODEL uses computer resources such as memory and the CPU so they can be used most efficiently.

Saving Time with Large Data Sets

If your input data set has many observations, the FIT statement does a large number of model program executions. A pass through the data is made at least once for each iteration and the model program is executed once for each observation in each pass. If you refine the starting estimates by using a smaller data set, the final estimation with the full data set may require fewer iterations.

For example, you can use

```
proc model;
   /* Model goes here */
   fit / data=a(obs=25);
   fit / data=a;
```

where OBS=25 selects the first 25 observations in A. The second FIT statement produces the final estimates using the full data set and starting values from the first run.

Fitting the Model in Sections to Save Space and Time

If you have a very large model (with several hundred parameters, for example), the procedure uses considerable space and time. You may be able to save resources by breaking the estimation process into several steps and estimating the parameters in subsets.

You can use the FIT statement to select for estimation only the parameters for selected equations. Do not break the estimation into too many small steps; the total computer time required is minimized by compromising between the number of FIT statements that are executed and the size of the crossproducts matrices that must be processed.

When the parameters are estimated for selected equations, the entire model program must be executed, even though only a part of the model program may be needed to compute the residuals for the equations selected for estimation. If the model itself can be broken into sections for estimation (and later combined for simulation and forecasting), then more resources can be saved.

For example, to estimate the following four-equation model in two steps, you could use

```
proc model data=a outmodel=part1;
   parms a0-a2 b0-b2 c0-c3 d0-d3;
   y1 = a0 + a1*y2 + a2*x1;
   y2 = b0 + b1*y1 + b2*x2;
   y3 = c0 + c1*y1 + c2*y4 + c3*x3;
   y4 = d0 + d1*y1 + d2*y3 + d3*x4;
   fit y1 y2;
   fit y3 y4;
   fit y1 y2 y3 y4;
run;
```

You should try estimating the model in pieces to save time only if there are more than 14 parameters; the preceding example takes more time, not less, and the difference in memory required is trivial.

Memory Requirements for Parameter Estimation

PROC MODEL is a large program, and it requires much memory. Memory is also required for the SAS System, various data areas, the model program and associated tables and data vectors, and a few crossproducts matrices. For most models, the memory required for PROC MODEL itself is much larger than that required for the model program, and the memory required for the model program is larger than that required for the crossproducts matrices.

The number of bytes needed for two crossproducts matrices, four **S** matrices, and three parameter covariance matrices is

$$8 \times (2 + k + m + g)^2 + 16 \times g^2 + 12 \times (p + 1)^2$$

plus lower-order terms. m is the number of unique nonzero derivatives of each residual with respect to each parameter, g is the number of equations, k is the number of instruments, and p is the number of parameters. This formula is for the memory required for 3SLS. If you are using OLS, a reasonable estimate of the memory required for large problems (greater than 100 parameters) is to divide the value obtained from the formula in half.

Consider the following model program:

```
proc model data=test2 details;
   exogenous x1 x2;
   parms b1 100 a1 a2 b2 2.5 c2 55;
   y1 = a1 * y2 + b1 * x1 * x1;
   y2 = a2 * y1 + b2 * x2 * x2 + c2 / x2;
   fit y1 y2 / n3sls;
   inst b1 b2 c2 x1 ;
run;
```

The DETAILS option prints the storage requirements information shown in Figure 11.31.

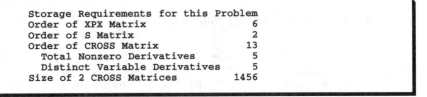

```
            Storage Requirements for this Problem
            Order of XPX Matrix               6
            Order of S Matrix                 2
            Order of CROSS Matrix            13
              Total Nonzero Derivatives       5
              Distinct Variable Derivatives   5
            Size of 2 CROSS Matrices       1456
```

Figure 11.31. Storage Requirements Information

The matrix $\mathbf{X'X}$ augmented by the residual vector is called the XPX matrix in the output, and it has the size $m + 1$. The order of the **S** matrix, 2 for this example, is the value of g. The CROSS matrix is made up of the k unique instruments, a constant column representing the intercept terms, followed by the m unique Jacobian variables plus a constant column representing the parameters with constant derivatives, followed by the g residuals.

The size of two CROSS matrices in bytes is

$$8 \times \left[(2 + k + m + g)^2 + 2 + k + m + g \right]$$

Note that the CROSS matrix is symmetric, so only the diagonal and the upper triangular part of the matrix is stored. For examples of the CROSS and XPX matrices see "Iteration History" in this section.

Heteroscedasticity

One of the key assumptions of regression is that the variance of the errors is constant across observations. If the errors have constant variance, the errors are called *homoscedastic*. Typically, residuals are plotted to assess this assumption. Standard estimation methods are inefficient when the errors are *heteroscedastic* or have nonconstant variance.

There are two methods for improving the efficiency of the parameter estimation in the presence of heteroscedastic errors. If the error variance relationships are known, weighted regression can be used. If the error variance relationship is unknown, GMM estimation can be used.

Weighted Regression

The WEIGHT statement can be used to correct for the heteroscedasticity. Consider the following model, which has a heteroscedastic error term:

$$y_t = 250 \left(e^{-0.2t} - e^{-0.8t} \right) + \sqrt{(9 / t)} \, \epsilon_t$$

The data for this model is generated with the following SAS statements:

```
data test;
   do t=1 to 25;
      y = 250 * (exp( -0.2 * t ) - exp( -0.8 * t )) +
          sqrt( 9 / t ) * rannor(1);
      output;
   end;
run;
```

If this model is estimated with OLS,

```
proc model data=test;
   parms b1 0.1 b2 0.9;
   y = 250 * ( exp( -b1 * t ) - exp( -b2 * t ) );
   fit y;
run;
```

the estimates shown in Figure 11.32 are obtained for the parameters.

Parameter	Estimate	Approx. Std Err	'T' Ratio	Approx. Prob>|T|
B1	0.200977	0.0010119	198.60	0.0001
B2	0.826236	0.0085334	96.82	0.0001

Figure 11.32. Unweighted OLS Estimates

If both sides of the model equation are multiplied by $t^{1/2}$, the model will have a homoscedastic error term. This multiplication or weighting is done through the WEIGHT statement. The WEIGHT statement variable operates on the squared residuals as

$$\epsilon_t' \, \epsilon_t = weight \times \mathbf{q}_t' \, \mathbf{q}_t$$

so that the WEIGHT statement variable represents the square of the model multiplier. The following PROC MODEL statements corrects the heteroscedasticity with a WEIGHT statement

```
proc model data=test;
   parms b1 0.1 b2 0.9;
   y = 250 * ( exp( -b1 * t ) - exp( -b2 * t ) );
   fit y;
   weight t;
run;
```

Note that the WEIGHT statement follows the FIT statement. The weighted estimates are shown in Figure 11.33.

Parameter	Estimate	Approx. Std Err	'T' Ratio	Approx. Prob>|T|
B1	0.200503	0.0008441	237.53	0.0001
B2	0.816710	0.01391	58.71	0.0001

Figure 11.33. Weighted OLS Estimates

The weighted OLS estimates are identical to the output produced by the following PROC MODEL example:

```
proc model data=test;
   parms b1 0.1 b2 0.9;
   y = 250 * ( exp( -b1 * t ) - exp( -b2 * t ) );
   _weight_ = t;
   fit y;
run;
```

If the WEIGHT statement is used in conjunction with the _WEIGHT_ variable, the two values are multiplied together to obtain the weight used.

The WEIGHT statement and the _WEIGHT_ variable operate on all the residuals in a system of equations. If a subset of the equations need to be weighted, the residuals for each equation can be modified through the RESID. variable for each equation. The following example demonstrates the use of the RESID. variable to make a homoscedastic error term:

```
proc model data=test;
   parms b1 0.1 b2 0.9;
   y = 250 * ( exp( -b1 * t ) - exp( -b2 * t ) );
   resid.y = resid.y * sqrt(t);
   fit y;
run;
```

These statements produce estimates of the parameters and standard errors that are identical to the weighted OLS estimates. The reassignment of the RESID.Y variable must be done after Y is assigned, otherwise it would have no effect. Also, note that the residual (RESID.Y) is multiplied by $\sqrt{t}$. Here the multiplier is acting on the residual before it is squared.

GMM Estimation

If the form of the heteroscedasticity is unknown, generalized method of moments estimation (GMM) can be used. The following PROC MODEL statements use GMM to estimate the example model used in the preceding section:

```
proc model data=test;
   parms b1 0.1 b2 0.9;
   y = 250 * ( exp( -b1 * t ) - exp( -b2 * t ) );
   fit y / gmm;
   instruments b1 b2;
run;
```

GMM is an instrumental method, so instrument variables must be provided.

GMM estimation generates estimates for the parameters shown in Figure 11.34.

Parameter	Estimate	Approx. Std Err	'T' Ratio	Approx. Prob>|T|
B1	0.200487	0.0008072	248.38	0.0001
B2	0.822148	0.01419	57.95	0.0001

Figure 11.34. GMM Estimation for Heteroscedasticity

Transformation of Error Terms

In PROC MODEL you can control the form of the error term. By default the error term is assumed to be additive. This section demonstrates how to specify nonadditive error terms and discusses the effects of these transformations.

Models with Nonadditive Errors

The estimation methods used by PROC MODEL assume that the error terms of the equations are independently and identically distributed with zero means and finite variances. Furthermore, the methods assume that the RESID.*name* equation variable for normalized form equations or the EQ.*name* equation variable for general form equations contains an estimate of the error term of the true stochastic model whose parameters are being estimated. Details on RESID.*name* and EQ.*name* equation variables are in the section "Equation Translations" later in this chapter.

To illustrate these points, consider the common loglinear model

$$y = \alpha x^\beta \tag{1}$$

Equations of this form are often estimated by linear regression, first *linearizing* the equation by taking logs of both sides:

$$\ln y = a + b \ln x \tag{2}$$

where $a = \ln(\alpha)$ and $b = \beta$. Equation (2) is called the *log form* of the equation in contrast to equation (1), which is called the *level form* of the equation. Using the SYSLIN procedure, you can estimate equation (2) by specifying

```
proc syslin data=in;
   model logy=logx;
run;
```

where LOGY and LOGX are the logs of Y and X computed in a preceding DATA step. The resulting values for INTERCEPT and LOGX correspond to a and b in equation (2).

Using the MODEL procedure, you can try to estimate the parameters in the level form (and avoid the DATA step) by specifying

```
proc model data=in;
   parms alpha beta;
   y = alpha * x ** beta;
   fit y;
run;
```

where ALPHA and BETA are the parameters in equation (1).

Unfortunately, at least one of the preceding is wrong; an ambiguity results because equations (1) and (2) contain no explicit error term. The SYSLIN and MODEL procedures both deal with additive errors; the residual used (the estimate of the error term in the equation) is the difference between the predicted and actual values (of LOGY for PROC SYSLIN and of Y for PROC MODEL in this example). If you perform the regressions discussed previously, PROC SYSLIN estimates equation (3) while PROC MODEL estimates equation (4).

$$\ln(y) = a + b \ln(x) + \epsilon \tag{3}$$

$$y = \alpha x^\beta + \xi \tag{4}$$

These are different statistical models. Equation (3) is the log form of equation (5)

$$y = \alpha x^\beta \mu \tag{5}$$

where $\mu = \exp(\epsilon)$. Equation (4), on the other hand, cannot be linearized because the error term ξ (different from μ) is additive in the level form.

You must decide whether your model is equation (4) or (5). If the model is equation (4), you should use PROC MODEL. If you linearize equation (1) without considering the error term and apply SYSLIN to MODEL LOGY=LOGX, the results will be wrong. On the other hand, if your model is equation (5) (in practice it usually is), and you want to use PROC MODEL to estimate the parameters in the *level* form, you must do something to account for the multiplicative error.

PROC MODEL estimates parameters by minimizing an objective function. The objective function is computed using either the RESID.-prefixed equation variable or the EQ.-prefixed equation variable. You must make sure that these prefixed equation variables are assigned an appropriate error term. If the model has additive errors that satisfy the assumptions, nothing needs to be done. In the case of equation (5), the error is nonadditive and the equation is in normalized form, so you must alter the value of RESID.Y.

The following assigns a valid estimate of μ to RESID.Y:

```
y = alpha * x ** beta;
resid.y = actual.y / pred.y;
```

However, $\mu = \exp(\epsilon)$ and, therefore, μ cannot have a mean of 0 and you cannot consistently estimate α and β by minimizing the sum of squares of an estimate of μ. Instead, you use $\epsilon = \ln(\mu)$.

```
proc model data=in;
   parms alpha beta;
   y = alpha * x ** beta;
   resid.y = log( actual.y / pred.y );
   fit y;
run;
```

If the model was expressed in general form, this transformation becomes

```
proc model data=in;
   parms alpha beta;
   EQ.trans = log( y / (alpha * x ** beta));
   fit trans;
run;
```

Both examples produce estimates of α and β of the level form that match the estimates of a and b of the log form. That is, ALPHA=exp(INTERCEPT) and BETA=LOGX, where INTERCEPT and LOGX are the PROC SYSLIN parameter estimates from the MODEL LOGY=LOGX. The standard error reported for ALPHA is different from that for the INTERCEPT in the log form.

The preceding example is not intended to suggest that loglinear models should be estimated in level form but, rather, to make the following points:

- Nonlinear transformations of equations involve the error term of the equation, and this should be taken into account when transforming models.

- The RESID.-prefixed and the EQ.-prefixed equation variables for models estimated by the MODEL procedure must represent additive errors with 0 means.

- You can use assignments to RESID.-prefixed and EQ.-prefixed equation variables to transform error terms.

- Some models do not have additive errors or 0 means, and many such models can be estimated using the MODEL procedure. The preceding approach applies not only to multiplicative models but to any model that can be manipulated to isolate the error term.

Predicted Values of Transformed Models

Nonadditive or transformed errors affect the distribution of the predicted values, as well as the estimates. For the preceding loglinear example, the MODEL procedure produces consistent parameter estimates. However, the predicted values for Y computed by PROC MODEL are not unbiased estimates of the expected values of Y, although they do estimate the conditional median Y values.

In general, the predicted values produced for a model with nonadditive errors are not unbiased estimates of the conditional means of the endogenous value. If the model can be transformed to a model with additive errors by using a *monotonic* transformation, the predicted values estimate the conditional medians of the endogenous variable.

For transformed models in which the biasing factor is known, you can use programming statements to correct for the bias in the predicted values as estimates of the endogenous means. In the preceding loglinear case, the predicted values will be biased by the factor $\exp\left(\sigma^2/2\right)$. You can produce approximately unbiased predicted values in this case by writing the model as

```
proc model data=in;
   parms alpha beta;
   control sigma2 0;
   y=alpha * x ** beta;
   resid.y = log( actual.y / pred.y );

   fit y;
run;

   control sigma2 MSE;
   pred.y = pred.y * exp( sigma2 / 2 );
   solve out=s;
run;
```

Before running the SOLVE step, you substitute the mean square error for Y reported by FIT step for *MSE* in the CONTROL statement. Refer to Miller (1984) for a discussion of bias factors for predicted values of transformed models.

Note that models with transformed errors are not appropriate for Monte Carlo simulation using the SDATA= option. PROC MODEL computes the OUTS= matrix from the transformed RESID.-prefixed equation variables, while it uses the SDATA= matrix to generate multivariate normal errors, which are added to the predicted values. This method of computing errors is inconsistent when the equation variables have been transformed.

Restrictions and Bounds on Parameters

Imposing Restrictions on Parameters

You can impose functional restrictions on parameters by reparameterizing the model to include fewer parameters. For example, suppose that in the following system of equations you want B2 to equal B1

```
parms a1 a2 b1 b2;
y1 = a1 + b1 * x;
y2 = a2 + b2 * x;
```

To do this, eliminate one of the parameters, as follows:

```
parms a1 a2 b;
y1 = a1 + b * x;
y2 = a2 + b * x;
```

A parameter associated with several dependent variables is called a *shared parameter*. A shared parameter is estimated with respect to the covariance matrix of the residuals across equations. This produces one parameter estimate.

The degree of freedom of a shared parameter is allocated among the several equations in which it appears: a parameter shared by m equations contributes $1/m$ degrees of freedom to each of the m equations. This often results in fractional degrees of freedom for the MSEs of the equations with shared parameters.

If you want to impose the nonlinear restriction that B2 is EXP(B1), then rewrite the model as

```
parms a1 a2 b1;
y1 = a1 + b1 * x;
y2 = a2 + exp(b1) * x;
```

You could also leave the expressions as they are and add a definition of B2. B2 is then taken out of the PARMS list and becomes a program variable.

```
parms a1 a2 b1;
b2 = exp(b1);
y1 = a1 + b1 * x;
y2 = a2 + b2 * x;
```

Suppose that in the following system of equations you want to impose the restriction A1 + A2 + A3 = 1

```
parms a1-a3 b1-b3;
y1 = a1 + b1 * x1;
y2 = a2 + b2 * x2;
y3 = a3 + b3 * x3;
```

Rewrite the model as follows:

```
parms a1-a2 b1-b3;
a3 = 1 - a1 - a2;
y1 = a1 + b1 * x1;
y2 = a2 + b2 * x2;
y3 = a3 + b3 * x3;
```

Imposing Bounds on Parameters

PROC MODEL can not compute optimal estimates subject to inequality constraints on the parameter estimates. However, bounds can sometimes be imposed by reparameterization or through the use of penalty functions.

Suppose that you have a parameter B that needs to be constrained to the interval 0 to 1. You can make B a function of an underlying parameter BB in the form

```
b = exp(bb) / ( 1 + exp(bb) );
```

This is called the *inverse logit transformation*. BB is declared in the PARMS list, and B becomes an undeclared program variable. B will be between 0 and 1.

Constraints can also be imposed on the untransformed model using *penalty functions*. Penalty functions modify the objective function so that it remains nearly the same in the feasible region and increases rapidly as it approaches the constraints. The jth constraint on the ith parameter θ_i is expressed as

$$h_j(\theta_i) \geq 0$$

One commonly used penalty function is the hyperbolic function. The hyperbolic penalty function is

$$\zeta_j = \frac{\alpha_j}{h_j(\theta_i)}$$

where α_j is a small positive constant. This penalty function is very small when θ_i is well inside the feasible region but grows exponentially as the parameter nears the boundary of this region. A collection of constraints can be imposed using a sum of penalty functions.

The objective function can be modified by adding the penalty functions to the error term. If

$$y = f(\mathbf{x}, \theta) + \epsilon$$

then ϵ^* is

$$\epsilon^* = \sqrt{\epsilon^2 + \frac{1}{n} \sum \frac{\alpha_j}{h_j(\theta_i)}}$$

where n is the number of observations used (_NUSED_). Refer to Bard (1974) for more information on penalty functions.

Consider the following pharmacokinetic model:

$$conc = \alpha\, e^{-\kappa_1 t} - \alpha\, e^{-\kappa_2 t}$$

where *conc* is the concentration of a drug, α is a scaling factor that should be positive, κ_1, and κ_2 are rate parameters for the inflow and outflow of the drug, and t is time. The estimation can produce several unrealistic values for the κ's. To avoid this, κ_1 needs to be restricted to a small positive value and κ_2 needs to be restricted so that

$$1 - e^{-\kappa_2} > 0$$

The following PROC MODEL statements estimate this model and enforce the restrictions:

```
proc model data=nl1ka ;

   /* define regression function */
   conc=a*exp(-k*time)-a*exp(-ka*time);

   /* deny infeasible set */
   if a <= 0 or ka <= 0 or ka >= 30 or 1 - exp(-k) <= 0
        then stop;

   /* add penalty functions to deflect search from boundary */
   penalty =   p1 / ( a )                /* a  >  0 */
             + p2 / ( ka )               /* ka >  0 */
             + p3 / ( 30 - ka )          /* ka < 30 */
             + p4 / ( 1 - exp(-k));    /* 1 - exp(-k)  >  0 */
   resid.conc = sqrt( resid.conc ** 2 +
                      scale * penalty/_NUSED_ );

   /* set initial parameter guess */
   parms a 5 ka 25 k .01;

   /* set initial penalty weights */
   control p1 1 p2 1 p3 1 p4 1 scale 1e-5;

   /* get initial estimates */
   fit conc;
run;

   /* iterate fit shrinking penalty weights towards 0 */
   control scale 1e-8;
   fit conc;
run;
```

The STOP programming statement signals that the function is not computable with the current parameter values and forces the estimation algorithm to try another parameter vector, halving the step size for the Gauss-Newton method or increasing λ for the Marquardt method. This prevents the change vector from jumping over the penalty function and trapping the iteration on the wrong side of the constraint.

The estimation is done in two stages. In the first stage, a large value of the SCALE control variable is used. A second estimation is done, using a much smaller scale value, to ensure that the penalty function is small relative to the residuals. If the parameter estimates are near the boundary, the second estimation could produce significantly different estimates than the first estimation. If this occurs, the penalty function associated with the active constraint should be sharpened.

Tests on Parameters

With single-equation models, you can test functions of the parameters by comparing the residual statistics from several runs.

Individual *t* tests for each parameter are printed, but for nonlinear models they are only asymptotically valid. You should be cautious in drawing any inferences from these *t* tests for small samples.

In general tests across several equations, you must force the covariance of equation errors matrices to be the same. The testing procedure is to run the unrestricted model, output the covariance matrix with the OUTSUSED= option, and input it to a restricted model with the SDATA= specification. Gallant and Jorgenson (1979) show how the change in the least-squares criterion function can be used as an asymptotically valid chi-square test.

This process is outlined as follows:

```
proc model data=a;
   .
   . full model specifications;
   .
   fit / sur outsused=smatrix;
run;
   reset purge;
   .
   . reduced model specifications;
   .
   fit / sur sdata=smatrix;
run;
```

The reduced model must be derivable by a set of parametric constraints on the full model. Now find the statistics labeled OBJECTIVE*N for both full and reduced models, subtract the full model OBJECTIVE*N (*full*) from the restricted model OBJECTIVE*N (*reduced*). Use the DATA step PROBCHI function on this difference, with degrees of freedom equal to the difference in the number of free parameters in the two models, to compute the significance of the test. For example,

```
p = 1 - probchi( reduced - full, df );
```

For information on testing parameter restrictions with methods that iterate the **S** matrix, refer to Gallant (1987, 367-70).

Choice of Instruments

Several of the estimation methods supported by PROC MODEL are instrumental variables methods. There is no standard method for choosing instruments for nonlinear regression. Few econometric textbooks discuss the selection of instruments for nonlinear models. Refer to Bowden and Turkington (1984, p. 180-182) for more information.

The purpose of the instrumental projection is to purge the regressors of their correlation with the residual. For nonlinear systems, the regressors are the partials of the residuals with respect to the parameters.

Possible instrumental variables include

- any variable in the model that is independent of the errors

- lags of variables in the system

- derivatives with respect to the parameters, if the derivatives are independent of the errors

- low degree polynomials in the exogenous variables

- variables from the data set or functions of variables from the data set.

Selected instruments must not

- depend on any variable endogenous with respect to the equations estimated

- depend on any of the parameters estimated

- be lags of endogenous variables if there is serial correlation of the errors.

If the preceding rules are satisfied and there are enough observations to support the number of instruments used, the results should be consistent and the efficiency loss held to a minimum.

You need at least as many instruments as the maximum number of parameters in any equation, or some of the parameters cannot be estimated. Note that *number of instruments* means linearly independent instruments. If you add an instrument that is a linear combination of other instruments, it has no effect and does not increase the effective number of instruments.

You can, however, use too many instruments. To get the benefit of instrumental variables, you must have more observations than instruments. Thus, there is a trade-off; the instrumental variables technique completely eliminates the simultaneous equation bias only in large samples. In finite samples, the larger the excess of observations over instruments, the more the bias is reduced. Adding more instruments can improve the efficiency, but after some point efficiency declines as the excess of observations over instruments becomes smaller and the bias grows.

The instruments used in an estimation are printed out at the beginning of the estimation. For example, the following statements produce the instruments list shown in Figure 11.35:

```
proc model data=test2;
   exogenous x1 x2;
   parms b1 a1 a2 b2 2.5 c2 55;
   y1 = a1 * y2 + b1 * exp(x1);
   y2 = a2 * y1 + b2 * x2 * x2 + c2 / x2;
   fit y1 y2 / n2sls;
   inst b1 b2 c2 x1 ;
run;
```

```
Instruments: 1 X1 @Y1/@B1 @Y2/@B2 @Y2/@C2
```

Figure 11.35. Instruments Used Message

This states that an intercept term, the exogenous variable X1, and the partial derivatives of the equations with respect to B1, B2, and C2, were used as instruments for the estimation.

Examples

Suppose that Y1 and Y2 are endogenous variables, that X1 and X2 are exogenous variables, and that A, B, C, D, E, F, and G are parameters. Consider the following model:

```
y1 = a + b * x1 + c * y2 + d * lag(y1);
y2 = e + f * x2 + g * y1;
fit y1 y2;
instruments exclude=(c g);
```

The INSTRUMENTS statement produces X1, X2, LAG(Y1), and an intercept as instruments.

To estimate the Y1 equation by itself, it is necessary to include X2 explicitly in the instruments since F, in this case, is not included in the estimation:

```
y1 = a + b * x1 + c * y2 + d * lag(y1);
y2 = e + f * x2 + g * y1;
fit y1;
instruments x2 exclude=(c);
```

This produces the same instruments as before. You can list the parameter associated with the lagged variable as an instrument instead of using the EXCLUDE= option. Thus, the following is equivalent to the previous example:

```
y1 = a + b * x1 + c * y2 + d * lag(y1);
y2 = e + f * x2 + g * y1;
fit y1;
instruments x1 x2 d;
```

For an example of declaring instruments when estimating a model involving identities, consider Klein's Model I

```
proc model data=klien;
   endogenous c p w i x wsum k y;
   exogenous  wp g t year;
   parms c0-c3 i0-i3 w0-w3;
   a: c = c0 + c1 * p + c2 * lag(p) + c3 * wsum;
   b: i = i0 + i1 * p + i2 * lag(p) + i3 * lag(k);
   c: w = w0 + w1 * x + w2 * lag(x) + w3 * year;
   x = c + i + g;
   y = c + i + g-t;
   p = x-w-t;
   k = lag(k) + i;
   wsum = w + wp;
```

The three equations to estimate are identified by the labels A, B, and C. The parameters associated with the predetermined terms are C2, I2, I3, W2, and W3 (and the intercepts, which are automatically added to the instruments). In addition, the system includes five identities that contain the predetermined variables G, T, LAG(K), and WP. Thus, the INSTRUMENTS statement can be written as

```
lagk = lag(k);
instruments c2 i2 i3 w2 w3 g t wp lagk;
```

where LAGK is a program variable used to hold LAG(K). However, this is more complicated than it needs to be. Except for LAG(K), all the predetermined terms in the identities are exogenous variables, and LAG(K) is already included as the coefficient of I3. There are also more parameters for predetermined terms than for endogenous terms, so you may prefer to use the EXCLUDE= option. Thus, you can specify the same instruments list with the simpler statement

```
instruments _exog_ exclude=(c1 c3 i1 w1);
```

To illustrate the use of polynomial terms as instrumental variables, consider the following model:

```
y1 = a + b * exp( c * x1 ) + d * log( x2 ) + e * exp( f * y2 );
```

The parameters are A, B, C, D, E, and F, and the right-hand variables are X1, X2, and Y2. Assume that X1 and X2 are exogenous (independent of the error), while Y2 is endogenous.

The equation for Y2 is not specified, but assume that it includes the variables X1, X3, and Y1, with X3 exogenous, so the exogenous variables of the full system are X1, X2, and X3. Using quadratic terms as instruments in the exogenous variables, the model is specified to PROC MODEL as

```
proc model;
   parms a b c d e f;
   y1 = a + b * exp( c * x1 ) + d * log( x2 ) + e * exp( f * y2 );
   instruments inst1-inst9;
   inst1 = x1; inst2 = x2; inst3 = x3;
   inst4 = x1 * x1; inst5 = x1 * x2; inst6 = x1 * x3;
   inst7 = x2 * x2; inst8 = x2 * x3; inst9 = x3 * x3;
   fit y1 / 2sls;
run;
```

It is not clear what degree polynomial should be used. There is no way to know how good the approximation is for any degree chosen, although the first-stage R^2 values may help the assessment.

First-Stage R^2

When the FSRSQ option is used in the FIT statement, the MODEL procedure prints a column of first-stage R^2 (FSRSQ) statistics along with the parameter estimates. The FSRSQ measures the fraction of the variation of the derivative column associated with the parameter that remains after projection through the instruments.

Ideally, the FSRSQ should be close to 1.00 for exogenous derivatives. If the FSRSQ is small for an endogenous derivative, it is unclear whether this reflects a poor choice of instruments or a large influence of the errors in the endogenous right-hand variables. When the FSRSQ for one or more parameters is small, the standard errors of the parameter estimates are likely to be large.

Note that you can make all the FSRSQs larger (or 1.00) by including more instruments, because of the disadvantage discussed previously. The FSRSQ statistics reported are unadjusted R^2s and do not include a degrees-of-freedom correction.

Autoregressive Moving Average Error Processes

Autoregressive moving average error processes (ARMA errors) and other models involving lags of error terms can be estimated using FIT statements and simulated or forecast using SOLVE statements. ARMA models for the error process are often used for models with autocorrelated residuals. The %AR macro can be used to specify models with autoregressive error processes. The %MA macro can be used to specify models with moving average error processes.

Autoregressive Errors

A model with first-order autoregressive errors, AR(1), has the form

$$y_t = f(x_t, \theta) + \mu_t$$
$$\mu_t = \phi \mu_{t-1} + \epsilon_t$$

while an AR(2) error process has the form

$$\mu_t = \phi_1 \mu_{t-1} + \phi_2 \mu_{t-2} + \epsilon_t$$

and so forth for higher-order processes. Note that the ϵ_t's are independent and identically distributed and have an expected value of 0.

An example of a model with an AR(2) component is

$$y = \alpha + \beta x_1 + \mu_t$$
$$\mu_t = \phi_1 \mu_{t-1} + \phi_2 \mu_{t-2} + \epsilon_t$$

You would write this model as follows:

```
proc model data=in;
   parms a b p1 p2;
   y = a + b * x1 + p1 * zlag1(y - (a + b * x1)) +
        p2 * zlag2(y - (a + b * x1));
   fit y;
run;
```

or equivalently using the %AR macro as

```
proc model data=in;
   parms a b;
   y = a + b * x1;
   %ar( y, 2 );
   fit y;
run;
```

Moving Average Models

A model with first-order moving average errors, MA(1), has the form

$$y_t = f(x_t) + \mu_t$$
$$\mu_t = \epsilon_t - \theta_1 \epsilon_{t-1}$$

where ϵ_t is identically and independently distributed with mean zero. An MA(2) error process has the form

$$\mu_t = \epsilon_t - \theta_1 \epsilon_{t-1} - \theta_2 \epsilon_{t-2}$$

and so forth for higher-order processes.

For example, you can write a simple linear regression model with MA(2) moving average errors as

```
proc model data=inma2;
   parms a b ma1 ma2;
   y = a + b * x + ma1 * zlag1( resid.y ) +
       ma2 * zlag2( resid.y );
   fit;
run;
```

where MA1 and MA2 are the moving average parameters.

Note that RESID.Y is automatically defined by PROC MODEL as

```
pred.y = a + b * x + ma1 * zlag1( resid.y ) +
         ma2 * zlag2( resid.y );
resid.y = actual.y - pred.y;
```

Note that RESID.Y is ϵ_t.

The ZLAG function must be used for MA models to truncate the recursion of the lags. This ensures that the lagged errors start at 0 in the lag-priming phase and do not propagate missing values when lag-priming period variables are missing, and ensures that the future errors are zero rather than missing during simulation or forecasting. For details on the lag functions, see "Lag Logic" in the section "Functions Across Time" earlier in this chapter.

This model written using the %MA macro is

```
proc model data=inma2;
   parms a b;
   y = a + b * x;
   %ma(y, 2);
   fit;
run;
```

General Form for ARMA Models

The general ARMA(p,q) process has the following form

$$\mu_t = \phi_1\mu_{t-1} + \ldots + \phi_p\mu_{t-p} + \epsilon_t - \theta_1\epsilon_{t-1} - \ldots - \theta_q\epsilon_{t-q}$$

An ARMA(p,q) model can be specified as follows

```
yhat = ... compute structural predicted value here ... ;
yarma = ar1 * zlag1( y - yhat ) + ...    /* ar part */
                                  + arp * zlagp( y - yhat )
      + ma1 * zlag1( resid.y )   + ...    /* ma part */
                                  + maq * zlagq( resid.y );
y = yhat + yarma;
```

where ARi and MAj represent the autoregressive and moving average parameters for the various lags. You can use any names you want for these variables, and there are many equivalent ways that the specification could be written.

Vector ARMA processes can also be estimated with PROC MODEL. For example, a two-variable AR(1) process for the errors of the two endogenous variables Y1 and Y2 can be specified as follows

```
y1hat = ... compute structural predicted value here ... ;

y1    = y1hat + ar1_1 * zlag1( y1 - y1hat )    /* ar part y1,y1 */
              + ar1_2 * zlag1( y2 - y2hat );   /* ar part y1,y2 */

y21hat = ... compute structural predicted value here ... ;

y2    = y2hat + ar2_2 * zlag1( y2 - y2hat )    /* ar part y2,y2 */
              + ar2_1 * zlag1( y1 - y1hat );   /* ar part y2,y1 */
```

Convergence Problems with ARMA Models

ARMA models can be difficult to estimate. If the parameter estimates are not within the appropriate range, a moving average model's residual terms will grow exponentially. The calculated residuals for later observations can be very large or can overflow. This can happen either because improper starting values were used or because the iterations moved away from reasonable values.

Care should be used in choosing starting values for ARMA parameters. Starting values of .001 for ARMA parameters usually work if the model fits the data well and the problem is well-conditioned. Note that an MA model can often be approximated by a high order AR model, and vice versa. This may result in high collinearity in mixed ARMA models, which in turn can cause serious ill-conditioning in the calculations and instability of the parameter estimates.

If you have convergence problems while estimating a model with ARMA error processes, try to estimate in steps. First, use a FIT statement to estimate only the structural parameters with the ARMA parameters held to zero (or to reasonable prior estimates if available). Next, use another FIT statement to estimate the ARMA parameters only, using the structural parameter values from the first run. Since the values of the structural parameters are likely to be close to their final estimates, the ARMA parameter estimates may now converge. Finally, use another FIT statement to produce simultaneous estimates of all the parameters. Since the initial values of the parameters are now likely to be quite close to their final joint estimates, the estimates should converge quickly if the model is appropriate for the data.

AR Initial Conditions

The initial lags of the error terms of AR(p) models can be modeled in different ways. The autoregressive error startup methods supported by SAS/ETS procedures are the following:

CLS   conditional least squares (ARIMA and MODEL procedures)

ULS   unconditional least squares (AUTOREG, ARIMA, and MODEL procedures)

ML   maximum likelihood (AUTOREG, ARIMA, and MODEL procedures)

YW   Yule-Walker (AUTOREG procedure only)

HL   Hildreth-Lu, which deletes the first p observations (MODEL procedure only)

See Chapter 4, for an explanation and discussion of the merits of various AR(p) startup methods.

The CLS, ULS, ML, and HL initializations can be performed by PROC MODEL. For AR(1) errors, these initializations can be produced as shown in Table 11.2. These methods are equivalent in large samples.

Table 11.2. Initializations Performed by PROC MODEL: AR(1) ERRORS

Method	Formula
conditional least squares	Y=YHAT+AR1*ZLAG1(Y-YHAT);
unconditional least squares	Y=YHAT+AR1*ZLAG1(Y-YHAT); IF _OBS_=1 THEN RESID.Y=SQRT(1-AR1**2)*RESID.Y;
maximum likelihood	Y=YHAT+AR1*ZLAG1(Y-YHAT); W=(1-AR1**2)**(-1/(2*_NUSED_)); IF _OBS_=1 THEN W=W*SQRT(1-AR1**2); RESID.Y=W*RESID.Y;
Hildreth-Lu	Y=YHAT+AR1*LAG1(Y-YHAT);

MA Initial Conditions

The initial lags of the error terms of MA(q) models can also be modeled in different ways. The following moving average error startup paradigms are supported by the ARIMA and MODEL procedures:

ULS   unconditional least squares

CLS   conditional least squares

ML   maximum likelihood

The conditional least-squares method of estimating moving average error terms is not optimal because it ignores the startup problem. This reduces the efficiency of the estimates, although they remain unbiased. The initial lagged residuals, extending before the start of the data, are assumed to be 0, their unconditional expected value. This introduces a difference between these residuals and the generalized least-squares residuals for the moving average covariance, which, unlike the autoregressive model, persists through the data set. Usually this difference converges quickly to 0, but for nearly noninvertible moving average processes the convergence is quite slow. To minimize this problem, you should have plenty of data, and the moving average parameter estimates should be well within the invertible range.

This problem can be corrected at the expense of writing a more complex program. Unconditional least-squares estimates for the MA(1) process can be produced by specifying the model as follows:

```
yhat = ... compute structural predicted value here ... ;
if _obs_ = 1 then do;
   h = sqrt( 1 + ma1 ** 2 );
   y = yhat;
   resid.y = ( y - yhat ) / h;
   end;
else do;
   g = ma1 / zlag1( h );
   h = sqrt( 1 + ma1 ** 2 - g ** 2 );
   y = yhat + g * zlag1( resid.y );
   resid.y = ( ( y - yhat) - g * zlag1( resid.y ) ) / h;
   end;
```

Moving-average errors can be difficult to estimate. You should consider using an AR(p) approximation to the moving average process. A moving average process can usually be well-approximated by an autoregressive process if the data have not been smoothed or differenced.

The %AR Macro

The SAS macro %AR generates programming statements for PROC MODEL for autoregressive models. The %AR macro is part of SAS/ETS software and no special options need to be set to use the macro. The autoregressive process can be applied to the structural equation errors or to the endogenous series themselves.

The %AR macro can be used for

- univariate autoregression

- unrestricted vector autoregression

- restricted vector autoregression

Univariate Autoregression

To model the error term of an equation as an autoregressive process, use the following statement after the equation:

```
%ar( varname, nlags )
```

For example, suppose that Y is a linear function of X1 and X2, and an AR(2) error. You would write this model as follows:

```
proc model data=in;
   parms a b c;
   y = a + b * x1 + c * x2;
   %ar( y, 2 )
   fit y / list;
run;
```

The calls to %AR must come *after* all of the equations that the process applies to.

The proceding macro invocation, %AR(y,2), produces the statements shown in the LIST output in Figure 11.36.

```
                       Listing of Program:

Stmt   Line:Col   Source Text
   1   15:1        PRED.Y = A + B * X1 + C * X2;

   1   15:1        RESID.Y = PRED.Y - ACTUAL.Y;

   1   15:1        ERROR.Y = PRED.Y - Y;

   2   2283:23     _PRED__Y = PRED.Y;

   3   2301:15     #OLD_PRED.Y = PRED.Y;
                   PRED.Y = #OLD_PRED.Y + Y_L1 * ZLAG1( Y -
                            _PRED__Y ) + Y_L2 * ZLAG2( Y - _PRED__Y );

   3   2301:15     RESID.Y = PRED.Y - ACTUAL.Y;

   3   2301:15     ERROR.Y = PRED.Y - Y;
```

Figure 11.36. LIST Option Output for an AR(2) Model

The _PRED_ prefixed variables are temporary program variables used so that the lags of the residuals are the correct residuals and not the ones redefined by this equation. Note that this is equivalent to the statements explicitly written in the "General Form for ARMA Models" earlier in this section.

You can also restrict the autoregressive parameters to 0 at selected lags. For example, if you wanted autoregressive parameters at lags 1, 12, and 13, you can use the following statements:

```
proc model data=in;
   parms a b c;
   y = a + b * x1 + c * x2;
   %ar( y, 13, , 1 12 13 )
   fit y / list;
run;
```

These statements generate the output shown in Figure 11.37.

```
                        Listing of Program:

Stmt  Line:Col  Source Text
   1  17:4       PRED.Y = A + B * X1 + C * X2;

   1  17:4       RESID.Y = PRED.Y - ACTUAL.Y;

   1  17:4       ERROR.Y = PRED.Y - Y;

   2  2344:23    _PRED__Y = PRED.Y;

   3  2362:15    #OLD_PRED.Y = PRED.Y;
                 PRED.Y = #OLD_PRED.Y + Y_L1 * ZLAG1( Y - _PRED__Y )
                          + Y_L12 * ZLAG12( Y - _PRED__Y ) + Y_L13 *
                          ZLAG13( Y - _PRED__Y );

   3  2362:15    RESID.Y = PRED.Y - ACTUAL.Y;

   3  2362:15    ERROR.Y = PRED.Y - Y;
```

Figure 11.37. LIST Option Output for an AR Model with Lags at 1, 12, and 13

There are variations on the conditional least-squares method, depending on whether observations at the start of the series are used to warm up the AR process. By default, the %AR conditional least-squares method uses all the observations and assumes zeros for the initial lags of autoregressive terms. By using the M= option, you can request that %AR use the unconditional least-squares (ULS) or maximum-likelihood (ML) method instead. For example,

```
proc model data=in;
   y = a + b * x1 + c * x2;
   %ar( y, 2, m=uls )
   fit y;
run;
```

Discussions of these methods is provided in the "AR Initial Conditions" earlier in this section.

By using the M=CLS*n* option, you can request that the first *n* observations be used to compute estimates of the initial autoregressive lags. In this case, the analysis starts with observation *n*+1. For example,

```
proc model data=in;
   y = a + b * x1 + c * x2;
   %ar( y, 2, m=cls2 )
   fit y;
run;
```

You can use the %AR macro to apply an autoregressive model to the endogenous variable instead of to the error term by using the TYPE=V option. For example, if you want to add the five past lags of Y to the equation in the previous example, you could use %AR to generate the parameters and lags using the following statements:

```
proc model data=in;
   parms a b c;
   y = a + b * x1 + c * x2;
   %ar( y, 5, type=v )
   fit y / list;
run;
```

The preceding statements generate the output shown in Figure 11.38.

```
                        Listing of Program:

Stmt  Line:Col  Source Text
  1   17:4      PRED.Y = A + B * X1 + C * X2;

  1   17:4      RESID.Y = PRED.Y - ACTUAL.Y;

  1   17:4      ERROR.Y = PRED.Y - Y;

  2   2304:15   #OLD_PRED.Y = PRED.Y;
                PRED.Y = #OLD_PRED.Y + Y_L1 * ZLAG1( Y ) + Y_L2 *
                        ZLAG2( Y ) + Y_L3 * ZLAG3( Y ) + Y_L4 *
                        ZLAG4( Y ) + Y_L5 * ZLAG5( Y );
  2   2304:15   RESID.Y = PRED.Y - ACTUAL.Y;

  2   2304:15   ERROR.Y = PRED.Y - Y;
```

Figure 11.38.   LIST Option Output for an AR model of Y

This model predicts Y as a linear combination of X1, X2, an intercept, and the values of Y in the most recent five periods.

Unrestricted Vector Autoregression

To model the error terms of a set of equations as a vector autoregressive process, use the following form of the %AR macro after the equations:

> %ar(*process_name, nlags, variable_list*)

The *process_name* value is any name that you supply for %AR to use in making names for the autoregressive parameters. You can use the %AR macro to model several different AR processes for different sets of equations by using different process names for each set. The process name ensures that the variable names used are unique. Use a short *process_name* value for the process if parameter estimates are to be written to an output data set. The %AR macro tries to construct parameter names less than or equal to eight characters, but this is limited by the length of *name*, which is used as a prefix for the AR parameter names.

The *variable_list* value is the list of endogenous variables for the equations.

For example, suppose that errors for equations Y1, Y2, and Y3 are generated by a second-order vector autoregressive process. You can use the following statements

```
proc model data=in;
   y1 = ... equation for y1 ...;
   y2 = ... equation for y2 ...;
   y3 = ... equation for y3 ...;
   %ar( name, 2, y1 y2 y3 )
   fit y1 y2 y3;
run;
```

which generate the following for Y1 and similar code for Y2 and Y3:

```
y1 = pred.y1 + name1_1_1*zlag1(y1-name_y1) +
     name1_1_2*zlag1(y2-name_y2) +
     name1_1_3*zlag1(y3-name_y3) +
     name2_1_1*zlag2(y1-name_y1) +
     name2_1_2*zlag2(y2-name_y2) +
     name2_1_3*zlag2(y3-name_y3) ;
```

Only the conditional least-squares (M=CLS or M=CLSn) method can be used for vector processes.

You can also use the same form with restrictions that the coefficient matrix be 0 at selected lags. For example, the statements

```
proc model data=in;
    y1 = ... equation for y1 ...;
    y2 = ... equation for y2 ...;
    y3 = ... equation for y3 ...;
    %ar( name, 3, y1 y2 y3, 1 3 )
    fit y1 y2 y3;
```

apply a third-order vector process to the equation errors with all the coefficients at lag 2 restricted to 0 and with the coefficients at lags 1 and 3 unrestricted.

You can model the three series Y1-Y3 as a vector autoregressive process in the variables instead of in the errors by using the TYPE=V option. If you want to model Y1-Y3 as a function of past values of Y1-Y3 and some exogenous variables or constants, you can use %AR to generate the statements for the lag terms. Write an equation for each variable for the nonautoregressive part of the model, and then call %AR with the TYPE=V option. For example,

```
proc model data=in;
    parms a1-a3 b1-b3;
    y1 = a1 + b1 * x;
    y2 = a2 + b2 * x;
    y3 = a3 + b3 * x;
    %ar( name, 2, y1 y2 y3, type=v )
    fit y1 y2 y3;
run;
```

The nonautoregressive part of the model can be a function of exogenous variables, or it may be intercept parameters. If there are no exogenous components to the vector autoregression model, including no intercepts, then assign 0 to each of the variables. There must be an assignment to each of the variables before %AR is called.

```
proc model data=in;
    y1=0;
    y2=0;
    y3=0;
    %ar( name, 2, y1 y2 y3, type=v )
    fit y1 y2 y3;
```

This example models the vector $\mathbf{Y} = (\text{Y1} \ \text{Y2} \ \text{Y3})'$ as a linear function only of its value in the previous two periods and a white-noise error vector. The model has $18 = (3 \times 3 + 3 \times 3)$ parameters.

Syntax of the %AR Macro

There are two cases of the syntax of the %AR macro. The first has the general form

%AR(*name, nlag* [*,endolist* [*, laglist*]] [**,M=** *method*] [**,TYPE= V**] **)**

where

name　　　specifies a prefix for %AR to use in constructing names of variables needed to define the AR process. If the *endolist* value is not specified, the endogenous list defaults to *name*, which must be the name of the equation to which the AR error process is to be applied. The *name* value cannot exceed eight characters.

nlag　　　is the order of the AR process.

endolist　　specifies the list of equations to which the AR process is to be applied. If more than one name is given, an unrestricted vector process is created with the structural residuals of all the equations included as regressors in each of the equations. If not specified, *endolist* defaults to *name*.

laglist　　specifies the list of lags at which the AR terms are to be added. The coefficients of the terms at lags not listed are set to 0. All of the listed lags must be less than or equal to *nlag*, and there must be no duplicates. If not specified, the *laglist* defaults to all lags 1 through *nlag*.

M=*method*　specifies the estimation method to implement. Valid values of the M= option are CLS (conditional least-squares estimates), ULS (unconditional least-squares estimates), and ML (maximum-likelihood estimates). M=CLS is the default. Only M=CLS is allowed when more than one equation is specified. The ULS and ML methods are not supported for vector AR models by %AR.

TYPE=V　　specifies that the AR process is to be applied to the endogenous variables themselves instead of to the structural residuals of the equations.

Restricted Vector Autoregression

You can control which parameters are included in the process, restricting those parameters that you do not include to 0. First, use %AR with the DEFER option to declare the variable list and define the dimension of the process. Then, use additional %AR calls to generate terms for selected equations with selected variables at selected lags. For example,

```
proc model data=d;
    y1 = ... equation for y1 ...;
    y2 = ... equation for y2 ...;
    y3 = ... equation for y3 ...;
    %ar( name, 2, y1 y2 y3, defer )
    %ar( name, y1, y1 y2 )
    %ar( name, y2 y3, , 1 )
    fit y1 y2 y3;
run;
```

The error equations produced are

```
y1 = pred.y1 + name1_1_1*zlag1(y1-name_y1) +
     name1_1_2*zlag1(y2-name_y2) + name2_1_1*zlag2(y1-name_y1) +
     name2_1_2*zlag2(y2-name_y2) ;
y2 = pred.y2 + name1_2_1*zlag1(y1-name_y1) +
     name1_2_2*zlag1(y2-name_y2) + name1_2_3*zlag1(y3-name_y3) ;
y3 = pred.y3 + name1_3_1*zlag1(y1-name_y1) +
     name1_3_2*zlag1(y2-name_y2) + name1_3_3*zlag1(y3-name_y3) ;
```

This model states that the errors for Y1 depend on the errors of both Y1 and Y2 (but not Y3) at both lags 1 and 2, and that the errors for Y2 and Y3 depend on the previous errors for all three variables, but only at lag 1.

%AR Macro Syntax for Restricted Vector AR

An alternative use of %AR is allowed to impose restrictions on a vector AR process by calling %AR several times to specify different AR terms and lags for different equations.

The first call has the general form

%AR(*name, nlag, endolist,* **DEFER)**

where

name   specifies a prefix for %AR to use in constructing names of variables needed to define the vector AR process

nlag   specifies the order of the AR process

endolist   specifies the list of equations to which the AR process is to be applied

DEFER   specifies that %AR is not to generate the AR process but is to wait for further information specified in later %AR calls for the same *name* value

The subsequent calls have the general form

```
%AR( name, eqlist [, varlist ] [, laglist ] [,TYPE= ] )
```

where

name   is the same as in the first call

eqlist   specifies the list of equations to which the specifications in this %AR call are to be applied. Only names specified in the *endolist* value of the first call for the *name* value can appear in the list of equations in *eqlist*.

varlist specifies the list of equations whose lagged structural residuals are to be included as regressors in the equations in *eqlist*. Only names in the *endolist* value of the first call for the *name* value can appear in *varlist*. If not specified, *varlist* defaults to *endolist*.

laglist specifies the list of lags at which the AR terms are to be added. The coefficients of the terms at lags not listed are set to 0. All of the listed lags must be less than or equal to the value of *nlag*, and there must be no duplicates. If not specified, *laglist* defaults to all lags 1 through *nlag*.

The %MA Macro

The SAS macro %MA generates programming statements for PROC MODEL for moving average models. The %MA macro is part of SAS/ETS software and no special options are needed to use the macro. The moving average error process can be applied to the structural equation errors. The syntax of the %MA macro is the same as the %AR macro except there is no TYPE= argument.

When you are using the %MA and %AR macros combined, the %MA macro must follow the %AR macro. The following SAS/IML statements produce an ARMA(1,(1 3)) error process and save it in the data set MADAT2.

```
    /* use IML module to simulate a MA process  */
proc iml;
   phi={1 .2};
   theta={ 1 .3 0 .5};
   y=armasim(phi, theta, 0,.1, 200,32565);
   create madat2 from y[colname='y'];
   append;
quit;
```

The following PROC MODEL statements are used to estimate the parameters of this model using maximum likelihood error structure:

```
title1 'Maximum Likelihood ARMA(1, (1 3))';
proc model data=madat2;
   y=0;
   %ar(y,1,,  M=ml)
   %ma(y,3,,1 3,  M=ml)  /* %MA always after %AR */
   fit y;
run;
```

The estimates of the parameters produced by this run are shown in Figure 11.39.

```
                   Maximum Likelihood  ARMA(1, (1 3))

                           MODEL Procedure
                           OLS Estimation

               Nonlinear OLS Summary of Residual Errors

              DF    DF
Equation    Model Error      SSE        MSE      Root MSE  R-Square  Adj R-Sq

Y             3    197     2.63825    0.01339     0.11572   -0.0067   -0.0169
RESID.Y            197     1.99570    0.01013     0.10065

                 Nonlinear OLS Parameter Estimates

                            Approx.    'T'    Approx.
Parameter     Estimate     Std Err    Ratio  Prob>|T|   Label

Y_L1         -0.100666     0.11866    -0.85    0.3973    AR(Y)  Y lag1 parameter
Y_M1         -0.193400     0.09393    -2.06    0.0408    MA(Y)  Y lag1 parameter
Y_M3         -0.593835     0.06011    -9.88    0.0001    MA(Y)  Y lag3 parameter
```

Figure 11.39.   Estimates from an ARMA(1, (1 3)) Process

Syntax of the %MA Macro

There are two cases of the syntax for the %MA macro. The first has the general form

%MA(*name, nlag* [*,endolist* [*, laglist*]] [**,M=** *method*] **)**

where

name   specifies a prefix for %MA to use in constructing names of variables needed to define the MA process and is the default *endolist*

nlag   is the order of the MA process

endolist   specifies the equations to which the MA process is to be applied. If more than one name is given, CLS estimation is used for the vector process.

laglist   specifies the lags at which the MA terms are to be added. All of the listed lags must be less than or equal to *nlag*, and there must be no duplicates. If not specified, the *laglist* defaults to all lags 1 through *nlag*.

M=*method* specifies the estimation method to implement. Valid values of the M= option are CLS (conditional least-squares estimates), ULS (unconditional least-squares estimates), and ML (maximum-likelihood estimates). M=CLS is the default. Only M=CLS is allowed when more than one equation is specified in *endolist*.

%MA Macro Syntax for Restricted Vector Moving Average

An alternative use of %MA is allowed to impose restrictions on a vector MA process by calling %MA several times to specify different MA terms and lags for different equations.

The first call has the general form

%MA(*name, nlag, endolist,* **DEFER)**

where

name   specifies a prefix for %MA to use in constructing names of variables needed to define the vector MA process

nlag   specifies the order of the MA process

endolist   specifies the list of equations to which the MA process is to be applied

DEFER   specifies that %MA is not to generate the MA process but is to wait for further information specified in later %MA calls for the same *name* value

The subsequent calls have the general form

```
%MA( name, eqlist [, varlist ] [, laglist ] )
```

where

name   is the same as in the first call

eqlist   specifies the list of equations to which the specifications in this %MA call are to be applied *varlist* specifies the list of equations whose lagged structural residuals are to be included as regressors in the equations in *eqlist*

laglist specifies the list of lags at which the MA terms are to be added

Distributed Lag Models and the %PDL Macro

In the following example, the variable y is modeled as a linear function of x, the first lag of x, the second lag of x, and so forth:

$$y_t = a + b_0 x_t + b_1 x_{t-1} + b_2 x_{t-2} + b_3 x_{t-3} + \ldots + b_n x_{t-l}$$

Models of this sort can introduce a great many parameters for the lags, and there may not be enough data to compute accurate independent estimates for them all. Often, the number of parameters is reduced by assuming that the lag coefficients follow some pattern. One common assumption is that the lag coefficients follow a polynomial in the lag length

$$b_i = \sum_{j=0}^{d} \alpha_j (i)^j$$

where d is the degree of the polynomial used. Models of this kind are called *Almon lag models*, *polynomial distributed lag models*, or *PDLs* for short. For example, Figure 11.40 shows the lag distribution that can be modeled with a low-order polynomial. Endpoint restrictions can be imposed on a PDL to require that the lag coefficients be 0 at the 0th lag, or at the final lag, or at both.

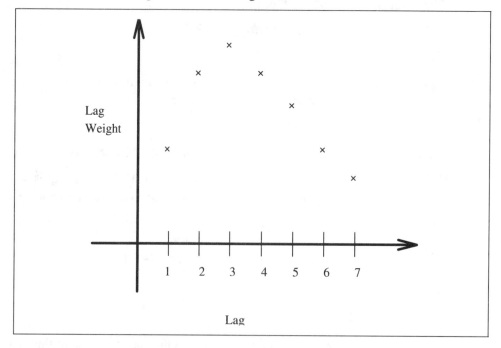

Figure 11.40. Polynomial Distributed Lags

For linear single-equation models, SAS/ETS software includes the PDLREG procedure for estimating PDL models. See Chapter 13, "The PDLREG Procedure," for a more detailed discussion of polynomial distributed lags and an explanation of endpoint restrictions.

Polynomial and other distributed lag models can be estimated and simulated or forecast with PROC MODEL. For polynomial distributed lags, the %PDL macro can generate the needed programming statements automatically.

The %PDL Macro

The SAS macro %PDL generates the programming statements to compute the lag coefficients of polynomial distributed lag models and to apply them to the lags of variables or expressions.

To use the %PDL macro in a model program, you first call it to declare the lag distribution; later, you call it again to apply the PDL to a variable or expression. The first call generates a PARMS statement for the polynomial parameters and assignment statements to compute the lag coefficients. The second call generates an expression that applies the lag coefficients to the lags of the specified variable or expression. A PDL can be declared only once, but it can be used any number of times (that is, the second call can be repeated).

The initial declaratory call has the general form

%PDL(*pdlname, nlags, degree,* **R** = *code* **)**

where *pdlname* is a name (up to eight characters) that you give to identify the PDL, *nlags* is the lag length, and *degree* is the degree of the polynomial for the distribution. The R=*code* is optional for endpoint restrictions. The value of *code* can be FIRST (for upper), LAST (for lower), or BOTH (for both upper and lower endpoints). See Chapter 13 for a discussion of endpoint restrictions.

The later calls to apply the PDL have the general form

```
%PDL( pdlname, expression )
```

where *pdlname* is the name of the PDL and *expression* is the variable or expression to which the PDL is to be applied. The *pdlname* given must be the same as the name used to declare the PDL.

Note the following example:

```
proc model data=in;
   parms int;
   %pdl( xpdl, 5, 3 )
   y = int + %pdl( xpdl, x );
   fit y / list;
run;
```

This example models Y as a linear function of X and five lags of X, using a cubic polynomial for the lag coefficients. The term XPDL is the name given to the lag distribution. Figure 11.41 shows the compressed LIST option output for this example.

```
                           Listing of Program:

Stmt  Line:Col   Source Text
   1  737:14      XPDL_L0 = XPDL_0 ;

   2  749:14      XPDL_L1 = XPDL_0 + XPDL_1 + XPDL_2 + XPDL_3 ;

   3  774:14      XPDL_L2 = XPDL_0 + XPDL_1 * 2 + XPDL_2 * 2**2 + XPDL_3 * 2**3 ;

   4  813:14      XPDL_L3 = XPDL_0 + XPDL_1 * 3 + XPDL_2 * 3**2 + XPDL_3 * 3**3 ;

   5  852:14      XPDL_L4 = XPDL_0 + XPDL_1 * 4 + XPDL_2 * 4**2 + XPDL_3 * 4**3 ;

   6  891:14      XPDL_L5 = XPDL_0 + XPDL_1 * 5 + XPDL_2 * 5**2 + XPDL_3 * 5**3 ;

   7  929:4       Y = INT + XPDL_L0*(X) + XPDL_L1*LAG1(X) + XPDL_L2*LAG2(X) +
                      XPDL_L3*LAG3(X) + XPDL_L4*LAG4(X) + XPDL_L5*LAG5(X);
```

Figure 11.41.   LIST Option Output for PDL

Note that six new program variables, XPDL_L0 through XPDL_L5, were defined using the four polynominal parameters XPDL_0 through XPDL_3. The estimate summary report, shown in Figure 11.42, contains only the estimates for the polynominal parameters.

```
                          MODEL Procedure
                          OLS Estimation

                Nonlinear OLS Summary of Residual Errors

              DF    DF
Equation    Model Error      SSE        MSE     Root MSE  R-Square  Adj R-Sq

Y             5     40     8.71859    0.21796    0.46687    0.9999    0.9999


                Nonlinear OLS Parameter Estimates

                                   Approx.     'T'      Approx.
            Parameter   Estimate   Std Err    Ratio    Prob>|T|

            INT          10.317962    7.80212    1.32    0.1935
            XPDL_0     -204.858040  172.46927   -1.19    0.2419
            XPDL_1      670.568215  567.42129    1.18    0.2443
            XPDL_2     -322.479831  276.87586   -1.16    0.2510
            XPDL_3       39.769539   34.44840    1.15    0.2552
```

Figure 11.42.   Estimates Summary Report for PDL

This second example models two variables, Y1 and Y2, and uses two PDLs:

```
proc model data=in;
   parms int1 int2;
   %pdl( logxpdl, 5, 3 )
   %pdl( zpdl, 6, 4 )
   y1 = int1 + %pdl( logxpdl, log(x) ) + %pdl( zpdl, z );
   y2 = int2 + %pdl( zpdl, z );
   fit y1 y2;
run;
```

A (5,3) PDL of the log of X is used in the equation for Y1. A (6,4) PDL of Z is used in the equations for both Y1 and Y2. Since the same ZPDL is used in both equations, the lag coefficients for Z are the same for the Y1 and Y2 equations, and the polynomial parameters for ZPDL are shared by the two equations. See Example 11.5 for a complete example and comparison with PDLREG.

Input Data Sets

DATA= *Input Data Set*

For FIT tasks, the DATA= option specifies which input data set to use in estimating parameters. Variables in the model program are looked up in the DATA= data set and, if found, their attributes (type, length, label, and format) are set to be the same as those in the DATA= data set (if not defined otherwise within PROC MODEL), and values for the variables in the program are read from the data set.

ESTDATA= *Input Data Set*

The ESTDATA= option specifies an input data set that contains an observation giving values for some or all of the model parameters. The data set can also contain observations giving the rows of a covariance matrix for the parameters.

Parameter values read from the ESTDATA= data set provide initial starting values for parameters estimated. Observations providing covariance values, if any are present in the ESTDATA= data set, are ignored.

The ESTDATA= data set is usually created by the OUTEST= option in a previous FIT statement. You can also create an ESTDATA= data set with a SAS DATA step program. The data set must contain a numeric variable for each parameter to be given a value or covariance column. The name of the variable in the ESTDATA= data set must match the name of the parameter in the model. Parameters with names longer than eight characters cannot be set from an ESTDATA= data set. The data set must also contain a character variable _NAME_ of length 8. _NAME_ has a blank value for the observation that gives values to the parameters. _NAME_ contains the name of a parameter for observations defining rows of the covariance matrix.

More than one set of parameter estimates and covariances can be stored in the ESTDATA= data set if the observations for the different estimates are identified by the variable _TYPE_. _TYPE_ must be a character variable of length 8. The TYPE= option is used to select for input the part of the ESTDATA= data set for which the _TYPE_ value matches the value of the TYPE= option.

The following SAS statements generate the ESTDATA= data set shown in Figure 11.43. The second FIT statement uses the TYPE= option to select the estimates from the GMM estimation as starting values for the FIML estimation.

```
          /* Generate test data */
data gmm2;
    do t=1 to 50;
        x1 = sqrt(t) ;
        x2 = rannor(10) * 10;
        y1 = -.002 * x2 * x2 - .05 / x2 - 0.001 * x1 * x1;
        y2 = 0.002* y1 + 2 * x2 * x2 + 50 / x2 + 5 * rannor(1);
        y1 = y1 + 5 * rannor(1);
        z1 = 1; z2 = x1 * x1; z3 = x2 * x2; z4 = 1.0/x2;
        output;
    end;
run;

proc model data=gmm2 ;
    exogenous x1 x2;
    parms a1 a2 b1 2.5 b2 c2 55 d1;
```

```
        inst b1 b2 c2 x1 x2;
        y1 = a1 * y2 + b1 * x1 * x1 + d1;
        y2 = a2 * y1 + b2 * x2 * x2 + c2 / x2 + d1;

        fit y1 y2 / 3sls gmm kernel=(qs,1,0.2) outest=gmmest;

        fit y1 y2 / fiml type=gmm estdata=gmmest;
    run;

    proc print data=gmmest;
    run;
```

OBS	_NAME_	_TYPE_	_NUSED_	A1	A2	B2	B1	C2	D1
1		3SLS	50	-.0022296	-1.25002	1.99609	0.025827	49.8119	-0.44533
2		GMM	50	-.0020131	-1.53882	1.99419	0.014908	49.8035	-0.64933

Figure 11.43.   ESTDATA= Data Set

PARMSDATA=   Input Data Set

The option PARMSDATA= reads values for all parameters whose names match the names of variables in the PARMSDATA= data set. Values for any or all of the parameters in the model can be reset using the PARMSDATA= option. The PARMSDATA= option goes in the PROC MODEL statement, and the data set is read before any FIT or SOLVE statements are executed.

Together, the OUTPARMS= and PARMSDATA= options enable you to change part of a model and recompile the new model program without the need to reestimate equations that were not changed.

Suppose you have a large model with parameters estimated and you now want to replace one equation, Y, with a new specification. Although the model program must be recompiled with the new equation, you do not need to reestimate all the equations, just the one that changed.

Using the OUTPARMS= and PARMSDATA= options, you can do the following:

```
proc model model=oldmod outparms=temp; run;
proc model outmodel=newmod parmsdata=temp data=in;
    ... include new model definition with changed y eq. here ...
    fit y;
run;
```

The model file NEWMOD will then contain the new model and its estimated parameters plus the old models with their original parameter values.

SDATA=   Input Data Set

The SDATA= option allows a cross-equation covariance matrix to be input from a data set. The **S** matrix read from the SDATA= data set, specified in the FIT statement, is used to define the objective function for the OLS, N2SLS, SUR, and N3SLS estimation methods and is used as the initial **S** for the methods that iterate the **S** matrix.

Most often, the SDATA= data set has been created by the OUTS= or OUTSUSED= option in a previous FIT statement. The OUTS= and OUTSUSED= data sets from a FIT statement can be read back in by a FIT statement in the same PROC MODEL step.

You can create an input SDATA= data set using the DATA step. PROC MODEL expects to find a character variable _NAME_ in the SDATA= data set as well as variables for the equations in the estimation or solution. For each observation with a _NAME_ value matching the name of an equation, PROC MODEL fills the corresponding row of the **S** matrix with the values of the names of equations found in the data set. If a row or column is omitted from the data set, a 1 is placed on the diagonal for the row or column. Missing values are ignored, and since the **S** matrix is symmetric, you can include only a triangular part of the **S** matrix in the SDATA= data set with the omitted part indicated by missing values. If the SDATA= data set contains multiple observations with the same _NAME_, the last values supplied for the _NAME_ are used. The structure of the expected data set is further described in "OUTS= Data Set" later in this chapter.

Use the TYPE= option in the PROC MODEL or FIT statement to specify the type of estimation method used to produce the **S** matrix you want to input.

The following SAS statements are used to generate an **S** matrix from a GMM and a 3SLS estimation and to store that estimate in the data set GMMS:

```
proc model data=gmm2 ;
    exogenous x1 x2;
    parms a1 a2 b1 2.5 b2 c2 55 d1;
    inst b1 b2 c2 x1 x2;
    y1 = a1 * y2 + b1 * x1 * x1 + d1;
    y2 = a2 * y1 + b2 * x2 * x2 + c2 / x2 + d1;

    fit y1 y2 / 3sls gmm kernel=(qs,1,0.2) outest=gmmest outs=gmms;
run;
```

The data set GMMS is shown in Figure 11.44.

OBS	_NAME_	_TYPE_	_NUSED_	Y1	Y2
1	Y1	3SLS	50	27.1032	38.1599
2	Y2	3SLS	50	38.1599	74.6253
3	Y1	GMM	50	27.4205	46.4028
4	Y2	GMM	50	46.4028	99.4656

Figure 11.44. SDATA= Data Set

VDATA= Input data set

The VDATA= option allows a variance matrix for GMM estimation to be input from a data set. When the VDATA= option is used in the PROC MODEL or FIT statement, the matrix that is input is used to define the objective function and is used as the initial **V** for the methods that iterate the **V** matrix.

Normally the VDATA= matrix is created from the OUTV= option in a previous FIT statement. Alternately an input VDATA= data set can be created using the DATA step. Each row and column of the **V** matrix is associated with an equation and an instrument. The position of each element in the **V** matrix can then be indicated by an equation name and an instrument name for the row of the element and an equation name and an instrument name for the column. Each observation in the VDATA= data set is an element in the **V** matrix. The row and column of the element are indicated by four variables (EQ_ROW, INST_ROW, EQ_COL, and INST_COL) that contain the equation name or instrument name. The variable name for an element is

VALUE. Missing values are set to 0. Because the variance matrix is symmetric, only a triangular part of the matrix needs to be input.

The following SAS statements are used to generate a **V** matrix estimation from GMM and to store that estimate in the data set GMMV:

```
proc model data=gmm2 ;
   exogenous x1 x2;
   parms a1 a2 b2 b1 2.5 c2 55 d1;
   inst b1 b2 c2 x1 x2;
   y1 = a1 * y2 + b1 * x1 * x1 + d1;
   y2 = a2 * y1 + b2 * x2 * x2 + c2 / x2 + d1;

   fit y1 y2 / gmm outv=gmmv;
run;
```

The data set GMM2 was generated by the example in the preceding section, "ESTDATA= Data Set." The **V** matrix stored in GMMV is selected for use in an additional GMM estimation by the following FIT statement:

```
fit y1 y2 / gmm vdata=gmmv;
run;

proc print data=gmmv(obs=15);
run;
```

A partial listing of the GMMV data set is shown in Figure 11.45. There are a total of 78 observations in this data set. The **V** matrix is 12 by 12 for this example.

OBS	_TYPE_	EQ_ROW	EQ_COL	INST_ROW	INST_COL	VALUE
1	GMM	Y1	Y1	1	1	1509.59
2	GMM	Y1	Y1	X1	1	8257.41
3	GMM	Y1	Y1	X1	X1	47956.08
4	GMM	Y1	Y1	X2	1	7136.27
5	GMM	Y1	Y1	X2	X1	44494.70
6	GMM	Y1	Y1	X2	X2	153135.59
7	GMM	Y1	Y1	@PRED.Y1/@B1	1	47957.10
8	GMM	Y1	Y1	@PRED.Y1/@B1	X1	289178.68
9	GMM	Y1	Y1	@PRED.Y1/@B1	X2	275074.36
10	GMM	Y1	Y1	@PRED.Y1/@B1	@PRED.Y1/@B1	1789176.56
11	GMM	Y1	Y1	@PRED.Y2/@B2	1	152885.91
12	GMM	Y1	Y1	@PRED.Y2/@B2	X1	816886.49
13	GMM	Y1	Y1	@PRED.Y2/@B2	X2	1121114.96
14	GMM	Y1	Y1	@PRED.Y2/@B2	@PRED.Y1/@B1	4576643.57
15	GMM	Y1	Y1	@PRED.Y2/@B2	@PRED.Y2/@B2	28818318.24

Figure 11.45.   The First 15 Observations in the VDATA= Data Set

Output Data Sets

OUT= *Data Set*

For normalized form equations, the OUT= data set specified in the FIT statement contains residuals, actuals, and predicted values of the dependent variables computed from the parameter estimates. For general form equations, actual values of the endogenous variables are copied for the residual and predicted values.

The variables in the data set are as follows:

- BY variables

- RANGE variable

- ID variables

- _ESTYPE_, a character variable of length 8 identifying the estimation method: OLS, SUR, N2SLS, N3SLS, ITOLS, ITSUR, IT2SLS, IT3SLS, GMM, IT-GMM, or FIML

- _TYPE_, a character variable of length 8 identifying the type of observation: RESIDUAL, PREDICT, or ACTUAL

- _WEIGHT_, the weight of the observation in the estimation. The _WEIGHT_ value is 0 if the observation was not used. It is equal to the product of the _WEIGHT_ model program variable and the variable named in the WEIGHT statement, if any, or 1 if weights were not used.

- the WEIGHT statement variable if used

- the model variables. The dependent variables for the normalized-form equations in the estimation contain residuals, actuals, or predicted values, depending on the _TYPE_ variable; whereas the model variables that are not associated with estimated equations always contain actual values from the input data set.

- any other variables named in the OUTVARS statement. These can be program variables computed by the model program, CONTROL variables, parameters, or special variables in the model program. Variable names longer than eight characters are truncated in the OUT= data set.

The following SAS statements are used to generate and print an OUT= data set:

```
proc model data=gmm2;
   exogenous x1 x2;
   parms a1 a2 b2 b1 2.5 c2 55 d1;
   inst b1 b2 c2 x1 x2;
   y1 = a1 * y2 + b1 * x1 * x1 + d1;
   y2 = a2 * y1 + b2 * x2 * x2 + c2 / x2 + d1;

   fit y1 y2 / 3sls gmm out=resid outall ;
run;

proc print data=resid(obs=20);
run;
```

The data set GMM2 was generated by the example in the preceding section "ESTDATA= Data Set." A partial listing of the RESID data set is shown in Figure 11.46.

OBS	_ESTYPE_	_TYPE_	_WEIGHT_	X1	X2	Y1	Y2
1	3SLS	ACTUAL	1	1.00000	-1.7339	-3.05812	-23.071
2	3SLS	PREDICT	1	1.00000	-1.7339	-0.36806	-19.351
3	3SLS	RESIDUAL	1	1.00000	-1.7339	-2.69006	-3.720
4	3SLS	ACTUAL	1	1.41421	-5.3046	0.59405	43.866
5	3SLS	PREDICT	1	1.41421	-5.3046	-0.49148	45.588
6	3SLS	RESIDUAL	1	1.41421	-5.3046	1.08553	-1.722
7	3SLS	ACTUAL	1	1.73205	-5.2826	3.17651	51.563
8	3SLS	PREDICT	1	1.73205	-5.2826	-0.48281	41.857
9	3SLS	RESIDUAL	1	1.73205	-5.2826	3.65933	9.707
10	3SLS	ACTUAL	1	2.00000	-0.6878	3.66208	-70.011
11	3SLS	PREDICT	1	2.00000	-0.6878	-0.18592	-76.502
12	3SLS	RESIDUAL	1	2.00000	-0.6878	3.84800	6.491
13	3SLS	ACTUAL	1	2.23607	-7.0797	0.29210	99.177
14	3SLS	PREDICT	1	2.23607	-7.0797	-0.53732	92.201
15	3SLS	RESIDUAL	1	2.23607	-7.0797	0.82942	6.976
16	3SLS	ACTUAL	1	2.44949	14.5284	1.86898	423.634
17	3SLS	PREDICT	1	2.44949	14.5284	-1.23490	421.969
18	3SLS	RESIDUAL	1	2.44949	14.5284	3.10388	1.665
19	3SLS	ACTUAL	1	2.64575	-0.6968	-1.03003	-72.214
20	3SLS	PREDICT	1	2.64575	-0.6968	-0.10353	-69.680

Figure 11.46.   The OUT= Data Set

OUTEST= Data Set

The OUTEST= data set contains parameter estimates and, if requested, estimates of the covariance of the parameter estimates.

The variables in the data set are as follows:

- BY variables

- _NAME_, a character variable of length 8, blank for observations containing parameter estimates or a parameter name for observations containing covariances

- _TYPE_, a character variable of length 8 identifying the estimation method: OLS, SUR, N2SLS, N3SLS, ITOLS, ITSUR, IT2SLS, IT3SLS, GMM, ITGMM, or FIML

- the parameters estimated.

If the COVOUT option is specified, an additional observation is written for each row of the estimate of the covariance matrix of parameter estimates, with the _NAME_ values containing the parameter names for the rows. Parameter names longer than 8 characters are truncated.

OUTPARMS= Data Set

The option OUTPARMS= writes all the parameter estimates to an output data set. This output data set contains one observation and is similar to the OUTEST= data set, but it contains all the parameters, is not associated with any FIT task, and contains no covariances. The OUTPARMS= option is used in the PROC MODEL statement, and the data set is written at the end, after any FIT or SOLVE statements have been performed.

OUTS= Data Set

The OUTS= SAS data set contains the estimate of the covariance matrix of the residuals across equations. This matrix is formed from the residuals that are computed using the parameter estimates.

The variables in the OUTS= data set are as follows:

- BY variables

- _NAME_, a character variable containing the name of the equation

- _TYPE_, a character variable of length 8 identifying the estimation method: OLS, SUR, N2SLS, N3SLS, ITOLS, ITSUR, IT2SLS, IT3SLS, GMM, ITGMM, or FIML

- variables with the names of the equations in the estimation.

Each observation contains a row of the covariance matrix. The data set is suitable for use with the SDATA= option in a subsequent FIT or SOLVE statement. (See "Tests on Parameters" earlier in this chapter for an example of the SDATA= option.)

OUTSUSED= Data Set

The OUTSUSED= SAS data set contains the covariance matrix of the residuals across equations that is used to define the objective function. The form of the OUTSUSED= data set is the same as that for the OUTS= data set.

Note that OUTSUSED= is the same as OUTS= for the estimation methods that iterate the **S** matrix (ITOLS, IT2SLS, ITSUR, and IT3SLS). If the SDATA= option is specified in the FIT statement, OUTSUSED= is the same as the SDATA= matrix read in for the methods that do not iterate the **S** matrix (OLS, SUR, N2SLS, and N3SLS).

OUTV= Data Set

The OUTV= data set contains the estimate of the variance matrix, **V**. This matrix is formed from the instruments and the residuals that are computed using the parameter estimates obtained from the initial 2SLS estimation when GMM estimation is selected. If an estimation method other than GMM or ITGMM is requested and OUTV= is specified, a **V** matrix is created using computed estimates. In the case that a VDATA= data set is used, this becomes the OUTV= data set. For ITGMM, the OUTV= data set is the matrix formed from the instruments and the residuals computed using the final parameter estimates.

Simulation Details

The *solution* given the vector **k**, of the following nonlinear system of equations is the vector **u** which satisfies this equation:

$$\mathbf{q}(\mathbf{u}, \mathbf{k}, \theta) = 0$$

A *simulation* is a set of solutions $\mathbf{u}_t$ for a specific sequence of vectors $\mathbf{k}_t$.

Model simulation can be performed to

- check how well the model predicts the actual values over the historical period

- investigate the sensitivity of the solution to changes in the input values or parameters

- examine the dynamic characteristics of the model

- check the stability of the simultaneous solution

- estimate the statistical distribution of the predicted values of the nonlinear model using Monte Carlo methods

By combining the various solution modes with different input data sets, model simulation can answer many different questions about the model. This section presents details of model simulation and solution.

Solution Modes

The following solution modes are commonly used:

- *Dynamic simultaneous forecast* mode is used for forecasting with the model. Collect the historical data on the model variables, the future assumptions of the exogenous variables, and any prior information on the future endogenous values, and combine them in a SAS data set. Use the FORECAST option in the SOLVE statement.

- *Dynamic simultaneous simulation* mode is often called *ex-post simulation*, *historical simulation*, or *ex-post forecasting*. Use the DYNAMIC option. This mode is the default.

- *Static simultaneous simulation* mode can be used to examine the within-period performance of the model without the complications of previous period errors. Use the STATIC option.

- *NAHEAD=n dynamic simultaneous simulation* mode can be used to see how well n-period-ahead forecasting would have performed over the historical period. Use the NAHEAD=n option.

The different solution modes are explained in detail in the following sections.

Dynamic and Static Simulations

In model simulation, either solved values or actual values from the data set can be used to supply lagged values of an endogenous variable. A *dynamic* solution refers to a solution obtained by using only solved values for the lagged values. Dynamic mode is used both for forecasting and for simulating the dynamic properties of the model.

A *static* solution refers to a solution obtained by using the actual values when available for the lagged endogenous values. Static mode is used to simulate the behavior of the model without the complication of previous period errors. Dynamic simulation is the default.

If you want to use static values for lags only for the first n observations, and dynamic values thereafter, specify the START=*n* option. For example, if you want a dynamic simulation to start after observation 24, specify START=24 in the SOLVE statement. If the model being simulated had a value lagged for four time periods, then this value would start using dynamic values when the simulation reached observation 28.

n-Period-Ahead Forecasting

Suppose you want to regularly forecast 12 months ahead and produce a new forecast each month as more data become available. *n*-period-ahead forecasting enables you to test how well you would have done over time had you been using your model to forecast one year ahead.

To see how well a model predicts *n* time periods in the future, perform an *n*-period-ahead forecast on real data and compare the forecast values with the actual values.

n-period-ahead forecasting refers to using dynamic values for the lagged endogenous variables only for lags 1 through $n - 1$. For example, 1-period-ahead forecasting, specified by the NAHEAD=1 option in the SOLVE statement, is the same as if a static solution had been requested. Specifying NAHEAD=2 produces a solution that uses dynamic values for lag one and static, actual, values for longer lags.

The following example is a 2-year-ahead dynamic simulation. The output is shown in Figure 11.47.

```
data yearly;
   input year x1 x2 x3 y1 y2 y3;
   cards;
84 1 4 9  0  7  4  5
85 2 5 6  1  1 27  4
86 3 3 8  2  5  8  2
87 4 2 10 3  0 10 10
88 1 4 7  6 20 60 40
89 2 5 4  8 40 40 40
90 3 3 2 10 50 60 60
91 4 2 5 11 40 50 60
;
run;

proc model data=yearly outmodel=foo;
   endogenous y1 y2 y3;
   exogenous  x1 x2 x3;

   y1 = 2 + 3*x1 - 2*x2 + 4*x3;
   y2 = 4 + lag2( y3 ) + 2*y1 + x1;
   y3 = lag3( y1 ) + y2 - x2;

   solve y1 y2 y3 / nahead=2 out=c;
run;

proc print data=c;
run;
```

```
                        MODEL Procedure
       Dynamic Simultaneous 2-Periods-Ahead Forecasting Simulation

                         Solution Summary

              Dataset Option        Dataset
              DATA=                 YEARLY
              OUT=                     C

              Variables Solved         3

              Simulation Lag Length    3

              Solution Method       NEWTON
              CONVERGE=              1E-8
              Maximum CC               0
              Maximum Iterations       1
              Total Iterations         8
              Average Iterations       1

                  Observations Processed
              Read                    20
              Lagged                  12
              Solved                   8
               First                   5
               Last                    8

          Variables Solved For: Y1 Y2 Y3
```

Figure 11.47. NAHEAD Summary Report

```
                          The SAS System                                 3

  OBS   _TYPE_    _MODE_    _LAG_   _ERRORS_   Y1    Y2    Y3   X1   X2   X3

   1    PREDICT   SIMULATE    0        0        0    10     7    2   10    3
   2    PREDICT   SIMULATE    1        0       24    58    52    4    7    6
   3    PREDICT   SIMULATE    1        0       41   101   102    5    4    8
   4    PREDICT   SIMULATE    1        0       47   141   139    3    2   10
   5    PREDICT   SIMULATE    1        0       42   130   145    2    5   11
```

Figure 11.48. C Data Set

The preceding 2-year-ahead simulation can be emulated without using the NA-
HEAD= option by the following PROC MODEL statements:

```
proc model data=test model=foo;
  range year = 87 to 88;
  solve y1 y2 y3 / dynamic solveprint;
run;

  range year = 88 to 89;
  solve y1 y2 y3 / dynamic solveprint;
run;

  range year = 89 to 90;
  solve y1 y2 y3 / dynamic solveprint;
run;

  range year = 90 to 91;
  solve y1 y2 y3 / dynamic solveprint;
run;
```

The totals shown under Observations Processed in Figure 11.47 are equal to the sum
of the four individual runs.

Simulation and Forecasting

You can perform a simulation of your model or use the model to produce forecasts. *Simulation* refers to the determination of the endogenous or dependent variables as a function of the input values of the other variables, even when actual data for some of the solution variables are available in the input data set. The simulation mode is useful for verifying the fit of the model parameters. Simulation is selected by the SIMULATE option in the SOLVE statement. Simulation mode is the default.

In forecast mode, PROC MODEL solves only for those endogenous variables that are missing in the data set. The actual value of an endogenous variable is used as the solution value whenever nonmissing data for it are available in the input data set. Forecasting is selected by the FORECAST option in the SOLVE statement.

For example, an econometric forecasting model can contain an equation to predict future tax rates, but tax rates are usually set in advance by law. Thus, for the first year or so of the forecast, the predicted tax rate should really be exogenous. Or, you may want to use a prior forecast of a certain variable from a short-run forecasting model to provide the predicted values for the earlier periods of a longer-range forecast of a long-run model. A common situation in forecasting is when historical data needed to fill the initial lags of a dynamic model are available for some of the variables but have not yet been obtained for others. In this case, the forecast must start in the past to supply the missing initial lags. Clearly, you should use the actual data that are available for the lags. In all the preceding cases, the forecast should be produced by running the model in the FORECAST mode; simulating the model over the future periods would not be appropriate.

Monte Carlo Simulation

The accuracy of the forecasts produced by PROC MODEL depends on four sources of error (Pindyck 1981, 405-406):

- The system of equations contains an implicit random error term ϵ

$$\mathbf{g}\left(\mathbf{y}, \mathbf{x}, \widehat{\theta}\right) = \epsilon$$

where $\mathbf{y}$, $\mathbf{x}$, $\mathbf{g}$, $\widehat{\theta}$, and ϵ are vector valued.

- The estimated values of the parameters, $\widehat{\theta}$, are themselves random variables.

- The exogenous variables may have been forecast themselves and therefore may contain errors.

- The system of equations may be incorrectly specified; the model only approximates the process modeled.

The RANDOM= option is used to request Monte Carlo (or stochastic) simulations to generate confidence intervals for errors arising from the first two sources. The Monte Carlo simulations can be performed with ϵ, θ, or both vectors represented as random variables. The SEED= option is used to control the random number generator for the simulations. SEED=0 forces the random number generator to use the system clock as its seed value.

In Monte Carlo simulations, repeated simulations are performed on the model for random perturbations of the parameters and the additive error term. The random perturbations follow a multivariate normal distribution with expected value of 0 and covariance described by a covariance matrix of the parameter estimates in the case of θ, or a covariance matrix of the equation residuals for the case of ϵ. PROC MODEL can generate both covariance matrices, or you can provide them.

The ESTDATA= option specifies a data set containing an estimate of the covariance matrix of the parameter estimates to use for computing perturbations of the parameters. The ESTDATA= data set is usually created by the FIT statement with the OUTEST= and OUTCOV options. When the ESTDATA= option is specified, the matrix read from the ESTDATA= data set is used to compute vectors of random shocks or perturbations for the parameters. These random perturbations are computed at the start of each repetition of the solution and added to the parameter values. The perturbed parameters are fixed throughout the solution range. If the covariance matrix of the parameter estimates is not provided, the parameters are not perturbed.

The SDATA= option specifies a data set containing the covariance matrix of the residuals to use for computing perturbations of the equations. The SDATA= data set is usually created by the FIT statement with the OUTS= option. When the SDATA= option is specified, the matrix read from the SDATA= data set is used to compute vectors of random shocks or perturbations for the equations. These random perturbations are computed at each observation. The simultaneous solution satisfies the model equations plus the random shocks. That is, the solution is not a perturbation of a simultaneous solution of the structural equations; rather, it is a simultaneous solution of the stochastic equations using the simulated errors. If the SDATA= option is not specified, the random shocks are not used.

The different random solutions are identified by the _REP_ variable in the OUT= data set. An unperturbed solution with _REP_=0 is also computed when the RANDOM= option is used. RANDOM=n produces $n + 1$ solution observations for each input observation in the solution range. If the RANDOM= option is not specified, the SDATA= and ESTDATA= options are ignored, and no Monte Carlo simulation is performed.

PROC MODEL does not have an automatic way of modeling the exogenous variables as random variables for Monte Carlo simulation. If the exogenous variables have been forecast, the error bounds for these variables should be included in the error bounds generated for the endogenous variables. If the models for the exogenous variables are included in PROC MODEL, then the error bounds created from a Monte Carlo simulation will contain the uncertainty due to the exogenous variables.

Alternatively, if the distribution of the exogenous variables is known, the built-in random number generator functions can be used to perturb these variables appropriately for the Monte Carlo simulation. For example, if you knew the forecast of an exogenous variable, X, had a standard error of 5.2 and the error was normally distributed, then the following statements could be used to generate random values for X:

```
x_new = x + 5.2 * rannor(456);
```

During a Monte Carlo simulation the random number generator functions produce one value at each observation. It is important to use a different seed value for all the random number generator functions in the model program; otherwise, the perturbations will be correlated. For the unperturbed solution, _REP_=0, the random number generator functions return 0.

PROC UNIVARIATE can be used to create confidence intervals for the simulation (see the Monte Carlo simulation example in "Getting Started" earlier in this chapter).

Solution Mode Output

The following SAS statements dynamically forecast the solution to a nonlinear equation:

```
proc model data=sashelp.citimon;
   parameters a 0.010708  b  -0.478849 c 0.929304;
   lhur = 1/(a * ip) + b + c * lag(lhur);
   solve lhur / out=sim forecast dynamic;
run;
```

The first page of output produced by the SOLVE step is shown in Figure 11.49. This is the summary description of the model. The error message states that the simulation was aborted at observation 144 because of missing input values.

```
                        MODEL Procedure

                        Model Summary

                Model Variables       1
                Parameters            3
                Equations             1

                Number of Statements  1

                Program Lag Length    1

        Model Variables: LHUR

        Parameters: A: 0.01071  B: -0.4788  C: 0.9293

        Equations: LHUR

ERROR: Solution values are missing because of missing input values for
       observation 144 at NEWTON iteration 0.
```

Figure 11.49. Solve Step Summary Output

The second page of output, shown in Figure 11.50, gives more information on the failed observation.

```
                         MODEL Procedure
                  Dynamic Single-Equation Forecast
ERROR: Solution values are missing because of missing input values for
       observation 144 at NEWTON iteration 0.

NOTE: Additional information on the values of the variables at this
      observation, which may be helpful in determining the cause of the
      failure of the solution process, is printed below.

Observation 144. Iteration 0. Missing=1 NEWTON CC=-1
Iteration Errors: Missing.

                   --- Listing of Program Data Vector ---
_N_:               287     A:        0.01071    ACTUAL.LHUR:        .
B:            -0.47885     C:        0.92930    ERROR.LHUR:         .
IP:                  .     LHUR:     7.10000    PRED.LHUR:          .
RESID.LHUR:          .

NOTE: Simulation aborted.
```

Figure 11.50. Solve Step Error Message

From the program data vector you can see the variable IP is missing for observation 144. LHUR could not be computed, so the simulation aborted.

The solution summary table is shown in Figure 11.51.

```
                    Solution Summary

          Dataset Option        Dataset
          DATA=            SASHELP.CITIMON
          OUT=                      SIM

          Variables Solved            1

          Forecast Lag Length         1

          Solution Method        NEWTON
          CONVERGE=                1E-8
          Maximum CC                  0
          Maximum Iterations          1
          Total Iterations          143
          Average Iterations          1
              Observations Processed
          Read                      145
          Lagged                      1
          Solved                    143
           First                      2
           Last                     145
           Failed                     1

          Variables Solved For: LHUR
```

Figure 11.51. Solution Summary Report

This solution summary table includes the names of the input data set and the output data set, followed by a description of the model. The table also indicates the solution method defaulted to Newton's method. The remaining output is defined as follows:

Maximum CC is the maximum convergence value accepted by the Newton procedure. This number is always less than the value for the CONVERGE= option.

Maximum   is the maximum number of Newton iterations performed at each ob-
Iterations servation and each replication of Monte Carlo simulations.

Total   is the sum of the number of iterations required for each observation
Iterations   and each Monte Carlo simulation.

Average   is the average number of Newton iterations required to solve the sys-
Iterations   tem at each step.

Solved   is the number of observations used times the number of random repli-
             cations selected plus one, for Monte Carlo simulations. The one ad-
             ditional simulation is the original unperturbed solution. For simula-
             tions not involving Monte Carlo, this number is the number of obser-
             vations used.

Summary Statistics

The STATS and THEIL options are used to select goodness of fit statistics. Actual
values must be provided in the input data set for these statistics to be printed. When
the RANDOM= option is specified, the statistics do not include the unperturbed
($\_REP\_=0$) solution.

STATS Option Output

If the STATS and THEIL options are added to the model in the previous section

```
proc model data=sashelp.citimon;
   parameters a 0.010708  b  -0.478849 c 0.929304;
   lhur= 1/(a * ip) + b + c * lag(lhur) ;
   solve lhur / out=sim dynamic stats theil;
   range date to '01nov91'd;
run;
```

the STATS output in Figure 11.52 and the THEIL output in Figure 11.53 are generated.

```
                         Descriptive Statistics

                             Actual              Predicted

   Variable    Nobs     N     Mean      Std      Mean      Std
   LHUR         142    142    7.0887    1.4509   7.2473    1.1465


                         Statistics of Fit

                             Mean     Mean %   Mean Abs Mean Abs %
            Variable     N   Error    Error    Error    Error
            LHUR        142  0.1585   3.5289   0.6937   10.00013

                         Statistics of Fit

             RMS       RMS %
Variable     Error     Error R-Square Label
LHUR         0.7854    11.2452  0.7049 UNEMPLOYMENT RATE: ALL WORKERS, 16 YEARS
```

Figure 11.52. STATS Output

The number of observations (Nobs), the number of observations with both predicted
and actual values nonmissing (N), and the mean and standard deviation of the actual
and predicted values of the determined variables are printed first.

The next set of columns in the output are defined as follows:

Mean Error $\qquad \frac{1}{N}\sum_{j=1}^{N}\left(\hat{y}_j - y_j\right)$

Mean % Error $\qquad \frac{100}{N}\sum_{j=1}^{N}\left(\hat{y}_j - y_j\right)/y_j$

Mean Abs Error $\qquad \frac{1}{N}\sum_{j=1}^{N}\left|\hat{y}_j - y_j\right|$

Mean Abs % Error $\quad \frac{100}{N}\sum_{j=1}^{N}\left|\left(\hat{y}_j - y_j\right)/y_j\right|$

RMS Error $\qquad \sqrt{\frac{1}{N}\sum_{j=1}^{N}\left(\hat{y}_j - y_j\right)^2}$

RMS % Error $\qquad 100\sqrt{\frac{1}{N}\sum_{j=1}^{N}\left(\left(\hat{y}_j - y_j\right)/y_j\right)^2}$

R-square $\qquad 1 - SSE/CSSA$

SSE $\qquad \sum_{j=1}^{N}\left(\hat{y}_j - y_j\right)^2$

SSA $\qquad \sum_{j=1}^{N}y_j^2$

CSSA $\qquad SSA - \left(\sum_{j=1}^{N}y_j\right)^2$

$\hat{y}$ $\qquad$ predicted value

y $\qquad$ actual value

When the RANDOM= option is specified, the statistics do not include the unperturbed (_REP_=0) solution.

THEIL Option Output

The THEIL option specifies that Theil forecast error statistics be computed for the actual and predicted values and for the relative changes from lagged values. Mathematically, the quantities are

$$\widehat{yc}_t = \frac{\hat{y}_t - y_{t-1}}{y_{t-1}} \qquad\qquad yc_t = \frac{y_t - y_{t-1}}{y_{t-1}}$$

where $\widehat{yc}_t$ is the relative change for the predicted value and yc_t is the relative change for the actual value.

```
                    Theil Forecast Error Statistics

                              MSE Decomposition Proportions Inequality Coef

Variable    N       MSE   Corr   Bias   Reg   Dist   Var  Covar    U1      U
                          (R)    (UM)  (UR)  (UD)   (US)  (UC)

Y1          50   0.22634 0.999  0.003 0.043 0.954 0.034 0.963   0.0367 0.0183
Y2          50   0.22081 0.909  0.006 0.002 0.992 0.069 0.925   0.4098 0.2170

              Theil Relative Change Forecast Error Statistics

            Relative Change   MSE Decomposition Proportions Inequality Coef

Variable    N       MSE   Corr   Bias   Reg   Dist   Var  Covar    U1      U
                          (R)    (UM)  (UR)  (UD)   (US)  (UC)

Y1          49   2.05716 1.000  0.039 0.264 0.697 0.258 0.703   0.0176 0.0088
Y2          49   0.65032 0.872  0.012 0.374 0.614 0.166 0.822   0.6239 0.2765
```

Figure 11.53.   THEIL Output

The columns have the following meaning:

Corr (R)   is the correlation coefficient, ρ, between the actual and predicted values.

$$\rho = \frac{\text{cov}(y, \hat{y})}{\sigma_a \, \sigma_p}$$

where σ_p and σ_a are the standard deviations of the predicted and actual values.

Bias (UM)   is an indication of systematic error and measures the extent to which the average values of the actual and predicted deviate from each other.

$$\frac{(E(y) - E(\hat{y}))^2}{\frac{1}{N} \sum_{t=1}^{N} (y_t - \hat{y}_t)^2}$$

Reg (UR)   is defined as $(\sigma_p - \rho \times \sigma_a)^2 / MSE$. Consider the regression

$$y = \alpha + \beta \hat{y}$$

If $\hat{\beta} = 1$, UR will equal 0.

Dist (UD)   is defined as $(1 - \rho^2) \, \sigma_a \sigma_a / MSE$ and represents the variance of the residuals obtained by regressing yc on $\widehat{yc}$.

Var (US)   is the variance proportion. US indicates the ability of the model to replicate the degree of variability in the endogenous variable.

$$US = \frac{(\sigma_p - \sigma_a)^2}{MSE}$$

Covar (UC)   represents the remaining error after deviations from average values and average variabilities have been accounted for.

$$UC = \frac{2(1 - \rho) \, \sigma_p \sigma_a}{MSE}$$

U1   is a statistic measuring the accuracy of a forecast.

$$U1 = \frac{MSE}{\sqrt{\frac{1}{N} \sum_{t=1}^{N} y_t^2}}$$

U   is the Theil's inequality coefficient, defined as follows:

$$U = \frac{MSE}{\sqrt{\frac{1}{N} \sum_{t=1}^{N} y_t^2} + \sqrt{\frac{1}{N} \sum_{t=1}^{N} \hat{y}_t^2}}$$

MSE   is the mean square error

$$MSE = \frac{1}{N} \sum_{t=1}^{N} \left(\widehat{yc} - yc \right)^2$$

More information on these statistics can be found in Maddala (1977, 344–347) and Pindyck and Rubinfeld (1981, 364–365).

Goal Seeking: Solving for Right-Hand Variables

The process of computing input values needed to produce target results is often called *goal seeking*. To compute a goal-seeking solution, use a SOLVE statement that lists the variables you want to solve for and provide a data set containing values for the remaining variables.

Consider the following demand model for packaged rice

$$quantity\,demanded = \alpha_1 + \alpha_2\,price^{2/3} + \alpha_3 income$$

where *price* is the price of the package and *income* is disposable personal income. The only variable the company has control over is the price it charges for rice. This model is estimated using the following simulated data and PROC MODEL statements:

```
data demand;
   do t=1 to 40;
       price = (rannor(10) +5) * 10;
       income = 8000 * t ** (1/8);
       demand = 7200 - 1054 * price ** (2/3) +
                 1746 * income + 100 * rannor(1);
       output;
   end;
run;
proc model data=demand ;
   demand = a1 - a2 * price ** (2/3) + a3 * income;
   fit demand / outest=demest;
run;
```

The goal is to find the price the company would have to charge to meet a sales target of 85,000 units. To do this, a data set is created with a DEMAND variable set to 85000 and with an INCOME variable set to 12686, the last income value.

```
data goal;
    demand = 85000;
    income = 12686;
run;
```

The desired price is then determined using the following PROC MODEL statements:

```
proc model ;
    demand = a1 - a2 * price ** (2/3) + a3 * income;
    solve price / estdata=demest data=goal solveprint;
run;
```

The SOLVEPRINT option prints the solution values, the number of iterations, and the final residuals at each observation. The SOLVEPRINT output from this solve is shown in Figure 11.54.

```
                        MODEL Procedure
                   Single-Equation Simulation

Observation 1. NEWTON Iterations=6 CC=1.601E-10(ERROR.DEMAND=16E-11)

Solution Values:
PRICE:    33.5902
```

Figure 11.54. Goal Seeking, SOLVEPRINT Output

The output indicates that it took six Newton iterations to determine the PRICE of 33.5902, which makes the DEMAND value within 16E-11 of the goal of 85,000 units.

Consider a more ambitious goal of 100,000 units. The output shown in Figure 11.55 indicates that the sales target of 100,000 units is not attainable according to this model.

```
                        MODEL Procedure
                   Single-Equation Simulation

ERROR: The solution did not converge for observation 1 after 50 NEWTON
       iterations using the convergence criterion CONVERGE=1E-8.

NOTE: Additional information on the values of the variables at this
      observation, which may be helpful in determining the cause of the
      failure of the solution process, is printed below.

Observation 1. Iteration 50. NEWTON CC=4164(ERROR.DEMAND=-4164)
Iteration Errors:
DEMAND:      -4164

                  --- Listing of Program Data Vector ---
 _N_:              255  A1:        7126.437997  A2:        1040.841492
A3:           6.992694  ACTUAL.DEMAND:   100000  DEMAND:          100000
ERROR.DEMAND:    -4164  INCOME:           12686  PRED.DEMAND:      95836
PRICE:    4.462312E-22  RESID.DEMAND:     -4164
@PRED.DEMAND/@PRI: -9.08044E9
```

Figure 11.55. Goal Seeking, Convergence Failure

The program data vector indicates that even with the value of PRICE nearly 0 (4.462312E-22) the demand is still 4,164 less than the goal. You may need to reformulate your model or collect more data to more accurately reflect the market response.

Numerical Solution Methods

If the SINGLE option is not used, PROC MODEL computes values that simultaneously satisfy the model equations for the variables named in the SOLVE statement. PROC MODEL provides three iterative methods (Newton, Jacobi, and Seidel) for computing a simultaneous solution of the system of nonlinear equations.

Single-Equation Solution

For normalized-form equation systems, the solution can either simultaneously satisfy all the equations or can be computed for each equation separately, using the actual values of the solution variables in the current period to compute each predicted value. Normally, PROC MODEL computes a simultaneous solution. The SINGLE option in the SOLVE statement selects single-equation solutions.

Single-equation simulations are often made to produce residuals (which estimate the random terms of the stochastic equations) rather than the predicted values themselves. If the input data and range are the same as that used for parameter estimation, a static single-equation simulation will reproduce the residuals of the estimation.

Newton's Method

The METHOD=NEWTON option in the SOLVE statement requests Newton's method to simultaneously solve the equations for each observation. Newton's method is the default solution method. Newton's method is an iterative scheme that uses the derivatives of the equations with respect to the solution variables, $\mathbf{J}$, to compute a change vector as

$$\Delta \mathbf{y}^i = \mathbf{J}^{-1} \mathbf{q}\left(\mathbf{y}^i, \mathbf{x}, \theta\right)$$

PROC MODEL builds and solves $\mathbf{J}$ using efficient sparse matrix techniques. The solution variables $\mathbf{y}^i$ at the ith iteration are then updated as

$$\mathbf{y}^{i+1} = \mathbf{y}^i + d \times \Delta \mathbf{y}^i$$

d is a damping factor between 0 and 1 chosen iteratively so that

$$\| \mathbf{q}\left(\mathbf{y}^{i+1}, \mathbf{x}, \theta\right) \| < \| \mathbf{q}\left(\mathbf{y}^i, \mathbf{x}, \theta\right) \|$$

The number of subiterations allowed for finding a suitable d is controlled by the MAXSUBITER= option. The number of iterations of Newton's method allowed for each observation is controlled by MAXITER= option. Refer to Ortega and Rheinbolt (1970) for more details.

Jacobi Method

The METHOD=JACOBI option in the SOLVE statement selects a derivative-free alternative to Newton's method. This method is referred to as the Jacobi method even though it is not the traditional nonlinear Jacobi method found in the literature. The Jacobi method as implemented in PROC MODEL substitutes predicted values for the endogenous variables and iterates until a fixed point is reached. The METHOD=JACOBI option is only for normalized-form equation systems.

If the normalized-form equation is

$$\mathbf{y} = \mathbf{f}(\mathbf{y}, \mathbf{x}, \theta)$$

the Jacobi iteration has the form

$$\mathbf{y}^{i+1} = \mathbf{f}\left(\mathbf{y}^i, \mathbf{x}, \theta\right)$$

Seidel Method

The Seidel method is an order-dependent alternative to the Jacobi method. The Seidel method is selected by the METHOD=SEIDEL option in the SOLVE statement and is applicable only to normalized-form equations. The Seidel method is like the Jacobi method, except that in the Seidel method the model is further edited to substitute the predicted values into the solution variables immediately after they are computed. Seidel thus differs from the other methods in that the values of the solution variables are not fixed within an iteration. With the other methods, the order of the equations in the model program makes no difference, but the Seidel method may work much differently when the equations are specified in a different sequence. Note that this fixed-point method is not the traditional nonlinear Seidel method found in the literature.

The iteration has the form

$$\mathbf{y}_j^{i+1} = \mathbf{f}(\hat{\mathbf{y}}^i, \mathbf{x}, \theta)$$

where $\mathbf{y}_j^{i+1}$ is the *j*th equation variable at the *i*th iteration and

$$\hat{\mathbf{y}}^i = \left(y_1^{i+1}, y_2^{i+1}, y_3^{i+1}, \ \dots, \ y_{j-1}^{i+1}, y_j^i, y_{j+1}^i, \ \dots, \ y_g^i \right)'$$

If the model is recursive, and if the equations are in recursive order, the Seidel method will converge at once. If the model is block-recursive, the Seidel method may converge faster if the equations are grouped by block and the blocks are placed in block-recursive order. The BLOCK option can be used to determine the block-recursive form.

Comparison of Methods

Newton's method is the default and should work better than the others for most small-to medium-sized models. The Seidel method is always fastest for recursive models with equations in recursive order. For very large models and some highly nonlinear smaller models, the Jacobi or Seidel methods can sometimes be faster. Newton's method uses more memory than the Jacobi or Seidel methods.

Both the Newton's method and the Jacobi method are order-invariant in the sense that the order in which equations are specified in the model program has no effect on the operation of the iterative solution process. In order-invariant methods, the values of the solution variables are fixed for the entire execution of the model program. Assignments to model variables are automatically changed to assignments to corresponding equation variables. Only after the model program has completed execution are the results used to compute the new solution values for the next iteration.

Troubleshooting Problems

In solving a simultaneous nonlinear dynamic model, you may encounter some of the following problems.

Missing Values

For SOLVE tasks, there can be no missing parameter values. If there are missing right-hand variables, this will result in a missing left-hand variable for that observation.

Unstable Solutions

A solution may exist but be unstable. An unstable system can cause the Jacobi and Seidel methods to diverge.

Explosive Dynamic Systems

A model may have well-behaved solutions at each observation but be dynamically unstable. The solution may oscillate wildly or grow rapidly with time.

Propagation of Errors

During the solution process, solution variables can take on values that cause computational errors. For example, a solution variable that appears in a LOG function may be positive at the solution but may be given a negative value during one of the iterations. When computational errors occur, missing values are generated and propagated, and the solution process may collapse.

Convergence Problems

The following items can cause convergence problems:

- illegal function values (for example, $\sqrt{-1}$)

- local minima in the model equation

- no solution exists

- multiple solutions exist

- initial values too far from the solution

- the CONVERGE= value too small

When PROC MODEL fails to find a solution to the system, the current iteration information and the program data vector are printed. The simulation halts if actual values are not available for the simulation to proceed. Consider the following program:

```
data test1;
   do t=1 to 50;
      x1 = sqrt(t) ;
      y = .;
      output;
   end;

proc model data=test1;
   exogenous x1 ;
   control a1 -1 b1 -29 c1 -4 ;
   y = a1 * sqrt(y) + b1 * x1 * x1 + c1 * lag(x1);
   solve y / out=sim forecast dynamic ;
run;
```

which produces the output shown in Figure 11.56.

```
ERROR: The solution did not converge for observation 1 after 50 NEWTON
       iterations using the convergence criterion CONVERGE=1E-8.

NOTE: Additional information on the values of the variables at this
      observation, which may be helpful in determining the cause of the
      failure of the solution process, is printed below.

Observation 1. Iteration 50. NEWTON CC=12039176(ERROR.Y=-62)
Iteration Errors:
Y:  -62.0020

                       --- Listing of Program Data Vector ---
   _N_:            601    A1:                -1    ACTUAL.X1:    1.41421
   ACTUAL.Y:         .    B1:               -29    C1:                -4
   ERROR.Y:   -62.00204   PRED.Y:      -62.00204   RESID.Y:            .
   X1:          1.41421   Y:          4.15002E-6
   @PRED.Y/@Y: -245.43965 @ERROR.Y/@Y: -246.43965
```

Figure 11.56.   SOLVE Convergence Problems

At the first observation, the procedure attempts to solve the following equation:

$$y = -\sqrt{y} - 62$$

There is no solution to this problem. The iterative solution process got as close as it could to making Y negative (from the program data vector Y=4.15002E-6) while still being able to evaluate the model. This problem can be avoided in this case by altering the equation.

In other models, the problem of missing values can be avoided by either altering the data set to provide better starting values for the solution variables or by altering the equations.

You should be aware that, in general, a nonlinear system can have any number of solutions, and the solution found may not be the one that you want. When multiple solutions exist, the solution that is found is usually determined by the starting values for the iterations. If the value from the input data set for a solution variable is missing, the starting value for it is taken from the solution of the last period (if nonmissing) or else the solution estimate is started at 0.

Iteration Output

The iteration output, produced by the ITPRINT option, is useful in determining the cause of a convergence problem. The ITPRINT option forces the printing of the solution approximation and equation errors at each iteration for each observation. A portion of the ITPRINT output from

```
proc model data=test1;
    exogenous x1 ;
    control a1 -1 b1 -29 c1 -4 ;
    y = a1 * sqrt(abs(y)) + b1 * x1 * x1 + c1 * lag(x1);
    solve y / out=sim forecast dynamic itprint;
run;
```

is shown in Figure 11.57.

```
Observation 1. Iteration 0. NEWTON CC=613961(ERROR.Y=-62)
Predicted Values:
Y:   0.000100
Iteration Errors:
Y:  -62.0101

Observation 1. Iteration 1. NEWTON CC=50.9(ERROR.Y=-61.9)
Predicted Values:
Y:    -1.2158
Iteration Errors:
Y:   -61.8868

Observation 1. Iteration 2. NEWTON CC=0.3648(ERROR.Y=41.8)
Predicted Values:
Y:  -114.4503
Iteration Errors:
Y:    41.7521

Observation 1. Iteration 3. NEWTON CC=0.003477(ERROR.Y=0.246)
Predicted Values:
Y:   -70.6511
Iteration Errors:
Y:     0.2457

Observation 1. Iteration 4. NEWTON CC=2.044E-7(ERROR.Y=0.0000144)
Predicted Values:
Y:   -70.3899
Iteration Errors:
Y: 0.0000144

Observation 1. Iteration 5. NEWTON CC=6.057E-16(ERROR.Y=4.26E-14)
Predicted Values:
Y:   -70.3899
Iteration Errors:
Y: 4.263E-14
```

Figure 11.57. SOLVE, ITPRINT Output

For each iteration, the equation with the largest error is listed in parentheses after the Newton convergence criteria measure. From this output, you can determine which equation or equations in the system are not converging well.

SOLVE Data Sets

SDATA= Input Data Set

The SDATA= option reads a cross-equation covariance matrix from a data set. The covariance matrix read from the SDATA= data set specified in the SOLVE statement is used to generate random equation errors when the RANDOM= option specifies Monte Carlo simulation.

Typically, the SDATA= data set is created by the OUTS= in a previous FIT statement. (The OUTS= data set from a FIT statement can be read back in by a SOLVE statement in the same PROC MODEL step.)

You can create an input SDATA= data set using the DATA step. PROC MODEL expects to find a character variable _NAME_ in the SDATA= data set as well as variables for the equations in the estimation or solution. For each observation with a _NAME_ value matching the name of an equation, PROC MODEL fills the corresponding row of the S matrix with the values of the names of equations found in the data set. If a row or column is omitted from the data set, an identity matrix row or column is assumed. Missing values are ignored. Since the S matrix is symmetric, you can include only a triangular part of the S matrix in the SDATA= data set with the omitted part indicated by missing values. If the SDATA= data set contains multiple observations with the same _NAME_, the last values supplied for the _NAME_ variable are used. The section "OUTS= Data Set" earlier in this chapter contains more details on the format of this data set.

Use the TYPE= option to specify the type of estimation method used to produce the S matrix you want to input.

ESTDATA= Input Data Set

The ESTDATA= option specifies an input data set that contains an observation with values for some or all of the model parameters. It can also contain observations with the rows of a covariance matrix for the parameters.

When the ESTDATA= option is used, parameter values are set from the first observation. If the RANDOM= option is used and the ESTDATA= data set contains a covariance matrix, the covariance matrix of the parameter estimates is read and used to generate pseudo-random shocks to the model parameters for Monte Carlo simulation. These random perturbations have a multivariate normal distribution with the covariance matrix read from the ESTDATA= data set.

The ESTDATA= data set is usually created by the OUTEST= option in a FIT statement. The OUTEST= data set contains the parameter estimates produced by the FIT statement and also contains the estimated covariance of the parameter estimates if the OUTCOV option is used. This OUTEST= data set can be read in by the ESTDATA= option in a SOLVE statement.

You can also create an ESTDATA= data set with a SAS DATA step program. The data set must contain a numeric variable for each parameter to be given a value or covariance column. The name of the variable in the ESTDATA= data set must match the name of the parameter in the model. Parameters with names longer than 8 characters cannot be set from an ESTDATA= data set. The data set must also contain a character variable _NAME_ of length 8. _NAME_ has a blank value for the observation that gives values to the parameters. _NAME_ contains the name of a parameter for observations defining rows of the covariance matrix.

More than one set of parameter estimates and covariances can be stored in the ESTDATA= data set if the observations for the different estimates are identified by the variable _TYPE_. _TYPE_ must be a character variable of length 8. The TYPE= option is used to select for input the part of the ESTDATA= data set for which the value of the _TYPE_ variable matches the value of the TYPE= option.

OUT= Data Set

The OUT= data set contains solution values, residual values, and actual values of the solution variables.

The OUT= data set contains the following variables:

- BY variables
- RANGE variable
- ID variables

- _TYPE_, a character variable of length 8 identifying the type of observation. Values for the _TYPE_ variable can be PREDICT, RESIDUAL, ACTUAL, or ERROR.

- _MODE_, a character variable of length 8 identifying the solution mode. _MODE_ takes the value FORECAST or SIMULATE.

- if lags are used, a numeric variable, _LAG_, containing the number of dynamic lags that contribute to the solution. The value of _LAG_ is always 0 for STATIC mode solutions. _LAG_ is set to a missing value for lag-starting observations.

- _REP_, a numeric variable containing the replication number, if the RANDOM= option is used. For example, if RANDOM=10, each input observation results in eleven output observations with _REP_ values 0 through 10. The observations with _REP_=0 are from the unperturbed solution. (The random-number generator functions are suppressed, and the parameter and endogenous perturbations are 0 when _REP_=0.)

- _ERRORS_, a numeric variable containing the number of errors that occurred during the execution of the program for the last iteration for the observation. If the solution failed to converge, this is counted as one error, and the _ERRORS_ variable is made negative.

- solution and other variables. The solution variables contain solution or predicted values for _TYPE_=PREDICT observations, residuals for _TYPE_=RESIDUAL observations, or actual values for _TYPE_=ACTUAL observations. The other model variables, and any other variables read from the input data set, are always actual values from the input data set.

- any other variables named in the OUTVARS statement. These can be program variables computed by the model program, CONTROL variables, parameters, or special variables in the model program. Compound variable names longer than 8 characters are truncated in the OUT= data set.

By default only the predicted values are written to the OUT= data set. The OUT-RESID, OUTACTUAL, and OUTERROR options are used to add the residual, actual, and ERROR. values to the data set.

For examples of the OUT= data set, see Example 11.6 at the end of this chapter.

DATA= *Input Data Set*

The input data set should contain all of the exogenous variables and should supply nonmissing values for them for each period to be solved.

Solution variables can be supplied in the input data set and are used as follows:

- to supply initial lags. For example, if the lag length of the model is 3, three observations are read in to feed the lags before any solutions are computed.

- to evaluate the goodness of fit. Goodness-of-fit measures are computed based on the difference between the solved values and the actual values supplied from the data set.

- to supply starting values for the iterative solution. If the value from the input data set for a solution variable is missing, the starting value for it is taken from the solution of the last period (if nonmissing) or else the solution estimate is started at 0.

- For STATIC mode solutions, actual values from the data set are used by the lagging functions for the solution variables.

- for FORECAST mode solutions, actual values from the data set are used as the solution values when nonmissing.

Programming Language Overview

Variables in the Model Program

Variable names are alphanumeric but must start with a letter. The length of a variable name is limited to 32 characters for non-SAS data set variables, while the length of the names of data set variables are restricted to 8 characters. If you use a variable name longer than 8 characters for a variable to be output to a data set, that name is truncated to 8 characters in the output data set. Uppercase and lowercase letters are treated as the same.

PROC MODEL uses several classes of variables, and different variable classes are treated differently. Variable class is controlled by *declaration statements*. These are the VAR, ENDOGENOUS, and EXOGENOUS statements for model variables, the PARAMETERS statement for parameters, and the CONTROL statement for control class variables. These declaration statements have several valid abbreviations. Various *internal variables* are also made available to the model program to enable communication between the model program and the procedure. RANGE, ID, and BY variables are also available to the model program. Those variables not declared as any of the preceding classes are *program variables*.

Some classes of variables can be lagged; that is, their value at each observation is remembered, and previous values can be referred to by the lagging functions. Other classes have only a single value and are not affected by lagging functions. For example, parameters have only one value and are not affected by lagging functions; therefore, if P is a parameter, DIFn(P) is always 0, and LAGn(P) is always the same as P for all values of n.

The different variable classes and their roles in the model are described in the following sections.

Model Variables

Model variables are declared by VAR, ENDOGENOUS, or EXOGENOUS statements, or by FIT and SOLVE statements. The model variables are the variables that the model is intended to explain or predict.

PROC MODEL treats assignments to model variables in the model program as defining model equations and automatically replaces the model variable on the left side of an equal sign with a corresponding equation variable.

Equation Variables

An equation variable is one of several special variables used by PROC MODEL to control the evaluation of model equations. An equation variable name consists of one of the prefixes EQ, RESID, ERROR, PRED, or ACTUAL, followed by a period and the name of a model equation.

Equation variable names can appear on parts of the PROC MODEL printed output, and they can be used in the model program. For example, RESID-prefixed variables can be used in LAG functions to define equations with moving-average error terms. See "Autoregressive Moving Average Error Processes" earlier in this chapter, for details.

The meaning of these prefixes is detailed in "Equation Translations" later in this chapter.

Parameters

Parameters are variables that have the same value for each observation. Parameters can be given values or can be estimated by fitting the model to data. During the SOLVE stage, parameters are treated as constants. If no estimation is performed, the SOLVE stage uses the initial value provided in either the ESTDATA= data set, the MODEL= file, or on the PARAMETER statement, as the value of the parameter.

The PARAMETERS statement declares the parameters of the model. Parameters are not lagged, and they cannot be changed by the model program.

Control Variables

Control variables supply constant values to the model program that can be used to control the model in various ways. The CONTROL statement declares control variables and specifies their values. A control variable is like a parameter except it has a fixed value and is not estimated from the data.

Control variables are not reinitialized before each pass through the data and, thus, can be used to retain values between passes. You can use control variables to vary the program logic. Control variables are not affected by lagging functions.

For example, if you have two versions of an equation for a variable Y, you can put both versions in the model and, using a CONTROL statement to select one of them, produce two different solutions to explore the effect the choice of equation has on the model:

```
select (case);
    when (1) y = ...first version of equation... ;
    when (2) y = ...second version of equation... ;
end;
control case 1;
solve / out=case1;
run;

control case 2;
solve / out=case2;
run;
```

RANGE, ID, and BY Variables

The RANGE statement controls the range of observations in the input data set that is processed by PROC MODEL. The ID statement lists variables in the input data set that are used to identify observations on the printout and in the output data set. The BY statement can be used to make PROC MODEL perform a separate analysis for each BY group. The variable in the RANGE statement, the ID variables, and the BY variables are available for the model program to examine, but their values should not be changed by the program. The BY variables are not affected by lagging functions.

Internal Variables

You can use several internal variables in the model program to communicate with the procedure. For example, if you wanted PROC MODEL to list the values of all the variables when more than 10 iterations are performed and the procedure is past the 20th observation, you can write

```
if _obs_ > 20 then if _iter_ > 10 then _list_ = 1;
```

Internal variables are not affected by lagging functions, and they cannot be changed by the model program except as noted. The following internal variables are available. The variables are all numeric except where noted.

ERROR   a flag that is set to 0 at the start of program execution and is set to a nonzero value whenever an error occurs. The program can also set the _ERROR_ variable.

ITER   the iteration number. For FIT tasks, the value of _ITER_ is negative for preliminary grid-search passes. The iterative phase of the estimation starts with iteration 0. After the estimates have converged, a final pass is made to collect statistics with _ITER_ set to a missing value. Note that at least one pass, and perhaps several subiteration passes as well, is made for each iteration. For SOLVE tasks, _ITER_ counts the iterations used to compute the simultaneous solution of the system.

LAG   the number of dynamic lags that contribute to the solution at the current observation. _LAG_ is always 0 for FIT tasks and for STATIC solutions. _LAG_ is set to a missing value during the lag starting phase.

LIST   list flag that is set to 0 at the start of program execution. The program can set _LIST_ to a nonzero value to request a listing of the values of all the variables in the program after the program has finished executing.

METHOD   is the solution method in use for SOLVE tasks. _METHOD_ is set to a blank value for FIT tasks. _METHOD_ is a character-valued variable. Values are NEWTON, JACOBI, SIEDEL, or ONEPASS.

MODE   takes the value ESTIMATE for FIT tasks and the value SIMULATE or FORECAST for SOLVE tasks. _MODE_ is a character-valued variable.

NMISS the number of missing or otherwise unusable observations during the model estimation. For FIT tasks, _NMISS_ is initially set to 0; at the start of each iteration, _NMISS_ is set to the number of unusable observations for the previous iteration. For SOLVE tasks, _NMISS_ is set to a missing value.

NUSED the number of nonmissing observations used in the estimation. For FIT tasks, PROC MODEL initially sets _NUSED_ to the number of parameters; at the start of each iteration, _NUSED_ is reset to the number of observations used in the previous iteration. For SOLVE tasks, _NUSED_ is set to a missing value.

OBS counts the observations being processed. _OBS_ is negative or 0 for observations in the lag starting phase.

REP the replication number for Monte Carlo simulation when the RANDOM= option is specified in the SOLVE statement. _REP_ is 0 when the RANDOM= option is not used and for FIT tasks. When _REP_=0, the random-number generator functions always return 0.

WEIGHT the weight of the observation. For FIT tasks, _WEIGHT_ provides a weight for the observation in the estimation. _WEIGHT_ is initialized to 1.0 at the start of execution for FIT tasks. For SOLVE tasks, _WEIGHT_ is ignored.

Program Variables

Variables not in any of the other classes are called program variables. Program variables are used to hold intermediate results of calculations. Program variables are reinitialized to missing values before each observation is processed. Program variables can be lagged. The RETAIN statement can be used to give program variables initial values and to enable them to keep their values between observations.

Character Variables

PROC MODEL supports both numeric and character variables. Character variables are not involved in the model specification but can be used to label observations, to write debugging messages, or for documentation purposes. All variables are numeric unless they are

- character variables in a DATA= SAS data set
- program variables assigned a character value
- declared to be character by a LENGTH or ATTRIB statement.

Equation Translations

Equations written in normalized form are always automatically converted to general-form equations. For example, when a normalized-form equation such as

```
y = a + b*x;
```

is encountered, it is translated into the equations

```
PRED.y = a + b*x;
RESID.y = PRED.y - ACTUAL.y;
ERROR.y = PRED.y - y;
```

If the same system is expressed as the following general-form equation, then this equation is used unchanged.

```
EQ.y = y -  a + b*x;
```

This makes it easy to solve for arbitrary variables and to modify the error terms for autoregressive or moving average models.

Use the LIST option to see how this transformation is performed. For example, the following statements produce the listing shown in Figure 11.58.

```
proc model data=line list;
    y = a1 + b1*x1 + c1*x2;
    fit y;
run;
```

```
                 Listing of Compiled Program Code:

Stmt  Line:Col  Statement as Parsed
   1  23:5      PRED.Y = A1 + B1 * X1 + C1 * X2;

   1  23:5      RESID.Y = PRED.Y - ACTUAL.Y;

   1  23:5      ERROR.Y = PRED.Y - Y;
```

Figure 11.58. LIST Output

PRED.Y is the predicted value of Y, and ACTUAL.Y is the value of Y in the data set. The predicted value minus the actual value, RESID.Y, is then the error term, ϵ, for the original Y equation. ACTUAL.Y and Y have the same value for parameter estimation. For solve tasks, ACTUAL.Y is still the value of Y in the data set, but Y becomes the solved value, the value that satisfies PRED.Y - Y = 0.

The following are the equation variable definitions:

EQ.   The value of an EQ-prefixed equation variable (normally used to define a general-form equation) represents the failure of the equation to hold. When the EQ.*name* variable is 0, the *name* equation is satisfied.

RESID.   The RESID.*name* variables represent the stochastic parts of the equations and are used to define the objective function for the estimation process. A RESID-prefixed equation variable is like an EQ-prefixed variable, but it makes it possible to use or transform the stochastic part of the equation without affecting the model solution process.

ERROR.   An ERROR.*name* variable is like an EQ-prefixed variable, except that it is used only for model solution and does not affect parameter estimation.

PRED. For a normalized-form equation (specified by assignment to a model variable), the PRED.*name* equation variable holds the predicted value, where *name* is the name of both the model variable and the corresponding equation. (PRED-prefixed variables are not created for general-form equations.)

ACTUAL. For a normalized-form equation (specified by assignment to a model variable), the ACTUAL.*name* equation variable holds the value of the *name* model variable read from the input data set.

The three equation variable prefixes, RESID., ERROR., and EQ. allow for control over the objective function for the FIT, the SOLVE, or both the FIT and the SOLVE stages. For FIT tasks, PROC MODEL looks first for a RESID.*name* variable for each equation. If defined, the RESID-prefixed equation variable is used to define the objective function for the parameter estimation process. Otherwise, PROC MODEL looks for an EQ-prefixed variable for the equation and uses it instead.

For SOLVE tasks, PROC MODEL looks first for an ERROR.*name* variable for each equation. If defined, the ERROR-prefixed equation variable is used for the solution process. Otherwise, PROC MODEL looks for an EQ-prefixed variable for the equation and uses it instead. To solve the simultaneous equation system, PROC MODEL computes values of the solution variables (the model variables being solved for) that make all of the ERROR.name and EQ.*name* variables close to 0.

Derivatives

Nonlinear modeling techniques require the calculation of derivatives of certain variables with respect to other variables. The MODEL procedure includes an analytic differentiator that determines the model derivatives and generates program code to compute these derivatives. When parameters are estimated, the MODEL procedure takes the derivatives of the equation with respect to the parameters. When the model is solved, Newton's method requires the derivatives of the equations with respect to the variables solved for.

PROC MODEL uses exact mathematical formulas for derivatives of non-user-defined functions. For other functions, numerical derivatives are computed and used.

The differentiator differentiates the entire model program, including conditional logic and flow of control statements. Delayed definitions, as when the LAG of a program variable is referred to before the variable is assigned a value, are also differentiated correctly.

The differentiator includes optimization features that produce efficient code for the calculation of derivatives. However, when flow of control statements such as GOTO statements are used, the optimization process is impeded, and less efficient code for derivatives may be produced. Optimization is also reduced by conditional statements, iterative DO loops, and multiple assignments to the same variable.

The table of derivatives is printed with the LISTDER option. The code generated for the computation of the derivatives is printed with the LISTCODE option.

Derivative Variables

When the differentiator needs to generate code to evaluate the expression for the derivative of a variable, the result is stored in a special derivative variable. Derivative variables are not created when the derivative expression reduces to a previously computed result, a variable, or a constant. The names of derivative variables, which may sometimes appear in the printed output, have the form *@obj/@wrt*, where *obj* is the variable whose derivative is being taken and *wrt* is the variable that the differentiation is with respect to. For example, the derivative variable for the derivative of Y with respect to X is named @Y/@X.

The derivative variables cannot be accessed or used as part of the model program.

Mathematical Functions

The following is a brief summary of SAS functions useful for defining models. Additional functions and details are in *SAS Language: Reference, Version 6, First Edition*. Information on creating new functions can be found in *SAS/TOOLKIT Software: Usage and Reference, Version 6, First Edition*, Chapter 15, "Writing a SAS Function or Call Routine."

ABS(x)	the absolute value of x
ARCOS(x)	the arccosine in radians of x. x should be between -1 and 1.
ARSIN(x)	the arcsine in radians of x. x should be between -1 and 1.
ATAN(x)	the arctangent in radians of x
COS(x)	the cosine of x. x is in radians.
COSH(x)	the hyperbolic cosine of x
EXP(x)	e^x
LOG(x)	the natural logarithm of x
LOG10(x)	the log base ten of x
LOG2(x)	the log base two of x
SIN(x)	the sine of x. x is in radians.
SINH(x)	the hyperbolic sine of x
SQRT(x)	the square root of x
TAN(x)	the tangent of x. x is in radians and is not an odd multiple of $\pi/2$.
TANH(x)	the hyperbolic tangent of x

Random-Number Functions

The MODEL procedure provides several functions for generating random numbers for Monte Carlo simulation. These functions use the same generators as the corresponding SAS DATA step functions.

The following random-number functions are supported: RANBIN, RANCAU, RANEXP, RANGAM, RANNOR, RANPOI, RANTBL, RANTRI, and RANUNI. For more information, refer to *SAS Language: Reference*.

Each reference to a random-number function sets up a separate pseudo-random sequence. Note that this means that two calls to the same random function with the same seed produce identical results. This is different from the behavior of the random-number functions used in the SAS DATA step. For example, the statements

```
x=rannor(123);
y=rannor(123);
z=rannor(567);
```

produce identical values for X and Y, but Z is from an independent pseudo-random sequence.

For FIT tasks, all random-number functions always return 0. For SOLVE tasks, when Monte Carlo simulation is requested, a random-number function computes a new random number on the first iteration for an observation (if it is executed on that iteration) and returns that same value for all later iterations of that observation. When Monte Carlo simulation is not requested, random-number functions always return 0.

Functions Across Time

PROC MODEL provides four types of special built-in functions that refer to the values of variables and expressions in previous time periods. These functions have the form

LAGn(x)   the nth lag of x

DIFn(x)   difference of x at lag n

ZLAGn(x) lag with lag length truncated and missing values converted to 0

ZDIFn(x)   difference with lag length truncated and missing values converted to 0

In these functions, n represents the number of periods, and x is any expression.

If you do not specify n, the number of periods is assumed to be 1. For example, LAG(X) is the same as LAG1(X). No more than four digits can be used with a lagging function; that is, LAG9999 is the greatest LAG function, ZDIF9999 is the greatest ZDIF function, and so on.

The LAG functions get values from previous observations and make them available to the program. For example, LAG(X) returns the value of the variable X as it was computed in the execution of the program for the preceding observation. The expression LAG2(X+2*Y) returns the value of the expression X+2*Y, computed using the values of the variables X and Y that were computed by the execution of the program for the observation two periods ago.

The DIF functions return the difference between the current value of a variable or expression and the value of its LAG. For example, DIF2(X) is a short way of writing X-LAG2(X), and DIF15(SQRT(2*Z)) is a short way of writing SQRT(2*Z)-LAG15(SQRT(2*Z)).

The ZLAG and ZDIF functions are like the LAG and DIF functions, but they are not counted in the determination of the program lag length, and they replace missing values with 0. The ZLAG function returns the lagged value if the lagged value is nonmissing, or 0 if the lagged value is missing. The ZDIF function returns the differenced value if the differenced value is nonmissing, or 0 if the value of the differenced value is missing. The ZLAG function is especially useful for models with ARMA error processes. See the next section, "Lag Logic," for details.

Lag Logic

The LAG and DIF lagging functions in the MODEL procedure are different from the queuing functions with the same names in the DATA step. Lags are determined by the final values that are set for the program variables by the execution of the model program for the observation.

This can have upsetting consequences for programs that take lags of program variables that are given different values at various places in the program, for example,

```
temp = x + w;
t    = lag( temp );
temp = q - r;
s    = lag( temp );
```

The expression LAG(TEMP) always refers to LAG(Q-R), never to LAG(X+W), since Q-R is the final value assigned to the variable TEMP by the model program. If LAG(X+W) is wanted for T, it should be computed as T=LAG(X+W) and not T=LAG(TEMP), as in the preceding example.

Care should also be exercised in using the DIF functions with program variables that may be reassigned later in the program. For example, the program

```
temp =  x ;
s    = dif( temp );
temp = 3 * y;
```

computes values for S equivalent to

```
s =  x  - lag( 3 * y );
```

Note that in the preceding examples, TEMP is a program variable, *not* a model variable. If it were a model variable, the assignments to it would be changed to assignments to a corresponding equation variable.

Note that whereas LAG1(LAG1(X)) is the same as LAG2(X), DIF1(DIF1(X)) is *not* the same as DIF2(X). The DIF2 function is the difference between the current period value at the point in the program where the function is executed and the final value at the end of execution two periods ago; DIF2 is not the second difference. In contrast, DIF1(DIF1(X)) is equal to DIF1(X)-LAG1(DIF1(X)), which equals X-2*LAG1(X)+LAG2(X), which is the second difference of X.

More information on the differences between PROC MODEL and the DATA step LAG and DIF functions is found in Chapter 2, "Working with Time Series Data."

Lag Lengths

The lag length of the model program is the number of lags needed for any relevant equation. The program lag length controls the number of observations used to initialize the lags.

PROC MODEL keeps track of the use of lags in the model program and automatically determines the lag length of each equation and of the model as a whole. PROC MODEL sets the program lag length to the maximum number of lags needed to compute any equation to be estimated, solved, or needed to compute any instrument variable used.

In determining the lag length, the ZLAG and ZDIF functions are treated as always having a lag length of 0. For example, if Y is computed as

```
y = lag2( x + zdif3( temp ) );
```

then Y has a lag length of 2 (regardless of how TEMP is defined). If Y is computed as

```
y = zlag2( x + dif3( temp ) );
```

then Y has a lag length of 0.

This is so ARMA errors can be specified without causing the loss of additional observations to the lag starting phase and so that recursive lag specifications, such as moving-average error terms, can be used. Recursive lags are not permitted unless the ZLAG or ZDIF functions are used to truncate the lag length. For example, the following statement produces an error message:

```
t = a + b * lag( t );
```

The program variable T depends recursively on its own lag, and the lag length of T is therefore undefined.

In the following equation RESID.Y depends on the predicted value for the Y equation but the predicted value for the Y equation depends on the LAG of RESID.Y, and, thus, the predicted value for the Y equation depends recursively on its own lag.

```
y = yhat + ma * lag( resid.y );
```

The lag length is infinite, and PROC MODEL prints an error message and stops. Since this kind of specification is allowed, the recursion must be truncated at some point. The ZLAG and ZDIF functions do this.

The following equation is legal and results in a lag length for the Y equation equal to the lag length of YHAT:

```
y = yhat + ma * zlag( resid.y );
```

Initially, the lags of RESID.Y are missing, and the ZLAG function replaces the missing residuals with 0s, their unconditional expected values.

The ZLAG0 function can be used to 0 the lag length of an expression. $ZLAG0(x)$ returns the current period value of the expression x, if nonmissing, or else returns 0, and prevents the lag length of x from contributing to the lag length of the current statement.

Initializing Lags

At the start of each pass through the data set or BY group, the lag variables are set to missing values and an initialization is performed to fill the lags. During this phase, observations are read from the data set, and the model variables are given values from the data. If necessary, the model is executed to assign values to program variables that are used in lagging functions. The results for variables used in lag functions are saved. These observations are not included in the estimation or solution.

If, during the execution of the program for the lag starting phase, a lag function refers to lags that are missing, the lag function returns missing. Execution errors that occur while starting the lags are not reported unless requested. The modeling system automatically determines whether the program needs to be executed during the lag starting phase.

If L is the maximum lag length of any equation being fit or solved, then the first L observations are used to prime the lags. If a BY statement is used, the first L observations in the BY group are used to prime the lags. If a RANGE statement is used, the first L observations prior to the first observation requested in the RANGE statement are used to prime the lags. Therefore, there should be at least L observations in the data set.

Initial values for the lags of model variables can also be supplied in VAR, ENDOGENOUS, and EXOGENOUS statements. This feature provides initial lags of solution variables for dynamic solution when initial values for the solution variable are not available in the input data set. For example, the statement

```
var x 2 3 y 4 5 z 1;
```

feeds the initial lags exactly like these values in an input data set:

Lag	X	Y	Z
2	3	5	.
1	2	4	1

If initial values for lags are available in the input data set and initial lag values are also given in a declaration statement, the values in the VAR, ENDOGENOUS, or EXOGENOUS statements take priority.

The RANGE statement is used to control the range of observations in the input data set that are processed by PROC MODEL. In the statement

```
range date = '01jan1924'd to '01dec1943'd;
```

'01jan1924' specifies the starting period of the range, and '01dec1943' specifies the ending period. The observations in the data set immediately prior to the start of the range are used to initialize the lags.

Language Differences

For the most part, PROC MODEL programming statements work the same as they do in the DATA step, as documented in the *SAS Language: Reference.* However, there are several differences that should be noted.

DO Statement Differences

The DO statement in PROC MODEL does not allow a character index variable. Thus, the following DO statement is not valid in PROC MODEL, although it is supported in the DATA step:

```
do i = 'A', 'B', 'C';                          /* invalid PROC MODEL code */
```

IF Statement Differences

The IF statement in PROC MODEL does not allow a character-valued condition. For example, the following IF statement is not supported by PROC MODEL:

```
if 'this' then statement;
```

Comparisons of character values are supported in IF statements, so the following IF statement is acceptable:

```
if 'this' < 'that' then statement;
```

PROC MODEL allows for embedded conditionals in expressions. For example, the following two statements are equivalent:

```
flag = if time = 1 or time = 2 then conc+30/5 + dose*time
            else if time > 5 then (0=1) else (patient * flag);
```

```
if time = 1 or time = 2 then flag= conc+30/5 + dose*time;
        else if time > 5 then flag=(0=1); else flag=patient*flag;
```

Note that the ELSE operator only involves the first object or token after it, so the following assignments are not equivalent:

```
total = if sum > 0 then sum else sum + reserve;
total = if sum > 0 then sum else (sum + reserve);
```

The first assignment makes TOTAL always equal to SUM plus RESERVE.

PUT Statement Differences

The PUT statement, mostly used in PROC MODEL for program debugging, only supports some of the features of the DATA step PUT statement. It also has some new features that the DATA step PUT statement does not support.

The PROC MODEL PUT statement does not support line pointers, factored lists, iteration factors, overprinting, the _INFILE_ option, or the colon (:) format modifier.

The PROC MODEL PUT statement does support expressions, but an expression must be enclosed in parentheses. For example, the following statement prints the square root of x:

```
put (sqrt(x));
```

The PUT statement supports the print item _PDV_ to print a formatted listing of all the variables in the program. For example, the following statement prints a much more readable listing of the variables than does the _ALL_ print item:

```
put _pdv_;
```

To print all the elements of the array A, use the following statement:

```
put a;
```

To print all the elements of A with each value labeled by the name of the element variable, use the statement

```
put a=;
```

IN Operator Difference

The IN operator is not supported in the MODEL procedure.

ABORT Statement Difference

In the MODEL procedure, the ABORT statement does not allow any arguments.

SELECT/WHEN/OTHERWISE Statement Differences

The WHEN and OTHERWISE statements allow more than one target statement. That is, DO groups are not necessary for multiple statement WHEN targets. For example, in PROC MODEL, the following syntax is valid:

```
select;
    when(exp1)
        stmt1;
        stmt2;
    when(exp2)
        stmt3;
        stmt4;
end;
```

The ARRAY Statement

> **ARRAY** *arrayname* [\{ *dimensions* \}] [$ [*length*]]
> [*variables and constants*] ;

The ARRAY statement is used to associate a name with a list of variables and constants. The array name can then be used with subscripts in the model program to refer to the items in the list.

In PROC MODEL, the ARRAY statement does not support all the features of the DATA step ARRAY statement. With PROC MODEL, the ARRAY statement cannot be used to initialize array elements. Implicit indexing cannot be used; all array references must have explicit subscript expressions. Only exact array dimensions are allowed; lower-bound specifications are not supported. A maximum of six dimensions is allowed.

On the other hand, the ARRAY statement supported by PROC MODEL does permit both variables and constants to be used as array elements. You cannot make assignments to constant array elements. Both dimension specification and the list of elements are optional, but at least one must be supplied. When the list of elements is not given or fewer elements than the size of the array are listed, array variables are created by suffixing element numbers to the array name to complete the element list.

The following are valid PROC MODEL ARRAY statements:

```
array x[120];              /* array X of length 120          */
array q[2,2];              /* Two dimensional array Q         */
array b[4] va vb vc vd;    /* B[2] = VB, B[4] = VD            */
array x x1-x30;            /* array X of length 30, X[7] = X7 */
```

RETAIN Statement

RETAIN *variables initial-values* ;

The RETAIN statement causes a program variable to hold its value from a previous observation until the variable is reassigned. The RETAIN statement can be used to initialize program variables.

The RETAIN statement does not work for model variables, parameters, or control variables because the values of these variables are under the control of PROC MODEL and not programming statements. Use the PARMS and CONTROL statements to initialize parameters and control variables. Use the VAR, ENDOGENOUS, or EXOGENOUS statement to initialize model variables.

Storing Programs in Model Files

Models can be saved and recalled from SAS catalog files. SAS catalogs are special files that can store many kinds of data structures as separate units in one SAS file. Each separate unit is called an entry, and each entry has an entry type that identifies its structure to the SAS system.

In general, to save a model, use the OUTMODEL=*name* option in the PROC MODEL statement, where *name* is specified as *libref.catalog.entry*, *libref.entry*, or *entry*. The *libref*, *catalog*, and *entry* names must be valid SAS names no more than 8 characters long. The *catalog* name is restricted to 7 characters on the CMS operating system. If not given, the *catalog* name defaults to MODELS, and the *libref* defaults to WORK. The entry type is always MODEL. Thus, OUTMODEL=X writes the model to the file WORK.MODELS.X.MODEL.

The MODEL= option is used to read in a model. A list of model files can be specified in the MODEL= option, and a range of names with numeric suffixes can be given, as in MODEL=(MODEL1-MODEL10). When more than one model file is given, the list must be placed in parentheses, as in MODEL=(A B C), except in the case of a single name. If more than one model file is specified, the files are combined in the order listed in the MODEL= option.

When the MODEL= option is specified in the PROC MODEL statement and model definition statements are also given later in the PROC MODEL step, the model files are read in first, in the order listed, and the model program specified in the PROC MODEL step is appended after the model program read from the MODEL= files. The class assigned to a variable, when multiple model files are used, is the last declaration of that variable. For example, if Y1 was declared endogenous in the model file M1 and exogenous in the model file M2, the following statement will cause Y1 to be declared exogenous.

```
proc model model=(m1 m2);
```

The INCLUDE statement can be used to append model code to the current model code. In contrast, when the MODEL= option is used in the RESET statement, the current model is deleted before the new model is read.

No model file is output by default if the PROC MODEL step performs any FIT or SOLVE tasks, or if the MODEL= option or the NOSTORE option is used. However, to ensure compatibility with previous versions of SAS/ETS software, when the PROC MODEL step does nothing but compile the model program, no input model file is read, and the NOSTORE option is not used, a model file is written. This model file is the default input file for a later PROC SYSNLIN or PROC SIMNLIN step. The default output model filename in this case is WORK.MODELS._MODEL_.MODEL.

If FIT statements are used to estimate model parameters, the parameter estimates written to the output model file are the estimates from the last estimation performed for each parameter.

Diagnostics and Debugging

PROC MODEL provides several features to aid in finding errors in the model program. These debugging features are not usually needed; most models can be developed without them.

The example model program that follows will be used in the following sections to illustrate the diagnostic and debugging capabilities. This example is the estimation of a segmented model.

```
*---------Fitting a Segmented Model using MODEL----*
|   |                                              |
| y | quadratic            plateau                 |
|   | y=a+b*x+c*x*x        y=p                      |
|   |                      ....................     |
|   |                   .  :                        |
|   |                .     :                        |
|   |             .        :                        |
|   |          .           :                        |
|   |       .              :                        |
|   +------------------------------------------X    |
|                      x0                           |
|                                                   |
| continuity restriction: p=a+b*x0+c*x0**2          |
| smoothness restriction: 0=b+2*c*x0 so x0=-b/(2*c) |
*-------------------------------------------------*;
```

```
title 'QUADRATIC MODEL WITH PLATEAU';
data a;
   input y x @@;
   cards;
.46 1  .47  2 .57  3 .61  4 .62  5 .68  6 .69  7
.78 8  .70  9 .74 10 .77 11 .78 12 .74 13 .80 13
.80 15 .78 16
;
proc model data=a;
parms a 0.45 b 0.5 c -0.0025;

x0 = -.5*b / c;                 /* join point */
if x < x0 then        /* Quadratic part of model */
   y = a + b*x + c*x*x;
else                     /* Plateau part of model */
   y = a + b*x0 + c*x0*x0;

fit y;
run;
```

Program Listing

The LIST option produces a listing of the model program. The statements are printed one per line with the original line number and column position of the statement.

The program listing from the example program is shown in Figure 11.59.

```
                Listing of Compiled Program Code:

Stmt  Line:Col  Statement as Parsed
   1  14:4      X0 = (-0.5 * B) / C;

   2  16:4      IF X < X0 THEN

   3  18:7          PRED.Y = A + B * X + C * X * X;

   3  18:7          RESID.Y = PRED.Y - ACTUAL.Y;

   3  18:7          ERROR.Y = PRED.Y - Y;

   4  19:4      ELSE

   5  21:7          PRED.Y = A + B * X0 + C * X0 * X0;

   5  21:7          RESID.Y = PRED.Y - ACTUAL.Y;

   5  21:7          ERROR.Y = PRED.Y - Y;
```

Figure 11.59. LIST Output for Segmented Model

The LIST option also shows the model translations that PROC MODEL performs. LIST output is useful for understanding the code generated by the %AR and the %MA macros.

Cross-Reference

The XREF option produces a cross-reference listing of the variables in the model program. The XREF listing is usually used in conjunction with the LIST option. The XREF listing does not include derivative (@-prefixed) variables. The XREF listing does not include generated assignments to equation variables, PRED, RESID, and ERROR-prefixed variables, unless the DETAILS option is used.

The cross-reference from the example program is shown in Figure 11.60.

```
    Cross Reference Listing For Program
Symbol-----------   Kind   Type   References (statement)/(line):(col)[lag]

A                   Var    Num    Used: 3/33:13 5/36:13
B                   Var    Num    Used: 1/29:12 3/33:16 5/36:16
C                   Var    Num    Used: 1/29:15 3/33:22 5/36:23
X0                  Var    Num    Assigned: 1/29:15   Used: 2/31:11 5/36:16 5/36:
                                  23 5/36:26
X                   Var    Num    Used: 2/31:11 3/33:16 3/33:22 3/33:24
PRED.Y              Var    Num    Assigned: 3/33:19 5/36:20
```

Figure 11.60.   XREF Output for Segmented Model

Compiler Listing

The LISTCODE option lists the model code and derivatives tables produced by the compiler. This listing is useful only for debugging and should not normally be needed.

LISTCODE prints the operator and operands of each operation generated by the compiler for each model program statement. Many of the operands are temporary variables generated by the compiler and given names such as #temp1. When derivatives are taken, the code listing includes the operations generated for the derivatives calculations. The derivatives tables are also listed.

A LISTCODE option prints the transformed equations from the example shown in Figure 11.61 and Figure 11.62.

```
                 Listing of Compiled Program Code:
Stmt  Line:Col  Statement as Parsed
  1   48:4      X0 = (-0.5 * B) / C;
                @X0/@B = -0.5 / C;
                @X0/@C = (0 - X0) / C;

  2   50:4      IF X < X0 THEN

  3   52:7          PRED.Y = A + B * X + C * X * X;
                    @PRED.Y/@A = 1;
                    @PRED.Y/@B = X;
                    @PRED.Y/@C = X * X;

  3   52:7          RESID.Y = PRED.Y - ACTUAL.Y;
                    @RESID.Y/@A = @PRED.Y/@A;
                    @RESID.Y/@B = @PRED.Y/@B;
                    @RESID.Y/@C = @PRED.Y/@C;
  3   52:7          ERROR.Y = PRED.Y - Y;

  4   53:4      ELSE

  5   55:7          PRED.Y = A + B * X0 + C * X0 * X0;
                    @PRED.Y/@A = 1;
                    @PRED.Y/@B = X0 + B * @X0/@B + C * @X0/@B * X0 + C * X0 *
                        @X0/@B;
                    @PRED.Y/@C = B * @X0/@C + (X0 + C * @X0/@C) * X0 + C * X0
                        * @X0/@C;

  5   55:7          RESID.Y = PRED.Y - ACTUAL.Y;
                    @RESID.Y/@A = @PRED.Y/@A;
                    @RESID.Y/@B = @PRED.Y/@B;
                    @RESID.Y/@C = @PRED.Y/@C;

  5   55:7          ERROR.Y = PRED.Y - Y;
```

Figure 11.61.   LISTCODE Output for Segmented Model - Statements as Parsed

```
1 Stmt ASSIGN    line 23 column 4. (1) arg=X0 argsave=X0
                 Source Text: X0 = -.5*B / C;
  Oper *         at 23:12 (30,0,2).           * : #temp1   <- -0.5 B
  Oper /         at 23:15 (31,0,2).           / : X0       <- #temp1 C

2 Stmt IF        line 24 column 4. (2) arg=#temp1 argsave=#temp1
                 ref.st=ASSIGN stmt number 5 at 27:7
                 Source Text: IF X < X0 THEN
  Oper <         at 24:11 (36,0,2).           < : #temp1   <- X X0

3 Stmt ASSIGN    line 25 column 7. (1) arg=PRED.Y argsave=Y
                 Source Text: Y = A + B*X + C*X*X;
  Oper *         at 25:16 (30,0,2).           * : #temp1   <- B X
  Oper +         at 25:13 (32,0,2).           + : #temp2   <- A #temp1
  Oper *         at 25:22 (30,0,2).           * : #temp3   <- C X
  Oper *         at 25:24 (30,0,2).           * : #temp4   <- #temp3 X
  Oper +         at 25:19 (32,0,2).           + : PRED.Y   <- #temp2 #temp4

3 Stmt Assign    line 25 column 7. (1) arg=RESID.Y argsave=Y
  Oper -         at 25:7 (33,0,2).            - : RESID.Y  <- PRED.Y ACTUAL.Y

3 Stmt Assign    line 25 column 7. (1) arg=ERROR.Y argsave=Y
  Oper -         at 25:7 (33,0,2).            - : ERROR.Y  <- PRED.Y Y

4 Stmt ELSE      line 26 column 4. (9)
                 Source Text: ELSE

5 Stmt ASSIGN    line 27 column 7. (1) arg=PRED.Y argsave=Y
                 Source Text: Y = A + B*X0 + C*X0*X0;
  Oper *         at 27:16 (30,0,2).           * : #temp1   <- B X0
  Oper +         at 27:13 (32,0,2).           + : #temp2   <- A #temp1
  Oper *         at 27:23 (30,0,2).           * : #temp3   <- C X0
  Oper *         at 27:26 (30,0,2).           * : #temp4   <- #temp3 X0
  Oper +         at 27:20 (32,0,2).           + : PRED.Y   <- #temp2 #temp4

5 Stmt Assign    line 27 column 7. (1) arg=RESID.Y argsave=Y
  Oper -         at 27:7 (33,0,2).            - : RESID.Y  <- PRED.Y ACTUAL.Y

5 Stmt Assign    line 27 column 7. (1) arg=ERROR.Y argsave=Y
  Oper -         at 27:7 (33,0,2).            - : ERROR.Y  <- PRED.Y Y
```

Figure 11.62. LISTCODE Output for Segmented Model - Compiled Code

Analyzing the Structure of Large Models

PROC MODEL provides several features to aid in analyzing the structure of the model program. These features summarize properties of the model in various forms.

The following Klein's model program is used to introduce the LISTDEP, BLOCK, and GRAPH options.

```
proc model  out=m data=klein listdep graph block;
   endogenous c p w i x wsum k y;
   exogenous  wp g t year;
   parms c0-c3 i0-i3 w0-w3;
   a: c = c0 + c1 * p + c2 * lag(p) + c3 * wsum;
   b: i = i0 + i1 * p + i2 * lag(p) + i3 * lag(k);
   c: w = w0 + w1 * x + w2 * lag(x) + w3 * year;
   x = c + i + g;
   y = c + i + g-t;
   p = x-w-t;
   k = lag(k) + i;
   wsum = w + wp;
   id year;
run;
```

Dependency List

The LISTDEP option produces a dependency list for each variable in the model program. For each variable, a list of variables that depend on it and a list of variables it depends on is given. The dependency list produced by the example program is shown in Figure 11.63.

```
    Dependency Listing For Program

Symbol-----------  Dependencies

C                  Current values affect: ERROR.C PRED.X PRED.Y RESID.X
                   ERROR.X RESID.Y ERROR.Y
P                  Current values affect: PRED.C PRED.I ERROR.P RESID.C
                   ERROR.C RESID.I ERROR.I
                   Lagged values affect: PRED.C PRED.I
W                  Current values affect: ERROR.W PRED.P PRED.WSUM RESID.P
                   ERROR.P RESID.WSUM ERROR.WSUM
I                  Current values affect: ERROR.I PRED.X PRED.Y PRED.K
                   RESID.X ERROR.X RESID.Y ERROR.Y RESID.K ERROR.K
X                  Current values affect: PRED.W ERROR.X PRED.P RESID.W
                   ERROR.W RESID.P ERROR.P
                   Lagged values affect: PRED.W
WSUM               Current values affect: PRED.C ERROR.WSUM RESID.C ERROR.C
K                  Current values affect: ERROR.K
```

Figure 11.63. A Portion of the LISTDEP Output for Klein's Model

BLOCK Listing

The BLOCK option prints an analysis of the program variables based on the assignments in the model program. The output produced by the example is shown in Figure 11.64.

```
                   Model Structure Analysis
         (Based on Assignments to Endogenous Model Variables)

              Exogenous Variables: WP G T YEAR

              Endogenous Variables: C P W I X WSUM K Y

NOTE: The System Consists of 2 Recursive Equations and 1 Simultaneous Blocks.


              Block Structure of the System

              Block 1: C P W I X WSUM


         Dependency Structure of the System

      Block 1 Depends On: All_Exogenous
         K       Depends On: Block 1 All_Exogenous
         Y       Depends On: Block 1 All_Exogenous
```

Figure 11.64. The BLOCK Output for Klein's Model

One use for the block output is to put a model in recursive form. Simulations of the model can be done with the SEIDEL method, which is efficient if the model is recursive and if the equations are in recursive order. By examining the block output, you can determine how to reorder the model equations for the most efficient simulation.

Adjacency Graph

The GRAPH option displays the same information as the BLOCK option with the addition of an adjacency graph. An X in a column in an adjacency graph indicates that the variable associated with the row depends on the variable associated with the column. The output produced by the example is shown in Figure 11.65.

```
                    Adjacency Matrix for Graph of System

                                              1 1 1
              Variable      1 2 3 4 5 6 7 8 9 0 1 2
                                              * * * *
         C          1:   X X . . . X . . . . . .
         P          2:   . X X . X . . . . . X .
         W          3:   . . X . X . . . . . . X
         I          4:   . X . X . . . . . . . .
         X          5:   X . . X X . . . . X . .
         WSUM       6:   . . X . . X . . X . . .
         K          7:   . . . X . . X . . . . .
         Y          8:   X . . X . . . X . X X .
         WP         9:   *. . . . . . . . X . . .
         G         10:   *. . . . . . . . X . . .
         T         11:   *. . . . . . . . . X .
         YEAR      12:   *. . . . . . . . . . X

                   (Note: * = Exogenous Variable.)

          Transitive Closure Matrix of Sorted System

          Block   Variable      1 2 3 4 5 6 7 8

             1    C          1:   X X X X X X . .
             1    P          2:   X X X X X X . .
             1    W          3:   X X X X X X . .
             1    I          4:   X X X X X X . .
             1    X          5:   X X X X X X . .
             1    WSUM       6:   X X X X X X . .
                  K          7:   X X X X X X X .
                  Y          8:   X X X X X X . X

   Adjacency Matrix for Graph of System Including Lagged Impacts

                                              1 1 1
          Block   Variable      1 2 3 4 5 6 7 8 9 0 1 2
                                              * * * *
             1    C          1:   X L . . . X . . . . . .
             1    P          2:   . X X . X . . . . . X .
             1    W          3:   . . X . L . . . . . . X
             1    I          4:   . L . X . . L . . . . .
             1    X          5:   X . . X X . . . . X . .
             1    WSUM       6:   . . X . . X . . X . . .
                  K          7:   . . . X . . L . . . . .
                  Y          8:   X . . X . . . X . X X .
                  WP         9:   *. . . . . . . . X . . .
                  G         10:   *. . . . . . . . X . . .
                  T         11:   *. . . . . . . . . X .
                  YEAR      12:   *. . . . . . . . . . X

                   (Note: * = Exogenous Variable.)
```

Figure 11.65.   The GRAPH Output for Klein's Model

The first and last graphs are straightforward. The middle graph represents the dependencies of the nonexogenous variables after transitive closure has been performed (that is, A depends on B, and B depends on C, so A depends on C). The preceding transitive closure matrix indicates that K and Y do not directly or indirectly depend on each other.

Examples

Example 11.1.   OLS Single Nonlinear Equation

This example illustrates the use of the MODEL procedure for nonlinear ordinary least-squares (OLS) regression. The model is a logistic growth curve for the population of the United States. The data are the population in millions recorded at ten year intervals starting in 1790 and ending in 1990. For an explanation of the starting values given by the START= option, see "Troubleshooting Convergence Problems" earlier in this chapter. Portions of the output from the following code is shown in Output 11.1.1 and Output 11.1.2.

```
title 'Logistic Growth Curve Model of U.S. Population';
data uspop;
   input pop :6.3 @@;
   retain year 1780;
   year=year+10;
   label pop='U.S. Population in Millions';
   cards;
3929  5308  7239   9638  12866  17069  23191  31443  39818 50155
62947 75994 91972 105710 122775 131669 151325 179323 203211
226542 248710
;

proc model data=uspop;
   label a = 'Maximum Population'
         b = 'Location Parameter'
         c = 'Initial Growth Rate';
   pop = a / ( 1 + exp( b - c * (year-1790) ) );
   fit pop start=(a 1000  b 5.5  c .02)/ out=resid outresid;
run;
```

Output 11.1.1.   Logistic Growth Curve Model Summary

```
         Logistic Growth Curve Model of U.S. Population

                    MODEL Procedure

                     Model Summary

          Model Variables          1
          Parameters               3
          Equations                1

          Number of Statements     1

     Model Variables: POP

     Parameters: A: 1000  B: 5.5  C: 0.02

     Equations: POP
```

Output 11.1.1.   (Continued)

```
        Logistic Growth Curve Model of U.S. Population

                       MODEL Procedure

                 The Equation to Estimate is:

                    POP = F( A, B, C )
```

Output 11.1.2.   Logistic Growth Curve Estimation Summary

```
            Logistic Growth Curve Model of U.S. Population

                         MODEL Procedure
                          OLS Estimation

              Nonlinear OLS Summary of Residual Errors

                DF    DF
Equation     Model  Error       SSE         MSE     Root MSE  R-Square  Adj R-Sq

POP              3     18   345.63550    19.20197    4.38201    0.9972    0.996

                Nonlinear OLS Parameter Estimates

                             Approx.      'T'     Approx.
   Parameter    Estimate     Std Err    Ratio    Prob>|T|   Label
   A          387.985007    30.05363    12.91     0.0001    Maximum Population
   B            3.990212     0.06946    57.45     0.0001    Location Parameter
   C            0.022700   0.0010700    21.22     0.0001    Initial Growth Rate
```

The adjusted R^2 value indicates the model fits the data well. There are only 21 observations and the model is nonlinear, so significance tests on the parameters are only approximate. The significance tests and associated approximate probabilities indicate that all the parameters are significantly different from 0.

The FIT statement included the options OUT=RESID and OUTRESID so that the residuals from the estimation are saved to the data set RESID. The residuals are plotted to check for heteroscedasticity using PROC GPLOT as follows:

```
proc gplot data=resid;
    plot pop*year / vref=0;
    title "Residual";
    symbol1 v=plus;
run;
```

The plot is shown in Output 11.1.3.

Example 11.1. OLS Single Nonlinear Equation □ □ □ 659

Output 11.1.3. Residual for Population Model (Actual - Predicted)

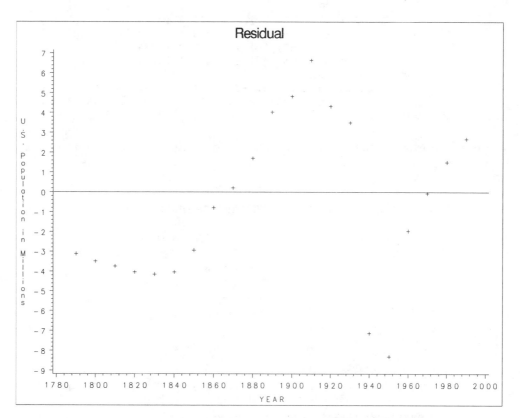

The residuals do not appear to be independent, and the model could be modified to explain the remaining nonrandom errors.

Example 11.2. A Consumer Demand Model

This example shows the estimation of a system of nonlinear consumer demand equations based on the translog functional form using seemingly unrelated regression (SUR). Expenditure shares and corresponding normalized prices are given for three goods.

Since the shares add up to one, the system is singular; therefore, one equation is omitted from the estimation process. The choice of which equation to omit is arbitrary. The parameter estimates of the omitted equation (share3) can be recovered from the other estimated parameters. The nonlinear system is first estimated in unrestricted form.

```
title1 'Consumer Demand--Translog Functional Form';
title2 'Nonsymmetric Model';
proc model data=tlog1;
   var share1 share2 p1 p2 p3;
   parms a1 a2 b11 b12 b13 b21 b22 b23 b31 b32 b33;
   bm1 = b11 + b21 + b31;
   bm2 = b12 + b22 + b32;
   bm3 = b13 + b23 + b33;
   lp1 = log(p1);
```

```
            lp2 = log(p2);
            lp3 = log(p3);
            share1 = ( a1 + b11 * lp1 + b12 * lp2 + b13 * lp3 ) /
                     ( -1 + bm1 * lp1 + bm2 * lp2 + bm3 * lp3 );
            share2 = ( a2 + b21 * lp1 + b22 * lp2 + b23 * lp3 ) /
                     ( -1 + bm1 * lp1 + bm2 * lp2 + bm3 * lp3 );
            fit share1 share2
                start=( a1 -.14 a2 -.45 b11 .03 b12 .47 b22 .98 b31 .20
                       b32 1.11 b33 .71 ) / outsused = smatrix sur;
        run;
```

A portion of the printed output produced in the preceding example is shown in Output 11.2.1 .

Output 11.2.1. Estimation Results from the Unrestricted Model

```
          Consumer Demand--Translog Functional Form
                     Nonsymmetric Model

                      MODEL Procedure

                       Model Summary

               Model Variables        5
               Parameters            11
               Equations              2

               Number of Statements   8

      Model Variables: SHARE1 SHARE2 P1 P2 P3

      Parameters: A1: -0.14  A2: -0.45  B11: 0.03  B12: 0.47  B13 B21
                  B22: 0.98  B23 B31: 0.2  B32: 1.11  B33: 0.71

      Equations: SHARE1 SHARE2
```

```
          Consumer Demand--Translog Functional Form
                     Nonsymmetric Model

                      MODEL Procedure

             The 2 Equations to Estimate are:

      SHARE1 = F( A1, B11, B12, B13, B21, B22, B23, B31, B32, B33 )
      SHARE2 = F( A2, B11, B12, B13, B21, B22, B23, B31, B32, B33 )

NOTE: At OLS Iteration 21 CONVERGE=0.001 Criteria Met.
NOTE: At SUR Iteration 2 CONVERGE=0.001 Criteria Met.
```

```
          Consumer Demand--Translog Functional Form
                     Nonsymmetric Model

                      MODEL Procedure
                       SUR Estimation

           Nonlinear SUR Summary of Residual Errors

            DF    DF
Equation  Model  Error      SSE        MSE     Root MSE  R-Square  Adj R-Sq

SHARE1     5.5   38.5     0.00166  0.00004305  0.0065616   0.8067    0.7841
SHARE2     5.5   38.5     0.00135  0.00003501  0.0059166   0.9445    0.9380


              Nonlinear SUR Parameter Estimates

                                Approx.      'T'     Approx.
           Parameter   Estimate  Std Err    Ratio    Prob>|T|

           A1          -0.148806  0.0022520  -66.08   0.0001
```

Example 11.2. A Consumer Demand Model □ □ □ 661

Output 11.2.1. (Continued)

```
            A2          -0.457757    0.0029668   -154.29    0.0001
            B11          0.048381    0.04984        0.97    0.3379
            B12          0.436551    0.05018        8.70    0.0001
            B13          0.248586    0.05163        4.82    0.0001
            B21          0.586321    0.20892        2.81    0.0079
            B22          0.759784    0.25647        2.96    0.0052
            B23          1.303815    0.23277        5.60    0.0001
            B31          0.297804    0.15042        1.98    0.0550
            B32          0.961556    0.16335        5.89    0.0001
            B33          0.829097    0.15560        5.33    0.0001

            Number of Observations        Statistics for System
            Used                   44     Objective         1.7493
            Missing                 0     Objective*N      76.9695
NOTE: The data set WORK.SMATRIX has 2 observations and 5 variables.
```

The model is then estimated under the restriction of symmetry ($b_{ij}=b_{ji}$).

Hypothesis testing requires that the **S** matrix from the unrestricted model be imposed on the restricted model, as explained in "Tests on Parameters" earlier in this chapter. The **S** matrix saved in the data set SMATRIX is requested by the SDATA= option.

A portion of the printed output produced in the following example is shown in Output 11.2.2.

```
title2 'Symmetric Model';
proc model data=tlog1;
   var share1 share2 p1 p2 p3;
   parms a1 a2 b11 b12 b22 b31 b32 b33;
   bm1 = b11 + b12 + b31;
   bm2 = b12 + b22 + b32;
   bm3 = b31 + b32 + b33;
   lp1 = log(p1);
   lp2 = log(p2);
   lp3 = log(p3);
   share1 = ( a1 + b11 * lp1 + b12 * lp2 + b31 * lp3 ) /
            ( -1 + bm1 * lp1 + bm2 * lp2 + bm3 * lp3 );
   share2 = ( a2 + b12 * lp1 + b22 * lp2 + b32 * lp3 ) /
            ( -1 + bm1 * lp1 + bm2 * lp2 + bm3 * lp3 );
   fit share1 share2
       start=( a1 -.14 a2 -.45 b11 .03 b12 .47 b22 .98 b31 .20
               b32 1.11 b33 .71 ) / sdata=smatrix sur;
run;
```

A chi-square test is used to see if the hypothesis of symmetry is accepted or rejected. ($Oc-Ou$) has a chi-square distribution asymptotically, where Oc is the constrained OBJECTIVE*N and Ou is the unconstrained OBJECTIVE*N. The degrees of freedom is equal to the difference in the number of free parameters in the two models.

In this example, Ou is 76.9695 and Oc is 78.4094, resulting in a difference of 1.4399 with 3 degrees of freedom. You can obtain the probability value by using the following statements:

```
data _null_;
                      /* reduced-full, nrestrictions */
    p = 1-probchi( 1.4399, 3 );
    put p=;
run;
```

The output from this DATA step run is 'P=0.6962091749'. With this probability you cannot reject the hypothesis of symmetry. This test is asymptotically valid.

Output 11.2.2.   Estimation Results from the Restricted Model

```
          Consumer Demand--Translog Functional Form
                       Symmetric Model

                       MODEL Procedure

              The 2 Equations to Estimate are:

          SHARE1 = F( A1, B11, B12, B22, B31, B32, B33 )
          SHARE2 = F( A2, B11, B12, B22, B31, B32, B33 )

NOTE: At SUR Iteration 5 CONVERGE=0.001 Criteria Met.
```

```
            Consumer Demand--Translog Functional Form
                        Symmetric Model

                        MODEL Procedure
                        SUR Estimation

           Nonlinear SUR Summary of Residual Errors

             DF    DF
Equation  Model  Error      SSE        MSE    Root MSE   R-Square  Adj R-Sq

SHARE1       4     40    0.00166  0.00004148  0.0064402    0.8066    0.7920
SHARE2       4     40    0.00139  0.00003475  0.0058952    0.9428    0.9385


              Nonlinear SUR Parameter Estimates

                                Approx.      'T'     Approx.
           Parameter  Estimate  Std Err     Ratio   Prob>|T|
           A1         -0.146838  0.0013473  -108.99   0.0001
           A2         -0.459703  0.0016696  -275.34   0.0001
           B11         0.028860  0.0074104     3.89   0.0004
           B12         0.467827  0.01153      40.57   0.0001
           B22         0.970080  0.01768      54.87   0.0001
           B31         0.208143  0.0061432    33.88   0.0001
           B32         1.102416  0.01274      86.51   0.0001
           B33         0.694245  0.01678      41.38   0.0001


           Number of Observations     Statistics for System
           Used              44       Objective      1.7820
           Missing            0       Objective*N   78.4094
```

Example 11.3.   Vector AR(1) Estimation   □ □ □   663

Example 11.3.   Vector AR(1) Estimation

This example shows the estimation of a two-variable vector AR(1) error process for the Grunfeld model (Grunfeld 1960) using the %AR macro. First, the full model is estimated. Second, the model is estimated with the restriction that the errors are univariate AR(1) instead of a vector process. The following produces Output 11.3.1 and Output 11.3.2.

```
data grunfeld;
   input year gei gef gec whi whf whc;
   label gei = 'Gross Investment GE'
         gec = 'Capital Stock Lagged GE'
         gef = 'Value of Outstanding Shares GE Lagged'
         whi = 'Gross Investment WH'
         whc = 'Capital Stock Lagged WH'
         whf = 'Value of Outstanding Shares Lagged WH';
   cards;
1935    33.1     1170.6    97.8     12.93    191.5     1.8
1936    45.0     2015.8    104.4    25.90    516.0     .8
1937    77.2     2803.3    118.0    35.05    729.0     7.4
1938    44.6     2039.7    156.2    22.89    560.4     18.1
1939    48.1     2256.2    172.6    18.84    519.9     23.5
1940    74.4     2132.2    186.6    28.57    628.5     26.5
1941    113.0    1834.1    220.9    48.51    537.1     36.2
1942    91.9     1588.0    287.8    43.34    561.2     60.8
1943    61.3     1749.4    319.9    37.02    617.2     84.4
1944    56.8     1687.2    321.3    37.81    626.7     91.2
1945    93.6     2007.7    319.6    39.27    737.2     92.4
1946    159.9    2208.3    346.0    53.46    760.5     86.0
1947    147.2    1656.7    456.4    55.56    581.4     111.1
1948    146.3    1604.4    543.4    49.56    662.3     130.6
1949    98.3     1431.8    618.3    32.04    583.8     141.8
1950    93.5     1610.5    647.4    32.24    635.2     136.7
1951    135.2    1819.4    671.3    54.38    723.8     129.7
1952    157.3    2079.7    726.1    71.78    864.1     145.5
1953    179.5    2371.6    800.3    90.08    1193.5    174.8
1954    189.6    2759.9    888.9    68.60    1188.9    213.5
;

title1 'Example of Vector AR(1) Error Process Using Grunfeld''s Model';
    /* Note: GE stands for General Electric and WH for Westinghouse */

proc model outmodel=grunmod;
   var gei whi gef gec whf whc;
   parms ge_int ge_f ge_c wh_int wh_f wh_c;
   label ge_int = 'GE Intercept'
         ge_f   = 'GE Lagged Share Value Coef'
         ge_c   = 'GE Lagged Capital Stock Coef'
         wh_int = 'WH Intercept'
         wh_f   = 'WH Lagged Share Value Coef'
         wh_c   = 'WH Lagged Capital Stock Coef';
   gei = ge_int + ge_f * gef + ge_c * gec;
   whi = wh_int + wh_f * whf + wh_c * whc;
run;
```

The preceding PROC MODEL step defines the structural model and stores it in the model file named GRUNMOD.

The following PROC MODEL step reads in the model, adds the vector autoregressive terms using %AR, and requests SUR estimation using the FIT statement.

```
title2 'With Unrestricted Vector AR(1) Error Process';
proc model data=grunfeld model=grunmod;
   %ar( ar, 1, gei whi )
   fit gei whi / sur;
run;
```

The final PROC MODEL step estimates the restricted model.

```
title2 'With restricted AR(1) Error Process';
proc model data=grunfeld model=grunmod;
   %ar( gei, 1 )
   %ar( whi, 1)
   fit gei whi / sur;
run;
```

Output 11.3.1. Results for the Unrestricted Model (Partial Output)

```
       Example of Vector AR(1) Error Process Using Grunfeld's Model
             With Unrestricted Vector AR(1) Error Process

                       MODEL Procedure

                       Model Summary

              Model Variables          6
              Parameters              10
              Equations                2

              Number of Statements     6

   Model Variables: GEI WHI GEF GEC WHF WHC

   Parameters: GE_INT GE_F GE_C WH_INT WH_F WH_C AR_1_1_1: 0
               AR_1_1_2: 0  AR_1_2_1: 0  AR_1_2_2: 0

   Equations: GEI WHI
```

```
       Example of Vector AR(1) Error Process Using Grunfeld's Model
             With Unrestricted Vector AR(1) Error Process

                       MODEL Procedure

              The 2 Equations to Estimate are:

      GEI = F( GE_INT, GE_F, GE_C, WH_INT, WH_F, WH_C, AR_1_1_1,
               AR_1_1_2 )
      WHI = F( GE_INT, GE_F, GE_C, WH_INT, WH_F, WH_C, AR_1_2_1,
               AR_1_2_2 )
NOTE: At OLS Iteration 5 CONVERGE=0.001 Criteria Met.
NOTE: At SUR Iteration 9 CONVERGE=0.001 Criteria Met.
```

Example 11.3. Vector AR(1) Estimation □ □ □ 665

Output 11.3.1. (Continued)

```
       Example of Vector AR(1) Error Process Using Grunfeld's Model
               With Unrestricted Vector AR(1) Error Process

                           MODEL Procedure
                           SUR Estimation

                Nonlinear SUR Summary of Residual Errors

              DF    DF
Equation    Model  Error       SSE         MSE      Root MSE   R-Square  Adj R-Sq

GEI          5     15         9374      624.96467   24.99929    0.7910    0.7352
WHI          5     15         1429       95.28070    9.76118    0.7940    0.7391


                   Nonlinear SUR Parameter Estimates

                          Approx.      'T'   Approx.
Parameter    Estimate     Std Err    Ratio  Prob>|T|  Label

GE_INT      -42.285817   30.52838    -1.39   0.1863   GE Intercept
GE_F          0.049894    0.01525     3.27   0.0051   GE Lagged Share Value Coef
GE_C          0.123946    0.04585     2.70   0.0163   GE Lagged Capital Stock Coef
WH_INT       -4.689309    8.96783    -0.52   0.6087   WH Intercept
WH_F          0.068979    0.01817     3.80   0.0018   WH Lagged Share Value Coef
WH_C          0.019308    0.07544     0.26   0.8015   WH Lagged Capital Stock Coef
AR_1_1_1      0.990902    0.39227     2.53   0.0233   AR(AR) GEI: LAG1 PARM FOR GEI
AR_1_1_2     -1.562524    1.08818    -1.44   0.1716   AR(AR) GEI: LAG1 PARM FOR WHI
AR_1_2_1      0.244161    0.17829     1.37   0.1910   AR(AR) WHI: LAG1 PARM FOR GEI
AR_1_2_2     -0.238639    0.49571    -0.48   0.6372   AR(AR) WHI: LAG1 PARM FOR WHI
```

Output 11.3.2. Results for the Restricted Model (Partial Output)

```
       Example of Vector AR(1) Error Process Using Grunfeld's Model
               With Unrestricted Vector AR(1) Error Process

                           MODEL Procedure

                           Model Summary

                Model Variables          6
                Parameters               8
                Equations                2

                Number of Statements     6

      Model Variables: GEI WHI GEF GEC WHF WHC

      Parameters: GE_INT GE_F GE_C WH_INT WH_F WH_C GEI_L1: 0   WHI_L1: 0

      Equations: GEI WHI
```

```
       Example of Vector AR(1) Error Process Using Grunfeld's Model
               With Unrestricted Vector AR(1) Error Process

                           MODEL Procedure
                           SUR Estimation

                Nonlinear SUR Summary of Residual Errors

              DF    DF
Equation    Model  Error       SSE         MSE      Root MSE   R-Square  Adj R-Sq

GEI          4     16        10559      659.92540   25.68901    0.7646    0.7204
WHI          4     16         1670      104.36017   10.21568    0.7594    0.7142


                   Nonlinear SUR Parameter Estimates

                          Approx.      'T'   Approx.
Parameter    Estimate     Std Err    Ratio  Prob>|T|  Label

GE_INT      -30.123897   29.72274    -1.01   0.3259   GE Intercept
```

Output 11.3.2. (Continued)

```
GE_F       0.043527   0.01488    2.93    0.0099 GE Lagged Share Value Coef
GE_C       0.119206   0.04229    2.82    0.0124 GE Lagged Capital Stock Coef
WH_INT     3.112671   9.27653    0.34    0.7416 WH Intercept
WH_F       0.053932   0.01539    3.50    0.0029 WH Lagged Share Value Coef
WH_C       0.038246   0.08046    0.48    0.6410 WH Lagged Capital Stock Coef
GEI_L1     0.482397   0.21490    2.24    0.0393 AR(GEI) GEI LAG1 PARAMETER
WHI_L1     0.455711   0.24239    1.88    0.0784 AR(WHI) WHI LAG1 PARAMETER
```

Example 11.4. MA(1) Estimation

This example estimates parameters for an MA(1) error process for the Grunfeld model, using both the unconditional least-squares and the maximum-likelihood methods. The ARIMA procedure estimates for Westinghouse equation are shown for comparison. The output of the following code is summarized in Output 11.4.1:

```
title1 'Example of MA(1) Error Process Using Grunfeld''s Model';
title2 'MA(1) Error Process Using Unconditional Least Squares';
proc model data=grunfeld model=grunmod;
   %ma(gei,1, m=uls);
   %ma(whi,1, m=uls);
   fit whi gei start=( gei_m1 0.8 -0.8) / startiter=2;
run;
```

Output 11.4.1. PROC MODEL Results Using ULS Estimation

```
         Example of MA(1) Error Process Using Grunfeld's Model
         MA(1) Error Process Using Unconditional Least Squares

                          MODEL Procedure
                          OLS Estimation

              Nonlinear OLS Summary of Residual Errors

             DF    DF
Equation  Model  Error      SSE          MSE      Root MSE  R-Square  Adj R-Sq

WHI          4     16       1874    117.12324     10.82235    0.7299    0.6793
RESID.WHI          16       1296     80.97535      8.99863
GEI          4     16      13835    864.68552     29.40554    0.6915    0.6337
RESID.GEI          16       7646    477.89001     21.86070


              Nonlinear OLS Parameter Estimates

                        Approx.     'T'   Approx.
Parameter   Estimate    Std Err   Ratio  Prob>|T| Label

GE_INT     -26.838955  32.09082   -0.84   0.4153  GE Intercept
GE_F         0.038226   0.01503    2.54   0.0217  GE Lagged Share Value Coef
GE_C         0.137099   0.03516    3.90   0.0013  GE Lagged Capital Stock Coef
WH_INT       3.681539   9.54464    0.39   0.7048  WH Intercept
WH_F         0.049154   0.01724    2.85   0.0115  WH Lagged Share Value Coef
WH_C         0.067280   0.07077    0.95   0.3559  WH Lagged Capital Stock Coef
GEI_M1      -0.876148   0.16143   -5.43   0.0001  MA(GEI) GEI lag1 parameter
WHI_M1      -0.749960   0.23681   -3.17   0.0060  MA(WHI) WHI lag1 parameter
```

The estimation summary from the following PROC ARIMA statements is shown in

Example 11.4. MA(1) Estimation □ □ □ **667**

Output 11.4.2.

```
title2 'PROC ARIMA Using Unconditional Least Squares';

proc arima data=grunfeld;
    identify var=whi cross=(whf whc ) noprint;
    estimate q=1 input=(whf whc) method=uls maxiter=40;
run;
```

Output 11.4.2. PROC ARIMA Results Using ULS Estimation

```
               Example of MA(1) Error Process Using Grunfeld's Model
                   PROC ARIMA Using Unconditional Least Squares

                              ARIMA Procedure

                    Unconditional Least Squares Estimation
                                   Approx.
    Parameter     Estimate      Std Error    T Ratio   Lag  Variable Shift
    MU             3.68608        9.54425       0.39     0   WHI          0
    MA1,1         -0.75005        0.23704      -3.16     1   WHI          0
    NUM1           0.04914        0.01723       2.85     0   WHF          0
    NUM2           0.06731        0.07077       0.95     0   WHC          0

    Constant Estimate  = 3.68607684
```

The model stored in Example 11.3 is read in using the MODEL= option and the moving average terms are added using the %MA macro.

The MA(1) model using maximum likelihood is estimated using the following:

```
title2 'MA(1) Error Process Using Maximum Likelihood ';
proc model data=grunfeld model=grunmod;
    %ma(gei,1, m=ml);
    %ma(whi,1, m=ml);
    fit whi gei;
run;
```

For comparison, the model is estimated using PROC ARIMA as follows:

```
title2 'PROC ARIMA Using Maximum Likelihood ';
proc arima data=grunfeld;
    identify var=whi cross=(whf whc) noprint;
    estimate q=1 input=(whf whc) method=ml;
run;
```

PROC ARIMA does not estimate systems so only one equation is evaluated.

The estimation results are shown in Output 11.4.3 and Output 11.4.4. The small differences in the parameter values between PROC MODEL and PROC ARIMA can be eliminated by tightening the convergence criteria for both procedures.

Output 11.4.3. PROC MODEL Results Using ML Estimation

```
         Example of MA(1) Error Process Using Grunfeld's Model
             MA(1) Error Process Using Maximum Likelihood

                           MODEL Procedure
                           OLS Estimation

                Nonlinear OLS Summary of Residual Errors

              DF    DF
  Equation  Model Error       SSE         MSE      Root MSE  R-Square  Adj R-Sq

  GEI         4    16        13743     858.90696    29.30711   0.6936   0.6361
  RESID.GEI        16         8095     505.95617    22.49347
  WHI         4    16         1857     116.09133    10.77457   0.7323   0.6821
  RESID.WHI        16         1344      84.00119     9.16522


                   Nonlinear OLS Parameter Estimates

                          Approx.      'T'  Approx.
  Parameter   Estimate    Std Err    Ratio Prob>|T|  Label

  GE_INT    -25.002016   34.29330    -0.73  0.4765  GE Intercept
  GE_F        0.037120    0.01613     2.30  0.0351  GE Lagged Shared Value Coef
  GE_C        0.137788    0.03799     3.63  0.0023  GE Lagged Capital Stock Coef
  WH_INT      2.946761    9.56382     0.31  0.7620  WH Intercept
  WH_F        0.050395    0.01743     2.89  0.0106  WH Lagged Share Value Coef
  WH_C        0.066531    0.07289     0.91  0.3749  WH Lagged Capital Stock Coef
  GEI_M1     -0.785157    0.19415    -4.04  0.0009  MA(GEI) GEI lag1 parameter
  WHI_M1     -0.693888    0.25396    -2.73  0.0148  MA(WHI) WHI lag1 parameter
```

Output 11.4.4. PROC ARIMA Results Using ML Estimation

```
         Example of MA(1) Error Process Using Grunfeld's Model
              PROC ARIMA Using Maximum Likelihood

                           ARIMA Procedure


                  Maximum Likelihood Estimation

                             Approx.
  Parameter     Estimate    Std Error   T Ratio  Lag  Variable  Shift
  MU            2.95645      9.20752      0.32     0    WHI       0
  MA1,1        -0.69305      0.25307     -2.74     1    WHI       0
  NUM1          0.05036      0.01686      2.99     0    WHF       0
  NUM2          0.06672      0.06939      0.96     0    WHC       0

  Constant Estimate  = 2.95644882
```

Example 11.5. Polynomial Distributed Lags Using %PDL

This example shows the use of the %PDL macro for polynomial distributed lag models. Simulated data is generated so that Y is a linear function of six lags of X, with the lag coefficients following a quadratic polynomial. The model is estimated using a fourth-degree polynomial, both with and without endpoint constraints. The example uses simulated data generated from the following model:

$$y_t = 10 + \sum_{z=0}^{6} f(z) x_{t-z} + \epsilon$$

$$f(z) = -5 z^2 + 1.5 z$$

Example 11.5. Polynomial Distributed Lags Using %PDL □ □ □ 669

The LIST option prints the model statements added by the %PDL macro.

```
/*------------------------------------------------------------------*/
/*  Generate Simulated Data for a Linear Model with a PDL on X  */
/*          y = 10 + x(6,2) + e                                 */
/*          pdl(x) = -5.*(lg)**2 + 1.5*(lg) + 0.                */
/*------------------------------------------------------------------*/
data pdl;
   pdl2=-5.; pdl1=1.5; pdl0=0;
   array zz(i) z0-z6;
   do i=1 to 7;
      z=i-1;
      zz=pdl2*z**2 + pdl1*z + pdl0;
      end;
   do n=-11 to 30;
      x  =10*ranuni(1234567)-5;
      pdl=z0*x + z1*x11 + z2*x12 + z3*x13 + z4*x14 + z5*x15 + z6*x16;
      e  =10*rannor(123);
      y  =10+pdl+e;
      if n>=1 then output;
      x16=x15; x15=x14; x14=x13; x13=x12; x12=x11; x11=x;
      end;
run;

title1 'Polynomial Distributed Lag Example';

title3 'Estimation of PDL(6,4) Model-- No Endpoint Restrictions';
proc model data=pdl;
   parms int;                  /* declare the intercept parameter */
   %pdl( xpdl, 6, 4 )          /* declare the lag distribution */
   y = int + %pdl( xpdl, x );  /* define the model equation */
   fit y / list;               /* estimate the parameters */
run;
```

Output 11.5.1. PROC MODEL Listing of Generated Program

```
                 Listing of Compiled Program Code:

Stmt  Line:Col  Statement as Parsed
  1   767:14    XPDL_L0 = XPDL_0;

  2   779:14    XPDL_L1 = XPDL_0 + XPDL_1 + XPDL_2 + XPDL_3 + XPDL_4;

  3   808:14    XPDL_L2 = XPDL_0 + XPDL_1 * 2 + XPDL_2 * 2 ** 2 + XPDL_3 * 2
                          ** 3 + XPDL_4 * 2 ** 4;

  4   856:14    XPDL_L3 = XPDL_0 + XPDL_1 * 3 + XPDL_2 * 3 ** 2 + XPDL_3 * 3
                          ** 3 + XPDL_4 * 3 ** 4;

  5   904:14    XPDL_L4 = XPDL_0 + XPDL_1 * 4 + XPDL_2 * 4 ** 2 + XPDL_3 * 4
                          ** 3 + XPDL_4 * 4 ** 4;

  6   952:14    XPDL_L5 = XPDL_0 + XPDL_1 * 5 + XPDL_2 * 5 ** 2 + XPDL_3 * 5
                          ** 3 + XPDL_4 * 5 ** 4;

  7  1000:14    XPDL_L6 = XPDL_0 + XPDL_1 * 6 + XPDL_2 * 6 ** 2 + XPDL_3 * 6
                          ** 3 + XPDL_4 * 6 ** 4;

  8  1048:4     PRED.Y = INT + XPDL_L0 * X + XPDL_L1 * LAG1( X ) + XPDL_L2 *
                          LAG2( X ) + XPDL_L3 * LAG3( X ) + XPDL_L4 * LAG4( X ) +
                          XPDL_L5 * LAG5( X ) + XPDL_L6 * LAG6( X );

  8  1048:4     RESID.Y = PRED.Y - ACTUAL.Y;

  8  1048:4     ERROR.Y = PRED.Y - Y;
```

Output 11.5.2. PROC MODEL Results Specifying No Endpoint Restrictions

```
              Polynomial Distributed Lag Example

       Estimation of PDL(6,4) Model-- No Endpoint Restrictions

                     MODEL Procedure
                     OLS Estimation

            Nonlinear OLS Summary of Residual Errors

            DF    DF
Equation  Model  Error      SSE       MSE     Root MSE  R-Square  Adj R-Sq

Y           6     18       1570    87.19560   9.33786    0.9997    0.9996



               Nonlinear OLS Parameter Estimates

                                Approx.      'T'    Approx.
          Parameter   Estimate  Std Err     Ratio   Prob>|T|

          INT        11.514134  1.94946      5.91    0.0001
          XPDL_0     -0.297951  0.68364     -0.44    0.6681
          XPDL_1      5.078412  1.75962      2.89    0.0098
          XPDL_2     -7.984183  1.35881     -5.88    0.0001
          XPDL_3      0.741345  0.35345      2.10    0.0503
          XPDL_4     -0.057755  0.02912     -1.98    0.0628
```

The LIST output for the model without endpoint restrictions is shown in Output 11.5.1 and Output 11.5.2. The first seven statements in the generated program are the polynomial expressions for lag parameters XPDL_L0 through XPDL_L6. The estimated parameters are INT, XPDL_0, XPDL_1, XPDL_2, XPDL_3, and XPDL_4.

Portions of the output produced by the following PDL model with endpoints of the model restricted to 0 are presented in Output 11.5.3 and Output 11.5.4.

```
title3 'Estimation of PDL(6,4) Model-- Both Endpoint Restrictions';
proc model data=pdl ;
   parms int;                      /* declare the intercept parameter */
   %pdl( xpdl, 6, 4, r=both )      /* declare the lag distribution */
   y = int + %pdl( xpdl, x );      /* define the model equation */
   fit y /list;                    /* estimate the parameters */
run;
```

Output 11.5.3. PROC MODEL Results Specifying Both Endpoint Restrictions

```
              Polynomial Distributed Lag Example

     Estimation of PDL(6,4) Model-- Both Endpoint Restrictions

                     MODEL Procedure
                     OLS Estimation

           Nonlinear OLS Summary of Residual Errors

            DF    DF
Equation  Model  Error      SSE       MSE     Root MSE  R-Square  Adj R-Sq

Y           4     20      601048   30052.4  173.35630    0.8867    0.8697


              Nonlinear OLS Parameter Estimates

                                Approx.      'T'    Approx.
          Parameter   Estimate  Std Err     Ratio   Prob>|T|

          INT         7.020876  36.17692     0.19    0.8481
```

Example 11.5. Polynomial Distributed Lags Using %PDL □ □ □ 671

Output 11.5.3. (Continued)

```
        XPDL_2       14.237766      6.11352      2.33    0.0305
        XPDL_3       -9.337813      1.87752     -4.97    0.0001
        XPDL_4        1.025098      0.15624      6.56    0.0001
```

Note that XPDL_0 and XPDL_1 are not shown in the estimate summary. They were used to satisfy the endpoint restrictions analytically by the generated %PDL macro code. Their values can be determined by back substitution.

To estimate the PDL model with one or more of the polynomial terms dropped, specify the largest degree of the polynomial desired with the %PDL macro and use the DROP= option in the FIT statement to remove the unwanted terms. The dropped parameters should be set to 0. The following PROC MODEL code demonstrates estimation with a PDL of degree 2 without the 0th order term.

```
title3 'Estimation of PDL(6,2) Model-- With XPDL_0 Dropped';
proc model data=pdl list;
    parms int;                    /* declare the intercept parameter */
    %pdl( xpdl, 6, 2 )            /* declare the lag distribution */
    y = int + %pdl( xpdl, x );    /* define the model equation */
    xpdl_0 =0;
    fit y drop=xpdl_0;           /* estimate the parameters */
run;
```

The results from this estimation are shown in Output 11.5.4.

Output 11.5.4. PROC MODEL Results Specifying %PDL(XPDL, 6, 2)

```
                 Nonlinear OLS Summary of Residual Errors

            DF    DF
Equation  Model Error     SSE       MSE     Root MSE  R-Square  Adj R-Sq

Y           3    21       2009    95.66646   9.78092   0.9996    0.9996


                 Nonlinear OLS Parameter Estimates

                                  Approx.     'T'    Approx.
           Parameter   Estimate   Std Err    Ratio   Prob>|T|

           INT        11.387721   2.02452     5.62    0.0001
           XPDL_1      1.381208   0.35757     3.86    0.0009
           XPDL_2     -5.008195   0.06816   -73.48    0.0001
```

Example 11.6.   General-Form Equations

Data for this example are generated. General-form equations are estimated and forecast using PROC MODEL. The system is a basic supply-demand model. Portions of the output from the following code is shown in Output 11.6.1 through Output 11.6.4.

```
title1 "General Form Equations for Supply-Demand Model";

proc model;
    var price quantity income unitcost;
    parms d0-d2 s0-s2;
    eq.demand=d0+d1*price+d2*income-quantity;
    eq.supply=s0+s1*price+s2*unitcost-quantity;

/* estimate the model parameters */
    fit supply demand / data=history outest=est n2sls;
    instruments income unitcost year;
run;

/* produce forecasts for income and unitcost assumptions */
    solve price quantity / data=assume out=pq;
run;

/* produce goal-seeking solutions for income and quantity assumptions*/
    solve price unitcost / data=goal out=pc;
run;

title2 "Parameter Estimates for the System";
proc print data=est;
run;

title2 "Price Quantity Solution";
proc print data=pq;
run;

title2 "Price Unitcost Solution";
proc print data=pc;
run;
```

Three data sets were used in this example. The first data set, HISTORY, was used to estimate the parameters of the model. The ASSUME data set was used to produce a forecast of PRICE and QUANTITY. Notice that the ASSUME data set does not have to contain the variables PRICE and QUANTITY.

```
data history;
    input year income unitcost price quantity;
    cards;
1976    2221.87    3.31220    0.17903    266.714
1977    2254.77    3.61647    0.06757    276.049
1978    2285.16    2.21601    0.82916    285.858
1979    2319.37    3.28257    0.33202    295.034
1980    2369.38    2.84494    0.63564    310.773
1981    2395.26    2.94154    0.62011    319.185
1982    2419.52    2.65301    0.80753    325.970
1983    2475.09    2.41686    1.01017    342.470
1984    2495.09    3.44096    0.52025    348.321
1985    2536.72    2.30601    1.15053    360.750
;

data assume;
```

Example 11.6. General-Form Equations □ □ □ 673

```
    input year income unitcost;
    cards;
1986    2571.87    2.31220
1987    2609.12    2.45633
1988    2639.77    2.51647
1989    2667.77    1.65617
1990    2705.16    1.01601
;
```

The output produced by the first SOLVE statement is shown in Output 11.6.3.

The third data set, GOAL, is used in a forecast of PRICE and UNITCOST as a function of INCOME and QUANTITY.

```
data goal;
    input year income quantity;
    cards;
1986    2571.87    371.4
1987    2721.08    416.5
1988    3327.05    597.3
1989    3885.85    764.1
1990    3650.98    694.3
;
```

The output from the final SOLVE statement is shown in Output 11.6.4.

Output 11.6.1. Printed Output from the FIT Statement

```
        General Form Equations for Supply-Demand Model

                    MODEL Procedure

            The 2 Equations to Estimate are:

        SUPPLY = F( S0(1), S1(PRICE), S2(UNITCOST) )
        DEMAND = F( D0(1), D1(PRICE), D2(INCOME) )

            Instruments: 1 INCOME UNITCOST YEAR
```

```
        General Form Equations for Supply-Demand Model

                    MODEL Procedure
                    2SLS Estimation

        Nonlinear 2SLS Summary of Residual Errors

              DF    DF
Equation   Model  Error      SSE        MSE     Root MSE  R-Square  Adj R-Sq

SUPPLY       3      7      3.32401    0.47486   0.68910
DEMAND       3      7      1.08290    0.15470   0.39332


            Nonlinear 2SLS Parameter Estimates

                              Approx.     'T'     Approx.
        Parameter   Estimate  Std Err    Ratio   Prob>|T|

        D0       -395.886693   4.18412   -94.62   0.0001
        D1          0.717328   0.56733     1.26   0.2466
        D2          0.298061   0.0018670  159.65   0.0001
        S0       -107.620381   4.17799   -25.76   0.0001
        S1        201.571081   1.59774   126.16   0.0001
        S2        102.211583   1.12171    91.12   0.0001
```

Output 11.6.2.   Listing of OUTEST= Data Set Created in the FIT Statement

```
                General Form Equations for Supply-Demand Model
                      Parameter Estimates for the System

    OBS _NAME_  _TYPE_  _NUSED_    D0       D1       D2       S0       S1      S2

     1            2SLS     10    -395.887 0.71733  0.29806  -107.620 201.571 102.212
```

Output 11.6.3.   Listing of OUT= Data Set Created in the First SOLVE Statement

```
                General Form Equations for Supply-Demand Model
                            Price Quantity Solution

    OBS  _TYPE_    _MODE_    _ERRORS_    PRICE    QUANTITY   INCOME   UNITCOST   YEAR

     1   PREDICT   SIMULATE     0       1.20473   371.552   2571.87   2.31220    1986
     2   PREDICT   SIMULATE     0       1.18666   382.642   2609.12   2.45633    1987
     3   PREDICT   SIMULATE     0       1.20154   391.788   2639.77   2.51647    1988
     4   PREDICT   SIMULATE     0       1.68089   400.478   2667.77   1.65617    1989
     5   PREDICT   SIMULATE     0       2.06214   411.896   2705.16   1.01601    1990
```

Output 11.6.4.   Listing of OUT= Data Set Created in the Second SOLVE
Statement

```
                General Form Equations for Supply-Demand Model
                            Price Unitcost Solution

    OBS  _TYPE_    _MODE_    _ERRORS_    PRICE    QUANTITY   INCOME   UNITCOST   YEAR

     1   PREDICT   SIMULATE     0       0.99284    371.4    2571.87   2.72857    1986
     2   PREDICT   SIMULATE     0       1.86594    416.5    2721.08   1.44798    1987
     3   PREDICT   SIMULATE     0       2.12230    597.3    3327.05   2.71130    1988
     4   PREDICT   SIMULATE     0       2.46166    764.1    3885.85   3.67395    1989
     5   PREDICT   SIMULATE     0       2.74831    694.3    3650.98   2.42576    1990
```

Example 11.7.   Spring and Damper Continuous System

This model simulates the mechanical behavior of a spring and damper system shown in Figure 11.66.

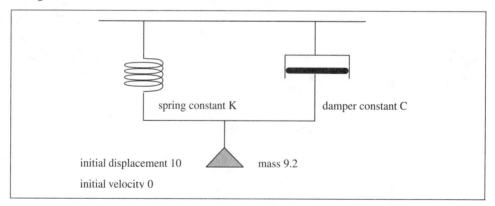

Figure 11.66.   Spring and Damper System Model

A mass is hung from a spring with spring constant K. The motion is slowed by a

Example 11.7. Spring and Damper Continuous System □ □ □ 675

damper with damper constant C. The damping force is proportional to the velocity, while the spring force is proportional to the displacement.

This is actually a continuous system; however, the behavior can be approximated by a discrete time model. We approximate the differential equation

$$\frac{\partial \, disp}{\partial \, time} = velocity$$

with the difference equation

$$\frac{\Delta \, disp}{\Delta \, time} = velocity$$

This is rewritten

$$\frac{disp - \text{LAG}(disp)}{dt} = velocity$$

where *dt* is the time step used. In PROC MODEL, this is expressed with the program statement

```
disp = lag(disp) + vel * dt;
```

This statement is simply a computing formula for Euler's approximation for the integral

$$disp = \int velocity \, dt$$

If the time step is small enough with respect to the changes in the system, the approximation is good. Although PROC MODEL does not have the variable step-size and error-monitoring features of simulators designed for continuous systems, the procedure is a good tool to use for less challenging continuous models.

This model is unusual because there are no exogenous variables, and endogenous data are not needed. Although you still need a SAS data set to count the simulation periods, no actual data are brought in.

Since the variables DISP and VEL are lagged, initial values specified in the VAR statement determine the starting state of the system. The mass, time step, spring constant, and damper constant are declared and initialized by a CONTROL statement.

```
title1 'Simulation of Spring-Mass-Damper System';

/*- Generate some obs. to drive the simulation time periods ---*/
data one;
   do n=1 to 100;
      output;
   end;
run;

proc model data=one;
   var      force -200  disp 10  vel  0  accel -20  time 0;
   control  mass  9.2   c   1.5  dt  .1  k        20;
   force = -k * disp -c * vel;
   disp  = lag(disp) + vel * dt;
```

```
vel   = lag(vel) + accel * dt;
accel = force / mass;
time  = lag(time) + dt;
```

The displacement scale is zeroed at the point where the force of gravity is offset, so the acceleration of the gravity constant is omitted from the force equation. The control variable C and K represent the damper and the spring constants respectively.

The model is simulated three times, and the simulation results are written to output data sets. The first run uses the original initial conditions specified in the VAR statement. In the second run, the time step is reduced by half. Notice that the path of the displacement is close to the old path, indicating that the original time step is short enough to yield an accurate solution. In the third run, the initial displacement is doubled; the results show that the period of the motion is unaffected by the amplitude. These simulations are performed by the following statements:

```
/*- Simulate the model for the base case -------------------*/
   control run '1';
   solve / out=a;
run;

/*- Simulate the model with half the time step -------------*/
   control run '2' dt .05;
   solve / out=b;
run;

/*- Simulate the model with twice the initial displacement -*/
   control run '3';
   var disp 20;
   solve / out=c;
run;
```

The output SAS data sets containing the solution results are merged and the displacement time paths for the three simulations are plotted. The three runs are identified on the plot as 1, 2, and 3. The following code produces Output 11.7.1 through Output 11.7.2.

```
/*- Plot the results -------------------------------------*/
data p;
   set a b c;
run;

title2 'Overlay Plot of All Three Simulations';
proc gplot data=p;
   plot disp*time=run;
run;
```

Example 11.7. Spring and Damper Continuous System □ □ □ **677**

Output 11.7.1. Printed Output Produced by PROC MODEL SOLVE Statements

```
            Simulation of Spring-Mass-Damper System

                       MODEL Procedure

                       Model Summary

                  Model Variables          5
                  CONTROL Variables        5
                  Equations                5

                  Number of Statements     5

                  Program Lag Length       1

    Model Variables: FORCE -200 DISP 10 VEL 0 ACCEL -20 TIME 0

    CONTROL Variables: MASS 9.2 C 1.5 DT 0.1 K 20 RUN '1'

    Equations: FORCE DISP VEL ACCEL TIME
```

```
            Simulation of Spring-Mass-Damper System

                       MODEL Procedure
                 Dynamic Simultaneous Simulation

                       Solution Summary

            Dataset Option        Dataset
            DATA=                     ONE
            OUT=                        A

            Variables Solved            5

            Simulation Lag Length       1

            Solution Method        NEWTON
            CONVERGE=                1E-8
            Maximum CC                  0
            Maximum Iterations          1
            Total Iterations           99
            Average Iterations          1

               Observations Processed
            Read                      100
            Lagged                      1
            Solved                     99
             First                      2
             Last                     100

    Variables Solved For: FORCE DISP VEL ACCEL TIME
```

```
            Simulation of Spring-Mass-Damper System

                       MODEL Procedure
                 Dynamic Simultaneous Simulation

                       Solution Summary

            Dataset Option        Dataset
            DATA=                     ONE
            OUT=                        B

            Variables Solved            5

            Simulation Lag Length       1

            Solution Method        NEWTON
            CONVERGE=                1E-8
            Maximum CC                  0
            Maximum Iterations          1
            Total Iterations           99
            Average Iterations          1

               Observations Processed
```

Output 11.7.1.   (Continued)

```
                        Read              100
                        Lagged              1
                        Solved             99
                         First              2
                         Last             100

            Variables Solved For: FORCE DISP VEL ACCEL TIME
```

```
              Simulation of Spring-Mass-Damper System

                        MODEL Procedure
                 Dynamic Simultaneous Simulation

                        Solution Summary

                Dataset Option       Dataset
                DATA=                    ONE
                OUT=                       C

                Variables Solved          5

                Simulation Lag Length     1

                Solution Method       NEWTON
                CONVERGE=               1E-8
                Maximum CC                 0
                Maximum Iterations         1
                Total Iterations          99
                Average Iterations         1

                    Observations Processed
                Read                     100
                Lagged                     1
                Solved                    99
                 First                     2
                 Last                    100

            Variables Solved For: FORCE DISP VEL ACCEL TIME
```

Example 11.7. Spring and Damper Continuous System □ □ □ 679

Output 11.7.2. Overlay Plot of all Three Simulations

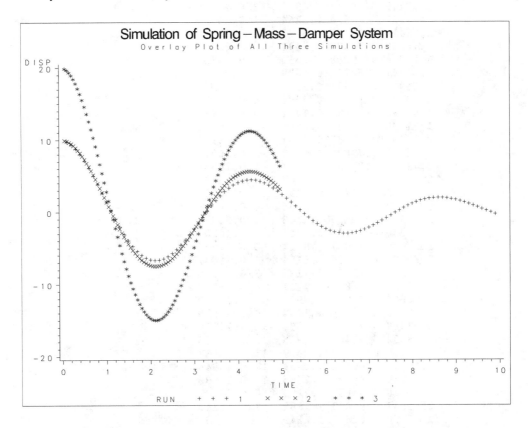

Example 11.8. Nonlinear FIML Estimation

The data and model for this example were obtained from Bard (1974, p.133-138). The example is a two-equation econometric model used by Bodkin and Klein to fit U.S production data for the years 1909-1949. The model is the following:

$$g_1 = c_1 \, 10^{c_2 z_4} \left(c_5 \, z^{-c_4} + (1 - c_5) z^{-c_4} \right)^{-c_3/c_4} - z_3 = 0$$

$$g_2 = \frac{c_5}{1 - c_5} \left(\frac{z_1}{z_2} \right)^{(-1-c_4)} - z_5 = 0$$

where z_1 is capital input, z_2 is labor input, z_3 is real output, z_4 is time in years with 1929 as year zero, and z_5 is the ratio of price of capital services to wage scale. The c_i's are the unknown parameters. z_1 and z_2 are considered endogenous variables. A FIML estimation is performed.

```
data bodkin;
   input z1 z2 z3 z4 z5;
cards;
1.33135 0.64629 0.4026 -20 0.24447
1.39235 0.66302 0.4084 -19 0.23454
1.41640 0.65272 0.4223 -18 0.23206
1.48773 0.67318 0.4389 -17 0.22291
1.51015 0.67720 0.4605 -16 0.22487
1.43385 0.65175 0.4445 -15 0.21879
```

```
1.48188 0.65570 0.4387 -14 0.23203
1.67115 0.71417 0.4999 -13 0.23828
1.71327 0.77524 0.5264 -12 0.26571
1.76412 0.79465 0.5793 -11 0.23410
1.76869 0.71607 0.5492 -10 0.22181
1.80776 0.70068 0.5052  -9 0.18157
1.54947 0.60764 0.4679  -8 0.22931
1.66933 0.67041 0.5283  -7 0.20595
1.93377 0.74091 0.5994  -6 0.19472
1.95460 0.71336 0.5964  -5 0.17981
2.11198 0.75159 0.6554  -4 0.18010
2.26266 0.78838 0.6851  -3 0.16933
2.33228 0.79600 0.6933  -2 0.16279
2.43980 0.80788 0.7061  -1 0.16906
2.58714 0.84547 0.7567   0 0.16239
2.54865 0.77232 0.6796   1 0.16103
2.26042 0.67880 0.6136   2 0.14456
1.91974 0.58529 0.5145   3 0.20079
1.80000 0.58065 0.5046   4 0.18307
1.86020 0.62007 0.5711   5 0.18352
1.88201 0.65575 0.6184   6 0.18847
1.97018 0.72433 0.7113   7 0.20415
2.08232 0.76838 0.7461   8 0.18847
1.94062 0.69806 0.6981   9 0.17800
1.98646 0.74679 0.7722  10 0.19979
2.07987 0.79083 0.8557  11 0.21115
2.28232 0.88462 0.9925  12 0.23453
2.52779 0.95750 1.0877  13 0.20937
2.62747 1.00285 1.1834  14 0.19843
2.61235 0.99329 1.2565  15 0.18898
2.52320 0.94857 1.2293  16 0.17203
2.44632 0.97853 1.1889  17 0.18140
2.56478 1.02591 1.2249  18 0.19431
2.64588 1.03760 1.2669  19 0.19492
2.69105 0.99669 1.2708  20 0.17912
;

proc model data=bodkin;
   parms c1-c5;
   endogenous z1 z2;
   exogenous z3 z4 z5;

   eq.g1 = c1 * 10 **(c2 * z4) * (c5*z1**(-c4)+
           (1-c5)*z2**(-c4))**(-c3/c4) - z3;
   eq.g2 = (c5/(1-c5))*(z1/z2)**(-1-c4) -z5;

   fit g1 g2 / fiml ;
run;
```

When FIML estimation is selected, the log likelihood of the system is output as the objective value. The results of the estimation are show in Output 11.8.1.

Example 11.8. Nonlinear FIML Estimation □ □ □ 681

Output 11.8.1. FIML Estimation Results for U.S. Production Data

```
                         MODEL Procedure
                          FIML Estimation

             Nonlinear FIML Summary of Residual Errors

              DF    DF
Equation    Model Error      SSE         MSE      Root MSE  R-Square  Adj R-Sq

G1            4    37      0.05291    0.0014299    0.03781
G2            1    40      0.01729    0.0004322    0.02079

                Nonlinear FIML Parameter Estimates

                                   Approx.      'T'     Approx.
           Parameter   Estimate    Std Err     Ratio    Prob>|T|

           C1          0.583889    0.02186      26.71    0.0001
           C2          0.00588198  0.0006716     8.76    0.0001
           C3          1.362873    0.11469      11.88    0.0001
           C4          0.474993    0.27047       1.76    0.0871
           C5          0.447049    0.05974       7.48    0.0001


           Number of Observations       Statistics for System
           Used                41       Log Likelihood  -110.7774
           Missing              0
```

References

Amemiya, T. (1974), "The Nonlinear Two-stage Least-squares Estimator," *Journal of Econometrics*, 2, 105–110.

Amemiya, T. (1977), "The Maximum Likelihood Estimator and the Nonlinear Three-Stage Least Squares Estimator in the General Nonlinear Simultaneous Equation Model," *Econometrica*, 45(4), 955–968.

Amemiya, T. (1985), *Advanced Econometrics*, Cambridge, MA: Harvard University Press.

Andrews, D.W.K. (1991), "Heteroscedasticity and Autocorrelation Consistent Covariance Matrix Estimation," *Econometrica*, 59(3), 817–858.

Andrews, D.W.K., and Monahan, J.C. (1992), "An Improved Heteroscedasticity and Autocorrelation Consistent Covariance Matrix Estimator," *Econometrica*, 60(4), 953–966.

Bard, Yonathan (1974), *Nonlinear Parameter Estimation*, New York: Academic Press, Inc.

Bates, D.M. and Watts, D.G. (1981), "A Relative Offset Orthogonality Convergence Criterion for Nonlinear Least Squares," *Technometrics*, 23, 2, 179–183.

Belsley, D.A.; Kuh, E.; and Welsch, R.E. (1980), *Regression Diagnostics*, New York: John Wiley & Sons, Inc.

Binkley, J.K. and Nelson, G. (1984), "Impact of Alternative Degrees of Freedom Corrections in Two and Three Stage Least Squares," *Journal of Econometrics*, 24, 3, 223–233.

Bowden, R.J. and Turkington, D.A. (1984), *Instrumental Variables*, New York: Cambridge University Press.

Calzolari, G. and Panattoni, L. (1988),"Alternative Estimators of FIML Covariance Matrix: A Monte Carlo Study," *Econometrica*, 56(3), 701–714.

Christensen, L.R.; Jorgenson, D.W.; and Lau, L.J. (1975), "Transcendental Logarithmic Utility Functions," *American Economic Review*, 65, 367–383.

Dagenais, M. G. (1978), "The Computation of FIML Estimates as Iterative Generalized Least Squares Estimates in Linear and Nonlinear Simultaneous Equation Models," *Econometrica*, 46, 6, 1351–1362.

Ferson, Wayne E. and Foerster, Stephen R. (1993), "Finite Sample Properties of the Generalized Method of Moments in Tests of Conditional Asset Pricing Models," Working Paper No. 77, University of Washington.

Gallant, A.R. (1977), "Three-Stage Least Squares Estimation for a System of Simultaneous, Nonlinear, Implicit Equations," *Journal of Econometrics*, 5, 71–88.

Gallant, A.R. (1987), *Nonlinear Statistical Models*, New York: John Wiley and Sons, Inc.

Gallant, A.R. and Holly, Alberto (1980),"Statistical Inference in an Implicit, Nonlinear, Simultaneous Equation Model in the Context of Maximum Likelihood Estimation," *Econometrica*, 48(3), 697–720.

Gallant, A.R. and Jorgenson, D.W. (1979), "Statistical Inference for a System of Simultaneous, Nonlinear, Implicit Equations in the Context of Instrumental Variables Estimation," *Journal of Econometrics*, 11, 275–302.

Goodnight, J.H. (1979), "A Tutorial on the SWEEP Operator," *The American Statistician*, 33, 149–158.

Grunfeld, Y. and Griliches, Z. (1960), "Is Aggregation Necessarily Bad ?" *Review of Economics and Statistics*, February, 113–134.

Hansen, L.P. (1982), "Large Sample Properties of Generalized Method of Moments Estimators," *Econometrica*, 50(4), 1029–1054.

Hansen, L.P. (1985),"A Method for Calculating Bounds on the Asymptotic Covariance Matrices of Generalized Method Of Moments Estimators," *Journal of Econometrics*, 30, 203–238.

Hatanaka, M. (1978),"On the Efficient Estimation Methods for the Macro-Economic Models Nonlinear in Variables," *Journal of Econometrics*, 8, 323–356.

Johnston, J. (1984), *Econometric Methods*, Third Edition, New York: McGraw-Hill Inc.

Jorgenson, D.W. and Laffont, J. (1974), "Efficient Estimation of Nonlinear Simultaneous Equations With Additive Disturbances," *Annals of Social and Economic Measurement*, 3, 615–640.

Maddala, G.S. (1977), *Econometrics*, New York: McGraw-Hill Inc.

Mikhail, W.M. (1975), "A Comparative Monte Carlo Study of the Properties of Economic Estimators," *Journal of the American Statistical Association*, 70, 94–104.

Miller, D.M. (1984), "Reducing Transformation Bias in Curve Fitting," *The American Statistician*, 38(2), 124–126.

Newey, W.K, and West, D. W. (1987),"A Simple, Positive Semi-Definite, Heteroscedasticity and Autocorrelation Consistent Covariance Matrix," *Econometrica*, 55, 703–708.

Ortega, J. M. and Rheinbolt, W.C. (1970), "Iterative Solution of Nonlinear Equations in Several Variables," New York: Academic Press, Inc.

Parzen, E. (1957),"On Consistent Estimates of the Spectrum of a Stationary Time Series," *Annals of Mathematical Statistics*, 28, 329–348.

Pearlman, J. G. (1980), "An Algorithm for Exact Likelihood of a High-Order Autoregressive-Moving Average Process," *Biometrika*, 67(1), 232–233.

Pindyck, R.S. and Rubinfeld, D.L. (1981), *Econometric Models and Economic Forecasts*, Second Edition, New York: McGraw-Hill Inc.

Savin, N.E. and White, K.J. (1978), "Testing for Autocorrelation with Missing Observations," *Econometrics*, 46, 59–67.

Theil, H. (1971), *Principles of Econometrics*, New York: John Wiley & Sons, Inc.

Chapter 12
The MORTGAGE Procedure

Chapter Table of Contents

Chapter 12
The MORTGAGE Procedure

Overview

The MORTGAGE procedure calculates the variables associated with equal payment, fixed-rate installment loans and produces amortization schedules. Various payment and compounding periods are allowed, including continuous compounding.

The MORTGAGE procedure has been superseded by the LOAN procedure. PROC MORTGAGE can only provide amortization for one simple fixed-rate loan. PROC LOAN can process any number of loans, analyze adjustable rate, buydown rate, and balloon payment loans, handle prepayments, points, and other issues, and compare different loan terms on various economic criteria. See Chapter 10, "The LOAN Procedure," for more information.

Getting Started

Given any three out of four quantities used in the calculation of installment loans (interest rate, life of the loan, principal amount, and payment), the MORTGAGE procedure calculates the fourth quantity. PROC MORTGAGE then prints a loan summary table and an amortization schedule, either for each payment or as a yearly summary.

For example, the following PROC MORTGAGE statement finds the monthly payment for a 120-month (ten-year) mortgage with principal amount of $100,000 at 10.5%. It also prints an amortization schedule showing the status of the loan after each payment.

```
proc mortgage rate=10.5 amount=100000 life=120;
run;
```

The loan summary table is shown in Figure 12.1, and the first year of the amortization schedule is shown in Figure 12.2.

```
                    L O A N   S U M M A R Y

  Payment:              1349.35     Principal Amount:    100000.00

  Total Interest:      61922.09     Nominal Rate:          10.500%
  Total Payment:      161922.09     Effective Rate:        11.020%

  Pay Interval:         MONTHLY     Compound Interval:     MONTHLY
  Number of Payments:       120

  Note: The computed quantity is PAYMENT.
```

Figure 12.1. Loan Summary Table

```
                        Loan Repayment Schedule

                 BEGINNING              INTEREST  PRINCIPAL     ENDING
YEAR  MONTH    OUTSTANDING   PAYMENT     PAYMENT  REPAYMENT  OUTSTANDING
  1   JAN      100000.00     1349.35      875.00     474.35    99525.65
  1   FEB       99525.65     1349.35      870.85     478.50    99047.15
  1   MAR       99047.15     1349.35      866.66     482.69    98564.46
  1   APR       98564.46     1349.35      862.44     486.91    98077.55
  1   MAY       98077.55     1349.35      858.18     491.17    97586.38
  1   JUN       97586.38     1349.35      853.88     495.47    97090.91
  1   JUL       97090.91     1349.35      849.55     499.80    96591.11
  1   AUG       96591.11     1349.35      845.17     504.18    96086.93
  1   SEP       96086.93     1349.35      840.76     508.59    95578.34
  1   OCT       95578.34     1349.35      836.31     513.04    95065.30
  1   NOV       95065.30     1349.35      831.82     517.53    94547.77
  1   DEC       94547.77     1349.35      827.29     522.06    94025.71

  1   ***      100000.00    16192.20    10217.91    5974.29    94025.71
```

Figure 12.2. Amortization Schedule

Suppose you want to know how much you can borrow with a 24-month fixed rate installment loan at 12% if you can only pay $350 per month. The following PROC MORTGAGE statement produces the answer to this question. The NYEARS=0 option is used to suppress printing of the amortization schedule. The loan summary table is shown in Figure 12.3.

```
proc mortgage rate=12 payment=350 life=24 nyears=0;
run;
```

```
                   L O A N   S U M M A R Y

   Payment:              350.00    Principal Amount:     7435.19

   Total Interest:       964.82    Nominal Rate:         12.000%
   Total Payment:       8400.01    Effective Rate:       12.683%

   Pay Interval:        MONTHLY    Compound Interval:    MONTHLY
   Number of Payments:       24

   Note: The computed quantity is AMOUNT.
```

Figure 12.3. Loan Summary Report

Syntax

The MORTGAGE procedure uses the following statement:

PROC MORTGAGE *options*;

Functional Summary

The following table summarizes the statements and options controlling the MORT-GAGE procedure.

Description	Statement	Option
Data Set Options		
specify output data set for loan summary	PROC MORTGAGE	OUTSUM=
specify output data set for amortization	PROC MORTGAGE	OUT=
Loan Specifications Options		
specify the principal amount of the loan	PROC MORTGAGE	AMOUNT=
specify the number of payments	PROC MORTGAGE	LIFE=
specify the periodic payment	PROC MORTGAGE	PAYMENT=
specify the initial annual nominal interest rate	PROC MORTGAGE	RATE=
Other Options		
specify the date of the first payment	PROC MORTGAGE	FIRSTPAYMENT=
specify the payment interval	PROC MORTGAGE	INTERVAL=
specify the compounding interval	PROC MORTGAGE	COMPOUND=
specify the life of the loan in months	PROC MORTGAGE	MONTH=
Printing Control Options		
suppress all printed output	PROC MORTGAGE	NOPRINT
print only part of the amortization schedule	PROC MORTGAGE	NYEARS=
print the loan summary table in the SAS log	PROC MORTGAGE	PRINTLOG
print a yearly summary amortization schedule	PROC MORTGAGE	YEARLY

PROC MORTGAGE Statement

> **PROC MORTGAGE** *options*;

You can use the following options with the PROC MORTGAGE statement:

Loan Specifications Options

AMOUNT= *value*

specifies the principal amount of the loan.

The AMOUNT= option can be abbreviated A=.

LIFE= *n*

specifies the life of the loan in number of payments. For example, if the payment interval is quarterly, the life of a 10-year loan is specified as LIFE=40.

The LIFE= option can be abbreviated L=.

PAYMENT= *value*

specifies the periodic payment amount.

The PAYMENT= option can be abbreviated P=.

RATE= *value*

specifies the fixed annual (nominal) percentage rate. The rate can be given in decimal notation or as a percent value. For example, use either R=.1275 or R=12.75 for a 12.75% loan. If the RATE= value is greater than or equal to 1, it is assumed to be a percent value and PROC MORTGAGE divides it by 100. The maximum value for the RATE= option is 120%.

The RATE= option can be abbreviated R=.

You must specify three of the four options AMOUNT=, LIFE=, RATE=, and PAYMENT=. The MORTGAGE procedure calculates the fourth value based on the values you give to the other three options.

Data Set Options

OUT= *SAS-data-set*

writes the amortization schedule to an output data set. See the section "OUT= Data Set" later in this chapter for details.

OUTSUM= *SAS-data-set*

writes the loan summary information to an output data set. See the section "OUTSUM= Data Set" later in this chapter for details.

Printing Control Options

NOPRINT

suppresses all printed output. The NOPRINT option may be useful when the MORTGAGE procedure is used only to create output data sets. The NOPRINT option can be abbreviated NOP.

NYEARS= *n*

specifies the number of years the amortization schedule covers. If NYEARS= is omitted, the schedule is printed for the full term of the loan. Fractional values are permitted for *n*. The NYEARS= option can be abbreviated N=.

PRINTLOG

prints the loan summary table in the SAS log. The amortization schedule is not printed when you specify PRINTLOG. The PRINTLOG option can be abbreviated PRINTL.

YEARLY

prints a yearly summary table rather than the full amortization schedule. The YEARLY option can be abbreviated Y.

Other Options

COMPOUND= *time-unit*

specifies the time interval between compoundings. The following time units are valid COMPOUND= values: CONTINUOUS, DAY, SEMIMONTH, MONTH, QUARTER, SEMIYEAR, and YEAR. The default is the time unit given by the INTERVAL= option. If the INTERVAL= option is not used, the default is COMPOUND=MONTH.

FIRSTPAYMENT= *yyyy:n*

specifies the date of the first payment, where *yyyy* is the year and *n* is the period within the year. The valid values of *n* depend on the INTERVAL= specification. For example, if a quarterly loan begins in the third quarter of 1977, use the specification INTERVAL=QUARTER FIRSTPAYMENT=1977:3. For this example, any value of *n* greater than 4 is invalid. The FIRSTPAYMENT= option can be abbreviated FIRSTP=.

INTERVAL= *time-unit*

specifies the time interval between periodic payments. The following time units are valid INTERVAL= values: SEMIMONTH, MONTH, QUARTER, SEMIYEAR, and YEAR. The default is INTERVAL=MONTH.

MONTH= *n*

specifies the life of the loan as the number of monthly payments (as in previous releases of the MORTGAGE procedure). You can specify the MONTH= option instead of the LIFE= option only if INTERVAL=MONTH. The MONTH= option can be abbreviated M=.

Details

Computational Details

For computational details, see the section "Details" in Chapter 10, "The LOAN Procedure."

OUT= Data Set

The OUT= data set contains the amortization schedule. The variables in the OUT= data set contain the values of the corresponding columns in the printed amortization schedule. The OUT= data set contains an observation for each payment period or, if the YEARLY option is specified, an observation for each year.

The OUT= data set contains the following variables:

- YEAR, a numeric variable containing the year of the payment or summary

- A numeric variable giving the period within the year. This variable is named according to the INTERVAL= specification and can be SEMIMON, MONTH, QTR, or SEMIYEAR. This variable is not included if you use the YEARLY option.

- BEGPRI, a numeric variable containing the beginning outstanding balance

- PAYMENT, a numeric variable containing the payments for this observation

- INT, a numeric variable containing the interest payment

- REPAY, a numeric variable containing the part of the PAYMENT going to principal repayment

- ENDPRI, a numeric variable containing the ending outstanding balance

OUTSUM= Data Set

The OUTSUM= data set contains the loan summary information. The OUTSUM= data set contains the following variables:

- AMOUNT, a numeric variable containing the principal amount

- BEGIN, a numeric variable containing the SAS date of the beginning of the loan. BEGIN is included in the OUTSUM= data set only if you specify the FIRSTPAYMENT= option.

- COMPOUND, a character variable containing the compounding interval

- COMPUTE, a character variable containing the name of the computed quantity

- EFFRATE, a numeric variable containing the effective interest rate

- END, a numeric variable containing the SAS date of the end of the loan. END is included in the OUTSUM= data set only if you specify the FIRSTPAYMENT= option.

- INTEREST, a numeric variable containing the total interest

- INTERVAL, a character variable containing the payment interval

- LIFE, a numeric variable containing the life of the loan in number of payments. LIFE is in the units specified by the INTERVAL= option.

- PAYMENT, a numeric variable containing the periodic payment amount

- RATE, a numeric variable containing the nominal interest rate

- TOTAL, a numeric variable containing the total payments over the life of the loan

The OUTSUM= data set contains one observation.

Printed Output

The output from the MORTGAGE procedure consists of two parts: a loan summary table and an amortization schedule.

The loan summary table shows the periodic payment, principal amount, total payment and interest, the nominal annual and effective interest rate, payment and compounding interval, and the length of the loan in the time units specified. The computed parameter is also shown in this summary table.

The remainder of the output from PROC MORTGAGE is the amortization schedule, which includes the following for each payment period (or for each year if the YEARLY option is specified): the year and period within the year; the principal balance at the beginning of the period; the total payment, interest payment, and principal repayment for the period; and the principal balance at the end of the period.

Examples

Example 12.1.   Calculating Monthly Payment for a Mortgage

This example shows an analysis of a 15-year fixed-rate mortgage loan. The amount borrowed is $74,600, and the interest rate is 8.75%. The loan started in September 1984, and you want to compute the loan payment and see the amortization schedule for the first three years. In addition, you want to produce an output data set containing the schedule information.

Note that, because the payment period is monthly, you do not need to specify the INTERVAL= option since the default value for INTERVAL= is MONTH. To specify the length of the loan, convert the 15 years into 180 months and specify either MONTHS=180 or LIFE=180.

The amortization summary and schedule produced by the MORTGAGE procedure are shown in Output 12.1.1. The PRINT procedure lists the first five observations of the output SAS data set, SCHEDULE, as shown in Output 12.1.2.

```
title 'Calculating the payment for a fixed-rate mortgage';
proc mortgage amount=74600 rate=.0875 life=180
     nyears=3 out=schedule firstpayment=1984:9;
run;

title2 'Partial Listing of PROC MORTGAGE OUT= Data Set';
proc print data=schedule(obs=6);
run;
```

Output 12.1.1. PROC MORTGAGE Output

```
              Calculating the payment for a fixed-rate mortgage

                          MORTGAGE Procedure

                        L O A N   S U M M A R Y


   Payment:              745.59      Principal Amount:      74600.00

   Total Interest:     59605.58      Nominal Rate:            8.750%
   Total Payment:     134205.58      Effective Rate:          9.110%

   Pay Interval:        MONTHLY      Compound Interval:      MONTHLY
   Number of Payments:      180


   First Payment:       SEP1984      Last Payment:          AUG1999

   Note: The computed quantity is PAYMENT.
```

```
              Calculating the payment for a fixed-rate mortgage

                          MORTGAGE Procedure

                        Loan Repayment Schedule
```

YEAR	MONTH	BEGINNING OUTSTANDING	PAYMENT	INTEREST PAYMENT	PRINCIPAL REPAYMENT	ENDING OUTSTANDING
1984	SEP	74600.00	745.59	543.96	201.63	74398.37
1984	OCT	74398.37	745.59	542.49	203.10	74195.27
1984	NOV	74195.27	745.59	541.01	204.58	73990.69
1984	DEC	73990.69	745.59	539.52	206.07	73784.62
1984	***	74600.00	2982.36	2166.98	815.38	73784.62
1985	JAN	73784.62	745.59	538.01	207.58	73577.04
1985	FEB	73577.04	745.59	536.50	209.09	73367.95
1985	MAR	73367.95	745.59	534.97	210.62	73157.33
1985	APR	73157.33	745.59	533.44	212.15	72945.18
1985	MAY	72945.18	745.59	531.89	213.70	72731.48
1985	JUN	72731.48	745.59	530.33	215.26	72516.22
1985	JUL	72516.22	745.59	528.76	216.83	72299.39
1985	AUG	72299.39	745.59	527.18	218.41	72080.98
1985	SEP	72080.98	745.59	525.59	220.00	71860.98
1985	OCT	71860.98	745.59	523.99	221.60	71639.38
1985	NOV	71639.38	745.59	522.37	223.22	71416.16
1985	DEC	71416.16	745.59	520.74	224.85	71191.31
1985	***	73784.62	8947.08	6353.77	2593.31	71191.31
1986	JAN	71191.31	745.59	519.10	226.49	70964.82
1986	FEB	70964.82	745.59	517.45	228.14	70736.68
1986	MAR	70736.68	745.59	515.79	229.80	70506.88
1986	APR	70506.88	745.59	514.11	231.48	70275.40
1986	MAY	70275.40	745.59	512.42	233.17	70042.23
1986	JUN	70042.23	745.59	510.72	234.87	69807.36
1986	JUL	69807.36	745.59	509.01	236.58	69570.78
1986	AUG	69570.78	745.59	507.29	238.30	69332.48
1986	SEP	69332.48	745.59	505.55	240.04	69092.44

Example 12.1. Calculating Monthly Payment for a Mortgage □ □ □ 695

Output 12.1.1. (Continued)

```
           Calculating the payment for a fixed-rate mortgage

                        MORTGAGE Procedure

                     Loan Repayment Schedule

                 BEGINNING              INTEREST   PRINCIPAL      ENDING
YEAR   MONTH    OUTSTANDING   PAYMENT    PAYMENT   REPAYMENT   OUTSTANDING

1986    OCT       69092.44    745.59     503.80     241.79      68850.65
1986    NOV       68850.65    745.59     502.04     243.55      68607.10
1986    DEC       68607.10    745.59     500.26     245.33      68361.77

1986    ***       71191.31   8947.08    6117.54    2829.54      68361.77

1987    JAN       68361.77    745.59     498.47     247.12      68114.65
1987    FEB       68114.65    745.59     496.67     248.92      67865.73
1987    MAR       67865.73    745.59     494.85     250.74      67614.99
1987    APR       67614.99    745.59     493.03     252.56      67362.43
1987    MAY       67362.43    745.59     491.18     254.41      67108.02
1987    JUN       67108.02    745.59     489.33     256.26      66851.76
1987    JUL       66851.76    745.59     487.46     258.13      66593.63
1987    AUG       66593.63    745.59     485.58     260.01      66333.62
```

Output 12.1.2. Partial Listing of the OUT= Data Set

```
              Calculating the payment for a fixed-rate mortgage
                 Partial Listing of PROC MORTGAGE OUT= Data Set

OBS    YEAR    MONTH     BEGPRI      PAYMENT      INT      REPAY      ENDPRI

 1     1984      9      74600.00     745.59     543.96    201.63     74398.37
 2     1984     10      74398.37     745.59     542.49    203.10     74195.27
 3     1984     11      74195.27     745.59     541.01    204.58     73990.69
 4     1984     12      73990.69     745.59     539.52    206.07     73784.62
 5     1985      1      73784.62     745.59     538.01    207.58     73577.04
 6     1985      2      73577.04     745.59     536.50    209.09     73367.95
```

Example 12.2. Quarterly versus Continuous Compounding

Suppose you are given a choice of two loans. The first is for a nominal annual rate of 15.0% compounded and paid quarterly. The other is for a nominal annual rate of 14.75%, but compounded continuously and paid quarterly. Assume the loan is for $100,000 over a five-year period. Which is more advantageous in terms of total interest paid?

In this example, the NYEARS=0 option is used to suppress printing of the amortization schedule. The two loan summary tables are shown in Output 12.2.1.

Note that, despite the larger nominal rate, the loan that is compounded and paid quarterly has a lower total interest than the continuously compounded one. This is consistent with the effective interest rates computed for the two loans. In fact, the effective interest rate is a means of comparing loans with different payment or compounding frequencies.

The LOAN procedure is much better for performing this kind of comparison. See Chapter 10 for details.

```
proc mortgage nyears=0 amount=100000 rate=.15 life=20
    interval=quarter;
run;

proc mortgage nyears=0 amount=100000 rate=.1475 life=20
    interval=quarter compound=continuous;
run;
```

Output 12.2.1. Comparing Quarterly and Continuous Compounding

```
                          MORTGAGE Procedure

                     L O A N   S U M M A R Y


Payment:              7196.21      Principal Amount:     100000.00

Total Interest:      43924.18      Nominal Rate:           15.000%
Total Payment:      143924.18      Effective Rate:         15.865%

Pay Interval:        QUARTERLY      Compound Interval:    QUARTERLY
Number of Payments:        20


Note: The computed quantity is PAYMENT.
```

```
                          MORTGAGE Procedure

                     L O A N   S U M M A R Y


Payment:              7200.29      Principal Amount:     100000.00

Total Interest:      44005.76      Nominal Rate:           14.750%
Total Payment:      144005.76      Effective Rate:         15.893%

Pay Interval:        QUARTERLY      Compound Interval:    CONTINUOUS
Number of Payments:        20


Note: The computed quantity is PAYMENT.
```

Reference

Muksian, R. (1984), *Financial Mathematics Handbook*, Englewood Cliffs, New Jersey: Prentice-Hall.

Chapter 13
The PDLREG Procedure

Chapter Table of Contents

Chapter 13
The PDLREG Procedure

Overview

The PDLREG procedure estimates regression models for time series data in which the effects of some of the regressor variables are distributed across time. The distributed lag model assumes that the effect of an input variable X on an output Y is distributed over time. If you change the value of X at time t, Y will experience some immediate effect at time t, and it will also experience a delayed effect at times $t + 1$, $t + 2$, and so on up to time $t + p$ for some limit p.

The regression model supported by PROC PDLREG can include any number of regressors with distribution lags and any number of covariates. (Simple regressors without lag distributions are called covariates.) For example, the two-regressor model with a distributed lag effect for one regressor is written

$$y_t = \alpha + \sum_{i=0}^{p} \beta_i \, x_{t-i} + \gamma z_t + u_t$$

Here, x_t is the regressor with a distributed lag effect, z_t is a simple covariate, and u_t is an error term.

The distribution of the lagged effects is modeled by Almon lag polynomials. The coefficients b_i of the lagged values of the regressor are assumed to lie on a polynomial curve. That is,

$$b_i = \alpha_0^* + \sum_{j=1}^{d} \alpha_j^* i^j$$

where $d \, (\leq p)$ is the degree of the polynomial. For the numerically efficient estimation, the PDLREG procedure uses *orthogonal polynomials*. The preceding equation can be transformed into orthogonal polynomials.

$$b_i = \alpha_0 + \sum_{j=1}^{d} \alpha_j \, f_j(i)$$

where $f_j(i)$ is a polynomial of degree j in the lag length i, and α_j is a coefficient estimated from the data.

The PDLREG procedure supports endpoint restrictions for the polynomial. That is, you can constrain the estimated polynomial lag distribution curve so that $b_{-1} = 0$ or

$b_{p+1} = 0$, or both. You can also impose linear restrictions on the parameter estimates for the covariates.

You can specify a minimum degree and a maximum degree for the lag distribution polynomial, and the procedure fits polynomials for all degrees in the specified range. (However, if distributed lags are specified for more that one regressor, you can specify a range of degrees for only one of them.)

The PDLREG procedure can also test for autocorrelated residuals and perform auto-correlated error correction using the autoregressive error model. You can specify any order autoregressive error model and can specify several different estimation methods for the autoregressive model, including exact maximum likelihood.

The PDLREG procedure computes generalized Durbin-Watson statistics to test for autocorrelated residuals. For models with lagged dependent variables, the procedure can produce Durbin h and Durbin t statistics. You can request significance level p-values for the Durbin-Watson, Durbin h, and Durbin t statistics. See Chapter 4, "The AUTOREG Procedure," for details about these statistics.

The PDLREG procedure assumes that the input observations form a time series. Thus, the PDLREG procedure should be used only for ordered and equally spaced time series data.

Getting Started

Use the MODEL statement to specify the regression model. The PDLREG procedure's MODEL statement is written like MODEL statements in other SAS regression procedures, except that a regressor can be followed by a lag distribution specification enclosed in parentheses.

For example, the following MODEL statement regresses Y on X and Z and specifies a distributed lag for X:

```
model y = x(4,2) z;
```

The notation X(4,2) specifies that the model includes X and 4 lags of X, with the coefficients of X and its lags constrained to follow a second-degree (quadratic) polynomial. Thus, the regression model specified by this MODEL statement is

$$y_t = a + b_0 x_t + b_1 x_{t-1} + b_2 x_{t-2} + b_3 x_{t-3} + b_4 x_{t-4} + c z_t + u_t$$

$$b_i = \alpha_0 + \alpha_1 f_1(i) + \alpha_2 f_2(i)$$

where $f_1(i)$ is a polynomial of degree 1 in i and $f_2(i)$ is a polynomial of degree 2 in i.

Lag distribution specifications are enclosed in parentheses and follow the name of the regressor variable. The general form of the lag distribution specification is

$$regressor\text{-}name\ (\ length,\ degree,\ minimum\text{-}degree,\ end\text{-}constraint\ )$$

where:

length	is the length of the lag distribution; that is, the number of lags of the regressor to use
degree	is the degree of the distribution polynomial
minimum-degree	is an optional minimum degree for the distribution polynomial
end-constraint	is an optional endpoint restriction specification, which can have the values FIRST, LAST, or BOTH

If the *minimum-degree* option is specified, the PDLREG procedure estimates models for all degrees between *minimum-degree* and *degree*.

Introductory Example

The following statements generate simulated data for variables Y and X. Y depends on the first three lags of X, with coefficients .25, .5, and .25. Thus, the effect of changes of X on Y takes effect 25% after one period, 75% after two periods, and 100% after three periods.

```
data test;
   xl1 = 0; xl2 = 0; xl3 = 0;
   do t = -3 to 100;
      x = ranuni(1234);
      y = 10 + .25 * xl1 + .5 * xl2 + .25 * xl3 + .1 * rannor(1234);
      if t > 0 then output;
      xl3 = xl2; xl2 = xl1; xl1 = x;
      end;
run;
```

The following statements use the PDLREG procedure to regress Y on a distributed lag of X. The length of the lag distribution is 4, and the degree of the distribution polynomial is specified as 3.

```
proc pdlreg data=test;
   model y = x( 4, 3 );
run;
```

The PDLREG procedure first prints a table of statistics for the residuals of the model, as shown in Figure 13.1. See Chapter 4 for an explanation of these statistics.

```
                         PDLREG Procedure

Dependent Variable = Y


                 Ordinary Least Squares Estimates

            SSE            1.158126   DFE                91
            MSE            0.012727   Root MSE     0.112813
            SBC            -128.826   AIC          -141.648
            Reg Rsq          0.7531   Total Rsq      0.7531
            Durbin-Watson    2.0801
```

Figure 13.1. Residual Statistics

The PDLREG procedure next prints a table of parameter estimates, standard errors, and *t*-tests, as shown in Figure 13.2.

Variable	DF	B Value	Std Error	t Ratio	Approx Prob
Intercept	1	9.91006671	0.04911	201.785	0.0001
X**0	1	0.52414843	0.04340	12.076	0.0001
X**1	1	0.00213572	0.04017	0.053	0.9577
X**2	1	-0.45867857	0.03930	-11.672	0.0001
X**3	1	0.04251484	0.03654	1.164	0.2476

Figure 13.2.   Parameter Estimates

The preceding table shows the model intercept and the estimated parameters of the lag distribution polynomial. The parameter labeled X**0 is the constant term, α_0, of the distribution polynomial. X**1 is the linear coefficient, α_1, X**2 is the quadratic coefficient, α_2, and X**3 is the cubic coefficient, α_3.

The parameter estimates for the distribution polynomial are not of interest in themselves. Since the PDLREG procedure does not print the orthogonal polynomial basis that it constructs to represent the distribution polynomial, these coefficient values cannot be interpreted.

However, because these estimates are for an orthogonal basis, you can use these results to test the degree of the polynomial. For example, this table shows that the X**3 estimate is not significant; the *p*-value for its *t* ratio is .2476, while the X**2 estimate is highly significant ($p < .0001$). This indicates that a second-degree polynomial may be more appropriate for this data.

The PDLREG procedure next prints the lag distribution coefficients, as shown in Figure 13.3.

Variable	Parameter Value	Std Error	t Ratio	Approx Prob
X(0)	-0.02556	0.039	-0.65	0.5180
X(1)	0.38321	0.036	10.66	0.0001
X(2)	0.47958	0.029	16.56	0.0001
X(3)	0.33078	0.035	9.56	0.0001
X(4)	0.00403	0.039	0.10	0.9173

Figure 13.3.   Coefficients of Estimated Lag Distribution

These are the coefficients of the lagged values of X in the regression model. These coefficients lie on the polynomial curve defined by the parameters shown in Figure 13.2. Note that the estimated values for X(1), X(2), and X(3) are highly significant, while X(0) and X(4) are not significantly different from 0. These estimates are reasonably close to the true values used to generate the simulated data.

The last part of the PDLREG procedure output is a graphical display of the lag distribution coefficients, shown in Figure 13.4. This graph plots the estimated lag distribution polynomial reported in Figure 13.2. The roughly quadratic shape of this plot is another indication that a third-degree distribution curve is not needed for this data.

```
                              Estimate of Lag Distribution
          Variable     -0.026                                      0.4796

          X(0)       |*|                                         |
          X(1)       | |*****************************            |
          X(2)       | |***************************************  |
          X(3)       | |**************************               |
          X(4)       | |                                         |
```

Figure 13.4.   Graph of Lag Distribution Coefficients

Syntax

The following statements can be used with the PDLREG procedure:

PROC PDLREG *option* ;
    BY *variables* ;
    MODEL *dependents* = *effects* / *options* ;
    OUTPUT OUT= *SAS-data-set keyword* = *variables* ;
    RESTRICT *restrictions* ;

Functional Summary

The statements and options used with the PDLREG procedure are summarized in the following table:

Description	Statement	Option
Data Set Options		
specify the input data set	PDLREG	DATA=
write predicted values to an output data set	OUTPUT	OUT=
BY-Group Processing		
specify BY-group processing	BY	
Printing Control Options		
request all print options	MODEL	ALL
print correlations of the estimates	MODEL	CORRB
print covariances of the estimates	MODEL	COVB
print DW statistics up to order j	MODEL	DW=j
print the marginal probability of DW statistics	MODEL	DWPROB

Description	Statement	Option
print inverse of the crossproducts matrix	MODEL	I
print details at each iteration step	MODEL	ITPRINT
print Durbin *t* statistic	MODEL	LAGDEP
print Durbin *h* statistic	MODEL	LAGDEP=
suppress printed output	MODEL	NOPRINT
print partial autocorrelations	MODEL	PARTIAL
print standardized parameter estimates	MODEL	STB
print crossproducts matrix	MODEL	XPX

Model Estimation Options

specify order of autoregressive process	MODEL	NLAG=
suppress intercept parameter	MODEL	NOINT
specify convergence criterion	MODEL	CONVERGE=
specify maximum number of iterations	MODEL	MAXITER=
specify estimation method	MODEL	METHOD=

Output Control Options

specify confidence limit size	OUTPUT	ALPHACLI=
specify confidence limit size for structural predicted values	OUTPUT	ALPHACLM=
output transformed intercept variable	OUTPUT	CONSTANT=
output lower confidence limit for predicted values	OUTPUT	LCL=
output lower confidence limit for structural predicted values	OUTPUT	LCLM=
output predicted values	OUTPUT	P=
output predicted values of the structural part	OUTPUT	PM=
output residuals from the predicted values	OUTPUT	R=
output residuals from the structural predicted values	OUTPUT	RM=
output transformed variables	OUTPUT	TRANSFORM=
output upper confidence limit for the predicted values	OUTPUT	UCL=
output upper confidence limit for the structural predicted values	OUTPUT	UCLM=

PROC PDLREG Statement

> **PROC PDLREG** *option* ;

The PROC PDLREG statement has the following option:

DATA= *SAS-data-set*
> specifies the name of the SAS data set containing the input data. If you do not specify the DATA= option, the most recently created SAS data set is used.

In addition, you can place any of the following MODEL statement options in the PROC PDLREG statement, which is equivalent to specifying the option for every MODEL statement: ALL, CONVERGE=, CORRB, COVB, DW=, DWPROB, IT-PRINT, MAXITER=, METHOD=, NOINT, NOPRINT, and PARTIAL.

BY Statement

> **BY** *variables* ;

A BY statement can be used with PROC PDLREG to obtain separate analyses on observations in groups defined by the BY variables.

MODEL Statement

> **MODEL** *dependent* = *effects* / *options* ;

The MODEL statement specifies the regression model. The keyword MODEL is followed by the dependent variable name, an equal sign, and a list of independent effects. Only one MODEL statement is allowed.

Every variable in the model must be a numeric variable in the input data set. Specify an independent effect with a variable name optionally followed by a polynomial lag distribution specification.

Specifying Independent Effects

The general form of an effect is

> *variable* (*length, degree, minimum-degree, constraint*)

The term in parentheses following the variable name specifies a polynomial distributed lag (PDL) for the variable. The PDL specification is as follows:

length
> specifies the number of lags of the variable to include in the lag distribution.

degree
> specifies the maximum degree of the distribution polynomial. If not specified, the degree defaults to the lag length.

minimum-degree
> specifies the minimum degree of the polynomial. By default *minimum-degree* is the same as *degree*.

constraint
> specifies endpoint restrictions on the polynomial. The value of *constraint* can be FIRST, LAST, or BOTH. If a value is not

specified, there are no endpoint restrictions.

If you do not specify the *degree* or *minimum-degree* parameter, but you do specify endpoint restrictions, you must use commas to show which parameter, *degree* or *minimum-degree*, is left out.

MODEL Statement Options

The following options can appear in the MODEL statement after a slash (/):

ALL

prints all the matrices computed during the analysis of the model.

CORRB

prints the matrix of estimated correlations between the parameter estimates.

COVB

prints the matrix of estimated covariances between the parameter estimates.

DW= *j*

prints the generalized Durbin-Watson statistics up to the order of *j*. The default is DW=1. When you specify the LAGDEP or LAGDEP=*name* option, the Durbin-Watson statistic is not printed unless you specify the DW= option.

DWPROB

prints the marginal probability of the Durbin-Watson statistic.

CONVERGE= *value*

sets the convergence criterion. If the maximum absolute value of the change in the autoregressive parameter estimates between iterations is less than this amount, then convergence is assumed. The default is CONVERGE=.001.

I

prints $(X'X)^{-1}$, the inverse of the crossproducts matrix for the model; or, if restrictions are specified, prints $(X'X)^{-1}$ adjusted for the restrictions.

ITPRINT

prints information on each iteration.

LAGDEP
LAGDV

prints the *t* statistic for testing residual autocorrelation when regressors contain lagged dependent variables.

LAGDEP= *name*
LAGDV= *name*

prints the Durbin *h* statistic for testing the presence of first-order autocorrelation when regressors contain the lagged dependent variable whose name is specified as LAGDEP=*name*. When the *h* statistic cannot be computed, the asymptotically equivalent *t* statistic is given.

MAXITER= *number*

sets the maximum number of iterations allowed. The default is MAXITER=50.

METHOD= *value*

specifies the type of estimates for the autoregressive component. The values of the METHOD= option are as follows:

METHOD=ML   specifies the maximum likelihood method

METHOD=ULS   specifies unconditional least squares

METHOD=YW   specifies the Yule-Walker method

METHOD=ITYW   specifies iterative Yule-Walker estimates

The default is METHOD=ML if you specified the LAGDEP or LAGDEP= option; otherwise, METHOD=YW is the default.

NLAG= *m*
NLAG= (*number-list*)

specifies the order of the autoregressive process or the subset of autoregressive lags to be fit. If you do not specify the NLAG= option, PROC PDLREG does not fit an autoregressive model.

NOINT

suppresses the intercept parameter from the model.

NOPRINT

suppresses the printed output.

PARTIAL

prints partial autocorrelations if the NLAG= option is specified.

STB

prints standardized parameter estimates. Sometimes known as a standard partial regression coefficient, a *standardized parameter estimate* is a parameter estimate multiplied by the standard deviation of the associated regressor and divided by the standard deviation of the regressed variable.

XPX

prints the crossproducts matrix, $\mathbf{X}'\mathbf{X}$, used for the model. $\mathbf{X}$ refers to the transformed matrix of regressors for the regression.

OUTPUT Statement

OUTPUT OUT= *SAS-data-set keyword= option* ... ;

The OUTPUT statement creates an output SAS data set with variables as specified by the following keyword options. The associated computations for these options are described in the section "Predicted Values" in Chapter 4.

ALPHACLI= *number*

sets the confidence limit size for the estimates of future values of the current realization of the response time series to *number*, where *number* is less than one and greater than zero. The resulting confidence interval has 1-*number* confidence. The default value for *number* is .05, corresponding to a 95% confidence interval.

ALPHACLM= *number*

sets the confidence limit size for the estimates of the structural or regression part of the model to *number*, where *number* is less than one and greater than zero. The resulting confidence interval has 1-*number* confidence. The default value for *number* is .05, corresponding to a 95% confidence interval.

OUT= *SAS-data-set*

names the output data.

The following specifications are of the form *KEYWORD=names*, where *KEYWORD=* specifies the statistic to include in the output data set and *names* gives names to the variables that contain the statistics.

CONSTANT= *variable*

writes the transformed intercept to the output data set.

LCL= *name*

requests that the lower confidence limit for the predicted value (specified in the PREDICTED= option) be added to the output data set under the name given.

LCLM= *name*

requests that the lower confidence limit for the structural predicted value (specified in the PREDICTEDM= option) be added to the output data set under the name given.

PREDICTED= *name*
P= *name*

stores the predicted values in the output data set under the name given.

PREDICTEDM= *name*
PM= *name*

stores the structural predicted values in the output data set under the name given. These values are formed from only the structural part of the model.

RESIDUAL= *name*
R= *name*

stores the residuals from the predicted values based on both the structural and time series parts of the model in the output data set under the name given.

RESIDUALM= *name*
RM= *name*

requests that the residuals from the structural prediction be given.

TRANSFORM= *variables*

requests that the specified variables from the input data set be transformed by the autoregressive model and put in the output data set. If you need to reproduce the data suitable for reestimation, you must also transform an intercept variable. To do this, transform a variable that only takes the value 1 or use the CONSTANT= option.

UCL= *name*

stores the upper confidence limit for the predicted value (specified in the PREDICTED= option) in the output data set under the name given.

UCLM= *name*

stores the upper confidence limit for the structural predicted value (specified in the PREDICTEDM= option) in the output data set under the name given.

For example, the SAS statements

```
proc pdlreg data=a;
   model y=x1 x2;
   output out=b p=yhat r=resid;
```

create an output data set named B. In addition to the input data set variables, the data set B contains the variable YHAT, whose values are predicted values of the dependent variable Y, and RESID, whose values are the residual values of Y.

RESTRICT Statement

RESTRICT *equation* , ... , *equation* ;

The RESTRICT statement places restrictions on the parameter estimates for covariates in the preceding MODEL statement. A parameter produced by a distributed lag cannot be restricted with the RESTRICT statement.

Each restriction is written as a linear equation. If you specify more than one restriction in a RESTRICT statement, the restrictions are separated by commas.

You can refer to parameters by the name of the corresponding regressor variable. Each name used in the equation must be a regressor in the preceding MODEL statement. Use the keyword INTERCEPT to refer to the intercept parameter in the model.

RESTRICT statements can be given labels. You can use labels to distinguish results for different restrictions in the printed output. Labels are specified as follows:

label : **RESTRICT ... ;**

The following is an example of the use of the RESTRICT statement, in which the coefficients of the regressors X1 and X2 are required to sum to 1.

```
proc pdlreg data=a;
   model y = x1 x2;
   restrict x1 + x2 = 1;
run;
```

Parameter names can be multiplied by constants. When no equal sign appears, the linear combination is set equal to 0. Note that the parameters associated with the variables are restricted, not the variables themselves. Here are some examples of valid RESTRICT statements:

```
restrict x1 + x2 = 1;
restrict x1 + x2 - 1;
restrict 2 * x1 = x2 + x3 , intercept + x4 = 0;
restrict x1 = x2 = x3 = 1;
restrict 2 * x1 - x2;
```

Restricted parameter estimates are computed by introducing a Lagrangian parameter

λ for each restriction (Pringle and Raynor 1971). The estimates of these Lagrangian parameters are printed in the parameter estimates table. If a restriction cannot be applied, its parameter value and degrees of freedom are listed as 0.

The Lagrangian parameter, λ, measures the sensitivity of the SSE to the restriction. If the restriction is changed by a small amount ϵ, the SSE is changed by $2\lambda\epsilon$.

The t ratio tests the significance of the restrictions. If λ is zero, the restricted estimates are the same as the unrestricted ones.

You can specify any number of restrictions on a RESTRICT statement, and you can use any number of RESTRICT statements. The estimates are computed subject to all restrictions specified. However, restrictions should be consistent and not redundant.

Details

Missing Values

The PDLREG procedure skips any observations at the beginning of the data set that have missing values. The procedure uses all observations with nonmissing values for all the independent and dependent variables such that the lag distribution has sufficient nonmissing lagged independent variables.

Polynomial Distributed Lag Estimation

The simple finite distributed lag model is expressed in the form

$$y_t = \alpha + \sum_{i=0}^{p} \beta_i x_{t-i} + \epsilon_t$$

When the lag length p is long, a severe multicollinearity can occur. Use the Almon or *polynomial distributed lag* model to avoid this problem, since the relatively low degree $d \ (\leq p)$ polynomials can capture the true lag distribution. The lag coefficient can be written in the Almon polynomial lag

$$\beta_i = \alpha_0^* + \sum_{j=1}^{d} \alpha_j^* i^j$$

Emerson (1968) proposed an efficient method of constructing orthogonal polynomials from the preceding polynomial equation as

$$\beta_i = \alpha_0 + \sum_{j=1}^{d} \alpha_j f_j(i)$$

where $f_j(i)$ is a polynomial of degree j in the lag length i.

The polynomials $f_j(i)$ are chosen so that they are orthogonal:

$$\sum_{i=1}^{n} w_i f_j(i) f_k(i) = \begin{cases} 1 & \text{if } j = k \\ 0 & \text{if } j \neq k \end{cases}$$

where w_i is the weighting factor, and $n = p + 1$. PROC PDLREG uses the equal weights ($w_i = 1$) for all i. To construct the orthogonal polynomials, the following recursive relation is used:

$$f_j(i) = (A_j i + B_j) f_{j-1}(i) - C_j f_{j-2}(i) \qquad j = 1, \dots, d$$

The constants A_j, B_j, and C_j are determined as follows:

$$\begin{aligned} \mathbf{A}_j = \Bigg\{ &\sum_{i=1}^{n} w_i i^2 f_{j-1}^2(i) - \left(\sum_{i=1}^{n} w_i f_{j-1}^2(i) \right)^2 \\ &- \left(\sum_{i=1}^{n} w_i i\, f_{j-1}(i) f_{j-2}(i) \right)^2 \Bigg\}^{-1/2} \end{aligned}$$

$$B_j = -A_j \sum_{i=1}^{n} w_i i\, f_{j-1}^2(i)$$

$$C_j = A_j \sum_{i=1}^{n} w_i i\, f_{j-1}(i) f_{j-2}(i)$$

where $f_{-1}(i) = 0$ and $f_0(i) = \left(\sum_{i=1}^{n} w_i \right)^{-1/2}$.

PROC PDLREG estimates the orthogonal polynomial coefficients, $\alpha_0, \dots, \alpha_d$, to compute the coefficient estimate of each independent variable (X) with distributed lags. For example, if an independent variable is specified as X(9,3), a third-degree polynomial is used to specify the distributed lag coefficients. The third-degree polynomial is fit as a constant term, a linear term, a quadratic term, and a cubic term. The four terms are constructed to be orthogonal. In the output produced by the PDLREG procedure for this case, parameter estimates with names X**0, X**1, X**2, and X**3 correspond to $\hat{\alpha}_0, \hat{\alpha}_1, \hat{\alpha}_2$, and $\hat{\alpha}_3$, respectively. A test using the t statistic and the p-value (PROB > $|t|$) associated with X**3 can determine whether a second-degree polynomial rather than a third-degree polynomial is appropriate. The estimates of the ten lag coefficients associated with the specification X(9,3) are labeled X(0), X(1), X(2), X(3), X(4), X(5), X(6), X(7), X(8), and X(9).

Autoregressive Error Model Estimation

The PDLREG procedure uses the same autoregressive error model estimation methods as the AUTOREG procedure. These two procedures share the same computational resources for computing estimates. See Chapter 4 for details about estimation methods for autoregressive error models.

OUT= Data Set

The OUT= data set produced by the PDLREG procedure's OUTPUT statement is similar in form to the OUT= data set produced by the AUTOREG procedure. See Chapter 4 for details on the OUT= data set.

Printed Output

The PDLREG procedure prints the following items:

1. the name of the dependent variable

2. the ordinary least squares (OLS) estimates

3. the estimates of autocorrelations and of the autocovariance, and if line size permits, a graph of the autocorrelation at each lag. The autocorrelation for lag 0 is 1. These items are printed if you specify the NLAG= option.

4. the partial autocorrelations if the PARTIAL and NLAG= options are specified. The first partial autocorrelation is the autocorrelation for lag 1.

5. the preliminary mean square error, which results from solving the Yule-Walker equations if you specify the NLAG= option

6. the estimates of the autoregressive parameters, their standard errors, and the ratios of estimates to standard errors (t) if you specify the NLAG= option

7. the statistics of fit for the final model if you specify the NLAG= option. These include the error sum of squares (SSE), the degrees of freedom for error (DFE), the mean square error (MSE), the root mean square error (Root MSE), the Schwarz information criterion (SBC), the Akaike's information criterion (AIC), the regression R^2 (Reg Rsq), and the total R^2 (Total Rsq). See Chapter 4 for details of the regression R^2 and the total R^2.

8. the parameter estimates for the structural model (B), a standard error estimate, the ratio of estimate to standard error (t), and an approximation to the significance probability for the parameter being 0 (PROB > $|t|$)

9. a plot of the lag distribution (estimate of lag distribution)

10. the covariance matrix of the parameter estimates if the COVB option is specified

Examples

Example 13.1.   Industrial Conference Board Data

In the following example, a second-degree Almon polynomial lag model is fit to a model with a five-period lag, and dummy variables are used for quarter effects. The PDL model is estimated using capital appropriations data series for the period 1952 to 1967. The estimation model is written

$$CE_t = a_0 + b_1 Q1_t + b_2 Q2_t + b_3 Q3_t \\ + c_0 CA_t + c_1 CA_{t-1} + \ldots + c_5 CA_{t-5}$$

where CE represents capital expenditures and CA represents capital appropriations.

```
title 'National Industrial Conference Board Data';
title2 'Quarterly Series - 1952Q1 to 1967Q4';

data a;
   input ce ca @@;
   qtr = mod( _n_-1, 4 ) + 1;
   q1  = qtr=1;
   q2  = qtr=2;
   q3  = qtr=3;
cards;
   2072 1660 2077 1926 2078 2181 2043 1897 2062 1695
   2067 1705 1964 1731 1981 2151 1914 2556 1991 3152
   2129 3763 2309 3903 2614 3912 2896 3571 3058 3199
   3309 3262 3446 3476 3466 2993 3435 2262 3183 2011
   2697 1511 2338 1631 2140 1990 2012 1993 2071 2520
   2192 2804 2240 2919 2421 3024 2639 2725 2733 2321
   2721 2131 2640 2552 2513 2234 2448 2282 2429 2533
   2516 2517 2534 2772 2494 2380 2596 2568 2572 2944
   2601 2629 2648 3133 2840 3449 2937 3764 3136 3983
   3299 4381 3514 4786 3815 4094 4093 4870 4262 5344
   4531 5433 4825 5911 5160 6109 5319 6542 5574 5785
   5749 5707 5715 5412 5637 5465 5383 5550 5467 5465
;

proc pdlreg data=a;
   model ce = q1 q2 q3 ca(5,2) / dwprob;
run;
```

The printed output produced by the PDLREG procedure is shown in Output 13.1.1. The small Durbin-Watson test indicates autoregressive errors.

Output 13.1.1. Printed Output Produced by PROC PDLREG

```
                National Industrial Conference Board Data
                    Quarterly Series - 1952Q1 to 1967Q4

                          PDLREG Procedure

Dependent Variable = CE


                      Ordinary Least Squares Estimates

            SSE             1205186    DFE                 48
            MSE            25108.05    Root MSE      158.4552
            SBC           733.8492     AIC           719.7979
            Reg Rsq         0.9834     Total Rsq       0.9834
            Durbin-Watson   0.6157     PROB<DW         0.0001


    Variable      DF        B Value    Std Error    t Ratio  Approx Prob

    Intercept      1     210.010941       73.252      2.867       0.0061
    Q1             1     -10.551513       61.063     -0.173       0.8635
    Q2             1     -20.988685       59.939     -0.350       0.7277
    Q3             1     -30.433738       59.900     -0.508       0.6137
    CA**0          1       0.375986     0.007318     51.379       0.0001
    CA**1          1       0.129650        0.025      5.156       0.0001
    CA**2          1    0.0246588297        0.059      0.416       0.6794


                  Parameter     Std       t      Approx
    Variable          Value    Error   Ratio       Prob

    CA(0)           0.08947    0.036    2.49     0.0165
    CA(1)           0.10432    0.011    9.56     0.0001
    CA(2)           0.12724    0.025    5.00     0.0001
    CA(3)           0.15823    0.025    6.24     0.0001
    CA(4)           0.19729    0.011   17.69     0.0001
    CA(5)           0.24443    0.037    6.60     0.0001
```

```
                National Industrial Conference Board Data
                    Quarterly Series - 1952Q1 to 1967Q4

                          PDLREG Procedure

                      Estimate of Lag Distribution
    Variable      0                                         0.2444

    CA(0)    |***************                              |
    CA(1)    |*****************                            |
    CA(2)    |********************                         |
    CA(3)    |**************************                   |
    CA(4)    |*******************************              |
    CA(5)    |*****************************************    |
```

The following statements use the REG procedure to fit the same polynomial distributed lag model. A DATA step computes lagged values of the regressor X, and RESTRICT statements are used to impose the polynomial lag distribution. Refer to Judge, Griffiths, Hill, Lutkepohl, and Lee (1985, pp 357–359) for the restricted least squares estimation of the Almon distributed lag model.

Example 13.1. Industrial Conference Board Data   □ □ □   715

```
data b;
   set a;
   ca_1 = lag( ca );
   ca_2 = lag2( ca );
   ca_3 = lag3( ca );
   ca_4 = lag4( ca );
   ca_5 = lag5( ca );
run;

proc reg data=b;
   model  ce = q1 q2 q3 ca ca_1 ca_2 ca_3 ca_4 ca_5;
   restrict  - ca + 5*ca_1 - 10*ca_2 + 10*ca_3 - 5*ca_4 +   ca_5;
   restrict    ca - 3*ca_1 +  2*ca_2 +  2*ca_3 - 3*ca_4 +   ca_5;
   restrict  -5*ca + 7*ca_1 +  4*ca_2 -  4*ca_3 - 7*ca_4 + 5*ca_5;
run;
```

The REG procedure output is shown in Output 13.1.2.

Output 13.1.2. Printed Output Produced by PROC REG

```
Model: MODEL1
NOTE: Restrictions have been applied to parameter estimates.
Dependent Variable: CE

                        Analysis of Variance

                          Sum of        Mean
      Source      DF      Squares       Square      F Value    Prob>F

      Model        6  71343377.342  11890562.89     473.576    0.0001
      Error       48  1205186.4038  25108.05008
      C Total     54  72548563.745

           Root MSE      158.45520     R-square      0.9834
           Dep Mean     3185.69091     Adj R-sq      0.9813
           C.V.            4.97397

                        Parameter Estimates

                   Parameter      Standard     T for H0:
      Variable  DF  Estimate         Error    Parameter=0    Prob > |T|

      INTERCEP  1   210.010941    73.25236219      2.867        0.0061
      Q1        1   -10.551513    61.06340747     -0.173        0.8635
      Q2        1   -20.988685    59.93859513     -0.350        0.7277
      Q3        1   -30.433738    59.90044939     -0.508        0.6137
      CA        1     0.089467     0.03599137      2.486        0.0165
      CA_1      1     0.104317     0.01090799      9.563        0.0001
      CA_2      1     0.127237     0.02546930      4.996        0.0001
      CA_3      1     0.158230     0.02537073      6.237        0.0001
      CA_4      1     0.197294     0.01115096     17.693        0.0001
      CA_5      1     0.244429     0.03704441      6.598        0.0001
      RESTRICT -1   623.632420 12696.603349        0.049        0.9610
      RESTRICT -1        18933 44802.588622        0.423        0.6745
      RESTRICT -1        10303 18422.143797        0.559        0.5786
```

Example 13.2. Money Demand Model

This example estimates the demand for money using the following dynamic specification:

$$m_t = a_0 + b_0 m_{t-1} + \sum_{i=0}^{5} c_i y_{t-i} + \sum_{i=0}^{2} d_i r_{t-i} + \sum_{i=0}^{3} f_i p_{t-i} + u_t$$

where

m_t = log of real money stock (M1)
y_t = log of real GNP
r_t = interest rate (commercial paper rate)
p_t = inflation rate
$c_i, d_i,$ and f_i $(i > 0)$ are coefficients for the lagged variables

The following DATA step reads the data and transforms the real money and real GNP variables using the natural logarithm. Refer to Balke and Gordon (1986) for a description of the data.

```
data a;
   input m1 gnp gdf r @@;
   m    = log( 100 * m1 / gdf );
   lagm = lag( m );
   y    = log( gnp );
   p    = log( gdf / lag( gdf ) );
   date = intnx( 'qtr', '1jan1968'd, _n_-1 );
   format date yyqc6.;
   label m    = 'Real Money Stock (M1)'
         lagm = 'Lagged Real Money Stock'
         y    = 'Real GNP'
         r    = 'Commercial Paper Rate'
         p    = 'Inflation Rate';
cards;
   ... data lines are omitted ...
;

proc print data=a(obs=5);
   var date m lagm y r p;
run;
```

Output 13.2.1 shows a partial list of the data set.

Example 13.2. Money Demand Model □ □ □ 717

Output 13.2.1. Partial List of the Data Set A

OBS	DATE	M	LAGM	Y	R	P
1	1968:1	5.44041	.	6.94333	5.58	.
2	1968:2	5.44732	5.44041	6.96226	6.08	0.011513
3	1968:3	5.45815	5.44732	6.97422	5.96	0.008246
4	1968:4	5.46492	5.45815	6.97661	5.96	0.014865
5	1969:1	5.46980	5.46492	6.98855	6.66	0.011005

The regression model is written for the PDLREG procedure with a MODEL statement. The LAGDEP= option is specified to test for the serial correlation in disturbances since regressors contain the lagged dependent variable LAGM.

```
title 'Money Demand Estimation using Distributed Lag Model';
title2 'Quarterly Data - 1968Q2 to 1983Q4';

proc pdlreg data=a;
   model m = lagm y(5,3) r(2,,,first) p(3,2) / lagdep=lagm;
run;
```

The estimated model is shown in Output 13.2.2 and Output 13.2.3.

Output 13.2.2. Parameter Estimates

```
            Money Demand Estimation using Distributed Lag Model
                    Quarterly Data - 1968Q2 to 1983Q4

                           PDLREG Procedure

Dependent Variable = M          Real Money Stock (M1)


                  Ordinary Least Squares Estimates

            SSE         0.001698    DFE              48
            MSE         0.000035    Root MSE    0.005948
            SBC         -404.602    AIC         -427.455
            Reg Rsq       0.9712    Total Rsq     0.9712
            Durbin h    -0.75332    PROB<h        0.2256


   Variable      DF      B Value    Std Error   t Ratio Approx Prob

   Intercept      1   -0.14074118     0.26248    -0.536     0.5943
   LAGM           1    0.98745650     0.04254    23.212     0.0001
   Y**0           1    0.01318355     0.00453     2.909     0.0055
   Y**1           1   -0.07037822     0.05283    -1.332     0.1891
   Y**2           1    0.12609284     0.07865     1.603     0.1154
   Y**3           1   -0.40890183     0.12648    -3.233     0.0022
   R**0           1   -0.000186163    0.00034    -0.555     0.5816
   R**1           1    0.00219982     0.00077     2.844     0.0065
   R**2           1    0.0007883663   0.00025     3.160     0.0027
   P**0           1   -0.66016172     0.11317    -5.834     0.0001
   P**1           1    0.40360645     0.23214     1.739     0.0885
   P**2           1   -1.00644499     0.22880    -4.399     0.0001


   Restriction   DF      L Value    Std Error   t Ratio Approx Prob

   R(-1)         -1   -0.01642126     0.00727    -2.257     0.0286
```

Output 13.2.3. Estimates for Lagged Variables

```
           Money Demand Estimation using Distributed Lag Model
                    Quarterly Data - 1968Q2 to 1983Q4

                           PDLREG Procedure

               Parameter      Std       t      Approx
   Variable      Value       Error    Ratio     Prob

   Y(0)         0.26862       0.091     2.95    0.0049
   Y(1)        -0.19648       0.061    -3.21    0.0024
   Y(2)        -0.16315       0.054    -3.04    0.0038
   Y(3)         0.06385       0.045     1.42    0.1632
   Y(4)         0.17973       0.059     3.06    0.0036
   Y(5)        -0.12028       0.068    -1.77    0.0827


                        Estimate of Lag Distribution
   Variable        -0.196           0                      0.2686

   Y(0)           |                 |***********************|
   Y(1)           |***************|                        |
   Y(2)           |  *************|                        |
   Y(3)           |                 |******                |
   Y(4)           |                 |****************      |
   Y(5)           |        ********|                       |


               Parameter      Std       t      Approx
   Variable      Value       Error    Ratio     Prob

   R(0)         -.001341      0.0004   -3.45    0.0012
   R(1)         -.000751      0.0002   -3.22    0.0023
   R(2)         0.001770      0.0008    2.35    0.0230
```

```
           Money Demand Estimation using Distributed Lag Model
                    Quarterly Data - 1968Q2 to 1983Q4

                           PDLREG Procedure

                        Estimate of Lag Distribution
   Variable        -0.001           0                      0.0018

   R(0)           |*****************|                      |
   R(1)           |        ********|                       |
   R(2)           |                 |**********************|


               Parameter      Std       t      Approx
   Variable      Value       Error    Ratio     Prob

   P(0)         -1.1041       0.203    -5.45    0.0001
   P(1)          0.0829       0.126     0.66    0.5128
   P(2)          0.2634       0.138     1.91    0.0624
   P(3)         -0.5626       0.208    -2.71    0.0093


                        Estimate of Lag Distribution
   Variable        -1.104               0              0.2634

   P(0)           |*******************************|      |
   P(1)           |                               |***   |
   P(2)           |                               |******|
   P(3)           |              ****************|        |
```

References

Balke, N.S. and Gordon, R.J. (1986), "Historical Data," in *The American Business Cycle*, ed. R.J. Gordon, Chicago: The University of Chicago Press.

Emerson, P.L. (1968), "Numerical Construction of Orthogonal Polynomials from a General Recurrence Formula," *Biometrics*, 24, 695–701.

Gallant, A.R. and Goebel, J.J. (1976), "Nonlinear Regression with Autoregressive Errors," *Journal of the American Statistical Association*, 71, 961–967.

Harvey, A.C. (1981), *The Econometric Analysis of Time Series*, New York: John Wiley & Sons, Inc.

Johnston, J. (1972), *Econometric Methods*, Second Edition, New York: McGraw-Hill Book Co.

Judge, G.G.; Griffiths, W.E.; Hill, R.C.; Lütkepohl, H.; and Lee, T.C. (1985), *The Theory and Practice of Econometrics*, Second Edition, New York: John Wiley & Sons, Inc.

Park, R.E. and Mitchell, B.M. (1980), "Estimating the Autocorrelated Error Model with Trended Data," *Journal of Econometrics*, 13, 185–201.

Pringle, R.M. and Raynor, A.A. (1971), *Generalized Inverse Matrices with Applications to Statistics*, New York: Hafner Publishing Company.

Chapter 14
The SIMLIN Procedure

Chapter Table of Contents

Chapter 14
The SIMLIN Procedure

Overview

The SIMLIN procedure reads the coefficients for a set of linear structural equations, which are usually produced by the SYSLIN procedure. PROC SIMLIN then computes the reduced form and, if input data are given, uses the reduced form equations to generate predicted values. PROC SIMLIN is especially useful when dealing with sets of structural difference equations. The SIMLIN procedure can perform simulation or forecasting of the endogenous variables.

The SIMLIN procedure can be applied only to models that are

- linear with respect to the parameters

- linear with respect to the variables

- square (equal number of equations and endogenous variables)

- nonsingular (the coefficients of the endogenous variables form an invertible matrix)

Getting Started

The SIMLIN procedure processes the coefficients in a data set created by the SYSLIN procedure using the OUTEST= option or by another regression procedure such as PROC REG. To use PROC SIMLIN, you must first produce the coefficient data set and then specify this data set on the EST= option of the PROC SIMLIN statement. You must also tell PROC SIMLIN which variables are endogenous and which variables are exogenous. List the endogenous variables in an ENDOGENOUS statement, and list the exogenous variables in an EXOGENOUS statement.

The following example illustrates the creation of an OUTEST= data set with PROC SYSLIN and the computation and printing of the reduced form coefficients for the model with PROC SIMLIN:

```
proc syslin data=in outest=e;
   model y1 = y2 x1;
   model y2 = y1 x2;
run;

proc simlin est=e;
   endogenous y1 y2;
   exogenous x1 x2;
run;
```

If the model contains lagged endogenous variables, you must also use a LAGGED statement to tell PROC SIMLIN which variables contain lagged values, which endogenous variables they are lags of, and the number of periods of lagging. For dynamic models, the TOTAL and INTERIM= options can be used on the PROC SIMLIN statement to compute and print total and impact multipliers. (See the section "Dynamic Multipliers" later in this chapter for an explanation of multipliers.)

In the following example, the variables Y1LAG1, Y2LAG1, and Y2LAG2 contain lagged values of the endogenous variables Y1 and Y2. Y1LAG1 and Y2LAG1 contain values of Y1 and Y2 for the previous observation, while Y2LAG2 contains two period lags of Y2. The LAGGED statement specifies the lagged relationships, and the TOTAL and INTERIM= options request multiplier analysis. The INTERIM=2 option prints matrices showing the impact that changes to the exogenous variables have on the endogenous variables after one and two periods.

```
data in; set in;
  y1lag1 = lag(y1);
  y2lag1 = lag(y2);
  y2lag2 = lag2(y2);
run;

proc syslin data=in outest=e;
   model y1 = y2 y1lag1 y2lag2 x1;
   model y2 = y1 y2lag1 x2;
run;

proc simlin est=e total interim=2;
   endogenous y1 y2;
   exogenous x1 x2;
   lagged y1lag1 y1 1 y2lag1 y2 1 y2lag2 y2 2;
run;
```

After the reduced form of the model is computed, the model can be simulated by specifying an input data set on the PROC SIMLIN statement and using an OUTPUT statement to write the simulation results to an output data set. The following example modifies the PROC SIMLIN step from the preceding example to simulate the model and stores the results in an output data set:

```
proc simlin est=e total interim=2 data=in;
   endogenous y1 y2;
   exogenous x1 x2;
   lagged y1lag1 y1 1 y2lag1 y2 1 y2lag2 y2 2;
   output out=sim predicted=y1hat y2hat
                  residual=y1resid y2resid;
run;
```

Prediction and Simulation

If you specify an input data set with the DATA= option in the PROC SIMLIN statement, the procedure reads the data and uses the reduced form equations to compute predicted and residual values for each of the endogenous variables. (If you do not specify a data set with the DATA= option, no simulation of the system is performed, and only the reduced form and multipliers are computed.)

The character of the prediction is based on the START= value. Until PROC SIMLIN encounters the START= observation, actual endogenous values are found and fed into the lagged endogenous terms. After the START= observation is reached, dynamic simulation begins, where predicted values are fed into lagged endogenous terms until the end of the data set is reached.

The predicted and residual values generated here are different from those produced by the SYSLIN procedure since PROC SYSLIN uses the structural form with actual endogenous values. The predicted values computed by the SIMLIN procedure solve the simultaneous equation system. These reduced-form predicted values are functions only of the exogenous and lagged endogenous variables and do not depend on actual values of current-period endogenous variables.

Syntax

The following statements can be used with PROC SIMLIN:

> **PROC SIMLIN** *options*;
>   **BY** *variables*;
>   **ENDOGENOUS** *variables*;
>   **EXOGENOUS** *variables*;
>   **ID** *variables*;
>   **LAGGED** *lag-var endogenous-var number* ... ;
>   **OUTPUT OUT=** *SAS-data-set options*;

Functional Summary

The statements and options controlling the SIMLIN procedure are summarized in the following table:

Description	Statement	Option
Data Set Options		
specify input data set containing structural coefficients	PROC SIMLIN	EST=
specify type of estimates read from EST= data set	PROC SIMLIN	TYPE=
write reduced form coefficients and multipliers to an output data set	PROC SIMLIN	OUTEST=
specify the input data set for simulation	PROC SIMLIN	DATA=
write predicted and residual values to an output data set	OUTPUT	
Printing Control Options		
print the structural coefficients	PROC SIMLIN	ESTPRINT
suppress printing of reduced form coefficients	PROC SIMLIN	NORED
suppress all printed output	PROC SIMLIN	NOPRINT

Description	Statement	Option
Dynamic Multipliers		
compute interim multipliers	PROC SIMLIN	INTERIM=
compute total multipliers	PROC SIMLIN	TOTAL
Declaring the Role of Variables		
specify BY-group processing	BY	
specify the endogenous variables	ENDOGENOUS	
specify the exogenous variables	EXOGENOUS	
specify identifying variables	ID	
specify lagged endogenous variables	LAGGED	
Controlling the Simulation		
specify the starting observation for dynamic simulation	PROC SIMLIN	START=

The PROC SIMLIN Statement

> **PROC SIMLIN** *options*;

The following options can be used in the PROC SIMLIN statement:

DATA= *SAS-data-set*

   specifies the SAS data set containing input data for the simulation. If you use the DATA= option, the data set you specify must supply values for all exogenous variables throughout the simulation. If you do not specify the DATA= option, no simulation of the system is performed, and only the reduced form and multipliers are computed.

EST= *SAS-data-set*

   specifies the input data set containing the structural coefficients of the system. If you omit the EST= option, the most recently created SAS data set is used. The EST= data set is normally a TYPE=EST data set produced by the OUTEST= option of PROC SYSLIN. However, you can also build the EST= data set with a SAS DATA step. See the section "The EST= Data Set" later in this chapter for details.

ESTPRINT

   prints the structural coefficients read from the EST= data set.

INTERIM= *n*

requests that interim multipliers be computed for interims one through *n*. If not specified, no interim multipliers are computed. This feature is available only if there are no lags greater than one.

NOPRINT

suppresses all printed output.

NORED

suppresses the printing of the reduced form coefficients.

OUTEST= *SAS-data-set*

specifies an output SAS data set to contain the reduced form coefficients and multipliers in addition to the structural coefficients read from the EST= data set. The OUTEST= data set has the same form as the EST= data set. If you do not specify the OUTEST= option, the reduced form coefficients and multipliers are not written to a data set.

START= *n*

specifies the observation number in the DATA= data set where the dynamic simulation is to be started. By default, the dynamic simulation starts with the first observation in the DATA= data set for which all variables (including lags) are not missing.

TOTAL

requests that the total multipliers be computed. This feature is available only if there are no lags greater than one.

TYPE= *value*

specifies the type of estimates to be read from the EST= data set. The TYPE= value must match the value of the _TYPE_ variable for the observations that you want to select from the EST= data set (TYPE=2SLS, for example).

The BY Statement

BY *variables*;

A BY statement can be used with PROC SIMLIN to obtain separate analyses for groups of observations defined by the BY variables.

The BY statement can be applied to one or both of the EST= and the DATA= input data sets. When you use a BY statement and you specify both an EST= and a DATA= input data set, PROC SIMLIN checks to see if one or both of the data sets contain the BY variables.

Thus, there are three ways of using the BY statement with PROC SIMLIN:

• If the BY variables are found in the EST= data set only, PROC SIMLIN simulates over the entire DATA= data set once for each set of coefficients read from the BY groups in the EST= data set.

• If the BY variables are found in the DATA= data set only, PROC SIMLIN performs separate simulations over each BY group in the DATA= data set, using the single set of coefficients in the EST= data set.

- If the BY variables are found in both the EST= and the DATA= data sets, PROC SIMLIN performs separate simulations over each BY group in the DATA= data set using the coefficients from the corresponding BY group in the EST= data set.

The ENDOGENOUS Statement

ENDOGENOUS *variables*;

List the names of the endogenous (jointly dependent) variables in the ENDOGENOUS statement. The ENDOGENOUS statement can be abbreviated ENDOG or ENDO.

The EXOGENOUS Statement

EXOGENOUS *variables*;

List the names of the exogenous (independent) variables in the EXOGENOUS statement. The EXOGENOUS statement can be abbreviated EXOG or EXO.

The ID Statement

ID *variables*;

You can use the ID statement to restrict the variables copied from the DATA= data set to the OUT= data set. Use the ID statement to list the variables you want to copy to the OUT= data set in addition to the exogenous, endogenous, lagged endogenous, and BY variables. If you omit the ID statement, all the variables in the DATA= data set are copied to the OUT= data set.

The LAGGED Statement

LAGGED *lag-var endogenous-var number* ... ;

For each lagged endogenous variable, specify the name of the lagged variable, the name of the endogenous variable that was lagged, and the degree of the lag. Only one LAGGED statement is allowed.

The following is an example of the use of the LAGGED statement:

```
proc simlin est=e;
   endog y1 y2;
   lagged y1lag1 y1 1  y2lag1 y2 1  y2lag3 y2 3;
```

This statement specifies that the variable Y1LAG1 contains the values of the endogenous variable Y1 lagged one period; the variable Y2LAG1 refers to the values of Y2 lagged one period; and the variable Y2LAG3 refers to the values of Y2 lagged three periods.

The OUTPUT Statement

OUTPUT OUT= *SAS-data-set options*;

The OUTPUT statement specifies that predicted and residual values be put in an output data set. A DATA= input data set must be supplied if the OUTPUT statement is used, and only one OUTPUT statement is allowed. The following options can be used in the OUTPUT statement:

OUT= *SAS-data-set*

names the output SAS data set to contain the predicted values and residuals. If you do not specify the OUT= option, the output data set is named using the DATA*n* convention.

PREDICTED= *names*
P= *names*

names the variables in the output data set that contain the predicted values of the simulation. These variables correspond to the endogenous variables in the order in which you specify them in the ENDOGENOUS statement. Specify up to as many names as there are endogenous variables. If you specify names on the PREDICTED= option for only some of the endogenous variables, predicted values for the remaining variables are not output. The names must not match any variable name in the input data set.

RESIDUAL= *names*
R= *names*

names the variables in the output data set that contain the residual values from the simulation. The residuals are the differences between the actual values of the endogenous variables from the DATA= data set and the predicted values from the simulation. These variables correspond to the endogenous variables in the order in which you specify them in the ENDOGENOUS statement. Specify up to as many names as there are endogenous variables. The names must not match any variable name in the input data set.

The following is an example of the use of the OUTPUT statement. This example outputs predicted values for Y1 and Y2 and outputs residuals for Y1.

```
proc simlin est=e;
    endog y1 y2;
    output out=b predicted=y1hat y2hat residual=y1resid;
```

Details

The following sections explain the structural and reduced forms, dynamic multipliers, input data sets, and the model simulation process in more detail.

Defining the Structural Form

An EST= input data set supplies the coefficients of the equation system. The data set containing the coefficients is normally a "TYPE=EST" data set created by the OUTEST= option of PROC SYSLIN or another regression procedure. The data set contains the special variables _TYPE_, _DEPVAR_, and INTERCEP. You can also supply the structural coefficients of the system to PROC SIMLIN in a data set produced by a SAS DATA step as long as the data set is of the form TYPE=EST. Refer to SAS/STAT software documentation for a discussion of the special TYPE=EST type of SAS data set.

Suppose that there is a $g \times 1$ vector of endogenous variables $\mathbf{y}_t$, an $l \times 1$ vector of lagged endogenous variables $\mathbf{y}_t^L$, and a $k \times 1$ vector of exogenous variables $\mathbf{x}_t$, including the intercept. Then, there are g structural equations in the simultaneous system that can be written

$$\mathbf{G}\,\mathbf{y}_t = \mathbf{C}\,\mathbf{y}_t^L + \mathbf{B}\,\mathbf{x}_t$$

where $\mathbf{G}$ is the matrix of coefficients of current-period endogenous variables, $\mathbf{C}$ is the matrix of coefficients of lagged endogenous variables, and $\mathbf{B}$ is the matrix of coefficients of exogenous variables. $\mathbf{G}$ is assumed to be nonsingular.

Computing the Reduced Form

First, the SIMLIN procedure computes reduced form coefficients by premultiplying by $\mathbf{G}^{-1}$:

$$\mathbf{y}_t = \mathbf{G}^{-1}\mathbf{C}\,\mathbf{y}_t^L + \mathbf{G}^{-1}\mathbf{B}\,\mathbf{x}_t$$

This can be written

$$\mathbf{y}_t = \Pi_1 \mathbf{y}_t^L + \Pi_2 \mathbf{x}_t$$

where $\Pi_1 = \mathbf{G}^{-1}\mathbf{C}$ and $\Pi_2 = \mathbf{G}^{-1}\mathbf{B}$ are the reduced form coefficient matrices.

The reduced form matrices $\Pi_1 = \mathbf{G}^{-1}\mathbf{C}$ and $\Pi_2 = \mathbf{G}^{-1}\mathbf{B}$ are printed unless you specify the NORED option in the PROC SIMLIN statement. The structural coefficient matrices $\mathbf{G}$, $\mathbf{C}$, and $\mathbf{B}$ are printed when you specify the ESTPRINT option.

Dynamic Multipliers

For models that have only first-order lags, the equation of the reduced form of the system can be rewritten

$$\mathbf{y}_t = \mathbf{D}\mathbf{y}_{t-1} + \Pi_2 \mathbf{x}_t$$

$\mathbf{D}$ is a matrix formed from the columns of Π_1 plus some columns of zeros, arranged in the order in which the variables meet the lags. The elements of Π_2 are called *im-*

pact multipliers because they show the immediate effect of changes in each exogenous variable on the values of the endogenous variables. This equation can be rewritten

$$\mathbf{y}_t = \mathbf{D}^2 \mathbf{y}_{t-2} + \mathbf{D\Pi}_2 \mathbf{x}_{t-1} + \mathbf{\Pi}_2 \mathbf{x}_t$$

The matrix formed by the product $\mathbf{D\Pi}_2$ shows the effect of the exogenous variables one lag back; the elements in this matrix are called *interim multipliers* and are computed and printed when you specify the INTERIM= option in the PROC SIMLIN statement. The ith period interim multipliers are formed by $\mathbf{D}^i \mathbf{\Pi}_2$.

The series can be expanded as

$$\mathbf{y}_t = \mathbf{D}^\infty \mathbf{y}_{t-\infty} + \sum_{i=0}^{\infty} \mathbf{D}^i \mathbf{\Pi}_2 \mathbf{x}_{t-i}$$

A permanent and constant setting of a value for x has the following cumulative effect:

$$\left(\sum_{i=0}^{\infty} \mathbf{D}^i \right) \mathbf{\Pi}_2 \mathbf{x} = (\mathbf{I} - \mathbf{D})^{-1} \mathbf{\Pi}_2 \mathbf{x}$$

The elements of $(\mathbf{I} - \mathbf{D})^{-1} \mathbf{\Pi}_2$ are called *total multipliers*. Assuming that the sum converges and that $(\mathbf{I} - \mathbf{D})$ is invertible, PROC SIMLIN computes the total multipliers when you specify the TOTAL option in the PROC SIMLIN statement.

Multipliers for Higher-Order Lags

The dynamic multiplier options require the system to have no lags of order greater than one. This limitation can be circumvented, since any system with lags greater than one can be rewritten as a system where no lag is greater than one by forming new endogenous variables that are single-period lags.

For example, suppose you have the third-order single equation

$$y_t = a\, y_{t-3} + b\, \mathbf{x}_t$$

This can be converted to a first-order three-equation system by introducing two additional endogenous variables, $y_{1,t}$ and $y_{2,t}$, and computing corresponding first-order lagged variables for each endogenous variable: $y_{t-1}, y_{1,t-1}$, and $y_{2,t-1}$. The higher-order lag relations are then produced by adding identities to link the endogenous and identical lagged endogenous variables:

$$y_{1,t} = y_{t-1}$$
$$y_{2,t} = y_{1,t-1}$$
$$y_t = a\, y_{2,t-1} + b\, \mathbf{x}_t$$

This conversion using the SYSLIN and SIMLIN procedures requires three steps:

1. Add the extra endogenous and lagged endogenous variables to the input data set

using a DATA step. Note that you need two copies of each lagged endogenous variable for each lag reduced, one to serve as an endogenous variable and one to serve as a lagged endogenous variable in the reduced system.

2. Add IDENTITY statements to the PROC SYSLIN step to equate each added endogenous variable to its lagged endogenous variable copy.

3. In the PROC SIMLIN step, declare the added endogenous variables in the ENDOGENOUS statement and define the lag relations in the LAGGED statement.

See Example 14.2 for an illustration of how to convert an equation system with higher-order lags into a larger system with only first-order lags.

EST= Data Set

Normally, PROC SIMLIN uses an EST= data set produced by PROC SYSLIN with the OUTEST= option. This data set is in the form expected by PROC SIMLIN. If there is more than one set of estimates produced by PROC SYSLIN, you must use the TYPE= option in the PROC SIMLIN statement to select the set to be simulated. Then PROC SIMLIN reads from the EST= data set only those observations with a _TYPE_ value corresponding to the TYPE= option (for example, TYPE=2SLS) or with a _TYPE_ value of IDENTITY.

The SIMLIN procedure can only solve square, nonsingular systems. If you have fewer equations than endogenous variables, you must specify IDENTITY statements in the PROC SYSLIN step to bring the system up to full rank. If there are g endogenous variables and $m < g$ stochastic equations with unknown parameters, then you use m MODEL statements to specify the equations with parameters to be estimated; you must use $g - m$ IDENTITY statements to complete the system.

You can build your own EST= data set with a DATA step rather than using PROC SYSLIN. The EST= data set must contain the endogenous variables, the lagged endogenous variables (if any), and the exogenous variables in the system (if any). If any of the equations have intercept terms, the variable INTERCEP must supply these coefficients. The EST= data set should also contain the special character variable _DEPVAR_ to label the equations.

The EST= data set must contain one observation for each equation in the system. The values of the lagged endogenous variables must contain the **C** coefficients. The values of the exogenous variables and the INTERCEP variable must contain the **B** coefficients. The values of the endogenous variables, however, must contain the negatives of the **G** coefficients. This is because the SYSLIN procedure writes the coefficients to the OUTEST= data set in the form

$$0 = \mathbf{H}\mathbf{y}_t + \mathbf{C}\mathbf{y}_t^L + \mathbf{B}\mathbf{x}_t$$

where $\mathbf{H} = -\mathbf{G}$.

See the section "Multipliers for Higher-Order Lags" and Example 14.2 later in this chapter for more information on building the EST= data set.

DATA= Data Set

The DATA= data set must contain all the exogenous variables. Values for all the exogenous variables are required for each observation for which you want predicted endogenous values. To forecast past the end of the historical data, the DATA= data set should contain nonmissing values for all of the exogenous variables and missing values for the endogenous variables for the forecast periods, in addition to the historical data. (See Example 14.1 for an illustration.)

In order for PROC SIMLIN to output residuals and compute statistics of fit, the DATA= data set must also contain the endogenous variables with nonmissing actual values for each observation for which residuals and statistics are to be computed.

If the system contains lags, initial values must be supplied for the lagged variables. This can be done by including either the lagged variables or the endogenous variables, or both, in the DATA= data set. If the lagged variables are not in the DATA= data set or if they have missing values in the early observations, PROC SIMLIN prints a warning and uses the endogenous variable values from the early observations to initialize the lags.

OUTEST= Data Set

The OUTEST= data set contains all the variables read from the EST= data set. The variables in the OUTEST= data set are as follows:

- the BY statement variables, if any
- _TYPE_, a character variable that identifies the type of observation
- _DEPVAR_, a character variable containing the name of the dependent variable for the observation
- the endogenous variables
- the lagged endogenous variables
- the exogenous variables
- INTERCEP, a numeric variable containing the intercept values
- _MODEL_, a character variable containing the name of the equation
- _SIGMA_, a numeric variable containing the estimated error variance of the equation (output only if present in the EST= data set)

The observations read from the EST= data set that supply the structural coefficients are copied to the OUTEST= data set, and the signs of endogenous coefficients are reversed. For these observations, the _TYPE_ variable values are the same as in the EST= data set.

In addition, the OUTEST= data set contains observations with the following _TYPE_ values:

REDUCED the reduced form coefficients. The endogenous variables for this group of observations contain the inverse of the endogenous coefficient matrix $\mathbf{G}$. The lagged endogenous variables contain the matrix $\Pi_1 = \mathbf{G}^{-1}\mathbf{C}$. The exogenous variables contain the matrix $\Pi_2 = \mathbf{G}^{-1}\mathbf{B}$.

IMULT*i* the interim multipliers, if you specify the INTERIM= option. There are $g \times n$ observations for the interim multipliers, where g is the number of endogenous variables and n is the value of the INTERIM=n option. For these observations, the _TYPE_ variable has the value IMULT*i*, where the interim number i ranges from one to n.

The exogenous variables in groups of g observations that have a _TYPE_ value of IMULT*i* contain the matrix $\mathbf{D}^i\Pi_2$ of multipliers at interim i. The endogenous and lagged endogenous variables for this group of observations are set to missing.

TOTAL the total multipliers, if you specify the TOTAL option. The exogenous variables in this group of observations contain the matrix $(\mathbf{I} - \mathbf{D})^{-1}\Pi_2$. The endogenous and lagged endogenous variables for this group of observations are set to missing.

OUT= Data Set

The OUT= data set normally contains all of the variables in the input DATA= data set, plus the variables named in the PREDICTED= and RESIDUAL= options in the OUTPUT statement.

You can use an ID statement to restrict the variables that are copied from the input data set. If you use an ID statement, the OUT= data set contains only the BY variables (if any), the ID variables, the endogenous and lagged endogenous variables (if any), the exogenous variables, plus the PREDICTED= and RESIDUAL= variables.

The OUT= data set contains an observation for each observation in the DATA= data set. When the actual value of an endogenous variable is missing in the DATA= data set, or when the DATA= data set does not contain the endogenous variable, the corresponding residual is missing.

Printed Output

Structural Form

The following items are printed as they are read from the EST= input data set. Structural zeros are printed as dots in the listing of these matrices.

1. Structural Coefficients for Endogenous Variables. This is the $\mathbf{G}$ matrix with g rows and g columns.

2. Structural Coefficients for Lagged Endogenous Variables. These coefficients make up the $\mathbf{C}$ matrix with g rows and l columns.

3. Structural Coefficients for Exogenous Variables. These coefficients make up the **B** matrix with g rows and k columns.

Reduced Form

The reduced form coefficients are determined by inverting **G** so that the endogenous variables can be directly expressed as functions of only lagged endogenous and exogenous variables.

1. Inverse Coefficient Matrix for Endogenous Variables. This is the inverse of the **G** matrix.

2. Reduced Form for Lagged Endogenous Variables. This is $\Pi_1 = \mathbf{G}^{-1}\mathbf{C}$, with g rows and l columns. Each value is a dynamic multiplier that shows how past values of lagged endogenous variables affect values of each of the endogenous variables.

3. Reduced Form for Exogenous Variables. This is $\Pi_2 = \mathbf{G}^{-1}\mathbf{B}$, with g rows and k columns. Its values are called *impact multipliers* because they show the immediate effect of each exogenous variable on the value of the endogenous variables.

Multipliers

Interim and total multipliers show the effect of a change in an exogenous variable over time.

1. Interim Multipliers. These are the interim multiplier matrices. They are formed by multiplying Π_2 by powers of **D**. The ith interim multiplier is $\mathbf{D}^i\Pi_2$. The interim multiplier of order i shows the effects of a change in the exogenous variables after i periods. Interim multipliers are only available if the maximum lag of the endogenous variables is 1.

2. Total Multipliers. This is the matrix of total multipliers, $\mathbf{T} = (\mathbf{I} - \mathbf{D})^{-1}\Pi_2$. This matrix shows the cumulative effect of changes in the exogenous variables. Total multipliers are only available if the maximum lag is one.

Statistics of Fit

If you use the DATA= option and the DATA= data set contains endogenous variables, PROC SIMLIN prints a statistics-of-fit report for the simulation. The statistics printed include the following. (Summations are over the observations for which both y_t and $\hat{y}_t$ are nonmissing.)

1. the number of nonmissing errors. (Number of observations for which both y_t and $\hat{y}_t$ are nonmissing.)

2. the mean error: $\frac{1}{n} \sum (y_t - \hat{y}_t)$

3. the mean percent error: $\frac{100}{n} \sum \frac{y_t - \hat{y}_t}{y_t}$

4. the mean absolute error: $\frac{1}{n} \sum |y_t - \hat{y}_t|$

5. the mean absolute percent error $\frac{100}{n} \sum \left| \frac{y_t - \hat{y}_t}{y_t} \right|$

6. the root mean square error: $\sqrt{\frac{1}{n} \sum (y_t - \hat{y}_t)^2}$

7. the root mean square percent error: $100 \sqrt{\frac{1}{n} \sum ((y_t - \hat{y}_t)/y_t)^2}$

Examples

Example 14.1. Simulating Klein's Model I

In this example, the SIMLIN procedure simulates a model of the U.S. economy called Klein's Model I. The SAS data set KLEIN, shown in Output 14.1.1, is used as input to the SYSLIN and SIMLIN procedures.

Output 14.1.1. PROC PRINT Listing of Input Data Set KLEIN

OBS	C	P	W	I	K	Y	X	WSUM	KLAG	PLAG	XLAG	WP	G	T	YR
1	41.9	12.4	25.5	-0.2	182.6	37.9	45.6	28.2	182.8	12.7	44.9	2.7	3.9	7.7	-10
2	45.0	16.9	29.3	1.9	184.5	46.2	50.1	32.2	182.6	12.4	45.6	2.9	3.2	3.9	-9
3	49.2	18.4	34.1	5.2	189.7	52.5	57.2	37.0	184.5	16.9	50.1	2.9	2.8	4.7	-8
4	50.6	19.4	33.9	3.0	192.7	53.3	57.1	37.0	189.7	18.4	57.2	3.1	3.5	3.8	-7
5	52.6	20.1	35.4	5.1	197.8	55.5	61.0	38.6	192.7	19.4	57.1	3.2	3.3	5.5	-6
6	55.1	19.6	37.4	5.6	203.4	57.0	64.0	40.7	197.8	20.1	61.0	3.3	3.3	7.0	-5
7	56.2	19.8	37.9	4.2	207.6	57.7	64.4	41.5	203.4	19.6	64.0	3.6	4.0	6.7	-4
8	57.3	21.1	39.2	3.0	210.6	60.3	64.5	42.9	207.6	19.8	64.4	3.7	4.2	4.2	-3
9	57.8	21.7	41.3	5.1	215.7	63.0	67.0	45.3	210.6	21.1	64.5	4.0	4.1	4.0	-2
10	55.0	15.6	37.9	1.0	216.7	53.5	61.2	42.1	215.7	21.7	67.0	4.2	5.2	7.7	-1
11	50.9	11.4	34.5	-3.4	213.3	45.9	53.4	39.3	216.7	15.6	61.2	4.8	5.9	7.5	0
12	45.6	7.0	29.0	-6.2	207.1	36.0	44.3	34.3	213.3	11.4	53.4	5.3	4.9	8.3	1
13	46.5	11.2	28.5	-5.1	202.0	39.7	45.1	34.1	207.1	7.0	44.3	5.6	3.7	5.4	2
14	48.7	12.3	30.6	-3.0	199.0	42.9	49.7	36.6	202.0	11.2	45.1	6.0	4.0	6.8	3
15	51.3	14.0	33.2	-1.3	197.7	47.2	54.4	39.3	199.0	12.3	49.7	6.1	4.4	7.2	4
16	57.7	17.6	36.8	2.1	199.8	54.4	62.7	44.2	197.7	14.0	54.4	7.4	2.9	8.3	5
17	58.7	17.3	41.0	2.0	201.8	58.3	65.0	47.7	199.8	17.6	62.7	6.7	4.3	6.7	6
18	57.5	15.3	38.2	-1.9	199.9	53.5	60.9	45.9	201.8	17.3	65.0	7.7	5.3	7.4	7
19	61.6	19.0	41.6	1.3	201.2	60.6	69.5	49.4	199.9	15.3	60.9	7.8	6.6	8.9	8
20	65.0	21.1	45.0	3.3	204.5	66.1	75.7	53.0	201.2	19.0	69.5	8.0	7.4	9.6	9
21	69.7	23.5	53.3	4.9	209.4	76.8	88.4	61.8	204.5	21.1	75.7	8.5	13.8	11.6	10
22	.	.	.	.	.	.	.	.	209.4	23.5	88.4	8.5	13.8	11.6	11
23	.	.	.	.	.	.	.	.	.	.	.	8.5	13.8	12.6	12
24	.	.	.	.	.	.	.	.	.	.	.	8.5	13.8	11.6	13
25	.	.	.	.	.	.	.	.	.	.	.	8.5	13.8	11.6	14
26	.	.	.	.	.	.	.	.	.	.	.	8.5	13.8	11.6	15
27	.	.	.	.	.	.	.	.	.	.	.	8.5	13.8	11.6	16

First, the model is specified and estimated using the SYSLIN procedure, and the parameter estimates are written to an OUTEST= data set. The printed output produced by the SYSLIN procedure is not shown here; see Example 17.1 in Chapter 17, "The SYSLIN Procedure," for the printed output of the PROC SYSLIN step.

```
title1 'Simulation of Klein''s Model I using SIMLIN';
proc syslin 3sls data=klein outest=a;

   instruments klag plag xlag wp g t yr;
   endogenous c p w i x wsum k y;

   consume: model    c = p plag wsum;
   invest:  model    i = p plag klag;
   labor:   model    w = x xlag yr;

   product: identity x = c + i + g;
   income:  identity y = c + i + g - t;
   profit:  identity p = x - w - t;
   stock:   identity k = klag + i;
   wage:    identity wsum = w + wp;
```

Example 14.1. Simulating Klein's Model I □□□ 737

```
run;

proc print data=a;
run;
```

The OUTEST= data set A created by the SYSLIN procedure contains parameter estimates to be used by the SIMLIN procedure. The OUTEST= data set is shown in Output 14.1.2.

Output 14.1.2. The OUTEST= Data Set Created by PROC SYSLIN

```
               Simulation of Klein's Model I using SIMLIN
```

OBS	_TYPE_	_MODEL_	_DEPVAR_	_SIGMA_	INTERCEP	KLAG	PLAG	XLAG
1	INST	FIRST	C	2.11403	58.3018	-0.14654	0.74803	0.23007
2	INST	FIRST	P	2.18298	50.3844	-0.21610	0.80250	0.02200
3	INST	FIRST	W	1.75427	43.4356	-0.12295	0.87192	0.09533
4	INST	FIRST	I	1.72376	35.5182	-0.19251	0.92639	-0.11274
5	INST	FIRST	X	3.77347	93.8200	-0.33906	1.67442	0.11733
6	INST	FIRST	WSUM	1.75427	43.4356	-0.12295	0.87192	0.09533
7	INST	FIRST	K	1.72376	35.5182	0.80749	0.92639	-0.11274
8	INST	FIRST	Y	3.77347	93.8200	-0.33906	1.67442	0.11733
9	2SLS	CONSUME	C	1.13566	16.5548	.	0.21623	.
10	2SLS	INVEST	I	1.30715	20.2782	-0.15779	0.61594	.
11	2SLS	LABOR	W	0.76716	1.5003	.	.	0.14667
12	3SLS	CONSUME	C	1.04956	16.4408	.	0.16314	.
13	3SLS	INVEST	I	1.60796	28.1778	-0.19485	0.75572	.
14	3SLS	LABOR	W	0.80149	1.7972	.	.	0.18129
15	IDENTITY	PRODUCT	X	.	0.0000	.	.	.
16	IDENTITY	INCOME	Y	.	0.0000	.	.	.
17	IDENTITY	PROFIT	P	.	0.0000	.	.	.
18	IDENTITY	STOCK	K	.	0.0000	1.00000	.	.
19	IDENTITY	WAGE	WSUM	.	0.0000	.	.	.

OBS	WP	G	T	YR	C	P	W	I	X	WSUM	K	Y
1	0.19327	0.20501	-0.36573	0.70109	-1	.	.	.	.	.	.	.
2	-0.07961	0.43902	-0.92310	0.31941	.	-1.00000	.	.	.	.	.	.
3	-0.44373	0.86622	-0.60415	0.71358	.	.	-1	.	.	.	.	.
4	-0.71661	0.10023	-0.16152	0.33190	.	.	.	-1	.	.	.	.
5	-0.52334	1.30524	-0.52725	1.03299	.	.	.	.	-1.00000	.	.	.
6	0.55627	0.86622	-0.60415	0.71358	.	.	.	.	.	-1.00000	.	.
7	-0.71661	0.10023	-0.16152	0.33190	.	.	.	.	.	.	-1	.
8	-0.52334	1.30524	-1.52725	1.03299	.	.	.	.	.	.	.	-1
9	.	.	.	.	-1	0.01730	.	.	.	0.81018	.	.
10	.	.	.	.	.	0.15022	.	-1	.	.	.	.
11	.	.	.	0.13040	.	.	-1	.	0.43886	.	.	.
12	.	.	.	.	-1	0.12489	.	.	.	0.79008	.	.
13	.	.	.	.	.	-0.01308	.	-1	.	.	.	.
14	.	.	.	0.14967	.	.	-1	.	0.40049	.	.	.
15	.	1.00000	.	.	1	.	.	1	-1.00000	.	.	.
16	.	1.00000	-1.00000	.	1	.	.	1	.	.	.	-1
17	.	.	-1.00000	.	.	-1.00000	-1	.	1.00000	.	.	.
18	.	.	.	.	.	.	.	1	.	.	-1	.
19	1.00000	.	.	.	.	.	1	.	.	-1.00000	.	.

Using the OUTEST= data set A produced by the SYSLIN procedure, the SIMLIN procedure can compute the reduced form and simulate the model. The following statements perform the simulation:

```
proc simlin est=a data=klein type=3sls
             estprint total interim=2 outest=b;
   endogenous c p w i x wsum k y;
   exogenous  wp g t yr;
   lagged  klag k 1    plag p 1    xlag x 1;
   id year;
   output out=c p=chat phat what ihat xhat wsumhat khat yhat
                r=cres pres wres ires xres wsumres kres yres;
run;
```

The reduced form coefficients and multipliers are added to the information read from EST= data set and written to the OUTEST= data set B. The predicted and residual values from the simulation are written to the OUT= data set C specified in the OUTPUT statement.

The SIMLIN procedure first prints the structural coefficient matrices read from the EST= data set, as shown in Output 14.1.3.

Output 14.1.3. SIMLIN Procedure Output–Structural Coefficients

```
            Simulation of Klein's Model I using SIMLIN

                         SIMLIN Procedure


        Structural Coefficients for Endogenous Variables

                    C            P            W            I

    C           1.0000      -0.1249            .            .
    I                .       0.0131            .       1.0000
    W                .            .       1.0000            .
    X          -1.0000            .            .      -1.0000
    Y          -1.0000            .            .      -1.0000
    P                .       1.0000       1.0000            .
    K                .            .            .      -1.0000
    WSUM             .            .      -1.0000            .


                    X         WSUM            K            Y

    C                .      -0.7901            .            .
    I                .            .            .            .
    W          -0.4005            .            .            .
    X           1.0000            .            .            .
    Y                .            .            .       1.0000
    P          -1.0000            .            .            .
    K                .            .       1.0000            .
    WSUM             .       1.0000            .            .
```

Example 14.1.   Simulating Klein's Model I   □ □ □   739

Output 14.1.3.   (Continued)

```
                Simulation of Klein's Model I using SIMLIN

                            SIMLIN Procedure

          Structural Coefficients for Lagged Endogenous Variables

                          KLAG            PLAG            XLAG

                C            .            0.1631            .
                I        -0.1948          0.7557            .
                W            .              .            0.1813
                X            .              .               .
                Y            .              .               .
                P            .              .               .
                K         1.0000            .               .
             WSUM           .              .               .


              Structural Coefficients for Exogenous Variables

                WP          G            T            YR        INTERCEP

      C          .          .            .            .         16.4408
      I          .          .            .            .         28.1778
      W          .          .            .         0.1497        1.7972
      X          .       1.0000          .            .              0
      Y          .       1.0000      -1.0000          .              0
      P          .          .        -1.0000          .              0
      K          .          .            .            .              0
   WSUM      1.0000          .            .            .              0
```

The SIMLIN procedure then prints the inverse of the endogenous variables coefficient matrix, as shown in Output 14.1.4.

Output 14.1.4.   SIMLIN Procedure Output–Inverse Coefficient Matrix

```
                Simulation of Klein's Model I using SIMLIN

                            SIMLIN Procedure

            Inverse Coefficient Matrix for Endogenous Variables

                     C            I            W            X

         C         1.6347       0.6347       1.0957       0.6347
         P         0.9724       0.9724      -0.3405       0.9724
         W         0.6496       0.6496       1.4406       0.6496
         I        -0.0127       0.9873       0.004453    -0.0127
         X         1.6219       1.6219       1.1001       1.6219
       WSUM        0.6496       0.6496       1.4406       0.6496
         K        -0.0127       0.9873       0.004453    -0.0127
         Y         1.6219       1.6219       1.1001       0.6219


                     Y            P            K            WSUM

         C            0         0.1959          0          1.2915
         P            0         1.1087          0          0.7682
         W            0         0.0726          0          0.5132
         I            0        -0.0145          0         -0.0100
         X            0         0.1814          0          1.2815
       WSUM           0         0.0726          0          1.5132
         K            0        -0.0145       1.0000       -0.0100
         Y         1.0000       0.1814          0          1.2815
```

The reduced form coefficient matrices are then printed, as shown in Output 14.1.5.

Output 14.1.5. SIMLIN Procedure Output – Reduced Form Coefficients

```
              Simulation of Klein's Model I using SIMLIN

                           SIMLIN Procedure


                Reduced Form for Lagged Endogenous Variables

                          KLAG            PLAG            XLAG

              C          -0.1237          0.7463          0.1986
              P          -0.1895          0.8935         -0.0617
              W          -0.1266          0.5969          0.2612
              I          -0.1924          0.7440         0.000807
              X          -0.3160          1.4903          0.1994
              WSUM       -0.1266          0.5969          0.2612
              K           0.8076          0.7440         0.000807
              Y          -0.3160          1.4903          0.1994


                   Reduced Form for Exogenous Variables

               WP             G              T             YR        INTERCEP

C            1.2915         0.6347        -0.1959        0.1640       46.7273
P            0.7682         0.9724        -1.1087       -0.0510       42.7736
W            0.5132         0.6496        -0.0726        0.2156       31.5721
I           -0.0100        -0.0127         0.0145       0.000667      27.6184
X            1.2815         1.6219        -0.1814        0.1647       74.3457
WSUM         1.5132         0.6496        -0.0726        0.2156       31.5721
K           -0.0100        -0.0127         0.0145       0.000667      27.6184
Y            1.2815         1.6219        -1.1814        0.1647       74.3457
```

The multiplier matrices (requested by the INTERIM=2 and TOTAL options) are printed next, as shown in Output 14.1.6.

Output 14.1.6. SIMLIN Procedure Output–Multipliers

```
              Simulation of Klein's Model I using SIMLIN

                           SIMLIN Procedure


                  Interim Multipliers for Interim 1

               WP             G              T             YR        INTERCEP

C            0.829130      1.049424       -0.865262    -.0054080     43.27442
P            0.609213      0.771077       -0.982167    -.0558215     28.39545
W            0.794488      1.005578       -0.710961    0.0125018     41.45124
I            0.574572      0.727231       -0.827867    -.0379117     26.57227
X            1.403702      1.776655       -1.693129    -.0433197     69.84670
WSUM         0.794488      1.005578       -0.710961    0.0125018     41.45124
K            0.564524      0.714514       -0.813366    -.0372452     54.19068
Y            1.403702      1.776655       -1.693129    -.0433197     69.84670


                  Interim Multipliers for Interim 2

               WP             G              T             YR        INTERCEP

C            0.663671      0.840004       -0.968727    -.0456589     28.36428
P            0.350716      0.443899       -0.618929    -.0401446     10.79216
W            0.658769      0.833799       -0.925467    -.0399178     28.33114
I            0.345813      0.437694       -0.575669    -.0344035     10.75901
X            1.009485      1.277698       -1.544396    -.0800624     39.12330
WSUM         0.658769      0.833799       -0.925467    -.0399178     28.33114
K            0.910337      1.152208       -1.389035    -.0716486     64.94969
Y            1.009485      1.277698       -1.544396    -.0800624     39.12330
```

Example 14.1. Simulating Klein's Model I □ □ □ 741

Output 14.1.6. (Continued)

```
            Simulation of Klein's Model I using SIMLIN

                         SIMLIN Procedure


                        Total Multipliers

            WP            G            T            YR         INTERCEP

C        1.881667     1.381613    -0.685987     0.1789624      41.3045
P        0.786945     0.996031    -1.286891    -.0748290       15.4770
W        1.094722     1.385582    -0.399095     0.2537914      25.8275
I        0.000000     0.000000    -0.000000     0.0000000       0.0000
X        1.881667     2.381613    -0.685987     0.1789624      41.3045
WSUM     2.094722     1.385582    -0.399095     0.2537914      25.8275
K        2.999365     3.796275    -4.904859    -.2852032      203.6035
Y        1.881667     2.381613    -1.685987     0.1789624      41.3045
```

The last part of the SIMLIN procedure output is a table of statistics of fit for the simulation, as shown in Output 14.1.7.

Output 14.1.7. SIMLIN Procedure Output – Simulation Statistics

```
            Simulation of Klein's Model I using SIMLIN

                         SIMLIN Procedure


                        Statistics of Fit

                        Mean       Mean %     Mean Abs     Mean Abs
      Variable    N     Error      Error       Error       % Error

         C       21    0.1367     -0.3827      3.5011       6.69769
         P       21    0.1422     -4.0671      2.9355      19.61400
         W       21    0.1282     -0.8939      3.1247       8.92110
         I       21    0.1337    105.8529      2.4983     127.13736
         X       21    0.2704     -0.9553      5.9622      10.40057
         WSUM    21    0.1282     -0.6669      3.1247       7.88988
         K       21   -0.1424     -0.1506      3.8879       1.90614
         Y       21    0.2704     -1.3476      5.9622      11.74177

                        Statistics of Fit

                        RMS        RMS %
      Variable          Error      Error     Label

         C              4.3155     8.1701    consumption
         P              3.4257    26.0265    profits
         W              4.0930    11.4709    private wage bill
         I              2.9980   252.3497    investment
         X              7.1881    12.5653    private production
         WSUM           4.0930    10.1724    total wage bill
         K              5.0036     2.4209    capital stock
         Y              7.1881    14.2214    national income
```

The OUTEST= output data set contains all the observations read from the EST= data set and also contains observations for the reduced form and multiplier matrices. The following statements produce a partial listing of the OUTEST= data set, as shown in Output 14.1.8:

```
proc print data=b;
   where _type_ = 'REDUCED' | _type_ = 'IMULT1';
run;
```

Output 14.1.8.   Partial Listing of OUTEST= Data Set

```
              Simulation of Klein's Model I using SIMLIN
```

OBS	_TYPE_	_DEPVAR_	_MODEL_	_SIGMA_	C	P	W	I	X	WSUM	K	Y
9	REDUCED	C	.	1.63465	0.63465	1.09566	0.63465	0	0.19585	0	1.29151
10	REDUCED	P	.	0.97236	0.97236	-0.34048	0.97236	0	1.10872	0	0.76825
11	REDUCED	W	.	0.64957	0.64957	1.44059	0.64957	0	0.07263	0	0.51321
12	REDUCED	I	.	-0.01272	0.98728	0.00445	-0.01272	0	-0.01450	0	-0.01005
13	REDUCED	X	.	1.62194	1.62194	1.10011	1.62194	0	0.18135	0	1.28146
14	REDUCED	WSUM	.	0.64957	0.64957	1.44059	0.64957	0	0.07263	0	1.51321
15	REDUCED	K	.	-0.01272	0.98728	0.00445	-0.01272	0	-0.01450	1	-0.01005
16	REDUCED	Y	.	1.62194	1.62194	1.10011	0.62194	1	0.18135	0	1.28146
17	IMULT1	C	.	.	.	.	.	.	.	.	.
18	IMULT1	P	.	.	.	.	.	.	.	.	.
19	IMULT1	W	.	.	.	.	.	.	.	.	.
20	IMULT1	I	.	.	.	.	.	.	.	.	.
21	IMULT1	X	.	.	.	.	.	.	.	.	.
22	IMULT1	WSUM	.	.	.	.	.	.	.	.	.

OBS	KLAG	PLAG	XLAG	WP	G	T	YR	INTERCEP
9	-0.12366	0.74631	0.19863	1.29151	0.63465	-0.19585	0.16399	46.7273
10	-0.18946	0.89347	-0.06173	0.76825	0.97236	-1.10872	-0.05096	42.7736
11	-0.12657	0.59687	0.26117	0.51321	0.64957	-0.07263	0.21562	31.5721
12	-0.19237	0.74404	0.00081	-0.01005	-0.01272	0.01450	0.00067	27.6184
13	-0.31603	1.49034	0.19944	1.28146	1.62194	-0.18135	0.16466	74.3457
14	-0.12657	0.59687	0.26117	1.51321	0.64957	-0.07263	0.21562	31.5721
15	0.80763	0.74404	0.00081	-0.01005	-0.01272	0.01450	0.00067	27.6184
16	-0.31603	1.49034	0.19944	1.28146	1.62194	-1.18135	0.16466	74.3457
17	.	.	.	0.82913	1.04942	-0.86526	-0.00541	43.2744
18	.	.	.	0.60921	0.77108	-0.98217	-0.05582	28.3955
19	.	.	.	0.79449	1.00558	-0.71096	0.01250	41.4512
20	.	.	.	0.57457	0.72723	-0.82787	-0.03791	26.5723
21	.	.	.	1.40370	1.77666	-1.69313	-0.04332	69.8467
22	.	.	.	0.79449	1.00558	-0.71096	0.01250	41.4512

Example 14.1. Simulating Klein's Model I □ □ □ 743

The actual and predicted values for the variable C are plotted in Output 14.1.9.

```
title2 h=1 'Plots of Simulation Results';
symbol1 i=none v=star;
symbol2 i=join v=plus h=2;
proc gplot data=c;
   plot c*year=1 chat*year=2 / overlay href=1941.5;
run;
```

Output 14.1.9. Plot of Actual and Predicted Consumption

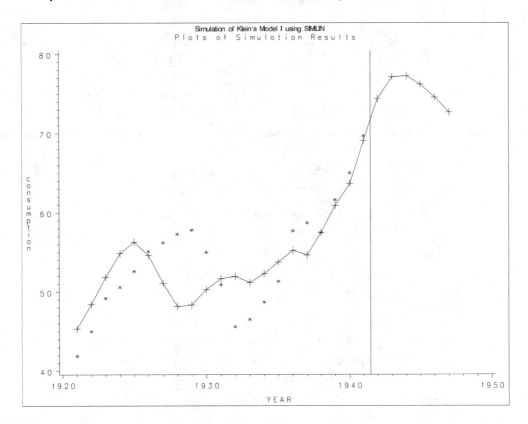

Example 14.2.   Multipliers for a Third-Order System

This example shows how to fit and simulate a single equation dynamic model with third-order lags. It then shows how to convert the third-order equation into a three-equation system with only first-order lags, so that the SIMLIN procedure can compute multipliers. (See the section "Multipliers for Higher-Order Lags" earlier in this chapter for more information.)

The input data set TEST is created from simulated data. A partial listing of the data set TEST produced by PROC PRINT is shown in Output 14.2.1.

```
title1 'Simulate Equation with Third-Order Lags';
title2 'Listing of Simulated Input Data';
proc print data=test(obs=10);
run;
```

Output 14.2.1.   Partial Listing of Input Data Set

```
                  Simulate Equation with Third-Order Lags
                       Listing of Simulated Input Data

      OBS        Y        YLAG1      YLAG2      YLAG3        X        N

        1      8.2369     8.5191     6.9491     7.8800    -1.2593     1
        2      8.6285     8.2369     8.5191     6.9491    -1.6805     2
        3     10.2223     8.6285     8.2369     8.5191    -1.9844     3
        4     10.1372    10.2223     8.6285     8.2369    -1.7855     4
        5     10.0360    10.1372    10.2223     8.6285    -1.8092     5
        6     10.3560    10.0360    10.1372    10.2223    -1.3921     6
        7     11.4835    10.3560    10.0360    10.1372    -2.0987     7
        8     10.8508    11.4835    10.3560    10.0360    -1.8788     8
        9     11.2684    10.8508    11.4835    10.3560    -1.7154     9
       10     12.6310    11.2684    10.8508    11.4835    -1.8418    10
```

The REG procedure in the following statements processes the input data and writes
the parameter estimates to the OUTEST= data set A:

```
title2 'Estimated Parameters';
proc reg data=test outest=a;
    model y=ylag3 x;
run;

title2 'Listing of OUTEST= Data Set';
proc print data=a;
run;
```

Output 14.2.2 shows the printed output produced by the REG procedure, and
Output 14.2.3 displays the OUTEST= data set A produced.

Output 14.2.2.   Estimates and Fit Information from PROC REG

```
                   Simulate Equation with Third-Order Lags
                             Estimated Parameters

Model: MODEL1
Dependent Variable: Y

                          Analysis of Variance

                              Sum of        Mean
        Source        DF      Squares      Square     F Value      Prob>F

        Model          2     173.98377    86.99189   1691.984      0.0001
        Error         27       1.38818     0.05141
        C Total       29     175.37196

            Root MSE        0.22675     R-square       0.9921
            Dep Mean       13.05234     Adj R-sq       0.9915
            C.V.            1.73721

                          Parameter Estimates

                         Parameter     Standard     T for H0:
        Variable   DF     Estimate       Error     Parameter=0    Prob > |T|

        INTERCEP    1     0.142386     0.23656658       0.602       0.5523
        YLAG3       1     0.771210     0.01722616      44.770       0.0001
        X           1    -1.776682     0.10842661     -16.386       0.0001
```

Example 14.2. Multipliers for a Third-Order System □ □ □ 745

Output 14.2.3. The OUTEST= Data Set Created by PROC REG

```
                 Simulate Equation with Third-Order Lags
                       Listing of OUTEST= Data Set

OBS    _MODEL_    _TYPE_    _DEPVAR_    _RMSE_    INTERCEP    YLAG3        X       Y

 1     MODEL1     PARMS        Y       0.22675    0.14239    0.77121   -1.77668   -1
```

The SIMLIN procedure processes the TEST data set using the estimates from PROC REG. The following statements perform the simulation and write the results to the OUT= data set OUT2:

```
title2 'Simulation of Equation';
proc simlin est=a data=test nored;
   endogenous y;
   exogenous  x;
   lagged ylag3 y 3;
   id n;
   output out=out1 predicted=yhat residual=yresid;
run;
```

The printed output from the SIMLIN procedure is shown in Output 14.2.4.

Output 14.2.4. Output Produced by PROC SIMLIN

```
                 Simulate Equation with Third-Order Lags
                        Simulation of Equation

                           SIMLIN Procedure


                          Statistics of Fit

                      Mean    Mean %   Mean Abs   Mean Abs     RMS     RMS %
Variable      N      Error    Error      Error     % Error    Error    Error

Y            30     -0.0233  -0.2268    0.2662     2.05684    0.3408   2.6159
```

The following statements plot the actual and predicted values, as shown in Output 14.2.5:

```
title2 'Plots of Simulation Results';
symbol1 i=none v=star;
symbol2 i=join v=plus h=2;
proc gplot data=out1;
   plot yhat*n=1 y*n=2 / overlay;
run;
```

Output 14.2.5. Plot of Predicted and Actual Values

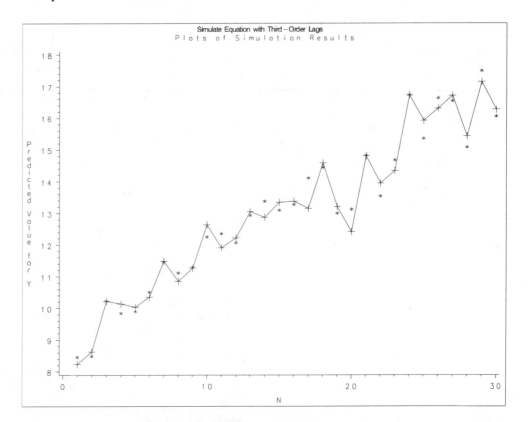

Next, you can modify the input data set TEST by creating two new variables, YLAG1X and YLAG2X, that are equal to YLAG1 and YLAG2. These variables are used in the SYSLIN procedure. (The estimates produced by PROC SYSLIN are the same as the estimates shown in Output 14.2.2 and are not shown.) A listing of the OUTEST= data set B created by PROC SYSLIN is shown in Output 14.2.6.

```
data test2;
   set test;
   ylag1x=ylag1;
   ylag2x=ylag2;
run;

title2 'Estimation of parameters and definition of identities';
proc syslin data=test2 outest=b;
   endogenous y ylag1x ylag2x;
   model y=ylag3 x;
   identity ylag1x=ylag1;
   identity ylag2x=ylag2;
run;

title2 'Listing of OUTEST= data set from PROC SYSLIN';
proc print data=b;
run;
```

Example 14.2. Multipliers for a Third-Order System □ □ □ 747

Output 14.2.6. Listing of OUTEST= Data Set Created from PROC SYSLIN

```
                  Simulate Equation with Third-Order Lags
                   Listing of OUTEST= data set from PROC SYSLIN

                        _                 I
                     _  D           _     N
                     M  E        S        T                          Y    Y
         _           O  P        I        E        Y        Y   Y    L    L
         T           D  V        G        R        L        L   L    A    A
   O     Y           E  A        M        C        A        A   A    G    G
   B     P           L  R        A        E        G        G   G    1    2
   S     E     _  _           _  P        3     X  1   2  Y X    X

   1  OLS      Y  Y     0.22675   0.14239  0.77121  -1.77668  .  . -1   .    .
   2  IDENTITY    YLAG1X  .       0.00000  .         .        1  .  . -1    .
   3  IDENTITY    YLAG2X  .       0.00000  .         .        .  1  .  . -1
```

The SIMLIN procedure is used to compute the reduced form and multipliers. The OUTEST= data set B from PROC SYSLIN is used as the EST= data set for the SIMLIN procedure. The following statements perform the multiplier analysis:

```
title2 'Simulation of transformed first-order equation system';

proc simlin est=b data=test2 total interim=2;
   endogenous y ylag1x ylag2x;
   exogenous  x;
   lagged  ylag1 y 1  ylag2 ylag1x 1  ylag3 ylag2x 1;
   id n;
   output out=out2 predicted=yhat residual=yresid;
run;
```

Output 14.2.7 shows the interim 2 and total multipliers printed by the SIMLIN procedure.

Output 14.2.7. Interim 2 and Total Multipliers

```
               Simulate Equation with Third-Order Lags
           Simulation of transformed first-order equation system

                          SIMLIN Procedure

               Interim Multipliers for Interim 2

                              X          INTERCEP

            Y          0.000000      0.0000000
            YLAG1X     0.000000      0.0000000
            YLAG2X    -1.776682      0.1423865


                   Total Multipliers

                              X          INTERCEP

            Y         -7.765556      0.6223455
            YLAG1X    -7.765556      0.6223455
            YLAG2X    -7.765556      0.6223455
```

References

Maddala, G.S (1977), *Econometrics*, New York: McGraw-Hill Book Co.

Pindyck, R.S. and Rubinfeld, D.L. (1991), *Econometric Models and Economic Forecasts*, Third Edition, New York: McGraw-Hill Book Co.

Theil, H. (1971), *Principles of Econometrics*, New York: John Wiley & Sons, Inc.

Chapter 15
The SPECTRA Procedure

Chapter Table of Contents

Chapter 15
The SPECTRA Procedure

Overview

The SPECTRA procedure performs spectral and cross-spectral analysis of time series. You can use spectral analysis techniques to look for periodicities or cyclical patterns in data.

The SPECTRA procedure produces estimates of the spectral and cross-spectral densities of a multivariate time series. Estimates of the spectral and cross-spectral densities of a multivariate time series are produced using a finite Fourier transform to obtain periodograms and cross-periodograms. The periodogram ordinates are smoothed by a moving average to produce estimated spectral and cross-spectral densities. PROC SPECTRA can also test whether or not the data are white noise.

PROC SPECTRA uses the finite Fourier transform to decompose data series into a sum of sine and cosine waves of different amplitudes and wavelengths. The Fourier transform decomposition of the series x_t is

$$x_t = \frac{a_0}{2} + \sum_{k=1}^{m} \left[a_k \cos(\omega_k t) + b_k \sin(\omega_k t) \right]$$

where

t is the time subscript, $t = 1, 2, \ldots, n$

x_t are the data

n is the number of observations in the time series

m is the number of frequencies in the Fourier decomposition: $m = \frac{n}{2}$ if n is even; $m = \frac{n-1}{2}$ if n is odd

a_0 is the mean term: $a_0 = 2\,\overline{x}$

a_k are the cosine coefficients

b_k are the sine coefficients

ω_k are the Fourier frequencies: $\omega_k = \frac{2\pi k}{n}$

Functions of the Fourier coefficients a_k and b_k can be plotted against frequency or against wavelength to form *periodograms*. The amplitude periodogram J_k is defined as follows:

$$J_k = \frac{n}{2} \left(a_k^2 + b_k^2 \right)$$

The spectral analysis literature uses several definitions of the term periodogram. The following discussion refers to the J_k sequence as the periodogram.

The periodogram can be interpreted as the contribution of the kth harmonic ω_k to the total sum of squares, in an analysis of variance sense, for the decomposition of the process into two-degree-of-freedom components for each of the m frequencies. When n is even, $\sin(\omega_{n/2})$ is zero, and thus the last periodogram value is a one-degree-of-freedom component.

The periodogram is a volatile and inconsistent estimator of the spectrum. The spectral density estimate is produced by smoothing the periodogram. Smoothing reduces the variance of the estimator but introduces a bias. The weight function used for the smoothing process, W(), often called the kernel or spectral window, is specified with the WEIGHTS statement. It is related to another weight function, $w()$, the lag window, which is used in other methods to taper the correlogram rather than to smooth the periodogram. Many specific weighting functions have been suggested (Fuller 1976, Jenkins and Watts 1968, Priestly 1981). Table 15.1 later in this chapter gives the formulas relevant when the WEIGHTS statement is used.

Letting i represent the imaginary unit $\sqrt{-1}$, the cross-periodogram is defined as follows:

$$J_k^{xy} = \frac{n}{2}\left(a_k^x a_k^y + b_k^x b_k^y\right) + i \frac{n}{2}\left(a_k^x b_k^y - b_k^x a_k^y\right)$$

The cross-spectral density estimate is produced by smoothing the cross-periodogram in the same way the periodograms are smoothed using the spectral window specified by the WEIGHTS statement.

The SPECTRA procedure creates an output SAS data set with variables that contain values of the periodograms, cross-periodograms, estimates of spectral densities, and estimates of cross-spectral densities. The section "OUT= Data Set" later in this chapter describes the form of the output data set.

Getting Started

To use the SPECTRA procedure, specify the input and output data sets and options for the analysis you want on the PROC SPECTRA statement, and list the variables you want to analyze in the VAR statement.

For example, to take the Fourier transform of a variable X in a data set A, use the following statements:

```
proc spectra data=a out=b coef;
   var x;
run;
```

This PROC SPECTRA step writes the Fourier coefficients a_k and b_k to the variables COS_01 and SIN_01 in the output data set B.

When you specify a WEIGHT statement, the periodogram is smoothed by a weighted moving average to produce an estimate for the spectral density of the series. The following statements write a spectral density estimate for X to the variable S_01 in the output data set B:

```
proc spectra data=a out=b s;
   var x;
   weight 1 2 3 4 3 2 1;
run;
```

When you specify more than one variable in the VAR statement, you can perform cross-spectral analysis by specifying the CROSS option. The CROSS option by itself produces the cross-periodograms. For example, the following statements write the real and imaginary parts of the cross-periodogram of X and Y to the variable RP_01_02 and IP_01_02 in the output data set B:

```
proc spectra data=a out=b cross;
   var x y;
run;
```

To produce cross-spectral density estimates, combine the CROSS option and the S option. The cross-periodogram is smoothed using the weights specified by the WEIGHTS statement in the same way as the spectral density. The squared coherency and phase estimates of the cross-spectrum are computed when you specify the K and PH options.

The following example computes cross-spectral density estimates for the variables X and Y:

```
proc spectra data=a out=b cross s;
   var x y;
   weight 1 2 3 4 3 2 1;
run;
```

The real part and imaginary part of the cross-spectral density estimates are written to the variable CS_01_02 and QS_01_02, respectively.

Syntax

The following statements are used with the SPECTRA procedure:

PROC SPECTRA *options*;
  BY *variables*;
  VAR *variables*;
  WEIGHTS *constants*;

Functional Summary

The statements and options controlling the SPECTRA procedure are summarized in the following table:

Description	Statement	Option
Statements		
specify BY-group processing	BY	
specify the variables to be analyzed	VAR	
specify weights for spectral density estimates	WEIGHTS	
Data Set Options		
specify the input data set	PROC SPECTRA	DATA=
specify the output data set	PROC SPECTRA	OUT=
Output Control Options		
output the amplitudes of the cross-spectrum	PROC SPECTRA	A
output the Fourier coefficients	PROC SPECTRA	COEF
output the periodogram	PROC SPECTRA	P
output the spectral density estimates	PROC SPECTRA	S
output cross-spectral analysis results	PROC SPECTRA	CROSS
output squared coherency of the cross-spectrum	PROC SPECTRA	K
output the phase of the cross-spectrum	PROC SPECTRA	PH
Other Options		
subtract the series mean	PROC SPECTRA	ADJMEAN
request tests for white noise	PROC SPECTRA	WHITETEST

PROC SPECTRA Statement

PROC SPECTRA *options*;

The following options can be used in the PROC SPECTRA statement:

A

outputs the amplitude variables (A_*nn_mm*) of the cross-spectrum.

ADJMEAN
CENTER

subtracts the series mean before performing the Fourier decomposition. This sets the first periodogram ordinate to 0 rather than $2n$ times the squared mean. This option is commonly used when the periodograms are to be plotted to prevent a large first periodogram ordinate from distorting the scale of the plot.

COEF

outputs the Fourier cosine and sine coefficients of each series, in addition to the periodogram.

CROSS

is used with the P and S options to output cross-periodograms and cross-spectral densities.

DATA= *SAS-data-set*

names the SAS data set containing the input data. If you omit the DATA= option, the most recently created SAS data set is used.

K

outputs the squared coherency variables (K_*nn_mm*) of the cross-spectrum. The K_*nn_mm* variables are identically 1 unless you specify weights in the WEIGHTS statement and specify the S option.

OUT= *SAS-data-set*

names the output data set created by PROC SPECTRA to store the results. If you omit the OUT= option, the output data set is named using the DATA*n* convention.

P

outputs the periodogram variables. The variables are named P_*nn*, where *nn* is an index of the original variable with which the periodogram variable is associated. When you specify both the P and CROSS options, the cross-periodogram variables RP_*nn_mm* and IP_*nn_mm* are also output.

PH

outputs the phase variables (PH_*nn_mm*) of the cross-spectrum.

S

outputs the spectral density estimates. The variables are named S_*nn*, where *nn* is an index of the original variable with which the estimate variable is associated. When you specify both the S and CROSS options, the cross-spectral variables CS_*nn_mm* and QS_*nn_mm* are also output.

WHITETEST

prints a test of the hypothesis that the series are white noise. See the section "White Noise Test" later in this chapter for details.

Note that the CROSS, A, K, and PH options are only meaningful if you specify more than one variable in the VAR statement.

BY Statement

BY *variables*;

A BY statement can be used with PROC SPECTRA to obtain separate analyses for groups of observations defined by the BY variables.

VAR Statement

> **VAR** *variables*;

The VAR statement specifies one or more numeric variables containing the time series to analyze. The order of the variables in the VAR statement list determines the index, *nn*, used to name the output variables. The VAR statement is required.

WEIGHTS Statement

> **WEIGHTS** *constants*;

The WEIGHTS statement specifies the relative weights used in the moving average applied to the periodogram ordinates to form the spectral density estimates. A WEIGHTS statement must be used to produce smoothed spectral density estimates. If you do not use the WEIGHTS statement, only the periodogram is produced.

You can specify any number of weighting constants. The constants should be positive and symmetric about the middle weight. The middle constant (or the constant to the right of the middle if you specify an even number of weight constants) is the relative weight of the current periodogram ordinate. The constant immediately following the middle one is the relative weight of the next periodogram ordinate, and so on. The actual weights used in the smoothing process are the weights you specify in the WEIGHTS statement scaled so that they sum to $\frac{1}{4\pi}$.

The moving average reflects at each end of the periodogram. The first periodogram ordinate is not used; the second periodogram ordinate is used in its place.

For example, you can specify a simple triangular weighting using the following WEIGHTS statement:

```
weights 1 2 3 2 1;
```

Details

Input Data

Observations in the data set analyzed by the SPECTRA procedure should form ordered, equally spaced time series. No more than 99 variables can be included in the analysis.

Data are often de-trended before analysis by the SPECTRA procedure; this can be done using SAS regression procedures to output residuals. Optionally, the data can be centered using the ADJMEAN option in the PROC SPECTRA statement, since the zero periodogram ordinate corresponding to the mean is of little interest from the point of view of spectral analysis.

Computational Method

If the number of observations, n, factors into prime integers that are less than or equal to 23, and the product of the square-free factors of n is less than 210, then PROC SPECTRA uses the Fast Fourier Transform developed by Cooley and Tukey and implemented by Singleton (1969). If n cannot be factored this way, then PROC SPECTRA uses a Chirp-Z algorithm similar to that proposed by Monro and Branch (1976). To reduce memory requirements, when n is small the Fourier coefficients are computed directly using the defining formulas.

White Noise Test

PROC SPECTRA prints two test statistics for white noise when the WHITETEST option is specified: Fisher's Kappa statistic (Davis 1941, Fuller 1976) and Bartlett's Kolmogorov-Smirnov statistic (Bartlett 1966, Fuller 1976, Durbin 1967).

If the time series is a sequence of independent random variables with mean 0 and variance σ^2, then the periodogram J_k will have the same expected value for all k. For a time series with nonzero autocorrelation, each ordinate of the periodogram J_k will have different expected values. The Fisher's Kappa statistic tests whether the largest J_k can be considered different from the mean of the J_k. Critical values for the Fisher's Kappa test can be found in Fuller 1976 and *SAS/ETS Software: Applications Guide 1, Version 6, First Edition*.

The Kolmogorov-Smirnov statistic reported by PROC SPECTRA has the same asymtotic distribution as Bartlett's test (Durbin 1967). The Kolmogorov-Smirnov statistic compares the normalized cumulative periodogram and the cumulative distribution function of a uniform(0,1) random variable. The normalized cumulative periodogram, F_j, of the series is

$$F_j = \frac{\sum_{k=1}^{j} J_k}{\sum_{k=1}^{m} J_k}, j = 1, 2, ..., m - 1$$

where $m = \frac{n}{2}$ if n is even or $m = \frac{n-1}{2}$ if n is odd. The test statistic is the maximum absolute difference of the normalized cumulative periodogram and the uniform cumulative distribution function. For $m - 1 > 100$, if Bartlett's Kolmogorov-Smirnov statistic exceeds the critical value $a/(m-1)^{1/2}$ then reject the null hypothesis that the series represents white noise. The values $a = 1.36$ or $a = 1.63$ corresponding to 5% or 1% significance levels, respectively. Critical values for $m - 1 < 100$ can be found in a table of significance points of the Kolmogorov-Smirnov statistics with sample size $m - 1$ (Miller 1956, Owen 1962).

Transforming Frequencies

The variable FREQ in the data set created by the SPECTRA procedure ranges from 0 to π. Sometimes it is preferable to express frequencies in cycles per observation period, which is equal to $\frac{2}{\pi}$FREQ.

To express frequencies in cycles per unit of time (for example, in cycles per year), multiply FREQ by $\frac{d}{2\pi}$, where d is the number of observations per unit of time. For example, for monthly data, if the desired time unit is years, then d is 12. The period of the cycle is $\frac{2\pi}{d \times \text{FREQ}}$, which ranges from $\frac{2}{d}$ to infinity.

Missing Values

The SPECTRA procedure does not support missing values. If the SPECTRA procedure encounters a missing value for any variable listed in the VAR statement, it prints an error message and stops.

OUT= Data Set

The OUT= data set contains $\frac{n}{2} + 1$ observations, if n is even, or $\frac{n+1}{2}$ observations, if n is odd, where n is the number of observations in the time series.

The variables in the new data set are named according to the following conventions. Each variable to be analyzed is associated with an index. The first variable listed in the VAR statement is indexed as 01, the second variable as 02, and so on. Output variables are named by combining indices with prefixes. The prefix always identifies the nature of the new variable, and the indices identify the original variables from which the statistics were obtained.

Variables containing spectral analysis results have names consisting of a prefix, an underscore, and the index of the variable analyzed. For example, the variable S_01 contains spectral density estimates for the first variable in the VAR statement. Variables containing cross-spectral analysis results have names consisting of a prefix, an underscore, the index of the first variable, another underscore, and the index of the second variable. For example, the variable A_01_02 contains the amplitude of the cross-spectral density estimate for the first and second variables in the VAR statement.

Table 15.1 shows the formulas and naming conventions used for the variables in the OUT= data set. Let X be variable number *nn* in the VAR statement list and let Y be variable number *mm* in the VAR statement list. Table 15.1 shows the output variables containing the results of the spectral and cross-spectral analysis of X and Y.

Table 15.1 uses the following notation. Let $\mathbf{W}_j$ be the vector of $2p + 1$ smoothing weights given by the WEIGHTS statement, normalized to sum to $\frac{1}{4\pi}$. The subscript of $\mathbf{W}_j$ runs from $\mathbf{W}_{-p}$ to $\mathbf{W}_p$, so that $\mathbf{W}_0$ is the middle weight in the WEIGHTS statement list. Let $\omega_k = \frac{2\pi k}{n}$, where $k = 0, 1, \ldots, \text{floor}\left(\frac{n}{2}\right)$.

Table 15.1.   Variables Created by PROC SPECTRA

Variable	Description
FREQ	frequency in radians from 0 to π (Note: Cycles per observation is $\frac{\text{FREQ}}{2\pi}$.)
PERIOD	period or wavelength: $\frac{2\pi}{\text{FREQ}}$ (Note: PERIOD is missing for FREQ=0.)
COS_*nn*	cosine transform of X: $a_k^x = \frac{2}{n} \sum_{t=1}^n \mathbf{X}_t \cos(\omega_k(t-1))$
SIN_*nn*	sine transform of X: $b_k^x = \frac{2}{n} \sum_{t=1}^n \mathbf{X}_t \sin(\omega_k(t-1))$
P_*nn*	periodogram of X: $J_k^x = \frac{n}{2}\left[\left(a_k^x\right)^2 + \left(b_k^x\right)^2\right]$
S_*nn*	spectral density estimate of X: $F_k^x = \sum_{j=-p}^{p} \mathbf{W}_j J_{k+j}^x$ (except across endpoints)
RP_*nn*_*mm*	real part of cross-periodogram X and Y: $\text{real}(J_k^{xy}) = \frac{n}{2}\left(a_k^x a_k^y + b_k^x b_k^y\right)$
IP_*nn*_*mm*	imaginary part of cross-periodogram of X and Y: $\text{imag}(J_k^{xy}) = \frac{n}{2}\left(a_k^x b_k^y - b_k^x a_k^y\right)$
CS_*nn*_*mm*	cospectrum estimate (real part of cross-spectrum) of X and Y: $C_k^{xy} = \sum_{j=-p}^{p} \mathbf{W}_j \, \text{real}\left(J_{k+j}^{xy}\right)$ (except across endpoints)
QS_*nn*_*mm*	quadrature spectrum estimate (imaginary part of cross-spectrum) of X and Y: $Q_k^{xy} = \sum_{j=-p}^{p} \mathbf{W}_j \, \text{imag}\left(J_{k+j}^{xy}\right)$ (except across endpoints)
A_*nn*_*mm*	amplitude (modulus) of cross-spectrum of X and Y: $A_k^{xy} = \sqrt{C_k^{xy\,2} + Q_k^{xy\,2}}$
K_*nn*_*mm*	coherency squared of X and Y: $K_k^{xy} = \left(A_k^{xy}\right)^2 / \left(F_k^x F_k^y\right)$
PH_*nn*_*mm*	phase spectrum in radians of X and Y: $\Phi_k^{xy} = \arctan\left(Q_k^{xy}/C_k^{xy}\right)$

Printed Output

When you specify the WHITETEST option, the SPECTRA procedure prints the following statistics for each variable in the VAR statement:

1. the name of the variable

2. $M-1$, the number of two-degree-of-freedom periodogram ordinates used in the tests

3. MAX(P(*)), the maximum periodogram ordinate

4. SUM(P(*)), the sum of the periodogram ordinates

5. Fisher's Kappa statistic

6. Bartlett's Kolmogorov-Smirnov test statistic

If you do not specify the WHITETEST option, PROC SPECTRA produces no printed output. See the section "White Noise Test" earlier in this chapter for details.

Examples

Example 15.1.   Spectral Analysis of Sunspot Activity

This example analyzes Wolfer's sunspot data (Anderson 1971). The following statements read and plot the data:

```
title "Wolfer's Sunspot Data";
data sunspot;
   input year wolfer @@;
   cards;
1749  809 1750  834 1751  477 1752  478 1753  307 1754  122 1755   96
1756  102 1757  324 1758  476 1759  540 1760  629 1761  859 1762  612
1763  451 1764  364 1765  209 1766  114 1767  378 1768  698 1769 1061
1770 1008 1771  816 1772  665 1773  348 1774  306 1775   70 1776  198
1777  925 1778 1544 1779 1259 1780  848 1781  681 1782  385 1783  228
1784  102 1785  241 1786  829 1787 1320 1788 1309 1789 1181 1790  899
1791  666 1792  600 1793  469 1794  410 1795  213 1796  160 1797   64
1798   41 1799   68 1800  145 1801  340 1802  450 1803  431 1804  475
1805  422 1806  281 1807  101 1808   81 1809   25 1810    0 1811   14
1812   50 1813  122 1814  139 1815  354 1816  458 1817  411 1818  304
1819  239 1820  157 1821   66 1822   40 1823   18 1824   85 1825  166
1826  363 1827  497 1828  625 1829  670 1830  710 1831  478 1832  275
1833   85 1834  132 1835  569 1836 1215 1837 1383 1838 1032 1839  858
1840  632 1841  368 1842  242 1843  107 1844  150 1845  401 1846  615
1847  985 1848 1243 1849  959 1850  665 1851  645 1852  542 1853  390
1854  206 1855   67 1856   43 1857  228 1858  548 1859  938 1860  957
1861  772 1862  591 1863  440 1864  470 1865  305 1866  163 1867   73
1868  373 1869  739 1870 1391 1871 1112 1872 1017 1873  663 1874  447
1875  171 1876  113 1877  123 1878   34 1879   60 1880  323 1881  543
1882  597 1883  637 1884  635 1885  522 1886  254 1887  131 1888   68
1889   63 1890   71 1891  356 1892  730 1893  849 1894  780 1895  640
1896  418 1897  262 1898  267 1899  121 1900   95 1901   27 1902   50
1903  244 1904  420 1905  635 1906  538 1907  620 1908  485 1909  439
1910  186 1911   57 1912   36 1913   14 1914   96 1915  474 1916  571
1917 1039 1918  806 1919  636 1920  376 1921  261 1922  142 1923   58
1924  167
;

symbol1 i=splines v=plus;
proc gplot data=sunspot;
   plot wolfer*year;
run;
```

Output 15.1.1 shows the plot of the sunspot series.

Example 15.1. Spectral Analysis of Sunspot Activity □ □ □ 761

Output 15.1.1. Plot of Original Data

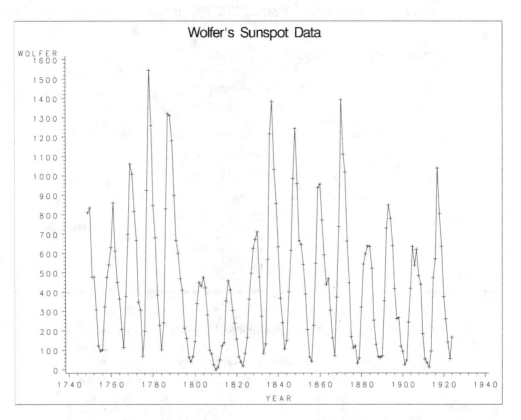

The spectral analysis of the sunspot series is performed by the following statements:

```
proc spectra data=sunspot out=b p s adjmean whitetest;
   var wolfer;
   weights 1 2 3 4 3 2 1;
run;

proc print data=b(obs=12);
run;
```

The PROC SPECTRA statement specifies the P and S options to write the periodogram and spectral density estimates to the OUT= data set B. The WEIGHTS statement specifies a triangular spectral window for smoothing the periodogram to produce the spectral density estimate. The ADJMEAN option zeros the frequency 0 value and avoids the need to exclude that observation from the plots. The WHITETEST option prints tests for white noise.

The Fisher's Kappa test statistic 16.070 is larger than the 5% critical value 7.2, so the null hypothesis that the sunspot series is white noise is rejected.

The Bartlett's Kolmogorov-Smirnov statistic 0.6501 is greater than

$$a\sqrt{1/(m-1)} = 1.36\sqrt{1/87} = 0.1458$$

so reject the null hypothesis that the spectrum represents white noise.

The printed output produced by PROC SPECTRA is shown in Output 15.1.2. The output data set B created by PROC SPECTRA is shown in part in Output 15.1.3.

Output 15.1.2. White Noise Test Results

```
                     Wolfer's Sunspot Data

                       SPECTRA Procedure


      ----- Test for White Noise for variable WOLFER -----

      Fisher's Kappa: (M-1)*MAX(P(*))/SUM(P(*))
      Parameters:    M-1      =        87
                     MAX(P(*)) =4062266.95
                     SUM(P(*)) =21156512.1
      Test Statistic: Kappa    =   16.7049

      Bartlett's Kolmogorov-Smirnov Statistic:
                  Maximum absolute difference of the standardized
                  partial sums of the periodogram and the CDF of a
                  uniform(0,1) random variable.

      Test Statistic =    0.6501
```

Output 15.1.3. First 12 Observations of the OUT= Data Set

```
                     Wolfer's Sunspot Data

       OBS     FREQ      PERIOD         P_01       S_01

         1   0.00000        .           0.00     59327.52
         2   0.03570    176.000      3178.15     61757.98
         3   0.07140     88.000   2435433.22     69528.68
         4   0.10710     58.667   1077495.76     66087.57
         5   0.14280     44.000    491850.36     53352.02
         6   0.17850     35.200      2581.12     36678.14
         7   0.21420     29.333    181163.15     20604.52
         8   0.24990     25.143    283057.60     15132.81
         9   0.28560     22.000    188672.97     13265.89
        10   0.32130     19.556    122673.94     14953.32
        11   0.35700     17.600     58532.93     16402.84
        12   0.39270     16.000    213405.16     18562.13
```

The following statements plot the periodogram and spectral density estimate:

```
proc gplot data=b;
   plot p_01 * freq;
   plot p_01 * period;
   plot s_01 * freq;
   plot s_01 * period;
run;
```

The periodogram is plotted against frequency in Output 15.1.4 and plotted against period in Output 15.1.5. The spectral density estimate is plotted against frequency in Output 15.1.6 and plotted against period in Output 15.1.7.

Example 15.1. Spectral Analysis of Sunspot Activity □ □ □ 763

Output 15.1.4. Plot of Periodogram by Frequency

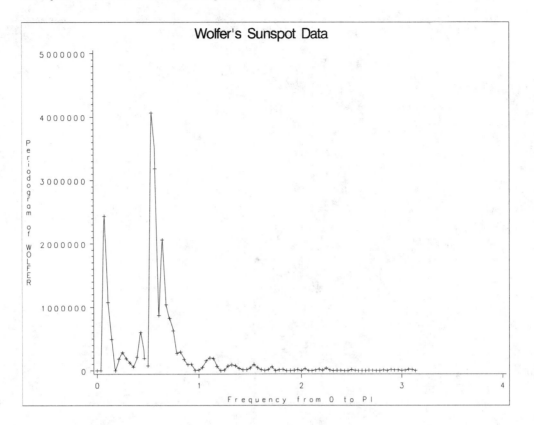

Output 15.1.5. Plot of Periodogram by Period

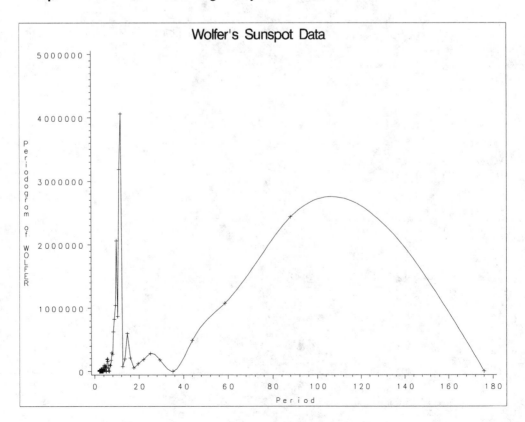

Output 15.1.6. Plot of Spectral Density Estimate by Frequency

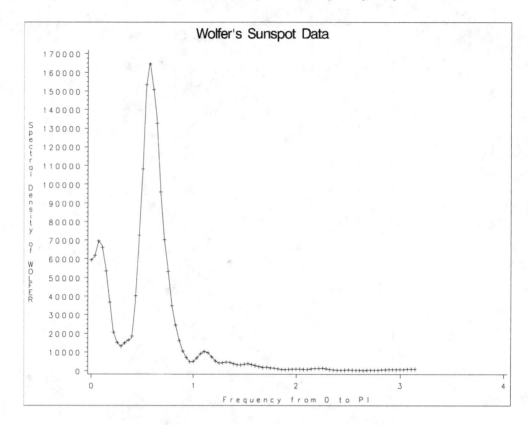

Output 15.1.7. Plot of Spectral Density Estimate by Period

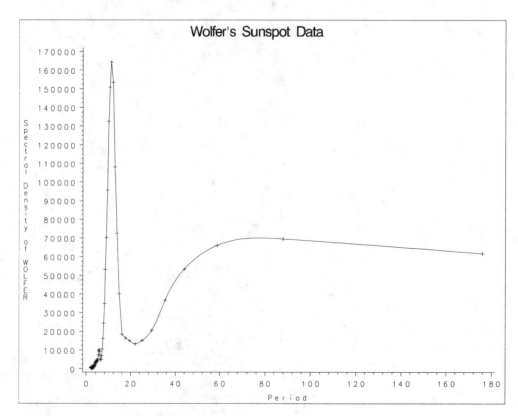

Example 15.1. Spectral Analysis of Sunspot Activity □ □ □ 765

Since PERIOD is the reciprocal of frequency, the plot axis for PERIOD is stretched for low frequencies and compressed at high frequencies. One way to correct this is to use a WHERE statement to restrict the plots and exclude the low frequency components. The following statements plot the spectral density for periods less than 50:

```
proc gplot data=b;
   where period < 50;
   plot s_01 * period / href=11;
run;
```

The spectral analysis of the sunspot series confirms a strong 11-year cycle of sunspot activity. The plot makes this clear by drawing a reference line at the 11-year period, which highlights the position of the main peak in the spectral density.

Output 15.1.8 shows the plot. Compare Output 15.1.8 and Output 15.1.7.

Output 15.1.8. Plot of Spectral Density Estimate by Period to 50 Years

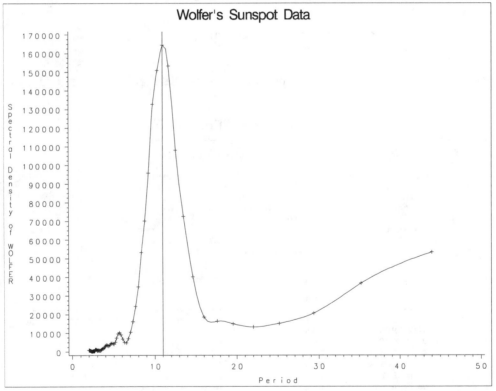

Example 15.2.   Cross-Spectral Analysis

This example shows cross-spectral analysis for two variables X and Y using simulated data. X is generated by an AR(1) process; Y is generated as white noise plus an input from X lagged 2 periods. All output options are specified on the PROC SPECTRA statement. PROC CONTENTS shows the contents of the OUT= data set.

```
data a;
   xl = 0; xll = 0;
   do i = - 10 to 100;
      x = .4 * xl  + rannor(123);
      y = .5 * xll + rannor(123);
      if i > 0 then output;
      xll = xl; xl = x;
      end;
run;

proc spectra data=a out=b cross coef a k p ph s;
   var x y;
   weights 1 1.5 2 4 8 9 8 4 2 1.5 1;
run;

proc contents data=b position;
run;
```

The PROC CONTENTS report for the output data set B is shown in Output 15.2.1.

Output 15.2.1.   Contents of PROC SPECTRA OUT= Data Set

```
                          CONTENTS PROCEDURE

Data Set Name: WORK.B                   Observations:           51
Member Type:   DATA                     Variables:              17
Engine:        SASEB                    Indexes:                0
Created:       DDMMMYY:00:00:00         Observation Length:     136
Last Modified: DDMMMYY:00:00:00         Deleted Observations:   0
Protection:                             Compressed:             NO
Data Set Type: DATA                     Sorted:                 NO
Label:         Spectral Density Estimates


               -----Variables Ordered by Position-----

   #   Variable   Type   Len   Pos   Label
   ------------------------------------------------------------------
   1   FREQ       Num     8     0    Frequency from 0 to PI
   2   PERIOD     Num     8     8    Period
   3   COS_01     Num     8    16    Cosine Transform of X
   4   SIN_01     Num     8    24    Sine Transform of X
   5   COS_02     Num     8    32    Cosine Transform of Y
   6   SIN_02     Num     8    40    Sine Transform of Y
   7   P_01       Num     8    48    Periodogram of X
   8   P_02       Num     8    56    Periodogram of Y
   9   S_01       Num     8    64    Spectral Density of X
  10   S_02       Num     8    72    Spectral Density of Y
  11   RP_01_02   Num     8    80    Real Periodogram of X by Y
  12   IP_01_02   Num     8    88    Imag Periodogram of X by Y
  13   CS_01_02   Num     8    96    Cospectra of X by Y
  14   QS_01_02   Num     8   104    Quadrature of X by Y
  15   K_01_02    Num     8   112    Coherency**2 of X by Y
  16   A_01_02    Num     8   120    Amplitude of X by Y
  17   PH_01_02   Num     8   128    Phase of X by Y
```

Example 15.2. Cross-Spectral Analysis □ □ □ 767

The following statements plot the amplitude of the cross-spectrum estimate against frequency and against period for periods less than 25:

```
symbol1 i=splines v=plus;
proc gplot data=b;
   plot a_01_02 * freq;
run;

proc gplot data=b;
   plot a_01_02 * period;
   where period < 25;
run;
```

Output 15.2.2 shows the plot of the amplitude of the cross-spectrum estimate against frequency. Output 15.2.3 shows the plot of the cross-spectrum amplitude against period for periods less than 25 observations.

Output 15.2.2. Plot of Cross-Spectrum Amplitude by Frequency

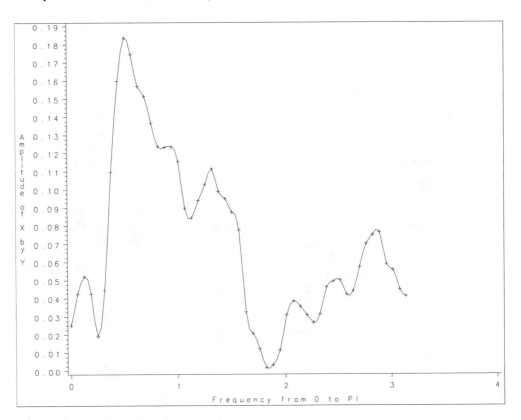

Output 15.2.3.   Plot of Cross-Spectrum Amplitude by Period

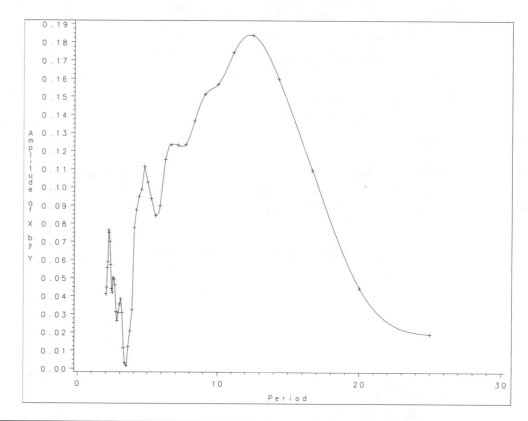

References

Anderson, T.W. (1971), *The Statistical Analysis of Time Series*, New York: John Wiley & Sons, Inc.

Bartlett, M.S. (1966), *An Introduction to Stochastic Processes*, Second Edition, Cambridge: Cambridge University Press.

Brillinger, D.R. (1975), *Time Series: Data Analysis and Theory*, New York: Holt, Rinehart and Winston, Inc.

Davis, H.T. (1941), *The Analysis of Economic Time Series*, Bloomington, IN: Principia Press.

Durbin, J. (1967), "Tests of Serial Independence Based on the Cumulated Periodogram," *Bulletin of International Statistics Institute*, 42, 1039–1049.

Fuller, W.A. (1976), *Introduction to Statistical Time Series*, New York: John Wiley & Sons, Inc.

Gentleman, W.M. and Sande, G. (1966), "Fast Fourier transforms—for fun and profit," *AFIPS Proceedings of the Fall Joint Computer Conference*, 19, 563–578.

Jenkins, G.M. and Watts, D.G. (1968), *Spectral Analysis and Its Applications*, San Francisco: Holden-Day.

Miller, L. H. (1956), "Tables of Percentage Points of Kolmogorov Statistics," *Journal of American Statistic Association*, 51, 111.

Monro, D.M. and Branch, J.L. (1976), "Algorithm AS 117. The chirp discrete Fourier transform of general length," *Applied Statistics*, 26, 351–361.

Nussbaumer, H.J. (1982), *Fast Fourier Transform and Convolution Algorithms*, Second Edition, New York: Springer-Verlag.

Owen, D. B. (1962), *Handbook of Statistical Tables*, Addison Wesley.

Priestly, M.B. (1981), *Spectral Analysis and Time Series*, New York: Academic Press, Inc.

Singleton, R.C. (1969), "An Algorithm for Computing the Mixed Radix Fast Fourier Transform," *IEEE Transactions of Audio and Electroacoustics*, AU-17, 93–103.

Chapter 16
The STATESPACE Procedure

Chapter Table of Contents

Chapter 16
The STATESPACE Procedure

Overview

The STATESPACE procedure analyzes and forecasts multivariate time series using the state space model. The STATESPACE procedure is appropriate for jointly forecasting several related time series that have dynamic interactions. By taking into account the autocorrelations among the whole set of variables, the STATESPACE procedure may give better forecasts than methods that model each series separately.

By default, the STATESPACE procedure automatically selects a state space model appropriate for the time series, making the procedure a good tool for automatic forecasting of multivariate time series. Alternatively, you can specify the state space model by giving the form of the state vector and the state transition and innovation matrices.

The methods used by the STATESPACE procedure assume that the time series are jointly stationary. Nonstationary series must be made stationary by some preliminary transformation, usually by differencing. The STATESPACE procedure enables you to specify differencing of the input data. When you specify differencing, the STATESPACE procedure automatically integrates forecasts of the differenced series to produce forecasts of the original series.

The State Space Model

The *state space model* represents a multivariate time series through auxiliary variables, some of which may not be directly observable. These auxiliary variables are called the state vector. The *state vector* summarizes all the information from the present and past values of the time series relevant to the prediction of future values of the series. The observed time series are expressed as linear combinations of the state variables. The state space model is also called a Markovian representation, or a canonical representation, of a multivariate time series process. The state space approach to modeling a multivariate stationary time series is summarized by Akaike (1976).

The state space form encompasses a very rich class of models. Any Gaussian multivariate stationary time series can be written in a state space form, provided that the dimension of the predictor space is finite. In particular, any autoregressive moving average (ARMA) process has a state space representation and, conversely, any state space process can be expressed in an ARMA form (Akaike 1974). More details on the relation of the state space and ARMA forms are given in the section "Relation of ARMA and State Space Forms" later in this chapter.

Let $\mathbf{x}_t$ be the $r \times 1$ vector of observed variables, after differencing (if you specified differencing) and subtracting the sample mean. Let $\mathbf{z}_t$ be the state vector of dimension s, $s \geq r$, where the first r components of $\mathbf{z}_t$ consist of $\mathbf{x}_t$. Let the notation $\mathbf{x}_{t+k|t}$

represent the conditional expectation (or prediction) of $\mathbf{x}_{t+k}$ based on the information available at time t. Then the last $s - r$ elements of $\mathbf{z}_t$ consist of elements of $\mathbf{x}_{t+k|t}$, where $k > 0$ is specified or determined automatically by the procedure.

There are various forms of the state space model in use. The form of the state space model used by the STATESPACE procedure is based on Akaike (1976). The model is defined by the following *state transition equation*:

$$\mathbf{z}_{t+1} = \mathbf{F} \mathbf{z}_t + \mathbf{G} \mathbf{e}_{t+1}$$

In the state transition equation, the $s \times s$ coefficient matrix $\mathbf{F}$ is called the *transition matrix*; it determines the dynamic properties of the model.

The $s \times r$ coefficient matrix $\mathbf{G}$ is called the *input matrix*; it determines the variance structure of the transition equation. For model identification, the first r rows and columns of $\mathbf{G}$ are set to an $r \times r$ identity matrix.

The input vector $\mathbf{e}_t$ is a sequence of independent normally distributed random vectors of dimension r with mean $\mathbf{0}$ and covariance matrix $\Sigma_{\mathbf{ee}}$. The random error $\mathbf{e}_t$ is sometimes called the innovation vector or shock vector.

In addition to the state transition equation, state space models usually include a *measurement equation* or *observation equation* that gives the observed values $\mathbf{x}_t$ as a function of the state vector $\mathbf{z}_t$. However, since PROC STATESPACE always includes the observed values $\mathbf{x}_t$ in the state vector $\mathbf{z}_t$, the measurement equation in this case merely represents the extraction of the first r components of the state vector.

The measurement equation used by the STATESPACE procedure is

$$\mathbf{x}_t = \begin{bmatrix} \mathbf{I}_r & \mathbf{0} \end{bmatrix} \mathbf{z}_t$$

where $\mathbf{I}_r$ is an $r \times r$ identity matrix. In practice, PROC STATESPACE performs the extraction of $\mathbf{x}_t$ from $\mathbf{z}_t$ without reference to an explicit measurement equation.

In summary

- $\mathbf{x}_t$　is an observation vector of dimension r.
- $\mathbf{z}_t$　is a state vector of dimension s, whose first r elements are $\mathbf{x}_t$ and whose last $s - r$ elements are conditional prediction of future $\mathbf{x}_t$.
- $\mathbf{F}$　is an $s \times s$ transition matrix.
- $\mathbf{G}$　is an $s \times r$ input matrix, with the identity matrix $\mathbf{I}_r$ forming the first r rows and columns.
- $\mathbf{e}_t$　is a sequence of independent normally distributed random vectors of dimension r with mean $\mathbf{0}$ and covariance matrix $\Sigma_{\mathbf{ee}}$.

How PROC STATESPACE Works

The design of the STATESPACE procedure closely follows the modeling strategy proposed by Akaike (1976). This strategy employs canonical correlation analysis for the automatic identification of the state space model.

Following Akaike (1976), the procedure first fits a sequence of unrestricted vector autoregressive (VAR) models and computes Akaike's information criterion (AIC) for each model. The vector autoregressive models are estimated using the sample autocovariance matrices and the Yule-Walker equations. The order of the VAR model producing the smallest Akaike information criterion is chosen as the order (number of lags into the past) to use in the canonical correlation analysis.

The elements of the state vector are then determined via a sequence of canonical correlation analyses of the sample autocovariance matrices through the selected order. This analysis computes the sample canonical correlations of the past with an increasing number of steps into the future. Variables that yield significant correlations are added to the state vector; variables that yield insignificant correlations are excluded from further consideration. The importance of the correlation is judged on the basis of another information criterion proposed by Akaike. See the section "Canonical Correlation Analysis" later in this chapter for details. If you specify the state vector explicitly, these model identification steps are omitted.

Once the state vector is determined, the state space model is fit to the data. The free parameters in the $\mathbf{F}$, $\mathbf{G}$, and Σ_{ee} matrices are estimated by approximate maximum likelihood. By default, the $\mathbf{F}$ and $\mathbf{G}$ matrices are unrestricted, except for identifiability requirements. Optionally, conditional least-squares estimates can be computed. You can impose restrictions on elements of the $\mathbf{F}$ and $\mathbf{G}$ matrices.

After the parameters are estimated, forecasts are produced from the state space model using the Kalman filtering technique. If you specify differencing, the forecasts are integrated to produce forecasts of the original input variables.

Getting Started

The following introductory example uses simulated data for two variables X and Y. The following statements generate the X and Y series:

```
data in;
   x=10;  y=40;
   x1=0; y1=0;
   a1=0; b1=0;
   iseed=123;
   do t=-100 to 200;
      a=rannor(iseed);
      b=rannor(iseed);
      dx = 0.5*x1 + 0.3*y1 + a - 0.2*a1 - 0.1*b1;
      dy = 0.3*x1 + 0.5*y1 + b;
      x = x + dx + .25;
      y = y + dy + .25;
      if t >= 0 then output;
      x1 = dx; y1 = dy;
      a1 = a; b1 = b;
   end;
   keep t x y;
run;
```

The simulated series X and Y are shown in Figure 16.1.

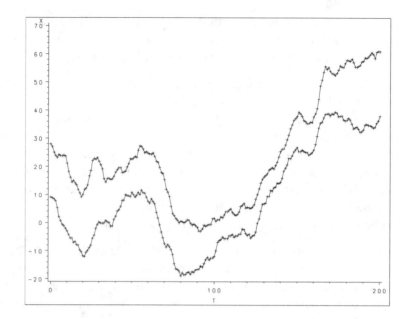

Figure 16.1.   Example Series

Automatic State Space Model Selection

The STATESPACE procedure is designed to automatically select the best state space model for forecasting the series. You can specify your own model if you wish, and you can use the output from PROC STATESPACE to help you identify a state space model. However, the easiest way is to let PROC STATESPACE choose the model.

Stationarity and Differencing

Although PROC STATESPACE selects the state space model automatically, it does assume that the input series are stationary. If the series are nonstationary, then the process may fail. Therefore, the first step is to examine your data and test to see if differencing is required.

The series shown in Figure 16.1 are nonstationary. In order to forecast X and Y with a state space model, you must difference them (or use some other de-trending method). If you fail to difference when needed and try to use PROC STATESPACE with nonstationary data, an inappropriate state space model may be selected, and the model estimation may fail to converge.

The following statements identify and fit a state space model for the first differences of X and Y, and forecast X and Y 10 periods ahead:

```
proc statespace data=in out=out lead=10;
   var x(1) y(1);
   id t;
run;
```

The DATA= option specifies the input data set and the OUT= option specifies the output data set for the forecasts. The LEAD= option specifies forecasting 10 observations past the end of the input data. The VAR statement specifies the variables to forecast and specifies differencing. The notation X(1) Y(1) specifies that the state space model analyzes the first differences of X and Y.

Descriptive Statistics and Preliminary Autoregressions

The first page of the printed output produced by the preceding statements is shown in Figure 16.2.

```
                        STATESPACE Procedure

                          Nobs = 200

                Variable      Mean        Std
                X           0.144316   1.233457
                Has been differenced.
                With period(s) = 1.
                Y           0.164871   1.304358
                Has been differenced.
                With period(s) = 1.


           Information Criterion for Autoregressive Models


         Lag=0          Lag=1          Lag=2          Lag=3          Lag=4
      149.696973      8.387786       5.517099      12.059863      15.369515


         Lag=5          Lag=6          Lag=7          Lag=8          Lag=9
      21.795384      24.006379      29.888743      33.557081      41.176060


         Lag=10
      47.702222



           Schematic Representation of Correlations

        Name/Lag   0   1   2   3   4   5   6   7   8   9  10
        X          ++  ++  ++  ++  ++  ++  +.  ..  +.  +.  ..
        Y          ++  ++  ++  ++  ++  +.  +.  +.  +.  ..  ..

    + is > 2*std error,   - is < -2*std error,   . is between
```

Figure 16.2. Descriptive Statistics and VAR Order Selection

Descriptive statistics are printed first, giving the number of nonmissing observations after differencing, and the sample means and standard deviations of the differenced series. The sample means are subtracted before the series are modeled (unless you specify the NOCENTER option), and the sample means are added back when the forecasts are produced.

Let $\mathbf{X}_t$ and $\mathbf{Y}_t$ be the observed values of X and Y, and let x_t and y_t be the values of X and Y after differencing and subtracting the mean difference. The series $\mathbf{x}_t$ modeled by the STATEPSACE procedure is

$$\mathbf{x}_t = \begin{bmatrix} x_t \\ y_t \end{bmatrix} = \begin{bmatrix} (1 - B)\mathbf{X}_t - 0.144316 \\ (1 - B)\mathbf{Y}_t - 0.164871 \end{bmatrix}$$

where B represents the backshift operator.

After the descriptive statistics, the PROC STATESPACE prints Akaike's information criterion (AIC) values for the autoregressive models fit to the series. The smallest AIC value, in this case 5.517 at lag 2, determines the number of autocovariance matrices analyzed in the canonical correlation phase.

A schematic representation of the autocorrelations is printed next. This indicates which elements of the autocorrelation matrices at different lags are significantly greater or less than 0.

The second page of the STATESPACE printed output is shown in Figure 16.3.

```
                        STATESPACE Procedure

        Schematic Representation of Partial Autocorrelations

            Name/Lag  1   2   3   4   5   6   7   8   9  10
            X         ++  +.  ..  ..  ..  ..  ..  ..  ..
            Y         ++  ..  ..  ..  ..  ..  ..  ..  ..

    + is > 2*std error,   - is < -2*std error,  . is between


                Yule-Walker Estimates for the Min AIC


                  Lag=1                     Lag=2
                  X          Y              X          Y
            X     0.25744    0.20224        0.17081    0.13355
            Y     0.29218    0.46930       -0.00537   -0.00048
```

Figure 16.3. Partial Autocorrelations and VAR Model

Figure 16.3 shows a schematic representation of the partial autocorrelations, similar to the autocorrelations shown in Figure 16.2. The selection of a second-order autoregressive model by the AIC statistic looks reasonable in this case because the partial autocorrelations for lags greater than 2 are not significant.

Next, the Yule-Walker estimates for the selected autoregressive model are printed. This output shows the coefficient matrices of the vector autoregressive model at each lag.

Selected State Space Model Form and Preliminary Estimates

After the autoregressive order selection process has determined the number of lags to consider, the canonical correlation analysis phase selects the state vector. By default, output for this process is not printed. You can use the CANCORR option to print details of the canonical correlation analysis. See the section "Canonical Correlation Analysis" later in this chapter for an explanation of this process.

After the state vector is selected, the state space model is estimated by approximate maximum likelihood. Information from the canonical correlation analysis and from the preliminary autoregression is used to form preliminary estimates of the state space model parameters. These preliminary estimates are used as starting values for the iterative estimation process.

The form of the state vector and the preliminary estimates are printed next, as shown in Figure 16.4.

```
                    STATESPACE Procedure
        Selected Statespace Form and Preliminary Estimates
                         State Vector
   X(T;T)               Y(T;T)                X(T+1;T)
              Estimate of the Transition Matrix
                        0       0      1
                      0.292   0.469  -0.004
                      0.249   0.245   0.204

                Input Matrix for the Innovation
                           1        0
                           0        1
                        0.257    0.202

              Variance Matrix for the Innovation
                    0.94519606 0.10078597
                    0.10078597 1.01470299
```

Figure 16.4. Preliminary Estimates of State Space Model

Figure 16.4 first prints the state vector as X[T;T] Y[T;T] X[T+1;T]. This notation indicates that the state vector is

$$\mathbf{z}_t = \begin{bmatrix} x_{t|t} \\ y_{t|t} \\ x_{t+1|t} \end{bmatrix}$$

The notation $x_{t+1|t}$ indicates the conditional expectation or prediction of x_{t+1} based on the information available at time t, and $x_{t|t}$ and $y_{t|t}$ are x_t and y_t, respectively.

The remainder of Figure 16.4 shows the preliminary estimates of the transition matrix **F**, the input matrix **G**, and the covariance matrix Σ_{ee}.

Estimated State Space Model

The next page of the STATESPACE output prints the final estimates of the model, as shown in Figure 16.5. This output has the same form as in Figure 16.4, but shows the maximum likelihood estimates instead of the preliminary estimates.

```
                        STATESPACE Procedure
                 Selected Statespace Form and Fitted Model
                            State Vector
         X(T;T)               Y(T;T)                X(T+1;T)
                 Estimate of the Transition Matrix
                          0        0        1
                        0.297    0.474    -0.020
                        0.230    0.228     0.256

                  Input Matrix for the Innovation
                                  1        0
                                  0        1
                               0.257    0.202

                  Variance Matrix for the Innovation
                        0.94518766  0.10075239
                        0.10075239  1.01471215
```

Figure 16.5. Fitted State Space Model

The estimated state space model shown in Figure 16.5 is

$$\begin{bmatrix} x_{t+1|t+1} \\ y_{t+1|t+1} \\ x_{t+2|t+1} \end{bmatrix} = \begin{bmatrix} 0 & 0 & 1 \\ .297 & .474 & -.020 \\ .230 & .228 & .256 \end{bmatrix} \begin{bmatrix} x_t \\ y_t \\ x_{t+1|t} \end{bmatrix} + \begin{bmatrix} 1 & 0 \\ 0 & 1 \\ .257 & .202 \end{bmatrix} \begin{bmatrix} e_{t+1} \\ n_{t+1} \end{bmatrix}$$

$$\operatorname{var}\begin{bmatrix} e_{t+1} \\ n_{t+1} \end{bmatrix} = \begin{bmatrix} .945 & .101 \\ .101 & 1.015 \end{bmatrix}$$

The next page of the STATESPACE output lists the estimates of the free parameters in the **F** and **G** matrices with standard errors and *t* statistics, as shown in Figure 16.6.

```
                        STATESPACE Procedure
                        Parameter Estimates
          Parameter  Estimate   Std. Err.   T value
            F(2,1)    0.297273   0.129995    2.286799
            F(2,2)    0.47376    0.115688    4.095148
            F(2,3)   -0.01998    0.313025   -0.06384
            F(3,1)    0.2301     0.126226    1.822917
            F(3,2)    0.228425   0.112978    2.021849
            F(3,3)    0.256031   0.305256    0.838742
            G(3,1)    0.257284   0.07106     3.620644
            G(3,2)    0.202273   0.068593    2.948911
```

Figure 16.6. Final Parameter Estimates

Convergence Failures

The maximum likelihood estimates are computed by an iterative nonlinear maximization algorithm, which may not converge. If the estimates fail to converge, warning messages are printed in the output.

If you encounter convergence problems, you should recheck the stationarity of the data and ensure that the specified differencing orders are correct. Attempting to fit state space models to nonstationary data is a common cause of convergence failure. You can also use the MAXIT= option to increase the number of iterations allowed or experiment with the convergence tolerance options DETTOL= and PARMTOL=.

Forecast Data Set

The following statements print the output data set. The WHERE statement excludes the first 190 observations from the output, so only the forecasts and the last 10 actual observations are printed.

```
proc print data=out;
   id t;
   where t > 190;
run;
```

The PROC PRINT output is shown in Figure 16.7.

T	X	FOR1	RES1	STD1	Y	FOR2	RES2	STD2
191	34.8159	33.6299	1.18600	0.97221	58.7189	57.9916	0.72728	1.00733
192	35.0656	35.6598	-0.59419	0.97221	58.5440	59.7718	-1.22780	1.00733
193	34.7034	35.5530	-0.84962	0.97221	59.0476	58.5723	0.47522	1.00733
194	34.6626	34.7597	-0.09707	0.97221	59.7774	59.2241	0.55330	1.00733
195	34.4055	34.8322	-0.42664	0.97221	60.5118	60.1544	0.35738	1.00733
196	33.8210	34.6053	-0.78434	0.97221	59.8750	60.8260	-0.95102	1.00733
197	34.0164	33.6230	0.39333	0.97221	58.4698	59.4502	-0.98046	1.00733
198	35.3819	33.6251	1.75684	0.97221	60.6782	57.9167	2.76150	1.00733
199	36.2954	36.0528	0.24256	0.97221	60.9692	62.1637	-1.19450	1.00733
200	37.8945	37.1431	0.75142	0.97221	60.8586	61.4085	-0.54984	1.00733
201	.	38.5068	.	0.97221	.	61.3161	.	1.00733
202	.	39.0428	.	1.59125	.	61.7509	.	1.83678
203	.	39.4619	.	2.28028	.	62.1546	.	2.62366
204	.	39.8284	.	2.97824	.	62.5099	.	3.38839
205	.	40.1474	.	3.67689	.	62.8275	.	4.12805
206	.	40.4310	.	4.36299	.	63.1139	.	4.84149
207	.	40.6861	.	5.03040	.	63.3755	.	5.52744
208	.	40.9185	.	5.67548	.	63.6174	.	6.18564
209	.	41.1330	.	6.29673	.	63.8435	.	6.81655
210	.	41.3332	.	6.89383	.	64.0572	.	7.42114

Figure 16.7. OUT= Data Set Produced by PROC STATESPACE

The OUT= data set produced by PROC STATESPACE contains the VAR and ID statement variables. In addition, for each VAR statement variable, the OUT= data set contains the variables FORi, RESi, and STDi. These variables contain the predicted values, residuals, and forecast standard errors for the ith variable in the VAR statement list. In this case, X is listed first in the VAR statement, so FOR1 contains the forecasts of X, while FOR2 contains the forecasts of Y.

The following statements plot the forecasts and actuals for the series:

```
proc gplot data=out;
   plot for1*t=1 for2*t=1 x*t=2 y*t=2 /
        overlay href=200.5;
   symbol1 v=plus i=join;
   symbol2 v=star i=none;
   where t > 150;
run;
```

The forecast plot is shown in Figure 16.8. The last 50 observations are also plotted to provide context, and a reference line is drawn between the historical and forecast periods. The actual values are plotted with asterisks.

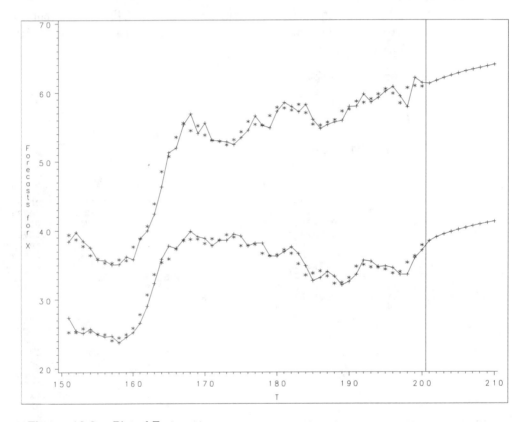

Figure 16.8. Plot of Forecasts

Controlling Printed Output

By default, the STATESPACE procedure produces a large amount of printed output. You can suppress the printed output for the autoregressive model selection process with the PRINTOUT=NONE option. The descriptive statistics and state space model estimation output are still printed when you specify PRINTOUT=NONE. You can produce more detailed output by specifying the PRINTOUT=LONG option and the printing control options CANCORR, COVB, and PRINT.

Specifying the State Space Model

Instead of allowing the STATESPACE procedure to select the model automatically, you can use FORM and RESTRICT statements to specify a state space model.

Specifying the State Vector

Use the FORM statement to control the form of the state vector. You can use this feature to force PROC STATESPACE to estimate and forecast a model different from the model it would select automatically. You can also use this feature to reestimate the automatically selected model (possibly with restrictions) without repeating the canonical correlation analysis.

The FORM statement specifies the number of lags of each variable to include in the state vector. For example, the statement FORM X 3; forces the state vector to include $x_{t|t}$, $x_{t+1|t}$, and $x_{t+2|t}$. The following statement specifies the state vector $\left(x_{t|t}, y_{t|t}, x_{t+1|t}\right)$, which is the same state vector selected in the preceding example:

```
form x 2 y 1;
```

You can specify the form for only some of the variables and allow PROC STATES-PACE to select the form for the other variables. If you specify only some of the variables in the FORM statement, canonical correlation analysis is used to determine the number of lags included in the state vector for the remaining variables not specified by the FORM statement. If the FORM statement includes specifications for all the variables listed in the VAR statement, the state vector is completely defined and the canonical correlation analysis is not performed.

Restricting the F and G matrices

After you know the form of the state vector, you can use the RESTRICT statement to fix some parameters in the **F** and **G** matrices to specified values. One use of this feature is to remove insignificant parameters by restricting them to 0.

In the introductory example shown in the preceding section, the F[2,3] parameter is not significant. (The parameters estimation output shown in Figure 16.6 gives the t statistic for F[2,3] as -0.06. F[3,3] and F[3,1] also have low significance with $t < 2$.)

The following statements reestimate this model with F[2,3] restricted to 0. The FORM statement is used to specify the state vector and thus bypass the canonical correlation analysis.

```
proc statespace data=in out=out lead=10;
   var x(1) y(1);
   id t;
   form x 2 y 1;
   restrict f(2,3)=0;
run;
```

The final estimates produced by these statements are shown in Figure 16.9.

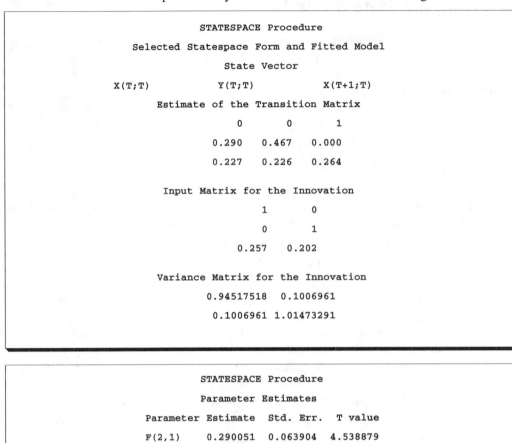

```
                     STATESPACE Procedure
              Selected Statespace Form and Fitted Model
                         State Vector
   X(T;T)              Y(T;T)                X(T+1;T)
              Estimate of the Transition Matrix
                     0        0        1
                  0.290    0.467    0.000
                  0.227    0.226    0.264

              Input Matrix for the Innovation
                         1        0
                         0        1
                     0.257    0.202

              Variance Matrix for the Innovation
                  0.94517518  0.1006961
                  0.1006961  1.01473291
```

```
                     STATESPACE Procedure
                     Parameter Estimates
        Parameter  Estimate  Std. Err.  T value
          F(2,1)   0.290051  0.063904  4.538879
          F(2,2)   0.467468   0.06043  7.735687
          F(3,1)   0.227051  0.125221    1.8132
          F(3,2)   0.226139  0.111711  2.024319
          F(3,3)    0.26436  0.299537  0.882562
          G(3,1)   0.256826  0.070994  3.617548
          G(3,2)   0.202022  0.068507  2.948915
```

Figure 16.9. Results using RESTRICT Statement

Syntax

The STATESPACE procedure uses the following statements:

PROC STATESPACE *options*;
    BY *variable* ... ;
    FORM *variable value* ... ;
    ID *variable*;
    INITIAL **F**(*row,column*)= *value* ... **G**(*row,column*)= *value* ... ;
    RESTRICT **F**(*row,column*)= *value* ... **G**(*row,column*)= *value* ... ;
    VAR *variable* (*difference, difference, ...*) ... ;

Functional Summary

The statements and options used by PROC STATESPACE are summarized in the following table:

Description	Statement	Option
Input Data Set Options		
specify the input data set	PROC STATESPACE	DATA=
prevent subtraction of sample mean	PROC STATESPACE	NOCENTER
specify the ID variable	ID	
specify the observed series and differencing	VAR	
Options for Autoregressive Estimates		
specify the maximum order	PROC STATESPACE	ARMAX=
specify maximum lag for autocovariances	PROC STATESPACE	LAGMAX=
output only minimum AIC model	PROC STATESPACE	MINIC
specify the amount of detail printed	PROC STATESPACE	PRINTOUT=
write preliminary AR models to a data set	PROC STATESPACE	OUTAR=
Options for Canonical Correlation Analysis		
print the sequence of canonical correlations	PROC STATESPACE	CANCORR
specify upper limit of dimension of state vector	PROC STATESPACE	DIMMAX=
specify the minimum number of lags	PROC STATESPACE	PASTMIN=
specify the multiplier of the degrees of freedom	PROC STATESPACE	SIGCORR=
Options for State Space Model Estimation		
specify starting values	INITIAL	
print covariance matrix of parameter estimates	PROC STATESPACE	COVB
specify the convergence criterion	PROC STATESPACE	DETTOL=
specify the convergence criterion	PROC STATESPACE	PARMTOL=
print the details of the iterations	PROC STATESPACE	ITPRINT
specify an upper limit of the number of lags	PROC STATESPACE	KLAG=
specify maximum number of iterations allowed	PROC STATESPACE	MAXIT=
suppress the final estimation	PROC STATESPACE	NOEST
write the state space model parameter estimates to an output data set	PROC STATESPACE	OUTMODEL=
use conditional least squares for final estimates	PROC STATESPACE	RESIDEST
specify criterion for testing for singularity	PROC STATESPACE	SINGULAR=
Options for Forecasting		
start forecasting before end of the input data	PROC STATESPACE	BACK=

Description	Statement	Option
specify the time interval between observations	PROC STATESPACE	INTERVAL=
specify multiple periods in the time series	PROC STATESPACE	INTPER=
specify how many periods to forecast	PROC STATESPACE	LEAD=
specify the output data set for forecasts	PROC STATESPACE	OUT=
print forecasts	PROC STATESPACE	PRINT

Options to Specify the State Space Model

specify the state vector	FORM	
specify the parameter values	RESTRICT	

BY Groups

specify BY-group processing	BY	

PROC STATESPACE Statement

PROC STATESPACE *options*;

The following options can be specified in the PROC STATESPACE statement:

Input Data Options

DATA= *SAS-data-set*

specifies the name of the SAS data set to be used by the procedure. If you omit the DATA= option, the most recently created SAS data set is used.

LAGMAX= *k*

specifies the number of lags for which the sample autocovariance matrix is computed. The LAGMAX= option controls the number of lags printed in the schematic representation of the autocorrelations.

The sample autocovariance matrix of lag i, denoted $\mathbf{C}_i$, is computed as

$$\mathbf{C}_i = \frac{1}{N-1} \sum_{t=1+i}^{N} \mathbf{x}_t \, \mathbf{x}'_{t-i}$$

where $\mathbf{x}_t$ is the differenced and centered data and N is the number of observations. (If the NOCENTER option is specified, 1 is not subtracted from N.) LAGMAX=k specifies that $\mathbf{C}_0$ through $\mathbf{C}_k$ are computed. The default is LAGMAX=10.

NOCENTER

prevents subtraction of the sample mean from the input series (after any specified differencing) before the analysis.

Options for Preliminary Autoregressive Models

ARMAX= *n*

specifies the maximum order of the preliminary autoregressive models. The AR-MAX= option controls the autoregressive orders for which information criteria are printed and controls the number of lags printed in the schematic representation of partial autocorrelations. The default is ARMAX=10. See the section "Preliminary Autoregressive Models" later in this chapter for details.

MINIC

writes to the OUTAR= data set only the preliminary Yule-Walker estimates for the VAR model producing the minimum AIC. See the section "OUTAR= Data Set" later in this chapter for details.

OUTAR= *SAS-data-set*

writes the Yule-Walker estimates of the preliminary autoregressive models to a SAS data set. See the section "OUTAR= Data Set" later in this chapter for details.

PRINTOUT= SHORT | LONG | NONE

determines the amount of detail printed. PRINTOUT=LONG prints the lagged covariance matrices, the partial autoregressive matrices, and estimates of the residual covariance matrices from the sequence of autoregressive models. PRINTOUT=NONE suppresses the output for the preliminary autoregressive models. The descriptive statistics and state space model estimation output are still printed when you specify PRINTOUT=NONE. PRINTOUT=SHORT is the default.

Canonical Correlation Analysis Options

CANCORR

prints the canonical correlations and information criterion for each candidate state vector considered. See the section "Canonical Correlation Analysis" later in this chapter for details.

DIMMAX= *n*

specifies the upper limit to the dimension of the state vector. You can use the DIMMAX= option to limit the size of the model selected. The default is DIM-MAX=10.

PASTMIN= *n*

specifies the minimum number of lags to include in the canonical correlation analysis. The default is PASTMIN=0. See the section "Canonical Correlation Analysis" later in this chapter for details.

SIGCORR= *value*

specifies the multiplier of the degrees of freedom for the penalty term in the information criterion used to select the state space form. The default is SIGCORR=2. The larger the value of the SIGCORR= option, the smaller the state vector tends to be. Hence, a large value causes a simpler model to be fit. See the section "Canonical Correlations Analysis" later in this chapter for details.

State Space Model Estimation Options

COVB

prints the inverse of the observed information matrix for the parameter estimates. This matrix is an estimate of the covariance matrix for the parameter estimates.

DETTOL= *value*

specifies the convergence criterion. You can use the DETTOL= and PARM-TOL= option values together to test for convergence of the estimation process. If, during an iteration, the relative change of the parameter estimates is less than the PARMTOL= value and the relative change of the determinant of the innovation variance matrix is less than the DETTOL= value, then iteration ceases and the current estimates are accepted. The default is DETTOL=1E-5.

ITPRINT

prints the iterations during the estimation process.

KLAG= *n*

sets an upper limit for the number of lags of the sample autocovariance matrix used in computing the approximate likelihood function. If the data have a strong moving average character, a larger KLAG= value may be necessary to obtain good estimates. The default is KLAG=15. See the section "Parameter Estimation" later in this chapter for details.

MAXIT= *n*

sets an upper limit to the number of iterations in the maximum likelihood or conditional least-squares estimation. The default is MAXIT=50.

NOEST

suppresses the final maximum likelihood estimation of the selected model.

OUTMODEL= *SAS-data-set*

writes the parameter estimates and their standard errors to a SAS data set. See the section "OUTMODEL= Data Set" later in this chapter for details.

PARMTOL= *value*

specifies the convergence criterion. You can use the DETTOL= and PARM-TOL= option values together to test for convergence of the estimation process. If, during an iteration, the relative change of the parameter estimates is less than the PARMTOL= value and the relative change of the determinant of the innovation variance matrix is less than the DETTOL= value, then iteration ceases and the current estimates are accepted. The default is PARMTOL=.001.

RESIDEST

computes the final estimates using conditional least squares on the raw data. This type of estimation may be more stable than the default maximum likelihood method but is usually more computationally expensive. See the section "Parameter Estimation" later in this chapter for details of the conditional least squares method.

SINGULAR= *value*

specifies the criterion for testing for singularity of a matrix. A matrix is declared singular if a scaled pivot is less than the SINGULAR= value when sweeping the matrix. The default is SINGULAR=1E-7.

Forecasting Options

BACK= *n*

starts forecasting *n* periods before the end of the input data. The BACK= option value must not be greater than the number of observations. The default is BACK=0.

INTERVAL= *interval*

specifies the time interval between observations. PROC STATESPACE uses the INTERVAL= value in conjunction with the ID variable to check whether the input data are in order and have no missing periods. The INTERVAL= option is also used to extrapolate the ID values for forecast observations. See Chapter 21, "Date Intervals, Formats, and Functions," for details on the INTERVAL= values allowed.

INTPER= *n*

specifies that each input observation corresponds to *n* time periods. For example, the options INTERVAL=MONTH and INTPER=2 specify bimonthly data and are equivalent to specifying INTERVAL=MONTH2. If you do not specify the INTERVAL= option, the INTPER= option controls the increment used to generate ID values for the forecast observations. The default is INTPER=1.

LEAD= *n*

specifies how many forecast observations are produced. The forecasts start at the point set by the BACK= option. The default is LEAD=0, which produces no forecasts.

OUT= *SAS-data-set*

writes the residuals, actual values, forecasts, and forecast standard errors to a SAS data set. See the section "OUT= Data Set" later in this chapter for details.

PRINT

prints the forecasts.

BY Statement

BY *variable* ... ;

You can use a BY statement with the STATESPACE procedure to obtain separate analyses on observations in groups defined by the BY variables.

FORM Statement

FORM *variable value* ... ;

You can use the FORM statement to specify the number of times a variable is included in the state vector. You can specify values for any variable listed in the VAR statement. If you specify a value for each variable in the VAR statement, the state vector for the state space model is entirely specified, and automatic selection of the state space model is not performed.

The FORM statement forces the state vector, $\mathbf{z}_t$, to contain a specific variable a given number of times. For example, if Y is one of the variables in $\mathbf{x}_t$, then the statement

```
form y 3;
```

forces the state vector to contain $\mathbf{Y}_t$, $\mathbf{Y}_{t+1|t}$, and $\mathbf{Y}_{t+2|t}$, possibly along with other variables.

The following statements illustrate the use of the FORM statement:

```
proc statespace data=in;
   var x y;
   form x 3 y 2;
run;
```

These statements fit a state space model with the following state vector:

$$
\mathbf{z}_t = \begin{bmatrix} x_{t|t} \\ y_{t|t} \\ x_{t+1|t} \\ y_{t+1|t} \\ x_{t+2|t} \end{bmatrix}
$$

ID Statement

ID *variable*;

The ID statement specifies a variable that identifies observations in the input data set. The variable specified in the ID statement is included in the OUT= data set. The values of the ID variable are extrapolated for the forecast observations based on the values of the INTERVAL= and INTPER= options.

INITIAL Statement

INITIAL F(*row,column*)= *value* ...   **G**(*row, column*)= *value* ... ;

The INITIAL statement gives initial values to the specified elements of the **F** and **G** matrices. These initial values are used as starting values for the iterative estimation.

Parts of the **F** and **G** matrices represent fixed structural identities. If you specify a fixed structural element instead of a free parameter, the corresponding initialization is ignored.

The following is an example of an INITIAL statement:

```
initial f(3,2)=0 g(4,1)=0 g(5,1)=0;
```

RESTRICT Statement

> **RESTRICT F**(*row,column*)= *value* ...   **G**(*row,column*)= *value* ... ;

The RESTRICT statement restricts the specified elements of the **F** and **G** matrices to the specified values.

To use the restrict statement, you need to know the form of the model. Either specify the form of the model with the FORM statement, or do a preliminary run, perhaps with the NOEST option, to find the form of the model that PROC STATESPACE selects for the data.

The following is an example of a RESTRICT statement:

```
restrict f(3,2)=0 g(4,1)=0 g(5,1)=0;
```

Parts of the **F** and **G** matrices represent fixed structural identities. If you specify a restriction for a fixed structural element instead of a free parameter, the restriction is ignored.

VAR Statement

> **VAR** *variable* (*difference, difference, ...) ... ;*

The VAR statement specifies the variables in the input data set to model and forecast. The VAR statement also specifies differencing of the input variables. The VAR statement is required.

You can specify differencing by following the variable name with a list of difference periods separated by commas. See the section "Stationarity and Differencing" later in this chapter for more information on differencing of input variables.

The order in which you list variables in the VAR statement controls the order in which variables are included in the state vector. Usually, you should list potential inputs before potential outputs.

For example, assuming the input data are monthly, the following VAR statement specifies the modeling and forecasting of the one period and seasonal second difference of X and Y:

```
var x(1,12) y(1,12);
```

In this example, the vector time series analyzed is

$$
\mathbf{x}_t = \begin{bmatrix} (1 - B)(1 - B^{12})\mathbf{X}_t \ - \ \bar{x} \\ (1 - B)(1 - B^{12})\mathbf{Y}_t \ - \ \bar{y} \end{bmatrix}
$$

where B represents the back shift operator, and $\bar{x}$ and $\bar{y}$ represent the means of the differenced series. If you specify the NOCENTER option, the mean differences are not subtracted.

Details

Missing Values

The STATESPACE procedure does not support missing values. The STATESPACE procedure uses the first contiguous group of observations with no missing values for any of the VAR statement variables. Observations at the beginning of the data set with missing values for any VAR statement variable are not used or included in the output data set.

Stationarity and Differencing

The state space model used by the STATESPACE procedure assumes that the time series are stationary. Hence, the data should be checked for stationarity. One way to check for stationarity is to plot the series. A graph of series over time can show a time trend or variability changes.

You can also check stationarity by using the sample autocorrelation functions displayed by the ARIMA procedure. The autocorrelation functions of nonstationary series tend to decay slowly. See Chapter 3, "The ARIMA Procedure," for more information.

Another alternative is to use the %DFTEST macro to apply Dickey-Fuller tests for unit roots in the time series. See Chapter 20, "SAS Macros," for more information on Dickey-Fuller unit root tests and the %DFTEST macro.

The most popular way to transform a nonstationary series to stationarity is by differencing. Differencing of the time series is specified in the VAR statement. For example, to take a simple first difference of the series X, use this statement:

```
var x(1);
```

In this example, the change in X from one period to the next is analyzed. When the series has a seasonal pattern, differencing at a period equal to the length of the seasonal cycle may be desirable. For example, suppose the variable X is measured quarterly and shows a seasonal cycle over the year. You can use the following statement to analyze the series of changes from the same quarter in the previous year:

```
var x(4);
```

To difference twice, add another differencing period to the list. For example, the following statement analyzes the series of second differences $\left(x_t - x_{t-1}\right) - \left(x_{t-1} - x_{t-2}\right) = x_t - 2x_{t-1} + x_{t-2}$:

```
var x(1,1);
```

The following statement analyzes the seasonal second difference series:

```
var x(1,4);
```

The series modeled is the one-period difference of the four-period difference: $(x_t - x_{t-4}) - (x_{t-1} - x_{t-5}) = x_t - x_{t-1} - x_{t-4} + x_{t-5}$.

Another way to obtain stationary series is to use a regression on time to de-trend the data. If the time series has a deterministic linear trend, regressing the series on time produces residuals that should be stationary. The following statements write residuals of X and Y to the variable RX and RY in the output data set DETREND:

```
data a;
   set a;
   t=_n_;
run;

proc reg data=a;
   model x y = t;
   output out=detrend r=rx ry;
run;
```

Then, use PROC STATESPACE to forecast the de-trended series RX and RY. A disadvantage of this method is that you need to add the trend back to the forecast series in an additional step. A more serious disadvantage of the de-trending method is that it assumes a deterministic trend. In practice, most time series appear to have a stochastic rather than a deterministic trend. Differencing is a more flexible and often more appropriate method.

There are several other methods to handle nonstationary time series. For more information and examples, refer to Brockwell and Davis (1991).

Preliminary Autoregressive Models

After computing the sample autocovariance matrices, PROC STATESPACE fits a sequence of vector autoregressive models. These preliminary autoregressive models are used to estimate the autoregressive order of the process and limit the order of auto-covariances considered in the state vector selection process.

Yule-Walker Equations for Forward and Backward Models

Unlike a univariate autoregressive model, a multivariate autoregressive model has different forms, depending on whether the present observation is being predicted from the past observations or from the future observations.

Let x_t be the r-component stationary time series given by the VAR statement after differencing and subtracting the vector of sample means. (If you specify the NOCEN-TER option, the mean is not subtracted.) Let n be the number of observations of x_t from the input data set.

Let e_t be a vector white noise sequence with mean vector $\mathbf{0}$ and variance matrix Σ_p, and let n_t be a vector white noise sequence with mean vector $\mathbf{0}$ and variance matrix Ω_p. Let p be the order of the vector autoregressive model for x_t.

The forward autoregressive form based on the past observations is written as follows:

$$\mathbf{x}_t = \sum_{i=1}^{p} \Phi_i^p \mathbf{x}_{t-i} + \mathbf{e}_t$$

The backward autoregressive form based on the future observations is written as follows:

$$\mathbf{x}_t = \sum_{i=1}^{p} \Psi_i^p \mathbf{x}_{t+i} + \mathbf{n}_t$$

Letting E denote the expected value operator, the autocovariance sequence for the $\mathbf{x}_t$ series, Γ_i, is

$$\Gamma_i = \mathrm{E}\, \mathbf{x}_t \mathbf{x}_{t-i}'$$

The Yule-Walker equations for the autoregressive model that matches the first p elements of the autocovariance sequence are

$$
\begin{bmatrix}
\Gamma_0 & \Gamma_1 & \cdots & \Gamma_{p-1} \\
\Gamma_1' & \Gamma_0 & \cdots & \Gamma_{p-2} \\
\vdots & \vdots & & \vdots \\
\Gamma_{p-1}' & \Gamma_{p-2}' & \cdots & \Gamma_0
\end{bmatrix}
\begin{bmatrix}
\Phi_1^p \\
\Phi_2^p \\
\vdots \\
\Phi_p^p
\end{bmatrix}
=
\begin{bmatrix}
\Gamma_1 \\
\Gamma_2 \\
\vdots \\
\Gamma_p
\end{bmatrix}
$$

and

$$
\begin{bmatrix}
\Gamma_0 & \Gamma_1' & \cdots & \Gamma_{p-1}' \\
\Gamma_1 & \Gamma_0 & \cdots & \Gamma_{p-2}' \\
\vdots & \vdots & & \vdots \\
\Gamma_{p-1} & \Gamma_{p-2} & \cdots & \Gamma_0
\end{bmatrix}
\begin{bmatrix}
\Psi_1^p \\
\Psi_2^p \\
\vdots \\
\Psi_p^p
\end{bmatrix}
=
\begin{bmatrix}
\Gamma_1' \\
\Gamma_2' \\
\vdots \\
\Gamma_p'
\end{bmatrix}
$$

Here, Φ_i^p are the coefficient matrices for the past observation form of the vector autoregressive model, and Ψ_i^p are the coefficient matrices for the future observation form. For more information on the Yule-Walker equations in the multivariate setting, see Whittle (1963) and Ansley and Newbold (1979).

The innovation variance matrices for the two forms can be written as follows:

$$\Sigma_p = \Gamma_0 - \sum_{i=1}^{p} \Phi_i^p \, \Gamma_i'$$

$$\Omega_p = \Gamma_0 - \sum_{i=1}^{p} \Psi_i^p \Gamma_i$$

The autoregressive models are fit to the data using the preceding Yule-Walker equations with Γ_i replaced by the sample covariance sequence C_i. The covariance matrices are calculated as

$$\mathbf{C}_i = \frac{1}{N-1} \sum_{t=i+1}^{N} \mathbf{x}_t \, \mathbf{x}'_{t-i}$$

Let $\widehat{\Phi}_p$, $\widehat{\Psi}_p$, $\widehat{\Sigma}_p$, and $\widehat{\Omega}_p$ represent the Yule-Walker estimates of Φ_p, Ψ_p, Σ_p, and Ω_p, respectively. These matrices are written to an output data set when you specify the OUTAR= option.

When you specify the PRINTOUT=LONG option, the sequence of matrices $\widehat{\Sigma}_p$ and the corresponding correlation matrices are printed. The sequence of matrices $\widehat{\Sigma}_p$ is used to compute Akaike's information criteria for selection of the autoregressive order of the process.

Akaike Information Criterion

Akaike's information criterion (AIC) is defined as $-2(maximum\ of\ log\ likelihood) + 2(number\ of\ parameters)$. Since the vector autoregressive models are estimates from the Yule-Walker equations, not by maximum likelihood, the exact likelihood values are not available for computing the AIC. However, for the vector autoregressive model, the maximum of the log likelihood can be approximated as

$$\ln(L) \approx -\frac{n}{2} \ln\left(\left| \widehat{\Sigma}_p \right| \right)$$

Thus, the AIC for the order p model is computed as

$$AIC_p = n \ln\left(\left| \widehat{\Sigma}_p \right| \right) + 2pr^2$$

You can use the printed AIC array to compute a likelihood ratio test of the autoregressive order. The log-likelihood ratio test statistic for testing the order p model against the order $p - 1$ model is

$$-n \ln\left(\left| \widehat{\Sigma}_p \right| \right) + n \ln\left(\left| \widehat{\Sigma}_{p-1} \right| \right)$$

This quantity is asymptotically distributed as a χ^2 with r^2 degrees of freedom if the series is autoregressive of order $p - 1$. It can be computed from the AIC array as

$$AIC_{p-1} - AIC_p + 2r^2$$

You can evaluate the significance of these test statistics with the PROBCHI function in a SAS DATA step or with a χ^2 table.

Determining the Autoregressive Order

Although the autoregressive models can be used for prediction, their primary value is to aid in the selection of a suitable portion of the sample covariance matrix for use in computing canonical correlations. If the multivariate time series $\mathbf{x}_t$ is of autoregressive order p, then the vector of past values to lag p is considered to contain essentially all the information relevant for prediction of future values of the time series.

By default, PROC STATESPACE selects the order, p, producing the autoregressive model with the smallest AIC_p. If the value p for the minimum AIC_p is less than the value of the PASTMIN= option, then p is set to the PASTMIN= value. Alternatively, you can use the ARMAX= and PASTMIN= options to force PROC STATESPACE to use an order you select.

Significance Limits for Partial Autocorrelations

The STATESPACE procedure prints a schematic representation of the partial autocorrelation matrices indicating which partial autocorrelations are significantly greater or significantly less than 0. Figure 16.10 shows an example of this table.

```
Schematic Representation of Partial Autocorrelations

Name/Lag    1    2    3    4    5    6    7    8    9    10
X          ++   +.   ..   ..   ..   ..   ..   ..   ..   ..
Y          ++   ..   ..   ..   ..   ..   ..   ..   ..   ..

+ is > 2*std error,   - is < -2*std error,   . is between
```

Figure 16.10. Significant Partial Autocorrelations

The partial autocorrelations are from the sample partial autoregressive matrices $\widehat{\Phi}_p^p$. The standard errors used for the significance limits of the partial autocorrelations are computed from the sequence of matrices Σ_p and Ω_p.

Under the assumption that the observed series arises from an autoregressive process of order $p - 1$, the pth sample partial autoregressive matrix $\widehat{\Phi}_p^p$ has an asymptotic variance matrix $\frac{1}{n} \Omega_p^{-1} \otimes \Sigma_p$. The significance limits for $\widehat{\Phi}_p^p$ used in the schematic plot of the sample partial autoregressive sequence are derived by replacing Ω_p and Σ_p with their sample estimators to produce the variance estimate, as follows:

$$\widehat{\mathrm{Var}}\left(\widehat{\Phi}_p^p\right) = \left(\frac{1}{n - rp}\right) \widehat{\Omega}_p^{-1} \otimes \widehat{\Sigma}_p$$

Canonical Correlation Analysis

Given the order p, let $\mathbf{p}_t$ be the vector of current and past values relevant to prediction of $\mathbf{x}_{t+1}$, as follows:

$$\mathbf{p}_t = \left(\mathbf{x}_t', \mathbf{x}_{t-1}', \cdots, \mathbf{x}_{t-p}'\right)'$$

Let $\mathbf{f}_t$ be the vector of current and future values:

$$\mathbf{f}_t = \left(\mathbf{x}_t', \mathbf{x}_{t+1}', \cdots, \mathbf{x}_{t+p}'\right)'$$

In the canonical correlation analysis, consider submatrices of the sample covariance matrix of $\mathbf{p}_t$ and $\mathbf{f}_t$. This covariance matrix, $\mathbf{V}$, has a block Hankel form:

$$
\mathbf{V} = \begin{bmatrix}
\mathbf{C}_0 & \mathbf{C}_1' & \mathbf{C}_2' & \cdots & \mathbf{C}_p' \\
\mathbf{C}_1' & \mathbf{C}_2' & \mathbf{C}_3' & \cdots & \mathbf{C}_{p+1}' \\
\vdots & \vdots & \vdots & & \vdots \\
\mathbf{C}_p' & \mathbf{C}_{p+1}' & \mathbf{C}_{p+2}' & \cdots & \mathbf{C}_{2p}'
\end{bmatrix}
$$

State Vector Selection Process

The canonical correlation analysis forms a sequence of potential state vectors, $\mathbf{z}_t^j$. Examine a sequence, $\mathbf{f}_t^j$, of subvectors of $\mathbf{f}_t$, and form the submatrix, $\mathbf{V}^j$, consisting of the rows and columns of $\mathbf{V}$ corresponding to the components of $\mathbf{f}_t^j$, and compute its canonical correlations.

The smallest canonical correlation of $\mathbf{V}^j$ is then used in the selection of the components of the state vector. The selection process is described in the following discussion. For more details about this process, refer to Akaike (1976).

In the following discussion, the notation $\mathbf{x}_{t+k|t}$ denotes the wide sense conditional expectation (best linear predictor) of $\mathbf{x}_{t+k}$, given all $\mathbf{x}_s$ with s less than or equal to t. In the notation $x_{i,t+1}$, the first subscript denotes the ith component of $\mathbf{x}_{t+1}$.

The initial state vector $\mathbf{z}_t^1$ is set to $\mathbf{x}_t$. The sequence $\mathbf{f}_t^j$ is initialized by setting

$$
\mathbf{f}_t^1 = \left(\mathbf{z}_t^{1\,\prime}, x_{1,\,t+1|t} \right)' = \left(\mathbf{x}_t', x_{1,\,t+1|t} \right)'
$$

That is, start by considering whether to add $x_{1,t+1|t}$ to the initial state vector $\mathbf{z}_t^1$.

The procedure forms the submatrix $\mathbf{V}^1$ corresponding to $\mathbf{f}_t^1$ and computes its canonical correlations. Denote the smallest canonical correlation of $\mathbf{V}^1$ as ρ_{min}. If ρ_{min} is significantly greater than 0, $x_{1,t+1|t}$ is added to the state vector.

If the smallest canonical correlation of $\mathbf{V}^1$ is not significantly greater than 0, then a linear combination of $\mathbf{f}_t^1$ is uncorrelated with the past, $\mathbf{p}_t$. Assuming that the determinant of $\mathbf{C}_0$ is not 0, (that is, no input series is a constant), you can take the coefficient of $x_{1,t+1|t}$ in this linear combination to be 1. Denote the coefficients of $\mathbf{z}_t^1$ in this linear combination as ℓ. This equation gives the relationship:

$$
x_{1,t+1|t} = \ell' \mathbf{x}_t
$$

Therefore, the current state vector already contains all the past information useful for predicting $x_{1,t+1}$ and any greater leads of $x_{1,t}$. The variable $x_{1,t+1|t}$ is not added to the state vector, and no terms $x_{1,t+k|t}$ are considered possible components of the state vector. The variable x_1 is no longer active for state vector selection.

The process described for $x_{1,t+1|t}$ is repeated for the remaining elements of $\mathbf{f}_t$. The next candidate for inclusion in the state vector is the next component of $\mathbf{f}_t$ corresponding to an active variable. Components of $\mathbf{f}_t$ corresponding to inactive variables that produced a zero ρ_{min} in a previous step are skipped.

Denote the next candidate as $x_{l,t+k|t}$. The vector $\mathbf{f}_t^j$ is formed from the current state vector and $x_{l,t+k|t}$ as follows:

$$\mathbf{f}_t^j = \left(\mathbf{z}_t^{j\,\prime}, x_{l,t+k|t} \right)^{\prime}$$

The matrix $\mathbf{V}^j$ is formed from $\mathbf{f}_t^j$ and its canonical correlations are computed. The smallest canonical correlation of $\mathbf{V}^j$ is judged to be either greater than or equal to 0. If it is judged to be greater than 0, $x_{l,t+k|t}$ is added to the state vector. If it is judged to be 0, then a linear combination of $\mathbf{f}_t^j$ is uncorrelated with the $\mathbf{p}_t$, and the variable x_l is now inactive.

The state vector selection process continues until no active variables remain.

Testing Significance of Canonical Correlations

For each step in the canonical correlation sequence, the significance of the smallest canonical correlation, ρ_{min}, is judged by an information criterion from Akaike (1976). This information criterion is

$$-n \ln\left(1 - \rho_{min}^2 \right) - \lambda(r\,(p+1) - q + 1)$$

where q is the dimension of $\mathbf{f}_t^j$ at the current step, r is the order of the state vector, p is the order of the vector autoregressive process, and λ is the value of the SIG-CORR= option. The default is SIGCORR=2. If this information criterion is less than or equal to 0, ρ_{min} is taken to be 0; otherwise, it is taken to be significantly greater than 0. (Do not confuse this information criterion with the AIC.)

Variables in $\mathbf{x}_{t+p|t}$ are not added in the model, even with positive information criterion, because of the singularity of $\mathbf{V}$. You can force the consideration of more candidate state variables by increasing the size of the $\mathbf{V}$ matrix by specifying a PASTMIN= option value larger than p.

Printing the Canonical Correlations

To print the details of the canonical correlation analysis process, specify the CAN-CORR option in the PROC STATESPACE statement. The CANCORR option prints the candidate state vectors, the canonical correlations, and the information criteria for testing the significance of the smallest canonical correlation.

Bartlett's χ^2 and its degrees of freedom are also printed when you specify the CAN-CORR option. The formula used for Bartlett's χ^2 is

$$\chi^2 = -(n - .5\,(r\,(p+1) - q + 1))\ln\left(1 - \rho_{min}^2 \right)$$

with $r\,(p+1) - q + 1$ degrees of freedom.

Figure 16.11 shows the output of the CANCORR option for the introductory example shown in the section "Getting Started" earlier in this chapter.

```
                    Canonical Correlations Analysis
      State vector               Correlations          Infor.    Chisq  D.F.

X(T;T),Y(T;T),X(T+1;T)       1.0000 1.0000 0.2370    3.566167  11.4505   4

X(T;T),Y(T;T),X(T+1;T),      1.0000 1.0000 0.2382   -5.35906  0.636134   3
Y(T+1;T)                     0.0566

X(T;T),Y(T;T),X(T+1;T),      1.0000 1.0000 0.2376   -4.46312  1.525353   3
X(T+2;T)                     0.0875
```

Figure 16.11. Canonical Correlations Analysis

New variables are added to the state vector if the information criteria are positive. In this example, $y_{t+1|t}$ and $x_{t+2|t}$ are not added to the state space vector because the information criteria for these models are negative.

If the information criterion is nearly 0, then you may want to investigate models that arise if the opposite decision is made regarding ρ_{min}. This investigation can be accomplished by using a FORM statement to specify part or all of the state vector.

Preliminary Estimates of F

When a candidate variable $x_{l,t+k|t}$ yields a zero ρ_{min} and is not added to the state vector, a linear combination of $\mathbf{f}_t^j$ is uncorrelated with the $\mathbf{p}_t$. Because of the method used to construct the $\mathbf{f}_t^j$ sequence, the coefficient of $x_{l,t+k|t}$ in $\mathbf{l}$ can be taken as 1. Denote the coefficients of $\mathbf{z}_t^j$ in this linear combination as $\mathbf{l}$.

This gives the relationship

$$x_{l,t+k|t} = \mathbf{l}' \mathbf{z}_t^j$$

The vector $\mathbf{l}$ is used as a preliminary estimate of the first r columns of the row of the transition matrix $\mathbf{F}$ corresponding to $x_{l,t+k-1|t}$.

Parameter Estimation

The model is $\mathbf{z}_{t+1} = \mathbf{F}\mathbf{z}_t + \mathbf{G}\mathbf{e}_{t+1}$, where $\mathbf{e}_t$ is a sequence of independent multivariate normal innovations with mean vector $\mathbf{0}$ and variance Σ_{ee}. The observed sequence, $\mathbf{x}_t$, composes the first r components of $\mathbf{z}_t$ and, thus, $\mathbf{x}_t = \mathbf{H}\mathbf{z}_t$, where $\mathbf{H}$ is the $r \times s$ matrix $[\mathbf{I}_r \ \mathbf{0}]$.

Let $\mathbf{E}$ be the $r \times n$ matrix of innovations, as follows:

$$\mathbf{E} = \begin{bmatrix} \mathbf{e}_1 & \cdots & \mathbf{e}_n \end{bmatrix}$$

If the number of observations, n, is reasonably large, the log likelihood, L, can be approximated up to an additive constant, as follows:

$$L = -\frac{n}{2} \ln(|\Sigma_{ee}|) - \frac{1}{2} \text{trace}(\Sigma_{ee}^{-1} \mathbf{E}\mathbf{E}')$$

The elements of Σ_{ee} are taken as free parameters and are estimated, as follows:

$$\mathbf{S}_0 = \tfrac{1}{n}\mathbf{EE}'$$

Replacing Σ_{ee} by $\mathbf{S}_0$ in the likelihood equation, the log likelihood, up to an additive constant, is

$$\mathrm{L} = -\tfrac{n}{2}\ln(\,|\,\mathbf{S}_0\,|\,)$$

Letting B be the backshift operator, the formal relation between $\mathbf{x}_t$ and $\mathbf{e}_t$ is

$$\mathbf{x}_t = \mathbf{H}(\mathbf{I} - \mathbf{BF})^{-1}\mathbf{Ge}_t$$

$$\mathbf{e}_t = \left(\mathbf{H}(\mathbf{I} - \mathbf{BF})^{-1}\mathbf{G}\right)^{-1}\mathbf{x}_t = \sum_{i=0}^{\infty} \Xi_i \mathbf{x}_{t-i}$$

Letting $\mathbf{C}_i$ be the ith lagged sample covariance of $\mathbf{x}_t$, and neglecting end effects, the matrix $\mathbf{S}_0$ is

$$\mathbf{S}_0 = \sum_{i,j=0}^{\infty} \Xi_i \mathbf{C}_{-i+j}\, \Xi_j'$$

For the computation of $\mathbf{S}_0$, the infinite sum is truncated at the value of the KLAG= option. The value of the KLAG= option should be large enough that the sequence Ξ_i is approximately 0 beyond that point.

Let θ be the vector of free parameters in the $\mathbf{F}$ and $\mathbf{G}$ matrices. The derivative of the log likelihood with respect to the parameter θ is

$$\frac{\partial\mathrm{L}}{\partial\theta} = -\tfrac{n}{2}\,\mathrm{trace}\left(\mathbf{S}_0^{-1}\,\frac{\partial\mathbf{S}_0}{\partial\theta}\right)$$

The second derivative is

$$\frac{\partial^2\mathrm{L}}{\partial\theta\partial\theta'} = \tfrac{n}{2}\mathrm{trace}\left(\mathbf{S}_0^{-1}\,\frac{\partial\mathbf{S}_0}{\partial\theta'}\,\mathbf{S}_0^{-1}\,\frac{\partial\mathbf{S}_0}{\partial\theta}\right) - \tfrac{n}{2}\mathrm{trace}\left(\mathbf{S}_0^{-1}\,\frac{\partial^2\mathbf{S}_0}{\partial\theta\partial\theta'}\right)$$

Near the maximum, the first term is unimportant and the second term can be approximated to give the following second derivative approximation:

$$\frac{\partial^2\mathrm{L}}{\partial\theta\partial\theta'} \cong -n\,\mathrm{trace}\left(\mathbf{S}_0^{-1}\,\frac{\partial\mathbf{E}}{\partial\theta}\,\frac{\partial\mathbf{E}'}{\partial\theta'}\right)$$

The first derivative matrix and this second derivative matrix approximation are computed from the sample covariance matrix $\mathbf{C}_0$ and the truncated sequence Ξ_i. The approximate likelihood function is maximized by a modified Newton-Raphson algorithm employing these derivative matrices.

The matrix $\mathbf{S}_0$ is used as the estimate of the innovation covariance matrix, Σ_{ee}. The negative of the inverse of the second derivative matrix at the maximum is used as an approximate covariance matrix for the parameter estimates. The standard errors of the parameter estimates printed in the parameter estimates tables are taken from the diagonal of this covariance matrix. The parameter covariance matrix is printed when you specify the COVB option.

If the data are nearly nonstationary, a better estimate of Σ_{ee} and the other parameters can sometimes be obtained by specifying the RESIDEST option. The RESIDEST option estimates the parameters using conditional least squares instead of maximum likelihood.

The residuals are computed using the state space equation and the sample mean values of the variables in the model as start-up values. The estimate of $\mathbf{S}_0$ is then computed using the residuals from the ith observation on, where i is the maximum number of times any variable occurs in the state vector. A multivariate Gauss-Marquardt algorithm is used to minimize $|\mathbf{S}_0|$. Refer to Harvey (1981a) for a further description of this method.

Forecasting

Given estimates of $\mathbf{F}$, $\mathbf{G}$, and Σ_{ee}, forecasts of $\mathbf{x}_t$ are computed from the conditional expectation of $\mathbf{z}_t$.

In forecasting, the parameters $\mathbf{F}$, $\mathbf{G}$, and Σ_{ee} are replaced with the estimates or by values you specify in the RESTRICT statement. One-step-ahead forecasting is performed for the observation $\mathbf{x}_t$, where $t \leq n - b$. Here, n is the number of observations and b is the value of the BACK= option. For the observation $\mathbf{x}_t$, where $t > n - b$, m-step-ahead forecasting is performed for $m = t - n + b$. The forecasts are generated recursively with the initial condition $\mathbf{z}_0 = 0$.

The m-step-ahead forecast of $\mathbf{z}_{t+m}$ is $\mathbf{z}_{t+m|t}$, where $\mathbf{z}_{t+m|t}$ denotes the conditional expectation of $\mathbf{z}_{t+m}$ given the information available at time t. The m-step-ahead forecast of $\mathbf{x}_{t+m}$ is $\mathbf{x}_{t+m|t} = \mathbf{H}\mathbf{z}_{t+m|t}$, where the matrix $\mathbf{H} = [\mathbf{I}_r \; \mathbf{0}]$.

Let $\Psi_i = \mathbf{F}^i \mathbf{G}$. Note that the last $s - r$ elements of $\mathbf{z}_t$ consist of the elements of $\mathbf{x}_{u|t}$ for $u > t$.

The state vector $\mathbf{z}_{t+m}$ can be represented as

$$\mathbf{z}_{t+m} = \mathbf{F}^m \mathbf{z}_t + \sum_{i=0}^{m-1} \Psi_i \mathbf{e}_{t+m-i}$$

Since $\mathbf{e}_{t+i|t} = \mathbf{0}$ for $i > 0$, the m-step-ahead forecast $\mathbf{z}_{t+m|t}$ is

$$\mathbf{z}_{t+m|t} = \mathbf{F}^m \mathbf{z}_t = \mathbf{F} \mathbf{z}_{t+m-1|t}$$

Therefore, the m-step-ahead forecast of $\mathbf{x}_{t+m}$ is

$$\mathbf{x}_{t+m|t} = \mathbf{H}\mathbf{z}_{t+m|t}$$

The *m*-step-ahead forecast error is

$$\mathbf{z}_{t+m} - \mathbf{z}_{t+m|t} = \sum_{i=0}^{m-1} \Psi_i \, \mathbf{e}_{t+m-i}$$

The variance of the *m*-step-ahead forecast error is

$$\mathbf{V}_{z,m} = \sum_{i=0}^{m-1} \Psi_i \, \Sigma_{\mathbf{ee}} \, \Psi_i'$$

Letting $\mathbf{V}_{z,0} = \mathbf{0}$, the variance of the *m*-step-ahead forecast error of $\mathbf{z}_{t+m}$, $\mathbf{V}_{z,m}$, can be computed recursively as follows:

$$\mathbf{V}_{z,m} = \mathbf{V}_{z,m-1} + \Psi_{m-1} \, \Sigma_{\mathbf{ee}} \, \Psi_{m-1}'$$

The variance of the *m*-step-ahead forecast error of $\mathbf{x}_{t+m}$ is the $r \times r$ left upper submatrix of $\mathbf{V}_{z,m}$; that is,

$$\mathbf{V}_{x,m} = \mathbf{H}\mathbf{V}_{z,m}\mathbf{H}'$$

Unless you specify the NOCENTER option, the sample mean vector is added to the forecast. When you specify differencing, the forecasts $\mathbf{x}_{t+m|t}$ plus the sample mean vector are integrated back to produce forecasts for the original series.

Let $\mathbf{y}_t$ be the original series specified by the VAR statement, with some 0 values appended corresponding to the unobserved past observations. Let B be the backshift operator, and let $\Delta(\mathrm{B})$ be the $s \times s$ matrix polynomial in the backshift operator corresponding to the differencing specified by the VAR statement. The off-diagonal elements of Δ_i are 0. Note that $\Delta_0 = \mathbf{I}_s$, where $\mathbf{I}_s$ is the $s \times s$ identity matrix. Then $\mathbf{z}_t = \Delta(\mathrm{B})\mathbf{y}_t$.

This gives the relationship:

$$\mathbf{y}_t = \Delta^{-1}(\mathrm{B}) \, \mathbf{z}_t = \sum_{i=0}^{\infty} \Lambda_i \mathbf{z}_{t-i}$$

where $\Delta^{-1}(\mathrm{B}) = \sum_{i=0}^{\infty} \Lambda_i \, \mathrm{B}^i$ and $\Lambda_0 = \mathbf{I}_s$.

The *m*-step-ahead forecast of $\mathbf{y}_{t+m}$ is

$$\mathbf{y}_{t+m|t} = \sum_{i=0}^{m-1} \Lambda_i \, \mathbf{z}_{t+m-i|t} + \sum_{i=m}^{\infty} \Lambda_i \, \mathbf{z}_{t+m-i}$$

The *m*-step-ahead forecast error of $\mathbf{y}_{t+m}$ is

$$\sum_{i=0}^{m-1} \Lambda_i \left(\mathbf{z}_{t+m-i} - \mathbf{z}_{t+m-i|t} \right) = \sum_{i=0}^{m-1} \left(\sum_{u=0}^{i} \Lambda_u \, \Psi_{i-u} \right) \mathbf{e}_{t+m-i}$$

Letting $\mathbf{V}_{y,0} = \mathbf{0}$, the variance of the *m*-step-ahead forecast error of $\mathbf{y}_{t+m}$, $\mathbf{V}_{y,m}$, is

$$
\mathbf{V}_{y,m} = \sum_{i=0}^{m-1} \left(\sum_{u=0}^{i} \Lambda_u \Psi_{i-u} \right) \Sigma_{\mathbf{ee}} \left(\sum_{u=0}^{i} \Lambda_u \Psi_{i-u} \right)'
$$

$$
= \mathbf{V}_{y,m-1} + \left(\sum_{u=0}^{m-1} \Lambda_u \Psi_{m-1-u} \right) \Sigma_{\mathbf{ee}} \left(\sum_{u=0}^{m-1} \Lambda_u \Psi_{m-1-u} \right)'
$$

Relation of ARMA and State Space Forms

Every state space model has an ARMA representation; conversely, every ARMA model has a state space representation. This section discusses this equivalence. The following material is adapted from Akaike (1974), where there is a more complete discussion. Pham-Dinh-Tuan (1978) also contains a discussion of this material.

Suppose you are given the following ARMA model:

$$
\Phi(B)\mathbf{x}_t = \Theta(B)\mathbf{e}_t
$$

or, in more detail

$$
\mathbf{x}_t - \Phi_1 \mathbf{x}_{t-1} - \cdots - \Phi_p \mathbf{x}_{t-p} = \mathbf{e}_t + \Theta_1 \mathbf{e}_{t-1} + \cdots + \Theta_q \mathbf{e}_{t-q} \quad (1)
$$

where $\mathbf{e}_t$ is a sequence of independent multivariate normal random vectors with mean $\mathbf{0}$ and variance matrix $\Sigma_{\mathbf{ee}}$; B is the backshift operator ($B\mathbf{x}_t = \mathbf{x}_{t-1}$); $\Phi(B)$ and $\Theta(B)$ are matrix polynomials in B; and $\mathbf{x}_t$ is the observed process.

If the roots of the determinantial equation $|\Phi(B)| = 0$ are outside the unit circle in the complex plane, the model can also be written

$$
\mathbf{x}_t = \Phi^{-1}(B)\Theta(B)\mathbf{e}_t = \sum_{i=0}^{\infty} \Psi_i \mathbf{e}_{t-i}
$$

The Ψ_i matrices are known as the impulse response matrices and can be computed as $\Phi^{-1}(B)\Theta(B)$.

You can assume $p > q$ since, if this is not initially true, you can add more terms Φ_i that are identically 0 without changing the model.

To write this set of equations in a state space form, proceed as follows. Let $\mathbf{x}_{t+i|t}$ be the conditional expectation of $\mathbf{x}_{t+i}$ given $\mathbf{x}_w$ for $w \leq t$. The following relations hold:

$$
\mathbf{x}_{t+i|t} = \sum_{j=i}^{\infty} \Psi_j \mathbf{e}_{t+i-j}
$$

$$
\mathbf{x}_{t+i|t+1} = \mathbf{x}_{t+i|t} + \Psi_{i-1} \mathbf{e}_{t+1}
$$

However, from equation (1) you can derive the following relationship:

$$\mathbf{x}_{t+p|t} = \Phi_1\mathbf{x}_{t+p-1|t} + \cdots + \Phi_p\mathbf{x}_t \tag{2}$$

Hence, when $i = p$, you can substitute for $\mathbf{x}_{t+p|t}$ in the right-hand side of equation (2) and close the system of equations.

This substitution results in the following model in the state space form $\mathbf{z}_{t+1} = \mathbf{F}\mathbf{z}_t + \mathbf{G}\mathbf{e}_{t+1}$:

$$
\begin{bmatrix} \mathbf{x}_{t+1} \\ \mathbf{x}_{t+2|t+1} \\ \vdots \\ \mathbf{x}_{t+p|t+1} \end{bmatrix} = \begin{bmatrix} 0 & \mathbf{I} & 0 & \cdots & 0 \\ 0 & 0 & \mathbf{I} & \cdots & 0 \\ \vdots & \vdots & \vdots & & \vdots \\ \Phi_p & \Phi_{p-1} & & \cdots & \Phi_1 \end{bmatrix} \begin{bmatrix} \mathbf{x}_t \\ \mathbf{x}_{t+1|t} \\ \vdots \\ \mathbf{x}_{t+p-1|t} \end{bmatrix} + \begin{bmatrix} \mathbf{I} \\ \Psi_1 \\ \vdots \\ \Psi_{p-1} \end{bmatrix} \mathbf{e}_{t+1}
$$

Note that the state vector $\mathbf{z}_t$ is composed of conditional expectations of $\mathbf{x}_t$ and the first r components of $\mathbf{z}_t$ are equal to $\mathbf{x}_t$.

The state space form can be cast into an ARMA form by solving the system of difference equations for the first r components.

When converting from an ARMA form to a state space form, you can generate a state vector larger than needed; that is, the state space model may not be a minimal representation. When converting from a state space form to an ARMA form, you can have nontrivial common factors in the autoregressive and moving average operators that yield an ARMA model larger than necessary.

If the state space form used is not a minimal representation, some but not all components of $\mathbf{x}_{t+i|t}$ may be linearly dependent. This situation corresponds to $\begin{bmatrix} \Phi_p & \Theta_{p-1} \end{bmatrix}$ being of less than full rank when $\Phi(\mathbf{B})$ and $\Theta(\mathbf{B})$ have no common nontrivial left factors. In this case, $\mathbf{z}_t$ consists of a subset of the possible components of $\begin{bmatrix} \mathbf{x}_{t+i|t} \end{bmatrix}$ $i = 1, 2, \cdots, p-1$. However, once a component of $\mathbf{x}_{t+i|t}$ (for example, the jth one) is linearly dependent on the previous conditional expectations, then all subsequent jth components of $\mathbf{x}_{t+k|t}$ for $k > i$ must also be linearly dependent. Note that in this case, equivalent but seemingly different structures can arise if the order of the components within $\mathbf{x}_t$ is changed.

OUT= Data Set

The forecasts are contained in the output data set specified by the OUT= option on the PROC STATESPACE statement. The OUT= data set contains the following variables:

- the BY variables

- the ID variable

- the VAR statement variables. These variables contain the actual values from the input data set.

- FORi, numeric variables containing the forecasts. The variable FORi contains the forecasts for the ith variable in the VAR statement list. Forecasts are one-step-ahead predictions until the end of the data or until the observation specified by the BACK= option.

- RESi, numeric variables containing the residual for the forecast of the ith variable in the VAR statement list. For forecast observations, the actual values are missing and the RESi variables contain missing values.

- STDi, numeric variables containing the standard deviation for the forecast of the ith variable in the VAR statement list. The values of the STDi variables can be used to construct univariate confidence limits for the corresponding forecasts. However, such confidence limits do not take into account the covariance of the forecasts.

OUTAR= Data Set

The OUTAR= data set contains the estimates of the preliminary autoregressive models. The OUTAR= data set contains the following variables:

- ORDER, a numeric variable containing the order p of the autoregressive model that the observation represents

- AIC, a numeric variable containing the value of the information criterion $\mathbf{AIC}_p$

- SIGFl, numeric variables containing the estimate of the innovation covariance matrices for the forward autoregressive models. The variable SIGFl contains the lth column of $\widehat{\Sigma}_p$ in the observations with ORDER=p.

- SIGBl, numeric variables containing the estimate of the innovation covariance matrices for the backward autoregressive models. The variable SIGBl contains the lth column of $\widehat{\Omega}_p$ in the observations with ORDER=p.

- FORk_l, numeric variables containing the estimates of the autoregressive parameter matrices for the forward models. The variable FORk_l contains the lth column of the lag k autoregressive parameter matrix $\widehat{\Phi}_k^p$ in the observations with ORDER=p.

- BACk_l, numeric variables containing the estimates of the autoregressive parameter matrices for the backward models. The variable BACk_l contains the lth column of the lag k autoregressive parameter matrix $\widehat{\Psi}_k^p$ in the observations with ORDER=p.

You can extract the estimates for the order p autoregressive model by selecting those observations with ORDER=p. Within these observations, the k,lth element of Φ_i^p is given by the value of the FORi_l variable in the kth observation. The k,lth element of Ψ_i^p is given by the value of BACi_l variable in the kth observation. The k,lth element of Σ_p is given by SIGFl in the kth observation. The k,lth element of Ω_p is given by SIGBl in the kth observation.

Table 16.1 shows an example of the OUTAR= data set, with ARMAX=3 and $\mathbf{x}_t$ of dimension 2. In Table 16.1, (i,j) indicate the i,jth element of the matrix.

Table 16.1. Values in the OUTAR= Data Set

Obs	ORDER	AIC	SIGF1	SIGF2	SIGB1	SIGB2	FOR1_1	FOR1_2	FOR2_1	FOR2_2	FOR3_1
1	0	AIC_0	$\Sigma_{0(1,1)}$	$\Sigma_{0(1,2)}$	$\Omega_{0(1,1)}$	$\Omega_{0(1,2)}$	.	.	.	.	.
2	0	AIC_0	$\Sigma_{0(2,1)}$	$\Sigma_{0(2,2)}$	$\Omega_{0(2,1)}$	$\Omega_{0(2,2)}$	.	.	.	.	.
3	1	AIC_1	$\Sigma_{1(1,1)}$	$\Sigma_{1(1,2)}$	$\Omega_{1(1,1)}$	$\Omega_{1(1,2)}$	$\Phi^1_{1(1,1)}$	$\Phi^1_{1(1,2)}$	.	.	.
4	1	AIC_1	$\Sigma_{1(2,1)}$	$\Sigma_{1(2,2)}$	$\Omega_{1(2,1)}$	$\Omega_{1(2,2)}$	$\Phi^1_{1(2,1)}$	$\Phi^1_{1(2,2)}$	.	.	.
5	2	AIC_2	$\Sigma_{2(1,1)}$	$\Sigma_{2(1,2)}$	$\Omega_{2(1,1)}$	$\Omega_{2(1,2)}$	$\Phi^2_{1(1,1)}$	$\Phi^2_{1(1,2)}$	$\Phi^2_{2(1,1)}$	$\Phi^2_{2(1,2)}$	.
6	2	AIC_2	$\Sigma_{2(2,1)}$	$\Sigma_{2(2,2)}$	$\Omega_{2(2,1)}$	$\Omega_{2(2,2)}$	$\Phi^2_{1(2,1)}$	$\Phi^2_{1(2,2)}$	$\Phi^2_{2(2,1)}$	$\Phi^2_{2(2,2)}$	.
7	3	AIC_3	$\Sigma_{3(1,1)}$	$\Sigma_{3(1,2)}$	$\Omega_{3(1,1)}$	$\Omega_{3(1,2)}$	$\Phi^3_{1(1,1)}$	$\Phi^3_{1(1,2)}$	$\Phi^3_{2(1,1)}$	$\Phi^3_{2(1,2)}$	$\Phi^3_{3(1,1)}$
8	3	AIC_3	$\Sigma_{3(2,1)}$	$\Sigma_{3(1,2)}$	$\Omega_{3(2,1)}$	$\Omega_{3(1,2)}$	$\Phi^3_{1(2,1)}$	$\Phi^3_{1(2,2)}$	$\Phi^3_{2(2,1)}$	$\Phi^3_{2(2,2)}$	$\Phi^3_{3(2,1)}$

Obs	FOR3_2	BACK1_1	BACK1_2	BACK2_1	BACK2_2	BACK3_1	BACK3_2
1	.	.	.	.	.	.	.
2	.	.	.	.	.	.	.
3	.	$\Psi^1_{1(1,1)}$	$\Psi^1_{1(1,2)}$	.	.	.	.
4	.	$\Psi^1_{1(2,1)}$	$\Psi^1_{1(2,2)}$	.	.	.	.
5	.	$\Psi^2_{1(1,1)}$	$\Psi^2_{1(1,2)}$	$\Psi^2_{2(1,1)}$	$\Psi^2_{2(1,2)}$	.	.
6	.	$\Psi^2_{1(2,1)}$	$\Psi^2_{1(2,2)}$	$\Psi^2_{2(2,1)}$	$\Psi^2_{2(2,2)}$	.	.
7	$\Phi^3_{3(1,2)}$	$\Psi^3_{1(1,1)}$	$\Psi^3_{1(1,2)}$	$\Psi^3_{2(1,1)}$	$\Psi^3_{2(1,2)}$	$\Psi^3_{3(1,1)}$	$\Psi^3_{3(1,2)}$
8	$\Phi^3_{3(2,2)}$	$\Psi^3_{1(2,1)}$	$\Psi^3_{1(2,2)}$	$\Psi^3_{2(2,1)}$	$\Psi^3_{2(2,2)}$	$\Psi^3_{3(2,1)}$	$\Psi^3_{3(2,2)}$

You can use the estimated autoregressive parameters in the IML procedure to obtain autoregressive estimates of the spectral density function or forecasts based on the autoregressive models.

OUTMODEL= Data Set

The OUTMODEL= data set contains the estimates of the **F** and **G** matrices and their standard errors, the names of the components of the state vector, and the estimates of the innovation covariance matrix. The variables contained in the OUTMODEL= data set are as follows:

- the BY variables

- STATEVEC, a character variable containing the name of the component of the state vector corresponding to the observation. The STATEVEC variable has the value STD for standard deviations observations, which contain the standard errors for the estimates given in the preceding observation.

- F_j, numeric variables containing the columns of the **F** matrix. The variable F_j contains the jth column of **F**. The number of F_j variables is equal to the value of the DIMMAX= option. If the model is of smaller dimension, the extraneous variables are set to missing.

- G_j, numeric variables containing the columns of the **G** matrix. The variable G_j contains the jth column of **G**. The number of G_j variables is equal to r, the dimension of $\mathbf{x}_t$ given by the number of variables in the VAR statement.

- SIG_*j*, numeric variables containing the columns of the innovation covariance matrix. The variable SIG_*j* contains the *j*th column of Σ_{ee}. There are *r* variables SIG_*j*.

Table 16.2 shows an example of the OUTMODEL= data set, with $\mathbf{x}_t = (x_t, y_t)'$, $\mathbf{z}_t = (x_t, y_t, x_{t+1|t})'$, and DIMMAX=4. In Table 16.2, $\mathbf{F}_{i,j}$ and $\mathbf{G}_{i,j}$ are the *i,j*th elements of **F** and **G**, respectively. Note that all elements for F_4 are missing because **F** is a 3×3 matrix.

Table 16.2. Value in the OUTMODEL= Data Set

Obs	STATEVEC	F_1	F_2	F_3	F_4	G_1	G_2	SIG_1	SIG_2
1	X(T;T)	0	0	1	.	1	0	$\Sigma_{1,1}$	$\Sigma_{1,2}$
2	STD	.	.	.	.	.	.	.	.
3	Y(T;T)	$\mathbf{F}_{2,1}$	$\mathbf{F}_{2,2}$	$\mathbf{F}_{2,3}$	.	0	1	$\Sigma_{2,1}$	$\Sigma_{2,2}$
4	STD	std $\mathbf{F}_{2,1}$	std $\mathbf{F}_{2,2}$	std $\mathbf{F}_{2,3}$	.	.	.	.	.
5	X(T+1;T)	$\mathbf{F}_{3,1}$	$\mathbf{F}_{3,2}$	$\mathbf{F}_{3,3}$	.	$\mathbf{G}_{3,1}$	$\mathbf{G}_{3,2}$	.	.
6	STD	std $\mathbf{F}_{3,1}$	std $\mathbf{F}_{3,2}$	std $\mathbf{F}_{3,3}$	.	std $\mathbf{G}_{3,1}$	std $\mathbf{G}_{3,2}$	.	.

Printed Output

The printed output produced by the STATESPACE procedure is described in the following list:

1. descriptive statistics, which include the number of observations used, labeled "Nobs," the names of the variables, their means and standard deviations (Std), and the differencing operations used

2. Akaike's information criteria for the sequence of preliminary autoregressive models

3. if you specified the PRINTOUT=LONG option, the sample autocovariance matrices of the input series at various lags

4. if you specified the PRINTOUT=LONG option, the sample autocorrelation matrices of the input series

5. a schematic representation of the autocorrelation matrices, showing the significant autocorrelations

6. if you specified the PRINTOUT=LONG option, the partial autoregressive matrices. (These are Φ_p^p as described in "Preliminary Autoregressive Models" earlier in this chapter.)

7. a schematic representation of the partial autocorrelation matrices, showing the significant partial autocorrelations

8. the Yule-Walker estimates of the autoregressive parameters for the autoregressive model with the minimum AIC

9. if you specified the PRINTOUT=LONG option, the autocovariance matrices of the residuals of the minimum AIC model. This is the sequence of estimated inno-

vation variance matrices for the solutions of the Yule-Walker equations.

10. if you specified the PRINTOUT=LONG option, the autocorrelation matrices of the residuals of the minimum AIC model

11. if you specified the CANCORR option, the canonical correlations analysis for each potential state vector considered in the state vector selection process. This includes the potential state vector, the canonical correlations, the information criterion for the smallest canonical correlation, Bartlett's χ^2 statistic ("Chisq") for the smallest canonical correlation, and the degrees of freedom of Bartlett's χ^2.

12. the components of the chosen state vector

13. the preliminary estimate of the transition matrix, **F**, the input matrix, **G**, and the variance matrix for the innovations, Σ_{ee}

14. if you specified the ITPRINT option, the iteration history of the likelihood maximization. For each iteration, this shows the iteration number, the number of step halvings, the determinant of the innovation variance matrix, the damping factor Lambda, and the values of the parameters.

15. the state vector, printed again to aid interpretation of the following listing of **F** and **G**

16. the final estimate of the transition matrix, **F**

17. the final estimate of the input matrix, **G**

18. the final estimate of the variance matrix for the innovations, Σ_{ee}

19. a table listing the estimates of the free parameters in **F** and **G** and their standard errors and *t* statistics

20. if you specified the COVB option, the covariance matrix of the parameter estimates

21. if you specified the COVB option, the correlation matrix of the parameter estimates

22. if you specified the PRINT option, the forecasts and their standard errors

Example

Example 16.1.   Series J from Box and Jenkins

This example analyzes the gas furnace data (series J) from Box and Jenkins. (The data are not shown. Refer to Box and Jenkins (1976) for the data.)

First, a model is selected and fit automatically using the following statements:

```
title1 'Gas Furnace Data';
title2 'Box & Jenkins Series J';
title3 'Automatically Selected Model';

proc statespace data=seriesj cancorr;
   var x y;
run;
```

The results for the automatically selected model are shown in Output 16.1.1.

Output 16.1.1.   Results for Automatically Selected Model

```
                     Gas Furnace Data
                   Box & Jenkins Series J
                 Automatically Selected Model

                    STATESPACE Procedure

                        Nobs = 296

              Variable      Mean        Std
              X          -0.05683    1.072766
              Y          53.50912    3.202121


        Information Criterion for Autoregressive Models


      Lag=0         Lag=1         Lag=2         Lag=3         Lag=4
  651.386156   -1033.57211   -1632.95659   -1645.12498   -1651.52305


      Lag=5         Lag=6         Lag=7         Lag=8         Lag=9
 -1648.91248   -1649.34335   -1643.15323   -1638.55591   -1634.79898


      Lag=10
 -1633.58501



        Schematic Representation of Correlations

        Name/Lag   0   1   2   3   4   5   6   7   8   9  10
        X             +-  +-  +-  +-  +-  +-  +-  +-  +-  +-  +-
        Y             -+  -+  -+  -+  -+  -+  -+  -+  -+  -+  -+

        + is > 2*std error,  - is < -2*std error,  . is between
```

Output 16.1.1. (Continued)

```
                          Gas Furnace Data
                        Box & Jenkins Series J
                      Automatically Selected Model

                        STATESPACE Procedure

              Schematic Representation of Partial Autocorrelations

         Name/Lag   1   2   3   4   5   6   7   8   9   10
             X          +.  -.  +.  ..  ..  -.  ..  ..  ..  ..
             Y          -+  --  -.  .+  ..  ..  ..  ..  ..  .+

         + is > 2*std error,   - is < -2*std error,   . is between


                      Yule-Walker Estimates for the Min AIC


                  Lag=1                      Lag=2
                X          Y                X          Y
        X    1.92589   -0.00124       -1.20166    0.00422
        Y    0.05050    1.29979       -0.02046   -0.32770


                  Lag=3                      Lag=4
                X          Y                X          Y
        X    0.11692   -0.00867        0.10424    0.00327
        Y   -0.71182   -0.25701        0.19541    0.13342
```

```
                          Gas Furnace Data
                        Box & Jenkins Series J
                      Automatically Selected Model

                        STATESPACE Procedure

                   Canonical Correlations Analysis
```

State vector	Correlations	Infor.	Chisq	D.F.
X(T;T),Y(T;T),X(T+1;T)	1.0000 1.0000 0.8049	292.9228	304.7481	8
X(T;T),Y(T;T),X(T+1;T), Y(T+1;T)	1.0000 1.0000 0.9067 0.6075	122.3358	134.7237	7
X(T;T),Y(T;T),X(T+1;T), Y(T+1;T),X(T+2;T)	1.0000 1.0000 0.9094 0.6103 0.1863	-1.54701	10.34705	6
X(T;T),Y(T;T),X(T+1;T), Y(T+1;T),Y(T+2;T)	1.0000 1.0000 0.9101 0.6189 0.2068	0.940392	12.80924	6
X(T;T),Y(T;T),X(T+1;T), Y(T+1;T),Y(T+2;T),Y(T+3;T)	1.0000 1.0000 0.9130 0.6288 0.2266 0.0833	-7.94103	2.041584	5

```
                          Gas Furnace Data
                        Box & Jenkins Series J
                      Automatically Selected Model

                        STATESPACE Procedure

             Selected Statespace Form and Preliminary Estimates

                           State Vector

        X(T;T)         Y(T;T)          X(T+1;T)         Y(T+1;T)
        Y(T+2;T)

                  Estimate of the Transition Matrix

                       0       0       1       0       0

                       0       0       0       1       0

                  -0.847   0.027   1.712  -0.050       0
```

Example 16.1. Series J from Box and Jenkins □ □ □ 811

Output 16.1.1. (Continued)

```
          0      0      0      0      1
       -0.198  0.334  -0.182  -1.236  1.787
```

```
              Input Matrix for the Innovation
                        1        0
                        0        1
                     1.926   -0.001
                     0.050    1.300
                     0.142    1.362
```

```
                   Gas Furnace Data
                 Box & Jenkins Series J
                Automatically Selected Model

                   STATESPACE Procedure

      Selected Statespace Form and Preliminary Estimates

             Variance Matrix for the Innovation
                 0.0352738  -0.0073378
                -0.0073378   0.09756908
```

```
                   Gas Furnace Data
                 Box & Jenkins Series J
                Automatically Selected Model

                   STATESPACE Procedure

        Selected Statespace Form and Fitted Model
                      State Vector
X(T;T)          Y(T;T)           X(T+1;T)          Y(T+1;T)
Y(T+2;T)

            Estimate of the Transition Matrix
            0      0      1      0      0
            0      0      0      1      0
        -0.862  0.031  1.724  -0.055    0
            0      0      0      0      1
        -0.348  0.292  -0.094  -1.098  1.671

              Input Matrix for the Innovation
                        1        0
                        0        1
                     1.924   -0.004
                     0.016    1.258
                     0.081    1.353
```

Output 16.1.1. (Continued)

```
                        Gas Furnace Data
                     Box & Jenkins Series J
                   Automatically Selected Model

                       STATESPACE Procedure

            Selected Statespace Form and Fitted Model


                 Variance Matrix for the Innovation

                    0.03557876   -0.007285

                        -0.007285 0.09557739


                     Parameter Estimates

           Parameter  Estimate   Std. Err.   T value

             F(3,1)    -0.86192   0.072961   -11.8135
             F(3,2)     0.030609  0.026167    1.16975
             F(3,3)     1.724235  0.061599   27.99136
             F(3,4)    -0.05483   0.030169   -1.81726
             F(5,1)    -0.34839   0.135253   -2.57582
             F(5,2)     0.292124  0.046299    6.309469
             F(5,3)    -0.09435   0.096527   -0.9774
             F(5,4)    -1.09823   0.109525  -10.0272
             F(5,5)     1.671418  0.083737   19.9604
             G(3,1)     1.92442   0.058162   33.08744
             G(3,2)    -0.00416   0.035255   -0.11812
             G(4,1)     0.015621  0.095771    0.163107
             G(4,2)     1.258495  0.055742   22.57733
             G(5,1)     0.08058   0.151622    0.531452
             G(5,2)     1.353204  0.091388   14.80719
```

The two series are believed to have a transfer function relation with the gas rate (variable X) as the input and the CO_2 concentration (variable Y) as the output. Since the parameter estimates shown in Output 16.1.1 support this kind of model, the model is reestimated with the feedback parameters restricted to 0. The following statements fit the transfer function (no feedback) model:

```
title3 'Transfer Function Model';
proc statespace data=seriesj printout=none;
   var x y;
   restrict f(3,2)=0  f(3,4)=0
            g(3,2)=0  g(4,1)=0  g(5,1)=0;
run;
```

The last two pages of the output are shown in Output 16.1.2.

Example 16.1. Series J from Box and Jenkins □ □ □ 813

Output 16.1.2. STATESPACE Output for Transfer Function Model

```
                         Gas Furnace Data
                      Box & Jenkins Series J
                      Transfer Function Model

                       STATESPACE Procedure

              Selected Statespace Form and Fitted Model

                           State Vector

   X(T;T)          Y(T;T)              X(T+1;T)         Y(T+1;T)
   Y(T+2;T)

                 Estimate of the Transition Matrix

                    0      0      1      0      0

                    0      0      0      1      0

                 -0.689  0.000  1.599  0.000    0

                    0      0      0      0      1

                 -0.359  0.284 -0.096 -1.073  1.650


                 Input Matrix for the Innovation

                           1      0

                           0      1

                         1.923  0.000

                         0.000  1.261

                         0.000  1.346
```

```
                         Gas Furnace Data
                      Box & Jenkins Series J
                      Transfer Function Model

                       STATESPACE Procedure

              Selected Statespace Form and Fitted Model

                 Variance Matrix for the Innovation

                    0.03699488 -0.0072039

                   -0.0072039 0.09571217


                       Parameter Estimates

          Parameter Estimate  Std. Err.   T value

            F(3,1)   -0.68882  0.050549  -13.6267
            F(3,3)    1.598717 0.050924   31.39431
            F(5,1)   -0.35944  0.229044   -1.56928
            F(5,2)    0.284179 0.096944    2.931354
            F(5,3)   -0.0963   0.140876   -0.6836
            F(5,4)   -1.07313  0.250385   -4.28592
            F(5,5)    1.650047 0.188533    8.752033
            G(3,1)    1.923446 0.056328   34.14737
            G(4,2)    1.260856 0.056464   22.33017
            G(5,2)    1.346332 0.091086   14.78096
```

References

Akaike, H. (1974), "Markovian Representation of Stochastic Processes and Its Application to the Analysis of Autoregressive Moving Average Processes," *Annals of the Institute of Statistical Mathematics*, 26, 363–387.

Akaike, H. (1976), "Canonical Correlations Analysis of Time Series and the Use of an Information Criterion," in *Advances and Case Studies in System Identification*, eds. R. Mehra and D.G. Lainiotis, New York: Academic Press.

Anderson, T.W. (1971), *The Statistical Analysis of Time Series*, New York: John Wiley & Sons.

Ansley, C.F. and Newbold, P. (1979), "Multivariate Partial Autocorrelations," *Proceedings of the Business and Economic Statistics Section*, American Statistical Association, 349–353.

Box, G.E.P. and Jenkins, G. (1976), *Time Series Analysis: Forecasting and Control*, San Francisco: Holden-Day.

Brockwell, P.J. and Davis, R.A. (1991), *Time Series: Theory and Methods*, 2nd Edition, Springer-Verlag.

Hannan, E.J. (1970), *Multiple Time Series*, New York: John Wiley & Sons.

Hannan, E.J. (1976), "The Identification and Parameterization of ARMAX and State Space Forms," *Econometrica*, 44, 713–722.

Harvey, A.C. (1981a), *The Econometric Analysis of Time Series*, New York: John Wiley & Sons.

Harvey, A.C. (1981b), *Time Series Models*, New York: John Wiley & Sons.

Jones, R.H. (1974), "Identification and Autoregressive Spectrum Estimation," *IEEE Transactions on Automatic Control*, AC-19, 894–897.

Pham-Dinh-Tuan (1978), "On the Fitting of Multivariate Processes of the Autoregressive-Moving Average Type," *Biometrika*, 65, 99–107.

Priestley, M.B. (1980), "System Identification, Kalman Filtering, and Stochastic Control," in *Directions in Time Series*, eds. D.R. Brillinger and G.C. Tiao, Institute of Mathematical Statistics.

Whittle, P. (1963), "On the Fitting of Multivariate Autoregressions and the Approximate Canonical Factorization of a Spectral Density Matrix," *Biometrika*, 50, 129–134.

Chapter 17
The SYSLIN Procedure

Chapter Table of Contents

Chapter 17
The SYSLIN Procedure

Overview

The SYSLIN procedure estimates parameters in an interdependent system of linear regression equations.

Ordinary least squares (OLS) estimates are biased and inconsistent when current period endogenous variables appear as regressors in other equations in the system. The errors of a set of related regression equations are often correlated, and the efficiency of the estimates can be improved by taking these correlations into account. The SYSLIN procedure provides several techniques which produce consistent and asymptotically efficient estimates for systems of regression equations.

The SYSLIN procedure provides the following estimation methods:

- ordinary least squares (OLS)
- two-stage least squares (2SLS)
- limited information maximum likelihood (LIML)
- K-class
- seemingly unrelated regressions (SUR)
- iterated seemingly unrelated regressions (ITSUR)
- three-stage least squares (3SLS)
- iterated three-stage least squares (IT3SLS)
- full information maximum likelihood (FIML)
- minimum expected loss (MELO)

Other features of the SYSLIN procedure enable you to

- impose linear restrictions on the parameter estimates
- test linear hypotheses about the parameters
- write predicted and residual values to an output SAS data set
- write parameter estimates to an output SAS data set
- write the crossproducts matrix (SSCP) to an output SAS data set
- use raw data, correlations, covariances, or cross products as input

Getting Started

This section introduces the use of the SYSLIN procedure. The problem of dependent regressors is introduced using a supply-demand example. This section explains the terminology used for variables in a system of regression equations and introduces the SYSLIN procedure statements for declaring the roles the variables play. The syntax used for the different estimation methods and the output produced is shown.

Simultaneous Equation Bias

In simultaneous systems of equations, endogenous variables are determined jointly rather than sequentially. Consider the following demand and supply functions for some product:

$$Q_D = a_1 + b_1 P + c_1 Y + d_1 S + \epsilon_1 \quad \text{(demand)}$$

$$Q_S = a_2 + b_2 P + c_2 U + \epsilon_2 \quad \text{(supply)}$$

$$Q = Q_D = Q_S \qquad \text{(market equilibrium)}$$

The variables in this system are as follows:

Q_D quantity demanded
Q_S quantity supplied
Q the observed quantity sold, which equates quantity supplied and quantity demanded in equilibrium
P price per unit
Y income
S price of substitutes
U unit cost
ϵ_1 the random error term for the demand equation
ϵ_2 the random error term for the supply equation

In this system, quantity demanded depends on price, income, and the price of substitutes. Consumers normally purchase more of a product when prices are lower and when income and the price of substitute goods are higher. Quantity supplied depends on price and the unit cost of production. Producers will supply more when price is high and when unit cost is low. The actual price and quantity sold are determined jointly by the values that equate demand and supply.

Since price and quantity are jointly endogenous variables, both structural equations are necessary to adequately describe the observed values. A critical assumption of OLS is that the regressors are uncorrelated with the residual. When current endogenous variables appear as regressors in other equations (endogenous variables depend on each other), this assumption is violated and the OLS parameter estimates are biased and inconsistent. Neither the demand nor supply equation can be estimated consistently by OLS.

Variables in a System of Equations

Before explaining how to use the SYSLIN procedure, it is useful to define some terms. The variables in a system of equations can be classified as follows:

- *Endogenous variables*, which are also called *jointly dependent* or *response variables*, are the variables determined by the system. Endogenous variables can also appear on the right-hand side of equations.

- *Exogenous variables* are independent variables that do not depend on any of the endogenous variables in the system.

- *Predetermined variables* include both the exogenous variables and *lagged endogenous variables*, which are past values of endogenous variables determined at previous time periods. PROC SYSLIN does not compute lagged values; any lagged endogenous variables must be computed in a preceding DATA step.

- *Instrumental variables* are predetermined variables used in obtaining predicted values for the current period endogenous variables by a first-stage regression. The use of instrumental variables characterizes estimation methods such as two-stage least squares and three-stage least squares. Instrumental variables estimation methods substitute these first-stage predicted values for endogenous variables when they appear as regressors in model equations.

Using PROC SYSLIN

First specify the input data set and estimation method in the PROC SYSLIN statement. If any model uses dependent regressors and you are using an instrumental variables regression method, declare the dependent regressors with an ENDOGENOUS statement and declare the instruments with an INSTRUMENTS statement. Next, use MODEL statements to specify the structural equations of the system.

The use of different estimation methods is shown by the following examples. These examples use simulated data (not shown).

OLS Estimation

PROC SYSLIN performs OLS regression if you do not specify a method of estimation in the PROC SYSLIN statement. OLS does not use instruments, so the ENDOGENOUS and INSTRUMENTS statements can be omitted.

The following statements estimate the supply-and-demand model shown previously:

```
proc syslin data=in;
   demand: model q = p y s;
   supply: model q = p u;
run;
```

The PROC SYSLIN output for the demand equation is shown in Figure 17.1, and the output for the supply equation is shown in Figure 17.2.

```
                            SYSLIN Procedure
                    Ordinary Least Squares Estimation

Model: DEMAND
Dependent variable: Q Quantity

                            Analysis of Variance

                             Sum of      Mean
            Source      DF   Squares     Square    F Value    Prob>F

            Model        3   9.58789    3.19596    398.308    0.0001
            Error       56   0.44934    0.00802
            C Total     59  10.03723

                 Root MSE     0.08958   R-Square    0.9552
                 Dep Mean     1.30095   Adj R-SQ    0.9528
                 C.V.         6.88541

                          Parameter Estimates

                   Parameter    Standard   T for H0:              Variable
Variable   DF      Estimate      Error    Parameter=0   Prob > |T|  Label

INTERCEP    1     -0.476769     0.210239    -2.268      0.0272   Intercept
P           1      0.123324     0.105177     1.173      0.2459   Price
Y           1      0.201282     0.032403     6.212      0.0001   Income
S           1      0.167258     0.024091     6.943      0.0001   Price of Substitutes
```

Figure 17.1.   OLS Results for Demand Equation

```
                            SYSLIN Procedure
                    Ordinary Least Squares Estimation

Model: SUPPLY
Dependent variable: Q Quantity

                            Analysis of Variance

                             Sum of      Mean
            Source      DF   Squares     Square    F Value    Prob>F

            Model        2   9.03389    4.51694    256.610    0.0001
            Error       57   1.00334    0.01760
            C Total     59  10.03723

                 Root MSE     0.13267   R-Square    0.9000
                 Dep Mean     1.30095   Adj R-SQ    0.8965
                 C.V.        10.19821

                          Parameter Estimates

                   Parameter    Standard   T for H0:              Variable
Variable   DF      Estimate      Error    Parameter=0   Prob > |T|  Label

INTERCEP    1     -0.303895     0.471397    -0.645      0.5217   Intercept
P           1      1.218743     0.053914    22.605      0.0001   Price
U           1     -1.077566     0.234150    -4.602      0.0001   Unit Cost
```

Figure 17.2.   OLS Results for Supply Equation

For each MODEL statement, the output first shows the model label and dependent variable name and label. This is followed by an analysis of variance table for the model, which shows the model, error, and total mean squares, and an F-test for the no-regression hypothesis. Next, the procedure prints the root mean square error, dependent variable mean and coefficient of variation, and the R^2 and adjusted R^2 statistics.

Finally, the table of parameter estimates shows the estimated regression coefficients, standard errors, and *t*-tests. You would expect the price coefficient in a demand equation to be negative. However, note that the OLS estimate of the price coefficient P in the demand equation (.1233) has a positive sign. This could be caused by simultaneous equation bias.

Two-Stage Least Squares Estimation

In the supply-and-demand model, P is an endogenous variable, and consequently the OLS estimates are biased. The following example estimates this model using two-stage least squares:

```
proc syslin data=in 2sls;
   endogenous  p;
   instruments y u s;
   demand: model q = p y s;
   supply: model q = p u;
run;
```

The 2SLS option in the PROC SYSLIN statement specifies the two-stage least-squares method. The ENDOGENOUS statement specifies that P is an endogenous regressor for which first-stage predicted values are substituted. You only need to declare an endogenous variable in the ENDOGENOUS statement if it is used as a regressor; thus although Q is endogenous in this model, it is not necessary to list it in the ENDOGENOUS statement.

Usually, all predetermined variables that appear in the system are used as instruments. The INSTRUMENTS statement specifies that the exogenous variables Y, U, and S are used as instruments for the first-stage regression to predict P.

The 2SLS results are shown in Figure 17.3 and Figure 17.4. The first-stage regressions are not shown. To see the first-stage regression results, use the FIRST option in the MODEL statement.

```
                         SYSLIN Procedure
                 Two-Stage Least Squares Estimation

Model: DEMAND
Dependent variable: Q Quantity

                        Analysis of Variance

                             Sum of       Mean
         Source        DF    Squares      Square     F Value     Prob>F

         Model          3    9.67088     3.22363     115.576     0.0001
         Error         56    1.56194     0.02789
         C Total       59   10.03723

                  Root MSE      0.16701    R-Square     0.8609
                  Dep Mean      1.30095    Adj R-SQ     0.8535
                  C.V.         12.83740

                        Parameter Estimates

              Parameter    Standard    T for H0:                Variable
Variable  DF   Estimate      Error     Parameter=0   Prob > |T|   Label

INTERCEP   1   1.901040     1.171224     1.623       0.1102    Intercept
P          1  -1.115183     0.607391    -1.836       0.0717    Price
Y          1   0.419544     0.117954     3.557       0.0008    Income
S          1   0.331475     0.088472     3.747       0.0004    Price of Substitutes
```

Figure 17.3. 2SLS Results for Demand Equation

```
                              SYSLIN Procedure
                       Two-Stage Least Squares Estimation

Model: SUPPLY
Dependent variable: Q Quantity

                              Analysis of Variance

                              Sum of        Mean
               Source    DF   Squares       Square    F Value    Prob>F

               Model      2   9.64610       4.82305   253.961    0.0001
               Error     57   1.08250       0.01899
               C Total   59  10.03723

                      Root MSE    0.13781   R-Square    0.8991
                      Dep Mean    1.30095   Adj R-SQ    0.8956
                      C.V.       10.59291

                           Parameter Estimates

                   Parameter    Standard    T for H0:           Variable
  Variable   DF     Estimate      Error    Parameter=0  Prob > |T|   Label

  INTERCEP    1    -0.518782    0.490999     -1.057      0.2952   Intercept
  P           1     1.333080    0.059271     22.491      0.0001   Price
  U           1    -1.146233    0.243491     -4.707      0.0001   Unit Cost
```

Figure 17.4. 2SLS Results for Supply Equation

The 2SLS output is similar in form to the OLS output. However, the 2SLS results are based on predicted values for the endogenous regressors from the first stage instrumental regressions. This makes the analysis of variance table and the R^2 statistics difficult to interpret. See the sections "ANOVA Table for Instrumental Variables Methods" and "The R^2 Statistics" later in this chapter for details.

Note that, unlike the OLS results, the 2SLS estimate for the P coefficient in the demand equation (-1.115) is negative.

LIML, K-Class, and MELO Estimation

To obtain limited information maximum likelihood, general K-class, or minimum expected loss estimates, use the ENDOGENOUS, INSTRUMENTS, and MODEL statements as in the 2SLS case, but specify the LIML, K=, or MELO option instead of 2SLS in the PROC SYSLIN statement. The following statements show this for K-class estimation:

```
proc syslin data=in k=.5;
   endogenous p;
   instruments y u s;
   demand: model q = p y s;
   supply: model q = p u;
run;
```

For more information on these estimation methods see "Estimation Methods" in the section "Details" later in this chapter and consult econometrics textbooks.

SUR, 3SLS, and FIML Estimation

In a multivariate regression model, the errors in different equations may be correlated. In this case the efficiency of the estimation may be improved by taking these cross-equation correlations into account.

Seemingly Unrelated Regression

Seemingly unrelated regression (SUR), also called joint generalized least squares (JGLS) or Zellner estimation, is a generalization of OLS for multi-equation systems. Like OLS, the SUR method assumes that all the regressors are independent variables, but SUR uses the correlations among the errors in different equations to improve the regression estimates. The SUR method requires an initial OLS regression to compute residuals. The OLS residuals are used to estimate the cross-equation covariance matrix.

The SUR option in the PROC SYSLIN statement specifies seemingly unrelated regression, as shown in the following statements:

```
proc syslin data=in sur;
   demand: model q = p y s;
   supply: model q = p u;
run;
```

INSTRUMENTS and ENDOGENOUS statements are not needed for SUR, since the SUR method assumes there are no endogenous regressors. For SUR to be effective, the models must use different regressors. SUR produces the same results as OLS unless the model contains at least one regressor not used in the other equations.

Three-Stage Least Squares

The three-stage least-squares method generalizes the two-stage least-squares method to take account of the correlations between equations in the same way that SUR generalizes OLS. Three-stage least squares requires three steps: first-stage regressions to get predicted values for the endogenous regressors; a two-stage least-squares step to get residuals to estimate the cross-equation correlation matrix; and the final 3SLS estimation step.

The 3SLS option in the PROC SYSLIN statement specifies the three-stage least-squares method, as shown in the following statements:

```
proc syslin data=in 3sls;
   endogenous  p;
   instruments y u s;
   demand: model q = p y s;
   supply: model q = p u;
run;
```

The 3SLS output begins with a two-stage least-squares regression to estimate the cross-model correlation matrix. This output is the same as the 2SLS results shown in Figure 17.3 and Figure 17.4, and is not repeated here. The next part of the 3SLS output prints the cross-model correlation matrix computed from the 2SLS residuals. This output is shown in Figure 17.5 and includes the cross-model covariances, correlations, the inverse of the correlation matrix, and the inverse covariance matrix.

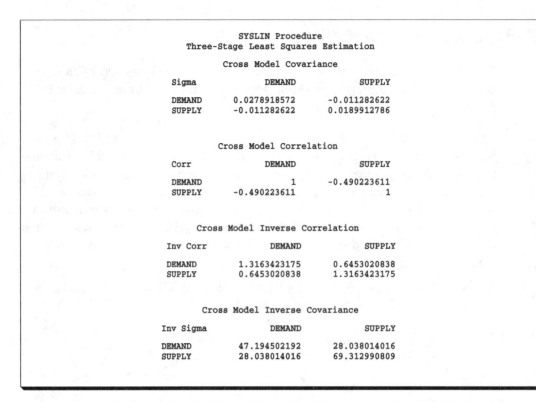

```
                         SYSLIN Procedure
                Three-Stage Least Squares Estimation
                      Cross Model Covariance

           Sigma              DEMAND              SUPPLY

           DEMAND         0.0278918572        -0.011282622
           SUPPLY        -0.011282622          0.0189912786


                      Cross Model Correlation

           Corr               DEMAND              SUPPLY

           DEMAND                  1            -0.490223611
           SUPPLY        -0.490223611                     1


                  Cross Model Inverse Correlation

           Inv Corr           DEMAND              SUPPLY

           DEMAND         1.3163423175        0.6453020838
           SUPPLY         0.6453020838        1.3163423175


                   Cross Model Inverse Covariance

           Inv Sigma          DEMAND              SUPPLY

           DEMAND         47.194502192        28.038014016
           SUPPLY         28.038014016        69.312990809
```

Figure 17.5. Estimated Cross-Model Covariances used for 3SLS Estimates

The final 3SLS estimates are shown in Figure 17.6.

```
                              SYSLIN Procedure
                     Three-Stage Least Squares Estimation

                System Weighted MSE:  0.57106 with 113 degrees of freedom.
                System Weighted R-Square:  0.9627


Model: DEMAND
Dependent variable: Q Quantity

                            Parameter Estimates

                      Parameter    Standard    T for H0:              Variable
      Variable  DF     Estimate      Error    Parameter=0   Prob > |T|  Label

      INTERCEP   1     1.980261    1.169169       1.694       0.0959   Intercept
      P          1    -1.176539    0.605012      -1.945       0.0568   Price
      Y          1     0.404115    0.117179       3.449       0.0011   Income
      S          1     0.359204    0.085077       4.222       0.0001   Price of Substitutes


Model: SUPPLY
Dependent variable: Q Quantity

                            Parameter Estimates

                      Parameter    Standard    T for H0:              Variable
      Variable  DF     Estimate      Error    Parameter=0   Prob > |T|  Label

      INTERCEP   1    -0.518782    0.490999      -1.057       0.2952   Intercept
      P          1     1.333080    0.059271      22.491       0.0001   Price
      U          1    -1.146233    0.243491      -4.707       0.0001   Unit Cost
```

Figure 17.6. Three-Stage Least Squares Results

This output first prints the system weighted mean square error and system weighted R^2 statistics. The system weighted MSE and system weighted R^2 measure the fit of the joint model obtained by stacking all the models together and performing a single regression with the stacked observations weighted by the inverse of the model error variances. See "The R^2 Statistics" later in this chapter for details.

Next, the table of 3SLS parameter estimates for each model is printed. This output has the same form as for the other estimation methods.

Note that the 3SLS and 2SLS results may be the same in some cases. This results from the same principle that causes OLS and SUR results to be identical unless an equation includes a regressor not used in the other equations of the system. However, the application of this principle is more complex when instrumental variables are used. When all the exogenous variables are used as instruments, linear combinations of all the exogenous variables appear in the third-stage regressions through substitution of first-stage predicted values.

In this example, 3SLS produces different (and, it is hoped, more efficient) estimates for the demand equation. However, the 3SLS and 2SLS results for the supply equation are the same. This is because the supply equation has one endogenous regressor and one exogenous regressor not used in other equations. In contrast, the demand equation has fewer endogenous regressors than exogenous regressors not used in other equations in the system.

Full Information Maximum Likelihood

The FIML option in the PROC SYSLIN statement specifies the full information maximum likelihood method, as shown in the following statements:

```
proc syslin data=in fiml;
   endogenous p q;
   instruments y u s;
   demand: model q = p y s;
   supply: model q = p u;
run;
```

The FIML results are shown in Figure 17.7.

```
                              SYSLIN Procedure
                  Full-Information Maximum Likelihood Estimation

Model: DEMAND
Dependent variable: Q Quantity

                               Parameter Estimates

                    Parameter     Standard    T for H0:                Variable
   Variable   DF     Estimate        Error    Parameter=0   Prob > |T|   Label

   INTERCEP    1     1.988529     1.233625          1.612       0.1126   Intercept
   P           1    -1.181474     0.652274         -1.811       0.0755   Price
   Y           1     0.402310     0.107269          3.750       0.0004   Income
   S           1     0.361345     0.103816          3.481       0.0010   Price of Substitutes


Model: SUPPLY
Dependent variable: Q Quantity

                               Parameter Estimates

                    Parameter     Standard    T for H0:                Variable
   Variable   DF     Estimate        Error    Parameter=0   Prob > |T|   Label

   INTERCEP    1    -0.524427     0.479522         -1.094       0.2787   Intercept
   P           1     1.336083     0.057939         23.060       0.0001   Price
   U           1    -1.148037     0.237793         -4.828       0.0001   Unit Cost
```

Figure 17.7. FIML Results

Computing Reduced Form Estimates

A system of structural equations with endogenous regressors can be represented as functions only of the predetermined variables. For this to be possible, there must be as many equations as endogenous variables. If there are more endogenous variables than regression models, you can use IDENTITY statements to complete the system. See "Reduced Form Estimates" in the section "Computational Details" later in this chapter for details.

The REDUCED option in the PROC SYSLIN statement prints reduced form estimates. The following statements show this using the 3SLS estimates of the structural parameters:

```
proc syslin data=in 3sls reduced;
   endogenous  p;
   instruments y u s;
   demand: model q = p y s;
   supply: model q = p u;
run;
```

The first four pages of this output were as shown previously and are not repeated here. (See Figure 17.3, Figure 17.4, Figure 17.5, and Figure 17.6.) The final page of the output from this example contains the reduced form coefficients from the 3SLS structural estimates, as shown in Figure 17.8.

```
                            SYSLIN Procedure
                  Three-Stage Least Squares Estimation

                        Endogenous Variables

                                  P                Q

              DEMAND     1.1765386989              1
              SUPPLY    -1.333079576               1


                        Exogenous Variables

              INTERCEP            Y            S               U

 DEMAND     1.9802610538   0.4041152398   0.3592037323               0
 SUPPLY    -0.51878208              0              0    -1.146233345


                    Inverse Endogenous Variables

              G Inv         DEMAND        SUPPLY

                P       0.3984669741   -0.398466974
                Q       0.5311881848    0.4688118152


                          Reduced Form

         INTERCEP            Y             S               U

 P     0.9957861555   0.1610265768   0.1431308243   0.4567361326
 Q     0.808680106    0.2146612407   0.1908047785   -0.537367735
```

Figure 17.8. Reduced Form 3SLS Results

Restricting Parameter Estimates

You can impose restrictions on the parameter estimates with RESTRICT and SRE-STRICT statements. The RESTRICT statement imposes linear restrictions on parameters in the equation specified by the preceding MODEL statement. The SRE-STRICT statement imposes linear restrictions that relate parameters in different models.

To impose restrictions involving parameters in different equations, use the SRE-STRICT statement. Specify the parameters in the linear hypothesis as *model-label.regressor-name*. (If the MODEL statement does not have a label, you can use the dependent variable name as the label for the model, provided the dependent variable uniquely labels the model.)

Tests for the significance of the restrictions are printed when RESTRICT or SRE-STRICT statements are used. You can label RESTRICT and SRESTRICT statements to identify the restrictions in the output.

The RESTRICT statement in the following example restricts the price coefficient in the demand equation to equal .015. The SRESTRICT statement restricts the estimate of the income coefficient in the demand equation to be .01 times the estimate of the unit cost coefficient in the supply equation.

```
proc syslin data=in 3sls;
    endogenous  p;
    instruments y u s;
    demand: model q = p y s;
    peq015: restrict p = .015;
    supply: model q = p u;
    yeq01u: srestrict demand.y = .01 * supply.u;
run;
```

The restricted estimation results are shown in Figure 17.9.

```
                          SYSLIN Procedure
                 Three-Stage Least Squares Estimation

Model: DEMAND
Dependent variable: Q Quantity

                         Parameter Estimates

                  Parameter     Standard     T for H0:                Variable
  Variable  DF     Estimate        Error   Parameter=0  Prob > |T|    Label

  INTERCEP   1    -0.465837     0.053307        -8.739      0.0001  Intercept
  P          1     0.015000            0             .           .  Price
  Y          1    -0.006789     0.002357        -2.881      0.0056  Income
  S          1     0.325589     0.009872        32.980      0.0001  Price of Substitutes
  RESTRICT  -1    50.593407     7.464990         6.777      0.0001  PEQ015


Model: SUPPLY
Dependent variable: Q Quantity

                         Parameter Estimates

                  Parameter     Standard     T for H0:                Variable
  Variable  DF     Estimate        Error   Parameter=0  Prob > |T|    Label

  INTERCEP   1    -1.318944     0.477633        -2.761      0.0077  Intercept
  P          1     1.291718     0.059101        21.856      0.0001  Price
  U          1    -0.678874     0.235679        -2.881      0.0056  Unit Cost
```

```
Cross Model Restrictions:

                            Parameter Estimates

                  Parameter      Standard   T for H0:                Variable
 Variable    DF    Estimate         Error  Parameter=0   Prob > |T|    Label

 RESTRICT    -1   342.361074    38.121026       8.981       0.0001    YEQ01U
```

Figure 17.9. Restricted Estimates

The standard error for P in the demand equation is 0, since the value of the P coefficient was specified by the RESTRICT statement and not estimated from the data. The parameter estimates table for the demand equation contains an additional row for the restriction specified by the RESTRICT statement. The parameter estimate for the restriction is the value of the Lagrange multiplier used to impose the restriction. The restriction is highly significant ($t = 6.777$), which means that the data are not consistent with the restriction, and the model does not fit as well with the restriction imposed. See "RESTRICT Statement" later in this chapter for more information.

After the parameter estimates table for the supply equation, the results for the cross-model restrictions are printed. This shows that the restriction specified by the SRESTRICT statement is not consistent with the data ($t = 8.98$). See the section "SRESTRICT Statement" for more information.

Testing Parameters

You can test linear hypotheses about the model parameters with TEST and STEST statements. The TEST statement tests hypotheses about parameters in the equation specified by the preceding MODEL statement. The STEST statement tests hypotheses that relate parameters in different models.

For example, the following statements test the hypothesis that the price coefficient in the demand equation is equal to .015:

```
proc syslin data=in 3sls;
   endogenous  p;
   instruments y u s;
   demand: model q = p y s;
   test_1: test p = .015;
   supply: model q = p u;
run;
```

The TEST statement results are shown in Figure 17.10. This reports an F-test for the hypothesis specified by the TEST statement. In this case the F statistic is 6.79 (3.879/.571) with 1 and 113 degrees of freedom. The p-value for this F statistic is .0104, which indicates that the hypothesis tested is almost, but not quite, rejected at the .01 level. See "TEST Statement" later in this chapter for more information.

```
                              SYSLIN Procedure
                      Three-Stage Least Squares Estimation

              System Weighted MSE:  0.57106 with 113 degrees of freedom.
              System Weighted R-Square:  0.9627


Model: DEMAND
Dependent variable: Q Quantity

                                  Parameter Estimates

                     Parameter      Standard    T for H0:                  Variable
     Variable   DF    Estimate        Error    Parameter=0   Prob > |T|     Label

     INTERCEP    1    1.980261      1.169169       1.694       0.0959   Intercept
     P           1   -1.176539      0.605012      -1.945       0.0568   Price
     Y           1    0.404115      0.117179       3.449       0.0011   Income
     S           1    0.359204      0.085077       4.222       0.0001   Price of Substitutes


Test: TEST_1
     Numerator:  3.878718   DF:     1   F Value:   6.7921
     Denominator: 0.571062  DF:   113   Prob>F:    0.0104
```

Figure 17.10. TEST Statement Results

To test hypotheses involving parameters in different equations, use the STEST statement. Specify the parameters in the linear hypothesis as *model-label.regressor-name*. (If the MODEL statement does not have a label, you can use the dependent variable name as the label for the model, provided the dependent variable uniquely labels the model.)

For example, the following statements test the hypothesis that the income coefficient in the demand equation is .01 times the unit cost coefficient in the supply equation:

```
proc syslin data=in 3sls;
   endogenous  p;
   instruments y u s;
   demand: model q = p y s;
   supply: model q = p u;
   stest1: stest demand.y = .01 * supply.u;
run;
```

The STEST statement results are shown in Figure 17.11. The form and interpretation of the STEST statement results is like the TEST statement results. In this case, the *F*-test produces a *p*-value less than .0001, and strongly rejects the hypothesis tested. See "STEST Statement" later in this chapter for more information.

```
                              SYSLIN Procedure
                      Three-Stage Least Squares Estimation

              System Weighted MSE:  0.57106 with 113 degrees of freedom.
              System Weighted R-Square:  0.9627


Model: DEMAND
Dependent variable: Q Quantity

                                  Parameter Estimates

                     Parameter      Standard    T for H0:                  Variable
     Variable   DF    Estimate        Error    Parameter=0   Prob > |T|     Label

     INTERCEP    1    1.980261      1.169169       1.694       0.0959   Intercept
     P           1   -1.176539      0.605012      -1.945       0.0568   Price
     Y           1    0.404115      0.117179       3.449       0.0011   Income
     S           1    0.359204      0.085077       4.222       0.0001   Price of Substitutes
```

```
Model: SUPPLY
Dependent variable: Q Quantity

                           Parameter Estimates

                  Parameter    Standard    T for H0:                  Variable
   Variable  DF    Estimate       Error   Parameter=0   Prob > |T|     Label

   INTERCEP   1   -0.518782    0.490999      -1.057       0.2952    Intercept
   P          1    1.333080    0.059271      22.491       0.0001    Price
   U          1   -1.146233    0.243491      -4.707       0.0001    Unit Cost


Test: STEST1
   Numerator:   12.82816   DF:     1  F Value:  22.4637
   Denominator:  0.571062   DF:   113  Prob>F:    0.0001
```

Figure 17.11.　STEST Statement Results

You can combine TEST and STEST statements with RESTRICT and SRESTRICT statements to perform hypothesis tests for restricted models. Of course, the validity of the TEST and STEST statement results will depend on the correctness of any restrictions you impose on the estimates.

Saving Residuals and Predicted Values

You can store predicted values and residuals from the estimated models in a SAS data set. Specify the OUT= option in the PROC SYSLIN statement and use the OUTPUT statement to specify names for new variables to contain the predicted and residual values.

For example, the following statements store the predicted quantity from the supply and demand equations in the data set PRED:

```
proc syslin data=in out=pred 3sls;
   endogenous  p;
   instruments y u s;
   demand: model q = p y s;
   output predicted=q_demand;
   supply: model q = p u;
   output predicted=q_supply;
run;
```

Plotting Residuals

You can plot the residuals against the regressors by specifying the PLOT option in the MODEL statement. For example, the following statements plot the 2SLS residuals for the demand model against price, income, price of substitutes, and the intercept.

```
proc syslin data=in 2sls;
   endogenous  p;
   instruments y u s;
   demand: model q = p y s / plot;
run;
```

The plot for price is shown in Figure 17.12. The other plots are not shown.

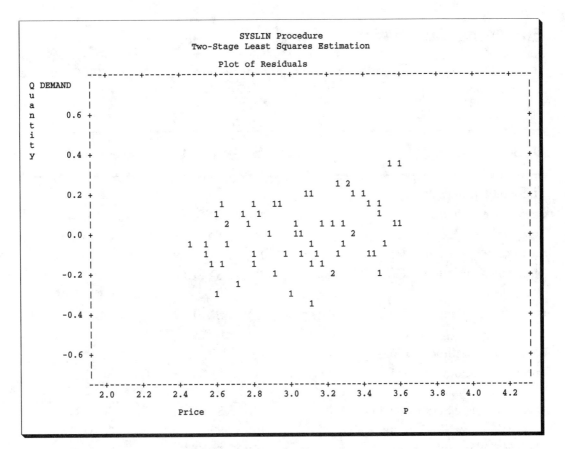

Figure 17.12. PLOT Option Output for P

Syntax

The SYSLIN procedure uses the following statements:

PROC SYSLIN *options* ;
    BY *variables* ;
    ENDOGENOUS *variables* ;
    IDENTITY *identities* ;
    INSTRUMENTS *variables* ;
    MODEL *response* = *regressors* / *options* ;
    OUTPUT PREDICTED= *variable* **RESIDUAL**= *variable* ;
    RESTRICT *restrictions* ;
    SRESTRICT *restrictions* ;
    STEST *equations* ;
    TEST *equations* ;
    VAR *variables* ;
    WEIGHT *variable* ;

Functional Summary

The SYSLIN procedure statements and options are summarized in the following table:

Description	Statement	Option
Data Set Options		
specify the input data set	PROC SYSLIN	DATA=
specify the output data set	PROC SYSLIN	OUT=
write parameter estimates to an output data set	PROC SYSLIN	OUTEST=
write covariances to the OUTEST= data set	PROC SYSLIN	OUTCOV
		OUTCOV3
write the SSCP matrix to an output data set	PROC SYSLIN	OUTSSCP=
Estimation Method Options		
specify full information maximum likelihood estimation	PROC SYSLIN	FIML
specify iterative SUR estimation	PROC SYSLIN	ITSUR
specify iterative 3SLS estimation	PROC SYSLIN	IT3SLS
specify K-class estimation	PROC SYSLIN	K=
specify limited information maximum likelihood estimation	PROC SYSLIN	LIML
specify minimum expected loss estimation	PROC SYSLIN	MELO
specify ordinary least-squares estimation	PROC SYSLIN	OLS
specify seemingly unrelated estimation	PROC SYSLIN	SUR
specify two-stage least-squares estimation	PROC SYSLIN	2SLS
specify three-stage least-squares estimation	PROC SYSLIN	3SLS
specify Fuller's modification to LIML	PROC SYSLIN	ALPHA=
specify convergence criterion	PROC SYSLIN	CONVERGE=
specify maximum number of iterations	PROC SYSLIN	MAXIT=
use diagonal of **S** instead of **S**	PROC SYSLIN	SDIAG
exclude RESTRICT statements in final stage	PROC SYSLIN	NOINCLUDE
specify criterion for testing for singularity	PROC SYSLIN	SINGULAR=
specify denominator for variance estimates	PROC SYSLIN	VARDEF=
Printing Control Options		
print first-stage regression statistics	PROC SYSLIN	FIRST
print estimates and SSE at each iteration	PROC SYSLIN	ITPRINT
print the restricted reduced form estimates	PROC SYSLIN	REDUCED
print descriptive statistics	PROC SYSLIN	SIMPLE
print uncorrected SSCP matrix	PROC SYSLIN	USSCP

Description	Statement	Option
print correlations of the parameter estimates	MODEL	CORRB
print covariances of the parameter estimates	MODEL	COVB
print Durbin-Watson statistics	MODEL	DW
print Basmann's test	MODEL	OVERID
plot residual values against regressors	MODEL	PLOT
print standardized parameter estimates	MODEL	STB
print unrestricted parameter estimates	MODEL	UNREST
print the model crossproducts matrix	MODEL	XPX
print the inverse of the crossproducts matrix	MODEL	I
suppress printed output	MODEL	NOPRINT
suppress all printed output	PROC SYSLIN	NOPRINT

Model Specification

Description	Statement	Option
specify structural equations	MODEL	
suppress the intercept parameter	MODEL	NOINT
specify linear relationship among variables	IDENTITY	
perform weighted regression	WEIGHT	

Tests and Restrictions on Parameters

Description	Statement	Option
place restrictions on parameter estimates	RESTRICT	
place restrictions on parameter estimates	SRESTRICT	
test linear hypothesis	STEST	
test linear hypothesis	TEST	

Other Statements

Description	Statement	Option
specify BY-group processing	BY	
specify the endogenous variables	ENDOGENOUS	
specify instrumental variables	INSTRUMENTS	
write predicted and residual values to a data set	OUTPUT	
name variable for predicted values	OUTPUT	PREDICTED=
name variable for residual values	OUTPUT	RESIDUAL=
include additional variables in $X'X$ matrix	VAR	

PROC SYSLIN Statement

PROC SYSLIN *options*;

The following options can be used with the PROC SYSLIN statement:

Data Set Options

DATA= *SAS-data-set*

specifies the input data set. If the DATA= option is omitted, the most recently created SAS data set is used. In addition to ordinary SAS data sets, PROC SYS-LIN can analyze data sets of TYPE=CORR, TYPE=COV, TYPE=UCORR, TYPE=UCOV, and TYPE=SSCP. See "Special TYPE= Input Data Set" in the section "Input Data Set" later in this chapter for more information.

OUT= *SAS-data-set*

specifies an output SAS data set for residuals and predicted values. The OUT= option is used in conjunction with the OUTPUT statement. See "OUT= Data Set" later in this chapter for more details.

OUTEST= *SAS-data-set*

writes the parameter estimates to an output data set. See "OUTEST= Data Set" later in this chapter for details.

OUTCOV
COVOUT

writes the covariance matrix of the parameter estimates to the OUTEST= data set in addition to the parameter estimates.

OUTCOV3
COV3OUT

writes covariance matrices for each model in a system to the OUTEST= data set when the 3SLS, SUR, or FIML option is used.

OUTSSCP= *SAS-data-set*

writes the sum-of-squares-and-crossproducts matrix to an output data set. See "OUTSSCP= Data Set" later in this chapter for details.

Estimation Method Options

2SLS

specifies the two-stage least-squares estimation method.

3SLS

specifies the three-stage least-squares estimation method.

FIML

specifies the full information maximum likelihood estimation method.

ITSUR

specifies the iterative seemingly unrelated estimation method.

IT3SLS

specifies the iterative three-stage least-squares estimation method.

K= *value*

specifies the K-class estimation method.

LIML

specifies the limited information maximum likelihood estimation method.

MELO

specifies the minimum expected loss estimation method.

OLS

specifies the ordinary least-squares estimation method. This is the default.

SUR

specifies the seemingly unrelated estimation method.

Printing and Control Options

ALL

specifies the CORRB, COVB, DW, I, OVERID, PLOT, STB, and XPX options for every MODEL statement.

ALPHA= *value*

specifies Fuller's modification to the LIML estimation method. See "Fuller's Modification to LIML" later in this chapter for details.

CONVERGE= *value*

specifies the convergence criterion for the iterative estimation methods IT3SLS, ITSUR, and FIML. The default is CONVERGE=.0001.

FIRST

prints first-stage regression statistics for the endogenous variables regressed on the instruments. This output includes sums of squares, estimates, variances, and standard deviations.

ITPRINT

prints parameter estimates, system-weighted residual sum of squares, and R^2 at each iteration for the IT3SLS and ITSUR estimation methods. For the FIML method, the ITPRINT option prints parameter estimates, negative of log likelihood function, and norm of gradient vector at each iteration.

MAXITER= *n*

specifies the maximum number of iterations allowed for the IT3SLS, ITSUR, and FIML estimation methods. The MAXITER= option can be abbreviated as MAXIT=. The default is MAXITER=30.

NOINCLUDE

excludes the RESTRICT statements from the final stage for the 3SLS, IT3SLS, SUR, ITSUR estimation methods.

NOPRINT

suppresses all printed output. Specifying NOPRINT in the PROC SYSLIN statement is equivalent to specifying NOPRINT in every MODEL statement.

REDUCED

prints the reduced form estimates. If the REDUCED option is specified, you should specify any IDENTITY statements needed to make the system square. See "Reduced Form Estimates" in the section "Computational Details" later in this chapter for more information.

SDIAG

uses the diagonal of **S** instead of **S** to do the estimation, where **S** is the covariance matrix of equation errors. See "Uncorrelated Errors Across Equations" in the section "Computational Details" later in this chapter for more information.

SIMPLE

prints descriptive statistics for the dependent variables. The statistics printed include the sum, mean, uncorrected sum of squares, variance, and standard deviation.

SINGULAR= *value*

specifies a criterion for testing singularity of the crossproducts matrix. This is a tuning parameter used to make PROC SYSLIN more or less sensitive to singularities. The value must be between 0 and 1. The default is SINGULAR=1E-8.

USSCP

prints the uncorrected sum-of-squares-and-crossproducts matrix.

USSCP2

prints the uncorrected sum-of-squares-and-crossproducts matrix for all variables used in the analysis, including predicted values of variables generated by the procedure.

VARDEF= DF | N | WEIGHT | WGT

specifies the denominator to use in calculating cross-equation error covariances and parameter standard errors and covariances. The default is VARDEF=DF, which corrects for model degrees of freedom. VARDEF=N specifies no degrees-of-freedom correction. VARDEF=WEIGHT specifies the sum of the observation weights. VARDEF=WGT specifies the sum of the observation weights minus the model degrees of freedom. See "Computation of Standard Errors" in the section "Computational Details" later in this chapter for more information.

BY Statement

BY *variables* **;**

A BY statement can be used with PROC SYSLIN to obtain separate analyses on observations in groups defined by the BY variables.

ENDOGENOUS Statement

> **ENDOGENOUS** *variables* ;

The ENDOGENOUS statement declares the jointly dependent variables that are projected in the first-stage regression through the instrument variables. The ENDOGENOUS statement is not needed for the SUR, ITSUR, or OLS estimation methods. The default ENDOGENOUS list consists of all the dependent variables in the MODEL and IDENTITY statements that do not appear in the INSTRUMENTS statement.

IDENTITY Statement

> **IDENTITY** *equation* ;

The IDENTITY statement specifies linear relationships among variables to write to the OUTEST= data set. It provides extra information in the OUTEST= data set but does not create or compute variables. The OUTEST= data set can be processed by the SIMLIN procedure in a later step.

The IDENTITY statement is also used to compute reduced form coefficients when the REDUCED option in the PROC SYSLIN statement is specified. See "Reduced Form Estimates" in the section "Computational Details" later in this chapter for more information.

The *equation* given by the IDENTITY statement has the same form as equations in the MODEL statement. A label can be specified for an IDENTITY statement as follows:

> *label* : **IDENTITY ...** ;

INSTRUMENTS Statement

> **INSTRUMENTS** *variables* ;

The INSTRUMENTS statement declares the variables used in obtaining first-stage predicted values. All the instruments specified are used in each first-stage regression. The INSTRUMENTS statement is required for the 2SLS, 3SLS, IT3SLS, LIML, MELO, and K-class estimation methods. The INSTRUMENTS statement is not needed for the SUR, ITSUR, OLS, or FIML estimation methods.

MODEL Statement

> **MODEL** *response* = *regressors* / *options* ;

The MODEL statement regresses the response variable on the left side of the equal sign against the regressors listed on the right side.

Models can be given labels. Model labels are used in the printed output to identify the results for different models. Model labels are also used in SRESTRICT and STEST statements to refer to parameters in different models. If no label is specified, the response variable name is used as the label for the model. The model label is specified as follows:

label : **MODEL ... ;**

The following options can be used in the MODEL statement after a slash (/).

ALL

 specifies the CORRB, COVB, DW, I, OVERID, PLOT, STB, and XPX options.

ALPHA= *value*

 specifies the α parameter for Fuller's modification to the LIML estimation method. See "Fuller's Modification to LIML" in the section "Computational Details" later in this chapter for more information.

CORRB

 prints the matrix of estimated correlations between the parameter estimates.

COVB

 prints the matrix of estimated covariances between the parameter estimates.

DW

 prints Durbin-Watson statistics and autocorrelation coefficients for the residuals. If there are missing values, d' is calculated according to Savin and White (1978). Use the DW option only if the data set to be analyzed is an ordinary SAS data set with time series observations sorted in time order. The Durbin-Watson test is not valid for models with lagged dependent regressors.

I

 prints the inverse of the crossproducts matrix for the model, $(\mathbf{X}'\mathbf{X})^{-1}$. If restrictions are specified, the crossproducts matrix printed is adjusted for the restrictions. See "Computational Details" later in this chapter for more information.

K= *value*

 specifies K-class estimation.

NOINT

 suppresses the intercept parameter from the model.

NOPRINT

 suppresses the normal printed output.

OVERID

 prints Basmann's (1960) test for over identifying restrictions. See "Over Identification Restrictions" in the section "Computational Details" later in this chapter for more information.

PLOT

 plots residual values against regressors. A plot of the residuals for each regressor is printed.

STB

 prints standardized parameter estimates. Sometimes known as a standard partial regression coefficient, a standardized parameter estimate is a parameter estimate multiplied by the standard deviation of the associated regressor and divided by the standard deviation of the response variable.

UNREST

prints parameter estimates computed before restrictions are applied. The UN-REST option is valid only if a RESTRICT statement is specified.

XPX

prints the model crossproducts matrix, $\mathbf{X}'\mathbf{X}$. See "Computational Details" later in this chapter for more information.

OUTPUT Statement

OUTPUT PREDICTED= *variable* **RESIDUAL=** *variable* ;

The OUTPUT statement writes predicted values and residuals from the preceding model to the data set specified by the OUT= option on the PROC SYSLIN statement. An OUTPUT statement must come after the MODEL statement to which it applies. The OUT= option must be specified in the PROC SYSLIN statement.

The following options can be specified in the OUTPUT statement:

PREDICTED= *variable*

names a new variable to contain the predicted values for the response variable. The PREDICTED= option can be abbreviated as PREDICT=, PRED=, or P=.

RESIDUAL= *variable*

names a new variable to contain the residual values for the response variable. The RESIDUAL= option can be abbreviated as RESID= or R=.

For example, the following statements create an output data set named B. In addition to the variables in the input data set, the data set B contains the variable YHAT, with values that are predicted values of the response variable Y, and YRESID, with values that are the residual values of Y.

```
proc syslin data=a out=b;
   model y = x1 x2;
   output p=yhat r=yresid;
run;
```

For example, the following statements create an output data set named PRED. In addition to the variables in the input data set, the data set PRED contains the variables Q_DEMAND and Q_SUPPLY, with values that are predicted values of the response variable Q for the demand and supply equations respectively, and R_DEMAND and R_SUPPLY, with values that are the residual values of the demand and supply equations.

```
proc syslin data=in out=pred;
   demand: model q = p y s;
   output p=q_demand r=r_demand;
   supply: model q = p u;
   output p=q_supply r=r_supply;
run;
```

See "OUT= Data Set" later in this chapter for more details.

RESTRICT Statement

> **RESTRICT** *equation* , ... , *equation* ;

The RESTRICT statement places restrictions on the parameter estimates for the preceding MODEL statement. Any number of RESTRICT statements can follow a MODEL statement. Each restriction is written as a linear equation. If more than one restriction is specified in a single RESTRICT statement, the restrictions are separated by commas.

Parameters are referred to by the name of the corresponding regressor variable. Each name used in the equation must be a regressor in the preceding MODEL statement. The keyword INTERCEPT is used to refer to the intercept parameter in the model.

RESTRICT statements can be given labels. The labels are used in the printed output to distinguish results for different restrictions. Labels are specified as follows:

> *label* : **RESTRICT ... ;**

The following is an example of the use of the RESTRICT statement, in which the coefficients of the regressors X1 and X2 are required to sum to 1.

```
proc syslin data=a;
   model y = x1 x2;
   restrict x1 + x2 = 1;
run;
```

Variable names can be multiplied by constants. When no equal sign appears, the linear combination is set equal to 0. Note that the parameters associated with the variables are restricted, not the variables themselves. Here are some examples of valid RESTRICT statements:

```
restrict x1 + x2 = 1;
restrict x1 + x2 - 1;
restrict 2 * x1 = x2 + x3 , intercept + x4 = 0;
restrict x1 = x2 = x3 = 1;
restrict 2 * x1 - x2;
```

Restricted parameter estimates are computed by introducing a Lagrangian parameter λ for each restriction (Pringle and Raynor 1971). The estimates of these Lagrangian parameters are printed in the parameter estimates table. If a restriction cannot be applied, its parameter value and degrees of freedom are listed as 0.

The Lagrangian parameter, λ, measures the sensitivity of the SSE to the restriction. If the restriction is changed by a small amount ϵ, the SSE is changed by $2\lambda\epsilon$.

The *t*-ratio tests the significance of the restrictions. If λ is 0, the restricted estimates are the same as the unrestricted.

Any number of restrictions can be specified in a RESTRICT statement, and any number of RESTRICT statements can be used. The estimates are computed subject to all restrictions specified. However, restrictions should be consistent and not redundant.

Note: The RESTRICT statement is not supported for the FIML estimation method.

SRESTRICT Statement

SRESTRICT *equation* , ... , *equation* ;

The SRESTRICT statement imposes linear restrictions involving parameters in two or more MODEL statements. The SRESTRICT statement is like the RESTRICT statement but is used to impose restrictions across equations, whereas the RESTRICT statement only applies to parameters in the immediately preceding MODEL statement.

Each restriction is written as a linear equation. Parameters are referred to as *label.variable*, where *label* is the model label and *variable* is the name of the regressor to which the parameter is attached. (If the MODEL statement does not have a label, you can use the dependent variable name as the label for the model, provided the dependent variable uniquely labels the model.) Each variable name used must be a regressor in the indicated MODEL statement. The keyword INTERCEPT is used to refer to intercept parameters.

SRESTRICT statements can be given labels. The labels are used in the printed output to distinguish results for different restrictions. Labels are specified as follows:

label **: SRESTRICT ... ;**

The following is an example of the use of the SRESTRICT statement, in which the coefficient for the regressor X2 is constrained to be the same in both models.

```
proc syslin data=a 3sls;
    endogenous y1 y2;
    instruments x1 x2;
    model y1 = y2 x1 x2;
    model y2 = y1 x2;
    srestrict y1.x2 = y2.x2;
run;
```

When no equal sign is used, the linear combination is set equal to 0. Thus, the restriction in the preceding example can also be specified as

```
srestrict y1.x2 - y2.x2;
```

Any number of restrictions can be specified in an SRESTRICT statement, and any number of SRESTRICT statements can be used. The estimates are computed subject to all restrictions specified. However, restrictions should be consistent and not redundant.

The results of the SRESTRICT statements are printed after the parameter estimates for all the models in the system. The format of the SRESTRICT statement output is the same as the parameter estimates table. In this output, the parameter estimate is the Lagrangian parameter, λ, used to impose the restriction.

The Lagrangian parameter, λ, measures the sensitivity of the system sum of square errors to the restriction. The system SSE is the system MSE shown in the printed output multiplied by the degrees of freedom. If the restriction is changed by a small amount ϵ, the system SSE is changed by $2\lambda\epsilon$.

The *t*-ratio tests the significance of the restriction. If λ is 0, the restricted estimates are the same as the unrestricted estimates.

The model degrees of freedom are not adjusted for the cross-model restrictions imposed by SRESTRICT statements.

Note: The SRESTRICT statement is not supported for the FIML estimation method.

STEST Statement

> **STEST** *equation , … , equation / options* ;

The STEST statement performs an *F*-test for the joint hypotheses specified in the statement.

The hypothesis is represented in matrix notation as

$$\mathbf{L}\beta = \mathbf{c}$$

and the *F*-test is computed as

$$\frac{(\mathbf{L}b - \mathbf{c})' \left(\mathbf{L}(\mathbf{X}'\mathbf{X})^{-1}\mathbf{L}'\right)^{-1}(\mathbf{L}b - \mathbf{c})}{m\,\hat{\sigma}^2}$$

where b is the estimate of β, m is the number of restrictions, and $\hat{\sigma}^2$ is the system weighted mean square error. See the section "Computational Details" later in this chapter for information on the matrix $\mathbf{X}'\mathbf{X}$.

Each hypothesis to be tested is written as a linear equation. Parameters are referred to as *label.variable*, where *label* is the model label and *variable* is the name of the regressor to which the parameter is attached. (If the MODEL statement does not have a label, you can use the dependent variable name as the label for the model, provided the dependent variable uniquely labels the model.) Each variable name used must be a regressor in the indicated MODEL statement. The keyword INTERCEPT is used to refer to intercept parameters.

STEST statements can be given labels. The label is used in the printed output to distinguish different tests. Any number of STEST statements can be specified. Labels are specified as follows:

> *label* : **STEST** … ;

The following is an example of the STEST statement:

```
proc syslin data=a 3sls;
   endogenous y1 y2;
   instruments x1 x2;
   model y1 = y2 x1 x2;
   model y2 = y1 x2;
   stest y1.x2 = y2.x2;
run;
```

The test performed is exact only for ordinary least squares, given the OLS assumptions of the linear model. For other estimation methods, the *F*-test is based on large sample theory and is only approximate in finite samples.

If RESTRICT or SRESTRICT statements are used, the tests computed by the STEST statement are conditional on the restrictions specified. The validity of the tests may be compromised if incorrect restrictions are imposed on the estimates.

The following are examples of STEST statements:

```
stest a.x1 + b.x2 = 1;
stest 2 * b.x2 = c.x3 + c.x4 ,
      a.intercept + b.x2 = 0;
stest a.x1 = c.x2 = b.x3 = 1;
stest 2 * a.x1 - b.x2 = 0;
```

The PRINT option can be specified in the STEST statement after a slash (/):

PRINT

prints intermediate calculations for the hypothesis tests.

Note: The STEST statement is not supported for the FIML estimation method.

TEST Statement

TEST *equation , ... , equation / options* ;

The TEST statement performs *F*-tests of linear hypotheses about the parameters in the preceding MODEL statement. Each equation specifies a linear hypothesis to be tested. If more than one equation is specified, the equations are separated by commas.

Variable names must correspond to regressors in the preceding MODEL statement, and each name represents the coefficient of the corresponding regressor. The keyword INTERCEPT is used to refer to the model intercept.

TEST statements can be given labels. The label is used in the printed output to distinguish different tests. Any number of TEST statements can be specified. Labels are specified as follows:

label : **TEST ...** ;

The following is an example of the use of TEST statement, which tests the hypothesis that the coefficients of X1 and X2 are the same:

```
proc syslin data=a;
   model y = x1 x2;
   test x1 = x2;
run;
```

The following statements perform *F*-tests for the hypothesis that the coefficients of X1 and X2 are equal, and that the sum of the X1 and X2 coefficients is twice the intercept, and for the joint hypothesis.

```
proc syslin data=a;
   model y = x1 x2;
   x1eqx2:  test x1 = x2;
   sumeq2i: test x1 + x2 = 2 * intercept;
   joint:   test x1 = x2, x1 + x2 = 2 * intercept;
run;
```

The following are additional examples of TEST statements:

```
test x1 + x2 = 1;
test x1 = x2 = x3 = 1;
test 2 * x1 = x2 + x3, intercept + x4 = 0;
test 2 * x1 - x2;
```

The TEST statement performs an *F*-test for the joint hypotheses specified. The hypothesis is represented in matrix notation as follows:

$$\mathbf{L}\beta = \mathbf{c}$$

The *F*-test is computed as

$$\frac{(\mathbf{L}\,b - \mathbf{c})'\,\left(\mathbf{L}(\mathbf{X}'\mathbf{X})^{-}\mathbf{L}'\right)^{-1}\,(\mathbf{L}\,b - \mathbf{c})}{m\,\hat{\sigma}^2}$$

where b is the estimate of β, m is the number of restrictions, and $\hat{\sigma}^2$ is the model mean square error. See the section "Computational Details" later in this chapter for information on the matrix $\mathbf{X}'\mathbf{X}$.

The test performed is exact only for ordinary least squares, given the OLS assumptions of the linear model. For other estimation methods, the *F*-test is based on large sample theory and is only approximate in finite samples.

If RESTRICT or SRESTRICT statements are used, the tests computed by the TEST statement are conditional on the restrictions specified. The validity of the tests may be compromised if incorrect restrictions are imposed on the estimates.

The PRINT option can be specified in the TEST statement after a slash (/):

PRINT

    prints intermediate calculations for the hypothesis tests.

Note: The TEST statement is not supported for the FIML estimation method.

VAR Statement

      VAR *variables* ;

The VAR statement is used to include variables in the crossproducts matrix that are not specified in any MODEL statement. This statement is rarely used with PROC SYSLIN and is used only with the OUTSSCP= option in the PROC SYSLIN statement.

WEIGHT Statement

> **WEIGHT** *variable* ;

The WEIGHT statement is used to perform weighted regression. The WEIGHT statement names a variable in the input data set whose values are relative weights for a weighted least-squares fit. If the weight value is proportional to the reciprocal of the variance for each observation, the weighted estimates are the best linear unbiased estimates (BLUE).

Details

Input Data Set

PROC SYSLIN does not compute new values for regressors. For example, if you need a lagged variable, you must create it with a DATA step. No values are computed by IDENTITY statements; all values must be in the input data set.

Special TYPE= Input Data Set

The input data set for most applications of the SYSLIN procedure contains standard rectangular data. However, PROC SYSLIN can also process input data in the form of a crossproducts, covariance, or correlation matrix. Data sets containing such matrices are identified by values of the TYPE= data set option.

These special kinds of input data sets can be used to save computer time. It takes nk^2 operations, where n is the number of observations and k is the number of variables, to calculate cross products; the regressions are of the order k^3. When n is in the thousands and k is much smaller, you can save most of the computer time in later runs of PROC SYSLIN by reusing the SSCP matrix rather than recomputing it.

The SYSLIN procedure can process TYPE= CORR, COV, UCORR, UCOV, or SSCP data sets. TYPE=CORR and TYPE=COV data sets, usually created by the CORR procedure, contain means and standard deviations, and correlations or covariances. TYPE=SSCP data sets, usually created in previous runs of PROC SYSLIN, contain sums of squares and cross products. Refer to *SAS/STAT User's Guide, Version 6, Fourth Edition* for more information on special SAS data sets.

When special SAS data sets are read, you must specify the TYPE= data set option. PROC CORR and PROC SYSLIN automatically set the type for output data sets; however, if you create the data set by some other means, you must specify its type with the TYPE= data set option.

When the special data sets are used, the DW (Durbin-Watson test) and PLOT options in the MODEL statement cannot be performed, and the OUTPUT statements are not valid.

Estimation Methods

A brief description of the methods used by the SYSLIN procedure follows. For more information on these methods, see the references at the end of this chapter.

There are two fundamental methods of estimation for simultaneous equations: least squares and maximum likelihood. There are two approaches within each of these categories: single equation methods and system estimation. 2SLS, 3SLS, and IT3SLS use the least-squares method; LIML and FIML use the maximum likelihood method. 2SLS and LIML are single equation methods, which means that over identifying restrictions in other equations are not taken into account in estimating parameters in a particular equation. (See "Over Identification Restrictions" in the section "Computational Details" later in this chapter for more information.) As a result, 2SLS and LIML estimates are not asymptotically efficient. The system methods are 3SLS, IT3SLS, and FIML. These methods use information concerning the endogenous variables in the system and take into account error covariances across equations and hence are asymptotically efficient in the absence of specification error.

K-class estimation is a class of estimation methods that include the 2SLS, OLS, LIML, and MELO methods as special cases. A K-value less than 1 is recommended but not required.

MELO is a Bayesian K-class estimator. It yields estimates that can be expressed as a matrix weighted average of the OLS and 2SLS estimates.

The SUR and ITSUR methods use information about contemporaneous correlation among error terms across equations in an attempt to improve the efficiency of parameter estimates.

Instrumental Variables and K-Class Estimation Methods

Instrumental variable methods involve substituting a predicted variable for the endogenous variable Y when it appears as a regressor. The predicted variables are linear functions of the instrumental variables and the endogenous variable.

The 2SLS method substitutes $\widehat{\mathbf{Y}}$ for $\mathbf{Y}$, which results in consistent estimates. In 2SLS, the instrumental variables are used as regressors to obtain the projected value $\widehat{\mathbf{Y}}$, which is then substituted for $\mathbf{Y}$. Normally, the predetermined variables of the system are used as the instruments. It is possible to use variables other than predetermined variables from your system of equations as instruments; however, the estimation may not be as efficient. For consistent estimates, the instruments must be uncorrelated with the residual and correlated with the endogenous variable.

K-class estimators are instrumental variable estimators where the first-stage predicted values take a special form: $\mathbf{Y}^* = (1-k)\mathbf{Y} + k\widehat{\mathbf{Y}}$ for a specified value k. The probability limit of k must equal 1 for consistent parameter estimates.

The LIML method results in consistent estimates that are exactly equal to 2SLS estimates when an equation is exactly identified. LIML can be viewed as least-variance ratio estimators or as maximum likelihood estimators. LIML involves minimizing the ratio $\lambda = rvar\_eq/rvar\_sys$, where $rvar\_eq$ is the residual variance associated with regressing the weighted endogenous variables on all predetermined variables appearing in that equation, and $rvar\_sys$ is the residual variance associated with regressing weighted endogenous variables on all predetermined variables in the system. The K-class interpretation of LIML is that $k = \lambda$. Unlike OLS and 2SLS, where k is 0 and 1, respectively, k is stochastic in the LIML method.

The MELO method computes the minimum expected loss estimator. The MELO method computes estimates that "minimize the posterior expectation of generalized quadratic loss functions for structural coefficients of linear structural models" (Judge et al. 1985, 635). Other frequently used K-class estimators may not have finite moments under some commonly encountered circumstances and hence there can be infinite risk relative to quadratic and other loss functions. MELO estimators have finite second moments and hence finite risk.

One way of comparing K-class estimators is to note that when $k=1$, the correlation between regressor and the residual is completely corrected for. In all other cases, it is only partially corrected for.

SUR and 3SLS Estimation Methods

SUR may improve the efficiency of parameter estimates when there is contemporaneous correlation of errors across equations. In practice, the contemporaneous correlation matrix is estimated using OLS residuals. Under two sets of circumstances, SUR parameter estimates are the same as those produced by OLS: when there is no contemporaneous correlation of errors across equations (the estimate of contemporaneous correlation matrix is diagonal), and when the independent variables are the same across equations.

Theoretically, SUR parameter estimates will always be at least as efficient as OLS in large samples, provided that your equations are correctly specified. However, in small samples the need to estimate the covariance matrix from the OLS residuals increases the sampling variability of the SUR estimates, and this effect can cause SUR to be less efficient than OLS. If the sample size is small and the across-equation correlations are small, then OLS should be preferred to SUR. The consequences of specification error are also more serious with SUR than with OLS.

The 3SLS method combines the ideas of the 2SLS and SUR methods. Like 2SLS, the 3SLS method uses $\widehat{Y}$ instead of Y for endogenous regressors, which results in consistent estimates. Like SUR, the 3SLS method takes the cross-equation error correlations into account to improve large sample efficiency. For 3SLS, the 2SLS residuals are used to estimate the cross-equation error covariance matrix.

The SUR and 3SLS methods can be iterated by recomputing the estimate of the cross-equation covariance matrix from the SUR or 3SLS residuals and then computing new SUR or 3SLS estimates based on this updated covariance matrix estimate. Continuing this iteration until convergence produces ITSUR or IT3SLS estimates.

FIML Estimation Method

The FIML estimator is a system generalization of the LIML estimator. The FIML method involves minimizing the determinant of the covariance matrix associated with residuals of the reduced form of the equation system. From a maximum likelihood standpoint, the LIML method involves assuming that the errors are normally distributed and then maximizing the likelihood function subject to restrictions on a particular equation. FIML is similar, except that the likelihood function is maximized subject to restrictions on all of the parameters in the model, not just those in the equation being estimated. The FIML method is implemented as an instrumental variable method (Hausman 1975).

Note: the RESTRICT, SRESTRICT, TEST, and STEST statements are not supported when the FIML method is used.

Choosing a Method for Simultaneous Equations

A number of factors should be taken into account in choosing an estimation method. Although system methods are asymptotically most efficient in the absence of specification error, system methods are more sensitive to specification error than single equation methods.

In practice, models are never perfectly specified. It is a matter of judgment whether the misspecification is serious enough to warrant avoidance of system methods.

Another factor to consider is sample size. With small samples, 2SLS may be preferred to 3SLS. In general, it is difficult to say much about the small sample properties of K-class estimators because this depends on the regressors used.

LIML and FIML are invariant to the normalization rule imposed but are computationally more expensive than 2SLS or 3SLS.

If the reason for contemporaneous correlation among errors across equations is a common omitted variable, it is not necessarily best to apply SUR. SUR parameter estimates are more sensitive to specification error than OLS. OLS may produce better parameter estimates under these circumstances. SUR estimates are also affected by the sampling variation of the error covariance matrix. There is some evidence from Monte Carlo studies that SUR is less efficient than OLS in small samples.

ANOVA Table for Instrumental Variables Methods

In the instrumental variables methods (2SLS, LIML, K-class, MELO), first-stage predicted values are substituted for the endogenous regressors. As a result, the regression sum of squares (RSS) and the error sum of squares (ESS) do not sum to the total corrected sum of squares for the dependent variable (TSS). The analysis of variance table printed for the second-stage results displays these sums of squares and the mean squares used for the F-test, but this table is not a variance decomposition in the usual analysis of variance sense.

The F-test shown in the instrumental variables case is a valid test of the no-regression hypothesis that the true coefficients of all regressors are 0. However, because of the first-stage projection of the regression mean square, this is a Wald-type test statistic, which is asymptotically F but not exactly F-distributed in finite samples. Thus, for small samples the F-test is only approximate when instrumental variables are used.

The R2 Statistics

As explained in the section "ANOVA Table for Instrumental Variables Methods," when instrumental variables are used, the regression sum of squares (RSS) and the error sum of squares (ESS) do not sum to the total corrected sum of squares. In this case, there are several ways that the R^2 statistic can be defined.

The definition of R^2 used by the SYSLIN procedure is

$$R^2 = \frac{RSS}{RSS + ESS}$$

This definition is consistent with the F-test of the null hypothesis that the true coefficients of all regressors are 0. However, this R^2 may not be a good measure of the goodness of fit of the model.

System Weighted R2 and System Weighted Mean Square Error

The system weighted R^2, printed for the 3SLS, IT3SLS, SUR, ITSUR, and FIML methods, is computed as follows:

$$R^2 = \frac{\mathbf{Y'\,W\,R\,(X'X)}^{-1}\,\mathbf{R'\,W\,Y}}{\mathbf{Y'\,W\,Y}}$$

In this equation, the matrix $\mathbf{X'X}$ is $\mathbf{R'W\,R}$, and $\mathbf{W}$ is the projection matrix of the instruments:

$$\mathbf{W} = \mathbf{S}^{-1} \otimes \mathbf{Z}(\mathbf{Z'Z})^{-1}\,\mathbf{Z'}$$

The matrix $\mathbf{Z}$ is the instrument set, $\mathbf{R}$ is the the regressor set, and $\mathbf{S}$ is the estimated cross-model covariance matrix.

The system weighted MSE, printed for the 3SLS, IT3SLS, SUR, ITSUR, and FIML methods, is computed as follows:

$$MSE = \tfrac{1}{tdf}\left(\mathbf{Y'\,W\,Y} - \mathbf{Y'\,W\,R\,(X'X)}^{-1}\,\mathbf{R'\,W\,Y}\right)$$

In this equation, *tdf* is the sum of the error degrees of freedom for the equations in the system.

Computational Details

This section discusses various computational details.

Computation of Model Crossproduct Matrix

Model crossproduct matrix $\mathbf{X'X}$ is formed from projected values. For K-class estimation,

$$\mathbf{X'X} = (1 - k)\,\mathbf{R'R} + k\,\mathbf{R'Z}(\mathbf{Z'Z})^{-1}\mathbf{Z'R}$$

where $\mathbf{Z}$ is the instrument set and $\mathbf{R}$ is the the regressor set. Note that $k = 1$ for the 2SLS method and $k = 0$ for the OLS method.

In the 3SLS, IT3SLS, SUR, and ITSUR methods, $\mathbf{X'X}$ is formed as

$$\mathbf{X'X} = \mathbf{R'}\left(\mathbf{S}^{-1} \otimes \mathbf{Z}(\mathbf{Z'Z})^{-1}\mathbf{Z'}\right)\mathbf{R}$$

where $\mathbf{Z}$ and $\mathbf{R}$ are as defined previously and $\mathbf{S}$ is an estimate of the cross-equation covariance matrix. For SUR and ITSUR, $\mathbf{Z}$ is the identity matrix.

Computation of Standard Errors

The VARDEF= option in the PROC SYSLIN statement controls the denominator used in calculating the cross-equation covariance estimates and the parameter standard errors and covariances. The values of the VARDEF= option and the resulting denominator are as follows:

N   uses the number of nonmissing observations.

DF   uses the number of nonmissing observations less the degrees of freedom in the model.

WEIGHT   uses the sum of the observation weights given by the WEIGHTS statement.

WDF   uses the sum of the observation weights given by the WEIGHTS statement less the degrees of freedom in the model.

The VARDEF= option does not affect the model mean square error, root mean square error, or R^2 statistics. These statistics are always based on the error degrees of freedom, regardless of the VARDEF= option. The VARDEF= option also does not affect the dependent variable coefficient of variation (C.V.).

Reduced Form Estimates

The REDUCED option in the PROC SYSLIN statement computes estimates of the reduced form coefficients. The REDUCED option requires that the equation system be square. If there are fewer models than endogenous variables, IDENTITY statements can be used to complete the equation system.

The reduced form coefficients are computed as follows. Represent the equation system, with all endogenous variables moved to the left side of the equations and identities, as

$$\mathbf{B\,Y} = \mathbf{\Gamma\,X}$$

Here $\mathbf{B}$ is the estimated coefficient matrix for the endogenous variables $\mathbf{Y}$, and $\mathbf{\Gamma}$ is the estimated coefficient matrix for the exogenous (or predetermined) variables $\mathbf{X}$.

The system can be solved for $\mathbf{Y}$ as follows, provided $\mathbf{B}$ is square and nonsingular:

$$\mathbf{Y} = \mathbf{B}^{-1}\mathbf{\Gamma\,X}$$

The reduced form coefficients are the matrix $\mathbf{B}^{-1}\mathbf{\Gamma}$.

Uncorrelated Errors Across Equations

The SDIAG option in the PROC SYSLIN statement computes estimates assuming uncorrelated errors across equations. As a result, when the SDIAG option is used, the 3SLS estimates are identical to 2SLS estimates, and the SUR estimates are the same as the OLS estimates.

Over Identification Restrictions

The OVERID option in the MODEL statement can be used to test for over identifying restrictions on parameters of each equation. The null hypothesis is that the predetermined variables not appearing in any equation have zero coefficients. The alternative hypothesis is that at least one of the assumed zero coefficients is nonzero. The test is approximate and rejects the null hypothesis too frequently for small sample sizes.

The formula for the test is given as follows. Let $y_i = \beta_i \mathbf{Y}_i + \gamma_i \mathbf{Z}_i + e$ be the ith equation. $\mathbf{Y}_i$ are the endogenous variables that appear as regressors in the ith equation, and $\mathbf{Z}_i$ are the instrumental variables that appear as regressors in the ith equation. Let N_i be the number of variables in $\mathbf{Y}_i$ and $\mathbf{Z}_i$.

Let $v_i = y_i - \mathbf{Y}_i \widehat{\beta}_i$. Let $\mathbf{Z}$ represent all instrumental variables, T be the total number of observations, and K be the total number of instrumental variables. Define $\hat{l}$ as follows:

$$\hat{l} = \frac{v_i' \left(\mathbf{I} - \mathbf{Z}_i (\mathbf{Z}'_i \mathbf{Z}_i)^{-1} \mathbf{Z}'_i \right) v_i}{v_i' \left(\mathbf{I} - \mathbf{Z}(\mathbf{Z}'\mathbf{Z})^{-1}\mathbf{Z}' \right) v_i}$$

Then the test statistic

$$\frac{T - K}{K - N_i} \left(\hat{l} - 1 \right)$$

is distributed approximately as an F with $K - N_i$ and $T - K$ degrees of freedom. Refer to Basmann (1960) for more information.

Fuller's Modification to LIML

The ALPHA= option in the PROC SYSLIN and MODEL statements parameterizes Fuller's modification to LIML. This modification is $k = \gamma - (\alpha / (n - g))$, where α is the value of the ALPHA= option, γ is the LIML k value, n is the number of observations, and g is the number of predetermined variables. Fuller's modification is not used unless the ALPHA= option is specified. Refer to Fuller (1977) for more information.

Missing Values

Observations having a missing value for any variable in the analysis are excluded from the computations.

OUT= Data Set

The output SAS data set produced by the OUT= option in the PROC SYSLIN statement contains all the variables in the input data set and the variables containing predicted values and residuals specified by OUTPUT statements.

The residuals are computed as actual values minus predicted values. Predicted values never use lags of other predicted values, as would be desirable for dynamic simulation. For these applications, PROC SIMLIN is available to predict or simulate values from the estimated equations.

OUTEST= Data Set

The OUTEST= option produces a TYPE=EST output SAS data set containing estimates from the regressions. The variables in the OUTEST= data set are as follows:

BY variables   The BY statement variables are included in the OUTEST= data set.

TYPE   identifies the estimation type for the observations. The _TYPE_ value INST indicates first-stage regression estimates. Other values indicate the estimation method used: 2SLS indicates two-stage least squares results, 3SLS indicates three-stage least squares results, LIML indicates limited information maximum likelihood results, and so forth. Observations added by IDENTITY statements have the _TYPE_ value IDENTITY.

MODEL   the model label. The model label is the label specified in the MODEL statement, or it is the dependent variable name if no label is specified. For first-stage regression estimates, _MODEL_ has the value FIRST.

DEPVAR   the name of the dependent variable for the model

NAME   the names of the regressors for the rows of the covariance matrix, if the COVOUT option is specified. _NAME_ has a blank value for the parameter estimates observations. The _NAME_ variable is not included in the OUTEST= data set unless the COVOUT option is used to output the covariance of parameter estimates matrix.

SIGMA   contains the root mean square error for the model, which is an estimate of the standard deviation of the error term. The _SIGMA_ variable contains the same values reported as Root MSE in the printed output.

INTERCEP   the intercept parameter estimates

regressors   the regressor variables from all the MODEL statements are included in the OUTEST= data set. Variables used in IDENTIFY statements are also included in the OUTEST= data set.

The parameter estimates are stored under the names of the regressor variables. The intercept parameters are stored in the variable INTERCEP. The dependent variable of the model is given a coefficient of -1. Variables not in a model have missing values for the OUTEST= observations for that model.

Some estimation methods require computation of preliminary estimates. All estimates computed are output to the OUTEST= data set. For each BY group and each estimation, the OUTEST= data set contains one observation for each MODEL or IDENTITY statement. Results for different estimations are identified by the _TYPE_ variable.

For example, consider the following statements:

```
proc syslin data=a outest=est 3sls;
    by b;
    endogenous y1 y2;
    instruments x1-x4;
    model y1 = y2 x1 x2;
    model y2 = y1 x3 x4;
    identity x1 = x3 + x4;
run;
```

The 3SLS method requires both a preliminary 2SLS stage and preliminary first stage regressions for the endogenous variable. The OUTEST= data set thus contains 3 different kinds of estimates. The observations for the first-stage regression estimates have the _TYPE_ value INST. The observations for the 2SLS estimates have the _TYPE_ value 2SLS. The observations for the final 3SLS estimates have the _TYPE_ value 3SLS.

Since there are two endogenous variables in this example, there are two first-stage regressions and two _TYPE_=INST observations in the OUTEST= data set. Since there are two model statements, there are two OUTEST= observations with _TYPE_=2SLS and two observations with _TYPE_=3SLS. In addition, the OUTEST= data set contains an observation with the _TYPE_ value IDENTITY containing the coefficients specified by the IDENTITY statement. All these observations are repeated for each BY group in the input data set defined by the values of the BY variable B.

When the COVOUT option is specified, the estimated covariance matrix for the parameter estimates is included in the OUTEST= data set. Each observation for parameter estimates is followed by observations containing the rows of the parameter covariance matrix for that model. The row of the covariance matrix is identified by the variable _NAME_. For parameter estimates observations, _NAME_ is blank. For covariance observations, _NAME_ contains the regressor name for the row of the covariance matrix, and the regressor variables contain the covariances.

See Example 17.1 for an example of the OUTEST= data set.

OUTSSCP= Data Set

The OUTSSCP= option produces a TYPE=SSCP output SAS data set containing sums of squares and cross products. The data set contains all variables used in the MODEL, IDENTITY, and VAR statements. Observations are identified by the variable _NAME_.

The OUTSSCP= data set can be useful when a large number of observations are to be explored in many different SYSLIN runs. The sum-of-squares-and-crossproducts matrix can be saved with the OUTSSCP= option and used as the DATA= data set on subsequent SYSLIN runs. This is much less expensive computationally because PROC SYSLIN never reads the original data again. In the step that creates the OUTSSCP= data set, include in the VAR statement all the variables you expect to use.

Printed Output

The printed output produced by the SYSLIN procedure is as follows:

1. If the SIMPLE option is used, a table of descriptive statistics is printed showing the sum, mean, sum of squares, variance, and standard deviation for all the variables used in the models.

2. First-stage regression results are printed if the FIRST option is specified and an instrumental variables method is used. This shows the regression of each endogenous variable on the variables in the INSTRUMENTS list.

3. The results of the second-stage regression are printed for each model. (See "Printed Output for Each Model," which follows this section.)

4. If a systems method like 3SLS, SUR, or FIML is used, the cross-equation error covariance matrix is printed. This matrix is shown four ways: the covariance matrix itself, the correlation matrix form, the inverse of the correlation matrix, and the inverse of the covariance matrix.

5. If a systems method like 3SLS, SUR, or FIML is used, the system weighted mean square error and system weighted R^2 statistics are printed. The system weighted MSE and R^2 measure the fit of the joint model obtained by stacking all the models together and performing a single regression with the stacked observations weighted by the inverse of the model error variances.

6. If a systems method like 3SLS, SUR, or FIML is used, the final results are printed for each model.

7. If the REDUCED option is used, the reduced form coefficients are printed. This consists of the structural coefficient matrix for the endogenous variables, the structural coefficient matrix for the exogenous variables, the inverse of the endogenous coefficient matrix, and the reduced form coefficient matrix. The reduced form coefficient matrix is the product of the inverse of the endogenous coefficient matrix and the exogenous structural coefficient matrix.

Printed Output for Each Model

The results printed for each model include the analysis of variance table, the parameter estimates table, and optional items requested by TEST statements or by options in the MODEL statement.

The printed output produced for each model is described in the following.

The analysis of variance table includes the following:

- the model degrees of freedom, sum of squares, and mean square

- the error degrees of freedom, sum of squares, and mean square. The error mean square is computed by dividing the error sum of squares by the error degrees of freedom and is not effected by the VARDEF= option.

- the corrected total degrees of freedom and total sum of squares. Note that for instrumental variables methods, the model and error sums of squares do not add to the total sum of squares.

- the F-ratio, labeled F Value, and its significance, labeled PROB>F, for the test of the hypothesis that all the nonintercept parameters are 0

- the root mean square error. This is the square root of the error mean square.

- the dependent variable mean

- the coefficient of variation (C.V.) of the dependent variable

- the R^2 statistic. This R^2 is computed consistently with the calculation of the F statistic. It is valid for hypothesis tests but may not be a good measure of fit for models estimated by instrumental variables methods.

- the R^2 statistic adjusted for model degrees of freedom, labeled Adj R-SQ

The parameter estimates table includes the following:

- estimates of parameters for regressors in the model and the Lagrangian parameter for each restriction specified

- a degrees of freedom column labeled DF. Estimated model parameters have 1 degree of freedom. Restrictions have a DF of -1. Regressors or restrictions dropped from the model due to collinearity have a DF of 0.

- the standard errors of the parameter estimates

- the T ratios, which are the parameter estimates divided by the standard errors

- the significance of the t-tests for the hypothesis that the true parameter is 0, labeled PROB>|T|. As previously noted, the significance tests are strictly valid in finite samples only for OLS estimates but are asymptotically valid for the other methods.

- the standardized regression coefficients, if the STB option is specified. This is the parameter estimate multiplied by the ratio of the standard deviation of the regressor to the standard deviation of the dependent variable.

- the labels of the regressor variables or restriction labels

In addition to the analysis of variance table and the parameter estimates table, the results printed for each model may include the following:

1. If TEST statements are specified, the test results are printed.

2. If the DW option is specified, the Durbin-Watson statistic and first-order autocorrelation coefficient are printed.

3. If the OVERID option is specified, the results of Basmann's test for overidentifying restrictions are printed.

4. If the PLOT option is used, plots of residual against each regressor are printed.

5. If the COVB or CORB options are specified, the results for each model also in-

clude the covariance or correlation matrix of the parameter estimates. For systems methods like 3SLS and FIML, the COVB and CORB output is printed for the whole system after the output for the last model, instead of separately for each model.

The third stage output for 3SLS, SUR, IT3SLS, ITSUR, and FIML does not include the analysis of variance table. When a systems method is used, the second stage output does not include the optional output, except for the COVB and CORB matrices.

Examples

Example 17.1.   Klein's Model I

This example uses PROC SYSLIN to estimate the classic Klein Model I. For a discussion of this model, see Theil (1971). The following statements read the data.

```
data klein;
   input year c p w i x wp g t k wsum;
   date=mdy(1,1,year);
   format date monyy.;
   y   =c+i+g-t;
   yr  =year-1931;
   klag=lag(k);
   plag=lag(p);
   xlag=lag(x);
   label year='Year'
         date='Date'
         c   ='Consumption'
         p   ='Profits'
         w   ='Private Wage Bill'
         i   ='Investment'
         k   ='Capital Stock'
         y   ='National Income'
         x   ='Private Production'
         wsum='Total Wage Bill'
         wp  ='Govt Wage Bill'
         g   ='Govt Demand'
         i   ='Taxes'
         klag='Capital Stock Lagged'
         plag='Profits Lagged'
         xlag='Private Product Lagged'
         yr  ='YEAR-1931';
   cards;
1920   .    12.7   .    .    44.9   .     .     .    182.8   .
1921  41.9  12.4  25.5 -0.2  45.6  2.7   3.9   7.7  182.6  28.2
1922  45.0  16.9  29.3  1.9  50.1  2.9   3.2   3.9  184.5  32.2
1923  49.2  18.4  34.1  5.2  57.2  2.9   2.8   4.7  189.7  37.0
1924  50.6  19.4  33.9  3.0  57.1  3.1   3.5   3.8  192.7  37.0
1925  52.6  20.1  35.4  5.1  61.0  3.2   3.3   5.5  197.8  38.6
1926  55.1  19.6  37.4  5.6  64.0  3.3   3.3   7.0  203.4  40.7
1927  56.2  19.8  37.9  4.2  64.4  3.6   4.0   6.7  207.6  41.5
1928  57.3  21.1  39.2  3.0  64.5  3.7   4.2   4.2  210.6  42.9
1929  57.8  21.7  41.3  5.1  67.0  4.0   4.1   4.0  215.7  45.3
1930  55.0  15.6  37.9  1.0  61.2  4.2   5.2   7.7  216.7  42.1
1931  50.9  11.4  34.5 -3.4  53.4  4.8   5.9   7.5  213.3  39.3
1932  45.6   7.0  29.0 -6.2  44.3  5.3   4.9   8.3  207.1  34.3
```

Example 17.1. Klein's Model I □ □ □   857

```
1933  46.5  11.2  28.5  -5.1  45.1  5.6   3.7   5.4  202.0  34.1
1934  48.7  12.3  30.6  -3.0  49.7  6.0   4.0   6.8  199.0  36.6
1935  51.3  14.0  33.2  -1.3  54.4  6.1   4.4   7.2  197.7  39.3
1936  57.7  17.6  36.8   2.1  62.7  7.4   2.9   8.3  199.8  44.2
1937  58.7  17.3  41.0   2.0  65.0  6.7   4.3   6.7  201.8  47.7
1938  57.5  15.3  38.2  -1.9  60.9  7.7   5.3   7.4  199.9  45.9
1939  61.6  19.0  41.6   1.3  69.5  7.8   6.6   8.9  201.2  49.4
1940  65.0  21.1  45.0   3.3  75.7  8.0   7.4   9.6  204.5  53.0
1941  69.7  23.5  53.3   4.9  88.4  8.5  13.8  11.6  209.4  61.8
;
```

The following statements estimate the Klein model using the limited information maximum likelihood method. In addition, the parameter estimates are written to a SAS data set with the OUTEST= option.

```
proc syslin data=klein outest=b liml;
    endogenous c p w i x wsum k y;
    instruments klag plag xlag wp g t yr;
    consume: model c = p plag  wsum;
    invest:  model i = p plag  klag;
    labor:   model w = x xlag  yr;
run;

proc print data=b;
run;
```

The PROC SYSLIN estimates are shown in Output 17.1.1.

Output 17.1.1. LIML Estimates

```
                          SYSLIN Procedure
              Limited-Information Maximum Likelihood Estimation

Model: CONSUME
Dependent variable: C Consumption

                        Analysis of Variance

                             Sum of        Mean
     Source        DF       Squares       Square     F Value     Prob>F

     Model          3     854.35415    284.78472     118.416     0.0001
     Error         17      40.88419      2.40495
     C Total       20     941.42952

              Root MSE       1.55079    R-Square       0.9543
              Dep Mean      53.99524    Adj R-SQ       0.9463
              C.V.           2.87209

                        Parameter Estimates

                    Parameter      Standard    T for H0:
     Variable   DF   Estimate         Error   Parameter=0   Prob > |T|

     INTERCEP    1   17.147655      2.045374         8.384       0.0001
     P           1   -0.222513      0.224230        -0.992       0.3349
     PLAG        1    0.396027      0.192943         2.053       0.0558
     WSUM        1    0.822559      0.061549        13.364       0.0001

                    Variable
     Variable   DF    Label

     INTERCEP    1   Intercept
     P           1   Profits
     PLAG        1   Profits Lagged
     WSUM        1   Total Wage Bill

NOTE: K-Class Estimation with K=1.4987455056
```

Output 17.1.1. (Continued)

```
                          SYSLIN Procedure
             Limited-Information Maximum Likelihood Estimation

Model: INVEST
Dependent variable: I Taxes

                      Analysis of Variance

                         Sum of        Mean
      Source      DF     Squares       Square    F Value    Prob>F

      Model        3    210.37901    70.12634     34.065    0.0001
      Error       17     34.99649     2.05862
      C Total     20    252.32667

            Root MSE      1.43479     R-Square     0.8574
            Dep Mean      1.26667     Adj R-SQ     0.8322
            C.V.        113.27274

                       Parameter Estimates

                   Parameter    Standard    T for H0:
      Variable  DF  Estimate      Error    Parameter=0   Prob > |T|

      INTERCEP   1  22.590825    9.498146      2.378       0.0294
      P          1   0.075185    0.224712      0.335       0.7420
      PLAG       1   0.680386    0.209145      3.253       0.0047
      KLAG       1  -0.168264    0.045345     -3.711       0.0017

                      Variable
      Variable  DF    Label

      INTERCEP   1    Intercept
      P          1    Profits
      PLAG       1    Profits Lagged
      KLAG       1    Capital Stock Lagged

NOTE: K-Class Estimation with K=1.0859528454
```

```
                          SYSLIN Procedure
             Limited-Information Maximum Likelihood Estimation

Model: LABOR
Dependent variable: W Private Wage Bill

                      Analysis of Variance

                         Sum of        Mean
      Source      DF     Squares       Square    F Value    Prob>F

      Model        3    696.14848   232.04949    393.621    0.0001
      Error       17     10.02192     0.58952
      C Total     20    794.90952

            Root MSE      0.76781     R-Square     0.9858
            Dep Mean     36.36190     Adj R-SQ     0.9833
            C.V.          2.11156

                       Parameter Estimates

                   Parameter    Standard    T for H0:
      Variable  DF  Estimate      Error    Parameter=0   Prob > |T|

      INTERCEP   1   1.526187    1.320838      1.155       0.2639
      X          1   0.433941    0.075507      5.747       0.0001
      XLAG       1   0.151321    0.074527      2.030       0.0583
      YR         1   0.131593    0.035995      3.656       0.0020

                      Variable
      Variable  DF    Label

      INTERCEP   1    Intercept
      X          1    Private Production
      XLAG       1    Private Product Lagged
      YR         1    YEAR-1931

NOTE: K-Class Estimation with K=2.4685825667
```

Example 17.1. Klein's Model I □ □ □   859

The OUTEST= data set is shown in part in Output 17.1.2. Note that the data set contains the parameter estimates and root mean square errors, _SIGMA_, for the first stage instrumental regressions as well as the parameter estimates and σ for the LIML estimates for the three structural equations.

Output 17.1.2.   The OUTEST= Data Set

OBS	_TYPE_	_MODEL_	_DEPVAR_	_SIGMA_	INTERCEP	KLAG	PLAG	XLAG	WP
1	INST	FIRST	C	2.11403	58.3018	-0.14654	0.74803	0.23007	0.19327
2	INST	FIRST	P	2.18298	50.3844	-0.21610	0.80250	0.02200	-0.07961
3	INST	FIRST	W	1.75427	43.4356	-0.12295	0.87192	0.09533	-0.44373
4	INST	FIRST	I	1.72376	35.5182	-0.19251	0.92639	-0.11274	-0.71661
5	INST	FIRST	X	3.77347	93.8200	-0.33906	1.67442	0.11733	-0.52334
6	INST	FIRST	WSUM	1.75427	43.4356	-0.12295	0.87192	0.09533	0.55627
7	INST	FIRST	K	1.72376	35.5182	0.80749	0.92639	-0.11274	-0.71661
8	INST	FIRST	Y	3.77347	93.8200	-0.33906	1.67442	0.11733	-0.52334
9	LIML	CONSUME	C	1.55079	17.1477	.	0.39603	.	.
10	LIML	INVEST	I	1.43479	22.5908	-0.16826	0.68039	.	.
11	LIML	LABOR	W	0.76781	1.5262	.	.	0.15132	.

OBS	G	T	YR	C	P	W	I	X	WSUM	K	Y
1	0.20501	-0.36573	0.70109	-1	.	.	.	.	.	.	.
2	0.43902	-0.92310	0.31941	.	-1.00000	.	.	.	.	.	.
3	0.86622	-0.60415	0.71358	.	.	-1	.	.	.	.	.
4	0.10023	-0.16152	0.33190	.	.	.	-1	.	.	.	.
5	1.30524	-0.52725	1.03299	.	.	.	.	-1.00000	.	.	.
6	0.86622	-0.60415	0.71358	.	.	.	.	.	-1.00000	.	.
7	0.10023	-0.16152	0.33190	.	.	.	.	.	.	-1	.
8	1.30524	-1.52725	1.03299	.	.	.	.	.	.	.	-1
9	.	.	.	-1	-0.22251	.	.	.	0.82256	.	.
10	.	.	.	.	0.07518	.	-1	.	.	.	.
11	.	.	0.13159	.	.	-1	.	0.43394	.	.	.

The following statements estimate the model using the 3SLS method. The reduced form estimates are produced by the REDUCED option; IDENTITY statements are used to make the model complete.

```
proc syslin data=klein 3sls reduced;
    endogenous c p w i x wsum k y;
    instruments klag plag xlag wp g t yr;
    consume: model    c = p plag wsum;
    invest:  model    i = p plag klag;
    labor:   model    w = x xlag yr;
    product: identity x = c + i + g;
    income:  identity y = c + i + g - t;
    profit:  identity p = y - w - wp;
    stock:   identity k = klag + i;
    wage:    identity wsum = w + wp;
run;
```

The preliminary 2SLS results and estimated cross-model covariance matrix are not shown. The 3SLS estimates are shown in Output 17.1.3. The reduced form estimates are shown in Output 17.1.4.

Output 17.1.3.   3SLS Estimates

```
                            SYSLIN Procedure
                  Three-Stage Least Squares Estimation

        System Weighted MSE:  5.9342 with 51 degrees of freedom.
        System Weighted R-Square:  0.9550
```

Model: CONSUME
Dependent variable: C Consumption

Parameter Estimates

Variable	DF	Parameter Estimate	Standard Error	T for H0: Parameter=0	Prob > |T|
INTERCEP	1	16.440790	1.449925	11.339	0.0001
P	1	0.124890	0.120179	1.039	0.3133
PLAG	1	0.163144	0.111631	1.461	0.1621
WSUM	1	0.790081	0.042166	18.738	0.0001

Variable	DF	Variable Label
INTERCEP	1	Intercept
P	1	Profits
PLAG	1	Profits Lagged
WSUM	1	Total Wage Bill

```
                            SYSLIN Procedure
                  Three-Stage Least Squares Estimation
```

Model: INVEST
Dependent variable: I Taxes

Parameter Estimates

Variable	DF	Parameter Estimate	Standard Error	T for H0: Parameter=0	Prob > |T|
INTERCEP	1	28.177847	7.550853	3.732	0.0017
P	1	-0.013079	0.179938	-0.073	0.9429
PLAG	1	0.755724	0.169976	4.446	0.0004
KLAG	1	-0.194848	0.036156	-5.389	0.0001

Variable	DF	Variable Label
INTERCEP	1	Intercept
P	1	Profits
PLAG	1	Profits Lagged
KLAG	1	Capital Stock Lagged

```
                            SYSLIN Procedure
                  Three-Stage Least Squares Estimation
```

Model: LABOR
Dependent variable: W Private Wage Bill

Parameter Estimates

Variable	DF	Parameter Estimate	Standard Error	T for H0: Parameter=0	Prob > |T|
INTERCEP	1	1.797218	1.240203	1.449	0.1655
X	1	0.400492	0.035359	11.327	0.0001
XLAG	1	0.181291	0.037965	4.775	0.0002
YR	1	0.149674	0.031048	4.821	0.0002

Variable	DF	Variable Label
INTERCEP	1	Intercept
X	1	Private Production

Example 17.1. Klein's Model I   □ □ □   861

Output 17.1.3. (Continued)

```
    XLAG       1  Private Product Lagged
    YR         1  YEAR-1931
```

Endogenous Variables

	C	P	W	I
CONSUME	1	-0.124890475	0	0
INVEST	0	0.0130791824	0	1
LABOR	0	0	1	0
PRODUCT	-1	0	0	-1
INCOME	-1	0	0	-1
PROFIT	0	1	1	0
STOCK	0	0	0	-1
WAGE	0	0	-1	0

Output 17.1.4. Reduced Form Estimates

SYSLIN Procedure
Three-Stage Least Squares Estimation

Endogenous Variables

	X	WSUM	K	Y
CONSUME	0	-0.790080936	0	0
INVEST	0	0	0	0
LABOR	-0.40049188	0	0	0
PRODUCT	1	0	0	0
INCOME	0	0	0	1
PROFIT	0	0	0	-1
STOCK	0	0	1	0
WAGE	0	1	0	0

Exogenous Variables

	INTERCEP	PLAG	KLAG	XLAG
CONSUME	16.440790064	0.1631440928	0	0
INVEST	28.177846868	0.7557239621	-0.194848249	0
LABOR	1.7972177277	0	0	0.181291015
PRODUCT	0	0	0	0
INCOME	0	0	0	0
PROFIT	0	0	0	0
STOCK	0	0	1	0
WAGE	0	0	0	0

SYSLIN Procedure
Three-Stage Least Squares Estimation

Exogenous Variables

	YR	G	T	WP
CONSUME	0	0	0	0
INVEST	0	0	0	0
LABOR	0.1496741151	0	0	0
PRODUCT	0	1	0	0
INCOME	0	1	-1	0
PROFIT	0	0	0	-1
STOCK	0	0	0	0
WAGE	0	0	0	1

Inverse Endogenous Variables

Output 17.1.4. (Continued)

G Inv	CONSUME	INVEST	LABOR	PRODUCT
C	1.6346535005	0.6346535005	1.0956566655	0.4388015976
P	0.9723636697	0.9723636697	-0.34047524	-0.136357569
W	0.6495721089	0.6495721089	1.4405850431	0.5769426119
I	-0.012717722	0.9872822782	0.0044531378	0.0017834455
X	1.6219357787	1.6219357787	1.1001098033	1.4405850431
WSUM	0.6495721089	0.6495721089	1.4405850431	0.5769426119
K	-0.012717722	0.9872822782	0.0044531378	0.0017834455
Y	1.6219357787	1.6219357787	1.1001098033	0.4405850431

SYSLIN Procedure
Three-Stage Least Squares Estimation

Inverse Endogenous Variables

G Inv	INCOME	PROFIT	STOCK	WAGE
C	0.1958519029	0.1958519029	0	1.2915085684
P	1.1087212386	1.1087212386	0	0.7682459988
W	0.072629497	0.072629497	0	0.5132145401
I	-0.014501167	-0.014501167	0	-0.01004803
X	0.1813507355	0.1813507355	0	1.2814605388
WSUM	0.072629497	0.072629497	0	1.5132145401
K	-0.014501167	-0.014501167	1	-0.01004803
Y	1.1813507355	0.1813507355	0	1.2814605388

Reduced Form

	INTERCEP	PLAG	KLAG	XLAG
C	46.727297762	0.7463069203	-0.123661123	0.1986327089
P	42.77363341	0.8934739139	-0.189463359	-0.061725102
W	31.572067066	0.5968710602	-0.126567988	0.2611651246
I	27.618402714	0.7440380538	-0.192370223	0.0008073139
X	74.345700476	1.4903449741	-0.316031347	0.1994400228
WSUM	31.572067066	0.5968710602	-0.126567988	0.2611651246
K	27.618402714	0.7440380538	0.8076297765	0.0008073139
Y	74.345700476	1.4903449741	-0.316031347	0.1994400228

SYSLIN Procedure
Three-Stage Least Squares Estimation

Reduced Form

	YR	G	T	WP
C	0.1639914418	0.6346535005	-0.195851903	1.0956566655
P	-0.05096033	0.9723636697	-1.108721239	-0.34047524
W	0.2156182915	0.6495721089	-0.072629497	0.4405850431
I	0.0006665195	-0.012717722	0.0145011673	0.0044531378
X	0.1646579613	1.6219357787	-0.181350736	1.1001098033
WSUM	0.2156182915	0.6495721089	-0.072629497	1.4405850431
K	0.0006665195	-0.012717722	0.0145011673	0.0044531378
Y	0.1646579613	1.6219357787	-1.181350736	1.1001098033

Example 17.2. Grunfeld's Model □ □ □ 863

Example 17.2. Grunfeld's Model

The following example was used by Zellner in his classic 1962 paper on seemingly unrelated regressions. Different stock prices often move in the same direction at a given point in time. The SUR technique may provide more efficient estimates than OLS in this situation.

The following statements read the data. (The prefix GE stands for General Electric and WH stands for Westinghouse.)

```
data grunfeld;
   input year ge_i ge_f ge_c wh_i wh_f wh_c;
   label ge_i = 'Gross Investment, GE'
         ge_c = 'Capital Stock Lagged, GE'
         ge_f = 'Value of Outstanding Shares Lagged, GE'
         wh_i = 'Gross Investment, WH'
         wh_c = 'Capital Stock Lagged, WH'
         wh_f = 'Value of Outstanding Shares Lagged, WH';
   cards;
1935    33.1     1170.6    97.8     12.93     191.5     1.8
1936    45.0     2015.8    104.4    25.90     516.0     .8
1937    77.2     2803.3    118.0    35.05     729.0     7.4
1938    44.6     2039.7    156.2    22.89     560.4     18.1
1939    48.1     2256.2    172.6    18.84     519.9     23.5
1940    74.4     2132.2    186.6    28.57     628.5     26.5
1941    113.0    1834.1    220.9    48.51     537.1     36.2
1942    91.9     1588.0    287.8    43.34     561.2     60.8
1943    61.3     1749.4    319.9    37.02     617.2     84.4
1944    56.8     1687.2    321.3    37.81     626.7     91.2
1945    93.6     2007.7    319.6    39.27     737.2     92.4
1946    159.9    2208.3    346.0    53.46     760.5     86.0
1947    147.2    1656.7    456.4    55.56     581.4     111.1
1948    146.3    1604.4    543.4    49.56     662.3     130.6
1949    98.3     1431.8    618.3    32.04     583.8     141.8
1950    93.5     1610.5    647.4    32.24     635.2     136.7
1951    135.2    1819.4    671.3    54.38     723.8     129.7
1952    157.3    2079.7    726.1    71.78     864.1     145.5
1953    179.5    2371.6    800.3    90.08     1193.5    174.8
1954    189.6    2759.9    888.9    68.60     1188.9    213.5
;
```

The following statements compute the SUR estimates for the Grunfeld model.

```
proc syslin data=grunfeld sur;
   ge:      model ge_i = ge_f ge_c;
   westing: model wh_i = wh_f wh_c;
run;
```

The PROC SYSLIN output is shown in Output 17.2.1.

Output 17.2.1.   PROC SYSLIN Output for SUR

```
                            SYSLIN Procedure
                   Ordinary Least Squares Estimation

Model: GE
Dependent variable: GE_I Gross Investment, GE
                         Analysis of Variance

                              Sum of         Mean
           Source       DF    Squares       Square     F Value      Prob>F

           Model         2  31632.03023  15816.01511    20.344      0.0001
           Error        17  13216.58777    777.44634
           C Total      19  44848.61800

                  Root MSE      27.88272    R-Square      0.7053
                  Dep Mean     102.29000    Adj R-SQ      0.6706
                  C.V.          27.25850

                         Parameter Estimates

                      Parameter      Standard     T for H0:
           Variable  DF  Estimate       Error    Parameter=0    Prob > |T|

           INTERCEP   1  -9.956306    31.374249     -0.317        0.7548
           GE_F       1   0.026551     0.015566      1.706        0.1063
           GE_C       1   0.151694     0.025704      5.902        0.0001

                            Variable
           Variable  DF     Label

           INTERCEP   1  Intercept
           GE_F       1  Value of Outstanding Shares Lagged, GE
           GE_C       1  Capital Stock Lagged, GE
```

```
                            SYSLIN Procedure
                   Ordinary Least Squares Estimation

Model: WESTING
Dependent variable: WH_I Gross Investment, WH
                         Analysis of Variance

                              Sum of         Mean
           Source       DF    Squares       Square     F Value      Prob>F

           Model         2   5165.55292   2582.77646    24.761      0.0001
           Error        17   1773.23393    104.30788
           C Total      19   6938.78686

                  Root MSE      10.21312    R-Square      0.7444
                  Dep Mean      42.89150    Adj R-SQ      0.7144
                  C.V.          23.81153

                         Parameter Estimates

                      Parameter      Standard     T for H0:
           Variable  DF  Estimate       Error    Parameter=0    Prob > |T|

           INTERCEP   1  -0.509390     8.015289     -0.064        0.9501
           WH_F       1   0.052894     0.015707      3.368        0.0037
           WH_C       1   0.092406     0.056099      1.647        0.1179

                            Variable
           Variable  DF     Label

           INTERCEP   1  Intercept
           WH_F       1  Value of Outstanding Shares Lagged, WH
           WH_C       1  Capital Stock Lagged, WH
```

Example 17.2. Grunfeld's Model □ □ □ 865

Output 17.2.1. (Continued)

```
                        SYSLIN Procedure
            Seemingly Unrelated Regression Estimation

                    Cross Model Covariance

         Sigma                    GE             WESTING

         GE              777.44633943         207.58713102
         WESTING         207.58713102         104.30787826


                    Cross Model Correlation

         Corr                     GE             WESTING

         GE                        1          0.7289649707
         WESTING          0.7289649707                   1


                 Cross Model Inverse Correlation

         Inv Corr                 GE             WESTING

         GE               2.133970354         -1.555589637
         WESTING         -1.555589637          2.133970354


                 Cross Model Inverse Covariance

         Inv Sigma                GE             WESTING

         GE              0.0027448458         -0.005462624
         WESTING         -0.005462624         0.0204583814
```

```
                        SYSLIN Procedure
            Seemingly Unrelated Regression Estimation

      System Weighted MSE:  0.97187 with 34 degrees of freedom.
      System Weighted R-Square:  0.6284


Model: GE
Dependent variable: GE_I Gross Investment, GE

                    Parameter Estimates

                     Parameter     Standard    T for H0:
   Variable   DF     Estimate       Error    Parameter=0    Prob > |T|

   INTERCEP    1    -27.719317     29.321219     -0.945        0.3577
   GE_F        1      0.038310      0.014415      2.658        0.0166
   GE_C        1      0.139036      0.024986      5.565        0.0001

                       Variable
   Variable   DF       Label

   INTERCEP    1    Intercept
   GE_F        1    Value of Outstanding Shares Lagged, GE
   GE_C        1    Capital Stock Lagged, GE
```

Output 17.2.1. (Continued)

```
                        SYSLIN Procedure
             Seemingly Unrelated Regression Estimation

Model: WESTING
Dependent variable: WH_I Gross Investment, WH

                      Parameter Estimates

                   Parameter      Standard    T for H0:
   Variable   DF    Estimate        Error    Parameter=0    Prob > |T|

   INTERCEP   1    -1.251988       7.545217     -0.166        0.8702
   WH_F       1     0.057630       0.014546      3.962        0.0010
   WH_C       1     0.063978       0.053041      1.206        0.2443

                   Variable
   Variable   DF    Label

   INTERCEP   1    Intercept
   WH_F       1    Value of Outstanding Shares Lagged, WH
   WH_C       1    Capital Stock Lagged, WH
```

References

Basmann, R.L. (1960), "On Finite Sample Distributions of Generalized Classical Linear Identifiability Test Statistics," *Journal of the American Statistical Association*, 55, 650–659.

Fuller, W.A. (1977), "Some Properties of a Modification of the Limited Information Estimator," *Econometrica*, 45, 939–952.

Hausman, J.A. (1975), "An Instrumental Variable Approach to Full Information Estimators for Linear and Certain Nonlinear Econometric Models," *Econometrica*, 43, 727–738.

Johnston, J. (1984), *Econometric Methods*, Third Edition, New York: McGraw-Hill Inc.

Judge, George G.; Griffiths, W.E.; Hill, R. Carter; Lutkepohl, Helmut; and Lee, Tsoung-Chao (1985), *The Theory and Practice of Econometrics*, Second Edition, New York: John Wiley & Sons, Inc.

Maddala, G.S. (1977), *Econometrics*, New York: McGraw-Hill Book Company.

Park, S.B. (1982), "Some Sampling Properties of Minimum Expected Loss (MELO) Estimators of Structural Coefficients," *Journal of the Econometrics*, 18, 295–311.

Pindyck, R.S. and Rubinfeld, D.L. (1981), *Econometric Models and Economic Forecasts*, Second Edition, New York: McGraw-Hill Inc.

Pringle, R.M. and Raynor, A.A. (1971), *Generalized Inverse Matrices with Applications to Statistics*, New York: Hafner Publishing Company.

Rao, P. (1974), "Specification Bias in Seemingly Unrelated Regressions," in *Essays in Honor of Tinbergen*, Volume 2, New York: International Arts and Sciences Press.

Savin, N.E. and White, K.J. (1978), "Testing for Autocorrelation with Missing Observations," *Econometrics*, 46, 59–66.

Theil, H. (1971), *Principles of Econometrics*, New York: John Wiley & Sons, Inc.

Zellner, A. (1962), "An Efficient Method of Estimating Seemingly Unrelated Regressions and Tests for Aggregation Bias," *Journal of the American Statistical Association*, 57, 348–368.

Zellner, A. (1978), "Estimation of Functions of Population Means and Regression Coefficients: A Minimum Expected Loss (MELO) Approach," *Journal of the Econometrics*, 8, 127–158.

Zellner, A. and Park, S. (1979), "Minimum Expected Loss (MELO) Estimators for Functions of Parameters and Structural Coefficients of Econometric Models," *Journal of the American Statistical Association*, 74, 185–193.

Chapter 18
The TSCSREG Procedure

Chapter Table of Contents

Chapter 18
The TSCSREG Procedure

Overview

The TSCSREG (**T**ime **S**eries **C**ross **S**ection **Reg**ression) procedure analyzes a class of linear econometric models that commonly arise when time series and cross-sectional data are combined. The TSCSREG procedure deals with panel data sets that consist of time series observations on each of several cross-sectional units.

Such models can be viewed as two-way designs with covariates, as follows:

$$y_{it} = \sum_{k=1}^{p} \mathbf{X}_{itk}\beta_k + u_{it} \quad i = 1, \dots, N; \quad t = 1, \dots, T$$

where N is the number of cross sections, T is the length of the time series for each cross section, and p is the number of exogenous or independent variables.

The performance of any estimation procedure for the model regression parameters depends on the statistical characteristics of the error components in the model. The TSCSREG procedure estimates the regression parameters in the preceding model under three common error structures. The TSCSREG procedure uses the following error structures and corresponding methods to analyze the structures:

- variance components (or error components) model

$$u_{it} = v_i + e_t + \epsilon_{it}$$

  The Fuller-Battese method is used to estimate this model. This error structure is similar to the common two-way random effects model with covariates. The variance components are estimated by the fitting-of-constants method, and the regression parameters are estimated with generalized least squares (GLS).

- first-order autoregressive model with contemporaneous correlation

$$u_{it} = \rho_i u_{i,t-1} + \epsilon_{it}$$

  The Parks method is used to estimate this model. This model assumes a first-order autoregressive error structure with contemporaneous correlation between cross sections. The covariance matrix is estimated by a two-stage procedure leading to the estimation of model regression parameters by GLS.

- mixed variance-component moving average error process

$$u_{it} = a_i + b_t + e_{it}$$
$$e_{it} = \alpha_0 \epsilon_t + \alpha_1 \epsilon_{t-1} + \dots + \alpha_m \epsilon_{t-m}$$

The Da Silva method is used to estimate the mixed variance-component moving average model. The Da Silva method estimates the regression parameters using a two-step GLS-type estimator.

The TSCSREG procedure analyzes panel data sets that consist of multiple time series observations on each of several individuals or cross-sectional units. The input data set must be in time series cross-sectional form. See Chapter 2, "Working with Time Series Data," for a discussion of how time series related by a cross-sectional dimension are stored in SAS data sets. The TSCSREG procedure requires that the time series for each cross section have the same number of observations and cover the same time range.

Getting Started

Specifying the Input Data

The input data set used by the TSCSREG procedure must be sorted by cross section and by time within each cross section. Therefore, the first step in using PROC TSCSREG is to make sure that the input data set is sorted. Normally, the input data set contains a variable that identifies the cross section for each observation and a variable that identifies the time period for each observation.

To illustrate, suppose that you have a data set A containing data over time for each of several states. You want to regress the variable Y on regressors X1 and X2. Cross sections are identified by the variable STATE, and time periods are identified by the variable DATE. The following statements sort data set A appropriately:

```
proc sort data=a;
   by state date;
run;
```

The next step is to invoke the TSCSREG procedure and specify the cross section and time series variables in an ID statement. List the variables in the ID statement exactly as they are listed in the BY statement, as shown in the following statements:

```
proc tscsreg data=a;
   id state date;
```

Alternatively, you can omit the ID statement and use the CS= and TS= options on the PROC TSCSREG statement to specify the number of cross sections in the data set and the number of time series observations in each cross section.

Specifying the Regression Model

Next, specify the linear regression model with a MODEL statement. The MODEL statement in PROC TSCSREG is specified like the MODEL statement in other SAS regression procedures: the dependent variable is listed first, followed by an equal sign, followed by the list of regressor variables.

```
proc tscsreg data=a;
   id state date;
   model y = x1 x2;
run;
```

The reason for using PROC TSCSREG instead of other SAS regression procedures is that you can incorporate a model for the structure of the random errors. It is important to consider what kind of error structure model is appropriate for your data and to specify the corresponding option in the MODEL statement.

The error structure options supported by the TSCSREG procedure are FULLER, PARKS, and DASILVA. See the section "Details" later in this chapter for more information about these methods and the error structures they assume.

By default, the Fuller-Battese method is used. Thus, the preceding example is the same as specifying the FULLER option, as shown in the following statements:

```
proc tscsreg data=a;
   id state date;
   model y = x1 x2 / fuller;
run;
```

You can specify more than one error structure option in the MODEL statement; the analysis is repeated using each method specified. You can use any number of MODEL statements to estimate different regression models or estimate the same model using different options. See Example 18.1 later in this chapter.

Introductory Example

The following example uses the cost function data from Greene (1990) to estimate the variance components model. The variable OUTPUT is the log of output in millions of kilowatt-hours, and COST is the log of cost in millions of dollars. Refer to Greene (1990) for details.

```
data greene;
   input firm year output cost @@;
cards;
      1 1955    5.36598    1.14867   1 1960    6.03787    1.45185
      1 1965    6.37673    1.52257   1 1970    6.93245    1.76627
      2 1955    6.54535    1.35041   2 1960    6.69827    1.71109
      2 1965    7.40245    2.09519   2 1970    7.82644    2.39480
      3 1955    8.07153    2.94628   3 1960    8.47679    3.25967
      3 1965    8.66923    3.47952   3 1970    9.13508    3.71795
      4 1955    8.64259    3.56187   4 1960    8.93748    3.93400
      4 1965    9.23073    4.11161   4 1970    9.52530    4.35523
      5 1955    8.69951    3.50116   5 1960    9.01457    3.68998
      5 1965    9.04594    3.76410   5 1970    9.21074    4.05573
      6 1955    9.37552    4.29114   6 1960    9.65188    4.59356
      6 1965   10.21163    4.93361   6 1970   10.34039    5.25520
;

proc sort data=greene;
   by firm year;
run;
```

Usually, you cannot explicitly specify all the explanatory variables that affect the dependent variable. The omitted or unobservable variables are summarized in the error disturbances. The TSCSREG procedure used with the Fuller-Battese method adds the individual and time-specific random effects to the error disturbances, and the parameters are efficiently estimated using the GLS method. The variance components model used by the Fuller-Battese method is

$$y_{it} = \sum_{k=1}^{p} X_{itk}\beta_k + v_i + e_t + \epsilon_{it} \quad i = 1, \dots, N; \quad t = 1, \dots, T$$

The following statements fit this model. Since the Fuller-Battese is the default method, no options are required.

```
proc tscsreg data=greene;
   model cost = output;
   id firm year;
run;
```

The TSCSREG procedure output is shown in Figure 18.1. A model description is printed first, which reports the estimation method used and the number of cross sections and time periods. The variance components estimates are printed next. Finally, the table of regression parameter estimates shows the estimates, standard errors, and *t*-tests.

```
                           TSCSREG Procedure
                    Fuller and Battese Method Estimation

Dependent Variable: COST

                          Model Description

            Estimation Method          FULLER
            Number of Cross Sections   6
            Time Series Length         4


                     Variance Component Estimates

            SSE         0.348082   DFE               22
            MSE         0.015822   Root MSE    0.125785

        Variance Component for Cross Sections        0.046907
        Variance Component for Time Series           0.009060
        Variance Component for Error                 0.008749


                        Parameter Estimates

                 Parameter      Standard    T for H0:               Variable
Variable   DF    Estimate         Error     Parameter=0  Prob > |T|   Label

INTERCEP   1     -2.999917      0.647783    -4.631054      0.0001   Intercept
OUTPUT     1      0.746596      0.076183     9.800034      0.0001
```

Figure 18.1. The Variance Components Estimates

Syntax

The following statements are used with the TSCSREG procedure:

PROC TSCSREG *options*;
    BY *variables*;
    ID *cross-section-id-variable time-series-id-variable*;
    MODEL *dependent* = *regressor-variables* / *options*;

Functional Summary

The statements and options used with the TSCSREG procedure are summarized in the following table:

Description	Statement	Option
Data Set Options		
specify the input data set	TSCSREG	DATA=
write parameter estimates to an output data set	TSCSREG	OUTEST=
include correlations in the OUTEST= data set	TSCSREG	CORROUT
include covariances in the OUTEST= data set	TSCSREG	COVOUT
specify number of time series observations	TSCSREG	TS=
specify number of cross sections	TSCSREG	CS=
Declaring the Role of Variables		
specify BY-group processing	BY	
specify the cross section and time ID variables	ID	
Printing Control Options		
print correlations of the estimates	MODEL	CORRB
print covariances of the estimates	MODEL	COVB
suppress printed output	MODEL	NOPRINT
Model Estimation Options		
specify Fuller-Battese method	MODEL	FULLER
specify PARKS	MODEL	PARKS
specify Da Silva method	MODEL	DASILVA
specify order of moving average error	MODEL	M=
print Φ matrix for Parks method	MODEL	PHI
print autocorrelation coefficients	MODEL	RHO
suppress the intercept term	MODEL	NOINT
control check for singularity	MODEL	SINGULAR=

PROC TSCSREG Statement

> **PROC TSCSREG** *options*;

You can specify the following options on the PROC TSCSREG statement:

DATA= *SAS-data-set*
: names the input data set. The input data set must be sorted by cross section and by time period within cross section. If you omit DATA=, the most recently created SAS data set is used.

TS= *number*
: specifies the number of observations in the time series for each cross section. The TS= option value must be greater than 1. The TS= option is required unless you use an ID statement. Note that the number of observations for each time series must be the same for each cross section and must cover the same time period.

CS= *number*
: specifies the number of cross sections. The CS= option value must be greater than 1. The CS= option is required unless you use an ID statement.

OUTEST= *SAS-data-set*
: names an output data set to contain the parameter estimates. When you do not specify the OUTEST= option, the OUTEST= data set is not created. See the section "OUTEST= Data Set" later in this chapter for details on the structure of the OUTEST= data set.

OUTCOV
COVOUT
: writes the covariance matrix of the parameter estimates to the OUTEST= data set. See the section "OUTEST= Data Set" later in this chapter for details.

OUTCORR
CORROUT
: writes the correlation matrix of the parameter estimates to the OUTEST= data set. See the section "OUTEST= Data Set" later in this chapter for details.

In addition, you can specify any of the following MODEL statement options in the PROC TSCSREG statement:

CORRB	DASILVA	PHI
COVB	M=	RHO
FULLER	NOINT	SINGULAR=
PARKS	NOPRINT	

When specified in the PROC TSCSREG statement, these options are equivalent to specifying the options for every MODEL statement. See the section "MODEL Statement" later in this chapter for a complete description of each of these options.

BY Statement

BY *variables* ;

You can use a BY statement with PROC TSCSREG to obtain separate analyses on observations in groups defined by the BY variables. When a BY statement appears, the input data set must be sorted by the BY variables as well as by cross section and time period within the BY groups.

When you specify both an ID statement and a BY statement, the input data set must be sorted first with respect to BY variables and then with respect to the cross section and time series ID variables. For example,

```
proc sort data=a;
   by byvar1 byvar2 csid tsid;
run;

proc tscsreg data=a;
   by byvar1 byvar2;
   id csid tsid;
   ... etc. ...
run;
```

When both a BY statement and an ID statement are used, the data set may have a different number of cross sections or a different number of time periods in each BY group. If you did not use an ID statement, you must specify the CS=N and TS=T options, and each BY group must contain $N \times T$ observations.

ID Statement

ID *cross-section-id-variable time-series-id-variable*;

You can use the ID statement to specify variables in the input data set that identify the cross section and time period for each observation.

When you use an ID statement, the TSCSREG procedure verifies that the input data set is sorted by the cross section ID variable and by the time series ID variable within each cross section. The TSCSREG procedure also verifies that the time series ID values are the same for all cross sections.

To make sure the input data set is correctly sorted, use PROC SORT with a BY statement with the variables listed exactly as they are listed in the ID statement to sort the input data set.

```
proc sort data=a;
   by csid tsid;
run;

proc tscsreg data=a;
   id csid tsid;
   ... etc. ...
run;
```

If you do not use the ID statement, you must specify the TS= and CS= options on the PROC TSCSREG statement. Note that the input data must be sorted by time within cross section, regardless of whether the cross section structure is given by an ID statement or by the options TS= and CS=.

If you specify an ID statement, the time series length T is set to the minimum number of observations for any cross section, and only the first T observations in each cross section are used. If you specify both the ID statement and the TS= and CS= options, the TS= and CS= options are ignored.

MODEL Statement

> **MODEL** *response* = *regressors / options*;

The MODEL statement specifies the regression model and the error structure assumed for the regression residuals. The response variable on the left side of the equal sign is regressed on the independent variables listed after the equal sign. You can use any number of MODEL statements. For each model statement only one response variable can be specified on the left side of the equal sign.

You can specify the error structure by using the FULLER, PARKS, and DASILVA options. You can use more than one of these three options, in which case the analysis is repeated for each error structure model you specify.

You can label the models. Model labels appear in the printed output to identify the results for different models. If you do not specify labels, the response variable name is used as the label for the model. Specify the model label as follows:

> *label* : **MODEL ... ;**

You can specify the following options on the MODEL statement after a slash (/).

CORRB
CORR
  prints the matrix of estimated correlations between the parameter estimates.

COVB
  prints the matrix of estimated covariances between the parameter estimates.

FULLER
  specifies that the model be estimated using the Fuller-Battese method, which assumes a variance components model for the error structure. See the section "Fuller-Battese Method (Variance Components Model)" later in this chapter for details. FULLER is the default.

PARKS
  specifies that the model be estimated using the Parks method, which assumes a first-order autoregressive model for the error structure. See the section "Parks Method (Autoregressive Model)" later in this chapter for details.

DASILVA
  specifies that the model be estimated using the Da Silva method, which assumes a mixed variance-component moving average model for the error structure. See the section "Da Silva Method (Variance Components Model)" later in this chapter for details.

M= *number*

specifies the order of the moving average process in the Da Silva method. The M= value must be less than $T - 1$. The default is M=1.

PHI

prints the Φ matrix of estimated covariances of the observations for the Parks method. The PHI option is relevant only when you use the PARKS option. See the section "Parks Method (Autoregressive Model)" later in this chapter for details.

RHO

prints the estimated autocorrelation coefficients for the Parks method.

NOINT
NOMEAN

suppresses the intercept parameter from the model.

NOPRINT

suppresses the normal printed output.

SINGULAR= *number*

specifies a singularity criterion for the inversion of the matrix. The default depends on the precision of the computer system.

Details

Fuller-Battese Method (Variance Components Model)

Fuller and Battese (1974) studied the model in which the random errors u_{it} have the decomposition

$$u_{it} = v_i + e_t + \epsilon_{it} \quad i = 1, 2, \dots, N; \quad t = 1, 2, \dots, T$$

The errors v_i, e_t, and ϵ_{it} are independently distributed with zero means and positive variances σ_v^2, σ_e^2, and σ_ϵ^2.

The linear model with this error structure is written in matrix notation as

$$\mathbf{y} = \mathbf{X}\beta + \mathbf{u}$$

where

$$\mathbf{y} = (y_{11}, y_{12}, \dots, y_{1T}, \dots, y_{N1}, \dots, y_{NT})'$$
$$\mathbf{X} = (\mathbf{x}_{11}, \mathbf{x}_{12}, \dots, \mathbf{x}_{1T}, \dots, \mathbf{x}_{N1}, \dots, \mathbf{x}_{NT})'$$
$\mathbf{x}_{it}$ are $p \times 1$ vectors of independent variables
β is a $p \times 1$ parameter vector
$$\mathbf{u} = (u_{11}, u_{12}, \dots, u_{1T}, \dots, u_{N1}, \dots, u_{NT})'$$

The covariance matrix for the vector of random errors **u** can be expressed

$$\mathbf{V} = \mathrm{E}(\mathbf{uu'}) = \sigma_\epsilon^2 \mathbf{I}_{NT} + \sigma_v^2 \mathbf{A} + \sigma_e^2 \mathbf{B}$$

$$\mathbf{A} = \mathbf{I}_N \otimes \mathbf{J}_T$$

$$\mathbf{B} = \mathbf{J}_N \otimes \mathbf{I}_T$$

where $\mathbf{I}_{NT}$, $\mathbf{I}_N$, and $\mathbf{I}_T$ are identity matrices of order NT, N, and T; $\mathbf{J}_N$ and $\mathbf{J}_T$ are $N \times N$ and $T \times T$ matrices with all elements equal to one; and $\otimes$ represents the Kronecker product. The following square matrices are defined:

$$\mathbf{M}_{..} = \mathbf{J}_{NT} / NT$$

$$\mathbf{M}_{1.} = \mathbf{A} / T - \mathbf{M}_{..}$$

$$\mathbf{M}_{.2} = \mathbf{B} / N - \mathbf{M}_{..}$$

$$\mathbf{M}_{12} = \mathbf{I}_{NT} - \mathbf{A} / T - \mathbf{B} / N + \mathbf{M}_{..}$$

where $\mathbf{J}_{NT}$ is a $NT \times NT$ matrix with all elements equal to 1. Note that the row vectors of $\mathbf{M}_{..}\mathbf{X}$, $\mathbf{M}_{1.}\mathbf{X}$, $\mathbf{M}_{.2}\mathbf{X}$, and $\mathbf{M}_{12}\mathbf{X}$, which correspond to the ith cross-sectional unit and tth time series, are $\mathbf{x}_{..}'$, $(\mathbf{x}_{i.}' - \mathbf{x}_{..}')$, $(\mathbf{x}_{.t}' - \mathbf{x}_{..}')$, and $(\mathbf{x}_{it}' - \mathbf{x}_{i.}' - \mathbf{x}_{.t}' + \mathbf{x}_{..}')$, respectively,   where $\mathbf{x}_{..} = \sum_{i=1}^{N} \sum_{t=1}^{T} \mathbf{x}_{it} / NT$, $\mathbf{x}_{i.} = \sum_{t=1}^{T} \mathbf{x}_{it} / T$,   and $\mathbf{x}_{.t} = \sum_{i=1}^{N} \mathbf{x}_{it} / N$.

The estimators for variance components are obtained by the fitting-of-constants method (Searle 1971) with the provision that any negative variance component is set to 0 for parameter estimation purposes.

First, the least-squares residual vectors are defined as

$$\hat{\epsilon} = \mathbf{C}_1 \left(\mathbf{I}_{NT} - \mathbf{X}[\mathbf{X}'\mathbf{C}_1\mathbf{X}]^- \mathbf{X}'\mathbf{C}_1 \right) \mathbf{y}$$

$$\hat{\mathbf{v}} = \mathbf{C}_2 \left(\mathbf{I}_{NT} - \mathbf{X}[\mathbf{X}'\mathbf{C}_2\mathbf{X}]^- \mathbf{X}'\mathbf{C}_2 \right) \mathbf{y}$$

$$\hat{\mathbf{e}} = \mathbf{C}_3 \left(\mathbf{I}_{NT} - \mathbf{X}[\mathbf{X}'\mathbf{C}_3\mathbf{X}]^- \mathbf{X}'\mathbf{C}_3 \right) \mathbf{y}$$

where $\mathbf{A}^-$ denotes generalized inverse of $\mathbf{A}$, $\mathbf{C}_1 = \mathbf{M}_{12}$, $\mathbf{C}_2 = \mathbf{M}_{12} + \mathbf{M}_{1.}$, and $\mathbf{C}_3 = \mathbf{M}_{12} + \mathbf{M}_{.2}$.

Then unbiased estimators for variance components are computed using the following formula:

$$\hat{\sigma}_\epsilon^2 = \frac{\hat{\epsilon}' \hat{\epsilon}}{(N-1)(T-1) - \mathrm{rank}\,(\mathbf{X}'\mathbf{M}_{12}\mathbf{X})}$$

$$\hat{\sigma}_v^2 = \frac{\hat{\mathbf{v}}'\hat{\mathbf{v}} - [T(N-1) - \mathrm{rank}\,(\mathbf{X}'\mathbf{M}_{.2}\mathbf{X})]\hat{\sigma}_\epsilon^2}{T(N-1) - T\,\mathrm{trace}\left([\mathbf{X}'\mathbf{C}_2\mathbf{X}]^- \mathbf{X}'\mathbf{M}_{1.}\mathbf{X}\right)}$$

$$\hat{\sigma}_e^2 = \frac{\hat{\mathbf{e}}'\hat{\mathbf{e}} - [N(T-1) - \mathrm{rank}\,(\mathbf{X}'\mathbf{M}_{1.}\mathbf{X})]\hat{\sigma}_\epsilon^2}{N(T-1) - N\,\mathrm{trace}\left([\mathbf{X}'\mathbf{C}_3\mathbf{X}]^- \mathbf{X}'\mathbf{M}_{.2}\mathbf{X}\right)}$$

If the $\mathbf{X}$ matrix does not contain the intercept, the denominator of $\hat{\sigma}_\epsilon^2$ should be increased by one.

The generalized least-squares estimation takes the following steps:

1. Obtain the constants using the following estimators for variance components.

$$\hat{\alpha}_1 = 1 - \left[\hat{\sigma}_\epsilon^2 / \left(\hat{\sigma}_\epsilon^2 + T\hat{\sigma}_v^2\right)\right]^{\frac{1}{2}}$$

$$\hat{\alpha}_2 = 1 - \left[\hat{\sigma}_\epsilon^2 / \left(\hat{\sigma}_\epsilon^2 + N\hat{\sigma}_e^2\right)\right]^{\frac{1}{2}}$$

$$\hat{\alpha}_3 = \hat{\alpha}_1 + \hat{\alpha}_2 - 1 + \left[\hat{\sigma}_\epsilon^2 / \left(\hat{\sigma}_\epsilon^2 + T\hat{\sigma}_v^2 + N\hat{\sigma}_e\right)\right]^{\frac{1}{2}}$$

2. Transform the variables using constants $\hat{\alpha}_1$, $\hat{\alpha}_2$, and $\hat{\alpha}_3$, as follows:

$$y_{it}^* = y_{it} - \hat{\alpha}_1 y_{i.} - \hat{\alpha}_2 y_{.t} + \hat{\alpha}_3 y_{..}$$

$$\mathbf{x}_{it}^* = \mathbf{x}_{it} - \hat{\alpha}_1 \mathbf{x}_{i.} - \hat{\alpha}_2 \mathbf{x}_{.t} + \hat{\alpha}_3 \mathbf{x}_{..}$$

where $y_{..}$, $y_{i.}$, and $y_{.t}$ are defined the same way as $\mathbf{x}_{..}$, $\mathbf{x}_{i.}$, and $\mathbf{x}_{.t}$.

3. Regress y_{it}^* on $\mathbf{x}_{it}^*$ using OLS.

The estimated generalized least-squares (EGLS) estimator $\hat{\beta}_F$ and its standard error can be obtained from the OLS estimator in step 3. The EGLS estimator can be represented in matrix notation as

$$\hat{\beta}_F = \left(\mathbf{X}' \, \hat{\mathbf{V}}^{-1} \mathbf{X}\right)^{-1} \mathbf{X}' \, \hat{\mathbf{V}}^{-1} \mathbf{y}$$

where

$$\hat{\mathbf{V}}^{-1} = \frac{\mathbf{M}_{12}}{\hat{\sigma}_\epsilon^2} + \frac{\mathbf{M}_{1.}}{\left(\hat{\sigma}_\epsilon^2 + T\hat{\sigma}_v^2\right)} + \frac{\mathbf{M}_{.2}}{\left(\hat{\sigma}_\epsilon^2 + N\hat{\sigma}_e^2\right)} + \frac{\mathbf{M}_{..}}{\left(\hat{\sigma}_\epsilon^2 + T\hat{\sigma}_v^2 + N\hat{\sigma}_e^2\right)}$$

Refer to Fuller and Battese (1974) for details on deriving the inverse of the covariance matrix $\mathbf{V}$.

Substantial computational advantages are gained by presenting the fitting-of-constants estimators for the variance components in terms of deviations from appropriate means, instead of creating dummy variables for use in regressions.

Finally, Fuller and Battese give sufficient conditions that the estimator, $\hat{\beta}_F$, is unbiased and asymptotically normally distributed.

Parks Method (Autoregressive Model)

Parks (1967) considered the first-order autoregressive model in which the random errors u_{it}, $i = 1, 2, \ldots, N$, $t = 1, 2, \ldots, T$, have the structure

$$E\left(u_{it}^2\right) = \sigma_{ii} \qquad\qquad \text{(heteroscedasticity)}$$

$$E\left(u_{it}u_{jt}\right) = \sigma_{ij} \qquad\qquad \text{(contemporaneously correlated)}$$

$$u_{it} = \rho_i u_{i,t-1} + \epsilon_{it} \qquad\qquad \text{(autoregression)}$$

where

$$E\left(\epsilon_{it}\right) = 0$$

$$E\left(u_{i,t-1}\epsilon_{jt}\right) = 0$$

$$E\left(\epsilon_{it}\epsilon_{jt}\right) = \phi_{ij}$$

$$E\left(\epsilon_{it}\epsilon_{js}\right) = 0 \qquad (s \neq t)$$

$$E\left(u_{i0}\right) = 0$$

$$E\left(u_{i0}u_{j0}\right) = \sigma_{ij} = \phi_{ij} / \left(1 - \rho_i\rho_j\right)$$

The model assumed is first-order autoregressive with contemporaneous correlation between cross sections. In this model, the covariance matrix for the vector of random errors **u** can be expressed

$$E\left(\mathbf{uu}'\right) = \mathbf{V} = \begin{bmatrix} \sigma_{11}\mathbf{P}_{11} & \sigma_{12}\mathbf{P}_{12} & \cdots & \sigma_{1N}\mathbf{P}_{1N} \\ \sigma_{21}\mathbf{P}_{21} & \sigma_{22}\mathbf{P}_{22} & \cdots & \sigma_{2N}\mathbf{P}_{2N} \\ \vdots & \vdots & \vdots & \vdots \\ \sigma_{N1}\mathbf{P}_{N1} & \sigma_{N2}\mathbf{P}_{N2} & \cdots & \sigma_{NN}\mathbf{P}_{NN} \end{bmatrix}$$

where

$$\mathbf{P}_{ij} = \begin{bmatrix} 1 & \rho_j & \rho_j^2 & \cdots & \rho_j^{T-1} \\ \rho_i & 1 & \rho_j & \cdots & \rho_j^{T-2} \\ \rho_i^2 & \rho_i & 1 & \cdots & \rho_j^{T-3} \\ \vdots & \vdots & \vdots & \vdots & \vdots \\ \rho_i^{T-1} & \rho_i^{T-2} & \rho_i^{T-3} & \cdots & 1 \end{bmatrix}$$

The matrix **V** is estimated by a two-stage procedure, and β is then estimated by generalized least squares. The first step in estimating **V** involves the use of ordinary least squares to estimate β and obtain the fitted residuals, as follows:

$$\hat{\mathbf{u}} = \mathbf{y} - \mathbf{X}\hat{\beta}_{OLS}$$

A consistent estimator of the first-order autoregressive parameter is then obtained in the usual manner, as follows:

$$\widehat{\rho}_i = \left(\sum_{t=2}^{T} \widehat{u}_{it} \, \widehat{u}_{i,t-1} \right) \Big/ \left(\sum_{t=2}^{T} \widehat{u}_{i,t-1}^2 \right) \quad i = 1, 2, \ldots, N$$

Finally, the autoregressive characteristic of the data can be removed (asymptotically) by the usual transformation of taking weighted differences. That is, for $i = 1, \ldots, N$ and $t = 2, \ldots, T$

$$y_{it} - \widehat{\rho}_i y_{i,t-1} = \sum_{k=1}^{p} \left(\mathbf{X}_{itk} - \widehat{\rho}_i \, \mathbf{X}_{i,t-1,k} \right) \beta_k + u_{it} - \widehat{\rho}_i u_{i,t-1}$$

while for $i = 1, 2, \ldots, N$ and $t = 1$

$$y_{i1}\sqrt{1 - \widehat{\rho}_i^2} = \sum_{k=1}^{p} \mathbf{X}_{i1k} \beta_k \sqrt{1 - \widehat{\rho}_i^2} + u_{i1}\sqrt{1 - \widehat{\rho}_i^2}$$

This system is written as

$$y_{it}^* = \sum_{k=1}^{p} \mathbf{X}_{itk}^* \, \beta_k + u_{it}^* \quad i = 1, 2, \ldots, N \, ; \quad t = 1, 2, \ldots, T$$

Notice that the transformed model has not lost any observations (Seely and Zyskind 1971).

The second step in estimating the covariance matrix $\mathbf{V}$ is to apply ordinary least squares to the preceding transformed model, obtaining

$$\widehat{\mathbf{u}}^* = \mathbf{y}^* - \mathbf{X}^* \beta_{\text{OLS}}^*$$

from which the consistent estimator of σ_{ij} is calculated:

$$s_{ij} = \frac{\widehat{\phi}_{ij}}{\left(1 - \widehat{\rho}_i \, \widehat{\rho}_j \right)}$$

where

$$\widehat{\phi}_{ij} = \frac{1}{(T - p)} \sum_{t=1}^{T} \widehat{u}_{it}^* \, \widehat{u}_{jt}^*$$

EGLS then proceeds in the usual manner,

$$\widehat{\beta}_{\text{P}} = \left(\mathbf{X}' \widehat{\mathbf{V}}^{-1} \mathbf{X} \right)^{-1} \mathbf{X}' \widehat{\mathbf{V}}^{-1} \mathbf{y}$$

where $\widehat{\mathbf{V}}$ is the derived consistent estimator of $\mathbf{V}$. For computational purposes, it should be pointed out that $\widehat{\beta}_{\text{P}}$ is obtained directly from the transformed model,

$$\widehat{\beta}_{\text{P}} = \left(\mathbf{X}^{*\,\prime} \left(\widehat{\mathbf{\Phi}}^{-1} \otimes \mathbf{I}_T \right) \mathbf{X}^* \right)^{-1} \mathbf{X}^{*\,\prime} \left(\widehat{\mathbf{\Phi}}^{-1} \otimes \mathbf{I}_T \right) \mathbf{y}^*$$

where $\widehat{\boldsymbol{\Phi}} = \left[\widehat{\phi}_{ij}\right]_{i,j=1,\dots,N}$. The preceding procedure is equivalent to Zellner's two-stage methodology applied to the transformed model (Zellner 1962).

Parks demonstrates that his estimator is consistent and asymptotically, normally distributed with

$$\mathrm{Var}\left(\widehat{\beta}_{\mathrm{P}}\right) = \left(\mathbf{X}'\,\mathbf{V}^{-1}\mathbf{X}\right)^{-1}$$

Standard Corrections

For the PARKS option, the first-order autocorrelation coefficient must be estimated for each cross section. Let $\mathbf{r} = \left(r_1,\dots,r_N\right)'$ be the $N \times 1$ vector of autocorrelation estimates. To ensure that only range-preserving estimates are used, the following modification for $\mathbf{r}$ is made:

$$r_i = \begin{cases} r_i & \text{if } |r_i| < 1 \\ \max(.95, rmax) & \text{if } r_i \geq 1 \\ \min(-.95, rmin) & \text{if } r_i \leq -1 \end{cases}$$

where

$$rmax = \begin{cases} 0 & \text{if } r_i < 0 \text{ or } r_i \geq 1 \text{ for all } i \\ \max_{j}\left[\, r_j : 0 \leq r_j < 1 \,\right] & \text{otherwise} \end{cases}$$

and

$$rmin = \begin{cases} 0 & \text{if } r_i > 0 \text{ or } r_i \leq -1 \text{ for all } i \\ \min_{j}\left[\, r_j : -1 < r_j \leq 0 \,\right] & \text{otherwise} \end{cases}$$

Whenever this correction is made, a warning message is printed.

Da Silva Method (Variance-Component Moving Average Model)

Suppose you have a sample of observations at T time points on each of N cross-sectional units. The Da Silva method assumes that the observed value of the dependent variable at the tth time point on the ith cross-sectional unit can be expressed as

$$y_{it} = \mathbf{x}'_{it}\beta + a_i + b_t + e_{it} \quad i = 1,\,\dots,N\,;\quad t = 1,\,\dots,T$$

where

$\mathbf{x}'_{it} = \left(x_{it1},\,\dots,x_{itp}\right)$ is a vector of explanatory variables for the tth time point and ith cross-sectional unit

$\beta = (\beta_1,\,\dots,\beta_{\mathrm{P}})'$ is the vector of parameters

a_i is a time-invariant, cross-sectional unit effect

b_t is a cross-sectionally invariant time effect

e_{it} is a residual effect unaccounted for by the explanatory variables and the specific time and cross-sectional unit effects

Since the observations are arranged first by cross sections, then by time periods within cross sections, these equations can be written in matrix notation as

$$\mathbf{y} = \mathbf{X}\beta + \mathbf{u}$$

where

$$\mathbf{u} = (\mathbf{a} \otimes \mathbf{1}_T) + (\mathbf{1}_N \otimes \mathbf{b}) + \mathbf{e}$$
$$\mathbf{y} = (y_{11}, \ldots, y_{1T}, y_{21}, \ldots, y_{NT})'$$
$$\mathbf{X} = (\mathbf{x}_{11}, \ldots, \mathbf{x}_{1T}, \mathbf{x}_{21}, \ldots, \mathbf{x}_{NT})'$$
$$\mathbf{a} = (a_1 \ldots a_N)'$$
$$\mathbf{b} = (b_1 \ldots b_T)'$$
$$\mathbf{e} = (e_{11}, \ldots, e_{1T}, e_{21}, \ldots, e_{NT})'$$

Here $\mathbf{1}_N$ is an $N \times 1$ vector with all elements equal to 1, and $\otimes$ denotes the Kronecker product.

It is assumed that

1. $\mathbf{x}_{it}$ is a sequence of nonstochastic, known $p \times 1$ vectors in $\Re^p$ whose elements are uniformly bounded in $\Re^p$. The matrix $\mathbf{X}$ has a full column rank p.

2. β is a $p \times 1$ constant vector of unknown parameters.

3. $\mathbf{a}$ is a vector of uncorrelated random variables such that $\mathrm{E}(a_i) = 0$ and $\mathrm{var}(a_i) = \sigma_a^2, \sigma_a^2 > 0, i = 1, \ldots, N$.

4. $\mathbf{b}$ is a vector of uncorrelated random variables such that $\mathrm{E}(b_t) = 0$ and $\mathrm{var}(b_t) = \sigma_b^2, \sigma_b^2 > 0, t = 1, \ldots, T$.

5. $\mathbf{e}_i = (e_{i1}, \ldots, e_{iT})'$ is a sample of a realization of a finite moving average time series of order $m < T - 1$ for each i. Hence, for $i = 1, \ldots, N$ and $t = 1, \ldots, T$,

$$e_{it} = \alpha_0 \epsilon_t + \alpha_1 \epsilon_{t-1} + \ldots + \alpha_m \epsilon_{t-m}$$

where $\alpha_0, \alpha_1, \ldots, \alpha_m$ are unknown constants such that $\alpha_0 \neq 0$ and $\alpha_m \neq 0$, and $\{\epsilon_j\}_{j=-\infty}^{j=\infty}$ is a white noise process, that is, a sequence of uncorrelated random variables with $\mathrm{E}(\epsilon_t) = 0$, $\mathrm{E}(\epsilon_t^2) = \sigma_\epsilon^2$, and $\sigma_\epsilon^2 > 0$.

6. The sets of random variables $\{a_i\}_{i=1}^{N}$, $\{b_t\}_{t=1}^{T}$, and $\{e_{it}\}_{t=1}^{T}$ for $i = 1, \ldots, N$ are mutually uncorrelated.

7. The random terms have normal distributions: $a_i \sim \mathrm{N}(0, \sigma_a^2), b_t \sim \mathrm{N}(0, \sigma_b^2)$, and $\epsilon_{t-k} \sim \mathrm{N}(0, \sigma_\epsilon^2)$, for $i = 1, \ldots, N; t = 1, \ldots T; k = 1, \ldots, m$.

If assumptions 1-6 are satisfied, then

$$\mathrm{E}(\mathbf{y}) = \mathbf{X}\beta$$

and

$$\text{var}(\mathbf{y}) = \sigma_a^2 (\mathbf{I}_N \otimes \mathbf{J}_T) + \sigma_b^2 (\mathbf{J}_N \otimes \mathbf{I}_T) + (\mathbf{I}_N \otimes \Gamma_T)$$

where Γ_T is a $T \times T$ matrix with elements γ_{ts} as follows:

$$\text{cov}(e_{it}e_{is}) = \begin{cases} \gamma(|t-s|) & \text{if } |t-s| \leq m \\ 0 & \text{if } |t-s| > m \end{cases}$$

where $\gamma(k) = \sigma_\epsilon^2 \sum_{j=0}^{m-k} \alpha_j \alpha_{j+k}$ for $k = |t-s|$. For the definition of $\mathbf{I}_N, \mathbf{I}_T, \mathbf{J}_N$, and $\mathbf{J}_T$, see the section "Fuller-Battese Method (Variance Components Model)" earlier in this chapter.

The covariance matrix, denoted by $\mathbf{V}$, can be written in the form

$$\mathbf{V} = \sigma_a^2 (\mathbf{I}_N \otimes \mathbf{J}_T) + \sigma_b^2 (\mathbf{J}_N \otimes \mathbf{I}_T) + \sum_{k=0}^{m} \gamma(k)\left(\mathbf{I}_N \otimes \Gamma_T^{(k)}\right)$$

where $\Gamma_T^{(0)} = \mathbf{I}_T$, and, for $k = 1, \dots, m$, the matrix $\Gamma_T^{(k)}$ is a band matrix whose kth off-diagonal elements are 1's and all other elements are 0's.

Thus, the covariance matrix of the vector of observations $\mathbf{y}$ has the form

$$\text{var}(\mathbf{y}) = \sum_{k=1}^{m+3} \nu_k \mathbf{V}_k$$

where

$$\nu_1 = \sigma_a^2$$
$$\nu_2 = \sigma_b^2$$
$$\nu_k = \gamma(k-3) \qquad k = 3, \dots, m+3$$
$$\mathbf{V}_1 = \mathbf{I}_N \otimes \mathbf{J}_T$$
$$\mathbf{V}_2 = \mathbf{J}_N \otimes \mathbf{I}_T$$
$$\mathbf{V}_k = \mathbf{I}_N \otimes \Gamma_T^{(k-3)} \qquad k = 3, \dots, m+3$$

The estimator of β is a two-step GLS-type estimator, that is, GLS with the unknown covariance matrix replaced by a suitable estimator of $\mathbf{V}$. It is obtained by substituting Seely estimates for the scalar multiples $\nu_k, k = 1, 2, \dots, m+3$.

Seely (1969) presents a general theory of unbiased estimation when the choice of estimators is restricted to finite dimensional vector spaces, with a special emphasis on quadratic estimation of functions of the form $\sum_{i=1}^{n} \delta_i \nu_i$.

The parameters ν_i ($i = 1, \dots, n$) are associated with a linear model $\text{E}(\mathbf{y}) = \mathbf{X}\beta$ with covariance matrix $\sum_{i=1}^{n} \nu_i \mathbf{V}_i$ where $\mathbf{V}_i$ ($i = 1, \dots, n$) are real symmetric matrices. The method is also discussed by Seely (1970a,1970b) and Seely and Zyskind (1971). Seely and Soong (1971) consider the MINQUE principle, using an approach along the lines of Seely (1969).

Missing Values

The TSCSREG procedure does not allow missing values in the input data. If the value of any variable specified in the MODEL statement is missing, analysis of the current model terminates for the current BY group and an error message is printed.

OUTEST= Data Set

PROC TSCSREG writes the parameter estimates to an output data set when you specify the OUTEST= option. The OUTEST= data set contains the following variables:

MODEL   a character variable containing the label for the MODEL statement if you specify a label

METHOD   a character variable identifying the estimation method. Current methods are FULLER, PARKS, and DASILVA.

TYPE   a character variable that identifies the type of observation. Values of the _TYPE_ variable are CORRB, COVB, CSPARMS, and PARMS; the CORRB observation contains correlations of the parameter estimates; the COVB observation contains covariances of the parameter estimates; the CSPARMS observation contains cross-sectional parameter estimates; and the PARMS observation contains parameter estimates.

NAME   a character variable containing the name of a regressor variable for COVB and CORRB observations and left blank for other observations. Use the _NAME_ variable in conjunction with the _TYPE_ values COVB and CORRB to identify rows of the correlation or covariance matrix.

DEPVAR   a character variable containing the name of the response variable

MSE   the mean square error of the transformed model

CSID   the value of the cross section ID for CSPARMS observations. Use _CSID_ with the _TYPE_ value CSPARMS to identify the cross section for the first-order autoregressive parameter estimate contained in the observation. _CSID_ is missing for observations with other _TYPE_ values. (Currently only the _A_1 variable contains values for CSPARMS observations.)

VARCS   the variance component estimate due to cross sections. _VARCS_ is included in the OUTEST= data set when you specify either the FULLER or DASILVA option.

VARTS   the variance component estimate due to time series. _VARTS_ is included in the OUTEST= data set when you specify either the FULLER or DASILVA option.

VARERR   the variance component estimate due to error. _VARERR_ is included in the OUTEST= data set when you specify the FULLER option.

_A_1   the first-order autoregressive parameter estimate. _A_1 is included in the OUTEST= data set when you specify the PARKS option. The values of _A_1 are cross-sectional parameters, meaning that they are estimated for each cross section separately. _A_1 has a value only for _TYPE_=CSPARMS observations. The cross section to which the estimate belongs is indicated by the _CSID_ variable.

INTERCEP   the intercept parameter estimate. (INTERCEP will be missing for models for which you specify the NOINT option.)

regressors   the regressor variables you specify in the MODEL statement. The regressor variables in the OUTEST= data set contain the corresponding parameter estimates for the model identified by _MODEL_ for _TYPE_=PARMS observations, and the corresponding covariance or correlation matrix elements for _TYPE_=COVB and _TYPE_=CORRB observations. The response variable contains the value -1 for the _TYPE_=PARMS observation for its model.

Printed Output

For each MODEL statement, the printed output from PROC TSCSREG includes the following:

1. a model description, which gives the estimation method used, the model statement label if specified, the number of cross sections and the number of observations in each cross section, and the order of moving average error process for the DASILVA option

2. the estimates of the underlying error structure parameters

3. the regression parameter estimates and analysis. For each regressor, this includes the name of the regressor, the degrees of freedom, the parameter estimate, the standard error of the estimate, a t statistic for testing whether the estimate is significantly different from 0, and the significance probability of the t statistic. Whenever possible, the notation of the original reference is followed.

Optionally, PROC TSCSREG prints the following:

4. the covariance and correlation of the resulting regression parameter estimates for each model and assumed error structure

5. the $\widehat{\Phi}$ matrix that is the estimated contemporaneous covariance matrix for the PARKS option

Example

Example 18.1. Analyzing Demand for Liquid Assets

In this example, the demand equations for liquid assets are estimated. The demand function for the demand deposits is estimated under three error structures while demand equations for time deposits and savings and loan (S & L) association shares are calculated using the Parks method. The data for seven states (CA, DC, FL, IL, NY, TX, and WA) are selected out of 49 states. Refer to Feige (1964) for data description. All variables were transformed via natural logarithm. The first five observations of the data set A are shown in Output 18.1.1.

```
data a;
   input state $ year d t s y rd rt rs;
   label d = 'Per Capita Demand Deposits'
         t = 'Per Capita Time Deposits'
         s = 'Per Capita S & L Association Shares'
         y = 'Permanent Per Capita Personal Income'
         rd = 'Service Charge on Demand Deposits'
         rt = 'Interest on Time Deposits'
         rs = 'Interest on S & L Association Shares';
cards;
   ... data lines are omitted ...
;

proc print data=a(obs=5);
run;
```

Output 18.1.1. A Sample of Liquid Assets Data

OBS	STATE	YEAR	D	T	S	Y	RD	RT	RS
1	CA	1949	6.2785	6.1924	4.4998	7.2056	-1.0700	0.1080	1.0664
2	CA	1950	6.4019	6.2106	4.6821	7.2889	-1.0106	0.1501	1.0767
3	CA	1951	6.5058	6.2729	4.8598	7.3827	-1.0024	0.4008	1.1291
4	CA	1952	6.4785	6.2729	5.0039	7.4000	-0.9970	0.4492	1.1227
5	CA	1953	6.4118	6.2538	5.1761	7.4200	-0.8916	0.4662	1.2110

The SORT procedure is used to sort the data into the required time series cross-sectional format. Then PROC TSCSREG analyzes the data.

```
proc sort data=a;
   by state year;
run;

title 'Demand for Liquid Assets';
proc tscsreg data=a;
   model d = y rd rt rs / fuller parks dasilva m=7;
   model t = y rd rt rs / parks;
   model s = y rd rt rs / parks;
   id state year;
run;
```

The income elasticities for liquid assets are greater than 1 except for the demand deposit income elasticity (0.692757) estimated by the Da Silva method. In Output 18.1.2, Output 18.1.3, and Output 18.1.4, the coefficient estimates (−0.290940, − 0.435906, and −0.277361) of demand deposits (RD) imply that demand deposits increase significantly as the service charge decreases. The price elasticities (0.227152 and 0.408066) for time deposits (RT) and S & L association shares (RS) have the expected sign and thus an increase in the interest rate on time deposits or S & L shares will increase the demand for the corresponding liquid asset. Demand deposits and S & L shares appear to be substitutes (Output 18.1.2, Output 18.1.3, Output 18.1.4, and Output 18.1.6). Time deposits are also substitutes for S & L shares in the time deposit demand equation (Output 18.1.5), while these liquid assets are independent of each other in Output 18.1.6 (insignificant coefficient estimate of RT, −0.027054). Demand deposits and time deposits appear to be weak complements in Output 18.1.3 and Output 18.1.4, while the cross elasticities between demand deposits and time deposits are not significant in Output 18.1.2 and Output 18.1.5.

Output 18.1.2. Demand for Demand Deposits — Fuller-Battese Method

```
                            Demand for Liquid Assets

                                TSCSREG Procedure
                       Fuller and Battese Method Estimation

Dependent Variable: D    Per Capita Demand Deposits

                              Model Description

                      Estimation Method          FULLER
                      Number of Cross Sections   7
                      Time Series Length         11


                          Variance Component Estimates

             SSE          0.079541    DFE               72
             MSE          0.001105    Root MSE    0.033238

          Variance Component for Cross Sections        0.034270
          Variance Component for Time Series           0.000260
          Variance Component for Error                 0.001110


                             Parameter Estimates

              Parameter      Standard    T for H0:                Variable
    Variable  DF  Estimate      Error    Parameter=0  Prob > |T|    Label

    INTERCEP  1  -1.236056    0.725222    -1.704382     0.0926    Intercept
    Y         1   1.064058    0.104018    10.229508     0.0001    Permanent Per Capita Personal Income
    RD        1  -0.290940    0.052646    -5.526380     0.0001    Service Charge on Demand Deposits
    RT        1   0.039388    0.027761     1.418836     0.1603    Interest on Time Deposits
    RS        1  -0.326618    0.114046    -2.863924     0.0055    Interest on S & L Association Shares
```

Example 18.1.   Analyzing Demand for Liquid Assets   □ □ □   **891**

Output 18.1.3.   Demand for Demand Deposits — Parks Method

```
                              Demand for Liquid Assets

                                TSCSREG Procedure
                             Parks Method Estimation

Dependent Variable: D    Per Capita Demand Deposits

                               Model Description

                    Estimation Method          PARKS
                    Number of Cross Sections   7
                    Time Series Length         11

                          Variance Component Estimates

                    SSE        73.3696     DFE              72
                    MSE        1.019022    Root MSE   1.009466


                              Parameter Estimates

                 Parameter    Standard    T for H0:            Variable
     Variable DF  Estimate      Error    Parameter=0  Prob > |T|  Label

     INTERCEP  1  -2.665650    0.313910    -8.491764    0.0001   Intercept
     Y         1   1.222569    0.042340    28.874940    0.0001   Permanent Per Capita Personal Income
     RD        1  -0.435906    0.020080   -21.708190    0.0001   Service Charge on Demand Deposits
     RT        1   0.041237    0.020958     1.967620    0.0530   Interest on Time Deposits
     RS        1  -0.266826    0.065415    -4.078968    0.0001   Interest on S & L Association Shares
```

Output 18.1.4.   Demand for Demand Deposits — Da Silva Method

```
                              Demand for Liquid Assets

                                TSCSREG Procedure
                            Da Silva Method Estimation

Dependent Variable: D    Per Capita Demand Deposits

                               Model Description

                    Estimation Method          DASILVA
                    Number of Cross Sections   7
                    Time Series Length         11
                    Order of MA Error Process  7

                          Variance Component Estimates

                    SSE        21609.89    DFE              72
                    MSE        300.1374    Root MSE   17.32447

          Variance Component for Cross Sections        0.030630
          Variance Component for Time Series           0.000148


                          Estimates of Autocovariances

                          Lag      Gamma

                           0       0.0009
                           1       0.0009
                           2       0.0008
                           3       0.0008
                           4       0.0013
                           5       0.0011
                           6       0.0010
                           7       0.0008
```

Output 18.1.4. (Continued)

```
                              Demand for Liquid Assets

                                  TSCSREG Procedure
                             Da Silva Method Estimation

Dependent Variable: D    Per Capita Demand Deposits

                                  Parameter Estimates

                  Parameter     Standard     T for H0:                  Variable
       Variable DF  Estimate       Error    Parameter=0  Prob > |T|     Label

       INTERCEP  1   1.281084    0.082410     15.545338     0.0001   Intercept
       Y         1   0.692757    0.006765    102.395687     0.0001   Permanent Per Capita Personal Income
       RD        1  -0.277361    0.002741   -101.181798     0.0001   Service Charge on Demand Deposits
       RT        1   0.009378    0.001707      5.493070     0.0001   Interest on Time Deposits
       RS        1  -0.099417    0.006013    -16.534859     0.0001   Interest on S & L Association Shares
```

Output 18.1.5. Demand for Time Deposits — Parks Method

```
                              Demand for Liquid Assets

                                  TSCSREG Procedure
                               Parks Method Estimation

Dependent Variable: T   Per Capita Time Deposits

                                  Model Description

                        Estimation Method           PARKS
                        Number of Cross Sections     7
                        Time Series Length           11

                             Variance Component Estimates

                    SSE      63.38067    DFE              72
                    MSE       0.880287   Root MSE     0.938236

                                  Parameter Estimates

                  Parameter     Standard     T for H0:                  Variable
       Variable DF  Estimate       Error    Parameter=0  Prob > |T|     Label

       INTERCEP  1  -5.333339    0.500716    -10.651418     0.0001   Intercept
       Y         1   1.516344    0.081016     18.716507     0.0001   Permanent Per Capita Personal Income
       RD        1  -0.047906    0.029449     -1.626729     0.1082   Service Charge on Demand Deposits
       RT        1   0.227152    0.033181      6.845794     0.0001   Interest on Time Deposits
       RS        1  -0.425686    0.126152     -3.374376     0.0012   Interest on S & L Association Shares
```

Example 18.1. Analyzing Demand for Liquid Assets □ □ □ 893

Output 18.1.6. Demand for Savings and Loan Shares — Parks Method

```
                          Demand for Liquid Assets

                             TSCSREG Procedure
                            Parks Method Estimation

Dependent Variable: S   Per Capita S & L Association Shares

                             Model Description

                  Estimation Method          PARKS
                  Number of Cross Sections   7
                  Time Series Length         11

                       Variance Component Estimates

                SSE        71.96753   DFE               72
                MSE        0.999549   Root MSE    0.999774


                           Parameter Estimates

                Parameter   Standard    T for H0:              Variable
Variable   DF   Estimate    Error     Parameter=0  Prob > |T|  Label

INTERCEP   1    -8.096324   0.784965  -10.314254   0.0001  Intercept
Y          1     1.832988   0.115695   15.843250   0.0001  Permanent Per Capita Personal Income
RD         1     0.576723   0.043484   13.262900   0.0001  Service Charge on Demand Deposits
RT         1    -0.027054   0.031222   -0.866506   0.3891  Interest on Time Deposits
RS         1     0.408066   0.109192    3.737133   0.0004  Interest on S & L Association Shares
```

Acknowledgements

Douglas J. Drummond and A. Ronald Gallant developed the TSCSREG procedure and contributed to the Version 5 SUGI Supplemental Library in 1979.

Dr. Drummond, now deceased, was with the Center for Survey Statistics, Research Triangle Park, North Carolina. Dr. Drummond programmed the Parks and Fuller-Battese methods. Professor Gallant, who is with North Carolina State University, Raleigh, NC, programmed the Da Silva method and generously contributed his time to the support of PROC TSCSREG after Dr. Drummond's death.

The version of PROC TSCSREG documented here was produced by converting the older SUGI Supplemental Library version of the procedure to Version 6 of SAS software. This conversion work was performed by SAS Institute, which now supports the procedure. Although several features were added during the conversion (such as the OUTEST= option, ID statement, and BY statement), credit for the statistical aspects and general design of the TSCSREG procedure belongs to Dr. Drummond and Professor Gallant.

References

Da Silva, J.G.C. (1975), "The Analysis of Cross-Sectional Time Series Data," Ph.D. dissertation, Department of Statistics, North Carolina State University.

SAS Institute Inc. (1979), SAS Technical Report S-106, *TSCSREG: A SAS Procedure for the Analysis of Time-Series Cross-Section Data*, Cary, NC: SAS Institute Inc.

Feige, E.L. (1964), *The Demand for Liquid Assets: A Temporal Cross-Section*

Analysis, Englewood Cliffs: Prentice-Hall.

Fuller, W.A. and Battese, G.E. (1974), "Estimation of Linear Models with Crossed-Error Structure," *Journal of Econometrics*, 2, 67–78.

Greene, W.H. (1990), *Econometric Analysis*, New York: Macmillan Publishing Company.

Hsiao, C. (1986), *Analysis of Panel Data*, Cambridge: Cambridge University Press.

Judge, G.G.; Griffiths, W.E.; Hill, R.C.; Lütkepohl, H.; and Lee, T.C. (1985), *The Theory and Practice of Econometrics*, Second Edition, New York: John Wiley & Sons, Inc.

Kmenta, J. (1971), *Elements of Econometrics*, New York: MacMillan Publishing Company, Inc.

Maddala, G.S. (1977), *Econometrics*, New York: McGraw-Hill Co.

Parks, R.W. (1967), "Efficient Estimation of a System of Regression Equations when Disturbances Are Both Serially and Contemporaneously Correlated," *Journal of the American Statistical Association*, 62, 500–509.

Searle S.R. (1971), "Topics in Variance Component Estimation," *Biometrics*, 26, 1–76.

Seely, J. (1969), "Estimation in Finite-Dimensional Vector Spaces with Application to the Mixed Linear Model," Ph.D. dissertation, Department of Statistics, Iowa State University.

Seely, J. (1970a), "Linear Spaces and Unbiased Estimation," *Annals of Mathematical Statistics*, 41, 1725–1734.

Seely, J. (1970b), "Linear Spaces and Unbiased Estimation–Application to the Mixed Linear Model," *Annals of Mathematical Statistics*, 41, 1735–1748.

Seely, J. and Soong, S. (1971), "A Note on MINQUE's and Quadratic Estimability," Corvallis, Oregon: Oregon State University.

Seely, J. and Zyskind, G. (1971), "Linear Spaces and Minimum Variance Unbiased Estimation," *Annals of Mathematical Statistics*, 42, 691–703.

Zellner, A. (1962), "An Efficient Method of Estimating Seemingly Unrelated Regressions and Tests for Aggregation Bias," *Journal of the American Statistical Association*, 57, 348–368.

Chapter 19
The X11 Procedure

Chapter Table of Contents

Chapter 19
The X11 Procedure

Overview

The X11 procedure, an adaptation of the U.S. Bureau of the Census X-11 Seasonal Adjustment program, seasonally adjusts monthly or quarterly time series. The procedure makes additive or multiplicative adjustments and creates an output data set containing the adjusted time series and intermediate calculations.

The X11 procedure also provides the X-11-ARIMA method developed by Statistics Canada. This method fits an ARIMA model to the original series, then uses the model forecast to extend the original series. This extended series is then seasonally adjusted by the standard X-11 seasonal adjustment method. The extension of the series improves the estimation of the seasonal factors and reduces revisions to the seasonally adjusted series as new data becomes available.

Seasonal adjustment of a series is based on the assumption that seasonal fluctuations can be measured in the original series, $O_t, t = 1, ..., n$, and separated from trend cycle, trading-day, and irregular fluctuations. The seasonal component of this time series, S_t, is defined as the intrayear variation that is repeated constantly or in an evolving fashion from year to year. The trend cycle component, C_t, includes variation due to the long-term trend, the business cycle, and other long-term cyclical factors. The trading-day component, D_t, is the variation that can be attributed to the composition of the calendar. The irregular component, I_t, is the residual variation. Many economic time series are related in a multiplicative fashion ($O_t = S_t C_t D_t I_t$). A seasonally adjusted time series, $C_t I_t$, consists of only the trend cycle and irregular components.

Getting Started

The most common use of the X11 procedure is to produce a seasonally adjusted series. Eliminating the seasonal component from an economic series facilitates comparison among consecutive months or quarters. A plot of the seasonally adjusted series is often more informative about trends or location in a business cycle than a plot of the unadjusted series.

The following example shows how to use PROC X11 to produce a seasonally adjusted series, $C_t I_t$ from an original series $O_t = S_t C_t D_t I_t$.

In the multiplicative model, the trend cycle component C_t keeps the same scale as the original series O_t, while S_t, D_t, and I_t vary around 1.0. In all printed tables and in the output data set, these latter components are expressed as percentages, and, thus, will vary around 100.0 (in the additive case, they vary around 0.0).

The naming convention used in PROC X11 for the tables follows the original U.S. Bureau of the Census X-11 Seasonal Adjustment program specification; refer to the U.S. Bureau of the Census, 1967, and "Printed Output" later in this chapter.

The tables corresponding to parts A - C are intermediate calculations. The final estimates of the individual components are found in the D tables: table D10 contains the final seasonal factors, table D12 contains the final trend cycle, and table D13 contains the final irregular series. If you are primarily interested in seasonally adjusting a series without consideration of intermediate calculations or diagnostics, you only need to look at table D11, the final seasonally adjusted series.

Basic Seasonal Adjustment

Suppose you have monthly retail sales data starting in September, 1978, in a SAS data set named SALES. At this point, you do not suspect that any calendar effects are present, and there are no prior adjustments that need to be made to the data.

In this simplest case, you need only specify the DATE= variable in the MONTHLY statement, which associates a SAS date value to each observation. To see the results of the seasonal adjustment, you must request table D11, the final seasonally adjusted series, in a TABLES statement.

```
data sales;
   input sales @@;
   date = intnx( 'month', '01sep78'd, _n_-1 );
   format date monyy.;
   cards;
run;

proc x11 data=sales;
   monthly date=date;
   var sales;
   tables d11;
run;
```

```
                       X11 Procedure


                X-11 Seasonal Adjustment Program
                    U. S. Bureau of the Census
               Economic Research and Analysis Division
                        November 1, 1968

      The X-11 program is divided into seven major parts.
        Part          Description
         A.   Prior adjustments, if any
         B.   Preliminary estimates of irregular component weights
                 and regression trading day factors
         C.   Final estimates of above
         D.   Final estimates of seasonal, trend-cycle and
                 irregular components
         E.   Analytical tables
         F.   Summary measures
         G.   Charts


      Series - SALES
          Period covered - 9/1978 to 8/1990

          Type of run multiplicative seasonal adjustment.
```

```
        No printout.   No charts.
Sigma limits for graduating extreme values are 1.5 and 2.5
   Irregular values out side of 2.5-sigma limits are excluded
        from trading day regression
```

```
                        X11 Procedure

                Seasonal Adjustment of - SALES


D11 Final Seasonally Adjusted Series
Year      JAN       FEB       MAR       APR       MAY       JUN

1978       .         .         .         .         .         .
1979    124.935   126.533   125.282   125.650   127.754   129.648
1980    128.734   139.542   143.726   143.854   148.723   144.530
1981    176.329   166.264   167.433   167.509   173.573   175.541
1982    186.747   202.467   192.024   202.761   197.548   206.344
1983    233.109   223.345   218.179   226.389   224.249   227.700
1984    238.261   239.698   246.958   242.349   244.665   247.005
1985    275.766   282.316   294.169   285.034   294.034   296.114
1986    325.471   332.228   330.401   330.282   333.792   331.349
1987    363.592   373.118   368.670   377.650   380.316   376.297
1988    370.966   384.743   386.833   405.209   380.840   389.132
1989    428.276   418.236   429.409   446.467   437.639   440.832
1990    480.631   474.669   486.137   483.140   481.111   499.169

Avg     277.735   280.263   282.435   286.358   285.354   288.638

Total:  40324  Mean:  280.03  S.D.:   111.31
```

```
                        X11 Procedure

                Seasonal Adjustment of - SALES


D11 Final Seasonally Adjusted Series
Year      JUL       AUG       SEP       OCT       NOV       DEC      Total

1978       .         .       123.507   125.776   124.735   129.870   503.887
1979    127.880   129.285   126.562   134.905   133.356   136.117   1548
1980    140.120   153.475   159.281   162.128   168.848   165.159   1798
1981    179.301   182.254   187.448   197.431   184.341   184.304   2142
1982    211.690   213.691   214.204   218.060   228.035   240.347   2514
1983    222.045   222.127   222.835   212.227   230.187   232.827   2695
1984    251.247   253.805   264.924   266.004   265.366   277.025   3037
1985    294.196   309.162   311.539   319.518   318.564   323.921   3604
1986    337.095   341.127   346.173   350.183   360.792   362.333   4081
1987    379.668   375.607   374.257   372.672   368.135   364.150   4474
1988    385.479   377.147   397.404   403.156   413.843   416.142   4711
1989    450.103   454.176   460.601   462.029   427.499   485.113   5340
1990    485.370   485.103      .         .         .         .      3875

Avg     288.683   291.413   265.728   268.674   268.642   276.442

Total:  40324  Mean:  280.03  S.D.:   111.31
```

Figure 19.1. Basic Seasonal Adjustment

You can compare the original series, table B1, and the final seasonally adjusted series, table D11 by plotting them together. These tables are requested and named in the OUTPUT statement.

```
title 'Monthly Retail Sales Data (in $1000)';

proc x11 data=sales noprint;
   monthly date=date;
   var sales;
   output out=out b1=sales d11=adjusted;
run;

symbol1 i=join v='plus';
symbol2 i=join v='diamond';
legend1 label=none value=('original' 'adjusted');

proc gplot data=out;
   plot sales    * date = 1
        adjusted * date = 2 / overlay legend=legend1;
run;
```

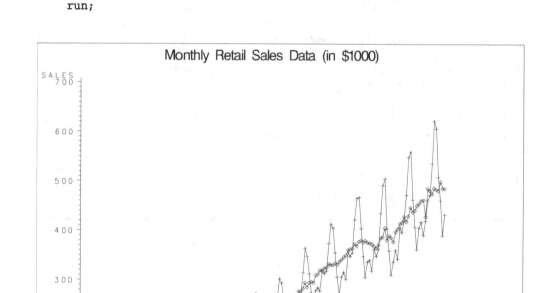

Figure 19.2. Plot of Original and Seasonally Adjusted Data

X-11-ARIMA

An inherent problem with the X-11 method is the revision of the seasonal factor estimates as new data become available. The X-11 method uses a set of centered moving averages to estimate the seasonal components. These moving averages apply symmetric weights to all observations except those at the beginning and end of the series, where asymmetric weights have to be applied. These asymmetric weights can cause poor estimates of the seasonal factors, which then can cause large revisions when new data become available.

While large revisions to seasonally adjusted values are not common, they can happen. When they do happen, they undermine the credibility of the X-11 method.

A method to address this problem was developed at Statistics Canada (Dagum, 1980, 1982b). This method, known as X-11-ARIMA, applies an ARIMA model to the original data (after adjustments, if any) to forecast the series one or more years. This extended series is then seasonally adjusted, allowing symmetric weights to be applied to the end of the original data. This method was tested against a large number of Canadian economic series and was found to greatly reduce the amount of revisions as new data were added.

The X-11-ARIMA method is available in PROC X11 through the use of the ARIMA statement. The ARIMA statement extends the original series either with a user-specified ARIMA model or by an automatic selection process in which the best model from a set of five predefined ARIMA models is used.

The following example illustrates the use of the ARIMA statement. The ARIMA statement does not contain a user-specified model, so the best model is chosen by the automatic selection process. Forecasts from this best model are then used to extend the original series by one year. The partial listing below shows parameter estimates and model diagnostics for the ARIMA model chosen by the automatic selection process.

```
proc x11 data=sales;
   monthly date=date;
   var sales;
   arima;
run;
```

```
                         X11 Procedure

                 Seasonal Adjustment of - SALES


              Conditional Least Squares Estimation

                                 Approx.
        Parameter    Estimate    Std Error   T Ratio   Lag
        MU          0.0001728    0.0009596    0.18     0
        MA1,1        0.37400     0.08934      4.19     1
        MA1,2        0.02315     0.08922      0.26     2
        MA2,1        0.57279     0.07908      7.24    12

        Constant Estimate  = 0.00017279

        Variance  Estimate = 0.00143131
        Std Error Estimate = 0.03783264
        AIC                = -482.24122*
        SBC                = -470.74043*
        Number of Residuals=       131
        * Does not include log determinant.



   Criteria Summary for Model 2: (0,1,2)(0,1,1)s, Log Transform

   Box-Ljung Chi-square: 22.03 with 21 df Prob= 0.40
   (Criteria prob > 0.05)
   Test for over-differencing: sum of MA parameters = 0.57
   (must be < 0.90)
   MAPE - Last Three Years:     2.84 (Must be < 15.00 %)
        - Last Year:            3.04
        - Next to Last Year:    1.96
        - Third from Last Year: 3.51
```

Figure 19.3. X-11-ARIMA Model Selection

Table D11 (final seasonally adjusted series) is now constructed using symmetric weights on observations at the end of the actual data. This should result in better estimates of the seasonal factors and, thus, smaller revisions in D11 as more data become available.

Syntax

The X11 procedure uses the following statements:

PROC X11 *options*;
　MONTHLY *options*;
　QUARTERLY *options*;
　ARIMA *options*;
　MACURVES *option*;
　OUTPUT OUT= *dataset options*;
　PDWEIGHTS *option*;
　TABLES *tablenames*;
　VAR *variables*;
　BY *variables*;
　ID *variables*;

Either the MONTHLY or QUARTERLY statement must be specified, depending on the type of time series data you have. The PDWEIGHTS and MACURVES statements can be used only with the MONTHLY statement. The TABLES statement controls the printing of tables, while the OUTPUT statement controls the creation of the OUT= data set.

Functional Summary

The statements and options controlling the X11 procedures are summarized in the following table.

Description	Statement	Option
Data Set Options		
specify input data set	PROC X11	DATA=
write the trading-day regression results to an output data set	PROC X11	OUTTDR=
write the stable seasonality test results to an output data set	PROC X11	OUTSTB=
write table values to an output data set	OUTPUT	OUT=
add extrapolated values to the output data set	ARIMA	OUTEX
add year-ahead estimates to the output data set	PROC X11	YRAHEADOUT

Description	Statement	Option
Printing Control Options		
suppress all printed output	PROC X11	NOPRINT
suppress all printed ARIMA output	ARIMA	NOPRINT
print all ARIMA output	ARIMA	PRINTALL
print selected tables and charts	TABLES	
print selected groups of tables	MONTHLY	PRINTOUT=
	QUARTERLY	PRINTOUT=
print selected groups of charts	MONTHLY	CHARTS=
	QUARTERLY	CHARTS=
print first pass tables	ARIMA	PRINTFP
specify number of decimals for printed tables	MONTHLY	NDEC=
	QUARTERLY	NDEC=
Date Information Options		
specify a SAS date variable	MONTHLY	DATE=
	QUARTERLY	DATE=
specify the beginning date	MONTHLY	START=
	QUARTERLY	START=
specify the ending date	MONTHLY	END=
	QUARTERLY	END=
specify beginning year for trading-day regression	MONTHLY	TDCOMPUTE=
Declaring the Role of Variables		
specify BY-group processing	BY	
specify the variables to be seasonally adjusted	VAR	
specify identifying variables	ID	
specify the prior monthly factor	MONTHLY	PMFACTOR=
Controlling the table computations		
use additive adjustment	MONTHLY	ADDITIVE
	QUARTERLY	ADDITIVE
specify seasonal factor moving average length	MACURVES	
specify the extreme value limit for trading-day regression	MONTHLY	EXCLUDE=
specify the lower bound for extreme irregulars	MONTHLY	FULLWEIGHT=
	QUARTERLY	FULLWEIGHT=
specify the upper bound for extreme irregulars	MONTHLY	ZEROWEIGHT=
	QUARTERLY	ZEROWEIGHT=
include the length-of-month in trading-day regression	MONTHLY	LENGTH

Description	Statement	Option
specify trading-day regression action	MONTHLY	TDREGR=
compute summary measure only	MONTHLY	SUMMARY
	QUARTERLY	SUMMARY
modify extreme irregulars prior to trend cycle estimation	MONTHLY	TRENDADJ
	QUARTERLY	TRENDADJ
specify moving average length in trend cycle estimation	MONTHLY	TRENDMA=
	QUARTERLY	TRENDMA=
specify weights for prior trading-day factors	PDWEIGHTS	

PROC X11 Statement

PROC X11 *options*;

The following options can appear in the PROC X11 statement:

DATA= *SAS-data-set*

specifies the input SAS data set used. If it is omitted, the most recently created SAS data set is used.

OUTEXTRAP

adds the extra observations used in ARIMA processing to the output data set.

When ARIMA forecasting/backcasting is requested, extra observations are appended on the ends of the series, and the calculations are carried out on this extended series. The appended observations are not normally written to the OUT= data set. However, if OUTEXTRAP is specified, these extra observations are written to the output data set. If a DATE= variable is specified in the MONTHLY/QUARTERLY statement, the date variable is extrapolated to identify forecasts/backcasts. The OUTEXTRAP option can be abbreviated as OUTEX.

NOPRINT

suppresses any printed output. The NOPRINT option overrides any PRINTOUT= option, any CHARTS= option, any TABLES statement, and any output associated with the ARIMA statement.

OUTSTB= *SAS-data-set*

Specifies the output data set to store the stable seasonality test results (table D8). All the information in the analysis of variance table associated with the stable seasonality test is contained in the variables written to this data set. See "OUTSTB Data Set" later in this chapter for details.

OUTTDR= *SAS-data-set*

Specifies the output data set to store the trading-day regression results (tables B15 and C15). All the information in the analysis of variance table associated with the trading-day regression is contained in the variables written to this data set. This option is valid only when the TDREGR= option specifies a value of AD-JUST, TEST, or PRINT in the MONTHLY statement. See "OUTTDR Data Set" later in this chapter for details.

YRAHEADOUT

adds one-year-ahead forecast values to the output data set for tables C16, C18 and D10. The original purpose of this option was to avoid recomputation of the seasonal adjustment factors when new data became available. While computing costs were an important factor when the X-11 method was developed, this is no longer the case and this option is obsolete. See "The YRAHEADOUT Option" later in this chapter for details.

ARIMA Statement

ARIMA *options*;

The ARIMA statement applies the X-11-ARIMA method to the series specified in the VAR statement. This method uses an ARIMA model estimated from the original data to extend the series one or more years. The ARIMA statement options control the ARIMA model used and the estimation, forecasting, and printing of this model.

There are two ways of obtaining an ARIMA model to extend the series. A model can be given explicitly with the MODEL= and TRANSFORM= options. Alternatively, the best fitting model from a set of five predefined models is found automatically whenever the MODEL= option is absent. See "Details of Model Selection" later in this chapter for details.

BACKCAST= *n*

Specifies the number of years to backcast the series. The default is BACKCAST= 0. See "Effect of Backcast and Forecast Length" later in this chapter for details.

CHICR= *value*

specifies the criteria for the significance level for the Box-Ljung chi-square test for lack of fit when testing the five predefined models. The default is CHICR= 0.05. The CHICR= option values must be between 0.01 and 0.90. The hypothesis being tested is that of model adequacy. Nonrejection of the hypothesis is evidence for an adequate model. Making the CHICR= value smaller makes it easier to accept the model. See "Criteria Details" in the section "Details of Model Selection" later in this chapter for further details on the CHICR= option.

CONVERGE= *value*

specifies the convergence criterion for the estimation of an ARIMA model. The default value is 0.001. The CONVERGE= value must be positive.

FORECAST= *n*

Specifies the number of years to forecast the series. The default is FORECAST= 1. See "Effect of Backcast and Forecast Length" later in this chapter for details.

MAPECR= *value*

specifies the criteria for the Mean Absolute Percent Error (MAPE) when testing the five predefined models. A small MAPE value is evidence for an adequate model; a large MAPE value results in the model being rejected. The MAPECR= value is the boundary for acceptance/rejection. Thus, a larger MAPECR= value makes it easier for a model to pass the criteria. The default is MAPECR= 15. The MAPECR= option values must be between 1 and 100. See "Criteria Details" in the section "Details of Model Selection" later in this chapter for further details on the MAPECR= option.

MAXITER= *n*

specifies the maximum number of iterations in the estimation process. MAXITER must be between 1 and 60; the default value is 15.

METHOD= CLS
METHOD= ULS
METHOD= ML

specifies the estimation method. ML requests maximum likelihood, ULS requests unconditional least-squares, and CLS requests conditional least-squares. METHOD=CLS is the default. The maximum likelihood estimates are more expensive to compute than the conditional least-squares estimates. In some cases, however, they may be preferable. For further information on the estimation methods, see "Estimation Details" in Chapter 3, "The ARIMA Procedure."

MODEL= (P= *n1* **Q=** *n2* **SP=** *n3* **SQ=** *n4* **DIF=** *n5* **SDIF=** *n6* **)**

specifies the ARIMA model. The AR and MA orders are given by P=$n1$ and Q=$n2$, respectively, while the seasonal AR and MA orders are given by SP=$n3$ and SQ=$n4$. The lag corresponding to seasonality is determined by the MONTHLY or QUARTERLY statement. Similarly, differencing and seasonal differencing are given by DIF=$n5$ and SDIF=$n6$, respectively.

For example

```
arima model=( p=2 q=1 sp=1 dif=1 sdif=1 );
```

specifies a $(2,1,1)(1,1,0)s$ model, where s, the seasonality is either 12 (monthly) or 4 (quarterly). More examples of the MODEL= syntax are given in the section "Details of Model Selection" later in this chapter.

NOPRINT

suppresses the normal printout generated by the ARIMA statement. Note that the effect of NOPRINT in the ARIMA statement is different from NOPRINT in the PROC statement, since the former only affects ARIMA output.

OVDIFCR= *value*

specifies the criteria for the over-differencing test when testing the five predefined models. When the MA parameters in one of these models sum to a number close to 1.0, this is an indication of over-parameterization and the model is rejected. The OVDIFCR= value is the boundary for this rejection; values greater than this value fail the over-differencing test. A larger OVDIFCR= value makes it easier for a model to pass the criteria. The default is OVDIFCR= 0.90. The OVDIFCR= option values must be between 0.80 and 0.99. See "Criteria Details" in the section "Details of Model Selection" later in this chapter for further details on the OVDIFCR= option.

PRINTALL

provides the same output as the default printing for all models fit and, in addition, prints an estimation summary and chi-square statistics for each model fit. See "Printed Output" later in this chapter for details.

PRINTFP

prints the results for the initial pass of X11 made to exclude trading-day effects. This option has an effect only when the TDREGR= option specifies a value of ADJUST, TEST, or PRINT. In these cases, an initial pass of the standard X11 method is required to get rid of calendar effects before doing any ARIMA estimation. Usually, this first pass is not of interest, and, by default, no tables are printed. However, specifying PRINTFP in the ARIMA statement causes any tables printed in the final pass to also be printed for this initial pass.

TRANSFORM= (LOG) | LOG
TRANSFORM= (*constant* ** *power*)

The ARIMA statement in PROC X11 allows certain transformations on the series before estimation. The specified transformation is applied only to a user-specified model. If the TRANSFORM= option is specified without the MODEL= option, the transformation request is ignored and a warning is printed.

The LOG transformation requests that the natural log of the series be used for estimation. The resulting forecasted values are transformed back to the original scale.

A general power transformation of the form $\mathbf{X}_t \rightarrow (\mathbf{X}_t + a)^b$ is obtained by specifying

```
transform= ( a ** b )
```

If the constant a is not specified, it is assumed to be 0. The specified ARIMA model is then estimated using the transformed series. The resulting forecasted values are transformed back to the original scale.

BY Statement

BY *variables*;

A BY statement can be used with PROC X11 to obtain separate analyses on observations in groups defined by the BY variables. When a BY statement appears, the procedure expects the input DATA= data set to be sorted in order of the BY variables.

ID Statement

ID *variables*;

If you are creating an output data set, use the ID statement to put values of the ID variables, in addition to the table values, into the output data set. The ID statement has no effect when an output data set is not created. If the DATE= variable is specified in the MONTHLY or QUARTERLY statement, this variable is included automatically in the OUTPUT data set. If no DATE= variable is specified, the variable _DATE_ is added.

The date variable (or _DATE_) values outside the range of the actual data (from ARIMA forecasting, backcasting, or from the YRAHEADOUT option) are extrapolated, while all other ID variables are missing.

MACURVES Statement

MACURVES *month= option* ...;

The MACURVES statement specifies the length of the moving average curves for estimating the seasonal factors for any month. This statement can be used only with monthly time series data.

The *month=option* specifications consist of the month name (or the first three letters of the month name), an equal sign, and one of the following option values:

'3'   specifies a three-term moving average for the month

'3X3'   specifies a three-by-three moving average

'3X5'   specifies a three-by-five moving average

'3X9'   specifies a three-by-nine moving average

STABLE   specifies a stable seasonal factor (average of all values for the month)

For example, the statement

```
macurves jan='3' feb='3x3' march='3x5' april='3x9';
```

specifies

- a three-term moving average to estimate seasonal factors for January

- a 3x3 (a three-term moving average of a three-term moving average) for February

- a 3x5 (a three-term moving average of a five-term moving average) for March

- a 3x9 (a three-term moving average of a nine-term moving average) for April

The numeric values used for the weights of the various moving averages and a discussion of the derivation of these weights are given in U.S. Bureau of Census (1967). A general discussion of moving average weights is given in Dagum (1985).

If the specification for a month is omitted, the X11 procedure uses a three-by-three moving average for the first estimate of each iteration and a three-by-five average for the second estimate.

MONTHLY Statement

MONTHLY *options*;

The MONTHLY statement must be used when the input data to PROC X11 are monthly time series. The MONTHLY statement specifies options that determine the computations performed by PROC X11 and what is included in its output. Either the DATE= or START= option must be used.

The following options can appear in the MONTHLY statement:

ADDITIVE

performs additive adjustments. If the ADDITIVE option is omitted, PROC X11 performs multiplicative adjustments.

CHARTS= STANDARD
CHARTS= FULL
CHARTS= NONE

specifies the charts produced by the procedure. The default is CHARTS=STANDARD, which specifies 12 monthly seasonal charts and a trend cycle chart. If you specify CHARTS=FULL (or CHARTS=ALL), the procedure prints additional charts of irregular and seasonal factors. To print no charts, specify CHARTS=NONE.

The TABLES statement can also be used to specify particular monthly charts to be printed. If no value for the CHARTS= option is specified, and a TABLES statement is specified, the TABLES statement overrides the default value of CHARTS=STANDARD; that is, no charts (or tables) are printed except those specified in the TABLES statement. However, if both the CHARTS= option and a TABLES statement are specified, the charts corresponding to the CHARTS= option and those requested by the TABLES statement are printed.

For example, suppose you wanted only charts G1, the final seasonally adjusted series and trend cycle, and G4, the final irregular and final modified irregular series. You would specify the following statements:

```
monthly date=date;
tables g1 g4;
```

DATE= *variable*

specifies a variable that gives the date for each observation. The starting and ending dates are obtained from the first and last values of the DATE= variable, which must contain SAS date values. The procedure checks values of the DATE= variable to ensure that the input observations are sequenced correctly. This variable is automatically added to the OUTPUT= data set, if one is requested, and extrapolated if necessary. If the DATE= option is not specified, the START= option must be specified.

The DATE= option and the START= and END= options can be used in combination to subset a series for processing. For example, suppose you have 12 years of monthly data (144 observations, no missing values) beginning in January, 1970 and ending in December, 1981, and you only want to seasonally adjust six years beginning in January of 1974. Specifying

```
monthly date=date start=jan74 end=dec79;
```

would seasonally adjust only this subset of the data. If, instead, you wanted to adjust the last eight years of data, only the START= option is needed:

```
monthly date=date start=jan74;
```

END= *mmmyy*

specifies that only the part of the input series ending with the month and year given be adjusted (for example, END=DEC70). See the DATE=*variable* option for using the START= and END= options to subset a series for processing.

EXCLUDE= *value*

excludes from the trading-day regression any irregular values that are more than *value* standard deviations from the mean. The value of the EXCLUDE= option must be between .1 and 9.9, with the default value being 2.5.

FULLWEIGHT= *value*

assigns weights to irregular values based on their distance from the mean in standard deviation units. The weights are used for estimating seasonal and trend cycle components. Irregular values less than the FULLWEIGHT= option value (in standard deviation units) are assigned full weights of 1, values that fall between the limits specified by the ZEROWEIGHT= and FULLWEIGHT= options are assigned weights linearly graduated between 0 and 1, and values greater than the limit specified by the ZEROWEIGHT= option are assigned a weight of 0.

For example, if ZEROWEIGHT=2 and FULLWEIGHT=1, a value 1.3 standard deviations from the mean is assigned a graduated weight. The value of the FULL-WEIGHT= option must be between .1 and 9.9 but must be less than the value of the ZEROWEIGHT= option. The default is FULLWEIGHT=1.5.

LENGTH

includes length-of-month allowance in computing trading-day factors. If this option is omitted, length-of-month allowances are included with the seasonal factors.

NDEC= *n*

specifies the number of decimal places shown on the printed tables on the listing. This option has no effect on the precision of the variables values in the output data set.

PMFACTOR= *variable*

specifies a variable containing the prior monthly factors. Use this option if you have previous knowledge of monthly adjustment factors. The PMFACTOR= option can be used to

- adjust the level of all or part of a series with discontinuities

- adjust for the influence of holidays that fall on different dates from year to year, such as the effect of Easter on certain retail sales

- adjust for unreasonable weather influence on series, such as housing starts

- adjust for changing starting dates of fiscal years (for budget series) or model years (for automobiles)

- adjust for temporary dislocating events, such as strikes

See "Prior Daily Weights and Trading-Day Regression" in the section "Details" later in this chapter for details and examples using the PMFACTOR= option.

PRINTOUT= STANDARD | LONG | FULL | NONE

specifies the tables to be printed by the procedure. If the PRINTOUT=STANDARD option is specified, between 17 and 27 tables are printed, depending on the other options that are specified. PRINTOUT=LONG prints between 27 and 39 tables, and PRINTOUT=FULL prints between 44 and 59 tables. Specifying PRINTOUT=NONE results in no tables being printed; however, charts are still printed. The default is PRINTOUT=STANDARD.

The TABLES statement can also be used to specify particular monthly tables to be printed. If no PRINTOUT= option is specified, and a TABLES statement is specified, the TABLES statement overrides the default value of PRINTOUT=STANDARD; that is, no tables (or charts) are printed except those specified in the TABLES statement. However, if both the PRINTOUT= option and a TABLES statement are specified, the tables corresponding to the PRINTOUT= option and those requested by the TABLES statement are printed.

START= *mmmyy*

adjusts only the part of the input series starting with the specified month and year. When the DATE= option is not used, the START= option gives the year and month of the first input observation (for example, START=JAN66). A value for the START= option must be specified if no DATE= option is specified. If the START= option is specified (and no DATE= option is specified), and an OUT= data set is requested, a variable named _DATE_ is added to the data set, giving the date value for each observation. See the DATE= option for using the START= and END= options to subset a series.

SUMMARY

specifies that the data are already seasonally adjusted and the procedure is to produce summary measures. If the SUMMARY option is omitted, the X11 procedure performs seasonal adjustment of the input data before calculating summary measures.

TDCOMPUTE= *year*

uses the part of the input series beginning with January of the specified year to derive trading-day weights. If this option is omitted, the entire series is used.

TDREGR= NONE | PRINT | ADJUST | TEST

specifies the treatment of trading-day regression. The value NONE omits the computation of the trading-day regression. The value PRINT computes and prints the trading-day regressions but does not adjust the series. The value ADJUST computes and prints the trading-day regression and adjusts the irregular components to obtain preliminary weights. The value TEST adjusts the final series if the trading-day regression estimates explain significant variation on the basis of an *F*-test (or residual trading-day variation if prior weights are used). The default is TDREGR=NONE.

See "Prior Daily Weights and Trading-Day Regression" in the section "Details" later in this chapter for details and examples using the TDREGR= option.

If ARIMA processing is requested, any value of TDREGR other than the default TDREGR=NONE will cause PROC X11 to perform an initial pass (see the section "Details" later in this chapter and the PRINTFP option in the section "ARIMA Statement" earlier in this chapter).

TRENDADJ

modifies extreme irregular values prior to computing the trend cycle estimates in the first iteration. If the TRENDADJ option is omitted, the trend cycle is computed without modifications for extremes.

TRENDMA= 9 | 13 | 23.

specifies the number of terms in the moving average to be used by the procedure in estimating the variable trend cycle component. The value of the TRENDMA= option must be 9, 13, or 23. If the TRENDMA= option is omitted, the procedure selects an appropriate moving average. For information concerning the number of terms in the moving average, see U.S. Bureau of the Census (1967).

ZEROWEIGHT= *value*

assigns weights to irregular values based on their distance from the mean in standard deviation units. The weights are used for estimating seasonal and trend cycle components. Irregular values beyond the standard deviation limit specified in the ZEROWEIGHT= option are assigned zero weights. Values that fall between the two limits (ZEROWEIGHT= and FULLWEIGHT=) are assigned weights linearly graduated between 0 and 1. For example, if ZEROWEIGHT=2 and FULLWEIGHT=1, a value 1.3 standard deviations from the mean would be assigned a graduated weight. The ZEROWEIGHT=value must be between .1 and 9.9 but must be greater than the FULLWEIGHT=value. The default is ZEROWEIGHT=2.5.

The ZEROWEIGHT option can be used in conjunction with the FULLWEIGHT= option to adjust outliers from a monthly or quarterly series. See Example 19.3 later in this chapter for an illustration of this use.

OUTPUT Statement

OUTPUT OUT= *SAS-data-set tablename= var1 var2 ... ;*

The OUTPUT statement creates an output data set containing specified tables. The data set is named by the OUT= option.

OUT= *SAS-data-set*

If OUT= is omitted, the SAS System names the new data set using the DATA*n* convention.

For each table to be included in the output data set, write the X11 table identification keyword, an equal sign, and a list of new variable names.

tablename = var1 var2 ...

The *tablename* keywords that can be used in the OUTPUT statement are listed in "Printed Output" later in this chapter. The following is an example of a VAR and OUTPUT statement.

```
var z1 z2 z3;
output out=out_x11  b1=s  d11=w x y;
```

The variable s contains the table B1 values for the variable z1, while the table D11 values for variables z1, z2, and z3 are contained in variables w, x, and y respectively. As this example shows, the list of variables following a *tablename=* keyword can be shorter than the VAR variable list.

In addition to the variables named by *tablename=var1 var2 ...*, the ID variables, and BY variables, the output data set contains a date identifier variable. If the DATE= option is specified in the MONTHLY or QUARTERLY statement, the DATE= variable is the date identifier. If no DATE= is specified, a variable named _DATE_ is the date identifier.

PDWEIGHTS Statement

PDWEIGHTS *day= w ... ;*

The PDWEIGHTS statement can be used to specify one to seven daily weights. The statement can only be used with monthly series. These weights are used to compute prior trading-day factors, which are then used to adjust the original series prior to the seasonal adjustment process. Only relative weights are needed; the X11 procedure adjusts the weights so that they sum to 7.0. The weights can also be corrected by the procedure on the basis of estimates of trading-day variation from the input data.

See "Prior Daily Weights and Trading-Day Regression" in the section "Details" later in this chapter for details and examples using the PDWEIGHTS statement.

Each *day=w* option specifies a weight (*w*) for the named day. The *day* can be any day, Sunday through Saturday. The *day* keyword can be the full spelling of the day or the three letter abbreviation. For example, SATURDAY=1.0 and SAT=1.0 are both valid. The weights *w* must be a numeric value between 0.0 and 10.0.

The following is an example of a PDWEIGHTS statement:

```
pdweights sun=.2 mon=.9 tue=1 wed=1 thu=1 fri=.8 sat=.3;
```

Any number of days can be specified with one PDWEIGHTS statement. The default weight value for any day that is not specified is 0. If you do not use a PDWEIGHTS statement, the program computes daily weights if TDREGR=ADJUST is specified. Refer to U.S. Bureau of the Census (1967) for details.

QUARTERLY Statement

QUARTERLY *options*;

The QUARTERLY statement must be used when the input data are quarterly time series. This statement includes options that determine the computations performed by the procedure and what is in the printed output. The DATE= option or the START= option must be used.

The following options can appear in the QUARTERLY statement:

ADDITIVE

performs additive adjustments. If this option is omitted, the procedure performs multiplicative adjustments.

CHARTS= STANDARD
CHARTS= FULL
CHARTS= NONE

specifies the charts to be produced by the procedure. The default value is CHARTS=STANDARD, which specifies four quarterly seasonal charts and a trend cycle chart. If you specify CHARTS=FULL (or CHARTS=ALL), the procedure prints additional charts of irregular and seasonal factors. To print no charts, specify CHARTS=NONE. The TABLES statement can also be used to specify particular charts to be printed. The presence of a TABLES statement overrides the default value of CHARTS=STANDARD, that is, if a TABLES statement is specified, and no CHARTS=option is specified, no charts (nor tables) are printed except those specified in the TABLES statement. However, if both the CHARTS= option and a TABLES statement are specified, the charts corresponding to the CHARTS= option and those requested by the TABLES statement are printed.

For example, suppose you only wanted charts G1, the final seasonally adjusted series and trend cycle, and G4, the final irregular and final modified irregular series. This is accomplished by specifying the following statements:

```
quarterly date=date;
tables g1 g4;
```

DATE= *variable*

specifies a variable that gives the date for each observation. The starting and ending dates are obtained from the first and last values of the DATE= variable, which must contain SAS date values. The procedure checks values of the DATE= variable to ensure that the input observations are sequenced correctly. This variable is automatically added to the OUTPUT= data set if one is requested, and extrapolated if necessary. If the DATE= option is not specified, the START= option must be specified.

The DATE= option and the START= and END= options can be used in combination to subset a series for processing. For example, suppose you have a series with 10 years of quarterly data (40 observations, no missing values) beginning in '70Q1' and ending in '79Q4', and you only want to seasonally adjust four years beginning in 74Q1 and ending in 77Q4. Specifying

```
quarterly date=variable start='74q1' end='77q4';
```

seasonally adjusts only this subset of the data. If, instead, you want to adjust the last six years of data, only the START= option is needed:

```
quarterly date=variable start='74q1';
```

END= '*yyQq*'

specifies that only the part of the input series ending with the quarter and year given be adjusted (for example, END='73Q4'). The specification must be enclosed in quotes and *q* must be 1, 2, 3, or 4. See the DATE= *variable* option for using the START= and END= options to subset a series.

FULLWEIGHT= *value*

assigns weights to irregular values based on their distance from the mean in standard deviation units. The weights are used for estimating seasonal and trend cycle components. Irregular values less than the value of the FULLWEIGHT= option (in standard deviation units) are assigned full weights of 1, values that fall between the limits specified by the ZEROWEIGHT= and FULLWEIGHT= options are assigned weights linearly graduated between 0 and 1, and values greater than the limit specified by the ZEROWEIGHT= option are assigned a weight of 0.

For example, if ZEROWEIGHT=2 and FULLWEIGHT=1, a value 1.3 standard deviations from the mean would be assigned a graduated weight. The default is FULLWEIGHT=1.5.

NDEC= *n*

specifies the number of decimal places shown on the output tables. This option has no effect on the precision of the variables in the output data set.

PRINTOUT= STANDARD
PRINTOUT= LONG
PRINTOUT= FULL
PRINTOUT= NONE

specifies the tables to print. If PRINTOUT=STANDARD is specified, between 17 and 27 tables are printed, depending on the other options that are specified. PRINTOUT=LONG prints between 27 and 39 tables, and PRINTOUT=FULL prints between 44 and 59 tables. Specifying PRINTOUT=NONE results in no tables being printed. The default is PRINTOUT=STANDARD.

The TABLES statement can also specify particular quarterly tables to be printed. If no value for the PRINTOUT= option is specified, and a TABLES statement is specified, the TABLES statement overrides the default value, PRINTOUT=STANDARD; that is, no tables (or charts) are printed except those specified in the TABLES statement. However, if both the PRINTOUT= option and a TABLES statement are specified, the tables corresponding to the PRINTOUT= option and those requested by the TABLES statement are printed.

START= '*yyQq*'

adjusts only the part of the input series starting with the quarter and year given. When the DATE= option is not specified, the START= option gives the year and quarter of the first input observation (for example, START='67Q1'). The specification must be enclosed in quotes, and *q* must be 1, 2, 3, or 4. The START= option must be specified if the DATE= option is not specified. If the START= option is specified (and no DATE= option is specified), and an OUTPUT= data set is requested, a variable named _DATE_ is added to the data set, giving the date value for a given observation. See the DATE= option for using the START= and END= options to subset a series.

SUMMARY

specifies that the input is already seasonally adjusted and that the procedure is to produce summary measures. If this option is omitted, the procedure performs seasonal adjustment of the input data before calculating summary measures.

TRENDADJ

modifies extreme irregular values prior to computing the trend cycle estimates. If this option is omitted, the trend cycle is computed without modification for extremes.

TRENDMA= 5 | 7.

specifies the number of terms in the moving average to be used by the procedure in estimating the variable trend cycle component. The value of the TRENDMA= option must be 5 or 7. If the TRENDMA= option is omitted, the procedure selects an appropriate moving average. For information concerning the number of terms in the moving average, see U.S. Bureau of the Census (1967).

ZEROWEIGHT= *value*

assigns weights to irregular values based on their distance from the mean in standard deviation units. The weights are used for estimating seasonal and trend cycle components. Irregular values beyond the standard deviation limit specified in the ZEROWEIGHT= option are assigned 0 weights. Values that fall between the two limits (of the ZEROWEIGHT= and FULLWEIGHT= options) are assigned weights linearly graduated between 0 and 1. For example, if ZEROWEIGHT=2 and FULLWEIGHT=1, a value 1.3 standard deviations from the mean would be assigned a graduated weight. The default is ZEROWEIGHT=2.5. The ZEROWEIGHT= option can be used in conjunction with the FULLWEIGHT= option to adjust outliers from a monthly or quarterly series. See Example 19.3 later in this chapter for an illustration of this use.

TABLES Statement

TABLES *tablenames*;

The TABLES statement prints the tables specified in addition to the tables that are printed as a result of the PRINTOUT= option in the MONTHLY or QUARTERLY statement. Table names are listed in Table 19.3 later in this chapter.

To print only selected tables, omit the PRINTOUT= option in the MONTHLY or QUARTERLY statement and list the tables to be printed in the TABLES statement.

For example, to print only the final seasonal factors and final seasonally adjusted series, use the statement

```
tables d10 d11;
```

VAR Statement

VAR *variables*;

The VAR statement is used to specify the variables in the input data set that are to be analyzed by the procedure. Only numeric variables can be specified. If the VAR statement is omitted, all numeric variables are analyzed except those appearing in a BY or ID statement or the variable named in the DATE= option in the MONTHLY or QUARTERLY statement.

Details

Historical Development of X-11

This section briefly describes the historical development of the standard X-11 seasonal adjustment method and the later development of the X-11-ARIMA method. Most of the following discussion is based on a comprehensive article by Bell and Hillmer (1984), which describes the history of X-11 and the justification of using seasonal adjustment methods, such as X-11, given the current availability of time series software. For further discussions on statistical problems associated with the X-11 method, refer to Ghysels (1990).

Seasonal adjustment methods began development in the 1920s and 1930s before there were suitable analytic models available and before electronic computing devices were developed. The lack of any suitable model led to methods that worked the same for any series, that is, methods that were not model-based and that could be applied to any series. Experience with economic series had shown that a given mathematical form could adequately represent a time series only for a fixed length; as more data were added, the model became inadequate. This suggested an approach using moving averages.

The basic method was to break up an economic time series into long-term trend, long-term cyclical movements, seasonal movements, and irregular fluctuations.

Early investigators found that it was not possible to uniquely decompose the trend and cyclical components. Thus, these two were grouped together; the resulting component is usually referred to as the "trend cycle component."

It was also found that estimating seasonal components in the presence of trend produced biased estimates of the seasonal components, but, at the same time, estimating trend in the presence of seasonality was difficult. This eventually lead to the iterative approach used in the X-11 method.

Two other problems were encountered by early investigators. First, some economic series appears to have changing or evolving seasonality. Secondly, moving averages were very sensitive to extreme values. The estimation method used in the X-11 method allows for evolving seasonal components. For the second problem, the X-11 method uses repeated adjustment of extreme values.

All of these problems encountered in the early investigation of seasonal adjustment methods suggested the use of moving averages in estimating components. Even with the use of moving averages instead of a model-based method, massive amounts of hand calculations were required. Only a small number of series could be adjusted, and little experimentation could be done to evaluate variations on the method.

With the advent of electronic computing in the 1950s, work on seasonal adjustment methods proceeded rapidly. These methods still used the framework previously described; variants of these basic methods could now be easily tested against a large number of series.

Much of the work was done by Julian Shiskin and others at the U.S. Bureau of the Census beginning in 1954 and culminated, after a number of variants, into the *X-11 Variant of the Census Method II Seasonal Adjustment Program*, which PROC X11 implements.

References for this work during this period include Shiskin and Eisenpress (1957), Shiskin (1958), and Marris (1960). The authoritative documentation for the X-11 Variant is in U.S. Bureau of the Census (1967). This document is not equivalent to a program specification; however the FORTRAN code implementing the X-11 Variant is in the public domain. A less detailed description of the X-11 Variant is given in U.S. Bureau of the Census (1969).

Development of the X-11-ARIMA Method

The X-11 method uses symmetric moving averages in estimating the various components. At the end of the series, however, these symmetric weights cannot be applied. Either asymmetric weights have to be used, or some method of extending the series must be found.

While various methods of extending a series have been proposed, the most important method to date has been the X-11-ARIMA method developed at Statistics Canada. This method uses Box-Jenkins ARIMA models to extend the series.

The Time Series Research and Analysis Division of Statistic Canada investigated 174 Canadian economic series and found five ARIMA models out of twelve that fit the majority of series well and reduced revisions for the most recent months. References giving details of various aspects of the X-11-ARIMA methodology include Dagum (1980, 1982a, 1982b, 1983, 1988); Laniel (1985); Lothian and Morry (1978); and Huot, Chui, Higginson, and Gait (1986).

Differences between X11ARIMA/88 and PROC X11

The original implementation of the X-11-ARIMA method was by Statistics Canada in 1980 (Dagum, 1980; X11ARIMA/80), with later changes and enhancements made in 1988 (Dagum, 1988; X11ARIMA/88). The calculations performed by PROC X11 differ from those in X11ARIMA/88, which result in differences in the final component estimates provided by these implementations.

There are three areas where Statistic Canada made changes to the original X-11 seasonal adjustment method in developing X11ARIMA/80 (refer to Monsell, 1984). These are

- selection of extreme values
- replacement of extreme values
- generation of seasonal and trend cycle weights

These changes have not been implemented in the current version of PROC X11. Thus the procedure produces identical results with previous versions of PROC X11 in the absence of an ARIMA statement.

Additional differences can result from the ARIMA estimation. X11ARIMA/88 uses Conditional Least Squares (CLS), while CLS, Unconditional Least Squares (ULS) and Maximum Likelihood (ML) are all available in PROC X11 by using the METHOD= option in the ARIMA statement. Generally, parameters estimates will differ for the different methods.

Implementation of the X-11 Seasonal Adjustment Method

The following steps describe the analysis of a monthly time series using multiplicative adjustments. Additional steps used by the X-11-ARIMA method are also indicated. Equivalent descriptions apply for an additive model by replacing *divide* by *subtract* where applicable.

In the multiplicative adjustment, the original series $\mathbf{O}_t$ is assumed to be of the form

$$\mathbf{O}_t = \mathbf{C}_t\, \mathbf{S}_t\, \mathbf{I}_t\, \mathbf{P}_t\, \mathbf{D}_t$$

where $\mathbf{C}_t$ is the trend cycle component, $\mathbf{S}_t$ is the seasonal component, $\mathbf{I}_t$ is the irregular component, $\mathbf{P}_t$ is the prior monthly factors component, and $\mathbf{D}_t$ is the trading-day component.

The trading-day component can be further factored as

$$\mathbf{D}_t = \mathbf{D}_{r,t}\, \mathbf{D}_{tr,t}$$

where $\mathbf{D}_{tr,t}$ are the trading-day factors derived from the prior daily weights, and $\mathbf{D}_{r,t}$ are the residual trading-day factors estimated from the trading-day regression.

Additional steps when using the X-11-ARIMA method

The X-11-ARIMA method consists of extending a given series by an ARIMA model and applying the usual X-11 seasonal adjustment method to this extended series. Thus, in the simplest case in which there are no prior factors or calendar effects in the series, the ARIMA model selection, estimation, and forecasting are performed, and the resulting extended series goes through the standard X-11 steps described later in the section "The Standard X-11 Seasonal Adjustment Method."

If prior factor or calendar effects are present, they must be eliminated from the series before the ARIMA estimation is done because these effects are not stochastic.

Prior factors, if present, are removed first. Calendar effects represented by prior daily weights are then removed. If there are no further calendar effects, the adjusted series is extended by the ARIMA model, and this extended series goes through the standard X-11 steps without repeating the removal of prior factors and calendar effects from prior daily weights.

If further calendar effects are present, a trading-day regression must be performed. In this case, it is necessary to go through an initial pass of the X-11 steps to obtain a final trading-day adjustment. In this initial pass, the series, adjusted for prior factors and prior daily weights, goes through the standard X-11 steps. At the conclusion of these steps, a final series adjusted for prior factors and all calendar effects is available. This adjusted series is then extended by the ARIMA model, and this extended series goes through the standard X-11 steps again without repeating the removal of prior factors and calendar effects from prior daily weights and trading-day regression.

The Standard X-11 Seasonal Adjustment Method

The following steps comprise the standard X-11 seasonal adjustment method. These steps are applied to the original data or the original data extended by an ARIMA model.

1. In step 1, the data are read, ignoring missing values until the first nonmissing value is found. If prior monthly factors are present, the procedure reads prior monthly $\mathbf{P}_t$ factors and divides them into the original series to obtain $\mathbf{O}_t / \mathbf{P}_t = \mathbf{C}_t \mathbf{S}_t \mathbf{I}_t \mathbf{D}_{tr,t} \mathbf{D}_{r,t}$. Seven daily weights can be specified to develop monthly factors to adjust the series for trading-day variation, $\mathbf{D}_{tr,t}$; these factors are then divided into the original or prior adjusted series to obtain $\mathbf{C}_t \mathbf{S}_t \mathbf{I}_t \mathbf{D}_{r,t}$.

2. In steps 2, 3, and 4, three iterations are performed, each of which provides estimates of the seasonal $\mathbf{S}_t$, trading-day $\mathbf{D}_{r,t}$, trend cycle $\mathbf{C}_t$, and irregular components $\mathbf{I}_t$. Each iteration refines estimates of the extreme values in the irregular components. After extreme values are identified and modified, final estimates of the seasonal component, seasonally adjusted series, trend cycle, and irregular components are produced.

   Step 2 consists of three substeps:

   a. During the first iteration, a centered, 12-term moving average is applied to the original series $\mathbf{O}_t$ to provide a preliminary estimate $\widetilde{\mathbf{C}}_t$ of the trend cycle curve $\mathbf{C}_t$. This moving average combines 13 (a 2 term moving average of a 12-term moving average) consecutive monthly values, removing the $\mathbf{S}_t$ and $\mathbf{I}_t$. Next, it obtains a preliminary estimate $\widehat{\mathbf{S}_t \mathbf{I}_t}$ by

$$\widehat{\mathbf{S}_t \mathbf{I}_t} = \frac{\mathbf{O}_t}{\widetilde{\mathbf{C}}_t}$$

   b. A moving average is then applied to the $\widehat{\mathbf{S}_t \mathbf{I}_t}$ to obtain an estimate $\hat{\mathbf{S}}_t$ of the seasonal factors. $\widehat{\mathbf{S}_t \mathbf{I}_t}$ is then divided by this estimate to obtain an estimate $\hat{\mathbf{I}}_t$ of the irregular component. Next, a moving standard deviation is calculated from the irregular component and is used in assigning a weight to each monthly value for measuring its degree of extremeness. These weights are used to modify extreme values in $\widehat{\mathbf{S}_t \mathbf{I}_t}$. New seasonal factors are estimated by applying a moving average to the modified value of $\widehat{\mathbf{S}_t \mathbf{I}_t}$. A preliminary seasonally adjusted series is obtained by dividing the original series by these new seasonal factors. A second estimate of the trend cycle is obtained by applying a weighted moving average to this seasonally adjusted series.

  c. The same process is used to obtain second estimates of the seasonally adjusted series and improved estimates of the irregular component. This irregular component is again modified for extreme values and then used to provide estimates of trading-day factors and refined weights for the identification of extreme values.

3. Using the same computations, a second iteration is performed on the original series that has been adjusted by the trading-day factors and irregular weights developed in the first iteration. The second iteration produces final estimates of the trading-day factors and irregular weights.

4. A third, and final, iteration is performed using the original series that has been adjusted for trading-day factors and irregular weights computed during the second iteration. During the third iteration, PROC X11 develops final estimates of seasonal factors, the seasonally adjusted series, the trend cycle, and the irregular components. The procedure computes summary measures of variation and produces a moving average of the final adjusted series.

Data Requirements

The input data set must contain either quarterly or monthly time series, and the data must be in chronological order. For the standard X-11 method, there must be at least three years of observations (12 for quarterly time series or 36 for monthly) in the input data sets or in each BY group in the input data set if a BY statement is used.

For the X-11-ARIMA method, there must be at least five years of observations (20 for quarterly time series or 60 for monthly) in the input data sets or in each BY group in the input data set if a BY statement is used.

Missing Values

Missing values at the beginning of a series to be adjusted are skipped. Processing starts with the first nonmissing value and continues until the end of the series or until another missing value is found.

Missing values are not allowed for the DATE= variable. The procedure terminates if missing values are found for this variable.

Missing values found in the PMFACTOR= variable are replaced by 100 for the multiplicative model (default) and by 0 for the additive model.

Missing values can occur in the output data set. If the time series specified in the OUTPUT statement is not computed by the procedure, the values of the corresponding variable are missing. If the time series specified in the OUTPUT statement is a moving average, the values of the corresponding variable are missing for the first n and last n observations, where n depends on the length of the moving average. Additionally, if the time series specified is an irregular component modified for extremes, only the modified values are given, and the remaining values are missing.

Prior Daily Weights and Trading-Day Regression

Suppose that a detailed examination of retail sales at ZXY Company indicates that certain days of the week have higher sales. In particular, Thursday, Friday and Saturday have approximately double the number of sales as Monday, Tuesday, and Wednesday, and no sales occur on Sunday. This means that months with five Saturdays would have higher sales than months with only four Saturdays.

This phenomenon is called a *calendar effect*; it can be handled in PROC X11 by using the PDWEIGHTS (Prior Daily WEIGHTS) statement or the TDREGR= option (Trading-Day Regression). The PDWEIGHTS statement and the TDREGR= option can be used separately or together.

If the relative weights are known (as in the preceding), it is appropriate to use the PDWEIGHTS statement. If further residual calendar variation is present, TDREGR=ADJUST should also be used. If you know that a calendar effect is present, but know nothing about the relative weights, use TDREGR=ADJUST without a PDWEIGHTS statement.

In this example, it is assumed that the calendar variation is due to both prior daily weights and residual variation. Thus, both a PDWEIGHTS statement and TDREGR=ADJUST are specified.

Note that only the relative weights are needed; in the actual computations, PROC X11 normalizes the weights to sum to 7.0. If a day of the week is not present in the PDWEIGHTS statement, it is given a value of 0. Thus, SUN=0 is not needed.

```
proc x11 data=sales;
   monthly date=date tdregr=adjust;
   var sales;
   tables a1 a4 b15 b16 C14 C15 c18 d11;
   pdweights mon=1 tue=1 wed=1 thu=2 fri=2 sat=2;
   output out=x11out a1=a1 a4=a4 b1=b1 c14=c14
                     c16=c16 c18=c18 d11=d11;
run;
```

Tables of interest include A1, A4, B15, B16, C14, C15, C18, and D11. Table A4 contains the adjustment factors derived from the prior daily weights, table C14 contains the extreme irregular values excluded from trading-day regression, table C15 contains the trading day-regression results, table C16 contains the monthly factors derived from the trading-day regression, and table C18 contains the final trading-day factors derived from the combined daily weights. Finally, table D11 contains the final seasonally adjusted series.

Adjustment for Prior Factors

Suppose now that a strike at ZXY Company during July and August of 1988 caused sales to decrease an estimated 50%. Since this is a one-time event with a known cause, it is appropriate to prior adjust the data to reflect the effects of the strike. This is done in PROC X11 through the use of PMFACTOR= *varname* (Prior Monthly Factor) in the MONTHLY statement.

In the following example, the PMFACTOR= variable is named PMF. Since the estimate of the decrease in sales is 50%, PMF has a value of 50.0 for the observations corresponding to July and August, 1988, and a value of 100.0 for the remaining observations.

This prior adjustment to SALES is performed by computing (SALES/PMF) * 100.0. A value of 100.0 for PMF leaves SALES unchanged, while a value of 50.0 for PMF doubles SALES. This value is the estimate of what SALES would have been without the strike. The following example shows how this prior adjustment is accomplished:

```
data sales; set sales;
   if '01jul88'd <= date <= '01aug88'd then pmf = 50;
   else pmf = 100;
run;

proc x11 data=sales;
   monthly date=date pmfactor=pmf;
   var sales;
   tables a1 a2 a3 d11;
   output out=x11out a1=a1 a2=a2 a3=a3 d11=d11;
run;
```

Table A2 contains the prior monthly factors (the values of PMF), and Table A3 contains the prior adjusted series.

The YRAHEADOUT Option

For monthly data, the YRAHEADOUT option affects only tables C16 (regression trading-day adjustment factors), C18 (trading-day factors from combined daily weights), and D10 (seasonal factors). For quarterly data, only D10 is affected. Variables for all other tables have missing values for the forecast observations. The forecast values for a table are included only if that table is specified in the OUTPUT statement.

Tables C16 and C18 are calendar effects that are extrapolated by calendar composition. These factors are independent of the data once trading-day weights have been calculated. Table D10 is extrapolated by a linear combination of past values. If N is the total number of nonmissing observations for the analysis variable, this linear combination is given by

$$\mathbf{D10}_t = \tfrac{1}{2}(3 \times \mathbf{D10}_{t-12} - \mathbf{D10}_{t-24}), \qquad t = N + 1, ..., N + 12$$

If the input data are monthly time series, 12 extra observations are added to the end of the output data set. (If a BY statement is used, 12 extra observations are added to the end of each BY group.) If the input data are quarterly time series, 4 extra observations are added to the end of the output data set. (If a BY statement is used, four extra observations are added to each BY group.)

The DATE= variable (or _DATE_) is extrapolated for the extra observations generated by the YRAHEADOUT option, while all other ID variables will have missing values.

If ARIMA processing is requested, and if both the OUTEXTRAP and YRAHEAD-

OUT options are specified in the PROC X11 statement, an additional 12 (4) observations are added to the end of output data set for monthly (quarterly) data after the ARIMA forecasts, using the same linear combination of past values as before.

Effect of Backcast and Forecast Length

Based on a number of empirical studies, (Dagum 1982a, 1982b, 1982c; Dagum and Laniel, 1987) one year of forecasts minimized revisions when new data become available. Two and three years of forecasts showed only small gains.

Backcasting improves seasonal adjustment but introduces permanent revisions at the beginning of the series and also at the end for series of length 8, 9 or 10 years. For series shorter than 7 years, the advantages of backcasting outweigh the disadvantages (Dagum, 1988).

Other studies (Pierce, 1980; Bobbit and Otto, 1990; and Buszuwski, 1987) suggest full forecasting, that is, using enough forecasts to allow symmetric weights for the seasonal moving averages for the most current data. For example, if a 3x9 seasonal moving average was specified for one or more months using the MACURVES statement, five years of forecasts would be required. This is because the seasonal moving averages are performed on calendar months separately, and the 3x9 is an eleven-term centered moving average, requiring five observations before and after the current observation. Thus, the following statement would require five additional December values to compute the seasonal moving average.

```
macurves dec='3x9';
```

Details of Model Selection

If an ARIMA statement is present, but no value for the MODEL= option is specified, PROC X11 estimates and forecasts five predefined models and selects the best. This section describes the details of the selection criteria and the selection process.

The five predefined models used by PROC X11 are the same as those used by X11ARIMA/88 from Statistics Canada. These particular models, shown in Table 19.1, were chosen on the basis of testing a large number of economics series (Dagum, 1988) and should provide reasonable forecasts for most economic series.

Table 19.1.   Five Predefined Models

Model #	Specification	Multiplicative	Additive
1	(0,1,1)(0,1,1)s	log transform	no transform
2	(0,1,2)(0,1,1)s	log transform	no transform
3	(2,1,0)(0,1,1)s	log transform	no transform
4	(0,2,2)(0,1,1)s	log transform	no transform
5	(2,1,2)(0,1,1)s	no transform	no transform

The selection process proceeds as follows. The five models are estimated and one-step-ahead forecasts are produced in the order shown in Table 19.1. As each model is estimated, the following three criteria are checked:

- The Mean Absolute Percent Error (MAPE) for the last three years of the series must be less than 15 %.

- The significance probability for the Box-Ljung Chi-square for up to lag 24 for monthly (8 for quarterly) must greater than 0.05.

- The over-differencing criteria must not exceed 0.9.

The description of these three criteria are given in "Criteria Details" later in this chapter. The default values for these criteria are those used by X11ARIMA/88 from Statistics Canada; these defaults can be changed by the MAPECR=, CHICR= and OVDIFCR= options.

A model that fails any one of these three criteria is excluded from further consideration. In addition, if the ARIMA estimation fails for a given model, a warning is issued, and the model is excluded. The final set of all models considered are those that pass all three criteria and are estimated successfully. From this set, the model with the smallest MAPE for the last three years is chosen.

If all five models fail, ARIMA processing is skipped for the variable being processed, and the standard X-11 seasonal adjustment is performed. A note is written to the log with this information.

The chosen model is then used to forecast the series one or more years (determined by the FORECAST= option in the ARIMA statement). These forecasts are appended on the original data (or the prior and calendar-adjusted data).

If a value for the BACKCAST= option is specified, the chosen model form is used, but the parameters are reestimated using the reversed series. Using these parameters, the reversed series is forecasted for the number of years specified by the BACKCAST= option. These forecasts are then reversed and appended to the beginning of the original series, or the prior and calendar-adjusted series, to produce the backcasts.

Note that the final selection rule (the smallest MAPE using the last three years) emphasizes the quality of the forecasts at the end of the series. This is consistent with the purpose of the X-11-ARIMA methodology, namely, to improve the estimates of seasonal factors and, thus, minimize revisions to recent past data as new data become available.

Criteria Details

The Mean Absolute Percent Error (MAPE)

For the MAPE criteria testing, only the last three years of the original series (or prior and calendar adjusted series) are used in computing the MAPE.

Let $y_t, t = 1, \ldots, n$ be the last three years of the series, and denote its one-step-ahead forecast by $\hat{y}_t$, where $n = 36$ for a monthly series, and $n = 12$ for a quarterly series.

With this notation, the MAPE criteria is computed as

$$MAPE = \frac{100}{n} \sum_{t=1}^{n} \frac{|y_t - \hat{y}_t|}{|y_t|}$$

Box-Ljung Chi-Square

The Box-Ljung Chi-Square is a lack of fit test using the model residuals. This test statistic is computed using the Ljung-Box formula

$$\chi_m^2 = n(n+2) \sum_{k=1}^{m} \frac{r_k^2}{n-k}$$

where n is the number of residuals that can be computed for the time series, and $m = 24$, for monthly series, or $m = 8$, for quarterly series.

$$r_k = \frac{\sum_{t=1}^{n-k} a_t \, a_{t+k}}{\sum_{t=1}^{n} a_t^2}$$

where the a_t's are the residual sequence. This formula has been suggested by Ljung and Box as yielding a better fit to the asymptotic chi-square distribution. Some simulation studies of the finite sample properties of this statistic are given by Davies, Triggs, and Newbold (1977) and by Ljung and Box (1978).

Over-Differencing Test

From Table 19.1 you can se that all models have a single seasonal MA factor and at most two nonseasonal MA factors. Also, all models have seasonal and nonseasonal differencing. Consider model 2 applied to a monthly series y_t with $E(y_t) = \mu$:

$$(1 - B)(1 - B^{12})(y_t - \mu) = (1 - \theta_1 B - \theta_2 B^2)(1 - \theta_3 B^{12})a_t$$

If $\theta_3 = 1.0$, then the factors $(1 - \theta_3 B^{12})$ and $(1 - B^{12})$ will cancel, resulting in a lower-order model.

Similarly, if $\theta_1 + \theta_2 = 1.0$,

$$(1 - \theta_1 B - \theta_2 B^2) = (1 - B)(1 - \alpha B)$$

for some $\alpha \neq 0.0$. Again, this results in cancellation and a lower-order model.

Since the parameters are not exact, it is not reasonable to require that

$$\theta_3 < 1.0 \text{ and } \theta_1 + \theta_2 < 1.0$$

Instead, an approximate test is performed by requiring that

$$\theta_3 \leq 0.9 \text{ and } \theta_1 + \theta_2 \leq 0.9$$

The default value of 0.9 can be changed by the OVDIFCR= option. Similar reasoning applies to the other models.

ARIMA Statement Options for the Five Predefined Models

The following table lists the five predefined models and gives the equivalent MODEL= parameters in a PROC X11 ARIMA statement.

In all models except the fifth, a log transformation is performed before the ARIMA estimation for the multiplicative case; no transformation is performed for the additive case. For the fifth model, no transformation is done for either case.

The multiplicative case is assumed in the following table. The indicated seasonality *s* in the specification is either 12 (monthly), or 4 (quarterly). The MODEL statement assumes a monthly series.

Table 19.2. ARIMA Statements Options for Predefined Models

Model	ARIMA Statement Options
(0,1,1)(0,1,1)s	MODEL=(Q=1 SQ=1 DIF=1 SDIF=1) TRANSFORM=LOG
(0,1,2)(0,1,1)s	MODEL=(Q=2 SQ=1 DIF=1 SDIF=1) TRANSFORM=LOG
(2,1,0)(0,1,1)s	MODEL=(P=2 SQ=1 DIF=1 SDIF=1) TRANSFORM=LOG
(0,2,2)(0,1,1)s	MODEL=(Q=2 SQ=1 DIF=2 SDIF=1) TRANSFORM=LOG
(2,1,2)(0,1,1)s	MODEL=(P=2 Q=2 SQ=1 DIF=1 SDIF=1)

OUT= Data Set

The OUT= data set specified in the OUTPUT statement contains the BY variables, if any; the ID variables, if any; and the DATE= variable if the DATE= option is given, or _DATE_ if the DATE= option is not specified.

In addition, the variables specified by the options

tablename= var1 var2 ... varn

are placed in the OUT= data set. A list of tables available for monthly and quarterly series is given in Table 19.3.

OUTSTB= Data Set

The output data set produced by the OUTSTB= option of the PROC X11 statement contains the information in the analysis of variance on table D8 (Final Unmodified S-I Ratios). This analysis of variance, following table D8 in the printed output, tests for stable seasonality (refer to U.S. Bureau of the Census, 1967, Appendix A). The variables in this data are

- NAME, a character variable containing the name of each variable in the VAR list

- TABLE, a character variable specifying the table from which the analysis of variance is performed. When ARIMA processing is requested, and two passes of X11 are required (when TDREGR=PRINT, TEST, or ADJUST), Table D8 and the stable seasonality test are computed twice; once in the initial pass, then again in the final pass. Both of these computations are put in the OUTSTB data set and are identified by D18.1 or D18.2 respectively.

- SOURCE, a character variable corresponding to the source column in the analysis of variance table following Table D8

- SS, a numeric variable containing the sum of squares associated with the corresponding source term

- DF, a numeric variable containing the degrees of freedom associated with the corresponding source term

- MS, a numeric variable containing the mean square associated with the corresponding source term. MS is missing for the source term Total.

- F, a numeric variable containing the F statistic for the Between source term. F will be missing for all other source terms.

- PROBF, a numeric variable containing the significance level for the F statistic. PROBF is missing for the source term Total and Error.

OUTTDR= Data Set

The trading-day regression results (tables B15 and C15) are written to the OUTTDR= data set, which contains the following variables:

- NAME, a character variable containing the name of the VAR variable being processed

- TABLE, a character variable containing the name of the table. It can only have values B15 (Preliminary Trading-Day Regression) or C15 (Final Trading-Day Regression).

- _TYPE_, a character variable whose value distinguishes the three distinct table format types. These types are (a) the regression, (b) the listing of the standard error associated with length-of-month, and (c) the Analysis of Variance. The first seven observations in the OUTTDR data set correspond to the regression on days of the week; thus, the _TYPE_ variable is given the value REGRESS (day-of-week regression coefficient). The next four observations correspond to 31, 30, 29, and 28 day months and are given the value _TYPE_=LOM_STD (length-of-month standard errors). Finally the last three observations correspond to the analysis of variance table, and _TYPE_=ANOVA.

- PARM, a character variable, further identifying the nature of the observation. PARM is set to blank for the three _TYPE_=ANOVA observations.

- SOURCE, a character variable containing the source in the regression. This variable is missing for all _TYPE_=REGRESS and LOM_STD.

- CWGT, a numeric variable containing the combined trading-day weight (prior weight + weight found from regression). The variable is missing for all _TYPE_=LOM_STD and _TYPE_=ANOVA.

- PRWGT, a numeric variable containing the prior weight. The prior weight is 1.0 if values for the PDWEIGHTS= option are not specified. This variable is missing for all _TYPE_=LOM_STD and _TYPE_=ANOVA.

- COEFF, a numeric variable containing the calculated regression coefficient for the given day. This variable is missing for all _TYPE_=LOM_STD and _TYPE_=ANOVA.

- STDERR, a numeric variable containing the standard errors. For observations with _TYPE_=REGRESS, this is the standard error corresponding to the regression coefficient. For observations with _TYPE_=LOM_STD, this is standard error for the corresponding length-of-month. This variable is missing for all _TYPE_=ANOVA.

- T1, a numeric variable containing the *t* statistic corresponding to the test that the combined weight is different from the prior weight. This variable is missing for all _TYPE_=LOM_STD and _TYPE_=ANOVA.

- T2, a numeric variable containing the *t* statistic corresponding to the test that the combined weight is different from 1.0 . This variable is missing for all _TYPE_=LOM_STD and _TYPE_=ANOVA.

- PROBT1, a numeric variable containing the significance level for *t* statistic T1. The variable is missing for all _TYPE_=LOM_STD and _TYPE_=ANOVA.

- PROBT2, a numeric variable containing the significance level for *t* statistic T2. The variable is missing for all _TYPE_=LOM_STD and _TYPE_=ANOVA.

- SS, a numeric variable containing the sum of squares associated with the corresponding source term. This variable is missing for all _TYPE_=REGRESS and LOM_STD.

- DF, a numeric variable containing the degrees of freedom associated with the corresponding source term. This variable is missing for all _TYPE_=REGRESS and LOM_STD.

- MS, a numeric variable containing the mean square associated with the corresponding source term. This variable is missing for the source term Total and for all _TYPE_=REGRESS and LOM_STD.

- F, a numeric variable containing the *F* statistic for the Regression source term. The variable is missing for the source terms Total and Error, and for all _TYPE_=REGRESS and LOM_STD.

- PROBF, a numeric variable containing the significance level for the *F* statistic. This variable is missing for the source term Total and Error and for all _TYPE_=REGRESS and LOM_STD.

Printed Output

The output from PROC X11, both printed tables and the series written to the OUT= data set, depends on whether the data are monthly or quarterly. For the printed tables, the output depends further on the value of the PRINTOUT= option and the TABLE statement, along with other options specified.

The printed output is organized into tables identified by a part letter and a sequence number within the part. The seven major parts of the X11 procedure are as follows:

A   prior adjustments (optional)
B   preliminary estimates of irregular component weights and regression trading-day factors
C   final estimates of irregular component weights and regression trading-day factors
D   final estimates of seasonal, trend cycle, and irregular components
E   analytical tables
F   summary measures
G   charts

Table 19.3 describes the individual tables and charts. Most tables apply both to quarterly and monthly series. Those that apply only to a monthly time series are indicated by an M in the notes section, while P indicates the table is not a time series, and is only printed, not output to the OUT= data set.

Table 19.3. Table Names and Descriptions

Table	Description	Notes
A1	original series	M
A2	prior monthly adjustment factors	M
A3	original series adjusted for prior monthly factors	M
A4	prior trading-day adjustments	M
A5	prior adjusted or original series	M
A13	ARIMA forecasts	
A14	ARIMA backcasts	
A15	prior adjusted or original series extended by ARIMA backcasts, forecasts	
B1	prior adjusted or original series	
B2	trend cycle	
B3	unmodified seasonal-irregular (S-I) ratios	
B4	replacement values for extreme S-I ratios	
B5	seasonal factors	
B6	seasonally adjusted series	
B7	trend cycle	
B8	unmodified S-I ratios	
B9	replacement values for extreme S-I ratios	
B10	seasonal factors	
B11	seasonally adjusted series	
B13	irregular series	
B14	extreme irregular values excluded from trading-day regression	M
B15	preliminary trading-day regression	M,P
B16	trading-day adjustment factors	M
B17	preliminary weights for irregular components	
B18	trading-day factors derived from combined daily weights	M
B19	original series adjusted for trading-day and prior variation	M
C1	original series modified by preliminary weights and adjusted for trading-day and prior variation	

Table	Description	Notes
C2	trend cycle	
C4	modified S-I ratios	
C5	seasonal factors	
C6	seasonally adjusted series	
C7	trend cycle	
C9	modified S-I ratios	
C10	seasonal factors	
C11	seasonally adjusted series	
C13	irregular series	
C14	extreme irregular values excluded from trading-day regression	M
C15	final trading-day regression	M,P
C16	final trading-day adjustment factors derived from regression coefficients	M
C17	final weight for irregular components	
C18	final trading-day factors derived from combined daily weights	M
C19	original series adjusted for trading-day and prior variation	M
D1	original series modified for final weights and adjusted for trading-day and prior variation	
D2	trend cycle	
D4	modified S-I ratios	
D5	seasonal factors	
D6	seasonally adjusted series	
D7	trend cycle	
D8	final unmodified S-I ratios	
D9	final replacement values for extreme S-I ratios	
D10	final seasonal factors	
D11	final seasonally adjusted series	
D12	final trend cycle	
D13	final irregular series	
E1	original series with outliers replaced	
E2	modified seasonally adjusted series	
E3	modified irregular series	
E4	ratios of annual totals	P
E5	percent changes in original series	
E6	percent changes in final seasonally adjusted series	
F1	MCD moving average	
F2	summary measures	P
G1	chart of final seasonally adjusted series and trend cycle	P
G2	chart of S-I ratios with extremes, S-I ratios without extremes, and final seasonal factors	P
G3	chart of S-I ratios with extremes, S-I ratios without extremes, and final seasonal factors in calendar order	P
G4	chart of final irregular and final modified irregular series	P

The PRINTOUT= Option

The PRINTOUT= option controls printing for groups of tables. See the "TABLES Statement" earlier in this chapter for details on specifying individual tables. The following list gives the tables printed for each value of the PRINTOUT= option.

STANDARD (26 tables)   A1-A4, B1, C13-C19, D8-D13, E1-E6, F1, F2.

LONG (40 tables)   A1-A5, A13-A15, B1, B2, B7, B10, B13-B15, C1, C7, C10, C13-C19, D1, D7-D11, D13, E1-E6, F1, F2.

FULL (62 tables)   A1-A5, A13-A15, B1-B11, B13-B19, C1-C11, C13-C19, D1, D2, D4-D12, E1-E6, F1, F2.

The actual number of tables printed depends on the options and statements specified. If a table is not computed, it is not printed. For example, if TDREGR=NONE is specified, none of the tables associated with the trading-day are printed.

The CHARTS= Option

Of the four charts listed in Table 19.3, G1 and G2 are printed by default (CHARTS=STANDARD). Charts G3 and G4 are printed when CHARTS=FULL is specified. See the "TABLES Statement" earlier in this chapter for details on specifying individual charts.

Tables Written to the OUT= data set

All tables that are time series can be written to the OUT= data set. However, depending on the specified options and statements, not all tables are computed. When a table is not computed, but is requested in the OUTPUT statement, the resulting variable has all missing values.

For example, if the PMFACTOR= option is not specified, table A2 is not computed, and requesting this table in the OUTPUT statement results in the corresponding variable having all missing values.

The trading-day regression results, tables B15 and C15, although not written to the OUT= data set, can be written to an output data set; see the "OUTTDR= Data Set" earlier in this chapter for details.

Printed Output from the ARIMA Statement

The information printed by default for the ARIMA model includes the parameter estimates, their approximate standard errors, t ratios, variances, the standard deviation of the error term, and the AIC and SBC statistics for the model. In addition, a criteria summary for the chosen model is given that shows the values for each of the three test criteria and the corresponding critical values.

If the PRINTALL option is specified, a summary of the Nonlinear Estimation Optimization and a table of Box-Ljung Statistics is also produced. If the automatic model selection is used, this information is printed for each of the five predefined models. Lastly, a Model Selection Summary is printed, showing the final model chosen.

Examples

Example 19.1. Component Estimation - Monthly Data

This example computes and plot the final estimates of the individual components for a monthly series. In the first plot, Output 19.1.1, an overlaid plot of the original and seasonally adjusted data is produced. The trend in the data is more evident in the seasonally adjusted data than in the original data. This trend is even more clear in Output 19.1.3, the plot of Table D12, the trend cycle. Note that both the seasonal factors and the irregular factors vary around 100, while the trend cycle and the seasonally adjusted data are in the scale of the original data.

From Output 19.1.2, the seasonal component appears to be slowly increasing, while no apparent pattern exists for the irregular series in Output 19.1.4.

```
data sales;
   input sales @@;
   date = intnx( 'month', '01sep78'd, _n_-1 );
   format date monyy.;
   cards;
run;

proc x11 data=sales noprint;
   monthly date=date;
   var sales;
   tables b1 d11;
   output out=out b1=series d10=d10 d11=d11
                  d12=d12 d13=d13;
run;

symbol1 i=join v='plus';
symbol2 i=join v='diamond';
legend1 label=none value=('original' 'adjusted');

proc gplot data=out;
   plot series * date = 1 d11 * date = 2 / overlay legend=lengend1;
run;

symbol1 i=join v=diamond;

proc gplot data=out;
   plot ( d10 d12 d13 ) * date;
run;
```

Output 19.1.1. Plot of Original and Seasonally Adjusted Data

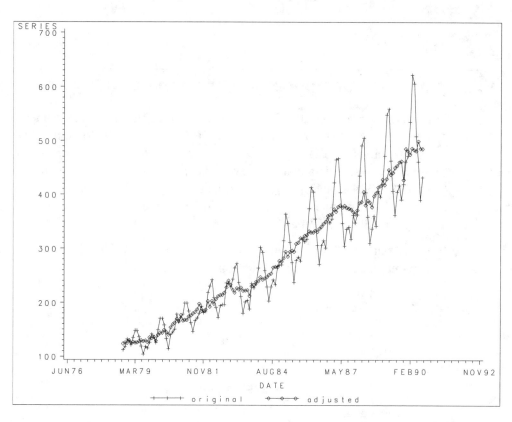
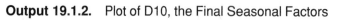

Output 19.1.2. Plot of D10, the Final Seasonal Factors

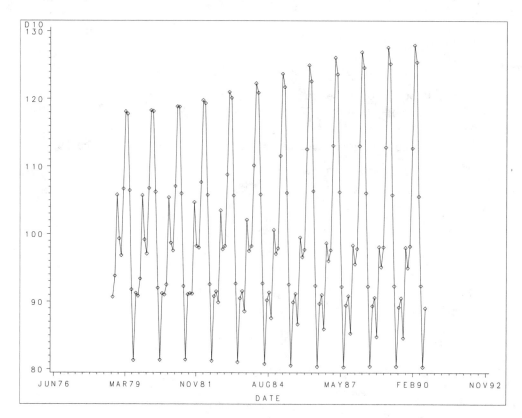

Example 19.1.   Component Estimation - Monthly Data   □ □ □   935

Output 19.1.3.   Plot of D12, the Final Trend Cycle

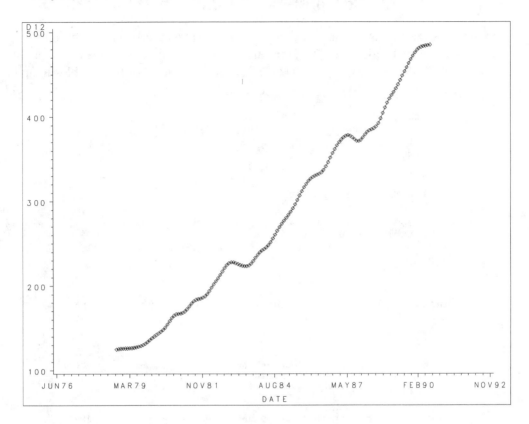

Output 19.1.4.   Plot of D13, the Final Irregular Series

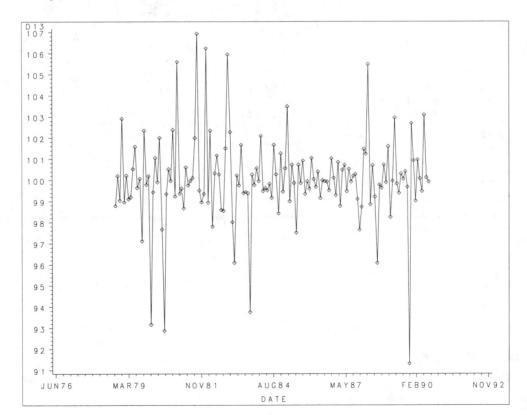

Example 19.2. Components Estimation - Quarterly Data

This example is similar to Example 19.1, except quarterly data are used. Tables B1, the original series, and D11, the final seasonally adjusted series, are printed by the TABLES statement. The OUTPUT statement writes the listed tables to an output data set.

```
data quarter;
    input date yyq4. +1 fy35rr 5.2;
    format date yyq4.;
cards;
run;

proc x11 data=quarter;
    var fy35rr;
    quarterly date=date;
    tables b1 d11;
    output out=out b1=b1 d10=d10 d11=d11 d12=d12 d13=d13;
run;
```

Output 19.2.1. Printed Output of PROC X11 Quarterly Example

```
                        X11 Procedure


                Quarterly Seasonal Adjustment Program
                     U. S. Bureau of the Census
                Economic Research and Analysis Division
                         November 1, 1968
             Series - FY35RR
                Period covered - 1st Quarter 1971 to 4th Quarter 1976

             Type of run multiplicative seasonal adjustment.
                 No printout.    No charts.
           Sigma limits for graduating extreme values are 1.5 and 2.5




B1 Original Series
Year      1st        2nd        3rd        4th       Total

1971     6.590      6.010      6.510      6.180     25.290
1972     5.520      5.590      5.840      6.330     23.280
1973     6.520      7.350      9.240     10.080     33.190
1974     9.910     11.150     12.400     11.640     45.100
1975     9.940      8.160      8.220      8.290     34.610
1976     7.540      7.440      7.800      7.280     30.060

Avg      7.670      7.617      8.335      8.300

Total:   191.53  Mean:   7.9804  S.D.:   1.9424
```

Example 19.2. Components Estimation - Quarterly Data □ □ □ 937

Output 19.2.1. (Continued)

```
                          X11 Procedure

                  Seasonal Adjustment of - FY35RR


D11 Final Seasonally Adjusted Series
Year      1st      2nd       3rd       4th      Total

1971     6.877    6.272     6.222     5.956     25.326
1972     5.762    5.836     5.583     6.089     23.271
1973     6.820    7.669     8.840     9.681     33.009
1974    10.370   11.655    11.855    11.160     45.040
1975    10.418    8.534     7.853     7.947     34.752
1976     7.901    7.793     7.444     6.979     30.116

Avg      8.025    7.960     7.966     7.969

Total:   191.51  Mean:   7.9797  S.D.:   1.9059
```

Example 19.3. Outlier Detection and Removal

PROC X11 can be used to detect and replace outliers in the irregular component of a monthly or quarterly series.

The weighting scheme used in measuring the extremeness of the irregulars is developed iteratively; thus, the statistical properties of this outlier adjustment method are unknown.

In this example, the data are simulated by generating a trend plus a random error. Two periods in the series were made extreme by multiplying one generated value by 2.0 and another by 0.10. The additive model is appropriate based on the way the data were generated. Note that the trend in the generated data was modeled automatically by the trend cycle component estimation.

The detection of outliers is accomplished by considering table D9, the final replacement values for extreme S-I ratios. This table indicates which observations had irregular component values more than FULLWEIGHT= standard deviation units from 0.0 (1.0 for the multiplicative model). The default value of the FULLWEIGHT= option is 1.5; a larger value would result in fewer observations being declared extreme.

In this example, FULLWEIGHT=3.0 is used to isolate the extreme inflated and deflated values generated in the DATA step. The value of the ZEROWEIGHT= option must be greater than the value of the FULLWEIGHT= option; it is given a value of 3.5.

A plot of the original and modified series, Output 19.3.2, shows that the deviation from the trend line for the modified series is greatly reduced compared with the original series.

```
data a;
   retain seed 99831;
   do kk = 1 to 48;
      x = kk + 100 + rannor( seed );
      date = intnx( 'month', '01jan70'd, kk-1 );
      if kk = 20 then x = 2 * x;
      else if kk = 30 then x = x / 10;
```

```
            output;
            end;
    run;

    proc x11 data=a;
       monthly date=date additive
               fullweight=3.0 zeroweight=3.5;
       var x;
       table d9;
       output out=b b1=original e1=e1;
    run;

    symbol1 i=join v=plus;
    symbol2 i=join v=diamond;
    legend1 label=none value=('unmodified' 'modified');

    proc gplot data= b;
       plot original * date = 1 e1 * date = 2 / overlay legend=legend1;
       format date monyy.;
    run;
```

Output 19.3.1.   Detection of Extreme Irregulars

```
                              X11 Procedure


    D9 Final Replacement Values for Extreme SI Ratios
    Year      JAN        FEB        MAR        APR        MAY        JUN

    1970       .          .          .          .          .          .
    1971       .          .          .          .          .          .
    1972       .          .          .          .          .       -10.671
    1973       .          .          .          .          .          .

    D9 Final Replacement Values for Extreme SI Ratios
    Year      JUL        AUG        SEP        OCT        NOV        DEC

    1970       .          .          .          .          .          .
    1971       .        11.180       .          .          .          .
    1972       .          .          .          .          .          .
    1973       .          .          .          .          .          .
```

Example 19.3. Outlier Detection and Removal □ □ □ 939

Output 19.3.2. Plot of Modified and Unmodified Values

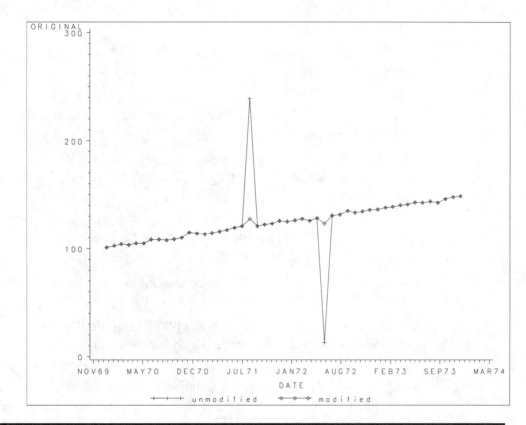

References

Bell, W.R. and Hillmer, S.C. (1984), "Issues Involved With the Seasonal Adjustment of Economic Time Series," *Journal of Business and Economic Statistics*, 2(4).

Bobbit, L.G. and Otto, M.C. (1990), "Effects of Forecasts on the Revisions of Seasonally Adjusted Data Using the X-11 Adjustment Procedure," *Proceedings of the Business and Economic Statistics Section of the American Statistical Association*, 449–453.

Buszuwski, J.A. (1987), "Alternative ARIMA Forecasting Horizons When Seasonally Adjusting Producer Price Data with X-11-ARIMA," *Proceedings of the Business and Economic Statistics Section of the American Statistical Association*, 488–493.

Cleveland, W.P. and Tiao, G.C. (1976), "Decomposition of Seasonal Time Series: A Model for Census X-11 Program," *Journal of the American Statistical Association*, 71(355).

Dagum, E.B. (1980), *The X-11-ARIMA Seasonal Adjustment Method*, Ottawa: Statistics Canada.

Dagum, E.B. (1982a), "Revisions of Time Varying Seasonal Filters," *Journal of Forecasting*, 1, 173–187.

Dagum, E.B. (1982b), "The Effects of Asymmetric Filters on Seasonal Factor Revision," *Journal of the American Statistical Association*, 77(380), 732–738.

Dagum, E.B. (1982c), "Revisions of Seasonally Adjusted Data Due to Filter Changes," *Proceedings of the Business and Economic Section, the American Statistical Association*, 39–45.

Dagum, E.B. (1983), "The X-11-ARIMA Seasonal Adjustment Method," Ottawa: Statistics Canada.

Dagum, E.B. (1985), "Moving Averages," in *Encyclopedia of Statistical Sciences*, eds. S. Kotz and N. L. Johnson, 5, New York: John Wiley & Sons, Inc.

Dagum, E.B. and Laniel, N. (1987), "Revisions of Trend Cycle Estimators of Moving Average Seasonal Adjustment Method," *Journal of Business and Economic Statistics*, 5(2), 177–189.

Dagum, E.B. (1988), *The X11ARIMA/88 Seasonal Adjustment Method*, Ottawa: Statistics Canada.

Davies, N., Triggs, C.M., and Newbold, P. (1977), "Significance Levels of the Box-Pierce Portmanteau Statistic in Finite Samples," *Biometrika*, 64, 517–522.

Ghysels, E. (1990), "Unit Root Tests and the Statistical Pitfalls of Seasonal Adjustment: The Case of U.S. Post War Real GNP," *Journal of Business and Economic Statistics*, 8(2), 145–152.

Hannan, E.J. (1963), "The Estimation of Seasonal Variation in Economic Time Series," *Journal of the American Statistical Association*, 58(301).

Huot, G.; Chui, L.; Higginson, J.; and Gait, N. (1986), "Analysis of Revisions in the Seasonal Adjustment of Data Using X11ARIMA Model-Based Filters," *International Journal of Forecasting*, 2, 217–229.

Laniel, N. (1985), "Design Criteria for the 13-term Henderson End-Weights," Working Paper, Methodology Branch, Ottawa: Statistics Canada.

Ljung, G.M. and Box, G.E.P. (1978), "On a Measure of Lack of Fit in Time Series Models," *Biometrika*, 65, 297–303.

Lothian, J. and Morry M. (1978), "Selection of Models for the Automated X-11-ARIMA Seasonal Adjustment Program," Ottawa: Statistics Canada.

Marris, S.N. (1960), "The Treatment of Moving Seasonality in Census Method II," *Seasonal Adjustments on Electronic Computers*, Organization for Economic Cooperation and Development.

Monsell, B.C. (1984), "The Substantive Changes in the X-11 Procedure of X-11-ARIMA," Bureau of the Census, Statistical Research Division, SRD Research Report Number Census/SRD/RR-84/10.

Nettheim, N.F. (1965), "A Spectral Study of Overadjustment for Seasonality," *1964 Proceedings of the Business and Economics Section: American Statisti-*

cal Association; republished as the Bureau of the Census Working Paper No. 21 (1965).

Pierce, D.A. (1980), "Data Revisions with Moving Average Seasonal Adjustment Procedures," *Journal of Econometrics*, 14, 95–114.

Shiskin, J., and Eisenpress, H. (1957), "Seasonal Adjustment by Electronic Computer Methods," JASA, 52(280).

Shiskin, J. (1958), "Decomposition of Economic Time Series," Science, 128 (3338).

U.S. Bureau of the Census (1965). "Estimating Trading Day Variation in Monthly Economic Time Series," Technical Paper No. 12, Washington, D.C.: U.S. Government Printing Office.

U.S. Bureau of the Census (1967). "The X-11 Variant of the Census Method II Seasonal Adjustment Program," Technical Paper No. 15, 1967 revision, Washington, D.C.: U.S. Government Printing Office.

U.S. Bureau of the Census (1969), *X-11 Information for the User*, U.S. Department of Commerce, Washington, DC: U.S. Government Printing Office.

Chapter 20
SAS Macros

Chapter Table of Contents

Chapter 20
SAS Macros

SAS Macros Provided with SAS/ETS Software

This chapter describes several SAS macros provided with SAS/ETS software. A SAS macro is a program that generates SAS statements. Macros make it easy to produce and execute complex SAS programs that would be time-consuming to write yourself.

SAS/ETS software includes the following macros:

%AR   generates statements to define autoregressive error models for the MODEL procedure

%BOXCOXAR   investigates Box-Cox transformations useful for modeling and forecasting a time series

%DFPVALUE   computes probabilities for Dickey-Fuller test statistics

%DFTEST   performs Dickey-Fuller tests for unit roots in a time series process

%LOGTEST   tests to see if a log transformation is appropriate for modeling and forecasting a time series

%MA   generates statements to define moving average error models for the MODEL procedure

%PDL   generates statements to define polynomial distributed lag models for the MODEL procedure

These macros are part of the SAS AUTOCALL facility and are automatically available for use in your SAS program. Refer to the *SAS Guide to Macro Processing, Version 6, Second Edition* for information about the SAS macro facility.

Since the %AR, %MA, and %PDL macros are used only with PROC MODEL, they are documented with the MODEL procedure. See the sections on the %AR, %MA, and %PDL macros in Chapter 11, "The MODEL Procedure," for more information about these macros. The %BOXCOXAR, %DFPVALUE, %DFTEST, and %LOGTEST macros are described in the following sections.

BOXCOXAR Macro

The %BOXCOXAR macro finds the optimal Box-Cox transformation for a time series.

Overview

Transformations of the dependent variable are a useful way of dealing with nonlinear relationships or heteroscedasticity. For example, the logarithmic transformation is often used for modeling and forecasting time series that show exponential growth or that show variability proportional to the level of the series.

The Box-Cox transformation is a general class of power transformations that include the log transformation and no-transformation as special cases. The Box-Cox transformation is

$$
\mathbf{Y}_t = \begin{cases} \dfrac{(\mathbf{X}_t + c)^\lambda - 1}{\lambda} & \text{for } \lambda \neq 0 \\[2ex] \ln(\mathbf{X}_t + c) & \text{for } \lambda = 0 \end{cases}
$$

The parameter λ controls the shape of the transformation. For example, $\lambda = 0$ produces a log transformation, while $\lambda = .5$ results in a square root transformation. When $\lambda = 1$, the transformed series differs from the original series by $c - 1$.

The constant c is optional. It can be used when some $\mathbf{X}_t$ values are negative or 0. You choose c so that the series $\mathbf{X}_t$ is always greater than $-c$.

The %BOXCOXAR macro tries a range of λ values and reports which of the values tried produces the optimal Box-Cox transformation. To evaluate different λ values, the %BOXCOXAR macro transforms the series with each λ value and fits an autoregressive model to the transformed series. It is assumed that this autoregressive model is a reasonably good approximation to the true time series model appropriate for the transformed series. The likelihood of the data under each autoregressive model is computed, and the λ value producing the maximum likelihood over the values tried is reported as the optimal Box-Cox transformation for the series.

The %BOXCOXAR macro prints and optionally writes to a SAS data set all of the λ values tried and the corresponding log likelihood value and related statistics for the autoregressive model.

You can control the range and number of λ values tried. You can also control the order of the autoregressive models fit to the transformed series. You can difference the transformed series before the autoregressive model is fit.

Syntax

The form of the %BOXCOXAR macro is

%BOXCOXAR(*SAS-data-set, variable* [*, options*] **)**

The first argument, *SAS-data-set*, specifies the name of the SAS data set containing the time series to be analyzed. The second argument, *variable*, specifies the time series variable name to be analyzed. The first two arguments are required.

The following options can be used with the %BOXCOXAR macro. Options must follow the required arguments and are separated by commas.

AR= *n*

specifies the order of the autoregressive model fit to the transformed series. The default is AR=5.

CONST= *value*

specifies a constant c to be added to the series before transformation. Use the CONST= option when some values of the series are 0 or negative. The default is CONST=0.

DIF= **(** *differencing-list* **)**

specifies the degrees of differencing to apply to the transformed series before the autoregressive model is fit. The *differencing-list* is a list of positive integers separated by commas and enclosed in parentheses. For example, DIF=(1,12) specifies that the transformed series be differenced once at lag 1 and once at lag 12. For more details, see "IDENTIFY Statement" in Chapter 3, "The ARIMA Procedure."

LAMBDAHI= *value*

specifies the maximum value of lambda for the grid search. The default is LAMBDAHI=1.

LAMBDALO= *value*

specifies the minimum value of lambda for the grid search. The default is LAMBDALO=0.

NLAMBDA= *n*

specifies the number of lambda values considered, including the LAMBDALO= and LAMBDAHI= option values. The default is NLAMBDA=2.

OUT= *SAS-data-set*

writes the results to an output data set. The output data set includes the λ values tried (LAMBDA), and for each λ value, the log likelihood (LOGLIK), residual mean square error (RMSE), Akaike Information Criterion (AIC), and Schwarz's Bayesian Criterion (SBC).

PRINT= YES | NO

specifies whether results are printed. The default is PRINT=YES. The printed output contains the λ values, log likelihoods, residual mean square errors, Akaike Information Criterion (AIC), and Schwarz's Bayesian Criterion (SBC).

Results

The value of λ producing the maximum log likelihood is returned in the macro variable &BOXCOXAR. The value of the variable &BOXCOXAR is ERROR if the %BOXCOXAR macro is unable to compute the best transformation due to errors.

Results are printed unless the PRINT=NO option is specified. Results are also stored in SAS data sets when the OUT= option is specified.

Details

Assume that the transformed series Y_t is a stationary pth order autoregressive process generated by independent normally distributed innovations.

$$(1 - \Theta(B))(Y_t - \mu) = \epsilon_t \qquad \epsilon_t \sim \text{iid } N(0, \sigma^2)$$

Given these assumptions, the log likelihood function of the transformed data Y_t is

$$l_Y(\,\cdot\,) = -\frac{n}{2}\ln(2\pi) - \frac{1}{2}\ln(\,|\Sigma|\,) - \frac{n}{2}\ln(\sigma^2)$$
$$- \frac{1}{2\sigma^2}(Y - 1\mu)' \Sigma^{-1}(Y - 1\mu)$$

In this equation, n is the number of observations, μ is the mean of Y_t, 1 is the n-dimensional column vector of 1s, σ^2 is the innovation variance, $Y = (Y_1, \cdots, Y_n)'$, and Σ is the covariance matrix of Y.

The log likelihood function of the original data $X_1, \cdots, X_n$ is

$$l_X(\,\cdot\,) = l_Y(\,\cdot\,) + (\lambda - 1)\sum_{t=1}^{n} \ln(X_t + c)$$

where c is the value of the CONST= option.

For each value of λ, the maximum log likelihood of the original data is obtained from the maximum log likelihood of the transformed data given the maximum likelihood estimate of the autoregressive model.

The maximum log likelihood values are used to compute the Akaike Information Criterion (AIC) and Schwarz's Bayesian Criterion (SBC) for each λ value. The residual mean square error based on the maximum likelihood estimator is also produced. To compute the mean square error, the predicted values from the model are retransformed to the original scale (Pankratz 1983, pp. 256-258; Taylor 1986).

After differencing as specified by the DIF= option, the process is assumed to be a stationary autoregressive process. You can check for stationarity of the series with the %DFTEST macro. If the process is not stationary, differencing with the DIF= option is recommended. For a process with moving average terms, a large value for the AR= option may be appropriate.

DFPVALUE Macro

Overview

The %DFPVALUE macro computes the significance of the Dickey-Fuller test. The %DFPVALUE macro evaluates the p-value for the Dickey-Fuller test statistic τ for the test of H_0: time series has a unit root vs. H_a: the time series is stationary, using tables published by Dickey (1976) and Dickey, Hasza, and Fuller (1984).

The %DFPVALUE macro can compute p-values for tests of a simple unit root with lag 1 or for seasonal unit roots at lags 2, 4, or 12. The %DFPVALUE macro takes into account whether an intercept or deterministic time trend is assumed for the series.

The %DFPVALUE macro is used by the %DFTEST macro, described later in this chapter.

Syntax

The %DFPVALUE macro has the following form:

%DFPVALUE(*tau* **,** *nobs* [**,** *options*] **)**

The first argument, *tau*, specifies the value of the Dickey-Fuller test statistic.

The second argument, *nobs*, specifies the number of observations on which the test statistic is based.

The first two arguments are required. The following options can be used with the %DFPVALUE macro. Options must follow the required arguments and are separated by commas.

DLAG= 1 | 2 | 4 | 12

specifies the lag period of the unit root to be tested. DLAG=1 specifies a 1-period unit root test. DLAG=2 specifies a test for a seasonal unit root with lag 2. DLAG=4 specifies a test for a seasonal unit root with lag 4. DLAG=12 specifies a test for a seasonal unit root with lag 12. The default is DLAG=1.

TREND= 0 | 1 | 2

specifies the degree of deterministic time trend included in the model. TREND=0 specifies no trend and assumes the series has a 0 mean. TREND=1 includes an intercept term. TREND=2 specifies both an intercept and a deterministic linear time trend term. The default is TREND=1. TREND=2 is not allowed with DLAG=2, 4, or 12.

Results

The computed *p*-value is returned in the macro variable &DFPVALUE. If the *p*-value is less than 0.01 or larger than 0.99, the macro variable &DFPVALUE is set to 0.01 or 0.99, respectively.

Details

Minimum Observations

The minimum number of observations required by the %DFPVALUE macro depends on the value of the DLAG= option. The minimum observations are as follows:

DLAG=	Min. Obs.
1	9
2	6
4	4
12	12

Background

Consider the following time series, where *d* is the value of the DLAG= option, and $Y_{1-d}, Y_{2-d}, \ldots Y_0$ are fixed initial values:

$$Y_t = \rho\, Y_{t-d} + e_t$$

With proper assumptions for the error e_t, the limiting distribution of the ordinary least squares estimator of ρ is the normal distribution when the absolute value of ρ is less than 1. If ρ is 1, the limiting distribution for the ordinary least squares estimator for ρ is not the normal distribution. Dickey and Fuller (1979) studied the limiting distribution with *d*=1, and Dickey, Hasza, and Fuller (1984) obtained the limiting distributions for *d*= 2, 4, and 12. For the model with an intercept or linear time trend term, the limiting distributions are also given in Dickey and Fuller (1979) and Dickey, Hasza, and Fuller (1984). For the *p*th order autoregressive time series with a unit root, the *t* statistic has the same limiting distribution as for the first order autoregressive time series. Therefore the same tables can be used. For details, see Fuller (1976) and Dickey, Hasza, and Fuller (1984).

Dickey (1976) and Dickey, Hasza, and Fuller (1984) provide tables of critical values for the test statistic for the test of H_0: time series with a unit root vs. H_a: stationary time series. However, these tables only provide critical values for selected sample sizes and significance levels. The %DFPVALUE macro uses these tables to obtain an approximate *p*-value in two steps.

First, critical values for the given sample size are linearly interpolated. This interpolation is made on the reciprocal of the sample size. The *p*-value is then obtained by cubic spline interpolation in the interpolated table row for the sample size from the first step. Note that the table used for DLAG=1 is from Dickey (1976) and, hence, the result can be a little different from the table in Fuller (1976, p. 373).

DFTEST Macro

Overview

The %DFTEST macro performs the Dickey-Fuller unit root test. You can use the %DFTEST macro to decide if a time series is stationary and to determine the order of differencing required for the time series analysis of a nonstationary series.

Most time series analysis methods require that the series analyzed be stationary. However, many economic time series are nonstationary processes. The usual approach to this problem is to difference the series. A time series that can be made stationary by differencing is said to have a *unit root*. For more information, see the discussion of this issue in the section "Getting Started" in Chapter 3.

The Dickey-Fuller test is a method for testing whether a time series has a unit root. The %DFTEST macro tests the hypothesis H_0: the time series has a unit root vs. H_a: the time series is stationary based on tables provided in Dickey (1976) and Dickey, Hasza, and Fuller (1984). The test can be applied for a simple unit root with lag 1 or for seasonal unit roots at lag 2, 4, or 12.

Syntax

The %DFTEST macro has the following form:

%DFTEST(*SAS-data-set* **,** *variable* [**,** *options*] **)**

The first argument, *SAS-data-set*, specifies the name of the SAS data set containing the time series variable to be analyzed.

The second argument, *variable*, specifies the time series variable name to be analyzed.

The first two arguments are required. The following options can be used with the %DFTEST macro. Options must follow the required arguments and are separated by commas.

AR= *n*

specifies the order of autoregressive model fit after any differencing specified by the DIF= and DLAG= options. The default is AR=3.

DIF= (*differencing-list*)

specifies the degrees of differencing to be applied to the series; *differencing-list* is a list of positive integers separated by commas and enclosed in parentheses. For example, DIF=(1,12) specifies that the series be differenced once at lag 1 and once at lag 12. For more details, see "IDENTIFY Statement" in Chapter 3.

If the option DIF=(d_1, $\cdots$, d_k) is specified, the series analyzed is $\left(1 - \mathbf{B}^{d_1}\right) \cdots \left(1 - \mathbf{B}^{d_k}\right) \mathbf{Y}_t$, where $\mathbf{Y}_t$ is the variable specified, and B is the backshift operator defined by $\mathbf{B}\mathbf{Y}_t = \mathbf{Y}_{t-1}$.

DLAG= 1 | 2 | 4 | 12
specifies the lag to be tested for a unit root. The default is DLAG=1.

OUT= *SAS-data-set*
writes residuals to an output data set.

OUTSTAT= *SAS-data-set*
writes the test statistic, parameter estimates, and other statistics to an output data set.

TREND= 0 | 1 | 2
specifies the degree of deterministic time trend included in the model. TREND=0 includes no deterministic term and assumes the series has a 0 mean. TREND=1 includes an intercept term. TREND=2 specifies an intercept and a linear time trend term. The default is TREND=1. TREND=2 is not allowed with DLAG=2, 4, or 12.

Results

The computed p-value is returned in the macro variable &DFTEST. If the p-value is less than 0.01 or larger than 0.99, the macro variable &DFTEST is set to 0.01 or 0.99, respectively. (The same value is given in the macro variable &DFPVALUE returned by the %DFPVALUE macro, which is used by the %DFTEST macro to compute the p-value.)

Results can be stored in SAS data sets with the OUT= and OUTSTAT= options.

Details

Minimum Observations

The minimum number of observations required by the %DFTEST macro depends on the value of the DLAG= option. Let s be the sum of the differencing orders specified by the DIF= option, let t be the value of the TREND= option, and let p be the value of the AR= option. The minimum number of observations required is as follows:

DLAG=	Min. Obs.
1	$1 + p + s + \max(9, p + t + 2)$
2	$2 + p + s + \max(6, p + t + 2)$
4	$4 + p + s + \max(4, p + t + 2)$
12	$12 + p + s + \max(12, p + t + 2)$

Observations are not used if they have missing values for the series or for any lag or difference used in the autoregressive model.

Theoretical Background

When a time series has a unit root, the series is nonstationary and the ordinary least squares (OLS) estimator is not normally distributed. Dickey (1976) and Dickey and Fuller (1979) studied the limiting distribution of the OLS estimator of autoregressive models for time series with a simple unit root. Dickey, Hasza, and Fuller (1984) obtained the limiting distribution for time series with seasonal unit roots.

Consider the $(p+1)$th order autoregressive time series

$$\mathbf{Y}_t = \alpha_1 \mathbf{Y}_{t-1} + \alpha_2 \mathbf{Y}_{t-2} + \cdots + \alpha_{p+1} \mathbf{Y}_{t-p-1} + e_t$$

and its characteristic equation

$$m^{p+1} - \alpha_1 m^p - \alpha_2 m^{p-1} - \cdots - \alpha_{p+1} = 0$$

If all the characteristic roots are less than 1 in absolute value, $\mathbf{Y}_t$ is stationary. $\mathbf{Y}_t$ is nonstationary if there is a unit root. If there is a unit root, the sum of the autoregressive parameters is 1, and, hence, you can test for a unit root by testing whether the sum of the autoregressive parameters is 1 or not. For convenience, the model is parameterized as

$$\nabla \mathbf{Y}_t = \delta \mathbf{Y}_{t-1} + \theta_1 \nabla \mathbf{Y}_{t-1} + \cdots + \theta_p \nabla \mathbf{Y}_{t-p} + e_t$$

where $\nabla \mathbf{Y}_t = \mathbf{Y}_t - \mathbf{Y}_{t-1}$ and

$$\delta = \alpha_1 + \cdots + \alpha_{p+1} - 1$$
$$\theta_k = -\alpha_{k+1} - \cdots - \alpha_{p+1}$$

The estimators are obtained by regressing $\nabla \mathbf{Y}_t$ on $\mathbf{Y}_{t-1}, \nabla \mathbf{Y}_{t-1}, \cdots, \nabla \mathbf{Y}_{t-p}$. The t statistic of the ordinary least squares estimator of δ is the test statistic for the unit root test.

If the TREND=1 option is used, the autoregressive model includes a mean term α_0. If TREND=2, the model also includes a time trend term, and the model is as follows:

$$\nabla \mathbf{Y}_t = \alpha_0 + \gamma t + \delta \mathbf{Y}_{t-1} + \theta_1 \nabla \mathbf{Y}_{t-1} + \cdots + \theta_p \nabla \mathbf{Y}_{t-p} + e_t$$

For testing for a seasonal unit root, consider the multiplicative model

$$\left(1 - \alpha_d \mathrm{B}^d\right)\left(1 - \theta_1 \mathrm{B} - \cdots - \theta_p \mathrm{B}^p\right)\mathbf{Y}_t = e_t$$

Let $\nabla^d \mathbf{Y}_t \equiv \mathbf{Y}_t - \mathbf{Y}_{t-d}$. The test statistic is calculated in the following steps:

1. Regress $\nabla^d \mathbf{Y}_t$ on $\nabla^d \mathbf{Y}_{t-1} \cdots \nabla^d \mathbf{Y}_{t-p}$ to obtain the initial estimators $\hat{\theta}_i$ and compute residuals $\hat{e}_t$. Under the null hypothesis that $\alpha_d = 1$, $\hat{\theta}_i$ are consistent estimators of θ_i.

2. Regress $\hat{e}_t$ on $\left(1 - \hat{\theta}_1 \mathrm{B} - \cdots - \hat{\theta}_p \mathrm{B}^p\right)\mathbf{Y}_{t-d}, \nabla^d \mathbf{Y}_{t-1}, \cdots, \nabla^d \mathbf{Y}_{t-p}$ to obtain estimates of $\delta = \alpha_d - 1$ and $\theta_i - \hat{\theta}_i$.

The t ratio for the estimate of δ produced by the second step is used as a test statistic for testing for a seasonal unit root. The estimates of θ_i are obtained by adding the estimates of $\theta_i - \hat{\theta}_i$ from the second step to $\hat{\theta}_i$ from the first step. The estimates of $\alpha_d - 1$ and θ_i are saved in the OUTSTAT= data set if the OUTSTAT= option is specified.

The series $\left(1 - B^d\right)\mathbf{Y}_t$ is assumed to be stationary, where d is the value of the DLAG= option.

If the OUTSTAT= option is specified, the OUTSTAT= data set contains estimates $\hat{\delta}, \hat{\theta}_1, \cdots, \hat{\theta}_p$.

If the series is an ARMA process, a large value of the AR= option may be desirable in order to obtain a reliable test statistic. To determine an appropriate value for the AR= option for an ARMA process, refer to Said and Dickey (1984).

LOGTEST Macro

Overview

The %LOGTEST macro tests whether a logarithmic transformation is appropriate for modeling and forecasting a time series. The logarithmic transformation is often used for time series that show exponential growth or variability proportional to the level of the series.

The %LOGTEST macro fits an autoregressive model to a series and fits the same model to the log of the series. Both models are estimated by the maximum likelihood method, and the maximum log likelihood values for both autoregressive models are computed. These log likelihood values are then expressed in terms of the original data and compared.

You can control the order of the autoregressive models. You can also difference the series and the log transformed series before the autoregressive model is fit.

You can print the log likelihood values and related statistics (AIC, SBC, and MSE) for the autoregressive models for the series and the log transformed series. You can also output these statistics to a SAS data set.

Syntax

The %LOGTEST macro has the following form:

%LOGTEST(*SAS-data-set* **,** *variable* [**,** *options*] **)**

The first argument, *SAS-data-set*, specifies the name of the SAS data set containing the time series variable to be analyzed. The second argument, *variable*, specifies the time series variable name to be analyzed.

The first two arguments are required. The following options can be used with the %LOGTEST macro. Options must follow the required arguments and are separated by commas.

AR= *n*

specifies the order of the autoregressive model fit to the series and the log transformed series. The default is AR=5.

CONST= *value*

specifies a constant to be added to the series before transformation. Use the CONST= option when some values of the series are 0 or negative. The series analyzed must be greater than the negative of the value of the CONST= option. The default is CONST=0.

DIF= (*differencing-list* **)**

specifies the degrees of differencing applied to the original and log transformed series before fitting the autoregressive model; *differencing-list* is a list of positive integers separated by commas and enclosed in parentheses. For example, DIF=(1,12) specifies that the transformed series be differenced once at lag 1 and once at lag 12. For more details, see "IDENTIFY Statement" in Chapter 3.

OUT= *SAS-data-set*

writes the results to an output data set. The output data set includes a variable TRANS identifying the transformation (LOG or NONE), the log likelihood value (LOGLIK), residual mean square error (RMSE), Akaike Information Criterion (AIC), and Schwarz's Bayesian Criterion (SBC) for the log transformed and untransformed cases.

PRINT= YES | NO

specifies whether the results are printed. The default is PRINT=NO. The printed output shows the log likelihood value, residual mean square error, Akaike Information Criterion (AIC), and Schwarz's Bayesian Criterion (SBC) for the log transformed and untransformed cases.

Results

The result of the test is returned in the macro variable &LOGTEST. The value of the &LOGTEST variable is LOG if the model fit to the log transformed data has a larger log likelihood than the model fit to the untransformed series. The value of the &LOGTEST variable is NONE if the model fit to the untransformed data has a larger log likelihood. The variable &LOGTEST is set to ERROR if the %LOGTEST macro is unable to compute the test due to errors.

Results are printed when the PRINT=YES option is specified. Results are stored in SAS data sets when the OUT= option is specified.

Details

Assume that a time series $\mathbf{X}_t$ is a stationary pth order autoregressive process with normally distributed white noise innovations. That is,

$$(1 - \Theta(B)) (\mathbf{X}_t - \mu_{\mathbf{X}}) = \epsilon_t$$

where $\mu_{\mathbf{X}}$ is the mean of $\mathbf{X}_t$.

The log likelihood function of $\mathbf{X}_t$ is

$$l_1(\,\cdot\,) = -\frac{n}{2}\ln(2\pi) - \frac{1}{2}\ln(\,|\Sigma_{\mathbf{XX}}|\,) - \frac{n}{2}\ln(\sigma_e^2)$$
$$-\frac{1}{2\sigma_e^2}(\mathbf{X} - \mathbf{1}\mu_{\mathbf{X}})'\Sigma_{\mathbf{XX}}^{-1}(\mathbf{X} - \mathbf{1}\mu_{\mathbf{X}})$$

where n is the number of observations, $\mathbf{1}$ is the n-dimensional column vector of 1s, σ_e^2 is the variance of the white noise, $\mathbf{X} = (\mathbf{X}_1, \cdots, \mathbf{X}_n)'$, and $\Sigma_{\mathbf{XX}}$ is the covariance matrix of $\mathbf{X}$.

On the other hand, if the log transformed time series $\mathbf{Y}_t = \ln(\mathbf{X}_t + c)$ is a stationary pth order autoregressive process, the log likelihood function of $\mathbf{X}_t$ is

$$l_0(\,\cdot\,) = -\frac{n}{2}\ln(2\pi) - \frac{1}{2}\ln(\,|\Sigma_{\mathbf{YY}}|\,) - \frac{n}{2}\ln(\sigma_e^2)$$
$$-\frac{1}{2\sigma_e^2}(\mathbf{Y} - \mathbf{1}\mu_{\mathbf{Y}})'\Sigma_{\mathbf{YY}}^{-1}(\mathbf{Y} - \mathbf{1}\mu_{\mathbf{Y}}) - \sum_{t=1}^{n}\ln(\mathbf{X}_t + c)$$

where $\mu_{\mathbf{Y}}$ is the mean of $\mathbf{Y}_t$, $\mathbf{Y} = (\mathbf{Y}_1, \cdots, \mathbf{Y}_n)'$, and $\Sigma_{\mathbf{YY}}$ is the covariance matrix of $\mathbf{Y}$.

The %LOGTEST macro compares the maximum values of $l_1(\,\cdot\,)$ and $l_0(\,\cdot\,)$ and determines which is larger.

The %LOGTEST macro also computes the Akaike Information Criterion (AIC), Schwarz's Bayesian Criterion (SBC), and residual mean square error based on the maximum likelihood estimator for the autoregressive model. For the mean square error, retransformation of forecasts is based on Pankratz (1983, pp. 256-258).

After differencing as specified by the DIF= option, the process is assumed to be a stationary autoregressive process. You may want to check for stationarity of the series using the %DFTEST macro. If the process is not stationary, differencing with the DIF= option is recommended. For a process with moving average terms, a large value for the AR= option may be appropriate.

References

Dickey, D. A. (1976), "Estimation and Testing of Nonstationary Time Series," Unpublished Ph.D. Thesis, Ames: Iowa State University.

Dickey, D. A. and Fuller, W. A. (1979), "Distribution of the Estimation for Autoregressive Time Series with a Unit Root," *Journal of The American Statistical Association*, 74, 427–431.

Dickey, D. A.; Hasza, D. P.; and Fuller, W. A. (1984), "Testing for Unit Roots in Seasonal Time Series," *Journal of The American Statistical Association*, 79, 355–367.

Fuller, W. A. (1976), *Introduction to Statistical Time Series.* New York: John Wiley & Sons, Inc.

Pankratz, A. (1983), *Forecasting with Univariate Box-Jenkins Models: Concepts and Cases.* New York: John Wiley & Sons, Inc.

Said, S. E. and Dickey, D. A. (1984), "Testing for Unit Roots in ARMA Models of Unknown Order," *Biometrika*, 71, 599–607.

Taylor, J. M. G. (1986) "The Retransformed Mean After a Fitted Power Transformation," *Journal of The American Statistical Association*, 81, 114–118.

Chapter 21
Date Intervals, Formats, and Functions

Chapter Table of Contents

Chapter 21
Date Intervals, Formats, and Functions

This chapter summarizes the time intervals, date and datetime informats, date and datetime formats, and date and datetime functions available in the SAS System. The use of these features is explained in Chapter 2, "Working with Time Series Data." The material in this chapter is also contained in the *SAS Language: Reference, Version 6, First Edition.* Because these features are useful for work with time series data, documentation of these features is consolidated and repeated here for easy reference.

Time Intervals

This section provides a reference for the different kinds of time intervals supported by the SAS System. How intervals are used is not discussed here; see Chapter 2 for an introduction to the use of time intervals.

Some interval names are for use with SAS date values, while other interval names are for use with SAS datetime values. The interval names used with SAS date values are YEAR, SEMIYEAR, QTR, MONTH, SEMIMONTH, TENDAY, WEEK, WEEKDAY, and DAY. The interval names used with SAS datetime or time values are HOUR, MINUTE, and SECOND. Various abbreviations of these names are also allowed, as described in the section "Summary of Interval Types" later in this chapter.

Interval names for use with SAS date values can be prefixed with DT to construct interval names for use with SAS datetime values. The interval names DTYEAR, DTSEMIYEAR, DTQTR, DTMONTH, DTSEMIMONTH, DTTENDAY, DTWEEK, DTWEEKDAY, and DTDAY are used with SAS datetime or time values.

Constructing Interval Names

Multipliers and shift indexes can be used with the basic interval names to construct more complex interval specifications. The general form of an interval name is as follows:

NAMEn.s

The three parts of the interval name are

NAME the name of the basic interval type. For example, YEAR specifies yearly intervals.

n an optional multiplier that specifies that the interval is a multiple of the period of the basic interval type. For example, the interval YEAR2 consists of two-year, or biennial, periods.

      s   an optional starting subperiod index that specifies that the intervals are shifted to later starting points. For example, YEAR.3 specifies yearly periods shifted to start on the first of March of each calendar year and to end in February of the following year.

Both the multiplier *n* and the shift index *s* are optional and default to 1. For example, YEAR, YEAR1, YEAR.1, and YEAR1.1 are all equivalent ways of specifying ordinary calendar years.

Shifted Intervals

Different kinds of intervals are shifted by different subperiods:

- YEAR, SEMIYEAR, QTR, and MONTH intervals are shifted by calendar months.

- WEEK, WEEKDAY, and DAY intervals are shifted by days.

- SEMIMONTH intervals are shifted by semimonthly periods.

- TENDAY intervals are shifted by ten-day periods.

- HOUR intervals are shifted by hours.

- MINUTE intervals are shifted by minutes.

- SECOND intervals are shifted by seconds.

If a subperiod is specified, the shift index cannot be greater than the number of subperiods in the whole interval. For example, you could use YEAR2.24, but YEAR2.25 would be an error because there is no twenty-fifth month in a two-year interval. For interval types that shift by subperiods that are the same as the basic interval type, only multiperiod intervals can be shifted.

For example, MONTH type intervals shift by MONTH subintervals; thus, monthly intervals cannot be shifted since there is only one month in MONTH. However, bimonthly intervals can be shifted, since there are two MONTH intervals in each MONTH2 interval. The interval name MONTH2.2 specifies bimonthly periods starting on the first day of even-numbered months.

Alignment of Intervals

Intervals that represent divisions of a year are aligned with the start of the year (January). MONTH2 periods begin with odd-numbered months (January, March, May, and so on). Likewise, intervals that represent divisions of a day are aligned with the start of the day (midnight). Thus, HOUR8.7 intervals divide the day into the periods 06:00 to 14:00, 14:00 to 22:00, and 22:00 to 06:00.

Intervals that do not nest within years or days are aligned relative to the SAS date or datetime value 0. The arbitrary reference time of midnight on January 1, 1960, is used as the origin for nonshifted intervals, and shifted intervals are defined relative to that reference point. For example, MONTH13 defines the intervals January 1, 1960, February 1, 1961, March 1, 1962, and so forth, and the intervals December 1, 1959, November 1, 1958, and so on before the base date January 1, 1960.

Similarly, WEEK2 interval beginning days are aligned relative to the Sunday of the week of January 1, 1960. The interval specification WEEK6.13 defines six-week periods starting on second Fridays, and the convention of alignment relative to the period containing January 1, 1960 tells where to start counting to find out what dates correspond to the second Fridays of six-week intervals.

Summary of Interval Types

The interval types are summarized as follows:

YEAR

specifies yearly intervals. Abbreviations are YEAR, YEARS, YEARLY, YR, ANNUAL, ANNUALLY, and ANNUALS. The starting subperiod s is in months.

SEMIYEAR

specifies semiannual intervals (every six months). Abbreviations are SEMIYEAR, SEMIYEARS, SEMIYEARLY, SEMIYR, SEMIANNUAL, and SEMIANN.

The starting subperiod s is in months. For example, SEMIYEAR.3 intervals are March–August and September–February.

QTR

specifies quarterly intervals (every three months). Abbreviations are QTR, QUARTER, QUARTERS, QUARTERLY, QTRLY, and QTRS. The starting subperiod s is in months.

MONTH

specifies monthly intervals. Abbreviations are MONTH, MONTHS, MONTHLY, and MON.

The starting subperiod s is in months. For example, MONTH2.2 intervals are February–March, April–May, June–July, August–September, October–November, and December–January of the following year.

SEMIMONTH

specifies semimonthly intervals. SEMIMONTH breaks each month into two periods, starting on the first and sixteenth day. Abbreviations are SEMIMONTH, SEMIMONTHS, SEMIMONTHLY, and SEMIMON.

The starting subperiod s is in SEMIMONTH periods. For example, SEMIMONTH2.2 specifies intervals from the sixteenth of one month through the fifteenth of the next month.

TENDAY

specifies ten-day intervals. TENDAY breaks the month into three periods, the first through the tenth day of the month, the eleventh through the twentieth day of the month, and the remainder of the month. (TENDAY is a special interval typically used for reporting automobile sales data.)

The starting subperiod s is in ten-day periods. For example, TENDAY4.2 defines forty-day periods starting at the second TENDAY period.

WEEK

specifies weekly intervals of seven days. Abbreviations are WEEK, WEEKS, WEEKLY.

The starting subperiod *s* is in days, with the days of the week numbered as 1=Sunday, 2=Monday, 3=Tuesday, 4=Wednesday, 5=Thursday, 6=Friday, and 7=Saturday. For example, WEEK.7 means weekly with Saturday as the first day of the week.

WEEKDAY
WEEKDAY17W

specifies daily intervals with weekend days included in the preceding week day. Abbreviations are WEEKDAY and WEEKDAYS.

The WEEKDAY interval is the same as DAY except that weekend days are absorbed into the preceding weekday. Thus, there are five WEEKDAY intervals in a calendar week: Monday, Tuesday, Wednesday, Thursday, and the three-day period Friday-Saturday-Sunday.

The default weekend days are Saturday and Sunday, but any one-to-six weekend days can be listed after the WEEKDAY string and followed by a W. Weekend days are specified as '1' for Sunday, '2' for Monday, and so forth. For example, WEEKDAY56W specifies a Friday-Saturday weekend. WEEKDAY7W specifies a six-day work week with a Sunday weekend. WEEKDAY17W is the same as WEEKDAY.

The starting subperiod *s* is in days.

DAY

specifies daily intervals. Abbreviations are DAY, DAYS, and DAILY. The starting subperiod *s* is in days.

HOUR

specifies hourly intervals. Abbreviations are HOUR, HOURS, HOURLY, and HR. The starting subperiod *s* is in hours.

MINUTE

specifies minute intervals. Abbreviations are MINUTE, MINUTES, and MIN. The starting subperiod *s* is in minutes.

SECOND

specifies second intervals. Abbreviations are SECOND, SECONDS, and SEC. The starting subperiod *s* is in seconds.

Examples of Interval Specifications

Table 21.1 shows examples of different kinds of interval specifications.

Table 21.1. Examples of Intervals

Name	Kind of Interval
YEAR	years starting in January
YEAR.10	fiscal years starting in October
YEAR2.7	biennial intervals starting in July of even years
YEAR2.19	biennial intervals starting in July of odd years
YEAR4.11	four-year intervals starting in November of leap years (frequency of U.S. presidential elections)
YEAR4.35	four-year intervals starting in November of even years between leap years (frequency of U.S. midterm elections)
WEEK	weekly intervals starting on Sundays
WEEK2	biweekly intervals starting on first Sundays
WEEK1.1	same as WEEK
WEEK.2	weekly intervals starting on Mondays
WEEK6.3	six-week intervals starting on first Tuesdays
WEEK6.11	six-week intervals starting on second Wednesdays
WEEKDAY	daily with Friday-Saturday-Sunday counted as the same day (five-day work week with a Saturday-Sunday weekend)
WEEKDAY67W	same as WEEKDAY
WEEKDAY56W	daily with Thursday-Friday-Saturday counted as the same day (five-day work week with a Friday-Saturday weekend)
WEEKDAY7W	daily with Saturday-Sunday counted as the same day (six-day work week with a Sunday weekend)
WEEKDAY3.2	three-weekday intervals (with Friday-Saturday-Sunday counted as one weekday) with the cycle three-weekday periods aligned to Monday 4 Jan 1960
HOUR8.7	eight-hour intervals starting at 6 a.m., 2 p.m., and 10 p.m. (might be used for work shifts)

Date and Datetime Informats

Table 21.2 summarizes the SAS date and datetime informats available in SAS software. See Chapter 2 for a discussion of the use of date and datetime informats. Refer to *SAS Language: Reference* for a complete description of these informats.

For each informat, Table 21.2 shows an example of a date or datetime value written in the style that the informat is designed to read. The date 17 October 1991 and the time 2:25:32 p.m. are used for the example in all cases. Table 21.2 shows the width range allowed by the informat and shows the default width.

Table 21.2. SAS Date and Datetime Informats

Informat Example	Description	Width Range	Default Width
DATE*w*. 17oct91	day, month abbreviation, and year: *ddMONyy*	7-32	7
DATETIME*w.d* 17oct91:14:45:32	date and time: *ddMONyy:hh:mm:ss*	13-40	18
DDMMYY*w*. 17/10/91	day, month, year: *ddmmyy, dd/mm/yy,* *dd-mm-yy,* or *dd mm yy*	6-32	6
JULIAN*w*. 91290	year and day of year (Julian dates): *yyddd*	5-32	5
MMDDYY*w*. 10/17/91	month, day, year: *mmddyy, mm/dd/yy,* *mm-dd-yy,* or *mm dd yy*	6-32	6
MONYY*w*. Oct91	month abbreviation and year	5-32	5
NENGO*w*. H.03/10/17	Japanese Nengo notation	7-32	10
TIME*w.d* 14:45:32	hours, minutes, seconds: *hh:mm:ss* or hours, minutes: *hh:mm.*	5-32	8
YYMMDD*w*. 91/10/17	year, month, day: *yymmdd, yy/mm/dd,* *yy-mm-dd,* or *yy mm dd*	6-32	6
YYQ*w*. 91Q4	year and quarter of year: *yyQq*	4-32	4

Date, Time, and Datetime Formats

The SAS date, time, and datetime formats are summarized in Table 21.3 and Table 21.4. A width value can be specified with each format. The tables list the range of width values allowed and the default width value for each format.

The notation used by a format is abbreviated in different ways, depending on the width option used. For example, the format MMDDYY8. writes the date 17 October 1991 as 10/17/91, while the format MMDDYY6. writes this date as 101791. In particular, formats that display the year show two-digit or four-digit year values, depending on the width option. The examples shown in the tables are for the default width.

Refer to *SAS Language: Reference* for a complete description of these formats, including the variations of the formats produced by different width options. See Chapter 2 for a discussion of the use of date, time, and datetime formats.

Date Formats

Table 21.3 lists the date formats available in SAS software. For each format, an example is shown of a date value in the notation produced by the format. The date 17OCT91 is used as the example.

Table 21.3. SAS Date Formats

Format Example	Description	Width Range	Default Width
DATE*w*. 17oct91	day, month abbreviation, year: *ddMONyy*	5-9	7
DAY*w*. 17	day of month	2-32	2
DDMMYY*w*. 17/10/91	day, month, year: *dd/mm/yy*	2-8	8
DOWNAME*w*. Thursday	name of day of the week	1-32	9
JULDAY*w*. 290	day of year	3-32	3
JULIAN*w*. 91290	year and day of year: *yyddd*	5-7	5
MMDDYY*w*. 10/17/91	month, day, year: *mm/dd/yy*	2-8	8
MMYY*w*. 10M1991	month and year: *mmMyy*	5-32	7
MMYYC*w*. 10:1991	month and year: *mm:yy*	5-32	7

Format Example	Description	Width Range	Default Width
MMYYD*w*. 10-1991	month and year: *mm-yy*	5-32	7
MMYYP*w*. 10.1991	month and year: *mm.yy*	5-32	7
MMYYS*w*. 10/1991	month and year: *mm/yy*	5-32	7
MMYYN*w*. 101991	month and year: *mmyy*	5-32	6
MONNAME*w*. October	name of month	1-32	9
MONTH*w*. 10	month of year	1-32	2
MONYY*w*. OCT91	month abbreviation and year: *MONyy*	5-7	5
QTR*w*. 4	quarter of year	1-32	1
QTRR*w*. IV	quarter in Roman numerals	3-32	3
NENGO*w*. H.03/10/17	Japanese Nengo notation	2-10	10
WEEKDATE*w*. Thursday, October 17, 1991	*day-of-week, month-name dd, yy*	3-37	29
WEEKDATX*w*. Thursday, 17 October 1991	*day-of-week, dd month-name yy*	3-37	29
WEEKDAY*w*. 5	day of week	1-32	1
WORDDATE*w*. October 17, 1991	*month-name dd, yy*	3-32	18
WORDDATX*w*. 17 October 1991	*dd month-name yy*	3-32	18
YEAR*w*. 1991	year	2-32	4
YYMM*w*. 1991M10	year and month: *yyMmm*	5-32	7
YYMMC*w*. 1991:10	year and month: *yy:mm*	5-32	7
YYMMD*w*. 1991-10	year and month: *yy-mm*	5-32	7
YYMMP*w*. 1991.10	year and month: *yy.mm*	5-32	7

Format Example	Description	Width Range	Default Width
YYMMS*w*. 1991/10	year and month: *yy/mm*	5-32	7
YYMMN*w*. 199110	year and month: *yymm*	5-32	7
YYMON*w*. 1991OCT	year and month abbreviation: *yyMON*	5-32	7
YYMMDD*w*. 91/10/17	year, month, day: *yy/mm/dd*	2-8	8
YYQ*w*. 91Q4	year and quarter: *yyQq*	4-6	4
YYQC*w*. 1991:4	year and quarter: *yy:q*	4-32	6
YYQD*w*. 1991-4	year and quarter: *yy-q*	4-32	6
YYQP*w*. 1991.4	year and quarter: *yy.q*	4-32	6
YYQS*w*. 1991/4	year and quarter: *yy/q*	4-32	6
YYQN*w*. 19914	year and quarter: *yyq*	3-32	5
YYQR*w*. 1991QIV	year and quarter in Roman numerals: *yyQrr*	6-32	8
YYQRC*w*. 1991:IV	year and quarter in Roman numerals: *yy:rr*	6-32	8
YYQRD*w*. 1991-IV	year and quarter in Roman numerals: *yy-rr*	6-32	8
YYQRP*w*. 1991.IV	year and quarter in Roman numerals: *yy.rr*	6-32	8
YYQRS*w*. 1991/IV	year and quarter in Roman numerals: *yy/rr*	6-32	8
YYQRN*w*. 1991IV	year and quarter in Roman numerals: *yyrr*	6-32	8

Datetime and Time Formats

Table 21.4 lists the datetime and time formats available. For each format, an example is shown of a datetime value in the notation produced by the format. The datetime value 17oct91:14:25:32 is used as the example.

Table 21.4. SAS Datetime and Time Formats

Format Example	Description	Width Range	Default Width
DATETIME*w.d* 17OCT91:14:25:32	*ddMONyy:hh:mm:ss*	7-40	16
HHMM*w.d* 14:25	hour and minute: *hh:mm*	2-20	5
HOUR*w.d* 14	hour	2-20	2
MMSS*w.d* 25:32	minutes and seconds: *mm:ss*	2-20	5
TIME*w.d* 14:25:32	time of day: *hh:mm:ss*	2-20	8
TOD*w.* 14:25:32	time of day: *hh:mm:ss*	2-20	8

Date, Time, and Datetime Functions

The SAS System provides functions to perform calculations with SAS date, time, and datetime values. SAS date, time, and datetime functions are used to

- compute date, time, and datetime values from calendar and time-of-day values
- compute calendar and time-of-day values from date and datetime values
- convert between date, time, and datetime values
- perform calculations involving time intervals

SAS date, time, and datetime functions are listed in alphabetical order in the following list. Refer to *SAS Language: Reference* for a complete description of these functions.

DATE()
    returns today's date as a SAS date value.

DATEJUL(*yyddd*)
    returns the SAS date value for a Julian date.

DATEPART(*datetime* **)**

returns the date part of a SAS datetime value as a date value.

DATETIME()

returns the current date and time of day as a SAS datetime value.

DAY(*date* **)**

returns the day of the month from a SAS date value.

DHMS(*date, hour, minute, second* **)**

returns a SAS datetime value for date, hour, minute, and second values.

HMS(*hour, minute, second* **)**

returns a SAS time value for hour, minute, and second values.

HOUR(*datetime* **)**

returns the hour from a SAS datetime or time value.

INTCK(*interval, date1, date2* **)**

returns the number of boundaries of intervals of the given kind that lie between the two date or datetime values.

INTNX(*interval, date, n* **)**

returns the date or datetime value of the beginning of the interval that is *n* intervals from the interval that contains the given date or datetime value.

JULDATE(*date* **)**

returns the Julian date from a SAS date value.

MDY(*month, day, year* **)**

returns a SAS date value for month, day, and year values.

MINUTE(*datetime* **)**

returns the minute from a SAS time or datetime value.

MONTH(*date* **)**

returns the month of the year from a SAS date value.

QTR(*date* **)**

returns the quarter of the year from a SAS date value.

SECOND(*date* **)**

returns the second from a SAS time or datetime value.

TIME()

returns the current time of day as a SAS time value.

TIMEPART(*datetime* **)**

returns the time part of a SAS datetime value.

TODAY()

returns the current date as a SAS date value. (TODAY is another name for the DATE function.)

WEEKDAY(*date* **)**

returns the day of the week from a SAS date value.

YEAR(*date* **)**

returns the year from a SAS date value.

YYQ(*year, quarter* **)**

returns a SAS date value for year and quarter values.

Chapter 22
Changes and Enhancements

Chapter Table of Contents

Chapter 22
Changes and Enhancements

This chapter summarizes the enhancements to SAS/ETS software made since the previous edition of the *SAS/ETS User's Guide, Version 6, First Edition.*

DATASOURCE Procedure

The DATASOURCE procedure extracts time series data from different kinds of data files distributed by various data vendors and stores them in a SAS data set. After they are stored in a SAS data set, the time series variables can be processed by other SAS procedures. PROC DATASOURCE also creates auxiliary SAS data sets containing descriptive information on the time series and on the key variables used to group time series.

The DATASOURCE procedure currently supports data files distributed by the following vendors:

- Citicorp Database Services (CITIBASE)
- Haver Analytics
- International Monetary Fund
- U.S. Bureau of Labor Statistics
- U.S. Bureau of Economic Analysis
- Standard & Poor's Compustat Services
- Center for Research in Security Prices (CRSP)
- Organization for Economic Cooperation and Development (OECD)

See Chapter 7, "The DATASOURCE Procedure," for details.

LOAN Procedure

The LOAN procedure analyzes a variety of periodic payment loans. The LOAN procedure supersedes the MORTGAGE procedure. Unlike PROC MORTGAGE, which only deals with a single fixed rate loan, PROC LOAN can analyze many different loans and can compare alternative loan contracts.

PROC LOAN handles fixed rate, adjustable rate, buydown rate, and balloon payment loans. Various payment and compounding intervals (including continuous compounding) are allowed. PROC LOAN supports prepayments, down payments, points, and loan initialization costs in the analysis. A variety of options to control interest rate changes for adjustable rate loans are provided.

Any number of different loans can be analyzed in a single PROC LOAN step. The LOAN procedure can compare alternative loans in terms of several different economic criteria, including after-tax or before-tax present worth of cost and true interest rate, break-even of payment and interest paid, and outstanding balance. These comparisons can be made for the life of the loan or for specified time periods. PROC LOAN reports which of several loan contracts is best based on the comparison criteria you select.

See Chapter 10, "The LOAN Procedure," for details.

TSCSREG Procedure

The TSCSREG (Time Series Cross-Section Regression) procedure analyzes regression models that arise when combining time series and cross-sectional data.

The TSCSREG procedure was developed by Douglas J. Drummond and A. Ronald Gallant and was contributed to the SUGI Supplemental Library in 1979. The TSCSREG procedure in SAS/ETS software was produced by converting the older SUGI Supplemental Library version of the procedure to Version 6 of SAS software. This conversion work was performed by SAS Institute, which now supports the procedure.

During the conversion process, several bugs were fixed and several new features were added. See Chapter 18, "The TSCSREG Procedure," for details.

ARIMA Procedure

The following are changes to the ARIMA procedure. See Chapter 3, "The ARIMA Procedure," for details.

OUTEST= Data Set

The OUTEST= option on the ESTIMATE statement writes the parameter estimates to an output data set.

OUTCORR and OUTCOV Options

The OUTCORR option on the ESTIMATE statement includes the correlations of the parameter estimates in the OUTEST= data set. The OUTCOV option includes the covariance matrix of the parameter estimates in the OUTEST= data set.

OUTMODEL= Data Set

The OUTMODEL= option on the ESTIMATE statement writes a representation of the ARIMA model and the parameter estimates to an output data set. The OUTMODEL= data set contains the parameter estimates, as does the OUTEST= data set, but in a different format that enables the ARIMA model to be reconstructed.

OUTSTAT= Data Set

The OUTSTAT= option on the ESTIMATE statement writes diagnostic statistics for the model to an output data set.

ALPHA= Option

The ALPHA= option on the FORECAST statement controls the size of the forecast confidence limits. (Previously, only the default 95% confidence limits were available.) For example, ALPHA=.01 specifies 99% forecast confidence limits.

NLAG= Option Default Changed

The NLAG= option now defaults to one-fourth the number of nonmissing observations. Previously, the NLAG= default was 24.

AUTOREG Procedure

The following are changes to the AUTOREG procedure. See Chapter 4, "The AUTOREG Procedure," for details.

Autoregressive Conditional Heteroscedasticity Models

The AUTOREG procedure now supports the family of generalized autoregressive conditional heteroscedasticity (GARCH) models. Using GARCH models you can jointly analyze and forecast both the expected value of a time series and its variability.

You can combine the regression with autoregressive errors model with the GARCH model for the error variance. The GARCH model features work with embedded missing values for the dependent or independent variables. Conditional prediction error variances, which measure the volatility of the data series at each time period, can be written to an output data set.

You can specify generalized autoregressive conditional heteroscedasticity models with the GARCH= option on the MODEL statement. The GARCH= option specifies a list of suboptions in parentheses.

With the various suboptions of the GARCH= option, you can specify many different kinds of conditional heteroscedasticity models from the GARCH family. The different kinds of GARCH type models supported include: ARCH(p) or GARCH(p,q) generalized autoregressive conditional heteroscedasticity, with or without intercept term; IGARCH(p,q), integrated generalized autoregressive conditional heteroscedasticity; constrained GARCH(p,q) with nonnegativity or stationarity restrictions; EGARCH(p,q), exponential generalized autoregressive conditional heteroscedasticity; and GARCH-M(p,q), the GARCH-in-mean model. You can also fit AR-GARCH models that combine an autoregressive error model with any of the supported GARCH type models for the innovation variance.

When GARCH models are estimated, the following diagnostic statistics are printed:

- Q statistics calculated using the squared residuals
- Lagrange multiplier test for the absence of ARCH effects
- normality test

See Chapter 4 for details on using GARCH models.

DWPROB Option: P-Values for the Durbin-Watson Statistic

The new DWPROB option computes the marginal probability of the Durbin-Watson statistic. With the DWPROB option, the procedure prints the exact *p*-value for your data, so that you do not need to refer to printed Durbin-Watson tables (which may yield inconclusive results).

DW= Option: Generalized Durbin-Watson Statistics

The new DW= option enables you to calculate the generalized Durbin-Watson statistics to test for autocorrelation at lags greater than one. Generalized Durbin-Watson statistics are requested with the new DW=*nlag* option in the MODEL statement.

LAGDEP= Option: Durbin *h* and Durbin *t* Statistics

The new LAGDEP= option tests for first-order autocorrelation when the regressors contain lagged dependent variables. The Durbin *h* statistic is computed by the LAGDEP= option. The LAGDEP option without a lagged dependent variable specified computes the Durbin *t* statistic.

COVOUT Option

The COVOUT option outputs the covariance matrix of parameter estimates to the OUTEST= data set.

The variable _SSE_ in the OUTEST= data set is replaced by _STDERR_, which contains the standard error of the parameter estimate.

Miscellaneous Changes

In previous releases, the likelihood value printed by the ITPRINT option was only the variable part of the likelihood that depends on the parameter values. The full likelihood value, including constant terms, is now printed in the ITPRINT output.

CITIBASE Procedure

The CITIBASE procedure was superseded by the DATASOURCE procedure. You can still use the CITIBASE procedure as before. However, the new DATASOURCE procedure can read CITIBASE files, as well as many other kinds of data files, and provides many additional features. See Chapter 7 for details.

EXPAND Procedure

The following are changes to the EXPAND procedure. See Chapter 8, "The EXPAND Procedure," for details.

TRANSFORMIN= and TRANSFORMOUT= Options

You can now apply various transformations to the input series using the new TRANSFORMIN= option on the CONVERT statement. You can apply transformations to the output series using the TRANSFORMOUT= option. These options are useful for modifying the interpolation process for series that must be restricted to a limited range.

For example, suppose you are interpolating missing values in a series of market share estimates. Market shares must be between 0% and 100%, but applying the spline interpolation to the raw series can produce estimates outside this range.

The following statements use the logistic transformation to transform proportions in the range 0 to 1 to values in the range $-\infty$ to $+\infty$. The TRANSFORMIN= option first divides the market shares by 100 to rescale percent values to proportions and then applies the LOGIT function. The TRANSFORMOUT= option applies the inverse logistic function ILOGIT to the interpolated values to convert back to proportions and then multiplies by 100 to rescale back to percentages.

```
proc expand data=a out=b;
   id date;
   convert mshare / transformin=( / 100 logit )
                    transformout=( ilogit * 100 );
run;
```

You can also use these options as a convenient way to do calculations normally performed with the SAS DATA step. For example, the following statements add the lead of X to the data set A:

```
proc expand data=a method=none;
   id date;
   convert x=xlead / transform=(lead);
run;
```

The METHOD= option value NONE was added to suppress interpolation when using PROC EXPAND to transform series without interpolation of missing values or frequency conversion.

EXTRAPOLATE Option, Extrapolation Changed

Previously, when extrapolation was required, the SPLINE method produced an extrapolation of the first and last cubic segments of the spline curve. Now, extrapolation is performed by a linear projection of the trend of the cubic spline curve fit to the input data, not by extrapolation of the first and last cubic segments. This is accomplished by appending linear segments to the ends of the spline curve.

These appended segments are also included in the OUTEST= data set, so the OUTEST= data set now contains additional observations for METHOD=SPLINE. The first and last observations in the OUTEST= data for a curve are now linear segments appended to the curve for use in extrapolating beyond the range of the input data.

The new EXTRAPOLATE option specifies that missing values at the beginning or the end of input series be replaced with values produced by a linear extrapolation of the interpolating curve fit to the input series. By default, PROC EXPAND only interpolates values within the range of the nonmissing input values and avoids extrapolating values beyond the first or last input value for a series, except as required to complete output intervals that overlap the end-points of the input data.

FORECAST Procedure

The following are changes to the FORECAST procedure. See Chapter 9, "The FORECAST Procedure," for details.

Starting Values

The FORECAST procedure has several new options to control the starting values for the exponential smoothing method, the Winters method, and the additive Winters method. These options are NSTART=, NSSTART=, ASTART=, BSTART=, and CSTART=.

With the addition of these features, the default starting values have been changed. In previous releases, the first nonmissing value was used as the starting value for the intercept (smoothed value), and the linear and quadratic trend parameters were initialized to zero. Now, the trend parameters are initialized with a time-trend regression over the beginning part of the series, with the number of periods included in the regression controlled by the NSTART= option. The start-up used in previous releases is similar to using NSTART=1.

The logic for computing the starting values for the seasonal factors in the WINTERS and ADDWINTERS methods when missing values are present has been improved. The computation of seasonal starting values is now controlled by the NSSTART= option. When missing values are present, PROC FORECAST now includes data in the seasonal startup until at least NSSTART= values are available for each season.

ASTART= , BSTART= , and CSTART= Options

The new options ASTART=, BSTART=, and CSTART= can be used to specify starting values for the trend parameters for each variable in the VAR statement list. ASTART= specifies the intercept or smoothed value at the first observation. BSTART= specifies the initial linear trend. CSTART= specifies the initial quadratic trend.

NSTART= Option

The new NSTART= option specifies that starting values are computed with a time-trend regression for the specified number of observations at the beginning of each series.

For exponential smoothing, NSTART= gives the number of observations to include in the trend regression. For the Winters and additive Winters methods, NSTART= specifies the number of complete seasonal cycles (for example, years) to include in the trend regression.

NSSTART= Option

The new NSSTART= option specifies the number of seasonal cycles to average to compute start values for the seasonal factors for the Winters and additive Winters methods. The NSSTART= option allows initialization of seasonal factors to be controlled separately from initialization of trend parameters. By default, NSSTART= is the same as NSTART=. If you do not specify the NSTART= option, the default is NSSTART=2, which is the same as in previous releases.

Calculation of Variance Estimate

In previous releases, the first TREND= residuals were ignored in computing the root mean square error. With the improvement in the default method of computing starting values, this is no longer desirable, and all residuals are now used in computing the error variance estimate. This change affects the confidence limits and the _TYPE_=SIGMA observations in the OUTEST= data set for these methods.

Statistics in the OUTEST= Data Set

The FORECAST procedure now includes more statistics of fit in the OUTEST= data set. The new statistics available in the OUTEST= are:

NRESID	number of residuals
SST	correct total sum of squares for the variable
SSE	sum of the squared residuals
MSE	mean squared error
RMSE	root mean squared error (square root of MSE)
MAPE	mean absolute percentage error
MPE	mean percentage error

MAE	mean absolute deviations
ME	mean error
MAXE	maximum residual value
MINE	minimum residual value
MAXPE	maximum percent error
MINPE	minimum percent error
RSQUARE	1-SSE/SST
ADJRSQ	R-square adjusted for model degrees of freedom
ARSQ	Amemiya's adjusted R-square
RW_RSQ	Harvey's R-square statistic for random walk null model
AIC	Akaike's information criterion
SBC	Schwarz's Bayesian criterion
APC	Amemiya's prediction criterion
CORR	correlation coefficient between actual and predicted values
THEILU	Theil's U statistic using original units
RTHEILU	Theil's U statistic calculated using relative changes
THEILUM	bias proportion of Theil's U statistic
THEILUS	variance proportion of Theil's U statistic
THEILUC	covariance proportion of Theil's U statistic
THEILUR	regression proportion of Theil's U statistic
THEILUD	disturbance proportion of Theil's U statistic
RTHEILUM	bias proportion of RTHEILU statistic
RTHEILUS	variance proportion of RTHEILU statistic
RTHEILUC	covariance proportion of RTHEILU statistic
RTHEILUR	regression proportion of RTHEILU statistic
RTHEILUD	disturbance proportion of RTHEILU statistic

OUTESTALL, OUTFITSTATS, and OUTESTTHEIL Options

Three new options have been added to control the statistics written to the OUTEST= data set. The OUTESTALL writes all available statistics. The OUTESTTHEIL option writes Theil forecast accuracy statistics to the OUTEST= data set. The OUTFITSTATS option writes various R^2 type forecast accuracy statistics in the OUTEST= data set.

Minimum Number of Observations

PROC FORECAST now produces forecasts based on fewer observations than was permitted previously. (Of course, forecasts produced from very few observations are likely to be unreliable.)

MODEL Procedure

The following are changes to the MODEL procedure. See Chapter 11, "The MODEL Procedure," for details.

Generalized Method of Moments Estimation

The new option GMM on the FIT statement requests the generalized method of moments estimation method. The GMM method is appropriate for models with heteroscedastic or correlated errors.

The iterated generalized method of moments method is also now available through the ITGMM option. ITGMM is similar to the iterated versions of 2SLS, SUR, and 3SLS. When you specify the ITGMM method, the variance matrix for GMM is reestimated at each iteration.

Several other new options are added to support the GMM method; these include the KERNEL=, VDATA=, and OUTV= options, which are described in the following sections.

KERNEL= Option

The new KERNEL= option selects the kernel function used by the GMM method to estimate the variance matrix. The general form of the KERNEL= option is

KERNEL= (PARZEN | QS | BART , [*c*] , [*e*])

The kernels supported are

BART   Bartlett kernel

PARZEN   Parzen weights kernel

QS   Quadratic spectral kernel

The values $e \geq 0$ and $c \geq 0$ are used to compute the bandwidth parameter $l(n)$ as a function of the number of nonmissing observations n. The bandwidth parameter $l(n)$ is computed based on e, c, and n as follows:

$$l(n) = c\, n^e$$

The default is KERNEL=(PARZEN, 1, 0.20).

VDATA= Data Set

The VDATA= option reads a variance matrix for GMM estimation from a SAS data set.

OUTV= Data Set

The OUTV= option writes the estimated variance matrix used by the generalized method of moments estimation method to an output data set. This matrix is formed from the instruments and the residuals that are computed using the parameter estimates obtained from the initial 2SLS estimation.

Full Information Maximum Likelihood Estimation

The new FIML option on the FIT statement requests the full information maximum likelihood estimation. The FIML method is a noninstrumental variables method for estimating parameters in a simultaneous system of regression equations.

COVBEST= Option

The COVBEST= option on the FIT statement controls the estimator of the covariance of the parameter estimates (COVB) used by the FIML method.

HESSIAN= Option

The new HESSIAN= option on the FIT statement controls the approximation of the Hessian matrix used in the minimization procedure for the FIML method. Alternate approximations can be used to improve convergence and execution time.

STARTITER= Option

The new STARTITER= option on the FIT statement controls how many minimization iterations are performed at each grid point when the START= option specifies an initial grid search for starting parameter values for the estimation process. The default is STARTITER=0, which performs no minimization iteration for the grid search.

MAXSUBITER= Option

The new MAXSUBITER= option on the SOLVE statement controls the number of damping subiterations that are performed in solving a nonlinear system using Newton's method. This enables you to simulate a larger class of models. Setting MAXSUBITER=0 causes no damping to be performed. The default is MAXSUBITER=10.

OUTPARMS= Data Set

The new OUTPARMS= option on the PROC MODEL statement writes all the parameters to an output data set. The OUTPARMS= data set contains one observation. The OUTPARMS= data set is written at the end of the PROC MODEL step, after any FIT or SOLVE statements are processed.

The OUTPARMS= data set is similar to the OUTEST= data set, but whereas the OUTEST= data set contains only the parameters estimated by a particular FIT task, the OUTPARMS= data set contains values of all the parameters in the model. The OUTPARMS= data set also does not contain covariances.

PARMSDATA= Data Set

The new PARMSDATA= option on the PROC MODEL statement reads values for all parameters whose names match the names of variables in the PARMSDATA= data set. Values for any or all of the parameters in the model can be reset using the PARMSDATA= option. The PARMSDATA= data set is read before any FIT or SOLVE statements are processed.

Together, the OUTPARMS= and PARMSDATA= options enable you to change part of a model and recompile the new model program without the need to reestimate equations that were not changed.

Suppose you have a large model with parameters estimated and you now want to replace one equation, Y, with a new specification. Since PROC MODEL does not have a model editor, the whole model program must be recompiled. Still, you don't want to have to reestimate all the equations, just the one that changed.

Using OUTPARMS= and PARMSDATA= options, you could do the following:

```
proc model model=oldmod outparms=temp;
run;
proc model outmodel=newmod parmsdata=temp data=in;
   ... include new model definition with changed y equation here ...
   fit y;
run;
```

The model file NEWMOD contains the corrected model with the parameter values from the old model.

Zero-Degrees-of-Freedom Fits

Previously, PROC MODEL required that there be at least one more nonmissing observation than parameters to be estimated. Now PROC MODEL requires only that the number of nonmissing observations be at least equal to the number of parameters estimated. Thus, it is possible to fit models even when there are no degrees of freedom for the residuals.

While such zero-degrees-of-freedom, perfect-fit "estimates" have no statistical meaning, you can use them to find initial values (by running a preliminary FIT on a minimal subset of the data) or when you use the FIT statement to calibrate coefficients of deterministic functions.

NDEC= Option

The NDEC= option enables you to control the precision of the format that PROC MODEL uses when printing various numbers. The default is NDEC=3, which means that PROC MODEL attempts to print values neatly (using the D format) but ensures that at least three significant digits are shown. If the NDEC= value is greater than nine, the BEST. format is used. The smallest value allowed is NDEC=2.

The NDEC= option affects the format of most, but not all, of the floating point numbers that PROC MODEL prints. For some values (such as parameter estimates), a precision limit one or two digits greater than the NDEC= value is used.

V5MODEL= Option

The V5MODEL= option reads model files written by Version 5 of SAS/ETS software.

LISTALL Option

The LISTALL option provides a quick way to request the LIST, LISTDEP, LISTDER, and LISTCODE options.

MAXERRORS= Option

The MAXERRORS= option now also limits diagnostic printing of the equation errors, the equation predicted values, and the program data vector when the solution fails. If the number of items (solution or *PDV* variables) is greater than the MAXERRORS= value, that part of the diagnostic output is suppressed. This feature prevents voluminous output when a SOLVE process fails.

MORTGAGE Procedure

The MORTGAGE procedure has been superseded by the LOAN procedure. You can still use the MORTGAGE procedure as before. However, the new LOAN procedure performs the same analysis as PROC MORTGAGE and provides many additional features. See Chapter 10 for details.

PDLREG Procedure

The PDLREG procedure supports the same Durbin-Watson statistics options, DW=, DWPROB, and LAGDEP=, as the AUTOREG procedure. See the section "AU-TOREG Procedure" earlier in this chapter and see Chapter 13, "The PDLREG Procedure," for details.

SIMLIN Procedure

The BY statement can now apply to both the EST= and DATA= data sets. Thus, there are now three ways of using the BY statement with the SIMLIN procedure:

- If the BY variables are found in the EST= data set only, PROC SIMLIN simulates over the whole DATA= data set once for each set of coefficients read from the BY groups in the EST= data set.

- If the BY variables are found in the DATA= data set only, PROC SIMLIN performs separate simulations over each BY group in the DATA= data set using the single set of coefficients in the EST= data set.

- If the BY variables are found in both the EST= and the DATA= data sets, PROC SIMLIN performs separate simulations over each BY group in the DATA= data sets using the coefficients from the corresponding BY group in the EST= data set.

See Chapter 14, "The SIMLIN Procedure," for details.

X11 Procedure

The following are changes to the X11 procedure. See Chapter 19, "The X11 Procedure," for details.

OUTSTB= Data Set

The OUTSTB= option on the PROC X11 statement writes the stable seasonality test results (table D8) to an output data set. The form of the OUTSTB= data set parallels the format of table D8.

OUTTDR= Data Set

The OUTTDR= option on the PROC X11 statement writes the trading day regression results (tables B15 and C15) to an output data set. The form of the OUTTDR= data set parallels the format of tables B15 and C15. Both tables B15 and C15 are written to the OUTTDR= data set, with the value of the variable TABLE identifying the two tables.

X11-ARIMA Method

PROC X11 now supports the X11-ARIMA methodology developed by Statistics Canada. The X11-ARIMA method overcomes a potential weakness in the usual X11 method.

The X11 method uses various moving averages with symmetric weights to decompose the actual series. However, symmetric weights cannot be applied at the ends of the series, and special asymmetric weights must be used instead. This adversely affects the quality of the results for values near the beginning or end of the series.

The X11-ARIMA method uses an ARIMA model to produce forecasts and backcasts of the series. These forecast and backcast values are added to the ends of the actual series to produce an extended series. The usual X11 method is then applied to this extended series, allowing symmetric weights for the various moving averages used in the X11 method to be applied for all periods within the time span of the actual data. The final X11-ARIMA results are that part of the X11 results for the extended series lying within the time span of the actual series. The ARIMA statement is used with the X11 procedure to specify the X11-ARIMA method.

ARIMA Statement

The ARIMA statement specifies the X11-ARIMA method. You can also use the ARIMA statement to specify the ARIMA model, to control the process by which the ARIMA model is automatically selected, or to specify other options. Features of the X11 procedure's ARIMA statement are described in the following sections.

By default, when the ARIMA statement is used, PROC X11 selects the best ARIMA model for each series according to the rules developed by Statistics Canada. However, you can specify a model to use for all series with the MODEL= and TRANSFORM= options.

The ARIMA statement also provides many other options for controlling the ARIMA model fitting and extrapolation process. See the section "ARIMA Statement" in Chapter 19 for more information.

NOPRINT Option

The NOPRINT option on the PROC X11 statement suppresses all printed output.

OUTEXTRAP Option

The OUTEXTRAP option on the PROC X11 statement extends the range of observations in the OUT= data set to included the entire series extended by ARIMA forecasts and backcasts. This option has no effect unless you specify the ARIMA statement.

By default, the OUT= data set contains requested tables for the range of the actual data. That is, the number of observations in the OUT= data set is the same as the number of observations in the input data set.

SAS Macros

Five new SAS macros are available in SAS/ETS software. These macros are part of the SAS AUTOCALL facility; they are automatically available for use in your SAS program.

The new macros are described in the following sections. See Chapter 20, "SAS Macros," for more information.

%BOXCOXAR Macro

The %BOXCOXAR macro investigates Box-Cox transformations for use in modeling and forecasting a time series.

%DFTEST Macro

The %DFTEST macro performs Dickey-Fuller tests for unit roots in a time series process.

%DFPVALUE Macro

The %DFPVALUE macro computes probabilities for Dickey-Fuller test statistics.

%LOGTEST Macro

The %LOGTEST macro tests to see if a time series should be log transformed for forecasting.

%MA Macro

The SAS macro %MA generates statements to define moving average error models for the MODEL procedure. The %MA macro complements the %AR macro for autoregressive error models. By using the %MA macro in conjunction with the %AR macro you can estimate nonlinear models with ARMA error structures.

See the "%MA Macro" section in Chapter 11 for more information about the %MA macro.

Time Intervals

WEEKDAY Interval

The new WEEKDAY interval type specifies daily data but with weekend days treated as part of the preceding weekday.

By default, the weekend days are Saturday and Sunday. Thus, WEEKDAY days have the sequence Monday, Tuesday, Wednesday, Thursday, Friday, Monday, and so on. You can control the weekend days by suffixing the weekend list to 'WEEKDAY' followed by a 'W'. Weekend days are coded as '1'=Sunday, '2'=Monday, and so on.

For example, WEEKDAY67W specifies weekdays with Friday and Saturday as weekend days (so the weekday cycle is Sunday, Monday, Tuesday, Wednesday, Thursday, Sunday, and so on.)

You can specify one to six weekend days. For example, WEEKDAY1W specifies a six-day week with only Sunday as a weekend day. The weekend days do not have to be consecutive. For example, WEEKDAY26W can be used to specify a five-day work-week with Mondays and Fridays off.

You can specify multiple-day WEEKDAY intervals. For example, WEEKDAY2 specifies the cycle of two-day intervals Monday–Tuesday, Wednesday–Thursday, Friday–Saturday–Sunday–Monday, Tuesday–Wednesday, Thursday–Friday–Saturday–Sunday, Monday–Tuesday, and so on. You can combine weekend specifications and multiday specifications. For example, WEEKDAY67W2 is similar to WEEKDAY2 but with Friday–Saturday weekends.

See Chapter 21, "Date Intervals, Formats, and Functions," for more information on time intervals.

Subject Index

N

O

observation equation
　　See measurement equation
OECD data files, DATASOURCE procedure
　　366, 367
omitted observations
　　contrasted with missing values 46
　　defined 46
　　replacing with missing values 76
operations research, SAS/OR software 24
order statistics
　　See RANK procedure
Organization for Economic Cooperation and
　　Development
　　See OECD data files
orthogonal polynomials, PDLREG procedure
　　699
output data sets
　　and the OUTPUT statement 51
　　ARIMA procedure 151-153, 155, 156
　　AUTOREG procedure 230
　　BOXCOXAR macro 947
　　CITIBASE procedure 266
　　COMPUTAB procedure 303
　　DATASOURCE procedure 327, 328,
　　　　330-332, 347-349, 351
　　DFTEST macro 952
　　different forms of 50, 51
　　EXPAND procedure 412, 413
　　FORECAST procedure 452, 454
　　in standard form 50
　　interleaved form 50
　　LOAN procedure 496-498
　　LOGTEST macro 955
　　MODEL procedure 612, 615-617, 634,
　　　　635
　　MORTGAGE procedure 692
　　PDLREG procedure 712
　　produced by SAS/ETS procedures 50,
　　　　51
　　SIMLIN procedure 733, 734
　　SPECTRA procedure 758
　　STATESPACE procedure 804-806
　　SYSLIN procedure 852, 853
　　TSCSREG procedure 887
　　X11 procedure 927, 928
OUTPUT statement, SAS/ETS procedures
　　using 51
over identification restrictions, SYSLIN pro-
　　cedure 851
over identifying restrictions, MODEL proce-
　　dure 557
overlay plots
　　of interleaved time series 57, 64
　　of time series 56, 63
　　TYPE variable and 57, 64

P

panel data
　　SAS/STAT software 26
　　TSCSREG procedure 871
parameter change vector, MODEL procedure
　　578
parameters, MODEL procedure 638
Pareto charts, SAS/QC software 25
Parks method, TSCSREG procedure 871,
　　882
partial autocorrelations, multivariate 796
path analysis, SAS/STAT software 27
PDL
　　See polynomial distributed lags
PDLREG procedure
　　BY groups 705
　　confidence limits 708
　　new features 987
　　orthogonal polynomials 699
　　output data sets 712
　　polynomial distributed lags 699
　　predicted values 708
　　residuals 708
　　restricted estimation 709
percent change calculations
　　at annual rates 82
　　introduced 82
　　moving averages 83
　　period-to-period 82
　　year-over-year 82
　　yearly averages 83
periodicity
　　changing by interpolation 94, 394
　　of time series observations 39, 51, 94
periodogram, SPECTRA procedure 751, 759
phase spectrum, SPECTRA procedure 759
PLOT procedure
　　base SAS software 20
　　plot axis for time series 60
　　plotting time series 59
　　reference lines 60
point-in-time values 394, 395
polynomial distributed lags
　　endpoint restrictions for 699, 705
　　MODEL procedure 608
　　PDLREG procedure 699
Prais-Winsten estimates, AUTOREG proce-
　　dure 217
predetermined variables, SYSLIN procedure
　　819
predicted values
　　ARIMA procedure 148
　　AUTOREG procedure 212, 226, 227
　　conditional variance 228
　　FORECAST procedure 453
　　PDLREG procedure 708
　　SIMLIN procedure 724, 729

Syntax Index